Physiology of Behavior

Physiology of Behavior

EIGHTH EDITION

Neil R. Carlson

University of Massachusetts, Amherst

PEARSON

Boston | New York | San Francisco
Mexico City | Montreal | Toronto | London | Madrid | Munich | Paris
Hong Kong | Singapore | Tokyo | Cape Town | Sydney

Series Editor: *Kelly May*
Series Editorial Assistant: *Marlana Voerster*
Marketing Manager: *Taryn Wahlquist*
Composition and Prepress Buyer: *Linda Cox*
Manufacturing Manager: *Megan Cochran*
Cover Coordinator: *Linda Knowles*
Photo Researcher: *Helane Manditch-Prottas*
Editorial-Production Coordinator: *Mary Beth Finch*
Editorial-Production Service: *Barbara Gracia*
Copyeditor: *Barbara Willette*
Text Designer: *Carol Somberg*
Illustrator: *Jay Alexander*
Electronic Composition: *Omegatype Typography, Inc.*

Library of Congress Cataloging-in-Publication Data
Carlson, Neil R., 1942–
    Physiology of behavior / Neil R. Carlson.—8th ed.
      p. cm.
    Includes bibliographical references and index.
    ISBN 0-205-38175-8
    1. Psychophysiology.   I. Title

QP360. C35 2003
612.8—dc21   200304352

Printed in the United States of America

10 9 8 7 6 5 4 3 2 1 VHP 07 06 05 04 03

Chapter Opener Art Credits
Page 1: David Hockney, *Pacific Coast Highway and Santa Monica* 1990 (Detail). Oil on canvas, 78 × 120". © David Hockney. Page 27: Alexandra Rozenman, from the series *Broken Windows*. Mixed media, 8 × 8". © Alexandra Rozenman. Page 66: Sam Francis, *Greenish Limb* 1970. © 2003 The Estate of Sam Francis/Artists Rights Society (ARS), New York. Copyright Giraudon/Art Resource, NY. Collection of Marie Noelle and Didier Sicard, Paris, France. Page 100: Howard Mehring, *Banner* 1957. Acrylic on canvas, 52 1/2 × 65 in. Gift from Vincent Melzac Collection. Copyright Smithsonian American Art Museum, Washington, DC/Art Resource, NY. Page 131: Bridget Riley, *Nataraja* 1993. Oil on linen, 65 × 89 in. (165 × 227 cm). © Bridget Riley. Copyright Tate Gallery, London/Art Resource, NY. Page 162: Alma Woodsey Thomas, *The Eclipse* 1970. Acrylic on canvas, 62 × 49 in. Gift of Alma W. Thomas. Copyright Smithsonian American Art Museum, Washington, DC/Art Resource, NY. Page 202: James Rosenquist, *Lady Dog Lizard* 1985. Oil on canvas, two panels, overall 9' 11 7/8" × 9' 11 7/8". Gift of Philip Johnson. (510.1998.a-b).

Photo credits are continued on page 698, which is considered an extension of the copyright page.

For old friends:

Wayne and Arlene, Ross and Pamela

Brief Contents

1 Introduction   1

2 Structure and Functions of Cells of the Nervous System   27

3 Structure of the Nervous System   66

4 Psychopharmacology   100

5 Methods and Strategies of Research   131

6 Vision   163

7 Audition, the Body Senses, and the Chemical Senses   202

8 Control of Movement   244

9 Sleep and Biological Rhythms   274

10 Reproductive Behavior   308

11 Emotion   342

12 Ingestive Behavior   373

13 Learning and Memory: Basic Mechanisms   410

14 Relational Learning and Amnesia   451

15 Human Communication   480

16 Schizophrenia and the Affective Disorders   515

17 Anxiety Disorders, Autistic Disorder, Attention-Deficit/ Hyperactivity Disorder, and Stress Disorders   546

18 Drug Abuse   572

Contents

Preface   *xvii*

C H A P T E R 1

Introduction   1

Understanding Human Consciousness:
A Physiological Approach   3
  Blindsight   3
  Split Brains   4
  Unilateral Neglect   6
  Interim Summary   7

The Nature of Physiological Psychology   8
  The Goals of Research   8
  Biological Roots of Physiological Psychology   9
  Interim Summary   12

Natural Selection and Evolution   13
  Functionalism and the Inheritance of Traits   13
  Evolution of the Human Species   16
  Evolution of Large Brains   19
  Interim Summary   20

Ethical Issues in Research with Animals   21

Careers in Neuroscience   22
  Interim Summary   23

Strategies for Learning   24

Suggested Readings   25

Suggested Web Sites   25

C H A P T E R 2

Structure and Functions of Cells of the Nervous System   27

Cells of the Nervous System   29
  Neurons   29
  Supporting Cells   35
  The Blood–Brain Barrier   38
  Interim Summary   39

Communication Within a Neuron   39
  Neural Communication: An Overview   39
  Measuring Electrical Potentials of Axons   41
  The Membrane Potential: Balance of Two Forces   42
  The Action Potential   45
  Conduction of the Action Potential   47
  Interim Summary   50

Communication Between Neurons   50
  The Concept of Chemical Transmission   51
  Structure of Synapses   51
  Release of Neurotransmitter   53
  Activation of Receptors   56
  Postsynaptic Potentials   57
  Termination of Postsynaptic Potentials   59
  Effects of Postsynaptic Potentials: Neural Integration   60
  Autoreceptors   61
  Other Types of Synapses   62
  Nonsynaptic Chemical Communication   62
  Interim Summary   64

Suggested Readings   64

Suggested Web Sites   65

C H A P T E R 3

Structure of the Nervous System   66

Basic Features of the Nervous System   67
  An Overview   70
  Meninges   70
  The Ventricular System and Production of CSF   70
  Interim Summary   74

The Central Nervous System   74
  Development of the Central Nervous System   75

The Forebrain   81

The Midbrain   89

The Hindbrain   91

The Spinal Cord   92

Interim Summary   **93**

The Peripheral Nervous System   94

Spinal Nerves   94

Cranial Nerves   95

The Autonomic Nervous System   96

Interim Summary   **98**

Suggested Readings   99

Suggested Web Sites   99

C H A P T E R   4

Psychopharmacology   100

Principles of Psychopharmacology   102

Pharmacokinetics   102

Drug Effectiveness   105

Effects of Repeated Administration   106

Placebo Effects   107

Interim Summary   **107**

Sites of Drug Action   108

Effects on Production of Neurotransmitters   108

Effects on Storage and Release of
Neurotransmitters   108

Effects on Receptors   108

Effects on Reuptake or Destruction of
Neurotransmitters   110

Interim Summary   **111**

Neurotransmitters and Neuromodulators   112

Acetylcholine   113

The Monoamines   116

Amino Acids   123

Lipids   127

Nucleosides   127

Soluble Gases   128

Interim Summary   **128**

Suggested Readings   130

Suggested Web Sites   130

C H A P T E R   5

Methods and Strategies of Research   131

Experimental Ablation   132

Evaluating the Behavioral Effects of Brain Damage   133

Producing Brain Lesions   134

Stereotaxic Surgery   135

Histological Methods   137

Tracing Neural Connections   139

Study of the Living Human Brain   143

Interim Summary   **144**

Recording and Stimulating Neural Activity   146

Recording of Neural Activity   146

Recording the Brain's Metabolic and Synaptic Activity   149

Measuring the Brain's Secretions   151

Stimulating Neural Activity   152

Behavioral Effects of Electrical Brain Stimulation   153

Interim Summary   **154**

Neurochemical Methods   155

Finding Neurons That Produce Particular
Neurochemicals   155

Localizing Particular Receptors   157

Interim Summary   **158**

Genetic Methods   159

Twin Studies   160

Adoption Studies   160

Targeted Mutations   160

Interim Summary   **160**

Suggested Readings   161

Suggested Web Sites   161

C H A P T E R   6

Vision   162

The Stimulus   164

Anatomy of the Visual System   165

The Eyes   165

Photoreceptors   168

Connections Between Eye and Brain   170

Interim Summary   **171**

Coding of Visual Information in the Retina   172

Coding of Light and Dark   172

Coding of Color   174

Interim Summary   **178**

**Analysis of Visual Information: Role of
the Striate Cortex   178**

Anatomy of the Striate Cortex   178

Orientation and Movement   179

Spatial Frequency   180

Texture   181

Retinal Disparity   182

Color   182

Modular Organization of the Striate Cortex   183

Blindsight   184

Interim Summary   **184**

**Analysis of Visual Information: Role of the Visual
Association Cortex   185**

Two Streams of Visual Analysis   185

Perception of Color   186

Analysis of Form   188

Perception of Movement   193

Perception of Spatial Location   197

Interim Summary   **200**

Suggested Readings   201

Suggested Web Sites   201

Behavioral Functions of the Auditory System   217

Interim Summary   **218**

Vestibular System   219

Anatomy of the Vestibular Apparatus   220

The Receptor Cells   221

The Vestibular Pathway   221

Interim Summary   **222**

Somatosenses   222

The Stimuli   222

Anatomy of the Skin and Its Receptive Organs   223

Perception of Cutaneous Stimulation   224

The Somatosensory Pathways   226

Perception of Pain   228

Interim Summary   **232**

Gustation   233

The Stimuli   233

Anatomy of the Taste Buds and Gustatory Cells   233

Perception of Gustatory Information   234

The Gustatory Pathway   237

Neural Coding of Taste   237

Interim Summary   **238**

Olfaction   238

The Stimulus   238

Anatomy of the Olfactory Apparatus   239

Transduction of Olfactory Information   240

Perception of Specific Odors   240

Interim Summary   **242**

Suggested Readings   243

Suggested Web Sites   243

C H A P T E R   7

Audition, the Body Senses, and the Chemical Senses   202

Audition   203

The Stimulus   203

Anatomy of the Ear   204

Auditory Hair Cells and the Transduction
of Auditory Information   207

The Auditory Pathway   209

Perception of Pitch   211

Perception of Loudness   213

Perception of Timbre   213

Perception of Spatial Location   214

C H A P T E R   8

Control of Movement   244

Muscles   245

Skeletal Muscle   245

Smooth Muscle   248

Cardiac Muscle   249

Interim Summary   **249**

Reflex Control of Movement   250

The Monosynaptic Stretch Reflex   250

The Gamma Motor System   250

Polysynaptic Reflexes   252

Interim Summary   254

Control of Movement by the Brain   254

Organization of Motor Cortex   255

Cortical Control of Movement:
The Descending Pathways   256

Deficits of Verbally Controlled Movements:
The Apraxias   259

The Basal Ganglia   262

The Cerebellum   268

The Reticular Formation   271

Interim Summary   272

Suggested Readings   272

Suggested Web Sites   273

C   H   A   P   T   E   R   9

Sleep and Biological Rhythms   274

**A Physiological and Behavioral Description
of Sleep   275**

Stages of Sleep   276

Mental Activity During Sleep   278

Interim Summary   279

Disorders of Sleep   280

Insomnia   280

Narcolepsy   280

REM Sleep Behavior Disorder   282

Problems Associated with Slow-Wave Sleep   283

Interim Summary   283

Why Do We Sleep?   283

Functions of Slow-Wave Sleep   283

Functions of REM Sleep   286

Interim Summary   287

**Physiological Mechanisms of Sleep
and Waking   288**

Chemical Control of Sleep   288

Neural Control of Arousal   289

Neural Control of Slow-Wave Sleep   292

Neural Control of REM Sleep   295

Interim Summary   299

Biological Clocks   299

Circadian Rhythms and Zeitgebers   300

The Suprachiasmatic Nucleus   301

Control of Seasonal Rhythms: The Pineal Gland
and Melatonin   305

Changes in Circadian Rhythms: Shift Work and Jet Lag   306

Interim Summary   306

Suggested Readings   307

Suggested Web Sites   307

C   H   A   P   T   E   R   10

Reproductive Behavior   308

Sexual Development   309

Production of Gametes and Fertilization   309

Development of the Sex Organs   310

Sexual Maturation   314

Interim Summary   315

Hormonal Control of Sexual Behavior   316

Hormonal Control of Female
Reproductive Cycles   316

Hormonal Control of Sexual Behavior
of Laboratory Animals   317

Organizational Effects of Androgens of Behavior:
Masculinization and Defeminization   319

Effects of Pheromones   319

Human Sexual Behavior   323

Sexual Orientation   326

Interim Summary   330

Neural Control of Sexual Behavior   331

Males   331

Females   334

Interim Summary   336

Parental Behavior   337

Maternal Behavior of Rodents   337

Hormonal Control of Maternal Behavior   338

Neural Control of Maternal Behavior   339

Neural Control of Paternal Behavior   340

Interim Summary   340

Suggested Readings   341

Suggested Web Sites   341

C H A P T E R 11

Emotion   342

Emotions as Response Patterns   343

Fear   344

Anger and Aggression   348

Hormonal Control of Aggressive Behavior   355

Interim Summary   359

Communication of Emotions   360

Facial Expression of Emotions:
Innate Responses   360

Neural Basis of the Communication of Emotions:
Recognition   361

Neural Basis of the Communication of Emotions:
Expression   365

Interim Summary   368

Feelings of Emotions   369

The James-Lange Theory   369

Feedback from Simulated Emotions   370

Interim Summary   371

Suggested Readings   372

Suggested Web Sites   372

C H A P T E R 12

Ingestive Behavior   373

Physiological Regulatory Mechanisms   375

Drinking   376

Some Facts About Fluid Balance   376

Two Types of Thirst   377

Neural Mechanisms of Thirst   380

Interim Summary   381

Eating: Some Facts About Metabolism   382

Absorption, Fasting, and the Two Nutrient
Reservoirs   382

Interim Summary   385

What Starts a Meal?   385

Social and Environmental Factors   385

Physiological Hunger Signals   386

Interim Summary   387

What Stops a Meal?   388

Head Factors   388

Gastric Factors   388

Intestinal Factors   389

Liver Factors   390

Metabolic Factors Present in the Blood   390

Long-Term Satiety: Signals from
Adipose Tissue   390

Interim Summary   392

Brain Mechanisms   393

Brain Stem   393

Hypothalamus   394

Interim Summary   400

Eating Disorders   400

Obesity   400

Anorexia Nervosa/Bulimia Nervosa   405

Interim Summary   407

Suggested Readings   409

Suggested Web Sites   409

C H A P T E R 13

Learning and Memory: Basic Mechanisms   410

The Nature of Learning   411

Interim Summary   415

Learning and Synaptic Plasticity   415

Induction of Long-Term Potentiation   415

Role of NMDA Receptors   418

Mechanisms of Synaptic Plasticity   422

Long-Term Depression   427

Other Forms of Long-Term Potentiation   428

Role of Long-Term Potentiation
in Learning   429

Interim Summary   429

Perceptual Learning   429

Learning to Recognize Particular Stimuli   430

Perceptual Short-Term Memory   433

Interim Summary   436

Classical Conditioning   436

Interim Summary   438

Instrumental Conditioning and Motor Learning   439

Basal Ganglia   439

Premotor Cortex   442

Reinforcement   444

Interim Summary   449

Suggested Readings   450

Suggested Web Sites   450

CHAPTER 14

Relational Learning and Amnesia   451

Human Anterograde Amnesia   452

Basic Description   453

Spared Learning Abilities   454

Declarative and Nondeclarative Memories   456

Anterograde Amnesia: Failure of Relational Learning   458

Anatomy of Anterograde Amnesia   459

Role of the Medial Temporal Lobe in Spatial Memory   464

Role of the Medial Temporal Lobe in Memory Retrieval   465

Confabulation: Role of the Prefrontal Cortex in Evaluating the Accuracy of Memories   466

Interim Summary   467

Relational Learning in Laboratory Animals   468

Remembering Places Visited   468

Spatial Perception and Learning   469

Role of the Hippocampal Formation in Memory Consolidation   471

Place Cells in the Hippocampal Formation   471

Role of Long-Term Potentiation in Relational Learning   474

Modulation of Hippocampal Functions by Monoaminergic and Acetylcholinergic Inputs   475

Theoretical Explanations of Hippocampal Functioning   477

Interim Summary   478

Suggested Readings   479

Suggested Web Sites   479

CHAPTER 15

Human Communication   480

Speech Production and Comprehension: Brain Mechanisms   481

Lateralization   482

Speech Production   482

Speech Comprehension   486

Aphasia in Deaf People   497

The Bilingual Brain   498

Prosody: Rhythm, Tone, and Emphasis in Speech   499

Interim Summary   500

Disorders of Reading and Writing   501

Relation to Aphasia   501

Pure Alexia   502

Toward an Understanding of Reading   505

Toward an Understanding of Writing   508

Developmental Dyslexias   511

Interim Summary   513

Suggested Readings   514

Suggested Web Sites   514

CHAPTER 16

Schizophrenia and the Affective Disorders   515

Schizophrenia   517

Description   517

Heritability   518

Pharmacology of Schizophrenia: The Dopamine Hypothesis   519

Schizophrenia as a Neurological Disorder   522

Interim Summary   531

Major Affective Disorders   532

Description   532

Heritability   533

Physiological Treatments   534

Role of Monoamines   536

A Role for Substance P?   538

Evidence for Brain Abnormalities   538

Role of Circadian Rhythms   541

Interim Summary   **544**

Suggested Readings   **544**

Suggested Web Sites   **545**

C H A P T E R   17

Anxiety Disorders, Autistic Disorder, Attention-Deficit/ Hyperactivity Disorder, and Stress Disorders   546

Anxiety Disorders   **548**

Panic Disorder   548

Obsessive-Compulsive Disorder   550

Interim Summary   **554**

Autistic Disorder   **555**

Description   555

Possible Causes   556

Interim Summary   **557**

Attention-Deficit/Hyperactivity Disorder   **558**

Description   558

Possible Causes   558

Interim Summary   **560**

Stress Disorders   **560**

Physiology of the Stress Response   560

Health Effects of Long-Term Stress   562

Posttraumatic Stress Disorder   564

Stress and Cardiovascular Disease   566

The Coping Response   566

Psychoneuroimmunology   567

Interim Summary   **570**

Suggested Readings   **571**

Suggested Web Sites   **571**

C H A P T E R   18

Drug Abuse   572

Common Features of Addiction   **573**

A Little Background   573

Physical Versus Psychological Addiction   574

Positive Reinforcement   575

Negative Reinforcement   576

Craving and Relapse   577

Interim Summary   **579**

Commonly Abused Drugs   **580**

Opiates   580

Cocaine and Amphetamine   584

Nicotine   586

Alcohol and Barbiturates   588

Cannabis   591

Interim Summary   **593**

Heredity and Drug Abuse   **594**

Heritability Studies of Humans   594

Animal Models of Drug Abuse   596

Interim Summary   **597**

Therapy for Drug Abuse   **597**

Interim Summary   **599**

Suggested Readings   **600**

Suggested Web Sites   **600**

References   **601**

Name Index   **661**

Subject Index   **671**

Preface

I wrote the first edition of *Physiology of Behavior* more than a quarter of a century ago. When I did so, I had no idea I would someday be writing the eighth edition. I'm still having fun, so I hope to do a few more. The interesting work coming out of my colleagues' laboratories—a result of their creativity and hard work—has given me something new to say with each edition. Because there was so much for me to learn (there are over 400 new references in this edition), I enjoyed writing this edition just as much as the first one. That is what makes writing new editions interesting: learning something new and then trying to find a way to convey the information to the reader.

In the preface to each of the previous editions, I mentioned some of the new research methods that had recently been developed. Investigators are continuing to develop new methods—for example, new staining techniques for specific substances, new imaging methods, new recording methods, and the means for analyzing the release of neurotransmitters and neuromodulators in restricted regions of the brains of freely moving animals. The research reported in this edition reflects the enormous advances made in research methods: targeted mutations against an enormous variety of genes, some of them specific to a particular region of the brain; insertion of genes that put fluorescent dyes on protein products; single-photon scanning laser microscopy that permits observation of biochemical and structural changes in living neurons; improved spatial and temporal resolution of functional imaging methods—and the list continues. Nowadays, as soon as a new method is developed in one laboratory, it is adopted by other laboratories and applied to a wide range of problems. And more and more, researchers are combining techniques that converge upon the solution to a problem. In the past, individuals tended to apply their particular research method to a problem; now they are more likely to use many methods, often in collaboration with other laboratories.

You will notice that the art in this book continues to evolve. Jay Alexander and I have worked together to redraw much of the anatomical art. Jay, an artist who also works as a technician in the Psychology Department at the University of Massachusetts, supplied the artistic talent. I think the result of our collaboration is a set of clear, consistent, and attractive illustrations.

The first part of the book is concerned with foundations: the history of the field, the structure and functions of neurons, neuroanatomy, psychopharmacology, and research methods. The second part is concerned with inputs and outputs: the sensory systems and the motor system. The third part deals with classes of species-typical behavior: sleep, reproduction, emotional behavior, and ingestion. The chapter on reproductive behavior includes parental behavior as well as mating. The chapter on emotion includes a discussion of fear, anger and aggression, communication of emotions, and feelings of emotions. Ingestive behavior—drinking and eating—is covered in a single chapter.

The fourth part of the book deals with learning. The first learning chapter discusses research on synaptic plasticity and the neural mechanisms that are responsible for perceptual learning and stimulus-response learning (including classical and operant conditioning). The second learning chapter discusses human amnesia and the role of the hippocampal formation in relational learning. The final part of the book deals with verbal communication and mental and behavioral disorders. The latter topic is covered in three chapters; the first discusses schizophrenia and the affective disorders; the second discusses the anxiety disorders, autism, attention deficit disorder, and stress; and the third discusses drug abuse.

Each chapter begins with a *Case History,* which describes an episode involving a neurological disorder or an issue in neuroscience. Other case histories are included in the text of the chapters. *Interim Summaries* follow each major section of the book. They not only provide useful reviews, but also break each chapter into manageable chunks. *Definitions of Key Terms* are printed in the margin near the places where the terms are first discussed. *Pronunciation Guides* for terms that might be difficult to pronounce are also found there. Each chapter ends with a list of *Suggested Readings* and *Suggested Websites* that provide more information about the topics discussed in the chapter.

The following list includes some of the information that is new to this edition:

- New research on the cannabinoids
- Transneuronal staining with pseudorabies virus
- Functional imaging studies on perception of form from motion
- New research on the role of outer hair cells in amplification of vibrations of the basilar membrane
- New research on the presence of dorsal and ventral streams in the auditory system
- New research on the capsaicin nociceptor in knockout mice

- "Olfactotopic" representation in olfactory cortex
- Deep brain stimulation for Parkinson's disease
- The discovery that narcolepsy is a neurodegenerative disease of hypocretinergic neurons
- New research on the role of adenosine as a sleep-promoting chemical
- The discovery of two families of pheromone receptor proteins
- New research on the effects of estradiol on women's sexual interest
- New research on the human amygdala and emotional memory
- New research on the role of the prefrontal cortex in decision making and moral judgments
- The role of serotonin in functions of prefrontal cortex and its relevance to anger and aggression
- The role of PYY$_{3-36}$ and malonyl CoA as satiety signals
- New research on the mechanisms of long-term potentiation and its role in learning
- The role of place cells in spatial memory
- Functional imaging studies of the human hippocampus
- New research on brain mechanisms of sign language
- A new section on the bilingual brain
- The role of languages with irregular orthography in the prevalence of developmental dyslexia
- The role of the father's age in susceptibility to schizophrenia
- Evidence for loss of cerebral gray matter in schizophrenia
- New research on the interactions between prefrontal cortex, ventral tegmental area, and nucleus accumbens in the development of schizophrenia
- Evidence that depression may result from hyperactivity activity of the amygdala and orbitofrontal cortex and hypoactivity of the subgenual prefrontal cortex
- The role of a duplicated region of chromosome 18 in susceptibility to panic disorder
- Lack of a fusiform face area in the brains of autistic adults
- A new section on attention-deficit/hyperactivity disorder
- The role of the amygdala in effects of short-term stress on hippocampal memory functions
- The role of increased sensitivity of brain glucocorticoid receptors in posttraumatic stress disorder
- The role of basolateral amygdala in classically conditioned drug craving
- Evidence that the orbitofrontal cortex and anterior cingulate cortex are involved in drug craving
- Evidence that stress early in life can increase susceptibility to drug addiction

Besides updating my discussion of research, I have updated my writing. Writing is a difficult, time-consuming endeavor, and I find that I am still learning how to do it well. I have said this in the preface of every edition of this book, and it is still true. I have worked with copy editors who have ruthlessly marked up my manuscript, showing me how to do it better the next time. I keep thinking, "This time there will be nothing for the copy editor to do," but I am always proved wrong: Most pages contain notes showing me how to improve my prose. But I do think that each time the writing is better organized, smoother, and more coherent.

Good writing means including all steps of a logical discourse. My teaching experience has taught me that an entire lecture can be wasted if the students do not understand all of the "obvious" conclusions of a particular experiment before the next one is described. Unfortunately, puzzled students sometimes write notes feverishly, in an attempt to get the facts down so they can study them—and understand them—later. A roomful of busy, attentive students tends to reinforce the lecturer's behavior. I am sure all my colleagues have been dismayed by a question from a student that reveals a lack of understanding of details long since passed, accompanied by quizzical looks from other students that confirm that they have the same question. Painful experiences such as these have taught me to examine the logical steps between the discussion of one experiment and the next and to make sure they are explicitly stated. A textbook writer must address the students who will read the book, not simply colleagues who are already acquainted with much of what he or she will say.

Because research on the physiology of behavior is an interdisciplinary effort, a textbook must provide the student with the background necessary for understanding a variety of approaches. I have been careful to provide enough biological background early in the book that students without a background in physiology can understand what is said later, while students with such a background can benefit from details that are familiar to them.

I designed this text for serious students who are willing to work. In return for their effort, I have endeavored to provide a solid foundation for further study. Those students who will not take subsequent courses in this or related fields should receive the satisfaction of a much better understanding of their own behavior. Also, they will have a greater appreciation for the forthcoming advances in medical practices related to disorders that affect a person's perception, mood, or behavior. I hope that students who read this book carefully will henceforth perceive human behavior in a new light.

Supplements for Students

I have prepared a revised CD-ROM, which contains the *Neuroscience Animations* and the *Computerized Study Guide.* The animations demonstrate some of the most important principles of neuroscience through movement and interaction. They include modules on neurophysiology (*Neurons and Supporting Cells, The Action Potential, Synapses,* and *Postsynaptic Potentials*), neuroanatomy, psychopharmacology, audition, sleep, emotion, ingestive behavior, memory, and verbal communication. The interactive *Computerized Study Guide,* accessible through the same menu, contains a set of *Self Tests* that include multiple-choice questions and an on-line review of *Terms and Definitions.* The questions and list of terms and definitions present questions and keep track of your progress, presenting missed items until you have answered all of them correctly. The computerized study guide also includes interactive *Figures and Diagrams* from the book that will help you learn terms and concepts. This CD-ROM is included *free* with the purchase of a new book.

A *Study Guide,* which my wife and I wrote, is also available. This workbook provides a framework for guiding study behavior. It promotes a thorough understanding of the principles of physiological psychology through active participation in the learning process. The study guide contains a set of *Concept Cards.* An important part of learning about physiological psychology is acquiring a new vocabulary, and the concept cards will help with this task. Terms are printed on one side of these cards, and definitions are printed on the other. A crossword puzzle, based on the vocabulary introduced in the text, finishes each chapter.

The publisher of this book, Allyn and Bacon, hosts a companion web site for this text: *www.abacon.com/carlson pob8e.* This site contains additional multiple-choice test questions for you, organized by chapter. This forum allows you to further practice exam taking. The web site also links to other relevant sites of interest, provided by Susan Shapiro at Indiana University–East. Allyn and Bacon also provides *Research Navigator with Guide,* a way for you to get started on a research paper. *Research Navigator* provides access to three databases of useful and reliable source material.

Supplements for Instructors

Several supplements are available for instructors who adopt *Physiology of Behavior.* An *Instructor's Manual* was written by Professor Shapiro. Each chapter of the Instructor's Manual includes an At-A-Glance Grid with detailed information about other supplements, teaching objectives, lecture material, demonstrations and activities, videos, suggested readings, and web resources. An appendix contains a comprehensive list of student handouts.

Grant McLaren, Edinboro University of Pennsylvania, has prepared a set of *PowerPoint Presentations* specifically for the eighth edition of the book. Available on CD-ROM, the presentations contain images from the textbook and provide a framework for lecture outlines. The CD-ROM also contains an electronic version of the Instructor's Manual.

Paul Wellman, Texas A&M University, has prepared a *Test Bank.* The test bank, available in print and also in Windows and Macintosh formats, includes over 80 multiple-choice, true/false, short answer, and essay questions, each with answer justification, page references, difficulty rating, and type designation.

The *Digital Image Archive* CD-ROM provides a comprehensive source for images useful in classroom presentations. A set of 145 full color acetate transparencies are also available.

Course Compass, a course management system, provides a set of tools that permit instructors to create an internet presence for the course.

Acknowledgments

Although I must accept the blame for any shortcomings of the book, I want to thank the many colleagues who helped me by responding to my requests for reprints of their work, suggesting topics that I should cover, sending photographs that have been reproduced in this book, and pointing out deficiencies in the previous edition.

Before I began work on the book, my publisher sent a questionnaire to colleagues who were familiar with the previous edition. Their responses to this questionnaire helped me to decide what changes to make in the revision. I thank:

John P. Broida, University of Southern Maine
Cheryl Conrad, Arizona State University
Donald V. Coscina, Wayne State University
Paul Haerich, Loma Linda University
James G. Holland, The University of Pittsburgh
Mary McNaughton-Cassill, University of Texas at San Antonio
June E. Millet, Los Angeles Valley College
William H. Overman, University of North Carolina at Wilmington
Beth Powell, Smith College

Rhea E. Steinpreis, University of Wisconsin
  at Milwaukee
Frank Webbe, Florida Institute of Technology

Several colleagues have reviewed the manuscript of
parts of this book and made suggestions for improving the
final drafts. I thank:

Giorgio Ascoli, George Mason University
Ronald Baenninger, Temple University
John P. Broida, University of Southern Maine
Michelle Butler, U.S. Air Force Academy
Cari Cannon, Santiago Canyon College
Clinton Chapman, Occidental College
Sherry Dingman, Marist College
Leonard W. Hamilton, Rutgers University
Norman Kinney, Southeast Missouri
  State University
Chuck Kutscher, Syracuse University
Grant McLaren, Edinboro University
  of Pennsylvania
Timothy Robinson, Gustavus Adolphus College
Margaret Ruddy, The College of New Jersey
Rebecca Tews, Virginia Commonwealth University
German Torres, New York College
  of Osteopathic Medicine
Janie Hamn Wilson, Georgia Southern University

I also want to thank the people at Allyn and Bacon.
Carolyn Merrill and Kelly May, my former and present
editors, provided assistance, support, and encouragement.
Kate Edwards and Marlana Voerster, editorial assistants,
helped to gather comments and suggestions from colleagues who have read the book, and Marlana helped to
coordinate the delivery of the manuscript to the people
involved in its production. Erin Liedel took charge of the
production of the study guide. Mary Beth Finch, the production editor, assembled the team that designed and produced the book. Barbara Gracia, of Woodstock Publishers'
Services, demonstrated her masterful organization skills
in managing the book's production. She got everything
done on time, despite an extremely tight schedule. Few
people realize what a difficult, demanding, and time-consuming job a production editor has with a project such as
this, with hundreds of illustrations and an author who
tends to procrastinate, but I do, and I thank her for all she
has done. Barbara Willette served as copy editor. Her
attention to detail surprised me again and again; she found
inconsistencies in my terminology and awkwardness in my
prose and gave me a chance to fix them before anyone
else saw them in print.

I must also thank my wife Mary for her support. Writing is a lonely pursuit, because one must be alone with
one's thoughts for many hours of the day. I thank her for
giving me the time to read, reflect, and write without feeling that I was neglecting her too much. I also thank her
for the superb job she did preparing the study guide.

I was delighted to hear from many students and colleagues who read previous editions of my book, and I hope
that the dialogue will continue. Please write to me and tell
me what you like and dislike about the book. My address
is Department of Psychology, Tobin Hall, University of
Massachusetts, Amherst, Massachusetts 01003. My e-mail
is nrc@psych.umass.edu. When I write, I like to imagine
that I am talking with you, the reader. If you write to me,
we can make the conversation a two-way exchange.

Physiology of Behavior

chapter 1

Introduction

David Hockney, *Pacific Coast Highway and Santa Monica*, 1990 (Detail). © David Hockney.

outline

■ **Understanding Human Consciousness: A Physiological Approach**
Blindsight
Split Brains
Unilateral Neglect
Interim Summary

■ **The Nature of Physiological Psychology**

The Goals of Research
Biological Roots of Physiological Psychology
Interim Summary

■ **Natural Selection and Evolution**
Functionalism and the Inheritance of Traits
Evolution of the Human Species
Evolution of Large Brains

Interim Summary

■ **Ethical Issues in Research with Animals**

■ **Careers in Neuroscience**
Interim Summary

■ **Strategies for Learning**

Miss S. was a sixty-year-old woman with a history of high blood pressure, which was not responding well to the medication she was taking. One evening she was sitting in her reclining chair reading the newspaper when the phone rang. She got out of her chair and walked to the phone. As she did, she began feeling giddy and stopped to hold onto the kitchen table. She has no memory of what happened after that.

The next morning, a neighbor, who usually stopped by to have coffee with Miss S., found her lying on the floor, mumbling incoherently. The neighbor called an ambulance, which took Miss S. to a hospital.

Two days after her admission, I visited her in her room, along with a group of neuropsychologists and neurological residents being led by the chief of neurology. We had already been told by the neurological resident in charge of her case that Miss S. had had a stroke in the back part of the right side of the brain. He had attached a CT scan to an illuminated viewer mounted on the wall and had showed us a white spot caused by the accumulation of blood in a particular region of her brain. (You can look at the scan yourself if you like; it is shown in Figure 5.18.)

About a dozen of us entered Miss S.'s room. She was awake but seemed a little confused. The resident greeted her and asked how she was feeling. "Fine, I guess," she said. "I still don't know why I'm here."

"Can you see the other people in the room?"

"Why, sure."

"How many are there?"

She turned her head to the right and began counting. She stopped when she had counted the people at the foot of her bed. "Seven," she reported. "What about us?" asked a voice from the left of her bed. "What?" she said, looking at the people she had already counted. "Here, to your left. No, toward your left!" the voice repeated.

Slowly, rather reluctantly, she began turning her head to the left. The voice kept insisting, and finally, she saw who was talking. "Oh," she said, "I guess there are more of you."

The resident approached the left side of her bed and touched her left arm. "What is this?" he asked. "Where?" she said. "Here," he answered, holding up her arm and moving it gently in front of her face.

"Oh, that's an arm."

"An arm? Whose arm?"

"I don't know. . . .I guess it must be yours."

"No, it's yours. Look, it's a part of you." He traced with his fingers from her arm to her shoulder.

"Well, if you say so," she said, still sounding unconvinced.

When we returned to the residents' lounge, the chief of neurology said that we had seen a classic example of unilateral neglect, caused by damage to a particular part of the right side of the brain. "I've seen many cases like this," he explained. "People can still perceive sensations from the left side of their body, but they just don't pay attention to them. A woman will put makeup on only the right side of her face, and a man will shave only half of his beard. When they put on a shirt or a coat, they will use their left hand to slip it over their right arm and shoulder, but then they'll just forget about their left arm and let the garment hang from one shoulder. They also don't look at things located toward the left or even the left halves of things. Once I visited a man in his hospital room who had just finished eating breakfast. He was sitting in his bed, with a tray in front of him. There was half of a pancake on his plate. 'Are you all done?' I asked. 'Sure,' he said. When he wasn't looking, I turned the plate around so that the uneaten part was on his right. He saw it, look startled, and said, 'Where the hell did that come from?'"

The last frontier in this world—and perhaps the greatest one—lies within us. The human nervous system makes possible all that we can do, all that we can know, and all that we can experience. Its complexity is immense, and the task of studying it and understanding it dwarfs all previous explorations our species has undertaken.

One of the most universal of all human characteristics is curiosity. We want to explain what makes things happen. In ancient times, people believed that natural phenomena were caused by animating spirits. All moving objects—animals, the wind and tides, the sun, moon, and stars—were assumed to have spirits that caused them to move. For example, stones fell when they were dropped because their animating spirits wanted to be reunited with Mother Earth. As our ancestors became more sophisticated and learned more about nature, they abandoned this approach (which we call *animism*) in favor of physical explanations for inanimate moving objects. But they still used spirits to explain human behavior.

From the earliest historical times, people have believed that they possess something intangible that animates them— a mind, or a soul, or a spirit. This belief stems from the fact that each of us is aware of his or her own existence. When we think or act, we feel as though something inside us is thinking or deciding to act. But what is the nature of the human mind? We have physical bodies, with muscles that move it and sensory organs such as eyes and ears that perceive information about the world around us. Within our bodies the nervous system plays a central role, receiving information from the sensory organs and controlling the movements of the muscles. But what role does the mind play? Does it *control* the nervous system? Is it a *part of* the nervous system? Is it physical and tangible, like the rest of the body, or is it a spirit that will always remain hidden?

This puzzle has historically been called the *mind–body question*. Philosophers have been trying to answer it for many centuries, and more recently, scientists have taken up the task. Basically, people have followed two different approaches: dualism and monism. **Dualism** is a belief in the dual nature of reality. Mind and body are separate; the body is made of ordinary matter, but the mind is not. **Monism** is a belief that everything in the universe consists of matter and energy and that the mind is a phenomenon produced by the workings of the nervous system.

Mere speculation about the nature of the mind can get us only so far. If we could answer the mind–body question simply by thinking about it, philosophers would have done so long ago. Physiological psychologists take an empirical, practical, and monistic approach to the study of human nature. Most of us believe that once we understand the workings of the human body—and, in particular, the workings of the nervous system—the mind–body problem will have been solved. We will be able to explain how we perceive, how we think, how we remember, and how we act. We will even be able to explain the nature of our own self-awareness. Of course, we are far from understanding the workings of the nervous system, so only time will tell whether this belief is justified. In any event there is no way to study nonphysical phenomena in the laboratory. All that we can detect with our sense organs and our laboratory instruments are manifestations of the physical world: matter and energy.

Understanding Human Consciousness: A Physiological Approach

As you will learn from subsequent chapters, scientists have discovered much about the physiology of behavior: of perception, motivation, emotion, memory, and control of specific movements. But before addressing these problems, I want to show you that a scientific approach to perhaps the most complex phenomenon of all—human consciousness—is at least possible.

The term *consciousness* can be used to refer to a variety of concepts, including simple wakefulness. Thus, a researcher may write about an experiment using "conscious rats," referring to the fact that the rats were awake and not anesthetized. However, in this context I am using the word *consciousness* to refer to the fact that we humans are aware of—and can tell others about—our thoughts, perceptions, memories, and feelings.

We know that consciousness can be altered by changes in the structure or chemistry of the brain; therefore, we may hypothesize that consciousness is a physiological function, just like behavior. We can even speculate about the origins of this self-awareness. Consciousness and the ability to communicate seem to go hand in hand. Our species, with its complex social structure and enormous capacity for learning, is well served by our ability to communicate: to express intentions to one another and to make requests of one another. Verbal communication makes cooperation possible and permits us to establish cus-

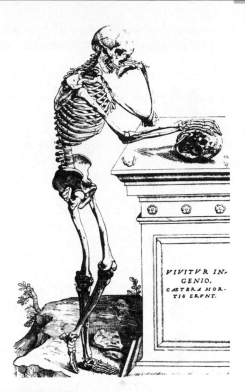

Will the human brain ever completely understand its own workings? A sixteenth-century woodcut from the first edition of *De humani corporis fabrica (On the Workings of the Human Body)* by Andreas Vesalius.
(Courtesy, National Library of Medicine.)

toms and laws of behavior. Perhaps the evolution of this ability is what has given rise to the phenomenon of consciousness. That is, our ability to send and receive messages with other people enables us to send and receive our own messages—in other words, to think and to be aware of our own existence. (See ***Figure 1.1.***)

Blindsight

A particularly interesting phenomenon known as **blindsight** has some implications for our understanding of consciousness (Weiskrantz et al., 1974). This phenomenon suggests that the common belief that perceptions must

---

dualism The belief that the body is physical but the mind (or soul) is not.

monism (*mahn ism*) The belief that the world consists only of matter and energy and that the mind is a phenomenon produced by the workings of the nervous system.

blindsight The ability of a person who cannot see objects in his or her blind field to accurately reach for them while remaining unconscious of perceiving them; caused by damage to the "mammalian" visual system of the brain.

enter consciousness to affect our behavior is incorrect—our behavior can be guided by sensory information of which we are completely unaware.

> Natalie J. had brought her grandfather to see Dr. M., a neuropsychologist. Mr. J.'s stroke had left him almost completely blind; all he could see was a tiny spot in the middle of his visual field. Dr. M. had learned about Mr. J.'s condition from his neurologist and had asked him to come to his laboratory so that he could do some tests for his research project.
>
> Dr. M. helped Mr. J. find a chair and sit down. Mr. J., who walked with the aid of a cane, gave it to his granddaughter to hold for him. "May I borrow that?" asked Dr. M. Natalie nodded and handed it to him. "The phenomenon I'm studying is called blindsight," he said. "Let me see if I can show you what it is.
>
> "Mr. J., please look straight ahead. Keep looking that way, and don't move your eyes or turn your head. I know that you can see a little bit straight ahead of you, and I don't want you to use that piece of vision for what I'm going to ask you to do. Fine. Now, I'd like you to reach out with your right hand and point to what I'm holding."
>
> "But I don't see anything—I'm blind!" said Mr. J., obviously exasperated.
>
> "I know, but please try, anyway."
>
> Mr. J. shrugged his shoulders and pointed. He looked startled when his finger encountered the end of the cane, which Dr. M. was pointing toward him.
>
> "Gramps, how did you do that?" asked Natalie, amazed. "I thought you were blind."
>
> "I am!" he said, emphatically. "It was just luck."
>
> "Let's try it just a couple more times, Mr. J.," said Dr. M. "Keep looking straight ahead. Fine." He reversed the cane, so that the handle was pointing toward Mr. J. "Now I'd like you to grab hold of the cane."
>
> Mr. J. reached out with an open hand and grabbed hold of the cane.
>
> "Good. Now put your hand down, please." He rotated the cane 90 degrees, so that the handle was oriented vertically. "Now reach for it again."
>
> Mr. J. did so. As his arm came up, he turned his wrist so that his hand matched the orientation of the handle, which he grabbed hold of again.
>
> "Good. Thank you, you can put your hand down." Dr. M. turned to Natalie. "I'd like to test your grandfather now, but I'll be glad to talk with you later."

As Dr. M. explained to Natalie afterwards, the brain contains not one but several mechanisms involved in vision. To simplify matters somewhat, let's consider two systems, which evolved at different times. The more primitive one, which resembles the visual system of animals such as fish and frogs, evolved first. The more complex one, which is possessed by mammals, evolved later. This second, "mammalian" system seems to be the one that is responsible for our ability to perceive the world around us. The first, "primitive" visual system, is mainly devoted to controlling eye movements and bringing our attention to sudden movements that occur off to the side of our field of vision.

Mr. J.'s stroke had damaged the mammalian visual system: the visual cortex of the brain and some of the nerve fibers that bring information to it from the eyes. Cases like his show that after the mammalian visual system is damaged, people can use the primitive visual system of their brains to guide hand movements toward an object even though they cannot see what they are reaching for. In other words, visual information can control behavior without producing a conscious sensation. The phenomenon of blindsight suggests that *consciousness is not a general property of all parts of the brain;* some parts of the brain, but not others, play a special role in consciousness. Although we are not sure just where these parts are or exactly how they work, they seem to be related to our ability to communicate—with others and with ourselves. The primitive system, which evolved before the development of consciousness, does not have these connections, so we are not conscious of the visual information it detects. It *does* have connections with those parts of the brain responsible for controlling hand movements. Only the mammalian visual system has direct connections with the parts of the brain responsible for consciousness. (See *Figure 1.2.*)

Split Brains

Studies of humans who have undergone a particular surgical procedure demonstrate dramatically how disconnecting parts of the brain involved with perceptions from parts that are involved with verbal behavior also disconnects them from consciousness. These results suggest that the parts of the brain involved in verbal behavior may be the ones responsible for consciousness.

The surgical procedure is one that has been used for people with very severe epilepsy that cannot be controlled by drugs. In these people, nerve cells in one side of the brain become overactive, and the overactivity is transmitted to the other side of the brain by the corpus callosum. The **corpus callosum** is a large bundle of nerve fibers that connect corresponding parts of one side of the brain with those of the other. Both sides of the brain then engage in wild activity and stimulate each other, causing a generalized epileptic seizure. These seizures can occur many times each day, preventing the patient from leading a normal life. Neurosurgeons discovered that cutting

---

corpus callosum (*core* pus ka **low** sum) The largest commissure of the brain, interconnecting the areas of neocortex on each side of the brain.

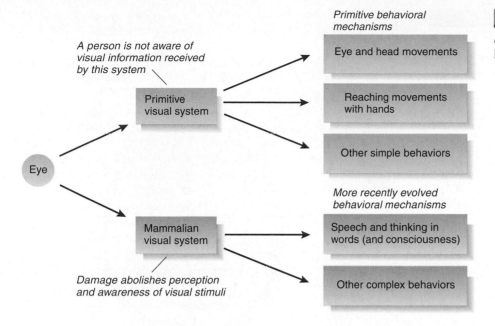

figure 1.2

An explanation of the blindsight phenomenon.

the corpus callosum (the **split-brain operation**) greatly reduced the frequency of the epileptic seizures.

Figure 1.3 shows a drawing of the split-brain operation. We see the brain being sliced down the middle, from front to back, dividing it into its two symmetrical halves. A "window" has been opened in the left side of the brain so that we can see the corpus callosum being cut by the neurosurgeon's special knife. (See *Figure 1.3.*)

Sperry (1966) and Gazzaniga and his associates (Gazzaniga, 1970; Gazzaniga and LeDoux, 1978) have studied these patients extensively. The largest part of the brain consists of two symmetrical parts, called the **cerebral hemispheres,** which receive sensory information from the opposite sides of the body. They also control movements of the opposite sides. The corpus callosum permits the two hemispheres to share information so that each side knows what the other side is perceiving and doing. After the split-brain operation is performed, the two hemispheres are disconnected and operate independently; their sensory mechanisms, memories, and motor systems can no longer exchange information. The effects of these disconnections are not obvious to the casual observer, for the simple reason that only one hemisphere—in most people, the left—controls speech. The right hemisphere of an epileptic person with a split brain appears able to understand verbal instructions reasonably well, but it is totally incapable of producing speech.

Because only one side of the brain can talk about what it is experiencing, people speaking with a person with a split brain are conversing with only one hemisphere: the left. The operations of the right hemisphere are more difficult to detect. Even the patient's left hemisphere has to learn about the independent existence of the right

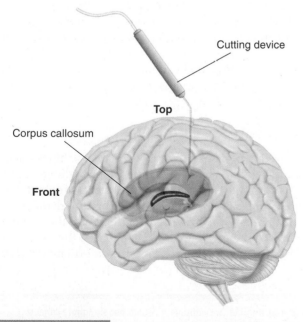

figure 1.3

The split-brain operation. A "window" has been opened in the side of the brain so that we can see the corpus callosum being cut at the midline of the brain.

split-brain operation Brain surgery that is occasionally performed to treat a form of epilepsy; the surgeon cuts the corpus callosum, which connects the two hemispheres of the brain.

cerebral hemispheres The two symmetrical halves of the brain; constitute the major part of the brain.

figure 1.4

Identification of an object in response to an olfactory stimulus by a person with a split brain.

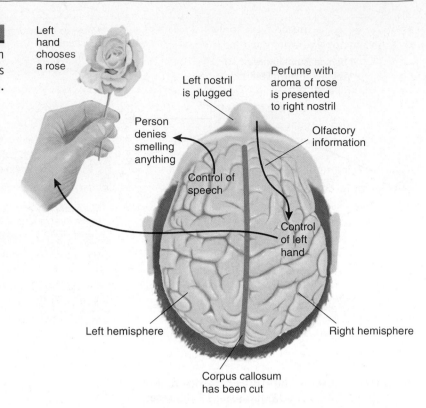

Left hand chooses a rose

Left nostril is plugged

Perfume with aroma of rose is presented to right nostril

Person denies smelling anything

Olfactory information

Control of speech

Control of left hand

Left hemisphere

Right hemisphere

Corpus callosum has been cut

hemisphere. One of the first things that these patients say they notice after the operation is that their left hand seems to have a "mind of its own." For example, patients may find themselves putting down a book held in the left hand, even if they have been reading it with great interest. This conflict occurs because the right hemisphere, which controls the left hand, cannot read and therefore finds the book boring. At other times these patients surprise themselves by making obscene gestures (with the left hand) when they had not intended to. A psychologist once reported that a man with a split brain attempted to beat his wife with one hand and protect her with the other. Did he *really* want to hurt her? Yes and no, I guess.

One exception to the crossed representation of sensory information is the olfactory system. That is, when a person sniffs a flower through the left nostril, only the left brain receives a sensation of the odor. Thus, if the right nostril of a patient with a split brain is closed, leaving only the left nostril open, the patient will be able to tell us what the odors are (Gordon and Sperry, 1969). However, if the odor enters the right nostril, the patient will say that he or she smells nothing. But, in fact, the right brain *has* perceived the odor and *can* identify it. To show that this is so, we ask the patient to smell an odor with the right nostril and then reach for some objects that are hidden from view by a partition. If asked to use the left hand, controlled by the hemisphere that detected the smell, the patient will select the object that corresponds to the odor—a plastic flower for a floral odor, a toy fish for a fishy odor, a model tree for the odor of pine, and so forth. But if asked

to use the right hand, the patient fails the test because the right hand is connected to the left hemisphere, which did not smell the odor. (See *Figure 1.4.*)

The effects of cutting the corpus callosum reinforce the conclusion that we become conscious of something only if information about it is able to reach the parts of the brain responsible for verbal communication, which are located in the left hemisphere. If the information does not reach these parts of the brain, then that information does not reach consciousness. We still know very little about the physiology of consciousness, but studies of people with brain damage are beginning to provide us with some useful insights. This issue is discussed in later chapters.

Unilateral Neglect

The phenomenon described in the case history at the beginning of this chapter—failure to notice things located to a person's left—is known as **unilateral neglect.** Unilateral ("one-sided") neglect is produced by damage to a particular part of the right side of the brain: the cortex of the parietal lobe. (Chapter 3 will describe the location of this region.) The parietal lobe receives information directly

unilateral neglect A syndrome in which people ignore objects located toward their left and the left sides of objects located anywhere; most often caused by damage to the right parietal lobe.

from the skin, the muscles, the joints, the internal organs, and the part of the inner ear that is concerned with balance. Thus, it is concerned with the body and its position. But that is not all; the parietal cortex indirectly receives auditory and visual information as well. Its most important function seems to be to put together information about the movements and location of the parts of the body with the locations of objects in space around us. The right and left parietal cortex handle somewhat different tasks: The left concerns itself with the position of the parts of the body, and the right concerns itself with the three-dimensional space around the body and the contents of that space.

If unilateral neglect simply consisted of blindness in the left side of the visual field and anesthesia of the left side of the body, it would not be nearly as interesting. But individuals with unilateral neglect are neither half blind nor half numb. Under the proper circumstances, they *can* see things located to their left, and they *can* tell when someone touches the left side of their bodies. But normally, they ignore such stimuli and act as if the left side of the world and of their bodies did not exist. In other words, their inattention to things to the left means that they normally do not become conscious of them.

Volpe, LeDoux, and Gazzaniga (1979) presented pairs of visual stimuli to people with unilateral neglect—one stimulus in the left visual field and one stimulus in the right. Invariably, the people reported seeing only the right-hand stimulus. But when the investigators asked the people to say whether or not the two stimuli were identical, they answered correctly, *even though they said that they were unaware of the left-hand stimulus.*

If you think about the story that the chief of neurology told about the man who ate only the right half of a pancake, you will realize that people with unilateral neglect *must* be able to perceive more than the right visual field. Remember that people with unilateral neglect fail to notice not only things to their left but also the *left halves* of things. But to distinguish between the left and right halves of an object, you first have to perceive the entire object—otherwise, how would you know where the middle was?

People with unilateral neglect also demonstrate their unawareness of the left half of things when they draw pictures. For example, when asked to draw a clock, they almost always successfully draw a circle; but then when they fill in the numbers, they scrunch them all in on the right side. Sometimes they simply stop after reaching 6 or 7, and sometimes they write the rest of the numbers underneath the circle. When asked to draw a daisy, they begin with a stem and a leaf or two and then draw all the petals to the right. When asked to draw a bicycle, they draw wheels and then put in spokes, but only on the right.

Bisiach and Luzzatti (1978) demonstrated a similar phenomenon, which suggests that unilateral neglect extends even to a person's own visual imagery. The investigators asked two patients with unilateral neglect to

describe the Piazza del Duomo, a well-known landmark in Milan, the city in which they and the patients lived. They asked the patients to imagine that they were standing at the north end of the piazza and to describe what they saw. The patients duly named the buildings, but only those on the west to their right. Then the investigators asked them to imagine themselves at the south end of the piazza. This time, they named the buildings on the east—again, to their right. Obviously, they knew about *all* of the buildings and their locations, but they visualized them only when the buildings were located in the right side of their (imaginary) visual field.

You might wonder whether damage to the *left* parietal lobe causes unilateral *right* neglect. The answer is yes, but it is very slight, it is difficult to detect, and it seems to be temporary. For all practical purposes, then, there is no right neglect. But why not? The answer is still a mystery. To be sure, people have suggested some possible explanations, but they are still quite speculative. Not until we know a lot more about the brain mechanisms of attention will we be able to understand this discrepancy

interim summary

Understanding Human Consciousness

The mind–body question has puzzled philosophers for many centuries. Modern science has adopted a monistic position—the belief that the world consists of matter and energy and that nonmaterial entities such as minds are not a part of the universe. Studies of the functions of the human nervous system tend to support this position, as two specific examples show. Both phenomena show that brain damage, by damaging conscious brain functions or disconnecting them from the speech mechanisms in the left hemisphere, can reveal the presence of other functions, of which the person is *not* conscious.

Blindsight is a phenomenon seen after partial damage to the "mammalian" visual system on one side of the brain. Although the person is, in the normal meaning of the word, blind to anything presented to part of the visual field, the person can nevertheless reach out and point to objects whose presence he or she is not conscious of. Similarly, when sensory information about a particular object is presented to the right hemisphere of a person who has had a split-brain operation, the person is not aware of the object but can, nevertheless, indicate by movements of the left hand that the object has been perceived. Unilateral neglect—failure to become aware of the left half of objects or items located to a person's left—reveals the existence of brain mechanisms that control our attention to things and hence our ability to become aware of them. These phenomena suggest that consciousness involves operations of the verbal mechanisms of the left hemisphere. Indeed, consciousness may be, in large part, a matter of our "talking to ourselves." Thus, once we understand the language functions of the brain, we may have gone a long way toward understanding how the brain can be conscious of its own existence.

The Nature of Physiological Psychology

The field of physiological psychology grew out of psychology. Indeed, the first textbook of psychology, written by Wilhelm Wundt in the late nineteenth century, was titled *Principles of Physiological Psychology*. In recent years, with the explosion of information in experimental biology, scientists from other disciplines have become prominent contributors to the investigation of the physiology of behavior. The united effort of physiological psychologists, physiologists, and other neuroscientists is due to the realization that the ultimate function of the nervous system is behavior.

When I ask my students what they think the ultimate function of the brain is, they often say "thinking," or "logical reasoning," or "perceiving," or "remembering things." Certainly, the nervous system performs these functions, but they support the primary one: control of movement. The basic function of perception is to inform us of what is happening in our environment so that our behaviors will be adaptive and useful: Perception without the ability to act would be useless. Of course, once perceptual abilities have evolved, they can be used for purposes other than guiding behavior. For example, we can enjoy a beautiful sunset or a great work of art without the perception causing us to do anything in particular. And thinking can often take place without causing any overt behavior. However, the *ability to think* evolved because it permits us to perform complex behaviors that accomplish useful goals. And whereas reminiscing about things that happened in our past can be an enjoyable pastime, the ability to learn and remember evolved—again—because it permitted our ancestors to profit from experience and perform behaviors that were useful to them.

The modern history of investigating the physiology of behavior has been written by psychologists who have combined the experimental methods of psychology with those of physiology and have applied them to the issues that concern all psychologists. Thus, we have studied perceptual processes, control of movement, sleep and waking, reproductive behaviors, ingestive behaviors, emotional behaviors, learning, and language. In recent years we have begun to study the physiology of human pathological conditions, such as addictions and mental disorders.

All of these topics are discussed in subsequent chapters of this book.

The Goals of Research

The goal of all scientists is to explain the phenomena they study. But what do we mean by *explain*? Scientific explanation takes two forms: generalization and reduction. All scientists deal with **generalization.** For example, psychologists explain particular instances of behavior as examples of general laws, which they deduce from their experiments. For instance, most psychologists would explain a pathologically strong fear of dogs as an example of a particular form of learning called *classical conditioning*. Presumably, the person was frightened earlier in life by a dog. An unpleasant stimulus was paired with the sight of the animal (perhaps the person was knocked down by an exuberant dog or was attacked by a vicious one), and the subsequent sight of dogs evokes the earlier response—fear.

Most physiologists use an additional approach to explanation: **reduction.** They explain complex phenomena in terms of simpler ones. For example, they may explain the movement of a muscle in terms of the changes in the membranes of muscle cells, the entry of particular chemicals, and the interactions among protein molecules within these cells. By contrast, a molecular biologist would explain these events in terms of forces that bind various molecules together and cause various parts of the molecules to be attracted to one another. In turn, the job of an atomic physicist is to describe matter and energy themselves and to account for the various forces found in nature. Practitioners of each branch of science use reduction to call on sets of more elementary generalizations to explain the phenomena they study.

The task of the physiological psychologist is to explain behavior by studying the physiological processes that control it. But physiological psychologists cannot simply be reductionists. It is not enough to observe behaviors and correlate them with physiological events that occur at the same time. Identical behaviors may occur for different reasons and thus may be initiated by different physiological mechanisms. Therefore, we must understand "psychologically" why a particular behavior occurs before we can understand what physiological events made it occur.

---

generalization A type of scientific explanation; a general conclusion based on many observations of similar phenomena.

reduction A type of scientific explanation; a phenomenon is described in terms of the more elementary processes that underlie it.

Let me provide a specific example: Mice, like many other mammals, often build nests. Behavioral observations show that mice will build nests under two conditions: when the air temperature is low and when the animal is pregnant. A nonpregnant mouse will build a nest only if the weather is cool, whereas a pregnant mouse will build one regardless of the temperature. The same behavior occurs for different reasons. In fact, nest-building behavior is controlled by two different physiological mechanisms. Nest building can be studied as a behavior related to the process of temperature regulation, or it can be studied in the context of parental behavior. Although the same set of brain mechanisms will control the movements that a mouse makes in building a nest in both cases, these mechanisms will be activated by different parts of the brain. One part receives information from the body's temperature detectors, and the other part is influenced by hormones that are present in the body after a mouse has given birth.

Sometimes, physiological mechanisms can tell us something about psychological processes. This relationship is particularly true of complex phenomena such as language, memory, and mood, which are poorly understood psychologically. For example, damage to a specific part of the brain can cause very specific impairments in a person's language abilities. The nature of these impairments suggests how these abilities are organized. When the damage involves a brain region that is important in analyzing speech sounds, it also produces deficits in spelling. This finding suggests that the ability to recognize a spoken word and the ability to spell it call on related brain mechanisms. Damage to another region of the brain can produce extreme difficulty in reading unfamiliar words by sounding them out, but it does not impair the person's ability to read words with which he or she is already familiar. This finding suggests that reading comprehension can take two routes: one that is related to speech sounds and another that is primarily a matter of visual recognition of whole words.

In practice, the research efforts of physiological psychologists involve both forms of explanation: generalization and reduction. Ideas for experiments are stimulated by the investigator's knowledge both of psychological generalizations about behavior and of physiological mechanisms. A good physiological psychologist must therefore be both a good psychologist *and* a good physiologist.

Biological Roots of Physiological Psychology

Study of (or speculations about) the physiology of behavior has its roots in antiquity. Because its movement was necessary for life, and because emotions caused it to beat more strongly, many ancient cultures including the Egyptian, Indian, and Chinese, considered the heart to be the seat of thought and emotions. The ancient Greeks did, too, but Hippocrates (460–370 B.C.) concluded that this role should be assigned to the brain. Except for the somewhat flowery language, the following extract from *On the Sacred Disease* (epilepsy) could have been written by a modern neurobiologist:

> Men ought to know that from nothing else but the brain come joys, delights, laughter and sports, and sorrows, griefs, despondency, and lamentations. And by this, in an especial manner, we acquire wisdom and knowledge, and see and hear and know what are foul and what are fair, what are bad and what are good, what are sweet, and what are unsavory. . . . And by the same organ we become mad and delirious, and fears and terrors assail us. . . . All these things we endure from the brain when it is not healthy (Hippocrates, 1952 translation, p. 159).

Not all ancient Greek scholars agreed with Hippocrates. Aristotle did not; he thought the brain served to cool the passions of the heart. But Galen (A.D. 130–200), who had the greatest respect for Aristotle, concluded that Aristotle's role for the brain was "utterly absurd, since in that case Nature would not have placed the encephalon so far from the heart, . . . and she would not have attached the sources of all the senses [the sensory nerves] to it (Galen, 1968 translation, p. 387). Galen thought enough of the brain to dissect and study the brains of cattle, sheep, pigs, cats, dogs, weasels, monkeys, and apes (Finger, 1994).

René Descartes, a seventeenth-century French philosopher and mathematician, has been called the father of modern philosophy. Although he was not a biologist, his speculations concerning the roles of the mind and brain in the control of behavior provide a good starting point in the modern history of physiological psychology. Descartes assumed that the world was a purely mechanical entity that, once having been set in motion by God, ran its course without divine interference. Thus, to understand the world, one had only to understand how it was constructed. To Descartes, animals were mechanical devices; their behavior was controlled by environmental stimuli. His view of the human body was much the same: It was a machine. As Descartes observed, some movements of the human body were automatic and involuntary. For example, if a person's finger touched a hot object, the arm would immediately withdraw from the source of stimulation. Reactions like this did not require participation of the mind; they occurred automatically. Descartes called these actions **reflexes** (from the Latin *reflectere,* "to bend back upon

---

reflex An automatic, stereotyped movement that is produced as the direct result of a stimulus.

figure   1.5

Descartes's explanation of a reflex action to a painful stimulus.

itself"). Energy coming from the outside source would be reflected back through the nervous system to the muscles, which would contract. The term is still in use today, but, of course, we explain the operation of a reflex differently. (See *Figure 1.5.*)

Like most philosophers of his time, Descartes was a dualist; he believed that each person possessed a mind— a uniquely human attribute that was not subject to the laws of the universe. But his thinking differed from that of his predecessors in one important way: He was the first to suggest that a link exists between the human mind and its purely physical housing, the brain. He believed that the mind controlled the movements of the body, while the body, through its sense organs, supplied the mind with information about what was happening in the environment. In particular, he hypothesized that this interaction took place in the pineal body, a small organ situated on top of the brain stem, buried beneath the cerebral hemispheres. He noted that the brain contained hollow chambers (the *ventricles*) that were filled with fluid, and he hypothesized that this fluid was under pressure. When the

model   A mathematical or physical analogy for a physiological process; for example, computers have been used as models for various functions of the brain.

mind decided to perform an action, it tilted the pineal body in a particular direction like a little joystick, causing fluid to flow from the brain into the appropriate set of nerves. This flow of fluid caused the same muscles to inflate and move. (See *Figure 1.6.*)

As a young man, René Descartes was greatly impressed by the moving statues in the grottoes of the Royal Gardens, just west of Paris (Jaynes, 1970). He was fascinated by the hidden mechanisms that caused the statues to move when visitors stepped on hidden plates. For example, as a visitor approached a bronze statue of Diana, bathing in a pool of water, she would flee and hide behind a bronze rose bush. If the visitor pursued her, an imposing statue of Neptune would rise up and bar the way with his trident.

These devices served as models for Descartes in theorizing about how the body worked. The pressurized water of the moving statues was replaced by pressurized fluid in the ventricles; the pipes by nerves; the cylinders by muscles; and finally, the hidden valves by the pineal body. This story illustrates one of the first times that a technological device was used as a model for explaining how the nervous system works. In science a **model** is a relatively simple system that works on known principles and is able to do at least some of the things that a more complex system can do. For example, when scientists discovered that elements of the nervous system communicate by means of electrical impulses, researchers developed models of the brain based on telephone switchboards and, more recently, computers. Abstract models, which are

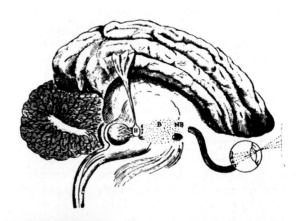

figure   1.6

Descartes's theory. Descartes believed that the "soul" (what we would today call the *mind*) controlled the movements of the muscles through its influence on the pineal body. His explanation is modeled on the mechanism that animated statues in the Royal Gardens near Paris.

(Courtesy of Historical Pictures Service, Chicago.)

completely mathematical in their properties, have also been developed.

Descartes's model was useful because, unlike purely philosophical speculations, it could be tested experimentally. In fact, it did not take long for biologists to prove that Descartes was wrong. For example, Luigi Galvani, a seventeenth-century Italian physiologist, found that electrical stimulation of a frog's nerve caused contraction of the muscle to which it was attached. Contraction occurred even when the nerve and muscle were detached from the rest of the body, so the ability of the muscle to contract and the ability of the nerve to send a message to the muscle were characteristics of these tissues themselves. Thus, the brain did not inflate muscles by directing pressurized fluid through the nerve. Galvani's experiment prompted others to study the nature of the message transmitted by the nerve and the means by which muscles contracted. The results of these efforts gave rise to an accumulation of knowledge about the physiology of behavior.

One of the most important figures in the development of experimental physiology was Johannes Müller, a nineteenth-century German physiologist. Müller was a forceful advocate of the application of experimental techniques to physiology. Previously, the activities of most natural scientists had been limited to observation and classification. Although these activities are essential, Müller insisted that major advances in our understanding of the workings of the body would be achieved only by experimentally removing or isolating animals' organs, testing their responses to various chemicals, and otherwise altering the environment to see how the organs responded. (See *Figure 1.7*) His most important contribution to the study of the physiology of behavior was his **doctrine of specific nerve energies.** Müller observed that although all nerves carry the same basic message—an electrical impulse—we perceive the messages of different nerves in different ways. For example, messages carried by the optic nerves produce sensations of visual images, and those carried by the auditory nerves produce sensations of sounds. How can different sensations arise from the same basic message?

The answer is that the messages occur in different channels. The portion of the brain that receives messages from the optic nerves interprets the activity as visual stimulation, even if the nerves are actually stimulated mechanically. (For example, when we rub our eyes, we see flashes of light.) Because different parts of the brain receive messages from different nerves, the brain must be functionally divided: Some parts perform some functions, while other parts perform others.

Müller's advocacy of experimentation and the logical deductions from his doctrine of specific nerve energies set the stage for performing experiments directly on the

figure 1.7

Johannes Müller (1801–1858).
(Courtesy of National Library of Medicine.)

brain. Indeed, Pierre Flourens, a nineteenth-century French physiologist, did just that. Flourens removed various parts of animals' brains and observed their behavior. By seeing what the animal could no longer do, he could infer the function of the missing portion of the brain. This method is called **experimental ablation** (from the Latin *ablatus,* "carried away"). Flourens claimed to have discovered the regions of the brain that control heart rate and breathing, purposeful movements, and visual and auditory reflexes.

Soon after Flourens performed his experiments, Paul Broca, a French surgeon, applied the principle of experimental ablation to the human brain. Of course, he did not intentionally remove parts of human brains to see how they worked but observed the behavior of people whose brains had been damaged by strokes. In 1861 he performed an autopsy on the brain of a man who had had a stroke that resulted in the loss of the ability to speak. Broca's observations led him to conclude that a portion

doctrine of specific nerve energies Müller's conclusion that because all nerve fibers carry the same type of message, sensory information must be specified by the particular nerve fibers that are active.

experimental ablation The research method in which the function of a part of the brain is inferred by observing the behaviors an animal can no longer perform after that part is damaged.

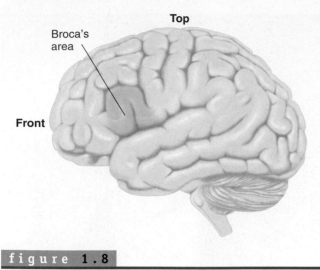

figure 1.8

Broca's area, a region of the brain named for French surgeon Paul Broca. Broca discovered that damage to a part of the left side of the brain disrupts a person's ability to speak.

of the cerebral cortex on the left side of the brain performs functions that are necessary for speech. (See *Figure 1.8.*) Other physicians soon obtained evidence supporting his conclusions. As you will learn in Chapter 15, the control of speech is not localized in a particular region of the brain. Indeed, speech requires many different functions, which are organized throughout the brain. Nonetheless, the method of experimental ablation remains important to our understanding of the brains of both humans and laboratory animals.

As I mentioned earlier, Luigi Galvani used electricity to demonstrate that muscles contain the source of the energy that powers their contractions. In 1870, German physiologists Gustav Fritsch and Eduard Hitzig used electrical stimulation as a tool for understanding the physiology of the brain. They applied weak electrical current to the exposed surface of a dog's brain and observed the effects of the stimulation. They found that stimulation of different portions of a specific region of the brain caused contraction of specific muscles on the opposite side of the body. We now refer to this region as the *primary motor cortex,* and we know that nerve cells there communicate directly with those that cause muscular contractions. We also know that other regions of the brain communicate with the primary motor cortex and thus control behaviors. For example, the region that Broca found necessary for speech communicates with, and controls, the portion of the primary motor cortex that controls the muscles of the lips, tongue, and throat, which we use to speak.

One of the most brilliant contributors to nineteenth-century science was the German physicist and physiologist Hermann von Helmholtz. Helmholtz devised a mathematical formulation of the law of conservation of energy, invented the ophthalmoscope (used to examine the retina of the eye), devised an important and influential theory of color vision and color blindness, and studied audition, music, and many physiological processes. Although Helmholtz had studied under Müller, he opposed Müller's belief that human organs are endowed with a vital nonmaterial force that coordinates their operations. Helmholtz believed that all aspects of physiology are mechanistic, subject to experimental investigation.

Helmholtz was also the first scientist to attempt to measure the speed of conduction through nerves. Scientists had previously believed that such conduction was identical to the conduction that occurs in wires, traveling at approximately the speed of light. But Helmholtz found that neural conduction was much slower—only about 90 feet per second. This measurement proved that neural conduction was more than a simple electrical message, as we will see in Chapter 2.

Twentieth-century developments in experimental physiology include many important inventions, such as sensitive amplifiers to detect weak electrical signals, neurochemical techniques to analyze chemical changes within and between cells, and histological techniques to see cells and their constituents. Because these developments belong to the modern era, they are discussed in detail in subsequent chapters.

i n t e r i m
s u m m a r y

The Nature of Physiological Psychology

All scientists hope to explain natural phenomena. In this context the term *explanation* has two basic meanings: generalization and reduction. Generalization refers to the classification of phenomena according to their essential features so that general laws can be formulated. For example, observing that gravitational attraction is related to the mass of two bodies and to the distance between them helps to explain the movement of planets. Reduction refers to the description of phenomena in terms of more basic physical processes. For example, gravitation can be explained in terms of forces and subatomic particles.

Physiological psychologists use both generalization and reduction to explain behavior. In large part, generalizations use the traditional methods of psychology. Reduction explains behaviors in terms of physiological events within the body—

primarily within the nervous system. Thus, physiological psychology builds on the tradition of both experimental psychology and experimental physiology.

A dualist, René Descartes, proposed a model of the brain on the basis of hydraulically activated statues. His model stimulated observations that produced important discoveries. The results of Galvani's experiments eventually led to an understanding of the nature of the message transmitted by nerves between the brain and the sensory organs and the muscles. Müller's doctrine of specific nerve energies paved the way for study of the functions of specific parts of the brain, through the methods of experimental ablation and electrical stimulation. Hermann von Helmholtz, a former student of Müller's, insisted that all aspects of human physiology were subject to the laws of nature. He also discovered that the conduction through nerves was slower than the conduction of electricity, which means that it was a physiological phenomenon.

Natural Selection and Evolution

Müller's insistence that biology must be an experimental science provided the starting point for an important tradition. However, other biologists continued to observe, classify, and think about what they saw, and some of them arrived at valuable conclusions. The most important of these scientists was Charles Darwin. (See *Figure 1.9.*) Darwin formulated the principles of *natural selection* and *evolution,* which revolutionized biology.

Functionalism and the Inheritance of Traits

Darwin's theory emphasized that all of an organism's characteristics—its structure, its coloration, its behavior—have functional significance. For example, the strong talons and sharp beaks that eagles possess permit the birds to catch and eat prey. Caterpillars that eat green leaves are themselves green, and their color makes it difficult for birds to see them against their usual background. Mother mice construct nests, which keep their offspring warm and out of harm's way. Obviously, the behavior itself is not inherited—how can it be? What *is* inherited is a brain that causes the behavior to occur. Thus, Darwin's theory gave rise to **functionalism,** a belief that characteristics of living organisms perform useful functions. So to understand the physiological basis of various behaviors, we must first

figure 1.9

Charles Darwin (1809–1882). His theory of evolution revolutionized biology and strongly influenced early psychologists.
(North Wind Picture Archives.)

understand what these behaviors accomplish. We must therefore understand something about the natural history of the species being studied so that the behaviors can be seen in context.

To understand the workings of a complex piece of machinery, we should know what its functions are. This principle is just as true for a living organism as it is for a mechanical device. However, an important difference exists between machines and organisms: Machines have inventors who had a purpose when they designed them, whereas organisms are the result of a long series of accidents. Thus, strictly speaking, we cannot say that any physiological mechanisms of living organisms have a *purpose.* But they do have *functions,* and these we can try to

functionalism The principle that the best way to understand a biological phenomenon (a behavior or a physiological structure) is to try to understand its useful functions for the organism.

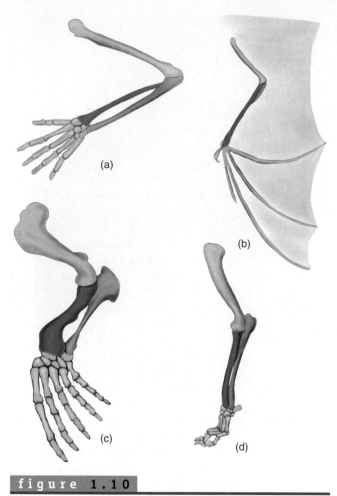

Bones of the forelimb: (a) human, (b) bat, (c) whale, (d) dog. Through the process of natural selection these bones have been adapted to suit many different functions.

determine. For example, the forelimbs shown in Figure 1.10 are adapted for different uses in different species of mammals. (See *Figure 1.10.*)

A good example of the functional analysis of an adaptive trait was demonstrated in an experiment by Blest (1957). Certain species of moths and butterflies have spots on their wings that resemble eyes—particularly the eyes of predators such as owls. (See *Figure 1.11.*) These insects normally rely on camouflage for protection; the backs of their wings, when folded, are colored like the bark of a tree. However, when a bird approaches, the insect's wings flip open, and the hidden eyespots are suddenly displayed.

natural selection The process by which inherited traits that confer a selective advantage (increase an animal's likelihood to live and reproduce) become more prevalent in a population.

The bird then tends to fly away rather than eat the insect. Blest performed an experiment to see whether the eyespots on a moth's or butterfly's wings really disturbed birds that saw them. He placed mealworms on different backgrounds and counted how many worms the birds ate. Indeed, when the worms were placed on a background that contained eyespots, the birds tended to avoid them.

Darwin formulated his theory of evolution to explain the means by which species acquired their adaptive characteristics. The cornerstone of this theory is the principle of **natural selection.** Darwin noted that members of a species were not all identical and that some of the differences they exhibited were inherited by their offspring. If an individual's characteristics permit it to reproduce more successfully, some of the individual's offspring will inherit the favorable characteristics and will themselves produce more offspring. As a result, the characteristics will become more prevalent in that species. He observed that animal breeders were able to develop strains that possessed particular traits by mating together only animals that possessed the desired traits. If *artificial selection,* controlled by animal breeders, could produce so many varieties of dogs, cats, and livestock, perhaps *natural selection* could be responsible for the development of species. Of course, it was the natural environment, not the hand of the animal breeder, that shaped the process of evolution.

Darwin and his fellow scientists knew nothing about the mechanism by which the principle of natural selection works. In fact, the principles of molecular genetics were not discovered until the middle of the twentieth century. Briefly, here is how the process works: Every sexually

f i g u r e   1 . 1 1

The owl butterfly. This butterfly displays its eyespots when approached by a bird. The bird usually will fly away.
(A. Cosmos Blank/Photo Researchers Inc.)

figure   1.12

An example of a maladaptive trait. Most mutations do not produce selective advantages, but those that do are passed on to future generations.

(J. H. Robinson/Animals Animals.)

reproducing multicellular organism consists of a large number of cells, each of which contains chromosomes. Chromosomes are large, complex molecules that contain the recipes for producing the proteins that cells need to grow and to perform their functions. In essence, the chromosomes contain the blueprints for the construction (that is, the embryological development) of a particular member of a particular species. If the plans are altered, a different organism is produced.

The plans do get altered; mutations occur from time to time. **Mutations** are accidental changes in the chromosomes of sperms or eggs that join together and develop into new organisms. For example, cosmic radiation might strike a chromosome in a cell of an animal's testis or ovary, thus producing a mutation that affects that animal's offspring. Most mutations are deleterious; the offspring either fails to survive or survives with some sort of deficit. (See *Figure 1.12.*) However, a small percentage of mutations are beneficial and confer a **selective advantage** to the organism that possesses them. That is, the animal is more likely than other members of its species to live long enough to reproduce and hence to pass on its chromosomes to its own offspring. Many different kinds of traits can confer a selective advantage: resistance to a particular disease, the ability to digest new kinds of food, more effective weapons for defense or for procurement of prey, and even a more attractive appearance to members of the opposite sex (after all, one must reproduce in order to pass on one's chromosomes).

Naturally, the traits that can be altered by mutations are physical ones; chromosomes make proteins, which

affect the structure and chemistry of cells. But the *effects* of these physical alterations can be seen in an animal's behavior. Thus, the process of natural selection can act on behavior indirectly. For example, if a particular mutation results in changes in the brain that cause a small animal to stop moving and freeze when it perceives a novel stimulus, that animal is more likely to escape undetected when a predator passes nearby. This tendency makes the animal more likely to survive and produce offspring, thus passing on its genes to future generations.

Other mutations are not immediately favorable, but because they do not put their possessors at a disadvantage, they are inherited by at least some members of the species. As a result of thousands of such mutations, the members of a particular species possess a variety of genes and are all at least somewhat different from one another. Variety is a definite advantage for a species. Different environments provide optimal habitats for different kinds of organisms. When the environment changes, species must adapt or run the risk of becoming extinct. If some members of the species possess assortments of genes that provide characteristics permitting them to adapt to the new environment, their offspring will survive, and the species will continue.

An understanding of the principle of natural selection plays some role in the thinking of every scientist who undertakes research in physiological psychology. Some researchers explicitly consider the genetic mechanisms of various behaviors and the physiological processes upon which these behaviors depend. Others are concerned with comparative aspects of behavior and its physiological basis; they compare the nervous systems of animals from a variety of species to make hypotheses about the evolution of brain structure and the behavioral capacities that correspond to this evolutionary development. But even though many researchers are not directly involved with the problem of evolution, the principle of natural selection guides the thinking of physiological psychologists. We ask ourselves what the selective advantage of a particular trait might be. We think about how nature might have used a physiological mechanism that already existed to perform more complex functions in more complex organisms. When we entertain hypotheses, we ask ourselves whether a particular explanation makes sense in an evolutionary perspective.

mutation A change in the genetic information contained in the chromosomes of sperms or eggs, which can be passed on to an organism's offspring; provides genetic variability.

selective advantage A characteristic of an organism that permits it to produce more than the average number of offspring of its species.

figure 1.13

Evolution of vertebrate species.
(Redrawn with permission from Carroll, R. Vertebrate Paleontology and Evolution. New York: W. H. Freeman, 1988.)

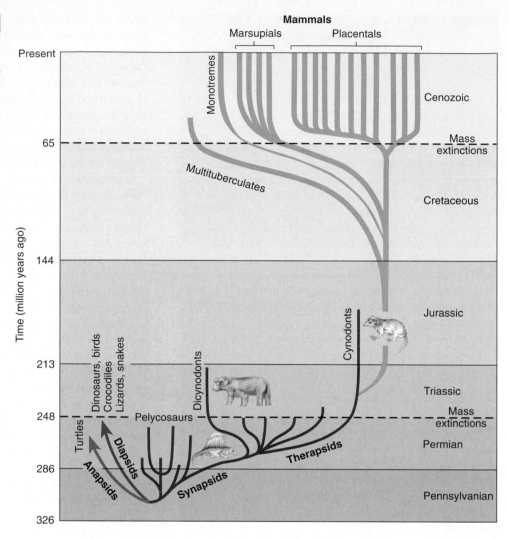

Evolution of the Human Species

To *evolve* means to develop gradually (from the Latin *evolvere*, "to unroll"). The process of **evolution** is a gradual change in the structure and physiology of plant and animal species as a result of natural selection. New species evolve when organisms develop novel characteristics that can take advantage of unexploited opportunities in the environment.

The first vertebrates to emerge from the sea—some 360 million years ago—were amphibians. In fact, amphibians have not entirely left the sea; they still lay their eggs in water, and the larvae that hatch from them have gills and only later transform into adults with air-breathing lungs. Seventy million years later, the first reptiles appeared. Reptiles had a considerable advantage over amphibians: Their eggs, enclosed in a shell just porous enough to permit the developing embryo to breathe, could be laid on land. Thus, reptiles could inhabit regions away from bodies of water, and they could bury their eggs where predators would be less likely to find them. Reptiles soon divided into three lines: the *anapsids,* the ancestors of today's tur-

tles; the *diapsids,* the ancestors of dinosaurs, birds, lizards, crocodiles, and snakes; and the *synapsids,* the ancestors of today's mammals. One group of synapsids, the *therapsids,* became the dominant land animal during the Permian period. Then, about 248 million years ago, the end of the Permian period was marked by a mass extinction. Dust from a catastrophic series of volcanic eruptions in present-day Siberia darkened the sky, cooled the earth, and wiped out approximately 95 percent of all animal species. Among those that survived was a small therapsid known as a *cynodont*—the direct ancestor of the mammal, which first appeared about 220 million years ago. (See *Figure 1.13.*)

The earliest mammals were small nocturnal predators that fed on insects. Their eyesight was poorer than that of the cynodonts from which they evolved, but their hear-

evolution A gradual change in the structure and physiology of plant and animal species—generally producing more complex organisms—as a result of natural selection.

ing was better. The middle ear of amphibians and reptiles contains a single tiny bone, the stapes ("stirrup"), which transmits sound vibrations to the receptive organ for hearing located in the inner ear. As a result of a series of mutations, the earliest mammals evolved a jaw that did away with two of the bones found in the jaws of reptiles. Rather than becoming altogether lost, these bones became incorporated into the mammalian middle ear. The chain of three tiny bones (the *ossicles*) in the middle ear makes it possible for mammals to hear very high frequencies. Presumably, this ability enabled the earliest mammals to hear sounds made by insects and prey on them at night, when larger predators could not see them. (See *Figure 1.14.*)

Mammals (and the other warm-blooded animals, birds) were only a modest success for many millions of years. Dinosaurs ruled, and mammals had to remain small and inconspicuous to avoid the large variety of agile and voracious predators. Then, around 65 million years ago, another mass extinction occurred. An enormous meteorite struck the Yucatan peninsula of present-day Mexico, producing a cloud of dust that destroyed many species, including the dinosaurs. Small, nocturnal mammals survived the cold and dark because they were equipped with insulating fur and a mechanism for maintaining their body temperature. The void left by the extinction of so many large herbivores and carnivores provided the opportunity for mammals to expand into new ecological niches, and expand they did.

The climate of the early Cenozoic period, which followed the mass extinction at the end of the Cretaceous period, was much warmer than it is today. Tropical forests covered much of the land areas, and in these forests our most direct ancestors, the primates, evolved. The first primates, like the first mammals, were small and preyed on insects and small cold-blooded vertebrates such as lizards and frogs. They had grasping hands that permitted them to climb about in small branches of the forest. Over time, larger species developed, with larger, forward-facing eyes (and the brains to analyze what the eyes saw), which facilitated arboreal locomotion and the capture of prey.

Plants evolved as well as animals. Dispersal of seeds is a problem inherent in forest life; if a tree's seeds fall at its base, they will be shaded by the parent and will not grow. Thus, natural selection favored trees that encased their seeds in sweet, nutritious fruit that would be eaten by animals and dropped on the ground some distance away, undigested, in the animals feces. (The feces even served to fertilize the young plants.) The evolution of fruit-bearing trees provided an opportunity for fruit-eating primates. In fact, the original advantage of color vision was probably the ability to discriminate ripe fruit from green leaves and eat the fruit before it spoiled—or some other animals got to it first. And because fruit is such a nutritious form of food, its availability provided an opportunity that could be exploited by larger primates, which were able to travel farther in quest of food.

The first *hominids* (humanlike apes) appeared in Africa. They appeared not in dense tropical forests, but in drier woodlands and in the savanna—vast areas of grasslands studded with clumps of trees and populated by large herbivorous animals and the carnivores that preyed on them. Our fruit-eating ancestors continued to eat fruit, of course, but they evolved characteristics that enabled them to gather roots and tubers as well, to hunt and kill game,

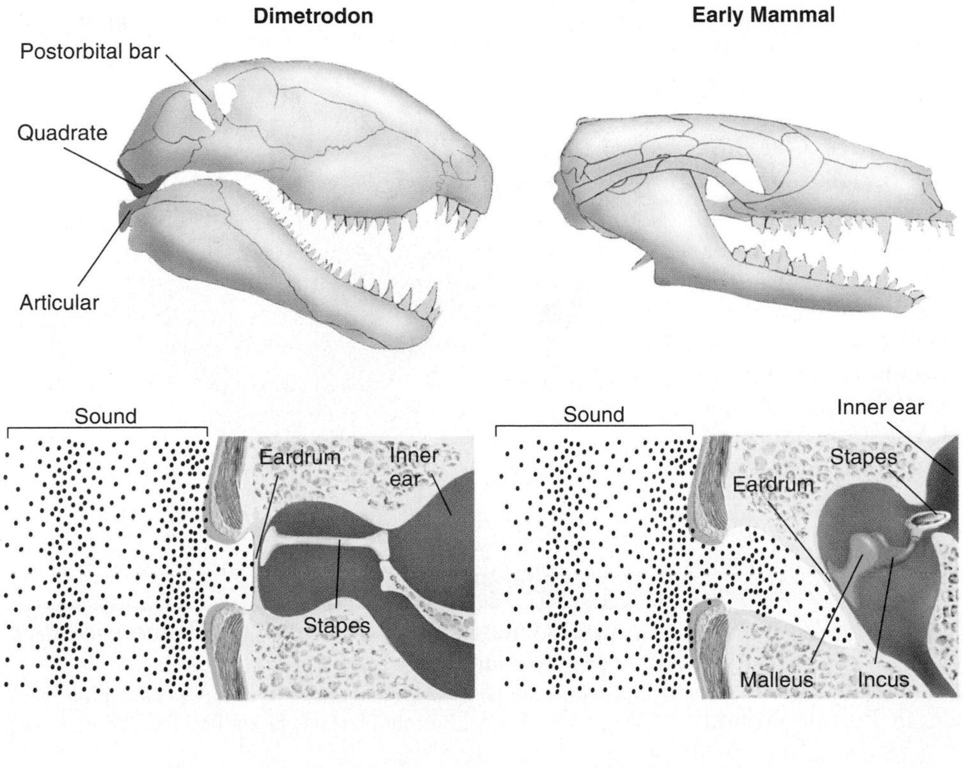

Dimetrodon

Postorbital bar

Quadrate

Articular

Early Mammal

Sound

Eardrum

Inner ear

Stapes

Sound

Inner ear

Stapes

Eardrum

Malleus   Incus

figure 1.14

The evolution of the mammalian middle ear bones (ossicles). The quadrate and articular bones of the reptilian jaw became the incus and the malleus.

(Adapted from Gould, S. J. *The Book of Life*. New York: W. W. Norton, 1993).

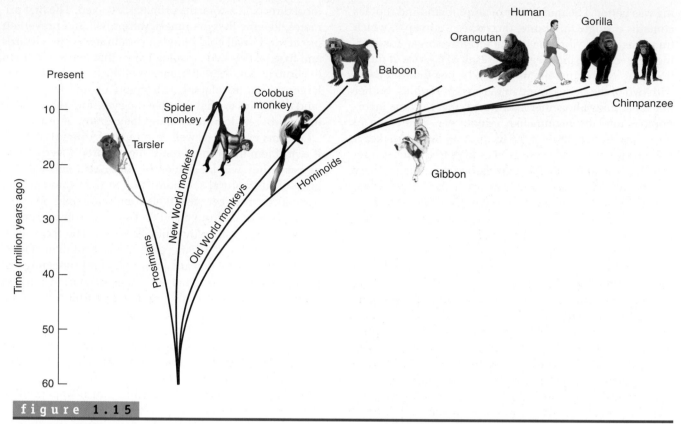

figure **1.15**

Evolution of primate species.

(Redrawn with permission from Lewin, R. *Human Evolution: An Illustrated Introduction,* 3rd ed. Boston: Blackwell Scientific Publications, 1993.)

and to defend themselves against other predators. They made tools that could be used to hunt, produce clothing, and construct dwellings; they discovered the many uses of fire; they domesticated dogs, which greatly increased their ability to hunt and helped warn of attacks by predators; and they developed the ability to communicate symbolically, by means of spoken words.

Figure 1.15 shows the primate family tree. Our closest living relatives—the only hominids besides ourselves who have survived—are the chimpanzees, gorillas, and orangutans. DNA analysis shows that genetically, there is very little difference between these four species. (See *Figure 1.15.*) For example, humans and chimpanzees share 98.8 percent of their DNA. (See *Figure 1.16.*)

The first hominid to leave Africa did so around 1.7 million years ago. This species, *Homo erectus* ("upright man"), scattered across Europe and Asia. One branch of *Homo erectus* appears to be the ancestor of *Homo neanderthalis,* which inhabited Western Europe between 120,000 and 30,000 years ago. Neanderthals resembled modern humans. They made tools out of stone and wood and discovered the use of fire. Our own species, *Homo sapiens,* evolved in East Africa around 100,000 years ago. They migrated to other parts of Africa and out of Africa to Asia, Polynesia, Australia, Europe, and the Americas. They encountered the Neanderthals in Europe around

40,000 years ago and coexisted with them for approximately 10,000 years. Eventually, the Neanderthals disappeared—perhaps through interbreeding with *Homo sapiens,* perhaps through competition for resources. Scientists have

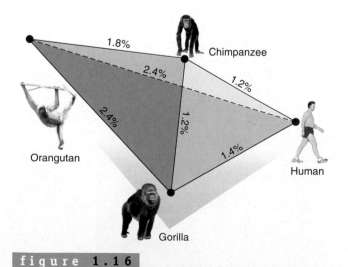

figure **1.16**

A pyramid illustrating the percentage differences in DNA among the four major species of hominids.

(Redrawn with permission from Lewin, R. *Human Evolution: An Illustrated Introduction.* Boston: Blackwell Scientific Publications, 1984.)

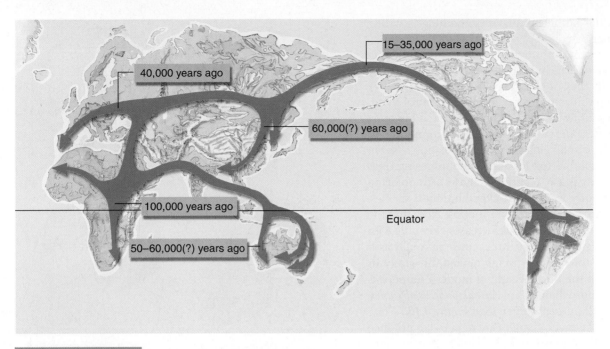

figure   1.17

Proposed migration routes of *Homo sapiens* after evolution of the species in East Africa. (Redrawn with permission from Cavalli-Sforza, L. L. Genes, peoples and languages. *Scientific American,* Nov. 1991, p. 75.)

not found evidence for warlike conflict between the two species. (See *Figure 1.17.*)

Evolution of Large Brains

Humans possessed several characteristics that enabled them to compete with other species. Their agile hands enabled them to make and use tools. Their excellent color vision helped them to spot ripe fruit, game animals, and dangerous predators. Their mastery of fire enabled them to cook food, provide warmth, and frighten nocturnal predators. Their upright posture and bipedalism made it possible for them to walk long distances efficiently, with their eyes far enough from the ground to see long distances across the plains. Bipedalism also permitted them to carry tools and food with them, which meant that they could bring fruit, roots, and pieces of meat back to their tribe. Their linguistic abilities enabled them to combine the collective knowledge of all the members of the tribe, to make plans, to pass information on to subsequent generations, and to establish complex civilizations that established their status as the dominant species. All of these characteristics required a larger brain.

A large brain requires a large skull, and an upright posture limits the size of a woman's birth canal. A newborn baby's head is about as large as it can be. As it is, the birth of a baby is much more arduous than the birth of mammals with proportionally smaller heads, including those of our closest primate relatives. Because a baby's brain is not large or complex enough to perform the physical and

intellectual abilities of an adult, it must continue to grow after the baby is born. In fact, all mammals (and all birds, for that matter) require parental care for a period of time while the nervous system develops. (In contrast, fish and reptiles resemble small adults and are able to move around and navigate on their own as soon as they hatch.) The fact that young mammals (particularly young humans) are guaranteed to be exposed to the adults who care for them means that a period of apprenticeship is possible. Consequently, the evolutionary process did not have to produce a brain with specialized circuits that performed specialized tasks. Instead, it could simply produce a larger brain with an abundance of neural circuits that could be modified by experience. Adults would nourish and protect their offspring and provide them with the skills they would need as adults. Some specialized circuits were necessary, of course (for example, those involved in analyzing the complex sounds we use for speech), but by and large, the brain is a general-purpose, programmable computer.

How does the human brain compare with the brains of other animals? In absolute size, our brains are dwarfed by those of elephants or whales. However, we might expect such large animals to have large brains to match their large bodies. Indeed, the human brain makes up 2.3 percent of our total body weight, while the elephant brain makes up only 0.2 percent of the animal's total body weight, which makes our brains seem very large in comparison. However, the shrew, which weighs only 7.5 g, has a brain that weighs 0.25 g, or 3.3 percent of its total body weight. Certainly, the shrew brain is much less complex than the human brain, so something is wrong with this comparison.

The answer is that although bigger bodies require bigger brains, the size of the brain does not have to go up proportionally with that of the body. For example, larger muscles do not require more nerve cells to control them. What counts, as far as intellectual ability goes, is having a brain with plenty of nerve cells that are not committed to moving muscles or analyzing sensory information—nerve cells that are available for learning, remembering, reasoning, and making plans. Figure 1.18 shows a graph of the brain sizes and body weights of several hominid species, including the ancestors of our own species. Note that the brain size of nonhuman hominids increases very little with size: A gorilla weighs almost three times as much as a chimpanzee, but their brains weigh almost the same. In contrast, although the body weight of modern humans is only 29 percent more than that of *Australopithecus africanus,* our brains are 242 percent larger. (See *Figure 1.18.*)

What types of genetic changes are required to produce a larger brain? This question will be addressed in more detail in Chapter 3, but the most important principle appears to be a slowing of the process of maturation, allowing more time for growth. This phenomenon is known as **neoteny** (roughly translated as "extended youth"). The brains of newborn mammals are larger than those of humans, relative to their body weight. After birth, the body grows proportionally faster than the brain. However, the mature human head and brain retain some infantile characteristics, including their disproportionate size.

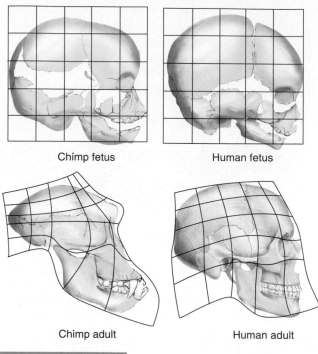

Chimp fetus Human fetus

Chimp adult Human adult

Neoteny in evolution of the human skull. The skulls of fetal humans and chimpanzees are much more similar than are those of the adults. The grid lines show the pattern of growth, indicating much less change in the human skull from birth to adulthood.

(Redrawn with permission from Lewin, R. *Human Evolution: An Illustrated Introduction,* 3rd ed. Boston: Blackwell Scientific Publications, 1993.)

Figure 1.19 shows fetal and adult skulls of chimpanzees and humans. As you can see, the fetal skulls are much more similar than those of the adults. The grid lines show the pattern of growth, indicating much less change in the human skull from birth to adulthood. (See *Figure 1.19.*)

Natural Selection and Evolution

Darwin's theory of evolution, which was based on the concept of natural selection, provided an important contribution to modern physiological psychology. The theory asserts that we must understand the functions that are performed by an organ or body part or by a behavior. Through random mutations, changes in an individual's genetic material cause different proteins to be produced, which results in the alteration of some physical characteristics. If the changes con-

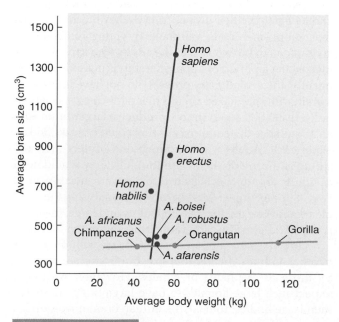

Average brain size as a function of body weight for several species of hominids.

(Redrawn with permission from Lewin, R. *Human Evolution: An Illustrated Introduction,* 3rd ed. Boston: Blackwell Scientific Publications, 1993.)

neoteny A slowing of the process of maturation, allowing more time for growth; an important factor in the development of large brains.

fer a selective advantage on the individual, the new genes will be transmitted to more and more members of the species. Even behaviors can evolve, through the selective advantage of alterations in the structure of the nervous system.

Amphibians emerged from the sea 360 million years ago. One branch, the therapsids, became the dominant land animal until a catastrophic series of volcanic eruptions wiped out most animal species. A small therapsid, the cynodont, survived the disaster and became the ancestor of the mammals. The earliest mammals were small, nocturnal insectivores who lived in trees. They remained small and inconspicuous until the extinction of the dinosaurs, which occurred around 65 million years ago. Mammals quickly filled the vacant ecological niches. Primates also began as small, nocturnal, tree-dwelling insectivores. Larger fruit-eating primates, with forward-facing eyes and larger brains, eventually evolved.

The first hominids appeared in Africa around 25 million years ago, eventually evolving into four major species: orangutans, gorillas, chimpanzees, and humans. Our ancestors acquired bipedalism around 3.7 million years ago and discovered tool making around 2.5 million years ago. The first hominids to leave Africa, *Homo erectus,* did so around 1.7 million years ago and scattered across Europe and Asia. *Homo neanderthalis* evolved in Western Europe, eventually to be replaced by *Homo sapiens,* which evolved in Africa around 100,000 years and spread throughout the world. By 30,000 years ago *Homo sapiens* had replaced *Homo neanderthalis.*

The evolution of large brains made possible the development of tool making, fire building, and language, which in turn permitted the development of complex social structures. Large brains also provided a large memory capacity and the abilities to recognize patterns of events in the past and to plan for the future. Because an upright posture limits the size of a woman's birth canal and therefore the size of the head that can pass through it, much of the brain's growth must take place after birth, which means that children require an extended period of parental care. This period of apprenticeship enabled the developing brain to be modified by experience.

Although human DNA differs from that of chimpanzees by only 1.2 percent, our brains are more than three times larger, which means that a small number of genes is responsible for the increase in the size of our brains. As we will see in Chapter 3, these genes appear to retard the events that stop brain development, resulting in a phenomenon known as neoteny.

Ethical Issues in Research with Animals

Most of the research described in this book involves experimentation on living animals. Any time we use another species of animals for our own purposes, we should be sure that what we are doing is both humane and worthwhile. I believe that a good case can be made that research on the physiology of behavior qualifies on both counts.

Humane treatment is a matter of procedure. We know how to maintain laboratory animals in good health in comfortable, sanitary conditions. We know how to administer anesthetics and analgesics so that animals do not suffer during or after surgery, and we know how to prevent infections with proper surgical procedures and the use of antibiotics. Most industrially developed societies have very strict regulations about the care of animals and require approval of the experimental procedures used on them. There is no excuse for mistreating animals in our care. In fact, the vast majority of laboratory animals *are* treated humanely.

Whether an experiment is *worthwhile* can be difficult to say. We use animals for many purposes. We eat their meat and eggs, and we drink their milk; we turn their hides into leather; we extract insulin and other hormones from their organs to treat people's diseases; we train them to do useful work on farms or to entertain us. Even having a pet is a form of exploitation; it is we—not they—who decide that they will live in our homes. The fact is, we have been using other animals throughout the history of our species.

Pet owning causes much more suffering among animals than scientific research does. As Miller (1983) notes, pet owners are not required to receive permission from a board of experts that includes a veterinarian to house their pets, nor are they subject to periodic inspections to be sure that their home is clean and sanitary, that their pets have enough space to exercise properly, or that their pets' diets are appropriate. Scientific researchers are. Miller also notes that fifty times more dogs and cats are killed by humane societies each year because they have been abandoned by former pet owners than are used in scientific research.

If a person believes that it is wrong to use another animal in any way, regardless of the benefits to humans, there is nothing anyone can say to convince that person of the value of scientific research with animals. For that person the issue is closed from the very beginning. Moral absolutes cannot be settled logically; like religious beliefs they can be accepted or rejected, but they cannot be proved or disproved. My arguments in support of scientific research with animals are based on an evaluation of the benefits the research has to humans. (We should also remember that research with animals often helps *other animals;* procedures used by veterinarians, as well as those used by physicians, come from such research.)

Before describing the advantages of research with animals, let me point out that the use of animals in research and teaching is a special target of animal rights activists. Nicholl and Russell (1990) examined twenty-one books written by such activists and counted the number of pages devoted to concern for different uses of animals. Next, they compared the relative concern the authors showed for these uses to the numbers of animals actually involved in each of these categories. The results indicate that the authors showed relatively little concern for animals that are used for food, hunting, or furs or for those killed in pounds; but although only 0.3 percent of the animals are used for research and education, 63.3 percent of the pages were devoted to this use. In terms of pages per million animals used, the authors devoted 0.08 to food, 0.23 to hunting, 1.27 to furs, 1.44 to killing in pounds—and 53.2 to research and education. The authors showed 665 times more concern for research and education compared with food and 231 times compared with hunting. Even the use of animals for furs (which consumes two-thirds as many animals as research and education) attracted 41.9 times less attention per animal.

The disproportionate amount of concern that animal rights activists show toward the use of animals in research and education is puzzling, particularly because this is the one *indispensable* use of animals. We *can* survive without eating animals, we *can* live without hunting, we *can* do without furs, but without using animals for research and for training future researchers, we *cannot* make progress in understanding and treating diseases. In not too many years our scientists will probably have developed a vaccine that will prevent the further spread of AIDS. Some animal rights activists believe that preventing the deaths of laboratory animals in the pursuit of such a vaccine is a more worthy goal than the prevention of the deaths of millions of humans that will occur as a result of the disease if a vaccine is not found. Even diseases that we have already conquered would take new victims if drug companies could no longer use animals. If they were deprived of animals, these companies could no longer extract hormones used to treat human diseases, and they could not prepare many of the vaccines we now use to prevent them.

Our species is beset by medical, mental, and behavioral problems, many of which can be solved only through biological research. Let us consider some of the major neurological disorders. Strokes, caused by bleeding or occlusion of a blood vessel within the brain, often leave people partly paralyzed, unable to read, write, or converse with their friends and family. Basic research on the means by which nerve cells communicate with each other has led to important discoveries about the causes of the death of brain cells. This research was not directed toward a specific practical goal; the potential benefits actually came as a surprise to the investigators.

Experiments based on these results have shown that if a blood vessel leading to the brain is blocked for a few minutes, the part of the brain that is nourished by that vessel will die. However, the brain damage can be prevented by first administering a drug that interferes with a particular kind of neural communication. This research is important, because it may lead to medical treatments that can help to reduce the brain damage caused by strokes. But it involves operating on a laboratory animal, such as a rat, and pinching off a blood vessel. (The animals are anesthetized, of course.) Some of the animals will sustain brain damage, and all will be killed so that their brains can be examined. However, you will probably agree that research like this is just as legitimate as using animals for food.

As you will learn later in this book, research with laboratory animals has produced important discoveries about the possible causes or potential treatments of neurological and mental disorders, including Parkinson's disease, schizophrenia, manic-depressive illness, anxiety disorders, obsessive-compulsive disorders, anorexia nervosa, obesity, and drug addictions. Although much progress has been made, these problems are still with us, and they cause much human suffering. Unless we continue our research with laboratory animals, they will not be solved. Some people have suggested that instead of using laboratory animals in our research, we could use tissue cultures or computers. Unfortunately, tissue cultures or computers are not substitutes for living organisms. We have no way to study behavioral problems such as addictions in tissue cultures, nor can we program a computer to simulate the workings of an animal's nervous system. (If we could, that would mean we already had all the answers.)

This book will discuss some of the many important discoveries that have helped to reduce human suffering. For example, the discovery of a vaccine for polio, a serious disease of the nervous system, involved the use of rhesus monkeys. As you will learn in Chapter 4, Parkinson's disease, an incurable, progressive neurological disorder, has been treated for years with a drug called L-DOPA, discovered through animal research. Now, because of research with rats, mice, rabbits, and monkeys stimulated by the accidental poisoning of several young people with a contaminated batch of synthetic heroin, patients are being treated with a drug that actually slows down the rate of brain degeneration. Researchers have hopes that a drug will be found to prevent the degeneration altogether.

The easiest way to justify research with animals is to point to actual and potential benefits to human health, as I have just done. However, we can also justify this research with a less practical, but perhaps equally important, argument. One of the things that characterizes our species is a quest for an understanding of our world. For example, astronomers study the universe and try to uncover its mysteries. Even if their discoveries never lead to practical benefits such as better drugs or faster methods of transportation, the fact that they enrich our understanding of the beginning and the fate of our universe justifies their efforts. The pursuit of knowledge is itself a worthwhile endeavor. Surely the attempt to understand the universe within us—our nervous system, which is responsible for all that we are or can be—is also valuable.

Careers in Neuroscience

What is physiological psychology, and what do physiological psychologists do? By the time you finish this book, you will have as complete an answer as I can give to these questions, but perhaps it is worthwhile for me to describe the field—and careers open to those who specialize in it—before we begin our study in earnest.

Physiological psychologists study all behavioral phenomena that can be observed in nonhuman animals. Some study humans, as well, using noninvasive physiological research methods. They attempt to understand the physiology of behavior: the role of the nervous system, interacting with the rest of the body (especially the endocrine system, which secretes hormones), in controlling behavior. They study such topics as sensory processes, sleep, emotional behavior, ingestive behavior, aggressive behavior, sexual behavior, parental behavior, and learning and memory. They also study animal models of disorders that afflict humans, such as anxiety, depression, obsessions and compulsions, phobias, psychosomatic illnesses, and schizophrenia.

Although physiological psychology is the original name for this field, several other terms are now in general use, such as *biological psychology, biopsychology, psychobiology,* and *behavioral neuroscience.* Most professional physiological psychologists have received a Ph.D. from a graduate program in psychology or from an interdisciplinary program. (My own university awards a Ph.D. in Neuroscience and Behavior. The program includes faculty members from the departments of psychology, biology, biochemistry, and computer science.)

Physiological psychology belongs to the larger field of *neuroscience.* Neuroscientists concern themselves with all aspects of the nervous system: its anatomy, chemistry, physiology, development, and functioning. The research of neuroscientists ranges from the study of molecular genetics to the study of social behavior. The field has grown enormously in the last few years; the most recent meeting of the Society for Neuroscience was attended by over thirty thousand members and graduate students.

Most professional physiological psychologists are employed by colleges and universities, where they are engaged in teaching and research. Others are employed by institutions devoted to research—for example, in laboratories owned and operated by national governments or by private philanthropic organizations. A few work in industry, usually for pharmaceutical companies that are interested in assessing the effects of drugs on behavior. To become a professor or independent researcher, one must receive a doctorate—usually a Ph.D., although some people turn to research after receiving an M.D. Nowadays, most physiological psychologists spend two years or more in a temporary postdoctoral position, working in the laboratory of a senior scientist to gain more research experience. During this time they write articles describing their research findings and submit them for publication in scientific journals. These publications are an important factor in obtaining a permanent position.

Two other fields often overlap with that of physiological psychology: *neurology* and *experimental neuropsychology* (often called *cognitive neuroscience*). Neurologists are physicians who are involved in the diagnosis and treatment of diseases of the nervous system. Most neurologists are solely involved in the practice of medicine, but a few engage in research devoted to advancing our understanding of the physiology of behavior. They study the behavior of people whose brains have been damaged by natural causes, using advanced brain-scanning devices to study the activity of various regions of the brain as a subject participates in various behaviors. This research is also carried out by experimental neuropsychologists (or cognitive neuroscientists)—scientists with a Ph.D. (usually in psychology) and specialized training in the principles and procedures of neurology.

Not all people engaged in neuroscience research have doctoral degrees. Many research technicians perform essential—and intellectually rewarding—services for the scientists with whom they work. Some of these technicians gain enough experience and education on the job to enable them to collaborate with their employers on their research projects rather than simply work for them.

---

interim
summary

Ethical Issues in Research with Animals *and* Careers in Neuroscience

Research on the physiology of behavior necessarily involves the use of laboratory animals. It is incumbent on all scientists using these animals to ensure that they are housed comfortably and treated humanely, and laws have been enacted to ensure that they are. Such research has already produced many benefits to humankind and promises to continue to do so.

Physiological psychology (also called biological psychology, biopsychology, psychobiology, and behavioral neuroscience) is a field devoted to our understanding of the physiology of behavior. Physiological psychologists are allied with other scientists in the broader field of neuroscience. To pursue a career in physiological psychology (or in the sister field of experimental neuropsychology), one must obtain a graduate degree and (usually) serve two years or more as a "postdoc"—a junior scientist.

---

physiological psychologist A scientist who studies the physiology of behavior, primarily by performing physiological and behavioral experiments with laboratory animals.

Strategies for Learning

The brain is a complicated organ. After all, it is responsible for all our abilities and all our complexities. Scientists have been studying this organ for a good many years and (especially in recent years) have been learning a lot about how it works. It is impossible to summarize this progress in a few simple sentences; therefore, this book contains a lot of information. I have tried to organize this information logically, telling you what you need to know in the order in which you need to know it. (After all, to understand some things, you sometimes need to understand other things first.) I have also tried to write as clearly as possible, making my examples as simple and as vivid as I can. Still, you cannot expect to master the information in this book by simply giving it a passive read; you will have to do some work.

Learning about the physiology of behavior involves much more than memorizing facts. Of course, there *are* facts to be memorized: names of parts of the nervous system, names of chemicals and drugs, scientific terms for particular phenomena and procedures used to investigate them, and so on. But the quest for information is nowhere near completed; we know only a small fraction of what we have to learn. And almost certainly, many of the "facts" that we now accept will some day be shown to be incorrect. If all you do is learn facts, where will you be when these facts are revised?

The antidote to obsolescence is knowledge of the process by which facts are obtained. In science, facts are the conclusions scientists make about their observations. If you learn only the conclusions, obsolescence is almost guaranteed. You will have to remember which conclusions are overturned and what the new conclusions are, and that kind of rote learning is hard to do. But if you learn about the research strategies the scientists use, the observations they make, and the reasoning that leads to the conclusions, you will develop an understanding that is easily revised when new observations (and new "facts") emerge. If you understand what lies behind the conclusions, then you can incorporate new information into what you already know and revise these conclusions yourself.

In recognition of these realities about learning, knowledge, and the scientific method, this book presents not just a collection of facts, but a description of the procedures, experiments, and logical reasoning that scientists have used in their attempt to understand the physiology of behavior. If, in the interest of expediency, you focus on the conclusions and ignore the process that leads to them, you run the risk of acquiring information that will quickly become obsolete. On the other hand, if you try to understand the experiments and see how the conclusions follow from the results, you will acquire knowledge that lives and grows.

Enough said. Now let me offer some practical advice about studying. You have been studying throughout your academic career, and you have undoubtedly learned some useful strategies along the way. Even if you have developed efficient and effective study skills, at least consider the possibility that there might be some ways to improve them.

If possible, the first reading of an assignment should be as uninterrupted as you can make it; that is, read the chapter without worrying much about remembering details. Next, after the first class meeting devoted to the topic, read the assignment again in earnest. Use a pen or pencil as you go, making notes. *Don't use a highlighter.* Sweeping the felt tip of a highlighter across some words on a page provides some instant gratification; you can even imagine that the highlighted words are somehow being transferred to your knowledge base. You have selected what is important, and when you review the reading assignment, you have only to read the highlighted words. But this is an illusion.

Be active, not passive. Force yourself to write down whole words and phrases. The act of putting the information into your own words will not only give you something to study shortly before the next exam but also put something into your head (which is helpful at exam time). Using a highlighter puts off the learning until a later date; rephrasing the information in your own words starts the learning process *right then.*

A good way to get yourself to put the information into your own words (and thus into your own brain) is to answer the questions in the study guide. If you cannot answer a question, look up the answer in the book, *close the book,* and write the answer down. The phrase *close the book* is important. If you *copy* the answer, you will get very little out of the exercise. However, if you make yourself remember the information long enough to write it down, you have a good chance of remembering it later. The importance of the study guide is *not* to have a set of short answers in your own handwriting that you can study before the quiz. The behaviors that lead to long-term learning are doing enough thinking about the material to summarize it in your own words, then going through the mechanics of writing those words down.

Before you begin reading the next chapter, let me say a few things about the design of the book that may help you with your studies. The text and illustrations are integrated as closely as possible. In my experience, one of the most annoying aspects of reading some books is not knowing when to look at an illustration. Therefore, in this book you will find figure references in boldfaced italics (like this: ***Figure 5.6***), which means "stop reading and look at the figure." These references appear in locations I think will be optimal. If you look away from the text then, you will be assured that you will not be interrupting a line of reasoning in a crucial place and will not have to reread several sentences to get going again. You will find sections like this:

"Figure 3.1 shows an alligator and a human. This alligator is certainly laid out in a linear fashion; we can draw a straight line that starts between its eyes and continues down the center of its spinal cord. (See *Figure 3.1.*)" This particular example is a trivial one and will give you no problems no matter when you look at the figure. But in other cases the material is more complex, and you will have less trouble if you know what to look for before you stop reading and examine the illustration.

You will notice that some words in the text are *italicized* and others are printed in **boldface.** Italics mean one of two things: Either the word is being stressed for emphasis and is not a new term or I am pointing out a new term that is not necessary for you to learn. On the other hand, a word in boldface is a new term that you should try to learn. Most of the boldfaced terms in the text are part of the vocabulary of the physiological psychologist. Often, they will be used again in a later chapter. As an aid to your studying, definitions of these terms are printed at the bottom of the page, along with pronunciation guides for terms whose pronunciation is not obvious. In addition, a comprehensive index at the end of the book provides a list of terms and topics, with page references.

At the end of each major section (there are usually three to five of them in a chapter), you will find an *Interim Summary,* which provides a place for you to stop and think again about what you have just read to make sure that you understand the direction the discussion has gone. Taken together, these sections provide a detailed summary of the information introduced in the chapter. My students tell me that they review the interim summaries just before taking a test.

One more thing. As you have undoubtedly noticed, a CD-ROM is included with your textbook. I prepared this CD-ROM to help you learn some of the material presented in this book. The CD-ROM (which works on both Windows and Apple operating systems) contains exercises and animations. Once you select a chapter from the opening menu, you will see what options are available. The exercises supplement the study guide: They will help you learn and remember definitions of new terms, and they contain multiple-choice questions for you to test yourself. They also contain many of the figures that appear in the book in a format that lets you practice putting the right labels in the right places. The animations contain illustrated presentations of things I talk about in the text, and in some cases they introduce new informaiton. I urge you to put the disk in your computer and see what's there. I always say this to my own students, but some never bother. Others do so late in the semester and then tell me that they wish they had used the CD-ROM earlier, because if they had done so, they probably would have gotten better grades on their exams. I have even received e-mails from students urging me to add reminders to the text to encourage readers to consult the CD-ROM. As you can see, I have taken their advice.

Okay, the preliminaries are over. The next chapter starts with something you can sink your (metaphorical) teeth into: the structure and functions of neurons, the most important elements of the nervous system.

Suggested Readings

Allman, J. M. *Evolving Brains.* New York: Scientific American Library, 1999.

Butterfield, H. *The Origins of Modern Science: 1300–1800.* New York: Macmillan, 1959.

Damasio, A. R. *Descartes's Error: Emotion, Reason, and the Human Brain.* New York: G. P. Putnam, 1994.

Finger, S. *Origins of Neuroscience: A History of Explorations into Brain Function.* New York: Oxford University Press, 1994.

Schultz, D., and Schultz, S. E. *A History of Modern Psychology.* New York: Academic Press, 1996.

Suggested Web Sites

Brain and Behavior Course

http://www.nyu.edu/classes/azmitia/lectures/

The Brain and Behavior site contains a series of 22 online lectures developed at New York University, including two lectures devoted to the history of neuroscience. The site also contains sample quizzes as well as links to other neuroscience sites.

Broca's Classic Paper on the Patient Tan

http://www.yorku.ca/dept/psych/classics/Broca/perte-e.htm

In 1861, Pierre Paul Broca published a case report relating the loss of language to damage to the left anterior hemisphere of the brain. This site provides a translation of Broca's report.

The Descent of Man by Charles Darwin

http://www.yorku.ca/dept/psych/classics/Darwin/Descent/index.htm

This site provides access to seven of the chapters published by Charles Darwin in his book The Descent of Man *(1871) in which he lays out his view on the evolution of humans.*

Mendel's Garden

http://www.unb.ca/web/units/psych/likely/mendel/call_mgarden.htm

This site will link students to a demonstration of the principles of genetic determination as examined by Gregor Mendel in his garden.

Split-Brain Syndrome

http://www.uwm.edu/~johnchay/sb.htm

An online demonstration of the study of split-brain patients is the focus of this site.

Split-Brain Consciousness

http://www.macalester.edu/~psych/whathap/UBNRP/Split_Brain/Split_Brain_Consciousness.html

This site provides a series of modules relating to the study of the split-brain including essays on consciousness, the history of the split-brain operation, and the behavior of split-brain patients.

Structure and Functions of Cells of the Nervous System

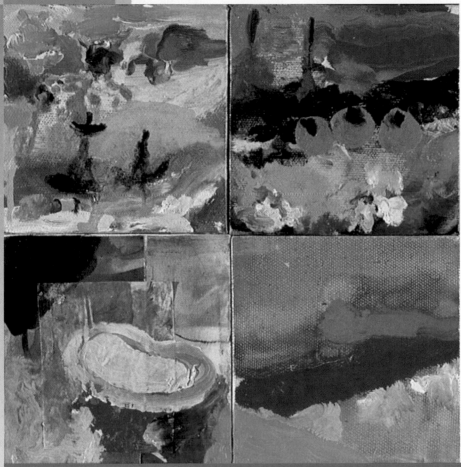

Alexandra Rozenman, from the series *Broken Windows*. © Alexandra Rozenman.

outline

- **Cells of the Nervous System**
Neurons
Supporting Cells
The Blood–Brain Barrier
Interim Summary

- **Communication Within a Neuron**
Neural Communication: An Overview
Measuring Electrical Potentials of Axons

The Membrane Potential:
   Balance of Two Forces
The Action Potential
Conduction of the Action Potential
Interim Summary

- **Communication Between Neurons**
The Concept of Chemical Transmission
Structure of Synapses
Release of Neurotransmitter

Activation of Receptors
Postsynaptic Potentials
Termination of Postsynaptic Potentials
Effects of Postsynaptic Potentials:
   Neural Integration
Autoreceptors
Other Types of Synapses
Nonsynaptic Chemical Communication
Interim Summary

Kathryn D. was getting desperate. All her life she had been healthy and active, eating wisely and keeping fit with sports and regular exercise. She went to her health club almost every day for a session of low-impact aerobics, followed by a swim. But several months ago, she began having trouble keeping up with her usual schedule. At first, she found herself getting tired toward the end of her aerobics class. Her arms, particularly, seemed to get heavy. Then when she entered the pool and started swimming, she found that it was hard to lift her arms over her head; she abandoned the crawl and the backstroke and did the sidestroke and breaststroke instead. She did not have any flulike symptoms, so she told herself that she needed more sleep and perhaps she should eat a little more.

Over the next few weeks, however, things only got worse. Aerobics classes were becoming an ordeal. Her instructor became concerned and suggested that Kathryn see her doctor. She did so, but he could find nothing wrong with her. She was not anemic, showed no signs of an infection, and seemed to be well nourished. He asked how things were going at work.

"Well, lately I've been under some pressure," she said. "The head of my department quit a few weeks ago, and I've taken over his job temporarily. I think I have a chance of getting the job permanently, but I feel as if my bosses are watching me to see whether I'm good enough for the job." Kathryn and her physician agreed that increased stress could be the cause of her problem. "I'd prefer not to give you any medication at this time," he said, "but if you don't feel better soon we'll have a closer look at you."

She *did* feel better for a while, but then all of a sudden her symptoms got worse. She quit going to the health club and found that she even had difficulty finishing a

day's work. She was certain that people were noticing that she was no longer her lively self, and she was afraid that her chances for the promotion were slipping away. One afternoon she tried to look up at the clock on the wall and realized that she could hardly see—her eyelids were drooping, and her head felt as if it weighed a hundred pounds. Just then, one of her supervisors came over to her desk, sat down, and asked her to fill him in on the progress she had been making on a new project. As she talked, she found herself getting weaker and weaker. Her jaw was getting tired, even her tongue was getting tired, and her voice was getting weaker. With a sudden feeling of fright she realized that the act of breathing seemed to take a lot of effort. She managed to finish the interview, but immediately afterward she packed up her briefcase and left for home, saying that she had a bad headache.

She telephoned her physician, who immediately arranged for her to go to the hospital to be seen by Dr. T., a neurologist. Dr. T. listened to a description of her symptoms and examined her briefly. She said to Kathryn, "I think I know what may be causing your symptoms. I'd like to give you an injection and watch your reaction." She gave some orders to the nurse, who left the room and came back with a syringe. Dr. T. took it, swabbed Kathryn's arm, and injected the drug. She started questioning Kathryn about her job. Kathryn answered slowly, her voice almost a whisper. As the questions continued, she realized that it was getting easier and easier to talk. She straightened her back and took a deep breath. Yes, she was sure. Her strength was returning! She stood up and raised her arms above her head. "Look," she said, her excitement growing. "I can do this again. I've got my strength back! What was that you gave me? Am I cured?"

T he brain is the organ that moves the muscles. That might sound simplistic, but ultimately, movement—or, more accurately, behavior—is the primary function of the nervous system. To make useful movements, the brain must know what is happening outside, in the environment. Thus, the body also contains cells that are specialized for detecting environmental events. Of course, complex animals such as we do not react automatically to events in our environment; our brains are flexible enough that we behave in different ways, according to present circumstances and those we experienced in the past. Besides perceiving and acting, we can remember and decide. All these abilities are made possible by the billions of cells found in the nervous system or controlled by them.

This chapter describes the structure and functions of the most important cells of the nervous system. Information, in the form of light, sound waves, odors, tastes, or contact with objects, is gathered from the environment by specialized cells called **sensory neurons.** Movements are accomplished by the contraction of muscles, which are controlled by **motor neurons.** (The term *motor* is used here in its orig-

inal sense to refer to movement, not to a mechanical engine.) And in between sensory neurons and motor neurons come the **interneurons**—neurons that lie entirely within the central nervous system. *Local interneurons* form circuits with nearby neurons and analyze small pieces of information *Relay interneurons* connect circuits of local interneurons in one region of the brain with those in other regions. Through these connections, circuits of neurons throughout the brain perform functions essential to tasks such as perceiving, learning, remembering, deciding, and controlling complex behaviors. How many neurons are there in the human ner-

sensory neuron A neuron that detects changes in the external or internal environment and sends information about these changes to the central nervous system.

motor neuron A neuron located within the central nervous system that controls the contraction of a muscle or the secretion of a gland.

interneuron A neuron located entirely within the central nervous system.

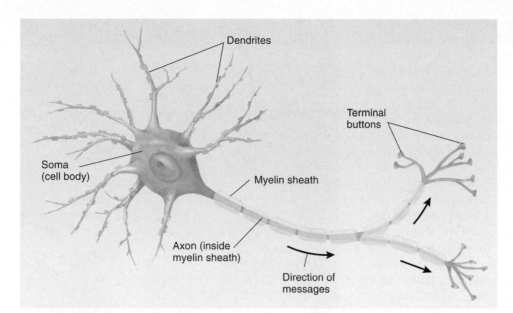

figure 2.1

The principal parts of a multipolar neuron.

vous system? I have seen estimates of between 100 billion and 1000 billion, but no one has counted them yet.

To understand how the nervous system controls behavior, we must first understand its parts—the cells that compose it. Because this chapter deals with cells, you need not be familiar with the structure of the nervous system, which is presented in Chapter 3. However, you need to know that the nervous system consists of two basic divisions: the central nervous system and the peripheral nervous system. The **central nervous system** (**CNS**) consists of the parts that are encased by the bones of the skull and spinal column: the brain and the spinal cord. The **peripheral nervous system** (**PNS**) is found outside these bones and consists of the nerves and most of the sensory organs.

Cells of the Nervous System

The first part of this chapter is devoted to a description of the most important cells of the nervous system—neurons and their supporting cells—and to the blood–brain barrier, which provides neurons in the central nervous system with chemical isolation from the rest of the body.

Neurons

Basic Structure

The neuron (nerve cell) is the information-processing and information-transmitting element of the nervous system. Neurons come in many shapes and varieties, according to the specialized jobs they perform. Most neurons have, in one form or another, the following four structures or regions: (1) cell body, or soma; (2) dendrites; (3) axon; and (4) terminal but-

See the interactive CD for more on neurons and supporting cells.

tons. (***Animation 2.1, Neurons and Supporting Cells,*** illustrates the information presented in the following section.)

■ **Soma** The **soma** (cell body) contains the nucleus and much of the machinery that provides for the life processes of the cell. (See ***Figure 2.1.***) Its shape varies considerably in different kinds of neurons.

■ **Dendrites** *Dendron* is the Greek word for tree, and the **dendrites** of the neuron look very much like trees. (See ***Figure 2.1.***) Neurons "converse" with one another, and dendrites serve as important recipients of these messages. The messages that pass from neuron to neuron are transmitted across the **synapse,** a junction between the terminal buttons (described later) of the sending cell and a portion of the somatic or dendritic membrane of the receiving cell. (The word *synapse* derives from the Greek *sunaptein,* "to join together.") Communication at a synapse proceeds in one direction: from the terminal button to the membrane of the other cell. (Like many general rules, this one has some exceptions. As we will see in Chapter 4, some synapses pass information in both directions.)

■ **Axon** The **axon** is a long, slender tube, often covered by a *myelin sheath.* (The myelin sheath is described

---

central nervous system (CNS) The brain and spinal cord.

peripheral nervous system (PNS) The part of the nervous system outside the brain and spinal cord, including the nerves attached to the brain and spinal cord.

soma The cell body of a neuron, which contains the nucleus.

dendrite A branched, treelike structure attached to the soma of a neuron; receives information from the terminal buttons of other neurons.

synapse A junction between the terminal button of an axon and the membrane of another neuron.

axon The long, thin, cylindrical structure that conveys information from the soma of a neuron to its terminal buttons.

later.) The axon carries information from the cell body to the terminal buttons. (See *Figure 2.1.*) The basic message it carries is called an *action potential.* This function is an important one and will be described in more detail later in the chapter. For now, it suffices to say that an action potential is a brief electrical/chemical event that starts at the end of the axon next to the cell body and travels toward the terminal buttons. The action potential is like a brief pulse; in a given axon the action potential is always of the same size and duration. When it reaches a point where the axon branches, it splits but does not diminish in size. Each branch receives a *full-strength* action potential.

Like dendrites, axons and their branches come in different shapes. In fact, the three principal types of neurons are classified according to the way in which their axons and dendrites leave the soma. The neuron depicted in Figure 2.1 is the most common type found in the central nervous system; it is a **multipolar neuron.** In this type of neuron the somatic membrane gives rise to one axon but to the trunks of many dendritic trees. **Bipolar neurons** give rise to one axon and one dendritic tree, at opposite ends of the soma. (See *Figure 2.2a.*) Bipolar neurons are usually sensory; that is, their dendrites detect events occur-

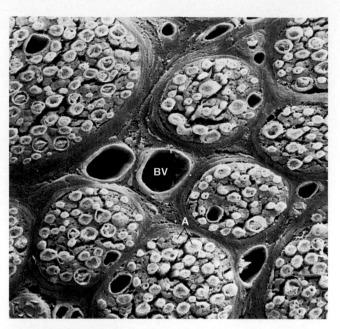

figure 2.3

Nerves. A nerve consists of a sheath of tissue that encases a bundle of individual nerve fibers (also known as axons). BV = blood vessel; A = individual axons.

(From *Tissues and Organs: A Text-Atlas of Scanning Electron Microscopy,* by Richard G. Kessel and Randy H. Kardon. Copyright © 1979 by W. H. Freeman and Co. Reprinted by permission.)

ring in the environment and communicate information about these events to the central nervous system.

The third type of nerve cell is the **unipolar neuron.** It has only one stalk, which leaves the soma and divides into two branches a short distance away. (See *Figure 2.2b.*) Unipolar neurons, like bipolar neurons, transmit sensory information from the environment to the CNS. The arborizations (treelike branches) outside the CNS are dendrites; the arborizations within the CNS end in terminal buttons. The dendrites of most unipolar neurons detect touch, temperature changes, and other sensory events that affect the skin. Other unipolar neurons detect events in our joints, muscles, and internal organs.

The central nervous system communicates with the rest of the body through nerves attached to the brain and to the spinal cord. Nerves are bundles of many thousands of individual fibers, all wrapped in a tough, protective membrane. Under a microscope nerves look something like telephone cables, with their bundles of wires. (See *Figure 2.3.*)

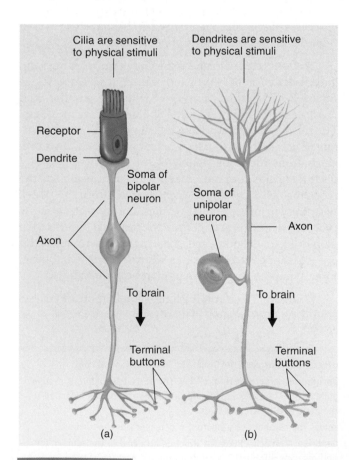

(a)   (b)

figure 2.2

Neurons. (a) A bipolar neuron, primarily found in sensory systems (for example, vision and audition). (b) A unipolar neuron, found in the somatosensory system (touch, pain, and the like).

multipolar neuron A neuron with one axon and many dendrites attached to its soma.

bipolar neuron A neuron with one axon and one dendrite attached to its soma.

unipolar neuron A neuron with one axon attached to its soma; the axon divides, with one branch receiving sensory information and the other sending the information into the central nervous system.

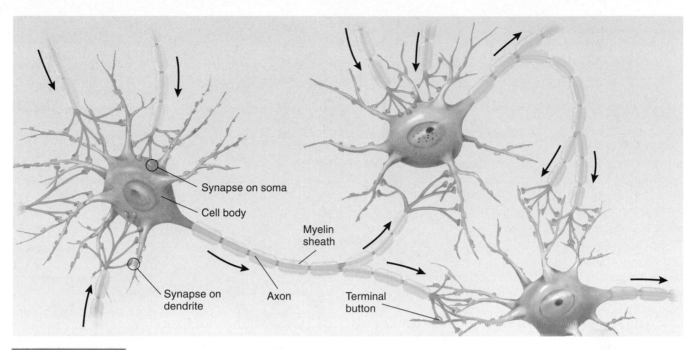

figure 2.4

An overview of the synaptic connections between neurons. The arrows represent the directions of the flow of information.

Like the individual wires in a telephone cable, nerve fibers transmit messages through the nerve, from a sense organ to the brain or from the brain to a muscle or gland.

■ **Terminal Buttons** Most axons divide and branch many times. At the ends of the twigs are found little knobs called **terminal buttons.** (Some neuroscientists prefer the original French word *bouton,* and others simply refer to them as *terminals.*) Terminal buttons have a very special function: When an action potential traveling down the axon reaches them, they secrete a chemical called a **neurotransmitter.** This chemical (there are many different ones in the CNS) either excites or inhibits the receiving cell and thus helps to determine whether an action potential occurs in its axon. Details of this process will be described later in this chapter.

An individual neuron receives information from the terminal buttons of axons of other neurons—and the terminal buttons of *its* axons form synapses with other neurons. A neuron may receive information from dozens or even hundreds of other neurons, each of which can form a large number of synaptic connections with it. Figure 2.4 illustrates the nature of these connections. As you can see, terminal buttons can form synapses on the membrane of the dendrites or the soma. (See *Figure 2.4.*)

Internal Structure

Figure 2.5 illustrates the internal structure of a typical multipolar neuron. (See *Figure 2.5.*) The **membrane** defines the boundary of the cell. It consists of a double layer of lipid (fatlike) molecules. Embedded in the membrane are a vari-

ety of protein molecules that have special functions. Some proteins detect substances outside the cell (such as hormones) and pass information about the presence of these substances to the interior of the cell. Other proteins control access to the interior of the cell, permitting some substances to enter but barring others. Still other proteins act as transporters, actively carrying certain molecules into or out of the cell. Because the proteins that are found in the membrane of the neuron are especially important in the transmission of information, their characteristics will be discussed in more detail later in this chapter.

The **nucleus** ("nut") of the cell is round or oval and is enclosed by the nuclear membrane. The nucleolus and the chromosomes reside here. The **nucleolus** is responsible for the production of **ribosomes,** small structures that

---

terminal button The bud at the end of a branch of an axon; forms synapses with another neuron; sends information to that neuron.

neurotransmitter A chemical that is released by a terminal button; has an excitatory or inhibitory effect on another neuron.

membrane A structure consisting principally of lipid molecules that defines the outer boundaries of a cell and also constitutes many of the cell organelles, such as the Golgi apparatus.

nucleus A structure in the central region of a cell, containing the nucleolus and chromosomes.

nucleolus (*new clee o lus*) A structure within the nucleus of a cell that produces the ribosomes.

ribosome (*ry bo soam*) A cytoplasmic structure, made of protein, that serves as the site of production of proteins translated from mRNA.

figure 2.5

The principal internal structures of a multipolar neuron.

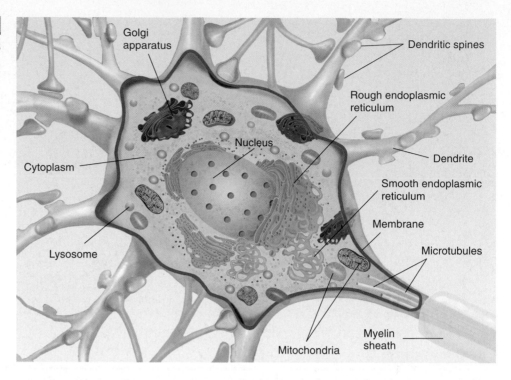

are involved in protein synthesis. The **chromosomes,** which consist of long strands of **deoxyribonucleic acid (DNA),** contain the organism's genetic information. When they are active, portions of the chromosomes (**genes**) cause production of another complex molecule, **messenger ribonucleic acid (mRNA),** which receives a copy of the information stored at that location. The mRNA leaves the nucleus and attaches to ribosomes, where it causes the production of a particular protein. (See *Figure 2.6.*)

Proteins are important in cell functions. As well as providing structure, proteins serve as **enzymes,** which direct the chemical processes of a cell by controlling chemical reactions. Enzymes are special protein molecules that act as catalysts; that is, they cause a chemical reaction to take place without becoming a part of the final product themselves. Because cells contain the ingredients needed to synthesize an enormous variety of compounds, the ones that cells actually do produce depend primarily on the particular enzymes that are present. Furthermore, there are enzymes that break molecules apart as well as put them together; the enzymes that are present in a particular region of a cell thus determine which molecules remain intact. For example,

$$A + B \overset{X}{\underset{Y}{\rightleftharpoons}} AB$$

In this reversible reaction the relative concentrations of enzymes X and Y determine whether the complex substance AB or its constituents, A and B, will predominate. Enzyme X makes A and B join together; enzyme Y splits AB apart. (Energy may also be required to make the reactions proceed.)

The bulk of the cell consists of cytoplasm. **Cytoplasm** is complex and varies considerably across types of cells, but it can most easily be characterized as a jellylike, semi-liquid substance that fills the space outlined by the membrane. It contains small, specialized structures, just as the body contains specialized organs. The generic term for these structures is *organelle,* "little organ." The most important organelles are described next.

Mitochondria (singular: mitochondrion) are shaped like oval beads and are formed of a double membrane. The inner membrane is wrinkled, and the wrinkles make up a set of shelves (*cristae*) that fill the inside of the bead. Mitochondria perform a vital role in the economy of the cell; many of the biochemical steps involved in the extraction

chromosome A strand of DNA, with associated proteins, found in the nucleus; carries genetic information.

deoxyribonucleic acid (DNA) (*dee ox ee ry bo new clay ik*) A long, complex macromolecule consisting of two interconnected helical strands; along with associated proteins, strands of DNA constitute the chromosomes.

gene The functional unit of the chromosome, which directs synthesis of one or more proteins.

messenger ribonucleic acid (mRNA) A macromolecule that delivers genetic information concerning the synthesis of a protein from a portion of a chromosome to a ribosome.

enzyme A molecule that controls a chemical reaction, combining two substances or breaking a substance into two parts.

cytoplasm The viscous, semiliquid substance contained in the interior of a cell.

mitochondria An organelle that is responsible for extracting energy from nutrients.

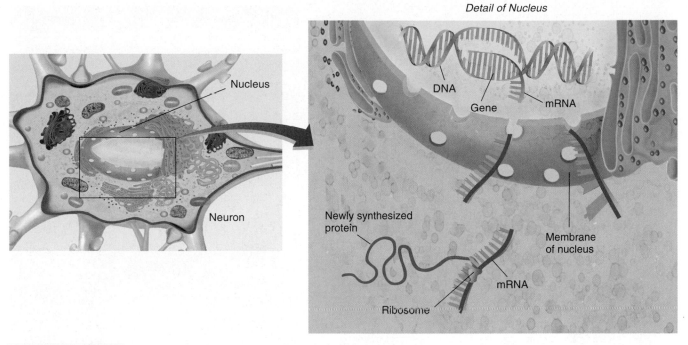

figure 2.6

Protein synthesis. When a gene is active, a copy of the information is made onto a molecule of messenger RNA. The mRNA leaves the nucleus and attaches to a ribosome, where the protein is produced.

of energy from the breakdown of nutrients take place on the cristae, controlled by enzymes located there. Most cell biologists believe that many eons ago mitochondria were free-living organisms that came to "infect" larger cells. Because the mitochondria could extract energy more efficiently than the cells they infected, they became useful to them and eventually became a permanent part of the cells. Cells provide mitochondria with nutrients, and mitochondria provide cells with a special molecule—**adenosine triphosphate (ATP)**—that they use as their immediate source of energy. Mitochondria contain their own DNA and reproduce independently of the cells in which they reside.

Endoplasmic reticulum, which serves as a storage reservoir and as a channel for transporting chemicals through the cytoplasm, appears in two forms: rough and smooth. Both types consist of parallel layers of membrane, arranged in pairs, of the sort that encloses the cell. Rough endoplasmic reticulum contains ribosomes. The protein produced by the ribosomes that are attached to the rough endoplasmic reticulum is destined to be transported out of the cell or used in the membrane. Unattached ribosomes are also distributed around the cytoplasm; the unattached variety appears to produce protein for use within the neuron. Smooth endoplasmic reticulum provides channels for the segregation of molecules involved in various cellular processes. Lipid (fatlike) molecules are produced here.

The **Golgi apparatus** is a special form of smooth endoplasmic reticulum. Some complex molecules, made up of simpler individual molecules, are assembled here. The Golgi apparatus also serves as a wrapping or pack-

aging agent. For example, secretory cells (such as those that release hormones) wrap their product in a membrane produced by the Golgi apparatus. When the cell secretes its products, it uses a process called **exocytosis** (*exo,* "outside"; *cyto,* "cell";*-osis,* "process"). Briefly stated, the container migrates to the inside of the outer membrane of the cell, fuses with it, and bursts, spilling its contents into the fluid surrounding the cell. As we will see, neurons communicate with one another by secreting chemicals by this means. Therefore, I will describe the process of exocytosis in more detail later in this chapter. The Golgi apparatus also produces **lysosomes,** small sacs that contain

adenosine triphosphate (ATP) (*ah* **den** *o seen*) A molecule of prime importance to cellular energy metabolism; its breakdown liberates energy.

endoplasmic reticulum Parallel layers of membrane found within the cytoplasm of a cell. Rough endoplasmic reticulum contains ribosomes and is involved with production of proteins that are secreted by the cell. Smooth endoplasmic reticulum is the site of synthesis of lipids and provides channels for the segregation of molecules involved in various cellular processes.

Golgi apparatus (*goal jee*) A complex of parallel membranes in the cytoplasm that wraps the products of a secretory cell.

exocytosis (*ex o sy* **toe** *sis*) The secretion of a substance by a cell through means of vesicles; the process by which neurotransmitters are secreted.

lysosome (*lye so soam*) An organelle surrounded by membrane; contains enzymes that break down waste products.

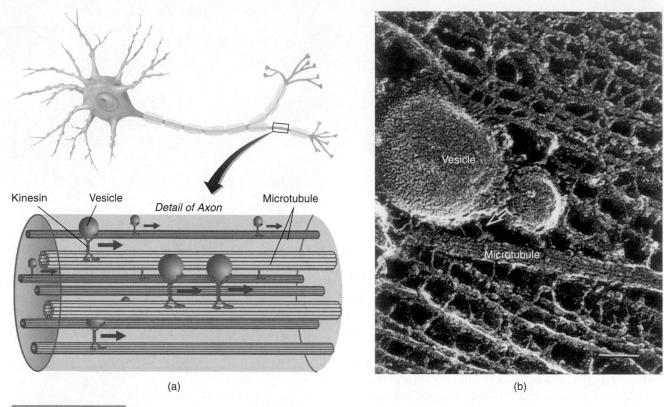

(a)

(b)

figure 2.7

Fast axoplasmic transport. (a) Kinesin molecules "walk" like an inchworm down a microtubule, carrying their cargo from the soma to the terminal buttons. Another protein, dynein, carries substances from the terminal buttons to the soma. (b) A photomicrograph of a mouse axon, showing an organelle being transported along a microtubule. The arrow points to what appears to be a kinesin molecule. (From Hirokawa, N. *Science,* 1998, *279,* 519–526.)

enzymes that break down substances no longer needed by the cell. These products are then recycled or excreted from the cell.

If a neuron grown in a tissue culture is exposed to a detergent, the lipid membrane and much of the interior of the cell dissolve away, leaving a matrix of insoluble strands of protein. This matrix, called the **cytoskeleton,** gives the neuron its shape. The cytoskeleton is made of three kinds of protein strands, linked to each other and forming a cohesive mass. The thickest of these strands, **microtubules,** are bundles of thirteen protein filaments arranged around a hollow core.

Axons can be extremely long, relative to their diameter and the size of the soma. For example, the longest axon in a human stretches from the foot to a region located in the base of the brain. Because terminal buttons need some items that can be produced only in the soma, there must be a system that can transport these items rapidly and efficiently through the axoplasm (that is, the cytoplasm of the axon). This system is referred to as **axoplasmic transport,** an active process by which substances are propelled along microtubules that run the length of the axon. Movement from the soma to the terminal buttons is called **anterograde** axoplasmic transport. (*Antero-* means "toward the front.") This

form of transport is accomplished by molecules of a protein called *kinesin*. In the cell body, kinesin molecules, which resemble a pair of legs and feet, attach to the item being transported down the axon. The kinesin molecule then walks like an inchworm down a microtubule, carrying the cargo to its destination. Energy is supplied by ATP molecules produced by the mitochondria. (See *Figure 2.7*.) Another protein, *dynein,* carries substances from the terminal buttons to the soma, a process known as **retrograde** axoplasmic transport. Anterograde axoplasmic transport is remarkably

cytoskeleton Formed of microtubules and other protein fibers, linked to each other and forming a cohesive mass that gives a cell its shape.

microtubule (*my kro **too** byool*) A long strand of bundles of protein filaments arranged around a hollow core; part of the cytoskeleton and involved in transporting substances from place to place within the cell.

axoplasmic transport An active process by which substances are propelled along microtubules that run the length of the axon.

anterograde In a direction along an axon from the cell body toward the terminal buttons.

retrograde In a direction along an axon from the terminal buttons toward the cell body.

fast: up to 500 mm per day. Retrograde axoplasmic transport is about half as fast as anterograde transport.

Supporting Cells

Neurons constitute only about half the volume of the CNS. The rest consists of a variety of supporting cells. Because neurons have a very high rate of metabolism but have no means of storing nutrients, they must constantly be supplied with nutrients and oxygen or they will quickly die. Thus, the role played by the cells that support and protect neurons is very important to our existence.

Glia

The most important supporting cells of the central nervous system are the *neuroglia,* or "nerve glue." **Glia** (also called *glial cells*) do indeed glue the CNS together, but they do much more than that. Neurons lead a very sheltered existence; they are buffered physically and chemically from the rest of the body by the glial cells. Glial cells surround neurons and hold them in place, controlling their supply of nutrients and some of the chemicals they need to exchange messages with other neurons; they insulate neurons from one another so that neural messages do not get scrambled; and they even act as housekeepers, destroying and removing the carcasses of neurons that are killed by disease or injury.

There are several types of glial cells, each of which plays a special role in the CNS. The three most important types are *astrocytes, oligodendrocytes,* and *microglia.* **Astrocyte** means "star cell," and this name accurately describes the shape of these cells. Astrocytes (or *astroglia*) provide physical support to neurons and clean up debris within the brain. They produce some chemicals that neurons need to fulfill their functions. They help to control the chemical composition of the fluid surrounding neurons by actively taking up or releasing substances whose concentrations must be kept within critical levels. Finally, astrocytes are involved in providing nourishment to neurons.

Some of the astrocyte's processes (the arms of the star) are wrapped around blood vessels; other processes are wrapped around parts of neurons, so the somatic and dendritic membranes of neurons are largely surrounded by astrocytes. This arrangement suggested to the Italian histologist Camillo Golgi (1844–1926) that astrocytes supplied neurons with nutrients from the capillaries and disposed of their waste products (Golgi, 1903). He thought that nutrients passed from capillaries to the cytoplasm of the astrocytes and then through the cytoplasm to the neurons.

Recent evidence suggests that Golgi was right. Reviews of the current literature (Tsacopoulos and Magistretti, 1996; Magistretti et al., 1999) suggests that astrocytes do more than pass glucose on to neurons: They receive glucose from capillaries and break it down to *lactate,* the chemical produced during the first step of glucose metabolism. They then release lactate into the extracellular fluid that surrounds neurons, and neurons take up the lactate, transport it to their mitochondria, and use it for energy. Presumably,

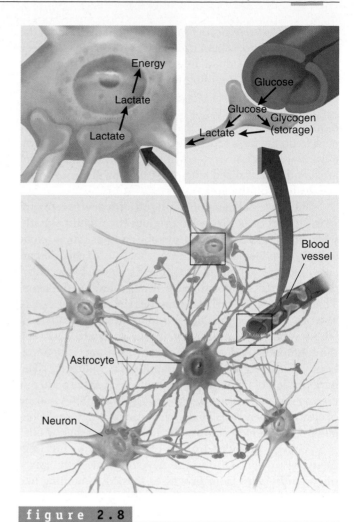

figure 2.8

Structure and location of astrocytes, whose processes surround capillaries and neurons of the central nervous system.

this process provides neurons with a fuel that they can metabolize even more rapidly than glucose. (See *Figure 2.8.*) In addition, astrocytes store a small amount of a carbohydrate called *glycogen* that can be broken down to glucose and then to lactate when the metabolic rate of neurons in their vicinity is especially high.

Besides transporting chemicals to neurons, astrocytes serve as the matrix that holds neurons in place—the "nerve glue," so to speak. These cells also surround and isolate synapses, limiting the dispersion of neurotransmitters that are released by the terminal buttons.

When neurons die, certain kinds of astrocytes take up the task of cleaning away the debris. These cells are able to travel around the CNS; they extend and retract their

glia (*glee* ah) The supporting cells of the central nervous system.

astrocyte A glial cell that provides support for neurons of the central nervous system, provides nutrients and other substances, and regulates the chemical composition of the extracellular fluid.

processes (*pseudopodia,* or "false feet") and glide about the way amoebas do. When these astrocytes contact a piece of debris from a dead neuron, they push themselves against it, finally engulfing and digesting it. We call this process **phagocytosis** (*phagein,* "to eat"; *kutos,* "cell"). If there is a considerable amount of injured tissue to be cleaned up, astrocytes will divide and produce enough new cells to do the task. Once the dead tissue is broken down, a framework of astrocytes will be left to fill in the vacant area, and a specialized kind of astrocyte will form scar tissue, walling off the area.

The principal function of **oligodendrocytes** is to provide support to axons and to produce the **myelin sheath,** which insulates most axons from one another. (Some axons are not myelinated and lack this sheath.) Myelin, 80 percent lipid and 20 percent protein, is produced by the oligodendrocytes in the form of a tube surrounding the axon. This tube does not form a continuous sheath; rather, it consists of a series of segments, each approximately 1 mm long, with a small (1–2 µm) portion of uncoated axon between the segments. (A *micrometer,* abbreviated µm, is one-millionth of a meter, or one-thousandth of a millimeter.) The bare portion of axon is called a **node of Ranvier,** after its discoverer. The myelinated axon, then, resembles a string of elongated beads. (Actually, the beads are *very much* elongated—their length is approximately 80 times their width.)

A given oligodendrocyte produces up to fifty segments of myelin. During the development of the CNS, oligodendrocytes form processes shaped something like canoe paddles. Each of these paddle-shaped processes then wraps itself many times around a segment of an axon and, while doing so, produces layers of myelin. Each paddle thus becomes a segment of an axon's myelin sheath. (See *Figures 2.9* and *2.10a.*)

As their name indicates, **microglia** are the smallest of the glial cells. Like some types of astrocytes, they act as phagocytes, engulfing and breaking down dead and dying neurons. But in addition, they serve as one of the representatives of the immune system in the brain, protecting the brain from invading microorganisms. They are primarily responsible for the inflammatory reaction in response to brain damage.

---

phagocytosis (*fagg o sy toe sis*) The process by which cells engulf and digest other cells or debris caused by cellular degeneration.

oligodendrocyte (*oh li go den droh site*) A type of glial cell in the central nervous system that forms myelin sheaths.

myelin sheath (*my a lin*) A sheath that surrounds axons and insulates them, preventing messages from spreading between adjacent axons.

node of Ranvier (*raw vee ay*) A naked portion of a myelinated axon, between adjacent oligodendroglia or Schwann cells.

microglia The smallest of glial cells; act as phagocytes and protect the brain from invading microorganisms.

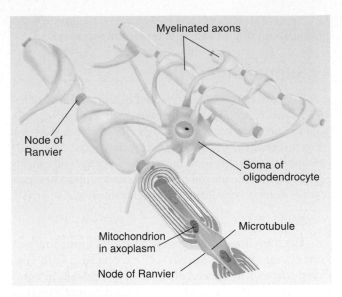

figure 2.9

An oligodendrocyte, which forms the myelin that surrounds many axons in the central nervous system. Each cell forms one segment of myelin for several adjacent axons.

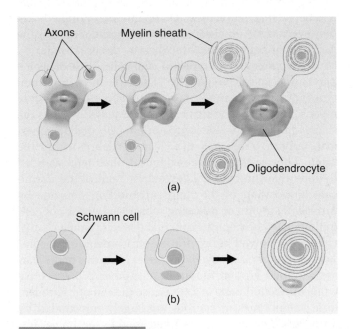

figure 2.10

Formation of myelin. During development a process of an oligodendrocyte or an entire Schwann cell tightly wraps itself many times around an individual axon and forms one segment of the myelin sheath. (a) Oligodendrocyte. (b) Schwann cell.

Dr. C., a retired neurologist, had been afflicted with multiple sclerosis for more than two decades when she died of a heart attack. One evening, twenty-three years previously, she and her husband had dinner at their favorite restaurant. As they were leaving, she stumbled and almost fell. Her husband joked, "Hey honey, you shouldn't have had that last glass of wine." She smiled at his attempt at humor, but she knew better—her clumsiness wasn't brought on by the two glasses of wine she had drunk with dinner. She suddenly realized that she had been ignoring some symptoms that she should have recognized.

The next day she consulted with one of her colleagues, who agreed that her own tentative diagnosis was probably correct: Her symptoms fit those of multiple sclerosis. She had experienced fleeting problems with double vision, she sometimes felt unsteady on her feet, and she occasionally noticed tingling sensations in her right hand. None of these symptoms was serious, and they lasted for only a short while, so she ignored them—or perhaps denied to herself that they were important.

A few weeks after Dr. C.'s death, a group of medical students and neurological residents gathered in an autopsy room at the medical school. Dr. D., the school's neuropathologist, displayed a stainless-steel tray on which were lying a brain and a spinal cord. "These belonged to Dr. C.," he said. "Several years ago she donated her organs to the medical school." Everyone looked at the brain more intently, knowing that it had animated an esteemed clinician and teacher whom they all knew by reputation, if not personally. Dr. D. led his audience to a set of light boxes on the wall, to which several MRI scans had been clipped. He pointed out some white spots that appeared on one scan. "This scan clearly shows some white-matter lesions, but they are gone on the next one, taken six months later. And here is another one, but it's gone on the next scan. The immune system attacked the myelin sheaths in a particular region, and then glial cells cleaned up the debris. MRI doesn't show the lesions then, but the axons can no longer conduct their messages."

He picked up Dr. C.'s brain and cut it in several slices. He picked one up. "Here, see this?" He pointed out a spot of discoloration in a band of white matter. This is a sclerotic plaque—a patch that feels harder than the surrounding tissue. There are many of them, located throughout the brain and spinal cord, which is why the disease is called multiple sclerosis." He picked up the spinal cord, felt along its length with his thumb and forefinger, and then stopped and said, "Yes, I can feel a plaque right here."

Dr. D. put the spinal cord down and said, "Who can tell me the etiology of this disorder?"

One of the students spoke up. "It's an autoimmune disease. The immune system gets sensitized to the body's own myelin protein and periodically attacks it, causing a variety of different neurological symptoms. Some say that a childhood viral illness somehow causes the immune system to start seeing the protein as foreign."

"That's right," said Dr. D. "The primary criterion for the diagnosis of multiple sclerosis is the presence of neurological symptoms disseminated in time and space. The symptoms don't all occur at once, and they can be caused only by damage to several different parts of the nervous system, which means that they can't be the result of a stroke."

Schwann Cells

In the central nervous system the oligodendrocytes support axons and produce myelin. In the peripheral nervous system the **Schwann cells** perform the same functions. Most axons in the PNS are myelinated. The myelin sheath occurs in segments, as it does in the CNS; each segment consists of a single Schwann cell, wrapped many times around the axon. In the CNS the oligodendrocytes grow a number of paddle-shaped processes that wrap around a number of axons. In the PNS a Schwann cell provides myelin for only one axon, and the entire Schwann cell—not merely a part of it—surrounds the axon. (See *Figure 2.10b.*)

Schwann cells also differ from their CNS counterparts, the oligodendrocytes, in an important way. As we saw, a nerve consists of a bundle of many myelinated axons, all covered in a sheath of tough, elastic connective tissue. If damage occurs to such a nerve, Schwann cells aid in the digestion of the dead and dying axons. Then the Schwann cells arrange themselves in a series of cylinders that act as guides for regrowth of the axons. The distal portions of the severed axons die, but the stump of each severed axon grows sprouts, which then spread in all directions. If one of these sprouts encounters a cylinder provided by a Schwann cell, the sprout will grow through the tube quickly (at a rate of up to 3–4 mm a day), while the other, nonproductive sprouts wither away. If the cut ends of the nerve are still located close enough to each other, the axons will reestablish connections with the muscles and sense organs they previously served.

Unfortunately, the glial cells of the CNS are not as cooperative as the supporting cells of the PNS. If axons in the brain or spinal cord are damaged, new sprouts will form, as in the PNS. However, the budding axons encounter scar tissue produced by the astrocytes, and they cannot penetrate this barrier. Even if the sprouts could get through, the axons would not reestablish their original connections without guidance similar to that provided by the Schwann cells of the PNS. During development axons have two modes of growth. The first mode causes them to elongate so that they reach their target, which could be as far away as the other end of the brain or spinal cord. Schwann cells provide this signal to injured axons. The second mode causes axons to stop elongating and begin sprouting terminal buttons because they have reached their target. Liuzzi and Lasek (1987) found that even when astrocytes do not produce scar tissue, they appear to produce a chemical signal that instructs regenerating axons to begin the second mode of growth: to stop elongating and start sprouting terminal buttons. Thus, the difference

---

Schwann cell A cell in the peripheral nervous system that is wrapped around a myelinated axon, providing one segment of its myelin sheath.

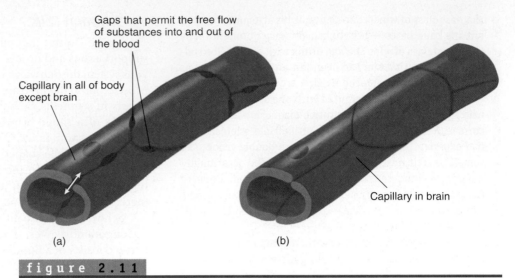

Gaps that permit the free flow of substances into and out of the blood

Capillary in all of body except brain

Capillary in brain

(a)

(b)

figure 2.11

The blood–brain barrier. (a) The cells that form the walls of the capillaries in the body outside the brain have gaps that permit the free passage of substances into and out of the blood. (b) The cells that form the walls of the capillaries in the brain are tightly joined.

in the regenerative properties of axons in the CNS and the PNS results from differences in the characteristics of the supporting cells, not from differences in the axons.

There is another difference between oligodendrocytes of the CNS and Schwann cells of the PNS: the chemical composition of the myelin protein they produce. The immune system of people with multiple sclerosis attacks only the myelin protein produced by oligodendrocytes; thus, the myelin of the peripheral nervous system is spared.

The Blood–Brain Barrier

Over one hundred years ago, Paul Ehrlich discovered that if a blue dye is injected into an animal's bloodstream, all tissues except the brain and spinal cord will be tinted blue. However, if the same dye is injected into the fluid-filled ventricles of the brain, the blue color will spread throughout the CNS (Bradbury, 1979). This experiment demonstrates that a barrier exists between the blood and the fluid that surrounds the cells of the brain—the **blood–brain barrier.**

Some substances can cross the blood–brain barrier; others cannot. Thus, it is *selectively permeable* (*per,* "through"; *meare,* "to pass"). In most of the body the cells that line the capillaries do not fit together absolutely tightly. Small gaps are found between them that permit the free exchange of most substances between the blood plasma and the fluid outside the capillaries that surrounds the cells of the body. In the central nervous system the capillaries lack these gaps, and therefore many substances cannot leave the blood. Thus, the walls of the

capillaries in the brain constitute the blood–brain barrier. (See *Figure 2.11.*) Other substances must be actively transported through the capillary walls by special proteins. For example, glucose transporters bring the brain its fuel, and other transporters rid the brain of toxic waste products (Rubin and Staddon, 1999).

What is the function of the blood–brain barrier? As we will see, transmission of messages from place to place in the brain depends on a delicate balance between substances within neurons and in the extracellular fluid that surrounds them. If the composition of the extracellular fluid is changed even slightly, the transmission of these messages will be disrupted—which means that brain functions will be disrupted. The presence of the blood–brain barrier makes it easier to regulate the composition of this fluid. In addition, many of the foods that we eat contain chemicals that would interfere with the transmission of information between neurons. The blood–brain barrier prevents these chemicals from reaching the brain.

The blood–brain barrier is not uniform throughout the nervous system. In several places the barrier is relatively permeable, allowing substances that are excluded elsewhere to cross freely. For example, the **area postrema** is

---

blood–brain barrier A semipermeable barrier between the blood and the brain produced by the cells in the walls of the brain's capillaries.

area postrema (*poss **tree** ma*) A region of the medulla where the blood–brain barrier is weak; poisons can be detected there and can initiate vomiting.

a part of the brain that controls vomiting. The blood–brain barrier is much weaker there, permitting neurons in this region to detect the presence of toxic substances in the blood. A poison that enters the circulatory system from the stomach can thus stimulate this area to initiate vomiting. If the organism is lucky, the poison can be expelled from the stomach before it causes too much damage.

interim summary

Cells of the Nervous System

Neurons are the most important cells of the nervous system. The central nervous system (CNS) includes the brain and spinal cord; the peripheral nervous system (PNS) includes nerves and some sensory organs.

Neurons have four principal parts: dendrites, soma (cell body), axon, and terminal buttons. They communicate by means of synapses, junctions between the terminal buttons of one neuron and the somatic or dendritic membrane of another. When an action potential travels down an axon, its terminal buttons secrete a chemical that has either an excitatory or an inhibitory effect on the neurons with which they communicate. Ultimately, the effects of these excitatory and inhibitory synapses cause behavior, in the form of muscular contractions.

Neurons contain a quantity of cytoplasm, enclosed in a membrane. Embedded in the membrane are protein molecules that have special functions, such as the detection of hormones or neurotransmitters or transport of particular substances into and out of the cell. The cytoplasm contains the nucleus, which contains the genetic information; the nucleolus (located in the nucleus), which manufactures ribosomes; the ribosomes, which serve as sites of protein synthesis; the endoplasmic reticulum, which serves as a storage reservoir and as a channel for transportation of chemicals through the cytoplasm; the Golgi apparatus, which wraps substances that the cell secretes in a membrane; the lysosomes, which contain enzymes that destroy waste products; microtubules and other protein fibers, which compose the cytoskeleton and help to transport chemicals from place to place; and the mitochondria, which serve as the location for most of the chemical reactions through which the cell extracts energy from nutrients.

The withdrawal reflex illustrates how neurons can be connected to accomplish useful behaviors. The circuit responsible for this reflex consists of three sets of neurons: sensory neurons, interneurons, and motor neurons. The reflex can be suppressed when neurons in the brain activate inhibitory interneurons that form synapses with the motor neurons.

Neurons are supported by the glial cells of the central nervous system and the supporting cells of the peripheral nervous system. In the CNS astrocytes provide support and nourishment and also remove debris and form scar tissue in the event of tissue damage. Microglia are phagocytes that serve as the representatives of the immune system. Oligodendrocytes form myelin, the substance that insulates axons, and also support unmyelinated axons. In the PNS, support and myelin are provided by the Schwann cells.

In most organs molecules freely diffuse between the blood within the capillaries that serve them and the extracellular fluid that bathes their cells. The molecules pass through gaps between the cells that line the capillaries. The walls of the capillaries of the CNS lack these gaps; consequently, fewer substances can enter or leave the brain across the blood–brain barrier.

Communication Within a Neuron

This section describes the nature of communication *within* a neuron—the way an action potential is sent from the cell body down the axon to the terminal buttons, informing them to release some neurotransmitter. The

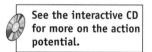 **See the interactive CD for more on the action potential.**

details of synaptic transmission—the communication between neurons—will be described in the next section. As we will see in this section, an action potential consists of a series of alterations in the membrane of the axon that permit various substances to move between the interior of the axon and the fluid surrounding it. These exchanges produce electrical currents. (***Animation 2.2, The Action Potential,*** illustrates the information presented in the following section.)

Neural Communication: An Overview

Before I begin my discussion of the action potential, let's step back and see how neurons can interact to produce a useful behavior. We begin by examining a simple assembly of three neurons and a muscle that control a withdrawal reflex. In the next two figures (and in subsequent figures that illustrate simple neural circuits), multipolar neurons are depicted in shorthand fashion as several-sided stars. The points of these stars represent dendrites, and only one or two terminal buttons are shown at the end of the axon. The sensory neuron in this example detects painful stimuli. When its dendrites are stimulated by a noxious stimulus (such as contact with a hot object), it sends messages down the axon to the terminal buttons, which are located in the spinal cord. (You will recognize this cell as

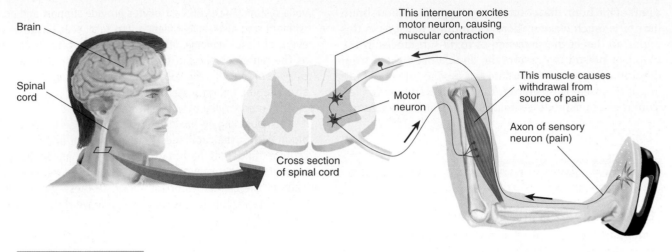

This interneuron excites
motor neuron, causing
muscular contraction

Brain

Spinal
cord

Motor
neuron

This muscle causes
withdrawal from
source of pain

Axon of sensory
neuron (pain)

Cross section
of spinal cord

figure 2.12

A withdrawal reflex, a simple example of a useful function of the nervous system.
The painful stimulus causes the hand to pull away from the hot iron.

a unipolar neuron; see *Figure 2.12.*) The terminal buttons of the sensory neuron release a neurotransmitter that excites the interneuron, causing it to send messages down its axon. The terminal buttons of the interneuron release a neurotransmitter that excites the motor neuron, which sends messages down its axon. The axon of the motor neuron joins a nerve and travels to a muscle. When the terminal buttons of the motor neuron release their neurotransmitter, the muscle cells contract, causing the hand to move away from the hot object. (See *Figure 2.12.*)

So far, all of the synapses have had excitatory effects. Now let us complicate matters a bit to see the effect of inhibitory synapses. Suppose you have removed a hot casserole from the oven. As you start walking over to the table to put it down, the heat begins to penetrate the rather thin potholders you are using. The pain caused by the hot

casserole triggers a withdrawal reflex that tends to make you drop it. Yet you manage to keep hold of it long enough to get to the table and put it down. What prevented your withdrawal reflex from making you drop the casserole on the floor?

The pain from the hot casserole increases the activity of excitatory synapses on the motor neurons, which tends to cause the hand to pull away from the casserole. However, this excitation is counteracted by *inhibition,* supplied by another source: the brain. The brain contains neural circuits that recognize what a disaster it would be if you dropped the casserole on the floor. These neural circuits send information to the spinal cord that prevents the withdrawal reflex from making you drop the dish.

Figure 2.13 shows how this information reaches the spinal cord. As you can see, an axon from a neuron in the

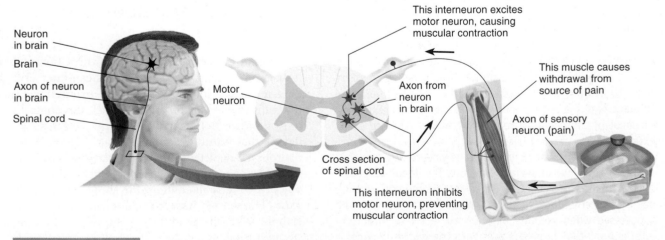

Neuron
in brain

Brain

Axon of neuron
in brain

Spinal cord

Motor
neuron

Axon from
neuron
in brain

Cross section
of spinal cord

This interneuron excites
motor neuron, causing
muscular contraction

This muscle causes
withdrawal from
source of pain

Axon of sensory
neuron (pain)

This interneuron inhibits
motor neuron, preventing
muscular contraction

figure 2.13

The role of inhibition. Inhibitory signals arising from the brain can prevent the
withdrawal reflex from causing the person to drop the casserole.

brain reaches the spinal cord, where its terminal buttons form synapses with an inhibitory interneuron. When the neuron in the brain becomes active, its terminal buttons excite this inhibitory interneuron. The interneuron releases an inhibitory neurotransmitter, which *decreases* the activity of the motor neuron, blocking the withdrawal reflex. This circuit provides an example of a contest between two competing tendencies: to drop the casserole and to hold onto it. (See *Figure 2.13.*)

Of course, reflexes are more complicated than this description, and the mechanisms that inhibit them are even more so. And thousands of neurons are involved in this process. The five neurons shown in Figure 2.13 represent many others: Dozens of sensory neurons detect the hot object, hundreds of interneurons are stimulated by their activity, hundreds of motor neurons produce the contraction—and thousands of neurons in the brain must become active if the reflex is to be inhibited. Yet this simple model provides an overview of the process of neural communication, which is described in more detail later in this chapter.

Measuring Electrical Potentials of Axons

Let's examine the nature of the message that is conducted along the axon. To do so, we obtain an axon that is large enough to work with. Fortunately, nature has provided the neuroscientist with the giant squid axon (the giant axon of a squid, not the axon of a giant squid!). This axon is about 0.5 mm in diameter, which is hundreds of times larger than the largest mammalian axon. (This large axon controls an emergency response: sudden contraction of the mantle, which squirts water through a jet and propels the squid away from a source of danger.) We place an isolated giant squid axon in a dish of seawater, in which it can exist for a day or two.

To measure the electrical charges generated by an axon, we will need to use a pair of electrodes. **Electrodes** are electrical conductors that provide a path for electricity to enter or leave a medium. One of the electrodes is a simple wire that we place in the seawater. The other one, which we use to record the message from the axon, has to be special. Because even a giant squid axon is rather small, we must use a tiny electrode that will record the membrane potential without damaging the axon. To do so, we use a microelectrode.

A **microelectrode** is simply a very small electrode, which can be made of metal or glass. In this case we will use one made of thin glass tubing, which is heated and drawn down to an exceedingly fine point, less than a thousandth of a millimeter in diameter. Because glass will not conduct electricity, the glass microelectrode is filled with a liquid that conducts electricity, such as a solution of potassium chloride.

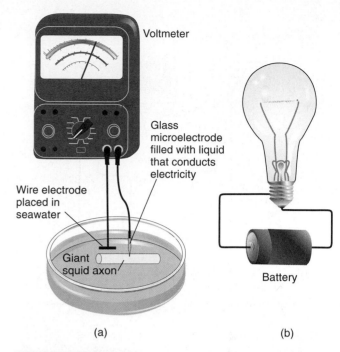

(a)   (b)

figure 2.14

Measuring electrical charge. (a) A voltmeter detecting the charge across a membrane of an axon. (b) A light bulb detecting the charge across the terminals of a battery.

We place the wire electrode in the seawater and insert the microelectrode into the axon. (See *Figure 2.14a.*) As soon as we do so, we discover that the inside of the axon is negatively charged with respect to the outside; the difference in charge being 70 mV (millivolts, or thousandths of a volt). Thus, the inside of the membrane is –70 mV. This electrical charge is called the **membrane potential.** The term *potential* refers to a stored-up source of energy—in this case, electrical energy. For example, a flashlight battery that is not connected to an electrical circuit has a *potential* charge of 1.5 V between its terminals. If we connect a light bulb to the terminals, the potential energy is tapped and converted into radiant energy (light). (See *Figure 2.14b.*) Similarly, if we connect our electrodes—one inside the axon and one outside it—to a very sensitive voltmeter, we will convert the potential energy to movement of the meter's needle. Of course, the potential electrical energy

---

electrode A conductive medium that can be used to apply electrical stimulation or to record electrical potentials.

microelectrode A very fine electrode, generally used to record activity of individual neurons.

membrane potential The electrical charge across a cell membrane; the difference in electrical potential inside and outside the cell.

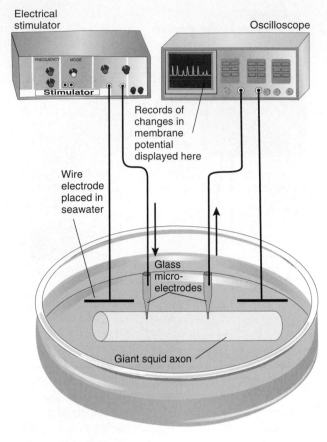

Electrical stimulator

Oscilloscope

Records of changes in membrane potential displayed here

Wire electrode placed in seawater

Glass micro-electrodes

Giant squid axon

The means by which an axon can be stimulated while its membrane potential is being recorded.

of the axonal membrane is very weak compared with that of a flashlight battery.

As we will see, the message that is conducted down the axon consists of a brief change in the membrane potential. However, this change occurs very rapidly—too rapidly for us to see if we were using a voltmeter. Therefore, to study the message, we will use an **oscilloscope.** This device, like a voltmeter, measures voltages, but it also produces a record of these voltages, graphing them as a function of time. These graphs are displayed on a screen, much like the one found in a television. The vertical axis represents voltage, and the horizontal axis represents time, going from left to right.

Once we insert our microelectrode into the axon, the oscilloscope draws a straight horizontal line at –70 mV, as long as the axon is not disturbed. This electrical charge across the membrane is called, quite appropriately, the **resting potential.** Now let us disturb the resting potential and see what happens. To do so, we will use another device—an electrical stimulator that allows us to alter the membrane potential at a specific location. (See *Figure 2.15.*) The stimulator can pass current through another microelectrode that

we have inserted into the axon. Because the inside of the axon is negative, a positive charge applied to the inside of the membrane produces a **depolarization.** That is, it takes away some of the electrical charge across the membrane near the electrode, reducing the membrane potential.

Let us see what happens to an axon when we artificially change the membrane potential at one point. Figure 2.16 shows a graph drawn by an oscilloscope that has been monitoring the effects of brief depolarizing stimuli. The graphs of the effects of these separate stimuli are superimposed on the same drawing so that we can compare them. We deliver a series of depolarizing stimuli, starting with a very weak stimulus (number 1) and gradually increasing their strength. Each stimulus briefly depolarizes the membrane potential a little more. Finally, after we present depolarization number 4, the membrane potential suddenly reverses itself, so that the inside becomes *positive* (and the outside becomes negative). The membrane potential quickly returns to normal, but first it overshoots the resting potential, becoming **hyperpolarized**—more polarized than normal—for a short time. The whole process takes about 2 msec (milliseconds). (See *Figure 2.16.*)

This phenomenon, a very rapid reversal of the membrane potential, is called the **action potential.** It constitutes the message carried by the axon from the cell body to the terminal buttons. The voltage level that triggers an action potential—which was achieved only by depolarizing shock number 4—is called the **threshold of excitation.**

The Membrane Potential: Balance of Two Forces

To understand what causes the action potential to occur, we must first understand the reasons for the existence of the membrane potential. As we will see, this elec-

oscilloscope A laboratory instrument that is capable of displaying a graph of voltage as a function of time on the face of a cathode ray tube.

resting potential The membrane potential of a neuron when it is not being altered by excitatory or inhibitory postsynaptic potentials; approximately –70 mV in the giant squid axon.

depolarization Reduction (toward zero) of the membrane potential of a cell from its normal resting potential.

hyperpolarization An increase in the membrane potential of a cell, relative to the normal resting potential.

action potential The brief electrical impulse that provides the basis for conduction of information along an axon.

threshold of excitation The value of the membrane potential that must be reached to produce an action potential.

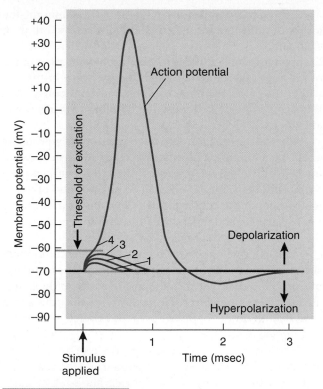

figure 2.16

An action potential. These results would be seen on an oscilloscope screen if depolarizing stimuli of varying intensities were delivered to the axon shown in Figure 2.15.

trical charge is the result of a balance between two opposing forces: diffusion and electrostatic pressure.

The Force of Diffusion

When a spoonful of sugar is carefully poured into a container of water, it settles to the bottom. After a time the sugar dissolves, but it remains close to the bottom of the container. After a much longer time (probably several days), the molecules of sugar distribute themselves evenly throughout the water, even if no one stirs the liquid. The process whereby molecules distribute themselves evenly throughout the medium in which they are dissolved is called **diffusion.**

When there are no forces or barriers to prevent them from doing so, molecules will diffuse from regions of high concentration to regions of low concentration. Molecules are constantly in motion, and their rate of movement is proportional to the temperature. Only at absolute zero [0 K (kelvin) $= -273.15°C = -459.7°F$] do molecules cease their random movement. At all other temperatures they move about, colliding and veering off in different directions, thus pushing one another away. The result of these collisions in the example of sugar and water is to force sugar molecules upward (and to force water molecules downward), away from the regions in which they are most concentrated.

The Force of Electrostatic Pressure

When some substances are dissolved in water, they split into two parts, each with an opposing electrical charge. Substances with this property are called **electrolytes;** the charged particles into which they decompose are called **ions.** Ions are of two basic types: *Cations* have a positive charge, and *anions* have a negative charge. For example, when sodium chloride (NaCl, table salt) is dissolved in water, many of the molecules split into sodium cations (Na^+) and chloride anions (Cl^-). (I find that the easiest way to keep the terms *cation* and *anion* straight is to think of the cation's plus sign as a cross, and remember the superstition of a black *cat* crossing your path.)

As you have undoubtedly learned, particles with the same kind of charge repel each other (+ repels +, and – repels –), but particles with different charges are attracted to each other (+ and – attract). Thus, anions repel anions, cations repel cations, but anions and cations attract each other. The force exerted by this attraction or repulsion is called **electrostatic pressure.** Just as the force of diffusion moves molecules from regions of high concentration to regions of low concentration, electrostatic pressure moves ions from place to place: Cations are pushed away from regions with an excess of cations, and anions are pushed away from regions with an excess of anions.

Ions in the Extracellular and Intracellular Fluid

The fluid within cells (**intracellular fluid**) and the fluid surrounding them (**extracellular fluid**) contain different ions. The forces of diffusion and electrostatic

---

diffusion Movement of molecules from regions of high concentration to regions of low concentration.

electrolyte An aqueous solution of a material that ionizes—namely, a soluble acid, base, or salt.

ion A charged molecule. *Cations* are positively charged, and *anions* are negatively charged.

electrostatic pressure The attractive force between atomic particles charged with opposite signs or the repulsive force between atomic particles charged with the same sign.

intracellular fluid The fluid contained within cells.

extracellular fluid Body fluids located outside of cells.

pressure contributed by these ions give rise to the membrane potential. Because the membrane potential is produced by a balance between the forces of diffusion and electrostatic pressures, understanding what produces this potential requires that we know the concentration of the various ions in the extracellular and intracellular fluids.

There are several important ions in these fluids. I will discuss four of them here: organic anions (symbolized by A$^-$), chloride ions (Cl$^-$), sodium ions (Na$^+$), and potassium ions (K$^+$). The Latin words for sodium and potassium are *natrium* and *kalium;* hence, they are abbreviated *Na* and *K,* respectively. Organic anions—negatively charged proteins and intermediate products of the cell's metabolic processes—are found only in the intracellular fluid. Although the other three ions are found in both the intracellular and extracellular fluids, K$^+$ is found predominantly in the intracellular fluid, whereas Na$^+$ and Cl$^-$ are found predominantly in the extracellular fluid. The sizes of the boxes in Figure 2.17 indicate the relative concentrations of these four ions. (See *Figure 2.17.*) The easiest way to remember which ion is found where is to recall that the fluid that surrounds our cells is similar to seawater, which is predominantly a solution of salt, NaCl. The primitive ancestors of our cells lived in the ocean; thus, the seawater was their extracellular fluid. Our extracellular fluid thus resembles seawater, produced and maintained by regulatory mechanisms that are described in Chapter 12.

Let us consider the ions in Figure 2.17, examining the forces of diffusion and electrostatic pressure exerted on each and reasoning why each is located where it is. A$^-$, the organic anion, is unable to pass through the membrane of the axon; therefore, although the presence of this ion within the cell contributes to the membrane potential, it is located where it is because the membrane is impermeable to it.

The potassium ion K$^+$ is concentrated within the axon; thus, the force of diffusion tends to push it out of the cell. However, the outside of the cell is charged positively with respect to the inside, so electrostatic pressure tends to force the cation inside. Thus, the two opposing forces balance, and potassium ions tend to remain where they are. (See *Figure 2.17.*)

The chloride ion Cl$^-$ is in greatest concentration outside the axon. The force of diffusion pushes this ion inward. However, because the inside of the axon is negatively charged, electrostatic pressure pushes the anion outward. Again, two opposing forces balance each other. (See *Figure 2.17.*)

The sodium ion Na$^+$ is also in greatest concentration outside the axon, so it, like Cl$^-$, is pushed into the cell by the force of diffusion. But unlike chloride, the sodium ion is *positively* charged. Therefore, electrostatic pressure does *not* prevent Na$^+$ from entering the cell; indeed, the negative charge inside the axon *attracts* Na$^+$. (See *Figure 2.17.*)

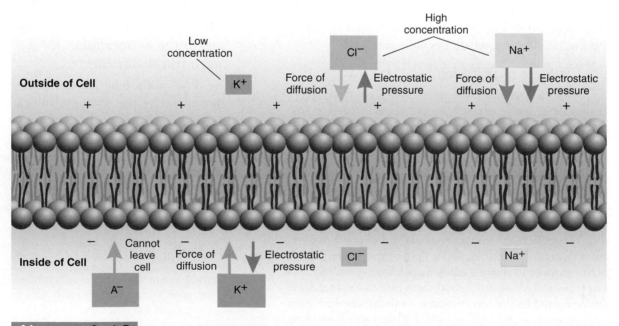

figure 2.17

The relative concentration of some important ions inside and outside the neuron and the forces acting on them.

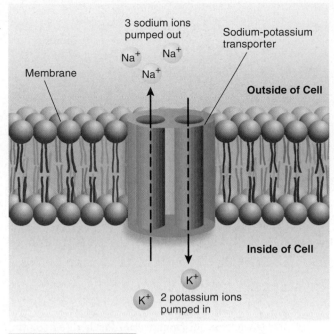

figure 2.18

A sodium-potassium transporter, situated in the cell membrane.

The Action Potential

As we saw, the forces of both diffusion and electrostatic pressure tend to push Na^+ into the cell. However, the membrane is not very permeable to this ion, and sodium-potassium transporters continuously pump out Na^+, keeping the intracellular level of Na^+ low. But imagine what would happen if the membrane suddenly became permeable to Na^+. The forces of diffusion and electrostatic pressure would cause Na^+ to rush into the cell. This sudden influx (inflow) of positively charged ions would drastically change the membrane potential. Indeed, experiments have shown that this mechanism is precisely what causes the action potential: A brief increase in the permeability of the membrane to Na^+ (allowing these ions to rush into the cell) is immediately followed by a transient increase in the permeability of the membrane to K^+ (allowing these ions to rush out of the cell). What is responsible for these transient increases in permeability?

We already saw that one type of protein molecule embedded in the membrane—the sodium-potassium transporter—actively pumps sodium ions out of the cell and pumps potassium ions into it. Another type of protein molecule provides an opening that permits ions to enter or leave the cells. These molecules provide **ion channels,** which contain passages ("pores") that can open or close. When an ion channel is open, a particular type of ion can flow through the pore and thus can enter or leave the cell. (See *Figure 2.19.*) Neural membranes contain many thousands of ion channels. For example, the giant squid axon contains several hundred sodium channels in each square micrometer of membrane. (There are one million square micrometers in a square millimeter; thus, a patch of axonal membrane the size of a lowercase letter "o" in this book would contain several hundred million sodium channels.) Each sodium channel can admit up to 100 million ions per second when it is open. Thus, the permeability of a membrane to a particular ion at a given moment is determined by the number of ion channels that are open.

The following numbered paragraphs describe the movements of ions through the membrane during the action potential. The numbers on the figure correspond

How can Na^+ remain in greatest concentration in the extracellular fluid, despite the fact that both forces (diffusion and electrostatic pressure) tend to push it inside? The answer is this: Another force, provided by the *sodium-potassium pump,* continuously pushes Na^+ out of the axon. The sodium-potassium pump consists of a large number of protein molecules embedded in the membrane, driven by energy provided by molecules of ATP produced by the mitochondria. These molecules, known as **sodium-potassium transporters,** exchange Na^+ for K^+, pushing three sodium ions out for every two potassium ions they push in. (See *Figure 2.18.*)

Because the membrane is not very permeable to Na^+, sodium-potassium transporters very effectively keep the intracellular concentration of Na^+ low. By transporting K^+ into the cell, they also increase the intracellular concentration of K^+ somewhat. The membrane is approximately 100 times more permeable to K^+ than to Na^+, so the increase is slight; but as we will see when we study the process of neural inhibition later in this chapter, it is very important. The transporters that make up the sodium-potassium pump use considerable energy: Up to 40 percent of a neuron's metabolic resources are used to operate them. Neurons, muscle cells, glia—in fact, most cells of the body—have sodium-potassium transporters in their membrane.

sodium-potassium transporter A protein found in the membrane of all cells that extrudes sodium ions from and transports potassium ions into the cell.

ion channel A specialized protein molecule that permits specific ions to enter or leave cells.

figure 2.19

Ion channels. When they are open, ions can pass through them, entering or leaving the cell.

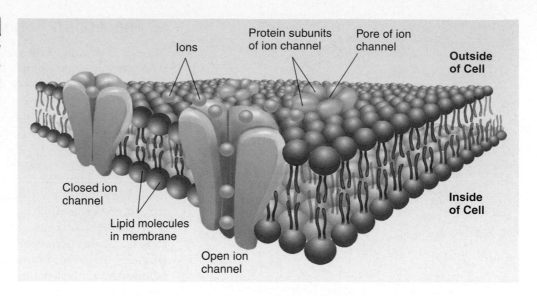

to the numbers of the paragraphs that follow. (See *Figure 2.20*.)

1. As soon as the threshold of excitation is reached, the sodium channels in the membrane open and Na$^+$ rushes in, propelled by the forces of diffusion and electrostatic pressure. The opening of these channels is triggered by reduction of the membrane potential (depolarization); they open at the point at which an action potential begins: the threshold of excitation. Because these channels are opened by changes in the membrane potential, they are called **voltage-dependent ion channels.** The influx of positively charged sodium ions produces a rapid change in the membrane potential, from –70 mV to +40 mV.

2. The membrane of the axon contains voltage-dependent potassium channels, but these channels are less sensitive than voltage-dependent sodium channels. That is, they require a greater level of depolarization before they begin to open. Thus, they begin to open later than the sodium channels.

3. At about the time the action potential reaches its peak (in approximately 1 msec), the sodium channels become *refractory*—the channels become blocked and cannot open again until the membrane once more reaches the resting potential. At this time, then, no more Na$^+$ can enter the cell.

4. By now, the voltage-dependent potassium channels in the membrane are open, letting K$^+$ ions move freely through the membrane. At this time, the inside of the axon is *positively* charged, so K$^+$ is driven out of the cell by diffusion and by electrostatic pressure. This outflow of cations causes the membrane potential to return toward its normal value. As it does so, the potassium channels begin to close again.

5. Once the membrane potential returns to normal, the potassium channels are closed, and no more potassium leaves the cell. At around this time, the sodium channels reset so that another depolarization can cause them to open again.

6. The membrane actually overshoots its resting value (–70 mV) and only gradually returns to normal. The accumulation of K$^+$ ions outside the membrane are responsible for this temporary hyperpolarization. The extra ions K$^+$ soon diffuse away, and the membrane potential returns to –70 mV. Eventually, sodium-potassium transporters remove the Na$^+$ ions that leaked in and retrieve the K$^+$ ions that leaked out.

Figure 2.21 illustrates the changes in permeability of the membrane to sodium and potassium ions during the action potential. (See *Figure 2.21*.)

How much ionic flow is there? The increased permeability of the membrane to Na$^+$ is brief, and diffusion over any appreciable distance takes some time. Thus, when I say, "Na$^+$ rushes in," I do not mean that the axoplasm becomes flooded with Na$^+$. At the peak of the action potential a very thin layer of fluid immediately inside the axon becomes full of newly arrived Na$^+$ ions; this amount is indeed enough to reverse the membrane potential. However, not enough time has

---

voltage-dependent ion channel An ion channel that opens or closes according to the value of the membrane potential.

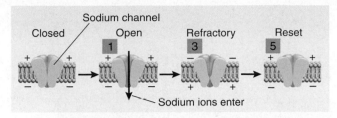

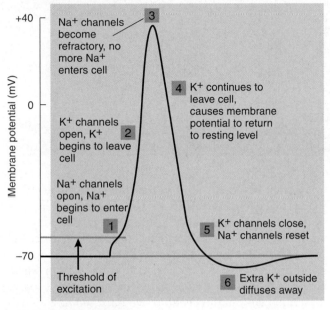

The movements of ions during the action potential. The shaded box at the top shows the opening of sodium channels at the threshold of excitation, their refractory condition at the peak of the action potential, and their resetting when the membrane potential returns to normal.

elapsed for these ions to fill the entire axon. Before that event can take place, the Na$^+$ channels close and K$^+$ starts flowing out.

Experiments have shown that an action potential temporarily increases the number of Na$^+$ ions inside the giant squid axon by 0.0003 percent. Although the concentration just inside the membrane is high, the total number of ions entering the cell is very small relative to the number already there. This means that on a short-term basis, sodium-potassium transporters are not very important. The few Na$^+$ ions that manage to leak in diffuse into the rest of the axoplasm, and the slight increase in Na$^+$ concentration is hardly noticeable. However, sodium-potassium transporters are important on a *long-term* basis. Without the activity of sodium-potassium transporters, the concentration of sodium ions in the axoplasm would eventually increase enough that the axon would no longer be able to function.

Conduction of the Action Potential

Now that we have a basic understanding of the resting membrane potential and the production of the action potential, we can consider the movement of the message down the axon, or *conduction of the action potential*. To study this phenomenon, we again make use of the giant squid axon. We attach an electrical stimulator to an electrode at one end of the axon and place recording electrodes, attached to oscilloscopes, at different distances from the stimulating electrode. Then we apply a depolarizing stimulus to the end of the axon and trigger an action potential. We record the action potential from each of the electrodes, one after the other. Thus, we see that the action

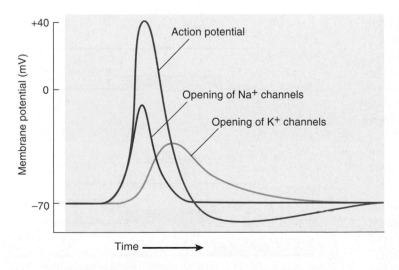

Changes in the permeability of the membrane to Na$^+$ and K$^+$ during the action potential.

figure 2.22

Conduction of the action potential. When an action potential is triggered, its size remains undiminished as it travels down the axon. The speed of conduction can be calculated from the delay between the stimulus and the action potential.

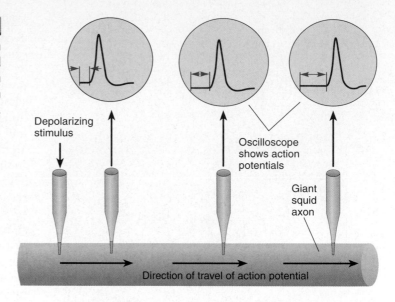

Depolarizing stimulus

Oscilloscope shows action potentials

Giant squid axon

Direction of travel of action potential

potential is conducted down the axon. As the action potential travels, it remains constant in size. (See *Figure 2.22.*)

This experiment establishes a basic law of axonal conduction: the **all-or-none law.** This law states that an action potential either occurs or does not occur; and once triggered, it is transmitted down the axon to its end. An action potential always remains the same size, without growing or diminishing. And when an action potential reaches a point where the axon branches, it splits but does not diminish in size. An axon will transmit an action potential in either direction, or even in both directions, if it is started in the middle of the axon's length. However, because action potentials in living animals always start at the end attached to the soma, axons normally carry one-way traffic.

As you know, the strength of a muscular contraction can vary from very weak to very forceful, and the strength of a stimulus can vary from barely detectable to very intense. We know that the occurrence of action potentials in axons controls the strength of muscular contractions and represents the intensity of a physical stimulus. But if the action potential is an all-or-none event, how can it represent information that can vary in a continuous fashion? The answer is simple: A single action potential is not the basic element of information; rather, variable information is represented by an axon's *rate of firing.* (In this context, *firing* refers to the production of action potentials.) A high rate of firing causes a strong muscular contraction, and a strong stimulus (such as a bright light) causes a high rate of firing in axons that serve the eyes. Thus, the all-or-none law is supplemented by the **rate law.** (See *Figure 2.23.*)

all-or-none law The principle that once an action potential is triggered in an axon, it is propagated, without decrement, to the end of the fiber.

rate law The principle that variations in the intensity of a stimulus or other information being transmitted in an axon are represented by variations in the rate at which that axon fires.

Action potentials are not the only kind of electrical signals that occur in neurons. As we will see in the last section of this chapter, when a message is sent across a synapse, a small electrical signal is produced in the membrane of the neuron that receives the message. To understand this process, and to understand the way in which action potentials are conducted in myelinated axons (described later in this section), we must see how signals other than action potentials are conducted. To do so, we produce a weak, subthreshold depolarization (too small to produce an action potential) at one end of an axon and record its effects from electrodes placed along the axon. We find that the stimulus produces a disturbance in the membrane potential that becomes smaller as it moves away from the point of stimulation. (See *Figure 2.24.*)

The transmission of the weak, subthreshold depolarization is *passive.* Neither sodium channels nor potassium channels open or close. The axon is acting like an electri-

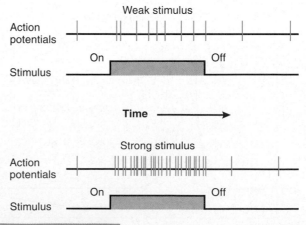

Weak stimulus

Action potentials

On   Off

Stimulus

Time

Strong stimulus

Action potentials

On   Off

Stimulus

figure 2.23

The rate law. The strength of a stimulus is represented by the rate of firing of an axon. The size of each action potential is always constant.

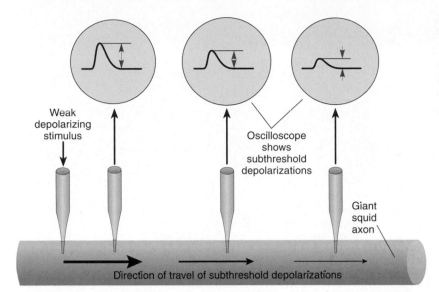

Weak depolarizing stimulus

Oscilloscope shows subthreshold depolarizations

Giant squid axon

Direction of travel of subthreshold depolarizations

figure 2.24

Decremental conduction. When a subthreshold depolarization is applied to the axon, the disturbance in the membrane potential is largest near the stimulating electrode and gets progressively smaller at distances farther along the axon.

cal cable, carrying along the current that started at one end. This property of the axon follows laws discovered in the nineteenth century that describe the conduction of electricity through telegraph cables laid along the ocean floor. As a signal passes through an undersea cable, the signal gets smaller because of the electrical characteristics of the cable, including leakage through the insulator and resistance in the wire. Because the signal decreases in size (decrements), it is referred to as *decremental conduction*. We say that the conduction of a weak depolarization by the axon follows the laws that describe the **cable properties** of the axon—the same laws that describe the electrical properties of an undersea cable. And because hyperpolarizations never trigger action potentials, these disturbances, too, are transmitted by means of the passive cable properties of an axon.

Recall that all but the smallest axons in mammalian nervous systems are myelinated; segments of the axons are covered by a myelin sheath produced by the oligodendrocytes of the CNS or the Schwann cells of the PNS. These segments are separated by portions of naked axon, the nodes of Ranvier. Conduction of an action potential in a myelinated axon is somewhat different from conduction in an unmyelinated axon.

Schwann cells (and the oligodendrocytes of the CNS) wrap tightly around the axon, leaving no measurable extracellular fluid between them and the axon. The only place where a myelinated axon comes into contact with the extracellular fluid is at a node of Ranvier, where the axon is naked. In the myelinated areas there can be no inward flow of Na^+ when the sodium channels open, because there *is* no extracellular sodium. How, then, does the "action potential" travel along the area of axonal membrane covered by myelin sheath? You guessed it—by cable properties. The axon passively conducts the electrical disturbance from the action potential to the next node of Ranvier. The disturbance gets smaller, but it is still large enough to trigger an action potential at the node. The action potential gets retrig-

gered, or repeated, at each node of Ranvier and is passed, by means of cable properties of the axon, along the myelinated area to the next node. Such conduction, appearing to hop from node to node, is called **saltatory conduction,** from the Latin *saltare,* "to dance." (See *Figure 2.25.*)

Saltatory conduction confers two advantages. The first is economic. Sodium ions enter axons during action potentials, and these ions must eventually be removed. Sodium-potassium transporters must be located along the entire length of unmyelinated axons because Na^+ enters everywhere. However, because Na^+ can enter myelinated axons only at the nodes of Ranvier, much less gets in, and consequently, much less has to be pumped out again. Therefore, myelinated axons expend much less energy to maintain their sodium balance.

The second advantage to myelin is speed. Conduction of an action potential is faster in a myelinated axon because the transmission between the nodes, which occurs by means of the axon's cable properties, is very fast. Increased speed enables an animal to react faster and (undoubtedly) to think faster. One of the ways to increase the speed of conduction is to increase size. Because it is so large, the unmyelinated squid axon, with a diameter of 500 µm, achieves a conduction velocity of approximately 35 m/sec (meters per second). However, the same speed is achieved by a myelinated cat axon with a diameter of a mere 6 µm. The fastest myelinated axon, 20 µm in diameter, can conduct action potentials at a speedy 120 m/sec, or 432 km/h (kilometers per hour). At that speed, a signal can get from one end of an axon to the other without much delay.

cable properties The passive conduction of electrical current, in a decremental fashion, down the length of an axon.

saltatory conduction Conduction of action potentials by myelinated axons. The action potential appears to jump from one node of Ranvier to the next.

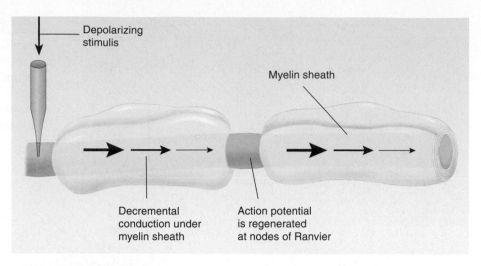

Depolarizing
stimulis

Myelin sheath

Decremental
conduction under
myelin sheath

Action potential
is regenerated
at nodes of Ranvier

figure 2.25

Saltatory conduction, showing propagation of an action potential down a myelinated axon.

Communication Within a Neuron

The message conducted down an axon is called an action potential. The membranes of all cells of the body are electrically charged, but only axons can produce action potentials. The resting membrane potential occurs because various ions are located in different concentrations in the fluid inside and outside the cell. The extracellular fluid (like seawater) is rich in Na$^+$ and Cl$^-$, and the intracellular fluid is rich in K$^+$ and various organic anions, designated as A$^-$.

The cell membrane is freely permeable to water, but its permeability to various ions—in particular, Na$^+$ and K$^+$—is regulated by ion channels. When the membrane potential is at its resting value (–70 mV), the voltage-dependent sodium and potassium channels are closed. The experiment with radioactive seawater showed us that some Na$^+$ continuously leaks into the axon but is promptly forced out of the cell again by the sodium-potassium transporters (which also pump potassium *into* the axon). When an electrical stimulator depolarizes the membrane of the axon so that its potential reaches the threshold of excitation, voltage-dependent sodium channels open and Na$^+$ rushes into the cell, driven by the force of diffusion and by electrostatic pressure. The entry of the positively charged ions further reduces the membrane potential and, indeed, causes it to reverse, so the inside becomes positive. The opening of the sodium channels is temporary; they soon close again. The depolarization caused by the influx of Na$^+$ activates voltage-dependent potassium channels, and K$^+$ leaves the axon, traveling down

its concentration gradient. This efflux (outflow) of K$^+$ quickly brings the membrane potential back to its resting value.

Because an action potential of a given axon is an all-or-none phenomenon, neurons represent intensity by their rate of firing. The action potential normally begins at one end of the axon, where the axon attaches to the soma. The action potential travels continuously down unmyelinated axons, remaining constant in size, until it reaches the terminal buttons. (If the axon divides, an action potential continues down each branch.) In myelinated axons ions can flow through the membrane only at the nodes of Ranvier, because the axons are covered everywhere else with myelin, which isolates them from the extracellular fluid. Thus, the action potential is conducted from one node of Ranvier to the next by means of passive cable properties. When the electrical message reaches a node, voltage-dependent sodium channels open, and a new action potential is triggered. This mechanism saves a considerable amount of energy because sodium-potassium transporters are not needed along the myelinated portions of the axon, and saltatory conduction is faster.

Communication Between Neurons

Now that you know about the basic structure of neurons and the nature of the action potential, it is time to describe the ways in which neurons can communicate with each other and with muscles and sensory organs. As we have seen, neurons communicate by means of synapses, and the medium used for these messages is the neurotransmitter released by terminal buttons. Neurotransmitters diffuse across the fluid-filled gap between terminal buttons and the membranes of the neurons with which they form synapses (the *postsynaptic* neurons). As we will see in this

> See the interactive CD for more information on synapses.

section, neurotransmitters produce **postsynaptic potentials**—brief depolarizations or hyperpolarizations—that increase or decrease the rate of firing of the axons of the postsynaptic neurons. (*Animation 2.3, Synapses,* illustrates the information presented in the following section.)

The Concept of Chemical Transmission

Chemicals are used to transmit information between cells. These chemicals—neurotransmitters, neuromodulators, and hormones—control the behavior of cells or organs. All these methods of transmission require cells that release the chemicals and specialized protein molecules (receptors) that detect the presence of these chemicals. These methods differ primarily in the distance between the cell that secretes the chemical and the receptors that detect its presence.

Neurotransmitters are released by terminal buttons of neurons and are detected by receptors in the membrane of another cell located a very short distance away. The communication at each synapse is private. Neuromodulators travel farther and are dispersed more widely than are neurotransmitters. **Neuromodulators,** too, are released by terminal buttons but are secreted in larger amounts and diffuse for longer distances, modulating the activity of many neurons in a particular part of the brain. Most neuromodulators are composed of proteinlike molecules called *peptides,* which are described later in this chapter.

Most hormones are produced in cells located in the **endocrine glands** (from the Greek *endo-,* "within," and *krinein,* "to secrete"). Others are produced by specialized cells located in various organs, such as the stomach, the intestines, the kidneys, and the brain. Cells that secrete hormones release these chemicals into the extracellular fluid. The hormones are then taken up by capillaries and distributed to the rest of the body through the bloodstream. Hormones affect the activity of cells (including neurons) that contain specialized receptors located either on the surface of their membrane or deep within their nuclei. (Both types are described later in this chapter.) Cells that contain receptors for a particular hor-

mone are referred to as **target cells** for that hormone; only these cells respond to its presence. Many neurons contain hormone receptors, and hormones are able to affect behavior by stimulating the receptors and changing the activity of these neurons. For example, a sex hormone, testosterone, increases the aggressiveness of most male mammals.

Neurotransmitters, neuromodulators, and hormones exert their effects on cells by attaching to a particular region of a receptor molecule called the **binding site.** A molecule of the chemical fits into the binding site the way a key fits into a lock; the shape of the binding site and the shape of the molecule of the neurotransmitter are complementary. (A chemical that attaches to a binding site is called a **ligand,** from the Latin *ligare,* "to bind.") Neurotransmitters, neuromodulators, or hormones are natural ligands, produced by cells of the body. But other chemicals found in nature (primarily in plants or in the poisonous venoms of animals) can serve as ligands, too. In addition, artificial ligands can be produced in the laboratory. These chemicals are discussed in Chapter 4, which deals with drugs and their effects.

Structure of Synapses

As you have already learned, synapses are junctions between the terminal buttons at the ends of the axonal branches of one neuron and the membrane of another. Synapses can occur in three places: on dendrites, on the soma, and on other axons. These synapses are referred to as *axodendritic, axosomatic,* and *axoaxonic.* Axodendritic synapses can occur on the smooth surface of a dendrite or on **dendritic spines**—small protrusions that stud the

---

postsynaptic potential Alterations in the membrane potential of a postsynaptic neuron, produced by liberation of neurotransmitter at the synapse.

neuromodulator A naturally secreted substance that acts like a neurotransmitter except that it is not restricted to the synaptic cleft but diffuses through the extracellular fluid.

endocrine gland A gland that liberates its secretions into the extracellular fluid around capillaries and hence into the bloodstream.

target cell The type of cell that is directly affected by a hormone or nerve fiber.

binding site The location on a receptor protein to which a ligand binds.

ligand (*ligh* gand or **ligg** and) A chemical that binds with the binding site of a receptor.

dendritic spine A small bud on the surface of a dendrite, with which a terminal button of another neuron forms a synapse.

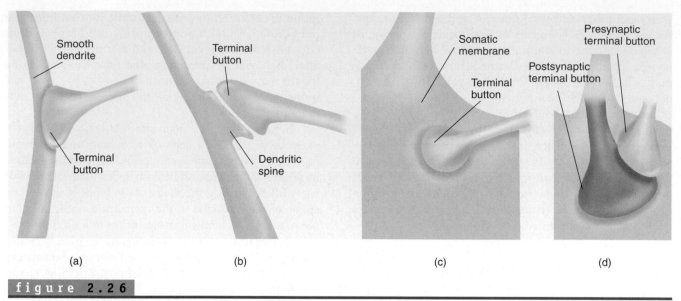

Smooth dendrite

Terminal button

Terminal button

Terminal button

Dendritic spine

Somatic membrane

Terminal button

Presynaptic terminal button

Postsynaptic terminal button

(a)   (b)   (c)   (d)

figure 2.26

Types of synapses. Axodendritic synapses can occur on the smooth surface of a dendrite (a) or on dendritic spines (b). Axosomatic synapses occur on somatic membrane (c). Axoaxonic synapses consist of synapses between two terminal buttons (d).

dendrites of several types of large neurons in the brain. (See *Figure 2.26.*)

Figure 2.27 illustrates a synapse. The **presynaptic membrane,** located at the end of the terminal button, faces the **postsynaptic membrane,** located on the neuron that receives the message (the *postsynaptic* neuron). These two membranes face each other across the **synaptic cleft,** a gap that varies in size from synapse to synapse but is usually around 20 nm wide. (A nanometer (nm) is one billionth of a meter.) The synaptic cleft contains extracellular fluid, through which the neurotransmitter diffuses. A meshwork of filaments crosses the synaptic cleft and keeps the presynaptic and postsynaptic membranes in alignment. (See *Figure 2.27.*)

As you may have noticed in Figure 2.27, three prominent structures are located in the cytoplasm of the terminal button: mitochondria, synaptic vesicles, and a cisterna. We also see microtubules, which are responsible for transporting material between the soma and terminal button. The presence of mitochondria implies that the terminal button needs energy to perform its functions. **Synaptic vesicles** are small, rounded objects in the shape of spheres or ovoids. (The term *vesicle* means "little bladder.") Many terminal buttons contain two types of synaptic vesicles: large and small. Small synaptic vesicles (found in all terminal buttons) contain molecules of the neurotransmitter. They range in number from a few dozen to several hundred. The membrane of small synaptic vesicles consists of approximately 10,000 lipid molecules into which are inserted about 200 protein molecules. These proteins serve to help transport the vesicles within the terminal button and to fill them

with the neurotransmitter. These vesicles are found in greatest numbers around the part of the presynaptic membrane that faces the synaptic cleft—near the **release zone,** the region from which the neurotransmitter is released. In many terminal buttons we see a scattering of large, dense-core synaptic vesicles. These vesicles contain one of a number of different peptides, the functions of which are described later in this chapter. (See *Figures 2.27* and *2.28.*)

Small synaptic vesicles are produced in the Golgi apparatus located in the soma and are carried by fast axoplasmic transport to the terminal button. As we will see, they are also produced from recycled material in the terminal button by the **cisternae,** collections of membrane similar to the Golgi apparatus. Large synaptic vesicles are

presynaptic membrane The membrane of a terminal button that lies adjacent to the postsynaptic membrane and through which the neurotransmitter is released.

postsynaptic membrane The cell membrane opposite the terminal button in a synapse; the membrane of the cell that receives the message.

synaptic cleft The space between the presynaptic membrane and the postsynaptic membrane.

synaptic vesicle (*vess i kul*) A small, hollow, beadlike structure found in terminal buttons; contains molecules of a neurotransmitter.

release zone A region of the interior of the presynaptic membrane of a synapse to which synaptic vesicles attach and release their neurotransmitter into the synaptic cleft.

cisterna A part of the Golgi apparatus; through the process of pinocytosis, it receives portions of the presynaptic membrane and recycles them into synaptic vesicles.

Detail of Synapse

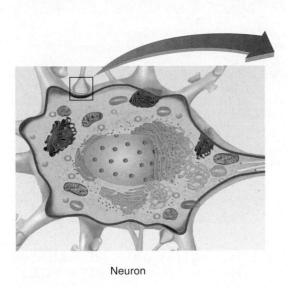

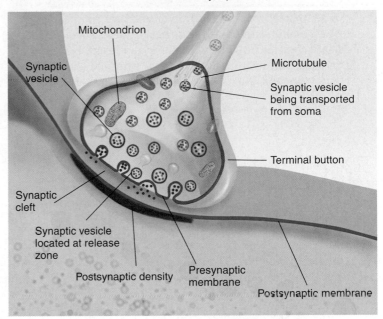

Neuron

figure **2.27**

Details of a synapse.

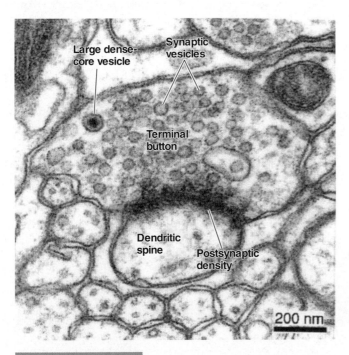

figure **2.28**

A photograph from an electron microscope, showing a cross section of a synapse. The terminal button contains many synaptic vesicles, filled with the neurotransmitter, and a single large dense-core vesicle, filled with a peptide. (From De Camilli, P., et al., in *Synapses,* edited by W. M. Cowan, T. C. Südhof, and C. F. Stevens. Baltimore, MD: Johns Hopkins University Press, 2001.)

produced only in the soma and transported through the axoplasm to the terminal buttons.

In an electron micrograph the postsynaptic membrane under the terminal button appears somewhat thicker and more dense than the membrane elsewhere. This postsynaptic density is caused by the presence of receptors—specialized protein molecules that detect the presence of neurotransmitters in the synaptic cleft. (See *Figures 2.27* and *2.28.*)

Release of Neurotransmitter

When action potentials are conducted down an axon (and down all of its branches), something happens inside all of the terminal buttons: A number of small synaptic vesicles located just inside the presynaptic membrane fuse with the membrane and then break open, spilling their contents into the synaptic cleft.

Heuser and colleagues (Heuser, 1977; Heuser et al., 1979) obtained photomicrographs that illustrate this process. Because the release of neurotransmitter is a very rapid event, taking only a few milliseconds to occur, special procedures are needed to stop the action so that the details can be studied. The experimenters electrically stimulated the nerve attached to an isolated frog muscle and then dropped the muscle against a block of pure copper that had been cooled to 4 K (approximately –453°F). Contact with the supercooled metal froze the outer layer of tissue in 2 msec or less. The ice held the components of the terminal buttons

figure 2.29

A photograph from an electron microscope, showing a cross section of a synapse. The omega-shaped figures are synaptic vesicles fusing with the presynaptic membranes of terminal buttons that form synapses with frog muscle.

(From Heuser, J. E., in *Society for Neuroscience Symposia, Vol. II*, edited by W. M. Cowan and J. A. Ferrendelli. Bethesda, MD: Society for Neuroscience, 1977.)

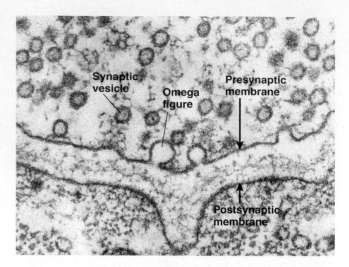

in place until they could be chemically stabilized and examined with an electron microscope. Figure 2.29 shows a portion of the synapse in cross section; note the vesicles that appear to be fused with the presynaptic membrane, forming the shape of an omega (Ω). (See *Figure 2.29*.)

How does an action potential cause synaptic vesicles to release the neurotransmitter? On the basis of experi-

ments with secretory cells in a variety of different species, Almers (1990) suggested the following model. Some synaptic vesicles are "docked" against the presynaptic membrane, ready to release their neurotransmitter into the synaptic cleft. Docking is accomplished when clusters of protein molecules attach to other protein molecules located in the presynaptic membrane. (See *Figure 2.30*.)

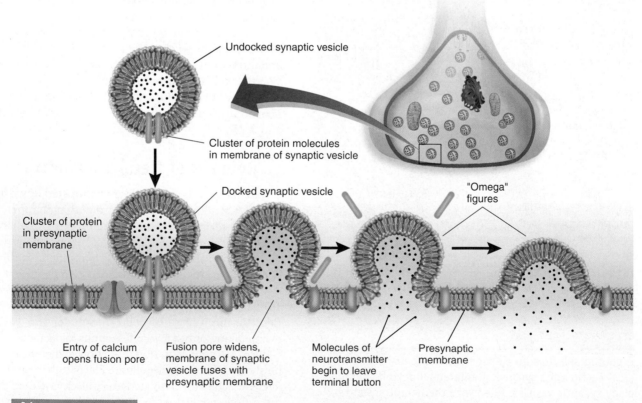

figure 2.30

Release of neurotransmitter. An action potential opens calcium channels. Calcium ions enter and bind with the protein embedded in the membrane of synaptic vesicles docked at the release zone. The fusion pores open, and the neurotransmitter is released into the synaptic cleft. The membrane of the vesicles fuses with that of the terminal button.

Calcium channels, when open,
cause release of neurotransmitter

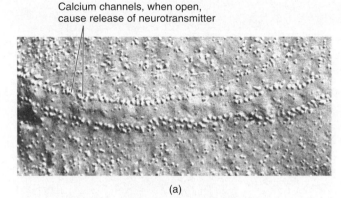

(a)

Synaptic vesicles fused with the presynaptic
membrane, releasing the neurotransmitter

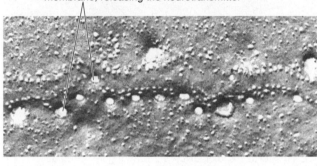

(b)

figure 2.31

Photomicrographs of the release of neurotransmitter by a terminal button that forms a synapse with a frog muscle. The views are of the surface of the fusion zone of the terminal button. (a) Just before release. The two rows of dots are probably calcium channels. (b) During release. The larger circles are holes in the presynaptic membrane, revealing the contents of the synaptic vesicles that have fused with it.
(From Heuser, J., and Reese, T. *Journal of Cell Biology,* 1981, *88,* 564–580.)

The release zone of the presynaptic membrane contains voltage-dependent calcium channels. When the membrane of the terminal button is depolarized by an arriving action potential, the calcium channels open. Like sodium ions, calcium ions (Ca^{2+}) are located in highest concentration in the extracellular fluid. Thus, when the voltage-dependent calcium channels open, Ca^{2+} flows into the cell, propelled by electrostatic pressure and the force of diffusion. The entry of Ca^{2+} is an essential step; if neurons are placed in a solution that contains no calcium ions, an action potential no longer causes the release of the neurotransmitter. (Calcium transporters, similar in operation to sodium-potassium transporters, later remove the intracellular Ca^{2+}.)

As we will see later in this chapter and in subsequent chapters of this book, calcium ions play many important roles in biological processes within cells. Calcium ions can bind with various types of proteins, changing their characteristics. According to Almers (1990), the calcium ions that enter the terminal button bind with the clusters of protein molecules that join the membrane of the synaptic vesicles with the presynaptic membrane. This event makes the segments of the clusters of protein molecules move apart, producing a *fusion pore*—a hole through both membranes that enables them to fuse together. The process of fusion takes approximately 0.1 msec. (See *Figure 2.30.*)

Figure 2.31 shows two photomicrographs of the presynaptic membrane, before and after the fusion pores have opened. We see the face of the presynaptic membrane as it would be viewed from the postsynaptic membrane. As

you can see, the synaptic vesicles are aligned in a row along the release zone. The small bumps arranged in lines on each side of the synaptic vesicles appear to be voltage-dependent calcium channels. (See *Figure 2.31.*)

What happens to the membrane of the synaptic vesicles after they have broken open and released the neurotransmitter they contain? Every time some neurotransmitter is released, the membrane of the terminal button gains the membrane of the synaptic vesicles that fuse with it and becomes slightly larger. Obviously, this process cannot go on indefinitely, or else the terminal buttons would get enormously big. The answer is that the membrane is recycled. Heuser and Reese (1973) proposed that as the synaptic vesicles fuse with the presynaptic membrane and burst open, their membrane becomes incorporated into that of the terminal button, which consequently becomes larger. Therefore, if the proper size of the terminal button is to be maintained, some membrane must be removed. Heuser and Reese obtained evidence that suggested that at the point of junction between the axon and the terminal button, little buds of membrane pinch off into the cytoplasm, in a process called **pinocytosis.** The buds of membrane migrate to the cisternae and fuse with them, pooling the lipid molecules in their membrane with that of the cisternae. Then new

pinocytosis (*pee no sy* **toh** *sis*) The pinching off of a bud of cell membrane, which travels to the interior of the cell.

synaptic vesicles are produced as beads of membrane break off from the cisternae. The appropriate proteins are inserted into the membrane of these vesicles, the vesicles are filled with molecules of the neurotransmitter, and they are transported toward the presynaptic membrane. The entire recycling process appears to take approximately one minute (Betz and Berwick, 1992). (See *Figure 2.32.*)

Activation of Receptors

How do molecules of the neurotransmitter produce a depolarization or hyperpolarization in the postsynaptic membrane? They do so by diffusing across the synaptic cleft and attaching to the binding sites of special protein molecules located in the postsynaptic membrane, called **postsynaptic receptors.** Once binding occurs, the postsynaptic receptors open **neurotransmitter-dependent ion channels,** which permit the passage of specific ions into or out of the cell. Thus, the presence of the neurotransmitter in the synaptic cleft allows particular ions to pass through the membrane, changing the local membrane potential.

Neurotransmitters open ion channels by at least two different methods, direct and indirect. The direct method

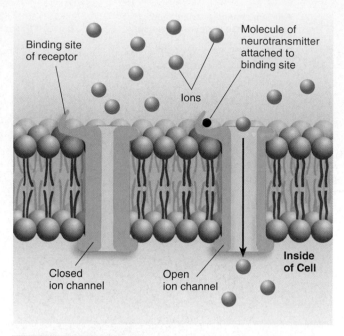

figure 2.33

Ionotropic receptors. The ion channel opens when a molecule of neurotransmitter attaches to the binding site. For purposes of clarity the drawing is schematic; molecules of neurotransmitter are actually much larger than individual ions.

is simpler, so I will describe it first. Figure 2.33 illustrates a neurotransmitter-dependent ion channel that is equipped with its own binding site. When a molecule of the appropriate neurotransmitter attaches to it, the ion channel opens. The formal name for this combination receptor/ion channel is an **ionotropic receptor.** (See *Figure 2.33.*)

Ionotropic receptors were first discovered in the organ that produces electrical current in *Torpedo,* the electric ray, where they occur in great number. (The electric ray is a fish that generates a powerful electrical current, not some kind of Star Wars weapon.) These receptors, which are sensitive to a neurotransmitter called *acetylcholine,* contain sodium channels. When these channels are open, sodium ions enter the cell and depolarize the membrane.

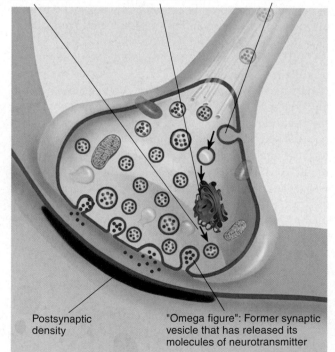

figure 2.32

Recycling of the membrane of synaptic vesicles that have released neurotransmitter into the synaptic cleft.

postsynaptic receptor A receptor molecule in the postsynaptic membrane of a synapse that contains a binding site for a neurotransmitter.

neurotransmitter-dependent ion channel An ion channel that opens when a molecule of a neurotransmitter binds with a postsynaptic receptor.

ionotropic receptor (*eye on oh **trow** pik*) A receptor that contains a binding site for a neurotransmitter and an ion channel that opens when a molecule of the neurotransmitter attaches to the binding site.

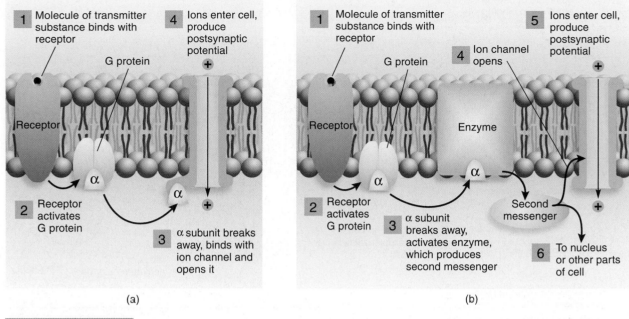

figure 2.34

Metabotropic receptors. (a) The ion channel is opened directly by the α subunit of an activated G protein. (b) The α subunit of the G protein activates an enzyme, which produces a second messenger that opens the ion channel.

The indirect method is more complicated. Some receptors do not open ion channels directly but instead start a chain of chemical events. These receptors are called **metabotropic receptors** because they involve steps that require that the cell expend metabolic energy. Metabotropic receptors are located in close proximity to another protein attached to the membrane—a **G protein.** When a molecule of the neurotransmitter binds with the receptor, the receptor activates a G protein situated inside the membrane next to the receptor. When activated, the G protein activates an enzyme that stimulates the production of a chemical called a **second messenger.** (The neurotransmitter is the first messenger.) Molecules of the second messenger travel through the cytoplasm, attach themselves to nearby ion channels, and cause them to open. Compared with postsynaptic potentials produced by ionotropic receptors, those produced by metabotropic receptors take longer to begin and last longer. (See *Figure 2.34.*)

The first second messenger to be discovered was *cyclic AMP,* a chemical that is synthesized from ATP. Since then, several other second messengers have been discovered. As you will see in later chapters, second messengers play an important role in both synaptic and nonsynaptic communication. And they can do more than open ion channels. For example, they can travel to the nucleus or other regions of the neuron and initiate biochemical changes that

affect the functions of the cell. They can even turn specific genes on or off, thus initiating or terminating production of particular proteins.

Postsynaptic Potentials

As I mentioned earlier, postsynaptic potentials can be either depolarizing (excitatory) or hyperpolarizing (inhibitory). What determines the nature of the postsynaptic potential at a particular synapse is not the neurotransmitter itself. Instead, it is determined by the characteristics of the postsynaptic receptors—in particular, *by the particular type of ion channel they open.*

---

metabotropic receptor (*meh tab oh **trow** pik*) A receptor that contains a binding site for a neurotransmitter; activates an enzyme that begins a series of events that opens an ion channel elsewhere in the membrane of the cell when a molecule of the neurotransmitter attaches to the binding site.

G protein A protein coupled to a metabotropic receptor; conveys messages to other molecules when a ligand binds with and activates the receptor.

second messenger A chemical produced when a G protein activates an enzyme; carries a signal that results in the opening of the ion channel or causes other events to occur in the cell.

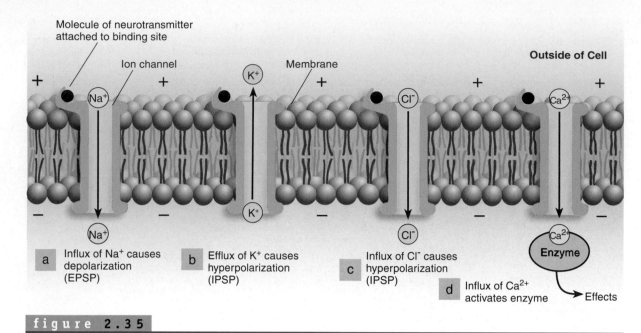

a Influx of Na⁺ causes depolarization (EPSP)

b Efflux of K⁺ causes hyperpolarization (IPSP)

c Influx of Cl⁻ causes hyperpolarization (IPSP)

d Influx of Ca²⁺ activates enzyme → Effects

Enzyme

figure 2.35

Ionic movements during postsynaptic potentials.

As Figure 2.35 shows, there are four major types of neurotransmitter-dependent ion channels found in the postsynaptic membrane: sodium (Na^+), potassium (K^+), chloride (Cl^-), and calcium (Ca^{2+}). Although the figure depicts only directly activated (ionotropic) ion channels, you should realize that many ion channels are activated indirectly, by metabotropic receptors coupled to G proteins.

The neurotransmitter-dependent sodium channel is the most important source of excitatory postsynaptic potentials. As we saw, sodium-potassium transporters keep sodium outside the cell, waiting for the forces of diffusion and electrostatic pressure to push it in. Obviously, when sodium channels are opened, the result is a depolarization—an **excitatory postsynaptic potential (EPSP)**. (See *Figure 2.35a*.)

We also saw that sodium-potassium transporters maintain a small surplus of potassium ions inside the cell. If potassium channels open, some of these cations will follow this gradient and leave the cell. Because K^+ is positively charged, its efflux will hyperpolarize the membrane, producing an **inhibitory postsynaptic potential (IPSP)**. (See *Figure 2.35b*.)

At many synapses inhibitory neurotransmitters open the chloride channels, instead of (or in addition to) potassium channels. The effect of opening chloride channels depends on the membrane potential of the neuron. If the membrane is at the resting potential, nothing happens, because (as we saw earlier) the forces of diffusion and electrostatic pressure balance perfectly for the chloride ion.

However, if the membrane potential has already been depolarized by the activity of excitatory synapses located nearby, then the opening of chloride channels will permit Cl^- to enter the cell. The influx of anions will bring the membrane potential back to its normal resting condition. Thus, the opening of chloride channels serves to neutralize EPSPs. (See *Figure 2.35c*.)

The fourth type of neurotransmitter-dependent ion channel is the calcium channel. Calcium ions (Ca^{2+}), being positively charged and being located in highest concentration outside the cell, act like sodium ions; that is, the opening of calcium channels depolarizes the membrane, producing EPSPs. But calcium does even more. As we saw earlier in this chapter, the entry of calcium into the terminal button triggers the migration of synaptic vesicles and the release of the neurotransmitter. In the dendrites of the postsynaptic cell, calcium binds with and activates special enzymes. These enzymes have a variety of effects, including the production of biochemical and structural changes in the postsynaptic neuron. As we will see in

excitatory postsynaptic potential (EPSP) An excitatory depolarization of the postsynaptic membrane of a synapse caused by the liberation of a neurotransmitter by the terminal button.

inhibitory postsynaptic potential (IPSP) An inhibitory hyperpolarization of the postsynaptic membrane of a synapse caused by the liberation of a neurotransmitter by the terminal button.

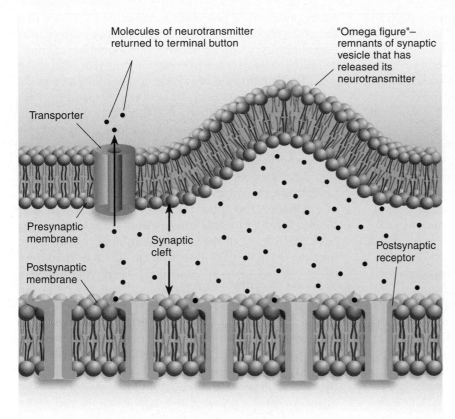

Molecules of neurotransmitter returned to terminal button

"Omega figure"– remnants of synaptic vesicle that has released its neurotransmitter

Transporter

Presynaptic membrane

Synaptic cleft

Postsynaptic membrane

Postsynaptic receptor

figure 2.36

Reuptake. Molecules of a neurotransmitter that has been released into the synaptic cleft are transported back into the terminal button.

Chapter 13, one of the ways that learning affects the connections between neurons involves changes in dendritic spines initiated by the opening of calcium channels. (See *Figure 2.35d.*)

Termination of Postsynaptic Potentials

Postsynaptic potentials are brief depolarizations or hyperpolarizations caused by the activation of postsynaptic receptors with molecules of a neurotransmitter. They are kept brief by two mechanisms: reuptake and enzymatic deactivation.

The postsynaptic potentials produced by almost all neurotransmitters are terminated by **reuptake.** This process is simply an extremely rapid removal of neurotransmitter from the synaptic cleft by the terminal button. The neurotransmitter does not return in the vesicles that get pinched off the membrane of the terminal button. Instead, the membrane contains special transporter molecules that draw on the cell's energy reserves to force molecules of the neurotransmitter from the synaptic cleft directly into the cytoplasm—just as sodium-potassium transporters move Na^+ and K^+ across the membrane. When an action potential arrives, the terminal button releases a small amount of neurotransmitter into the synaptic cleft and then takes it back, giving the postsynaptic receptors only a brief exposure to the neurotransmitter. (See *Figure 2.36.*)

Enzymatic deactivation is accomplished by an enzyme that destroys molecules of the neurotransmitter. As far as we know, postsynaptic potentials are terminated in this way for only one neurotransmitter: **acetylcholine (ACh).** Transmission at synapses on muscle fibers and at some synapses between neurons in the central nervous system is mediated by ACh. Postsynaptic potentials produced by ACh are short-lived because the postsynaptic membrane at these synapses contains an enzyme called

reuptake The reentry of a neurotransmitter just liberated by a terminal button back through its membrane, thus terminating the postsynaptic potential.

enzymatic deactivation The destruction of a neurotransmitter by an enzyme after its release—for example, the destruction of acetylcholine by acetylcholinesterase.

acetylcholine (ACh) (*a see tul koh leen*) A neurotransmitter found in the brain, spinal cord, and parts of the peripheral nervous system; responsible for muscular contraction.

acetylcholinesterase (AChE). AChE destroys ACh by cleaving it into its constituents: choline and acetate. Because neither of these substances is capable of activating postsynaptic receptors, the postsynaptic potential is terminated once the molecules of ACh are broken apart. AChE is an extremely energetic destroyer of ACh; one molecule of AChE will chop apart more that five thousand molecules of ACh each second.

You will recall that Kathryn, the woman featured in the case history that opened this chapter, suffered from progressive muscular weakness. As her neurologist discovered, Kathryn had myasthenia gravis. This disease was first described in 1672 by Thomas Willis, an English physician. The term literally means "grave muscle weakness." It is not a very common disorder, but most experts believe that many mild cases go undiagnosed.

In 1934 Dr. Mary Walker remarked that the symptoms of myasthenia gravis resembled the effects of curare, a poison that blocks neural transmission at the synapses on muscles. A drug called *physostigmine,* which deactivates acetylcholinesterase, serves as an antidote for curare poisoning. As we just saw, AChE is an enzyme that destroys the ACh and terminates the postsynaptic potentials it produces. By deactivating AChE, physostigmine greatly increases and prolongs the effects of ACh on the postsynaptic membrane. Thus, it increases the strength of synaptic transmission at the synapses on muscles and reverses the effects of curare. (Chapter 4 will say more about both curare and physostigmine.)

Dr. Walker reasoned that if physostigmine reversed the effects of curare poisoning, perhaps it would also reverse the symptoms of myasthenia gravis. She tried it, and it did within a matter of a few minutes. Later, pharmaceutical companies discovered drugs that could be taken orally and that produced longer-lasting effects. Nowadays, an injectable drug is used to make the diagnosis (as in Kathryn's case), and an oral drug is used to treat it. Unfortunately, no cure has yet been found for myasthenia gravis.

Like multiple sclerosis, myasthenia gravis is an autoimmune disease. For some reason, the immune system becomes sensitized against the protein that makes up acetylcholine receptors. Almost as fast as new ACh receptors are produced, the immune system destroys them.

Effects of Postsynaptic Potentials: Neural Integration

We have seen how neurons are interconnected by means of synapses, how action potentials trigger the release of neurotransmitters, and how these chemicals initiate excitatory or inhibitory postsynaptic potentials. Exci-

tatory postsynaptic potentials increase the likelihood that the postsynaptic neuron will fire; inhibitory postsynaptic potentials decrease this likelihood. (Remember, "firing" refers to the occurrence of an action potential.) Thus, the rate at which an axon fires is determined by the relative activity of the excitatory and inhibitory synapses on the soma and dendrites of that cell. If there are no active excitatory synapses or if the activity of inhibitory synapses is particularly high, that rate could be close to zero.

Let us look at the elements of this process. (***Animation 2.4, Postsynaptic Potentials,*** illustrates the material presented in this section.) The interaction of the effects of excitatory and inhibitory synapses on a particular neuron is called **neural integration.** (*Integration* means "to make whole," in the sense of combining two or more functions.) Figure 2.37 illustrates the effects of excitatory and inhibitory synapses on a postsynaptic neuron. The top panel shows what happens when several excitatory synapses become active. The release of the neurotransmitter produces depolarizing EPSPs in the dendrites of the neuron. These EPSPs (represented in red) are then transmitted, by means of passive cable properties, down the dendrites, across the soma, to the *axon hillock* located at the base of the axon. If the depolarization is still strong enough when it reaches this point, the axon will fire. (See ***Figure 2.37a.***)

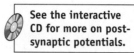
See the interactive CD for more on postsynaptic potentials.

Now let's consider what would happen if, at the same time, inhibitory synapses also become active. Inhibitory postsynaptic potentials are hyperpolarizing—they bring the membrane potential away from the threshold of excitation. Thus, they tend to cancel the effects of excitatory postsynaptic potentials. (See ***Figure 2.37b.***)

The rate at which a neuron fires is controlled by the relative activity of the excitatory and inhibitory synapses on its dendrites and soma. If the activity of excitatory synapses goes up, the rate of firing will go up. If the activity of inhibitory synapses goes up, the rate of firing will go down.

Note that *neural* inhibition (that is, an inhibitory postsynaptic potential) does not always produce *behavioral* inhibition. For example, suppose a group of neurons

---

acetylcholinesterase (AChE) (*a see tul koh lin **ess** ter ace*) The enzyme that destroys acetylcholine soon after it is liberated by the terminal buttons, thus terminating the postsynaptic potential.

neural integration The process by which inhibitory and excitatory postsynaptic potentials summate and control the rate of firing of a neuron.

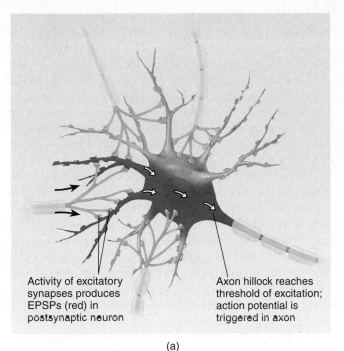

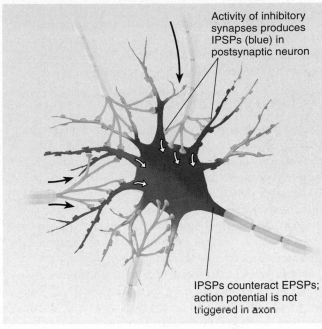

Activity of excitatory
synapses produces
EPSPs (red) in
postsynaptic neuron

Axon hillock reaches
threshold of excitation;
action potential is
triggered in axon

(a)

Activity of inhibitory
synapses produces
IPSPs (blue) in
postsynaptic neuron

IPSPs counteract EPSPs;
action potential is not
triggered in axon

(b)

figure 2.37

Neural integration. (a) If several excitatory synapses are active at the same time, the
EPSPs they produce (shown in red) summate as they travel toward the axon, and the
axon fires. (b) If several inhibitory synapses are active at the same time, the IPSPs they
produce (shown in blue) diminish the size of the EPSPs and prevent the axon from firing.

inhibits a particular movement. If these neurons are inhibited, they will no longer suppress the behavior. Thus, inhibition of the inhibitory neurons makes the behavior more likely to occur. Of course, the same is true for neural excitation. *Excitation* of neurons that *inhibit* a behavior suppresses that behavior. For example, when we are dreaming, a particular set of inhibitory neurons in the brain becomes active and prevents us from getting up and acting out our dreams. (As we will see in Chapter 9, if these neurons are damaged, people *will* act out their dreams.) Neurons are elements in complex circuits; without knowing the details of these circuits, one cannot predict the effects of the excitation or inhibition of one set of neurons on an organism's behavior.

Autoreceptors

Postsynaptic receptors detect the presence of a neurotransmitter in the synaptic cleft and initiate excitatory or inhibitory postsynaptic potentials. But the postsynaptic membrane is not the only location of receptors that respond to neurotransmitters. Many neurons also possess

receptors that respond to the neurotransmitter that *they themselves* release, called **autoreceptors.**

Autoreceptors can be located on the membrane of any part of the cell, but in this discussion we will consider those located on the terminal button. In most cases these autoreceptors do not control ion channels. Thus, when stimulated by a molecule of the neurotransmitter, autoreceptors do not produce changes in the membrane potential of the terminal button. Instead, they regulate internal processes, including the synthesis and release of the neurotransmitter. (As you may have guessed, autoreceptors are metabotropic; the control they exert on these processes is accomplished through G proteins and second messengers.) In most cases the effects of autoreceptor activation are inhibitory; that is, the presence of the neurotransmitter in the extracellular fluid in the vicinity of the neuron causes a decrease in the rate of synthesis or release of the neurotransmitter. Most

autoreceptor A receptor molecule located on a neuron that responds to the neurotransmitter released by that neuron.

investigators believe that autoreceptors are part of a regulatory system that controls the amount of neurotransmitter that is released. If too much is released, the autoreceptors inhibit both production and release; if not enough is released, the rates of production and release go up.

Other Types of Synapses

So far, the discussion of synaptic activity has referred only to the effects of postsynaptic excitation or inhibition. These effects occur at axosomatic or axodendritic synapses. Axoaxonic synapses work differently. Axoaxonic synapses do not contribute directly to neural integration. Instead, they alter the amount of neurotransmitter released by the terminal buttons of the postsynaptic axon. They can produce presynaptic modulation: presynaptic inhibition or presynaptic facilitation.

As you know, the release of a neurotransmitter by a terminal button is initiated by an action potential. Normally, a particular terminal button releases a fixed amount of neurotransmitter each time an action potential arrives. However, the release of neurotransmitter can be modulated by the activity of axoaxonic synapses. If the activity of the axoaxonic synapse decreases the release of the neurotransmitter, the effect is called **presynaptic inhibition.** If it increases the release, it is called **presynaptic facilitation.** (See *Figure 2.38.*)

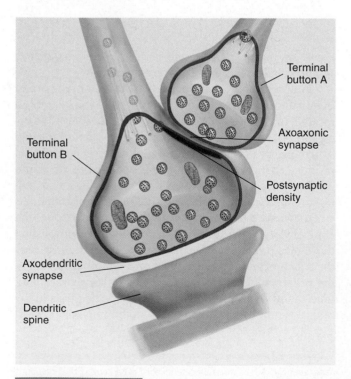

figure 2.38

An axoaxonic synapse. The activity of terminal button A can increase or decrease the amount of neurotransmitter released by terminal button B.

Many very small neurons have extremely short processes and apparently lack axons. These neurons form *dendrodendritic synapses,* or synapses between dendrites. Because these neurons lack long axonal processes, they do not transmit information from place to place within the brain. Most investigators believe that they perform regulatory functions, perhaps helping to organize the activity of groups of neurons. Because these neurons are so small, they are difficult to study; therefore, little is known about their function.

Some larger neurons, as well, form dendrodendritic synapses. Some of these synapses are chemical, indicated by the presence of synaptic vesicles in one of the juxtaposed dendrites and a postsynaptic thickening in the membrane of the other. Other synapses are *electrical;* the membranes meet and almost touch, forming a **gap junction.** The membranes on both sides of a gap junction contain channels that permit ions to diffuse from one cell to another. Thus, changes in the membrane potential of one neuron induce changes in the membrane of the other. (See *Figure 2.39.*) Although most gap junctions in vertebrate synapses are dendrodendritic, axosomatic and axodendritic gap junctions also occur. Gap junctions are common in invertebrates; their function in the vertebrate nervous system is not known.

Nonsynaptic Chemical Communication

Not all chemical communication takes place at synapses. Neurons possess receptors for a variety of substances in the membrane of all parts of the cell—and even in their nucleus. These receptors are sensitive to neuromodulators and to hormones.

First, let's consider neuromodulators. Neuromodulators do not elicit postsynaptic potentials; instead, they modulate the activity of a large number of neurons. Most neuromodulators are **peptides,** chains of amino acids that are linked together by special chemical attachments called *peptide bonds* (hence their name). Peptides

presynaptic inhibition The action of a presynaptic terminal button in an axoaxonic synapse; reduces the amount of neurotransmitter released by the postsynaptic terminal button.

presynaptic facilitation The action of a presynaptic terminal button in an axoaxonic synapse; increases the amount of neurotransmitter released by the postsynaptic terminal button.

gap junction A special junction between cells that permits direct communication by means of electrical coupling.

peptide A chain of amino acids joined together by peptide bonds. Most neuromodulators, and some hormones, consist of peptide molecules.

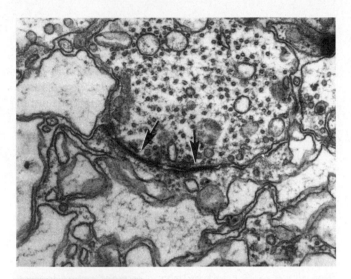

figure 2.39

A gap junction (arrows), which permits direct electrical coupling between the membranes of adjacent neurons. (From Bennett, M. V. L., and Pappas, G. D. *The Journal of Neuroscience,* 1983, *3,* 748–761.)

are released by the large dense-core vesicles found in many terminal buttons or by the terminals of specialized neurons that release *only* peptides. Neuromodulators diffuse through the brain's extracellular space, coming in contact with many neurons in the vicinity of the location in which they are released. As we will see in Chapter 4, several drugs affect behavior by mimicking the effects of neuromodulators. For example, opiates such as morphine and heroin mimic the effects of peptides produced in the brain.

Hormones are secreted by endocrine glands or by specialized cells located in other organs. Hormones consist of two types of molecules. Peptide hormones exert their effects on target cells by stimulating metabotropic receptors located in the membrane. The second messenger that is generated travels to the nucleus of the cell, where it initiates changes in the cell's physiological processes.

Steroid hormones consist of very small fat-soluble molecules. (*Steroid* derives from the Greek *stereos,* "solid," and Latin *oleum,* "oil." They are synthesized from cho-le*sterol.*) Examples of steroid hormones include the sex hormones secreted by the ovaries and testes and the hormones secreted by the adrenal cortex. Because steroid hormones are soluble in lipids, they pass easily through the cell membrane. They travel to the nucleus, where they attach themselves to receptors located there. The receptors, stimulated by the hormone, then direct the machinery of the cell to alter its protein production. (See *Figure 2.40.*)

In the past few years investigators have discovered the presence of steroid receptors in terminal buttons and around the postsynaptic membrane of some neurons.

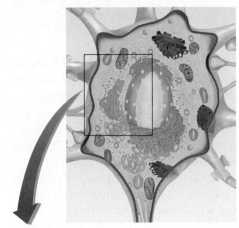

Detail of Cell

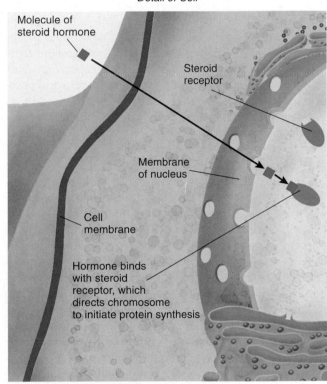

Molecule of steroid hormone

Steroid receptor

Membrane of nucleus

Cell membrane

Hormone binds with steroid receptor, which directs chromosome to initiate protein synthesis

figure 2.40

Action of steroid hormones. Steroid hormones affect their target cells by means of specialized receptors in the nucleus. Once a receptor binds with a molecule of a steroid hormone, it causes genetic mechanisms to initiate protein synthesis.

These steroid receptors influence synaptic transmission, and they do so rapidly. Exactly how these steroid receptors work is still not known.

steroid A chemical of low molecular weight, derived from cholesterol. Steroid hormones affect their target cells by attaching to receptors found within the nucleus.

interim summary

Communication Between Neurons

Synapses consist of junctions between the terminal buttons of one neuron and the membrane; another neuron, a muscle cell, or a gland cell. When an action potential is transmitted down an axon, the terminal buttons at the end release a neurotransmitter, a chemical that produces either depolarizations (EPSPs) or hyperpolarizations (IPSPs) of the postsynaptic membrane. The rate of firing of the axon of the postsynaptic neuron is determined by the relative activity of the excitatory and inhibitory synapses on the membrane of its dendrites and soma—a phenomenon known as *neural integration*.

Chemical communication takes place between a cell that secretes a chemical and one that contains receptors for that chemical. The communication can involve neurotransmitters, neuromodulators, or hormones; the distance varies from the space that separates the presynaptic and postsynaptic membrane to the space that separates cells at different locations in the body. Neurotransmitters, neuromodulators, and hormones act on cells by attaching to the binding sites of receptors and initiating chemical changes in these cells.

Terminal buttons contains synaptic vesicles. Most terminal buttons contain two sizes of vesicles, the smaller of which are found in greatest numbers around the release zone of the presynaptic membrane. When an action potential is transmitted down an axon, the depolarization opens voltage-dependent calcium channels, which permit Ca^{2+} to enter. The calcium ions bind with the clusters of protein molecules in the membranes of synaptic vesicles already docked at the release zone. The protein clusters spread apart, causing the vesicles to break open and fuse their membrane with that of the terminal button, thus releasing the neurotransmitter. The extra membrane pinches off into the cytoplasm and travels to the cisternae, where it is recycled in the production of new vesicles.

The activation of postsynaptic receptors by molecules of a neurotransmitter causes neurotransmitter-dependent ion channels to open, resulting in postsynaptic potentials. Ionotropic receptors contain ion channels, which are directly opened when a ligand attaches to the binding site. Metabotropic receptors are linked to G proteins, which, when activated, open ion channels—usually by producing a chemical called a second messenger.

The nature of the postsynaptic potential depends on the type of ion channel that is opened by the postsynaptic receptors at a particular synapse. Excitatory postsynaptic potentials occur when Na^+ enters the cell. Inhibitory postsynaptic potentials are produced when K^+ leaves the cell or Cl^- enters it. The entry of Ca^{2+} produces EPSPs, but even more important, it activates special enzymes that cause physiological changes in the postsynaptic cell.

Postsynaptic potentials are normally very brief. They are terminated by two means. Acetylcholine is deactivated by the enzyme acetylcholinesterase. In all other cases (as far as we know) molecules of the neurotransmitter are removed from the synaptic cleft by means of transporters located in the presynaptic membrane. This retrieval process is called reuptake.

The presynaptic membrane, as well as the postsynaptic membrane, contains receptors that detect the presence of a neurotransmitter. Presynaptic receptors, also called autoreceptors, monitor the quantity of neurotransmitter that a neuron releases and, apparently, regulate the amount that is synthesized and released.

Axosomatic and axodendritic synapses are not the only kinds found in the nervous system. Axoaxonic synapses either reduce or enhance the amount of neurotransmitter released by the postsynaptic terminal button, producing presynaptic inhibition or presynaptic facilitation. Dendrodendritic synapses also exist, but their role in neural communication is not yet understood.

Nonsynaptic chemical transmission is similar to synaptic transmission. Peptide neuromodulators and hormones activate metabotropic peptide receptors located in the membrane; their effects are mediated through the production of second messengers. Steroid hormones enter the nucleus, where they bind with receptors capable of altering the synthesis of proteins that regulate the cell's physiological processes. These hormones also bind with receptors located elsewhere in the cell, but less is known about their functions.

Suggested Readings

Aidley, D. J. *The Physiology of Excitable Cells,* 4th ed. Cambridge, England: Cambridge University Press, 1998.

Cowan, W. M., Südhof, T. C., and Stevens, C. F. *Synapses.* Baltimore, MD: Johns Hopkins University Press, 2001.

Kandel, E. R., Schwartz, J. H., and Jessell, T. M. *Principles of Neural Science,* 4th ed. New York: McGraw-Hill, 2000.

Nicholls, J. G., Martin, A. R., Fuchs, P. A., and Wallace, B. G. *From Neuron to Brain,* 4th ed. Sunderland, MA: Sinauer, 2001.

Suggested Web Sites

Action Potential Animation

http://www.fiu.edu/orgs/psych/psb_4003/figures/a_p.htm

This site provides a colorful animation of the ionic events that occur during an action potential.

Tutorial on the Action Potential

http://pavlov.psyc.queensu.ca/~symonsl/brains/actpot.html

A tutorial with an animation of the action potential is the focus of this site.

Action Potential Simulator

http://www.phypc.med.wayne.edu/jeffram/axon3.htm

This site provides a powerful simulation program of the ionic and electrical events that occur during an action potential. The simula- *tor allows the instructor to demonstrate EPSPs, IPSPs, and the effects of toxins such as TTX and TEA on the membrane potential.*

Synapse Web

http://synapses.bu.edu/

This site is devoted to the anatomy of synapses and includes images of synaptic connections as well as links to other sites relating to synapses.

Cell Membrane Animations

http://www.emile-21.com/VRML/membPot0.html

This site provides a series of animations relating to the cell membrane potential. The animations require the installation of a VRML plug-in.

Structure of the Nervous System

Sam Francis, *Greenish Limb*, 1970. © 2003 The Estate of Sam Francis/Artists Rights Society (ARS), New York. © Giraudon/Art Resource, NY.

outline

■ **Basic Features of the Nervous System**
An Overview
Meninges
The Ventricular System and Production of CSF
Interim Summary

■ **The Central Nervous System**
Development of the Central Nervous System
The Forebrain
The Midbrain
The Hindbrain
The Spinal Cord

Interim Summary
■ **The Peripheral Nervous System**
Spinal Nerves
Cranial Nerves
The Autonomic Nervous System
Interim Summary

Ryan B., a college freshman, had suffered from occasional epileptic seizures since childhood. He had been taking drugs for his seizures for many years, but lately the medication wasn't helping—his seizures were becoming more frequent. His neurologist increased the dose of the medication, but the seizures persisted, and the drug made it difficult for Ryan to concentrate on his studies. He was afraid that he would have to drop out of school.

He made an appointment with his neurologist and asked whether another drug was available that might work better and not affect his ability to concentrate. "No," said the neurologist, "you're taking the best medication we have right now. But I want to send you to Dr. L., a neurosurgeon at the medical school. I think you might be a good candidate for seizure surgery."

Ryan had a focal-seizure disorder. His problems were caused by a localized region of the brain that contained some scar tissue. Periodically, this region would irritate the surrounding areas, triggering epileptic seizures—wild, sustained firing of cerebral neurons that result in cognitive disruption and, sometimes, uncontrolled movements. Ryan's focus was probably a result of brain damage that occurred when he was born. Dr. L. ordered some tests that indicated that the seizure focus was located in the left side of his brain, in a region known as the medial temporal lobe.

Ryan was surprised to learn that he would remain awake during his surgery. In fact, he would be called on to provide information that the surgeon would need to remove a region of his brain that included the seizure focus. As you might expect, he was nervous when he was wheeled into the surgery, but after the anesthesiologist injected something through the tube in one of his veins, Ryan relaxed and thought to himself, "This won't be too bad."

Dr. L. marked something on his scalp, which had previously been shaved, and then made several injections of a local anesthetic. Then he cut the scalp and injected some more anesthetic. Finally, he used a drill and a saw to remove a piece of skull. He then cut and folded back the thick membrane that covers the brain, exposing the surface of the brain.

When removing a seizure focus, the surgeon wants to cut away all the abnormal tissue while sparing brain tissue that performs important functions, such as the comprehension and production of speech. For this reason Dr. L. began stimulating parts of the brain to determine which regions he could safely remove. To do so, he placed a metal probe against the surface of Ryan's brain and pressed a pedal that delivered a weak electrical current. The stimulation disrupts the firing patterns of the neurons located near the probe, preventing them from carrying out their normal functions. Dr. L. found that stimulation of parts of the temporal lobe disrupted Ryan's ability to understand what he and his associates were saying. When he removed the part of the brain containing the seizure focus, he was careful not to damage these regions.

The operation was successful. Ryan continued to take his medication but at a much lower dose. His seizures disappeared, and he found it easier to concentrate in class. I met Ryan during his junior year, when he took a course I was teaching. I described seizure surgery to the class one day, and after the lecture he approached me and told me about his experience. He received the third highest grade in the class.

The goal of neuroscience research is to understand how the brain works. To understand the results of this research, you must be acquainted with the basic structure of the nervous system. The number of terms introduced in this chapter is kept to a minimum (but as you will see, the minimum is still a rather large number). The exercise on the animations CD-ROM entitled "Figures and Diagrams" will help you learn the names and locations of the major structures of the nervous system. (See *Chapter 3 Animations: Figures and Diagrams.*) With the framework you will receive from this chapter and from the animations, you should have no trouble learning the material presented in subsequent chapters.

Basic Features of the Nervous System

Before beginning a description of the nervous system, I want to discuss the terms that are used to describe it. The gross anatomy of the brain was described long ago, and everything that could be seen without the aid of a microscope was given a name. Early anatomists named most brain structures according to their similarity to commonplace objects: amygdala, or "almond-shaped object"; hippocampus, or "sea horse"; genu, or "knee"; cortex, or "bark"; pons, or "bridge"; uncus, or "hook," to give a few examples. Throughout this book I will translate the names of anatomical terms as I introduce them, because the translation makes the terms more memorable. For example, knowing that *cortex* means "bark" (like the bark of a tree) will help you to remember that the cortex is the outer layer of the brain.

When describing features of a structure as complex as the brain, we need to use terms denoting directions. Directions in the nervous system are normally described relative to the **neuraxis,** an imaginary line drawn through the spinal cord up to the front of the brain. For simplicity's

---

neuraxis An imaginary line drawn through the center of the length of the central nervous system, from the bottom of the spinal cord to the front of the forebrain.

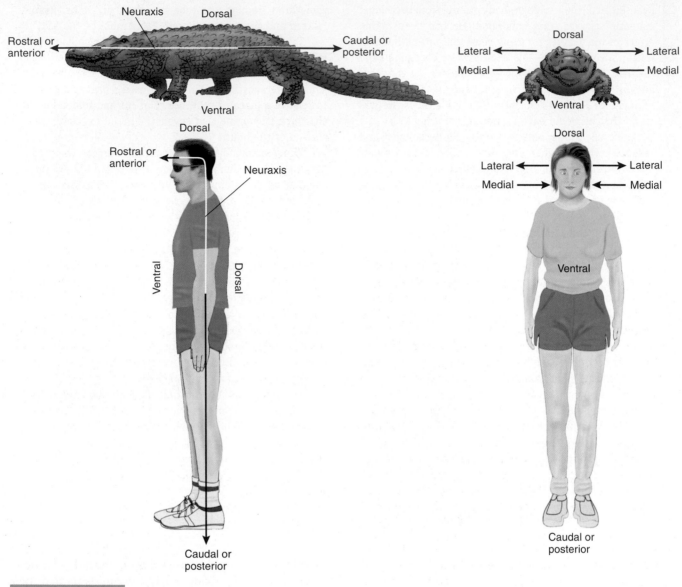

figure 3.1

Side and frontal views of alligator and human, showing the terms used to denote
anatomical directions.

sake let us consider an animal with a straight neuraxis. Figure 3.1 shows an alligator and two humans. This alligator
is certainly laid out in a linear fashion; we can draw a
straight line that starts between its eyes and continues
down the center of its spinal cord. (See *Figure 3.1.*) The
front end is **anterior,** and the tail is **posterior.** The terms
rostral (toward the beak) and **caudal** (toward the tail) are
also employed, especially when referring specifically to the
brain. The top of the head and the back are part of the
dorsal surface, while the **ventral** (front) surface faces the
ground. (*Dorsum* means "back," and *ventrum* means
"belly.") These directions are somewhat more complicated in the human; because we stand upright, our neuraxis bends, so the top of the head is perpendicular to the
back. (You will also encounter the terms *superior* and *inferior.* When referring to the brain, *superior* means "above,"

anterior With respect to the central nervous system, located near or
toward the head.

posterior With respect to the central nervous system, located near
or toward the tail.

rostral "Toward the beak"; with respect to the central nervous system, in a direction along the neuraxis toward the front of the face.

caudal "Toward the tail"; with respect to the central nervous system,
in a direction along the neuraxis away from the front of the face.

dorsal "Toward the back"; with respect to the central nervous system, in a direction perpendicular to the neuraxis toward the top of
the head or the back.

ventral "Toward the belly"; with respect to the central nervous system, in a direction perpendicular to the neuraxis toward the bottom
of the skull or the front surface of the body.

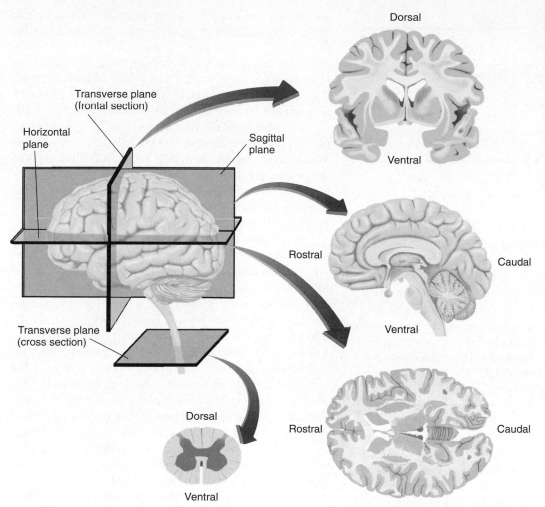

figure 3.2

Planes of section as they pertain to the human central nervous system.

and *inferior* means "below." For example, the *superior colliculi* are located above the *inferior colliculi*.) The frontal views of both the alligator and the human illustrate the terms **lateral** and **medial:** toward the side and toward the midline, respectively. (See *Figure 3.1*.)

Two other useful terms are *ipsilateral* and *contralateral*. **Ipsilateral** refers to structures on the same side of the body. If we say that the olfactory bulb sends axons to the *ipsilateral* hemisphere, we mean that the left olfactory bulb sends axons to the left hemisphere and the right olfactory bulb sends axons to the right hemisphere. **Contralateral** refers to structures on opposite sides of the body. If we say that a particular region of the left cerebral cortex controls movements of the *contralateral* hand, we mean that the region controls movements of the right hand.

To see what is in the nervous system, we have to cut it open; to be able to convey information about what we find, we slice it in a standard way. Figure 3.2 shows a human nervous system. We can slice the nervous system in three ways:

1. Transversely, like a salami, giving us **cross sections** (also known as **frontal sections** when referring to the brain).
2. Parallel to the ground, giving us **horizontal sections.**

3. Perpendicular to the ground and parallel to the neuraxis, giving us **sagittal sections.** The **midsagittal plane** divides the brain into two symmetrical halves. The sagittal section in Figure 3.2 lies in the midsagittal plane.

Note that because of our upright posture, cross sections of the spinal cord are parallel to the ground. (See *Figure 3.2*.)

---

lateral Toward the side of the body, away from the middle.

medial Toward the middle of the body, away from the side.

ipsilateral Located on the same side of the body.

contralateral Located on the opposite side of the body.

cross section With respect to the central nervous system, a slice taken at right angles to the neuraxis.

frontal section A slice through the brain parallel to the forehead.

horizontal section A slice through the brain parallel to the ground.

sagittal section (*sadj i tul*) A slice through the brain parallel to the neuraxis and perpendicular to the ground.

midsagittal plane The plane through the neuraxis perpendicular to the ground; divides the brain into two symmetrical halves.

table **3.1**

The Major Divisions of the Nervous System	
CENTRAL NERVOUS SYSTEM (CNS)	**PERIPHERAL NERVOUS SYSTEM (PNS)**
Brain	Nerves
Spinal cord	Peripheral ganglia

An Overview

The nervous system consists of the brain and spinal cord, which make up the *central nervous system (CNS),* and the cranial nerves, spinal nerves, and peripheral ganglia, which constitute the *peripheral nervous system (PNS).* The CNS is encased in bone: The brain is covered by the skull, and the spinal cord is encased by the vertebral column. (See *Table 3.1.*)

Figure 3.3 illustrates the relation of the brain and spinal cord to the rest of the body. Do not be concerned with unfamiliar labels on this figure; these structures will be described later. (See *Figure 3.3.*) The brain is a large mass of neurons, glia, and other supporting cells. It is the most protected organ of the body, encased in a tough, bony skull and floating in a pool of cerebrospinal fluid. The brain receives a copious supply of blood and is chemically guarded by the blood–brain barrier.

The brain receives approximately 20 percent of the blood flow from the heart, and it receives it continuously. Other parts of the body, such as the skeletal muscles or digestive system, receive varying quantities of blood, depending on their needs, relative to those of other regions. But the brain always receives its share. The brain cannot store its fuel (primarily glucose), nor can it temporarily extract energy without oxygen, as the muscles can; therefore, a consistent blood supply is essential. A 1-second interruption of the blood flow to the brain uses up much of the dissolved oxygen; a 6-second interruption produces unconsciousness. Permanent damage begins within a few minutes.

Meninges

The entire nervous system—brain, spinal cord, cranial and spinal nerves, and peripheral ganglia—is covered by tough connective tissue. The protective sheaths around the brain and spinal cord are referred to as the **meninges** (singular: *meninx*). The meninges consist of three layers, which are shown in Figure 3.3. The outer layer is thick, tough, and flexible but unstretchable; its name, **dura mater,** means "hard mother." The middle layer of the meninges, the **arachnoid membrane,** gets its name from the weblike appearance of the *arachnoid trabeculae* that protrude from it (from the Greek *arachne,* meaning "spider"; *trabecula* means "track"). The arachnoid membrane, soft and spongy, lies beneath the dura mater. Closely attached to the brain and spinal cord, and following every surface convolution, is the **pia mater** ("pious mother"). The smaller surface blood vessels of the brain and spinal cord are contained within this layer. Between the pia mater and arachnoid membrane is a gap called the **subarachnoid space.** This space is filled with a liquid called **cerebrospinal fluid (CSF).** (See *Figure 3.3.*)

The peripheral nervous system (PNS) is covered with two layers of meninges. The middle layer (arachnoid membrane), with its associated pool of CSF, covers only the brain and spinal cord. Outside the central nervous system, the outer and inner layers (dura mater and pia mater) fuse and form a sheath that covers the spinal and cranial nerves and the peripheral ganglia.

In the first edition of this book I said that I did not know why the outer and inner layers of the meninges were referred to as "mothers." I received a letter from medical historians at the Department of Anatomy at UCLA that explained the name. (Sometimes, it pays to proclaim one's ignorance.) A tenth-century Persian physician, Ali ibn Abbas, used the Arabic term *al umm* to refer to the meninges. The term literally means "mother" but was used to designate any swaddling material, because Arabic lacked a specific term for the word *membrane.* The tough outer membrane was called *al umm al djafiya,* and the soft inner one was called *al umm al rigiga.* When the writings of Ali ibn Abbas were translated into Latin during the eleventh century, the translator, who was probably not familiar with the structure of the meninges, made a literal translation of *al umm.* He referred to the membranes as the "hard mother" and the "pious mother" (*pious* in the sense of "delicate"), rather than using a more appropriate Latin word.

The Ventricular System and Production of CSF

The brain is very soft and jellylike. The considerable weight of a human brain (approximately 1400 g), along with its delicate construction, necessitates that it be protected

---

meninges (singular: **meninx**) (*men in jees*) The three layers of tissue that encase the central nervous system: the dura mater, arachnoid membrane, and pia mater.

dura mater The outermost of the meninges; tough and flexible.

arachnoid membrane (*a rak noyd*) The middle layer of the meninges, located between the outer dura mater and inner pia mater.

pia mater The layer of the meninges that clings to the surface of the brain; thin and delicate.

subarachnoid space The fluid-filled space that cushions the brain; located between the arachnoid membrane and the pia mater.

cerebrospinal fluid (CSF) A clear fluid, similar to blood plasma, that fills the ventricular system of the brain and the subarachnoid space surrounding the brain and spinal cord.

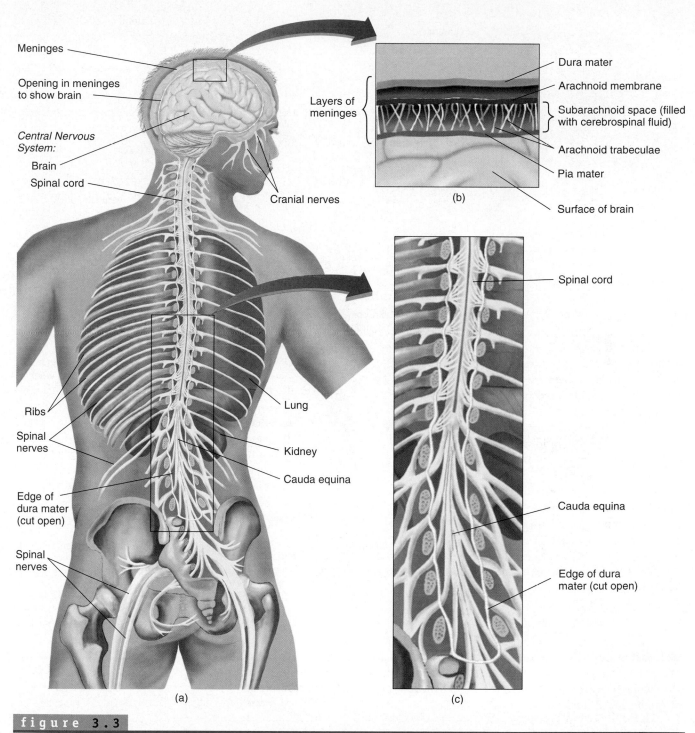

figure 3.3

(a) The relation of the nervous system to the rest of the body. (b) Detail of the meninges that cover the central nervous system. (c) A closer view of the lower spinal cord and cauda equina.

from shock. A human brain cannot even support its own weight well; it is difficult to remove and handle a fresh brain from a recently deceased human without damaging it.

Fortunately, the intact brain within a living human is well protected. It floats in a bath of CSF contained within the subarachnoid space. Because the brain is completely immersed in liquid, its net weight is reduced to approximately 80 g; thus, pressure on the base of the brain is considerably diminished. The CSF surrounding the brain and spinal cord also reduces the shock to the

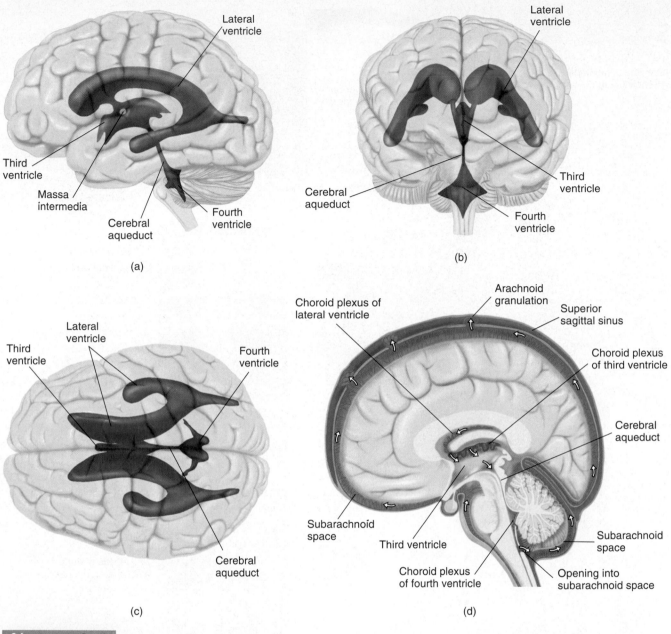

The ventricular system of the brain. (a) Lateral view of the left side of the brain.
(b) Frontal view. (c) Dorsal view. (d) The production, circulation, and reabsorption
of cerebrospinal fluid.

central nervous system that would be caused by sudden head movement.

The brain contains a series of hollow, interconnected chambers called **ventricles** ("little bellies"), which are filled with CSF. (See *Figure 3.4.*) The largest chambers are the **lateral ventricles,** which are connected to the **third ventricle.** The third ventricle is located at the midline of the brain; its walls divide the surrounding part of the brain

ventricle (*ven trik ul*) One of the hollow spaces within the brain, filled with cerebrospinal fluid.

lateral ventricle One of the two ventricles located in the center of the telencephalon.

third ventricle The ventricle located in the center of the diencephalon.

A scanning-electron micrograph of the choroid plexus.
BV = blood vessel, CE = choroid plexus, V = ventricle.

(From *Tissues and Organs: A Text-Atlas of Scanning Electron Microscopy,* by Richard G. Kessel and Randy H. Kardon. Copyright © 1979 by W. H. Freeman and Co. Reprinted by permission.)

into symmetrical halves. A bridge of neural tissue called the *massa intermedia* crosses through the middle of the third ventricle and serves as a convenient reference point. The **cerebral aqueduct,** a long tube, connects the third ventricle to the **fourth ventricle.** The lateral ventricles constitute the first and second ventricles, but they are never referred to as such. (See *Figure 3.4.*)

Cerebrospinal fluid is extracted from the blood and resembles blood plasma in its composition. CSF is manufactured by special tissue with an especially rich blood supply called the **choroid plexus,** which protrudes into all four of the ventricles. CSF is produced continuously; the total volume of CSF is approximately 125 ml, and the half-life (the time it takes for half of the CSF present in the ventricular system to be replaced by fresh fluid) is about 3 hours. Therefore, several times this amount is produced by the choroid plexus each day. The continuous production of CSF means that there must be a mechanism for its removal. The production, circulation, and reabsorption of CSF are illustrated in *Figure 3.4d.* A scanning electron micrograph of the choroid plexus is shown in *Figure 3.5.*

Figure 3.4(d) shows a slightly rotated midsagittal view of the central nervous system, which shows only the right lateral ventricle (because the left hemisphere has been removed). Cerebrospinal fluid is produced by the choroid plexus of the lateral ventricles, and it flows into the third

ventricle. More CSF is produced in this ventricle, which then flows through the cerebral aqueduct to the fourth ventricle, where still more CSF is produced. The CSF leaves the fourth ventricle through small openings that connect with the subarachnoid space surrounding the brain. The CSF then flows through the subarachnoid space around the central nervous system, where it is reabsorbed into the blood supply through the **arachnoid granulations.** These pouch-shaped structures protrude into the **superior sagittal sinus,** a blood vessel that drains into the veins serving the brain. (See *Figure 3.4d* and *Animation 3.1, Meninges and CSF.*)

 See the interactive CD for more on meninges and CSF.

Occasionally, the flow of CSF is interrupted at some point in its route of passage. For example, a brain tumor growing in the midbrain may push against the cerebral aqueduct, blocking its flow, or an infant may be born with a cerebral aqueduct that it too small to accommodate a normal flow of CSF. This occlusion results in greatly increased pressure within the ventricles, because the choroid plexus continues to produce CSF. The walls of the ventricles then expand and produce a condition known as **obstructive hydrocephalus** (*hydrocephalus* literally means "water-head"). If the obstruction remains and if nothing is done to reverse the increased intracerebral pressure, blood vessels will be occluded, and permanent—perhaps fatal—brain damage will occur. Fortunately, a surgeon can usually operate on the person, drilling a hole through the skull and inserting a shunt tube into one of the ventricles. The tube is then placed beneath the skin and connected to a pressure relief valve that is

cerebral aqueduct A narrow tube interconnecting the third and fourth ventricles of the brain, located in the center of the mesencephalon.

fourth ventricle The ventricle located between the cerebellum and the dorsal pons, in the center of the metencephalon.

choroid plexus The highly vascular tissue that protrudes into the ventricles and produces cerebrospinal fluid.

arachnoid granulation Small projections of the arachnoid membrane through the dura mater into the superior sagittal sinus; CSF flows through them to be reabsorbed into the blood supply.

superior sagittal sinus A venous sinus located in the midline just dorsal to the corpus callosum, between the two cerebral hemispheres.

obstructive hydrocephalus A condition in which all or some of the brain's ventricles are enlarged; caused by an obstruction that impedes the normal flow of CSF.

f i g u r e   3 . 6

Hydrocephalus in an infant. A surgeon places a shunt tube in a lateral ventricle, which permits cerebrospinal fluid to escape to the abdominal cavity, where it is absorbed into the blood supply. A pressure valve regulates the flow of CSF through the shunt.

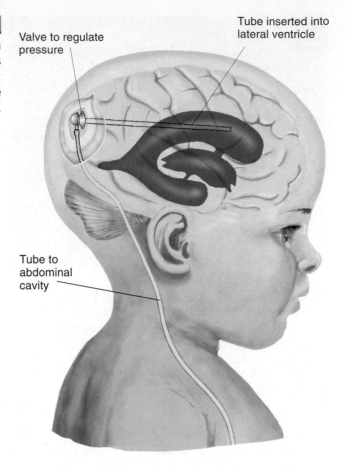

Valve to regulate pressure

Tube inserted into lateral ventricle

Tube to abdominal cavity

implanted in the abdominal cavity. When the pressure in the ventricles becomes excessive, the valve permits the CSF to escape into the abdomen, where eventually it is reabsorbed into the blood supply. (See *Figure 3.6.*)

i n t e r i m
s u m m a r y

Basic Features of the Nervous System

Anatomists have adopted a set of terms to describe the locations of parts of the body. *Anterior* is toward the head, *posterior* is toward the tail, *lateral* is toward the side, *medial* is toward the middle, *dorsal* is toward the back, and *ventral* is toward the front surface of the body. In the special case of the nervous system, *rostral* means toward the beak (or nose), and *caudal* means toward the tail. *Ipsilateral* means "same side," and *contralateral* means "other side." A cross section (or, in the case of the brain, a frontal section) slices the nervous system at right angles to the neuraxis, a horizontal section slices the brain parallel to the ground, and a sagittal section slices it perpendicular to the ground, parallel to the neuraxis.

The central nervous system consists of the brain and spinal cord, and the peripheral nervous system consists of the spinal and cranial nerves and peripheral ganglia. The CNS is covered with the meninges: dura mater, arachnoid membrane, and pia mater. The space under the arachnoid membrane is filled with cerebrospinal fluid, in which the brain floats. The PNS is covered with only the dura mater and pia mater. Cerebrospinal fluid is produced in the choroid plexus of the lateral, third, and fourth ventricles. It flows from the two lateral ventricles into the third ventricle, through the cerebral aqueduct into the fourth ventricle, then into the subarachnoid space, and finally back into the blood supply through the arachnoid granulations. If the flow of CSF is blocked by a tumor or other obstruction, the result is hydrocephalus: enlargement of the ventricles and subsequent brain damage.

The Central Nervous System

Although the brain is exceedingly complicated, an understanding of the basic features of brain development makes it easier to learn and remember the location of the most important structures. With that end in mind, I introduce these features here in the context of development of the central nervous system. Two animations will help you learn and remember the structure of the brain. ***Animation 3.2, The Rotatable Brain*** is just what the title implies: a drawing of the human brain that you can rotate in three dimensions. You can choose

>
> **See the interactive CD for a view of the rotatable brain.**

whether to see some internal structures or see specialized regions of the cerebral cortex. ***Animation 3.3, Brain Slices*** is even more comprehensive. It consists of two sets of photographs of human brain slices, taken in the transverse (frontal) and horizontal planes. As you move the cursor across each slice, brain regions are outlined and their names appear. If you want to know how to pronounce these names, you can click on the region. You

> **See the interactive CD for more information on brain slices.**

can also see magnified views of the slices and move them around by clicking and dragging. Finally, you can test yourself: The computer will present names of the regions shown in each slice, and you try to click on the correct region.

Development of the Central Nervous System

The central nervous system begins early in embryonic life as a hollow tube, and it maintains this basic shape even after it is fully developed. During development parts of the tube elongate, pockets and folds form, and the tissue around the tube thickens until the brain reaches its final form.

An Overview of Brain Development

Development of the nervous system begins around the eighteenth day after conception. Part of the *ectoderm* (outer layer) of the back of the embryo thickens and forms a plate. The edges of this plate form ridges that curl toward each other along a longitudinal line, running in a rostral–caudal direction. By the twenty-first day these ridges touch each other and fuse together, forming a tube—the **neural tube**—which gives rise to the brain and spinal cord. The top part of the ridges break away from the neural tube and become the ganglia of the autonomic nervous system, described later in this chapter. (See ***Figure 3.7***.)

By the twenty-eighth day of development the neural tube is closed, and its rostral end has developed three interconnected chambers. These chambers become ventricles, and the tissue that surrounds them becomes the

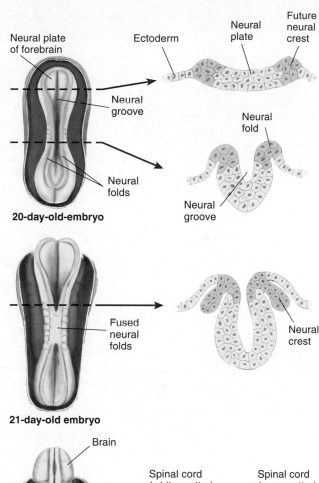

20-day-old-embryo

21-day-old embryo

24-day-old embryo

figure 3.7

Development of the neural plate into the neural tube, which gives rise to the brain and spinal cord. *Left:* Dorsal views. *Right:* Cross section at levels indicated by dotted lines.

neural tube A hollow tube, closed at the rostral end, that forms from ectodermal tissue early in embryonic development; serves as the origin of the central nervous system.

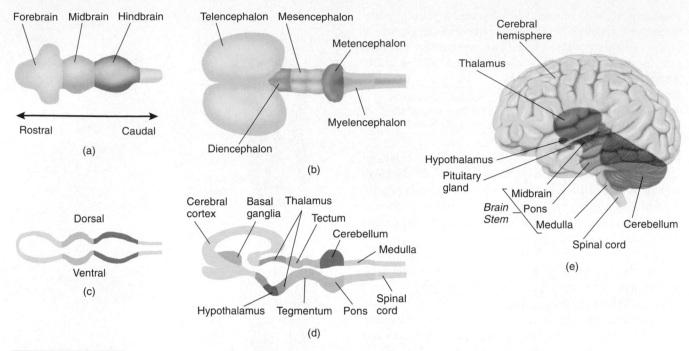

figure 3.8

A schematic outline of brain development, showing its relation to the ventricles. (a) and (c) Early development. (b) and (d) Later in development. (e) A lateral view of the left side of a semitransparent human brain, showing the brain stem "ghosted in." The colors of all figures denote corresponding regions.

three major parts of the brain: the forebrain, the midbrain, and the hindbrain. (See *Figures 3.8a* and *3.8c.*) As development progresses, the rostral chamber (the forebrain) divides into three separate parts, which become the two lateral ventricles and the third ventricle. The region around the lateral ventricles becomes the telencephalon ("end brain"), and the region around the third ventricle becomes the diencephalon ("interbrain"). (See *Figures 3.8b* and *3.8d.*) In its final form, the chamber inside the midbrain (mesencephalon) becomes narrow, forming the cerebral aqueduct, and two structures develop in the hindbrain: the metencephalon ("afterbrain") and the myelencephalon ("marrowbrain"). (See *Figure 3.8e.*)

Table 3.2 summarizes the terms I have introduced here and mentions some of the major structures found in each part of the brain. The colors in the table match those in Figure 3.8. These structures will be described in the remainder of the chapter. (See *Table 3.2.*)

Details of Brain Development

Brain development begins with a thin tube and ends with a structure weighing approximately 1400 g (about 3 lb) and consisting of several hundreds of billions of cells. Where do these cells come from, and what controls their growth?

The cells that line the inside of the neural tube—the **ventricular zone**—give rise to the cells of the central nervous system. These cells divide, producing neurons and glia, which then migrate away from the center. Ten weeks after conception, the brain of the human fetus is about 1.25 cm (0.5 in.) long and, in cross section, is mostly ventricle—in other words, hollow space. By 20 weeks, the brain is about 5 cm (2 in.) long and has the basic shape of the mature brain. In cross section, we see more brain tissue than ventricle.

Let's consider the development of the cerebral cortex, about which most is known. *Cortex* means "bark," and the **cerebral cortex,** approximately 3 mm thick, surrounds the cerebral hemispheres like the bark of a tree.

ventricular zone A layer of cells that line the inside of the neural tube; contains founder cells that divide and give rise to cells of the central nervous system.

cerebral cortex The outermost layer of gray matter of the cerebral hemispheres.

Anatomical Subdivisions of the Brain

MAJOR DIVISION	VENTRICLE	SUBDIVISION	PRINCIPAL STRUCTURES
Forebrain	Lateral	Telencephalon	Cerebral cortex
			Basal ganglia
			Limbic system
	Third	Diencephalon	Thalamus
			Hypothalamus
Midbrain	Cerebral aqueduct	Mesencephalon	Tectum Tegmentum
Hindbrain	Fourth	Metencephalon	Cerebellum
			Pons
		Myelencephalon	Medulla oblongata

Corrected for body size, the cerebral cortex is larger in humans than in any other species. As we will see, circuits of neurons in the cerebral cortex play a vital role in cognition and control of movement.

One of the ways in which investigators study brain development is through labeling studies. To perform these studies, investigators inject pregnant animals with a radioactive substance that is incorporated into cells that are in the process of division. Thus, only cells that are born at the time of the injection contain the radioactive label. Later, the investigators examine the brains of the fetuses to see where these cells are located. These studies have shown that the cerebral cortex develops from the inside out. That is, the first cells to be produced by the ventricular zone migrate a short distance and establish the first layer. The next cells pass through the first layer and form the second one. The last cells to be produced must pass through all the ones born before them.

What guides neurons to their final resting place? Rakic (1972, 1988) discovered that a special form of glial cell provides pathways that neurons follow during their migration. These cells, **radial glia,** extended fibers radially outward from the ventricular zone, like spokes in a wheel. These fibers end in cuplike feet that attach to the surface of the cortex, and as the cortex grows thicker, these fibers grow along with it.

The cells in the ventricular zone that give rise to neurons are known as **founder cells.** During the first phase of development, founder cells divide, making new founder cells and increasing the size of the ventricular zone. This phase is referred to as **symmetrical division,** because the division of each founder cell produces two identical cells. Then, seven weeks after conception, founder cells receive a signal to begin a period of **asymmetrical division.** During this phase, founder cells divide asymmetrically, producing another founder cell, which remains in place, and a neuron, which travels outward into the cerebral cortex, guided by the fiber of a radial glial cell. Neurons crawl along radial fibers like amoebas, pushing their way

radial glia Special glia with fibers that grow radially outward from the ventricular zone to the surface of the cortex; provide guidance for neurons migrating outward during brain development.

founder cells Cells of the ventricular zone that divide and give rise to cells of the central nervous system.

symmetrical division Division of a founder cell that gives rise to two identical founder cells; increases the size of the ventricular zone and hence the brain that develops from it.

asymmetrical division Division of a founder cell that gives rise to another founder cell and a neuron, which migrates away from the ventricular zone toward its final resting place in the brain.

figure 3.9

A cross section through the nervous system early in its development. Radially oriented glial cells help to guide the migration of newly formed neurons.

(Adapted from Rakic, P. A small step for the cell, a giant leap for mankind: A hypothesis of neocortical expansion during evolution. *Trends in Neuroscience,* 1995, *18,* 383–388.)

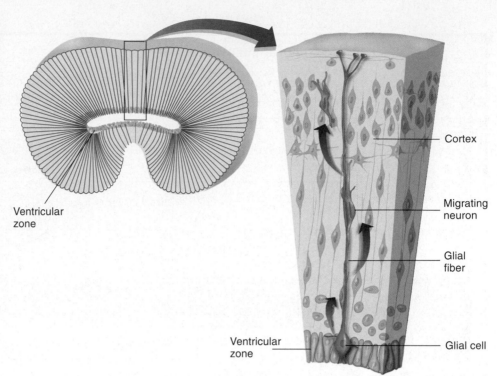

Ventricular zone

Cortex

Migrating neuron

Glial fiber

Ventricular zone

Glial cell

through neurons that were born earlier and finally coming to rest. (See *Figure 3.9.*)

The period of asymmetrical division lasts about three months. Because the human cerebral cortex contains about 100 billion neurons, there are about one billion neurons migrating along radial glial fibers on a given day. The migration path of the earliest neurons is the shortest and takes about one day. The last neurons have the longest distance to go, because the cortex is thicker by then. Their migration takes about two weeks. The end of cortical development occurs when the founder cells receive a chemical signal that causes them to die—a phenomenon known as **apoptosis** (literally, a "falling away"). Molecules of the chemical that conveys this signal bind with receptors that activate killer genes within the cells. (All cells have these genes, but only certain cells respond to the chemical signal that turns them on.)

Once neurons have migrated to their final locations, they begin forming connections with other neurons. They grow dendrites, which receive the terminal buttons from the axons of other neurons, and they grow axons of their own. The growth of axons is guided by physical and chemical factors. Once the growing ends of the axons (the *growth cones*) reach their targets, they form numerous branches. Each of these branches finds a vacant place on the membrane of the appropriate type of postsynaptic cell, grows a terminal button, and establishes a synaptic connection. Apparently, different types of cells—or even different parts of a single cell—secrete different chemicals, which attract different types of axons (Benson, Colman, and Huntley, 2001). Of course, the establishment of a synaptic connection also requires efforts on the part of the postsynaptic cell; this cell must contribute its parts of the synapse, including the postsynaptic receptors. The chemical signals that the cells exchange to tell one another to establish these connections are just now being discovered.

The ventricular zone gives rise to more neurons than are needed. In fact, these neurons must compete to survive. The axons of approximately 50 percent of these neurons do not find vacant postsynaptic cells of the right type with which to form synaptic connections, so they die by apoptosis. This phenomenon, too, involves a chemical signal; when a presynaptic neuron establishes synaptic connections, it receives a signal from the postsynaptic cell that permits it to survive. The neurons that come too late do not find any available space and therefore do not receive this life-sustaining signal. This scheme might seem wasteful, but apparently the evolutionary process found that the safest strategy was to produce too many neurons and let them fight to establish synaptic connections rather than try to produce exactly the right number of each type of neuron.

---

apoptosis (*ay po **toe** sis*) Death of a cell caused by a chemical signal that activates a genetic mechanism inside the cell.

As we will see later in this chapter, different regions of the cerebral cortex perform specialized functions. Some receive and analyze visual information, some receive and analyze auditory information, some control movement of the muscles, and so on. Thus, different regions receive different inputs, contain different types of circuits of neurons, and have different outputs. What factors control this pattern of development?

Some of the specialization is undoubtedly programmed genetically. The neurons produced by the asymmetrical division of a particular founder cell all follow a particular radial glial fiber, so they end up somewhere in a single column extending outward from the ventricular zone. Thus, if the founder cells in different regions of the ventricular zone are themselves different, the neurons they produce will reflect these differences.

Experiments suggest that the specialization of a particular region of the cerebral cortex can also be induced by the axons that provide input to that region. For example, Krubitzer and her colleagues (see Krubitzer, 1998) removed some of the cerebral cortex of an opossum early in development, before the cortex had received its input from the thalamus. (As we will see later in this chapter, the *thalamus* is a structure located in the depths of the brain. Particular groups of neurons in the thalamus send axons to particular regions of the cerebral cortex and provide information from the sense organs.) The investigators used opossums because they are born during an early stage of brain development. After brain development was complete, the investigators used microelectrodes to record the activity of neurons in various regions of the cortex and examined the neural circuitry in these regions under a microscope. They found that the boundaries of the specialized regions were different from those seen in a normal brain: All regions were present, but they were squeezed into the available space. Thus, the growth of axons from particular regions of the thalamus to particular regions of the cerebral cortex appeared to affect the development of the cortical regions that they served. (See *Figure 3.10*.)

Experience also affects brain development. For example, one cue for depth perception arises from the fact that each eye gets a slightly different view of the world (Poggio and Poggio, 1984). This form of depth perception, *stereopsis* ("solid appearance"), is the kind obtained from a stereoscope or a three-dimensional movie. The particular neural circuits that are necessary for stereopsis, which are located in the cerebral cortex, will not develop unless an infant has experience viewing objects with both eyes during a critical period early in life. If an infant's eyes do not move together properly—if they are not directed toward the same place in the environment (that is, if the eyes are "crossed")—the infant never develops stereoscopic vision, even if the eye movements are later corrected by surgery on the eye muscles. This critical period occurs some time between one

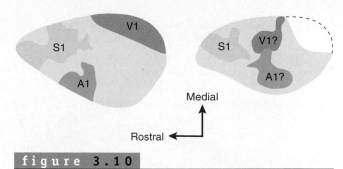

figure 3.10

The visual, auditory, and somatosensory areas of the cerebral cortex of the opossum *(Monodelphis domestica)*, drawn as if they were flattened out. Removal of the region that normally develops into visual cortex early in cortical development caused the sensory areas to develop in new locations, reduced in size.

(Adapted from Krubitzer, L. in *Brain and Mind: Evolutionary Perspectives,* edited by M. S. Gazzaniga and J. S. Altmann. Strasbourg, France: Human Frontier Science Program, 1998.)

and three years of age (Banks, Aslin, and Letson, 1975). Similar phenomena have been studied in laboratory animals and have confirmed that sensory input affects the connections established between cortical neurons.

Evidence indicates that a certain amount of neural rewiring can even be accomplished in the adult brain. For example, after a person's arm is amputated, the region of the cerebral cortex that previously analyzed sensory information from the missing limb soon begins analyzing information from adjacent regions of the body, such as the stump of the arm, the trunk, or the face. In fact, the person becomes more sensitive to touch in these regions after the changes in the cortex take place (Elbert et al., 1994; Kew et al., 1994; Yang et al., 1994). In addition, musicians who play stringed instruments have a larger cortical region devoted to analysis of sensory information from the fingers of the left hand (which they use to press the strings), and when a blind person who can read Braille touches objects with his or her fingertips, an enlarged region of the cerebral cortex is activated (Elbert et al., 1995; Sadato et al., 1996).

For many years, researchers have believed that *neurogenesis* (production of new neurons) does not take place in the fully developed brain. However, recent studies have shown this belief to be incorrect—the adult brain contains some stem cells (similar to the founder cells that give rise to the cells of the developing brain) that can divide and produce neurons. Detection of newly produced cells is done by administering a small amount of a radioactive form of one of the nucleotide bases that cells use to produce the DNA that is needed for neurogenesis. The next day, the animals' brains are removed and examined with methods described in Chapter 5. Such studies have found evidence for neurogenesis in the adult brain (Cameron and

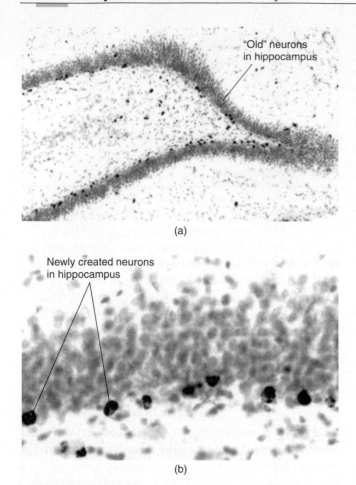

(a)

(b)

figure 3.11

Evidence of neurogenesis. (a) A section through a part of the hippocampus, showing cells containing DNA labeled with a radioactive nucleotide. (b) A magnified view of part of the same section.

(From Cameron, H. A. and McKay, R. D. G. *Journal of Comparative Neurology,* 2001, *435,* 406–417. By permission.)

McKay, 2001. See *Figure 3.11.*) However, although the mature brain can produce new neurons, there is no evidence yet that indicates that these neurons can establish connections to replace neural circuits that have been destroyed through injury, stroke, or disease (Horner and Gage, 2000).

Evolution of the Human Brain

The brains of the earliest vertebrates were smaller than those of later animals, and they were simpler as well. The evolutionary process brought about genetic changes that were responsible for the development of more complex brains, with more parts and more interconnections. An important factor in the evolution of more complex brains is genetic duplication (Allman, 1999). As Lewis (1992) noted, most of the genes that a species possesses perform important functions. If a mutation causes one of these genes to do something new, the previous function would be lost, and the animal might not survive. However, geneticists have discovered that genes can sometimes duplicate themselves, and

the duplication is passed on to the organism's offspring. This means that the animals have one gene to perform the important functions and another one to "experiment" with. If a mutation of the extra gene occurs, the old gene is still present, and its important function is still performed.

Research with a variety of species, from fruit flies to mammals, has shown that the evolution of more complex bodies and more complex brains involved duplication and modification of genes—in particular, *master genes* that control the activity of sets of other genes that are active during development. For example, the vertebrate hindbrain is made of six to eight segments known as *rhombomeres* (segments of the *rhombencephalon,* a structure that gives rise to the metencephalon and myelencephalon). Development of each of the rhombomeres appears to be controlled by a different master gene. Over the course of vertebrate brain evolution the original gene was duplicated several times and then modified. (See *Figure 3.12.*)

As we saw in Chapter 1, the human brain is larger than that of any other large animal when corrected for body size— more than three times larger than that of a chimpanzee, our

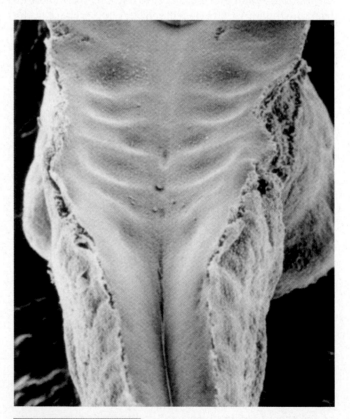

figure 3.12

Rhombomeres. A scanning electron micrograph of the dorsal surface of a chick embryo. The rhombomeres appear as a series of segments marked by swellings and grooves. Each rhombomere appears to be the product of a duplicated and mutated control gene.

(From Keynes, R., and Lumsden, A. Segmentation and the origin of regional diversity in the vertebrate central nervous system. *Neuron,* 1990, *4,* 1–9. Reprinted by permission.)

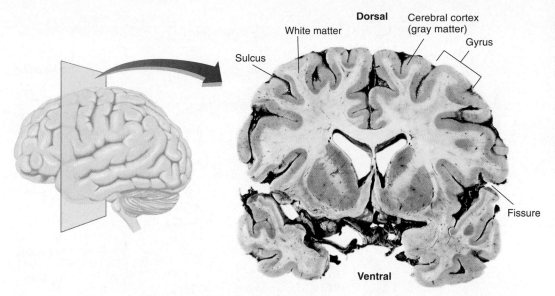

White matter
Dorsal
Cerebral cortex
(gray matter)
Gyrus
Sulcus
Fissure
Ventral

figure 3.13

A slice of a human brain showing fissures and gyri and the layer of cerebral cortex that follows these convolutions.

closest relative. What types of genetic changes are required to produce a large brain? Considering the fact that the difference between the genes of humans and chimpanzees is only 1.2 percent, the number of genes responsible for the differences between the chimpanzee brain and the human brain must be small. After all, only a small percentage of the 1.2 percent is devoted to brain development. In fact, Rakic (1988) suggests that the size differences between these two brains could be caused by a very simple process.

We just saw that the size of the ventricular zone increases during symmetrical division of the founder cells located there. The ultimate size of the brain is determined by the size of the ventricular zone. As Rakic notes, each symmetrical division doubles the number of founder cells and thus doubles the size of the brain. The human brain is 10 times larger than that of a rhesus macaque monkey. Thus, between three and four additional symmetrical divisions of founder cells would account for the difference in the size of these two brains. In fact, the stage of symmetrical division lasts about two days longer in humans, which provides enough time for three more divisions. The period of asymmetrical division is longer, too, which accounts for the fact that the human cortex is 15 percent thicker. Thus, delays in the termination of the symmetrical and asymmetrical periods of development could be responsible for the increased size of the human brain. A few simple mutations of the genes that control the timing of brain development could be responsible for these delays.

The Forebrain

As we saw, the **forebrain** surrounds the rostral end of the neural tube. Its two major components are the telencephalon and the diencephalon.

Telencephalon

The telencephalon includes most of the two symmetrical **cerebral hemispheres** that make up the cere-

brum. The cerebral hemispheres are covered by the cerebral cortex and contain the limbic system and the basal ganglia. The latter two sets of structures are primarily in the **subcortical regions** of the brain—those located deep within it, beneath the cerebral cortex.

■ **Cerebral Cortex**   As we saw in the previous section, the cerebral cortex surrounds the cerebral hemispheres like the bark of a tree. In humans the cerebral cortex is greatly convoluted; these convolutions, consisting of **sulci** (small grooves), **fissures** (large grooves), and **gyri** (bulges between adjacent sulci or fissures), greatly enlarge the surface area of the cortex, compared with a smooth brain of the same size. In fact, two-thirds of the surface of the cortex is hidden in the grooves; thus, the presence of gyri and sulci triples the area of the cerebral cortex. The total surface area is approximately 2360 cm^2 (2.5 ft^2), and the thickness is approximately 3 mm. The cerebral cortex consists mostly of glia and the cell bodies, dendrites, and interconnecting axons of neurons. Because cell bodies predominate, giving the cerebral cortex a grayish brown appearance, it is referred to as *gray matter*. (See *Figure 3.13.*) Beneath the cerebral cortex run millions of axons that connect the neurons of the cerebral cortex

---

forebrain   The most rostral of the three major divisions of the brain; includes the telencephalon and diencephalon.

cerebral hemisphere (*sa ree brul*)   One of the two major portions of the forebrain, covered by the cerebral cortex.

subcortical region   The region located within the brain, beneath the cortical surface.

sulcus (plural: sulci) (*sul kus, sul sigh*)   A groove in the surface of the cerebral hemisphere, smaller than a fissure.

fissure   A major groove in the surface of the brain, larger than a sulcus.

gyrus (plural: gyri) (*jye russ, jye rye*)   A convolution of the cortex of the cerebral hemispheres, separated by sulci or fissures.

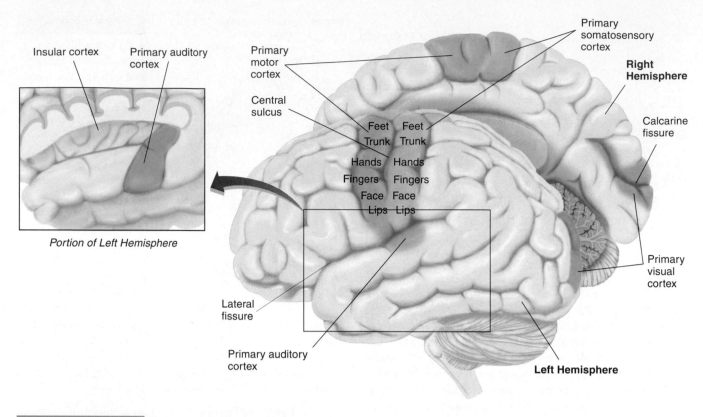

Insular cortex
Primary auditory cortex
Portion of Left Hemisphere

Primary motor cortex
Central sulcus
Feet Feet
Trunk Trunk
Hands Hands
Fingers Fingers
Face Face
Lips Lips
Lateral fissure
Primary auditory cortex

Primary somatosensory cortex
Right Hemisphere
Calcarine fissure
Primary visual cortex
Left Hemisphere

A lateral view of the left side of a human brain and part of the inner surface of the right side. The inset shows a cutaway of part of the frontal lobe of the left hemisphere, permitting us to see the primary auditory cortex on the dorsal surface of the temporal lobe, which forms the ventral bank of the lateral fissure.

with those located elsewhere in the brain. The large concentration of myelin gives this tissue an opaque white appearance—hence the term *white matter.*

Three areas of the cerebral cortex receive information from the sensory organs. The **primary visual cortex,** which receives visual information, is located at the back of the brain, on the inner surfaces of the cerebral hemispheres—primarily, on the upper and lower banks of the **calcarine fissure.** (*Calcarine* means "spur-shaped." See *Figure 3.14.*) The **primary auditory cortex,** which receives auditory information, is located on the lower surface of a deep fissure in the side of the brain—the **lateral fissure.** (See the inset in *Figure 3.14.*) The **primary somatosensory cortex,** a vertical strip of cortex just caudal to the **central sulcus,** receives information from the body senses. As Figure 3.14 shows, different regions of the primary somatosensory cortex receive information from different regions of the body. In addition, the base of the somatosensory cortex and a portion of the **insular cortex,** which is normally hidden from view by the frontal and temporal lobes, receives information concerning taste. (See *Figure 3.14.*)

With the exception of olfaction and gustation (taste), sensory information from the body or the environment is sent to primary sensory cortex of the contralateral hemisphere. Thus, the primary somatosensory cortex of the left

hemisphere learns what the right hand is holding, the left primary visual cortex learns what is happening toward the person's right, and so on.

The region of the cerebral cortex that is most directly involved in the control of movement is the **primary motor**

primary visual cortex The region of the posterior occipital lobe whose primary input is from the visual system.

calcarine fissure (*kal ka rine*) A fissure located in the occipital lobe on the medial surface of the brain; most of the primary visual cortex is located along its upper and lower banks.

primary auditory cortex The region of the superior temporal lobe whose primary input is from the auditory system.

lateral fissure The fissure that separates the temporal lobe from the overlying frontal and parietal lobes.

primary somatosensory cortex The region of the anterior parietal lobe whose primary input is from the somatosensory system.

central sulcus (*sul kus*) The sulcus that separates the frontal lobe from the parietal lobe.

insular cortex (*in sue lur*) A sunken region of the cerebral cortex that is normally covered by the rostral superior temporal lobe and caudal inferior frontal lobe.

primary motor cortex The region of the posterior frontal lobe that contains neurons that control movements of skeletal muscles.

cortex, located just in front of the primary somatosensory cortex. Neurons in different parts of the primary motor cortex are connected to muscles in different parts of the body. The connections, like those of the sensory regions of the cerebral cortex, are contralateral; the left primary motor cortex controls the right side of the body and vice versa. Thus, if a surgeon places an electrode on the surface of the primary motor cortex and stimulates the neurons there with a weak electrical current, the result will be movement of a particular part of the body. Moving the electrode to a different spot will cause a different part of the body to move. (See *Figure 3.14.*) I like to think of the strip of primary motor cortex as the keyboard of a piano, with each key controlling a different movement. (We will see shortly who the "player" of this piano is.)

The regions of primary sensory and motor cortex occupy only a small part of the cerebral cortex. The rest of the cerebral cortex accomplishes what is done between sensation and action: perceiving, learning and remembering, planning, and acting. These processes take place in the *association areas* of the cerebral cortex. The central sulcus provides an important dividing line between the rostral and caudal regions of the cerebral cortex. (See *Figure 3.14.*) The rostral region is involved in movement-related activities, such as planning and executing behaviors. The caudal region is involved in perceiving and learning.

Discussing the various regions of the cerebral cortex is easier if we have names for them. In fact, the cerebral cortex is divided into four areas, or *lobes,* named for the bones of the skull that cover them: the frontal lobe, parietal lobe, temporal lobe, and occipital lobe. Of course, the brain contains two of each lobe, one in each hemisphere. The **frontal lobe** (the "front") includes everything in front of the central sulcus. The **parietal lobe** (the "wall") is located on the side of the cerebral hemisphere, just behind the central sulcus, caudal to the frontal lobe. The **temporal lobe** (the "temple") juts forward from the base of the brain, ventral to the frontal and parietal lobes. The **occipital lobe** (from the Latin *ob,* "in back of," and *caput,* "head") lies at the very back of the brain, caudal to the parietal and temporal lobes. Figure 3.15 shows these lobes in three views of the cerebral hemispheres: a ventral view (a view from the bottom), a midsagittal view (a view of the inner surface of the right hemisphere after the left hemisphere has been removed), and a lateral view. (See *Figure 3.15.*)

frontal lobe The anterior portion of the cerebral cortex, rostral to the parietal lobe and dorsal to the temporal lobe.

parietal lobe (*pa rye i tul*) The region of the cerebral cortex caudal to the frontal lobe and dorsal to the temporal lobe.

temporal lobe (*tem por ul*) The region of the cerebral cortex rostral to the occipital lobe and ventral to the parietal and frontal lobes.

occipital lobe (*ok sip i tul*) The region of the cerebral cortex caudal to the parietal and temporal lobes.

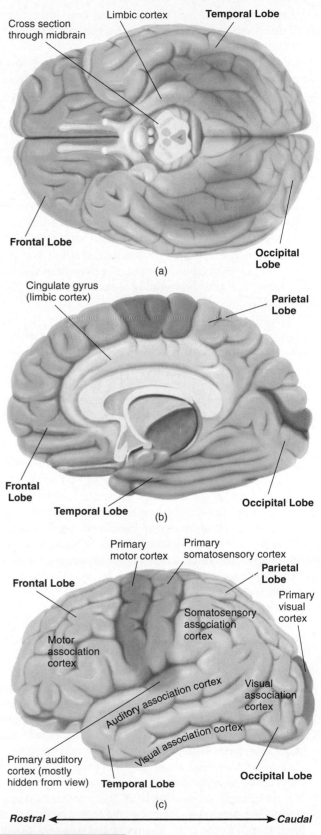

figure 3.15

The four lobes of the cerebral cortex, the primary sensory and motor cortex, and the association cortex. (a) Ventral view, from the base of the brain. (b) Midsagittal view, with the cerebellum and brain stem removed. (c) Lateral view.

Each primary sensory area of the cerebral cortex sends information to adjacent regions, called the **sensory association cortex.** Circuits of neurons in the sensory association cortex analyze the information received from the primary sensory cortex; perception takes place there, and memories are stored there. The regions of the sensory association cortex located closest to the primary sensory areas receive information from only one sensory system. For example, the region closest to the primary visual cortex analyzes visual information and stores visual memories. Regions of the sensory association cortex located far from the primary sensory areas receive information from more than one sensory system; thus, they are involved in several kinds of perceptions and memories. These regions make it possible to integrate information from more than one sensory system. For example, we can learn the connection between the sight of a particular face and the sound of a particular voice. (See *Figure 3.15.*)

If people sustain damage to the somatosensory association cortex, their deficits are related to somatosensation and to the environment in general; for example, they may have difficulty perceiving the shapes of objects that they can touch but not see, they may be unable to name parts of their bodies (see the case below), or they may have trouble drawing maps or following them. Destruction of the primary visual cortex causes blindness. However, although people who sustain damage to the visual association cortex will not become blind, they may be unable to recognize objects by sight. People who sustain damage to the auditory association cortex may have difficulty perceiving speech or even producing meaningful speech of their own. People who sustain damage to regions of the association cortex at the junction of the three posterior lobes, where the somatosensory, visual, and auditory functions overlap, may have difficulty reading or writing.

Mr. M., a city bus driver, stopped to let a passenger climb board. The passenger asked him a question, and Mr. M. suddenly realized that he didn't understand what she was saying. He could hear her, but her words made no sense. He opened his mouth to reply. He made some sounds, but the look on the woman's face told him that she couldn't understand what he was trying to say. He turned off the engine and looked around at the passengers and tried to tell them to get some help. Although he was unable to say anything, they understood that something was wrong, and one of them called an ambulance.

An MRI scan showed that Mr. M. had sustained an intracerebral hemorrhage—a kind of stroke caused by rupture of blood vessels in the brain. The stroke had damaged his left parietal lobe. Mr. M. gradually regained the ability to talk and understand the speech of others, but some deficits remained. A colleague, Dr. D., and I studied Mr. M. several weeks after his stroke. The dialogue went something like this:

"Show me your hand."

"My hand . . . my hand." Looks at has arms, then touches his left forearm.

"Show me your chin."

"My chin." Looks at his arms, looks down, puts his hand on his abdomen.

"Show me your right elbow."

"My right . . . " (points to the right with his right thumb) "elbow." Looks up and down his right arm, finally touches his right shoulder.

As you can see, Mr. M. could understand that we were asking him to point out parts of his body and could repeat the names of the body parts when we spoke them, but he could not identify which body parts these names referred to. This strange deficit, which sometimes follows damage to the left parietal lobe, is called *autotopagnosia,* or "poor knowledge of one's own topography." (A better term would be *autotopanomia,* or "poor knowledge of the names of one's own topography," but then, no one asked me to choose the term.) The parietal lobes are involved with space: the right primarily with external space, and the left with one's body and personal space. I'll say more about disorders such as this one in Chapter 15, which deals with brain mechanisms of language.

Just as regions of the sensory association cortex of the posterior part of the brain are involved in perceiving and remembering, the frontal association cortex is involved in the planning and execution of movements. The **motor association cortex** (also known as the *premotor cortex*) is located just rostral to the primary motor cortex. This region controls the primary motor cortex; thus, it directly controls behavior. If the primary motor cortex is the keyboard of the piano, then the motor association cortex is the piano player. The rest of the frontal lobe, rostral to the motor association cortex, is known as the **prefrontal cortex.** This region of the brain is less involved with the control of movement and more involved in formulating plans and strategies.

Although the two cerebral hemispheres cooperate with each other, they do not perform identical functions. Some functions are *lateralized*—located primarily on one side of the brain. In general, the left hemisphere participates in the *analysis* of information—the extraction of the elements that make up the whole of an experience. This ability makes the left hemisphere particularly good at recognizing *serial events*—events whose elements occur one after the other—and controlling sequences of behav-

sensory association cortex Those regions of the cerebral cortex that receive information from the regions of primary sensory cortex.

motor association cortex The region of the frontal lobe rostral to the primary motor cortex; also known as the premotor cortex.

prefrontal cortex The region of the frontal lobe rostral to the motor association cortex.

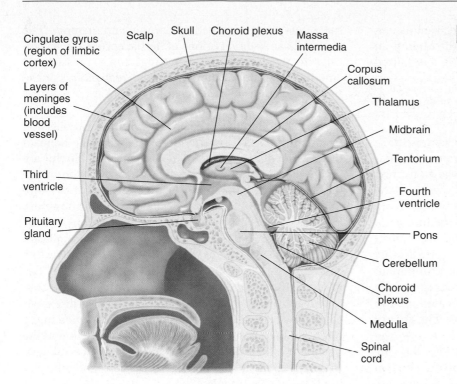

Cingulate gyrus (region of limbic cortex)
Scalp
Skull
Choroid plexus
Massa intermedia
Corpus callosum
Thalamus
Midbrain
Tentorium
Fourth ventricle
Pons
Cerebellum
Choroid plexus
Medulla
Spinal cord
Layers of meninges (includes blood vessel)
Third ventricle
Pituitary gland

figure 3.16

A midsagittal view of the brain and part of the spinal cord.

ior. (In a few people the functions of the left and right hemispheres are reversed.) The serial functions that are performed by the left hemisphere include verbal activities, such as talking, understanding the speech of other people, reading, and writing. These abilities are disrupted by damage to the various regions of the left hemisphere. (I will say more about language and the brain in Chapter 15.)

In contrast, the right hemisphere is specialized for *synthesis;* it is particularly good at putting isolated elements together to perceive things as a whole. For example, our ability to draw sketches (especially of three-dimensional objects), read maps, and construct complex objects out of smaller elements depends heavily on circuits of neurons that are located in the right hemisphere. Damage to the right hemisphere disrupts these abilities.

We are not aware of the fact that each hemisphere perceives the world differently. Although the two cerebral hemispheres perform somewhat different functions, our perceptions and our memories are unified. This unity is accomplished by the **corpus callosum,** a large band of axons that connects corresponding parts of the association cortex of the left and right hemispheres: The left and right temporal lobes are connected, the left and right parietal lobes are connected, and so on. Because of the corpus callosum, each region of the association cortex knows what is happening in the corresponding region of the opposite side of the brain.

Figure 3.16 shows a *midsagittal* view of the brain. The brain (and part of the spinal cord) has been sliced down the middle, dividing it into its two symmetrical halves.

The left half has been removed, so we see the inner surface of the right half. The cerebral cortex that covers most of the surface of the cerebral hemispheres (including the frontal, parietal, occipital, and temporal lobes) is called the **neocortex** ("new" cortex, because it is of relatively recent evolutionary origin). Another form of cerebral cortex, the **limbic cortex,** is located around the medial edge of the cerebral hemispheres (*limbus* means "border"). The **cingulate gyrus,** an important region of the limbic cortex, can be seen in this figure. (See ***Figure 3.16.***) In addition, if you look back at the top two drawings of Figure 3.15, you will see that the limbic cortex occupies the regions that have not been colored in. (Refer to ***Figure 3.15.***)

Figure 3.16 also shows the corpus callosum. To slice the brain into its two symmetrical halves, one must slice through the middle of the corpus callosum. (Recall that I described the split-brain operation, in which the corpus callosum is severed, in Chapter 1.) (See ***Figure 3.16.***)

corpus callosum (*ka loh sum*) A large bundle of axons that interconnects corresponding regions of the association cortex on each side of the brain.

neocortex The phylogenetically newest cortex, including the primary sensory cortex, primary motor cortex, and association cortex.

limbic cortex Phylogenetically old cortex, located at the medial edge ("limbus") of the cerebral hemispheres; part of the limbic system.

cingulate gyrus (*sing yew lett*) A strip of limbic cortex lying along the lateral walls of the groove separating the cerebral hemispheres, just above the corpus callosum.

As I mentioned earlier, one of the Chapter 3 animations on the CD-ROM will permit you to view the brain from various angles and see the locations of the specialized regions of the cerebral cortex. (See *Animation 3.2, The Rotatable Brain.*)

■ **Limbic System** A neuroanatomist, Papez (1937), suggested that a set of interconnected brain structures formed a circuit whose primary function was motivation and emotion. This system included several regions of the limbic cortex (already described) and a set of interconnected structures surrounding the core of the forebrain. A physiologist, MacLean (1949), expanded the system to include other structures and coined the term **limbic system.** Besides the limbic cortex, the most important parts of the limbic system are the **hippocampus** ("sea horse") and the **amygdala** ("almond"), located next to the lateral ventricle in the temporal lobe. The **fornix** ("arch") is a bundle of axons that connects the hippocampus with other regions of the brain, including the **mammillary** ("breast-shaped") **bodies,** protrusions on the base of the brain that contain parts of the hypothalamus. (See *Figure 3.17.*)

MacLean noted that the evolution of this system, which includes the first and simplest form of cerebral cortex, appears to have coincided with the development of emotional responses. As you will see in Chapter 14, we now know that parts of the limbic system (notably, the hippocampal formation and the region of limbic cortex that

surrounds it) are involved in learning and memory. The amygdala and some regions of limbic cortex are specifically involved in emotions: feelings and expressions of emotions, emotional memories, and recognition of the signs of emotions in other people.

■ **Basal Ganglia** The **basal ganglia** are a collection of subcortical nuclei in the forebrain, which lie beneath the anterior portion of the lateral ventricles. **Nuclei** are groups of neurons of similar shape. (The word *nucleus,* from the Greek "nut," can refer to the inner portion of an atom, to the structure of a cell that contains the chromosomes, and—as in this case—to a collection of neurons located within the brain.) The major parts of the basal ganglia are the *caudate nucleus,* the *putamen,* and the *globus pallidus* (the "nucleus with a tail," the "shell," and the "pale globe." See *Figure 3.18*). The basal ganglia are involved in the control of movement. For example, Parkinson's disease is caused by degeneration of certain neurons located in the midbrain that send axons to the caudate nucleus and the putamen. The symptoms of this disease are of weakness, tremors, rigidity of the limbs, poor balance, and difficulty in initiating movements.

Diencephalon

The second major division of the forebrain, the **diencephalon,** is situated between the telencephalon and the mesencephalon; it surrounds the third ventricle. Its two most important structures are the thalamus and the hypothalamus. (See *Figure 3.18.*)

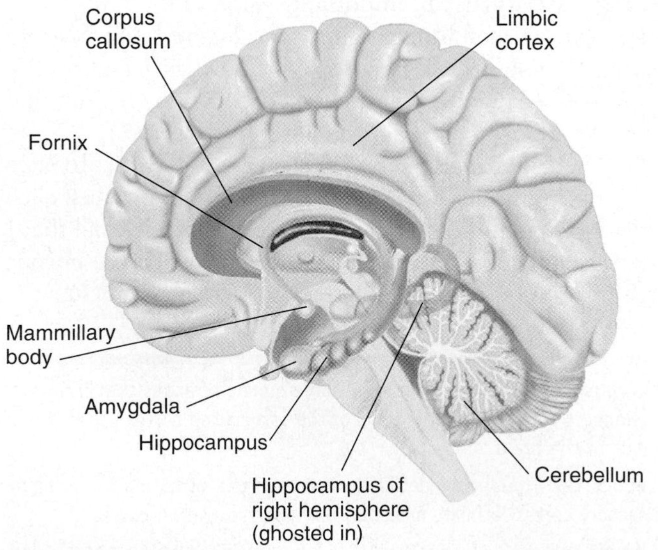

figure **3.17**

The major components of the limbic system. All of the left hemisphere except for the limbic system has been removed.

limbic system A group of brain regions including the anterior thalamic nuclei, amygdala, hippocampus, limbic cortex, and parts of the hypothalamus, as well as their interconnecting fiber bundles.

hippocampus A forebrain structure of the temporal lobe, constituting an important part of the limbic system; includes the hippocampus proper (Ammon's horn), dentate gyrus, and subiculum.

amygdala (*a mig da la*) A structure in the interior of the rostral temporal lobe, containing a set of nuclei; part of the limbic system.

fornix A fiber bundle that connects the hippocampus with other parts of the brain, including the mammillary bodies of the hypothalamus; part of the limbic system.

mammillary bodies (*mam i lair ee*) A protrusion of the bottom of the brain at the posterior end of the hypothalamus, containing some hypothalamic nuclei; part of the limbic system.

basal ganglia A group of subcortical nuclei in the telencephalon, the caudate nucleus, the globus pallidus, and the putamen, important parts of the motor system.

nucleus (plural: **nuclei**) An identifiable group of neural cell bodies in the central nervous system.

diencephalon (*dy en seff a lahn*) A region of the forebrain surrounding the third ventricle; includes the thalamus and the hypothalamus.

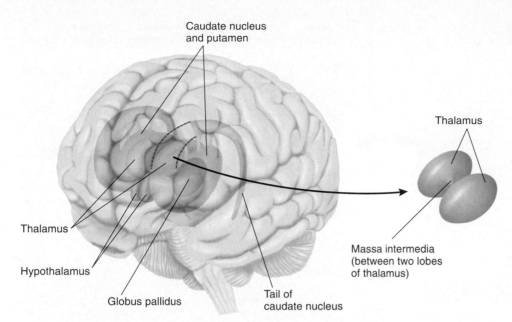

Caudate nucleus
and putamen

Thalamus

Thalamus

Hypothalamus

Globus pallidus

Tail of
caudate nucleus

Massa intermedia
(between two lobes
of thalamus)

figure 3.18

The location of the basal ganglia
and diencephalon, ghosted in
to a semitransparent brain.

■ **Thalamus** The **thalamus** (from the Greek *thalamos,* "inner chamber") makes up the dorsal part of the diencephalon. It is situated near the middle of the cerebral hemispheres, immediately medial and caudal to the basal ganglia. The thalamus has two lobes, connected by a bridge of gray matter called the *massa intermedia,* which pierces the middle of the third ventricle. (See *Figure 3.18.*) The massa intermedia is probably not an important structure, because it is absent in the brains of many people. However, it serves as a useful reference point in looking at diagrams of the brain; it appears in Figures 3.4, 3.16, 3.17, 3.18, and 3.19.

Most neural input to the cerebral cortex is received from the thalamus; indeed, much of the cortical surface can be divided into regions that receive projections from specific parts of the thalamus. **Projection fibers** are sets of axons that arise from cell bodies located in one region of the brain and synapse on neurons located within another region (that is, they *project to* these regions).

The thalamus is divided into several nuclei. Some thalamic nuclei receive sensory information from the sensory systems. The neurons in these nuclei then relay the sensory information to specific sensory projection areas of the cerebral cortex. For example, the **lateral geniculate nucleus** receives information from the eye and sends axons to the primary visual cortex, and the **medial geniculate nucleus** receives information from the inner ear and sends axons to the primary auditory cortex. Other thalamic nuclei project to specific regions of the cerebral cortex, but they do not relay sensory information. For example, the **ventrolateral nucleus** receives information from the cerebellum and projects it to the primary motor cortex. And as we will see in Chapter 9, several nuclei are involved in controlling the general excitability of the cere-

bral cortex. To accomplish this task, these nuclei have widespread projections to all cortical regions.

■ **Hypothalamus** As its name implies, the **hypothalamus** lies at the base of the brain, under the thalamus. Although the hypothalamus is a relatively small structure, it is an important one. It controls the autonomic nervous system and the endocrine system and organizes behaviors related to survival of the species—the so-called four F's: fighting, feeding, fleeing, and mating.

The hypothalamus is situated on both sides of the ventral portion of the third ventricle. The hypothalamus is a complex structure, containing many nuclei and fiber tracts.

thalamus The largest portion of the diencephalon, located above the hypothalamus; contains nuclei that project information to specific regions of the cerebral cortex and receive information from it.

projection fiber An axon of a neuron in one region of the brain whose terminals form synapses with neurons in another region.

lateral geniculate nucleus A group of cell bodies within the lateral geniculate body of the thalamus that receives fibers from the retina and projects fibers to the primary visual cortex.

medial geniculate nucleus A group of cell bodies within the medial geniculate body of the thalamus; receives fibers from the auditory system and projects fibers to the primary auditory cortex.

ventrolateral nucleus A nucleus of the thalamus that receives inputs from the cerebellum and sends axons to the primary motor cortex.

hypothalamus The group of nuclei of the diencephalon situated beneath the thalamus; involved in regulation of the autonomic nervous system, control of the anterior and posterior pituitary glands, and integration of species-typical behaviors.

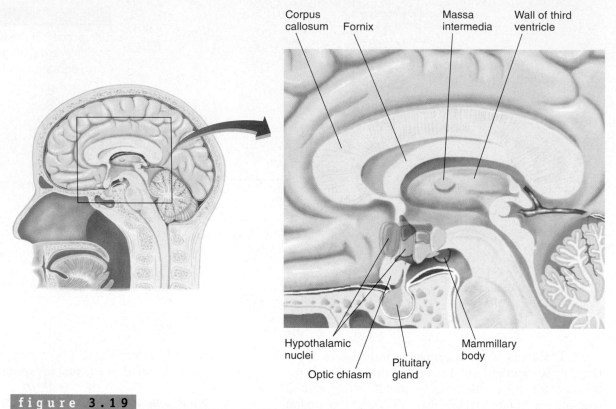

Corpus callosum   Fornix   Massa intermedia   Wall of third ventricle

Hypothalamic nuclei   Optic chiasm   Pituitary gland   Mammillary body

figure 3.19

A midsagittal view of part of the brain, showing some of the nuclei of the hypothalamus. The nuclei are situated on the far side of the wall of the third ventricle, inside the right hemisphere.

Figure 3.19 indicates its location and size. Note that the pituitary gland is attached to the base of the hypothalamus via the pituitary stalk. Just in front of the pituitary stalk is the **optic chiasm,** where half of the axons in the optic nerves (from the eyes) cross from one side of the brain to the other. (See *Figure 3.19.*) The role of the hypothalamus in the control of the four F's (and other behaviors, such as drinking and sleeping) will be considered in several chapters later in this book.

Much of the endocrine system is controlled by hormones produced by cells in the hypothalamus. A special system of blood vessels directly connects the hypothalamus with the **anterior pituitary gland.** (See *Figure 3.20.*) The hypothalamic hormones are secreted by specialized neurons called **neurosecretory cells,** located near the base of the pituitary stalk. These hormones stimulate the anterior pituitary gland to secrete its hormones. For example, *gonadotropin-releasing hormone* causes the anterior pituitary gland to secrete the *gonadotropic hormones,* which play a role in reproductive physiology and behavior.

Most of the hormones secreted by the anterior pituitary gland control other endocrine glands. Because of this function, the anterior pituitary gland has been called the body's "master gland." For example, the gonadotropic hormones stimulate the gonads (ovaries and testes) to release

male or female sex hormones. These hormones affect cells throughout the body, including some in the brain. Two other anterior pituitary hormones—prolactin and somatotropic hormone (growth hormone)—do not control other glands but act as the final messenger. The behavioral effects of many of the anterior pituitary hormones are discussed in later chapters.

The hypothalamus also produces the hormones of the **posterior pituitary gland** and controls their secretion.

optic chiasm (*kye az'm*) An X-shaped connection between the optic nerves, located below the base of the brain, just anterior to the pituitary gland.

anterior pituitary gland The anterior part of the pituitary gland; an endocrine gland whose secretions are controlled by the hypothalamic hormones.

neurosecretory cell A neuron that secretes a hormone or hormone-like substance.

posterior pituitary gland The posterior part of the pituitary gland; an endocrine gland that contains hormone-secreting terminal buttons of axons whose cell bodies lie within the hypothalamus.

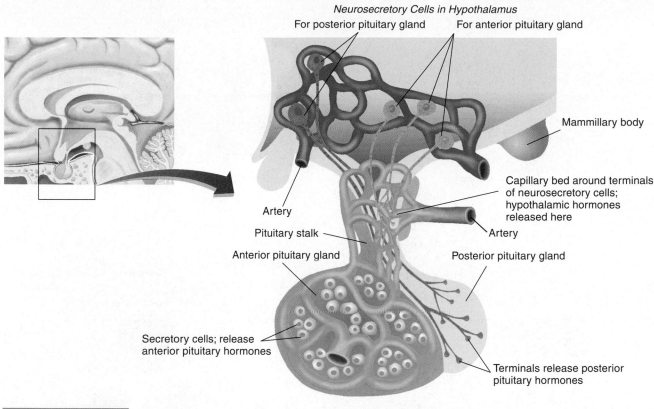

figure 3.20

The pituitary gland. Hormones released by the neurosecretory cells in the hypothalamus enter capillaries and are conveyed to the anterior pituitary gland, where they control its secretion of hormones. The hormones of the posterior pituitary gland are produced in the hypothalamus and carried there in vesicles by means of axoplasmic transport.

These hormones include oxytocin, which stimulates ejection of milk and uterine contractions at the time of childbirth, and vasopressin, which regulates urine output by the kidneys. They are produced by neurons in the hypothalamus whose axons travel down the pituitary stalk and terminate in the posterior pituitary gland. The hormones are carried in vesicles through the axoplasm of these neurons and collect in the terminal buttons in the posterior pituitary gland. When these axons fire, the hormone contained within their terminal buttons is liberated and enters the circulatory system.

The Midbrain

The **midbrain** (also called the **mesencephalon**) surrounds the cerebral aqueduct and consists of two major parts: the tectum and the tegmentum.

Tectum

The **tectum** ("roof") is located in the dorsal portion of the mesencephalon. Its principal structures are the **superior colliculi** and the **inferior colliculi,** which appear as four bumps on the dorsal surface of the **brain stem.** The brain stem includes the diencephalon, midbrain, and hindbrain, and it is so called because it looks

midbrain The mesencephalon; the central of the three major divisions of the brain.

mesencephalon (*mezz en **seff** a lahn*) The midbrain; a region of the brain that surrounds the cerebral aqueduct; includes the tectum and the tegmentum.

tectum The dorsal part of the midbrain; includes the superior and inferior colliculi.

superior colliculi (*ka **lik** yew lee*) Protrusions on top of the midbrain; part of the visual system.

inferior colliculi Protrusions on top of the midbrain; part of the auditory system.

brain stem The "stem" of the brain, from the medulla to the diencephalon, excluding the cerebellum.

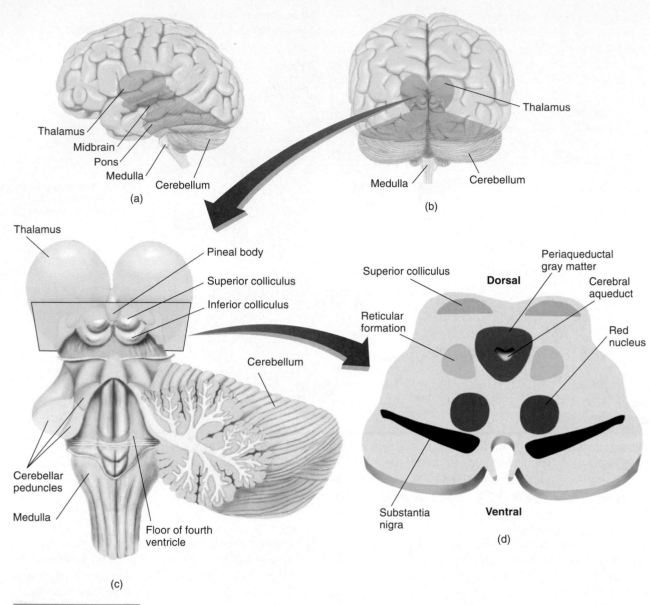

Thalamus
Midbrain
Pons
Medulla
Cerebellum

(a)

Thalamus
Medulla
Cerebellum

(b)

Thalamus
Pineal body
Superior colliculus
Inferior colliculus
Cerebellum
Cerebellar peduncles
Medulla
Floor of fourth ventricle

(c)

Superior colliculus
Reticular formation
Substantia nigra
Periaqueductal gray matter
Dorsal
Cerebral aqueduct
Red nucleus
Ventral

(d)

> **figure 3.21**
>
> The cerebellum and brain stem. (a) Lateral view of a semitransparent brain, showing the cerebellum and brain stem ghosted in. (b) View from the back of the brain. (c) A dorsal view of the brain stem. The left hemisphere of the cerebellum and part of the right hemisphere have been removed to show the inside of the fourth ventricle and the cerebellar peduncles. (d) A cross section of the midbrain.

just like that—a stem. Figure 3.21 shows several views of the brain stem: lateral and posterior views of the brain stem inside a semitransparent brain, an enlarged view of the brain stem with part of the cerebellum cut away to reveal the inside of the fourth ventricle, and a cross section through the midbrain. (See *Figure 3.21.*) The inferior colliculi are a part of the auditory system. The superior colliculi are part of the visual system. In mammals they are primarily involved in visual reflexes and reactions to moving stimuli.

Tegmentum

The **tegmentum** ("covering") consists of the portion of the mesencephalon beneath the tectum. It includes the rostral end of the reticular formation, several nuclei con-

---

tegmentum The ventral part of the midbrain; includes the periaqueductal gray matter, reticular formation, red nucleus, and substantia nigra.

trolling eye movements, the periaqueductal gray matter, the red nucleus, the substantia nigra, and the ventral tegmental area. (See *Figure 3.21d.*)

The **reticular formation** is a large structure consisting of many nuclei (over ninety in all). It is also characterized by a diffuse, interconnected network of neurons with complex dendritic and axonal processes. (Indeed, *reticulum* means "little net"; early anatomists were struck by the netlike appearance of the reticular formation.) The reticular formation occupies the core of the brain stem, from the lower border of the medulla to the upper border of the midbrain. (See *Figure 3.21d.*) The reticular formation receives sensory information by means of various pathways and projects axons to the cerebral cortex, thalamus, and spinal cord. It plays a role in sleep and arousal, attention, muscle tonus, movement, and various vital reflexes. Its functions will be described more fully in later chapters.

The **periaqueductal gray matter** is so called because it consists mostly of cell bodies of neurons ("gray matter," as contrasted with the "white matter" of axon bundles) that surround the cerebral aqueduct as it travels from the third to the fourth ventricle. The periaqueductal gray matter contains neural circuits that control sequences of movements that constitute species-typical behaviors, such as fighting and mating. As we will see in Chapter 7, opiates such as morphine decrease an organism's sensitivity to pain by stimulating receptors on neurons located in this region.

The **red nucleus** and **substantia nigra** ("black substance") are important components of the motor system. A bundle of axons that arises from the red nucleus constitutes one of the two major fiber systems that bring motor information from the cerebral cortex and cerebellum to the spinal cord. The substantia nigra contains neurons whose axons project to the caudate nucleus and putamen, parts of the basal ganglia. As we will see in Chapter 4, degeneration of these neurons causes Parkinson's disease.

The Hindbrain

The **hindbrain,** which surrounds the fourth ventricle, consists of two major divisions: the metencephalon and the myelencephalon.

Metencephalon

The metencephalon consists of the pons and the cerebellum.

■ **Cerebellum** The **cerebellum** ("little brain"), with its two hemispheres, resembles a miniature version of the cerebrum. It is covered by the **cerebellar cortex** and has a set of **deep cerebellar nuclei.** These nuclei receive projections from the cerebellar cortex and themselves send projections out of the cerebellum to other parts of the brain. Each hemisphere of the cerebellum is attached to the dorsal surface of the pons by bundles of axons: the superior, middle, and inferior **cerebellar peduncles** ("little feet"). (See *Figure 3.21c.*)

Damage to the cerebellum impairs standing, walking, or performance of coordinated movements. (A virtuoso pianist or other performing musician owes much to his or her cerebellum.) The cerebellum receives visual, auditory, vestibular, and somatosensory information, and it also receives information about individual muscle movements being directed by the brain. The cerebellum integrates this information and modifies the motor outflow, exerting a coordinating and smoothing effect on the movements. Cerebellar damage results in jerky, poorly coordinated, exaggerated movements; extensive cerebellar damage makes it impossible even to stand. Chapter 8 discusses the anatomy and functions of the cerebellum in more detail.

■ **Pons** The **pons,** a large bulge in the brain stem, lies between the mesencephalon and medulla oblongata, immediately ventral to the cerebellum. *Pons* means "bridge," but it does not really look like one. (Refer to *Figures 3.16* and *3.21a.*) The pons contains, in its core, a portion of the reticular formation, including some nuclei that appear to be important in sleep and arousal. It also contains a large nucleus that relays information from the cerebral cortex to the cerebellum.

---

reticular formation A large network of neural tissue located in the central region of the brain stem, from the medulla to the diencephalon.

periaqueductal gray matter The region of the midbrain surrounding the cerebral aqueduct; contains neural circuits involved in species-typical behaviors.

red nucleus A large nucleus of the midbrain that receives inputs from the cerebellum and motor cortex and sends axons to motor neurons in the spinal cord.

substantia nigra A darkly stained region of the tegmentum that contains neurons that communicate with the caudate nucleus and putamen in the basal ganglia.

hindbrain The most caudal of the three major divisions of the brain; includes the metencephalon and myelencephalon.

cerebellum (*sair a **bell** um*) A major part of the brain located dorsal to the pons, containing the two cerebellar hemispheres, covered with the cerebellar cortex; an important component of the motor system.

cerebellar cortex The cortex that covers the surface of the cerebellum.

deep cerebellar nuclei Nuclei located within the cerebellar hemispheres; receive projections from the cerebellar cortex and send projections out of the cerebellum to other parts of the brain.

cerebellar peduncle (*pee dun kul*) One of three bundles of axons that attach each cerebellar hemisphere to the dorsal pons.

pons The region of the metencephalon rostral to the medulla, caudal to the midbrain, and ventral to the cerebellum.

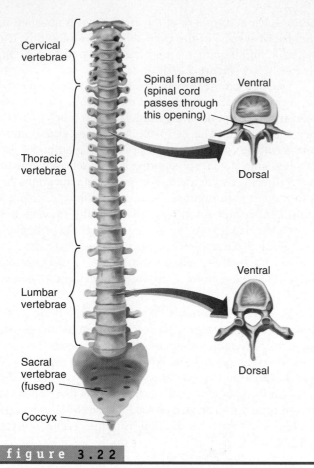

Cervical vertebrae

Spinal foramen (spinal cord passes through this opening)

Ventral

Dorsal

Thoracic vertebrae

Ventral

Lumbar vertebrae

Dorsal

Sacral vertebrae (fused)

Coccyx

figure 3.22

A ventral view of the human spinal column, with details showing the anatomy of the vertebrae.

Myelencephalon

The myelencephalon contains one major structure, the **medulla oblongata** (literally, "oblong marrow"), usually just called the *medulla*. This structure is the most caudal portion of the brain stem; its lower border is the rostral end of the spinal cord. (Refer to *Figures 3.16* and *3.21a.*) The medulla contains part of the reticular formation, including nuclei that control vital functions such as regulation of the cardiovascular system, respiration, and skeletal muscle tonus.

The Spinal Cord

The **spinal cord** is a long, conical structure, approximately as thick as our little finger. The principal function of the spinal cord is to distribute motor fibers to the effector organs of the body (glands and muscles) and to collect somatosensory information to be passed on to the brain. The spinal cord also has a certain degree of autonomy from the brain; various reflexive control circuits (some of which are described in Chapter 8) are located there.

The spinal cord is protected by the vertebral column, which is composed of twenty-four individual ver-

tebrae of the *cervical* (neck), *thoracic* (chest), and *lumbar* (lower back) regions and the fused vertebrae making up the *sacral* and *coccygeal* portions of the column (located in the pelvic region). The spinal cord passes through a hole in each of the vertebrae (the *spinal foramens*). Figure 3.22 illustrates the divisions and structures of the spinal cord and vertebral column. (See *Figure 3.22.*) Note that the spinal cord is only about two-thirds as long as the vertebral column; the rest of the space is filled by a mass of **spinal roots** composing the **cauda equina** ("horse's tail"). (Refer to *Figure 3.3c.*)

Early in embryological development the vertebral column and spinal cord are the same length. As development progresses, the vertebral column grows faster than the spinal cord. This differential growth rate causes the spinal roots to be displaced downward; the most caudal roots travel the farthest before they emerge through openings between the vertebrae and thus compose the cauda equina. To produce the **caudal block** that is sometimes used in pelvic surgery or childbirth, a local anesthetic can be injected into the CSF contained within the sac of dura mater surrounding the cauda equina. The drug blocks conduction in the axons of the cauda equina.

Figure 3.23(a) shows a portion of the spinal cord, with the layers of the meninges that wrap it. Small bundles of fibers emerge from each side of the spinal cord in two straight lines along its dorsolateral and ventrolateral surfaces. Groups of these bundles fuse together and become the thirty-one paired sets of **dorsal roots** and **ventral roots.** The dorsal and ventral roots join together as they pass through the intervertebral foramens and become spinal nerves. (See *Figure 3.23a.*)

Figure 3.23(b) shows a cross section of the spinal cord. Like the brain, the spinal cord consists of white matter and gray matter. Unlike the brain's, its white matter (consisting of ascending and descending bundles of myelinated

medulla oblongata (*me doo la*) The most caudal portion of the brain; located in the myelencephalon, immediately rostral to the spinal cord.

spinal cord The cord of nervous tissue that extends caudally from the medulla.

spinal root A bundle of axons surrounded by connective tissue that occurs in pairs, which fuse and form a spinal nerve.

cauda equina (*ee kwye na*) A bundle of spinal roots located caudal to the end of the spinal cord.

caudal block The anesthesia and paralysis of the lower part of the body produced by injection of a local anesthetic into the cerebrospinal fluid surrounding the cauda equina.

dorsal root The spinal root that contains incoming (afferent) sensory fibers.

ventral root The spinal root that contains outgoing (efferent) motor fibers.

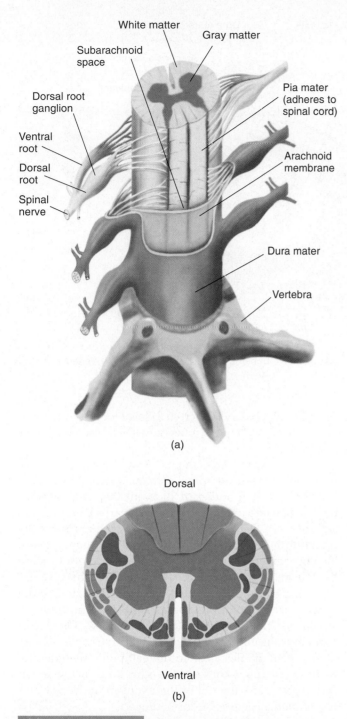

(a)

Dorsal

Ventral

(b)

figure 3.23

The spinal cord. (a) A portion of the spinal cord, showing the layers of the meninges and the relation of the spinal cord to the vertebral column. (b) A cross section through the spinal cord. Ascending tracts are shown in blue; descending tracts are shown in red.

axons) is on the outside; the gray matter (mostly neural cell bodies and short, unmyelinated axons) is on the inside. In Figure 3.23(b), ascending tracts are indicated in blue; descending tracts are indicated in red. (See *Figure 3.23b*.)

i n t e r i m
s u m m a r y

The Central Nervous System

The brain consists of three major divisions, organized around the three chambers of the tube that develops early in embryonic life: the forebrain, the midbrain, and the hindbrain. The development of the neural tube into the mature central nervous system is illustrated in Figure 3.7, and Table 3.2 outlines the major divisions and subdivisions of the brain.

During the first phase of brain development, symmetrical division of the founder cells of the ventricular zone, which lines the neural tube, increases its size. During the second phase, asymmetrical division of these cells gives rise to neurons, which migrate up the fibers of radial glial cells to their final resting places. There, neurons develop dendrites and axons and establish synaptic connections with other neurons. Later, neurons that fail to develop a sufficient number of synaptic connections are killed through apoptosis. Although the basic development of the nervous system is genetically controlled, sensory stimulation plays a role in refining the details. In addition, the neural circuitry of even a fully mature brain can be modified through experience.

The duplication of genes—in particular, master genes that control groups of other genes—facilitated the increase in complexity of the brain during the process of evolution. When a gene is duplicated, one of the copies can continue to perform vital functions, leaving the other copy for "experimentation" through mutations. The large size of the human brain, relative to the brains of other primates, appears to be accomplished primarily by lengthening the first and second periods of brain development.

The forebrain, which surrounds the lateral and third ventricles, consists of the telencephalon and diencephalon. The telencephalon contains the cerebral cortex, the limbic system, and the basal ganglia. The cerebral cortex is organized into the frontal, parietal, temporal, and occipital lobes. The central sulcus divides the frontal lobe, which deals specifically with movement and the planning of movement, from the other three lobes, which deal primarily with perceiving and learning. The limbic system, which includes the limbic cortex, the hippocampus, and the amygdala, is involved in emotion, motivation, and learning. The basal ganglia participate in the control of movement. The diencephalon consists of the thalamus, which directs information to and from the cerebral cortex, and the hypothalamus, which controls the endocrine system and modulates species-typical behaviors.

The midbrain, which surrounds the cerebral aqueduct, consists of the tectum and tegmentum. The tectum is involved in audition and the control of visual reflexes and reactions to moving stimuli. The tegmentum contains the reticular formation, which is important in sleep, arousal, and movement; the periaqueductal gray matter, which controls various species-typical behaviors; and the red nucleus

figure 3.24

A cross section of the spinal cord, showing the route taken by afferent and efferent axons through the dorsal and ventral roots.

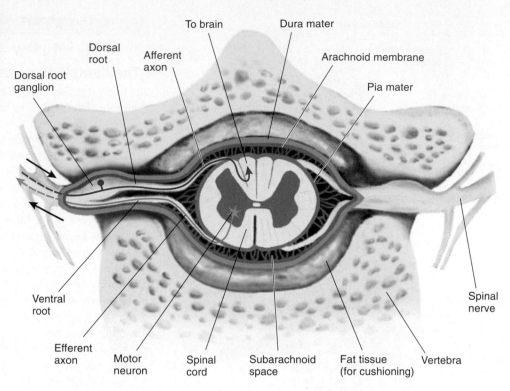

and the substantia nigra, both parts of the motor system. The hindbrain, which surrounds the fourth ventricle, contains the cerebellum, the pons, and the medulla. The cerebellum plays an important role in integrating and coordinating movements. The pons contains some nuclei that are important in sleep and arousal. The medulla oblongata, too, is involved in sleep and arousal, but it also plays a role in control of movement and in control of vital functions such as heart rate, breathing, and blood pressure.

The outer part of the spinal cord consists of white matter: axons conveying information up or down. The central gray matter contains cell bodies.

The Peripheral Nervous System

The brain and spinal cord communicate with the rest of the body via the cranial nerves and spinal nerves. These nerves are part of the peripheral nervous system, which conveys sensory information to the central nervous system and conveys messages from the central nervous system to the body's muscles and glands.

Spinal Nerves

The **spinal nerves** begin at the junction of the dorsal and ventral roots of the spinal cord. The nerves leave the vertebral column and travel to the muscles or sensory receptors they innervate, branching repeatedly as they go.

Branches of spinal nerves often follow blood vessels, especially those branches that innervate skeletal muscles. (Refer to *Figure 3.3.*)

Now let us consider the pathways by which sensory information enters the spinal cord and motor information leaves it. The cell bodies of all axons that bring sensory information into the brain and spinal cord are located outside the CNS. (The sole exception is the visual system; the retina of the eye is actually a part of the brain.) These incoming axons are referred to as **afferent axons** because they "bear toward" the CNS. The cell bodies that give rise to the axons that bring somatosensory information to the spinal cord reside in the **dorsal root ganglia,** rounded swellings of the dorsal root. (See *Figure 3.24.*) These neurons are of the unipolar type (described in Chapter 2). The axonal stalk divides close to the cell body, sending one limb into the spinal cord and the other limb out to the sensory organ. Note that all of the axons in the dorsal root convey somatosensory information.

Cell bodies that give rise to the ventral root are located within the gray matter of the spinal cord. The axons of these multipolar neurons leave the spinal cord via a ventral root, which joins a dorsal root to make a spinal nerve. The axons that leave the spinal cord through the ventral

spinal nerve A peripheral nerve attached to the spinal cord.

afferent axon An axon directed toward the central nervous system, conveying sensory information.

dorsal root ganglion A nodule on a dorsal root that contains cell bodies of afferent spinal nerve neurons.

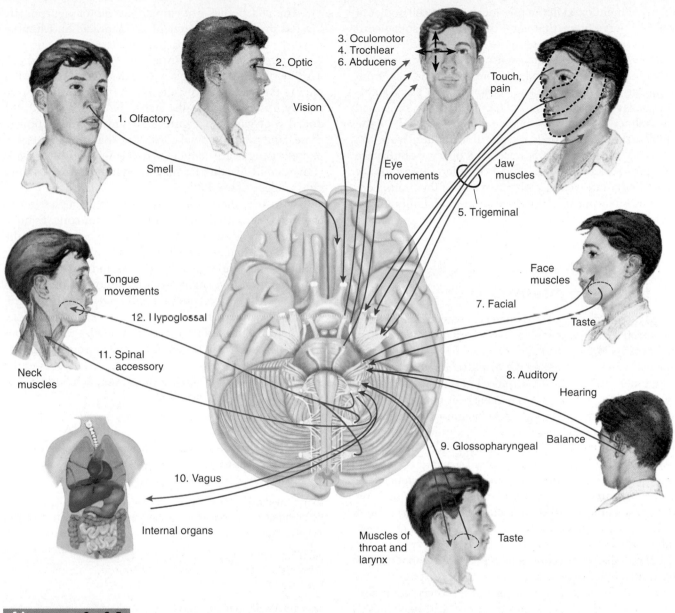

1. Olfactory — Smell
2. Optic — Vision
3. Oculomotor
4. Trochlear
6. Abducens — Eye movements
5. Trigeminal — Touch, pain; Jaw muscles
7. Facial — Face muscles; Taste
8. Auditory — Hearing; Balance
9. Glossopharyngeal — Muscles of throat and larynx; Taste
10. Vagus — Internal organs
11. Spinal accessory — Neck muscles
12. Hypoglossal — Tongue movements

figure 3.25

The twelve pairs of cranial nerves and the regions and functions they serve. Red lines denote axons that control muscles or glands; blue lines denote sensory axons.

roots control muscles and glands. They are referred to as **efferent axons** because they "bear away from" the CNS. (See *Figure 3.24.*)

Cranial Nerves

Twelve pairs of **cranial nerves** are attached to the ventral surface of the brain. Most of these nerves serve sensory and motor functions of the head and neck region. One of them, the *tenth,* or **vagus nerve,** regulates the functions of organs in the thoracic and abdominal cavities. It is called the *vagus* ("wandering") nerve because its branches wander throughout the thoracic and abdominal cavities. (The word *vagabond* has the same

root.) Figure 3.25 presents a view of the base of the brain and illustrates the cranial nerves and the structures they serve. Note that efferent (motor) fibers are drawn in red and that afferent (sensory) fibers are drawn in blue. (See *Figure 3.25.*)

efferent axon (*eff* ur ent) An axon directed away from the central nervous system, conveying motor commands to muscles and glands.

cranial nerve A peripheral nerve attached directly to the brain.

vagus nerve The largest of the cranial nerves, conveying efferent fibers of the parasympathetic division of the autonomic nervous system to organs of the thoracic and abdominal cavities.

As I mentioned in the previous section, cell bodies of sensory nerve fibers that enter the brain and spinal cord (except for the visual system) are located outside the central nervous system. Somatosensory information (and the sense of taste) is received, via the cranial nerves, from unipolar neurons. Auditory, vestibular, and visual information is received via fibers of bipolar neurons (described in Chapter 2). Olfactory information is received via the **olfactory bulbs,** which receive information from the olfactory receptors in the nose. The olfactory bulbs are complex structures containing a considerable amount of neural circuitry; actually, they are part of the brain. Sensory mechanisms are described in more detail in Chapters 6 and 7.

The Autonomic Nervous System

The part of the peripheral nervous system that I have discussed so far—which receives sensory information from the sensory organs and that controls movements of the skeletal muscles—is called the **somatic nervous system.** The other branch of the peripheral nervous system—the **autonomic nervous system** (ANS)—is concerned with regulation of smooth muscle, cardiac muscle, and glands. (*Autonomic* means "self-governing.") Smooth muscle is found in the skin (associated with hair follicles), in blood vessels, in the eyes (controlling pupil size and accommodation of the lens), and in the walls and sphincters of the gut, gallbladder, and urinary bladder. Merely describing the organs innervated by the autonomic nervous system suggests the function of this system: regulation of "vegetative processes" in the body.

The ANS consists of two anatomically separate systems: the *sympathetic division* and the *parasympathetic division.* With few exceptions organs of the body are innervated by both of these subdivisions, and each has a different effect. For example, the sympathetic division speeds the heart rate, whereas the parasympathetic division slows it.

Sympathetic Division of the ANS

The **sympathetic division** is most involved in activities associated with expenditure of energy from reserves that are stored in the body. For example, when an organism is excited, the sympathetic nervous system increases blood flow to skeletal muscles, stimulates the secretion of epinephrine (resulting in increased heart rate and a rise in blood sugar level), and causes piloerection (erection of fur in mammals that have it and production of "goose bumps" in humans).

The cell bodies of sympathetic motor neurons are located in the gray matter of the thoracic and lumbar regions of the spinal cord (hence the sympathetic nervous system is also known as the *thoracolumbar system*). The fibers of these neurons exit via the ventral roots. After joining the spinal nerves, the fibers branch off and pass into **sympathetic ganglia** (not to be confused with the dorsal root ganglia). Figure 3.26 shows the relation of these ganglia to the spinal cord. Note that individual sympathetic ganglia are connected to the neighboring ganglia above and below, thus forming the **sympathetic ganglion chain.** (See *Figure 3.26.*)

The axons that leave the spinal cord through the ventral root belong to the **preganglionic neurons.** Sympathetic preganglionic axons enter the ganglia of the sympathetic chain. Most of the axons form synapses there, but others pass through these ganglia and travel to one of the sympathetic ganglia located among the internal organs. With one exception (mentioned in the next paragraph), all sympathetic preganglionic axons form synapses with neurons located in one of the ganglia. The neurons with which they form synapses are called **postganglionic neurons.** The postganglionic neurons send axons to the target organs, such as the intestines, stomach, kidneys, or sweat glands. (See *Figure 3.26.*)

olfactory bulb The protrusion at the end of the olfactory nerve; receives input from the olfactory receptors.

somatic nervous system The part of the peripheral nervous system that controls the movement of skeletal muscles or transmits somatosensory information to the central nervous system.

autonomic nervous system (ANS) The portion of the peripheral nervous system that controls the body's vegetative functions.

sympathetic division The portion of the autonomic nervous system that controls functions that accompany arousal and expenditure of energy.

sympathetic ganglia Nodules that contain synapses between preganglionic and postganglionic neurons of the sympathetic nervous system.

sympathetic ganglion chain One of a pair of groups of sympathetic ganglia that lie ventrolateral to the vertebral column.

preganglionic neuron The efferent neuron of the autonomic nervous system whose cell body is located in a cranial nerve nucleus or in the intermediate horn of the spinal gray matter and whose terminal buttons synapse upon postganglionic neurons in the autonomic ganglia.

postganglionic neuron Neurons of the autonomic nervous system that form synapses directly with their target organ.

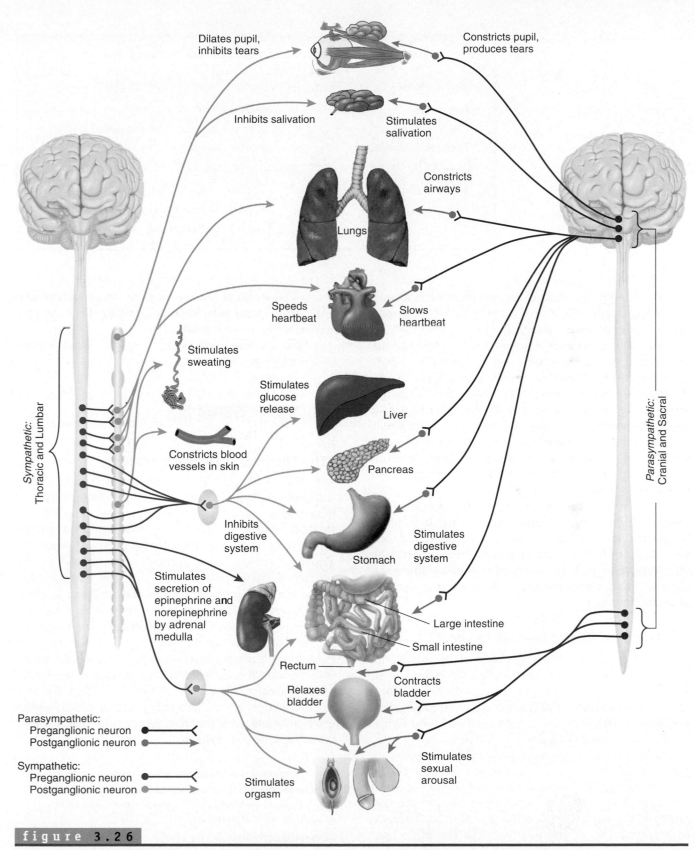

Dilates pupil, inhibits tears

Constricts pupil, produces tears

Inhibits salivation

Stimulates salivation

Constricts airways

Lungs

Speeds heartbeat

Slows heartbeat

Stimulates sweating

Stimulates glucose release

Liver

Constricts blood vessels in skin

Pancreas

Inhibits digestive system

Stimulates digestive system

Stomach

Sympathetic:
Thoracic and Lumbar

Parasympathetic:
Cranial and Sacral

Stimulates secretion of epinephrine and norepinephrine by adrenal medulla

Large intestine

Small intestine

Rectum

Contracts bladder

Relaxes bladder

Parasympathetic:
   Preganglionic neuron
   Postganglionic neuron

Sympathetic:
   Preganglionic neuron
   Postganglionic neuron

Stimulates orgasm

Stimulates sexual arousal

figure 3.26

The autonomic nervous system and the target organs and functions served by the sympathetic and parasympathetic branches.

table **3.3**

The Major Divisions of the Peripheral Nervous System	
SOMATIC NERVOUS SYSTEM	**AUTONOMIC NERVOUS SYSTEM (ANS)**
Spinal nerves	*Sympathetic branch*
Afferents from sense organs	Spinal nerves (from thoracic and lumbar regions)
Efferents to muscles	Sympathetic ganglia
Cranial nerves	*Parasympathetic branch*
Afferents from sense organs	Cranial nerves (3rd, 7th, 9th, and 10th)
Efferents to muscles	Spinal nerves (from sacral region)
	Parasympathetic ganglia (adjacent to target organs)

The sympathetic nervous system controls the **adrenal medulla,** a set of cells located in the center of the adrenal gland. The adrenal medulla closely resembles a sympathetic ganglion. It is innervated by preganglionic axons, and its secretory cells are very similar to postganglionic sympathetic neurons. These cells secrete epinephrine and norepinephrine when they are stimulated. These hormones function chiefly as an adjunct to the direct neural effects of sympathetic activity; for example, they increase blood flow to the muscles and cause stored nutrients to be broken down into glucose within skeletal muscle cells, thus increasing the energy available to these cells.

The terminal buttons of sympathetic preganglionic axons secrete acetylcholine. The terminal buttons on the target organs, belonging to the postganglionic axons, secrete another neurotransmitter: norepinephrine. (An exception to this rule is provided by the sweat glands, which are innervated by acetylcholine-secreting terminal buttons.)

Parasympathetic Division of the ANS

The **parasympathetic division** of the autonomic nervous system supports activities that are involved with increases in the body's supply of stored energy. These activities include salivation, gastric and intestinal motility, secretion of digestive juices, and increased blood flow to the gastrointestinal system.

Cell bodies that give rise to preganglionic axons in the parasympathetic nervous system are located in two regions: the nuclei of some of the cranial nerves (especially the vagus nerve) and the intermediate horn of the gray matter in the sacral region of the spinal cord. Thus, the parasympathetic division of the ANS has often been referred to as the *craniosacral system.* Parasympathetic ganglia are located in the immediate vicinity of the target organs; the postganglionic fibers are therefore relatively

short. The terminal buttons of both preganglionic and postganglionic neurons in the parasympathetic nervous system secrete acetylcholine.

Table 3.3 summarizes the major divisions of the peripheral nervous system.

interim
s u m m a r y

The Peripheral Nervous System

The spinal nerves and the cranial nerves convey sensory axons into the central nervous system and motor axons out from it. Spinal nerves are formed by the junctions of the dorsal roots, which contain incoming (afferent) axons, and the ventral roots, which contain outgoing (efferent) axons. The autonomic nervous system consists of two divisions: the sympathetic division, which controls activities that occur during excitement or exertion, such as increased heart rate, and the parasympathetic division, which controls activities that occur during relaxation, such as decreased heart rate and increased activity of the digestive system. The pathways of the autonomic nervous system contain preganglionic axons, from the brain or spinal cord to the sympathetic or parasympathetic ganglia, and postganglionic axons, from the ganglia to the target organ. The adrenal medulla, which secretes epinephrine and norepinephrine, is controlled by axons of the sympathetic nervous system.

adrenal medulla The inner portion of the adrenal gland, located atop the kidney, controlled by sympathetic nerve fibers; secretes epinephrine and norepinephrine.

parasympathetic division The portion of the autonomic nervous system that controls functions that occur during a relaxed state.

Suggested Readings

Diamond, M. C., Scheibel, A. B., and Elson, L. M. *The Human Brain Coloring Book.* New York: Barnes & Noble, 1985.

Gluhbegovic, N., and Williams, T. H. *The Human Brain: A Photographic Guide.* New York: Harper & Row, 1980.

Heimer, L. *The Human Brain and Spinal Cord: Functional Neuroanatomy and Dissection Guide,* 2nd ed. New York: Springer-Verlag, 1995.

Nauta, W. J. H., and Feirtag, M. *Fundamental Neuroanatomy.* New York: W. H. Freeman, 1986.

Netter, F. H. *The CIBA Collection of Medical Illustrations. Vol. 1: Nervous System. Part 1: Anatomy and Physiology.* Summit, NJ: CIBA Pharmaceutical Products Co., 1991.

Suggested Web Sites

Neuroscience Images

http://synergy.mcg.edu/pt/PT413/images/image.html

Color images of the external surface of the human brain are provided by this site.

The Global Spinal Cord

http://www.anatomy.wisc.edu/sc97/text/SC/contents.htm

The ascending and descending fibers of the spinal cord are the focus of this Web site.

Harvard Brain Atlas

http://www.med.harvard.edu/AANLIB/home.html

This link provides access to the Whole Brain Atlas page that provides images of normal as well as damaged human brains.

Insights from a Broken Brain

http://science-education.nih.gov/nihHTML/ose/snapshots/multimedia/ritn/Gage/Broken_brain1.html

Phineas Gage is the subject of this Web site. The site briefly describes the accident that resulted in damage to his frontal lobes and the personality changes that followed the accident. The site contains several graphics and a description of two recent imaging techniques (PET and MRI).

Medical Neuroscience

http://www.indiana.edu/~m555/

This Web site provides a large number of sections of human brain. Each section can be viewed in either a labeled or unlabeled mode. A unique feature of the site relates to a series of clinical cases relating brain damage to function.

chapter 4

Psychopharmacology

Howard Mehring, *Banner,* 1957. © Smithsonian
American Art Museum, Washington, DC/Art
Resource, NY.

outline

- **Principles of
  Psychopharmacology**
  Pharmacokinetics
  Drug Effectiveness
  Effects of Repeated Administration
  Placebo Effects
  Interim Summary

- **Sites of Drug Action**
  Effects on Production
     of Neurotransmitters
  Effects on Storage and Release
     of Neurotransmitters
  Effects on Receptors
  Effects on Reuptake or Destruction
     of Neurotransmitters
  Interim Summary

- **Neurotransmitters and
  Neuromodulators**
  Acetylcholine
  The Monoamines
  Amino Acids
  Peptides
  Lipids
  Nucleosides
  Soluble Gases
  Interim Summary

In July 1982, some people in northern California began showing up at neurology clinics displaying dramatic, severe symptoms (Langston, Ballard, Tetrud, and Irwin, 1983). The most severely affected patients were almost totally paralyzed. They were unable to speak intelligibly, they drooled constantly, and their eyes were open with a fixed stare. Others, less severely affected, walked with a slow, shuffling gait and moved slowly and with great difficulty. The symptoms looked like those of Parkinson's disease, but that disorder has a very gradual onset. In addition, it rarely strikes people before late middle age, and the patients were all in their twenties or early thirties.

The common factor linking these patients was intravenous drug use; all of them had been taking a "new heroin," a synthetic opiate related to meperidine (*Demerol*). Because the symptoms looked like those of Parkinson's disease, the patients were given L-DOPA, the drug used to treat this disease, and they all showed significant improvement in their symptoms. But even with this treatment the symptoms were debilitating. In normal cases of Parkinson's disease L-DOPA therapy works for a time, but as the degeneration of dopamine-secreting neurons continues, the drug loses its effectiveness. This pattern of response also appears to have occurred in the young patients (Langston and Ballard, 1984).

Some detective work revealed that the chemical that caused the neurological symptoms was not the synthetic opiate itself but another chemical with which it was contaminated. According to researcher William Langston, the mini-epidemic appears to have started "when a young man in Silicon Valley was sloppy in his synthesis of synthetic heroin. That sloppiness led to the presence of MPTP, which by an extraordinary trick of fate is highly toxic to the very same neurons that are lost in Parkinson's disease" (Lewin, 1989, p. 467). Because of the research that followed up on that "trick of fate," patients with Parkinson's disease are now receiving a drug that appears to slow the rate of degeneration of their dopamine-secreting neurons. There is hope that new drugs may even halt the degeneration, giving patients many more years of useful, productive lives and preventing others from ever developing the disease.

C hapter 2 introduced you to the cells of the nervous system, and Chapter 3 described its basic structure. Now it is time to build on this information by introducing the field of psychopharmacology. **Psychopharmacology** is the study of the effects of drugs on the nervous system and (of course) on behavior. (*Pharmakon* is the Greek word for "drug.")

But what *is* a drug? Like many words, this one has several different meanings. In one context it refers to a medication that we would obtain from a pharmacist—a chemical that has a therapeutic effect on a disease or its symptoms. In another context the word refers to a chemical that people are likely to abuse, such as heroin or cocaine. The meaning that will be used in this book (and the one generally accepted by pharmacologists) is "an exogenous chemical not necessary for normal cellular functioning that significantly alters the functions of certain cells of the body when taken in relatively low doses." Because the topic of this chapter is *psycho*pharmacology, we will concern ourselves here only with chemicals that alter the functions of cells within the nervous system. The word *exogenous* rules out chemical messengers produced by the body, such as neurotransmitters, neuromodulators, or hormones. (*Exogenous* means "produced from without"—that is, from outside the body.) Chemical messengers produced by the body are not drugs, although synthetic chemicals that mimic their effects are classified as drugs. The definition of a drug also rules out essential nutrients, such as proteins, fats, carbohydrates, minerals, and vitamins that are a necessary constituent of a healthy diet. Finally, it states that drugs are effective in low doses. This qualification is important, because large quantities of almost any substance—even common ones such as table salt—will alter the functions of cells.

As we will see in this chapter, drugs have *effects* and *sites of action*. **Drug effects** are the changes we can observe in an animal's physiological processes and behavior. For example, the effects of morphine, heroin, and other opiates include decreased sensitivity to pain, slowing of the digestive system, sedation, muscular relaxation, constriction of the pupils, and euphoria. The **sites of action** of drugs are the points at which molecules of drugs interact with molecules located on or in cells of the body, thus affecting some biochemical processes of these cells. For example, the sites of action of the opiates are specialized receptors situated in the membrane of certain neurons. When molecules of opiates attach to and activate these receptors, the drugs alter the activity of these neurons and produce their effects. This chapter considers both the effects of drugs and their sites of action.

Psychopharmacology is an important field of neuroscience. It has been responsible for the development of psychotherapeutic drugs, which are used to treat psychological and behavioral disorders. It has also provided tools that have enabled other investigators to study the functions of cells of the nervous system and the behaviors controlled by particular neural circuits.

---

psychopharmacology The study of the effects of drugs on the nervous system and on behavior.

drug effect The changes a drug produces in an animal's physiological processes and behavior.

sites of action The locations at which molecules of drugs interact with molecules located on or in cells of the body, thus affecting some biochemical processes of these cells.

This chapter does not contain all this book has to say about the subject of psychopharmacology. Throughout the book you will learn about the use of drugs to investigate the nature of neural circuits involved in the control of perception, memory, and behavior. In addition, Chapters 16 and 17 discuss the use of drugs to study and treat mental disorders such as schizophrenia, depression, and the anxiety disorders, and Chapter 18 discusses the nature of reinforcement and the physiology of drug abuse.

Principles of Psychopharmacology

This chapter begins with a description of the basic principles of psychopharmacology: the routes of administration of drugs and their fate in the body. The second section discusses the sites of drug actions. The final section discusses specific neurotransmitters and neuromodulators and the physiological and behavioral effects of specific drugs that interact with them.

Pharmacokinetics

To be effective, a drug must reach its sites of action. To do so, molecules of the drug must enter the body and then enter the bloodstream so that they can be carried to the organ (or organs) they act on. Once there, they must leave the bloodstream and come into contact with the molecules with which they interact. For almost all of the drugs we are interested in, this means that the molecules of the drug must enter the central nervous system. Some behaviorally active drugs exert their effects on the peripheral nervous system, but these drugs are less important to us than those that affect cells of the CNS.

Molecules of drugs must cross several barriers to enter the body and find their way to their sites of action. Some molecules pass through these barriers easily and quickly; others do so very slowly. And once molecules of drugs enter the body, they begin to be metabolized—broken down by enzymes—or excreted in the urine (or both). In time, the molecules either disappear or are transformed into inactive fragments. The process by which drugs are absorbed, distributed within the body, metabolized, and excreted is referred to as **pharmacokinetics** ("movements of drugs").

Routes of Administration

First, let's consider the routes by which drugs can be administered. For laboratory animals the most common route is injection. The drug is dissolved in a liquid (or, in some cases, suspended in a liquid in the form of fine particles) and injected through a hypodermic needle. The

fastest route is **intravenous (IV) injection**—injection into a vein. The drug immediately enters the bloodstream, and it reaches the brain within a few seconds. The disadvantages of IV injections are the increased care and skill they require in comparison to most other forms of injection and the fact that the entire dose reaches the bloodstream at once. If an animal is especially sensitive to the drug, there may be little time to administer another drug to counteract its effects.

An **intraperitoneal (IP) injection** is rapid, but not as rapid as an IV injection. The drug is injected through the abdominal wall into the *peritoneal cavity*—the space that surrounds the stomach, intestines, liver, and other abdominal organs. IP injections are the most common route for administering drugs to small laboratory animals. An **intramuscular (IM) injection** is made directly into a large muscle, such as those found in the upper arm, thigh, or buttocks. The drug is absorbed into the bloodstream through the capillaries that supply the muscle. If very slow absorption is desirable, the drug can be mixed with another drug (such as ephedrine) that constricts blood vessels and retards the flow of blood through the muscle. A drug can also be injected into the space beneath the skin, by means of a **subcutaneous (SC) injection.** A subcutaneous injection is useful only if small amounts of drug need to be administered, because large amounts would be painful. Some fat-soluble drugs can be dissolved in vegetable oil and administered subcutaneously. In this case, molecules of the drug will slowly leave the deposit of oil over a period of several days. If *very* slow and prolonged absorption of a drug is desirable, the drug can be formed into a dry pellet or placed in a sealed silicone rubber capsule and implanted beneath the skin.

Oral administration is the most common form of administering medicinal drugs to humans. Because of the difficulty of getting laboratory animals to eat something that does not taste good to them, researchers seldom use this route. Some chemicals cannot be administered orally because they will be destroyed by stomach acid or digestive enzymes or because they are not absorbed from

pharmacokinetics The process by which drugs are absorbed, distributed within the body, metabolized, and excreted.

intravenous (IV) injection Injection of a substance directly into a vein.

intraperitoneal (IP) injection (*in tra pair i toe* **nee** *ul*) Injection of a substance into the *peritoneal cavity*—the space that surrounds the stomach, intestines, liver, and other abdominal organs.

intramuscular (IM) injection Injection of a substance into a muscle.

subcutaneous (SC) injection Injection of a substance into the space beneath the skin.

oral administration Administration of a substance into the mouth, so that it is swallowed.

the digestive system into the bloodstream. For example, insulin, a peptide hormone, must be injected. **Sublingual administration** of certain drugs can be accomplished by placing them beneath the tongue. The drug is absorbed into the bloodstream by the capillaries that supply the mucous membrane that lines the mouth. (Obviously, this method works only with humans, who will cooperate and leave the capsule beneath their tongue.) Nitroglycerine, a drug that causes blood vessels to dilate, is taken sublingually by people who suffer the pains of angina pectoris, caused by obstructions in the coronary arteries.

Drugs can also be administered at the opposite end of the digestive tract, in the form of suppositories. **Intrarectal administration** is rarely used to give drugs to experimental animals. For obvious reasons this process would be difficult with a small animal. In addition, when agitated, small animals such as rats tend to defecate, which would mean that the drug would not remain in place long enough to be absorbed. And I'm not sure I would want to try to administer a rectal suppository to a large animal. Rectal suppositories are most commonly used to administer drugs that might upset a person's stomach.

The lungs provide another route for drug administration: **inhalation.** Nicotine, freebase cocaine, and marijuana are usually smoked. In addition, drugs used to treat lung disorders are often inhaled in the form of a vapor or fine mist. The route from the lungs to the brain is very short, and drugs administered this way have very rapid effects.

Some drugs can be absorbed directly through the skin, so they can be given by means of **topical administration.** Natural or artificial steroid hormones can be administered this way, as can nicotine (as a treatment to make it easier for a person to stop smoking). The mucous membrane lining the nasal passages also provides a route for topical administration. Commonly abused drugs such as cocaine hydrochloride are often sniffed so that they come into contact with the nasal mucosa. This route delivers the drug to the brain very rapidly. (The technical, rarely used name for this route is *insufflation.* And note that sniffing is not the same as inhalation; when powdered cocaine is sniffed, it ends up in the mucous membrane of the nasal passages, not in the lungs.)

Finally, drugs can be administered directly into the brain. As we saw in Chapter 2, the blood–brain barrier prevents certain chemicals from leaving capillaries and entering the brain. Some drugs cannot cross the blood–brain barrier. If these drugs are to reach the brain, they must be injected directly into the brain or into the cerebrospinal fluid in the brain's ventricular system. To study the effects of a drug in a specific region of the brain (for example, in a particular nucleus of the hypothalamus), a researcher will inject a very small amount of the drug directly into the brain. This procedure, known as **intracerebral administration,** is described in more detail in Chapter 5. To achieve a widespread distribution of

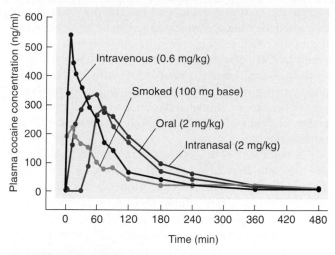

figure 4.1

The concentration of cocaine in blood plasma after intravenous injection, inhalation, sniffing, and oral administration.

(Adapted from Feldman, Meyer, and Quenzer, 1997; after Jones, 1990.)

a drug in the brain, a researcher will get past the blood–brain barrier by injecting the drug into a cerebral ventricle. The drug is then absorbed into the brain tissue, where it can exert its effects. This route, **intracerebroventricular (ICV) administration,** is used very rarely in humans—primarily to deliver antibiotics directly to the brain to treat certain types of infections.

Figure 4.1 shows the time course of blood levels of a commonly abused drug, cocaine, after intravenous injection, inhalation, sniffing, and oral administration. The amounts received were not identical, but the graph illustrates the relative rapidity with which the drug reaches the blood. (See *Figure 4.1.*)

Distribution of Drugs Within the Body

As we saw, drugs exert their effects only when they reach their sites of action. In the case of drugs that affect behavior, most of these sites are located on or in particular

---

sublingual administration (*sub ling wul*) Administration of a substance by placing it beneath the tongue.

intrarectal administration Administration of a substance into the rectum.

inhalation Administration of a vaporous substance into the lungs.

topical administration Administration of a substance directly onto the skin or mucous membrane.

intracerebral administration Administration of a substance directly into the brain.

intracerebroventricular (ICV) administration Administration of a substance into one of the cerebral ventricles.

cells in the central nervous system. The previous section described the routes by which drugs can be introduced into the body. With the exception of intracerebral or intracerebroventricular administration the differences in the routes of drug administration vary only in the rate at which a drug reaches the blood plasma (that is, the liquid part of the blood). But what happens next? All the sites of action of drugs of interest to psychopharmacologists lie outside the blood vessels.

Several factors determine the rate at which a drug in the bloodstream reaches sites of action within the brain. The first is lipid solubility. The blood–brain barrier is a barrier only for water-soluble molecules. Molecules that are soluble in lipids pass through the cells that line the capillaries in the central nervous system, and they rapidly distribute themselves throughout the brain. For example, diacetylmorphine (more commonly known as heroin) is more lipid soluble than morphine is. Thus, an intravenous injection of heroin produces more rapid effects than does one of morphine. Even though the molecules of the two drugs are equally effective when they reach their sites of action in the brain, the fact that heroin molecules get there faster means that they produce a more intense "rush" and thus explains why drug addicts prefer heroin to morphine.

Many drugs bind with various tissues of the body or with proteins in the blood—a phenomenon known as **depot binding.** As long as the molecules of the drug are bound to a depot, they cannot reach their sites of action and cannot exert their effects. One source of such binding is **albumin,** a protein found in the blood. Albumin serves to transport free fatty acids, a source of nutrients for most cells of the body, but this protein can also bind with some lipid-soluble drugs. Depot binding can both delay and prolong the effects of a drug. Consider a lipid-soluble drug taken orally. As molecules of the drug are absorbed from the stomach, they begin to bind with albumin in the blood. For a while, very little of the drug reaches the brain. Finally, the albumin molecules can hold no more of the drug, so it begins to enter the brain. Eventually, all the drug is absorbed from the stomach. Then, perhaps over a period of several hours, the albumin molecules gradually release the molecules of the drug as the plasma concentration of the drug falls. (See *Figure 4.2.*)

Other sources of depot binding include fat tissue, bones, muscles, and the liver. Of course, drugs bind with these depots more slowly than they do with albumin, because they must leave the blood vessels to do so. Thus, these sources of binding are less likely to interfere with the initial effects of a drug. For example, thiopental, a barbiturate that is sometimes used to anesthetize the brain, has high lipid solubility. An intravenous injection of this drug reaches the brain within a few seconds after being injected intravenously. The drug also binds very well with muscles and fat tissue, so it soon is taken out of circulation, and the levels of the drug in the brain fall rapidly. Within 30 minutes or so, the drug's anesthetic effect is gone. Eventually, the drug is destroyed by enzymes and excreted by the kidneys.

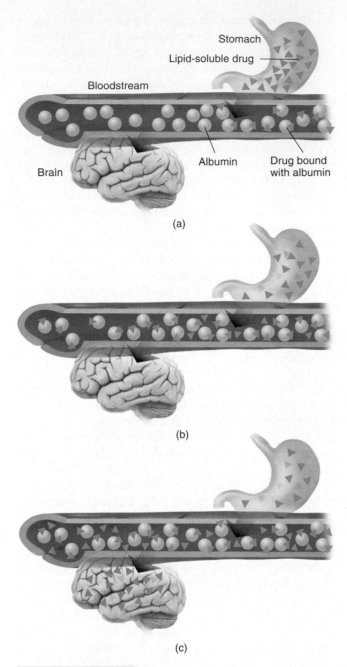

Stomach

Lipid-soluble drug

Bloodstream

Brain

Albumin

Drug bound with albumin

(a)

(b)

(c)

figure 4 . 2

Depot binding with blood albumin protein. (a) The drug begins to be absorbed from the stomach into the bloodstream, where it binds with albumin. (b) The albumin molecules are saturated with the drug and can hold no more. (c) Unbound molecules of the drug begin to enter the brain. Eventually, molecules of the drug will break away from the molecules of albumin and enter the brain.

depot binding Binding of a drug with various tissues of the body or with proteins in the blood.

albumin (*al bew min*) A protein found in the blood; serves to transport free fatty acids and can bind with some lipid-soluble drugs.

Inactivation and Excretion

Drugs do not remain in the body indefinitely. Many are deactivated by enzymes, and all are eventually excreted, primarily by the kidneys. The liver plays an especially active role in enzymatic deactivation of drugs, but some deactivating enzymes are also found in the blood. The brain also contains enzymes that destroy some drugs. In some cases enzymes transform molecules of a drug into other forms that themselves are biologically active. Occasionally, the transformed molecules is *even more* active than the one that is administered. In such cases the effects of a drug can have a very long duration.

Drug Effectiveness

Drugs vary widely in their effectiveness. A small dose of a relatively effective drug can equal or exceed the effects of larger amounts of a relatively ineffective drug. The best way to measure the effectiveness of a drug is to plot a **dose-response curve.** To do this, subjects are given various doses of a drug, usually defined as milligrams of drug per kilogram of a subject's body weight, and the effects of the drug are plotted. Because the molecules of most drugs distribute themselves throughout the blood and then throughout the rest of the body, a heavier subject (human or laboratory animal) will require a larger quantity of a drug to achieve the same concentration as a smaller subject. As Figure 4.3 shows, increasingly stronger doses of a drug cause increasingly larger effects, until the point of maximum effect is reached. At this point, increasing the dose of the drug does not produce any more effect. (See *Figure 4.3.*)

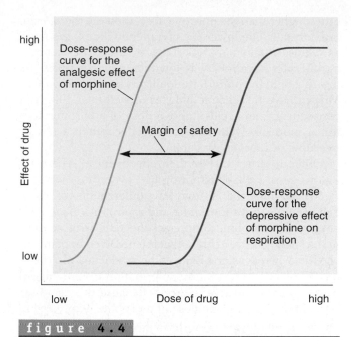

figure   4.4

Dose-response curves for the analgesic effect of morphine and for the drug's adverse side effects, its depressant effect on respiration. A drug's margin of safety is reflected by the difference between the dose-response curve for its therapeutic effects and its adverse side effects.

Most drugs have more than one effect. Opiates such as morphine and codeine produce analgesia (reduced sensitivity to pain), but they also depress the activity of neurons in the medulla that control heart rate and respiration. A physician who prescribes an opiate to relieve a patient's pain wants to administer a dose that is large enough to produce analgesia but not enough to depress heart rate and respiration—effects that could be fatal. Figure 4.4 shows two dose-response curves, one for the analgesic effects of a painkiller and one for the drug's depressant effects on respiration. The difference between these curves indicates the drug's margin of safety. Obviously, the most desirable drugs have a large margin of safety. (See *Figure 4.4.*)

One measure of a drug's margin of safety is its **therapeutic index.** This measure is obtained by administering varying doses of the drug to a group of laboratory animals such as mice. Two numbers are obtained: the dose that produces the desired effects in 50 percent of the animals and the dose that produces toxic effects in 50 percent of the animals. The therapeutic index is the ratio of these two numbers. For example, if the toxic dose is five

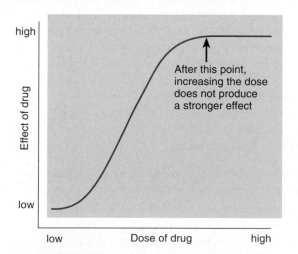

figure   4.3

A dose-response curve. Increasingly stronger doses of the drug produce increasingly larger effects until the maximum effect is reached. After that point, increments in the dose do not produce any increments in the drug's effect. However, the risk of adverse side effects increases.

dose-response curve A graph of the magnitude of an effect of a drug as a function of the amount of drug administered.

therapeutic index The ratio between the dose that produces the desired effect in 50 percent of the animals and the dose that produces toxic effects in 50 percent of the animals.

times higher than the effective dose, then the therapeutic index is 5.0. The lower the therapeutic index, the more care must be taken in prescribing the drug. For example, barbiturates have relatively low therapeutic indexes—as low as 2 or 3. In contrast, tranquilizers such as Librium or Valium have therapeutic indexes of well over 100. As a consequence, an accidental overdose of a barbiturate is much more likely to have tragic effects than a similar overdose of Librium or Valium.

Why do drugs vary in their effectiveness? There are two reasons. First, different drugs—even those with the same behavioral effects—may have different sites of action. For example, both morphine and aspirin have analgesic effects, but morphine suppresses the activity of neurons in the spinal cord and brain that are involved in pain perception, whereas aspirin reduces the production of a chemical involved in transmitting information from damaged tissue to pain-sensitive neurons. Because the drugs act very differently, a given dose of morphine (expressed in terms of milligrams of drug per kilogram of body weight) produces much more pain reduction than the same dose of aspirin.

The second reason that drugs vary in their effectiveness has to do with the affinity of the drug with its site of action. As we will see in the next major section of this chapter, most drugs of interest to psychopharmacologists exert their effects by binding with other molecules located in the central nervous system—with presynaptic or postsynaptic receptors, with transporter molecules, or with enzymes involved in the production or deactivation of neurotransmitters. Drugs vary widely in their **affinity** for the molecules to which they attach—the readiness with which the two molecules join together. A drug with a high affinity will produce effects at a relatively low concentration, whereas one with a low affinity must be administered in relatively high doses. Thus, even two drugs with identical sites of action can vary widely in their effectiveness if they have different affinities for their binding sites. In addition, because most drugs have multiple effects, a drug can have high affinities for some of its sites of action and low affinities for others. The most desirable drug has a high affinity for sites of action that produce therapeutic effects and a low affinity for sites of action that produce toxic side effects. One of the goals of research by drug companies is to find chemicals with just this pattern of effects.

Effects of Repeated Administration

Often, when a drug is administered repeatedly, its effects will not remain constant. In most cases its effects will diminish—a phenomenon known as **tolerance.** In other cases a drug becomes more and more effective—a phenomenon known as **sensitization.**

Let's consider tolerance first. Tolerance is seen in many drugs that are commonly abused. For example, a regular user of heroin must take larger and larger amounts of the drug for it to be effective. And once a person has taken an opiate regularly enough to develop tolerance, that individual will suffer **withdrawal symptoms** if he or she suddenly stops taking the drug. Withdrawal symptoms are primarily the opposite of the effects of the drug itself. For example, heroin produces euphoria; withdrawal from it produces *dysphoria*—a feeling of anxious misery. (*Euphoria* and *dysphoria* mean "easy to bear" and "hard to bear," respectively.) Heroin produces constipation; withdrawal from it produces nausea and cramping. Heroin produces relaxation; withdrawal from it produces agitation.

Withdrawal symptoms are caused by the same mechanisms that are responsible for tolerance. Tolerance is the result of the body's attempt to compensate for the effects of the drug. That is, most systems of the body, including those controlled by the brain, are regulated so that they stay at an optimal value. When the effects of a drug alter these systems for a prolonged time, compensatory mechanisms begin to produce the opposite reaction, at least partially compensating for the disturbance from the optimal value. These mechanisms account for the fact that more and more of the drug must be taken to achieve a given level of effects. Then, when the person stops taking the drug, the compensatory mechanisms make themselves felt, unopposed by the action of the drug.

Research suggests that there are several types of compensatory mechanisms. As we will see, many drugs that affect the brain do so by binding with receptors and activating them. The first compensatory mechanism involves a decrease in the effectiveness of such binding. Either the receptors become less sensitive to the drug (that is, their affinity for the drug decreases) or the receptors decrease in number. The second compensatory mechanism involves the process that couples the receptors to ion channels in the membrane or to the production of second messengers. After prolonged stimulation of the receptors, one or more steps in the coupling process become less effective. (Of course, *both* effects can occur.) The details of these compensatory mechanisms are described in Chapter 18, which discusses the causes and effects of drug abuse.

---

affinity The readiness with which two molecules join together.

tolerance A decrease in the effectiveness of a drug that is administered repeatedly.

sensitization An increase in the effectiveness of a drug that is administered repeatedly.

withdrawal symptom The appearance of symptoms opposite to those produced by a drug when the drug is administered repeatedly and then suddenly no longer taken.

As we saw, many drugs have several different sites of action and thus produce several different effects. This means that some of the effects of a drug may show tolerance but others may not. For example, barbiturates cause sedation and also depress neurons that control respiration. The sedative effects show tolerance, but the respiratory depression does not. This means that if larger and larger doses of a barbiturate are taken to achieve the same level of sedation, the person begins to run the risk of taking a dangerously large dose of the drug.

Sensitization is, of course, the exact opposite of tolerance: Repeated doses of a drug produce larger and larger effects. Because compensatory mechanisms tend to correct for deviations away from the optimal values of physiological processes, sensitization is less common than tolerance. And some of the effects of a drug may show sensitization while others show tolerance. For example, repeated injections of cocaine become more and more likely to produce movement disorders and convulsions, whereas the euphoric effects of the drug do not show sensitization—and may even show tolerance.

Placebo Effects

A **placebo** is an innocuous substance that has no specific physiological effect. The word comes from the Latin *placere*, "to please." A physician may sometimes give a placebo to anxious patients to placate them. (You can see that *placate* also has the same root.) But although placebos have no *specific* physiological effect, it is incorrect to say that they have *no* effect. If a person thinks that a placebo has a physiological effect, then administration of the placebo may actually produce that effect.

When experimenters want to investigate the behavioral effects of drugs in humans, they must use control groups whose members receive placebos, or they cannot be sure that the behavioral effects they observe were caused by specific effects of the drug. Studies with laboratory animals must also use placebos, even though we need not worry about the animals's "beliefs" about the effects of the drugs we give them. Consider what you must do to give a rat an intraperitoneal injection of a drug. You reach into the animal's cage, pick the animal up, hold it in such a way that its abdomen is exposed and its head is positioned to prevent it from biting you, insert a hypodermic needle through its abdominal wall, press the plunger of the syringe, and replace the animal in its cage, being sure to let go of it quickly so that it cannot turn and bite you. Even if the substance you inject is innocuous, the experience of receiving the injection would activate the animal's autonomic nervous system, cause the secretion of stress hormones, and have other physiological effects. If we want to know what the behavioral effects of a drug are, we must compare the drug-treated animals with other animals who receive a placebo, administered in exactly the same way as the drug. (By the way, a skilled and experienced researcher can handle a rat so gently that it shows very little reaction to a hypodermic injection.)

interim summary

Principles of Psychopharmacology

Psychopharmacology is the study of the effects of drugs on the nervous system and behavior. Drugs are exogenous chemicals that are not necessary for normal cellular functioning that significantly alter the functions of certain cells of the body when taken in relatively low doses. Drugs have *effects,* physiological and behavioral, and they have *sites of action*—molecules with which they interact to produce these effects.

Pharmacokinetics is the fate of a drug as it is absorbed into the body, circulates throughout the body, and reaches its sites of action. Drugs may be administered by intravenous, intraperitoneal, intramuscular, and subcutaneous injection; they may be administered orally, sublingually, intrarectally, by inhalation, and topically (on skin or mucous membrane); and they may be injected intracerebrally or intracerebroventricularly. Lipid-soluble drugs easily pass through the blood–brain barrier, whereas others pass this barrier slowly or not at all.

The time courses of various routes of drug administration are different. And once molecules of a drug reach the blood, they may bind with albumin protein, and they may bind with storage depots in fat tissue, muscles, or bones. Eventually, drugs disappear from the body. Some are deactivated by enzymes, especially in the liver, and others are simply excreted.

The dose-response curve represents a drug's effectiveness; it relates the amount administered (usually in milligrams per kilogram of the subject's body weight) to the resulting effect. Most drugs have more than one site of action and thus more than one effect. The safety of a drug is measured by the difference between doses that produce desirable effects and those that produce toxic side effects. Drugs vary in their effectiveness because of the nature of their sites of actions and the affinity between molecules of the drug and these sites of action.

Repeated administration of a drug can cause either tolerance, often resulting in withdrawal symptoms, or sensitization. Tolerance can be caused by decreased affinity of a drug with its receptors, by decreased numbers of receptors, or by decreased coupling of receptors with the biochemical steps it controls. Some of the effects of a drug may show tolerance, while others may not—or may even show sensitization.

placebo (*pla see boh*) An inert substance that is given to an organism in lieu of a physiologically active drug; used experimentally to control for the effects of mere administration of a drug.

Sites of Drug Action

Throughout the history of our species, people have discovered that plants—and a few animals—produce chemicals that act on synapses. (Of course, the people who discovered these chemicals knew nothing about neurons and synapses.) Some of these chemicals have been used for their pleasurable effects; others have been used to treat illness, reduce pain, or poison other animals (or enemies). More recently, scientists have learned to produce completely artificial drugs, some with potencies far greater than the naturally occurring ones. The traditional uses of drugs remain, but in addition, they can be used in research laboratories to investigate the operations of the nervous system. Most drugs that affect behavior do so by affecting synaptic transmission. Drugs that affect synaptic transmission are classified into two general categories. Those that block or inhibit the postsynaptic effects are called **antagonists.** Those that facilitate them are called **agonists.** (The Greek word *agon* means "contest." Thus, an *agonist* is one who takes part in the contest.)

This section will describe the basic effects of drugs on synaptic activity. Recall from Chapter 2 that the sequence of synaptic activity goes like this: Neurotransmitters are synthesized and stored in synaptic vesicles. The synaptic vesicles travel to the presynaptic membrane, where they become docked. When an axon fires, voltage-dependent calcium channels in the presynaptic membrane open, permitting the entry of calcium ions. The calcium ions interact with the docking proteins and initiate the release of the neurotransmitters into the synaptic cleft. Molecules of the neurotransmitter bind with postsynaptic receptors, causing particular ion channels to open, which produces excitatory or inhibitory postsynaptic potentials. The effects of the neurotransmitter are kept relatively brief by their reuptake by transporter molecules in the presynaptic membrane or by their destruction by enzymes. In addition, the stimulation of presynaptic autoreceptors regulates the synthesis and release of the neurotransmitter. The discussion of the effects of drugs in this section follows the same basic sequence. All of the effects I will describe are summarized in Figure 4.5, with some details shown in additional figures. I should warn you that some of the effects are complex, so the discussion that follows bears careful reading. I recommend that you study **Animation 4.1,** *Actions of Drugs,* which reviews this material.

> See the interactive CD for more on the actions of drugs.

Effects on Production of Neurotransmitters

The first step is the synthesis of the neurotransmitter from its precursors. In some cases the rate of synthesis and release of a neurotransmitter is increased when a precursor is administered; in these cases the precursor itself serves as an agonist. (See step 1 in *Figure 4.5.*)

The steps in the synthesis of neurotransmitters are controlled by enzymes. Therefore, if a drug inactivates one of these enzymes, it will prevent the neurotransmitter from being produced. Such a drug serves as an antagonist. (See step 2 in *Figure 4.5.*)

Effects on Storage and Release of Neurotransmitters

Neurotransmitters are stored in synaptic vesicles, which are transported to the presynaptic membrane, where the chemicals are released. The storage of neurotransmitters in vesicles is accomplished by the same kind of transporter molecules that are responsible for reuptake of a neurotransmitter into a terminal button. The transporter molecules are located in the membrane of synaptic vesicles, and their action is to pump molecules of the neurotransmitter across the membrane, filling the vesicles. Some of the transporter molecules that fill synaptic vesicles are capable of being blocked by a drug. Molecules of the drug bind with a particular site on the transporter and inactivate it. Because the synaptic vesicles remain empty, nothing is released when the vesicles eventually rupture against the presynaptic membrane. The drug serves as an antagonist. (See step 3 in *Figure 4.5.*)

Some drugs act as antagonists by preventing the release of neurotransmitters from the terminal button. They do so by deactivating the proteins that cause docked synaptic vesicles to fuse with the presynaptic membrane and expel their contents into the synaptic cleft. Other drugs have just the opposite effect: They act as agonists by binding with these proteins and directly triggering release of the neurotransmitter. (See steps 4 and 5 in *Figure 4.5.*)

Effects on Receptors

The most important—and most complex—site of action of drugs in the nervous system is on receptors, both presynaptic and postsynaptic. Let's consider postsynaptic receptors first. (Here is where the careful reading should begin.) Once a neurotransmitter is released, it must stimulate the postsynaptic receptors. Some drugs bind with these receptors, just as the neurotransmitter does. Once a drug has

---

antagonist A drug that opposes or inhibits the effects of a particular neurotransmitter on the postsynaptic cell.

agonist A drug that facilitates the effects of a particular neurotransmitter on the postsynaptic cell.

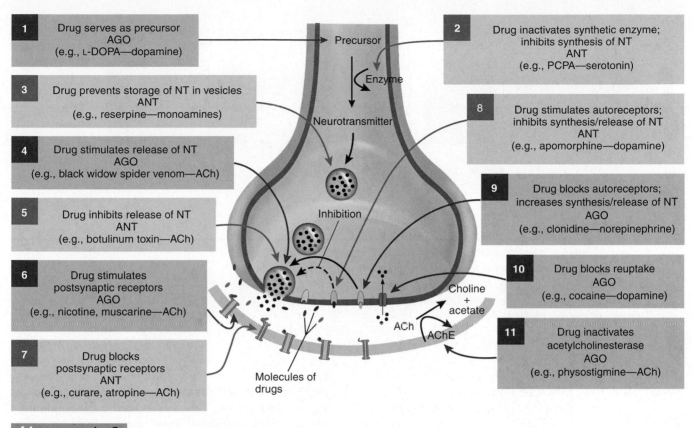

figure 4.5

A summary of the ways in which drugs can affect the synaptic transmission
(AGO = agonist; ANT = antagonist; NT = neurotransmitter). Drugs that act
as agonists are marked in blue; drugs that act as antagonists are marked in red.

bound with the receptor, it can serve as either an agonist
or an antagonist.

A drug that mimics the effects of a neurotransmitter
acts as a **direct agonist.** Molecules of the drug attach to
the binding site to which the neurotransmitter normally
attaches. This binding causes ion channels controlled by
the receptor to open, just as they do when the neurotransmitter is present. Ions then pass through these channels and produce postsynaptic potentials. (See step 6 in
Figure 4.5.)

Drugs that bind with postsynaptic receptors can also
serve as antagonists. Molecules of such drugs bind with
the receptors but do not open the ion channel. Because
they occupy the receptor's binding site, they prevent the
neurotransmitter from opening the ion channel. These
drugs are called **receptor blockers** or **direct antagonists.**
(See step 7 in *Figure 4.5.*)

Some receptors have multiple binding sites, to which
different ligands can attach. Molecules of the neurotransmitter bind with one site, and other substances (such
as neuromodulators and various drugs) bind with the others. Binding of a molecule with one of these alternative
sites is referred to as **noncompetitive binding,** because

the molecule does not compete with molecules of the
neurotransmitter for the same binding site. If a drug attaches
to one of these alternative sites and prevents the ion channel from opening, the drug is said to be an **indirect antagonist.** The ultimate *effect* of an indirect antagonist is similar
to that of a direct antagonist, but its site of action is different. If a drug attaches to one of the alternative sites

direct agonist A drug that binds with and activates a receptor.

receptor blocker A drug that binds with a receptor but does
not activate it; prevents the natural ligand from binding with
the receptor.

direct antagonist A synonym for receptor blocker.

noncompetitive binding Binding of a drug to a site on a receptor; does not interfere with the binding site for the principal
ligand.

indirect antagonist A drug that attaches to a binding site on a
receptor and interferes with the action of the receptor; does not
interfere with the binding site for the principal ligand.

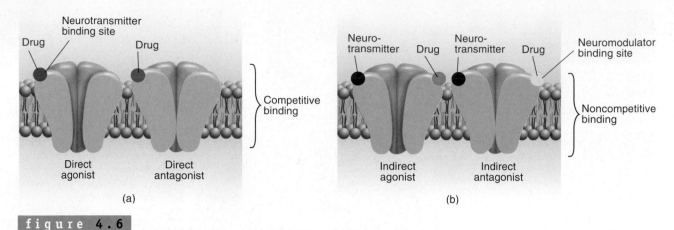

figure 4.6

Actions of drugs at binding sites on receptors. (a) Competitive binding. Direct agonists and antagonists act directly on the neurotransmitter binding site. (b) Noncompetitive binding. Indirect agonists and antagonists act on an alternative binding site and modify the effects of the neurotransmitter on opening of the ion channel.

and *facilitates* the opening of the ion channel, it is said to be an **indirect agonist.** (See *Figure 4.6.*)

As we saw in Chapter 2, the presynaptic membranes of some neurons contain autoreceptors that regulate the amount of neurotransmitter that is released. Because stimulation of these receptors causes less neurotransmitter to be released, drugs that selectively activate presynaptic receptors act as antagonists. Drugs that *block* presynaptic autoreceptors have the opposite effect: They *increase* the release of the neurotransmitter, acting as agonists. (Refer to steps 8 and 9 in *Figure 4.5.*)

We also saw in Chapter 2 that some terminal buttons form axoaxonic synapses—synapses of one terminal button with another. Activation of the first terminal button causes presynaptic inhibition or facilitation of the second one. The second terminal button contains **presynaptic heteroreceptors,** which are sensitive to the neurotransmitter released by the first one. (*Auto* means "self"; *hetero* means "other.") Presynaptic heteroreceptors that produce presynaptic inhibition do so by inhibiting the release of the neurotransmitter. Conversely, presynaptic heteroreceptors responsible for presynaptic facilitation *facilitate* the release of the neurotransmitter. So drugs can block or facilitate presynaptic inhibition or facilitation, depending on whether they block or activate presynaptic heteroreceptors. (See *Figure 4.7.*)

Finally (yes, this is the last site of action I will describe in this subsection), you will recall from Chapter 2 that autoreceptors are located in the membrane of dendrites of some neurons. When these neurons become active, their dendrites, as well as their terminal buttons, release neurotransmitter. The neurotransmitter released by the

dendrites stimulates autoreceptors located on these same dendrites, which decrease neural firing by producing hyperpolarizations. This mechanism has a regulatory effect, serving to prevent these neurons from becoming too active. Thus, drugs that bind with and *activate* dendritic autoreceptors will serve as *antagonists.* Those that bind with and *block* dendritic autoreceptors will serve as *agonists,* because they will prevent the inhibitory hyperpolarizations. (See *Figure 4.8.*)

As you will surely realize, the effects of a particular drug that binds with a particular type of receptor can be very complex. The effects depend on where the receptor is located, what its normal effects are, and whether the drug activates the receptor or blocks its actions.

Effects on Reuptake or Destruction of Neurotransmitters

The next step after stimulation of the postsynaptic receptor is termination of the postsynaptic potential. Two processes accomplish that task: Molecules of the neurotransmitter are taken back into the terminal button through

indirect agonist A drug that attaches to a binding site on a receptor and facilitates the action of the receptor; does not interfere with the binding site for the principal ligand.

presynaptic heteroreceptor A receptor located in the membrane of a terminal button that receives input from another terminal button by means of an axoaxonic synapse; binds with the neurotransmitter released by the presynaptic terminal button.

the process of reuptake, or they are destroyed by an enzyme. Drugs can interfere with either of these processes. In the first case molecules of the drug attach to the transporter molecules responsible for reuptake and inactivate them, thus blocking reuptake. In the second case molecules of the drug bind with the enzyme that normally destroys the neurotransmitter and prevents the enzymes from working. The most important example of such an enzyme is acetylcholinesterase, which destroys acetylcholine. Because both types of drugs prolong the presence of the neurotransmitter in the synaptic cleft (and hence in a location where they can stimulate postsynaptic receptors), they serve as *agonists*. (Refer to steps 10 and 11 in *Figure 4.5*.)

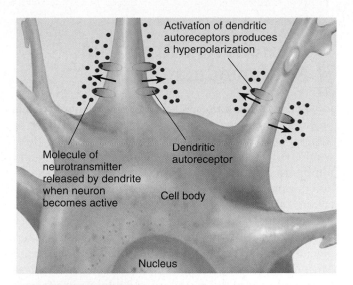

figure **4.8**

Dendritic autoreceptors. The dendrites of certain neurons release some neurotransmitter when the cell is active. Activation of dendritic autoreceptors by the neurotransmitter (or by a drug that binds with these receptors) hyperpolarizes the membrane, reducing the neuron's rate of firing. Blocking of dendritic autoreceptors by a drug prevents this effect.

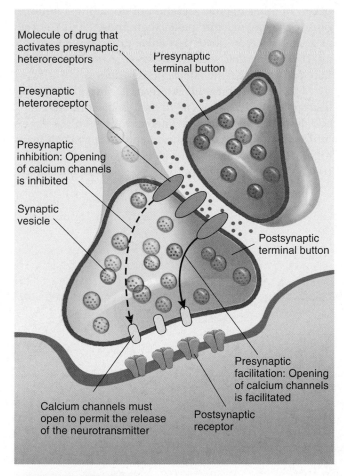

figure **4.7**

Presynaptic heteroreceptors. Presynaptic facilitation is caused by activation of receptors that facilitate the opening of calcium channels near the active zone of the postsynaptic terminal button, which promotes release of the neurotransmitter. Presynaptic inhibition is caused by activation of receptors that inhibit the opening of these calcium channels.

interim summary

Sites of Drug Action

The process of synaptic transmission entails the synthesis of the neurotransmitter, its storage in synaptic vesicles, its release into the synaptic cleft, its interaction with postsynaptic receptors, and the consequent opening of ion channels in the postsynaptic membrane. The effects of the neurotransmitter are then terminated by reuptake into the terminal button or, in the case of acetylcholine, by enzymatic deactivation.

Each of the steps necessary for synaptic transmission can be interfered with by drugs that serve as *antagonists,* and a few can be stimulated by drugs that serve as *agonists.* Thus, drugs can increase the pool of available precursor, block a biosynthetic enzyme, prevent the storage of neurotransmitter in synaptic vesicles, stimulate or block the release of the neurotransmitter, stimulate or block presynaptic or postsynaptic receptors, retard reuptake, or deactivate enzymes that destroy the neurotransmitter. A drug that activates postsynaptic receptors serves as an agonist, whereas one that activates presynaptic or dendritic autoreceptors or serves as an antagonist. A drug that blocks postsynaptic receptors serves as an antagonist, whereas one that blocks autoreceptors serves as an agonist. A drug that activates or blocks presynaptic heteroreceptors serves as an agonist or antagonist, depending on whether the heteroreceptors are responsible for presynaptic facilitation or inhibition.

Neurotransmitters and Neuromodulators

Because neurotransmitters have two general effects on postsynaptic membranes—depolarization (EPSP) or hyperpolarization (IPSP)—one might expect that there would be two kinds of neurotransmitters, excitatory and inhibitory. Instead, there are many different kinds—several dozen, at least. In the brain most synaptic communication is accomplished by two neurotransmitters: one with excitatory effects (glutamate) and one with inhibitory effects (GABA). (Another inhibitory neurotransmitter, glycine, is found in the spinal cord and lower brain stem.) Most of the activity of local circuits of neurons involves balances between the excitatory and inhibitory effects of these chemicals, which are responsible for most of the information transmitted from place to place within the brain. In fact, there are probably no neurons in the brain that do not receive excitatory input from glutamate-secreting terminal buttons and inhibitory input from neurons that secrete either GABA or glycine. And with the exception of neurons that detect painful stimuli, all sensory organs transmit information to the brain through axons whose terminals release glutamate. (Pain-detecting neurons secrete a peptide.)

What do all the other neurotransmitters do? In general, they have modulating effects rather than information-transmitting effects. That is, the release of neurotransmitters other than glutamate and GABA tends to activate or inhibit entire circuits of neurons that are involved in particular brain functions. For example, secretion of acetylcholine activates the cerebral cortex and facilitates learning, but the information that is learned and remembered is transmitted by neurons that secrete glutamate and GABA. Secretion of norepinephrine increases vigilance and enhances readiness to act when a signal is detected. Secretion of serotonin suppresses certain categories of species-typical behaviors and reduces the likelihood that the animal acts impulsively. Secretion of dopamine in some regions of the brain generally activates voluntary movements but does not specify which movements will occur. In other regions secretion of dopamine reinforces ongoing behaviors and makes them more likely to occur at a later time. Because particular drugs can selectively affect neurons that secrete particular neurotransmitters, they can have specific effects on behavior.

This section introduces the most important neurotransmitters, discusses some of their behavioral functions, and describes the drugs that interact with them. As we saw in the previous section of this chapter, drugs have many different sites of action. Fortunately for your information-processing capacity (and perhaps your sanity), not all types

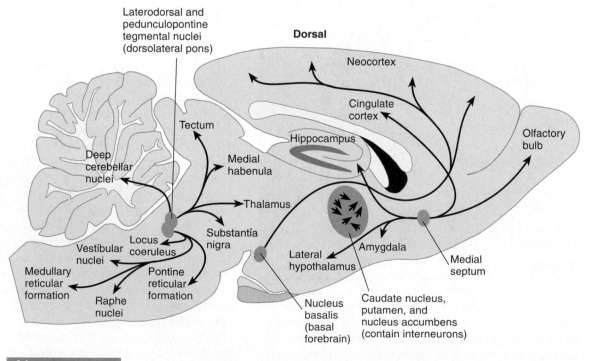

figure 4.9

A schematic midsagittal section of a rat brain, showing the locations of the most important groups of acetylcholinergic neurons and the distribution of their axons and terminal buttons.
(Adapted from Woolf, 1991.)

of neurons are affected by all types of drugs. As you will see, that still leaves a good number of drugs to be mentioned by name. Obviously, some are more important than others. Those whose effects I describe in some detail are more important than those I mention in passing. If you want to learn more details about these drugs (and many others), you should consult an up-to-date psychopharmacology text.

Acetylcholine

Acetylcholine is the primary neurotransmitter secreted by efferent axons of the central nervous system. All muscular movement is accomplished by the release of acetylcholine, and ACh is also found in the ganglia of the autonomic nervous system and at the target organs of the parasympathetic branch of the ANS. Because ACh is found outside the central nervous system in locations that are easy to study, this neurotransmitter was the first to be discovered, and it has received much attention from neuroscientists. Some terminology: These synapses are said to be *acetylcholinergic. Ergon* is the Greek word for "work." Thus, *dopaminergic* synapses release dopamine, *serotonergic* synapses release serotonin, and so on. (The suffix *-ergic* is pronounced *"ur jik".)*

The axons and terminal buttons of acetylcholinergic neurons are distributed widely throughout the brain. Three systems have received the most attention from neuroscientists: those originating in the dorsolateral pons, the basal forebrain, and the medial septum. The effects of ACh release in the brain are generally facilitatory. The acetylcholinergic neurons located in the dorsolateral pons are responsible for eliciting most of the characteristics of REM sleep (the phase of sleep during which dreaming occurs). Those located in the basal forebrain are involved in activating the cerebral cortex and facilitating learning, especially perceptual learning. Those located in the medial septum control the electrical rhythms of the hippocampus and modulate its functions, which include the formation of particular kinds of memories. These functions of acetylcholinergic neurons are described in more detail in Chapters 9 and 14.

Figure 4.9 shows a schematic midsagittal view of a rat brain. On it are indicated the most important sites of acetylcholinergic cell bodies and the regions served by the branches of their axons. The figure illustrates a rat brain because most of the neuroanatomical tracing studies have been performed with rats. Presumably, the location and projections of acetylcholinergic neurons in the human brain resemble those found in the rat brain, but we cannot yet be certain. The methods used for tracing particular systems of neurons in the brain, and the difficulty of doing such studies with the human brain, are described in Chapter 5. (See *Figure 4.9.*)

Acetylcholine is composed of two components: *choline,* a substance derived from the breakdown of lipids, and *acetate,* the anion found in vinegar, also called acetic acid. Acetate cannot be attached directly to choline; instead, it is transferred from a molecule of *acetyl-CoA.* CoA (coenzyme

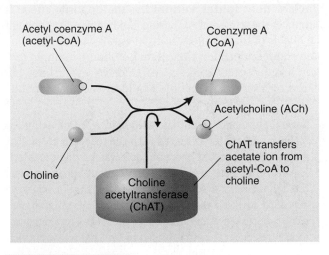

figure 4.10

The biosynthesis of acetylcholine.

A) is a complex molecule, consisting in part of the vitamin pantothenic acid (one of the B vitamins). CoA is produced by the mitochondria, and it takes part in many reactions in the body. **Acetyl-CoA** is simply CoA with an acetate ion attached to it. ACh is produced by the following reaction: In the presence of the enzyme **choline acetyltransferase (ChAT),** the acetate ion is transferred from the acetyl-CoA molecule to the choline molecule, yielding a molecule of ACh and one of ordinary CoA. (See *Figure 4.10.*)

A simple analogy will illustrate the role of coenzymes in chemical reactions. Think of acetate as a hot dog and choline as a bun. The task of the person (enzyme) who operates the hot dog vending stand is to put a hot dog into the bun (make acetylcholine). To do so, the vendor needs a fork (coenzyme) to remove the hot dog from the boiling water. The vendor inserts the fork into the hot dog (attaches acetate to CoA) and transfers the hot dog from fork to bun.

Two drugs, botulinum toxin and the venom of the black widow spider, affect the release of acetylcholine. **Botulinum toxin** is produced by *clostridium botulinum,* a bacterium that can grow in improperly canned food. This drug prevents the release of ACh (step 5 of Figure 4.5). The drug is an extremely potent poison; someone once calculated that a teaspoonful of pure botulinum toxin could kill the world's entire human population. In contrast,

---

acetyl-CoA (*a see tul*) A cofactor that supplies acetate for the synthesis of acetylcholine.

choline acetyltransferase (ChAT) (*koh leen a see tul trans fer ace*) The enzyme that transfers the acetate ion from acetyl coenzyme A to choline, producing the neurotransmitter acetylcholine.

botulinum toxin (*bot you lin um*) An acetylcholine antagonist; prevents release by terminal buttons.

black widow spider venom has the opposite effect: It stimulates the release of ACh (step 4 of Figure 4.5). Although the effects of black widow spider venom can also be fatal, the venom is much less toxic than botulinum toxin. In fact, most healthy adults would have to receive several bites, but infants or frail, elderly people would be more susceptible.

Several years ago I spent the academic year in a neurological research center affiliated with the teaching hospital at a medical center. One morning as I was having breakfast, I read a brief item in the newspaper about a man who had been hospitalized for botulism. Later that morning, I attended a weekly meeting during which the chief of neurology discussed interesting cases presented by the neurological residents. I was surprised to see that we would visit the man with botulism.

We entered the intensive care unit and saw that the man was clearly on his way to recovery. His face was pale and his voice was weak, but he was no longer on a respirator. There wasn't much to see, so we went back to the lounge and discussed his case.

Just before dinner a few days earlier, Mr. F. opened a jar of asparagus that his family had canned. He noted right away that it smelled funny. Because his family had grown the asparagus in their own garden, he was reluctant to throw it away. However, he decided that he wouldn't take any chances. He dipped a spoon into the liquid in the jar and touched it to his tongue. It didn't taste right, so he didn't swallow it. Instead, he stuck his tongue out and rinsed it under a stream of water from the faucet at the kitchen sink. He dumped the asparagus into the garbage disposal.

About an hour later, as the family was finishing dinner, Mr. F. discovered that he was seeing double. Alarmed, he asked his wife to drive him to the hospital. When he arrived at the emergency room, he was seen by one of the neurological residents, who asked him, "Mr. F., you haven't eaten some home-canned foods recently, have you?"

Learning that he had indeed let some liquid from a suspect jar of asparagus touch his tongue, the resident ordered a vial of botulinum antitoxin from the pharmacy. Meanwhile, he took a blood sample from Mr. F.'s vein and sent it to the lab for some in vivo testing in mice. He then administered the antitoxin, but already he could see that it was too late: Mr. F. was showing obvious signs of muscular weakness and was having some difficulty breathing. He was immediately sent to the intensive care unit, where he was put on a respirator. Although he became completely paralyzed, the life support system did what its name indicates, and eventually his acetylcholinergic terminal buttons repaired themselves and he regained control of his muscles. (By the way, the first symptom of his poisoning was double vision because the delicate balance between the muscles that move the eyes is upset by any interference with acetylcholinergic transmission.)

What fascinated me the most was the in vivo testing procedure for the presence of botulinum toxin in Mr. F.'s blood. The blood was spun in a centrifuge, and the plasma was injected into several mice, half of which had been pretreated with botulinum antitoxin. The pretreated mice survived; the others all died. Just think: Mr. F. had touched a few drops of the contaminated liquid on his tongue and then rinsed it off immediately, but enough of the toxin entered his bloodstream that a small amount of his blood plasma could kill a mouse.

You undoubtedly know that *botox* treatment has become fashionable. A dilute (obviously!) solution of botulinum toxin is injected into people's facial muscles to stop muscular contractions that are causing wrinkles. I'm not planning on getting a botox treatment, but if I did, I would want to be sure that the solution was sufficiently dilute.

You will recall from Chapter 2 that after being released by the terminal button, ACh is deactivated by the enzyme acetylcholinesterase (AChE), which is present in the postsynaptic membrane. The deactivation produces choline and acetate from ACh. Because the amount of choline that is picked up by the soma from the general circulation and then sent to the terminal buttons by means of axoplasmic flow is not sufficient to keep up with the loss of choline by an active synapse, choline must be recycled. After ACh is destroyed by the AChE in the postsynaptic membrane, the choline is returned to the terminal buttons by means of reuptake. There, it is converted back into ACh. This process has an efficiency of 50 percent; that is, half of the choline is retrieved and recycled. (See *Figure 4.11.*)

Drugs that deactivate AChE (step 11 of Figure 4.5) are used for several purposes. Some are used as insecticides. These drugs readily kill insects but not humans and other mammals, because our blood contains enzymes that destroy them. (Insects lack the enzyme.) Other AChE inhibitors are used medically. For example, a hereditary disorder called *myasthenia gravis* is caused by an attack of a person's immune system against acetylcholine receptors located on skeletal muscles. The person becomes weaker and weaker as the muscles become less responsive to the neurotransmitter. If the person is given an AChE inhibitor such as **neostigmine,** the person will regain some strength, because the acetylcholine that is released has a more prolonged effect on the remaining receptors. (Fortunately, neostigmine cannot cross the blood–brain barrier, so it does not affect the AChE found in the central nervous system.)

---

black widow spider venom A poison produced by the black widow spider that triggers the release of acetylcholine.

neostigmine (*nee o **stig** meen*) A drug that inhibits the activity of acetylcholinesterase.

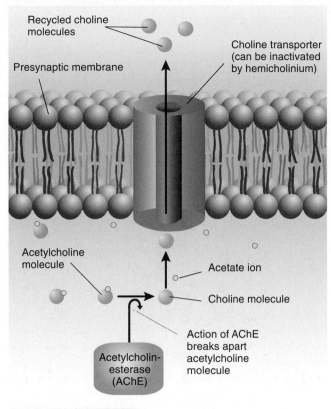

Recycled choline molecules

Presynaptic membrane

Choline transporter (can be inactivated by hemicholinium)

Acetylcholine molecule

Acetate ion

Choline molecule

Acetylcholinesterase (AChE)

Action of AChE breaks apart acetylcholine molecule

figure 4.11

The destruction of acetylcholine by acetylcholinesterase and the reuptake of choline. The drug hemicholinium blocks the reuptake of choline.

Reuptake of choline can be blocked by a drug called **hemicholinium.** Because this drug prevents the recycling of choline, the terminal button must rely solely on transport of this substance from the cell body. The result is production (and release) of less acetylcholine, which means that hemicholinium serves as an acetylcholine antagonist. (See *Figure 4.11.*)

There are two different types of ACh receptors—one ionotropic and one metabotropic. These receptors were identified when investigators discovered that different drugs activated them (step 6 of Figure 4.5). The ionotropic ACh receptor is stimulated by nicotine, a drug found in tobacco leaves. (The Latin name of the plant is *Nicotiniana tabacum.*) The metabotropic ACh receptor is stimulated by muscarine, a drug found in the poison mushroom *Amanita muscaria.* Consequently, these two ACh receptors are referred to as **nicotinic receptors** and **muscarinic receptors,** respectively. Because muscle fibers must be able to contract rapidly, they contain the rapid, ionotropic nicotinic receptors.

Because muscarinic receptors are metabotropic in nature and thus control ion channels through the production of second messengers, their actions are slower and

more prolonged than those of nicotinic receptors. The central nervous system contains both kinds of ACh receptors, but muscarinic receptors predominate. Some nicotinic receptors are found at axoaxonic synapses in the brain, where they produce presynaptic facilitation.

Just as two different drugs stimulate the two classes of acetylcholine receptors, two different drugs *block* them (step 7 of Figure 4.5). Both drugs were discovered in nature long ago, and both are still used by modern medicine. The first, **atropine,** blocks muscarinic receptors. The drug is named after *Atropos,* the Greek fate who cut the thread of life (which a sufficient dose of atropine will certainly do). Atropine is one of several *belladonna alkaloids* extracted from a plant called the deadly nightshade, and therein lies a tale. Many years ago, women who wanted to increase their attractiveness to men put drops containing belladonna alkaloids into their eyes. In fact, *belladonna* means "pretty lady." Why was the drug used this way? One of the unconscious responses that occurs when we are interested in something is dilation of our pupils. By blocking the effects of acetylcholine on the pupil, belladonna alkaloids such as atropine make the pupils dilate. This change makes a woman appear more interested in a man when she looks at him, and, of course, this apparent sign of interest makes him regard her as more attractive.

Another drug, **curare,** blocks nicotinic receptors. Because these receptors are the ones found on muscles, curare, like botulinum toxin, causes paralysis. However, the effects of curare are much faster. The drug is extracted from several different species of plants found in South America, where it was discovered long ago by people who used it to coat the tips of arrows and darts. Within minutes of being struck by one of these points, an animal collapses, ceases breathing, and dies. Nowadays, curare (and other drugs with the same site of action) are used to paralyze patients who are to undergo surgery so that their muscles will relax completely and not contract when they are cut with a scalpel. An anesthetic must also be used, because a person who receives only curare will remain perfectly conscious and sensitive to pain, even though paralyzed. And, of course, a respirator must be used to supply air to the lungs.

hemicholinium (*hem ee koh **lin** um*) A drug that inhibits the uptake of choline.

nicotinic receptor An ionotropic acetylcholine receptor that is stimulated by nicotine and blocked by curare.

muscarinic receptor (*muss ka **rin** ic*) A metabotropic acetylcholine receptor that is stimulated by muscarine and blocked by atropine.

atropine (*a tro peen*) A drug that blocks muscarinic acetylcholine receptors.

curare (*kew **rahr** ee*) A drug that blocks nicotinic acetylcholine receptors.

table 4.1	
Classification of the Monoamine Transmitter Substances	
CATECHOLAMINES	**INDOLAMINES**
Dopamine	Serotonin
Norepinephrine	
Epinephrine	

The Monoamines

Epinephrine, norepinephrine, dopamine, and serotonin are four chemicals that belong to a family of compounds called **monoamines.** Because the molecular structures of these substances are similar, some drugs affect the activity of all of them to some degree. The first three—epinephrine, norepinephrine, and dopamine—belong to a subclass of monoamines called **catecholamines.** It is worthwhile learning the terms in Table 4.1, because they will be used many times throughout the rest of this book. (See *Table 4.1.*)

The monoamines are produced by several systems of neurons in the brain. Most of these systems consist of a relatively small number of cell bodies located in the brain stem, whose axons branch repeatedly and give rise to an enormous number of terminal buttons distributed throughout many regions of the brain. Monoaminergic neurons thus serve to modulate the function of widespread regions of the brain, increasing or decreasing the activities of particular brain functions.

Dopamine

The first catecholamine in Table 4.1, **dopamine (DA),** produces both excitatory and inhibitory postsynaptic potentials, depending on the postsynaptic receptor. Dopamine is one of the more interesting neurotransmitters because it has been implicated in several important functions, including movement, attention, learning, and the reinforcing effects of drugs that people tend to abuse; therefore, it is discussed in Chapters 8, 9, 13, and 18.

The synthesis of the catecholamines is somewhat more complicated than that of ACh, but each step is a simple one. The precursor molecule is modified slightly, step by step, until it achieves its final shape. Each step is controlled by a different enzyme, which causes a small part to be added or taken off. The precursor for the two major catecholamine neurotransmitters (dopamine and norepinephrine) is *tyrosine,* an essential amino acid that we must obtain from our diet. Tyrosine receives a hydroxyl group (OH—an oxygen atom and a hydrogen atom) and becomes **L-DOPA** (L-3,4-dihydroxyphenylalanine). The enzyme that adds the hydroxyl group is called *tyrosine hydroxylase.*

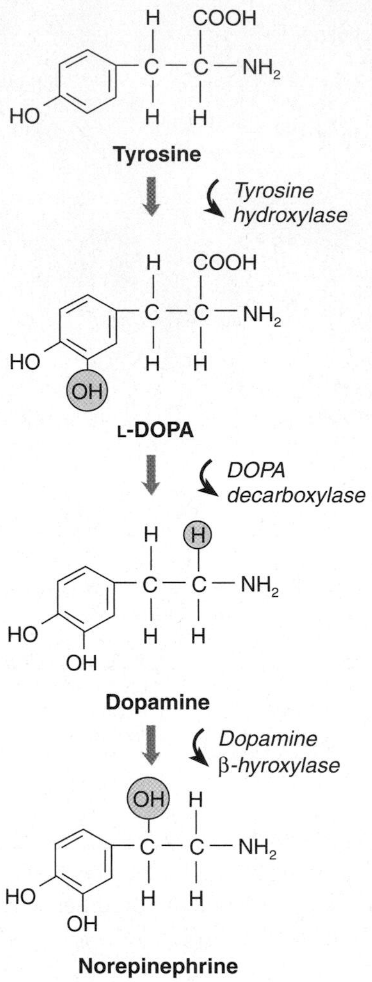

figure 4.12

Biosynthesis of the catecholamines.

L-DOPA then loses a carboxyl group (COOH—one carbon atom, two oxygen atoms, and one hydrogen atom) through the activity of the enzyme *DOPA decarboxylase* and becomes dopamine. Finally, the enzyme *dopamine β-hydroxylase* attaches a hydroxyl group to dopamine, which becomes norepinephrine. These reactions are shown in *Figure 4.12.*

monoamine (*mahn o a meen*) A class of amines that includes indolamines such as serotonin and catecholamines such as dopamine, norepinephrine, and epinephrine.

catecholamine (*cat a kohl a meen*) A class of amines that includes the neurotransmitters dopamine, norepinephrine, and epinephrine.

dopamine (DA) (*dope a meen*) A neurotransmitter; one of the catecholamines.

L-DOPA (*ell dope a*) The levorotatory form of DOPA; the precursor of the catecholamines; often used to treat Parkinson's disease because of its effect as a dopamine agonist.

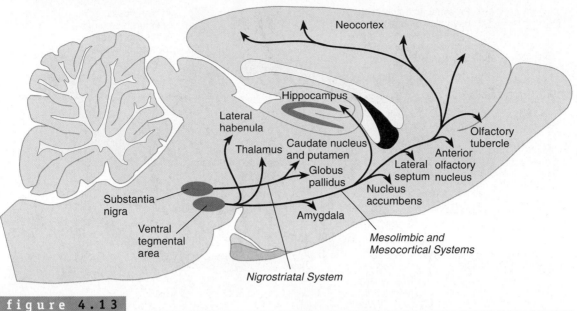

figure 4.13

A schematic midsagittal section of a rat brain, showing the locations of the most important groups of dopaminergic neurons and the distribution of their axons and terminal buttons.
(Adapted from Fuxe et al., 1985.)

The brain contains several systems of dopaminergic neurons. The three most important of these originate in the midbrain: in the substantia nigra and in the ventral tegmental area. (The substantia nigra was shown in Figure 3.21; the ventral tegmental area is located just below this region.) The cell bodies of neurons of the **nigrostriatal system** are located in the substantia nigra and project their axons to the neostriatum: the caudate nucleus and the putamen. The neostriatum is an important part of the basal ganglia, which is involved in the control of movement. The cell bodies of neurons of the **mesolimbic system** are located in the ventral tegmental area and project their axons to several parts of the limbic system, including the nucleus accumbens, amygdala, and hippocampus. The nucleus accumbens plays an important role in the reinforcing (rewarding) effects of certain categories of stimuli, including those of drugs that people abuse. The cell bodies of neurons of the **mesocortical system** are also located in the ventral tegmental area. Their axons project to the prefrontal cortex. These neurons have an excitatory effect on the frontal cortex and affect such functions as formation of short-term memories, planning, and strategy preparation for problem solving. These three systems of dopaminergic neurons are shown in *Figure 4.13.*

Degeneration of dopaminergic neurons that connect the substantia nigra with the caudate nucleus causes **Parkinson's disease,** a movement disorder characterized by tremors, rigidity of the limbs, poor balance, and difficulty in initiating movements. The cell bodies of these neurons are located in a region of the brain called the *substantia nigra* ("black

substance"). This region is normally stained black with melanin, the substance that gives color to skin. This compound is produced by the breakdown of dopamine. (The brain damage that causes Parkinson's disease was discovered by pathologists who observed that the substantia nigra of a deceased person who had had this disorder was pale rather than black.) People with Parkinson's disease are given L-DOPA, the precursor to dopamine. Although dopamine cannot cross the blood–brain barrier, L-DOPA can. Once L-DOPA reaches the brain, it is taken up by dopaminergic neurons and is converted to dopamine (step 1 of Figure 4.5). The increased synthesis of dopamine causes more dopamine to be released by the surviving dopaminergic neurons in patients with Parkinson's disease. As a consequence, the patients' symptoms are alleviated.

nigrostriatal system (*nigh grow stry **ay** tul*) A system of neurons originating in the substantia nigra and terminating in the neostriatum (caudate nucleus and putamen).

mesolimbic system (*mee zo **lim** bik*) A system of dopaminergic neurons originating in the ventral tegmental area and terminating in the nucleus accumbens, amygdala, and hippocampus.

mesocortical system (*mee zo **kor** ti kul*) A system of dopaminergic neurons originating in the ventral tegmental area and terminating in the prefrontal cortex.

Parkinson's disease A neurological disease characterized by tremors, rigidity of the limbs, poor balance, and difficulty in initiating movements; caused by degeneration of the nigrostriatal system.

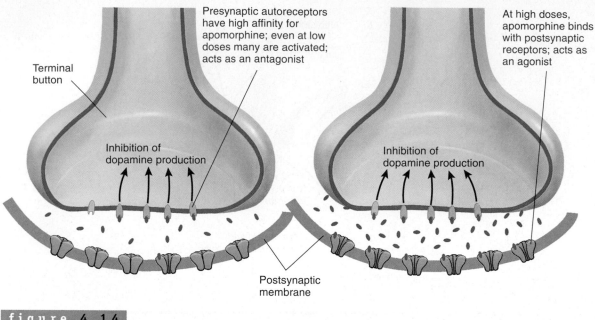

Presynaptic autoreceptors have high affinity for apomorphine; even at low doses many are activated; acts as an antagonist

At high doses, apomorphine binds with postsynaptic receptors; acts as an agonist

Terminal button

Inhibition of dopamine production

Inhibition of dopamine production

Postsynaptic membrane

figure 4.14

The effects of low and high doses of apomorphine. At low doses apomorphine serves as a dopamine antagonist; at high doses it serves as an agonist.

Another drug, **AMPT** (or α-methyl-*p*-tyrosine), inactivates tyrosine hydroxylase, the enzyme that converts tyrosine to L-DOPA (step 2 of Figure 4.5). Because this drug interferes with the synthesis of dopamine (and of norepinephrine, as well), it serves as a catecholamine antagonist. The drug is not normally used medically, but it has been used as a research tool in laboratory animals.

The drug **reserpine** prevents the storage of monoamines in synaptic vesicles by blocking the transporters in the membrane that pump monoamines into the vesicles (step 3 of Figure 4.5). Because the synaptic vesicles remain empty, no neurotransmitter is released when an action potential reaches the terminal button. Reserpine, then, is a monoamine antagonist. The drug, which comes from the root of a shrub, was discovered over three thousand years ago in India, where it was found to be useful in treating snakebite and seemed to have a calming effect. Pieces of the root are still sold in markets in rural areas of India. In Western medicine reserpine was previously used to treat high blood pressure, but it has been replaced by drugs with fewer side effects.

Several different types of dopamine receptors have been identified, all metabotropic. Of these, two are the most common: *D_1 receptors* and *D_2 receptors*. It appears that D_1 receptors are exclusively postsynaptic, whereas D_2 receptors are found both presynaptically and postsynaptically in the brain. Stimulation of D_1 receptors increases the production of the second messenger cyclic AMP, whereas stimulation of D_2 receptors decreases it, as does stimulation of D_3 and D_4 receptors. Several drugs stimulate or block specific types of dopamine receptors.

Autoreceptors are found in the dendrites, soma, and terminal buttons of dopaminergic neurons. Activation of the autoreceptors in the dendritic and somatic membrane decreases neural firing by producing hyperpolarizations. The presynaptic autoreceptors located in the terminal buttons suppress the activity of the enzyme tyrosine hydroxylase and thus decrease the production of dopamine—and ultimately its release. Dopamine autoreceptors resemble D_2 receptors, but there seem to be some differences. For example, the drug **apomorphine** is a D_2 agonist, but it seems to have a greater affinity for presynaptic D_2 receptors than for postsynaptic D_2 receptors. A low dose of apomorphine acts as an antagonist, because it stimulates the presynaptic receptors and inhibits the production and release of dopamine. Higher doses begin to stimulate postsynaptic D_2 receptors, and the drug begins to act as a direct agonist. (See *Figure 4.14.*)

Several drugs inhibit the reuptake of dopamine, thus serving as potent dopamine agonists (step 10 of Figure 4.5). The best known of these drugs are amphetamine, cocaine, and methylphenidate. Amphetamine has an interesting effect: It causes the release of both dopamine and norepinephrine by causing the transporters for these neurotransmitters to run in reverse, propelling DA and NE into the synaptic cleft. Of course, this action also blocks reuptake

AMPT A drug that blocks the activity of tyrosine hydroxylase and thus interferes with the synthesis of the catecholamines.

reserpine (*ree sur peen*) A drug that interferes with the storage of monoamines in synaptic vesicles.

apomorphine (*ap o more feen*) A drug that blocks dopamine autoreceptors at low doses; at higher doses blocks postsynaptic receptors as well.

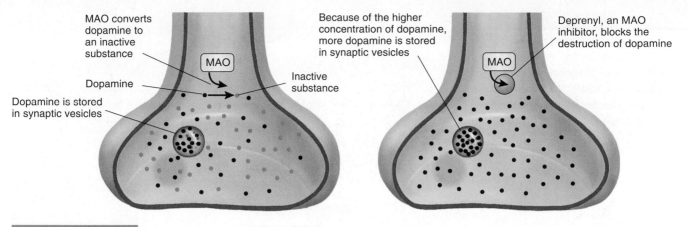

MAO converts dopamine to an inactive substance

figure 4.15

The role of monoamine oxidase in dopaminergic terminal buttons and the action of deprenyl.

of these neurotransmitters. Cocaine and **methylphenidate** simply block dopamine reuptake. Because cocaine also blocks voltage-dependent sodium channels, it is sometimes used as a topical anesthetic, especially in the form of eye drops for eye surgery. Methylphenidate (Ritalin) is used to treat children with attention deficit disorder.

The production of the catecholamines is regulated by an enzyme called **monoamine oxidase (MAO).** This enzyme is found within monoaminergic terminal buttons, where it destroys excessive amounts of neurotransmitter. A drug called **deprenyl** destroys the particular form of monoamine oxidase (MAO-B) that is found in dopaminergic terminal buttons. Because deprenyl prevents the destruction of dopamine, more dopamine is released when an action potential reaches the terminal button. Thus, deprenyl serves as a dopamine agonist. (See *Figure 4.15.*)

MAO is also found in the blood, where it deactivates amines that are present in foods such as chocolate and cheese; without such deactivation these amines could cause dangerous increases in blood pressure.

Dopamine has been implicated as a neurotransmitter that might be involved in schizophrenia, a serious mental disorder whose symptoms include hallucinations, delusions, and disruption of normal, logical thought processes. Drugs such as **chlorpromazine,** which block D_2 receptors, alleviate these symptoms (step 7 of Figure 4.5). Hence, investigators have speculated that schizophrenia is produced by overactivity of dopaminergic neurons. More recently discovered drugs, such as **clozapine,** may exert their therapeutic effects by blocking D_4 receptors. The physiology of schizophrenia is discussed in Chapter 16.

As we saw in the case reported at the beginning of this chapter, MPTP can damage the brain and cause the symptoms of Parkinson's disease. This discovery galvanized researchers interested in this disease. (I recently checked PubMed, a web site maintained by the U.S. National Institutes of Health, and found that 2,854 publications referred to MPTP.) The first step was to find out whether the drug would have the same effect in laboratory animals so that the details of the process could be studied. It did; Langston

and colleagues (1984) found that injections of MPTP produced parkinsonian symptoms in squirrel monkeys and that these symptoms could be reduced by L-DOPA therapy. And just as the investigators had hoped, examination of the animals' brains showed a selective loss of dopamine-secreting neurons in the substantia nigra.

It turns out that MPTP itself does not cause neural damage; instead, the drug is converted by an enzyme present in glial cells into another substance, MPP+. *That* chemical is taken up by dopamine-secreting neurons, by means of the reuptake mechanism that normally retrieves dopamine that is released by terminal buttons. MPP+ accumulates in mitochondria in these cells and blocks their ability to metabolize nutrients, thus killing the cells (Maret et al., 1990). The enzyme that converts MPTP into MPP+ is none other than monoamine oxidase (MAO), which, as you now know, is responsible for deactivating excess amounts of monoamines present in terminal buttons. Because pharmacologists had already developed MAO inhibitors, Langston and his colleagues decided to see whether one of these drugs (pargyline) would protect squirrel monkeys from the toxic effects of MPTP by preventing its conversion into MPP+ (Langston et al., 1984). It worked; when MAO was inhibited by pargyline, MPTP injections had no effects.

These results made researchers wonder whether MAO inhibitors might possibly protect against the degeneration of dopamine-secreting neurons in patients with

methylphenidate (*meth ul fen i date*) A drug that inhibits the reuptake of dopamine.

monoamine oxidase (MAO) (*mahn o a meen*) A class of enzymes that destroy the monoamines: dopamine, norepinephrine, and serotonin.

deprenyl (*depp ra nil*) A drug that blocks the activity of MAO-B; acts as a dopamine agonist.

chlorpromazine (*klor proh ma zeen*) A drug that reduces the symptoms of schizophrenia by blocking dopamine D_2 receptors.

clozapine (*kloz a peen*) A drug that reduces the symptoms of schizophrenia, apparently by blocking dopamine D_4 receptors.

figure 4.16

A schematic midsagittal section of a rat brain, showing the locations of the most important groups of noradrenergic neurons and the distribution of their axons and terminal buttons. (Adapted from Cotman and McGaugh, 1980.)

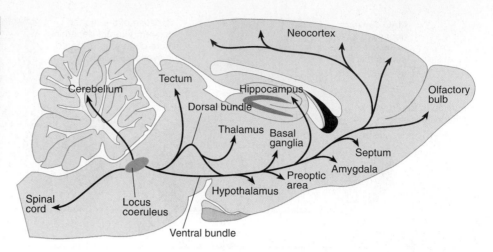

Parkinson's disease. No one thought that Parkinson's disease was caused by MPP+, but perhaps some other toxins were involved. Epidemiologists have found that Parkinson's disease is more common in highly industrialized countries, which suggests that environmental toxins produced in these societies may be responsible for the brain damage (Tanner, 1989; Veldman et al., 1998). Fortunately, several MAO inhibitors have been tested and approved for use in humans. One of them, deprenyl, was tested and appeared to slow down the progression of neurological symptoms (Tetrud and Langston, 1989).

As a result of this study, many neurologists are now treating their Parkinson's patients with deprenyl, especially during the early stages of the disease. More recent studies found that deprenyl does not protect dopaminergic neurons indefinitely (Shoulson et al., 2002), but researchers are trying to develop other drugs with more sustained neuroprotective effects.

Norepinephrine

Because **norepinephrine (NE),** like ACh, is found in neurons in the autonomic nervous system, this neurotransmitter has received much experimental attention. I should note that *Adrenalin* and *epinephrine* are synonymous, as are *noradrenalin* and *norepinephrine.* Let me explain why. **Epinephrine** is a hormone produced by the adrenal medulla, the central core of the adrenal glands, located just above the kidneys. Epinephrine also serves as a neurotransmitter in the brain, but it is of minor importance compared with norepinephrine. *Ad renal* is Latin for "toward kidney." In Greek one would say *epi nephron* ("upon the kidney"), hence the term *epinephrine.* The latter term has been adopted by pharmacologists, probably because the word *Adrenalin* was appropriated by a drug company as a proprietary name; therefore, to be consistent with general usage, I will refer to the neurotransmitter as *norepinephrine.* The accepted adjectival form is *noradrenergic;* I suppose that *norepinephrinergic* never caught on because it takes so long to pronounce.

We have already seen the biosynthetic pathway for norepinephrine in Figure 4.12. The drug AMPT, which prevents the conversion of tyrosine to L-DOPA, blocks the production of norepinephrine as well as dopamine (step 2 of Figure 4.5).

Most neurotransmitters are synthesized in the cytoplasm of the terminal button and then stored in newly formed synaptic vesicles. However, for norepinephrine the final step of synthesis occurs inside the vesicles themselves. The vesicles are first filled with dopamine. Then the dopamine is converted to norepinephrine through the action of the enzyme dopamine ß-hydroxylase located within the vesicles. The drug **fusaric acid** inhibits the activity of the enzyme dopamine-ß-hydroxylase and thus blocks the production of norepinephrine without affecting the production of dopamine.

Excess norepinephrine in the terminal buttons is destroyed by monoamine oxidase, type A. The drug **moclobemide** specifically blocks MAO-A and hence serves as a noradrenergic agonist.

Almost every region of the brain receives input from noradrenergic neurons. The cell bodies of most of these neurons are located in seven regions of the pons and medulla and one region of the thalamus. The cell bodies of the most important noradrenergic system begin in the **locus coeruleus,** a nucleus located in the dorsal pons. The axons of these neurons project to the regions shown in Figure 4.16.

norepinephrine (NE) (*nor epp i **neff** rin*) One of the catecholamines; a neurotransmitter found in the brain and in the sympathetic division of the autonomic nervous system.

epinephrine (*epp i **neff** rin*) One of the catecholamines; a hormone secreted by the adrenal medulla; serves also as a neurotransmitter in the brain.

fusaric acid (*few **sahr** ik*) A drug that inhibits the activity of the enzyme dopamine-ß-hydroxylase and thus blocks the production of norepinephrine.

moclobemide (*mok low **bem** ide*) A drug that blocks the activity of MAO-A; acts as a noradrenergic agonist.

locus coeruleus (*sur **oo** lee us*) A dark-colored group of noradrenergic cell bodies located in the pons near the rostral end of the floor of the fourth ventricle.

As we will see later, the primary effect of activation of these neurons is an increase in vigilance—attentiveness to events in the environment. (See *Figure 4.16.*)

Most neurons that release norepinephrine do not do so through terminal buttons on the ends of axonal branches. Instead, they usually release them through **axonal varicosities,** beadlike swellings of the axonal branches. These varicosities give the axonal branches of catecholaminergic neurons the appearance of beaded chains.

There are several types of noradrenergic receptors, identified by their differing sensitivities to various drugs. Actually, these receptors are usually called *adrenergic* receptors rather than *noradrenergic* receptors, because they are sensitive to epinephrine (Adrenalin) as well as norepinephrine. Neurons in the central nervous system contain β_1- and β_2-*adrenergic receptors* and α_1- and α_2-*adrenergic receptors*. All four kinds of receptors are also found in various organs of the body besides the brain and are responsible for the effects of the catecholamines when they act as hormones outside the central nervous system. A fifth type of adrenergic receptor, the β_3 receptor, is found only outside the central nervous system, primarily in adipose (fat) tissue. In the brain all autoreceptors appear to be of the α_2 type. (The drug **clonidine** stimulates α_2 autoreceptors and hence acts as an antagonist.) All adrenergic receptors are metabotropic, coupled to G proteins that control the production of second messengers.

Adrenergic receptors produce both excitatory and inhibitory effects. In general, the *behavioral* effects of the release of NE are excitatory. In the brain α_1 receptors produce a slow depolarizing (excitatory) effect on the postsynaptic membrane, while α_2 receptors produce a slow hyperpolarization. Both types of β receptors increase the responsiveness of the postsynaptic neuron to its excitatory inputs, which presumably related to the role this neurotransmitter plays in vigilance. Noradrenergic neurons—in particular, α_2 receptors—are also involved in sexual behavior and in the control of appetite.

Serotonin

The third monoamine neurotransmitter, **serotonin** (also called **5-HT,** or 5-hydroxytryptamine), has also received much experimental attention. Its behavioral effects are complex. Serotonin plays a role in the regulation of mood; in the control of eating, sleep, and arousal; and in the regulation of pain. Serotonergic neurons are involved somehow in the control of dreaming.

The precursor for serotonin is the amino acid *tryptophan*. The enzyme *tryptophan hydroxylase* adds a hydroxyl group, producing *5-HTP* (5-hydroxytryptophan). The enzyme *5-HTP decarboxylase* removes a carboxyl group from 5-HTP, and the result is 5-HT (serotonin). (See *Figure 4.17.*) The drug **PCPA** (*p*-chlorophenylalanine) blocks the activity of tryptophan hydroxylase and thus serves as a serotonergic antagonist.

The cell bodies of serotonergic neurons are found in nine clusters, most of which are located in the raphe nuclei

Tryptophan

Tryptophan hydroxylase

COOH

5-hydroxytryptophan (5-HTP)

5-HTP decarboxylase

5-hydroxytryptamine (5-HT, or serotonin)

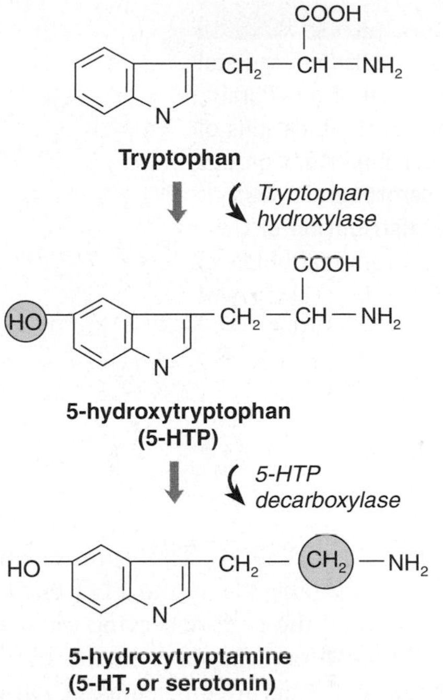

figure 4.17

Biosynthesis of serotonin (5-hydroxytryptamine, or 5-HT).

of the midbrain, pons, and medulla. The two most important clusters are found in the dorsal and medial raphe nuclei, and I will restrict my discussion to these clusters. The word *raphe* means "seam" or "crease" and refers to the fact that most of the raphe nuclei are found at or near the midline of the brain stem. Both the dorsal and median raphe nuclei project axons to the cerebral cortex. In addition, neurons in the dorsal raphe innervate the basal ganglia, and those in the median raphe innervate the dentate gyrus, a part of the hippocampal formation. These and other connections are shown in *Figure 4.18.*

Like norepinephrine, 5-HT is released from varicosities rather than terminal buttons. In fact, there are two types of serotonergic axonal fibers, which appear to have different functions. The **D system** originates in the dorsal raphe nucleus. Its axonal fibers are thin, with

axonal varicosity An enlarged region along the length of an axon that contains synaptic vesicles and releases a neurotransmitter or neuromodulator.

clonidine A drug that stimulates presynaptic noradrenergic α_2 receptors and hence acts as an antagonist, suppressing the synthesis and release of NE.

serotonin (5-HT) (*sair a toe nin*) An indolamine neurotransmitter; also called 5-hydroxytryptamine.

PCPA A drug that inhibits the activity of tryptophan hydroxylase and thus interferes with the synthesis of 5-HT.

D system A system of serotonergic neurons that originates in the dorsal raphe nucleus; its axonal fibers are thin, with spindle-shaped varicosities that do not appear to form synapses with other neurons.

figure 4.18

A schematic midsagittal section of a rat brain, showing the locations of the most important groups of serotonergic neurons and the distribution of their axons and terminal buttons. (Adapted from Consolazione and Cuello, 1982.)

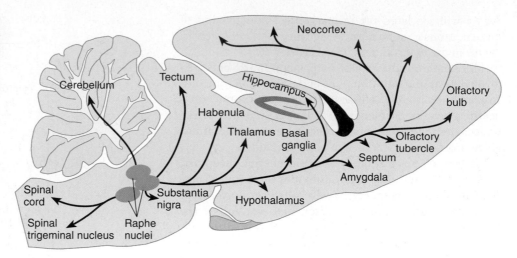

spindle-shaped varicosities. These varicosities do not appear to form synapses; that is, the 5-HT that they release diffuses throughout the region, serving as a neuromodulator. The **M system** originates in the median raphe nucleus. Its axonal fibers are thick, and the varicosities are rounded, appearing like beads on a chain. These varicosities appear to be located adjacent to postsynaptic membranes, forming conventional synapses. Figure 4.19 is a photomicrograph of both types of fibers, located in the forebrain. Fibers belonging to the D system are indicated with small arrows, and those belonging to the M system are indicated with large open arrows. Almost certainly, these two systems have different behavioral effects. (See *Figure 4.19*.)

Investigators have identified at least nine different types of serotonin receptors: $5\text{-HT}_{1A\text{-}1B}$, $5\text{-HT}_{1D\text{-}1F}$, $5\text{-HT}_{2A\text{-}2C}$, and 5-HT_3. Of these the 5-HT_{1B} and 5-HT_{1D} receptors serve as presynaptic autoreceptors. In the dorsal and median raphe nuclei, 5-HT_{1A} receptors serve as autoreceptors in the membrane of dendrites and soma. All 5-HT receptors are metabotropic except for the 5-HT_3 receptor, which is ionotropic. The 5-HT_3 receptor controls a chloride channel, which means that it produces inhibitory postsynaptic potentials. These receptors appear to play a role in nausea and vomiting, because 5-HT_3 antagonists have been found to be useful in treating the side effects of chemotherapy and radiotherapy for the treatment of cancer. Pharmacologists have discovered drugs that serve as agonists or antagonists for some, but not all, of the types of 5-HT receptors.

Drugs that inhibit the reuptake of serotonin have found a very important place in the treatment of mental disorders. The best known of these, **fluoxetine** (Prozac), is used to treat depression, some forms of anxiety disorders, and obsessive-compulsive disorder. These disorders—and their treatment—are discussed in Chapters 16 and 17. Another drug, **fenfluramine,** which causes the release of serotonin as well as inhibits its reuptake, has been used as an appetite suppressant in the treatment of obesity. Chapter 12 discusses the topic of obesity and its control by means of drugs.

Several hallucinogenic drugs appear to produce their effects by interacting with serotonergic transmission. **LSD** (lysergic acid diethylamide) produces distortions of visual perceptions that some people find awesome and fascinating but that simply frighten other people. This drug, which is effective in extremely small doses, is a direct agonist for postsynaptic 5-HT_{2A} receptors in the forebrain.

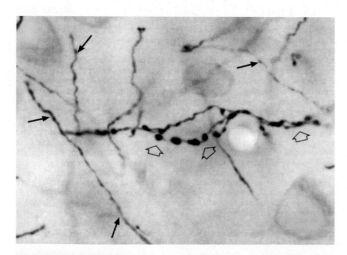

figure 4.19

A photomicrograph of axonal fibers belonging to the D system (small arrows) and M system (large open arrows) of serotonergic neurons.

(From Törk, I. *Annals of the New York Academy of Sciences,* 1990, *600,* 9–35.)

M system A system of serotonergic neurons that originates in the median raphe nucleus; its axonal fibers are thick and rounded and appear to form conventional synapses with other neurons.

fluoxetine (*floo ox i teen*) A drug that inhibits the reuptake of 5-HT.

fenfluramine (*fen fluor i meen*) A drug that stimulates the release of 5-HT.

LSD A drug that stimulates 5-HT_{2A} receptors.

Another drug, **MDMA** (methylenedioxymethamphetamine), is both a noradrenergic and serotonergic agonist and has both excitatory and hallucinogenic effects. Like its relative amphetamine, MDMA (popularly called "ecstasy") causes noradrenergic transporters to run backwards, this causing the release of norepinephrine and inhibiting its reuptake. This site of action is apparently responsible for the drug's excitatory effect. MDMA also causes serotonergic transporters to run backwards, and this site of action is apparently responsible for the drug's hallucinogenic effects. Unfortunately, research indicates that MDMA can damage serotonergic neurons and cause cognitive deficits. These effects are described in more detail in Chapter 18.

Amino Acids

So far, all of the neurotransmitters I have described are synthesized within neurons: acetylcholine from choline, the catecholamines from the amino acid tyrosine, and serotonin from the amino acid tryptophan. Some neurons secrete simple amino acids as neurotransmitters. Because amino acids are used for protein synthesis by all cells of the brain, it is difficult to prove that a particular amino acid is a neurotransmitter. However, investigators suspect that at least eight amino acids may serve as neurotransmitters in the mammalian central nervous system. As we saw in the introduction to this section, three of them are especially important because they are the most common neurotransmitters in the CNS: glutamate, gamma-aminobutyric acid (GABA), and glycine.

Glutamate

Because **glutamate** (also called *glutamic acid*) and GABA are found in very simple organisms, many investigators believe that these neurotransmitters are the first to have evolved. Besides producing postsynaptic potentials by activating postsynaptic receptors, they also have direct excitatory effects (glutamic acid) and inhibitory effects (GABA) on axons; they raise or lower the threshold of excitation, thus affecting the rate at which action potentials occur. These direct effects suggest that these substances had a general modulating role even before the evolutionary development of specific receptor molecules.

Glutamate is the principal excitatory neurotransmitter in the brain and spinal cord. It is produced in abundance by the cells' metabolic processes. There is no effective way to prevent its synthesis without disrupting other activities of the cell.

Investigators have discovered four types of glutamate receptors. Three of these receptors are ionotropic and are named after the artificial ligands that stimulate them: the **NMDA receptor,** the **AMPA receptor,** and the **kainate receptor.** The other glutamate receptor—the **metabotropic glutamate receptor**—is (obviously!) metabotropic. Actually, there appear to be at least seven different metabotropic glutamate receptors, but little is known about their functions except that some of them serve as

presynaptic autoreceptors. The AMPA receptor is the most common glutamate receptor. It controls a sodium channel, so when glutamate attaches to the binding site, it produces EPSPs. The kainate receptor has similar effects.

The NMDA receptor has some special—and very important—characteristics. It contains at least six different binding sites: four located on the exterior of the receptor and two located deep within the ion channel. When it is open, the ion channel controlled by the NMDA receptor permits both sodium and calcium ions to enter the cell. The influx of both of these ions causes a depolarization, of course, but the entry of calcium (Ca^{2+}) is especially important. Calcium serves as a second messenger, binding with—and activating—various enzymes within the cell. These enzymes have profound effects on the biochemical and structural properties of the cell. As we shall see, one important result is alteration in the characteristics of the synapse that provide one of the building blocks of a newly formed memory. These effects of NMDA receptors will be discussed in much more detail in Chapter 13. The drug **AP5** (2-amino-5-phosphonopentanoate) blocks the glutamate binding site on the NMDA receptor and impairs synaptic plasticity and certain forms of learning.

Figure 4.20 presents a schematic diagram of an NMDA receptor and its binding sites. Obviously, glutamate binds with one of these sites, or we would not call it a glutamate receptor. However, glutamate by itself cannot open the calcium channel. For that to happen, a molecule of glycine must be attached to the glycine binding site, located on the outside of the receptor. (We do not yet understand why glycine—which also serves as an inhibitory neurotransmitter in some parts of the central nervous system—is required for this ion channel to open.) (See *Figure 4.20.*)

An additional requirement for the opening of the calcium channel is that a magnesium ion *not* be attached to the magnesium binding site, located deep within the channel. Under normal conditions, when the postsynaptic membrane is at the resting potential, a magnesium ion (Mg^{2+}) is attracted to the magnesium binding site and blocks the

---

MDMA A drug that serves as a noradrenergic and serotonergic agonists, also knowns as "ecstasy"; has excitatory and hallucinogenic effects.

glutamate An amino acid; the most important excitatory neurotransmitter in the brain.

NMDA receptor A specialized ionotropic glutamate receptor that controls a calcium channel that is normally blocked by Mg^{2+} ions; has several other binding sites.

AMPA receptor An ionotropic glutamate receptor that controls a sodium channel; stimulated by AMPA.

kainate receptor (*kay in ate*) An ionotropic glutamate receptor that controls a sodium channel; stimulated by kainic acid.

metabotropic glutamate receptor (*meh tab a troh pik*) A category of metabotropic receptors that are sensitive to glutamate.

AP5 (2-amino-5-phosphonopentanoate) A drug that blocks the glutamate binding site on NMDA receptors.

calcium channel. If a molecule of glutamate attaches to its binding site, the channel widens, but the magnesium ion still blocks it, so no calcium can enter the postsynaptic neuron. However, if the postsynaptic membrane is partially depolarized, the magnesium ion is repelled from its binding site. Thus, the NMDA receptor opens only if glutamate is present *and* the postsynaptic membrane is depolarized. The NMDA receptor, then, is a voltage- and neurotransmitter-dependent ion channel. (See *Figure 4.20.*)

What about the other three binding sites? If a zinc ion (Zn^{2+}) binds with the zinc binding site, the activity of the NMDA receptor is decreased. On the other hand, the polyamine site has a facilitatory effect. (Polyamines are chemicals that have been shown to be important for tissue growth and development. The significance of the polyamine binding site is not yet understood.) The PCP site, located deep within the ion channel near the magnesium binding site, binds with a hallucinogenic drug, **PCP** (phencyclidine, also known as "angel dust"). PCP serves as an indirect antagonist; when it attaches to its binding site, calcium ions cannot pass through the ion channel. PCP is a synthetic drug and is not produced by the brain. Thus, it is not the natural ligand of the PCP binding site. What that ligand is and what useful functions it serves are not yet known. The behavioral symptoms of PCP are listed in *Table 4.2.*

Several drugs affect glutamatergic synapses. As you already know, NMDA, AMPA, and kainate serve as direct agonists at the receptors named after them. In addition, one of the most common drugs—alcohol—serves as an antagonist of NMDA receptors. As we will see in Chapter 18, this effect is responsible for the seizures that can be provoked by sudden withdrawal from heavy long-term alcohol intake.

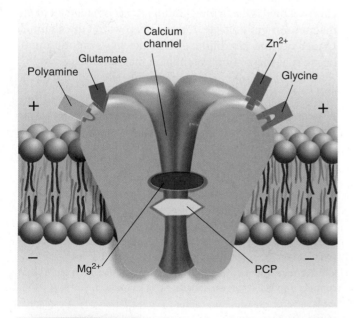

figure 4.20

A schematic illustration of an NMDA receptor, with its binding sites.

table 4.2
Behavioral Symptoms of Phencyclidine (PCP)
Altered body image
Feelings of isolation and aloneness
Cognitive disorganization
Drowsiness and apathy
Negativism and hostility
Feelings of euphoria and inebriation
Dreamlike states

Source: Adapted from Feldman, Meyer, and Quenzer, 1997.

GABA

GABA (gamma-aminobutyric acid) is produced from glutamic acid by the action of an enzyme (glutamic acid decarboxylase, or GAD) that removes a carboxyl group. The drug **allylglycine** inactivates GAD and thus prevents the synthesis of GABA (step 2 of Figure 4.5). GABA is an inhibitory neurotransmitter, and it appears to have a widespread distribution throughout the brain and spinal cord. Two GABA receptors have been identified: $GABA_A$ and $GABA_B$. The $GABA_A$ receptor is ionotropic and controls a chloride channel; the $GABA_B$ receptor is metabotropic and controls a potassium channel.

As you know, neurons in the brain are greatly interconnected. Without the activity of inhibitory synapses these interconnections would make the brain unstable. That is, through excitatory synapses neurons would excite their neighbors, which would then excite *their* neighbors, which would then excite the originally active neurons, and so on, until most of the neurons in the brain would be firing uncontrollably. In fact, this event does sometimes occur, and we refer to it as a *seizure.* (*Epilepsy* is a neurological disorder characterized by the presence of seizures.) Normally, an inhibitory influence is supplied by GABA-secreting neurons, which are present in large numbers in the brain. Some investigators believe that one of the causes of epilepsy is an abnormality in the biochemistry of GABA-secreting neurons or in GABA receptors.

Like NMDA receptors, $GABA_A$ receptors are complex; they contain at least five different binding sites. The

PCP Phencyclidine; a drug that binds with the PCP binding site of the NMDA receptor and serves as an indirect antagonist.
GABA An amino acid; the most important inhibitory neurotransmitter in the brain.
allylglycine A drug that inhibits the activity of GAD and thus blocks the synthesis of GABA.

primary binding site is, of course, for GABA. The drug **muscimol** (derived from the ACh agonist, muscarine) serves as a direct agonist for this site (step 6 of Figure 4.5). Another drug, **bicuculline,** blocks this GABA binding site, serving as a direct antagonist (step 7 of Figure 4.5). A second site on the GABA$_A$ receptor binds with a class of tranquilizing drugs called the **benzodiazepines.** These drugs include diazepam (Valium) and chlordiazepoxide (Librium), which are used to reduce anxiety, promote sleep, reduce seizure activity, and produce muscle relaxation. The third site binds with barbiturates. The fourth site binds with various steroids, including some steroids used to produce general anesthesia. The fifth site binds with picrotoxin, a poison found in an East Indian shrub. In addition, alcohol binds with one of these sites—probably the benzodiazepine binding site. (See *Figure 4.21.*)

Barbiturates, drugs that bind to the steroid site, and benzodiazepines all promote the activity of the GABA$_A$ receptor; thus, all these drugs serve as indirect agonists. The benzodiazepines are very effective **anxiolytics,** or "anxiety-dissolving" drugs. They are often used to treat people with anxiety disorders. In addition, some benzodiazepines serve as effective sleep medications, and others are used to treat some types of seizure disorder.

In low doses barbiturates have a calming effect. In progressively higher doses they produce difficulty in walking and talking, unconsciousness, coma, and death. Although veterinarians sometimes use barbiturates to produce anesthesia for surgery, the therapeutic index—the ratio between a dose that produces anesthesia and one that causes fatal depression of the respiratory centers of the brain—is small. As a consequence, these drugs are rarely used by themselves to produce surgical anesthesia in humans.

Picrotoxin has effects opposite to those of benzodiazepines and barbiturates: It *inhibits* the activity of the GABA$_A$ receptor, thus serving as an indirect antagonist. In high enough doses, this drug causes convulsions.

Various steroid hormones are normally produced in the body, and some hormones related to progesterone (the principal pregnancy hormone) act on the steroid binding site of the GABA$_A$ receptor, producing a sedative effect. However, the brain does not produce Valium, barbiturates, or picrotoxin. What are the natural ligands for these binding sites? So far, most research has concentrated on the benzodiazepine binding site. These binding sites are more complex than the others. They can be activated by drugs such as the benzodiazepines, which promote the activity of the receptor and thus serve as indirect agonists. They can also be activated by other drugs that have the opposite effect—that inhibit the activity of the receptor, thus serving as indirect antagonists. Presumably, the brain produces natural ligands that act as indirected agonists or antagonists at the benzodiazepine binding site, but so far, such a chemical has not been identified.

What about the GABA$_B$ receptor? This metabotropic receptor, coupled to a G protein, serves as both a postsynaptic receptor and a presynaptic autoreceptor. A GABA$_B$ agonist, baclofen, serves as a muscle relaxant. Another drug, CGP 335348, serves as an antagonist. The activation of GABA$_B$ receptors opens potassium channels, producing hyperpolarizing inhibitory postsynaptic potentials.

Glycine

The amino acid **glycine** appears to be the inhibitory neurotransmitter in the spinal cord and lower portions of the brain. Little is known about its biosynthetic pathway; there are several possible routes, but not enough is known to decide how neurons produce glycine. The bacteria that cause tetanus (lockjaw) release a chemical that prevents the release of glycine (and GABA as well); the removal of the inhibitory effect of these synapses causes muscles to contract continuously.

The glycine receptor is ionotropic, and it controls a chloride channel. Thus, when it is active, it produces

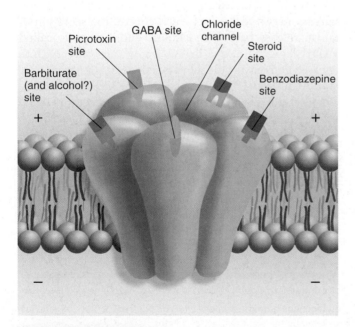

figure   **4.21**

A schematic illustration of a GABA$_A$ receptor, with its binding sites.

muscimol (*musk* i *mawl*) A direct agonist for the GABA binding site on the GABA$_A$ receptor.

bicuculline (by *kew* kew leen) A direct antagonist for the GABA binding site on the GABA$_A$ receptor.

benzodiazepine (ben zoe dy *azz* a peen) A category of anxiolytic drugs; an indirect agonist for the GABA$_A$ receptor.

anxiolytic (angz ee oh *lit* ik) An anxiety-reducing effect.

glycine (*gly* seen) An amino acid; an important inhibitory neurotransmitter in the lower brain stem and spinal cord.

inhibitory postsynaptic potentials. The drug **strychnine,** an alkaloid found in the seeds of the *Strychnos nux vomica,* a tree found in India, serves as a glycine antagonist. Strychnine is very toxic, and even relatively small doses cause convulsions and death. No drugs have yet been found that serve as specific glycine agonists.

Researchers have discovered that some terminal buttons in the brain release both glycine and GABA (Jonas, Bischofberger, and Sandkühler, 1998; Nicoll and Malenka, 1998). The apparent advantage for the corelease of these two inhibitory neurotransmitters is the production of rapid, longlasting postsynaptic potentials: The glycine stimulates rapid ionotropic receptors and the GABA stimulates long-lasting metabotropic receptors. Obviously, the postsynaptic membrane at these synapses contains both glycine and GABA receptors.

Peptides

Recent studies have discovered that the neurons of the central nervous system release a large variety of peptides. Peptides consist of two or more amino acids linked together by peptide bonds. All the peptides that have been studied so far are produced from precursor molecules. These precursors are large polypeptides that are broken into pieces by special enzymes. A neuron manufactures both the polypeptides and the enzymes that it needs to break them apart in the right places. The appropriate sections are retained, and the other ones are destroyed. Because the synthesis of peptides takes place in the soma, vesicles containing these chemicals must be delivered to the terminal buttons by axoplasmic transport.

Peptides are released from all parts of the terminal button, not just from the active zone; thus, only a portion of the molecules are released into the synaptic cleft. The rest presumably act on receptors belonging to other cells in the vicinity. Once released, peptides are destroyed by enzymes. There is no mechanism for reuptake and recycling of peptides.

Several different peptides are released by neurons. Although most peptides appear to serve as neuromodulators, some act as neurotransmitters. One of the best known families of peptides is the **endogenous opioids.** (*Endogenous* means "produced from within"; *opioid* means "like opium.") Several years ago it became clear that opiates (drugs such as opium, morphine, and heroin) reduce pain because they have direct effects on the brain. (Please note that the term *opioid* refers to endogenous chemicals, and *opiate* refers to drugs.) Pert, Snowman, and Snyder (1974) discovered that neurons in a localized region of the brain contain specialized receptors that respond to opiates. Then, soon after the discovery of the opiate receptor, other neuroscientists discovered the natural ligands for these receptors (Terenius and Wahlström, 1975; Hughes et al., 1975), which they called **enkephalins** (from the Greek word *enkephalos,* "in the head"). We now know that the enkephalins are only two members of a family of endogenous opioids, all of which are synthesized from one

of three large peptides that serve as precursors. In addition, we know that there are at least three different types of opiate receptors: μ (mu), δ (delta), and κ (kappa).

Several different neural systems are activated when opiate receptors are stimulated. One type produces analgesia, another inhibits species-typical defensive responses such as fleeing and hiding, and another stimulates a system of neurons involved in reinforcement ("reward"). The last effect explains why opiates are often abused. The situations that cause neurons to secrete endogenous opioids are discussed in Chapter 7, and the brain mechanisms of opiate addiction are discussed in Chapter 18.

So far, pharmacologists have developed only two types of drugs that affect neural communication by means of opioids: direct agonists and antagonists. Many synthetic opiates, including heroin (dihydromorphine) and Percodan (levorphanol), have been developed and are used clinically as analgesics (step 6 of Figure 4.5). Several opiate receptors blockers have also been developed (step 7 of Figure 4.5). One of them, **naloxone,** is used clinically to reverse opiate intoxication. This drug has saved the lives of many drug abusers who would otherwise have died of an overdose of heroin. And as we saw earlier in this chapter, naloxone was used to demonstrate that the administration of a placebo can cause analgesia by triggering the release of endogenous opioids.

As we saw in Chapter 2, many terminal buttons contain two different types of synaptic vesicles, each filled with a different substance. These terminal buttons release peptides in conjunction with a "classical" neurotransmitter (one of those I just described). The primary reason for the corelease of peptides is their ability to regulate the sensitivity of presynaptic or postsynaptic receptors to the neurotransmitter. For example, the terminal buttons of the salivary nerve of the cat (which control the secretion of saliva) release both acetylcholine and a peptide called VIP. When the axons fire at a low rate only ACh is released and only a little saliva is secreted. At a higher rate, both ACh and VIP are secreted, and the VIP dramatically increases the sensitivity of the muscarinic receptors in the salivary gland to ACh; thus, much saliva is released.

Several peptide hormones are also found in the brain, where they serve as neuromodulators. In some cases the peripheral and the central peptides perform related functions. For example, outside the nervous system the hormone angiotensin acts directly on the kidneys and blood vessels to produce effects that help the body cope with the loss of fluid, and inside the nervous system circuits of neurons that use angiotensin as a neurotransmitter perform

---

strychnine (*strik* neen) A direct antagonist for the glycine receptor.

endogenous opioid (en *dodge* en us *oh* pee oyd) A class of peptides secreted by the brain that act as opiates.

enkephalin (en *keff* a lin) One of the endogenous opioids.

naloxone (na *lox* own) A drug that blocks opiate receptors.

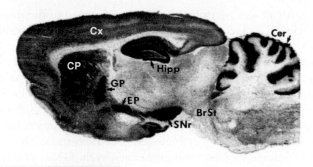

figure 4.22

An autoradiogram of a sagittal section of a rat brain that has been incubated in a solution containing a radioactive ligand for THC receptors. The receptors are indicated by dark areas. (Autoradiography is described in Chapter 5.) (Br St = brain stem, Cer = cerebellum, CP = caudate nucleus/putamen, Cx = cortex, EP = entopeduncular nucleus, GP = globus pallidus, Hipp = hippocampus, SNr = substantia nigra.)

(Courtesy of Miles Herkenham, National Institute of Mental Health, Bethesda, MD.)

similar functions, including the activation of neural circuits that produce thirst.

Many peptides produced in the brain have interesting behavioral effects, which will be discussed in subsequent chapters.

Lipids

Various substances derived from lipids can serve to transmit messages within or between cells. At least two of them appear to be **cannabinoids**—natural ligands for the receptors that are responsible for the physiological effects of the active ingredient in marijuana. Matsuda et al. (1990) discovered that THC (tetrahydrocannibinal, the active ingredient of marijuana) stimulates cannabinoid receptors located in specific regions of the brain. (See *Figure 4.22.*) Two types of cannabinoid receptors, CB_1 and CB_2, both metabotropic, have since been discovered. These receptors may affect both calcium and potassium channels (Mechoulam et al., 1998).

THC produces analgesia and sedation, stimulates appetite, reduces nausea caused by drugs used to treat cancer, relieves asthma attacks, decreases pressure within the eyes in patients with glaucoma, and reduces the symptoms of certain motor disorders. On the other hand, THC interferes with concentration and memory, alters visual and auditory perception, and distorts perceptions of the passage of time (Kunos and Batkai, 2001). Devane et al. (1992) discovered the first natural ligand for the THC receptor: a lipidlike substance that they named **anandamide,** from the Sanskrit word *ananda,* or "bliss." Anandamide seems to be synthesized on demand; that is, it is produced and released as it is needed and is not stored in synaptic vesicles. A few years after the discovery of anandamide, Mechoulam et al. (1995) discovered another natural ligand, 2-arachidonyl glycerol (2-AG).

Another of the effects of anandamide is interference with the functioning of 5-HT_3 receptors. As we saw earlier, these receptors are involved in vomiting; thus, THC serves as an antiemetic (antivomiting) drug. Fride and Mechoulam (1996) discovered that the behavioral effects of THC were not seen in young mice, which suggested that the immature brain lacked at least some of the neural mechanisms responsible for these effects. On the basis of this observation, they tried using THC to control the nausea and vomiting caused by chemotherapy for cancer in young children (Abrahamov et al., 1995). The drug successfully blocked the side effects of the chemotherapy without producing the psychotropic effects that THC produces in adults. In fact, the investigators were able to administer very high doses of THC that adults would not have been able to tolerate.

Recent research indicates that the endogenous cannabinoids modulate the synaptic changes that appear to be responsible for learning, which accounts for the effects of THC on memory (Baranaga, 2001). Cannabinoids also appear to play an essential role in the reinforcing effects of opiates: A targeted mutation that prevents the production of CB_1 receptors abolishes the reinforcing effects of morphine, but not of cocaine, amphetamine, or nicotine (Cossu et al., 2001). These effects of cannabinoids are discussed further in Chapter 18.

Nucleosides

A nucleoside is a compound that consists of a sugar molecule bound with a purine or pyrimidine base. One of these compounds, **adenosine** (a combination of ribose and adenine), serves as a neuromodulator in the brain.

Adenosine is known to be released, apparently by glial cells as well as neurons, when cells are short of fuel or oxygen. The release of adenosine activates receptors on nearby blood vessels and causes them to dilate, increasing the flow of blood and helping bring more of the needed substances to the region. Adenosine also acts as a neuromodulator, through its action on at least three different types of adenosine receptors. Adenosine receptors are coupled to G proteins, and their effect is to open potassium channels, producing inhibitory postsynaptic potentials. Because adenosine is present in all cells, investigators have not yet succeeded in distinguishing neurons that release this chemical as a neuromodulator. Thus, circuits of adenosinergic neurons have not yet been identified.

Because adenosine receptors suppress neural activity, adenosine and other adenosine receptor agonists have generally inhibitory effects on behavior. In fact, as we will

---

cannabinoid (*can ob in oid*) A lipid; an endogenous ligand for receptors that bind with THC, the active ingredient of marijuana.

anandamide (*a nan da mide*) The first cannabinoid to be discovered and probably the most important one.

adenosine (*a den oh seen*) A nucleoside; a combination of ribose and adenine; serves as a neuromodulator in the brain.

table 4.3	
Typical Caffeine Content of Chocolate and Several Beverages	
ITEM	**CAFFEINE CONTENT**
Chocolates	Baking chocolage, 35mg/oz
	Milk chocolate, 6mg/oz
Beverages	Coffee, 85 mg/5-oz cup
	Decaffeinated coffee, 3mg/5-oz cup
	Tea (brewed 3 minutes), 28 mg/5-oz cup
	Cocoa or hot chocolate, 30 mg/5-oz cup
	Cola drink, 30–46 mg/12-oz container

Source: Based on data from Somani and Gupta, 1988.

see in Chapter 9, some investigators believe that adenosine receptors may be involved in the control of sleep. A very common drug, **caffeine,** blocks adenosine receptors (step 7 of Figure 4.5) and hence produces excitatory effects. Caffeine is a bitter-tasting alkaloid found in coffee, tea, cocoa beans, and other plants. In much of the world a majority of the adult population ingests caffeine every day—fortunately, without apparent harm. (See *Table 4.3.*)

Prolonged use of caffeine leads to a moderate amount of tolerance, and people who suddenly stop taking caffeine complain of withdrawal symptoms, which include headaches, drowsiness, and difficulty in concentrating. If the person continues to abstain, the symptoms disappear within a few days. Caffeine does not produce the compulsive drug-taking behavior that is often seen in people who abuse amphetamine, cocaine, or the opiates. In addition, laboratory animals do not readily self-administer caffeine, as they do drugs that are commonly abused by humans.

Soluble Gases

Recently, investigators have discovered that neurons use at least two simple, soluble gases—nitric oxide and carbon monoxide—to communicate with one another. One of these, **nitric oxide (NO),** has received the most attention. Nitric oxide (not to be confused with nitrous oxide, or laughing gas) is a soluble gas that is produced by the activity of an enzyme found in certain neurons. Researchers have found that NO is used as a messenger in many parts of the body; for example, it is involved in the control of the muscles in the wall of the intestines, it dilates blood vessels in regions of the brain that become metabolically active, and it stimulates the changes in blood vessels that produce penile erections (Culotta and Koshland, 1992). As we will see in Chapter 13, it may also play a role in the establishment of neural changes that are produced by learning. And as we will see in Chapter 8, nitric oxide has also been implicated in the brain degeneration that accompanies Huntington's chorea, a hereditary disorder.

All of the neurotransmitters and neuromodulators discussed so far (with the exception of anandamide and perhaps adenosine) are stored in synaptic vesicles and released by terminal buttons. Nitric oxide is produced in several regions of a nerve cell—including dendrites—and is released as soon as it is produced. More accurately, it diffuses out of the cell as soon as it is produced. It does not activate membrane-bound receptors but enters neighboring cells, where it activates an enzyme responsible for the production of a second messenger, cyclic GMP. Within a few seconds of being produced, nitric oxide is converted into biologically inactive compounds.

Nitric oxide is produced from arginine, an amino acid, by the activation of an enzyme known as **nitric oxide synthase.** This enzyme can be inactivated (step 2 of Figure 4.5) by a drug called L-NAME (nitro-L-arginine methyl ester).

interim summary

Neurotransmitters and Neuromodulators

The nervous system contains a variety of neurotransmitters, each of which interacts with a specialized receptor. Those that have received the most study are acetylcholine and the monoamines: dopamine, norepinephrine, and 5-hydroxytryptamine (serotonin). The synthesis of these neurotransmitters is controlled by a series of enzymes. Several amino acids also serve as neurotransmitters, the most important of which are glutamate (glutamic acid), GABA, and glycine. Glutamate serves as an excitatory neurotransmitter; the others serve as inhibitory neurotransmitters.

Peptide neurotransmitters consist of chains of amino acids. Like proteins, peptides are synthesized at the ribosomes according to sequences coded for by the chromosomes. The best-known class of peptides in the nervous system includes the endogenous opioids, whose effects are mimicked by drugs such as opium and heroin. One lipid appears to serve as a chemical messenger: anandamide, the endogenous ligand for the THC (marijuana) receptor. Adenosine, a nucleoside that has inhibitory effects on synaptic transmission, is released by neurons and glial cells in the brain. In addition, two soluble gases—nitric oxide and carbon monoxide—can diffuse out of the cell in which they are produced and trigger the production of a second messenger in adjacent cells.

This chapter has mentioned many drugs and their effects. They are summarized for your convenience in *Table 4.4.*

caffeine A drug that blocks adenosine receptors.

nitric oxide (NO) A gas produced by cells in the nervous system; used as a means of communication between cells.

nitric oxide synthase The enzyme responsible for the production of nitric oxide.

table **4.4**

Drugs Mentioned in this Chapter

NEUROTRANSMITTER	NAME OF DRUG	EFFECT OF DRUG	EFFECT ON SYNAPTIC TRANSMISSION
Acetylcholine (ACh)	Botulinum toxin	Block release of ACh	Antagonist
	Black widow spider venom	Stimulate release of ACh	Agonist
	Nicotine	Stimulate nicotinic receptors	Agonist
	Curare	Block nicotinic receptors	Antagonist
	Muscarine	Stimulate muscarinic receptors	Agonist
	Atropine	Block muscarinic receptors	Antagonist
	Neostigmine	Inhibit acetylcholinesterase	Agonist
	Hemicholinium	Inhibit reuptake of choline	Antagonist
Dopamine (DA)	L-DOPA	Facilitate synthesis of DA	Agonist
	AMPT	Inhibit synthesis of DA	Antagonist
	Reserpine	Inhibit storage of DA in synaptic vesicles	Antagonist
	Cholorpromazine	Block D_2 receptors	Antagonist
	Chozapine	Block D_4 receptors	Antagonist
	Cocaine, methylphenidate	Block DA reuptake	Agonist
	Amphetamine	Stimulate release of DA	Agonist
	Deprenyl	Block MAO-B	Agonist
Norepinephrine (NE)	Fusaric acid	Inhibit synthesis of NE	Antagonist
	Reserpine	Inhibit storage of NE in synaptic vesicles	Antagonist
	Clonidine	Stimulate α_2 receptors	Antagonist
	Desipramine	Inhibit reuptake of NE	Agonist
	Moclobemide	Inhibit MAO-A	Agonist
	MDMA, amphetamine	Stimulate release of NE	Agonist
Serotonin (5-HT)	PCPA	Inhibit synthesis of 5-HT	Antagonist
	Reserpine	Inhibit storage of 5-HT in synaptic vesicles	Antagonist
	Fenfluramine	Stimulate release of 5-HT	Agonist
	Fluoxetine	Inhibit reuptake of 5-HT	Agonist
	LSD	Stimulate $5\text{-}HT_{2A}$ receptors	Agonist
	MDMA	Stimulate release of 5-HT	Agonist
Glutamate	AMPA	Stimulate AMPA receptor	Agonist
	Kainic acid	Stimulate kainate receptor	Agonist
	NMDA	Stimulate NMDA receptor	Agonist
	AP5	Block NMDA receptor	Antagonist
GABA	Allylglycine	Inhibit syntheses of GABA	Antagonist
	Muscimol	Stimulate GABA receptors	Agonist
	Bicuculline	Block GABA receptors	Antagonist
	Benzodiazepines	Serve as indirect GABA agonist	Agonist
Glycine	Strychnine	Block glycine receptors	Antagonist
Opioids	Opiates (morphine, heroin, etc.)	Stimulate opiate receptors	Agonist
	Naloxone	Block opiate receptors	Antagonist
Adenosine	Caffeine	Block adenosine receptors	Antagonist
Nitric oxide (NO)	L-Name	Inhibit synthesis of NO	Antagonist

Suggested Readings

Cooper, J. R., Bloom, F. E., and Roth, R. H. *The Biochemical Basis of Neuropharmacology,* 7th ed. New York: Oxford University Press, 1996.

Feldman, R. S., Meyer, J. S., and Quenzer, L. F. *Principles of Neuropsychopharmacology.* Sunderland, MA: Sinauer Associates, 1997.

Grilly, D. M. *Drugs and Human Behavior,* 4th ed. Boston: Allyn and Bacon, 2002.

Suggested Web Sites

Animations: How Drugs Work

http://www.pbs.org/wnet/closetohome/science/html/animations.html

This site provides a series of color animations that illustrate the action of drugs such as alcohol, opiates, and cocaine on synaptic function.

Internet Mental Health

www.mentalhealth.com

This site is a general resource that provides links to sites dealing with common mental disorders and the drugs that are used to treat mental disorders.

Drugs That Alter Anxiety

http://salmon.psy.plym.ac.uk/year2/anxiety.htm

This site provides student access to a comprehensive set of materials relating to the study of anxiety and the drugs that are used to treat anxiety.

The Search for Novel Antipsychotic Drugs

http://salmon.psy.plym.ac.uk/year2/schizo1.htm

This site provides student access to a comprehensive set of materials relating to the pharmacology of schizophrenia.

Pharmacology Information Network

http://pharminfo.com/

This site is a general resource site providing access to a database on common drugs.

Psychopharmacology Resources

http://www.psychwatch.com/psychopharm_page.htm

Links to sites dealing with the topic of psychopharmacology are provided by this site.

Classroom Psychopharmacology

http://www.unl.edu/tcweb/pharm/cpp.start.html

This site focuses on the topic of drugs that are used to treat children for problems within the classroom. The site provides an overview of synaptic function, of conditions that are treated by drugs, and of the drugs that are most commonly used for children.

Methods and Strategies of Research

Bridget Riley, *Nataraha*, 1993. © Bridget Riley. © Tate Gallery, London/Art Resource, NY.

o u t l i n e

■ **Experimental Ablation**
Evaluating the Behavioral Effects
    of Brain Damage
Producing Brain Lesions
Stereotaxic Surgery
Histological Methods
Tracing Neural Connections
Study of the Living
    Human Brain
Interim Summary

■ **Recording and Stimulating
Neural Activity**
Recording of Neural Activity
Recording the Brain's Metabolic
    and Synaptic Activity
Measuring the Brain's Secretions
Stimulating Neural Activity
Behavioral Effects of Electrical
    Brain Stimulation
Interim Summary

■ **Neurochemical Methods**
Finding Neurons That Produce
    Particular Neurochemicals
Localizing Particular Receptors
Interim Summary
■ **Genetic Methods**
Twin Studies
Adoption Studies
Targeted Mutations
Interim Summary

As we saw in Chapter 4, about twenty years ago, several young people injected themselves with an illicit drug that was contaminated with MPTP, a chemical that destroyed the dopaminergic neurons in their nigrostriatal system. As a result, they suffered from severe parkinsonism. Fetal transplantation, an experimental neurosurgical method of treating parkinsonism has shown some promise. The rationale for the procedure is this: The symptoms of parkinsonism, whether from Parkinson's disease or the toxic effects of MPTP, are caused by the lack of dopamine in the basal ganglia—specifically, in the caudate nucleus and putamen. There is at present no way to induce the brain to regrow the dopaminergic neurons of the nigrostriatal system. However, if dopamine-secreting neurons can be introduced into the caudate nucleus and putamen, and if they survive and secrete dopamine, then perhaps the parkinsonian symptoms will diminish. Because the implanted neurons must be healthy and vigorous and not trigger the recipient's immune system, the logical source for them is aborted human fetuses—or, perhaps some day, cultures of stem cells that have been induced to become dopamine-secreting neurons.

At least one of the people with MPTP poisoning received such a transplant. (Let's call him Mr. B.) Before the operation took place, Mr. B. was given an injection of radioactive L-DOPA, the precursor for dopamine. Then,

one hour later, he was wheeled into a small room that housed a PET scanner. His head was positioned in the scanner, and for the next several minutes the machine gathered data from positrons that were being emitted as the radioactive particles in his head broke down.

A few weeks later, Mr. B. entered the hospital for his surgery. Technicians removed dopaminergic neurons from the substantia nigra of several aborted fetuses and prepared them for implantation into Mr. B.'s brain. Mr. B. was anesthetized, and the surgeon made cuts in his scalp to expose parts of his skull. He attached the frame of a stereotaxic apparatus to his skull, made some measurements, and then drilled several holes. He used the stereotaxic apparatus to guide the injections of the fetal neurons into Mr. B.'s caudate nucleus and putamen. Once the injections were complete, the surgeon removed the stereotaxic frame and sutured the incisions he had made in the scalp.

The operation was quite successful; Mr. B. recovered much of his motor control. A little more than a year later, he was again given an injection of radioactive L-DOPA, and again his head was placed in the PET scanner. The results of the second scan showed what his recovery implied: The cells had survived and were secreting dopamine.

S tudy of the physiology of behavior involves the efforts of scientists in many disciplines, including physiology, neuroanatomy, biochemistry, psychology, endocrinology, and histology. Pursuing a research project in behavioral neuroscience requires competence in many experimental techniques. Because different procedures often produce contradictory results, investigators must be familiar with the advantages and limitations of the methods they employ. Scientific investigation entails a process of asking questions of nature. The method that is used frames the question. Often we receive a puzzling answer, only to realize later that we were not asking the question we thought we were. As we will see, the best conclusions about the physiology of behavior are made not by any single experiment, but by a program of research that enables us to compare the results of studies that approach the problem with different methods.

An enormous—and bewildering—array of research methods is available to the investigator. If I merely presented a catalog of them, it would not be surprising if you got lost—or simply lost interest. Instead, I will present only the most important and commonly used procedures, organized around a few problems that researchers have studied. This way, it should be easier to see the types of information provided by various research methods and to

understand their advantages and disadvantages. It will also permit me to describe the strategies that researchers employ as they follow up the results of one experiment by designing and executing another one.

Experimental Ablation

One of the most important research methods used to investigate brain functions involves destroying part of the brain and evaluating the animal's subsequent behavior. This method is called **experimental ablation** (from the Latin word *ablatus,* a "carrying away"). In most cases experimental ablation does not involve the removal brain tissue; instead, the researcher destroys some tissue and leaves it in place. Experimental ablation is the oldest method used in neuroscience, and it remains one of the most important ones today.

---

experimental ablation The removal or destruction of a portion of the brain of a laboratory animal; presumably, the functions that can no longer be performed are the ones the region previously controlled.

Evaluating the Behavioral Effects of Brain Damage

A *lesion* is a wound or injury, and a researcher who destroys part of the brain usually refers to the damage as a *brain lesion.* Experiments in which part of the brain is damaged and the animal's behavior is subsequently observed are called **lesion studies.** The rationale for lesion studies is that the function of an area of the brain can be inferred from the behaviors that the animal can no longer perform after the area is damaged. For example, if, after part of the brain is destroyed, an animal can no longer perform tasks that require vision, we can conclude that the animal is blind—and that the damaged area plays some role in vision.

We must be very careful in interpreting the effects of brain lesions. For example, how do we ascertain that the lesioned animal is blind? Does it bump into objects, or fail to run through a maze toward a light that signals the location of food, or no longer constrict its pupils to light? An animal could bump into objects because of deficits in motor coordination, it could have lost its appetite for food (and thus its motivation to run through the maze), or it could see quite well but could have lost its visual reflexes. Researchers can often be fooled. Years ago they thought that the albino rat was blind. (It isn't.) Think about it: How would you test whether a rat can see? Remember that rats have vibrissae (whiskers) that can be used to detect a wall before bumping into it or the edge of a table before walking off it. They can also find their way around a room by following odor trails.

Just what can we learn from lesion studies? Our goal is to discover what functions are performed by different regions of the brain and then to understand how these functions are combined to accomplish particular behaviors. The distinction between *brain function* and *behavior* is an important one. Circuits within the brain perform functions, not behaviors. No one brain region or neural circuit is solely responsible for a behavior; each region performs a function (or set of functions) that contributes to performance of the behavior. For example, the act of reading involves functions required for controlling eye movements, focusing the lens of the eye, perceiving and recognizing words and letters, comprehending the meaning of the words, and so on. Some of these functions also participate in other behaviors; for example, controlling eye movement and focusing are required for any task that involves looking, and brain mechanisms used for comprehending the meanings of words also participate in comprehending speech. The researcher's task is to understand the functions that are required for performing a particular behavior and to determine what circuits of neurons in the brain are responsible for each of these functions.

Let me give an example of how researchers try to deduce the nature of the functions performed by various parts of the brain. Neural circuits located in the cortex covering the parietal lobe perform functions involved in spatial perception and memory. Damage there disrupts people's ability to follow or draw maps, to remember the locations of objects that they have just seen, and so on. In addition, people with parietal lobe damage often have difficulty performing arithmetic calculations. At first glance there would not seem to be a relation between this deficit and the spatial functions of the parietal lobe, but in fact they are almost certainly related. To prove this to yourself, try to multiply 55 by 12 without using pencil and paper. Close your eyes and work on the problem for a while. Try to analyze how you did it.

Most people report that they try to imagine the numbers arranged one above the other as they would be if paper and pencil were being used. In other words, they "write" the problem out mentally. Apparently, damage to the parietal lobes makes it difficult for people to put each of the numbers in a particular location in an imaginary "space" and remember what they were.

The interpretation of lesion studies is complicated by the fact that all regions of the brain are interconnected. Suppose that we have a good understanding of the functions required for performance of a particular behavior. We find that damage to brain structure X impairs a particular behavior. Can we necessarily conclude that a function essential to this behavior is performed by circuits of neurons located in structure X? Unfortunately, we cannot. The functions we are interested in may actually be performed by neural circuits located elsewhere in the brain. Damage to structure X may simply interfere with the normal operation of the neural circuits in structure Y.

Let me cite a particular example that illustrates this complication. Damage to one part of the brain (the septum) completely disrupts the maternal behavior of a female rodent. The animal does not build a nest for her offspring, and she does not gather them together all in one place and nurse them. The result is that the pups end up scattered all over the cage, where they eventually starve unless the experimenter rescues them by giving them to a foster mother. What function does the septum perform that is so vital to normal maternal behavior? It happens that a connection between the septum and the hippocampal formation controls the activity of the latter structure—it turns some of the functions of the hippocampus on or off. Among these functions are some that are required for animals to perceive their location in space. When the septum is damaged, these functions are permanently turned off. Thus, the absence of nest building and pup gathering is almost certainly caused by disruption of the mother's spatial perception. The septum

lesion study A synonym for experimental ablation.

itself is not directly involved in spatial perception, but through its control of neural circuits located in the hippocampus, its damage disrupts maternal behavior.

Producing Brain Lesions

How do we produce brain lesions? It is easy to destroy parts of the brain immediately beneath the skull; we anesthetize the animal, cut its scalp, remove part of its skull, and cut through the dura mater, bringing the cortex into view. Then we can use a suction device to aspirate the brain tissue. To accomplish this tissue removal, we place a glass pipette on the surface of the brain and suck away brain tissue with a vacuum pump attached to the pipette.

More often, we want to destroy regions that are hidden away in the depths of the brain. Brain lesions of subcortical regions (regions located beneath the cortex) are usually produced by passing electrical current through a stainless steel wire that is coated with an insulating varnish except for the very tip. We guide the wire stereotaxically so that its end reaches the appropriate location. (Stereotaxic surgery is described in the next subsection.) Then we turn on a lesion-making device, which produces radio frequency (RF) current—alternating current of a very high frequency. The passage of the current through the brain tissue produces heat that kills cells in the region surrounding the tip of the electrode. (See *Figure 5.1.*)

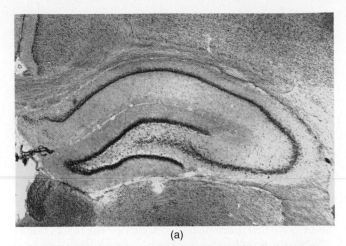

(a)

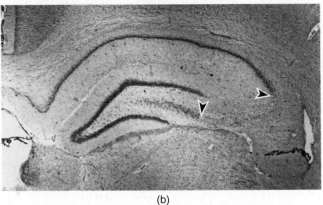

(b)

figure 5.2

Excitotoxic lesion. (a) Section through a normal hippocampus of a rat brain. (b) A lesion produced by infusion of an excitatory amino acid in a region of the hippocampus. Arrowheads mark the ends of the region in which neurons have been destroyed.

(Courtesy of Benno Roozendaal, University of California, Irvine.)

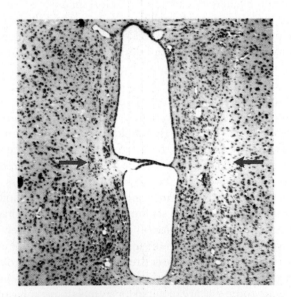

figure 5.1

Radio frequency lesion. The arrows point to very small lesions produced by passing radio frequency current through the tips of stainless steel electrodes placed in the medial preoptic nucleus of a rat brain. The oblong hole in the middle of the photograph is the third ventricle. (Frontal section, cell-body stain.)

(From Turkenburg, J. L., Swaab, D. F., Endert, E., Louwerse, A. L., and van de Poll, N. E. *Brain Research Bulletin,* 1988, *21,* 215–224.)

Lesions produced by these means destroy everything in the vicinity of the electrode tip, including neural cell bodies and the axons of neurons that pass through the region. A more selective method of producing brain lesions employs an excitatory amino acid such as *kainic acid,* which kills neurons by stimulating them to death. (As we saw in Chapter 4, kainic acid stimulates glutamate receptors.) Lesions produced this way are referred to as **excitotoxic lesions.** When an excitatory amino acid is injected through a cannula into a region of the brain, the chemical destroys neural cell bodies in the vicinity but spares axons that belong to different neurons that happen to pass nearby. (See *Figure 5.2.*) This selectivity permits

excitotoxic lesion (*ek sigh tow **tok** sik*) A brain lesion produced by intracerebral injection of an excitatory amino acid, such as kainic acid.

the investigator to determine whether the behavioral effects of destroying a particular brain structure are caused by the death of neurons located there or by the destruction of axons that pass nearby. For example, some researchers discovered that RF lesions of a particular region in the brain stem abolished REM sleep; therefore, they believed that this region was involved in the production of this stage of sleep. (REM sleep is the stage of sleep during which dreaming occurs.) But later studies showed that when kainic acid was used to destroy the neurons located there, the animals' sleep was *not* affected. Therefore, the RF lesions must have altered sleep by destroying the axons that pass through the area.

Even more specific methods of lesion production are available. For example, the drug **6-hydroxydopamine** (6-HD) resembles the catecholamines norepinephrine and dopamine. Because of this resemblance, 6-HD is taken up by transporter molecules in axons and terminal buttons of dopaminergic and noradrenergic neurons. Once inside, the chemical poisons and kills the neurons. Thus, 6-HD can be injected directly into particular regions of the brain to kill specific populations of dopaminergic and noradrenergic neurons.

Note that when we produce subcortical lesions by passing RF current through an electrode or infusing a chemical through a cannula, we always cause additional damage to the brain. When we pass an electrode or a cannula through the brain to get to our target, we inevitably cause a small amount of damage even before turning on the lesion maker or starting the infusion. Thus, we cannot simply compare the behavior of brain-lesioned animals with that of unoperated control animals; the incidental damage to the brain regions above the lesion may actually be responsible for some of the behavioral deficits we see. What we do is operate on a group of animals and produce **sham lesions.** To do so, we anesthetize each animal, put it in the stereotaxic apparatus (described below), cut open the scalp, drill the holes, insert the electrode or cannula, and lower it to the proper depth. In other words, we do everything we would do to produce the lesion except turn on the lesion maker or start the infusion. This group of animals serves as a control group; if the behavior of the animals with brain lesions is different from that of the sham-operated control animals, we can conclude that the lesions caused the behavioral deficits. (As you can see, a sham lesion serves the same purpose as a placebo does in a pharmacology study.)

Most of the time, investigators produce permanent brain lesions, but sometimes it is advantageous to disrupt the activity of a particular region of the brain temporarily. The easiest way to do so is to inject a local anesthetic or a drug called *muscimol* into the appropriate part of the brain. The anesthetic blocks action potentials in axons entering or leaving that region, thus effectively producing a temporary lesion (usually called a *reversible* brain lesion). Muscimol, a drug that stimulates GABA receptors, inactivates a

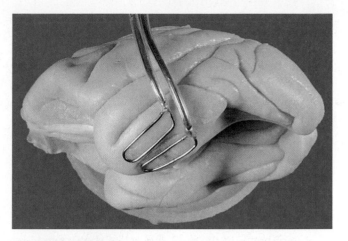

f i g u r e 5 . 3

A cryoloop, a device that produces temporary lesions of the cerebral cortex. The device is surgically implanted between the skull and the brain, and the temporary lesion can be produced while the animal is awake and alert. A chilled liquid is circulated through the stainless steel tubes. The cryoloop shown in the photograph was placed against a region of the visual association cortex of the left hemisphere of a monkey brain.
(Courtesy of James Horel, SUNY Upstate Medical Center.)

region of the brain by inhibiting the neurons located there. (You will recall that GABA is the most important inhibitory neurotransmitter in the brain.) Reversible lesions can also be produced by cooling brain tissue enough to suppress neural activity. Figure 5.3 shows a device called a *cryoloop*, which can be used to produce temporary lesions of a region of the cerebral cortex of the monkey brain. The device consists of a series of stainless steel tubes through which a chilled liquid can be circulated. It is implanted between the skull and the surface of the brain. (See ***Figure 5.3***.)

Stereotaxic Surgery

So how do we get the tip of an electrode or cannula to a precise location in the depths of an animal's brain? The answer is **stereotaxic surgery.** *Stereotaxis* literally means "solid arrangement"; more specifically, it refers to

6-hydroxydopamine (6-HD) A chemical that is selectively taken up by axons and terminal buttons of noradrenergic or dopaminergic neurons and acts as a poison, damaging or killing them.

sham lesion A "placebo" procedure that duplicates all the steps of producing a brain lesion except for the one that actually causes the brain damage.

stereotaxic surgery (*stair ee oh **tak** sik*) Brain surgery using a stereotaxic apparatus to position an electrode or cannula in a specified position of the brain.

the ability to locate objects in space. A *stereotaxic apparatus* contains a holder that fixes the animal's head in a standard position and a carrier that moves an electrode or a cannula through measured distances in all three axes of space. However, to perform stereotaxic surgery, one must first study a *stereotaxic atlas.*

The Stereotaxic Atlas

No two brains of animals of a given species are completely identical, but there is enough similarity among individuals to predict the location of particular brain structures relative to external features of the head. For instance, a subcortical nucleus of a rat might be so many millimeters ventral, anterior, and lateral to a point formed by the junction of several bones of the skull. Figure 5.4 shows two views of a rat skull: a drawing of the dorsal surface and, beneath it, a midsagittal view. (See *Figure 5.4.*) The skull is composed of several bones that grow together and form *sutures* (seams). The heads of newborn babies contain a soft spot at the junction of the coronal and sagittal sutures called the *fontanelle.* Once this gap closes, the junction is called **bregma,** from the Greek word meaning "front of head." We can find bregma on a rat's skull, too, and it serves as a convenient reference point. If the animal's skull is oriented as shown in the illustration, a particular region of the brain is found in a fairly constant position, relative to bregma.

A **stereotaxic atlas** contains photographs or drawings that correspond to frontal sections taken at various

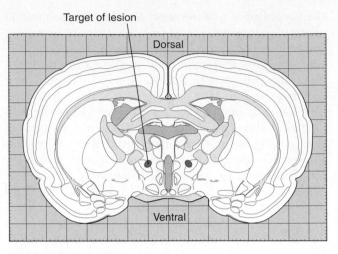

figure 5.5

A sample page from a stereotaxic atlas of the rat brain. The target (the fornix) is indicated in red. Labels have been removed for the sake of clarity.

(Adapted from Swanson, L. W. *Brain Maps: Structure of the Rat Brain.* New York: Elsevier, 1992.)

distances rostral and caudal to bregma. For example, the page shown in Figure 5.5 is a drawing of a slice of the brain that contains a brain structure (shown in red) that we are interested in. If we wanted to place the tip of a wire in this structure (the fornix), we would have to drill a hole through the skull immediately above it. (See *Figure 5.5.*) Each page of the stereotaxic atlas is labeled according to the distance of the section anterior or posterior to bregma. The grid on each page indicates distances of brain structures ventral to the top of the skull and lateral to the midline. To place the tip of a wire in the fornix, we would drill a hole above the target and then lower the electrode through the hole until the tip was at the correct depth, relative to the skull height at bregma. (See *Figures 5.4 and 5.5.*) Thus, by finding a neural structure (which we cannot see in our animal) on one of the pages of a stereotaxic atlas, we can determine the structure's location relative to bregma (which we can see). Note that, because of variations in different strains and ages of animals, the atlas gives only an approximate location. We always have to try out a new set of coordinates, slice and stain the animal's brain, see the actual location of the lesion, correct the numbers, and try again. (Slicing and staining of brains are described later.)

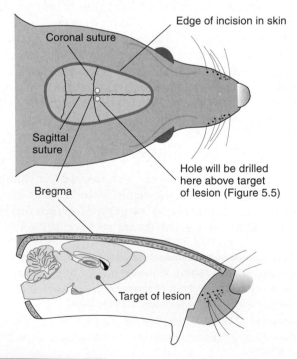

figure 5.4

Relation of the skull sutures to a rat's brain, and the location of a target for an electrode placement. *Top:* Dorsal view. *Bottom:* Midsagittal view.

bregma The junction of the sagittal and coronal sutures of the skull; often used as a reference point for stereotaxic brain surgery.

stereotaxic atlas A collection of drawings of sections of the brain of a particular animal with measurements that provide coordinates for stereotaxic surgery.

The Stereotaxic Apparatus

A **stereotaxic apparatus** operates on simple principles. The device includes a head holder, which maintains the animal's skull in the proper orientation, a holder for the electrode, and a calibrated mechanism that moves the electrode holder in measured distances along the three axes: anterior–posterior, dorsal–ventral, and lateral–medial. Figure 5.6 illustrates a stereotaxic apparatus designed for small animals; various head holders can be used to outfit this device for such diverse species as rats, mice, hamsters, pigeons, and turtles. (See *Figure 5.6.*)

Once we obtain the coordinates from a stereotaxic atlas, we anesthetize the animal, place it in the apparatus, and cut the scalp open. We locate bregma, dial in the appropriate numbers on the stereotaxic apparatus, drill a hole through the skull, and lower the device into the brain by the correct amount. Now the tip of the cannula or electrode is where we want it to be, and we are ready to produce the lesion.

Of course, stereotaxic surgery may be used for purposes other than lesion production. Wires placed in the brain may be used to stimulate neurons as well as destroy them, and drugs can be injected that stimulate neurons or block specific receptors. We can attach cannulas or wires permanently by following a procedure that will be described later in this chapter. In all cases, once surgery is complete, the wound is sewn together, and the animal is taken out of the stereotaxic apparatus and allowed to recover from the anesthetic.

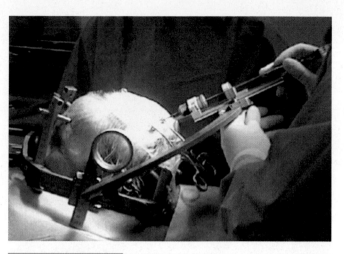

figure 5.7

Stereotaxic surgery being performed on a human patient. (Photograph courtesy of John W. Snell, Department of Neurological Surgery, University of Virginia.)

Stereotaxic apparatuses are made for humans, by the way. Sometimes a neurosurgeon produces subcortical lesions—for example, to reduce the symptoms of Parkinson's disease. Usually, the surgeon uses multiple landmarks and verifies the location of the wire (or other device) inserted into the brain by taking MRI scans before producing a brain lesion. (See *Figure 5.7.*)

Histological Methods

After producing a brain lesion and observing its effects on an animal's behavior, we must slice and stain the brain so that we can observe it under the microscope and see the location of the lesion. Brain lesions often miss the mark, so we have to verify the precise location of the brain damage after testing the animal behaviorally. To do so, we must fix, slice, stain, and examine the brain. Together, these procedures are referred to as *histological methods*. (The prefix *histo-* refers to body tissue.)

Fixation and Sectioning

If we hope to study the tissue in the form it had at the time of the organism's death, we must destroy the autolytic enzymes (*autolytic* means "self-dissolving"), which will otherwise turn the tissue into mush. The tissue must also be preserved to prevent its decomposition by bacteria or molds. To achieve both of these objectives, we place the neural tissue in a **fixative**. The most commonly used

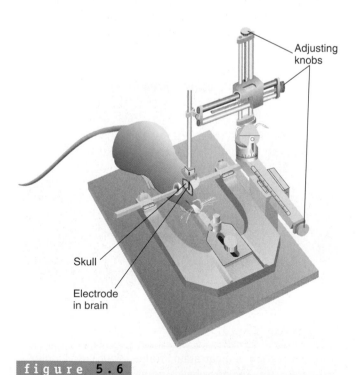

figure 5.6

A stereotaxic apparatus for performing brain surgery on rats.

stereotaxic apparatus A device that permits a surgeon to position an electrode or cannula into a specific part of the brain.

fixative A chemical such as formalin; used to prepare and preserve body tissue.

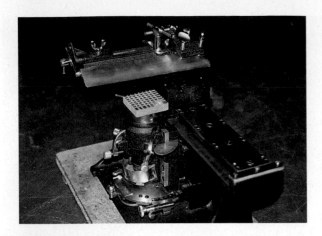

figure   5.8

A microtome.

fixative is **formalin,** an aqueous solution of formalde-hyde, a gas. Formalin halts autolysis, hardens the very soft and fragile brain, and kills any microorganisms that might destroy it.

Before the brain is fixed (that is, put into a fixative solution), it is usually perfused. **Perfusion** of tissue (literally, "a pouring through") entails removal of the blood and its replacement with another fluid. The animal's brain is perfused because better histological results are obtained when no blood is present in the tissue. The animal whose brain is to be studied is humanely killed with an overdose of a general anesthetic. Blood vessels are opened so that the blood can be drained from them and replaced with a dilute salt solution. The brain is removed from the skull and placed in a jar containing the fixative.

Once the brain has been fixed, we must slice it into thin sections and stain various cellular structures in order to see anatomical details. Slicing is done with a **microtome** (literally, "that which slices small"). Slices prepared for examination under a light microscope are typically 10 to 80 µm in thickness; those prepared for the electron microscope are generally cut at less than 1 µm. (For some reason, slices of brain tissue are usually referred to as *sections*.)

A microtome contains three parts: a knife, a platform on which to mount the tissue, and a mechanism that advances the knife (or the platform) the correct amount after each slice so that another section can be cut. In most cases the platform includes an attachment that freezes the brain to make it hard enough to be cut into thin sections. Figure 5.8 shows a microtome. The knife holder slides forward on an oiled rail and takes a section off the top of the tissue mounted on the platform. The platform automatically rises by a predetermined amount as the knife and holder are pushed back so that the next forward movement of the knife takes off another section. (See *Figure 5.8.*)

After the tissue is cut, we attach the slices to glass microscope slides. We can then stain the tissue by putting the entire slide into various chemical solutions. Finally, we cover the stained sections with a small amount of a transparent liquid known as a *mounting medium* and place a very thin glass coverslip over the sections. The mounting medium keeps the coverslip in position.

Staining

If you looked at an unstained section of brain tissue under a microscope, you would be able to see the outlines of some large cellular masses and the more prominent fiber bundles. However, no fine details would be revealed. For this reason the study of microscopic neuroanatomy requires special histological stains. Researchers have developed many different stains to identify specific substances within and outside of cells. For verifying the location of a brain lesion, we will use one of the simplest: a cell-body stain.

In the late nineteenth century Franz Nissl, a German neurologist, discovered that a dye known as methylene blue would stain the cell bodies of brain tissue. The material that takes up the dye, known as the *Nissl substance,* consists of RNA, DNA, and associated proteins located in the nucleus and scattered, in the form of granules, in the cytoplasm. Many dyes besides methylene blue can be used to stain cell bodies found in slices of the brain, but the most frequently used is cresyl violet. Incidentally, the dyes were not developed specifically for histological purposes but were originally formulated for use in dyeing cloth.

The discovery of cell-body stains made it possible to identify nuclear masses in the brain. Figure 5.9 shows a

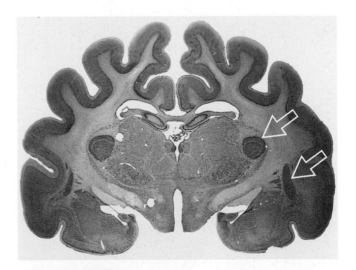

figure   5.9

A frontal section of a cat brain, stained with cresyl violet, a cell-body stain. The arrowheads point to *nuclei,* or groups of cell bodies.

(Histological material courtesy of Mary Carlson.)

frontal section of a cat brain stained with cresyl violet. Note that you can observe fiber bundles by their lighter appearance; they do not take up the stain. (See *Figure 5.9.*) The stain is not selective for *neural* cell bodies; all cells are stained, neurons and glia alike. It is up to the investigator to determine which is which—by size, shape, and location.

Electron Microscopy

The light microscope is limited in its ability to resolve extremely small details. Because of the nature of light itself, magnification of more than approximately 1500 times does not add any detail. To see such small anatomical structures as synaptic vesicles and details of cell organelles, investigators must use an electron microscope. A beam of electrons is passed through the tissue to be examined. A shadow of the tissue is then cast on a sheet of photographic film, which is exposed by the electrons. Electron photomicrographs produced in this way can provide information about structural details on the order of a few tens of nanometers. (See *Figure 5.10.*)

A **scanning electron microscope** provides less magnification than a standard transmission electron microscope, which transmits the electron beam through the tissue. However, it shows objects in three dimensions. The microscope scans the tissue with a moving beam of electrons. The information received from the reflection of the beam is used to produce a remarkably detailed three-dimensional view. (See *Figure 5.11.*)

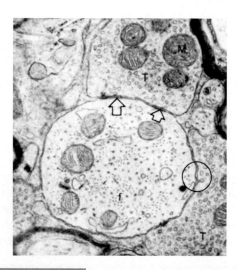

figure 5.10

An electron photomicrograph of a section through an axodendritic synapse. Two synaptic regions are indicated by arrows, and a circle points out a region of pinocytosis in an adjacent terminal button, presumably representing recycling of vesicular membrane. T = terminal button; f = microfilaments; M = mitochondrion.

(From Rockel, A. J., and Jones, E. G. *Journal of Comparative Neurology,* 1973, *147,* 61–92.)

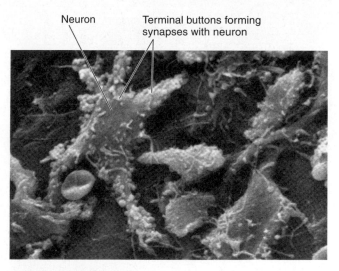

Neuron   Terminal buttons forming synapses with neuron

figure 5.11

A scanning electron micrograph of neurons and glia.

(From Kessel, R. G., and Kardon, R. H. *Tissues and Organs: A Text-Atlas of Scanning Electron Microscopy.* San Francisco: W. H. Freeman, 1979. By permission.)

Tracing Neural Connections

Let's suppose that we were interested in discovering the neural mechanisms responsible for reproductive behavior. To start out, we wanted to study the physiology of sexual behavior of female rats. On the basis of some hints we received by reading reports of experiments by other researchers published in scientific journals, we performed stereotaxic surgery on two groups of female rats. We made a lesion in the ventromedial nucleus of the hypothalamus (VMH) of the rats in the experimental group and performed sham surgery on the rats in the control group. After a few days' recovery we placed the animals (individually, of course) with male rats. The females in the control group responded positively to the males' attention; they engaged in courting behavior followed by copulation. However, the females with the VMH lesions rejected the males' attention and refused to copulate with

formalin (*for ma lin*) The aqueous solution of formaldehyde gas; the most commonly used tissue fixative.

perfusion (*per few zhun*) The process by which an animal's blood is replaced by a fluid such as a saline solution or a fixative in preparing the brain for histological examination.

microtome (*my krow tome*) An instrument that produces very thin slices of body tissues.

scanning electron microscope A microscope that provides three-dimensional information about the shape of the surface of a small object.

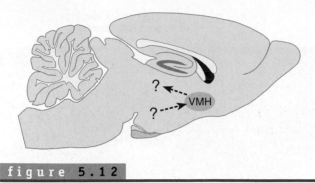

Once we know that a particular brain region is involved in a particular function, we may ask what structures provide inputs to the region and what structures receive outputs from it.

them. We confirmed with histology that the VMH was indeed destroyed in the brains of the experimental animals. (One experimental rat did copulate, but we discovered later that the lesion had missed the VMH in that animal, so we discarded the data from that subject.)

The results of our experiment indicate that neurons in the VMH appear to play a role in functions required for copulatory behavior in females. (By the way, it turns out that these lesions do not affect copulatory behavior in males.) So where do we go from here? What is the next step? In fact, there are many questions that we could pursue. One question concerns the system of brain structures that participate in female copulatory behavior. Certainly, the VMH does not stand alone; it receives inputs from other structures and sends outputs to still others. Copulation requires integration of visual, tactile, and olfactory perceptions and organization of patterns of movements in response to those of the partner. In addition, the entire network requires activation by the appropriate sex hormones. What is the precise role of the VMH in this complicated system?

Before we can hope to answer this question, we must know more about the connections of the VMH with the rest of the brain. What structures send their axons to the VMH, and to what structures does the VMH, in turn, send its axons? Once we know what the connections are, we can investigate the role of these structures and the nature of their interactions. (See *Figure 5.12.*)

How do we investigate the connections of the VMH? The question cannot be answered by means of histological procedures that stain all neurons, such as cell-body stains. If we look closely at a brain that has been prepared by these means, we see only a tangled mass of neurons. But in recent years researchers have developed very precise methods that make specific neurons stand out from all of the others.

Tracing Efferent Axons

Eventually, the VMH must affect behavior. That is, neurons in the VMH must send axons to parts of the brain that contain neurons that are responsible for muscular

movements. The pathway is probably not direct; more likely, neurons in the VMH affect neurons in other structures, which influence those in yet other structures, until, eventually, the appropriate motor neurons are stimulated. To discover this system, we want to be able to identify the paths followed by axons leaving the VMH. In other words, we want to trace the *efferent axons* of this structure.

We will use an **anterograde labeling method** to trace these axons. (*Anterograde* means "moving forward.") Anterograde labeling methods employ chemicals that are taken up by dendrites or cell bodies and are then transported through the axons toward the terminal buttons.

Over the years neuroscientists have developed several different methods for tracing the pathways followed by efferent axons. A recently developed method is replacing earlier ones, so this is what we will use. Cell biologists have discovered that a family of proteins produced by plants bind with specific complex molecules present in cells of the immune system. These proteins, called *lectins,* have also found a use in tracing neural pathways. A particular lectin produced by the kidney bean, **PHA-L** (*phaseolus vulgaris leukoagglutinin,* if you really want to know), is used to identify efferent axons.

To discover the destination of the efferent axons of neurons located within the VMH, we inject a minute quantity of PHA-L into that nucleus. (We use a stereotaxic apparatus to do so, of course.) The molecules of PHA-L are taken up by dendrites and are transported through the soma to the axon, where they travel by means of fast axoplasmic transport to the terminal buttons. Within a few days the cells are filled in their entirety with molecules of PHA-L: dendrites, soma, axons and all their branches, and terminal buttons. Then we kill the animal, slice the brain, and mount the sections on microscope slides. A special *immunocytochemical* method is used to make the molecules of PHA-L visible, and the slides are examined under a microscope. (See *Figure 5.13.*)

Immunocytochemical methods take advantage of the immune reaction. The body's immune system has the ability to produce antibodies in response to antigens. *Antigens* are proteins (or peptides), such as those found on the surface of bacteria or viruses. *Antibodies,* which are also proteins, are produced by white blood cells to destroy invading microorganisms. Antibodies either are secreted by white blood cells or are located on their surface, in the way

anterograde labeling method (*ann ter oh grade*) A histological method that labels the axons and terminal buttons of neurons whose cell bodies are located in a particular region.

PHA-L Phaseolus vulgaris leukoagglutinin; a protein derived from kidney beans and used as an anterograde tracer; taken up by dendrites and cell bodies and carried to the ends of the axons.

immunocytochemical method A histological method that uses radioactive antibodies or antibodies bound with a dye molecule to indicate the presence of particular proteins of peptides.

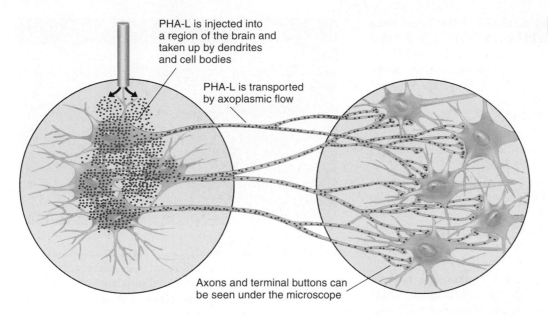

PHA-L is injected into
a region of the brain and
taken up by dendrites
and cell bodies

PHA-L is transported
by axoplasmic flow

Axons and terminal buttons can
be seen under the microscope

figure　5.13

The rationale for the
use of PHA-L to trace
efferent axons.

neurotransmitter receptors are located on the surface of neurons. When the antigens present on the surface of an invading microorganism come into contact with the antibodies that recognize them, the antibodies trigger an attack on the invader by the white blood cells.

Cell biologists have developed methods for producing antibodies to any peptide or protein. The antibody molecules are attached to various types of dye molecules. Some of these dyes react with other chemicals and stain the tissue a brown color. Others are fluorescent; they glow when they are exposed to light of a particular wavelength. To determine where the peptide or protein (the antigen) is

located in the brain, the investigator places fresh slices of brain tissue in a solution that contains the antibody/dye molecules. The antibodies attach themselves to their antigen. When the investigator examines the slices with a microscope (under light of a particular wavelength in the case of fluorescent dyes), he or she can see which parts of the brain—even which individual neurons—contain the antigen.

Figure 5.14 shows how PHA-L can be used to identify the efferents of a particular region of the brain. Molecules of this chemical were injected into the VMH. Two days later, after the PHA-L had been taken up by the neurons in this region and transported to the ends of their

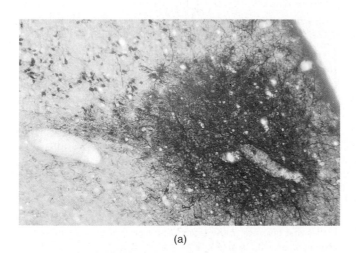

(a)

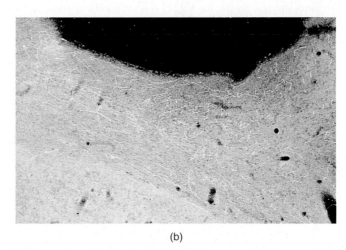

(b)

figure　5.14

An anterograde labeling method. PHA-L was injected into the ventromedial nucleus of the hypothalamus (VMH), where it was taken up by dendrites and carried through the cells' axons to their terminal buttons. (a) The injection site. (b) Labeled axons and terminal buttons in the periaqueductal gray matter (PAG).

(Courtesy of Kirsten Nielsen Ricciardi and Jeffrey Blaustein, University of Massachusetts.)

axons, the animal was killed. Slices of the brain were treated with an antibody to PHA-L, attached to a dye that stains the tissue a reddish brown color. Figure 5.14(a) shows the site of the injection; as you can see, the lectin fills nearby cell bodies and dendrites. (See *Figure 5.14a.*) Figure 5.14(b) shows a photomicrograph of the periaqueductal gray matter (PAG). This region contains some labeled axons and terminal buttons (gold color), which proves that some of the efferent axons of the VMH terminate in the PAG. (See *Figure 5.14b.*)

To continue our study of the role of the VMH in female sexual behavior, we would find the structures that receive information from neurons in the VMH (such as the PAG) and see what happens when each of them is destroyed. Let's suppose that damage to some of these structures also impairs female sexual behavior. We will inject these structures with PHA-L and see where *their* axons go. Eventually, we will discover the relevant pathways from the VMH to the motor neurons whose activity is necessary for copulatory behavior. (In fact, researchers have done so, and some of their results are presented in Chapter 10.)

Tracing Afferent Axons

Tracing efferent axons from the VMH will tell us only part of the story about the neural circuitry involved in female sexual behavior: the part between the VMH and the motor neurons. What about the circuits *before* the VMH? Is the VMH somehow involved in the analysis of sensory information (such as the sight, odor, or touch of the male)? Or perhaps the activating effect of a female's sex hormones on her behavior act through the VMH or through neurons whose axons form synapses there. To discover the parts of the brain that are involved in the "upstream" components of the neural circuitry, we need to find the inputs of the VMH—its afferent connections. To do so, we will employ a **retrograde labeling method.**

Retrograde means "moving backward." Retrograde labeling methods employ chemicals that are taken up by terminal buttons and carried back through the axons toward the cell bodies. The method for identifying the afferent inputs to a particular region of the brain is similar to the method used for identifying its efferents. First, we inject a small quantity of a chemical called **fluorogold** into the VMH. The chemical is taken up by terminal buttons and is transported back by means of retrograde axoplasmic transport to the cell bodies. A few days later we kill the animal, slice its brain, and examine the tissue under light of the appropriate wavelength. The molecules of fluorogold fluoresce under this light. We discover that the medial amygdala is one of the regions that provides input to the VMH. (See *Figure 5.15.*)

The anterograde and retrograde labeling methods that I have described identify a single link in a chain of neurons—neurons whose axons enter or leave a particular brain region. *Transneuronal* tracing methods identify a series of two, three, or more neurons that form serial

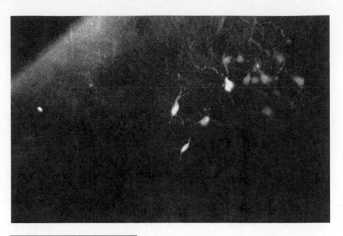

figure 5.15

A retrograde tracing method. Fluorogold was injected in the VMH, where it was taken up by terminal buttons and transported back through the axons to their cell bodies. The photograph shows these cell bodies, located in the medial amygdala.

(Courtesy of Yvon Delville, University of Massachusetts Medical School.)

synaptic connections with each other. The most effective transneuronal tracing method uses a **pseudorabies virus**—a weakened form of a pig herpes virus that was originally developed as a vaccine. The virus is injected directly into a brain region, is taken up by neurons there, and infects them. The virus spreads throughout the infected neurons and is eventually released, passing on the infection to neurons with which they form synaptic connections. Some neurons are killed by the virus; others survive the infection. This method can be used to trace circuits in either the anterograde or retrograde direction.

The longer the experimenter waits after injecting the virus, the larger the number of neurons that become infected. After the animal is killed and the brain is sliced, immunocytochemical methods are used to localize a protein produced by the virus. For example, Daniels, Miselis, and Flanagan-Cato (1999) injected pseudorabies virus in the muscles responsible for female rats' mating posture. After a few days, the rats were killed, and their brains were examined for evidence of viral infection. The study indicated that the virus found its way up the motor nerves to

---

retrograde labeling method A histological method that labels cell bodies that give rise to the terminal buttons that form synapses with cells in a particular region.

fluorogold (*flew roh gold*) A dye that serves as a retrograde label; taken up by terminal buttons and carried back to the cell bodies.

pseudorabies virus A weakened form of a pig herpes virus; used for transneuronal tracing, which labels a series of neurons that are interconnected synaptically.

the motor neurons in the spinal cord, then to the reticular formation of the medulla, then to the periaqueductal gray matter, and finally to the VMH. These results confirm the results of the anterograde and retrograde labeling methods I just described. (Infected neurons were found in other structures as well, but they are not relevant to this discussion.)

Together, anterograde and retrograde labeling methods—including transneuronal methods—enable us to discover circuits of interconnected neurons. Thus, these methods help to provide us with a "wiring diagram" of the brain. (See *Figure 5.16*.) Armed with other research methods (including some to be described later in this chapter), we can try to discover the functions of each component of this circuit.

Study of the Living Human Brain

There are many good reasons to investigate the functions of brains of animals other than humans. For one thing, we can compare the results of studies made with different species to make some inferences about the evolution of various neural systems. Even if our primary interest is in the functions of the human brain, we certainly cannot ask people to submit to brain surgery for the purposes of research. But diseases and accidents do occasionally damage the human brain, and if we know where the damage occurs, we can study the people's behavior and try to make the same sorts of inferences we make with deliber-

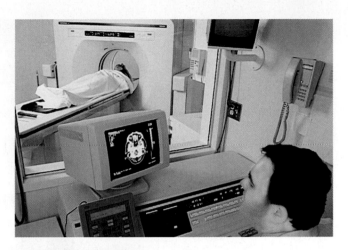

figure 5.17

A computerized tomography (CT) scanner.
(Larry Mulvihill/Rainbow.)

ately produced brain lesions in laboratory animals. The problem is, where is the lesion?

In past years a researcher might study the behavior of a person with brain damage and never find out exactly where the lesion was located. The only way to be sure was to obtain the patient's brain when he or she died and examine slices of it under a microscope. But it was often impossible to do so. Sometimes the patient outlived the researcher. Sometimes the patient moved out of town. Sometimes (often, perhaps) the family refused permission for an autopsy. Because of these practical problems, study of the behavioral effects of damage to specific parts of the human brain made rather slow progress.

Recent advances in X-ray techniques and computers have led to the development of several methods for studying the anatomy of the living brain. These advances permit researchers to study the location and extent of brain damage while the patient is still living. The first method that was developed is called **computerized tomography** **(CT)** (from the Greek for *tomos*, "cut," and *graphein*, "to write"). This procedure, usually referred to as a *CT scan*, works as follows: The patient's head is placed in a large doughnut-shaped ring. The ring contains an X-ray tube and, directly opposite it (on the other side of the patient's head), an X-ray detector. The X-ray beam passes through the patient's head, and the detector measures the amount of radioactivity that gets through it. The beam scans the head from all angles, and a computer translates the numbers it receives from the detector into pictures of the skull and its contents. (See *Figure 5.17.*)

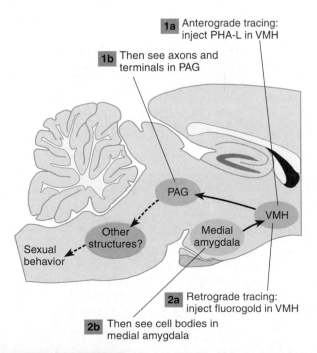

figure 5.16

One of the inputs to the VMH and one of the outputs, as revealed by anterograde and retrograde labeling methods.

computerized tomography (CT) The use of a device that employs a computer to analyze data obtained by a scanning beam of X-rays to produce a two-dimensional picture of a "slice" through the body.

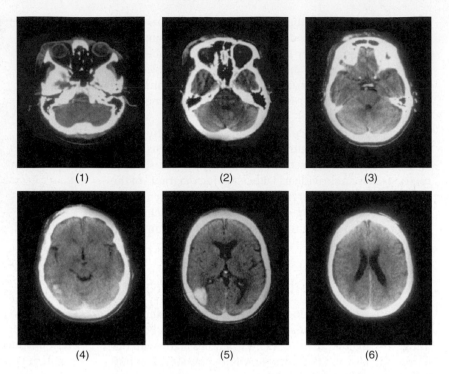

figure 5.18

A series of CT scans from a patient with a lesion in the right occipital-parietal area (scan 5). The lesion appears white because it was accompanied by bleeding; blood absorbs more radiation than the surrounding brain tissue. Rostral is up, caudal is down; left and right are reversed. Scan 1 shows a section through the eyes and the base of the brain.
(Courtesy of J. McA. Jones, Good Samaritan Hospital, Portland, Oregon.)

(1)   (2)   (3)

(4)   (5)   (6)

Figure 5.18 shows a series of these CT scans taken through the head of a patient who sustained a stroke. The stroke damaged a part of the brain involved in bodily awareness and perception of space. The patient lost her awareness of the left side of her body and of items located on her left. You can see the damage as a white spot in the lower left corner of scan 5. (See *Figure 5.18.*)

An even more detailed picture of what is inside a person's head is provided by a process called **magnetic resonance imaging (MRI).** The MRI scanner resembles a CT scanner, but it does not use X-rays. Instead, it passes an extremely strong magnetic field through the patient's head. When a person's body is placed in a strong magnetic field, the nuclei of some atoms in molecules in the body spin with a particular orientation. If a radio frequency wave is then passed through the body, these nuclei emit radio waves of their own. Different molecules emit energy at different frequencies. The MRI scanner is tuned to detect the radiation from hydrogen atoms. Because these atoms are present in different concentrations in different tissues, the scanner can use the information to prepare pictures of slices of the brain. Unlike CT scans, which are generally limited to the horizontal plane, MRI scans can be taken in the sagittal or frontal planes as well. (See *Figure 5.19.*)

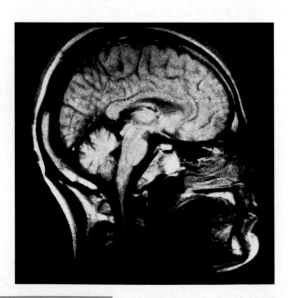

figure 5.19

A midsagittal MRI scan of a human brain.
(Photo courtesy of Philips Medical Systems.)

interim summary

Experimental Ablation

The goal of research in behavioral neuroscience is to understand the brain functions required for the performance of a particular behavior and then to learn the location of the neural circuits that perform these functions. The lesion method is the oldest one employed in such research, and it

magnetic resonance imaging (MRI) A technique whereby the interior of the body can be accurately imaged; involves the interaction between radio waves and a strong magnetic field.

remains one of the most useful. A subcortical lesion is made under the guidance of a stereotaxic apparatus. The coordinates are obtained from a stereotaxic atlas, and the tip of an electrode or cannula is placed at the target. A lesion is made by passing radio frequency current through the electrode or infusing an excitatory amino acid through the cannula, producing an excitotoxic lesion. The advantage of excitotoxic lesions is that they destroy only neural cell bodies; axons passing through the region are not damaged.

The location of a lesion must be determined after the animal's behavior is observed. The animal is killed by humane means, the brain is perfused with a saline solution, and the brain is removed and placed in a fixative such as formalin. A microtome is used to slice the brain, which is usually frozen to make it hard enough to cut into thin sections. These sections are mounted on glass slides, stained with a cell-body stain, and examined under a microscope.

Light microscopes enable us to see cells and their larger organelles, but an electron microscope is needed to see small details, such as individual mitochondria and synaptic vesicles. Scanning electron microscopes provide a three-dimensional view of tissue, but at a lower magnification than transmission electron microscopes.

The next step in a research program often requires the investigator to discover the afferent and efferent connections of the region of interest with the rest of the brain. Efferent connections (those that carry information from the region in question to other parts of the brain) are revealed with anterograde tracing methods, such as the one that uses PHA-L. Afferent connections (those that bring information to the region in question from other parts of the brain) are revealed with retrograde tracing methods, such as the one that uses fluorogold. Chains of neurons that form synaptic connections are revealed by the transneuronal tracing method, which uses the pseudorabies virus.

Although brain lesions are not deliberately made in the human brain for the purposes of research, diseases and accidents can cause brain damage, and if we know where the damage is located, we can study people's behavior and make inferences about the location of the neural circuits that perform relevant functions. If the patient dies and the brain is available for examination, ordinary histological methods can be used. Otherwise, the living brain can be examined with CT scanners and MRI scanners.

Table 5.1 summarizes the research methods presented in this section.

table 5.1

Research Methods: Part I

GOAL OF METHOD	METHOD	REMARKS
Destroy or inactivate specific brain region	Radio frequency lesion	Destroys all brain tissue near tip of electrode
	Exitotoxic lesion; uses excitatory amino acid such as kainic acid	Destroys only cell bodies near tip of cannula; spares axons passing through region
	6-HD lesion	Destroys catecholaminergic neurons near tip of cannula
	Infusion of local anesthetic; cryoloop	Temporarily inactivates specific brain region; animal can serve as its own control
Place electrode or cannula in specific region within brain	Stereotaxic surgery	Consult stereotaxic atlas for coordinates
Find location of lesion	Perfuse brain; fix brain; slice brain; stain sections	
Identify axons leaving a particular region and the terminal buttons of these axons	Anterograde tracing method, such as PHA-L	
Identify location of neurons whose axons terminate in a particular region	Retrograde tracing method, such as fluorogold	
Identify chain of neurons that are interconnected synaptically	Transneuronal tracing method; uses pseudorabies virus	Can be used for both anterograde and retrograde tracing
Find location of lesion in living human brain	Computerized tomography (CT scanner)	Slows "slice" of brain; uses X-rays
	Magnetic resonance imaging (MRI scanner)	Shows "slice" of brain; better detail than CT scan; uses a magnetic field and radio waves

Recording and Stimulating Neural Activity

The first section of this chapter dealt with the anatomy of the brain and the effects of damage to particular regions. This section considers a different approach: studying the brain by recording or stimulating the activity of particular regions. Brain functions involve activity of circuits of neurons; thus, different perceptions and behavioral responses involve different patterns of activity in the brain. Researchers have devised methods to record these patterns of activity or artificially produce them.

Recording of Neural Activity

Axons produce action potentials, and terminal buttons elicit postsynaptic potentials in the membrane of the cells with which they form synapses. These electrical events can be recorded (as we saw in Chapter 2), and changes in the electrical activity of a particular region can be used to determine whether that region plays a role in various behaviors. For example, recordings can be made during stimulus presentations, decision making, or motor activities.

Recordings can be made *chronically,* over an extended period of time after the animal recovers from surgery, or *acutely,* for a relatively short period of time during which the animal is kept anesthetized. Acute recordings, made while the animal is anesthetized, are usually restricted to studies of sensory pathways. Acute recordings seldom involve behavioral observations, since the behavioral capacity of an anesthetized animal is limited, to say the least.

Recordings with Microelectrodes

Drugs that affect serotonergic and noradrenergic neurons also affect REM sleep. Suppose that, knowing this fact, we wondered whether the activity of serotonergic and noradrenergic neurons would vary during different stages of sleep. To find out, we would record the activity of these neurons with microelectrodes. **Microelectrodes** have a very fine tip, small enough to record the electrical activity of individual neurons. This technique is usually called **single-unit recording** (a unit refers to an individual neuron).

Microelectrodes can be constructed of fine glass tubes. As we saw in Chapter 2, these electrodes can be used to record action potentials in giant squid axons. Glass tubes have an interesting property. If they are heated until soft and if the ends are pulled apart, the softened glass will stretch into a very fine filament. However, no matter how thin the filament becomes, it will still have a hole running through it. To construct glass microelectrodes, we heat the middle of a length of capillary tubing (glass with an outside diameter of approximately 1 mm) and then sharply pull the ends apart. The glass tube is drawn out

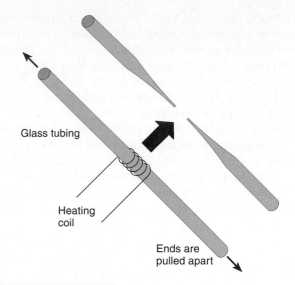

figure **5.20**

Microelectrodes produced by heating the center portion of a length of glass capillary tubing and pulling the ends apart.

and becomes finer and finer until the tube snaps apart. The result is two microelectrodes, as shown in *Figure 5.20.* (These devices are usually produced with the aid of a special machine, called a *microelectrode puller.*) Glass will not conduct electricity, so we fill the microelectrode with a conducting liquid, such as a solution of potassium chloride.

Because we want to record the activity of single neurons over a long period of time in unanesthetized animals, we want more durable electrodes. We can purchase arrays of very fine wires, gathered together in a bundle. The wires are insulated with a special varnish so that only their tips are bare. The wires are flexible enough that they can follow movements of the brain tissue caused by movements of the animal's head. As a result, they are less likely to damage the neurons whose signals they are receiving. In addition, we can record the activity of several individual neurons in a particular region of the brain.

We implant the electrodes in the brains of animals through stereotaxic surgery. We attach them to miniaturized electrical sockets and bond the sockets to the animals' skull, using plastics that were originally developed for the dental profession. Then, after recovery from surgery, the animal can be "plugged in" to the recording system. Laboratory animals pay no heed to the electrical sockets on their skulls and behave quite normally. (See *Figure 5.21.*)

microelectrode A very fine electrode, generally used to record activity of individual neurons.

single-unit recording Recording of the electrical activity of a single neuron.

Researchers often attach rather complex devices to the animals' skulls when they implant microelectrodes. These devices include screw mechanisms that permit the experimenter to move the electrode—or array of electrodes—deeper into the brain so that they can record from several different parts of the brain during the course of their observations.

The electrical signals detected by microelectrodes are quite small and must be amplified. Amplifiers used for this purpose work just like the amplifiers in a stereo system, converting the weak signals recorded at the brain into stronger ones. These signals can be displayed on an oscilloscope and stored in the memory of a computer for analysis at a later time.

What about the results of our recordings from serotonergic and noradrenergic neurons? As you will learn in Chapter 9, if we record the activity of these neurons during various stages of sleep, we will find that their firing rates fall almost to zero during REM sleep. This observation suggests that these neurons have an *inhibitory* effect on REM sleep. That is, REM sleep cannot occur until these neurons stop firing.

Recordings with Macroelectrodes

Sometimes, we want to record the activity of a region of the brain as a whole, not the activity of individual neurons located there. To do this, we would use macroelectrodes. **Macroelectrodes** do not detect the activity of individual neurons; rather, the records that are obtained with these devices represent the postsynaptic potentials of many thousands—or millions—of cells in the area of the electrode. These electrodes can consist of unsharpened wires inserted into the brain, screws attached to the skull, or even metal disks attached to the human scalp with a

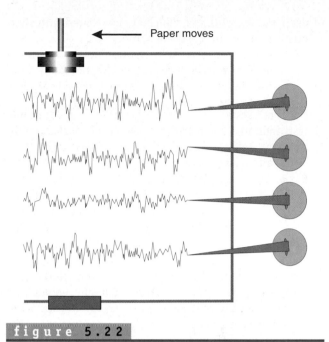

figure **5.22**

A record from an ink-writing oscillograph.

special paste that conducts electricity. Recordings taken from the scalp, especially, represent the activity of an enormous number of neurons, whose electrical signals pass through the meninges, skull, and scalp before reaching the electrodes.

Occasionally, neurosurgeons implant macroelectrodes directly into the human brain. The reason for doing so is to detect the source of abnormal electrical activity that is giving rise to frequent seizures. Once the source is determined, the surgeon can open the skull and remove the source of the seizures—usually scar tissue caused by brain damage that occurred earlier in life. Most often, the electrical activity of a human brain is recorded through electrodes attached to the scalp and displayed on an *ink-writing oscillograph,* commonly called a *polygraph.*

A polygraph contains a mechanism that moves a very long strip of paper past a series of pens. These pens are essentially the pointers of large voltmeters, moving up and down in response to the electrical signal sent to them by the biological amplifiers. Figure 5.22 illustrates a record of electrical activity recorded from macroelectrodes attached to various locations on a person's scalp. (See *Figure 5.22.*) Such records are called **electroencephalograms (EEGs),** or "writings of electricity from the head." They can be used to diagnose epilepsy or brain tumors or to study the stages

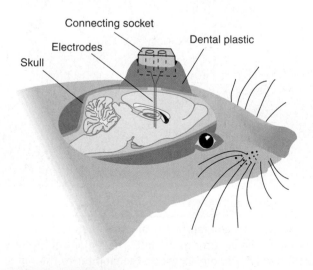

figure **5.21**

A permanently attached set of electrodes, with a connecting socket cemented to the skull.

macroelectrode An electrode used to record the electrical activity of large numbers of neurons in a particular region of the brain; much larger than a microelectrode.

electroencephalogram (EEG) An electrical brain potential recorded by placing electrodes on in the scalp.

of sleep and wakefulness, which are associated with characteristic patterns of electrical activity.

Another use of the EEG is to monitor the condition of the brain during procedures that could potentially damage it. I witnessed just such a procedure several years ago.

Mrs. F. had sustained one mild heart attack, and subsequent tests indicated a considerable amount of atherosclerosis, commonly referred to as "hardening of the arteries." Many of her arteries were narrowed by cholesterol-rich atherosclerotic plaque. A clot formed in a particularly narrow portion of one of her coronary arteries, which caused her heart attack. After that attack, her physician prescribed a drug that reduced the tendency for the platelets in her blood to form clots.

Knowing that atherosclerosis is not limited to the arteries in the heart, her physician used his stethoscope to listen to her carotid arteries, and sure enough, he heard—especially on the left side—the characteristic noises (they go by the French word *bruits*) that were made as the blood passed through her narrow, hardened blood vessels. As the months passed after her heart attack, Mrs. F. had several *transient ischemic attacks,* brief episodes of neurological symptoms that appear to be caused by blood clots forming and then dissolving in cerebral blood vessels. In her case, they caused numbness in her right arm and difficulty in talking. Her physician referred her to a neurologist, who ordered an angiogram. This procedure revealed that her left carotid artery was almost totally blocked. The neurologist referred Mrs. F. to a neurosurgeon, who urged her to have an operation that would remove the plaque from part of her left carotid artery and increase the blood flow to the left side of her brain.

The procedure is called a *carotid endarterectomy*. I was chatting with Mrs. F.'s neurosurgeon after a conference, and he happened to mention that he would be performing the operation later that morning. I asked whether I could watch, and he agreed. When I entered the operating room, scrubbed and gowned, I found Mrs. F. already anesthetized, and the surgical nurse had prepared the left side of her neck for the incision. In addition, several EEG electrodes had been attached to her scalp, and I saw that Dr. L., a neurologist who specializes in clinical neurophysiology, seated at his EEG machine.

The surgeon made an incision in Mrs. F.'s neck and exposed the carotid artery, at the point where the common carotid, coming from the heart, branched into the external and internal carotid arteries. He placed a plastic band around the common carotid artery and clamped it shut, stopping the flow of blood. "How does it look, Ken?" he asked Dr. L. "No good—I see some slowing. You'd better shunt."

The surgeon quickly removed the constricting band and asked the nurse for a shunt, a short length of plastic tubing a little thinner than the artery. He made two small incisions in the artery well above and well below the region that contained the plaque, and inserted the shunt. Now he could work on the artery without stopping the flow of blood to the brain. He made a longitudinal cut in the artery, exposing a yellowish mass that he dissected away and removed. He sewed up the incision, removed the shunt, and sutured the small cuts he had made to accommodate it. "Everything still okay?" he asked Dr. L. "Yes, her EEG is fine."

Most neurosurgeons prefer to do an endarterectomy by temporarily clamping the artery shut while they work on it. The work goes faster, and complications are less likely. Because the blood supply to the two hemispheres of the brain are interconnected (with special *communicating arteries*), it is often possible to shut down one of the carotid arteries for a few minutes without causing any damage. However, sometimes the blood flow from one side of the brain to the other is insufficient to keep the other side nourished with blood and oxygen. The only way the surgeon can know is to have the patient's EEG monitored. If the brain is not receiving a sufficient blood supply, the EEG will show the presence of characteristic "slow waves." That is what happened when Mrs. F.'s artery was clamped shut, and that is why the surgeon had to use a shunt tube. Without it, the procedure might have caused a stroke instead of preventing one.

By the way, Mrs. F. made a good recovery.

Magnetoencephalography

As you undoubtedly know, when electrical current flows through a conductor, it induces a magnetic field. This means that as action potentials pass down axons or

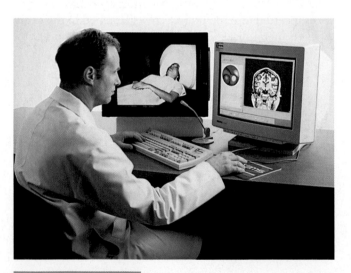

figure 5.23

Magnetoencephalography. The neuromagnetometer is shown on the monitor to the left. The regions of increased electrical activity are shown on the monitor to the right, superimposed on an image of the brain derived from an MRI scan.

(Courtesy of CTF Systems Inc.)

as postsynaptic potentials pass down dendrites or sweep across the somatic membrane of a neuron, magnetic fields are also produced. These fields are exceedingly small, but engineers have developed superconducting detectors (called SQUIDs, or "superconducting quantum interference devices") that can detect magnetic fields that are approximately one-billionth of the size of the earth's magnetic field. **Magnetoencephalography** is performed with *neuromagnetometers,* devices that contain an array of several SQUIDs, oriented so that a computer can examine their output and calculate the source of particular signals in the brain. The neuromagnetometer shown in Figure 5.23 contains 275 SQUIDs. These devices can be used clinically—for example, to find the sources of seizures so that they can be removed surgically. They can also be used in experiments to measure regional brain activity that accompanies the perception of various stimuli or the performance of various behaviors or cognitive tasks. (See *Figure 5.23.*)

Recording the Brain's Metabolic and Synaptic Activity

Electrical signals are not the only signs of neural activity. If the neural activity of a particular region of the brain increases, the metabolic rate of this region increases, too, largely as a result of increased operation of ion pumps in the membrane of the cells. This increased metabolic rate can be measured. The experimenter injects radioactive **2-deoxyglucose (2-DG)** into the animal's bloodstream. Because this chemical resembles glucose (the principal food for the brain), it is taken into cells. Thus, the most active cells, which use glucose at the highest rate, will take up the highest concentrations of radioactive 2-DG. But unlike normal glucose, 2-DG cannot be metabolized, so it stays in the cell. The experimenter then kills the animal, removes the brain, slices it, and prepares it for *autoradiography.*

Autoradiography can be translated roughly as "writing with one's own radiation." Sections of the brain are mounted on microscope slides. The slides are then taken into a darkroom, where they are coated with a photographic emulsion (the substance found on photographic film). Several weeks later, the slides, with their coatings of emulsion, are developed, just like photographic film. The molecules of radioactive 2-DG show themselves as spots of silver grains in the developed emulsion because the radioactivity exposes the emulsion, just as X-rays or light will do.

The most active regions of the brain contain the most radioactivity, showing this radioactivity in the form of dark spots in the developed emulsion. Figure 5.24 shows an autoradiograph of a slice of a rat brain; the dark spots at the bottom (indicated by the arrow) are nuclei of the hypothalamus with an especially high metabolic rate.

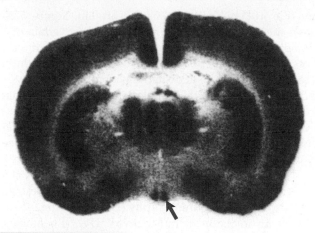

figure 5.24

A 2-DG autoradiogram of a rat brain (frontal section, dorsal is at top), showing especially high regions of activity in the pair of nuclei in the hypothalamus, at the base of the brain.

(From Schwartz, W. J., and Gainer, H. *Science,* 1977, *197,* 1089–1091.)

Chapter 9 describes these nuclei and their function. (See *Figure 5.24.*)

Another method of identifying active regions of the brain capitalizes on the fact that when neurons are activated (for example, by the terminal buttons that form synapses with them), particular genes in the nucleus called *immediate early genes* are turned on and particular proteins are produced. These proteins then bind with the chromosomes in the nucleus. The presence of these nuclear proteins indicates that the neuron has just been activated.

One of the nuclear proteins produced during neural activation is called **Fos.** You will remember that we already did some research on the neural circuitry involved in the sexual behavior of female rats. Suppose we want to use the Fos method in this research project to see what neurons are activated during a female rat's sexual activity. We place female rats with males and permit the animals to copulate. Then we remove the rats' brains, slice them, and

magnetoencephalography A procedure that detects groups of synchronously activated neurons by means of the magnetic field induced by their electrical activity; uses an array of superconducting quantum interference devices, or SQUIDs.

2-deoxyglucose (2-DG) (*dee ox ee gloo kohss*) A sugar that enters cells along with glucose but is not metabolized.

autoradiography A procedure that locates radioactive substances in a slice of tissue; the radiation exposes a photographic emulsion or a piece of film that covers the tissue.

Fos (*fahs*) A protein produced in the nucleus of a neuron in response to synaptic stimulation.

follow a procedure that stains Fos protein. Figure 5.25 shows the results: Neurons in the medial amygdala of a female rat that has just mated show the presence of dark spots, indicating the presence of Fos protein. Thus, these neurons appear to be activated by copulatory activity—perhaps by the physical stimulation of the genitals that occurs then. As you will recall, when we injected a retrograde tracer (fluorogold) into the VMH, we found that this region receives input from the medial amygdala. (See *Figure 5.25.*)

The metabolic activity of specific brain regions can be measured in human brains, too, using a method known as **positron emission tomography (PET).** First, the patient receives an injection of radioactive 2-DG. (Eventually, the chemical is broken down and leaves the cells. The dose given to humans is harmless.) The person's head is placed in a machine similar to a CT scanner. When the radioactive molecules of 2-DG decay, they emit subatomic particles called positrons, which are detected by the scanner. The computer determines which regions of the brain have taken up the radioactive substance, and it produces a picture of a slice of the brain, showing the activity level of various regions in that slice. (See *Figure 5.26.*)

One of the disadvantages of PET scanners is their operating cost. For reasons of safety the radioactive chemicals that are administered have very short half-lives; that is, they decay and lose their radioactivity very quickly. For example, the half-life of radioactive 2-DG is 110 minutes; the half-life of radioactive water (also used for PET scans) is only 2 minutes. Because these chemicals decay so

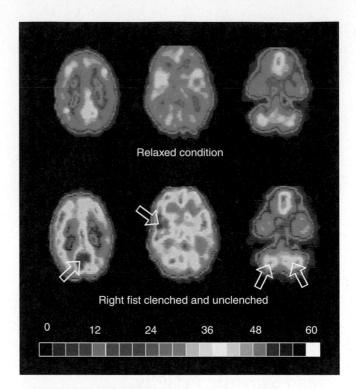

Relaxed condition

Right fist clenched and unclenched

0   12   24   36   48   60

figure 5.26

PET scans of a human brain (horizontal sections). The top row shows three scans from a person at rest. The bottom row shows three scans from the same person while he was clenching and unclenching his right fist. The scans show increased uptake of radioactive 2-deoxyglucose in regions of the brain that are devoted to the control of movement, which indicates increased metabolic rate in these areas. Different computer-generated colors indicate different rates of uptake of 2-DG, as shown in the scale at the bottom.

(Courtesy of the Brookhaven National Laboratory and the State University of New York, Stony Brook.)

quickly, they must be produced on site, in an atomic particle accelerator called a *cyclotron*. Therefore, to the cost of the PET scanner must be added the cost of the cyclotron and the salaries of the personnel who operate it.

The most recent development in brain imaging is **functional MRI (fMRI).** Engineers have devised modifications to existing MRI scanners that acquire images very rapidly and permit the measurement of regional metabolism by detecting levels of oxygen in the brain's blood vessels. Functional MRI scans have a higher resolution

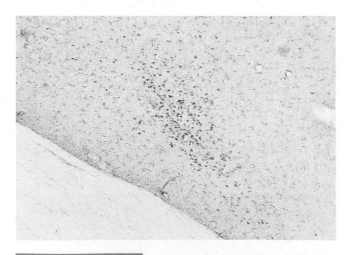

figure 5.25

Localization of Fos protein. The photomicrograph shows a frontal section of the brain of a female rat, taken through the medial amygdala. The dark spots indicate the presence of Fos protein, localized by means of immunocytochemistry. The synthesis of Fos protein was stimulated by permitting the animal to engage in copulatory behavior.

(Courtesy of Marc Tetel, Skidmore College.)

positron emission tomography (PET) The use of a device that reveals the localization of a radioactive tracer in a living brain.

functional MRI (fMRI) A modification of the MRI procedure that permits the measurement of regional metabolism in the brain.

than PET scans, and they can be acquired much faster. Thus, they reveal more detailed information about the activity of particular brain regions. (See *Figure 5.27.*)

Measuring the Brain's Secretions

Sometimes we are interested not in the general metabolic activity of particular regions of the brain, but in the secretion of specific neurotransmitters or neuromodulators in these regions. For example, suppose we know that acetylcholinergic neurons in the brain stem participate in the control of REM sleep. (The experiments that provided this knowledge are described in the next section of this chapter.) One of the characteristics of REM sleep is muscular paralysis, which prevents us from getting out of bed and acting out our dreams. We decide to measure the secretion of acetylcholine in a region of the medulla known to contain glycine-secreting neurons that inhibit motor neurons in the spinal cord. To do so, we use a procedure called **microdialysis.**

Dialysis is a process in which substances are separated by means of an artificial membrane that is permeable to some molecules but not others. A microdialysis probe consists of a small metal tube that introduces a solution into a section of dialysis tubing—a piece of artificial membrane shaped in the form of a cylinder, sealed at the bottom. Another small metal tube leads the solution away after it has circulated through the pouch. A drawing of such a probe is shown in *Figure 5.28.*

We use stereotaxic surgery to place a microdialysis probe in a rat's brain so that the tip of the probe is located in the region we are interested in. We pump a small amount of a solution similar to extracellular fluid through one of the small metal tubes into the dialysis tubing. The fluid cir-

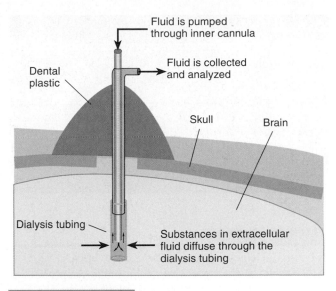

figure 5.28

Microdialysis. A dilute salt solution is slowly infused into the microdialysis tube, where it picks up molecules that diffuse in from the extracellular fluid. The contents of the fluid are then analyzed.

(Adapted from Hernandez, L., Stanley, B. G., and Hoebel, B. G. *Life Sciences,* 1986, *39,* 2629–2637.)

culates through the dialysis tubing and passes through the second metal tube, from which it is taken for analysis. As the fluid passes through the dialysis tubing, it collects molecules from the extracellular fluid of the brain, which are pushed across the membrane by the force of diffusion.

We analyze the contents of the fluid that has passed through the dialysis tubing by an extremely sensitive analytical method. This method is so sensitive that it can detect neurotransmitters (and their breakdown products) that have been released by the terminal buttons and have escaped from the synaptic cleft into the rest of the extracellular fluid. In fact, we find that the amount of acetylcholine present in the extracellular fluid of the nucleus in the medulla *does* increase during REM sleep.

In a few special cases (for example, in monitoring brain chemicals of people with intracranial hemorrhages or head trauma), the microdialysis procedure has been applied to study of the human brain, but ethical reasons prevent us from doing so for research purposes. Fortunately, there is a noninvasive way to measure neurochemicals in the human brain. Although PET scanners are expensive machines, they are also versatile. They can be used to localize *any* radioactive substance that emits positrons.

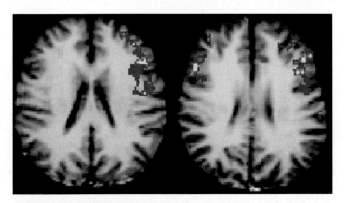

figure 5.27

A functional MRI scan of a human brain. Localized increases in neural activity of males (left) and females (right) while they were judging whether pairs of written words rhymed.

(From Shaywitz, B. A., et al., *Nature,* 1995, *373,* 607–609. By permission.)

microdialysis A procedure for analyzing chemicals present in the interstitial fluid through a small piece of tubing made of a semipermeable membrane that is implanted in the brain.

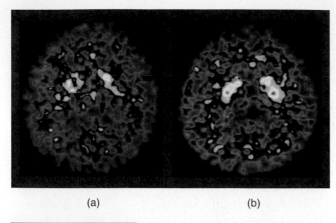

(a)   (b)

figure 5.29

PET scans showing uptake of radioactive L-DOPA in the basal ganglia of a patient with parkinsonian symptoms induced by a toxic chemical before and after receiving a transplant of fetal dopaminergic neurons. (a) Preoperative scan. (b) Scan taken 13 months postoperatively. The increased uptake of L-DOPA indicates that the fetal transplant was secreting dopamine.

(Adapted from Widner, H., Tetrud, J., Rehncrona, S., Snow, B., Brundin, P., Gustavii, B., Björklund, A., Lindvall, O., and Langston, J. W. *New England Journal of Medicine,* 1992, *327,* 1556–1563. Scans reprinted with permission.)

Figure 5.29 shows PET scans of the brain of Mr. B., the man described in the case that opened this chapter. A stereotaxic apparatus was used to transplant fetal dopamine-secreting neurons into his basal ganglia. As we saw, a PET scan was taken of his brain before his surgery and a little more than a year afterward. He was given an injection of radioactive L-DOPA one hour before each scan was made. As you learned in Chapter 4, L-DOPA is taken up by the terminals of dopaminergic neurons, where it is converted to

dopamine; thus, the radioactivity shown in the scans indicates the presence of dopamine-secreting terminals in the basal ganglia. The scans show the amount of radioactivity before (part a) and after (part b) he received the transplant. As you can see, the basal ganglia contained substantially more dopamine after the surgery. (See *Figure 5.29.*)

Stimulating Neural Activity

So far, this section has been concerned with research methods that measure the activity of specific regions of the brain. But sometimes we may want to artificially change the activity of these regions to see what effects these changes have on the animal's behavior. For example, female rats will copulate with males only if certain female sex hormones are present. If we remove the rats' ovaries, the loss of these hormones will abolish their sexual behavior. We found in our earlier studies that VMH lesions disrupt this behavior. Perhaps if we *activate* the VMH, we will make up for the lack of female sex hormones and the rats will copulate again.

How do we activate neurons? We can do so by electrical or chemical stimulation. Electrical stimulation simply involves passing an electrical current through a wire inserted into the brain, as you saw in Figure 5.21. Chemical stimulation is usually accomplished by injecting a small amount of an excitatory amino acid, such as kainic acid or glutamic acid, into the brain. As you learned in Chapter 4, the principal excitatory neurotransmitter in the brain is glutamic acid (glutamate), and both of these substances stimulate glutamate receptors, thus activating the neurons on which these receptors are located.

Injections of chemicals into the brain can be done through an apparatus that is permanently attached to the skull so that the animal's behavior can be observed several times. We place a metal cannula (a guide cannula) in

figure 5.30

An intracranial cannula. A guide cannula is permanently attached to the skull, and at a later time a thinner cannula can be inserted through the guide cannula into the brain. Chemicals can be infused into the brain through this device.

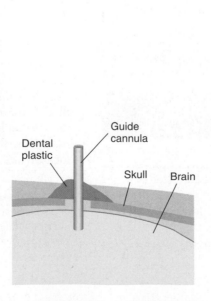

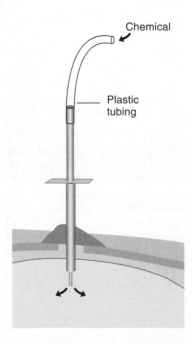

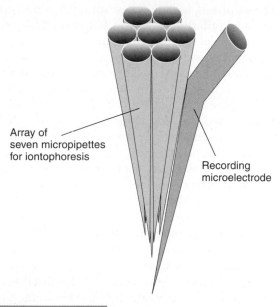

Array of
seven micropipettes
for iontophoresis

Recording
microelectrode

figure 5.31

Microiontophoresis. Molecules of different chemicals are carried out of the seven micropipettes by an electrical current. The recording microelectrode records the activity of the neuron and determines whether it responds to the chemicals.

an animal's brain and cement its top to the skull. At a later date we place a smaller cannula of measured length inside the guide cannula and then inject a chemical into the brain. Because the animal is free to move about, we can observe the effects of the injection on its behavior. (See *Figure 5.30.*)

The principal disadvantage of chemical stimulation is that it is slightly more complicated than electrical stimulation; chemical stimulation requires cannulas, tubes, special pumps or syringes, and sterile solutions of excitatory amino acids. However, it has a distinct advantage over electrical stimulation: It activates cell bodies but not axons. Because only cell bodies (and their dendrites, of course) contain glutamate receptors, we can be assured that an injection of an excitatory amino acid into a particular region of the brain excites the cells there, but not the axons of other neurons that happen to pass through the region. Thus, the effects of chemical stimulation are more localized than the effects of electrical stimulation.

You might have noticed that I just said that kainic acid, which I described earlier as a neurotoxin, can be used to stimulate neurons. These two uses are not really contradictory. Kainic acid produces excitotoxic lesions by stimulating neurons to death. Whereas large doses of a concentrated solution kill neurons, small doses of a dilute solution simply stimulate them.

What about the results of our experiment? In fact (as we shall see in Chapter 10), VMH stimulation *does* substitute for female sex hormones. Perhaps, then, the female sex hormones exert their effects in this nucleus. We

will see how to test this hypothesis in the final section of this chapter.

When drugs are injected into the brain through cannulas, the chemicals diffuse over a region that involves hundreds (or thousands) of neurons. Sometimes, we want to study the effect of chemicals on the activity of a single cell. To do that we use a technique known as *microiontophoresis.*

When neurotransmitters bind with postsynaptic receptors, ion channels open, producing excitatory or inhibitory postsynaptic potentials. These potentials increase or decrease the cell's firing rate. To determine the effects of transmitter substances (or drugs that stimulate or block particular receptors) on the activity of an individual neuron, an investigator uses a **multibarreled micropipette.** This device consists of two or more glass microelectrodes (also called *micropipettes*), bundled together so that their tips are close to one another.

Figure 5.31 illustrates a seven-barreled micropipette glued to a recording microelectrode. Each of the seven micropipettes can be filled with a neurotransmitter, neuro-modulator, hormone, or drug. The pH (acid–base balance) of the solutions in the micropipettes is adjusted so that the chemicals ionize. Then when an electrical current is passed through one of the micropipettes, some molecules of the substance will be discharged. The injection of extremely small quantities of a chemical this way is called **microiontophoresis** (*iontophoresis* means "ion carrying," from *pherein,* "to bear or carry"). (See *Figure 5.31.*)

The recording microelectrode detects the neural activity of the cell that is being exposed to one of the chemicals placed in the micropipettes—for example, a particular neurotransmitter. If the neuron changes its firing rate when some of the hormone is ejected from the micropipette, we can conclude that the neuron contains receptors for that neurotransmitter.

Behavioral Effects of Electrical Brain Stimulation

Stimulation of the brain of a freely moving animal often produces behavioral changes. For example, hypothalamic stimulation can elicit behaviors such as feeding, drinking, grooming, attack, or escape, a finding that suggests that the hypothalamus is involved in their control. Stimulation of part of the caudate nucleus often halts ongoing behavior, which suggests that this structure is

multibarreled micropipette A group of micropipettes attached together, used to infuse several different substances by means of iontophoresis while recording from a single neuron.

microiontophoresis A procedure that uses electricity to eject a chemical from a micropipette to determine the effects of the chemical on the electrical activity of a cell.

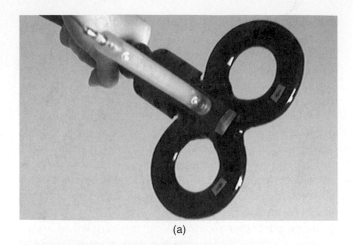

(a)

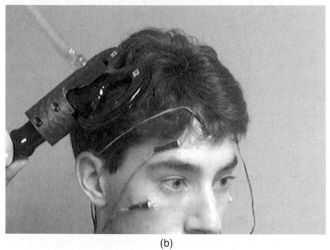

(b)

figure 5.32

Transcranial magnetic stimulation. (a) The coil used to apply the stimulation. (b) An illustration of the use of the coil. The wires on the man's face supply electrical current to light-emitting diodes, which provide reference points to keep track of head movements.

(Photographs courtesy of Michael Leventon and the MIT ΔI Laboratory.)

involved in motor inhibition. Brain stimulation can serve as a signal for a learned task or can even serve as a rewarding or punishing event, as we will see in Chapter 13.

There are problems in interpreting the significance of the effects of brain stimulation, especially when it is produced with electricity. An electrical stimulus (usually a series of pulses) can never duplicate the natural neural processes that go on in the brain. The normal interplay of spatial and temporal patterns of excitation and inhibition is destroyed by the artificial stimulation of an area. Electrical brain stimulation is probably as natural as attaching ropes to the arms of the members of an orchestra and then shaking all the ropes simultaneously to see what they can play. In fact, local stimulation is sometimes used to produce a "temporary lesion," by which the region is put out of commission by the meaningless artificial stimulation.

The surprising finding is that stimulation sometimes *does* produce orderly changes in behavior. This occurs when the stimulation takes place in regions of the brain that exert modulatory functions on neural circuits located in other parts of the brain. For example, the axons of acetylcholinergic neurons in the basal forebrain innervate much of the cerebral cortex. If these neurons are artificially stimulated, the widespread release of acetylcholine activates the cerebral cortex and facilitates information processing taking place there.

As we saw earlier in this chapter, neural activity induces magnetic fields that can be detected by means of magnetoencephalography. Similarly, magnetic fields can be used to stimulate neurons by inducing electrical currents in brain tissue. **Transcranial magnetic stimulation (TMS)** uses a coil of wires, usually arranged in the shape of the numeral 8, to stimulate neurons in the human cerebral cortex. The stimulating coil is placed on top of the skull so that the crossing point in the middle of the 8 is located immediately above the region to be stimulated. Pulses of electricity send magnetic fields that activate neurons in the cortex. The effects are very similar to those of direct stimulation of the exposed brain. For example, as we shall see in Chapter 6, stimulation of a particular region of the visual association cortex will disrupt a person's ability to detect movements in visual stimuli. In addition, TMS has been used to treat the symptoms of mental disorders such as depression.

Figure 5.32 shows an electromagnetic coil used in transcranial magnetic stimulation and its placement on a person's head. (See *Figure 5.32.*)

interim
summary

Recording and Stimulating Neural Activity

When circuits of neurons participate in their normal functions, their electrical activity, metabolic activity, and chemical secretions increase. Thus, by observing these processes as an animal perceives various stimuli or engages in various behaviors, we can make some inferences about the functions performed by various regions of the brain. Microelectrodes can be used to record the electrical activity of individual neurons. Chronic recordings require that the electrode be attached to an electrical socket, which is fastened to the skull with a plastic adhesive. Macroelectrodes record the activity of large groups of neurons. In rare cases macroelectrodes are placed in the depths of the human brain, but most often they are placed on the scalp and their activity is recorded on a polygraph.

transcranial magnetic stimulation Stimulation of the cerebral cortex by means of magnetic fields produced by passing pulses of electricity through a coil of wire placed next to the skull; interferes with the functions of the brain region that is stimulated.

Research Methods: Part II

GOAL OF METHOD	METHOD	REMARKS
Record electrical activity of single neurons	Glass or metal microelectrodes	Metal microelectrodes can be implanted permanently to record neural activity as animal moves
Record electrical activity of regions of brain	Metal macroelectrodes	In humans, usually attached to the scalp with a special paste
Record magnetic fields induced by neural activity	Magnetoencephalography; uses a neuromagnetometer, which contains an array of SQUIDs	Can determine the location of a group of neurons firing synchronously
Record metabolic activity of regions of brain	2-DG autoradiography	Measures local glucose utilization
	Measurements of Fos protein	Identifies neurons that have recently been stimulated
	2-DG PET scan Functional MRI	Measures regional metabolic activity of human brain
Measure neurotransmitters and neuromodulators released by neurons	Microdialysis	A wide variety of substances can be analyzed
Measure neurochemicals in the living human brain	PET scan	Can localize any radioactive substance in the human brain
Stimulate neural activity	Electrical stimulation	Stimulates neurons near the tip of the electrode and axons passing through region
	Chemical stimulation with excitatory amino acid	Stimulates only neurons near the tip of the cannula, not axons passing through region
	Transcranial magnetic stimulation	Stimulates neurons in the human cerebral cortex with an electromagnet placed on the head

Metabolic activity can be measured by giving an animal an injection of radioactive 2-DG, which accumulates in metabolically active neurons. The presence of the radioactivity is revealed through autoradiography: Slices of the brain are placed on microscope slides, covered with a photographic emulsion, left to sit a while, and then developed like photographic negatives. When neurons are stimulated, they synthesize the nuclear protein Fos. The presence of Fos, revealed by a special staining method, provides another way to discover active regions of the brain. The metabolic activity of various regions of the living human brain can be revealed by the 2-DG method, but a PET scanner is used to detect the active regions.

The secretions of neurotransmitters and neuromodulators can be measured by implanting the tip of a microdialysis probe in a particular region of the brain. A PET scanner can be used to perform similar observations of the human brain.

Researchers can stimulate various regions of the brain by implanting a macroelectrode and applying mild electrical stimulation. Alternatively, they can implant a guide cannula in the brain; after the animal has recovered from the surgery, they insert a smaller cannula and inject a weak solution of an excitatory amino acid into the brain. The advantage of this procedure is that only neurons whose cell bodies are located nearby will be stimulated; axons passing through the region will not be affected.

Table 5.2 summarizes the research methods presented in this section.

Neurochemical Methods

I have already described some neurochemical methods in the context of damaging or stimulating the brain or measuring neural activity. This section describes several other neurochemical methods that are useful in studying the physiology of behavior.

Finding Neurons That Produce Particular Neurochemicals

Suppose we learn that a particular drug affects behavior. How would we go about discovering the neural circuits that are responsible for the drug's effects? To answer this question, let's take a specific example. Physicians discovered several years ago that farm workers who had

figure 5.33

Localization of a peptide by means of immunocytochemistry. The photomicrograph shows a portion
of a frontal section through the rat forebrain.
The gold- and rust-colored fibers are axons and
terminal buttons that contain vasopressin, a peptide
neurotransmitter.

(Courtesy of Geert DeVries, University of Massachusetts.)

been exposed to certain types of insecticides (the organophosphates) had particularly intense and bizarre dreams
and even reported having hallucinations while awake. A
plausible explanation for these symptoms is that the drug
stimulates the neural circuits responsible for dreaming.
(After all, dreams are hallucinations that we have while
sleeping.) Alternatively, the drug could disrupt inhibitory
mechanisms that *prevent* dreaming while we are awake.
Other evidence (which will not be described here) indicates that the former hypothesis is true: Organophosphate
insecticides directly activate the neural circuits responsible for dreaming.

---

in situ hybridization (*in see too*) The production of DNA complementary to a particular messenger RNA in order to detect the presence of the RNA.

The first question to ask relates to how the organophosphate insecticides work. Pharmacologists have the answer:
These drugs are acetylcholinesterase inhibitors. As you
learned in Chapter 4, acetylcholinesterase inhibitors are
potent acetylcholine agonists. By inhibiting AChE, the
drugs prevent the rapid destruction of ACh after it is
released by terminal buttons and thus prolong the postsynaptic potentials at acetylcholinergic synapses.

Now that we understand the action of the insecticides, we know that these drugs act at acetylcholinergic
synapses. What neurochemical methods should we use to
discover the sites of action of the drugs in the brain? There
are three possibilities: We could look for neurons that
contain acetylcholine, we could look for the enzyme
acetylcholinesterase (which must be present in the postsynaptic membranes of cells that receive synaptic input
from acetylcholinergic neurons), or we could look for
acetylcholine receptors. Let's see how these three methods work.

First, let's consider methods by which we can localize particular neurochemicals, such as neurotransmitters
and neuromodulators. (In our case we are interested in
acetylcholine.) There are three basic ways of localizing
neurochemicals in the brain: localizing the *chemicals* themselves, localizing the *enzymes* that produce them, and localizing the *messenger RNA* involved in their synthesis.

Peptides (or proteins) can be localized directly by
means of immunocytochemical methods, which were
described in the first section of this chapter. Slices of brain
tissue are exposed to an antibody for the peptide, linked
to a dye (usually, a fluorescent dye). The slices are then

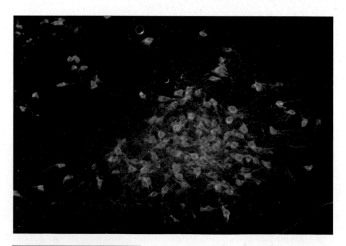

figure 5.34

Localization of an enzyme responsible for the synthesis of
a neurotransmitter, revealed by immunocytochemistry. The
photomicrograph shows a section through the pons. The
orange neurons contain choline acetyltransferase, which
implies that they produce (and thus secrete) acetylcholine.

(Courtesy of David A. Morilak and Roland Ciaranello, Nancy Pritzker
Laboratory of Developmental and Molecular Neurobiology, Depart-
ment of Psychiatry and Behavioral Sciences, Stanford University
School of Medicine.)

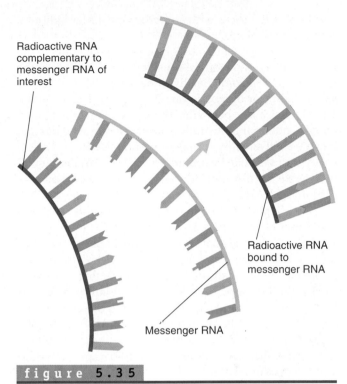

Radioactive RNA
complementary to
messenger RNA of
interest

Radioactive RNA
bound to
messenger RNA

Messenger RNA

figure 5.35

An explanation of the use of in situ hybridization to localize messenger RNA that is responsible for the synthesis of a particular protein or peptide.

examined under a microscope using light of a particular wavelength. For example, Figure 5.33 shows the location of axons in the forebrain that contain vasopressin, a peptide neurotransmitter. Two sets of axons are shown. One set, which forms a cluster around the third ventricle at the base of the brain, shows up as a rusty color. The other set, scattered through the lateral septum, looks like strands of gold fibers. (As you can see, a properly stained brain section can be beautiful. See *Figure 5.33.*)

But we are interested in acetylcholine, which is not a peptide. Therefore, we cannot use immunocytochemical methods to find this neurotransmitter. However, we can use these methods to localize the enzyme that produces it. The synthesis of acetylcholine is made possible by the enzyme choline acetyltransferase (ChAT). Thus, neurons that contain this enzyme almost certainly secrete ACh. Figure 5.34 shows acetylcholinergic neurons in the pons that have been identified by means of immunocytochemistry; the brain tissue was exposed to an antibody to ChAT attached to a fluorescent dye. (See *Figure 5.34.*)

Another indirect way to localize a substance uses a technique known as **in situ hybridization:** All peptides and proteins (which includes all enzymes, of course) are synthesized according to information contained on the chromosomes. As we saw in Chapter 2, when a particular protein is to be produced, the necessary information is copied from a chromosome onto a piece of messenger RNA, which then leaves the nucleus and travels to a ribosome, where protein synthesis takes place. (This process

was illustrated in Figure 2.6.) The recipe for the protein is coded as a particular sequence of nucleotides that make up the messenger RNA. If this code is known (and in most cases it is), molecular biologists can synthesize a piece of radioactive RNA that contains a sequence of nucleotides complementary to the sequence on the messenger RNA. We would expose slices of brain tissue to the radioactive RNA, which sticks to molecules of the appropriate messenger RNA. Then we would use autoradiographic methods (described in the second section of this chapter) to reveal the location of the messenger RNA and, by inference, the location of the cells producing the protein whose synthesis the RNA initiates.

Figure 5.35 explains the in situ hybridization method graphically, and Figure 5.36 shows the location of the messenger RNA responsible for the synthesis of a peptide, vasopressin, as revealed by this method. Side lighting of the microscope slide makes the silver grains in the photographic emulsion show up as white spots. (See *Figures 5.35* and *5.36.*)

Localizing Particular Receptors

As we saw in earlier chapters, neurotransmitters, neuromodulators, and hormones convey their messages to their target cells by binding with receptors. The location of these receptors can be determined by two different procedures.

The first procedure uses autoradiography. We expose slices of brain tissue to a solution containing a radioactive ligand for a particular receptor. Next, we rinse the slices so that the only radioactivity remaining in them is that of the molecules of the ligand bound to their receptors.

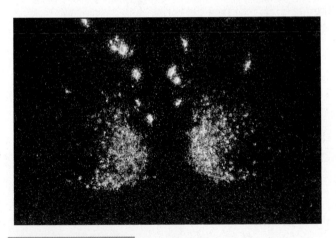

figure 5.36

In situ hybridization. The tissue was exposed to radioactive RNA that binds with the messenger RNA responsible for the synthesis of vasopressin, a peptide. The location of the radioactive RNA, revealed by means of autoradiography, shows up as white spots. The labeled neurons are located in a pair of nuclei in the hypothalamus.

(Courtesy of Geert DeVries, University of Massachusetts.)

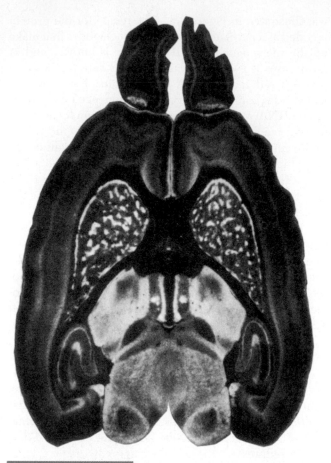

figure   5.37

An autoradiogram of a rat brain (horizontal section, rostral is at top) that was incubated in a solution containing radioactive morphine, a ligand for opiate receptors. The receptors are indicated by white areas.

(From Herkenham, M. A., and Pert, C. B. *Journal of Neuroscience,* 1982, *2,* 1129–1149.)

Finally, we use autoradiographic methods to localize the radioactive ligand—and thus the receptors. Figure 5.37 shows an example of the results of this procedure. We see an autoradiogram of a slice of a rat's brain that was soaked in a solution that contained radioactive morphine, which bound with the brain's opiate receptors. (See *Figure 5.37.*)

The second procedure uses immunocytochemistry. Receptors are proteins; therefore, we can produce antibodies against them. We expose slices of brain tissue to the appropriate antibody (labeled with a fluorescent dye)

double labeling   Labeling neurons in a particular region by two different means, for example, by using an anterograde tracer and a label for a particular enzyme.

and look at the slices with a microscope under light of a particular wavelength.

Let's apply the method for localizing receptors to the first line of investigation we considered in this chapter: the role of the ventromedial hypothalamus (VMH) in the sexual behavior of female rats. As we saw, lesions of the VMH abolish this behavior. We also saw that the behavior does not occur if the rat's ovaries are removed but that it can be activated by stimulation of the VMH with electricity or an excitatory amino acid. These results suggest that the sex hormones produced by the ovaries act on neurons in the VMH.

This hypothesis suggests two experiments. First, we could use the procedure shown in Figure 5.30 to place a small amount of the appropriate sex hormone directly into the VMH of female rats whose ovaries we had previously removed. As we shall see in Chapter 10, this procedure works; the hormone *does* reactivate the animals' sexual behavior. The second experiment would use autoradiography to look for the receptors for the sex hormone. We would expose slices of rat brain to the radioactive hormone, rinse them, and perform autoradiography. If we did so, we would indeed find radioactivity in the VMH. (And if we compared slices from the brains of female and male rats, we would find evidence of more hormone receptors in the females' brains.) We could also use immunocytochemistry to localize the hormone receptors, and we would obtain the same results.

A useful property of the various methods of localizing neurochemicals is that they can be combined with anterograde or retrograde tracers. Thus, investigators not only can determine what chemicals a particular neuron contains, but also can determine what connections these neurons have with other parts of the brain. This method is called **double labeling.** Figure 5.38 shows a group of neurons in the periaqueductal gray matter. The cells that appear brown have been stained with an immunocytochemical method that reveals the presence of estrogen receptors. The terminal buttons that form synapses with these neurons have been stained with PHA-L, which was injected into the VMH. These results tell us that neurons in the periaqueductal gray matter that are sensitive to estrogens (female sex hormones) also receive input from the ventromedial nucleus of the hypothalamus. (See *Figure 5.38.*)

i n t e r i m
s u m m a r y

Neurochemical Methods

Neurochemical methods can be used to determine the location of an enormous variety of substances in the brain. They can identify neurons that secrete a particular neuro-

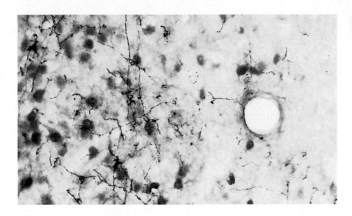

figure 5.38

Double labeling, using immunocytochemistry and anterograde tracing. The photomicrograph shows a slice through the periaqueductal gray matter of a guinea pig. The tissue has been treated with an antibody to estrogen receptor protein; a dye label attached to the antibody makes the cells that contain these receptors show up as brown. The purple-colored axons and terminal buttons are labeled with PHA-L, which was injected into the ventromedial nucleus of the hypothalamus.

(Courtesy of Kirsten Nielsen Ricciardi and Jeffrey Blaustein, University of Massachusetts.)

transmitter or neuromodulator and those that possess receptors that respond to the presence of these substances. Peptides and proteins can be directly localized, through immunocytochemical methods; the tissue is exposed to an antibody that is linked to a molecule that fluoresces under light of a particular wavelength. Other substances can be detected by immunocytochemical localization of an enzyme that is required for their synthesis. Peptides and proteins can also be detected by in situ hybridization methods that reveal the presence of the messenger RNA that directs their synthesis.

Receptors for neurochemicals can be localized by two means. The first method uses autoradiography to reveal the distribution of a radioactive ligand to which the tissue has been exposed. The second method uses immunocytochemistry to detect the presence of the receptors themselves, which are proteins. Combined staining methods can localize neurons that possess a particular receptor or a particular peptide and also have connections with particular regions of the brain.

Table 5.3 summarizes the research methods presented in this section.

Genetic Methods

All behavior is determined by interactions between an individual's brain and his or her environment. Many behavioral characteristics—such as talents, personality variables and mental disorders—seem to run in families. This fact suggests that genetic factors may play a role in the development of physiological differences that are ultimately responsible for these characteristics. In some cases the genetic link is very clear: A defective gene interferes with brain development, and a neurological abnormality causes behavioral deficits. In other cases the links between heredity and behavior are much more subtle, and special genetic methods must be used to reveal them.

table 5.3

Research Methods: Part III		
GOAL OF METHOD	**METHOD**	**REMARKS**
Identify neurons producing a particular neurotransmitter or neuromodulator	Immunocytochemical localization of peptide or protein	Requires a specific antibody
	Immunocytochemical localization of enzyme responsible for synthesis of substance	Useful if substance is not a peptide or protein
Identify neurons that contain a particular type of receptor	Autoradiographic localization of radioactive ligand	
	Immunocytochemical localization of receptor	Requires a specific antibody
Identify neurons that produce a particular neurotransmitter or contain a particular type of receptor; also communicate with other neurons in a specific brain region	Combination of any of the methods above with anterograde or retrograde tracing methods	Provides detailed information about the connections of specific types of neurons

Twin Studies

A powerful method for estimating the influence of heredity on a particular trait is to compare the *concordance rate* for this trait in pairs of monozygotic and dizygotic twins. Monozygotic twins (identical twins) have identical genotypes—that is, their chromosomes, and the genes they contain, are identical. In contrast, the genetic similarity between dizygotic twins (fraternal twins) is, on the average, 50 percent. Investigators study records to identify pairs of twins in which at least one member has the trait—for example, a diagnosis of a particular mental disorder. If both twins have been diagnosed with this disorder, they are said to be *concordant*. If only one has received this diagnosis, the twins are said to be *discordant*. Thus, if a disorder has a genetic basis, the percentage of monozygotic twins who are concordant for the diagnosis will be higher than that for dizygotic twins. For example, as we will see in Chapter 16, the concordance rate for schizophrenia in twins is at least four times higher for monozygotic twins than for dizygotic twins, a finding that provides strong evidence that schizophrenia is a heritable trait. Twin studies have found that many individual characteristics, including personality traits, prevalence of obesity, incidence of alcoholism, and a wide variety of mental disorders, are influenced by genetic factors.

Adoption Studies

Another method for estimating the heritability of a particular behavioral trait is to compare people who were adopted early in life with their biological and adoptive parents. All behavioral traits are affected to some degree by hereditary factors, environmental factors, and an interaction between hereditary and environmental factors. Environmental factors are both social and biological in nature. For example, the mother's health, nutrition, and drug-taking behavior during pregnancy are prenatal environmental factors, and the child's diet, medical care, and social environment (both inside and outside the home) are postnatal environmental factors. If a child is adopted soon after birth, most of the postnatal environmental factors will be associated with the adoptive parents, the genetic factors will be associated with the biological parents, and the prenatal environmental factors will be associated with the biological mother.

Adoption studies require that the investigator knows the identity of the parents of the people being studied and is able to measure the behavioral trait in the biological and adoptive parents. If the people being studied strongly resemble their biological parents, we conclude that the trait is probably influenced by genetic factors. To be certain, we will have to rule out possible differences in the prenatal environment of the adopted children. If, instead, the peo-ple resemble their adoptive parents, we conclude that the trait is influenced by environmental factors. (It would take further study to determine just what these environmental factors might be.) Of course, it is possible that both hereditary and environmental factors play a role, in which case the people being studied will resemble both their biological and adoptive parents.

Targeted Mutations

A recently developed method has put a powerful tool in the hands of neuroscientists. **Targeted mutations** are mutated genes produced in the laboratory and inserted into the chromosomes of mice. These mutated genes (also called knockout genes) are defective—They fail to produce a functional protein. In many cases the target of the mutation is an enzyme that controls a particular chemical reaction. For example, we will see in Chapter 13 that lack of a particular enzyme interferes with learning. This result suggests that the enzyme is partly responsible for changes in the structure of synapses required for learning to occur. In other cases the target of the mutation is a protein that itself serves useful functions in the cell. For example, we will see in Chapter 18 that a particular type of opiate receptor is involved in the reinforcing and analgesic effects of opiates.

---

i n t e r i m   s u m m a r y

Genetic Methods

Because genes direct an organism's development, genetic methods are very useful in studies of the physiology of behavior. Twin studies compare the concordance rates of monozygotic (identical) and dizygotic (fraternal) twins for a particular trait. A higher concordance rate for monozygotic twins provides evidence that the trait is influenced by heredity. Adoption studies compare people who were adopted during infancy with their biological and adoptive parents. If the people resemble their biological parents, evidence is seen for genetic factors. If the people resemble their adoptive parents, evidence is seen for a role of factors in the family environment.

Targeted mutations permit neuroscientists to study the effects of a lack of a particular protein—for example, an enzyme, structural protein, or receptor—on an animal's physiological and behavioral characteristics.

---

targeted mutation A mutated gene (also called a "knockout gene") produced in the laboratory and inserted into the chromosomes of mice; fails to produce a functional protein.

Suggested Readings

Laboratory Manual

Wellman, P. *Laboratory Exercises in Physiological Psychology.* Boston: Allyn and Bacon, 1994.

Stereotaxic Atlases

Paxinos, G., and Watson, C. *The Rat Brain in Stereotaxic Coordinates,* 4th ed. San Diego, CA: Academic Press, 1998.

Slotnick, B. M., and Leonard, C. M. *A Stereotaxic Atlas of the Albino Mouse Forebrain.* Rockville, MD: Public Health Service, 1975. (U.S. Government Printing Office Stock Number 017-024-00491-0)

Snider, R. S., and Niemer, W. T. *A Stereotaxic Atlas of the Cat Brain.* Chicago: University of Chicago Press, 1961.

Swanson, L. W. *Brain Maps: Structure of the Rat Brain.* Amsterdam: Elsevier, 1992.

Histological Methods

Heimer, L., and Záborsky, L. *Neuroanatomical Tract-Tracing Methods 2: Recent Progress.* New York: Plenum Press, 1989.

Suggested Web Sites

Online Mendelian Inheritance

http://www3.ncbi.nlm.nih.gov/Omim/

This site contains an online catalog of human genes and genetic disorders and links to other genetic inheritance sites.

Bioscience Research: Methods

http://biochemie.net/links/Methods/

Protocols for various techniques in molecular biology are the focus of this site.

Tutorial of Functional MRI

http://www.mhri.edu.au/~nab/gregg.html

This site provides an advanced overview of the functional MRI technique and provides comprehensive references for the technique.

Vision

o u t l i n e

■ **The Stimulus**

■ **Anatomy of the Visual System**
The Eyes
Photoreceptors
Connections Between Eye and Brain
Interim Summary

■ **Coding of Visual Information
in the Retina**
Coding of Light and Dark
Coding of Color
Interim Summary

■ **Analysis of Visual Information:
Role of the Striate Cortex**
Anatomy of the Striate Cortex
Orientation and Movement
Spatial Frequency
Texture
Retinal Disparity
Color
Modular Organization of the
   Striate Cortex
Blindsight
Interim Summary

■ **Analysis of Visual Information:
Role of the Visual Association
Cortex**
Two Streams of Visual Analysis
Perception of Color
Analysis of Form
Perception of Movement
Perception of Spatial Location
Interim Summary

Alma Woodsey Thomas, *The Eclipse*, 1970.
© Smithsonian American Art Museum,
Washington, DC/Art Resource, NY.

Dr. L., a young neuropsychologist, was presenting the case of Mrs. R. to a group of medical students doing a rotation in the neurology department at the medical center. The chief of the department had shown them Mrs. R.'s CT scans, and now Dr. L. was addressing the students. He told them that Mrs. R.'s stroke had not impaired her ability to talk or to move about, but it had affected her vision.

A nurse ushered Mrs. R. into the room and helped her find a seat at the end of the table.

"How are you, Mrs. R.?" asked Dr. L.

"I'm fine. I've been home for a month now, and I can do just about everything that I did before I had my stroke."

"Good. How is your vision?"

"Well, I'm afraid that's still a problem."

"What seems to give you the most trouble?"

"I just don't seem to be able to recognize things. When I'm working in my kitchen, I know what everything is as long as no one moves anything. A few times my husband tried to help me by putting things away, and I couldn't see them any more." She laughed. "Well, I could see them, but I just couldn't say what they were."

Dr. L. took some objects out of a paper bag and placed them on the table in front of her.

"Can you tell me what these are?" he asked. "No," he said, "please don't touch them."

Mrs. R. stared intently at the objects. "No, I can't rightly say what they are."

Dr. L. pointed to one of them, a wristwatch. "Tell me what you see here," he said.

Mrs. R. looked thoughtful, turning her head one way and then the other. "Well, I see something round, and it has two things attached to it, one on the top and one on the bottom." She continued to stare at it. "There are some things inside the circle, I think, but I can't make out what they are."

"Pick it up."

She did so, made a wry face, and said, "Oh. It's a wristwatch." At Dr. L.'s request, she picked up the rest of the objects, one by one, and identified each of them correctly.

"Do you have trouble recognizing people, too?" asked Dr. L.

"Oh, yes!" she sighed. "While I was still in the hospital, my husband and my son both came in to see me, and I couldn't tell who was who until my husband said something—then I could tell which direction his voice was coming from. Now I've trained myself to recognize my husband. I can usually see his glasses and his bald head, but I have to work at it. And I've been fooled a few times." She laughed. "One of our neighbors is bald and wears glasses, too, and one day when he and his wife were visiting us, I thought he was my husband, so I called him 'honey.' It was a little embarrassing at first, but everyone understood."

"What does a face look like to you?" asked Dr. L.

"Well, I know that it's a face, because I can usually see the eyes, and it's on top of a body. I can see a body pretty well, by how it moves." She paused a moment. "Oh, yes, I forgot, sometimes I can recognize a person by how he moves. You know, you can often recognize friends by the way they walk, even when they're far away. I can still do that. That's funny, isn't it? I can't see people's faces very well, but I can recognize the way they walk."

Dr. L. made some movements with his hands. "Can you tell what I'm doing?" he asked.

"Yes, you're mixing something—like some cake batter."

He mimed the gestures of turning a key, writing, and dealing out playing cards, and Mrs. R. recognized them without any difficulty.

"Do you have any trouble reading?" he asked.

"Well, a little, but I don't do too badly."

Dr. L. handed her a magazine, and she began to read the article aloud—somewhat hesitantly but accurately. "Why is it," she asked, "that I can see the *words* all right but have so much trouble with *things* and with people's faces?"

A s we saw in Chapter 3, the brain performs two major functions: It controls the movements of the muscles, producing useful behaviors, and it regulates the body's internal environment. To perform both these tasks, the brain must be informed about what is happening both in the external environment and within the body. Such information is received by the sensory systems. This chapter and the next are devoted to a discussion of the ways in which sensory organs detect changes in the environment and the ways in which the brain interprets neural signals from these organs.

We receive information about the environment from **sensory receptors**—specialized neurons that detect a variety of physical events. (Do not confuse *sensory receptors* with receptors for neurotransmitters, neuromodulators, and hormones. Sensory receptors are specialized neurons, and the other types of receptors are specialized proteins that bind with certain molecules.) Stimuli impinge on the receptors and, through various processes, alter their membrane potentials. This process is known as **sensory transduction**

---

sensory receptor A specialized neuron that detects a particular category of physical events.

sensory transduction The process by which sensory stimuli are transduced into slow, graded receptor potentials.

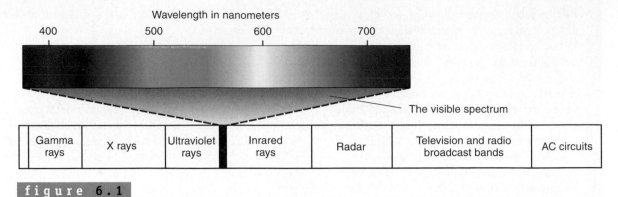

Wavelength in nanometers

| Gamma rays | X rays | Ultraviolet rays | Inrared rays | Radar | Television and radio broadcast bands | AC circuits |

The visible spectrum

figure   6.1

The electromagnetic spectrum.

because sensory events are *transduced* ("transferred") into changes in the cells' membrane potential. These electrical changes are called **receptor potentials.** Most receptors lack axons; a portion of their somatic membrane forms synapses with the dendrites of other neurons. Receptor potentials affect the release of neurotransmitters and hence modify the pattern of firing in neurons with which these cells form synapses. Ultimately, the information reaches the brain.

People often say that we have five senses: sight, hearing, smell, taste, and touch. Actually, we have more than five, but even experts disagree about how the lines between the various categories should be drawn. Certainly, we should add the vestibular senses; as well as providing us with auditory information, the inner ear supplies information about head orientation and movement. The sense of touch (or, more accurately, *somatosensation*) detects changes in pressure, warmth, cold, vibration, limb position, and events that damage tissue (that is, produce pain). Everyone agrees that we can detect these stimuli; the issue is whether we should say that they are detected by separate senses.

This chapter considers vision, the sensory modality that receives the most attention from psychologists, anatomists, and physiologists. One reason for this attention derives from the fascinating complexity of the sensory organs of vision and the relatively large proportion of the brain that is devoted to the analysis of visual information. Another reason, I am sure, is that vision is so important to us as individuals. A natural fascination with such a rich source of information about the world leads to curiosity about how this sensory modality works. Chapter 7 deals with the other sensory modalities: audition, the vestibular senses, the somatosenses, gustation, and olfaction.

receptor potential A slow, graded electrical potential produced by a receptor cell in response to a physical stimulus.

hue One of the perceptual dimensions of color; the dominant wavelength.

brightness One of the perceptual dimensions of color; intensity.

saturation One of the perceptual dimensions of color; purity.

The Stimulus

As we all know, our eyes detect the presence of light. For humans light is a narrow band of the spectrum of electromagnetic radiation. Electromagnetic radiation with a wavelength between 380 and 760 nm (a nanometer, nm, is one-billionth of a meter) is visible to us. (See *Figure 6.1*.) Other animals can detect different ranges of electromagnetic radiation. For example, honeybees can detect differences in ultraviolet radiation reflected by flowers that appear white to us. The range of wavelengths we call *light* is not qualitatively different from the rest of the electromagnetic spectrum; it is simply the part of the continuum that we humans can see.

The perceived color of light is determined by three dimensions: *hue, saturation,* and *brightness*. Light travels at a constant speed of approximately 300,000 kilometers (186,000 miles) per second. Thus, if the frequency of oscillation of the wave varies, the distance between the peaks of the waves will similarly vary, but in inverse fashion. Slower oscillations lead to longer wavelengths, and faster ones lead to shorter wavelengths. Wavelength determines

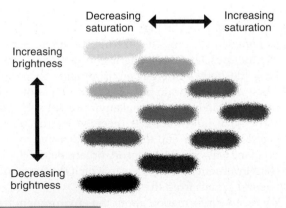

figure   6.2

Examples of colors with the same dominant wavelength (hue) but different levels of saturations or brightness.

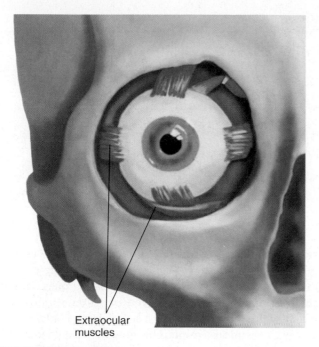

figure **6.3**

The extraocular muscles, which move the eyes.

the first of the three perceptual dimensions of light: **hue.** The visible spectrum displays the range of hues that our eyes can detect.

Light can also vary in intensity, which corresponds to the second perceptual dimension of light: **brightness.** If the intensity of the electromagnetic radiation is increased, the apparent brightness increases, too. The third dimension, **saturation,** refers to the relative purity of the light that is being perceived. If all the radiation is of one wavelength, the perceived color is pure, or fully saturated. Conversely, if the radiation contains all wavelengths, it

produces no sensation of hue—it appears white. Colors with intermediate amounts of saturation consist of different mixtures of wavelengths. Figure 6.2 shows some color samples, all with the same hue but with different levels of brightness and saturation. (See *Figure 6.2.*)

Anatomy of the Visual System

For an individual to see, an image must be focused on the retina, the inner lining of the eye. This image causes changes in the electrical activity of millions of neurons in the retina, which results in messages being sent through the optic nerves to the rest of the brain. (I said "the rest" because the retina is actually part of the brain; it and the optic nerve are in the central—not peripheral—nervous system.) This section describes the anatomy of the eyes, the photoreceptors in the retina that detect the presence of light, and the connections between the retina and the brain.

The Eyes

The eyes are suspended in the *orbits,* bony pockets in the front of the skull. They are held in place and moved by six extraocular muscles attached to the tough, white outer coat of the eye called the *sclera.* (See *Figure 6.3.*) Normally, we cannot look behind our eyeballs and see these muscles, because their attachments to the eyes are hidden by the *conjunctiva.* These mucous membranes line the eye lid and fold back to attach to the eye (thus preventing a contact lens that has slipped off the cornea from "falling behind the eye"). Figure 6.4 illustrates the anatomy of the eye. (See *Figure 6.4*.)

The eyes make three types of movements: vergence movements, saccadic movements, and pursuit movements.

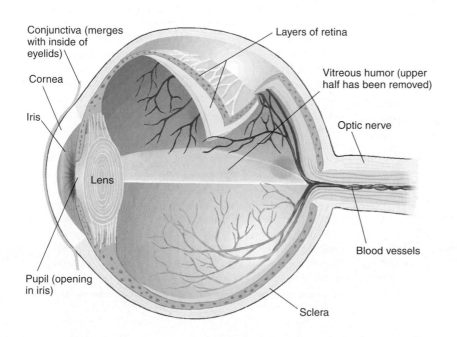

figure **6.4**

The human eye.

Locations and Response Characteristics of Photoreceptors

CONES	RODS
Most prevalent in the central retina; found in the fovea	Most prevalent in the peripheral retina; not found in the fovea
Sensitive to moderate-to-high levels of light	Sensitive to low levels of light
Provide information about hue	Provide only monochromatic information
Provide excellent acuity	Provide poor acuity

Vergence movements are cooperative movements that keep both eyes fixed on the same target—or, more precisely, that keep the image of the target object on corresponding parts of the two retinas. If you hold up a finger in front of your face, look at it, and then bring your finger closer to your face, your eyes will make vergence movements toward your nose. If you then look at an object on the other side of the room, your eyes will rotate outward, and you will see two separate blurry images of your finger.

When you scan the scene in front of you, your gaze does not roam slowly and steadily across its features. Instead, your eyes make jerky **saccadic movements**—you shift your gaze abruptly from one point to another. When you read a line in this book, your eyes stop several times, moving very quickly between each stop. You cannot consciously control the speed of movement between stops; during each *saccade* the eyes move as fast as they can. Only by performing a **pursuit movement**—say, by looking at your finger while you move it around—can you make your eyes move more slowly.

The outer layer of most of the eye, the sclera, is opaque and does not permit entry of light. However, the cornea, the outer layer at the front of the eye, is transparent and admits light. The amount of light that enters is regulated by the size of the pupil, which is an opening in the iris, the pigmented ring of muscles situated behind the cornea. The lens, situated immediately behind the iris, consists of a series of transparent, onionlike layers. Its shape can be altered by contraction of the ciliary muscles. These changes in shape permit the eye to focus images of near or distant objects on the retina—a process called **accommodation.**

After passing through the lens, light traverses the main part of the eye, which is filled with *vitreous humor* ("glassy liquid"), a clear, gelatinous substance. After passing through the vitreous humor, light falls on the **retina,** the interior lining of the back of the eye. In the retina are located the receptor cells, the **rods** and **cones** (named for their shapes), collectively known as **photoreceptors.**

The human retina contains approximately 120 million rods and 6 million cones. Although they are greatly outnumbered by rods, cones provide us with most of the information about our environment. In particular, they are responsible for our daytime vision. They provide us with information about small features in the environment and thus are the source of vision of the highest sharpness, or *acuity* (from *acus,* "needle"). The **fovea,** or central region of the retina, which mediates our most acute vision, contains only cones. Cones are also responsible for color vision—our ability to discriminate light of different wavelengths. Although rods do not detect different colors and provide vision of poor acuity, they are more sensitive to light. In a very dimly lighted environment we use our rod vision; therefore, in dim light we are color-blind and lack foveal vision. You may have noticed, while out on a dark night, that looking directly at a dim, distant light (that is, placing the image of the light on the fovea) causes it to disappear. (See *Table 6.1*.)

Another feature of the retina is the **optic disk,** where the axons conveying visual information gather together

vergence movement The cooperative movement of the eyes, which ensures that the image of an object falls on identical portions of both retinas.

saccadic movement (*suh kad ik*) The rapid, jerky movement of the eyes used in scanning a visual scene.

pursuit movement The movement that the eyes make to maintain an image of a moving object on the fovea.

accommodation Changes in the thickness of the lens of the eye, accomplished by the ciliary muscles, that focus images of near or distant objects on the retina.

retina The neural tissue and photoreceptive cells located on the inner surface of the posterior portion of the eye.

rod One of the receptor cells of the retina; sensitive to light of low intensity.

cone One of the receptor cells of the retina; maximally sensitive to one of three different wavelengths of light and hence encodes color vision.

photoreceptor One of the receptor cells of the retina; transduces photic energy into electrical potentials.

fovea (*foe vee a*) The region of the retina that mediates the most acute vision of birds and higher mammals. Color-sensitive cones constitute the only type of photoreceptor found in the fovea.

optic disk The location of the exit point from the retina of the fibers of the ganglion cells that form the optic nerve; responsible for the blind spot.

figure 6.5

A test for the blind spot. With your left eye closed, look at the + with your right eye and move the page nearer to and farther from you. When the page is about 20 cm from your face, the green circle disappears because its image falls on the blind spot of your right eye.

and leave the eye through the optic nerve. The optic disk produces a *blind spot* because no receptors are located there. We do not normally perceive our blind spots, but their presence can be demonstrated. If you have not found yours, you may want to try the exercise described in *Figure 6.5*.

Close examination of the retina shows that it consists of several layers of neuron cell bodies, their axons and dendrites, and the photoreceptors. Figure 6.6 illustrates a cross section through the primate retina, which is divided into three main layers: the photoreceptive layer, the bipolar cell layer, and the ganglion cell layer. Note that the photoreceptors are at the *back* of the retina; light must pass through the overlying layers to get to them. Fortunately, these layers are transparent. (See *Figure 6.6*.)

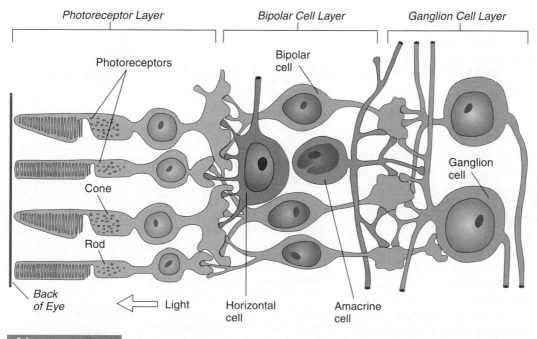

figure 6.6

Details of retinal circuitry.

(Adapted from Dowling, J. E., and Boycott, B. B. *Proceedings of the Royal Society of London, B,* 1966, *166,* 80–111.)

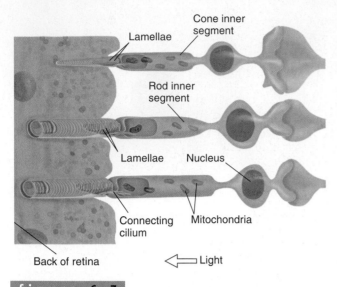

Cone inner segment

Lamellae

Rod inner segment

Lamellae Nucleus

Connecting cilium Mitochondria

Back of retina ⟸ Light

Photoreceptors.

The photoreceptors form synapses with **bipolar cells,** neurons whose two arms connect the shallowest and deepest layers of the retina. In turn, these neurons form synapses with the **ganglion cells,** neurons whose axons travel through the optic nerves (the second cranial nerves) and carry visual information into the brain. In addition, the retina contains **horizontal cells** and **amacrine cells,** both of which transmit information in a direction parallel to the surface of the retina and thus combine messages from adjacent photoreceptors. (See *Figure 6.6.*)

The primate retina contains approximately 55 different types of neurons: one type of rod, three types of cones, two types of horizontal cells, ten types of bipolar cells, 24–29 types of amacrine cells, and 10–15 types of ganglion cells (Masland, 2001).

Photoreceptors

Figure 6.7 shows a drawing of two rods and a cone. Note that each photoreceptor consists of an outer segment connected by a cilium to the inner segment, which contains the nucleus. (See *Figure 6.7.*) The outer segment contains several hundred **lamellae,** or thin plates of membrane. (*Lamella* is the diminutive form of *lamina,* "thin layer.")

Let's consider the nature of transduction of visual information. The first step in the chain of events that leads to visual perception involves a special chemical called a photopigment. **Photopigments** are special molecules embedded in the membrane of the lamellae; a single human rod contains approximately 10 million of them. The molecules consist of two parts: an **opsin** (a protein) and **retinal** (a lipid). There are several forms of opsin; for

example, the photopigment of human rods, **rhodopsin,** consists of *rod opsin* plus retinal. (*Rhod-* refers to the Greek *rhodon,* "rose," not to *rod.* Before it is bleached by the action of light, rhodopsin has a pinkish hue.) Retinal is synthesized from vitamin A, which explains why carrots, which are rich in this vitamin, are said to be good for your eyesight.

When a molecule of rhodopsin is exposed to light, it breaks into its two constituents: rod opsin and retinal. When that happens, the rod opsin changes from its rosy color to a pale yellow; hence, we say that the light *bleaches* the photopigment. The splitting of the photopigment causes a change in the membrane potential of the photoreceptor (the receptor potential), which changes the rate at which the photoreceptor releases its neurotransmitter, glutamate.

The membrane of photoreceptors is different from that of other neurons—it contains cation channels that are normally *open* (Baylor, 1996). In the dark these ion channels, which admit Na^+ and Ca^{2+}, are held open by molecules of cyclic GMP; thus, the resting membrane potential is less polarized than that of other neurons. As a consequence, photoreceptors continuously release glutamate when light is *not* falling on them. When light strikes a molecule of photopigment and causes it to split, the resulting series of chemical events activates a G protein known as *transducin.* In turn, molecules of transducin activate molecules of the enzyme *phosphodiesterase,* which destroy cyclic GMP, closing the ion channels. Because cations can no longer enter the cell, the membrane then becomes more polarized, and the release of glutamate decreases. (See *Figure 6.8.*)

bipolar cell A bipolar neuron located in the middle layer of the retina, conveying information from the photoreceptors to the ganglion cells.

ganglion cell A neuron located in the retina that receives visual information from bipolar cells; its axons give rise to the optic nerve.

horizontal cell A neuron in the retina that interconnects adjacent photoreceptors and the outer processes of the bipolar cells.

amacrine cell (*amm a krin*) A neuron in the retina that interconnects adjacent ganglion cells and the inner processes of the bipolar cells.

lamella A layer of membrane containing photopigments; found in rods and cones of the retina.

photopigment A protein dye bonded to retinal, a substance derived from vitamin A; responsible for transduction of visual information.

opsin (*opp sin*) A class of protein that, together with retinal, constitutes the photopigments.

retinal (*rett i nahl*) A chemical synthesized from vitamin A; joins with an opsin to form a photopigment.

rhodopsin (*roh dopp sin*) A particular opsin found in rods.

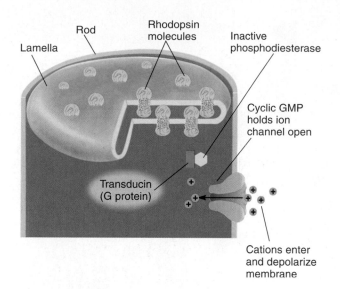

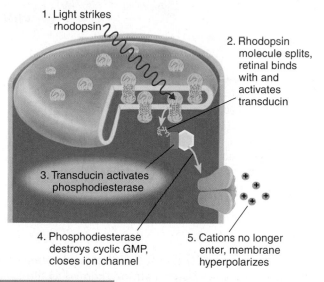

figure 6.8

Transduction. A hypothetical explanation for the production of receptor potentials in photoreceptors.

In the vertebrate retina, photoreceptors provide input to both bipolar cells and horizontal cells. Figure 6.9 shows the neural circuitry from a photoreceptor to a ganglion cell. The circuitry is much simplified and omits the horizontal cells and amacrine cells. The first two types of cells in the circuit—photoreceptors and bipolar cells—do not produce action potentials. Instead, their release of neurotransmitter is regulated by the value of their membrane potential; depolarizations increase the release, and hyperpolarizations decrease it. The circles indicate what would be seen on an oscilloscope screen recording changes in the cells' membrane potentials in response to a spot of light shining on the photoreceptor.

The hyperpolarizing effect of light on the membranes of photoreceptors is shown in the left graph. The hyperpolarization *reduces* the release of neurotransmitter by the photoreceptor. Because the neurotransmitter normally hyperpolarizes the dendrites of the bipolar cell, a *reduction* in its release causes the membrane of the bipolar cell to *depolarize*. Thus, light hyperpolarizes the photoreceptor and depolarizes the bipolar cell. (See ***Figure 6.9***.) The depolarization causes the bipolar cell to release more neurotransmitter, which depolarizes the membrane of the ganglion cell, causing it to increase its rate of firing. Thus, light shining on the photoreceptor causes excitation of the ganglion cell.

The circuit shown in Figure 6.9 illustrates a ganglion cell whose firing rate increases in response to light. As we will see, other ganglion cells *decrease* their firing rate in response to light. These neurons are connected to bipolar cells that form different types of synapses with the photoreceptors. The functions of these two types of circuits are discussed in a later section, "Coding of Visual Information in the Retina." If you would like to know more about the neural circuitry of the retina, you should consult the book by Rodieck (1998).

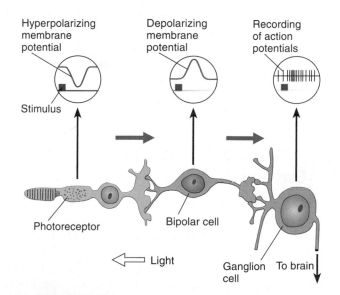

figure 6.9

Neural circuitry in the retina. Light striking a photoreceptor produces a hyperpolarization, so the photoreceptor releases *less* neurotransmitter. Because the neurotransmitter normally hyperpolarizes the membrane of the bipolar cell, the reduction causes a *depolarization*. This depolarization causes the bipolar cell to release *more* neurotransmitter, which excites the ganglion cell.

(Adapted from Dowling, J. E., in *The Neurosciences: Fourth Study Program,* edited by F. O. Schmitt and F. G. Worden. Cambridge, Mass.: MIT Press, 1979.)

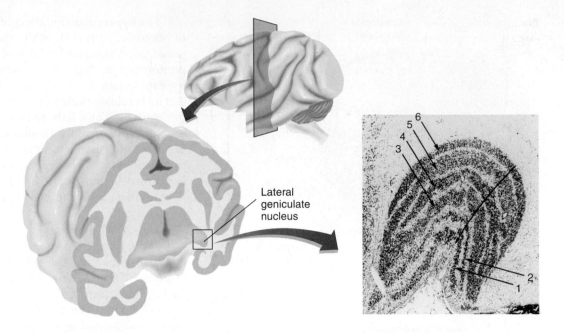

A photomicrograph of a section through the right lateral geniculate nucleus of a rhesus monkey (cresyl violet stain). Layers 1, 4, and 6 receive input from the contralateral (left) eye, and layers 2, 3, and 5 receive input from the ipsilateral (right) eye. Layers 1 and 2 are the magnocellular layers; layers 3–6 are the parvocellular layers. The koniocellular sublayers are found ventral to each of the parvocellular and magnocellular other layers. The receptive fields of all six principal layers are in almost perfect registration; cells located along the line of the unlabeled arrow have receptive fields centered on the same point.

(From Hubel, D. H., Wiesel, T. N., and Le Vay, S. *Philosophical Transactions of the Royal Society of London, B,* 1977, *278*, 131–163.)

Connections Between Eye and Brain

The axons of the retinal ganglion cells bring information to the rest of the brain. They ascend through the optic nerves and reach the **dorsal lateral geniculate nucleus** of the thalamus. This nucleus receives its name from its resemblance to a bent knee (*genu* is Latin for "knee"). It contains six layers of neurons, each of which receives input from only one eye. The neurons in the two inner layers contain cell bodies that are larger than those in the outer four layers. For this reason, the inner two layers are called the **magnocellular layers,** and the outer four layers are called the **parvocellular layers** (*parvo-* refers to the small size of the cells). A third set of neurons in the **koniocellular sublayers** are found ventral to each of the magnocellular and parvocellular layers. (*Konis* is the Greek word for "dust.") As we will see later, these three sets of layers belong to different systems, which are responsible for the analysis of different types of visual information. They receive input from different types of retinal ganglion cells. (See *Figure 6.10*.)

The neurons in the dorsal lateral geniculate nucleus send their axons through a pathway known as the *optic radiations* to the primary visual cortex—the region sur-

dorsal lateral geniculate nucleus A group of cell bodies within the lateral geniculate body of the thalamus; receives inputs from the retina and projects to the primary visual cortex.

magnocellular layer One of the inner two layers of neurons in the dorsal lateral geniculate nucleus; transmits information necessary for the perception of form, movement, depth, and small differences in brightness to the primary visual cortex.

parvocellular layer One of the four outer layers of neurons in the dorsal lateral geniculate nucleus; transmits information necessary for perception of color and fine details to the primary visual cortex.

koniocellular sublayer (*koh nee oh sell yew lur*) One of the sublayers of neurons in the dorsal lateral geniculate nucleus found ventral to each of the magnocellular and parvocellular layers; transmits information from short-wavelength ("blue") cones to the primary visual cortex.

rounding the **calcarine fissure** (*calcarine* means "spur-shaped"), a horizontal fissure located in the medial and posterior occipital lobe. The primary visual cortex is often called the **striate cortex** because it contains a dark-staining layer *(striation)* of cells. (See *Figure 6.11*.)

Figure 6.12 shows a diagrammatical view of a horizontal section of the human brain. The optic nerves join together at the base of the brain to form the X-shaped **optic chiasm** (*khiasma* means "cross"). There, axons from ganglion cells serving the inner halves of the retina (the nasal sides) cross through the chiasm and ascend to the dorsal lateral geniculate nucleus of the opposite side of the brain. The axons from the outer halves of the retina (the temporal sides) remain on the same side of the brain. (See *Figure 6.12*.) The lens inverts the image of the world projected on the retina (and similarly reverses left and right). Therefore, because the axons from the nasal halves of the retinas cross to the other side of the brain, each hemisphere receives information from the contralateral half (opposite side) of the visual scene. That is, if a person looks straight ahead, the right hemisphere receives information from the left half of the visual field, and the left hemisphere receives information from the right. (See *Figure 6.12*.)

Besides the primary retino-geniculo-cortical pathway, several other pathways are taken by fibers from the retina.

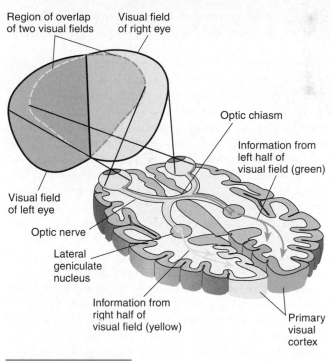

figure **6.12**

The primary visual pathway.

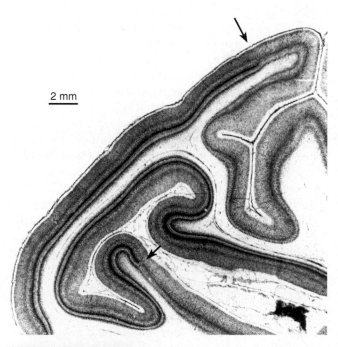

figure **6.11**

A photomicrograph of a cross section through the striate cortex of a rhesus macaque monkey. The ends of the striate cortex are shown by arrows.

(From Hubel, D. H., and Wiesel, T. N. *Proceedings of the Royal Society of London, B,* 1977, *198,* 1–59.)

For example, one pathway to the hypothalamus synchronizes an animal's activity cycles to the 24-hour rhythms of day and night. (We will study this system in Chapter 9.) Other pathways, especially those that travel to the optic tectum and the pretectal nuclei, coordinate eye movements, control the muscles of the iris (and thus the size of the pupil) and the ciliary muscles (which control the lens), and help to direct our attention to sudden movements in the periphery of our visual field.

interim
summary

The Stimulus and Anatomy of the Visual System

Light consists of electromagnetic radiation, similar to radio waves but of a different frequency and wavelength. Color can vary in three perceptual dimensions: hue, brightness, and sat-

calcarine fissure (*kal ka rine*) A horizontal fissure on the inner surface of the posterior cerebral cortex; the location of the primary visual cortex.

striate cortex (*stry ate*) The primary visual cortex.

optic chiasm A cross-shaped connection between the optic nerves, located below the base of the brain, just anterior to the pituitary gland.

uration, which correspond to the physical dimensions of wavelength, intensity, and purity.

The photoreceptors in the retina—the rods and the cones—detect light. Muscles move the eyes so that images of the environment fall on the retina. Accommodation is accomplished by the ciliary muscles, which change the shape of the lens. Photoreceptors communicate through synapses with bipolar cells, which communicate through synapses with ganglion cells. In addition, horizontal cells and amacrine cells combine messages from adjacent photoreceptors.

When light strikes a molecule of photopigment in a photoreceptor, the retinal molecule detaches from the opsin molecule. This detachment activates a G protein called transducin, which activates the enzyme phosphodiesterase, which in turn destroys the molecules of cyclic GMP that are holding cation channels open. The reduction in the influx of Na^+ and Ca^{2+} produces the receptor potential—hyperpolarization of the photoreceptor membrane. As a result, the rate of firing of the ganglion cell changes, signaling the detection of light.

Visual information from the retina reaches the striate cortex surrounding the calcarine fissure after being relayed through the magnocellular, parvocellular, and koniocellular layers of the dorsal lateral geniculate nuclei. Several other regions of the brain, including the hypothalamus and the tectum, also receive visual information. These regions help to regulate activity during the day–night cycle, coordinate eye and head movements, control attention to visual stimuli, and regulate the size of the pupils.

Coding of Visual Information in the Retina

This section describes the way in which cells of the retina encode information they receive from the photoreceptors.

Coding of Light and Dark

One of the most important methods for studying the physiology of the visual system is the use of microelectrodes to record the electrical activity of single neurons. As we saw in the previous section, some ganglion cells become excited when light falls on the photoreceptors with which they communicate. The **receptive field** of a neuron in the visual system is the part of the visual field that an individual neuron "sees"—that is, the part in which light must fall for the neuron to be stimulated. Obviously, the location of the receptive field of a particular neuron depends on the location of the photoreceptors that provide it with visual information. If a neuron receives information from photoreceptors located in the fovea, its receptive field will be at the fixation point—the point at which the eye is looking. If the neuron receives informa-

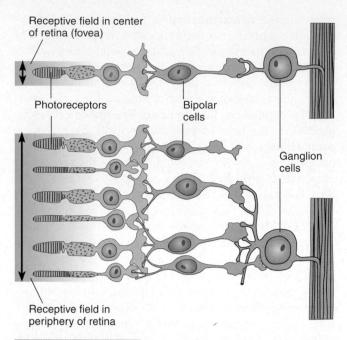

Receptive field in center of retina (fovea)

Photoreceptors

Bipolar cells

Ganglion cells

Receptive field in periphery of retina

figure 6.13

Central versus peripheral acuity. Ganglion cells in the fovea receive input from a smaller number of photoreceptors than in the periphery and hence provide more acute visual information.

tion from photoreceptors located in the periphery of the retina, its receptive field will be located off to one side.

At the periphery of the retina many individual receptors converge on a single ganglion cell, bringing information from a relatively large area of the retina—and hence a relatively large area of the visual field. However, foveal vision is more direct, with approximately equal numbers of ganglion cells and cones. These receptor-to-axon relationships explain the fact that our foveal (central) vision is very acute but our peripheral vision is much less precise. (See *Figure 6.13*.)

Over sixty years ago, Hartline (1938) discovered that the frog retina contained three types of ganglion cells. ON cells responded with an excitatory burst when the retina was illuminated, OFF cells responded when the light was turned off, and ON/OFF cells responded briefly when the light went on and again when it went off. Kuffler (1952, 1953), recording from ganglion cells in the retina of the cat, discovered that their receptive field consists of a roughly circular center, surrounded by a ring. Stimulation of the center or surrounding fields had contrary effects: ON cells were excited by light falling in the central field (*center*) and were inhibited by light falling in the

receptive field That portion of the visual field in which the presentation of visual stimuli will produce an alteration in the firing rate of a particular neuron.

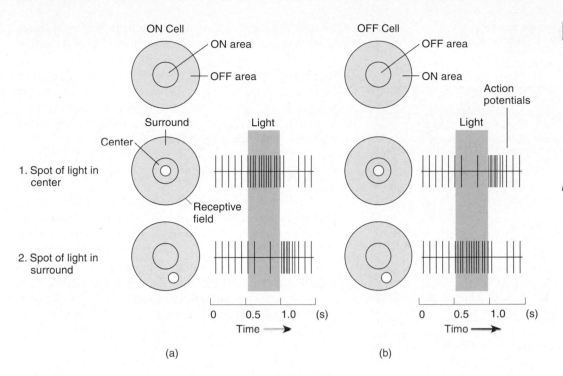

figure 6.14

Responses of ON and OFF ganglion cells to stimuli presented in the center or the surround of the receptive field.
(Adapted from Kuffler, S. W. *Cold Spring Harbor Symposium for Quantitative Biology*, 1952, *17*, 281–292.)

surrounding field (*surround*), whereas OFF cells responded in the opposite manner. ON/OFF ganglion cells were briefly excited when light was turned on or off. In primates these ON/OFF cells project primarily to the superior colliculus, which is primarily involved in visual reflexes (Schiller and Malpeli, 1977); thus, they do not appear to play a direct role in form perception. (See *Figure 6.14*.)

Figure 6.14 also illustrates a rebound effect that occurs when the light is turned off again. Neurons whose firing is inhibited while the light is on will show a brief burst of excitation when it is turned off. In contrast, neurons whose firing is increased will show a brief period of inhibition when the light is turned off. (See *Figure 6.14*.)

The two major categories of ganglion cells (ON and OFF) and the organization of their receptive fields into contrasting center and surround provide useful information to the rest of the visual system. Let us consider these two types of ganglion cells first. As Schiller (1992) notes, ganglion cells normally fire at a relatively low rate. Then, when the level of illumination in the center of their receptive field increases or decreases (for example, when an object moves or the eye makes a saccade), they signal the change. In particular, ON cells signal increases, and OFF cells signal decreases—but both signal them by an increased rate of firing. Such a system is particularly efficient. Theoretically, a single type of ganglion cell could fire at an intermediate rate and signal changes in the level of illumination by increases or decreases in rate of firing. However, in this case the average rate of firing of the one million axons in each optic nerve would have to be much higher.

Several studies have shown that ON cells and OFF cells do, indeed, signal different kinds of information. Schiller, Sandell, and Maunsell (1986) injected monkeys with APB

(2-amino-4-phosphonobutyrate), a drug that selectively blocks synaptic transmission in ON bipolar cells. They found that the animals had difficulty detecting spots that were made brighter than the background but had no difficulty detecting spots that were slightly darker than the background. In addition, Dolan and Schiller (1989) found that an injection of APB completely blocked vision in very dim light, which is normally mediated by rods. Thus, rod bipolar cells must all be of the ON type. (If you think about it, that arrangement makes sense; in very dim light we are more likely to see brighter objects against a dark background than dark objects against a light background.)

The second characteristic of the receptive fields of ganglion cells—their center-surround organization—enhances our ability to detect the outlines of objects even when the contrast between the object and the background is low. Figure 6.15 illustrates this phenomenon. This figure shows six gray squares arranged in order of brightness. The right side of each square looks lighter than the left side, which makes the borders between the squares stand out.

figure 6.15

Enhancement of contrast. Although each gray square is of uniform darkness, the right edge of each square looks somewhat lighter and the left edge looks somewhat darker. This effect appears to be caused by the opponent center-surround arrangement of the receptive fields of the retinal ganglion cells.

All of the surrounds of the ON cells whose receptive fields fall within the lighter gray are evenly illuminated; this illumination partially inhibits the firing of these cells

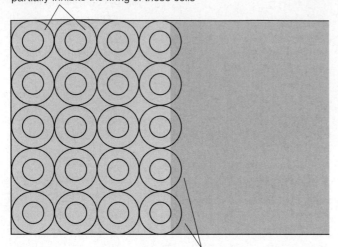

A portion of the inhibitory surrounds of the ON cells near the border receives less illumination; thus, these cells have the highest rate of firing

figure 6.16

A schematic explanation of the phenomenon shown in Figure 6.15. Only ON cells are shown; OFF cells are responsible for the darker appearance of the left side of the darker square.

But these exaggerated borders do not exist in the illustration; they are added by our visual system because of the center-surround organization of the receptive fields of the retinal ganglion cells. (See *Figure 6.15.*)

Figure 6.16 explains how this phenomenon works. We see the centers and surrounds of the receptive fields of several ganglion cells. (In reality these receptive fields would be overlapping, but the simplified arrangement is easier to understand. This example also includes only ON cells—again, for the sake of simplicity.) The image of the transition between lighter and darker regions falls across some of these receptive fields. The cells whose centers are located in the brighter region but whose surrounds are located at least partially in the darker region will have the highest rate of firing. (See *Figure 6.16.*)

Coding of Color

So far, we have been examining the monochromatic properties of ganglion cells—that is, their responses to light and dark. But, of course, objects in our environment selectively absorb some wavelengths of light and reflect others, which, to our eyes, gives them different colors. The retinas of humans, Old World monkeys, one species of New World monkey, and apes contain three different types of cones, which provides them (and us) with the most elaborate form of color vision (Jacobs, 1996; Hunt et al., 1998). Although monochromatic (black-and-white) vision is perfectly adequate for most purposes, color vision gave our primate ancestors the ability to distinguish ripe fruit from unripe fruit and made it more difficult for other animals to hide themselves by means of camouflage (Mollon, 1989). In fact, the photopigments of primates with three types of cones seem well suited for distinguishing red and yellow fruits against a background of green foliage (Regan et al., 2001).

Color Mixing

Various theories of color vision have been proposed for many years—long before it was possible to disprove or validate them by physiological means. In 1802 Thomas Young, a British physicist and physician, proposed that the eye detected different colors because it contained three types of receptors, each sensitive to a single hue. His theory was referred to as the *trichromatic* (three-color) *theory.*

figure 6.17

Additive color mixing and paint mixing. When blue, red, and green light of the proper intensity are all shone together, the result is white light. When red, blue, and yellow paints are mixed together, the result is a dark gray.

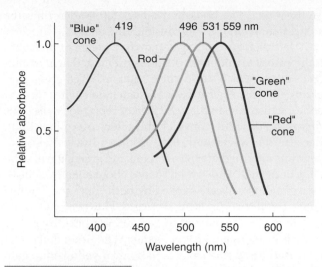

figure 6.18

Relative absorbance of light of various wavelengths by rods and the three types of cones in the human retina.

(From Dartnall, H. J. A., Bowmaker, J. K., and Mollon, J. D. Human visual pigments: Microspectrophotometric results from the eyes of seven persons. *Proceedings of the Royal Society of London, B*, 1983, *220*, 115–130.)

It was suggested by the fact that for a human observer any color can be reproduced by mixing various quantities of three colors judiciously selected from different points along the spectrum.

I must emphasize that *color mixing* is different from *pigment mixing*. If we combine yellow and blue pigments (as when we mix paints), the resulting mixture is green. Color mixing refers to the addition of two or more light sources. If we shine a beam of red light and a beam of bluish green light together on a white screen, we will see yellow light. If we mix yellow and blue light, we get white light. When white appears on a color television screen or computer monitor, it actually consists of tiny dots of red, blue, and green light. (See *Figure 6.17*.)

Another fact of color perception suggested to a German physiologist, Ewald Hering (1905/1965), that hue might be represented in the visual system as *opponent colors*. People interested in color perception have long regarded yellow, blue, red, and green as primary colors—colors that seem unique and do not appear to be blends of other colors. (Black and white are primary, too, but we perceive them as colorless.) All other colors can be described as mixtures of these primary colors. The trichromatic system cannot explain why *yellow* is included in this group—why it is perceived as a pure color. In addition, some colors appear to blend, whereas others do not. For example, one can speak of a bluish green or a yellowish green, and orange appears to have both red and yellow qualities. Purple resembles both red and blue. But try to imagine a reddish green or a bluish yellow. It is impossible; these colors seem to be opposite to each other. Again, these facts are not explained by the trichromatic theory. As we shall see in the following section, the visual system uses both trichromatic and opponent-color systems to encode information related to color.

Photoreceptors: Trichromatic Coding

Physiological investigations of retinal photoreceptors in higher primates have found that Young was right: Three different types of photoreceptors (three different types of cones) are responsible for color vision. Investigators have studied the absorption characteristics of individual photoreceptors, determining the amount of light of different wavelengths that is absorbed by the photopigments. These characteristics are controlled by the particular opsin a photoreceptor contains; different opsins absorb particular wavelengths more readily. Figure 6.18 shows the absorption characteristics of the four types of photoreceptors in the human retina: rods and the three types of cones. (See *Figure 6.18*.)

The peak sensitivities of the three types of cones are approximately 420 nm (blue-violet), 530 nm (green), and 560 nm (yellow-green). The peak sensitivity of the short-wavelength cone is actually 440 nm in the intact eye because the lens absorbs some short-wavelength light. For convenience the short-, medium-, and long-wavelength cones are traditionally called "blue," "green," and "red" cones, respectively. The retina contains approximately equal numbers of "red" and "green" cones but a much smaller number of "blue" cones (approximately 8 percent of the total).

Genetic defects in color vision appear to result from anomalies in one or more of the three types of cones (Boynton, 1979; Nathans et al., 1986; Wissinger and Sharpe, 1998). The first two kinds of defective color vision described here involve genes on the X chromosome; thus, because males have only one X chromosome, they are much more likely to have this disorder. (Females are likely to have a normal gene on one of their X chromosomes, which compensates for the defective one.) People with **protanopia** ("first-color defect") confuse red and green. They see the world in shades of yellow and blue; both red and green look yellowish to them. Their visual acuity is normal, which suggests that their retinas do not lack "red" or "green" cones. This fact, and their sensitivity to lights of different wavelengths, suggests that their "red" cones are filled with "green" cone opsin. People with **deuteranopia** ("second-color defect") also confuse red and green and also have normal visual acuity. Their "green" cones appear to be filled with "red" cone opsin.

protanopia (*pro tan owe pee a*) An inherited form of defective color vision in which red and green hues are confused; "red" cones are filled with "green" cone opsin.

deuteranopia (*dew ter an owe pee a*) An inherited form of defective color vision in which red and green hues are confused; "green" cones are filled with "red" cone opsin.

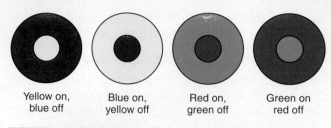

| Yellow on,
blue off | Blue on,
yellow off | Red on,
green off | Green on
red off |

figure 6.19

Receptive fields of color-sensitive ganglion cells. When a portion of the receptive field is illuminated with the color shown, the cell's rate of firing increases. When a portion is illuminated with the complementary color, the cell's rate of firing decreases.

Tritanopia ("third-color defect") is rare, affecting fewer than 1 in 10,000 people. This disorder involves a faulty gene that is not located on an X chromosome; thus, it is equally prevalent in males and females. People with tritanopia have difficulty with hues of short wavelengths and see the world in greens and reds. To them a clear blue sky is a bright green, and yellow looks pink. Their retinas lack "blue" cones. Because the retina contains so few of these cones, their absence does not noticeably affect visual acuity.

Retinal Ganglion Cells: Opponent-Process Coding

At the level of the retinal ganglion cell the three-color code gets translated into an opponent-color system. Daw (1968) and Gouras (1968) found that these neurons respond specifically to pairs of primary colors, with red opposing green and blue opposing yellow. Thus, the retina contains two kinds of color-sensitive ganglion cells: *red-green* and *yellow-blue*. Some color-sensitive ganglion cells respond in a center-surround fashion. For example, a cell might be excited by red and inhibited by green in the center of their receptive field while showing the opposite response in the surrounding ring. (See *Figure 6.19*.) Other ganglion cells that receive input from cones do not respond differentially to different wavelengths but simply encode relative brightness in the center and surround. These cells serve as "black-and-white detectors."

The response characteristics of retinal ganglion cells to light of different wavelengths are obviously determined by the particular circuits that connect the three types of cones with the two types of ganglion cells. These circuits involve different types of bipolar cells, amacrine cells, and horizontal cells.

Figure 6.20 helps to explain how particular hues are detected by the "red," "green," and "blue" cones and translated into excitation or inhibition of the red-green and yellow-blue ganglion cells. The diagram does not show the actual neural circuitry, which includes the retinal neurons that connect the cones with the ganglion cells. The arrows in Figure 6.20 refer merely to the *effects* of the light falling on the retina. The book by Rodieck (1998) describes the actual neural circuitry in considerable detail.

Detection and coding of pure red, green, or blue light is the easiest to understand. For example, red light excites "red" cones, which causes the excitation of red-green ganglion cells. (See *Figure 6.20a*.) Green light excites "green" cones, which causes the *inhibition* of red-green cells. (See *Figure 6.20b*.) But consider the effect of yellow light. Because the wavelength that produces the sensation of yellow is intermediate between red and green, it will stimulate both "red" and "green" cones about equally. Yellow-blue ganglion cells are excited by both "red" and "green" cones, so their rate of firing increases. However, red-green ganglion cells are excited by red and inhibited by green, so their firing rate does not change. The brain detects an increased firing rate from the axons of yellow-blue ganglion cells, which it interprets as yellow. (See *Figure 6.20c*.) Blue light simply inhibits the activity of yellow-blue ganglion cells. (See *Figure 6.20d*.)

The opponent-color system employed by the ganglion cells explains why we cannot perceive a reddish green or a bluish yellow: An axon that signals red or green (or yellow or blue) can either increase or decrease its rate of firing; it cannot do both at the same time. A reddish green would have to be signaled by a ganglion cell firing slowly and rapidly at the same time, which is obviously impossible.

Negative Afterimages

Figure 6.21 demonstrates an interesting property of the visual system: the formation of a **negative afterimage.** Stare at the cross in the center of the image on the left for approximately 30 seconds. Then quickly look at the cross in the center of the white rectangle to the right. You will have a fleeting experience of seeing the red and green colors of a radish—colors that are complementary, or opposite, to the ones on the left. (See *Figure 6.21*.) Complementary items go together to make up a whole. In this context **complementary colors** are those that make white (or shades of gray) when added together. (This phenomenon is demonstrated even more vividly in *Animation 6.1, Complementary Colors*.)

The most important cause of negative afterimages is adaptation in the rate of firing of retinal ganglion cells. When ganglion cells are excited or inhibited for a

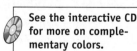

See the interactive CD for more on complementary colors.

---

tritanopia (*try tan owe pee a*) An inherited form of defective color vision in which hues with short wavelengths are confused; "blue" cones are either lacking or faulty.

negative afterimage The image seen after a portion of the retina is exposed to an intense visual stimulus; consists of colors complementary to those of the physical stimulus.

complementary colors Colors that make white or gray when mixed together.

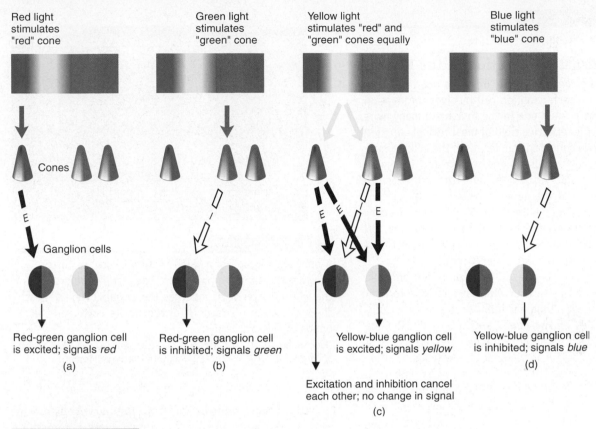

figure 6.20

Color coding in the retina. (a) Red light stimulating a "red" cone, which causes excitation of a red-green ganglion cell. (b) Green light stimulating a "green" cone, which causes inhibition of a red-green ganglion cell. (c) Yellow light stimulating "red" and "green" cones equally but not affecting "blue" cones. The stimulation of "red" and "green" cones causes excitation of a yellow-blue ganglion cell. (d) Blue light stimulating a "blue" cone, which causes inhibition of a yellow-blue ganglion cell. The arrows labeled E and I represent neural circuitry within the retina that translates excitation of a cone into excitation or inhibition of a ganglion cell. For clarity, only some of the circuits are shown.

prolonged period of time, they later show a *rebound effect,* firing faster or slower than normal. For example, the green of the radish in Figure 6.21 inhibits some red-green ganglion cells. When this region of the retina is then stimu- lated with the neutral-colored light reflected off the white rectangle, the red-green ganglion cells—no longer inhib- ited by the green light—fire faster than normal. Thus, we see a red afterimage of the radish.

figure 6.21

A negative afterimage. Stare for approximately 30 seconds at the cross in the center of the left figure; then quickly transfer your gaze to the cross in the center of the right figure. You will see colors that are complementary to the originals.

Coding of Visual Information in the Retina

Recordings of the electrical activity of single neurons in the retina indicate that each ganglion cell receives information from photoreceptors—just one in the fovea and many more in the periphery. The receptive field of most retinal ganglion cells consists of two concentric circles, with the cells becoming excited when light falls in one region and becoming inhibited when it falls in the other. This arrangement enhances the ability of the nervous system to detect contrasts in brightness. ON cells are excited by light in the center, and OFF cells are excited by light in the surround. ON cells detect light objects against dark backgrounds; OFF cells detect dark objects against light backgrounds.

Color vision occurs as a result of information provided by three types of cones, each of which is sensitive to light of a certain wavelength: long, medium, or short. The absorption characteristics of the cones are determined by the particular opsin that their photopigment contains. Most forms of defective color vision appear to be caused by alterations in cone opsins. The "red" cones of people with protanopia are filled with "green" cone opsin, and the "green" cones of people with deuteranopia are filled with "red" cone opsin. The retinas of people with tritanopia appear to lack "blue" cones.

Most color-sensitive ganglion cells respond in an opposing center-surround fashion to the pairs of primary colors: red and green, and blue and yellow. The responses of these neurons is determined by the retinal circuitry connecting them with the photoreceptors.

Analysis of Visual Information: Role of the Striate Cortex

The retinal ganglion cells encode information about the relative amounts of light falling on the center and surround regions of their receptive field and, in many cases, about the wavelength of that light. The striate cortex performs additional processing of this information, which it then transmits to the visual association cortex.

Anatomy of the Striate Cortex

The striate cortex consists of six principal layers (and several sublayers), arranged in bands parallel to the surface. These layers contain the nuclei of cell bodies and dendritic trees that show up as bands of light or dark in sections of tissue that have been dyed with a cell-body stain. (See *Figure 6.22*.)

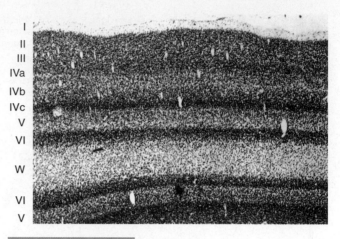

figure   6.22

A photomicrograph of a small section of striate cortex, showing the six principal layers. The letter W refers to the white matter that underlies the visual cortex; beneath the white matter is layer VI of the striate cortex on the opposite side of the gyrus.

(From Hubel, D. H., and Wiesel, T. N. *Proceedings of the Royal Society of London, B,* 1977, *198,* 1–59. Reprinted with permission.)

In primates information from the parvocellular and magnocellular layers of the dorsal lateral geniculate nucleus enters the middle layer (layer 4C) of the striate cortex. From there it is relayed to the upper layers, where it is analyzed by circuits of neurons. Axons bringing information from the koniocellular layers form synapses with neurons in layer 3.

If we consider the striate cortex of one hemisphere as a whole—if we imagine that we remove it and spread it out on a flat surface—we find that it contains a map of the contralateral half of the visual field. (Remember that each side of the brain sees the opposite side of the visual field.) The map is distorted; approximately 25 percent of the striate cortex is devoted to the analysis of information from the fovea, which represents a small part of the visual field. (The area of the visual field seen by the fovea is approximately the size of a large grape held at arm's length.)

The pioneering studies of David Hubel and Torsten Wiesel at Harvard University during the 1960s began a revolution in the study of the physiology of visual perception (see Hubel and Wiesel, 1977, 1979). Hubel and Wiesel discovered that neurons in the visual cortex did not simply respond to spots of light; they selectively responded to specific *features* of the visual world. That is, the neural circuitry within the visual cortex combines information from several sources (for example, from axons carrying information received from several different ganglion cells) in such a way as to detect features that are larger than the receptive field of a single ganglion cell. The following subsections describe the visual characteristics that researchers have studied so far: orientation and movement, spatial frequency, texture, retinal disparity, and color.

Orientation and Movement

Most neurons in the striate cortex are sensitive to *orientation*. That is, if a line is positioned in the cell's receptive field and rotated around its center, the cell will respond only when the line is in a particular position—a particular orientation. Some neurons respond best to a vertical line, some to a horizontal line, and some to a line oriented somewhere in between. Figure 6.23 shows the responses of a neuron in the striate cortex when lines were presented at various orientations. As you can see, this neuron responded best when a vertical line was presented in its receptive field. (See *Figure 6.23*.)

Some orientation-sensitive neurons have receptive fields organized in an opponent fashion. Hubel and Wiesel referred to them as **simple cells.** For example, a line of a particular orientation (say, a dark 45° line against a white background) might excite a cell if placed in the center of the receptive field but inhibit it if moved away from the center. (See *Figure 6.24a*.) Another type of neuron, which the researchers referred to as a **complex cell,** also responded best to a line of a particular orientation but did not show an inhibitory surround; that is, it continued to respond while the line was moved within the receptive field. In fact, many

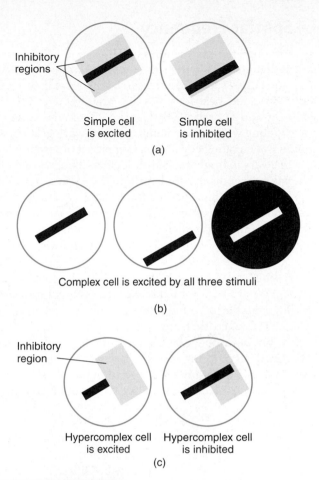

Simple cell is excited   Simple cell is inhibited

Inhibitory regions

(a)

Complex cell is excited by all three stimuli

(b)

Inhibitory region

Hypercomplex cell is excited   Hypercomplex cell is inhibited

(c)

figure 6.24

Response characteristics of neurons to orientation in the primary visual cortex. (a) Simple cell. (b) Complex cell. (c) Hypercomplex cell.

complex cells increased their rate of firing when the line was moved perpendicular to its angle of orientation—often only in one direction. Thus, these neurons also served as movement detectors. In addition, complex cells responded equally well to white lines against black backgrounds and black lines against white backgrounds. (See *Figure 6.24b*.) Finally, **hypercomplex cells** responded to lines of a particular orientation but had an inhibitory region at the end (or ends) of the lines, which meant that the cells detected the location of *ends* of lines of a particular orientation. (See *Figure 6.24c*.)

simple cell An orientation-sensitive neuron in the striate cortex whose receptive field is organized in an opponent fashion.

complex cell A neuron in the visual cortex that responds to the presence of a line segment with a particular orientation located within its receptive field, especially when the line moves perpendicularly to its orientation.

hypercomplex cell A neuron in the visual cortex that responds to the presence of a line segment with a particular orientation that ends at a particular point within the cell's receptive field.

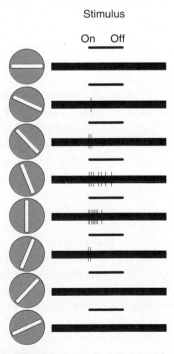

Stimulus

On   Off

figure 6.23

Orientation sensitivity. An orientation-sensitive neuron in the striate cortex will become active only when a line of a particular orientation appears within its receptive field. For example, the neuron depicted in this figure responds best to a bar that is vertically oriented.

(Adapted from Hubel, D. H., and Wiesel, T. N. *Journal of Physiology (London)*, 1959, *148*, 574–591.)

Spatial Frequency

Although the early studies by Hubel and Wiesel suggested that neurons in the primary visual cortex detected lines and edges, subsequent research found that they actually responded best to sine-wave gratings (De Valois, Albrecht, and Thorell, 1978). Figure 6.25 compares a sine-wave grating with a more familiar square-wave grating. A square-wave grating consists of a simple set of rectangular bars that vary in brightness; the brightness along the length of a line perpendicular to them would vary in a stepwise (square-wave) fashion. (See *Figure 6.25a*.) A **sine-wave grating** looks like a series of fuzzy, unfocused parallel bars. Along any line perpendicular to the long axis of the grating, the brightness varies according to a sine-wave function. (See *Figure 6.25b*.)

A sine-wave grating is designated by its spatial frequency. We are accustomed to the expression of frequencies (for example, of sound waves or radio waves) in terms of time or distance (such as cycles per second or cycles per meter). But because the image of a stimulus on the retina varies in size according to how close it is to the eye, the visual angle is generally used instead of the physical distance between adjacent cycles. Thus, the **spatial frequency** of a sine-wave grating is its variation in brightness measured in cycles per degree of visual angle. (See *Figure 6.26*.)

Most neurons in the striate cortex respond best when a sine-wave grating of a particular spatial frequency is placed in the appropriate part of the visual field. Different neurons detect different spatial frequencies. For orientation-sensitive neurons the grating must be aligned at the appropriate angle of orientation. Albrecht (1978) mapped the shapes of receptive fields of simple cells by observing their response while moving a very thin flickering line of the appropriate orientation through their receptive fields. He found that many of them had multiple inhibitory and excitatory regions surrounding the center. The profile of the excitatory and inhibitory regions of the receptive fields of such neurons looked like a modulated sine wave—precisely what would be needed to detect a few cycles of a sine-wave grating. (See *Figure 6.27*.) In most cases a neuron's receptive field is large enough to include between 1.5 and 3.5 cycles of the grating (De Valois, Thorell, and Albrecht, 1985).

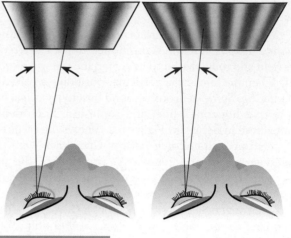

figure **6.26**

The concepts of visual angle and spatial frequency. Angles are drawn between the sine waves, with the apex at the viewer's eye. The *visual angle* between adjacent sine waves is smaller when the waves are closer together.

What is the point of having neural circuits that analyze spatial frequency? A complete answer requires some rather complicated mathematics, so I will give a simplified one here. (If you are interested, you can consult De Valois and De Valois, 1988.) Consider the types of information provided by high and low spatial frequencies. Small objects, details within a large object, and large objects with sharp edges provide a signal rich in high frequencies, whereas large areas of light and dark are represented by low frequencies. An image that is deficient in high-frequency information looks fuzzy and out of focus, like the image seen by a nearsighted person who is not wearing corrective lenses. This image still provides much information about forms and objects in the environment; thus, the most important visual information is that contained in *low spatial frequencies*. When low-frequency information is removed, the shapes of images are very difficult to perceive. (As we will see, the more primitive magnocellular system provides low-frequency information.)

Many experiments have confirmed that the concept of spatial frequency plays a central role in visual perception, and mathematical models have shown that the information present in a scene can be represented very efficiently if it is first encoded in terms of spatial frequency. Thus, the brain probably represents the information in a similar way. Here

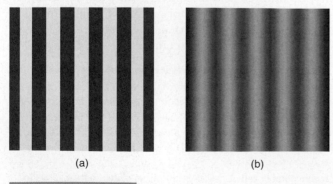

(a)	(b)

figure **6.25**

Parallel gratings. (a) Square-wave grating. (b) Sine-wave grating.

sine-wave grating A series of straight parallel bands varying continuously in brightness according to a sine-wave function, along a line perpendicular to their lengths.

spatial frequency The relative width of the bands in a sine-wave grating, measured in cycles per degree of visual angle.

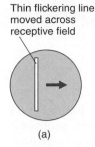

Thin flickering line moved across receptive field

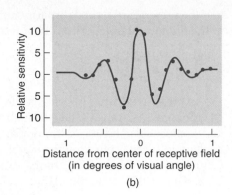

(a)

Distance from center of receptive field
(in degrees of visual angle)

(b)

figure 6.27

The experiment by Albrecht, 1978. (a) The stimulus presented to the animal. (b) The response of a simple cell in the primary visual cortex.

(Adapted from De Valois, R. L., and De Valois, K. K. *Spatial Vision.* New York: Oxford University Press, 1988.)

I will describe just one example to help show the validity of the concept. Look at the two pictures in *Figure 6.28.* You can see that the picture on the right looks much more like the face of Abraham Lincoln, the late U.S. President, than the one on the left does. Yet both pictures contain the same information. The creators of the pictures, Harmon and Julesz (1973), used a computer to construct the figure on the left, which consists of a series of squares, each representing the average brightness of a portion of a picture of Lincoln. The one on the right is simply a transformation of the first one in which high frequencies have been removed. Sharp edges contain high spatial frequencies, so the transformation eliminates them. In the case of the picture on the left, these frequencies have nothing to do with

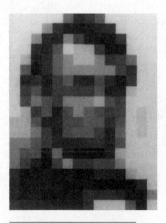

figure 6.28

Spatial filtering. Both pictures contain the same amount of low-frequency information, but extraneous high-frequency information has been filtered from the picture on the right. If you look at the pictures from across the room, they look identical.

(From Harmon, L. D., and Julesz, B. *Science,* 1973, *180,* 1191–1197. Copyright 1973 by the American Association for the Advancement of Science.)

the information contained in the original picture; thus, they can be seen as visual "noise." The filtration process (accomplished by a computer) removes this noise—and makes the image much clearer to the human visual system. Presumably, the high frequencies produced by the edges of the squares in the left figure stimulate neurons in the striate cortex that are tuned to high spatial frequencies. When the visual association cortex receives this noisy information, it has difficulty perceiving the underlying form.

If you want to watch the effect of filtering the extraneous high-frequency noise, try the following demonstration. Put the book down and look at the pictures in Figure 6.28 from across the room. The distance "erases" the high frequencies, because they exceed the resolving power of the eye, and the two pictures look identical. Now walk toward the book, focusing on the left figure. As you get closer, the higher frequencies reappear, and this picture looks less and less like the face of Lincoln. (See *Figure 6.28.*)

Texture

Several years ago, von der Heydt, Peterhans, and Duersteler (1992) discovered a new class of neurons in the monkey striate cortex. These neurons respond to "periodic patterns." They do not respond when single lines, bars, or edges are placed in their receptive fields, but they do respond vigorously when a grating (square-wave, sine-wave, or thin-line) of a particular spatial frequency and orientation is presented there. To provide a reliable response, these cells require a minimum of two to seven alternating dark and light bars. They are not spatial-frequency analyzers like the ones I just described. The proof of this fact is difficult to convey in a few words, because it requires an understanding of the underlying mathematics. Those of you who would like to know more should consult the article.

These neurons showed extreme sensitivity to deviations from their optimal frequency and orientation. Figure 6.29 shows three square-wave gratings. The middle one produced the optimal response in a particular neuron in striate cortex. The one on the left, which has a slightly higher spatial frequency, produced only half as much excitation. The one on the right, which is rotated slightly counterclockwise, also produced only half as much excitation. (See *Figure 6.29.*)

Von der Heydt and his colleagues estimate that approximately 4 million periodic-pattern-selective cells serve the central four degrees of vision in the monkey striate cortex. They suggest that the function provided by these cells is perception of surfaces. Most surfaces (especially those found in nature) have a rough texture, and many of them contain a repeating pattern. For example, tree trunks, grasslands, boulders, leaves of bushes and trees, pebble-strewn ground—even a close-up view of the fur of another animal—contain periodic patterns that potentially could be detected by these cells. These cells could help us discriminate surfaces that differ only in terms of their texture and could help us determine their orientation.

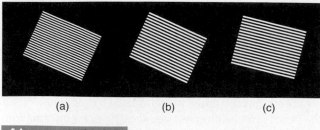

(a)   (b)   (c)

figure 6.29

Sensitivity of a "texture" cell. The center stimulus (b) produced the highest rate of firing. The firing rate decreased by 50 percent when the spatial frequency of the grating was slightly higher (a) or the grating was rotated slightly (c).

(Adapted from von der Heydt, R., Peterhans, E., and Duersteler, M. R. *Journal of Neuroscience,* 1992, *12,* 1416–1434.)

Retinal Disparity

We perceive depth by many means, most of which involve cues that can be detected monocularly, by one eye alone. For example, perspective, relative retinal size, loss of detail through the effects of atmospheric haze, and relative apparent movement of retinal images as we move our heads all contribute to depth perception and do not require binocular vision. However, binocular vision provides a vivid perception of depth through the process of stereoscopic vision, or *stereopsis.* If you have used a stereoscope (such as a View-Master) or have seen a three-dimensional movie, you know what I mean. Stereopsis is particularly important in the visual guidance of fine movements of the hands and fingers, such as we use when we thread a needle.

Most neurons in the striate cortex are *binocular*—that is, they respond to visual stimulation of either eye. Many of these binocular cells, especially those found in a layer that receives information from the magnocellular system, have response patterns that appear to contribute to the perception of depth (Poggio and Poggio, 1984). In most cases the cells respond most vigorously when each eye sees a stimulus in a slightly *different* location. That is, the neurons respond to **retinal disparity,** a stimulus that produces images on slightly different parts of the retina of each eye. This is exactly the information that is needed for stereopsis; each eye sees a three-dimensional scene slightly differently,

---

retinal disparity The fact that points on objects located at different distances from the observer will fall on slightly different locations on the two retinas; provides the basis for stereopsis.

cytochrome oxidase (CO) blob The central region of a module of the primary visual cortex, revealed by a stain for cytochrome oxidase; contains wavelength-sensitive neurons; part of the parvocellular system.

---

and the presence of retinal disparity indicates differences in the distance of objects from the observer.

Color

In the striate cortex information from color-sensitive ganglion cells is transmitted, through the parvocellular and koniocellular layers of the dorsal lateral geniculate nucleus, to special cells grouped together in **cytochrome oxidase (CO) blobs.** CO blobs were discovered by Wong-Riley (1978), who found that a stain for cytochrome oxidase, an enzyme that is present in mitochondria, showed a patchy distribution. Subsequent research with the stain (Horton and Hubel, 1980; Humphrey and Hendrickson, 1980) revealed the presence of a polka-dot pattern of dark columns extending through layers 2 and 3 and (more faintly) layers 5 and 6. The columns are oval in cross section, approximately 150×200 μm in diameter, and spaced at 0.5-mm intervals (Fitzpatrick, Itoh, and Diamond, 1983; Livingstone and Hubel, 1987).

Figure 6.30 shows a photomicrograph of a slice through a macaque monkey visual cortex that has been flattened out and stained for the mitochondrial enzyme. You can clearly see the CO blobs within the striate cortex. Because the curvature of the cortex prevents it from being perfectly flattened, some of the tissue is missing in the center of the slice. (See *Figure 6.30.*)

Until recently, researchers believed that the parvocellular system transmitted all information pertaining to color to the striate cortex. However, it now appears that the parvocellular system receives information only from "red" and "green" cones; additional information from "blue" cones is transmitted through the koniocellular sys-

figure 6.30

A photomicrograph of a slice through the primary visual cortex of a macaque monkey, parallel to the surface. The dark spots are the blobs, colored by a stain for cytochrome oxidase.

(From Hubel, D. H., and Livingstone, M. S. *Journal of Neuroscience,* 1989, *7,* 3378–3415.

tem (Hendry and Yoshioka, 1994; Martin et al., 1997; Komatsu, 1998).

To summarize, neurons in the striate cortex respond to several different features of a visual stimulus, including orientation, movement, spatial frequency, texture, retinal disparity, and color. Now let us turn our attention to the way this information is organized within the striate cortex.

Modular Organization of the Striate Cortex

Most investigators believe that the brain is organized in modules, which probably range in size from a hundred thousand to a few million neurons. Each module receives information from other modules, performs some calculations, and then passes the results to other modules. In recent years investigators have been learning the characteristics of the modules that are found in the visual cortex (De Valois and De Valois, 1988; Livingstone and Hubel, 1988).

The striate cortex is divided into approximately 2500 modules, each approximately 0.5 × 0.7 mm and containing approximately 150,000 neurons. The neurons in each module are devoted to the analysis of various features contained in one very small portion of the visual field. Collectively, these modules receive information from the entire visual field, the individual modules serving like the tiles in a mosaic mural. Input from the parvocellular, koniocellular, and magnocellular layers of the dorsal lateral geniculate nucleus is received by different sublayers of the striate cortex: The parvocellular input is received by layer 4Cβ, the magnocellular input is received by layer 4Cα, and the koniocellular input is received by layer 3.

The modules actually consist of two segments, each surrounding a CO blob. Neurons located within the blobs have a special function: They are sensitive to color and to low spatial frequencies but are relatively insensitive to other visual features. These neurons do not respond selectively to different orientations and have relatively large receptive fields, which means that they do not provide information useful for form perception (Kaas and Collins, 2001).

Outside the CO blob, neurons show sensitivity to orientation, movement, spatial frequency, texture, and binocular disparity, but most do not respond to color (Livingstone and Hubel, 1984; Born and Tootell, 1991; Edwards, Purpura, and Kaplan, 1995). Each half of the module receives input from only one eye, but the circuitry within the module combines the information from both eyes, which means that most of the neurons are binocular. Depending on their locations within the module, neurons receive varying percentages of input from each of the eyes.

If we record from neurons anywhere within a single module, we will find that all of their receptive fields overlap. Thus, all the neurons in a module analyze information from the same region of the visual field. Furthermore, if

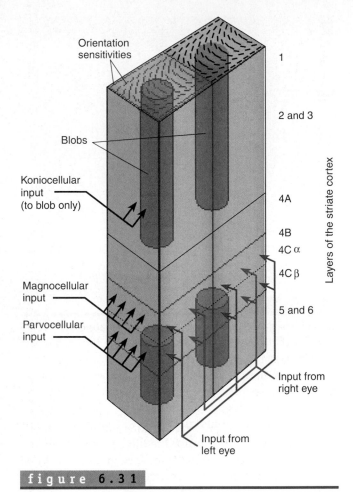

One of the modules of the primary visual cortex.

we insert a microelectrode straight down into an interblob region of the striate cortex (that is, in a location in a module outside one of the CO blobs), we will find both simple and complex cells, but all of the orientation-sensitive cells will respond to lines of the same orientation. In addition, they will all share the same **ocular dominance**—that is, the same percentage of input from each of the eyes. If we move our electrode around the module, we will find that these two characteristics—orientation sensitivity and ocular dominance—vary systematically and are arranged at right angles to each other. (See *Figure 6.31*.)

How does spatial frequency fit into this organization? Edwards, Purpura, and Kaplan (1995) found that neurons within the CO blobs responded to low spatial frequencies but were sensitive to small differences in brightness. Outside the blobs, sensitivity to spatial frequency varied with the distance from the center of the nearest blob. Higher frequencies were associated with greater distances.

ocular dominance The extent to which a particular neuron receives more input from one eye than from the other.

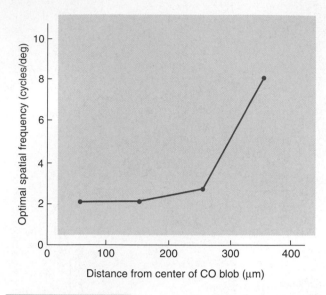

figure 6.32

Optimal spatial frequency of neurons in striate cortex as a function of the distance of the neuron from the center of the nearest cytochrome oxidase blob.

(Adapted from Edwards, D. P., Purpura, K. P., and Kaplan, E. *Vision Research,* 1995, *35,* 1501–1523.

(See *Figure 6.32*.) However, neurons outside the blobs were less sensitive to contrast; the difference between the bright and dark areas of the sine-wave grating had to be greater for these neurons than for neurons within the blobs.

Blindsight

Visual perception depends on the integrity of the connections between the retina and the striate cortex. Thus, damage to the eyes, optic nerves, optic tracts, lateral geniculate nucleus, optic radiations, or primary visual cortex itself results in loss of vision in particular portions of the visual field or in complete blindness if the damage is total. However, an interesting phenomenon is seen in people with **cortical blindness**—blindness caused by damage to the optic radiations or primary visual cortex.

It has long been recognized that damage to the optic radiations or primary visual cortex on one side of the brain causes blindness in the contralateral visual field. That is, if the right side of the brain is damaged, the patient will be blind to everything located to the left when he or she looks straight ahead. However, Weiskrantz and his colleagues (Weiskrantz et al., 1974; Weiskrantz, 1987) found that if an object is placed in the patient's blind field and the patient

---

cortical blindness Blindness caused by damage to the optic radiations or primary visual cortex.

blindsight The ability of a person to reach for objects located in his or her "blind" field; occurs after damage restricted to the primary visual cortex.

is asked to reach for it, he or she will be able to do so rather accurately. The patients are surprised to find their hands repeatedly coming into contact with an object in what appears to them as darkness; they say that they see nothing there. The patient is also sensitive to movement and, to a certain extent, the orientation of objects in the blind field.

This phenomenon, which Weiskrantz called **blindsight,** may depend on the connections that the visual association cortex receives from the superior colliculus, the dorsal lateral geniculate nucleus, and the pulvinar—another nucleus of the thalamus (Cowey and Stoerig, 1991; Rockland et al., 1999). The role of these connections in the intact brain is not known. Most of the inputs to the visual association cortex come directly from the striate cortex, and these connections are obviously necessary for normal visual perception.

Besides telling us something about the functions of the various parts of the visual system, the phenomenon of blindsight also shows that visual information can control behavior without producing a conscious sensation. Although the superior colliculi and pulvinar send visual information to parts of the brain that guide hand movements, they do not appear to send them to parts of the brain responsible for conscious awareness. Perhaps that connection is a more recent evolutionary development.

Incidentally, monkeys with lesions of the striate cortex also show the phenomenon of blindsight, but—obviously—we have no way of assessing the animals' awareness of their visual perceptions (Cowey and Stoerig, 1995).

interim summary

Analysis of Visual Information: Role of the Striate Cortex

The striate cortex consists of six layers and several sublayers. Visual information is received from the magnocellular, parvocellular, and koniocellular layers of the dorsal lateral geniculate nucleus. The magnocellular system is more primitive, color-blind, and sensitive to movement, depth, and small differences in brightness. The parvocellular system is more recent, color-sensitive (receiving information from "red" and "green" cones), and able to discriminate finer details. The koniocellular system provides additional information about color, received from "blue" cones.

The striate cortex is organized into modules, each surrounding a pair of CO blobs, which are revealed by a stain for cytochrome oxidase, an enzyme found in mitochondria. Each half of a module receives information from one eye; but because information is shared, most of the neurons respond to input to both eyes. The neurons in the CO blobs are sensitive to color and to low-frequency sine-wave gratings, whereas those between the blobs are sensitive to sine-wave gratings of higher spatial frequencies, orientation, retinal disparity, and movement. Some cells are specifically sensitive to orientation and frequency of gratings and probably are involved in detecting the texture of surfaces.

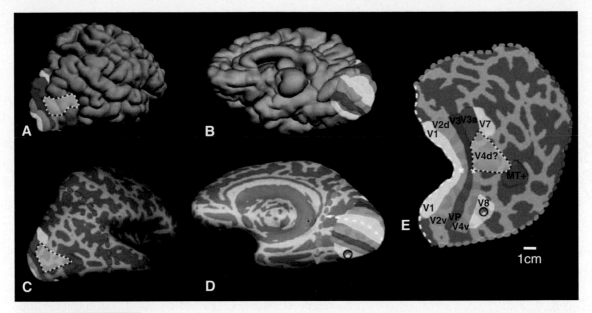

Striate cortex and regions of extrastriate cortex of the human brain. (a) A nearly normal lateral view. (b) A nearly normal midsagittal view. (c) An "inflated" lateral view. (d) An "inflated" midsagittal view. (e) An unrolling of the cortical surface caudal to the dotted red line and green lines shown in (c) and (d). (From Tootell, B. H., and Hadjikhani, N. *Cerebral Cortex*, 2001, *11*, 298–311.)

Damage to the visual system up to the striate cortex produces blindness in all or part of the visual field. However, damage limited to the striate cortex or to the optic radiations leading to them produces a syndrome called blindsight. People with blindsight deny seeing anything in the blind part of their visual field but can nevertheless point to objects located there and discriminate their size and orientation. They are also sensitive to movement. But although their behavior can be affected by objects in their blind field, they have no conscious awareness of the presence of these objects. Their ability to respond to visual stimuli apparently depends on connections from the superior colliculus, the lateral geniculate nucleus, and the pulvinar to the visual association cortex.

Analysis of Visual Information: Role of the Visual Association Cortex

Although the striate cortex is necessary for visual perception, perception of objects and of the totality of the visual scene does not take place there. Each module of the striate cortex sees only what is happening in one tiny part of the visual field. Thus, for us to perceive objects and entire visual scenes, the information from these individual modules must be combined. That combination takes place in the visual association cortex.

Two Streams of Visual Analysis

Visual information received from the striate cortex is analyzed in the visual association cortex. Neurons in the striate cortex send axons to the **extrastriate cortex,** the region of the visual association cortex that surrounds the striate cortex (Zeki and Shipp, 1988). The primate extrastriate cortex (sometimes called the prestriate cortex or circumstriate cortex) consists of several regions, each of which contains one or more independent maps of the visual field. Each region is specialized, containing neurons that respond to a particular feature of visual information, such as orientation, movement, spatial frequency, retinal disparity, or color. So far, investigators have identified twenty-five distinct regions and subregions of the visual cortex of the rhesus monkey. These regions are arranged hierarchically, beginning with the striate cortex (Van Essen, Anderson, and Felleman, 1992). Most of the information passes up the hierarchy; each region receives information from regions located beneath it in the hierarchy, analyzes the information, and passes the results on to "higher" regions for further analysis. Some information is also transmitted in the opposite direction, but axons that descend the hierarchy are much less numerous than those that ascend it.

Figure 6.33 shows the most important regions of the striate and extrastriate cortex of the human brain. The

extrastriate cortex A region of visual association cortex; receives fibers from the striate cortex and from the superior colliculi and projects to the inferior temporal cortex.

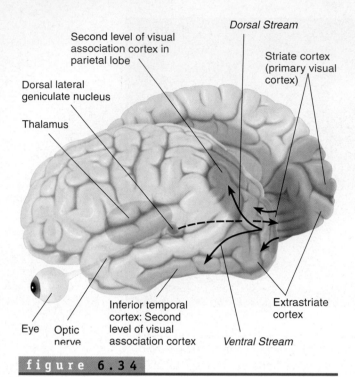

Dorsal lateral geniculate nucleus

Second level of visual association cortex in parietal lobe

Thalamus

Dorsal Stream

Striate cortex (primary visual cortex)

Eye Optic nerve

Inferior temporal cortex: Second level of visual association cortex

Extrastriate cortex

Ventral Stream

figure 6.34

The human visual system, from the eye to the two streams of visual association cortex.

views of brain in Figures 6.33(a) and 6.33(b) are nearly normal in appearance. Figures 6.33(c) and 6.33(d) show "inflated" cortical surfaces, enabling us to see regions that are normally hidden in the depths of sulci and fissures. The hidden regions are shown in dark gray, while regions normally visible (the surfaces of gyri) are shown in light gray. Figure 6.33(e) shows an unrolling of the cortical surface caudal to the dotted red line and green lines in Figure 6.33(c) and 6.33(d).

Most of the outputs of the striate cortex—often called V1, because it is the first region of visual cortex—are sent to area V2, a region of the extrastriate cortex just adjacent to V1. At this point, the pathways diverge. On the basis of their own research and a review of the literature, Ungerleider and Mishkin (1982) concluded that the visual association cortex contains two streams of analysis: the **dorsal stream** and the **ventral stream.** Subsequent anatomical studies have confirmed this conclusion (Baizer, Ungerleider, and Desimone, 1991). Some of the outputs of area V2 continue forward toward a series of regions that constitute the ventral

dorsal stream A system of interconnected regions of visual cortex involved in the perception of spatial location, beginning with the striate cortex and ending with the posterior parietal cortex.

ventral stream A system of intreconnected regions of visual cortex involved in the perception of form, beginning with the striate cortex and ending with the inferior temporal cortex.

stream; others ascend into regions of the dorsal stream. Some axons conveying information received from the magnocellular system bypass area V2: They project from area V1 directly to area V5, a region of the extrastriate cortex devoted to the analysis of movement. The ventral stream recognizes *what* an object is, and the dorsal stream recognizes *where* the object is located. (See *Figure 6.34.*)

As we saw, the parvocellular, koniocellular, and magnocellular systems provide different kinds of information. The magnocellular system is found in all mammals, whereas the parvocellular and koniocellular systems are found only in primates. These systems receive information from different types of ganglion cells, which are connected to different types of bipolar cells and photoreceptors. Only the cells in the parvocellular and koniocellular system receive information about wavelength from cones; thus, these systems analyze information concerning color. Cells in the parvocellular system also show high spatial resolution and low temporal resolution; that is, they are able to detect very fine details, but their response is slow and prolonged. The koniocellular system, which receives information only from "blue" cones, which are much less numerous than "red" and "green" cones, does not provide information about fine details. In contrast, neurons in the magnocellular system are color-blind. They are not able to detect fine details, but they can detect smaller contrasts between light and dark. They are also especially sensitive to movement. (See *Table 6.2.*)

At one time, researchers believed that the dorsal stream received its information solely from the magnocellular system and the ventral stream received its information solely from the parvocellular system. But more recent research has shown that both systems contribute information to both streams (Maunsell, 1992). The dorsal stream receives mostly magnocellular input, but the ventral stream receives approximately equal input from both of these systems and from the koniocellular system as well.

Perception of Color

As we saw earlier, neurons within the CO blobs in the striate cortex respond to colors. Like the ganglion cells in the retina (and the parvocellular and koniocellular neurons in the dorsal lateral geniculate nucleus), these neurons respond in opponent fashion. This information is analyzed by the regions of the visual association cortex that constitute the ventral stream.

Studies with Laboratory Animals

In the monkey brain neurons in the CO blobs send information about color to a specific subarea of the extrastriate cortex. Zeki (1980) found that neurons in this subarea (called *V4*) also respond selectively to colors, but their response characteristics are much more complex. Unlike the neurons we have encountered so far, these neurons respond to a variety of wavelengths, not just those that correspond to red, green, yellow, and blue.

Properties of the Magnocellular, Parvocellular, and Koniocellular Divisions of the Visual System

PROPERTY	MAGNOCELLULAR DIVISION	PARVOCELLULAR DIVISION	KONIOCELLULAR DIVISION
Color	No	Yes (from "red" and "green" cones)	Yes (from "blue" cones)
Sensitivity to contrast	High	Low	?
Spatial resolution (ability to detect fine details)	Low	High	Low
Temporal resolution	Fast (transient response)	Slow (sustained response)	?

The appearance of the colors of objects remains much the same whether we observe them under artificial light, under an overcast sky, or at noon on a cloudless day. This phenomenon is known as **color constancy.** Our visual system does not simply respond according to the wavelength of the light reflected by objects in each part of the visual field; instead, it compensates for the source of the light. This compensation appears to be made by simultaneously comparing the color composition of each point in the visual field with the average color of the entire scene. If the scene contains a particularly high level of long-wavelength light (as it would if an object were illuminated by the light of a setting sun), then some long-wavelength light is "subtracted out" of the perception of each point in the scene. This compensation helps us to see what is actually out there.

Schein and Desimone (1990) performed a careful study of the response characteristics of neurons in area V4 of the monkey extrastriate cortex. They found that these neurons responded to specific colors. Some also responded to colored bars of specific orientation; thus, area V4 seems to be involved in the analysis of form as well as color. The color-sensitive neurons had a rather unusual secondary receptive field—a large region surrounding the primary field. When stimuli were presented in the secondary receptive field, the neuron did not respond. However, stimuli presented there could suppress the neuron's response to a stimulus presented in the primary field. For example, if a cell would fire when a red spot was presented in the primary field, it would fire at a slower rate (or not at all) when an additional red stimulus was presented in the surrounding secondary field. In other words, these cells responded to particular wavelengths of light but subtracted out the amount of that wavelength that was present in the background. As Schein and Desimone point out, this subtraction could serve as the basis for color constancy.

Walsh et al. (1993) confirmed this prediction; damage to area V4 does disrupt color constancy. The investigators found that although monkeys could still discriminate between different colors after area V4 had been dam-

aged, their performance was impaired when the color of the overall illumination was changed. But the fact that the monkeys could still perform a color discrimination task under constant illumination means that some region besides area V4 must be involved in color vision.

A study by Heywood, Gaffan, and Cowey (1995) appears to have found that region—a portion of the inferior temporal cortex just anterior to area V4—a region of the monkey brain that is usually referred to as area TEO. The investigators destroyed area TEO, leaving area V4 intact, and observed severe impairment in color discrimination. The monkeys had no difficulty discriminating shades of gray, so the deficit on this task appeared to be restricted to color perception. (As we will see later, lesions of the inferior temporal cortex also disrupt the ability to perceive and recognize objects.)

When humans from a variety of cultures are asked to provide single names for colors, they universally chose eleven of them: red, orange, yellow, green, blue, purple, pink, brown, white, black, and gray (Boynton and Olson, 1987; Uchikawa and Boynton, 1987). Matuzawa (1985) found that chimpanzees appear to classify colors the same way, which suggests that the classification is based on the characteristics of neural mechanisms responsible for color perception. Indeed, Komatsu (1997) found a good correspondence between the eleven color categories and the responses of color-sensitive neurons in the inferior temporal cortex of the monkey.

Studies with Humans

Lesions of a restricted region of the human extrastriate cortex in the medial occipital lobe can cause loss of color vision without disruption of visual acuity. The patients describe their vision as resembling a black-and-white film

---

color constancy The relatively constant appearance of the colors of objects viewed under varying lighting conditions.

(Damasio et al., 1980; Kennard et al., 1995). The condition is known as **achromatopsia** ("vision without color"). If the brain damage is unilateral, people will lose color vision in only half of the visual field. In addition, they cannot even imagine colors or remember the colors of objects they saw before their brain damage occurred. As we just saw, Heywood, Gaffan, and Cowey (1995) found a region of the inferior temporal cortex of the monkey brain whose damage disrupted the ability to make color discriminations.

The analogous region appears to play a critical role in color perception in humans. A functional MRI study by Hadjikhani et al. (1998) found a color-sensitive region in the inferior temporal cortex, in a position corresponding to TEO in the monkey's cortex, which they called area V8. Indeed, lesions that cause achromatopsia damage V8 or other brain regions that provide input to V8. (Refer to *Figure 6.33*.)

Of course, perception of colors is useless in itself. The function of our ability to perceive different colors is to help us perceive different objects in our environment. Thus, to perceive and understand what is in front of us, we must have information about color combined with other forms of information. Some people with brain damage lose the ability to perceive shapes but can still perceive colors. For example, Zeki et al. (1999) described a patient who could identify colors but was otherwise blind. Patient P. B. received an electrical shock that caused both cardiac and respiratory arrest. He was revived, but the period of anoxia caused extensive damage to his extrastriate cortex. As a result, he lost all form perception. However, he could identify the colors of objects presented on a video monitor. He did *not* show blindsight. As we saw earlier, the residual visual abilities shown by people with blindsight are presumably mediated by projections from the superior colliculus and the thalamus to the extrastriate cortex, and Patient P. B.'s extrastriate cortex was severely damaged.

Analysis of Form

The analysis of form by the visual cortex begins with neurons in the striate cortex that are sensitive to orientation and spatial frequency. These neurons send information to the extrastriate cortex, which consists of several subregions. These subregions analyze the information and send it along the ventral stream toward the temporal neocortex.

Studies with Laboratory Animals

In primates the recognition of visual patterns and identification of particular objects take place in the **inferior temporal cortex,** located on the ventral part of the temporal lobe. This region of visual association cortex is located at the end of the ventral stream. It is here that analyses of form and color are put together and perceptions of three-dimensional objects and backgrounds are achieved. The

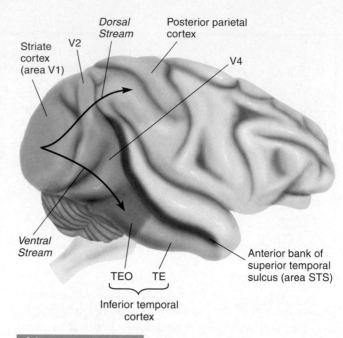

figure   6.35

Areas of visual cortex in the rhesus monkey brain.
(Adapted from Zeki, S. M. *Journal of Physiology*, 1978, *277*, 227–244.)

inferior temporal cortex consists of two major regions: areas TE and TEO. Damage to these regions causes severe deficits in visual discrimination (Mishkin, 1966; Gross, 1973; Dean, 1976). (See *Figures 6.35* and *6.36*.)

The receptive fields of neurons in area TEO are quite variable in size, but generally they are larger than those of neurons in area V4 and smaller than those of neurons in area TE (Boussaoud, Desimone, and Ungerleider, 1991). Their primary inputs come from area V4, and their primary outputs go to area TE, suggesting that "the neural coding of visual objects in TEO is based on object features that are more global than those in V4, but not quite as global as those in TE" (Boussaoud et al., 1991, p. 574). (As we saw, area TEO plays a critical role in perception of color.) Lesions of TEO make it almost impossible for monkeys to learn a task that requires them to discriminate between two simple two-dimensional patterns that differ in form, size, orientation, color, or brightness (Iwai and Mishkin, 1969; Gross, 1973; Dean, 1982; Ungerleider and Mishkin, 1982; Mishkin, Ungerleider, and Macko, 1983). Thus, this region serves as an essential link in the analysis of visual information.

achromatopsia (*ay krohm a **top** see a*) Inability to discriminate among different hues; caused by damage to the visual association cortex.

inferior temporal cortex In primates the highest level of the ventral stream of the visual association cortex; located on the inferior portion of the temporal lobe.

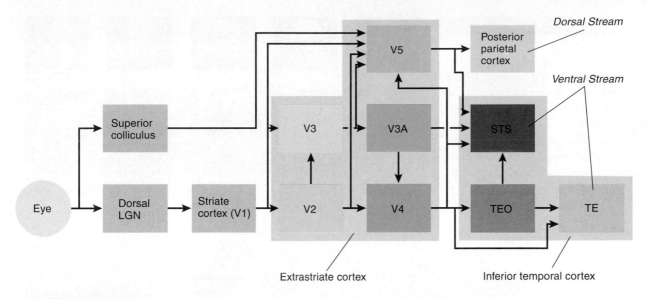

Interconnections of areas of visual cortex in the rhesus monkey brain. This diagram is greatly simplified; only the major areas and the most important connections are shown. The colors correspond to those shown in Figure 6.35. Some of the subareas are hidden in the depth of sulci and are therefore not visible in Figure 6.35.

Neurons in area TE have the largest receptive fields of all, often encompassing the entire contralateral half of the visual field. In general, these neurons respond best to three-dimensional objects (or photographs of them). They respond poorly to simple stimuli such as spots, lines, or sine-wave gratings. Most of them continue to respond even when these stimuli are moved to a different location, are changed in size, are placed against a different background, or are partially occluded by another object (Rolls and Baylis, 1986; Kovács, Vogels, and Orban, 1995). Thus, they appear to participate in the recognition of objects rather than the analysis of specific features.

Tanaka and his colleagues (reviewed by Tanaka, 1996) investigated the response characteristics of these neurons. First, they located a single neuron with a microelectrode. Then they presented a large number of three-dimensional items, such as toy animals, plants, and "junk" objects, until they found one that produced the best response. Then they used a computerized system to present a series of simplified versions of the picture to find the simplest pattern that would still excite the cell. Figure 6.37 illustrates this procedure. The cell responded when the tiger's head was presented and continued to respond to successively simplified patterns. The cell was activated by a pair of black rectangles superimposed on a white square but not by either of the two components of this stimulus (See *Figure 6.37*.)

Obviously, the fact that the cell responded to the tiger's face does not mean that it was a "tiger's face analyzer." As Tanaka observed, no single cell could recognize a complex stimulus found in nature. Instead, particular stimuli would be represented by the activity of a large

group of cells, each sensitive to slightly different patterns. It is the *pattern* of activity in circuits of neurons in area TE that represents the perception of particular objects.

Like other regions of the visual cortex, the inferior temporal cortex is arranged in columns. Neurons in adjacent regions usually respond to slightly different versions of the same stimuli. For example, several studies (for example, Desimone et al., 1984) have found neurons in the temporal lobe that are specifically excited by the sight of another face—either that of another monkey or that of a human. Some of these neurons respond to full-face views, and others respond to profiles. Most of these

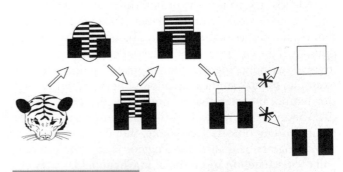

An analysis of the response characteristics of a neuron in area TE. The cell responded vigorously to the tiger's face and to the four simplified patterns selected by the computer. It did not respond to the white square or to the two black rectangles presented alone.

(From Tanaka, K. *Current Opinion in Neurobiology*, 1992, *2*, 502–505.)

figure 6.38

Results of the study by Wang, Tanaka, and Tanifuji (1996). *Top row:* Views of the doll's head shown to the monkey. *Middle row:* Computer-generated images of the surface of the inferior temporal cortex. The arrows point to dark spots indicating a cluster of activated neurons. *Bottom:* Superimposed drawings of the outline of the clusters of activated neurons.
(Adapted from Wang, G., Tanaka, K., and Tanifuji, M. *Science,* 1996, *272,* 1665–1668.)

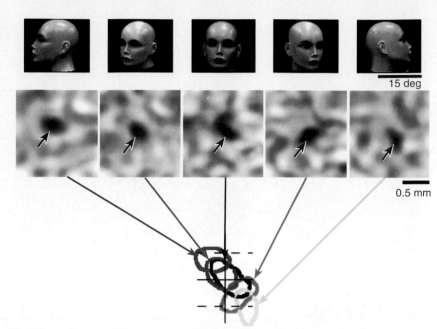

15 deg

0.5 mm

face-sensitive cells are located in area TE and in the cortex that lines the anterior bank of the superior temporal sulcus (area STS). (Refer to *Figure 6.35*.)

A study by Wang, Tanaka, and Tanifuji (1996) used an optical recording technique to study the functional organization of the inferior temporal cortex in monkeys. They placed transparent "windows" over the surface of the cortex that permitted them to monitor the surface of the brain. They used a special computer-driven video camera to record changes in the appearance of the cortex caused by changes in the oxidation level of hemoglobin in the cortical capillaries—changes that correlate with neural activity. Figure 6.38 shows the response to different view's of a doll's head as it rotated. As you can see from the movement of the dark spot (arrows) from frame to frame, adjacent clusters of neurons were activated by different views of the head. (See *Figure 6.38*.)

Clearly, neurons in the primate inferior temporal cortex respond to very complex shapes. The complexity and the specific nature of these features suggest that the development of the circuits responsible for detecting them must involve learning. Indeed, that seems to be the case. For example, several studies have found neurons in the inferior temporal cortex that respond specifically to objects that the monkeys have already seen many times but not to unfamiliar objects (Kobatake, Tanaka, and Tamori, 1992; Logothetis, Pauls, and Poggio, 1995). Such studies will be discussed in more detail in Chapter 13.

Studies with Humans

Damage to the human visual association cortex can cause a category of deficits known as **visual agnosia.** *Agnosia* ("failure to know") refers to an inability to perceive or identify a stimulus by means of a particular sensory modality, even though its details can be detected by means of that modality and the person retains relatively normal intellectual capac-

ity. *Apperceptive* visual agnosias are failures in high-level perception, whereas *associative* visual agnosias are disconnections between these perceptions and verbal systems. The distinction will be described in more detail later in this section.

■ **Apperceptive Visual Agnosia** Ms. L., whose case was described in the opening of this chapter, had **apperceptive visual agnosia.** As we saw, she could not identify common objects by sight, even though she had relatively normal visual acuity. However, she could still read—even small print. When she was permitted to hold an object that she could not recognize visually, she could immediately recognize it by touch and say what it is. This proves that she had not forgotten her memory for the object or simply forgotten how to say its name.

■ **Are Faces Special?** A common symptom of apperceptive visual agnosia is **prosopagnosia,** inability to recognize particular faces (*prosopon* is Greek for "face"). That is, patients with this disorder can recognize that they are looking at a face, but they cannot say whose face it is—even if it belongs to a relative or close friend. They see eyes, ears, a nose, a mouth—but cannot recognize the particular configuration of these features that identifies an individual face. They still remember who these people are and will usually recognize them when they hear their voice. As one patient said, "I have trouble recognizing people from just faces alone. I look at their hair color, listen to their voices . . . I use

visual agnosia (*ag no zha*) Deficits in visual perception in the absence of blindness; caused by brain damage.

apperceptive visual agnosia Failure to perceive objects, even though visual acuity is relatively normal.

prosopagnosia (*prah soh pag no zha*) Failure to recognize particular people by the sight of their faces.

clothing, voice, and hair. I try to associate something with a person one way or another . . . what they wear, how their hair is worn" (Buxbaum, Glosser, and Coslett, 1999, p. 43).

Some investigators believe that facial recognition is mediated by special circuits in the brain that are devoted to the specific analysis of facial features. The most recent evidence suggests that faces are indeed recognized by special circuits in the visual association cortex but that these circuits are not genetically programmed as a "face-recognizing device." Instead, they develop through experience and can be used for learning to recognize other types of visual stimuli.

To recognize a particular person's face, we must have neural circuits that can analyze subtle differences in the configuration of eyes, eyebrows, nose, cheekbones, lips, chin, and all the other features that distinguish one face from another. Studies with brain-damaged people and functional imaging studies suggest that these special face-recognizing circuits are found in the **fusiform face area,** a region of visual association cortex located in the extrastriate cortex at the base of the brain. (See Kanwisher, McDermott, and Chun, 1997, for a review.) Most studies indicate that the right hemisphere is more important than the left. For example, Wada and Yamamoto (2001) reported the case of a patient with brain damage limited almost exclusively to the right fusiform gyrus who showed a profound prosopagnosia, and Allison et al. (1994) found that electrical stimulation of this region often disrupted a person's ability to identify familiar faces. (See *Figure 6.39.*)

figure 6.40

Visual object agnosia without prosopagnosia. A patient could recognize the face in this painting but not the flowers and vegetables that compose it..
(Giuseppe Arcimboldo. 1527–1593. *Vertumnus*. Erich Lessing/ Art Resource, New York.)

Perhaps the strangest piece of evidence for a special face-recognition region comes from a report by Moscovitch, Winocur, and Behrmann (1997), who studied a man with a visual agnosia for objects but not for faces. For example, he recognized the face shown in Figure 6.40 but not the flowers and vegetables that compose it. (See *Figure 6.40.*) Presumably, his general-purpose object-recognition circuits were damaged, but the fusiform face region was not.

So there seems to be a special region devoted to recognition of faces. But must we conclude that the development of this region is a result of natural selection? Several kinds of evidence suggest that the answer is no—that the face-recognition circuits develop as a result of the experience we have seeing people's faces. First, consider the fact that some neural circuits appear to be devoted to the rapid and efficient recognition of written words. Damage to one part of the brain can impair people's ability to read but not affect their ability to recognize objects, and damage to another region can impair object recognition but not reading. (This

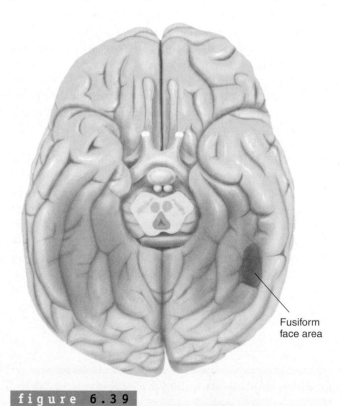

Fusiform face area

figure 6.39

The fusiform face area, located in the extrastriate cortex of the occipital lobe on the base of the brain.

fusiform face area A region of the extrastriate cortex located at the base of the brain; involved in perception of faces and other complex objects that require expertise to recognize

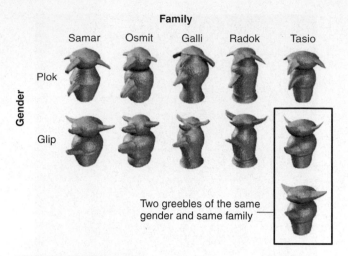

Gender

Family

Samar   Osmit   Galli   Radok   Tasio

Plok

Glip

Two greebles of the same gender and same family

figure 6.41

Some "greebles," computer-created objects from the study by Gauthier and Tarr (1997). Greebles were categorized by family and gender, and different individuals each had their own particular shapes. Two greebles of the same gender and family would resemble each other more closely than any other two greebles.

(From Gauthier, I., and Tarr, M. J. *Vision Research,* 1997, *37,* 1673–1682.)

evidence is reviewed in Chapter 15, which discusses the neural mechanisms of spoken and written language.) The process of natural selection cannot possibly be responsible for the development of these circuits because the invention of written languages occurred very recently—only a few thousand years ago. In addition, until *very* recently, the vast majority of the world's population was illiterate, so there has not been enough time for the evolution of innate word-recognition circuits to take place. So if experience looking at words can cause the development of circuits that recognize words, perhaps experience looking at faces can cause the development of face-recognition circuits.

Because of the extensive experience we have looking at faces, we are all experts at recognizing them. What about people who have become experts at recognizing other types of objects? It appears that recognition of specific complex stimuli by experts, too, is disrupted by lesions that cause prosopagnosia: inability of a farmer to recognize his cows, inability of a bird expert to recognize different species of birds, and inability of a driver to recognize his own car—except by reading its license plate (Bornstein, Stroka, and Munitz, 1969; Damasio, Damasio, and Van Hoesen, 1982).

In a functional imaging study, Gauthier et al. (2000) found that when bird or car experts (but not nonexperts) viewed pictures of birds or cars, the fusiform face area was activated. Another study (Gauthier et al., 1999) found that when people had spent a long time becoming familiar with computer-generated objects they called "greebles," viewing the greebles activated the fusiform face area. (See *Figure 6.41.*)

Another functional imaging study (Golby et al., 2001) found higher activation of the fusiform face area when people viewed pictures of faces of members of their own race (African Americans or European Americans). Presumably, this difference reflected the fact that people have more experience seeing other members of their own race. Indeed, the subjects in this study learned to recognize faces of people of their own race more accurately than those of people of the other race.

As we will see in Chapter 17, people with autistic disorder fail to develop normal social relations with other people. Indeed, in severe cases they give no signs that they recognize that other people exist. Grelotti, Dauthier, and Schultz (2002) found that people with autistic disorder showed a deficit in the ability to recognize faces and that looking at faces failed to activate the fusiform gyrus. The authors speculate that the lack of interest in other people, caused by the brain abnormalities responsible for autism, resulted in a lack of motivation that normally promotes the acquisition of expertise in recognizing faces as a child grows up.

In summary, a face-recognition region does appear to exist in the right fusiform gyrus, but the circuits there are specialized for acquiring expertise in recognizing a variety of closely related complex visual stimuli. The neural circuitry that is responsible for our ability to recognize faces does not seem to be genetically programmed for only one type of expertise.

■ **Associative Visual Agnosia** A person with apperceptive agnosia who cannot recognize common objects also cannot draw them or copy other people's drawings; therefore, we properly speak of a deficit in perception. However, the brains of people with an **associative visual agnosia** appear to contain the neural circuits necessary for object recognition, but the people seem to be unaware of these perceptions. For example, a patient studied by Ratcliff and Newcombe (1982) could copy a drawing of an anchor (better than I could have done). Therefore, he must have been able to perceive the shape of the anchor. However, he did not recognize either the sample or the copy that he had just drawn as being an anchor. When asked on another occasion to draw a picture of an anchor from memory (not from a picture), he could not do so. Even though he could copy a real image of an anchor, the word *anchor* failed to produce a mental image of one. (See *Figure 6.42.*) When asked on yet another occasion to define *anchor,* he said, "a brake for ships," so we can conclude that he knew what the word meant.

associative visual agnosia Inability to identify objects that are perceived visually, even though the form of the perceived object can be drawn or matched with similar objects.

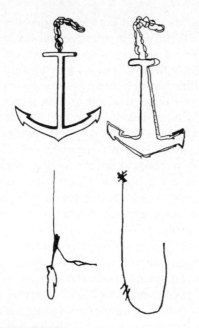

figure 6.42

Associative visual agnosia. The patient successfully copied an anchor (*top*) but failed on two attempts to comply with a request to "draw an anchor" (*bottom*).
(From Ratcliff, G., and Newcombe, F., in *Normality and Pathology in Cognitive Functions,* edited by A. W. Ellis. London: Academic Press, 1982.)

Associative agnosia also extends to prosopagnosia. For example, Sergent and Signoret (1992) reported the case of a patient who could match photos of different views of the same face but could not identify the faces—even when they were pictures of the patient herself. The lesion seems to have affected the ability to identify faces without severely damaging perceptual analysis.

Associative visual agnosia appears to involve difficulty in transferring visual information to verbal mechanisms. That is, the person perceives the object well enough to draw it (or to match it with similar stimuli), but his or her verbal mechanisms do not receive the necessary information to produce the appropriate word.

David Margolin and I studied a man who had sustained brain damage from an inflammatory disease that affected his cerebral blood vessels. (The damage was diffuse, so we could not make any conclusions about the anatomy of his disorder.) Suffering from an apparent visual agnosia, he failed to identify most pictures of objects. However, he sometimes made unintentional gestures when he was studying a picture that gave him enough of a clue that he could identify it. For example, on one occasion while puzzling over a picture of a cow, he started making movements with both hands that were unmistakably ones he would make if he were milking a cow. He looked at his hands and said, "Oh, a cow!" (He was a farmer, by the way.)

We might speculate that his perceptual mechanisms, in the visual association cortex, were relatively normal but that connections between these mechanisms and the speech mechanisms of the left hemisphere were disrupted. However, the connections between the perceptual mechanisms and the motor mechanisms of the frontal lobe were spared, permitting him to make appropriate movements when looking at some pictures. In fact, a particularly observant and conscientious speech therapist helped the patient learn how to read by these means. She taught him the manual alphabet used by deaf people, in which letters are represented by particular hand and finger movements. (This system is commonly called *finger spelling*.) He could then look at individual letters of words he could not read, make the appropriate movements, observe the sequence of letters that he spelled, and decode the word.

Recent studies suggest that associative visual agnosia is best explained as a disruption of connections between the ventral stream of the visual cortex from the brain's verbal mechanisms without damage to the connections between these mechanisms and the dorsal stream. I will say more about these studies in the next subsection.

Perception of Movement

We need to know not only what things are, but also where they are and where they are going. Without the ability to perceive the direction and velocity of movement of objects, we would have no way to predict where they will be. We would be unable to catch them (or avoid letting them catch us). This section examines the perception of movement; the final section examines the perception of location.

Studies with Laboratory Animals

One of the regions of the extrastriate cortex—area V5, also known as area MT, for *medial temporal*—contains neurons that respond to movement. Damage to this region severely disrupts a monkey's ability to perceive moving stimuli (Siegel and Andersen, 1986). Area V5 receives input directly from the striate cortex and from several regions of the extrastriate cortex. It also receives input from the superior colliculus.

Accurately determining the velocity and direction of movement of an object is an important ability. That moving object could be a prey animal trying to run away, a predator trying to catch you, or a projectile you are trying to catch (or keep from hitting you). If we are to accurately track moving objects, the information received by V5 must be up to date. In fact, the axons that transmit information from the magnocellular system are thick and heavily myelinated, which increases the rate at which they conduct action potentials. Petersen, Miezin, and Allman (1988) recorded the responses of neurons in areas V4 and

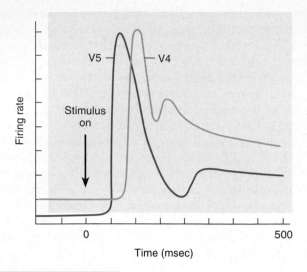

figure 6.43

Responses of neurons in areas V4 and V5 to stimuli presented in their receptive field. Note that neurons in the motion-sensitive area V5 responded sooner, and their firing ceased sooner, than neurons in the form- and color-sensitive area V4. The faster, briefer response is what one would expect of neurons involved in perceiving a moving object's velocity and direction of movement.

(Adapted from Petersen, S., Miezin, F., and Allman, J. Transient and sustained responses in four extrastriate visual areas of the owl monkey. *Experimental Brain Research,* 1988, *70,* 55–60.

V5. As you can see in Figure 6.43, visual information reached the V5 neurons sooner than it reached those in area V4, whose neurons are involved in the analysis of form and color. (See *Figure 6.43.*)

The input from the superior colliculus contributes in some way to the movement sensitivity of neurons in area V5. Rodman, Gross, and Albright (1989, 1990) found that destruction of the striate cortex or the superior colliculus alone does not eliminate the movement sensitivity of V5 neurons, but destruction of both areas does. The roles played by these two sources of input are not yet known. Clearly, both inputs provide useful information; Seagraves et al. (1987) found that monkeys still could detect movement after lesions of the striate cortex but had difficulty estimating its rate.

Albright, Desimone, and Gross (1984) mapped the characteristics of movement-sensitive neurons in area V5. They found that all V5 neurons responded better to moving stimuli than to stationary ones and that most of them gave the same response regardless of the color or shape of the test stimulus. Most neurons showed directional sensitivity; that is, they responded only to movements in a particular direction. They also found that, like the striate cortex, area V5 is divided into rectangular modules. Traveling along the long axis of a module, they encountered neurons with directional sensitivities that varied systematically, in a clockwise or counterclockwise fashion. The receptive fields of movement-sensitive neurons in area V5 are elongated, with most neurons showing movement sensitivity in a direction at right angles to the long axis. Some modules are surrounded by antagonistic surrounds, which show sensitivity to movement in the opposite direction. These modules seem best able to detect local movement—movement of isolated points within the visual field. Other modules respond best to coordinated movement of randomly placed dots in both the center of the receptive field and its surround, which suggests that they respond best to global movement—movement of large parts of the visual field (Born, 2000).

A region adjacent to area V5 (sometimes called V5a but more often referred to as MST, for *medial superior temporal*) receives information about movement from V5 and performs a further analysis. MST neurons respond to complex patterns of movement, including radial, circular, and spiral motion (see Vaina, 1998, for a review). One important function of this region—in particular, the dorsolateral MST, or MSTd—appears to be analysis of **optic flow.** As we move around in our environment or as objects in our environment move in relation to us, the sizes, shapes, and locations of environmental features on our retinas change. Imagine the image seen by a video camera as you walk along a street, pointing the lens of the camera straight in front of you. Suppose your path will pass just to the right of a mailbox. The image of the mailbox will slowly get larger. Finally, as you pass it, it will veer to the left and disappear. Points on the sidewalk will move downward, and branches of trees that you pass under will move upward. Analysis of the relative movement of the visual elements of your environment—the optic flow—will tell you where you are heading, how fast you are approaching different items in front of you, and whether you will pass to the left or right (or under or over) these items. The point toward which we are moving does not move, but all other points in the visual scene move away from it. Therefore, this point is called the *center of expansion*. If we keep moving in the same direction, we will eventually bump into an object that lies at the center of expansion. We can also use optic flow to determine whether an object approaching us will hit us or pass us by.

Bradley et al. (1996) recorded from single units in MSTd of monkeys and found that particular neurons responded selectively to expansion foci located in particular regions of the visual field. These neurons compen-

optic flow The complex motion of points in the visual field caused by relative movement between the observer and environment; provides information about the relative distance of objects from the observer and of the relative direction of movement.

sated for eye movements, which means that their activity identified the location in the environment toward which an animal was moving. (The ability of the visual system to compensate for eye movements is discussed in the next subsection of this chapter.) Britten and van Wezel (1998) found that electrical stimulation of MSTd disrupted monkeys' ability to perceive the apparent direction in which they were heading; thus, these neurons do indeed seem to play an essential role in heading estimation derived from optic flow.

Not all regions of cerebral cortex that analyze important aspects of visual information are located in the caudal part of the brain. Rizzolatti and his colleagues (Gallese et al., 1996; Rizzolatti et al., 1996) recorded from the frontal cortex of monkeys and found a group of neurons with particularly interesting response characteristics. These neurons, found in the rostral part of the ventral premotor cortex, responded when the monkeys either *saw* or *performed* various grasping, holding, or manipulating movements. For example, one of these neurons might respond when the monkey saw an experimenter pick up a piece of food from a tray. It would not respond to the sight of the experimenter's hand alone, to the sight of the tray alone, or to the sight of the experimenter picking up the piece of food with a pair of pliers. The same neuron would also respond when the monkey picked up a piece of food from the tray, whether it did so when the lights were on and its movement was guided by vision or when the lights were off so it had to pick up the piece of food in the dark. The investigators called the cells *mirror neurons* because they responded to a particular visual stimulus or to the movement that produces this stimulus. Presumably, they are involved in a monkey's ability to recognize and imitate gestures made by other monkeys.

Studies with Humans

Bilateral damage to parts of the visual association cortex of the human brain can produce an inability to perceive movement—**akinetopsia.** For example, Zihl et al. (1991) reported the case of a woman with bilateral lesions of the lateral occipital cortex and area V5.

> Patient L. M. had an almost total loss of movement perception. She was unable to cross a street without traffic lights, because she could not judge the speed at which cars were moving. Although she could perceive movements, she found moving objects very unpleasant to look at. For example, while talking with another person, she avoided looking at the person's mouth because she found its movements very disturbing. When the investigators asked her to try to detect movements of a visual target in the laboratory, she said, "First the target is completely at rest. Then it suddenly jumps upwards and downwards" (p. 2244). She was able to see that the target was constantly changing its position, but she was unaware of any sensation of movement.

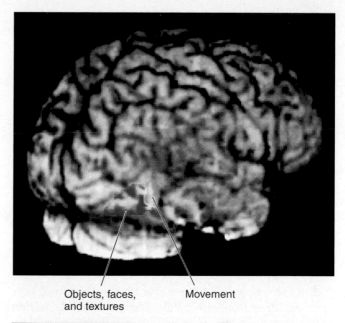

Objects, faces,   Movement
and textures

figure 6.44

Responses to shapes and movement. Averaged PET images of activation in the occipital lobe produced by pictures of objects, faces, and textures (red) and moving random patterns of dots (green).

(From Malach, R., Reppas, J. B., Benson, R. R., Kwong, K. K., Jiang, H., Kennedy, W. A., Ledden, P. J., Brady, T. J., Rosen, B. R., and Tootell, R. B. H. *Proceedings of the National Academy of Sciences, USA,* 1995, *92,* 8135–8139.)

As we saw in the previous subsection, area V5 is the one region of the monkey brain that is most important for perception of movement. Several PET and functional MRI studies suggest that the region of the human brain that performs this function is located near the junction of the lateral occipital and temporal lobes. For example, Malach et al. (1995) showed people two types of stimuli: (1) pictures of objects, faces, and textures and (2) moving random patterns of dots. As Figure 6.44 shows, these stimuli activated different regions of extrastriate cortex. The red region was activated by objects, faces, and textures, and the green region (presumably, corresponding to area V5) was activated by movement. (See *Figure 6.44.*)

Walsh et al. (1998) used transcranial magnetic stimulation (TMS) to temporarily inactivate area V5 in normal human subjects. As we saw in Chapter 5, the TMS procedure applies a strong localized magnetic field to the brain by passing an electrical current through a coil of wire placed on the scalp. The magnetic field induces a weak

akinetopsi Inability to perceive movement, caused by damage to area V5 (also called MST) of the visual association cortex.

electrical current in the brain that temporarily disrupts normal neural activity. The investigators found that during the stimulation, people were unable to detect which of several objects displayed on a computer screen was moving. When the current was off, the subjects had no trouble detecting the motion. The current had no effect on the subject's ability to detect stimuli that varied in their form.

As we saw in the previous subsection, neurons in area MSTd of the monkey brain respond to optic flow, an important source of information about the direction in which the animal is heading. A functional imaging study by Peuskens et al. (2001) found that the same region became active when subjects judged their heading while viewing a display showing optic flow. Vaina and her colleagues (Jornales et al., 1997; Vaina, 1998) found that people with lesions that included this region were able to perceive motion but could not perceive heading from optic flow. (**Animation 6.2, Motion Aftereffects,** illustrates movement-related phenomenon.)

> See the interactive CD for more on motion aftereffects.

Perception of movement can even help us perceive three-dimensional forms—a phenomenon known as *form from motion.* Johansson (1973) demonstrated just how much information we can derive from movement. He dressed actors in black and attached small lights to several points on their bodies, such as their wrists, elbows, shoulders, hips, knees, and feet. He made movies of the actors in a darkened room while they were performing various behaviors, such as walking, running, jumping, limping, doing push-ups, and dancing with a partner who was also equipped with lights. Even though observers who watched the films could see only a pattern of moving lights against a dark background, they could readily perceive the pattern as belonging to a moving human and could identify the behavior the actor was performing. Subsequent studies (Kozlowski and Cutting, 1977; Barclay, Cutting, and Kozlowski, 1978) showed that people could even tell, with reasonable accuracy, the sex of the actor wearing the lights. The cues appeared to be supplied by the relative amounts of movement of the shoulders and hips as the person walked.

McCleod et al. (1996) suggest that the ability to perceive form from motion does not involve area V5. They reported that Patient L. M. (studied by Zihl et al., 1991) could recognize people depicted solely by moving points of light *even though she could not perceive the movements themselves.* Vaina and her colleagues (reported by Vaina, 1998) found a patient with a lesion in the medial right occipital lobe who showed just the opposite deficits: Patient R. A. could perceive movement—even complex radial and circular optic flow—but could not perceive form from motion. Thus, perception of motion and perception of form from motion involve different regions of the visual association cortex.

A functional imaging study by Grossman et al. (2000) found that when people viewed a video that showed form from motion, a small region on the ventral bank of the posterior end of the superior temporal sulcus became active. More activity was seen in the right hemisphere, whether the images were presented to the left or right visual field.

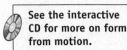

> See the interactive CD for more on form from motion.

(For a demonstration of this phenomenon, see **Animation 6.3, Form from Motion.**) Grossman and Blake (2001) found that this region became active even when people *imagined* that they were watching points of light representing form from motion. (See **Figure 6.45**.)

Perception of form from motion might not seem like a phenomenon that has any importance outside the laboratory. However, this phenomenon does occur under natural circumstances, and it appears to involve brain mechanisms different from those involved in normal object perception. For example, people with visual agnosia can often still perceive *actions* (such as someone pretending to stir something in a bowl or deal out some playing cards) even though they cannot recognize objects by sight. They may be able to recognize friends by the way they walk, even though they cannot recognize their faces. For example, Lê et al. (2002) reported the case of patient S. B., a 30-year-old man whose ventral stream was damaged extensively bilaterally by encephalitis when he was three years old. As a result, he was unable to recognize objects, faces, textures, or colors. However, he could perceive movement and could even catch a ball that was thrown to him. Furthermore, he could recognize other people's arm and hand movements that mimed common activities such as cutting something with a knife or brushing one's teeth, and he could recognize people he know by their gait.

So far, this discussion has been confined to movement of objects in the visual field. But if a person moves his or her eyes, head, or whole body, the image on the retina will move even if everything within the person's visual field remains stable. Often, of course, *both* kinds of movements will occur at the same time. The problem for the visual system is to determine which of these images are produced by movements of objects in the environment and which are produced by the person's own eye, head, and body movements.

To illustrate this problem, think about how the page of this book looks as you read it. If we could make a videotape of one of your retinas, we would see that the image of the page projected there is in constant movement as your eyes make several saccades along a line and then snap back to the beginning of the next line. Yet the page seems perfectly still to you. On the other hand, if you look at a single point on the page (say, a period at the end of a sentence) and then move the page around while following it with your eyes, you perceive the book as mov-

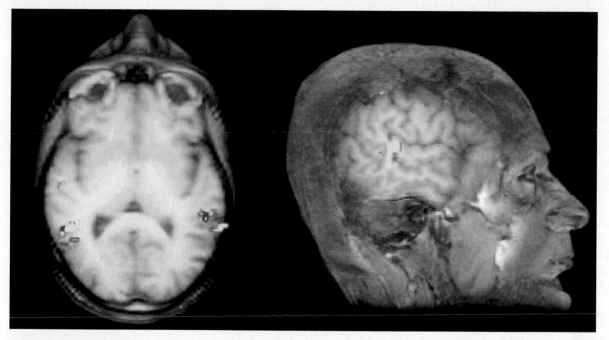

Responses to viewing form from motion. Horizontal and lateral views of neural activity while the subject was viewing videos of biological motion such as those shown in Animation 6.3. Maximum activity is seen in a small region on the ventral bank of the posterior end of the superior temporal sulcus, primarily in the right hemisphere. (From Grossman, E. D., and Blake, R. *Vision Research,* 2001, *41,* 1475–1482.)

ing, even though the image on your retina remains relatively stable. (Try it.) Then think about the images on your retina while you are driving in busy traffic, constantly moving your eyes around to keep track of your own location and that of other cars moving in different directions at different speeds. You are perceiving not only the simple movement of objects, but optic flow as well, which helps you keep track of the trajectories of the objects relative to each other and to yourself.

Haarmeier et al. (1997) reported the case of a patient with bilateral damage to the extrastriate cortex who could not compensate for image movement caused by head and eye movements. When the patient moved his eyes, it looked to him as if the world were moving in the same direction. Without the ability to compensate for head and eye movements, any movement of a retinal image was perceived as movement of the environment. On the basis of evidence from EEG and MEG (magnetoencephalography) studies in human subjects and single-unit recordings in monkeys, Thier et al. (2001) suggest that this compensation involves extrastriate cortex located at the junction of the temporal and parietal lobes near a region involved in the analysis of signals from the vestibular system. Indeed, the investigators note that when patients with damage to

this region move their eyes, the lack of compensation for these movements makes them feel very dizzy.

As we saw in the previous subsection, mirror neurons in the ventral premotor area of the monkey brain respond when the monkey either sees or performs a particular action. Functional imaging studies suggest that a region containing mirror neurons is also found in the human prefrontal cortex. Rizzolatti and Arbib (1998) suggest that these neurons might be involved in recognizing and imitating other people's gestures, including those made by deaf people when they communicate by sign language.

Perception of Spatial Location

As we just saw, all subareas of the extrastriate cortex send information to the inferior temporal cortex, the region in which object perception appears to take place. In addition, three subareas of the extrastriate cortex—those involved with color, orientation, and movement—send information through area V5 to the parietal cortex. (Refer to *Figures 6.35* and *6.36*.) The parietal lobe is involved in spatial perception, and it is through these connections that it receives its visual input. Damage to the parietal lobes disrupts performance on a variety of tasks

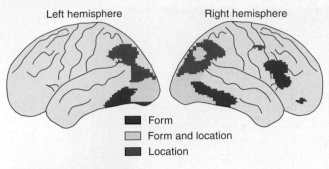

Left hemisphere   Right hemisphere

■ Form
□ Form and location
■ Location

figure 6.46

Responses to objects and location. Averaged PET images of cortical activation produced by performing an object discrimination (human faces and random patterns) or a spatial location discrimination of the same stimuli.

(Adapted from Haxby, J. V., Horwitz, B., Ungerleider, L. G., Maisog, J. M., Pietrini, P., and Grady, C. L. *Journal of Neuroscience,* 1994, *14,* 6336–6353.)

that require perceiving and remembering the locations of objects (Ungerleider and Mishkin, 1982).

Haxby et al. (1994) had human subjects perform two different discrimination tasks: one for form (human faces) and the other for spatial location (human faces and random patterns). In both cases the subjects saw a display showing a face or a pattern, followed by a second display. In the form discrimination task the subjects had to ignore the location of the faces but decide whether the second display contained the same face as the first. In the spatial location task they had to ignore the nature of the forms but decide whether the form shown in the second display was in the same *location* as the one shown in the first display. While the subjects were performing the discrimination tasks, the investigators used a PET scanner to record their regional cerebral blood flow. They found that performance of both tasks increased the metabolic activity of much of the extrastriate cortex. However, only the form discrimination task activated the ventral stream, and only the location discrimination task activated the dorsal stream. (See *Figure 6.46.*)

A functional imaging study by Mellet et al. (1996) showed that the dorsal stream is involved in the construction of mental images of three-dimensional objects according to verbal instructions. The investigators asked people to imagine an assembly of cube-shaped blocks, put together one by one. For example, the assembly in Figure 6.47 begins with the block shown in blue. The second block goes to the right of the first, the third goes below the second, the fourth goes below the third, and so on. (See *Figure 6.47a.*) Functional MRI images that were taken while the subjects were constructing the mental images of these objects found increased activity in a bilateral occipitoparietal-frontal network that included the superior extrastriate cortex of the occipital lobe, inferior parietal cortex, and dorsal premo-

tor cortex of the frontal lobe. Activity was also seen in the right inferior temporal cortex. (See *Figure 6.47b.*) Thus, imagining the construction of a three-dimensional assembly involves the dorsal stream (where spatial perception takes place) and the frontal lobes (where planning of movements takes place). The involvement of the ventral stream of the right hemisphere may reflect the people's recognition of the imaginary shape they had constructed.

A particularly interesting phenomenon called **Balint's syndrome** occurs in people with bilateral damage to the parieto-occipital region—the region bordering the parietal lobe and occipital lobe (Balint, 1909; Damasio, 1985). Balint's syndrome consists of three major symptoms: optic ataxia, ocular apraxia, and simultanagnosia. All three symptoms are related to spatial perception.

Optic ataxia is a deficit in reaching for objects under visual guidance (*ataxia* comes from the Greek word for "disorderly"). A person with Balint's syndrome might be able to perceive and recognize a particular object, but when he or she tries to reach for it, the movement is often misdirected. **Ocular apraxia** (literally "without visual action") is a deficit of visual scanning. If a person with Balint's syndrome looks around a room filled with objects, he or she will see an occasional item and will be able to perceive it normally. However, the patient will not be able to maintain fixation; his or her eyes will begin to wander, and another object will come into view for a time. The person is unable to make a systematic scan of the contents of the room and will not be able to perceive the location of the objects he or she sees. If an object moves or if a light flashes, the person may report seeing something but will not be able to make an eye movement that directs the gaze toward the target.

Simultanagnosia is the most interesting of the three symptoms (Rizzo and Robin, 1990). As I just mentioned, if the gaze of a person with Balint's syndrome happens to fall on an object, he or she will perceive it. But *only one object* will be perceived at a time. For example, if an examiner holds either a comb or a pen in front of a patient's eyes, the patient will recognize the object. But if the examiner holds a pen and a comb together (for example, so that they form the legs of an X), the patient will see either the comb or the pen but not both. The existence of simultanagnosia means that perception of separate objects takes

Balint's syndrome A syndrome caused by bilateral damage to the parieto-occipital region; includes optic ataxia, ocular apraxia, and simultanagnosia

optic ataxia (*ay tack see a*) Difficulty in reaching for objects under visual guidance.

ocular apraxia (*ay prak see a*) Difficulty in visual scanning.

simultanagnosia (*sime ul tane ag no zha*) Difficulty in perceiving more than one object at a time.

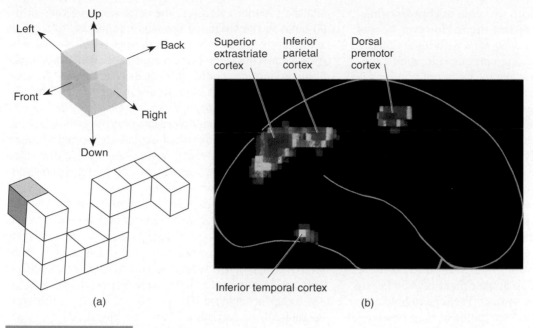

figure   6.47

Construction of a mental image. Subjects imagined the construction of an assembly of cubes as the experimenter indicated the location of each new block. (a) An assembly produced by the following directions: right, down, down, back, back, back, up, up, back, back, right. (b) Neural activity during the imaginary construction task, as measured by functional MRI.

(From Mellett, E., Tzourio, N., Crivello, F., Joliot, M., Denis, M., and Mazoyer, B. *Journal of Neuroscience,* 1996, *16,* 6504–6512.)

place at least somewhat independently, even when the outlines of the objects overlap in the visual field.

Goodale and his colleagues (Goodale and Milner, 1992; Goodale et al., 1994) suggested that the primary function of the dorsal stream of the visual cortex is to guide actions rather than simply to perceive spatial locations. As Ungerleider and Mishkin (1982) originally put it, the ventral and dorsal streams tell us "what" and "where." Goodale and his colleagues suggested that the better terms are "what" and *"how."* First, they noted that the visual cortex of the parietal lobe is extensively connected to regions of the frontal lobe involved in controlling eye movements, reaching movements of the limbs, and grasping movements of the hands and fingers (Cavada and Goldman-Rakic, 1989; Gentilucci and Rizzolatti, 1990; Broussaud, di Pellegrino, and Wise, 1996). Second, they noted that the optic ataxia and ocular apraxia of Balint's syndrome, which are caused by bilateral damage to the dorsal stream, are deficits in visually guided movements. They cited the case of a person with such lesions who had no difficulty recognizing line drawings (that is, the ventral stream was intact) but who had trouble picking up objects (Jakobson et al., 1991). The patient could easily perceive the difference in size of wooden blocks that were set out before her, but she failed to adjust the distance between her thumb and forefinger to the size of the block she was about to pick up. In contrast, a patient with profound visual agnosia could not distinguish between wooden blocks of different sizes but *could* adjust the distance between her thumb and forefinger when she picked them up. She made this adjustment by means of vision, before she actually touched them (Milner et al., 1991; Goodale et al., 1994).

The suggestion by Goodale and his colleagues seems a reasonable one. Of course, the dorsal stream is involved in perception of the location of object's space—but then, if its primary role is to direct movements, it *must* be involved in location of these objects, or else how could it direct movements toward them? In addition, it must contain information about the size and shape of objects, or else how could it control the distance between thumb and forefinger?

I mentioned earlier that I would attempt to explain associative visual agnosia as a disruption of the connections between the ventral stream and the brain's verbal mechanisms. As we saw, people with associative agnosia cannot verbally identify visually presented objects or pictures of them, but they can copy them, and sometimes they can make hand movements that enable them to guess what the object is. Sirigu, Duhamel, and Poncet (1991) reported the case of a patient with bilateral lesions of the anterior temporal cortex who was able to copy drawings of objects but was unable to name them. However, he was able to say or demonstrate *what to do* with these objects. For example, he said, "You open on one side, stick something on it, close it, and it stays in. I can tell you how it works, but I don't see its exact use" (p. 2555). And what had the investigators shown him? A safety pin. When they showed him a picture of a jackhammer, he acted as if he were holding one, and made shaking movements. What was it for? "Probably to make holes . . . in the wall . . . when you want to hang a picture" (p. 2566).

It is important to realize that the patient recognized *what to do* with objects he saw, not *what they were used for.* He was able to describe or mime behaviors, not functions. Certainly, one would not use a jackhammer to hang a picture on the wall. Consider what he said when shown a pair of pliers: "It is used manually, when you pull apart here [points to handle] it opens up at the other end." So far, so good. But then he went on to say, "Perhaps to hold several pieces of paper together" (p. 2566). When shown an iron, he said "You hold it in one hand, and move it back and forth horizontally." He then mimed the action, as if he were pressing some clothes on an ironing board. "Maybe you can spread glue evenly with it" (p. 2566).

Even though the patient could not identify most objects visually, he accurately answered questions about their physical properties, such as "Which one would feel the heaviest?," "Which one is the softest?," or "Which one would feel the coldest?" The fact that he could answer these questions (and could mime what to do with them) indicates that the circuits responsible for visual form perception (those in the ventral stream) were relatively intact but that they were no longer connected to the circuits responsible for speech (and for consciousness). His dorsal stream and its connections with speech mechanisms were undamaged, and it was apparently through these connections that he was able to describe how to use the objects. This interpretation is consistent with Goodale and Milner's conclusion that the dorsal stream is primarily occupied with controlling movements, not simply perceiving the location of objects.

interim summary

Analysis of Visual Information: Role of the Visual Association Cortex

The visual cortex consists of the striate cortex, the extrastriate cortex, and the visual association cortex of the inferior temporal lobe and the posterior parietal lobe. There are at least twenty-five different subregions of the visual cortex, arranged in a hierarchical fashion. The extrastriate cortex receives information from the striate cortex, the pulvinar,

and the superior colliculus. The color-sensitive cells in the CO blobs in the striate cortex send information to areas V4 and V8 of the extrastriate cortex. Damage to the area V4 abolishes color constancy (accurate perception of color under different lighting conditions), and damage to area V8 causes achromatopsia, a loss of color vision but not of form perception. A condition opposite to achromatopsia can also be seen: A patient with extensive damage to the extrastriate cortex was functionally blind but could still recognize colors. His brain damage apparently destroyed regions of the visual association cortex that are responsible for form perception but not those for color perception.

The visual cortex is organized into two streams. The ventral stream, which ends with the inferior temporal cortex, is involved with perception of objects. Lesions of this region disrupt visual object perception. Also, single neurons in the inferior temporal cortex respond best to complex stimuli and continue to do so even if the object is moved to a different location, changed in size, placed against a different background, or partially hidden. The dorsal stream, which ends with the posterior parietal cortex, is involved with perception of location, movement, and control of eye and hand movements.

Functional imaging studies indicate that specific regions of the cortex are involved in perception of form, movement, and color, and these studies are enabling us to discover the correspondences between the anatomy of the human visual system and that of laboratory animals. Studies of humans who have sustained damage to the visual association cortex have discovered two basic forms of visual agnosia. Apperceptive visual agnosia involves difficulty in perceiving the shapes of objects, even though fine details can often be detected. Prosopagnosia—failure to recognize faces—appears to be caused by damage to the fusiform face area, a region on the medial surface of the right occipital cortex. The development of this region appears to be a result of extensive experience looking at faces; expertise with other complex stimuli such as cows, birds, cars, or even artificial creatures (greebles) causes the development of circuits devoted to the perception of these stimuli as well. The fusiform face region fails to develop in people with autism, presumably because of insufficient motivation to become expert in recognizing other people's faces.

The second basic form of visual agnosia, associative visual agnosia, is characterized by relatively good object perception (shown by the fact that the patients can copy drawings of objects) but the inability to recognize what is perceived. This disorder is probably caused by damage to axons that connect the visual association cortex with regions of the brain that are important for verbalization and thinking in words. Some patients with this disorder can describe or mime actions appropriate to the objects they see but cannot recognize.

Damage to area V5 (also called area MT) disrupts an animal's ability to perceive movement, and damage to the posterior parietal cortex disrupts perception of the spatial location of objects. Damage to the human visual association cortex corresponding to area V5 disrupts perception of movement, producing a disorder known as akinetopsia. In addition, transcranial magnetic stimulation of V5 causes a temporary disruption, and functional imaging studies show that perception of moving stimuli activate this region. In both monkeys and humans, damage to area MSTd, a region of extrastriate cortex that receives information from area V5, appears to be specialized for perceiving optic flow, one of the cues we use to perceive the direction in which we are heading. The ability to perceive form from motion—recognition of complex movements of people indicated by lights attached to parts of their body—is probably related to the ability to recognize people by the way they walk. This ability apparently depends on a region of cerebral cortex on the ventral bank of the posterior end of the superior temporal sulcus. The visual association cortex receives information about eye movements from the motor system and information about movement of retinal images from the visual cortex and determines which movements are caused by head and eye movements and which are caused by movements in the environment. A patient with extrastriate damage was unable to compensate for eye movements; when he moved his eyes, he perceived movement in the environment. The location of the region responsible for this compensation appears to be in the extrastriate cortex at the junction of the temporal and parietal lobes.

Mirror cells in the ventral premotor cortex become active when a monkey sees a particular limb movement or makes the movement itself. This region (which appears to exist in humans as well) may play a role in learning to imitate the movement of others. Sometimes people with visual agnosia caused by damage to the ventral system can still perceive the meanings of mimed actions or recognize friends by the way they walk, which indicates that the dorsal stream of their visual cortex is largely intact. Balint's syndrome, which is caused by bilateral damage to the parieto-occipital region (the dorsal stream), includes the symptoms of optic ataxia, ocular apraxia, and simultanagnosia.

Suggested Readings

Gregory, R. L. *Eye and Brain: The Psychology of Seeing,* 5th ed. Princeton, NJ: Princeton University Press, 1997.

Oyster, C. W. *The Human Eye: Structure and Function.* Sunderland, MA: Sinauer Associates, 1999.

Rodieck, R. W. *The First Steps in Seeing.* Sunderland, MA: Sinauer Associates, 1998.

Tanaka, K. Inferotemporal cortex and object vision. *Annual Review of Neuroscience,* 1996, *19,* 100–139.

Wandell, B. A. *Foundations of Vision.* Sunderland, MA: Sinauer Associates, 1995.

Zeki, S. *A Vision of the Brain.* Oxford: Blackwell Scientific Publications, 1992.

Suggested Web Sites

Retina Reference

http://retina.anatomy.upenn.edu/~lance/retina/retina.html

The anatomy of the retina is the focus of this site. The site contains some marvelous images and diagrams of the retina and visual system.

Perception: An Introduction to the Gestalt-Theorie by Kurt Koffka (1922)

http://www.yorku.ca/dept/psych/classics/Koffka/Perception/perception.htm

This site contains a translation of portions of a book by Kurt Koffka (1922) which outlines the general Gestalt view of perception.

Tutorials in Sensation and Perception

http://psych.hanover.edu/Krantz/sen_tut.html

This perception site contains tutorials and demonstrations on visual perception including visual aftereffects, motion illusions, and receptive fields.

Blindsight Demonstration

http://serendip.brynmawr.edu/bb/blindsight.html

This site provides an online demonstration of the phenomenon known as blindsight.

chapter 7

Audition, the Body Senses, and the Chemical Senses

James Rosenquist, *Lady Dog Lizard*, 1985. © James Rosenquist/Licensed by VAGA, New York, NY. Digital Image © The Museum of Modern Art/Licensed by SCALA/Art Resource, NY.

outline

■ **Audition**
The Stimulus
Anatomy of the Ear
Auditory Hair Cells and the Transduction
    of Auditory Information
The Auditory Pathway
Perception of Pitch
Perception of Loudness
Perception of Timbre
Perception of Spatial Location
Behavioral Functions of the Auditory
    System
Interim Summary

■ **Vestibular System**
Anatomy of the Vestibular Apparatus
The Receptor Cells
The Vestibular Pathway
Interim Summary

■ **Somatosenses**
The Stimuli
Anatomy of the Skin and Its
    Receptive Organs
Perception of Cutaneous Stimulation
The Somatosensory Pathways
Perception of Pain
Interim Summary

■ **Gustation**
The Stimuli
Anatomy of the Taste Buds
    and Gustatory Cells
Perception of Gustatory Information
The Gustatory Pathway
Neural Coding of Taste
Interim Summary

■ **Olfaction**
The Stimulus
Anatomy of the Olfactory Apparatus
Transduction of Olfactory Information
Perception of Specific Odors
Interim Summary

Nine-year-old Sara tried to think of something else, but the throbbing pain in her thumb was relentless. Earlier in the day, her brother had slammed the car door on it.

"Why does it have to hurt so much, Daddy?" she asked piteously.

"I wish I could help you, sweetheart," he answered. "Pain may be useful, but it sure isn't fun."

"What do you mean, useful?" she asked in astonishment. "You mean it's good for me?" She looked at her father reproachfully.

"Well, this probably isn't the time to tell you about the advantages of pain, because it's hard to appreciate them when you're suffering." A glimmer of interest began to grow in her eyes. For as long as she could remember, Sara loved to have her father explain things to her, even when his explanations got a little confusing.

"You know," he said, "there are some people who never feel any pain. They are born that way."

"Really?" Her eyes widened. "They're lucky!"

"No, they really aren't. Without the sense of pain, they keep injuring themselves. When they touch something hot, they don't know enough to let go, even when their hand is getting burned. If the water in the shower gets too hot, they don't realize they're getting scalded. If their shoes don't fit right, they get huge blisters without knowing what's happening. If they fall and sprain their ankle—or even break a bone—they don't feel that something bad has happened to them, and their injury will just get worse. Some people who have no ability to feel pain have died when their appendix burst because they didn't know that something bad was happening inside them."

Sara looked thoughtful. Her father's explanation seemed to be distracting her from her pain.

"Parents of children who can't feel pain say that it's difficult to teach them to avoid danger. When a child does something that causes pain, she quickly learns to avoid repeating her mistake. Remember when you were three years old and walked on the grill of the heater in the cabin floor? You had just gotten out of the shower, and you burned the bottoms of your feet."

"I *think* so," she said. "Yes, you bought me a bag of candy corn to make me forget how much it hurt."

"That's right. Your mom and I had told you that the grill was dangerous when the heater was on, but it took an actual experience to teach you to stay away. We feel pain when parts of our bodies are damaged. The injured cells make a chemical that's picked up by nerve endings, and the nerves send messages to the brain to warn it that something bad is happening. Our brains automatically try to get us away from whatever it is that hurts us—and we also learn to become afraid of it. After you burned your feet on the grill, you stayed away from it even when you were wearing shoes. Kids who can't feel pain can learn to stay away from dangerous things, but it's not an automatic, gut-level kind of learning. They have to pay attention all the time, and if they let down their guard, it's easy for them to injure themselves. Pain isn't fun, but it's hard to survive without it."

"I guess so," said Sara reluctantly. She looked at her bandaged thumb, and the sudden realization of how much it hurt brought tears to her eyes again. "But the pain could go away now, because it's already taught me everything I need to know."

One chapter was devoted to vision, but the rest of the sensory modalities must share a chapter. This unequal allocation of space reflects the relative importance of vision to our species and the relative amount of research that has been devoted to it. This chapter is divided into five major sections, which discuss audition, the vestibular system, the somatosenses, gustation, and olfaction.

Audition

For most people audition is the second most important sense. The value of verbal communication makes it even more important than vision in some respects; for example, a blind person can join others in conversation far more easily than a deaf person can. (Of course, deaf people can use sign language to converse.) Acoustic stimuli also provide information about things that are hidden from view, and our ears work just as well in the dark. This section describes the nature of the stimulus, the sensory receptors, the brain mechanisms devoted to audition, and some of the details of the physiology of auditory perception.

The Stimulus

We hear sounds, which are produced by objects that vibrate and set molecules of air into motion. When an object vibrates, its movements cause molecules of air surrounding it alternately to condense and rarefy (pull apart), producing waves that travel away from the object at approximately 700 miles per hour. If the vibration ranges

figure 7.1

Sound waves. Changes in air pressure from sound waves move the eardrum in and out. Air molecules are closer together in regions of higher pressure and farther apart in regions of lower pressure.

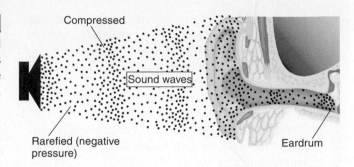

Compressed

Sound waves

Rarefied (negative pressure)

Eardrum

between approximately 30 and 20,000 times per second, these waves will stimulate receptor cells in our ears and will be perceived as sounds. (See *Figure 7.1.*)

In Chapter 6 we saw that light has three perceptual dimensions—hue, brightness, and saturation—that correspond to three physical dimensions. Similarly, sounds vary in their pitch, loudness, and timbre. The perceived **pitch** of an auditory stimulus is determined by the frequency of vibration, which is measured in **hertz (Hz),** or cycles per second. (The term honors Heinrich Hertz, a nineteenth-century German physicist.) **Loudness** is a function of intensity—the degree to which the condensations and rarefactions of air differ from each other. More vigorous vibrations of an object produce more intense sound waves and hence louder ones. **Timbre** provides information about the nature of the particular sound—for example, the sound of an oboe or a train whistle. Most natural acoustic stimuli are complex, consisting of several different frequencies of vibration. The particular mixture determines the sound's timbre. (See *Figure 7.2.*)

The eye is a *synthetic* organ (literally, "a putting together"). When two different wavelengths of light are mixed, we perceive a single color. For example, when we see a mixture of red and bluish green light, we perceive pure yellow light and cannot detect either of the two constituents. In contrast, the ear is an *analytical* organ (from *analyein,* "to undo"). When two different frequencies of sound waves are mixed, we do not perceive an intermediate tone; instead, we hear both original tones. As we will see, the ability of our auditory system to detect the individual component frequencies of a complex tone gives us the capacity to identify the nature of particular sounds, such as those of different musical instruments.

Anatomy of the Ear

Figure 7.3 shows a section through the ear and auditory canal and illustrates the apparatus of the middle and inner ear. (See *Figure 7.3.*) Sound is funneled via the *pinna* (external ear) through the ear canal to the **tympanic membrane** (eardrum), which vibrates with the sound.

The *middle ear* consists of a hollow region behind the tympanic membrane, approximately 2 ml in volume. It contains the bones of the middle ear, called the **ossicles,** which are set into vibration by the tympanic membrane. (As we saw in Chapter 1, two of these bones evolved from part of the reptilian jaw.) The **malleus** (hammer) connects with the tympanic membrane and transmits vibra-

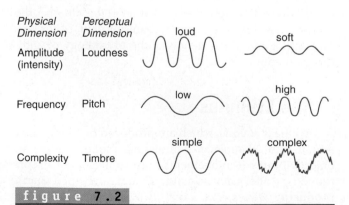

Physical Dimension	Perceptual Dimension		
Amplitude (intensity)	Loudness	loud	soft
Frequency	Pitch	low	high
Complexity	Timbre	simple	complex

figure 7.2

The physical and perceptual dimensions of sound waves.

pitch A perceptual dimension of sound; corresponds to the fundamental frequency.

hertz (Hz) Cycles per second.

loudness A perceptual dimension of sound; corresponds to intensity.

timbre (*tim* ber or *tamm* ber) A perceptual dimension of sound; corresponds to complexity.

tympanic membrane The eardrum.

ossicle (*ahss i kul*) One of the three bones of the middle ear.

malleus The "hammer"; the first of the three ossicles.

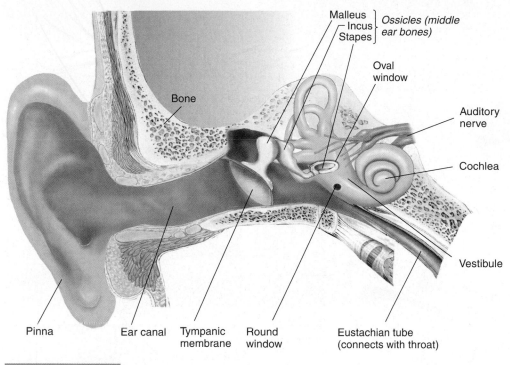

Malleus
Incus } Ossicles (middle
Stapes }   ear bones)

Oval
window

Auditory
nerve

Cochlea

Bone

Vestibule

Pinna   Ear canal   Tympanic   Round   Eustachian tube
                         membrane   window   (connects with throat)

The auditory apparatus.

tions via the **incus** (anvil) and **stapes** (stirrup) to the **cochlea,** the structure that contains the receptors. The baseplate of the stapes presses against the membrane behind the **oval window,** the opening in the bony process surrounding the cochlea. (See *Figure 7.3.*)

The cochlea is part of the *inner ear.* It is filled with fluid; therefore, sounds transmitted through the air must be transferred into a liquid medium. This process normally is very inefficient—99.9 percent of the energy of airborne sound would be reflected away if the air impinged directly against the oval window of the cochlea. The chain of ossicles serves as an extremely efficient means of energy transmission. The bones provide a mechanical advantage, with the baseplate of the stapes making smaller but more forceful excursions against the oval window than the tympanic membrane makes against the malleus.

The name *cochlea* comes from the Greek word *kokhlos,* or "land snail." It is indeed snail-shaped, consisting of two and three-quarters turns of a gradually tapering cylinder, 35 mm (1.37 in.) long. The cochlea is divided longitudinally into three sections, the *scala vestibuli* ("vestibular stairway"), the *scala media* ("middle stairway"), and the *scala tympani* ("tympanic stairway"), as shown in *Figure 7.4.* The receptive organ, known as the **organ of Corti,** consists of the *basilar membrane,* the *hair cells,* and the *tectorial membrane.* The auditory receptor cells are called **hair cells,**

and they are anchored, via rodlike **Deiters's cells,** to the **basilar membrane.** The cilia of the hair cells pass through the *reticular membrane,* and the ends of some of them attach to the fairly rigid **tectorial membrane,** which projects

incus The "anvil"; the second of the three ossicles.

stapes (*stay peez*) The "stirrup"; the last of the three ossicles.

cochlea (*cock lee uh*) The snail-shaped structure of the inner ear that contains the auditory transducing mechanisms.

oval window An opening in the bone surrounding the cochlea that reveals a membrane, against which the baseplate of the stapes presses, transmitting sound vibrations into the fluid within the cochlea.

organ of Corti The sensory organ on the basilar membrane that contains the auditory hair cells.

hair cell The receptive cell of the auditory apparatus.

Deiters's cell (*dye terz*) A supporting cell found in the organ of Corti; sustains the auditory hair cells.

basilar membrane (*bazz i ler*) A membrane in the cochlea of the inner ear; contains the organ of Corti.

tectorial membrane (*tek torr ee ul*) A membrane located above the basilar membrane; serves as a shelf against which the cilia of the auditory hair cells move.

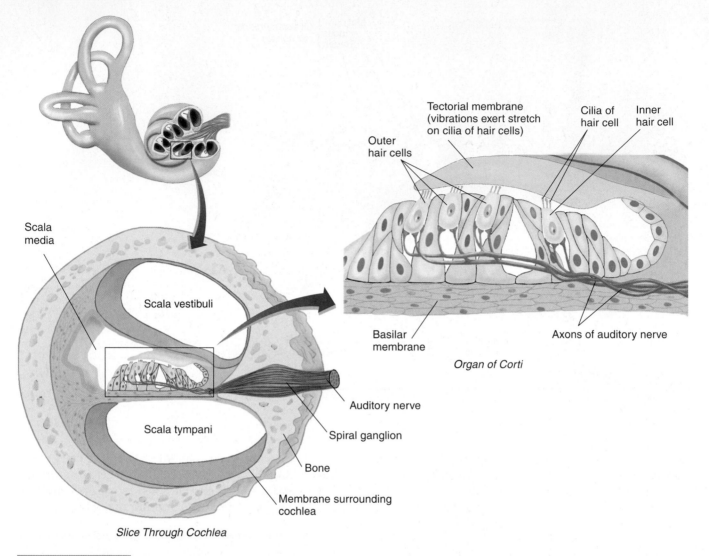

Scala
media

Scala vestibuli

Scala tympani

Auditory nerve

Spiral ganglion

Bone

Membrane surrounding
cochlea

Slice Through Cochlea

Tectorial membrane
(vibrations exert stretch
on cilia of hair cells)

Cilia of
hair cell

Inner
hair cell

Outer
hair cells

Basilar
membrane

Axons of auditory nerve

Organ of Corti

figure 7.4

A cross section through the cochlea, showing the organ of Corti.

overhead like a shelf. (See *Figure 7.4.*) Sound waves cause the basilar membrane to move relative to the tectorial membrane, which bends the cilia of the hair cells. This bending produces receptor potentials.

Georg von Békésy—in a lifetime of brilliant studies on the cochleas of various animals, from human cadavers to elephants—found that the vibratory energy exerted on the oval window causes the basilar membrane to bend (von Békésy, 1960). Because of the physical characteristics of the basilar membrane, the portion that bends the most is determined by the frequency of the sound: High-frequency sounds cause the end nearest the oval window to bend.

Figure 7.5 shows this process in a cochlea that has been partially straightened. If the cochlea were a closed system, no vibration would be transmitted through the oval window, because liquids are essentially incompressible. However, there is a membrane-covered opening, the **round window,** that allows the fluid inside the cochlea to move back and forth. The baseplate of the stapes vibrates against the membrane behind the oval window and introduces sound waves of high or low frequency into the cochlea. The vibrations cause part of the basilar membrane to flex back and forth. Pressure changes in the fluid underneath the basilar membrane are transmitted to the membrane of the round

round window An opening in the bone surrounding the cochlea of the inner ear that permits vibrations to be transmitted, via the oval window, into the fluid in the cochlea.

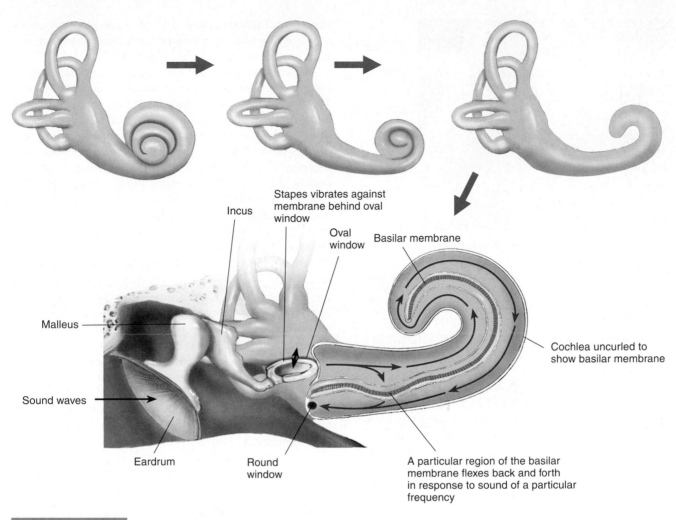

Incus

Stapes vibrates against
membrane behind oval
window

Oval
window

Basilar membrane

Malleus

Sound waves

Eardrum

Round
window

Cochlea uncurled to
show basilar membrane

A particular region of the basilar
membrane flexes back and forth
in response to sound of a particular
frequency

figure 7.5

Responses to sound waves. When the stapes pushes against the membrane behind the
oval window, the membrane behind the round window bulges outward. Different high-
frequency and medium-frequency sound vibrations cause flexing of different portions of
the basilar membrane. In contrast, low-frequency sound vibrations cause the tip of the
basilar membrane to flex in synchrony with the vibrations.

window, which moves in and out in a manner opposite
to the movements of the oval window. That is, when the
baseplate of the stapes pushes in, the membrane behind
the round window bulges out. As we will see in a later
subsection, different frequencies of sound vibrations cause
different portions of the basilar membrane to flex. (See
Figure 7.5.)

Some people suffer from a middle ear disease that
causes the bone to grow over the round window. Because
their basilar membrane cannot easily flex back and forth,
these people have a severe hearing loss. However, their
hearing can be restored by a surgical procedure called *fen-
estration* ("window making"), in which a tiny hole is drilled
in the bone where the round window should be.

Auditory Hair Cells
and the Transduction
of Auditory Information

Two types of auditory receptors, *inner* and *outer* auditory hair cells, lie on the inside and outside of the cochlear
coils, respectively. Hair cells contain **cilia** ("eyelashes"),

cilium A hairlike appendage of a cell involved in movement or in
transducing sensory information; found on the receptors in the
auditory and vestibular system.

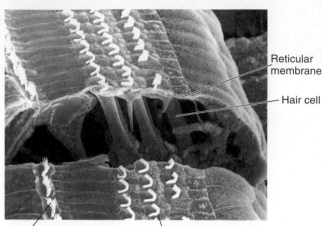

Reticular
membrane

Hair cell

Cilia of inner hair cells   Cilia of outer hair cells

figure 7.6

A scanning electron photomicrograph of a portion of the organ of Corti, showing the cilia of the inner and outer hair cells.

(Photomicrograph courtesy of I. Hunter-Duvar, The Hospital for Sick Children, Toronto, Ontario.)

fine hairlike appendages, arranged in rows, according to height. The human cochlea contains approximately 3500 inner hair cells and 12,000 outer hair cells. The hair cells form synapses with dendrites of bipolar neurons whose axons bring auditory information to the brain. Figure 7.6 shows the appearance of the inner and outer hair cells and the reticular membrane in a photograph taken by means of a scanning electron microscope. Note the three rows of outer hair cells on the right and the single row of inner hair cells on the left. (See *Figure 7.6.*)

Sound waves cause both the basilar membrane and the tectorial membrane to flex up and down. These movements bend the cilia of the hair cells in one direction or the other. The tips of the cilia of outer hair cells are attached directly to the tectorial membrane. The cilia of the inner hair cells do not touch the overlying tectorial membrane, but the relative movement of the two membranes causes the fluid within the cochlea to flow past them, making them bend back and forth, too.

Cilia contain a core of actin filaments surrounded by myosin filaments, and these proteins make the cilia stiff and rigid (Flock, 1977). Adjacent cilia are linked to each other by elastic filaments known as **tip links.** Each tip link is attached to the end of one cilium and to the side of an adjacent cilium. The points of attachment, known as

tip link An elastic filament that attaches the tip of one cilium to the side of the adjacent cilium.

insertional plaque The point of attachment of a tip link to a cilium.

insertional plaques, look dark under an electron microscope. As we will see, receptor potentials are triggered at the insertional plaques. (See *Figure 7.7*.)

Normally, tip links are slightly stretched, which means that they are under a small amount of tension. Thus, movement of the bundle of cilia in the direction of the tallest of them further stretches these linking fibers, whereas movement in the opposite direction relaxes them. The bending of the bundle of cilia causes receptor potentials (Pickles and Corey, 1992; Hudspeth and Gillespie, 1994; Gillespie, 1995; Jaramillo, 1995). Unlike the fluid that surrounds most neurons, the fluid that surrounds the auditory hair cells is rich in potassium. Each insertional plaque contains a single cation channel. When the bundle of cilia is straight, the probability of an individual ion channel being open is approximately 10 percent. This means that a small amount of the cations K^+ and Ca^{2+} diffuses into the cilium. When the bundle moves toward the tallest one, the increased tension on the tip links opens all the ion channels, the flow of cations into the cilium increases, and the membrane depolarizes. As a result, the release of neurotransmitter by the hair cell increases. When the bundle moves in the opposite direction, toward the shortest cilium, the relaxation of the tip links allows the opened ion channels to close. The influx of cations ceases, the membrane hyperpolarizes, and the release of neurotransmitter decreases. (See *Figure 7.8*.)

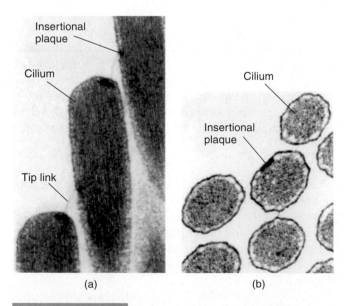

Insertional
plaque

Cilium   Cilium

Insertional
plaque

Tip link

(a)   (b)

figure 7.7

Electron micrographs of the transduction apparatus in hair cells. (a) Longitudinal section through three adjacent cilia. Tip links, elastic filaments attached to insertional plaques, link adjacent cilia. (b) A cross section through several cilia, showing an insertional plaque.

(From Hudspeth, A. J., and Gillespie, P. G. *Neuron,* 1994, *12,* 1–9.)

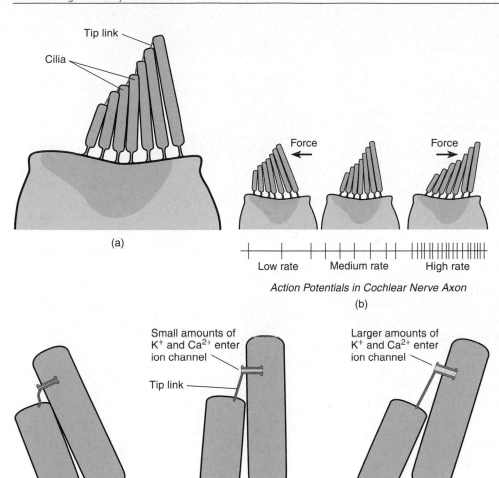

(a)

Low rate   Medium rate   High rate

Action Potentials in Cochlear Nerve Axon

(b)

Small amounts of K⁺ and Ca²⁺ enter ion channel

Tip link

Larger amounts of K⁺ and Ca²⁺ enter ion channel

Open probability = 0 percent   Open probability = 10 percent   Open probability = 100 percent

(c)

figure 7.8

Transduction in hair cells of the inner ear. (a) Appearance of the cilia of an auditory hair cell. (b) Movement of the bundle of cilia toward the tallest one increases the firing rate of the cochlear nerve axon attached to the hair cell, while movement away from the tallest one decreases it. (c) Movement toward the tallest cilium increases tension on the tip links, which opens the ion channels and increases the influx of K⁺ and Ca²⁺ ions. Movement toward the shortest cilium removes tension from the tip links, which permits the ion channels to close, stopping the influx of cations.

The Auditory Pathway

Connections with the Cochlear Nerve

The organ of Corti sends auditory information to the brain by means of the **cochlear nerve,** a branch of the auditory nerve (eighth cranial nerve). The neurons that give rise to the afferent axons that travel through this nerve are of the bipolar type. Their cell bodies reside in the *cochlear nerve ganglion*. (This ganglion is also called the *spiral ganglion* because it consists of clumps of cell bodies arranged in a spiral caused by the curling of the cochlea.) These neurons have axonal processes, capable of sustaining action potentials, that protrude from both ends of the soma. The end of one process acts like a dendrite, responding with excitatory postsynaptic potentials when the neurotransmitter is released by the auditory hair cells. The excitatory postsynaptic potentials trigger action poten-

tials in the auditory nerve axons, which form synapses with neurons in the medulla. (Refer to *Figure 7.4.*)

Each cochlear nerve contains approximately 50,000 afferent axons. The dendrites of approximately 95 percent of these axons form synapses with the inner hair cells. Most afferent fibers make contact with only one inner hair cell, but each inner hair cell forms synapses with approximately twenty fibers (Dallos, 1992). The axons that receive information from the inner hair cells are thick and myelinated. The other 5 percent of the sensory fibers in the cochlear nerve form synapses with the much more numerous outer hair cells, at a ratio of approximately one fiber per thirty outer hair cells. In addition, these axons are thin

cochlear nerve The branch of the auditory nerve that transmits auditory information from the cochlea to the brain.

and unmyelinated. Thus, although the inner hair cells represent only 29 percent of the total number of receptor cells, their connections with auditory nerves suggest that they are of primary importance in the transmission of auditory information to the central nervous system.

Physiological and behavioral studies confirm the inferences made from the synaptic connections of the two types of hair cells: The inner hair cells are necessary for normal hearing. In fact, Deol and Glucksohn-Waelsch (1979) found that a mutant strain of mice whose cochleas contain *only* outer hair cells apparently cannot hear at all. Subsequent research indicates that the outer hair cells are *effector* cells, involved in altering the mechanical characteristics of the basilar membrane and thus influencing the effects of sound vibrations on the inner hair cells. I will discuss the role of outer hair cells in the section on place coding of pitch.

The cochlear nerve contains efferent axons as well as afferent ones. The source of the efferent axons is the superior olivary complex, a group of nuclei in the medulla; thus, the efferent fibers constitute the **olivocochlear bundle.** The fibers form synapses directly on outer hair cells and on the dendrites that serve the inner hair cells. The neurotransmitter at the afferent synapses is glutamate. The efferent terminal buttons secrete acetylcholine, which appears to have an inhibitory effect on the hair cells.

The Central Auditory System

The anatomy of the auditory system is more complicated than that of the visual system. Rather than give a detailed verbal description of the pathways, I will refer you to *Figure 7.9.* Note that axons enter the **cochlear nucleus** of the medulla and synapse there. Most of the neurons in the cochlear nucleus send axons to the **superior olivary complex,** also located in the medulla. Axons of neurons in these nuclei pass through a large fiber bundle called the **lateral lemniscus** to the inferior colliculus, located in the dorsal midbrain. Neurons there send their axons to the medial geniculate nucleus of the thalamus, which sends its axons to the auditory cortex of the temporal lobe. As you can see, there are many synapses along the way to complicate the story. Each hemisphere receives information from both ears but primarily from the contralateral one. Auditory information is relayed to the cerebellum and reticular formation as well.

If we unrolled the basilar membrane into a flat strip and followed afferent axons serving successive points along its length, we would reach successive points in the nuclei of the auditory system and ultimately successive points along the surface of the primary auditory cortex. The *basal* end of the basilar membrane (the end toward the oval window) is represented most medially in the auditory cortex, and the *apical* end is represented most laterally there. Because, as we will see, different parts of the basilar membrane respond best to different frequencies of sound, this relationship between cortex and basilar membrane is referred to as **tonotopic representation** (*tonos* means "tone," and *topos* means "place").

As we saw in Chapter 6, the visual cortex is arranged in a hierarchy. Modules in the striate cortex (primary visual

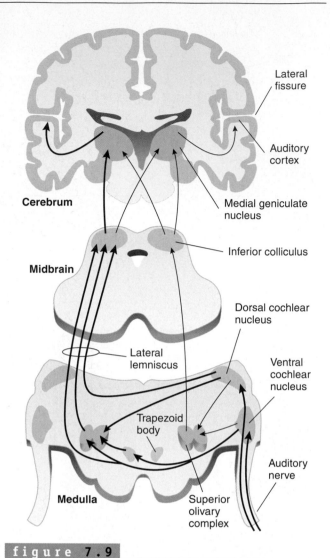

figure 7.9

The pathway of the auditory system. The major pathways are indicated by heavy arrows.

cortex) analyze features of visual information and pass the results of this analysis to subregions of the extrastriate cortex, which perform further analyses and pass information on to other regions, culminating in the highest levels of visual association cortex in the parietal and inferior temporal lobes. The dorsal stream, which ends in the pari-

olivocochlear bundle A bundle of efferent axons that travel from the olivary complex of the medulla to the auditory hair cells on the cochlea.

cochlear nucleus One of a group of nuclei in the medulla that receive auditory information from the cochlea.

superior olivary complex A group of nuclei in the medulla; involved with auditory functions, including localization of the source of sounds.

lateral lemniscus A band of fibers running rostrally through the medulla and pons; carries fibers of the auditory system.

tonotopic representation (*tonn oh top ik*) A topographically organized mapping of different frequencies of sound that are represented in a particular region of the brain.

etal cortex, is involved in perception of location ("where"), while the ventral stream, which ends in the inferior temporal cortex, is involved in perception of form ("what").

The auditory cortex seems to be similarly arranged. The primary auditory cortex lies hidden on the upper bank of the lateral fissure. The **core region,** which contains the primary auditory cortex, actually consists of three regions, each of which receives a separate tonotopic map of auditory information from the ventral division from the medial geniculate nucleus (Kaas, Hackett, and Tramo, 1999; Hackett, Preuss, and Kaas, 2001). The first level of auditory association cortex, the **belt region,** surrounds the primary auditory cortex, much as the extrastriate cortex surrounds the primary visual (striate) cortex. The belt region, which consists of at least seven divisions, receives information from both the primary auditory cortex and the dorsal and medial divisions of the medial geniculate nucleus. The highest level of auditory association cortex, the **parabelt region,** receives information from the belt region and from the divisions of the medial geniculate nucleus that project to the belt region. (*See Figure 7.10.*)

Like the visual cortex, the auditory cortex is arranged in two streams, dorsal and ventral. The dorsal stream, which terminates in the posterior parietal cortex, is involved with sound localization, and the ventral stream, which terminates in the parabelt region of the anterior tem-

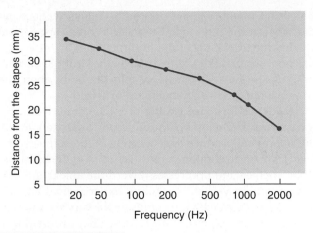

figure 7.11

Anatomical coding of pitch. Stimuli of different frequencies maximally deform different regions of the basilar membrane.
(From von Békésy, G. *Journal of the Acoustical Society of America,* 1949, *21,* 233–245.)

poral lobe, is involved with analysis of complex sounds (Rauschecker and Tian, 2000). Research on the functions of these streams is described later.

Perception of Pitch

As we have seen, the perceptual dimension of pitch corresponds to the physical dimension of frequency. The cochlea detects frequency by two means: moderate to high frequencies by place coding and low frequencies by rate coding. These two types of coding are described next.

Place Coding

The work of von Békésy has shown us that because of the mechanical construction of the cochlea and basilar membrane, acoustic stimuli of different frequencies cause different parts of the basilar membrane to flex back and forth. Figure 7.11 illustrates the amount of deformation along the length of the basilar membrane produced by stimulation with tones of various frequencies. Note that higher frequencies produce more displacement at the basal end of the membrane (the end closest to the stapes). (See *Figure 7.11.*)

These results suggest that at least some frequencies of sound waves are detected by means of a **place code.** In this context a code represents a means by which neurons can represent information. Thus, if neurons at one end of

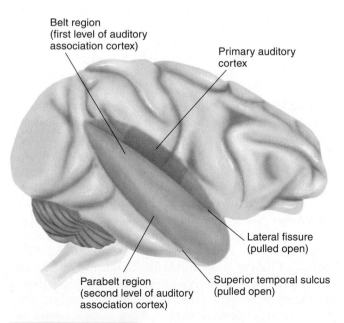

figure 7.10

A lateral view of the monkey brain, showing the location of the primary auditory cortex, the belt region (first level of auditory association cortex), and the parabelt region (second level of auditory association cortex). The temporal lobe has been pulled down to expose the cortex on the upper and lower banks of the lateral fissure, and the superior temporal sulcus has been pulled apart.
(Adapted from Kaas, J. H., Hackett, T. A., and Tramo, M. J. *Current Opinion in Neurobiology,* 1999, *9,* 164–170.)

core region The primary auditory cortex, located on a gyrus on the dorsal surface of the temporal lobe.

belt region The first level of auditory association cortex; surrounds the primary auditory cortex.

parabelt region The second level of auditory association cortex; surrounds the belt region.

place code The system by which information about different frequencies is coded by different locations on the basilar membrane.

the basilar membrane are excited by higher frequencies and those at the other end by lower frequencies, we can say that the frequency of the sound is *coded* by the particular neurons that are active. In turn, the firing of particular axons in the cochlear nerve tells the brain about the presence of particular frequencies of sound.

Evidence for place coding of pitch comes from several sources. High doses of the antibiotic drugs kanamycin and neomycin produce degeneration of the auditory hair cells. Damage to auditory hair cells begins at the basal end of the cochlea and progresses toward the apical end; this pattern can be verified by killing experimental animals after dosing them with the antibiotic for varying amounts of time. Longer exposures to the drug are associated with increased progress of hair cell damage down the basilar membrane. Stebbins et al. (1969) found that the progressive death of hair cells induced by an antibiotic closely parallels a progressive hearing loss: The highest frequencies are the first to go, and the lowest are the last.

Good evidence for place coding of pitch (at least, in humans) comes from the effectiveness of cochlear implants. **Cochlear implants** are devices that are used to restore hearing in people with deafness caused by damage to the hair cells. The external part of a cochlear implant consists of a microphone and a miniaturized electronic signal processor. The internal part contains a very thin, flexible array of electrodes, which the surgeon carefully inserts into the cochlea in such a way that it follows the snaillike curl and ends up resting along the entire length of the basilar membrane. Each electrode in the array stimulates a different part of the basilar membrane. Information from the signal processor is passed to the electrodes by means of flat coils of wire, implanted under the skin.

The primary purpose of a cochlear implant is to restore a person's ability to understand speech. Because most of the important acoustical information in speech is contained in frequencies that are too high to be accurately represented by a rate code, the multichannel electrode was developed in an attempt to duplicate the place coding of pitch on the basilar membrane (Loeb, 1990). When different regions of the basilar membrane are stimulated, the person perceives sounds with different pitches. The signal processor in the external device analyzes the sounds detected by the microphone and sends separate signals to the appropriate portions of the basilar membrane. This device can work well; some people with cochlear implants can understand speech well enough to use a telephone.

Most people in the Deaf community, who communicate with each other by means of signing, have negative feelings toward oral communication. The difficult task of deciphering lip movements makes them feel tense. They realize that their pronunciation is imperfect and that their voices sound strange to others. They feel at a disadvantage with respect to hearing people in a spoken conversation. In contrast, they feel relaxed and at ease when communicating with other deaf people.

Like other people who closely identify with their cultures, members of the Deaf community feel pride in their common heritage and react to perceived threats. Some deaf people say that if they were given the opportunity to hear, they would refuse it. Some deaf parents have expressed happiness when they learned that their children were born deaf, too. They no longer needed to fear that their children would not be a part of their own Deaf culture.

Some members of the Deaf community perceive the cochlear implant as a serious threat to their culture. This device is most useful for two groups: people who became deaf in adulthood and very young children. Cochlear implants in postlingually deaf adults pose no threat to the Deaf community because these people never were members of the culture. But putting a cochlear implant in a young child means that the child's early education will be committed to the oralist approach. In addition, many deaf people resent the implication that deafness is something that needs to be repaired. They see themselves as different but not at all defective.

The work of von Békésy indicated that although the basilar membrane codes for frequency along its length, the coding was not very specific. His studies and those of investigators who followed him indicated that a given frequency causes a large region of the basilar membrane to be deformed. This finding contrasted with the observation that people can detect changes in frequency of only 2 or 3 Hz.

The reason for this discrepancy is now clear. Because of technical limitations, von Békésy had to observe the cochleas of animals that were no longer living or, at best, cochleas that had been damaged by the procedure necessary to make the measurements. More recently, investigators have used much more sensitive—and less damaging—procedures to observe movements of the basilar membrane in response to different frequencies of sound. It appears that the point of maximum vibration of the basilar membrane to a particular frequency is very precisely localized—but only when the cells in the organ of Corti are alive and healthy (Evans, 1992; Ruggero, 1992; Narayan et al., 1998).

The fact that the tuning characteristics of the basilar membrane change when the cells in the organ of Corti die suggested that these cells somehow affect the mechanical properties of the basilar membrane. We now know that the outer hair cells are responsible for this selective tuning and for amplification of the vibration of the basilar membrane produced by sound waves. As I mentioned earlier, outer hair cells are capable of motion. They contain contractile proteins, just as muscle fibers do. When these cells are exposed to an electrical current or when acetylcholine is placed on them, they contract by up to 10 percent of their length (Brownell et al., 1985; Zenner, Zimmermann, and Schmitt, 1985). Because the tips of their cilia are embed-

cochlear implant An electronic device surgically implanted in the inner ear that can enable a deaf person to hear.

ded in the tectorial membrane, contraction alters the mechanical characteristics of the basilar membrane—and consequently the response properties of the inner hair cells.

When the basilar membrane vibrates, movement of the cilia of the outer hair cells opens and closes ion channels, causing changes in the membrane potential. These changes cause movements of the contractile proteins, thus lengthening and shortening the cells. These changes in length amplify the vibrations of the basilar membrane. As a consequence, the signal that is received by inner hair cells is enhanced, which greatly increases the sensitivity of the inner ear to sound waves. For a while, investigators questioned whether the mechanical response of the outer hair cells could be fast enough to follow high-frequency sounds, but a study by Frank, Hemmert, and Gummer (1999) found that they could do so.

Rate Coding

We have seen that the frequency of a sound can be detected by place coding. However, the lowest frequencies do not appear to be accounted for in this manner. Kiang (1965) was unable to find any cells that responded best to frequencies of less than 200 Hz. How, then, can animals distinguish low frequencies? It appears that lower frequencies are detected by neurons that fire in synchrony to the movements of the apical end of the basilar membrane. Thus, lower frequencies are detected by means of **rate coding.**

The most convincing evidence of rate coding of pitch comes from studies of people with cochlear implants. Pijl and Schwartz (1995a, 1995b) found that stimulation of a single electrode with pulses of electricity produced sensations of pitch that were proportional to the frequency of the stimulation. In fact, the subjects could even recognize familiar tunes produced by modulating the pulse frequency. (The subjects had become deaf later in life, after they had already learned to recognize the tunes.) As we would expect, the subjects' perceptions were best when the tip of the basilar membrane was stimulated, and only low frequencies could be distinguished by this method. (See *Animation 7.1, Perception of Pitch.*)

> See the interactive CD for more on perception of pitch.

Perception of Loudness

The cochlea is an extremely sensitive organ. Wilska (1935) used an ingenious procedure to estimate the smallest vibration needed to produce a perceptible sound. He glued a small wooden rod to a volunteer's tympanic membrane (temporarily, of course) and made the rod vibrate longitudinally by means of an electromagnetic coil that could be energized with alternating current. He could vary the frequency and intensity of the current, which consequently changed the perceived pitch and loudness of the stimulus. He found that subjects could detect a sound even when the eardrum was vibrated over a distance less than the diameter of a hydrogen atom—showing that the auditory system is very sensitive. Thus, in very quiet environments a young,

healthy ear is limited in its ability to detect sounds in the air by the masking noise of blood rushing through the cranial blood vessels rather than by the sensitivity of the auditory system itself. More recent studies using modern instruments (reviewed by Hudspeth, 1983) have essentially confirmed Wilska's measurements. The softest sounds that can be detected appear to move the tip of the hair cells between 1 and 100 picometers (pm; trillionths of a meter). They achieve their maximum response when the tips are moved 100 nm (Corwin and Warchol, 1991).

The axons of the cochlear nerve appear to inform the brain of the loudness of a stimulus by altering their rate of firing. Louder sounds produce more intense vibrations of the eardrum and ossicles, which produce a more intense shearing force on the cilia of the auditory hair cells. As a result, these cells release more neurotransmitter, producing a higher rate of firing by the cochlear nerve axons. This explanation seems simple for the axons involved in place coding of pitch; in this case pitch is signaled by which neurons fire, and loudness is signaled by their rate of firing. However, the neurons in the apex of the basilar membrane that signal the lowest frequencies do so by their rate of firing. If they fire more frequently, they signal a higher pitch. Therefore, most investigators believe that the loudness of low-frequency sounds is signaled by the *number* of axons arising from these neurons that are active at a given time.

Perception of Timbre

Although laboratory investigations of the auditory system often employ pure sine waves as stimuli, these waves are seldom encountered outside the laboratory. Instead, we hear sounds with a rich mixture of frequencies—sounds of complex timbre. For example, consider the sound of a clarinet playing a particular note. If we hear it, we can easily say that it is a clarinet and not a flute or a violin. The reason we can do so is that these three instruments produce sounds of different timbre, which our auditory system can distinguish.

Figure 7.12 shows the waveform from a clarinet playing a steady note (*top*). The shape of the waveform repeats itself regularly at the **fundamental frequency,** which corresponds to the perceived pitch of the note. A Fourier analysis of the waveform shows that it actually consists of a series of sine waves that includes the fundamental frequency and many **overtones,** multiples of the fundamental frequency. Different instruments produce overtones with different intensities. (See *Figure 7.12.*) Electronic

---

rate code The system by which information about different frequencies is coded by the rate of firing of neurons in the auditory system.

fundamental frequency The lowest, and usually most intense, frequency of a complex sound; most often perceived as the sound's basic pitch.

overtone The frequency of complex tones that occurs at multiples of the fundamental frequency.

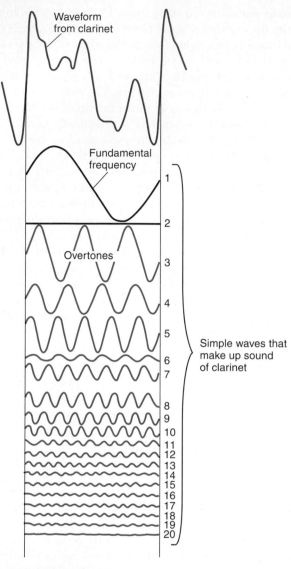

figure 7.12

The shape of a sound wave from a clarinet (*top*) and the individual frequencies into which it can be analyzed.

(Reprinted from *Stereo Review,* copyright © 1977 by Diamandis Communications Inc.)

synthesizers simulate the sounds of real instruments by producing a series of overtones of the proper intensities, mixing them, and passing them through a loudspeaker.

When the basilar membrane is stimulated by the sound of a clarinet, different portions respond to each of the overtones. This response produces a unique anatomically coded pattern of activity in the cochlear nerve, which is subsequently identified by circuits in the auditory association cortex.

Actually, the recognition of complex sounds is not quite that simple. Figure 7.12 shows the analysis of a *sustained* sound of a clarinet. But most sounds (including those produced by a clarinet) are dynamic; that is, their beginning, middle, and end are different from each other. The beginning of a note played on a clarinet (the *attack*) con-

tains frequencies that appear and disappear in a few milliseconds. And at the end of the note (the *decay*), some harmonics disappear before others. If we are to recognize different sounds, the auditory cortex must analyze a complex sequence of multiple frequencies that appear, change in amplitude, and disappear. And when you consider the fact that we can listen to an orchestra and identify several instruments that are playing simultaneously, you can appreciate the complexity of the analysis performed by the auditory system. We will revisit this process later in this chapter.

Perception of Spatial Location

So far, I have discussed coding of pitch, loudness, and timbre only (the last of which is actually a complex frequency analysis). The auditory system also responds to other qualities of acoustic stimuli. For example, our ears are very good at determining whether the source of a sound is to the right or left of us. Two separate physiological mechanisms detect the location of sound sources: We use phase differences for low frequencies (less than approximately 3000 Hz) and intensity differences for high frequencies. In addition, we use another mechanism—analysis of timbre—to determine whether the source of a sound is in front of us or behind us.

Localization by Means of Arrival Time and Phase Differences

If we are blindfolded, we can still determine with rather good accuracy the location of a stimulus that emits a click. We are most accurate at judging the *azimuth*—that is, the horizontal (left or right) angle of the source of the sound relative to the midline of our body. However, we can also do a reasonably good job at judging the *elevation* of the source of a sound—its location above or below the level of our ears. First, let's consider localization of the azimuth of a click. Neurons in our auditory system respond selectively to different *arrival times* of the sound waves at the left and right ears. If the source of the click is to the right or left of the midline, the sound pressure wave will reach one ear sooner and initiate action potentials there first. Only if the stimulus is straight ahead will the ears be stimulated simultaneously. Many neurons in the auditory system respond to sounds presented to either ear. Some of these neurons, especially those in the superior olivary complex of the medulla, respond according to the difference in arrival times of sound waves produced by clicks presented *binaurally* (that is, to both ears). Their response rates reflect differences as small as a fraction of a millisecond.

Of course, we can hear continuous sounds as well as clicks, and we can also perceive the location of their source. We detect the source of continuous low-pitched sounds by means of phase differences. **Phase differences**

---

phase difference The difference in arrival times of sound waves at each of the eardrums.

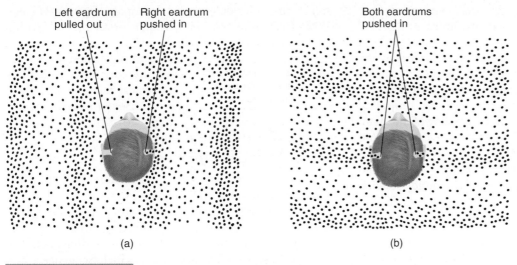

Left eardrum   Right eardrum   Both eardrums
pulled out   pushed in   pushed in

(a)   (b)

figure 7.13

Localizing the source of low-frequency and medium-frequency sounds through phase differences. (a) Source of a 1000-Hz tone to the right. The pressure waves on each eardrum are out of phase; one eardrum is pushed in while the other is pushed out. (b) Source of a sound directly in front. The vibrations of the eardrums are synchronized (in phase).

refer to the simultaneous arrival, at each ear, of different portions (phases) of the oscillating sound wave. For example, if we assume that sound travels at 700 miles per hour through the air, adjacent cycles of a 1000-Hz tone are 12.3 inches apart. Thus, if the source of the sound is located to one side of the head, one eardrum is pulled out while the other is pushed in. The movement of the eardrums will reverse, or be 180° *out of phase*. If the source were located directly in front of the head, the movements would be perfectly in phase (0° out of phase). (See *Figure 7.13*.) Because some auditory neurons respond only when the eardrums (and thus the bending of the basilar membrane) are at least somewhat out of phase, neurons in the superior olivary complex in the brain are able to

use the information they provide to detect the source of a continuous sound.

A possible mechanism to explain the ability of the nervous system to detect very short delays in the arrival times of two signals was first proposed by Jeffress (1948). He suggested that neurons received information from two sets of axons coming from the two ears. Each neuron served as a *coincidence detector;* it responded only if it received signals simultaneously from synapses belonging to both sets of axons. If a signal reached the two ears simultaneously, neurons in the middle of the array would fire. However, if the signal reached one ear before the other, then neurons farther away from the "early" ear would be stimulated. (See *Figure 7.14.*)

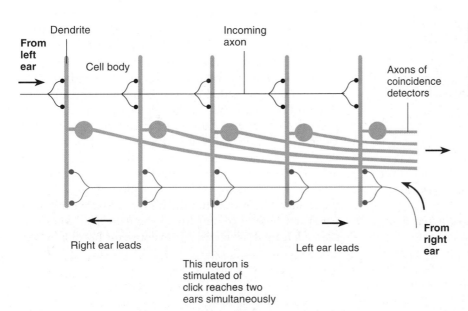

Dendrite   Incoming
                            axon
**From
left
ear**   Cell body   Axons of
                                                                 coincidence
                                                                 detectors

Right ear leads   Left ear leads
                                                    **From
                                                    right
                                                    ear**

This neuron is
stimulated of
click reaches two
ears simultaneously

figure 7.14

A model of a coincidence detector that can determine differences in arrival times at each ear of an auditory stimulus.

In fact, that is exactly how the mechanism works. Carr and Konishi (1989, 1990) obtained anatomical evidence in support of Jeffress's hypothesis from the brain of the barn owl, a nocturnal bird that can detect very accurately the source of a sound (such as that made by an unfortunate mouse). Figure 7.15 shows a drawing of the distribution of the branches of two axons, one from each ear, projecting to the nucleus laminaris, the barn owl analog of the mammalian medial superior olive. As you can see, axons from the ipsilateral and contralateral ears penetrate the nucleus from opposite directions; therefore, dorsally located neurons within the nucleus are stimulated by sounds that first

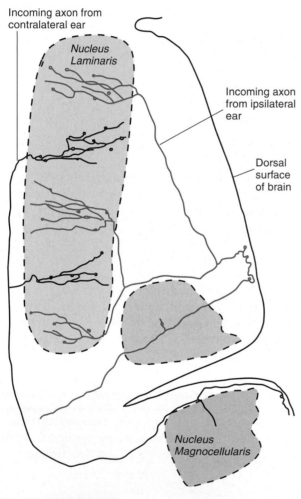

figure   7.15

Evidence for a coincidence detector in the brain of a barn owl. Compare the branches of the axons with those of Figure 7.14. The drawing was prepared from microscopic examination of sections of stained tissue.

(Adapted from Carr, C. E., and Konishi, M. *Proceedings of the National Academy of Sciences, USA,* 1989, *85,* 8311–8315.)

reach the contralateral ear. (Compare *Figures 7.14* and *7.15*.) Carr and Konishi recorded from single units within the nucleus and found that the response characteristics of the neurons located there were perfectly consistent with these anatomical facts. (See *Animation 7.2: Sound Localization*.)

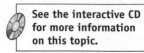

See the interactive CD for more information on this topic.

Localization by Means of Intensity Differences

The auditory system cannot readily detect binaural phase differences of high-frequency stimuli; the differences in phases of such rapid sine waves are just too short to be measured by the neurons. However, high-frequency stimuli that occur to the right or left of the midline stimulate the ears unequally. The head absorbs high frequencies, producing a "sonic shadow," so the ear closest to the source of the sound receives the most intense stimulation. Some neurons in the auditory system respond differentially to binaural stimuli of different intensity in each ear, which means that they provide information that can be used to detect the source of tones of high frequency.

The neurons that detect binaural differences in loudness are located in the superior olivary complex. But whereas neurons that detect binaural differences in phase or arrival time are located in the *medial* superior olivary complex, these neurons are located in the *lateral* superior olivary complex. Information from both sets of neurons is sent to other levels of the auditory system.

Localization by Means of Timbre

We just saw that left–right localization of the source of a high- and low-frequency sounds is accomplished by two different mechanisms. But how can we determine whether the source of a sound is in front of us or behind us? One answer is that we can turn our heads, thus transforming the discrimination into a left–right decision. But we have another means by which we can distinguish front from back: analysis of timbre. This method involves a part of the auditory system that I have not said much about: the external ear (pinna). If you look at someone's external ear, you will see that it contains several folds and ridges. Most of the sound waves that we hear bounce off the folds and ridges of the pinna before they enter the ear canal. This process changes the nature of the sounds that we hear. Depending on the angle at which the sound waves strike these folds and ridges, different frequencies will be enhanced or attenuated. In other words, the pattern of reflections will change with the location of the source of the sound, which will alter the timbre of the sound that is perceived. Sounds coming from behind the head will sound different from those coming from above the head or in front of it, and sounds coming from above will sound different from those coming from the level of our ears.

People's ears differ in shape; thus, the changes in the timbre of a sound coming from different locations will also differ from person to person. This means that each individual must learn to recognize the subtle changes in the timbre of sounds that originate in locations in front of the head, behind it, above it, or below it. The neural circuits that accomplish this task are not genetically programmed—they must be acquired as a result of experience.

An experiment by Zwiers, Van Opstal, and Cruysberg (2001) found evidence for the role of experience in calibrating the sensitivity of the auditory system to changes in elevation. They found that blind people had more difficulty judging the elevation of sounds than sighted people did—especially if some noise was present. Presumably, the increased accuracy of sighted people reflected the fact that they had had the opportunity to calibrate the changes in timbre of sounds caused by changes in the height of their sources, which they could see. In contrast, the ability of blind people to perceive the horizontal location of the sources of sounds was as good as that of sighted people. After all, blind people have much experience navigating to and around the sources of sounds located at ground level (and objects that reflect sounds, such as that of a tapping cane). These perceptions can be calibrated by physical contact with these objects.

Behavioral Functions of the Auditory System

Hearing has three primary functions: to detect sounds, to determine the location of their sources, and to recognize the identity of these sources—and thus their meaning and relevance to us (Heffner and Heffner, 1990; Yost, 1991). Let us consider the third function: recognizing the identity of a sound source. Unless you are in a completely silent location, pay attention to what you can hear. Right now, I am sitting in an office and can hear the sound of a fan in a computer, the tapping of the keys as I write this, the footsteps of someone passing outside the door, and the voices of some people talking in the hallway. How can I recognize these sources? The axons in my cochlear nerve contain a constantly changing pattern of activity corresponding to the constantly changing mixtures of frequencies that strike my eardrums. Somehow, the auditory system of my brain recognizes particular patterns that belong to particular sources, and I perceive each of them as an independent entity.

The task of the auditory system in identifying sound sources, then, is one of *pattern recognition*. The auditory system must recognize that particular patterns of constantly changing activity belong to different sound sources. And

as we saw, few patterns are simple mixtures of fixed frequencies. For example, the notes played on a clarinet have a characteristic attack and decay. And notes of different pitches produce different patterns of activity in our cochlear nerve, yet we recognize each of the notes as belonging to a clarinet. Needless to say, we are far from understanding how this pattern recognition works.

Although the subcortical components of the auditory system are often referred to as "relay nuclei," it is clear that these nuclei do much more than passively transmit information from the cochlear nerve to the auditory cortex. For example, as we saw earlier in this chapter, the superior olivary complex contains circuits that analyze the location of sound sources according to arrival time (or phase differences) and intensity differences.

Pattern recognition, however, appears to be accomplished by circuits of neurons in the auditory cortex. We know a little bit about the types of analyses that the auditory cortex accomplishes. Various studies (Whitfield and Evans, 1965; Saitoh, Maruyama, and Kudoh, 1981) have found neurons in the auditory cortex that respond only to the onset or cessation of a sound (or to both), to changes in pitch or intensity (sometimes only to changes in one direction), or to complex stimuli that contain a variety of frequencies. Winter and Funkenstein (1971) found neurons in the auditory cortex of the squirrel monkey that responded specifically to the vocalizations made by members of this species. McKenna, Weinberger, and Diamond (1989) found that when they presented a series of different tones, some neurons in the primary auditory cortex responded to a particular frequency only in a particular context; for example, they would respond if the tone were the last in a series but not if it were the first. Rauschecker, Tian, and Hauser (1995) found that neurons in the auditory association cortex of rhesus monkeys responded much better to sound mixtures than to pure tones. Thus, neurons in the auditory cortex encode rather complex features. Because data are scanty so far, we have no real conception of the coding mechanism that the brain uses for these changes or even of precisely what features are coded.

However the analysis of auditory information is accomplished, it is clear that the circuits that perform this analysis must receive accurate information. For example, recognition of complex sounds such as those found in speech requires that the timing of changes in the components of these sounds be preserved all the way to the auditory cortex. In fact, the neurons that convey information to the auditory cortex contain special features that permit them to conduct this information rapidly and accurately (Trussell, 1999). Their axons contain special low-threshold voltage-gated potassium channels that produce very short action potentials. Their terminal buttons are large and release large amounts of glutamate, and the

figure 7.16

Evidence for the existence of dorsal and ventral streams of analysis in the cerebral cortex. Regions of the brain that became activated when subjects made judgments about pitch of sounds (yellow and orange) or about their locations (blue).
(From Alain, C., Arnott, S. R., Hevenor, S., Graham, S., and Grady, C. L. *Proceedings of the National Academy of Science, USA,* 2001, *98,* 12301–12306.)

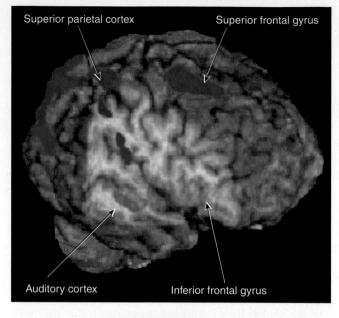

Location > Pitch   Pitch > Location

postsynaptic membrane contains neurotransmitter-dependent ion channels that act unusually rapidly; thus, these synapses produce very strong EPSPs. The terminal buttons form synapses with the somatic membrane of the postsynaptic neurons, which minimizes the distance between the synapses and the axon—and also the delay in conducting information to the axon of the postsynaptic neuron.

As we saw earlier, the auditory cortex, like the visual cortex, is organized into two streams: a dorsal stream, involved in perception of location, and a ventral stream, involved in perception of form. Anatomical studies have shown that the auditory cortex is similarly organized in two streams, with a similar dichotomy of functions (Romanski et al., 1999). In a single-unit recording study, Rauschecker and Tian (2000) found that neurons in the "what" system discriminated between different monkey calls, while neurons in the "where" system discriminated between different locations of loudspeakers presenting these calls.

Alain et al. (2001) found that the human auditory cortex shows a similar arrangement. In a functional-imaging study, they presented subjects with discrimination tasks that required them to determine the pitch of a sound or the location of its source. As Figure 7.16 shows, judgments of pitch activated ventral regions ("what"), and judgments of location activated dorsal regions ("where"). (See *Figure 7.16*.)

As we saw in Chapter 6, lesions of the visual association cortex in humans can produce visual agnosias—the inability to recognize objects even though the visual acuity may be good. Similarly, lesions of the auditory association cortex can produce auditory agnosias, the inability to comprehend the meaning of sounds even though the individuals are not deaf. If the lesion occurs in the left hemisphere, the person will sustain a particular form of language disorder. If it occurs in the right hemisphere, the person will be unable to recognize the nature or location of nonspeech sounds. Because of the importance of audition to language, these topics are discussed in much more detail in Chapter 15.

interim summary

Audition

The receptive organ for audition is the organ of Corti, located on the basilar membrane. When sound strikes the tympanic membrane, it sets the ossicles into motion, and the baseplate of the stapes pushes against the membrane behind the oval window. Pressure changes thus applied to the fluid within the cochlea cause a portion of the basilar membrane to flex, causing the basilar membrane to move laterally with respect to the tectorial membrane that overhangs it. This movement pulls directly on the cilia of the outer hair cells and changes their membrane potential. This change causes contractions or relaxations of contractile proteins within the cell, which amplify movements of the basilar membrane and sharpen their focus. These events cause movements in the fluid within the cochlea, which, in turn, causes the cilia of the inner hair cells to wave back and forth. These mechanical forces open potassium channels in the tips of the hair cells and thus produce receptor potentials.

The inner hair cells form synapses with the dendrites of the bipolar neurons whose axons give rise to the cochlear branch of the eighth cranial nerve. The central auditory system involves several brain stem nuclei, including the cochlear nuclei, superior olivary complexes, and inferior colliculi. The medial geniculate nucleus relays auditory information to the primary auditory cortex on the medial surface of the temporal lobe. The primary auditory cortex contains three separate tonotopic representations of auditory information and is surrounded by two levels of auditory association cortex: the belt region, which contains seven tonotopic maps, and the parabelt region. As we saw in Chapter 6, the visual association cortex is divided into two streams, one analyzing color and form, and the other analyzing location and movement. Similarly, the auditory association cortex is organized into streams that analyze the nature of sounds and the location of their sources.

Pitch is encoded by two means. High-frequency sounds cause the base of the basilar membrane (near the oval window) to flex; low-frequency sounds cause the apex (opposite end) to flex. Because high and low frequencies thus stimulate different groups of auditory hair cells, frequency is encoded anatomically. The lowest frequencies cause the apex of the basilar membrane to flex back and forth in time with the acoustic vibrations. The outer hair cells act as motive elements rather than as sensory transducers, contracting in response to activity of the efferent axons and modifying the mechanical properties of the basilar membrane.

The auditory system is analytical in its operation. That is, it can discriminate between sounds with different timbres by detecting the individual overtones that constitute the sounds and producing unique patterns of neural firing in the auditory system.

Left–right localization is performed by analyzing binaural differences in arrival time, in phase relations, and in intensity. The location of the azimuth of the sources of brief sounds (such as clicks) and sounds of frequencies below approximately 3000 Hz is detected by neurons in the medial superior olivary complex, which respond most vigorously when one ear receives the click first or when the phase of a sine wave received by one ear leads that received by the other. The location of the azimuth of the sources of high-frequency sounds is detected by neurons in the lateral superior olivary complex, which respond most vigorously when one organ of Corti is stimulated more intensely than the other. Localization of the elevation of the sources of sounds can be accomplished by turning the head or by perception of subtle differences in the timbre of sounds coming from different directions. The folds and ridges in the external ear (pinna) reflect different

frequencies into the ear canal, changing the timbre of the sound according to the location of its source.

To recognize the source of sounds, the auditory system must recognize the constantly changing patterns of activity received from the axons in the cochlear nerve. Studies have found neurons in the auditory cortex that respond to complex stimuli, such as ascending or descending pitches, series of tones, combinations of two or more tones, or even species-specific vocalizations. Like the visual cortex, the auditory cortex is organized into two streams. The ventral stream is involved in the analysis of the sound, and the dorsal stream is involved in perception of its location. Bilateral lesions of the auditory cortex of monkeys produce severe impairments in hearing, and lesions of the left auditory cortex impair the ability to discriminate the vocalizations of other monkeys. In humans, left-hemisphere damage to the auditory cortex impairs recognition of language, and right-hemisphere damage impairs the analysis of nonspeech sounds.

Vestibular System

The vestibular system has two components: the vestibular sacs and the semicircular canals. They represent the second and third components of the *labyrinths* of the inner ear. (We just studied the first component, the cochlea.) The **vestibular sacs** respond to the force of gravity and inform the brain about the head's orientation. The **semicircular canals** respond to angular acceleration—changes in the rotation of the head—but not to steady rotation. They also respond (but rather weakly) to changes in position or to linear acceleration.

The functions of the vestibular system include balance, maintenance of the head in an upright position, and adjustment of eye movement to compensate for head movements. Vestibular stimulation does not produce any readily definable sensation; certain low-frequency stimulation of the vestibular sacs can produce nausea, and stimulation of the semicircular canals can produce dizziness and rhythmic eye movements (*nystagmus*). However, we are not directly aware of the information received from these organs. This section describes the vestibular system: the vestibular apparatus, the receptor cells, and the vestibular pathway in the brain.

vestibular sac One of a set of two receptor organs in each inner ear that detect changes in the tilt of the head.

semicircular canal One of the three ringlike structures of the vestibular apparatus that detect changes in head rotation.

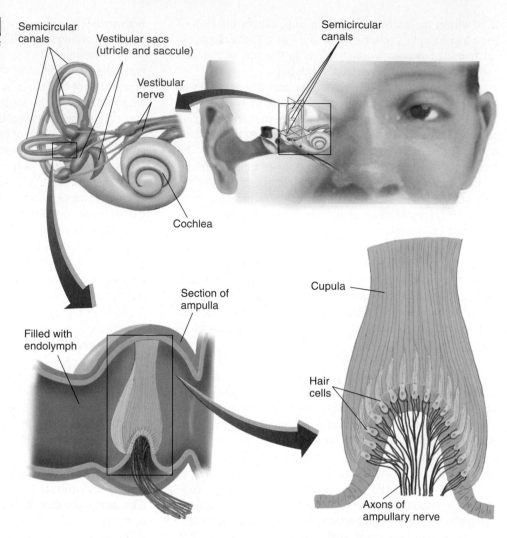

figure 7.17

The receptive organ of the semicircular canals.

Anatomy of the Vestibular Apparatus

Figure 7.17 shows the labyrinths of the inner ear, which include the cochlea, the semicircular canals, and the two vestibular sacs: the **utricle** ("little pouch") and the **saccule** ("little sack"). (See *Figure 7.17*.) The semicircular canals approximate the three major planes of the head: sagittal, transverse, and horizontal. Receptors in each canal respond maximally to angular acceleration in one plane. The semicircular canal consists of a membranous canal floating within a bony one; the membranous canal contains a fluid called *endolymph*. An enlargement called the **ampulla** contains the organ in which the sensory receptors reside. The sensory receptors are hair cells similar to those found in the cochlea. Their cilia are embedded in a gelatinous mass called the **cupula,** which blocks part of the ampulla. (See *Figure 7.17*.)

To explain the effects of angular acceleration on the semicircular canals, I will first describe an "experiment." If we place a glass of water on the exact center of a turntable and then start the turntable spinning, the water in the glass will, at first, remain stationary (the glass will move with respect to the water it contains). Eventually,

however, the water will begin rotating with the container. If we then stop the turntable, the water will continue spinning for a while because of its inertia.

The semicircular canals operate on the same principle. The endolymph within these canals, like the water in the glass, resists movement when the head begins to rotate. This inertial resistance pushes the endolymph against the cupula, causing it to bend, until the fluid begins to move at the same speed as the head. If the head rotation is then stopped, the endolymph, still circulating through the canal, pushes the cupula the other way. Angular acceleration is thus translated into bending of the cupula, which exerts a shearing force on the cilia of the hair cells. (Of course,

---

utricle (*you* trih kul) One of the vestibular sacs.

saccule (*sak* yule) One of the vestibular sacs.

ampulla (*am* **pull** uh) An enlargement in a semicircular canal; contains the cupula and the crista.

cupula (*kew* pew luh) A gelatinous mass found in the ampulla of the semicircular canals; moves in response to the flow of the fluid in the canals.

unlike the glass of water in my example, we do not normally spin around in circles; the semicircular canals measure very slight and very brief rotations of the head.)

The vestibular sacs (the utricle and saccule) work very differently. These organs are roughly circular, and each contains a patch of receptive tissue. The receptive tissue is located on the "floor" of the utricle and on the "wall" of the saccule when the head is in an upright position. The receptive tissue, like that of the semicircular canals and cochlea, contains hair cells. The cilia of these receptors are embedded in an overlying gelatinous mass, which contains something rather unusual: *otoconia,* which are small crystals of calcium carbonate. (See *Figure 7.18.*) The weight of the

(a)   (b)

figure 7.19

(a) Oblique view of a normal bundle of vestibular hair cells. (b) Top view of a bundle of hair cells from which the longest has been detached.

(From Hudspeth, A. J., and Jacobs, R. *Proceedings of the National Academy of Sciences, USA,* 1979, *76,* 1506–1509.)

crystals causes the gelatinous mass to shift in position as the orientation of the head changes. Thus, movement produces a shearing force on the cilia of the receptive hair cells.

The Receptor Cells

The hair cells of the semicircular canal and vestibular sacs are similar in appearance. Each hair cell contains several cilia, graduated in length from short to long. These hair cells resemble the auditory hair cells found in the cochlea, and their transduction mechanism is also similar: A shearing force of the cilia opens ion channels, and the entry of potassium ions depolarizes the ciliary membrane. Figure 7.19 shows two views of a hair cell of a bullfrog saccule made by a scanning electron microscope. (See *Figure 7.19.*)

The Vestibular Pathway

The vestibular and cochlear nerves constitute the two branches of the eighth cranial nerve (auditory nerve). The bipolar cell bodies that give rise to the afferent axons of the vestibular nerve are located in the **vestibular ganglion,** which appears as a nodule on the vestibular nerve.

Most of the axons of the vestibular nerve synapse within the vestibular nuclei in the medulla, but some axons travel directly to the cerebellum. Neurons of the vestibular nuclei send their axons to the cerebellum, spinal cord, medulla, and pons. There also appear to be vestibular

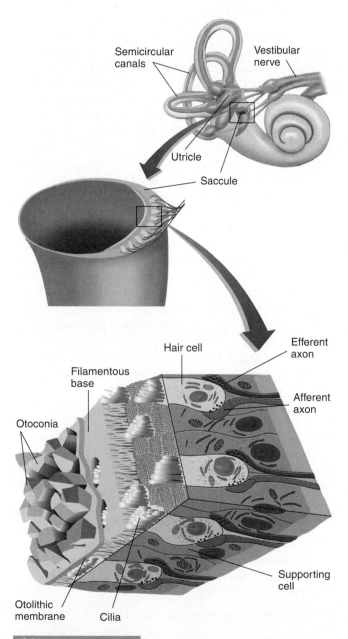

figure 7.18

The receptive tissue of the vestibular sacs: the utricle and the saccule.

vestibular ganglion A nodule on the vestibular nerve that contains the cell bodies of the bipolar neurons that convey vestibular information to the brain.

projections to the temporal cortex, but the precise pathways have not been determined. Most investigators believe that the cortical projections are responsible for feelings of dizziness; the activity of projections to the lower brain stem can produce the nausea and vomiting that accompany motion sickness. Projections to brain stem nuclei controlling neck muscles are clearly involved in maintaining an upright position of the head.

Perhaps the most interesting connections are those to the cranial nerve nuclei (third, fourth, and sixth) that control the eye muscles. As we walk or (especially) run, the head is jarred quite a bit. The vestibular system exerts direct control on eye movement, to compensate for the sudden head movements. This process, called the *vestibulo-ocular reflex,* maintains a fairly steady retinal image. Test this reflex yourself: Look at a distant object and hit yourself (gently) on the side of the head. Note that your image of the world jumps a bit, but not too much. People who have suffered vestibular damage and who lack the vestibulo-ocular reflex have difficulty seeing anything while walking or running. Everything becomes a blur of movement.

interim summary

Vestibular System

The semicircular canals are filled with fluid. When the head begins rotating or comes to rest after rotation, inertia causes the fluid to push the cupula to one side or the other. This movement exerts a shearing force on the cupula, the organ containing the vestibular hair cells. The vestibular sacs contain a patch of receptive tissue that contains hair cells whose cilia are embedded in a gelatinous mass. The weight of the otoconia in the gelatinous mass shifts when the head tilts, causing a shearing force on some of the cilia of the hair cells.

Each hair cell contains one long cilium and several shorter ones. These cells form synapses with dendrites of bipolar neurons whose axons travel through the vestibular nerve. The receptors also receive efferent terminal buttons from neurons located in the cerebellum and medulla, but the function of these connections is not known. Vestibular information is received by the vestibular nuclei in the medulla, which relay it on to the cerebellum, spinal cord, medulla, pons, and temporal cortex. These pathways are responsible for control of posture, head movements, and eye movements and the puzzling phenomenon of motion sickness.

Somatosenses

The somatosenses provide information about what is happening on the surface of our body and inside it. The **cutaneous senses** (skin senses) include several sub-

modalities commonly referred to as *touch.* **Kinesthesia** provides information about body position and movement and arises from receptors in joints, tendons, and muscles. The muscle receptors are discussed in this section and in Chapter 8. The **organic senses** arise from receptors in and around the internal organs, providing us with unpleasant sensations, such as stomachaches or gallbladder attacks, or pleasurable ones, such as those provided by a warm drink on a cold winter day. Because the cutaneous senses are the most studied of the somatosenses, both perceptually and physiologically, I will devote most of my discussion to them.

The Stimuli

The cutaneous senses respond to several different types of stimuli: pressure, vibration, heating, cooling, and events that cause tissue damage (and hence pain). Feelings of pressure are caused by mechanical deformation of the skin. Vibration is produced in the laboratory or clinic by tuning forks or mechanical devices, but it more commonly occurs when we move our fingers across a rough surface. Thus, we use vibration sensitivity to judge an object's roughness. Obviously, sensations of warmth and coolness are produced by objects that change skin temperature from normal. Sensations of pain can be caused by many different types of stimuli, but it appears that most cause at least some tissue damage.

Kinesthesia is provided by stretch receptors in skeletal muscles that report changes in muscle length to the central nervous system and by stretch receptors in tendons that measure the force being exerted by the muscles. Receptors within joints between adjacent bones respond to the magnitude and direction of limb movement. Muscle length detectors, located within the muscles, do not give rise to conscious sensations; their information is used to control movement. These receptors will be discussed separately in Chapter 8.

Additional information about the internal organs is provided by receptors in the linings of muscles, outer layers of the gastrointestinal system and other internal organs, and linings of the abdominal and thoracic cavities. Many of these tissues are sensitive only to stretch and do not report sensations when cut, burned, or crushed. In addition, the stomach and esophagus are responsive to heat and cold and to some chemicals.

---

cutaneous sense (*kew tane ee us*) One of the somatosenses; includes sensitivity to stimuli that involve the skin.

kinesthesia Perception of the body's own movements.

organic sense A sense modality that arises from receptors located within the inner organs of the body.

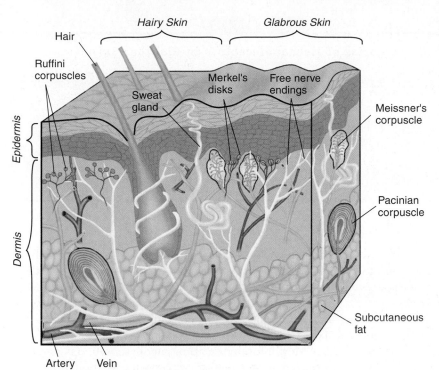

figure 7.20
Cutaneous receptors.

Anatomy of the Skin and Its Receptive Organs

The skin is a complex and vital organ of the body—one that we tend to take for granted. We cannot survive without it; extensive skin burns are fatal. Our cells, which must be bathed by a warm fluid, are protected from the hostile environment by the skin's outer layers. The skin participates in thermoregulation by producing sweat, thus cooling the body, or by restricting its circulation of blood, thus conserving heat. Its appearance varies widely across the body, from mucous membrane to hairy skin to the smooth, hairless skin of the palms and the soles of the feet.

Skin consists of subcutaneous tissue, dermis, and epidermis and contains various receptors scattered throughout these layers. Figure 7.20 shows cross sections through hairy and **glabrous skin** (hairless skin, found on our fingertips and palms and on the bottoms of our toes and feet). Hairy skin contains unencapsulated (free) nerve endings; **Ruffini corpuscles,** which respond to indentation of the skin; and **Pacinian corpuscles,** which respond to rapid vibrations. Pacinian corpuscles are the largest sensory end organs in the body. Their size, approximately 0.5×1.0 mm, makes them visible to the naked eye. They consist of up to seventy onionlike layers wrapped around the dendrite of a single myelinated axon. Free nerve endings, which detect painful stimuli and changes in temperature, are found just below the surface of the skin. Other free nerve endings are found in a basketwork around the base of hair follicles and around the emergence of hair shafts

from the skin. These fibers detect movement of hairs. (See *Figure 7.20.*)

Glabrous skin contains a more complex mixture of free nerve endings and axons that terminate within specialized end organs (Iggo and Andres, 1982). The increased complexity reflects the fact that we use the palms of our hands and the inside surfaces of our fingers to explore the environment actively: We use them to hold and touch objects. In contrast, the rest of our body most often contacts the environment passively; that is, other things come into contact with it.

Glabrous skin, like hairy skin, contains free nerve endings, Ruffini corpuscles and Pacinian corpuscles. (Pacinian corpuscles are also found in the joints and in various internal organs.) Glabrous skin also contains **Meissner's corpuscles,** which are found in *papillae* ("nipples"), small elevations of the dermis that project up into the epidermis. These end organs are innervated by between two and

---

glabrous skin (*glab russ*) Skin that does not contain hair; found on the palms and the soles of the feet.

Ruffini corpuscle A vibration-sensitive organ located in hairy skin.

Pacinian corpuscle (*pa chin ee un*) A specialized, encapsulated somatosensory nerve ending that detects mechanical stimuli, especially vibrations.

Meissner's corpuscle The touch-sensitive end organs located in the papillae, small elevations of the dermis that project up into the epidermis.

table **7.1**

Categories of Mechanoreceptors in Glabrous Skin		
SPEED OF ADAPTATION	**SIZE OF RECEPTIVE FIELD**	**IDENTITY OF RECEPTOR**
Slow	Small, sharp borders	Merkel's disk
Slow	Large, diffuse borders	Ruffini corpuscles
Rapid	Small, sharp borders	Meissner's corpuscles
Rapid	Large, diffuse borders	Pacinian corpuscles

six axons. They respond to low-frequency vibration or to brief taps on the skin. **Merkel's disks,** which respond to indentation of the skin, are found at the base of the epidermis, in the same general locations as Meissner's corpuscles, adjacent to sweat ducts. (See *Figure 7.20.*)

The *mechanoreceptors* in the skin (that is, those receptors that respond to mechanical stimulation) can be divided into four categories, depending on the size of their receptive field in the skin and the speed with which they adapt to a constant stimulus. (The process of adaptation is described in the next subsection.) Glabrous skin, with its increased cutaneous sensitivity, contains receptors with the smallest receptive fields: Meissner's corpuscles and Merkel's disks. (See *Table 7.1.*)

Perception of Cutaneous Stimulation

The three most important qualities of cutaneous stimulation are touch, temperature, and pain. These qualities are described in the sections that follow.

Touch

Sensitivity to pressure and vibration is caused by movement of the skin. The best-studied receptor is the Pacinian corpuscle, which primarily detects vibration. When the corpuscle is bent relative to the axon, the membrane becomes depolarized. If the threshold of excitation is exceeded, an action potential is produced at the first node of Ranvier. Loewenstein and Mendelson (1965) have shown that the layers of the corpuscle alter the mechanical characteristics of the organ, so the axon responds briefly when the intact organ is bent and again when it is released. Thus, this receptor is sensitive to vibration but not to steady pressure.

The bending of the tip of the nerve ending in a Pacinian corpuscle appears to produce a receptor potential by opening ion channels in the membrane. These channels appear to be anchored to protein filaments beneath the membrane and have long carbohydrate chains attached to them. When a mechanical stimulus changes the shape of the nerve ending, tension is exerted on the carbohydrate chains, pulling the channel open. (See *Figure 7.21.*) Most investigators believe that the encapsulated endings serve only to modify the physical stimulus transduced by the axons that enter them.

Most information about tactile sensation is precisely localized—that is, we can perceive the location on our skin where we are being touched. Until very recently, neuroscientists believed that in humans this information was transmitted to the central nervous system only by fast-conducting myelinated axons. However, a recent study discovered a new category of tactile sensation that is transmitted by small-diameter unmyelinated axons (Olausson et al., 2002).

> At age 31, patient G. L., a 54-year-old woman, "suffered a permanent and specific loss of large myelinated afferents after episodes of acute polyradiculitis and polyneuropathy that affected her whole body below the nose. A sural nerve biopsy indicated a complete loss of large-diameter myelinated fibers. . . . Before the present study, she denied having any touch sensibility below the nose, and she lost the ability to perceive tickle when she became ill. She states that her perceptions of temperature, pain and itch are intact" (Olausson et al., 2002, pp. 902–903).

Olausson and his colleagues found that patient G. L. could indeed detect the stimuli that are normally attributed to small-diameter unmyelinated axons—temperature, pain, and itch—but that she could not detect vibratory or normal tactile stimuli. But when the hairy skin on her forearm or the back of her hand was stroked with a soft brush, she reported a faint, pleasant sensation. However, she could not determine the direction of the stroking or its precise location. Functional MRI (fMRI) analysis showed that

---

Merkel's disk The touch-sensitive end organs found at the base of the epidermis, adjacent to sweat ducts.

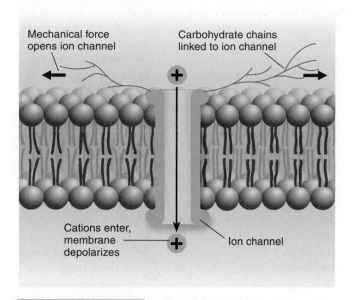

A hypothetical explanation of transduction of somatosensory information. Mechanical force on carbohydrate chains linked to ion channels opens the channels, permitting the entry of cations, which depolarizes the membrane potential.

this stimulation activated the insular cortex, a region that is known to be associated with emotional responses. The somatosensory cortex was not activated. When regions of hairy skin of control subjects were stimulated this way, fMRI showed activation of the primary and secondary somatosensory cortex as well as the insular cortex because the stimulation activated both large and small axons. The glabrous skin on the palm of the hand is served only by large-diameter, myelinated axons. When this region was stroked with a brush, G. L. reported no sensation at all, presumably because of the absence of these axons.

The investigators conclude that besides conveying information about noxious and thermal stimuli, small-diameter unmyelinated axons constitute a "system for limbic touch that may underlie emotional, hormonal and affiliative responses to caress-like, skin-to-skin contact between individuals." (Olausson et al., 2002, p. 900) And as we saw, G. L. could no longer perceive tickle. Olausson and his colleagues note that tickling sensations, which were previously believed to be transmitted by these small axons, are apparently transmitted by the large, myelinated axons that were destroyed in patient G. L.

■ **Adaptation** Investigators have known for a long time that a moderate, constant stimulus applied to the skin fails to produce any sensation after it has been present for a while. For example, we not only ignore the pressure of a wristwatch, but we cannot feel it at all if we keep our arm still (assuming that the band is not painfully

tight). Physiological studies have shown that the reason for the lack of sensation is the absence of receptor firing; the receptors adapt to a constant stimulus.

This adaptation is not caused by "fatigue" of physical or chemical processes within the receptor. Instead, adaptation occurs because of the physical construction of the skin and the cutaneous sensory organs. Nafe and Wagoner (1941) recorded the sensations reported by human subjects as a stimulus weight gradually moved downward, deforming the skin. Pressure was reported until the weight finally stopped moving. When the weight was increased, pressure was reported until downward movement stopped again. Pressure sensations were also briefly recorded when the weight was removed, while the surface of the skin regained its normal shape. (You might have noticed that when you first take your hat off, it feels for a few moments as if you were still wearing it.)

■ **Responsiveness to Moving Stimuli** A moderate, constant, nondamaging stimulus is rarely of any importance to an organism, so this adaptation mechanism is useful. Our cutaneous senses are used much more often to analyze shapes and textures of stimulus objects that are moving with respect to the surface of the skin. Sometimes, the object itself moves; but more often, we do the moving ourselves.

If I placed an object in your palm and asked you to keep your hand still, you would have a great deal of difficulty recognizing the object by touch alone. If I said you could now move your hand, you would manipulate the object, letting its surface slide across your palm and the pads of your fingers. You would be able to describe its three-dimensional shape, hardness, texture, slipperiness, and so on. Obviously, your motor system must cooperate, and you need kinesthetic sensation from your muscles and joints, besides the cutaneous information. If you squeeze the object and feel a lot of well-localized pressure in return, it is hard. If you feel a less intense, more diffuse pressure in return, it is soft. If it produces vibrations as it moves over the ridges on your fingers, it is rough. If very little effort is needed to move the object while pressing it against your skin, it is slippery. If it does not produce vibrations as it moves across your skin, but moves in a jerky fashion, and if it takes effort to remove your fingers from its surface, it is sticky. Thus, our somatosenses work dynamically with the motor system to provide useful information about the nature of objects that come into contact with our skin.

Temperature

Feelings of warmth and coolness are relative, not absolute (except at the extremes). There is a temperature level that, for a particular region of skin, will produce a sensation of temperature neutrality—neither warmth nor coolness. This neutral point is not an absolute value but depends on the prior history of thermal stimulation of that area. If the temperature of a region of skin is raised by a few degrees, the initial feeling of warmth is replaced by one of neutrality. If the skin temperature is lowered to its initial value, it now feels cool. Thus, increases in temperature lower the sensitivity of warmth receptors and raise the sensitivity of cold receptors. The converse holds for decreases in skin temperature. This adaptation to ambient temperature can be demonstrated easily by placing one hand in a bucket of warm water and the other in a bucket of cool water until some adaptation has taken place. If you then simultaneously immerse both hands in water at room temperature, it will feel warm to one hand and cool to the other.

There are two types of thermal receptors: one that responds to warmth and one that responds to coolness. (As we will see in the next section, another category of cutaneous receptor responds to intense heat and gives rise to a sensation of pain.) The transduction of temperature changes into the rate of axonal firing is not yet understood. Spray (1986) suggested that the sodium-potassium pump may be responsible for sensory transduction in coolness receptors. A drop in temperature would slow the action of the pump, which would permit sodium to accumulate in the free nerve ending and depolarize its membrane. In support of this suggestion he found that *ouabain,* a toxin that inactivates the sodium-potassium pump, produced a brief burst of activity in cold-receptive fibers in the skin of a frog. After that burst, the fibers became unresponsive to temperature changes. Obviously, detectors of warmth must operate by a different mechanism.

An ingenious experiment by Bazett et al. (1932) showed long ago that receptors for warmth and coolness lie at different depths in the skin. The investigators lifted the prepuce (foreskin) of uncircumcised males with dull fishhooks. They applied thermal stimuli on one side of the folded skin and recorded the rate at which the temperature changes were transmitted through the skin by placing small temperature sensors on the opposite side. They then correlated these observations with verbal reports of warmth and coolness. The investigators concluded that coolness receptors were close to the skin and that warmth receptors were located deeper in the tissue. (This experiment shows the extremities to which scientists will go to obtain information—pun intended.)

Pain

The story of pain is quite different from that of temperature and pressure; the analysis of this sensation is extremely difficult. It is obvious that our awareness of pain and our emotional reaction to it are controlled by mechanisms within the brain. For example, we can have a tooth removed painlessly under hypnosis, which has no effect on the sensitivity of pain receptors. Stimuli that produce pain also tend to trigger species-typical escape and withdrawal responses. Subjectively, these stimuli *hurt,* and

we try hard to avoid them. However, sometimes we are better off ignoring pain and getting on with other tasks. In fact, our brains possess mechanisms that can reduce pain, partly through the action of the endogenous opioids. These mechanisms are described in more detail in a later section of this chapter.

Pain reception, like thermosensation, is accomplished by the networks of free nerve endings in the skin. There appears to be at least three types of pain receptors (usually referred to as *nociceptors,* or "detectors of noxious stimuli"). High-threshold mechanoreceptors are free-nerve endings that respond to intense pressure, which might be caused by something striking, stretching, or pinching the skin. A second type of free nerve ending appears to respond to extremes of heat, to acids, and to the presence of *capsaicin,* the active ingredient in chile peppers. (Note that we say that chile peppers make food taste "hot.") This type of fiber contains VR1 receptors—ionotropic receptors that contain a cation channel (Kress and Zeilhofer, 1999). Caterina et al. (2000) found that mice with a targeted mutation against the VR1 receptor showed less sensitivity to painful high temperature stimuli and would drink water to which capsaicin had been added. They responded normally to noxious mechanical stimuli. Presumably, this receptor is responsible for pain produced by burning of the skin and for pain caused by inflammation, which is reduced by applying a cold compress.

Another type of nociceptive fiber contains receptors that are sensitive to ATP (Burnstock and Wood, 1996). These receptors are ionotropic and control channels that admit sodium and calcium ions. You will recall that ATP is produced by mitochondria and serves as an energy source for the cell's metabolic processes. ATP is also released when the blood supply to a region of the body is disrupted (a condition called *ischemia,* which occurs during the spasms of blood vessels that cause angina or migraine) or when a muscle is damaged. It is also released by rapidly growing tumors. Thus, these nociceptors may be at least partly responsible for the pain caused by angina, migraine, damage to muscles, and cancer.

The Somatosensory Pathways

Somatosensory axons from the skin, muscles, or internal organs enter the central nervous system via spinal nerves. Those located in the face and head primarily enter through the trigeminal nerve (fifth cranial nerve). The cell bodies of the unipolar neurons are located in the dorsal root ganglia and cranial nerve ganglia. Axons that convey precisely localized information, such as fine touch, ascend through the *dorsal columns* in the white matter of the spinal cord to nuclei in the lower medulla. From there axons cross the brain and ascend through the *medial lemniscus* to the *ventral posterior nuclei of the thalamus,* the relay nuclei for somatosensation. Axons from the thalamus project to the primary somatosensory cortex, which in turn sends axons to the secondary somatosensory cortex. In contrast, axons that convey poorly localized information, such as pain or temperature, form synapses with other neurons as soon as they enter the spinal cord. The axons of these neurons cross to the other side of the spinal cord and ascend through the *spinothalamic tract* to the ventral posterior nuclei of the thalamus. (See *Figure 7.22*.)

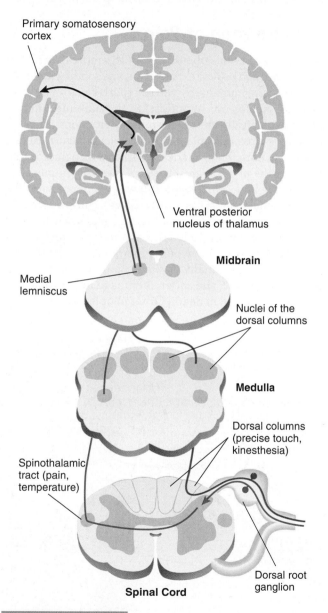

Primary somatosensory cortex

Ventral posterior nucleus of thalamus

Midbrain

Medial lemniscus

Nuclei of the dorsal columns

Medulla

Dorsal columns (precise touch, kinesthesia)

Spinothalamic tract (pain, temperature)

Dorsal root ganglion

Spinal Cord

figure 7.22

The somatosensory pathways from the spinal cord to the somatosensory cortex. Note that precisely localized information (such as fine touch) and imprecisely localized information (such as pain and temperature) are transmitted by different pathways.

Recall from Chapter 6 that the primary visual cortex contains columns of cells, each of which responds to particular features, such as orientation, ocular dominance, or spatial frequency. Within these columns are blobs that contain cells that respond to particular colors. The somatosensory cortex also has a columnar arrangement; in fact, cortical columns were discovered there by Mountcastle (1957) before they were found in the visual and auditory cortex. Within a column neurons respond to a particular type of stimulus (for example, temperature or pressure) applied to a particular part of the body.

Dykes (1983) has reviewed research indicating that the primary and secondary somatosensory cortical areas are divided into at least five (and perhaps as many as ten) different maps of the body surface. Within each map, cells respond to a particular submodality of somatosensory receptors. So far, separate areas have been identified that respond to slowly adapting cutaneous receptors, rapidly adapting cutaneous receptors, receptors that detect changes in muscle length, receptors located in the joints, and Pacinian corpuscles.

As you learned in Chapter 6, the extrastriate cortex consists of several subareas, each of which contains an independent representation of the visual field. For example, one area responds specifically to color and form, and another responds to movement. The somatosensory cortex appears to follow a similar scheme: Each cortical map of the body contains neurons that respond to a specific submodality of stimulation. Undoubtedly, further investigations will provide more accurate functional maps of the cortical subareas of both of these sensory systems.

As we saw in Chapter 6, damage to the visual association cortex can cause visual agnosia, and as we saw earlier in this chapter, damage to the auditory association cortex can cause auditory agnosia. You will not be surprised to learn that damage to the somatosensory association cortex can cause of tactile agnosia. For example, Reed, Caselli, and Farah (1996) described patient E. C., a woman with left parietal lobe damage who was unable to recognize common objects by touch. For example, the patient identified a pine cone as a brush, a ribbon as a rubber band, and a snail shell as a bottle cap. The deficit was not due to a simple loss of tactile sensitivity; the patient was still sensitive to light touch and to warm and cold objects, and she could easily discriminate objects by their size, weight, and roughness.

Nakamura et al. (1998) described patient M. T., who had a different type of tactile agnosia. Patient M. T. had bilateral lesions of the angular gyrus, a region of the parietal lobe surrounding the caudal end of the lateral fissure. This patient, like patient E. C., had normal tactile sensitivity, but he could not identify objects by touch. However, unlike patient E. C., he could *draw* objects that he touched even though he could not recognize what they are.

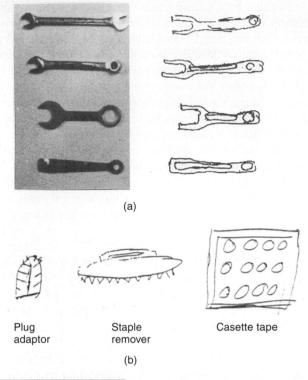

(a)

Plug adaptor   Staple remover   Casette tape

(b)

figure 7.23

Tactile agnosia. (a) Drawings of wrenches felt but not seen by M. T., a patient with associative tactile agnosia. Although the patient did not recognize the objects as wrenches, she was able to draw them accurately. (b) Drawings of objects felt but not seen by E. C., a patient with apperceptive tactile agnosia. The patient could neither recognize the objects by touch nor draw them accurately.

(From Nakamura, J., Endo, K., Sumida, T., and Hasegawa, T. *Cortex,* 1998, *34,* 375–388, and Reed, C. L., Caselli, R. J., and Farah, M. J. *Brain,* 1996, *119,* 875–888.)

(See *Figure 7.23.*) The fact that he could draw the objects means that his ability to perceive three-dimensional objects by touch must have been intact. However, the brain damage prevented the information analyzed by the somatosensory association cortex to be transmitted to parts of the brain responsible for control of language—and for consciousness. As you may have recognized, patient E. C.'s deficit resembles apperceptive visual agnosia and patient M. T.'s deficit resembles associative visual agnosia (both described in Chapter 6). Indeed, these deficits are referred to as apperceptive and associative tactile agnosias.

As I mentioned earlier, recognition of objects by touch requires cooperation between the somatosensory and motor systems. When we attempt to identify objects by touch alone, we explore them with moving fingers. Valenza et al. (2001) reported the case of a patient with brain damage to the right hemisphere that produced a disorder they called *tactile apraxia.* As we will see in Chapter 8, *apraxia* refers to a difficulty in carrying out purposeful

movements in the absence of paralysis or muscular weakness. When the experimenters gave the patient objects to identify by touch with her left hand, the patient explored it with her fingers in a disorganized fashion. (Exploration and identification using her right hand were normal.) If the experimenters guided the patient's fingers and explored the object the way people normally do, she was able to recognize the object's shape. Thus, her deficit was caused by a movement disorder and not by damage to brain mechanisms involved in tactile perception.

Perception of Pain

Pain is a curious phenomenon. It is more than a mere sensation; it can be defined only by some sort of withdrawal reaction or, in humans, by verbal report. Pain can be modified by opiates, by hypnosis, by the administration of pharmacologically inert sugar pills, by emotions, and even by other forms of stimulation, such as acupuncture. Recent research efforts have made remarkable progress in discovering the physiological bases of these phenomena.

We might reasonably ask *why* we experience pain. The answer is that in most cases pain serves a constructive role. For example, people who have congenital insensitivity to pain suffer an abnormally large number of injuries, such as cuts and burns. One woman did not make the shifts in posture that we normally do when our joints start to ache. As a consequence, she suffered damage to the spine that ultimately resulted in death. Other people have died from

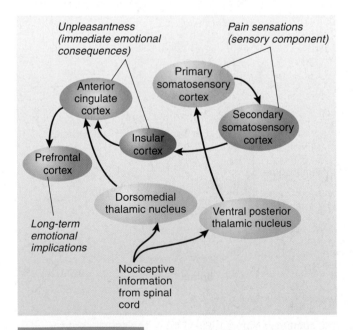

figure 7.24

A simplified, schematic diagram of the brain mechanisms involved in the three components of pain: the sensory component, the immediate emotional component, and the long-term emotional component.

(Adapted from Price, D. B., *Science,* 2000, *288,* 1769–1772.)

ruptured appendixes and ensuing abdominal infections that they did not feel (Sternbach, 1968). I am sure that a person who is passing a kidney stone would not find much comfort in the fact that pain does more good than ill; but pain is, nevertheless, very important to our existence.

As we saw earlier, the VR1 receptor, a pain receptor that is sensitive to capsaicin, heat, and acids, appears to be involved in the pain caused by inflammation. As Basbaum and Woolf (1999) note, inflammation, which often accompanies injuries to skin or muscle, greatly increases sensitivity of the inflamed region to painful stimuli. This effect motivates the individual to minimize movement of the injured part and avoid contact with other objects. The effect is to reduce the likelihood of further injury.

Some environmental events diminish the perception of pain. For example, Beecher (1959) noted that many wounded American soldiers back from the battle at Anzio, Italy, during World War II reported that they felt no pain from their wounds—They did not even want medication. It would appear that their perception of pain was diminished by the relief they felt from surviving such an ordeal. There are other instances in which people still report the perception of pain but are not bothered by it. Some tranquilizers have this effect, and damage to parts of the brain does, too.

Pain appears to have three different perceptual and behavioral effects (Price, 2000). First is the sensory component—the pure perception of the intensity of a painful stimulus. The second component is the immediate emotional consequences of pain—the unpleasantness or degree to which the individual is bothered by the painful stimulus. It is this characteristic that was reduced in some of the soldiers at Anzio. The third component is the long-term emotional implications of chronic pain—the threat that such pain represents to one's future comfort and well-being.

These three components of pain appear to involve different brain mechanisms. The purely sensory component of pain is mediated by a pathway from the spinal cord to the ventral posterolateral thalamus to the primary and secondary somatosensory cortex. The immediate emotional component of pain appears to be mediated by pathways that reach the anterior cingulate cortex and insular cortex. The long-term emotional component appears to be mediated by pathways that reach the prefrontal cortex. (See *Figure 7.24*.)

Let's look at some evidence for brain mechanisms involved in short-term and long-term emotional responses to pain. Several studies have found that painful stimuli activate the insular cortex and the anterior cingulate cortex. In addition, Ostrowsky et al. (2002) found that electrical stimulation of the insular cortex caused reports of painful burning and stinging sensations. Damage to this region decreases people's emotional response to pain (Berthier, Starkstein, and Leiguarda, 1933): They continue to feel the pain but do not seem to recognize that it is harmful. They do not withdraw from pain or the threat of pain.

Rainville et al. (1997) produced pain sensations in human subjects by having them put their arms in ice water. Under one condition they used hypnosis to diminish the unpleasantness of the pain. The hypnosis worked; the subjects said the pain was less unpleasant, even though it was still as intense. Meanwhile, the investigators used a PET scanner to measure regional activation of the brain. They found that the painful stimulus increased the activity of both the primary somatosensory cortex and the anterior cingulate cortex. When the subjects were hypnotized and found the pain less unpleasant, the activity of the anterior cingulate cortex decreased—but the activity of the primary somatosensory cortex remained high. Presumably, the primary somatosensory cortex is involved in the perception of pain, and the anterior cingulate cortex is involved in its immediate emotional effects—its unpleasantness. (See *Figure 7.25*.)

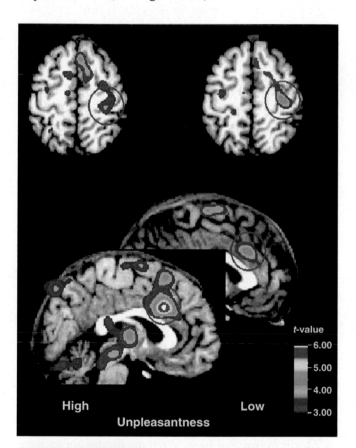

figure 7.25

PET scans showing brain regions that respond to sensory and emotional components of pain. *Top:* Dorsal views of the brain. Activation of the primary somatosensory cortex (circled in red) by a painful stimulus was not affected by a hypnotically suggested reduction in unpleasantness of a painful stimulus, indicating that this region responded to the sensory component of pain. *Bottom:* Midsagittal views of the brain. The anterior cingulate cortex (circled in red) showed much less activation when the unpleasantness of the painful stimulus was reduced by hypnotic suggestion. (From Rainville, P., Duncan, G. H., Price, D. D., Carrier, Benoit, and Bushnell, M. C. *Science,* 1997, *277*, 968–971.)

Another study from the same laboratory, Hofbauer et al. (2001) produced the opposite effect. They presented subjects with a painful stimulus and used hypnotic suggestion to reduce the perceived intensity of the pain. They found that the suggestion reduced subjects ratings of pain and also decreased the activation of the somatosensory cortex. Thus, changes in perceived *intensity* of pain is reflected in changes in activation of the somatosensory cortex, whereas changes in perceived *unpleasantness* of pain is reflected in changes in activation of the anterior cingulate cortex.

The final component of pain—the emotional consequences of chronic pain—appears to involve the prefrontal cortex. As we will see in Chapter 11, damage to the prefrontal cortex impairs people's ability to make plans for the future and to recognize the personal significance of situations in which they are involved. Along with the general lack of insight, people with prefrontal damage tend not to be concerned with the implications of chronic conditions—including chronic pain—for their future.

A particularly interesting form of pain sensation occurs after a limb has been amputated. After the limb is gone, up to 70 percent of amputees report that they feel as though the missing limb still exists and that it often hurts. This phenomenon is referred to as the **phantom limb** (Melzak, 1992). People with phantom limbs report that the limb feels very real, and they often say that if they try to reach out with it, it feels as though it were responding. Sometimes, they perceive it as sticking out, and they may feel compelled to avoid knocking it against the side of a doorframe or sleeping in a position that would make it come between them and the mattress. People have reported all sorts of sensations in phantom limbs, including pain, pressure, warmth, cold, wetness, itching, sweatiness, and prickliness.

The classic explanation for phantom limbs has been activity of the sensory axons belonging to the amputated limb. Presumably, the nervous system interprets this activity as coming from the missing limb. When nerves are cut and connections cannot be reestablished between the proximal and distal portions, the cut ends of the proximal portions form nodules known as *neuromas*. The treatment for phantom pain has been to cut the nerves above these neuromas, to cut the dorsal roots that bring the afferent information from these nerves into the spinal cord, or to make lesions in somatosensory pathways in the spinal cord, thalamus, or cerebral cortex. Sometimes these procedures work for a while, but often the pain returns.

Melzak suggested that the phantom limb sensation is inherent in the organization of the parietal cortex. As we saw in Chapter 3, the parietal cortex is involved in our awareness of our own bodies. Indeed, people with lesions of the parietal lobe (especially in the right hemisphere) have been known to push their own leg out of bed, believing that it actually belongs to someone else. Melzak reports that some people who were born with missing limbs nev-

ertheless experience phantom limb sensations, which would suggest that our brains are genetically programmed to provide sensations for all four limbs.

Endogenous Modification of Pain Sensitivity

For many years investigators have known that perception of pain can be modified by environmental stimuli. Recent work, beginning in the 1970s, has revealed the existence of neural circuits whose activity can produce analgesia. A variety of environmental stimuli can activate these analgesia-producing circuits. Most of these stimuli cause the release of the endogenous opioids, which were described in Chapter 4.

Electrical stimulation of particular locations within the brain can cause analgesia, which can even be profound enough to serve as an anesthetic for surgery in rats (Reynolds, 1969). The most effective locations appear to be within the periaqueductal gray matter and in the rostroventral medulla. For example, Mayer and Liebeskind (1974) reported that electrical stimulation of the periaqueductal gray matter produced analgesia in rats equivalent to that produced by at least 10 milligrams (mg) of morphine per kilogram of body weight, which is a large dose. The technique has even found an application in reducing severe, chronic pain in humans: Fine wires are surgically implanted in parts of the central nervous system and attached to a radio-controlled device that permits the patient to administer electrical stimulation when necessary (Kumar, Wyant, and Nath, 1990).

Analgesic brain stimulation apparently triggers the neural mechanisms that reduce pain, primarily by causing endogenous opioids to be released. Basbaum and Fields (1978, 1984), who summarized their work and that of others, proposed a neural circuit that mediates opiate-induced analgesia. Basically, they proposed the following: Endogenous opioids (released by environmental stimuli or administered as a drug) stimulate opiate receptors on neurons in the periaqueductal gray matter. Because the effect of opiates appears to be inhibitory (Nicoll, Alger, and Jahr, 1980), Basbaum and Fields proposed that the neurons that contain opiate receptors are themselves inhibitory interneurons. Thus, the administration of opiates activates the neurons on which these interneurons synapse. (See *Figure 7.26*.)

Neurons in the periaqueductal gray matter send axons to the **nucleus raphe magnus,** located in the medulla. The neurons in this nucleus send axons to the dorsal horn of the spinal cord gray matter; destruction of these

---

phantom limb Sensations that appear to originate in a limb that has been amputated.

nucleus raphe magnus A nucleus of the raphe that contains serotonin-secreting neurons that project to the dorsal gray matter of the spinal cord and is involved in analgesia produced by opiates.

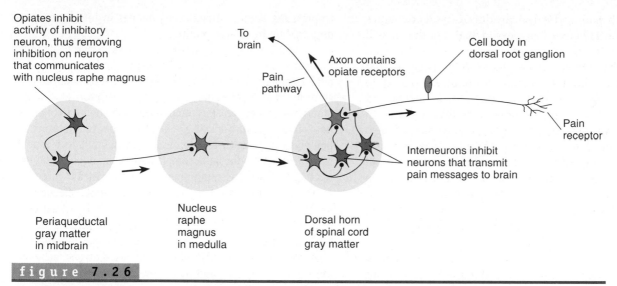

Opiates inhibit
activity of inhibitory
neuron, thus removing
inhibition on neuron
that communicates
with nucleus raphe magnus

To
brain

Axon contains
opiate receptors

Cell body in
dorsal root ganglion

Pain
pathway

Pain
receptor

Interneurons inhibit
neurons that transmit
pain messages to brain

Periaqueductal
gray matter
in midbrain

Nucleus
raphe
magnus
in medulla

Dorsal horn
of spinal cord
gray matter

figure 7.26

The neural circuit that mediates opiate-induced analgesia, as hypothesized by Basbaum and Fields (1978).

axons eliminates analgesia induced by an injection of morphine. The inhibitory effects of these neurons apparently involve one or two interneurons in the spinal cord. (See *Figure 7.26.*)

Pain sensitivity can be regulated by direct neural connections, as well as by secretion of the endogenous opioids. The periaqueductal gray matter receives inputs from the frontal cortex, amygdala, and hypothalamus (Beitz, 1982; Mantyh, 1983). These inputs permit learning and emotional reactions to affect an animal's responsiveness to pain even without the secretion of opioids.

Biological Significance of Analgesia

It appears that a considerable amount of neural circuitry is devoted to reducing the intensity of pain. What functions do these circuits perform? When an animal encounters a noxious stimulus, it usually stops what it is doing and engages in withdrawal or escape behaviors. Obviously, these responses are quite appropriate. However, they are sometimes counterproductive. For example, if an animal sustains a wound that causes chronic pain, a tendency to engage in withdrawal responses will interfere with its performance of everyday activities, such as obtaining food. Thus, chronic, unavoidable pain would best be diminished.

Another useful function of analgesia is the suppression of pain during important behaviors such as fighting or mating. For example, males fighting for access to females during mating season will fail to pass on their genes if pain elicits withdrawal responses that interfere with fighting. As we will see, these conditions *do* diminish pain.

First, let us consider the effects of unavoidable pain. Several experiments have shown that analgesia can be produced by the application of painful stimuli or even by the presence of nonpainful stimuli that have been paired with painful ones (that is, through classically conditioned analgesia). For example, Maier, Drugan, and Grau (1982) administered inescapable shocks to rats' tails or administered shocks that the animals could learn to escape by making a response. Although both groups of animals received the same amount of shock, only those that received *inescapable* shocks showed analgesia. That is, when their pain sensitivity was tested, it was found to be lower than that of control subjects. The analgesia was abolished by administration of naloxone, which indicates that it was mediated by the release of endogenous opioids. The results make good sense, biologically. If pain is escapable, it serves to motivate the animal to make appropriate responses. If it occurs whatever the animal does, then a reduction in pain sensitivity is in the animal's best interest. Defeat by another animal of the same species or exposure to the sound or smell of a predator all have been reported to produce analgesia (Kavaliers, 1985; Lester and Fanselow, 1985; Hendrie, 1991).

Pain can be reduced by stimulating regions other than those that hurt. For example, people often rub or scratch the area around a wound in an apparent attempt to diminish the severity of the pain. And as you know, acupuncturists insert needles into various parts of the body to reduce pain. The needle is usually then rotated, thus stimulating axons and nerve endings in the vicinity. Often, the region that is stimulated is far removed from the region that becomes less sensitive to pain.

Several experimental studies have shown that acupuncture does indeed produce analgesia (Kaptchuk, 2002). Mayer et al. (1976) reported that the analgesia produced by acupuncture—but not analgesia produced by hypnosis—could be blocked by naloxone. Thus, acupuncture, but not hypnosis, appears to cause analgesia through the release of endogenous opioids.

Although pain reduction produced by acupuncture may be more effective if a person believes that it will work, belief in its efficacy is not the only reason this procedure works. Many studies have demonstrated that acupuncture reduces the reaction of laboratory animals to pain, where "belief" can certainly not be an issue. Lee and Beitz (1992) reported that acupuncture that was able to reduce an animal's sensitivity to painful stimuli also reduced the production of Fos protein in somatosensory neurons in the dorsal horn of the spinal cord. (You will recall from Chapter 5 that the production of Fos protein in neurons indicates that they have been activated.)

There is evidence that engaging in behaviors that are important to survival also reduces sensitivity to pain. For example, Komisaruk and Larsson (1971) found that gentle probing of a rat's vagina with a glass rod produced analgesia. Such probing also increases the activity of neurons in the periaqueductal gray matter and decreases the responsiveness of neurons in the ventrobasal thalamus to painful stimulation (Komisaruk and Steinman, 1987). The phenomenon also occurs in humans; Whipple and Komisaruk (1988) found that self-administered vaginal stimulation reduces sensitivity to painful stimuli but not to neutral tactile stimuli. Presumably, copulation triggers analgesic mechanisms. The adaptive significance of this phenomenon is clear: Painful stimuli encountered during the course of copulation are less likely to cause the behavior to be interrupted; thus, the chances of pregnancy are increased.

Pain can also be reduced, at least in some people, by administering a pharmacologically inert placebo. When some people take a medication that they believe will reduce pain, it triggers the release of endogenous opioids and actually does so. This effect is eliminated if the people are given an injection of naloxone, a drug that blocks opiate receptors (Levine, Gordon, and Fields, 1979). Thus, for some people a placebo is not pharmacologically inert—it has a physiological effect. The placebo effect is probably mediated through connections of the frontal cortex with the periaqueductal gray matter.

interim summary

Somatosenses

Cutaneous sensory information is provided by specialized receptors in the skin. Pacinian corpuscles provide information about vibration. Ruffini corpuscles, similar to Pacinian corpuscles but considerably smaller, respond to indentation of the skin. Meissner's corpuscles, found in papillae and innervated by several axons, respond to low-frequency vibration or to brief taps on the skin. Merkel's disks, also found in papillae, consist of single, flattened dendritic endings next to specialized epithelial cells. These receptors respond

to pressure. Painful stimuli and changes in temperature are detected by free nerve endings.

Our somatosensory system is most sensitive to changes in mechanical stimuli. Unless the skin is moving, we do not detect nonpainful stimuli, because the receptors adapt to constant mechanical pressure. Temperature receptors also adapt; moderate changes in skin temperature are soon perceived as neutral, and deviations above or below this temperature are perceived as warmth or coolness. Transduction in temperature receptors might be accomplished by changes in the rate of the sodium-potassium pump. There are at least three different types of pain receptors: high-threshold mechanoreceptors: fibers with capsaicin receptors, which detect extremes of heat, acids, and the presence of capsaicin (and, undoubtedly, a yet-undiscovered natural ligand); and fibers with receptors sensitive to ATP, which is released during ischemia, after muscle damage, and by rapidly growing tumors.

Precise, well-localized somatosensory information is conveyed by a pathway through the dorsal columns and their nuclei and the medial lemniscus, connecting the dorsal column nuclei with the ventral posterior nuclei of the thalamus. Information about pain and temperature ascends the spinal cord through the spinothalamic system. Organic sensibility reaches the central nervous system by means of axons that travel through nerves of the autonomic nervous systems.

The neurons in the primary somatosensory cortex are topographically arranged, according to the part of the body from which they receive sensory information (somatotopic representation). Columns within the somatosensory cortex respond to a particular type of stimulus from a particular region of the body. Recent studies have shown that different types of somatosensory receptors send their information to separate areas of the somatosensory cortex.

Pain perception is not a simple function of stimulation of pain receptors; it is a complex phenomenon with sensory and emotional components that can be modified by experience and the immediate environment. The sensory component is mediated by the primary and secondary somatosensory cortex, the immediate emotional component appears to be mediated by the anterior cingulate cortex and the insular cortex, and the long-term emotional component appears to be mediated by the prefrontal cortex. Functional imaging studies using hypnotic suggestion found that a decrease in the sensory component of pain reduced activation of the somatosensory cortex, and reduction of the unpleasantness of pain reduced the activation of the anterior cingulate cortex. The phantom limb phenomenon, which often is accompanied by phantom pain, appears to be inherent in the organization of the parietal lobe.

Just as we have mechanisms to perceive pain, we have mechanisms to reduce it—to produce analgesia. Under the appropriate circumstances neurons in the periaqueductal gray matter are stimulated through synaptic connections with the frontal cortex, amygdala, and hypothalamus. In addition, some neurosecretory cells in the brain release enkephalins, a class of endogenous opioids. These neuro-modulators activate receptors on neurons in the periaqueductal gray matter and provide additional stimulation of neurons in this region. Connections from the periaqueductal gray matter to the nucleus raphe magnus of the medulla activate serotonergic neurons located there. These neurons send axons to the dorsal horn of the spinal cord gray matter, where they inhibit the transmission of pain information to the brain. In humans chronic pain is sometimes treated by implanting electrodes in the periaqueductal gray matter or the thalamus and permitting the patients to stimulate the brain through these electrodes when the pain becomes severe.

Analgesia occurs when it is important for an animal to continue a behavior that would tend to be inhibited by pain—for example, mating or fighting. In addition, inescapable pain activates brain mechanisms that produce analgesia, but escapable pain does not. This distinction makes sense: If the pain is escapable, its sensation should not be blunted but should serve to motivate the animal's efforts to escape. Because the endogenous opioids are found in several regions of the brain that are apparently not involved in pain perception, these neuromodulators undoubtedly serve functions besides analgesia. The fact that many people have chosen to self-administer opiates extracted from the opium poppy attests to its potency as a reinforcer of behavior.

Analgesia can also be produced by stimulating regions other than those that hurt, which is the basis for acupuncture. This phenomenon can be demonstrated in laboratory animals, which suggests that it has a physiological basis. The administration of a placebo can also produce analgesia. Because this effect is blocked by naloxone, it must involve the release of endogenous opioids.

Gustation

The stimuli we have encountered so far produce receptor potentials by imparting physical energy: thermal, photic (involving light), or kinetic. However, the stimuli received by the last two senses to be studied—gustation and olfaction—interact with their receptors chemically. This section discusses the first of them: gustation.

The Stimuli

Gustation is clearly related to eating; this sense modality helps us to determine the nature of things we put in our mouths. For a substance to be tasted, molecules of it must dissolve in the saliva and stimulate the taste receptors on the tongue. Tastes of different substances vary, but much less than we generally realize. There are only five qualities of taste: *bitterness, sourness, sweetness, saltiness,* and *umami.* You are familiar with the first four qualities, and I

will explain the fifth one later. Flavor, as opposed to taste, is a composite of olfaction and gustation. Much of the flavor of a steak depends on its odor; to an *anosmic* person (one who lacks the sense of smell) or to a person whose nostrils are stopped up, an onion tastes like an apple, and a steak tastes like salty cardboard.

Most vertebrates possess gustatory systems that respond to all five taste qualities. (An exception is the cat family; lions, tigers, leopards, and house cats do not detect sweetness—but then, none of the food they normally eat is sweet.) Clearly, sweetness receptors are food detectors. Most sweet-tasting foods, such as fruits and some vegetables, are safe to eat (Ramirez, 1990). Saltiness receptors detect the presence of sodium chloride. In some environments inadequate amounts of this mineral are obtained from the usual source of food, so sodium chloride detectors help the animal to detect its presence. Injuries that cause bleeding deplete an organism of its supply of sodium rapidly, so the ability to find it quickly can be critical.

Most species of animals will readily ingest substances that taste sweet or somewhat salty. However, they will tend to avoid substances that taste sour or bitter. Because of bacterial activity, many foods become acidic when they spoil. The acidity tastes sour and causes an avoidance reaction. (Of course, we have learned to make highly preferred mixtures of sweet and sour, such as lemonade.) Bitterness is almost universally avoided and cannot easily be improved by adding some sweetness. Many plants produce poisonous alkaloids, which protect them from being eaten by animals. Alkaloids taste bitter; thus, the bitterness receptor undoubtedly serves to warn animals away from these chemicals.

Anatomy of the Taste Buds and Gustatory Cells

The tongue, palate, pharynx, and larynx contain approximately 10,000 taste buds. Most of these receptive organs are arranged around *papillae,* small protuberances of the tongue. *Fungiform papillae,* located on the anterior two-thirds of the tongue, contain up to eight taste buds, along with receptors for pressure, touch, and temperature. *Foliate papillae* consist of up to eight parallel folds along each edge of the back of the tongue. Approximately 1300 taste buds are located in these folds. *Circumvallate papillae,* arranged in an inverted V on the posterior third of the tongue, contain approximately 250 taste buds. They are shaped like little plateaus surrounded by moatlike trenches. Taste buds consist of groups of twenty to fifty receptor cells, specialized neurons arranged somewhat like the segments of an orange. Cilia are located at the end of each cell and project through the opening of the taste bud (the pore) into the saliva that coats the tongue. Tight junctions between adjacent taste cells prevent substances in the saliva from

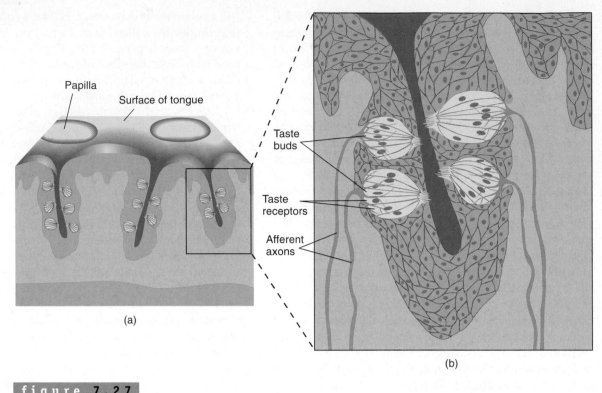

Papilla

Surface of tongue

Taste buds

Taste receptors

Afferent axons

(a)

(b)

figure 7.27

The tongue. (a) Papillae on the surface of the tongue. (b) Taste buds.

diffusing freely into the taste bud itself. Figure 7.27 shows the appearance of a circumvallate papilla; a cross section through the surrounding trench contains a taste bud. (See *Figure 7.27*.)

Taste receptor cells form synapses with dendrites of bipolar neurons whose axons convey gustatory information to the brain through the seventh, ninth, and tenth cranial nerves. The receptor cells have a life span of only ten days. They quickly wear out, being directly exposed to a rather hostile environment. As they degenerate, they are replaced by newly developed cells; the dendrite of the bipolar neuron is passed on to the new cell (Beidler, 1970).

Perception of Gustatory Information

Transduction of taste is similar to the chemical transmission that takes place at synapses: The tasted molecule binds with the receptor and produces changes in membrane permeability that cause receptor potentials. Different substances bind with different types of receptors, producing different taste sensations. In this section I will describe what we know about the nature of the molecules with particular tastes and the receptors that detect their presence. I should note that in some cases researchers have found that more than one type of receptor detects a par-

ticular taste and that different types of receptors may be found in different species. Thus, the following description, and the information in Figure 7.28, should be seen as representative rather than definitive.

To taste salty, a substance must ionize. Although the best stimulus for saltiness receptors is sodium chloride (NaCl), a variety of salts containing metallic cations (such as Na^+, K^+, and Li^+) with a small anion (such as Cl^-, Br^-, SO_4^{2-}, or NO_3^-) taste salty. The receptor for saltiness seems to be a simple sodium channel. When present in the saliva, sodium enters the taste cell and depolarizes it, triggering action potentials that cause the cell to release neurotransmitter (Avenet and Lindemann, 1989; Kinnamon and Cummings, 1992). (See *Figure 7.28a*.) The best evidence that sodium channels are involved is the fact that amiloride, a drug that is known to block sodium channels, prevents sodium chloride from activating taste cells and decreases sensations of saltiness. However, the drug does not completely block these sensations in humans, so most investigators believe that more than one type of receptor is involved (Schiffman, Lockhead, and Maes, 1983; Ossebaard, Polet, and Smith, 1997).

Sourness receptors appear to respond to the hydrogen ions present in acidic solutions. However, because the sourness of a particular acid is not simply a function of the concentration of hydrogen ions, the anions must have an effect, as well. The reason for this anion effect is not yet

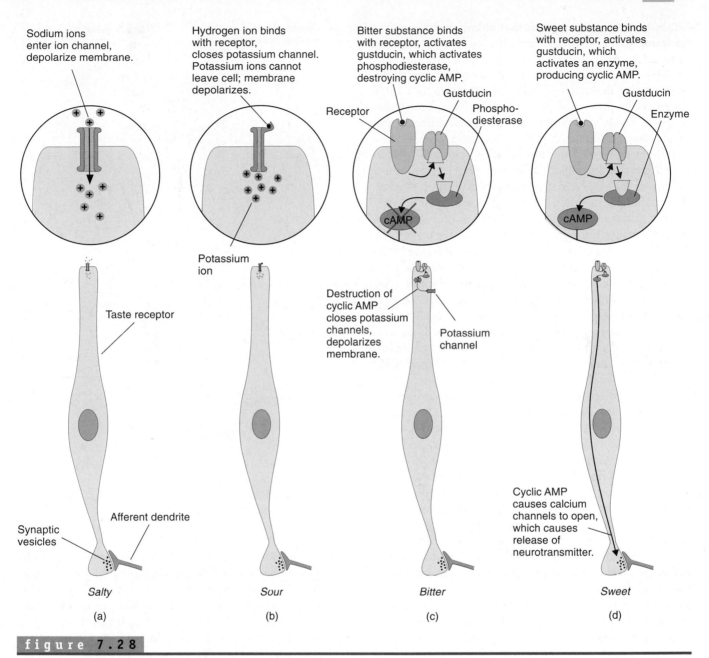

Sodium ions enter ion channel, depolarize membrane.

Hydrogen ion binds with receptor, closes potassium channel. Potassium ions cannot leave cell; membrane depolarizes.

Bitter substance binds with receptor, activates gustducin, which activates phosphodiesterase, destroying cyclic AMP.

Sweet substance binds with receptor, activates gustducin, which activates an enzyme, producing cyclic AMP.

Receptor   Gustducin   Phospho-diesterase   Gustducin   Enzyme

cAMP

Potassium ion

Taste receptor

Destruction of cyclic AMP closes potassium channels, depolarizes membrane.

Potassium channel

Cyclic AMP causes calcium channels to open, which causes release of neurotransmitter.

Synaptic vesicles

Afferent dendrite

Salty   *Sour*   *Bitter*   *Sweet*

(a)   (b)   (c)   (d)

figure 7.28

Transduction of taste information. (a) Salty taste. (b) Sour taste. (c) Bitter taste. (d) Sweet taste.

known. Kinnamon, Dionne, and Beam (1988) suggest that sourness is detected by sites on potassium channels in the membrane of taste cell cilia. These channels are normally open, permitting K$^+$ to flow out of the cell. Hydrogen ions bind with these sites and close the channels. Their closure prevents this outward current and depolarizes the membrane, producing action potentials. (See *Figure 7.28b*.)

Bitter and sweet substances are more difficult to characterize. The typical stimulus for bitterness is a plant alkaloid such as quinine; for sweetness it is a sugar such as glucose or fructose. The fact that some molecules elicit both sensations suggests that bitterness and sweetness

receptors may be similar. For example, the Seville orange rind contains a glycoside (complex sugar) that tastes extremely bitter; the addition of a hydrogen ion to the molecule makes it taste intensely sweet (Horowitz and Gentili, 1974). Some amino acids taste sweet. Indeed, the commercial sweetener aspartame consists simply of two amino acids: aspartate and phenylalanine.

Recent research suggests that bitterness is not detected by a single receptor. Instead, there appears to be a family of bitterness receptors whose genes are located on chromosomes 5, 7, and 12 (Matsunami, Montmayeur, and Buck, 2000). The apparent existence of at least 24 different bitterness receptors suggests that although different bitter compounds share a common taste quality, they are detected by different means. As we saw, many compounds found in nature that taste bitter to us are poisonous. Rather than entrust detection of these compounds to a single receptor, the process of evolution has given us the ability to detect a wide variety of compounds with different molecular shapes.

Bitterness receptors are coupled with a G protein called **gustducin,** which is very similar in structure to *transducin,* the G protein involved in transduction of photic information in the retina (McLaughlin et al., 1993). When a bitter molecule binds with the receptor, gustducin activates phosphodiesterase, an enzyme that destroys cyclic AMP. Thus, detection of a bitter-tasting molecule by the receptor causes a decrease in intracellular cyclic AMP. In taste receptor cells, as in photoreceptors, it appears that potassium channels in the body of the taste receptor cell are normally held open by the action of cyclic AMP, which permits a constant efflux of K^+ cations. Thus, a fall in the level of cyclic AMP causes potassium channels to close, and the membrane depolarizes. (See *Figure 7.28c*)

Most molecules that taste sweet have a hydrogen ion situated 0.3 nm from a site that will accept a hydrogen ion. Presumably, the sweetness receptor has sites that match these. Sweetness receptors, like bitterness receptors, appear to be coupled to gustducin. Wong, Gannon, and Margolskee (1996) produced a mutation in mice using genetic engineering techniques that permit investigators to "knock out" a particular gene—in this case the gene responsible for the production of gustducin. As expected, the mice did not respond to bitter substances. But in addition, they failed to respond to sweet substances. (They did respond to sour and salty substances.) The binding of sweet-tasting molecules with their receptors causes an increase in the level of cyclic AMP in the cell. This second messenger causes calcium channels to open, and the subsequent influx of calcium causes the cell to release its neurotransmitter (Lindemann, 1996). (See *Figure 7.28d*.)

In recent years, researchers have recognized the existence of a fifth taste quality: *umami*. **Umami,** a Japanese word that means "good taste," refers to the taste of monosodium glutamate (MSG), a substance that is often used as a flavor enhancer in Asian cuisine (Kurihara, 1987;

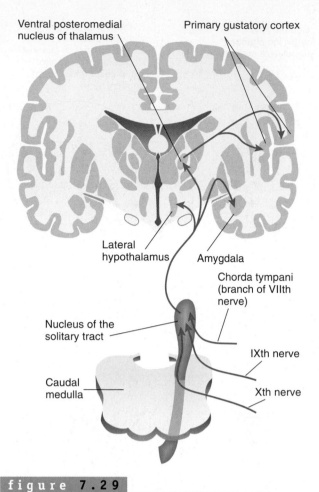

figure 7.29

Neural pathways of the gustatory system.

Scott and Plata-Salaman, 1991). MSG is present naturally in meats, cheeses, and some vegetables. Chaudhari et al. (1996) suggest that a specialized metabotropic glutamate receptor (mGluR4) may be responsible for detecting the taste of glutamate. The investigators found this receptor in taste buds but not in other parts of the tongue. They also reported that rats did not distinguish the taste of MSG from that of a ligand for this receptor, L-AP4. Activation of the mGluR4 receptor appears to close a cation channel, thus depolarizing the membrane (Bigiani et al., 1997).

A sixth taste quality has been proposed. Fats (triglycerides) consist of three fatty acids molecules joined to a molecule of glycerol, a carbohydrate. Because a gram of fat contains almost twice as many calories as a gram of protein or carbohydrate, it seems reasonable that there could have natural selection for receptors that identify fat. The fact that people show such strong preference for foods that are rich in fat suggests that we can detect the presence of this compound. However, until fairly recently, most investigators believed that we identify fats by their texture or "mouth feel" and perhaps by their odor. Now it appears that the tongue may indeed possess taste receptors that detect the presence of fats.

---

gustducin (*gust doo sin*) A G protein that plays a vital role in the transduction of sweetness and bitterness.

umami (*oo mah mee*) The taste sensation produced by glutamate.

chorda tympani A branch of the facial nerve that passes beneath the eardrum; conveys taste information from the anterior part of the tongue and controls the secretion of some salivary glands.

nucleus of the solitary tract A nucleus of the medulla that receives information from visceral organs and from the gustatory system.

Actually, these receptors, if they exist, appear to detect fatty acids. The tongue contains *lingual lipase,* an enzyme that breaks down fat molecules into their constituents (Lohse et al., 1997). Furthermore, the apical membranes of taste buds contain fatty-acid transporters, molecules that permit the entry of fatty acids into the cell (Fukuwatari et al., 1997). Gilbertson et al. (1997), using the patch-clamp method to record from individual taste cells, found that the presence of fatty acids closes a potassium channel that is normally open, depolarizing the membrane. Only essential fatty acids—those that must be obtained from an animal's diet—had this effect, suggesting that the receptors identify the fats that are nutritionally the most important.

The Gustatory Pathway

Gustatory information is transmitted through cranial nerves 7, 9, and 10. Information from the anterior part of the tongue travels through the **chorda tympani,** a branch of the seventh cranial nerve (facial nerve). Taste receptors in the posterior part of the tongue send information through the lingual (tongue) branch of the ninth cranial nerve (glossopharyngeal nerve); the tenth cranial nerve (vagus nerve) carries information from receptors of the palate and epiglottis. The chorda tympani gets its name because it passes through the middle ear just beneath the tympanic membrane. Because of its convenient location, it is accessible to a recording or stimulating electrode. Investigators have even recorded from this nerve during the course of human ear operations.

The first relay station for taste is the **nucleus of the solitary tract,** located in the medulla. In primates the taste-sensitive neurons of this nucleus send their axons to the ventral posteromedial thalamic nucleus, a nucleus that also receives somatosensory information received from the trigeminal nerve (Beckstead, Morse, and Norgren, 1980). Thalamic taste-sensitive neurons send their axons to the primary gustatory cortex, which is located in the base of the frontal cortex and in the insular cortex (Pritchard et al., 1986). Neurons in this region project to the secondary gustatory cortex, located in the caudolateral orbitofrontal cortex (Rolls, Yaxley, and Sienkiewicz, 1990). Unlike most other sense modalities, taste is ipsilaterally represented in the brain—that is, the right side of the tongue projects to the right side of the brain, and the left projects to the left. (See *Figure 7.29.*)

Gustatory information also reaches the amygdala and the hypothalamus and adjacent basal forebrain (Nauta, 1964; Russchen, Amaral, and Price, 1986). Many investigators believe that the hypothalamic pathway plays a role in mediating the reinforcing effects of sweet and salty tastes. In fact, some neurons in the hypothalamus respond to sweet stimuli only when the animal is hungry (Rolls et al., 1986).

Neural Coding of Taste

Almost all fibers in the chorda tympani respond to more than one taste quality, and many respond to changes in temperature as well. However, most show a preference for a particular taste quality. Figure 7.30 shows the average responses of fibers in the rat chorda tympani and glossopharyngeal nerve to sucrose (S), NaCl (N), HCl (H), quinine (Q), and water (W), as recorded by Nowlis and Frank (1977). (See *Figure 7.30.*)

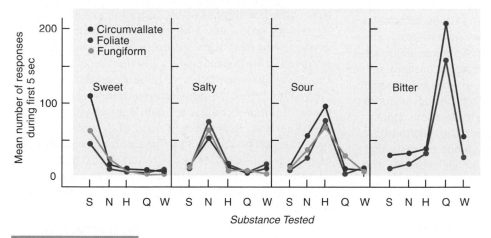

figure   7.30

Mean number of responses recorded from axons in rat chorda tympani and glosso-pharyngeal nerve during the first 5 seconds after the application of sugar (S), NaCl (N), HCl (H), quinine (Q), and water (W). The response characteristics of the axons are categorized as sweet, salty, sour, or bitter.

(From Nowlis, G. H., and Frank, M., in *Olfaction and Taste 6,* edited by J. Le Magnen and P. MacLeod. Washington, DC: Information Retrieval, 1977.)

Scott and his colleagues (Scott et al., 1991; Smith-Swintosky, Plata-Salaman, and Scott, 1991) operated on monkeys, attaching devices that permitted them to record the activity of single neurons in the primary gustatory cortex while the animals were awake and alert. Slightly over 3 percent of the cells they found responded to taste. Others responded to movement of the mouth or to various somatosensory stimuli. Many cells did not respond to any of the stimuli that the investigators tried.

Although the distribution of the taste-sensitive neurons in the nucleus of the solitary tract and the gustatory thalamus resembles that found on the surface of the tongue (Beckstead, Morse, and Norgren, 1980; Scott et al., 1986), their distribution in the gustatory cortex appears to be unsystematic. However, the investigators did find clusters of neurons with similar response characteristics, which suggests that like other regions of sensory cortex, the gustatory cortex may be organized in columns. They found two major groups of taste-sensitive neurons: sweet and salty. They found cells that were responsive to sour and bitter also, but the responses were less distinct. They noted that the minimum concentrations of salty, sweet, sour, and bitter substances that produced responses in these neurons were very close to the minimum concentrations of these substances that human subjects can detect. Recording in the secondary gustatory cortex, Rolls and his colleagues (reviewed by Rolls, 1995a) found both narrowly and broadly tuned neurons responding to single taste qualities or to several of them.

interim summary

Taste receptors detect only five sensory qualities: bitterness, sourness, sweetness, saltiness, and umami (umaminess?). Bitter foods often contain plant alkaloids, many of which are poisonous. Sour foods have usually undergone bacterial fermentation, which can produce toxins. On the other hand, sweet foods (such as fruits) are usually nutritious and safe to eat, and salty foods contain an essential cation: sodium. The fact that people in affluent cultures today tend to ingest excessive amounts of sweet and salty foods suggests that these taste qualities are naturally reinforcing. Umami, the taste of glutamate, identifies proteins.

Saltiness receptors appear to be simple sodium channels. Sourness receptors appear to detect the presence of hydrogen ions, which closes potassium channels located on the cilia and depolarizes the membrane of the cell. Both bitter and sweet tastes are detected by receptors bound to gustducin, a G protein. The structure of molecules that taste bitter appears to include a hydrophobic residue, and some also have a region with a positive charge. Bitter molecules activate phosphodiesterase, which destroys cyclic AMP and closes potassium channels, thus depolarizing the membrane of the cell. Most molecules that taste sweet have a hydrogen ion situated 0.3 nm from a site that will accept a hydrogen ion. Sweet molecules *increase* cyclic AMP levels, which opens calcium channels and thus causes the release of the neurotransmitter. The taste of glutamate (umami) is detected by a particular metabolic glutamate receptor (mGluR4). Fats, an important component of the diet, may also be tasted, at least indirectly. The tongue contains an enzyme that converts some of the fat in the mouth to fatty acids, which appear to be transported into taste cells, where they stimulate specialized receptors.

Gustatory information from the anterior part of the tongue travels through the chorda tympani, a branch of the facial nerve that passes beneath the eardrum on its way to the brain. The posterior part of the tongue sends gustatory information through the glossopharyngeal nerve, and the palate and epiglottis send gustatory information through the vagus nerve. Gustatory information is received by the nucleus of the solitary tract (located in the medulla) and is relayed by the ventral posteromedial thalamus to the primary gustatory cortex in the opercular and insular areas. The caudolateral orbitofrontal cortex contains the secondary gustatory cortex. Gustatory information is also sent to the amygdala, hypothalamus, and basal forebrain.

Olfaction

Olfaction, the second chemical sense, helps us to identify food and avoid food that has spoiled and is unfit to eat. It helps the members of many species to track prey or detect predators and to identify friends, foes, and receptive mates. For humans olfaction is the most enigmatic of all sensory modalities. Odors have a peculiar ability to evoke memories, often vague ones that seem to have occurred in the distant past—a phenomenon that Marcel Proust vividly described in his book *Remembrance of Things Past*. Although people can discriminate among many thousands of different odors, we lack a good vocabulary to describe them. It is relatively easy to describe sights we have seen or sounds we have heard, but the description of an odor is difficult. At best, we can say that it smells like something else. Thus, the olfactory system appears to be specialized for *identifying things*, not for analyzing particular qualities.

The Stimulus

The stimulus for odor (known formally as *odorants*) consists of volatile substances having a molecular weight in the range of approximately 15 to 300. Almost all odorous compounds are lipid soluble and of organic origin.

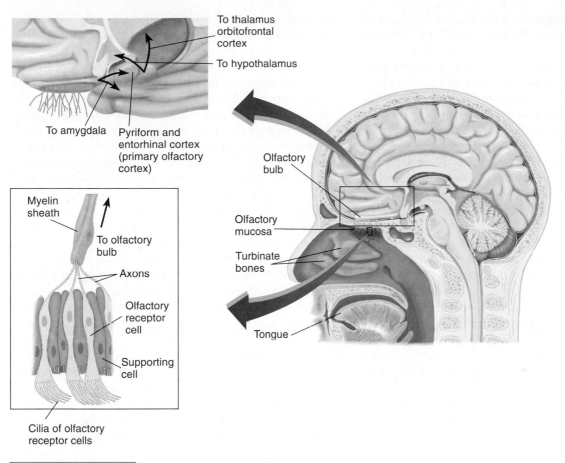

The olfactory system.

However, many substances that meet these criteria have no odor at all, so we still have much to learn about the nature of odorants.

Anatomy of the Olfactory Apparatus

Our six million olfactory receptor cells reside within two patches of mucous membrane (the **olfactory epithelium**), each having an area of about 1 square inch. The olfactory epithelium is located at the top of the nasal cavity, as shown in *Figure 7.31.* Less than 10 percent of the air that enters the nostrils reaches the olfactory epithelium; a sniff is needed to sweep air upward into the nasal cavity so that it reaches the olfactory receptors.

The inset in Figure 7.31 illustrates a group of olfactory receptor cells, along with their supporting cells. (See *inset, Figure 7.31.*) Olfactory receptor cells are bipolar neurons whose cell bodies lie within the olfactory mucosa that lines the *cribriform plate,* a bone at the base of the rostral part of the brain. There is a constant production of new olfactory receptor cells, but their life is considerably longer than those of gustatory receptor cells. Supporting cells contain enzymes that destroy odorant molecules and thus help to prevent them from damaging the olfactory receptor cells.

Olfactory receptor cells send a process toward the surface of the mucosa, which divides into 10 to 20 cilia that penetrate the layer of mucus. Odorous molecules must dissolve in the mucus and stimulate receptor molecules on the olfactory cilia. Approximately 35 bundles of axons, ensheathed by glial cells, enter the skull through small holes in the cribriform ("perforated") plate. The olfactory mucosa also contains free nerve endings of trigeminal nerve axons; these nerve endings presumably mediate sensations of pain that can be produced by sniffing some irritating chemicals, such as ammonia.

olfactory epithelium The epithelial tissue of the nasal sinus that covers the cribriform plate; contains the cilia of the olfactory receptors.

The **olfactory bulbs** lie at the base of the brain on the ends of the stalklike olfactory tracts. Each olfactory receptor cell sends a single axon into the olfactory bulb, where it forms synapses with dendrites of **mitral cells** (named for their resemblance to a bishop's miter). These synapses take place in the complex axonal and dendritic arborizations called **olfactory glomeruli** (from *glomus*, "ball"). There are approximately 10,000 glomeruli, each of which receives input from a bundle of approximately 2000 axons. The axons of the mitral cells travel to the rest of the brain through the olfactory tracts. Some of these axons terminate in other regions of the ipsilateral forebrain; others cross the brain and terminate in the contralateral olfactory bulb.

Olfactory tract axons project directly to the amygdala and to two regions of the limbic cortex: the pyriform cortex and the entorhinal cortex. (See *Figure 7.31.*) The amygdala sends olfactory information to the hypothalamus, the entorhinal cortex sends it to the hippocampus, and the pyriform cortex sends it to the hypothalamus and to the orbitofrontal cortex, via the dorsomedial nucleus of the thalamus (Buck, 1996; Shipley and Ennis, 1996). As you may recall, the orbitofrontal cortex also receives gustatory information; thus, it may be involved in the combining of taste and olfaction into flavor. The hypothalamus also receives a considerable amount of olfactory information, which is probably important for the acceptance or rejection of food and for the olfactory control of reproductive processes seen in many species of mammals.

Most mammals have another organ that responds to chemicals in the environment: the *vomeronasal organ*. Because it plays an important role in animals' responses to pheromones, chemicals produced by other animals that affect reproductive physiology and behavior, its structure and function are described in Chapter 10.

Efferent fibers from several locations in the brain enter the olfactory bulbs. These include acetylcholinergic, noradrenergic, dopaminergic, and serotonergic inputs (Shipley and Ennis, 1996). As we shall see in Chapter 10, the noradrenergic input appears to be involved in olfactory memories, particularly those involved in reproduction.

Transduction of Olfactory Information

For many years researchers have recognized that olfactory cilia contain receptors that are stimulated by molecules of odorants, but the nature of the receptors was unknown. Jones and Reed (1989) identified a particular G protein, which they called G_{olf}. This protein is able to activate an enzyme that catalyzes the synthesis of cyclic AMP, which, in turn, can open sodium channels and depolarize the membrane of the olfactory cell (Nakamura and Gold, 1987; Firestein, Zufall, and Shepherd, 1991; Menco et al., 1992).

As we saw in Chapter 2, G proteins serve as the link between metabotropic receptors and ion channels: When a ligand binds with a metabotropic receptor, the G protein either opens ion channels directly or does so indirectly, by triggering the production of a second messenger. The discovery of G_{olf} suggested that olfactory cilia contained odorant receptors linked to this G protein. Indeed, Buck and Axel (1991) used molecular genetics techniques and discovered a family of genes that code for a family of olfactory receptor proteins. So far, olfactory receptor genes have been isolated in more than twelve species of vertebrates, including mammals, birds, and amphibians (Mombaerts, 1999). In humans there appear to be between five hundred and one thousand different receptors, each sensitive to different odorants (Ressler, Sullivan, and Buck, 1994a). Thus, molecules of odorant bind with receptors, and the G proteins coupled to these receptors open sodium channels and produce depolarizing receptor potentials.

Perception of Specific Odors

For many years recognition of specific odors has been an enigma. Humans can recognize up to ten thousand different odorants, and other animals can probably recognize even more of them (Shepherd, 1994). Even if we have several hundred (or even one thousand) different olfactory receptors, that leaves many odors unaccounted for. And every year, chemists synthesize new chemicals, many with odors unlike those that anyone has previously detected. How can we use a relatively small number of receptors to detect so many different odorants?

Before I answer this question, we should look more closely at the relation between receptors, olfactory neurons, and the glomeruli to which the axons of these neurons project. First, the cilia of each olfactory neuron contain only one type of receptor (Nef et al., 1992; Vassar, Ngai, and Axel, 1993). As we saw, each glomerulus receives information from approximately two thousand different olfactory receptor cells. Using in situ hybridization methods to identify particular receptor proteins in individual cells, Ressler, Sullivan, and Buck (1994) discovered that although a given glomerulus receives information from approximately two thousand different olfactory receptor cells, each of these cells contains the same type of receptor molecule. Thus, there are as many types of

---

olfactory bulb The protrusion at the end of the olfactory tract; receives input from the olfactory receptors.

mitral cell A neuron located in the olfactory bulb that receives information from olfactory receptors; axons of mitral cells bring information to the rest of the brain.

olfactory glomerulus (*glow mare you luss*) A bundle of dendrites of mitral cells and the associated terminal buttons of the axons of olfactory receptors.

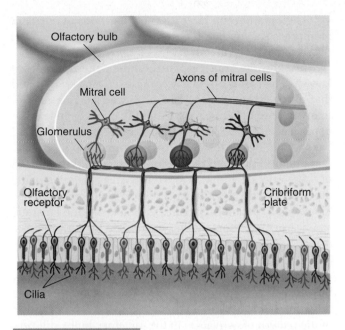

Details of the connections of olfactory receptor cells with the glomeruli of the olfactory bulb. Each glomerulus receives information from only one type of receptor cell. Olfactory receptor cells of different colors contain different types of receptor molecules.

glomeruli as there are types of receptor molecules. Furthermore, the location of particular types of glomeruli (defined by the type of receptor that sends information to them) appears to be the same in each of the olfactory bulbs in a given animal and may even be the same from one animal to another. (See *Figure 7.32*.)

An ingenious study by Zou et al. (2001) investigated the specificity of olfactory information in the pathway from olfactory receptors to olfactory glomeruli to the olfactory cortex. To accomplish this feat, they inserted a gene for a transneuronal tracer protein (barley lectin) into the DNA of mice adjacent to two different olfactory receptor genes. Because of the location of this gene, it was turned on only in olfactory receptor cells that produced one of the two selected receptor genes. Thus, two different types of olfactory receptor cells expressed barley lectin. This protein is transmitted from one neuron to others with which it forms synapses. Thus, it was carried to glomeruli and from there to a third set of neurons in olfactory cortex. The investigators found that just as retinotopic information is maintained in the visual system and tonotopic information is maintained in the auditory system, "olfactotopic" information is maintained in the olfactory system. That is, the particular glomeruli, which receiving information from particular olfactory receptors, send this information to specific regions of olfactory cortex. These regions appeared to occur in identical locations in different mice.

Now let's get back to the question I just posed: How can we use a relatively small number of receptors to detect so many different odorants? The answer is that a particular odorant binds to more than one receptor. Thus, because a given glomerulus receives information from only one type of receptor, different odorants produce different *patterns* of activity in different glomeruli. Recognizing a particular odor, then, is a matter of recognizing a particular pattern of activity in the glomeruli. The task of chemical recognition is transformed into a task of spatial recognition.

Figure 7.33 illustrates this process (Malnic et al., 1999). The left side of the figure shows the shapes of eight hypothetical odorants. The right side shows four hypothetical odorant receptor molecules. If a portion of the odorant molecule fits the binding site of the receptor molecule, it will activate it and stimulate the olfactory neuron. As you can see, each odorant molecule fits the binding site of at least one of the receptors and in most cases fits more than one of them. Notice also that the *pattern* of receptors activated by each of the eight odorants is different, which

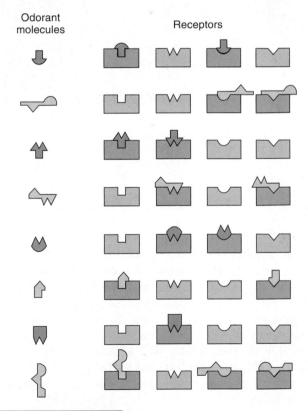

A hypothetical explanation of coding of olfactory information. Different odorant molecules attach to different combinations of receptor molecules. (Activated receptor molecules are shown in blue.) Unique patterns of activation represent particular odorants.

(Adapted from Malnic, B., Hirono, J., Sato, T., and Buck, L. B. *Cell,* 1999, *96,* 713–723.)

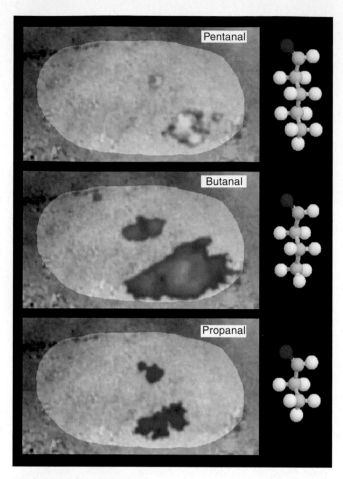

figure 7.34

Patterns of activation of glomeruli in the rat olfactory bulb produced by exposure of the olfactory mucosa to three different odorants.

(From Rubin, B. D., and Katz, L. C. *Neuron,* 1999, *23,* 499–511.)

means that if we know which pattern of receptors is activated, we know which odorant is present. Of course, even though a particular odorant might bind with several different types of receptor molecules, it might not bind equally well with each of them. For example, it might bind very well with one receptor molecule, moderately well with another, weakly with another, and so on. (See *Figure 7.33*.) As we just saw, the spatial pattern of "olfactotopic" information is maintained in the olfactory cortex. Presumably, the brain recognizes particular odors by recognizing different patterns of activation there.

Rubin and Katz (1999) obtained evidence to support this model. Figure 7.34 shows the patterns of activity in the olfactory bulbs produced by exposing the olfactory mucosa to three different odorants, pentanal, butanal, and propanal. The molecular structures of these odorants is shown to the right. The patterns were obtained by means of computerized optical analysis of the exposed surface of the olfactory bulbs. The small spots of color represent indi-

vidual glomeruli; the larger spots are groups of adjacent glomeruli. As you can see, the three odorants produced different patterns of activity. (See *Figure 7.34*.)

Just how the brain recognizes these patterns is not yet known. The task is obviously complex. Cain (1988) noted that although most odors are produced by mixtures of many different chemicals, we identify odors as belonging to particular objects. For example, the smells of coffee, fried bacon, and cigarette smoke are each made of up to several hundred different types of molecules. Although each of these odors is a mixture, we recognize them as being unique—We do not detect the individual components. However, if the smells of coffee, fried bacon, and cigarette smoke are mixed together (as they might be at a breakfast counter that permits smoking), we still recognize all three odors, even though each one of them is itself a mixture!

Another consideration is that animals whose olfactory bulbs are mostly destroyed can still discriminate between different odors (Lu and Slotnick, 1998). Clearly, a portion of the pattern of activation in the olfactory bulbs still provides enough information for the animals to perform olfactory discriminations. Whether the odors still smell the same to the animals after the surgery (that is, whether the destruction of part of the pattern changes the way particular odorants are perceived) is an open question.

interim summary

The olfactory receptors consist of bipolar neurons located in the olfactory epithelium that lines the roof of the nasal sinuses, on the bone that underlies the frontal lobes. The receptors send processes toward the surface of the mucosa, which divide into cilia. The membranes of these cilia contain receptors that detect aromatic molecules dissolved in the air that sweeps past the olfactory mucosa. The axons of the olfactory receptors pass through the perforations of the cribriform plate into the olfactory bulbs, where they form synapses in the glomeruli with the dendrites of the mitral cells. These neurons send axons through the olfactory tracts to the brain, principally to the amygdala, the pyriform cortex, and the entorhinal cortex. The hippocampus, hypothalamus, and orbitofrontal cortex receive olfactory information indirectly,

Aromatic molecules produce membrane potentials by interacting with a newly discovered family of receptor molecules, which may number up to one thousand. These receptor molecules are coupled to a special G protein, G_{olf}. When an odorant molecule bind with and stimulates one of these receptors, G_{olf} catalyzes the synthesis of cyclic AMP, which opens sodium channels and depolarizes the membrane. Each glomerulus receives information from only one type of olfactory receptor, and "olfactotopic" coding is maintained all the way to the olfactory cortex. This means that the task of detecting different odors is a spatial one; the brain recognizes odors by means of the patterns of activity created in the olfactory cortex.

Suggested Readings

Audition

Ehret, G., and Romand, R. *The Central Auditory System.* New York: Oxford University Press, 1997.

Moore, B. C. J. *Hearing: Handbook of Perception and Cognition,* 2nd ed. San Diego: Academic Press, 1995.

Yost, W. A. *Fundamentals of Hearing: An Introduction,* 3rd ed. San Diego: Academic Press, 1994.

Vestibular System

Cohen, B., Tomko, D. L., and Guedry, F. E. *Sensing and Controlling Motion: Vestibular and Sensorimotor Function.* New York: New York Academy of Sciences, 1992.

Somatosenses

Bromm, B., and Desmedt, J. E. *Pain and the Brain: From Nociception to Cognition.* New York: Raven Press, 1995.

García-Añoveros, J., and Corey, D. P. The molecules of mechanosensation. *Annual Review of Neuroscience,* 1997, *20,* 567–594.

Kruger, L. *Pain and Touch: Handbook of Perception and Cognition,* 2nd ed. San Diego: Academic Press, 1996.

Melzak, R. Phantom limbs. *Scientific American,* 1992, *266(4),* 120–126.

Olfaction and Gustation

Doty, R. L. Olfaction. *Annual Review of Psychology,* 2001, *52,* 423–452.

Herness, M. S., and Gilbertson, T. A. Cellular mechanisms of taste transduction. *Annual Review of Physiology,* 1999, *61,* 873–900.

Hildebrand, J. G., and Shepherd, G. M. Mechanisms of olfactory discrimination: Converging evidence for common principles across phyla. *Annual Review of Neuroscience,* 1997, *20,* 595–632.

Suggested Web Sites

Somatosensory Pathways

http://thalamus.wustl.edu/course/body.html

This site contains a tutorial on somatosensory pathways.

Relief of Pain and Suffering

http://www.library.ucla.edu/libraries/biomed/his/PainExhibit/

The measurement and treatment of pain is the focus of this site. Topics covered on the site include pain measurement, analgesia and anesthesia, and the phantom limb phenomenon.

The Nature of Pain

http://msnews.org/mchenryone.htm

The focus of this site is a general tutorial on pain.

Auditory System Function

http://penguin.d.umn.edu/undergrad/audsysfunctweb/sld001.htm

This site provides access to a PowerPoint slide set dealing with auditory system structure and function (30 slides).

Somatosensory Mapping

http://alpha.nmrlab.hscsyr.edu/nmr_lab/jake_home.html

This site contains an fMRI image showing the mapping of somatosensory cortex. The site also contains an image of a homunculus.

chapter 8

Control of Movement

Francis Picabia, *Dances at the Spring (Danses à la Source)*, 1912. © 2003 Artists Rights Society (ARS), New York/ADAGP, Paris. Digital Image © The Museum of Modern Art/Licensed by SCALA/Art Resource, NY.

outline

■ **Muscles**
Skeletal Muscle
Smooth Muscle
Cardiac Muscle
Interim Summary

■ **Reflex Control of Movement**
The Monosynaptic Stretch Reflex

The Gamma Motor System
Polysynaptic Reflexes
Interim Summary

■ **Control of Movement by the Brain**
Organization of Motor Cortex
Cortical Control of Movement:
    The Descending Pathways

Deficits of Verbally Controlled
    Movements: The Apraxias
The Basal Ganglia
The Cerebellum
The Reticular Formation
Interim Summary

Although Mr. J., a 48-year-old photographer, had just had a severe stroke that damaged much of his left parietal lobe, he was still a pleasant, cheerful, and likable man. His neurologist, Dr. R., introduced him to us, and he sat down in a chair in front of the room.

"Mr. J., will you please show us how to wave hello?" asked Dr. R. The patient made a clumsy movement with his right hand and smiled apologetically. "Hold up your index finger, like this," said Dr. R., pointing toward the ceiling. Mr. J. held up his hand, pursed his lips together, and, with a determined look on his face, clenched and unclenched his fist. Clearly, he was trying as hard as he could to point with his index finger, but he just could not move it without also moving his other fingers. "Can you hold your hand like this?" asked Dr. R., who held his hand in front of himself, palm down. Mr. J. watched him and, with obvious effort, copied the movement. "That's good! Now turn your hand over." Mr. J. grunted and began slapping his hand against his thigh. It looked to us as if he were trying to make the requested movement, but the wrong one was coming in its place. Dr. R. took hold of Mr. J.'s hand and, with great effort (Mr. J. was a strong man), managed to turn it over. "Good, now turn it over again." Mr. J. began slapping his thigh with the back of his hand. Several times, Dr. R. helped him turn his hand over; but despite his efforts, Mr. J. was unable to do so by himself. He appeared to have very poor control of his movements.

Dr. R. addressed the rest of us. "You can see that Mr. J.'s apraxia is severe. But now watch this." He turned to Mr. J. "Will you please take off your glasses?" Mr. J. reached up to his glasses, took hold of the earpieces, and smoothly removed them. "Fine. Now put them back on." He did so. Dr. R. then asked, "Do you know what a hammer is?" "Sure," answered Mr. J. "Okay, will you show us how you would use a hammer?" Mr. J. looked at his hand and then began slapping it against his thigh, as he had done before. "Okay, you can stop." Mr. J. continued slapping his thigh, harder and harder. "Stop! That's enough." With great effort Mr. J. finally ceased making the movements. "Now let's try this," said Dr. R., who placed a block of wood on the table in front of Mr. J. and handed him a hammer and a nail. "Can you pound the nail into the wood?" Mr. J. held the nail upright with the fingers of his left hand, grasped the hammer with his right hand, and skillfully drove the nail into the wood.

After Mr. J. had left, Dr. R. said, "Mr. J.'s problem is not that he cannot make skilled movements, but that he cannot make these movements when we ask him to. He can manipulate his glasses and he can use a hammer, but he can't make even the simplest voluntary movements out of context. Did you notice that he waved to you when I introduced him, even though he couldn't do so when I asked him to show us how to wave 'hello'?" We sheepishly admitted that we hadn't been that observant. "The movement was an automatic one that he had learned to make long ago, and it was triggered by the fact that he was meeting other people. The parietal lobe is involved in the control of movements—especially sequences of movements—that are not dictated by the context. Thus, he finds it almost impossible to follow verbal requests to make arbitrary movements."

S o far, I have described the nature of neural communication, the basic structure of the nervous system, and the physiology of perception. Now it is time to consider the ultimate function of the nervous system: control of behavior. The brain is the organ that moves the muscles. It does many other things, but all of them are secondary to making our bodies move. This chapter describes the principles of muscular contraction, some reflex circuitry within the spinal cord, and the means by which the brain initiates behaviors. The rest of the book describes the physiology of particular categories of behaviors and the ways in which our behaviors can be modified by experience.

Muscles

Mammals have three types of muscles: skeletal muscle, smooth muscle, and cardiac muscle.

Skeletal Muscle

Skeletal muscles are the ones that move us (our skeletons) around and thus are responsible for our behavior. Most of them are attached to bones at each end and move the bones when they contract. (Exceptions include eye muscles and some abdominal muscles, which are attached to bone at one end only.) Muscles are fastened to bones via *tendons*, strong bands of connective tissue. Several different classes of movement can be accomplished by the skeletal muscles, but I will refer principally to two of them: flexion and extension. Contraction of a flexor muscle produces **flexion,** the drawing in of a limb. **Extension,** which

skeletal muscle One of the striated muscles attached to bones.

flexion A movement of a limb that tends to bend its joints; opposite of extension.

extension A movement of a limb that tends to straighten its joints; the opposite of flexion.

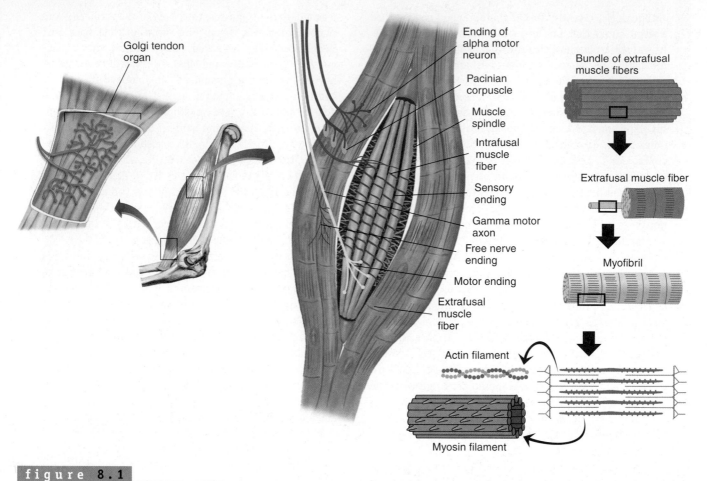

f i g u r e   8 . 1

Anatomy of skeletal muscle.

is the opposite movement, is produced by contraction of extensor muscles. These are the so-called *antigravity muscles*—the ones we use to stand up. When a four-legged animal lifts a paw, the movement is one of flexion. Putting it back down is one of extension. Sometimes, people say that they "flex" their muscles. This is an incorrect use of the term. Muscles *contract;* limbs *flex*. Bodybuilders show off their arm muscles by simultaneously contracting the flexor and extensor muscles of that limb.

Anatomy

The detailed structure of a skeletal muscle is shown in *Figure 8.1.* As you can see, it consists of two types of muscle fibers. The **extrafusal muscle fibers** are served by axons of the **alpha motor neurons.** Contraction of these fibers provides the muscle's motive force. The **intrafusal muscle fibers** are specialized sensory organs that are served by two axons, one sensory and one motor. These organs are also called *muscle spindles* because of their shape. In fact, the Latin word *fusus* means "spindle"; hence, *intrafusal* muscle fibers are found within the spindles, and *extrafusal* muscle fibers are found outside them.

The central region (*capsule*) of the intrafusal muscle fiber contains sensory endings that are sensitive to stretch applied to the muscle fiber. Actually, there are two types of intrafusal muscle fibers, but for simplicity's sake only one kind is shown here. The efferent axon of the **gamma motor neuron** causes the intrafusal muscle fiber to contract; however, this contraction contributes an insubstantial amount of force. As we will see, the function of this

extrafusal muscle fiber One of the muscle fibers that are responsible for the force exerted by contraction of a skeletal muscle.

alpha motor neuron A neuron whose axon forms synapses with extrafusal muscle fibers of a skeletal muscle; activation contracts the muscle fibers.

intrafusal muscle fiber A muscle fiber that functions as a stretch receptor, arranged parallel to the extrafusal muscle fibers, thus detecting changes in muscle length.

gamma motor neuron A neuron whose axons form synapses with intrafusal muscle fibers.

contraction is to modify the sensitivity of the fiber's afferent ending to stretch.

A single myelinated axon of an alpha motor neuron serves several extrafusal muscle fibers. In primates the number of muscle fibers served by a single axon varies considerably, depending on the precision with which the muscle can be controlled. In muscles that move the fingers or eyes the ratio can be less than one to ten; in muscles that move the leg it can be one to several hundred. An alpha motor neuron, its axon, and associated extrafusal muscle fibers constitute a **motor unit.**

A single muscle fiber consists of a bundle of **myofibrils,** each of which consists of overlapping strands of **actin** and **myosin.** Note the small protrusions on the myosin filaments; these structures (*myosin cross bridges*) are the motile elements that interact with the actin filaments and produce muscular contractions. (See *Figure 8.1*.) The regions in which the actin and myosin filaments overlap produce dark stripes, or *striations;* hence, skeletal muscle is often referred to as **striated muscle.**

The Physical Basis of Muscular Contraction

The synapse between the terminal button of an efferent neuron and the membrane of a muscle fiber is called a **neuromuscular junction.** The terminal buttons of the neurons synapse on **motor endplates,** located in grooves along the surface of the muscle fibers. When an axon fires, acetylcholine is liberated by the terminal buttons and produces a depolarization of the postsynaptic membrane—an **endplate potential.** The endplate potential is much larger than an excitatory postsynaptic potential in synapses between neurons; an endplate potential *always* causes the muscle fiber to fire, propagating the potential along its length. This action potential induces a contraction, or *twitch,* of the muscle fiber.

The depolarization of a muscle fiber opens the gates of voltage-dependent calcium channels, permitting calcium ions to enter the cytoplasm. This event triggers the contraction. Calcium acts as a cofactor that permits the myofibrils to extract energy from the ATP that is present in the cytoplasm. The myosin cross bridges alternately attach to the actin strands, bend in one direction, detach themselves, bend back, reattach to the actin at a point farther down the strand, and so on. Thus, the cross bridges "row" along the actin filaments. Figure 8.2 illustrates this rowing sequence and shows how this sequence results in shortening the muscle fiber. (See *Figure 8.2*.)

A single impulse of a motor neuron produces a single twitch of a muscle fiber. The physical effects of the twitch last considerably longer than will the action potential, because of the elasticity of the muscle and the time required to rid the cell of calcium. (Like sodium, calcium is actively extruded by a pump situated in the membrane.)

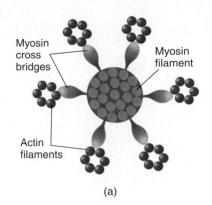

(a)

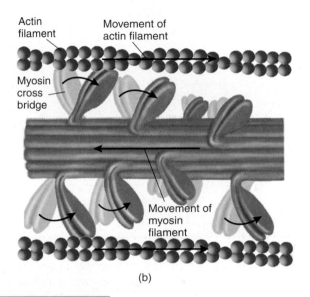

(b)

figure 8.2

The mechanism by which muscles contract. (a) Cross section through a myosin filament and the surrounding actin filaments. (b) The myosin cross bridges performing "rowing" movements, which cause the actin and myosin filaments to move relative to each other. For the sake of clarity, only two actin filaments are shown.

---

motor unit A motor neuron and its associated muscle fibers.

myofibril An element of muscle fibers that consists of overlapping strands of actin and myosin; responsible for muscular contractions.

actin One of the proteins (with myosin) that provide the physical basis for muscular contraction.

myosin One of the proteins (with actin) that provide the physical basis for muscular contraction.

striated muscle Skeletal muscle; muscle that contains striations.

neuromuscular junction The synapse between the terminal buttons of an axon and a muscle fiber.

motor endplate The postsynaptic membrane of a neuromuscular junction.

endplate potential The postsynaptic potential that occurs in the motor endplate in response to release of acetylcholine by the terminal button.

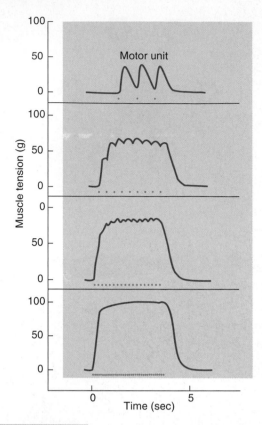

figure 8.3

Action potentials and contractions. A rapid succession of action potentials can cause a muscle fiber to produce a sustained contraction. Each dot represents an individual action potential.

(Adapted from Devanandan, M. S., Eccles, R. M., and Westerman, R. A. *Journal of Physiology (London)*, 1965, *178*, 359–367.)

Figure 8.3 shows how the physical effects of a series of action potentials can overlap, causing a sustained contraction by the muscle fiber. A single motor unit in a leg muscle of a cat can raise a 100-gram weight, which attests to the remarkable strength of the contractile mechanism. (See *Figure 8.3*.)

As you know from your own experience, muscular contraction is not an all-or-nothing phenomenon, as are the twitches of the constituent muscle fibers. Obviously, the strength of a muscular contraction is determined by the average rate of firing of the various motor units. If, at a given moment, many units are firing, the contraction will be forceful. If few are firing, the contraction will be weak.

Sensory Feedback from Muscles

As we saw, the intrafusal muscle fibers contain sensory endings that are sensitive to stretch. The intrafusal muscle fibers are arranged in parallel with the extrafusal muscle fibers. Therefore, they are stretched when the muscle lengthens and are relaxed when it shortens. Thus, even though these afferent neurons are *stretch receptors,* they serve as *muscle length detectors.* This distinction is important. Stretch receptors are also located within the tendons, in the **Golgi tendon organ.** These receptors detect the total amount of stretch exerted by the muscle, through its tendons, on the bones to which the muscle is attached. The stretch receptors of the Golgi tendon organ encode the degree of stretch by the rate of firing. They respond not to a muscle's length but to how hard it is pulling. In contrast, the receptors on intrafusal muscle fibers detect muscle length, not tension.

Figure 8.4 shows the response of afferent axons of the muscle spindles and Golgi tendon organ to various types of movements. Figure 8.4(a) shows the effects of passive lengthening of muscles, the kind of movement that would be seen if your forearm, held in a completely relaxed fashion, were slowly lowered by someone who was supporting it. The rate of firing of one type of muscle spindle afferent neuron (MS_1) increases, while the activity of the afferent of the Golgi tendon organ remains unchanged. (See *Figure 8.4a*.) Figure 8.4(b) shows the results when the arm is dropped quickly; note that this time the second type of muscle spindle afferent neuron (MS_2) fires a rapid burst of impulses. This fiber, then, signals rapid changes in muscle length. (See *Figure 8.4b*.) Figure 8.4(c) shows what would happen if a weight were suddenly dropped into your hand while your forearm was held parallel to the ground. Neurons MS_1 and MS_2 (especially MS_2, which responds to rapid changes in muscle length) briefly fire, because your arm lowers briefly and then comes back to the original position. The Golgi tendon organ, monitoring the strength of contraction, fires in proportion to the stress on the muscle, so it increases its rate of firing as soon as the weight is added. (See *Figure 8.4c*.)

Smooth Muscle

Our bodies contain two types of **smooth muscle,** both of which are controlled by the autonomic nervous system. *Multiunit smooth muscles* are found in large arteries, around hair follicles (where they produce *piloerection,* or fluffing of fur), and in the eye (controlling lens adjustment and pupillary dilation). This type of smooth muscle is normally inactive, but it will contract in response to neural stimulation or to certain hormones. In contrast,

Golgi tendon organ The receptor organ at the junction of the tendon and muscle that is sensitive to stretch.

smooth muscle Nonstriated muscle innervated by the autonomic nervous system, found in the walls of blood vessels, in the reproductive tracts, in sphincters, within the eye, in the digestive system, and around hair follicles.

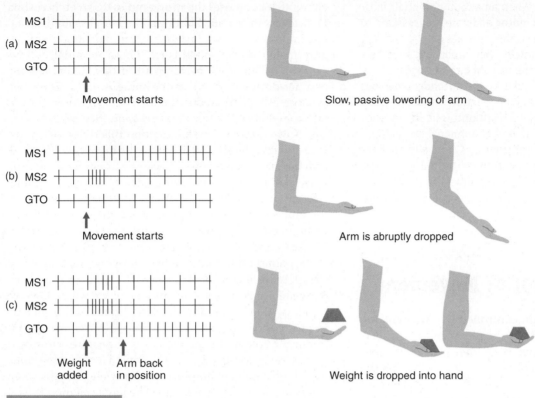

MS1
(a) MS2
GTO

↑
Movement starts

Slow, passive lowering of arm

MS1
(b) MS2
GTO

↑
Movement starts

Arm is abruptly dropped

MS1
(c) MS2
GTO

↑ Weight added   ↑ Arm back in position

Weight is dropped into hand

figure 8.4

Effects of arm movements on the firing of muscle and tendon afferent axons. (a) Slow passive extension of the arm. (b) Rapid extension of the arm. (c) Addition of a weight to an arm held in a horizontal position. MS_1 and MS_2 are two types of muscle spindles; GTO is an afferent fiber from the Golgi tendon organ.

single-unit smooth muscles normally contract in a rhythmical fashion. Some of these cells spontaneously produce *pacemaker potentials,* which we can regard as self-initiated excitatory postsynaptic potentials. These slow potentials elicit action potentials, which are propagated by adjacent smooth muscle fibers, causing a wave of muscular contraction. The efferent nerve supply (and various hormones) can modulate the rhythmical rate, increasing or decreasing it. Single-unit smooth muscles are found chiefly in the gastrointestinal system, uterus, and small blood vessels.

Cardiac Muscle

As its name implies, **cardiac muscle** is found in the heart. This type of muscle looks somewhat like striated muscle but acts like single-unit smooth muscle. The heart beats regularly, even if it is denervated. Neural activity and certain hormones (especially the catecholamines) serve to modulate the heart rate. A group of cells in the *pacemaker* of the heart are rhythmically active and initiate the contractions of cardiac muscle that constitute the heartbeat.

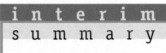

interim summary

Muscles

Our bodies possess skeletal muscle, smooth muscle, and cardiac muscle. Skeletal muscles contain extrafusal muscle fibers, which provide the force of contraction. The alpha motor neurons form synapses with the extrafusal muscle fibers and control their contraction. Skeletal muscles also contain intrafusal muscle fibers, which detect changes in muscle length. The length of the intrafusal muscle fiber, and hence its sensitivity to increases in muscle length, is controlled by the gamma motor neuron. Besides the intrafusal muscle fibers, the muscles contain stretch receptors in the Golgi tendon organs, located at the ends of the muscles.

The force of muscular contraction is provided by long protein molecules called actin and myosin, arranged in

---

cardiac muscle The muscle responsible for the contraction of the heart.

overlapping parallel arrays. When an action potential, initiated by the synapse at the motor endplate, causes Ca^{2+} to enter the muscle fiber, the myofibrils extract energy from ATP and cause a twitch of the muscle fiber, producing a ratchet-like "rowing" movement of the myosin cross bridges.

Smooth muscle is controlled by the autonomic nervous system through direct neural connections and indirectly through the endocrine system. Multiunit smooth muscles contract only in response to neural or hormonal stimulation. In contrast, single-unit smooth muscles normally contract rhythmically, but their rate is controlled by the autonomic nervous system. Cardiac muscle also contracts spontaneously, and its rate of contraction, too, is influenced by the autonomic nervous system.

Reflex Control of Movement

Although behaviors are controlled by the brain, the spinal cord possesses a certain degree of autonomy. Particular kinds of somatosensory stimuli can elicit rapid responses through neural connections located within the spinal cord. These reflexes constitute the simplest level of motor integration.

The Monosynaptic Stretch Reflex

The activity of the simplest functional neural pathway in the body is easy to demonstrate. Sit on a surface high enough to allow your legs to dangle freely, and have someone lightly tap your patellar tendon, just below the kneecap. This stimulus briefly stretches your quadriceps muscle, on the top of your thigh. The stretch causes the muscle to contract, which makes your leg kick forward. (I am sure few of you will bother with this demonstration, because you are already familiar with it; physical examinations often include a test of this reflex.) The time interval between the tendon tap and the start of the leg extension is about 50 milliseconds. That interval is too short for the involvement of the brain; it would take considerably longer for sensory information to be relayed to the brain and for motor information to be relayed back. For example, suppose a person is asked to move his or her leg as quickly as possible after being *touched* on the knee. This response would not be reflexive but would involve sensory and motor mechanisms of the brain. In this case the interval between the stimulus and the start of the response would be several times greater than the time required for the patellar reflex.

Obviously, the patellar reflex as such has no utility; no selective advantage is bestowed on animals that kick a limb when a tendon is tapped. However, if a more natural stimulus is applied, the utility of this mechanism becomes apparent. Figure 8.5 shows the effects of placing a weight in a person's hand. This time I have included a piece of the spinal cord, with its roots, to show the neural

circuit that composes the **monosynaptic stretch reflex.** First, follow the circuit: Starting at the muscle spindle, afferent impulses are conducted to terminal buttons in the gray matter of the spinal cord. These terminal buttons synapse on an alpha motor neuron that innervates the extrafusal muscle fibers of the same muscle. Only one synapse is encountered along the route from receptor to effector—hence the term *monosynaptic.* (See *Figure 8.5.*)

Now consider a useful function this reflex performs. If the weight the person is holding is increased, the forearm begins to move down. This movement lengthens the muscle and increases the firing rate of the muscle spindle afferent neurons, whose terminal buttons then stimulate the alpha motor neurons, increasing their rate of firing. Consequently, the strength of the muscular contraction increases, and the arm pulls the weight up. (See *Figure 8.5.*)

Another important role played by the monosynaptic stretch reflex is control of posture. To stand, we must keep our center of gravity above our feet, or we will fall. As we stand, we tend to oscillate back and forth and from side to side. Our vestibular sacs and our visual system play an important role in the maintenance of posture. However, these systems are aided by the activity of the monosynaptic stretch reflex. For example, consider what happens when a person begins to lean forward. The large calf muscle (gastrocnemius) is stretched, and this stretching elicits compensatory muscular contraction that pushes the toes down, thus restoring upright posture. (See *Figure 8.6.*)

The Gamma Motor System

The muscle spindles are very sensitive to changes in muscle length; they will increase their rate of firing when the muscle is lengthened by a very small amount. The interesting thing is that this detection mechanism is adjustable. Remember that the ends of the intrafusal muscle fibers can be contracted by activity of the associated efferent axons of the gamma motor neurons; their rate of firing determines the degree of contraction. When the muscle spindles are relaxed, they are relatively insensitive to stretch. However, when the gamma motor neurons are active, they become shorter and hence become much more sensitive to changes in muscle length. This property of adjustable sensitivity simplifies the role of the brain in controlling movement. The more control that can occur in the spinal cord, the fewer messages must be sent to and from the brain.

We already saw that the afferent axons of the muscle spindle help to maintain limb position even when the load carried by the limb is altered. Efferent control of the muscle spindles permits these muscle length detectors to assist

monosynaptic stretch reflex A reflex in which a muscle contracts in response to its being quickly stretched; involves a sensory neuron and a motor neuron, with one synapse between them.

figure **8.5**

The monosynaptic stretch reflex.
(a) Neural circuit. (b) A useful function.

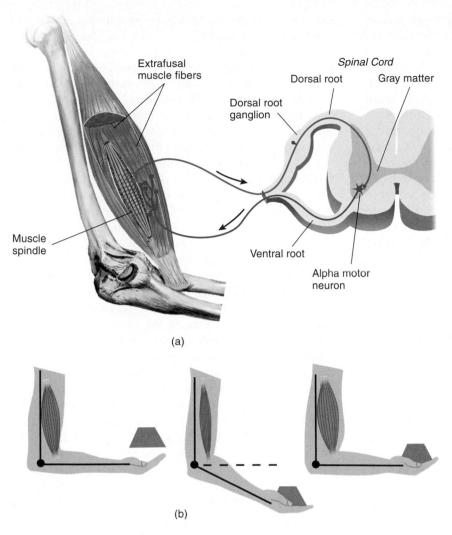

Extrafusal
muscle fibers

Spinal Cord

Dorsal root

Gray matter

Dorsal root
ganglion

Muscle
spindle

Ventral root

Alpha motor
neuron

(a)

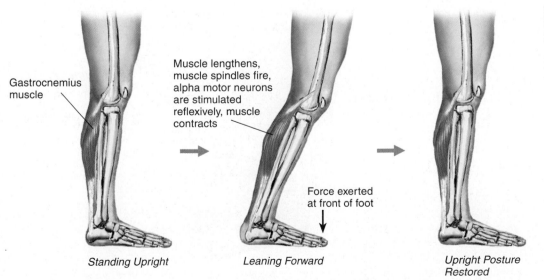

(b)

in changes in limb position as well. Consider a single muscle spindle. When its efferent axon is completely silent, the spindle is completely relaxed and extended. As the firing rate of the efferent axon increases, the spindle gets shorter and shorter. If, simultaneously, the rest of the entire muscle also gets shorter, there will be no stretch on the central region that contains the sensory endings, and the afferent axon will not respond. However, if the muscle spindle contracts faster than does the muscle as a whole, there will be a considerable amount of afferent activity.

Gastrocnemius
muscle

Muscle lengthens,
muscle spindles fire,
alpha motor neurons
are stimulated
reflexively, muscle
contracts

Force exerted
at front of foot

Standing Upright   *Leaning Forward*   *Upright Posture
Restored*

figure **8.6**

The role of the
monosynaptic stretch
reflex in postural control.

The motor system makes use of this phenomenon in the following way: When commands from the brain are issued to move a limb, both the alpha motor neurons and the gamma motor neurons are activated. The alpha motor neurons start the muscle contracting. If there is little resistance, both the extrafusal and intrafusal muscle fibers will contract at approximately the same rate, and little activity will be seen from the afferent axons of the muscle spindle. However, if the limb meets with resistance, the intrafusal muscle fibers will shorten more than the extrafusal muscle fibers, and hence sensory axons will begin to fire and cause the monosynaptic stretch reflex to strengthen the contraction. Thus, the brain makes use of the gamma motor system in moving the limbs. By establishing a rate of firing in the *gamma motor system,* the brain controls the length of the muscle spindles and, indirectly, the length of the entire muscle.

Polysynaptic Reflexes

The monosynaptic stretch reflex is the only spinal reflex we know of that involves only one synapse. All others are *polysynaptic.* Examples include relatively simple ones, such as limb withdrawal in response to noxious stimulation, and relatively complex ones, such as the ejaculation of semen. Spinal reflexes do not exist in isolation; they are normally controlled by the brain. For example, Chapter 2 described how inhibition from the brain can prevent a person from dropping a hot casserole dish, even though the painful stimuli received by the fingers serve to cause reflexive extension of the fingers. This section will describe some general principles by which polysynaptic spinal reflexes operate.

Before I begin the discussion, I should mention that the simple circuit diagrams used here (including the one you just looked at in Figure 8.6) are much too simple. Reflex circuits are typically shown as a single chain of neurons, but in reality most reflexes involve thousands of neurons. Each axon usually synapses on many neurons, and each neuron receives synapses from many different axons.

As we previously saw, the afferent axons from the Golgi tendon organ serve as detectors of muscle stretch. There are two populations of afferent axons from the Golgi tendon organ, with different sensitivities to stretch. The more sensitive afferent axons tell the brain how hard the muscle is pulling. The less sensitive ones have an additional function. Their terminal buttons synapse on spinal cord interneurons—neurons that reside entirely within the gray matter of the spinal cord and serve to interconnect other spinal neurons. These interneurons synapse on the alpha motor neurons serving the same muscle. The terminal buttons liberate glycine and hence produce inhibitory postsynaptic potentials on the motor neurons. (See *Figure 8.7.*) The function of this reflex pathway is to decrease the strength of muscular contraction when there is danger of damage to the tendons or bones to which the muscles are attached. Weight lifters can lift heavier weights if their Golgi tendon organs are deactivated with injections of a local anesthetic, but they run the risk of pulling the tendon away from the bone or even breaking the bone.

The discovery of the inhibitory Golgi tendon organ reflex provided the first real evidence of neural inhibition,

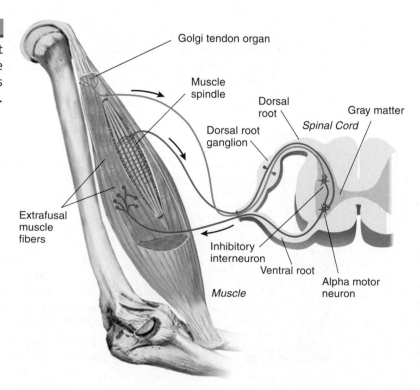

figure **8.7**

Polysynaptic inhibitory reflex. Input from the Golgi tendon organ can cause inhibitory postsynaptic potentials to occur on the alpha motor neuron.

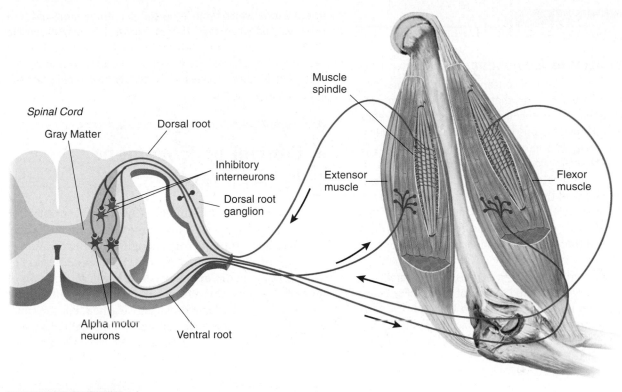

Secondary reflexes. Firing of the muscle spindle causes excitation on the alpha motor neuron of the agonist and inhibition on the antagonist.

long before the synaptic mechanisms were understood. A **decerebrate** cat, whose brain stem has been cut through, exhibits a phenomenon known as **decerebrate rigidity.** The animal's back is arched, and its legs are extended stiffly from its body. This rigidity results from excitation originating in the caudal reticular formation, which greatly facilitates all stretch reflexes, especially of extensor muscles, by increasing the activity of the gamma motor system. Rostral to the brain stem transection is an inhibitory region of the reticular formation, which normally counterbalances the excitatory one. The transection removes the inhibitory influence, leaving only the excitatory one. If you attempt to flex the outstretched leg of a decerebrate cat, you will meet with increasing resistance, which suddenly melts away, allowing the limb to flex. It almost feels as though you were closing the blade of a pocketknife—hence the term **clasp-knife reflex.** The sudden release is, of course, mediated by activation of the Golgi tendon organ reflex.

Even the monosynaptic stretch reflex serves as the basis of polysynaptic reflexes. Muscles are arranged in opposing pairs. The **agonist** moves the limb in the direction being studied, and because muscles cannot push back, the **antagonist** muscle must move the limb back in the opposite direction. Consider this finding: When a stretch reflex is elicited in the agonist, it contracts quickly, thus causing the antagonist to lengthen. It would appear, then,

that the antagonist is presented with a stimulus that should elicit *its* stretch reflex. Yet the antagonist relaxes instead. Let us see why.

Afferent axons of the muscle spindles, besides sending terminal buttons to the alpha motor neuron and to the brain, also synapse on inhibitory interneurons. The terminal buttons of these interneurons synapse on the alpha motor neurons that innervate the antagonistic muscle. (See *Figure 8.8*.) Thus, a stretch reflex excites the agonist and *inhibits the antagonist* so that the limb can move in the direction controlled by the stimulated muscle.

decerebrate Describes an animal whose brain stem has been transected.

decerebrate rigidity Simultaneous contraction of agonistic and antagonistic muscles; caused by decerebration or damage to the reticular formation.

clasp-knife reflex A reflex that occurs when force is applied to flex or extend the limb of an animal showing decerebrate rigidity; resistance is replaced by sudden relaxation.

agonist A muscle whose contraction produces or facilitates a particular movement.

antagonist A muscle whose contraction resists or reverses a particular movement.

Reflex Control of Movement

Reflexes are simple circuits of sensory neurons, interneurons (usually), and efferent neurons that control simple responses to particular stimuli. In the monosynaptic stretch reflex the terminal buttons of axons that receive sensory information from the intrafusal muscle fibers synapse with alpha motor neurons that innervate the same muscle. Thus, a sudden lengthening of the muscle causes the muscle to contract. By setting the length of the intrafusal muscle fibers, and hence their sensitivity to increases in muscle length, the motor system of the brain can control limb position. Changes in a weight being held that cause the limb to move will be quickly compensated for by means of the monosynaptic stretch reflex.

Polysynaptic reflexes contain at least one interneuron between the sensory neuron and the motor neuron. For example, when a strong muscular contraction threatens to damage muscles or limbs, the increased rate of firing of the afferent axons of Golgi tendon organs stimulates inhibitory

interneurons, which inhibit the alpha motor neurons of those muscles. And when the afferent axons of intrafusal muscle fibers fire, they excite inhibitory interneurons that slow the rate of firing of the alpha motor neurons that serve the antagonistic muscles, causing the antagonist to relax and the agonist to contract.

Control of Movement by the Brain

Movements can be initiated by several means. For example, rapid stretch of a muscle triggers the monosynaptic stretch reflex, a stumble triggers righting reflexes, and the rapid approach of an object toward the face causes a startle response, a complex reflex consisting of movements of several muscle groups. Other stimuli initiate sequences of movements that we have previously learned. For example, the presence of food causes eating, and the sight of a loved one evokes a hug and a kiss. Because there is no single cause

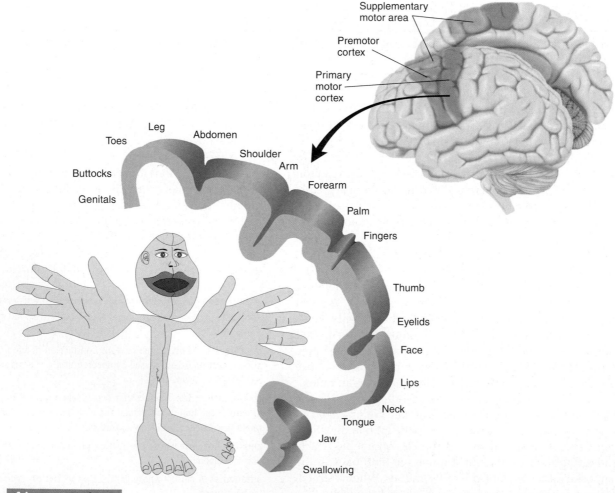

Motor cortex and a motor homunculus. Stimulation of various regions of the primary motor cortex causes movement in muscles of various parts of the body.

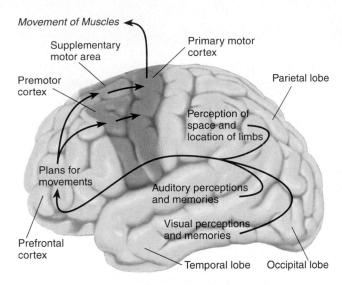

figure   8.10

Cortical control of movement. The posterior association cortex is involved with perceptions and memories, and the frontal association cortex is involved with plans for movement.

of behavior, we cannot find a single starting point in our search for the neural mechanisms that control movement.

The brain and spinal cord include several different motor systems, each of which can simultaneously control particular kinds of movements. For example, a person can walk and talk with a friend simultaneously. While doing so, he or she can gesture with the hands to emphasize a point, scratch an itch, brush away a fly, wipe sweat off his or her forehead, and so on. Walking, postural adjustments, talking, movement of the arms, and movements of the fingers all involve different specialized motor systems.

Organization of Motor Cortex

The primary motor cortex lies on the precentral gyrus, just rostral to the central sulcus. Stimulation studies (including those in awake humans) have shown that the activation of neurons located in particular parts of the primary motor cortex causes movements of particular parts of the body. In other words, the primary motor cortex shows **somatotopic organization** (from *soma,* "body," and *topos,* "place"). Figure 8.9 shows a *motor homunculus* based on the observations of Penfield and Rasmussen (1950). Note that a disproportionate amount of cortical area is devoted to movements of the fingers and the muscles used for speech. (See *Figure 8.9.*)

The principal cortical input to the primary motor cortex is the frontal association cortex, located rostral to it. Two regions immediately adjacent to the primary motor cortex—the *supplementary motor area* and the *premotor cortex*—are especially important in the control of movement. Both regions receive sensory information from the parietal and temporal lobes, and both send efferent axons to the primary motor cortex. The **supplementary motor area** is located on the medial surface of the brain, just rostral to the primary motor cortex. The **premotor cortex** is located primarily on the lateral surface, also just rostral to the primary motor cortex. (See *Figure 8.9.*)

The supplementary motor area and the premotor cortex are involved in the planning of movements, and they exe-

cute these plans through their connections with the primary motor cortex. Functional imaging studies show that when people execute sequences of movements—or even imagine them—these regions become activated (Roth et al., 1996). (More evidence for the functions of this region of the frontal lobe is discussed in Chapter 14.) The supplementary motor area and the premotor cortex receive information from association areas of the parietal and temporal cortex. As we saw in Chapter 6, the visual association cortex is organized in two streams: dorsal and ventral. The ventral stream, which terminates in the inferior temporal cortex, is involved in perceiving and recognizing particular objects—the "what" of visual perception. The dorsal stream, which terminates in the posterior parietal lobe, is involved in perception of location—the "where" of visual perception. In addition, the parietal lobes are involved in organizing visually guided movements—the "how" of visual perception. Besides receiving visual information about space, the parietal lobe receives information about spatial location from the somatosensory and auditory systems and integrates this information with visual information. Thus, the regions of the frontal cortex involved in planning movements receive the information they need about what is happening and where it is happening from the temporal and parietal lobes. Because the parietal lobes contain spatial information, the pathway from them to the frontal lobes is especially important in controlling both locomotion and arm and hand movements. After all, meaningful locomotion requires us to know where we are, and meaningful movements of our arms and hands require us to know where objects are located in space. (See *Figure 8.10.*)

---

somatotopic organization A topographically organized mapping of parts of the body that are represented in a particular region of the brain.

supplementary motor area A region of motor association cortex of the dorsal and dorsomedial frontal lobe, rostral to the primary motor cortex.

premotor cortex A region of motor association cortex of the lateral frontal lobe, rostral to the primary motor cortex.

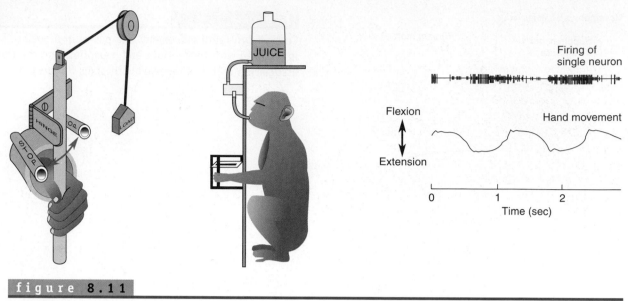

The relation between firing of single neurons in the motor cortex and hand movements. The single-unit records are redrawn from the original data and are therefore only approximate representations.

(Redrawn from Evarts, E. V. *Journal of Neurophysiology,* 1968, *31,* 14–27.)

The primary motor cortex also receives projections from the adjacent primary somatosensory cortex, located just across the central sulcus. The connections between these two areas are quite specific: Neurons in the primary somatosensory cortex that respond to stimuli applied to a particular part of the body send axons to neurons in the primary motor cortex that move muscles in the same part of the body. For example, Asanuma and Rosén (1972) and Rosén and Asanuma (1972) found that somatosensory neurons that respond to a touch on the back of the thumb send axons to motor neurons that cause thumb extension, and somatosensory neurons that respond to a touch on the ball of the thumb send axons to motor neurons that cause thumb flexion. This organization appears to provide rapid feedback to the motor system during manipulation of objects.

Evidence that supports this suggestion was obtained by Evarts (1974), who recorded the activity of single neurons in the precentral gyrus of monkeys. He trained his subjects to move a lever back and forth by means of wrist flexions and extensions. When the monkeys made the movements in the correct amount of time, they received a squirt of grape juice, a drink they appeared to enjoy. Figure 8.11 shows the experimental preparation as well as the relationship between lever movement and the firing of a cortical neuron. Note that the firing of this neuron is nicely related to the movement, with the rate increasing during flexion. (See *Figure 8.11.*) Evarts trained monkeys to produce a hand movement in response to a flash of a light or to a tactile stimulus delivered through the handle. He found that neurons in the motor cortex began firing 100 ms after a visual stimulus but responded as soon as 25 ms after a tactile stimulus. These results confirm the conclusion that hand and finger movements are controlled by somatosensory feedback received by neurons in the postcentral gyrus.

Cortical Control of Movement: The Descending Pathways

Neurons in the primary motor cortex control movements by two groups of descending tracts, the **lateral group** and the **ventromedial group,** named for their locations in the white matter of the spinal cord. The lateral group consists of the *corticospinal tract*, the *corticobulbar tract,* and the *rubrospinal tract.* This system is primarily involved in control of independent limb movements, particularly movements of the hands and fingers. *Independent* limb movements mean that the right and left limbs make different movements—or one limb moves while the other remains still. These movements contrast with coordinated limb movements, such as those involved in locomotion.

lateral group The corticospinal tract, the corticobulbar tract, and the rubrospinal tract.

ventromedial group The vestibulospinal tract, the tectospinal tract, the reticulospinal tract, and the ventral corticospinal tract.

The ventromedial group consists of the *vestibulospinal tract,* the *tectospinal tract,* the *reticulospinal tract,* and the *ventral corticospinal tract.* These tracts control more automatic movements: gross movements of the muscles of the trunk and coordinated trunk and limb movements involved in posture and locomotion.

Let's first consider the lateral group of descending tracts. The **corticospinal tract** consists of axons of cortical neurons that terminate in the gray matter of the spinal cord. The largest concentration of cell bodies responsible for these axons is located in the primary motor cortex, but neurons in the parietal and temporal lobes also send axons through the corticospinal pathway. The axons leave the cortex and travel through subcortical white matter to the ventral midbrain, where they enter the cerebral peduncles. They leave the peduncles in the medulla and form the **pyramidal tracts,** so-called because of their shape. At the level of the caudal medulla, most of the fibers decussate (cross over) and descend through the contralateral spinal cord, forming the **lateral corticospinal tract.** The rest of the fibers descend through the ipsilateral spinal cord, forming the **ventral corticospinal tract.** Because of its location and function, the ventral corticospinal tract is actually part of the ventromedial group. (See the light and dark blue lines in *Figure 8.12.*)

Most of the axons in the lateral corticospinal tract originate in the regions of the primary motor cortex and supplementary motor area that control the distal parts of the limbs: the arms, hands, and fingers and the lower legs, feet, and toes. They form synapses, directly or via interneurons, with motor neurons in the gray matter of the spinal cord—in the lateral part of the ventral horn. These motor neurons control muscles of the distal limbs, including those that move the arms, hands, and fingers. (See the light blue lines in *Figure 8.12.*)

The axons in the ventral corticospinal tract originate in the upper leg and trunk regions of the primary motor

---

corticospinal tract The system of axons that originates in the motor cortex and terminates in the ventral gray matter of the spinal cord.

pyramidal tract The portion of the corticospinal tract on the ventral border of the medulla.

lateral corticospinal tract The system of axons that originates in the motor cortex and terminates in the contralateral ventral gray matter of the spinal cord; controls movements of the distal limbs.

ventral corticospinal tract The system of axons that originates in the motor cortex and terminates in the ipsilateral ventral gray matter of the spinal cord; controls movements of the upper legs and trunk.

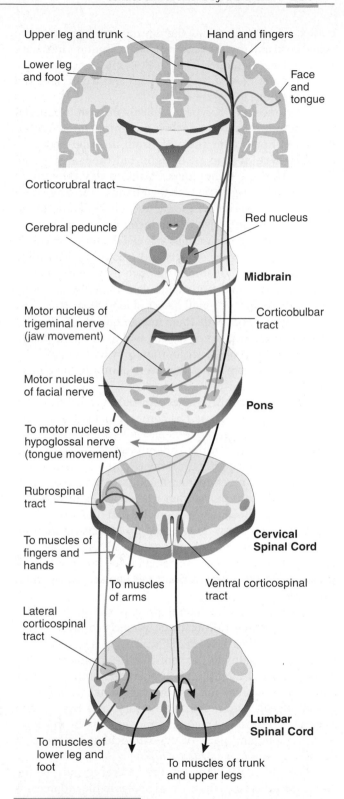

figure 8.12

The lateral group of descending motor tracts: the lateral corticospinal tract (light blue lines), corticobulbar tract (green lines), and rubrospinal tract (red lines). The ventral corticospinal tract (dark blue lines) is part of the ventromedial group.

cortex. They descend to the appropriate region of the spinal cord and divide, sending terminal buttons into both sides of the gray matter. They control motor neurons that move the muscles of the upper legs and trunk. (See the dark blue lines in *Figure 8.12*.)

Lawrence and Kuypers (1968a) cut both pyramidal tracts in monkeys to assess their motor functions. Within six to ten hours after recovery from the anesthesia the animals were able to sit upright, but their arms hung loosely from their shoulders. Within a day they could stand, hold the cage bars with their hands, and even climb a little. By six weeks the monkeys could walk and climb rapidly. Therefore, posture and locomotion were not disturbed. However, the animals' manual dexterity was poor. They could reach for objects and grasp them, but they used their fingers together as though they were wearing mittens; they could not manipulate their fingers independently to pick up small pieces of food. And once they had grasped food with their hand, they had difficulty releasing their grip. They usually had to use their mouth to pry their hand open. In contrast, they had no difficulty releasing their grip when they were climbing the bars of their cage.

The results confirm what we would predict from the anatomical connections: The corticospinal pathway controls hand and finger movements and is indispensable for moving the fingers independently when reaching and manipulating. Postural adjustments of the trunk and use of the limbs for reaching and locomotion are unaffected; therefore, these types of movements are controlled by other systems. Because the monkeys had difficulty releasing their grasp when they picked up objects but had no trouble doing so when climbing the walls of the cage, we can conclude that the same behavior (opening the hand) is controlled by different brain mechanisms in different contexts.

The second of the lateral group of descending pathways, the **corticobulbar tract,** projects to the medulla (sometimes called the *bulb*). This pathway is similar to the corticospinal pathway, except that it terminates in the motor nuclei of the fifth, seventh, ninth, tenth, eleventh, and twelfth cranial nerves (the trigeminal, facial, glossopharyngeal, vagus, spinal accessory, and hypoglossal nerves). These nerves control movements of the face, neck, tongue, and parts of the extraocular eye muscles. (See the green lines in *Figure 8.12*.)

The third member of the lateral group is the **rubrospinal tract.** This tract originates in the red nucleus (*nucleus ruber*) of the midbrain. The red nucleus receives its most important inputs from the motor cortex via the **corticorubral tract** and (as we shall see later) from the cerebellum. Axons of the rubrospinal tracts terminate on motor neurons in the spinal cord that control movements

of forelimb and hindlimb muscles. (They do not control the muscles that move the fingers.) (See the red lines in *Figure 8.12*.)

Lawrence and Kuypers (1968b) destroyed the rubrospinal tract *unilaterally* in some of the animals that had previously received bilateral lesions of the pyramidal tract. The rubrospinal tract lesion severely affected the animals' use of the ipsilateral arm. The arm tended to hang straight from the shoulder, with hand and fingers extended. If they could reach food only with the affected arm, they made a raking movement with the arm as a whole, bending their elbow and wrist as the food approached their mouth. The arm movement was accompanied by movements of the trunk. The monkeys did not hold the food with their hand, even with the mittenlike grasp that is produced by pyramidal tract lesions. The animals managed to hold onto cage bars with their affected hand, but the grip was weaker.

Lawrence and Kuypers concluded that the rubrospinal system controls independent movements of the forearms and hands—that is, movements that are independent of trunk movements. This control overlaps with that of the pyramidal system but does not include independent movements of the fingers.

Now let's consider the second set of pathways originating in the brain stem: the ventromedial group. This group includes the **vestibulospinal tracts,** the **tectospinal tracts,** and the **reticulospinal tracts,** as well as the ventral corticospinal tract (already described). These tracts control motor neurons in the ventromedial part of the spinal

corticobulbar tract A bundle of axons from the motor cortex to the fifth, seventh, ninth, tenth, eleventh, and twelfth cranial nerves; controls movements of the face, neck, tongue, and parts of the extraocular eye muscles.

rubrospinal tract The system of axons that travels from the red nucleus to the spinal cord; controls independent limb movements.

corticorubral tract The system of axons that travels from the motor cortex to the red nucleus.

vestibulospinal tract A bundle of axons that travels from the vestibular nuclei to the gray matter of the spinal cord; controls postural movements in response to information from the vestibular system.

tectospinal tract A bundle of axons that travels from the tectum to the spinal cord; coordinates head and trunk movements with eye movements.

reticulospinal tract A bundle of axons that travels from the reticular formation to the gray matter of the spinal cord; controls the muscles responsible for postural movements.

cord gray matter. Neurons of all these tracts receive input from the portions of the primary motor cortex that control movements of the trunk and proximal muscles (that is, the muscles located on the parts of the limbs close to the body). In addition, the reticular formation receives a considerable amount of input from the premotor cortex and from several subcortical regions, including the amygdala, hypothalamus, and basal ganglia. The cell bodies of neurons of the vestibulospinal tracts are located in the vestibular nuclei. As you might expect, this system plays a role in the control of posture. The cell bodies of neurons in the tectospinal tracts are located in the superior colliculus and are involved in coordinating head and trunk movements with eye movements. The cell bodies of neurons of the reticulospinal tracts are located in many nuclei in the brain stem and midbrain reticular formation. These neurons control several automatic functions, such as muscle tonus, respiration, coughing, and sneezing; but they are also involved in behaviors that are under direct neocortical control, such as walking. (See *Figure 8.13*.)

You will recall that Lawrence and Kuypers (1968a) found no deficits in postural movements after they had destroyed both the right and left pyramidal tracts. Presumably, the animals maintained their control of posture through the ventromedial pathways. Another study confirmed this speculation. Lawrence and Kuypers (1968b) cut the ventromedial fibers of some of the animals that had previously received bilateral pyramidal tract lesions. These animals showed severe impairments in posture. After a long recovery period they could eventually stand with great difficulty but could not take more than a few steps without falling. When they reached for food, their upper arms hung at their sides. Thus, we can conclude that the ventromedial pathways control the muscles of the trunk and proximal limbs, with supplementary control of the trunk muscles coming from the ventral corticospinal tract.

Table 8.1 summarizes the names of these pathways, their locations, and the muscle groups they control. (See *Table 8.1*.)

Deficits of Verbally Controlled Movements: The Apraxias

Damage to the corpus callosum, frontal lobe, or parietal lobe of the human brain produces a category of deficits called **apraxia**. Literally, the term means "without action," but apraxia differs from paralysis or weakness that occurs when motor structures such as the precentral gyrus, basal ganglia, brain stem, or spinal cord are damaged. Apraxia is the "inability to properly execute a learned skilled movement" (Heilman, Rothi, and Kertesz, 1983, p. 381). Neuropsychological studies of the apraxias have provided

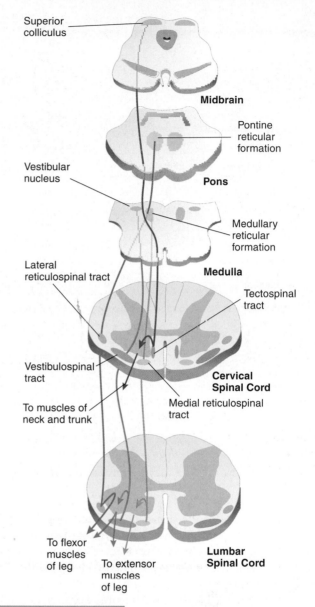

figure 8.13

The ventromedial group of descending motor tracts: the tectospinal tract (blue lines), lateral reticulospinal tract (purple lines), medial reticulospinal tract (orange lines), and vestibulospinal tract (green lines).

information about the way skilled behaviors are organized and initiated.

There are four major types of apraxia, two of which I will discuss in this chapter. *Limb apraxia* refers to problems

---

apraxia Difficulty in carrying out purposeful movements, in the absence of paralysis or muscular weakness.

Major Motor Pathways				
	ORIGIN	**TERMINATION**	**MUSCLE GROUP**	**FUNCTION**
Lateral Group				
Lateral corticospinal tract	Finger, hand, and arm region of motor cortex	Spinal cord	Fingers, hands, and arms	Grasping and manipulating objects
Rubrospinal tract	Red nucleus	Spinal cord	Hands (not fingers), lower arms, feet, and lower legs	Movement of forearms and hands independent from that of the trunk
Corticobulbar tract	Face region of motor cortex	Cranial nerve nuclei: 5, 7, 9, 10, 11, and 12	Face and tongue	Face and tongue movements
Ventromedial Group				
Vestibulospinal tract	Vestibular nuclei	Spinal cord	Trunk and legs	Posture
Tectospinal tract	Superior colliculi	Spinal cord	Neck and trunk	Coordination of eye movements with those of trunk and head
Lateral reticulospinal tract	Medullary reticular formation	Spinal cord	Flexor muscles of legs	Walking
Medial reticulospinal tract	Pontine reticular formation	Spinal cord	Extensor muscles of legs	Walking
Ventral corticospinal tract	Trunk and upper leg region of motor cortex	Spinal cord	Hands (not fingers), lower arms, feet, and lower legs.	Locomotion and posture

with movements of the arms, hands, and fingers. *Oral apraxia* refers to problems with movements of the muscles used in speech. *Apraxic agraphia* refers to a particular type of writing deficit. *Constructional apraxia* refers to difficulty in drawing or constructing objects. Because of their relation to language, I will describe oral apraxia and the agraphias in Chapter 16.

Limb Apraxia

Limb apraxia is characterized by movement of the wrong part of the limb, incorrect movement of the correct part, or correct movements but in the incorrect sequence. It is assessed by asking patients to perform movements. The most difficult movements involve pantomiming particular acts. For example, the examiner might ask the patient, "Pretend you have a key in your hand and open a door with it." In response, a patient with limb apraxia might wave his wrist back and forth rather than rotating it or might rotate his wrist first and then pretend to insert the key. Or if asked to pretend she is brushing her teeth, a patient might use her finger as though it were a toothbrush rather than pretending to hold a toothbrush in her hand.

To perform behaviors on verbal command without having a real object to manipulate, a person must comprehend the command and be able to imagine the missing article as well as to make the proper movements; therefore, these requests are the most difficult to carry out. Somewhat easier are tasks that involve imitating behaviors performed by the experimenter. Sometimes, a patient who cannot mime the use of a key can copy the examiner's hand movements. The easiest tasks involve the actual use of objects. For example, the examiner might give the patient a door key and ask him or her to demonstrate its use. If the brain lesion makes it impossible for the patient to understand speech, then the examiner cannot assess the ability to perform behaviors on verbal command. In this case the examiner can only measure the patient's ability to imitate movements or use actual objects. (See Heilman, Rothi, and Kertesz, 1983, for a review.)

Limb apraxia can be caused by three types of lesions. **Callosal apraxia** is apraxia of the left limb that is caused

callosal apraxia An apraxia of the left hand caused by damage to the anterior corpus callosum.

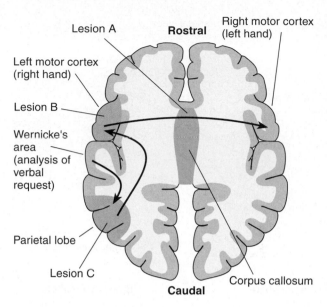

figure 8.14

Apraxias. Lesion A causes callosal apraxia of the left limb, lesion B causes sympathetic apraxia of the right limb, and lesion C causes left parietal apraxia of both limbs.

by damage to the anterior corpus callosum. The explanation for the deficit is the following: When a person hears a verbal request to perform a movement, the meaning of the speech is analyzed by circuits in the posterior left hemisphere (discussed in Chapter 15). A neural command to make the movement is conveyed through long transcortical axons to the prefrontal area. There, the command activates neural circuits that contain the memory of the movements that constitute the behavior. This information is transmitted through the corpus callosum to the right prefrontal cortex and from there to the right precentral gyrus. Neurons in this area control the individual movements. Damage to the anterior corpus callosum prevents communication between the left and right motor cortex. Thus, the right arm can perform the requested movement, but the left arm cannot. (See lesion A in *Figure 8.14*.)

A similar form of apraxia of the left limb is caused by damage to the anterior left hemisphere, sometimes called **sympathetic apraxia.** The damage causes a primary motor impairment of the right arm and hand: full or partial paralysis. As with anterior callosal lesions, the damage also causes apraxia of the left arm. The term *sympathetic* was originally adopted because the clumsiness of the left hand appeared to be a "sympathetic" response to the paralysis of the right one. (See lesion B in *Figure 8.14*.)

The third form of limb apraxia is **left parietal apraxia,** caused by lesions of the posterior left hemisphere. These lesions involve both limbs. The posterior parietal lobe contains areas of association cortex that receive information from the surrounding sensory association cortex of the occipital, temporal, and anterior parietal lobes. (See lesion C in *Figure 8.14*.)

From the effects of parietal lobe lesions in humans and monkeys, Mountcastle et al. (1975) suggested that this region contains a sensory representation of the surrounding environment and keeps track of the location of objects in the environment and the location of the organism's body parts in relation to them. Because the right parietal lobe is especially important for perception of three-dimensional space, information about location of objects external to the person is probably supplied from this region. According to Mountcastle and his colleagues, the left parietal region serves as a "command apparatus for the operation of the limbs, hands, and eyes within immediate extrapersonal space." For example, when a person hears a command to reach for a particular object, the left auditory association cortex decodes the meaning of the request and passes it on to the left parietal association cortex. Using information received from the right parietal association cortex about the spatial location of the object, neural circuits in the left parietal association cortex assess the relative location of the person's hand and the object and send information about the starting and ending coordinates to the left frontal association cortex. There, the sequence of muscular contractions necessary to perform the movement is organized and then is executed through the primary motor cortex and

sympathetic apraxia A movement disorder of the left hand caused by damage to the left frontal lobe; similar to callosal apraxia.

left parietal apraxia An apraxia caused by damage to the left parietal lobe; characterized by difficulty in producing sequences of movements by verbal request or in imitation of movements made by someone else.

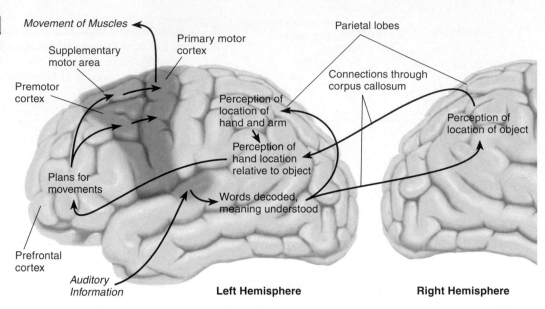

figure 8.15

The "command apparatus" of the left parietal lobe.

Movement of Muscles

Supplementary motor area

Primary motor cortex

Premotor cortex

Parietal lobes

Connections through corpus callosum

Perception of location of hand and arm

Perception of location of object

Perception of hand location relative to object

Plans for movements

Words decoded, meaning understood

Prefrontal cortex

Auditory Information

Left Hemisphere

Right Hemisphere

Perception of location of object

its connections with the spinal cord and subcortical motor systems. (See *Figure 8.15*.)

Constructional Apraxia

Constructional apraxia is caused by lesions of the right hemisphere, particularly the right parietal lobe. People with this disorder do not have difficulty making most types of skilled movements with their arms and hands. They have no trouble using objects properly, imitating their use, or pretending to use them. However, they have trouble drawing pictures or assembling objects from elements such as toy building blocks.

The primary deficit in constructional apraxia appears to involve the ability to perceive and imagine geometrical relations. Because of this deficit, a person cannot draw a picture, say, of a cube, because he or she cannot imagine what the lines and angles of a cube look like, not because of difficulty controlling the movements of his or her arm and hand. (See *Figure 8.16*.) Besides being unable to draw accurately, a person with constructional apraxia invariably has trouble with other tasks involving spatial perception, such as following a map.

The Basal Ganglia

Anatomy and Function

The basal ganglia constitute an important component of the motor system. We know that they are important because their destruction by disease or injury causes severe

motor deficits. The motor nuclei of the basal ganglia include the caudate nucleus, putamen, and globus pallidus. The basal ganglia receive most of their input from all regions of the cerebral cortex (but especially the primary motor cortex and primary somatosensory cortex) and the substantia

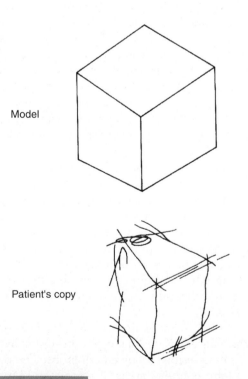

Model

Patient's copy

figure 8.16

Attempt to copy a cube by a patient with constructional apraxia caused by a lesion of the right parietal lobe.

(From *Fundamentals of Human Neuropsychology*, by B. Kolb and I. Q. Whishaw. W. H. Freeman and Company. Copyright © 1980.)

constructional apraxia Difficulty in drawing pictures or diagrams or in making geometrical constructions of elements such as building blocks or sticks; caused by damage to the right parietal lobe.

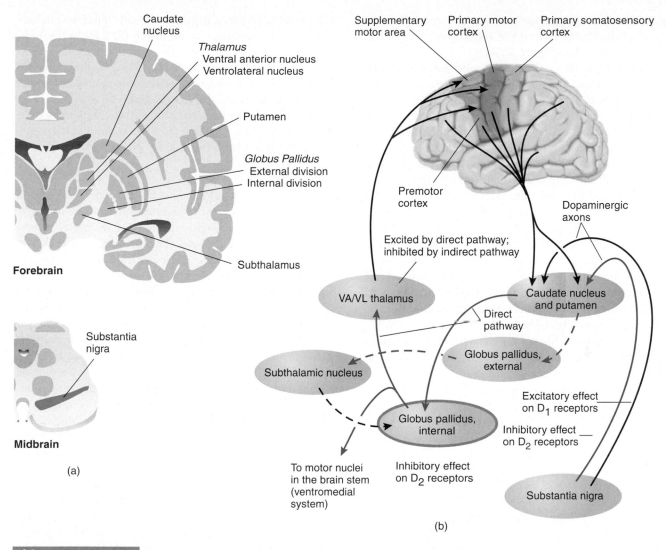

The basal ganglia. (a) The locations of the components of the basal ganglia and associated structures. (b) The major connections of the basal ganglia and associated structures. Excitatory connections are shown as black lines; inhibitory connections are shown as red lines. The indirect pathway is indicated by arrows with broken lines. Many connections, such as the inputs to the substantia nigra, are omitted for clarity. The internal division of the globus pallidus, the primary output of the basal ganglia and the target of stereotaxic surgery for Parkinson's disease, is outlined in gray.

nigra. They have two primary outputs: the primary motor cortex, supplementary motor area, and premotor cortex (via the thalamus) and motor nuclei of the brain stem that contribute to the ventromedial pathways. Through these connections the basal ganglia influence movements under the control of the primary motor cortex and exert some direct control over the ventromedial system.

Figure 8.17(a) illustrates the components of the basal ganglia: the **caudate nucleus,** the **putamen,** and the **globus pallidus.** It also shows some nuclei associated with the basal

caudate nucleus A telencephalic nucleus, one of the input nuclei of basal ganglia; involved with control of voluntary movement.

putamen A telencephalic nucleus; one of the input nuclei of the basal ganglia; involved with control of voluntary movement.

globus pallidus A telencephalic nucleus; the primary output nucleus of the basal ganglia; involved with control of voluntary movement.

ganglia: the **ventral anterior nucleus** and **ventrolateral nucleus** of the thalamus and the substantia nigra of the ventral midbrain. (See *Figure 8.17a*.)

Figure 8.17(b) shows some of the more important connections of the basal ganglia and helps to explain the role these structures play in the control of movement. For the sake of clarity this figure leaves out many connections, including inputs to the substantia nigra from the basal ganglia and other structures. First, let's take a quick look at the loop formed between the cortex and the basal ganglia. The frontal, parietal, and temporal cortex send axons to the caudate nucleus and the putamen, which then connect with the globus pallidus. The globus pallidus sends information back to the motor cortex via the ventral anterior and ventrolateral nuclei of the thalamus, completing the loop. Thus, the basal ganglia can monitor somatosensory information and are informed of movements being planned and executed by the motor cortex. Using this information (and other information they receive from other parts of the brain), they can then influence the movements controlled by the motor cortex. Throughout this circuit, information is represented somatotopically. That is, projections from neurons in the motor cortex that cause movements in particular parts of the body project to particular parts of the putamen, and this segregation is maintained all the way back to the motor cortex. (See *Figure 8.17b*.)

Another important input to the basal ganglia comes from the substantia nigra of the midbrain. We already saw in Chapter 4 that degeneration of the nigrostriatal bundle, the dopaminergic pathway from the substantia nigra to the caudate nucleus and putamen (the *neostriatum*), causes Parkinson's disease. (I will say more about this disorder later.) (See *Figure 8.17b*.)

Now let's consider some of the complexities of the cortical-basal ganglia loop. The links in the loop are made by both excitatory (glutamate-secreting) neurons and inhibitory (GABA-secreting) neurons. The caudate nucleus and putamen receive excitatory input from the cerebral cortex. They send inhibitory axons to the external and internal divisions of the globus pallidus (the GP_i and the GP_e, respectively). The pathway that includes the GP_I is known as the **direct pathway** (arrows with solid lines). Neurons in GP_i send inhibitory axons to the ventral anterior and ventrolateral thalamus (VA/VL thalamus), which send excitatory projections to the motor cortex. The net effect of the loop is excitatory because it contains two inhibitory links. Each inhibitory link (red arrow) reverses the sign of the input to that link. Thus, excitatory input to the caudate nucleus and putamen causes these structures to *inhibit* neurons in the GP_i. This inhibition *removes* the inhibitory effect of the connections between the GP_i on the VA/VL thalamus; in other words, neurons in the VA/VL thalamus become more excited. This excitation is passed on to the motor cortex. (See *Figure 8.17b*.)

The pathway that includes the GP_e is known as the **indirect pathway** (arrows with broken lines). Neurons in

GP_e send inhibitory input to the subthalamic nucleus, which sends excitatory input to the GP_i. From there on, the circuit is identical to the one we just examined—except that the ultimate effect of this loop on the thalamus and frontal cortex is *inhibitory*. And while we're at it, notice also that the globus pallidus sends axons to various motor nuclei in the brain stem that contribute to the ventromedial system. Also notice that the subthalamic nucleus sends excitatory input back to the GP_e. (See *Figure 8.17b*.)

Parkinson's Disease

Now that you understand the cortical-basal ganglia loop, you can understand the symptoms and treatment of two important neurological disorders: Parkinson's disease and Huntington's disease. The primary symptoms of Parkinson's disease are muscular rigidity, slowness of movement, a resting tremor, and postural instability. For example, once a person with Parkinson's disease is seated, he or she finds it difficult to arise. Once the person begins walking, he or she has difficulty stopping. Thus, a person with Parkinson's disease cannot easily pace back and forth across a room. Reaching for an object can be accurate, but the movement usually begins only after a considerable delay, and the individual components of the movement (a series of trunk, arm, hand, and finger movements) are poorly coordinated (Poizner et al., 2000). Writing is slow and labored, and as it progresses, the letters get smaller and smaller. Postural movements are impaired. A normal person who is bumped while standing will quickly move to restore balance—for example, by taking a step in the direction of the impending fall or by reaching out with the arms to grasp a piece of furniture. However, a person with Parkinson's disease fails to do so and simply falls. A person with this disorder is even unlikely to put out his or her arms to break the fall.

Parkinson's disease also produces a resting tremor—vibratory movements of the arms and hands that diminish somewhat when the individual makes purposeful

---

ventral anterior nucleus (of thalamus) A thalamic nucleus that receives projections from the basal ganglia and sends projections to the motor cortex.

ventrolateral nucleus (of thalamus) A thalamic nucleus that receives projections from the basal ganglia and sends projections to the motor cortex.

direct pathway (in basal ganglia) The pathway that includes the caudate nucleus and putamen, the internal division of the globus pallidus, and the ventral anterior/ventrolateral thalamic nuclei; has an excitatory effect on movement.

indirect pathway (in basal ganglia) The pathway that includes the caudate nucleus and putamen, the external division of the globus pallidus, the subthalamic nucleus, the internal division of the globus pallidus, and the ventral anterior/ventrolateral thalamic nuclei; has an inhibitory effect on movement.

movements. The tremor is accompanied by rigidity; the joints appear stiff. However, the tremor and rigidity are not the cause of the slow movements. In fact, some patients with Parkinson's disease show extreme slowness of movements but little or no tremor.

Let's look at Figure 8.17(b) again to see why damage to the nigrostriatal bundle causes slowness of movements and disrupts postural adjustments. Normal movements require an appropriate balance between the direct (excitatory) and indirect (inhibitory) pathways. The caudate nucleus and putamen consist of two different zones, both of which receive input from dopaminergic neurons of the substantia nigra. One of these zones contains D_1 dopamine receptors, which produce excitatory effects. Neurons in this zone send their axons to the GP_i. Neurons in the other zone contain D_2 receptors, which produce inhibitory effects. These neurons send their axons to the GP_e. (See *Figure 8.17b.*) The first of these circuits, beginning with the black arrow from the substantia nigra, goes through two inhibitory synapses (red arrows) before it reaches the VA/VL thalamus; thus, this circuit has an excitatory effect on behavior. The second of these circuits begins with an inhibitory input to the caudate nucleus and putamen, but it goes through *four* inhibitory synapses in the following pathway: substantia nigra → caudate/putamen → GP_e → subthalamic nucleus → GP_i → VA/VL thalamus. Thus, the effect of this pathway, too, is excitatory; thus, dopaminergic input to the caudate nucleus and putamen facilitate movements. And note that the GP_i also sends axons to the ventromedial system. A decrease in this inhibitory output is probably responsible for the muscular rigidity and poor control of posture seen in Parkinson's disease. (See *Figure 8.17b.*)

As we saw in Chapter 4, the standard treatment for Parkinson's disease is L-DOPA, the precursor of dopamine. When an increased amount of L-DOPA is present, the remaining nigrostriatal dopaminergic neurons in a patient with Parkinson's disease will produce and release more dopamine. But this compensation often produces *dyskinesias* and *dystonias*—involuntary movements and postures that are presumably caused by too much stimulation of dopamine receptors in the basal ganglia. In addition, L-DOPA does not work indefinitely; eventually, the number of nigrostriatal dopaminergic neurons declines to such a low level that the symptoms become worse. Some patients—especially those whose symptoms began when they were relatively young—eventually become bedridden, scarcely able to move.

Neurosurgeons have been developing three stereotaxic procedures designed to alleviate the symptoms of Parkinson's disease that no longer respond to treatment with L-DOPA. The first one, transplantation of fetal tissue, attempts to reestablish the secretion of dopamine in the neostriatum. The tissue is obtained from the substantia nigra of aborted human fetuses and implanted into the caudate nucleus and putamen by means of stereotaxically guided needles. Although the procedure is still experimental, some good results have been obtained. As we saw in Chapter 5, PET scans have shown that dopaminergic fetal cells are able to grow in their new host and secrete dopamine, reducing the patient's symptoms. In a study of 32 patients with fetal tissue transplants, Freed et al. (2002) found that those whose symptoms had previously responded to L-DOPA were most likely to benefit from the surgery. Presumably, these patients had a sufficient number of basal ganglia neurons with receptors that could be stimulated by the dopamine secreted by either the medication or the transplanted tissue.

Because of ethical and practical issues, investigators have continued to search for other sources of dopamine-secreting neurons. Fetal dopaminergic cells are difficult to obtain, and about 90 percent of them die through apoptosis once they are transplanted into the human brain. (*Apoptosis,* programmed cell death, was described in Chapter 3.) One potential source of neurons could come from cultures of fetal stem cells—undifferentiated cells that have the ability, if appropriately stimulated, to develop into a variety of types of cells, including dopaminergic neurons (Freed, 2002). A significant advantage of human stem cells is that large numbers of cells could be transplanted, thus increasing the numbers of surviving cells in the patients' brains.

Recent research suggests that another source of dopamine-secreting neurons may prove to be even more effective than cells taken from the substantia nigra. The carotid body is a small organ on the carotid arteries, located on each side of the neck. This organ contains receptor cells that measure how much oxygen the blood contains, and can increase a person's rate of breathing if that level falls. Some of the neurons in the carotid body—the *glomus cells,* secrete dopamine. Luquin et al. (1999) destroyed the dopaminergic neurons of the nigrostriatal pathway in monkeys by giving them an injection of MPTP, a neurotoxin. (MPTP is discussed later in this subsection.) Destruction of these neurons produced the symptoms of Parkinson's disease. Next, the investigators removed neurons from the animals' carotid bodies and transplanted them to the putamen. The grafts survived and secreted dopamine, and the animal's symptoms improved. A subsequent study by Toledo-Aral et al. (2002) obtained similar results.

The second stereotaxic procedure for treating Parkinson's disease has a long history, but only recently have technological developments in imaging methods and electrophysiological techniques led to an increase in its popularity. As we saw in Figure 8.17(b), the principal output of the basal ganglia comes from the internal division of the globus pallidus. This output, which is directed toward the motor cortex through the VA/VL thalamus and to components of the ventromedial system in the brain stem, is inhibitory. As we saw, a decrease in the activity of the dopaminergic input to the neostriatum causes an *increase* in the activity of the GP_i. Thus, damage to the GP_i might be expected to relieve the symptoms of Parkinson's disease.

In the 1950s Leksell and his colleagues performed pallidotomies (surgical destruction of the internal division of the globus pallidus) in patients with severe Parkinson's disease (Svennilson et al., 1960; Laitinen, Bergenheim, and Hariz, 1992). The surgery often reduced the rigidity and enhanced the patient's ability to move. Unfortunately, the surgery occasionally made the patient's symptoms worse and sometimes resulted in partial blindness. (The optic tract is located next to the GP_i.)

With the development of L-DOPA therapy in the late 1960s, pallidotomies were abandoned. However, it eventually became evident that L-DOPA worked for a limited time and that the symptoms of Parkinson's disease would eventually return. For that reason, in the 1990s neurosurgeons again began experimenting with pallidotomies, first with laboratory animals and then with humans (Graybiel, 1996). This time, they used MRI scans to find the location of the GP_i and then inserted an electrode into the target region. They could then pass low-intensity, high-frequency stimulation through the electrode, thus temporarily disabling the region around its tip. If the patient's rigidity disappeared (obviously, the patient was awake during the surgery), then the electrode was in the right place. To make the lesion, the surgeon passed radiofrequency current of sufficient strength to heat and destroy the brain tissue. The results of this procedure have been so promising that several neurological teams have begun promoting its use in the treatment of relatively young patients whose symptoms no longer respond to L-DOPA. PET studies have found that after pallidotomy the metabolic activity in the premotor and supplementary motor areas, normally depressed in patients with Parkinson's disease, returns to normal levels (Grafton et al., 1995), which indicates that lesions of the GP_i do indeed release the motor cortex from inhibition.

Neurosurgeons have also targeted the subthalamic nucleus in patients with advanced Parkinson's disease, especially those with disabling tremors. As Figure 8.17(b) shows, the subthalamic nucleus has an excitatory effect on the GP_i; thus, damage to the subthalamic nucleus decreases the activity of this region and removes some of the inhibition on motor output. (See *Figure 8.17b.*) Normally, damage to the subthalamic nucleus causes dyskinesias. However, in people with Parkinson's disease, damage to this region brings motor activity, which is normally depressed, back to normal (Guridi and Obeso, 2001).

Perkel and Farries (2000) suggest that the tremors that often accompany Parkinson's disease may be caused by abnormal activity in the reciprocal connections between the subthalamic nucleus and the GP_e. They note that cultures of neurons taken from the basal ganglia, subthalamic nucleus, and cortex show rhythmic bursting at frequencies similar to those of Parkinsonian tremors. These oscillations were abolished by cutting the connections between the subthalamic nucleus and the GP_e but not those between the cortex and caudate/putamen or caudate/putamen and GP_e (Plenz and Kitai, 1999). These findings may explain why subthalamic lesions are so successful in alleviating tremors.

The third stereotaxic procedure aimed at relieving the symptoms of Parkinson's disease involves implanting electrodes in the subthalamic nucleus and attaching a device that permits the patient to electrically stimulate the brain through the electrodes. (See *Figure 8.18.*) According to some studies, deep brain stimulation is as effective as brain lesions in suppressing tremors and has fewer adverse side effects (Simuni et al., 2002; Speelman et al., 2002). The fact that either lesions or stimulation alleviate tremors suggests that the stimulation has an inhibitory effect on subthalamic neurons, but this hypothesis has not yet been confirmed.

What causes Parkinson's disease? Research suggests that it may be caused by toxins—present in the environment, caused by faulty metabolism, or produced by unrecognized infectious disorders. As we saw in Chapter 4, several young people developed symptoms of Parkinson's disease after taking a drug contaminated with MPTP,

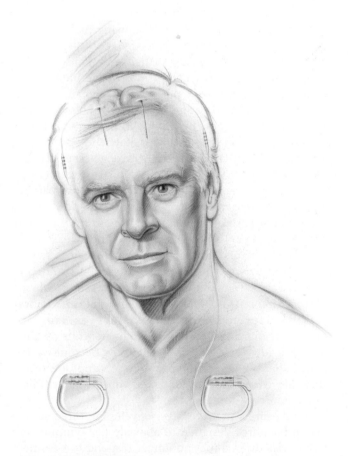

figure 8.18

Deep brain stimulation. Electrodes are implanted in the patient's brain, and wires are run under the skin to stimulation devices implanted near the collarbone. (Illustration used with permission by Medtronic, Inc.)

which destroyed dopaminergic neurons of the substantia nigra (Langston et al., 1983). This episode, and the fact that exposure to pesticides and herbicides appears to increase the incidence of Parkinson's disease (Di Monte, Lavasani, and Manning-Bog, 2002; Petrovitch et al., 2002) suggest that environmental toxins may play a role in the development of this disorder. Ironically, smoking and coffee drinking appear to have a small *protective* effect (Hernan et al., 2002).

Although most cases of Parkinson's disease do not appear to have a genetic basis, the cause of a rare genetic form of the disease—*autosomal recessive juvenile parkinsonism*—has been found. Kitada et al. (1998) discovered that mutation of a gene called *parkin* is responsible for this disorder. The parkin gene is normally highly active in dopaminergic neurons of the substantia nigra. The protein it produces appears to play a role in ferrying defective or degraded proteins to the *proteosomes*—organelles responsible for destroying these proteins (Fishman and Oyler, 2002). Perhaps, then, the disease permits toxic levels of proteins to accumulate in these cells. Whether this mechanism is related to the neurotoxic process that occurs in the more typical form of Parkinson's disease is not yet known.

Huntington's Disease

Another basal ganglia disease, **Huntington's disease,** is caused by degeneration of the caudate nucleus and putamen, especially of GABAergic and acetylcholinergic neurons. (See *Figure 8.19*.) Whereas Parkinson's disease causes a poverty of movements, Huntington's disease, formerly called *Huntington's chorea,* causes uncontrollable ones, especially jerky limb movements. (*Chorea* derives from the Greek *khoros,* meaning "dance.") The movements of Huntington's disease look like fragments of purposeful movements but occur involuntarily. This disease is progressive and eventually causes death.

The symptoms of Huntington's disease usually begin in the patient's thirties or forties but can sometimes begin in the early twenties. The first signs of neural degeneration occur in the caudate nucleus and the putamen—specifically, in the medium-sized spiny inhibitory neurons whose axons travel to the external division of the globus pallidus. The loss of inhibition provided by these GABA-secreting neurons increases the activity of the GP_e, which then inhibits the subthalamic nucleus. As a consequence, the activity level of the GP_i decreases and excessive movements occur. (Refer to *Figure 8.17b*.) As the disease progresses, the caudate nucleus and putamen degenerate until almost all of their neurons disappear. The patient dies from complications of immobility.

Huntington's disease is a hereditary disorder, caused by a dominant gene on chromosome 4. In fact, the gene has been located, and its defect has been identified as a repeated sequence of bases that code for the amino acid glutamine (Collaborative Research Group, 1993). This repeated sequence causes the gene product—a protein

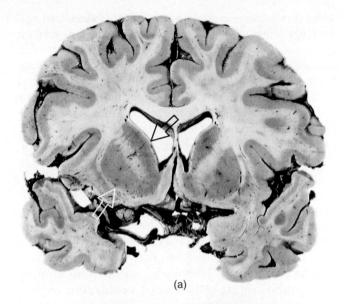

(a)

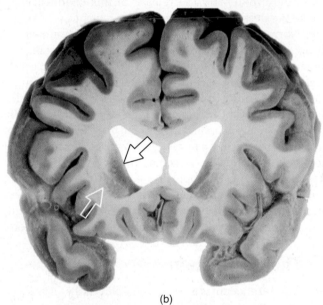

(b)

figure 8.19

Huntington's disease. (a) A slice through a normal human brain, showing the normal appearance of the caudate nuclei (arrowheads) and lateral ventricles. (b) A slice through the brain of a person who had Huntington's disease. The arrowheads indicate the location of the caudate nuclei, which are severely degenerated. As a consequence of the degeneration, the lateral ventricles (open spaces in the middle of the slice) have enlarged. (Courtesy of Harvard Medical School/Betty G. Martindale and Anthony D'Agostino, Good Samaritan Hospital, Portland, Oregon.)

Huntington's disease A fatal inherited disorder that causes degeneration of the caudate nucleus and putamen; characterized by uncontrollable jerking movements, writhing movements, and dementia.

called *huntingtin*—to contain an elongated stretch of glutamine. Longer stretches of glutamine are associated with patients whose symptoms began at a younger age, which strongly suggests that this abnormal portion of the huntingtin molecule is responsible for the disease.

Subsequent research discovered that other proteins interact with the elongated stretch of glutamine. Burke et al. (1996) found that GADPH, an enzyme that plays a critical role in glucose metabolism, interacts with huntingtin. Possibly, the abnormal huntingtin may somehow interfere with the action of GADPH and cause some cells to starve. Researchers in another laboratory (Li et al., 1995) discovered that huntingtin is associated with another protein found only in the brain, which they called HAP1 (huntingtin-associated protein 1). This team also discovered that HAP1 is found in neurons that contain nitric oxide synthase, the enzyme responsible for the production of nitric oxide (Li et al., 1996). As they noted, nitric oxide is extremely toxic, and the release of this chemical may cause the destruction of surrounding neurons.

Normal huntingtin is found in the cytoplasm, where it apparently plays a role in production of certain cell organelles (Hilditch-Maguire et al., 2000). In cells of genetically altered HD mice that express long huntingtin and develop a disorder that closely resembles Huntington's disease, fragments of huntingtin begin to accumulate in the nucleus, which apparently triggers the production of *caspase,* a "killer enzyme" that plays a role in apoptosis. Li et al. (2000) found that HD mice lived longer if they were given a caspase inhibitor, which suppresses apoptosis. Further research will undoubtedly clarify the role of faulty huntingtin protein in the neuropathology of Huntington's disease. Unfortunately, there is at present no treatment for the disorder.

The Cerebellum

The cerebellum is an important part of the motor system. It contains about 50 billion neurons, versus the approximately 22 billion neurons in the cerebral cortex (Robinson, 1995). Its outputs project to every major motor structure of the brain. When it is damaged, people's movements become jerky, erratic, and uncoordinated. The cerebellum consists of two hemispheres that contain several deep nuclei situated beneath the wrinkled and folded cerebellar cortex. Thus, the cerebellum resembles the cerebrum in miniature. The medial part of the cerebellum is phylogenetically older than the lateral part, and it participates in control of the ventromedial system. The **flocculonodular lobe,** located at the caudal end of the cerebellum, receives input from the vestibular system and projects axons to the vestibular nucleus. You will not be surprised to learn that this system is involved in postural reflexes. (See the green lines in *Figure 8.20*.) The **vermis** ("worm"), located on the midline, receives auditory and visual information from the tectum and cutaneous and kinesthetic information from the spinal cord. It sends its outputs to the **fastigial nucleus**

(one of the set of deep cerebellar nuclei). Neurons in the fastigial nucleus send axons to the vestibular nucleus and to motor nuclei in the reticular formation. Thus, these neurons influence behavior through the vestibulospinal and reticulospinal tracts, two of the three ventromedial pathways. (See the blue lines in *Figure 8.20*.)

The rest of the cerebellar cortex receives most of its input from the cerebral cortex, including the primary motor cortex and association cortex. This input is relayed to the cerebellar cortex through the pontine tegmental reticular nucleus. The intermediate zone of the cerebellar cortex projects to the **interposed nuclei,** which in turn project to the red nucleus. Thus, the intermediate zone influences the control of the rubrospinal system over movements of the arms and legs. The interposed nuclei also send outputs to the ventrolateral thalamic nucleus, which projects to the motor cortex. (See the red lines in *Figure 8.20*.)

The lateral zone of the cerebellum is involved in the control of independent limb movements, especially rapid, skilled movements. Such movements are initiated by neurons in the frontal association cortex, which control neurons in the primary motor cortex. But although the frontal cortex can plan and initiate movements, it does not contain the neural circuitry needed to calculate the complex, closely timed sequences of muscular contractions that are needed for rapid, skilled movements. That task falls to the lateral zone of the cerebellum.

Both the frontal association cortex and the primary motor cortex send information about intended movements to the lateral zone of the cerebellum via the **pontine nucleus.** The lateral zone also receives information from the somatosensory system, which informs it about the current position and rate of movement of the limbs—information that is necessary for computing the details of a movement. When the cerebellum receives information that the motor cortex has begun to initiate a movement, it computes the contribution that various muscles will have to make to perform that movement. The results of this computation are sent to the **dentate nucleus,** another

flocculonodular lobe A region of the cerebellum; involved in control of postural reflexes.

vermis The portion of the cerebellum located at the midline; receives somatosensory information and helps to control the vestibulospinal and reticulospinal tracts through its connections with the fastigial nucleus.

fastigial nucleus A deep cerebellar nucleus; involved in the control of movement by the reticulospinal and vestibulospinal tracts.

interposed nuclei A set of deep cerebellar nuclei; involved in the control of the rubrospinal system.

pontine nucleus A large nucleus in the pons that serves as an important source of input to the cerebellum.

dentate nucleus A deep cerebellar nucleus; involved in the control of rapid, skilled movements by the corticospinal and rubrospinal systems.

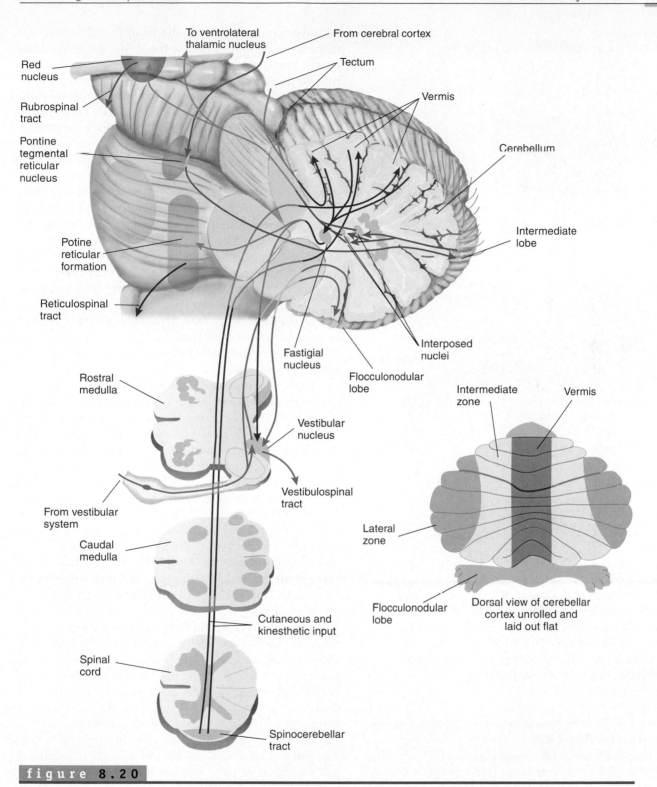

Inputs and outputs of three systems of the cerebellum: the flocculonodular lobe (green lines), the vermis (blue lines), and the intermediate zone of the cerebellar cortex (red lines).

of the deep cerebellar nuclei. Neurons in the dentate nucleus pass the information on to the ventrolateral thalamus, which projects to the primary motor cortex. The projection from the ventrolateral thalamus to the primary motor cortex enables the cerebellum to modify the ongoing movement that was initiated by the frontal cortex. The lateral zone of the cerebellum also sends efferents to the red nucleus (again, via the dentate nucleus); thus, it helps

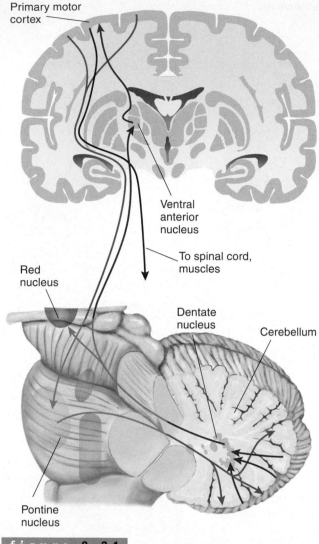

Primary motor cortex

Ventral anterior nucleus

To spinal cord, muscles

Red nucleus

Dentate nucleus

Cerebellum

Pontine nucleus

figure 8.21

Inputs and outputs of the lateral zone of the cerebellar cortex. This zone receives information about impending movements from the frontal lobes and helps to smooth and integrate the movements through its connections to the primary motor cortex and red nucleus through the dentate nucleus and ventral thalamus.

to control independent limb movements through this system as well. (See *Figure 8.21*.)

In humans lesions of different regions of the cerebellum produce different symptoms. Damage to the flocculonodular lobe or the vermis causes disturbances in posture and balance. Damage to the intermediate zone produces deficits in movements controlled by the rubrospinal system; the principal symptom of this damage is limb rigidity. Damage to the lateral zone causes weakness and *decomposition of movement*. For example, a

person attempting to bring the hand to the mouth will make separate movements of the joints of the shoulder, elbow, and wrist instead of performing simultaneous smooth movements.

Lesions of the lateral zone of the cerebellar cortex also appear to impair the timing of rapid *ballistic* movements. Ballistic (literally, "throwing") movements occur too fast to be modified by feedback. The sequence of muscular movements must then be programmed in advance, and the individual muscles must be activated at the proper times. You might like to try this common neurological test. Have a friend place his or her finger in front of your face, about three-quarters of an arm's length away. While your friend slowly moves his or her finger around to serve as a moving target, alternately touch your nose and your friend's finger as rapidly as you can. If your cerebellum is normal, you can successfully hit your nose and your friend's finger without too much trouble. People with lateral cerebellar damage have great difficulty; they tend to miss the examiner's hand and poke themselves in the eye. (I have often wondered why neurologists do not adopt a less dangerous test.)

When making rapid, aimed movements, we cannot rely on feedback to stop the movement when we reach the target. By the time we perceive that our finger has reached the proper place, it is too late to stop the movement, and we will overshoot the target if we try to stop it then. Instead of relying on feedback, the movement appears to be timed. We estimate the distance between our hand and the target, and our cerebellum calculates the amount of time that the muscles will have to be turned on. After the proper amount of time, the cerebellum briefly turns on antagonistic muscles to stop the movement. In fact, Kornhuber (1974) suggested that one of the primary functions of the cerebellum is timing the duration of rapid movements. Obviously, learning must play a role in controlling such movements.

Timmann, Watts, and Hore (1999) reported an interesting example of the role the cerebellum plays in timing sequences of muscular contractions. When tossing a ball at a target using an overarm throw, a person raises his or her hand above the shoulder, rotates the arm forward, and then releases the ball by extending the fingers—moving them apart. The timing of the release is critical: too soon and the ball goes too high, too late and it goes too low. The researchers found that normal subjects released the ball within an 11-msec window 95 percent of the time. Patients with cerebellar lesions did five times worse: Their window was 55 msec wide.

The cerebellum also appears to integrate successive *sequences* of movements that must be performed one after the other. For example, Holmes (1939) reported that one of his patients said, "The movements of my left arm are done subconsciously, but I have to think out each movement of the right [affected] arm. I come to a dead stop in turning and have to think before I start again." Thach (1978) obtained experimental evidence that corroborates this role. He found that many neurons in the dentate nuclei (which receive inputs from the lateral zone of the cerebellar cortex) showed response patterns that predicted the *next* movement in a sequence rather than the one that was currently taking place. Presumably, the cerebellum was planning these movements.

Dr. S., a professor of neurology at the medical school, stood on the stage of the auditorium as he presented a case to a group of physicians and students. He discussed the symptoms and possible causes of cerebellar-brain stem degeneration. "Now I'd like to present Mr. P.," he said, as a set of MRI scans appeared on the screen. "As you can see, Mr. P.'s cerebellum shows substantial degeneration, but we can't see evidence of any damage to the brain stem."

Dr. S. left the stage and returned, pushing Mr. P. onstage in a wheelchair.

"Mr. P., how are you feeling today?'

"I'm fine," he replied. "Of course, I'd feel better if I could have walked out here myself."

"Of course."

Dr. S. talked with Mr. P. for a few minutes, getting him to talk enough so that we could see that his mental condition was lucid and that he had no obvious speech or memory problems.

"Okay, Mr. P., I'd like you to make some movements." He faced Mr. P. and said, "Please stretch your hands out and hold them like this." Dr. S. suddenly raised his arms from his sides and held them out straight in front of him, palms down, fingers pointing forward.

Mr. P. did not respond immediately. He looked as if he were considering what to do. Suddenly, his arms straightened out and lifted from the armrests of the wheelchair. Instead of stopping when they were pointed straight ahead of him, they continued upward. Mr. P. grunted and his arms began flailing around—up, down, left, and right—until he finally managed to hold them outstretched in front of him. He was panting with the effort to hold them there.

"Thank you, Mr. P. Please put your arms down again. Now try this." Dr. S. very slowly raised his arms from his side until they were straight out in front of them. Mr. P. did the same, and this time there was no overshoot.

After a few more demonstrations, Dr. S. thanked Mr. P. and wheeled him offstage. When he returned, he reviewed what we had seen.

"When Mr. P. tried to quickly raise his arms in front of him, his primary motor cortex sent messages to the appropriate muscles, and his arms straightened out and began

to rise. Normally, the cerebellum is informed about the movement, and through its connections back to the motor cortex begins to contract the antagonistic muscles at the appropriate time, bringing the arms to rest in the intended position. Mr. P. could get the movement started just fine, but the damage to his cerebellum eliminated the help this structure gives to rapid movements and he couldn't stop his arms in time. When he tried to move slowly, he could use visual and kinesthetic feedback from the position of his arms to control the movement. Your cerebellum isn't nearly as important in the control of simple, slow movements. For that, you need your basal ganglia, but that's another story."

The Reticular Formation

The reticular formation consists of a large number of nuclei located in the core of the medulla, pons, and midbrain. The reticular formation controls the activity of the gamma motor system and hence regulates muscle tonus. In addition, the pons and medulla contain several nuclei with specific motor functions. For example, different locations in the medulla control automatic or semiautomatic responses such as respiration, sneezing, coughing, and vomiting. As we saw, the ventromedial pathways originate in the superior colliculi, vestibular nuclei, and reticular formation. Thus, the reticular formation plays a role in the control of posture.

The reticular formation also plays a role in locomotion. Stimulation of the **mesencephalic locomotor region,** located ventral to the inferior colliculus, causes a cat to make pacing movements (Shik and Orlovsky, 1976). The mesencephalic locomotor region does not send fibers directly to the spinal cord but apparently controls the activity of reticulospinal tract neurons.

Other motor functions of the reticular formation are also being discovered. Siegel and McGinty (1977) recorded from thirty-five single neurons in the reticular formation of unanesthetized, freely moving cats. Thirty-two of these neurons responded during *specific* movements of the head, tongue, facial muscles, ears, forepaw, or shoulder. The specific nature of the relations suggests that the neurons play some role in controlling the movements. For example, one neuron responded when the tongue moved out and to the left. The function of these neurons and the range of movements they control are not yet known.

---

mesencephalic locomotor region A region of the reticular formation of the midbrain whose stimulation causes alternating movements of the limbs normally seen during locomotion.

Control of Movement by the Brain

The motor systems of the brain are complex. (Having read this section, you do not need me to tell you that.) A good way to review the systems is through an example. While following my description, you might want to look at Table 8.1 and Figures 8.12 and 8.13 again. Suppose you see, out of the corner of your eye, that something is moving. You quickly turn your head and eyes toward the source of the movement and discover that a vase of flowers on a table someone has just bumped is ready to fall. You quickly reach forward, grab it, and restore it to a stable, upright position. (For simplicity's sake I will assume that you are right-handed.)

The rapid movement of your head and eyes is controlled by mechanisms that involve the superior colliculi and nearby nuclei. The head movement and corresponding movement of the trunk are mediated by the tectospinal tract. You perceive the tipping vase because of the activity of neurons in your visual association cortex. Your visual association cortex also contributes information about depth to your right parietal lobe, whose association cortex determines the exact spatial location of the vase. Your left parietal lobe uses the spatial information, together with its own record of the location of your hand, to compute the path your hand must travel to intercept the vase. The information is relayed to your left frontal lobe, where the motor association cortex starts the movement. Because the movement will have to be a ballistic one, the cerebellum controls its timing, on the basis of information it receives from the association cortex of the frontal and parietal lobes. Your hand stops just as it touches the vase, and connections between the somatosensory cortex and the primary motor cortex initiate a reflex that closes your hand around the vase.

The movement of your hand is controlled through a cooperation between the corticospinal, rubrospinal, and ventromedial pathways. Even before your hand moves, the ventral corticospinal tract and the ventromedial pathways (vestibulospinal and reticulospinal system, largely under the influence of the basal ganglia) begin adjusting your posture so that you will not fall forward when you suddenly reach in front of you. Depending on how far forward you will have to reach, the reticulospinal tract may even cause one leg to step forward to take your weight. The rubrospinal tract controls the muscles of your upper arm, and the lateral corticospinal tract controls your finger and hand movements. Perhaps you say, triumphantly, "I got it!" The corticobulbar pathway, under the control of speech mechanisms in the left hemisphere, causes the muscles of your vocal apparatus to say these words.

A person with apraxia will have difficulty making controlled movements of the limb in response to a verbal request. Most cases of apraxia are produced by lesions of the left parietal lobe, which sends information about the requested movement to the left frontal association cortex. This region directly controls movement of the right limb by activating neurons in the left primary motor cortex and indirectly controls movement of the left limb by sending information to the right frontal association cortex. Damage to the left frontal association cortex or to its connections with the right hemisphere also produces apraxia.

The basal ganglia are part of a circuit that includes the cerebral cortex, the subthalamic nucleus, thalamic motor nuclei, and the substantia nigra. This system is involved in coordinating and timing of movements slower than those controlled by the cerebellum. Parkinson's disease is caused by degeneration of dopamine-secreting neurons of the substantia nigra that send axons to the basal ganglia. It can be treated with L-DOPA, lesions of the internal division of the globus pallidus or subthalamic nucleus, stimulation of the subthalamic nucleus, or implants of fetal dopaminergic neurons in the caudate nucleus and putamen. Huntington's disease, a fatal disease caused by a mutation that caused production of abnormal huntingtin protein, causes degeneration of the caudate nucleus and putamen. Although identification of the faulty protein provides hope for understanding the causes of the neural degeneration, there is still no treatment for this disorder.

Suggested Readings

Kandel, E. R., Schwartz, J. H., and Jessell, T. M. *Principles of Neural Science*, 4th ed. New York: McGraw-Hill, 2000.

Kolb, B., and Whishaw, I. Q. *Fundamentals of Human Neuropsychology*, 4th ed. New York: W. H. Freeman, 1996.

Nicholls, J. G., Martin, A. R., Wallace, B. G., and Kuffler, S. W. *From Neuron to Brain*, 3rd ed. Sunderland, MA: Sinauer Associates, 1992.

Suggested Web Sites

Brain, Nerve, and Muscle Disorders

http://cpmcnet.columbia.edu/texts/guide/toc/toc26.html

This site provides a comprehensive treatment of muscle disorders.

Dana Brainweb Page

http://www.dana.org/brainweb/

The Dana Web site contains a series of links to disease states and to general neuroscience Web sites.

Neuromuscular Disease Site:

http://www.neuro.wustl.edu/neuromuscular/

This site provides a comprehensive review of evaluation of neuro-muscular disease and includes a number of images and diagrams of the motor system.

Motor Cortex Animation

http://www.fmrib.ox.ac.uk/~stuart/image_gallery/PManim.html

An animation of an fMRI view of motor cortex is provided on this site.

Lecture Notes on the Motor System

http://www.nyu.edu/classes/azmitia/lectures/lecture09/index.html

This site provides faculty/students with a lecture outline on the motor system and the site contains four color images relating to muscle fiber function and structure.

Sleep and Biological Rhythms

Roberto Matta-Echaurren, No title. © Artists Rights Society (ARS), New York/ADAGP, Paris. © Cameraphoto Arte, Venice/Art Resource, NY.

o u t l i n e

■ **A Physiological and Behavioral Description of Sleep**
Stages of Sleep
Mental Activity During Sleep
Interim Summary

■ **Disorders of Sleep**
Insomnia
Narcolepsy
REM Sleep Behavior Disorder
Problems Associated with
Slow-Wave Sleep
Interim Summary

■ **Why Do We Sleep?**
Functions of Slow-Wave Sleep
Functions of REM Sleep
Interim Summary

■ **Physiological Mechanisms of Sleep and Waking**
Chemical Control of Sleep
Neural Control of Arousal
Neural Control of
Slow-Wave Sleep
Neural Control of REM Sleep
Interim Summary

■ **Biological Clocks**
Circadian Rhythms
and Zeitgebers
The Suprachiasmatic Nucleus
Control of Seasonal Rhythms:
The Pineal Gland and Melatonin
Changes in Circadian Rhythms:
Shift Work and Jet Lag
Interim Summary

Lately, Michael felt almost afraid of going to bed because of the unpleasant experiences he had been having. His dreams seemed to have become more intense, in a rather disturbing way. Several times in the past few months, he felt as if he were paralyzed as he lay in bed, waiting for sleep to come. It was a strange feeling; was he *really* paralyzed, or was he just not trying hard enough to move? He always fell asleep before he was able to decide. A couple of times he woke up just before it was time for his alarm to go off and felt unable to move. Then the alarm would ring, and he would quickly shut it off. That meant that he really wasn't paralyzed, didn't it? Was he going crazy?

Last night brought the worst experience of all. As he was falling asleep, he felt again as if he were paralyzed. Then he saw his old roommate enter his bedroom. But that wasn't possible! Since the time he graduated from college, he had lived alone, and he always locked the door. He tried to say something, but he couldn't. His roommate was holding a hammer. He walked up to his bed, stood over Michael, and suddenly raised the hammer, as if to smash in his forehead. When he awoke in the morning, he shuddered with the remembrance. It had seemed so real! It must have been a dream, but he didn't think he was asleep. He was in bed. Can a person really dream that he is lying in bed, not yet asleep?

That day at the office he had trouble concentrating on his work. He forced himself to review his notes, because he had to present the details of the new project to the board of directors. This was his big chance; if the project were accepted, he would certainly be chosen to lead it, and that would mean a promotion and a substantial raise. Naturally, with so much at stake, he felt nervous when he entered the boardroom. His boss intro-duced Michael and asked him to begin. He glanced at his notes and opened his mouth to talk. Suddenly, he felt his knees buckle. All his strength seemed to slip away. He fell heavily to the floor. He could hear people running over and asking what had happened. He couldn't move anything except his eyes. His boss got down on his knees, looked into his face, and asked, "Michael, are you all right?" Michael looked at his boss and tried to answer, but he couldn't say a thing. A few seconds later, he felt his strength coming back. He opened his mouth and said, "I'm okay." He struggled to his knees and then sat in a chair, feeling weak and frightened.

"You undoubtedly have a condition known as narcolepsy," said the doctor who Michael visited. "It's a problem that concerns the way your brain controls sleep. I'll have you spend a night in the sleep clinic and get some recordings done to confirm my diagnosis, but I'm sure that I'll be proved correct. You told me that lately you've been taking short naps during the day. What were these naps like? Were you suddenly struck by an urge to sleep?" Michael nodded. "I just had to put my head on the desk, even though I was afraid that my boss might see me. But I don't think I slept more than five minutes or so." "Did you still feel sleepy when you woke?" "No," he replied, "I felt fine again." The doctor nodded. "All the symptoms you have reported—the sleep attacks, the paralysis you experienced before sleeping and after waking up, the spell you had today—they all fit together. Fortunately, we can usually control narcolepsy with medication. In fact, we have a new one that does an excellent job. I'm sure we'll have you back to normal, and there is no reason why you can't continue with your job. If you'd like, I can talk with your boss and reassure him, too."

W hy do we sleep? Why do we spend at least one-third of our lives doing something that provides most of us with only a few fleeting memories? I will attempt to answer this question in several ways. In the first two parts of this chapter I will describe what is known about the phenomenon of sleep and its disorders: How much do we sleep? What do we do while asleep? Are sleeping medications effective? What do we know about narcolepsy, sleepwalking, and other sleep-related disorders? In the third part I will discuss research on the causes of sleep: What happens if we do not get enough sleep? Does sleep perform a restorative function? In the fourth part of the chapter I will describe the search for the chemicals and the neural circuits that control sleep and wakefulness. In the final part of the chapter I will discuss the brain's biological clock—the mechanism that controls daily rhythms of sleep and activity.

A Physiological and Behavioral Description of Sleep

Sleep is a behavior. That statement might seem peculiar, because we usually think of behaviors as activities that involve movements, such as walking or talking. Except for the rapid eye movements that accompany a particular stage, sleep is not distinguished by movement. What characterizes sleep is that the insistent urge of sleepiness forces us to seek out a quiet, comfortable place, lie down, and remain there for several hours. Because we remember very little about what happens while we sleep, we tend to think of sleep more as a state of consciousness than as a behavior. The change in consciousness is undeniable, but it should not prevent us from noticing the behavioral changes.

Stages of Sleep

The best research on human sleep is conducted in a sleep laboratory. A sleep laboratory, usually located at a university or medical center, consists of one or several small bedrooms adjacent to an observation room, where the experimenter spends the night (trying to stay awake). The experimenter prepares the sleeper for electrophysiological measurements by attaching electrodes to the scalp to monitor the electroencephalogram (EEG) and to the chin to monitor muscle activity, recorded as the **electromyogram (EMG).** Electrodes attached around the eyes monitor eye movements, recorded as the **electro-oculogram (EOG).** In addition, other electrodes and transducing devices can be used to monitor autonomic measures such as heart rate, respiration, and skin conductance. Wires from the electrodes are bundled together in a "ponytail," which is then plugged into a junction box at the head of the bed. (See *Figure 9.1.*)

During wakefulness the EEG of a normal person shows two basic patterns of activity: *alpha activity* and *beta activity.* **Alpha activity** consists of regular, medium-frequency waves of 8–12 Hz. The brain produces this activity when a person is resting quietly, not particularly aroused or excited and not engaged in strenuous mental activity (such as problem solving). Although alpha waves sometimes occur when a person's eyes are open, they are much more prevalent when the eyes are closed. The other type

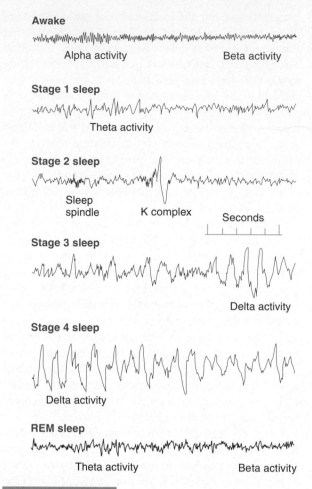

Awake

Alpha activity   Beta activity

Stage 1 sleep

Theta activity

Stage 2 sleep

Sleep
spindle   K complex   Seconds

Stage 3 sleep

Delta activity

Stage 4 sleep

Delta activity

REM sleep

Theta activity   Beta activity

figure 9.2

An EEG recording of the stages of sleep.
(From Horne, J. A. *Why We Sleep: The Functions of Sleep in Humans and Other Mammals.* Oxford, England: Oxford University Press, 1988.)

of waking EEG pattern, **beta activity,** consists of irregular, mostly low-amplitude waves of 13–30 Hz. This activity occurs when a person is alert and attentive to events in the environment or is thinking actively. (See *Figure 9.2.*)

Let us look at a typical night's sleep of a female college student on her third night in the laboratory. (Of course,

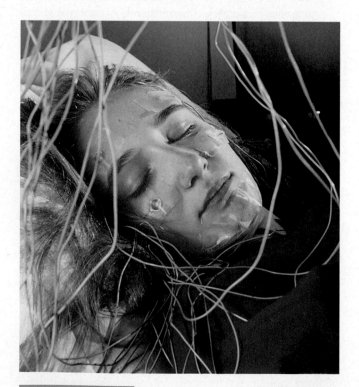

figure 9.1

A subject prepared for a night's sleep in a sleep laboratory.
(Philippe Platilly/Science Photo Library/Photo Researchers Inc.)

electromyogram (EMG) (*my oh gram*) An electrical potential recorded from an electrode placed on or in a muscle.

electro-oculogram (EOG) (*ah kew loh gram*) An electrical potential from the eyes, recorded by means of electrodes placed on the skin around them; detects eye movements.

alpha activity Smooth electrical activity of 8–12 Hz recorded from the brain; generally associated with a state of relaxation.

beta activity Irregular electrical activity of 13–30 Hz recorded from the brain; generally associated with a state of arousal.

we would obtain similar results from a male, with one exception, which is noted later.) The experimenter attaches the electrodes, turns the lights off, and closes the door. Our subject becomes drowsy and soon enters stage 1 sleep, marked by the presence of some **theta activity** (3.5–7.5 Hz). This stage is actually a transition between sleep and wakefulness; if we watch our volunteer's eyelids, we will see that from time to time they slowly open and close and that her eyes roll upward and downward. (See *Figure 9.2.*) About 10 minutes later she enters stage 2 sleep. The EEG during this stage is generally irregular but contains periods of theta activity, *sleep spindles,* and *K complexes.* Sleep spindles are short bursts of waves of 12–14 Hz that occur between two and five times a minute during stages 1–4 of sleep. Some investigators believe that sleep spindles represent the activity of a mechanism that is involved in keeping a person asleep (Bowersox, Kaitin, and Dement, 1985; Steriade, 1992; Nicolas et al., 2001). The sleep of older people contains fewer sleep spindles and is generally accompanied by more awakenings during the night. K complexes are sudden, sharp waveforms, which, unlike sleep spindles, are usually found only during stage 2 sleep. They spontaneously occur at the rate of approximately one per minute but often can be triggered by noises—especially unexpected noises. According to De Gennaro, Ferrara, and Bertini (2000), they appear to be the forerunner of delta waves, which appear in deeper levels of sleep. (See *Figure 9.2.*)

The subject is sleeping soundly now; but if awakened, she might report that she has not been asleep. This phenomenon often is reported by nurses who awaken loudly snoring patients early in the night (probably to give them a sleeping pill) and find that the patients insist they were lying there awake all the time. About 15 minutes later the subject enters stage 3 sleep, signaled by the occurrence of high-amplitude **delta activity** (less than 3.5 Hz). (See *Figure 9.2.*) The distinction between stage 3 and stage 4 is not clear-cut; stage 3 contains 20–50 percent delta activity, and stage 4 contains more than 50 percent. (See *Figure 9.2.*)

About 90 minutes after the beginning of sleep (and about 45 minutes after the onset of stage 4 sleep), we notice an abrupt change in a number of physiological measures recorded from our subject. The EEG suddenly becomes mostly desynchronized, with a sprinkling of theta waves, very similar to the record obtained during stage 1 sleep. (See *Figure 9.2.*) We also note that her eyes are rapidly darting back and forth beneath her closed eyelids. We can see this activity in the EOG, recorded from electrodes attached to the skin around her eyes, or we can observe the eye movements directly—the cornea produces a bulge in the closed eyelids that can be seen to move about. We also see that the EMG becomes silent; there is a profound loss of muscle tonus. In fact, physiological studies have shown that, aside from occasional twitching, a person actually becomes paralyzed during REM sleep.

This peculiar stage of sleep is quite distinct from the quiet sleep we saw earlier. It is usually referred to as **REM sleep** (for the **r**apid **e**ye **m**ovements that characterize it). It has also been called *paradoxical sleep,* because of the presence of beta activity, which is usually seen during wakefulness or stage 1 sleep. The term *paradoxical* merely reflects people's surprise at observing an unexpected phenomenon, but the years since its first discovery (reported by Aserinsky and Kleitman in 1953) have blunted the surprise value.

At this point I should introduce some terminology. Stages 1–4 are usually referred to as **non-REM sleep.** Stages 3 and 4 are referred to as **slow-wave sleep,** because of the presence of delta activity. As we will see, research has focused on the role of REM sleep and of slow-wave sleep; most investigators believe that the other stages of non-REM sleep, stages 1 and 2, are less important. (As we shall see, when people are sleep deprived, they make up most of their slow-wave sleep and REM sleep but not their stage 1 and stage 2 sleep.) By some criteria, stage 4 is the deepest stage of sleep; only loud noises will cause a person to awaken, and when awakened, the person acts groggy and confused. During REM sleep a person might not react to noises, but he or she is easily aroused by meaningful stimuli, such as the sound of his or her name. Also, when awakened from REM sleep, a person appears alert and attentive.

If we arouse our volunteer during REM sleep and ask her what was going on, she will almost certainly report that she had been dreaming. The dreams of REM sleep tend to be narrative in form; there is a storylike progression of events. If we wake her during slow-wave sleep and ask, "Were you dreaming?" she will most likely say, "No." However, if we question her more carefully, she might report the presence of a thought, an image, or some emotion.

During the rest of the night our subject's sleep alternates between periods of REM and non-REM sleep. Each cycle is approximately 90 minutes long, containing a 20- to 30-minute bout of REM sleep. Thus, an 8-hour sleep

---

theta activity EEG activity of 3.5–7.5 Hz that occurs intermittently during early stages of slow-wave sleep and REM sleep.

delta activity Regular, synchronous electrical activity of less than 4 Hz recorded from the brain; occurs during the deepest stages of slow-wave sleep.

REM sleep A period of desynchronized EEG activity during sleep, at which time dreaming, rapid eye movements, and muscular paralysis occur; also called *paradoxical sleep.*

non-REM sleep All stages of sleep except REM sleep.

slow-wave sleep Non-REM sleep, characterized by synchronized EEG activity during its deeper stages.

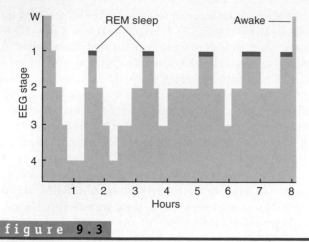

figure 9.3

A typical pattern of the stages of sleep during a single night. The dark blue shading indicates REM sleep.

will contain four or five periods of REM sleep. Figure 9.3 shows a graph of a typical night's sleep. The *x*-axis indicates the EEG activity that is being recorded; thus REM sleep and stage 1 sleep are placed on the same line because similar patterns of EEG activity occur at these times. Note that most slow-wave sleep (stages 3 and 4) occurs during the first half of night. Subsequent bouts of non-REM sleep contain more and more stage 2 sleep, and bouts of REM sleep (indicated by the horizontal bars) become more prolonged. (See *Figure 9.3*.)

The fact that REM sleep occurs at regular 90-minute intervals suggests that a brain mechanism alternately causes REM and slow-wave sleep. Normally, a period of slow-wave sleep must precede REM sleep. In addition, there seems to be a refractory period after each occurrence of REM sleep, during which time REM sleep cannot take place again. In fact, the cyclical nature of REM sleep appears to be controlled by a "clock" in the brain that also controls an activity cycle that continues through waking. The first suggestion that a 90-minute activity cycle occurs throughout the day came from the observation that infants who are fed on demand show regular feeding patterns (Kleitman, 1961). Later studies found 90-minute cycles of rest and activity, including such activities as eating, drinking, smoking, heart rate, oxygen consumption, stomach motility, urine production, and performance on various tasks that make demands upon a person's ability to pay attention. Kleitman termed this phenomenon the **basic rest–activity cycle** (Kleitman, 1982.) An internal "clock," as yet undiscovered, appears to cause regular changes in activity and alertness during the day and control periods of slow-wave and REM sleep at night.

basic rest-activity cycle A 90-minute cycle (in humans) of waxing and waning alertness, controlled by a biological clock in the caudal brain stem; controls cycles of REM sleep and slow-wave sleep.

As we saw, during REM sleep we become paralyzed; most of our spinal and cranial motor neurons are strongly inhibited. (Obviously, the ones that control respiration and eye movements are spared.) At the same time the brain is very active. Cerebral blood flow and oxygen consumption are accelerated. In addition, a male's penis will become at least partially erect, and a female's vaginal secretions will increase. However, Fisher, Gross, and Zuch (1965) found that in males, genital changes do not signify that the person is experiencing a dream with sexual content. (Of course, people can have dreams with frank sexual content. In males some dreams culminate in ejaculation—the so-called nocturnal emissions, or "wet dreams." Females, too, sometimes experience orgasm during sleep.)

The fact that penile erections occur during REM sleep, independent of sexual arousal, has been used clinically to assess the causes of impotence (Karacan, Salis, and Williams, 1978; Singer and Weiner, 1996). A subject sleeps in the laboratory with a device attached to his penis that measures its circumference. If penile enlargement occurs during REM sleep, then his failure to obtain an erection during attempts at intercourse is not caused by physiological problems such as nerve damage or a circulatory disorder. (A neurologist told me that there is a less expensive way to gather the same data. The patient obtains a strip of postage stamps, moistens them, and applies them around his penis before going to bed. In the morning he checks to see whether the perforations are broken.)

The important differences between REM and slow-wave sleep are listed in *Table 9.1*.

Mental Activity During Sleep

Although sleep is a period during which we do not respond very much to the environment, it is incorrect to refer to sleep as a state of unconsciousness. Consciousness during sleep certainly differs from waking consciousness, but we *are* conscious then. In the morning we usually for-

table 9.1

Principal Characteristics of REM and Slow-Wave Sleep	
REM SLEEP	**SLOW-WAVE SLEEP**
EEG desynchrony (rapid, irregular waves)	EEG synchrony (slow waves)
Lack of muscle tonus	Moderate muscle tonus
Rapid eye movements	Slow or absent eye movements
Penile erection or vaginal secretion	Lack of genital activity
Dreams	

get what we experienced while asleep, so in retrospect we conclude that we were unconscious. However, when experimenters wake sleeping subjects, the reports that the subjects give make it clear that they were conscious.

Madsen et al. (1991) found that the rate of cerebral blood flow in the human brain during REM sleep was high in the visual association cortex but low in the inferior frontal cortex. As we shall see in Chapter 14, the inferior frontal cortex is involved in making plans and keeping track of the organization of events in time. As Madsen and his colleagues noted, dreams are characterized by good visual images (undoubtedly involving the visual association cortex), but they are poorly organized with respect to time; for example, past, present, and future are often interchanged (Hobson, 1988). And as Melges (1982) put it, "the dreamer often has no feeling of striving for long-term goals but rather is carried along by the flow of time by circumstances that crop up in an unpredictable way." This quote could just as well be describing the daily life of a person whose inferior frontal cortex has been damaged.

Several investigators have suggested that the eye movements made during REM sleep are related to the visual imagery that occurs while we dream. Roffwarg et al. (1962) recorded the eye movements of subjects during REM sleep and then awakened them and asked them to describe what had been happening in their dreams. They found that the eye movements were similar to what would have been expected if the subjects had actually been watching these events. Miyauchi, Takino, and Azakami (1990) recorded the EEG of sleeping subjects and found that a particular wave accompanied eye movements during REM sleep. This wave was also seen when waking subjects scanned a scene, but it was *not* seen when they simply made eye movements in a dark room. Therefore, the EEG wave is not produced by eye movements themselves but may actually indicate that the subjects had been scanning a visual image during a dream.

Evidence indicates that the particular brain mechanisms that become active during a dream are those that would become active if the events in the dream were actually occurring. For example, cortical and subcortical motor mechanisms become active during a dream that contains movement—as if the person were actually moving (McCarley and Hobson, 1979). In addition, if a dream involves talking and listening, regions of the dreamer's brain that are involved in speaking and listening become especially active (Hong et al., 1996). (Brain mechanisms of verbal communication are discussed in Chapter 15.)

Although narrative, storylike dreaming occurs during REM sleep, mental activity can also accompany slow-wave sleep. Some of the most terrifying nightmares occur during slow-wave sleep, especially stage 4 sleep (Fisher et al., 1970). Although narrative, storylike dreaming occurs during REM sleep, mental activity can also accompany slow-wave sleep. Some of the most terrifying nightmares occur during slow-wave sleep, especially stage 4 sleep

The Nightmare, 1781, by Henry Fuseli, Swiss, 1741–1825. (Gift of Mr. and Mrs. Bert L. Smokler and Mr. and Mrs. Lawrence A. Fleischman, Acc. No. 55.5. Courtesy of The Detroit Institute of Arts.)

(Fisher et al., 1970). In French the word for nightmare is *cauchemar,* or "pressing devil." Figure 9.4 shows a victim of a nightmare (undoubtedly in the throes of stage 4 slow-wave sleep) being squashed by an *incubus* (from the Latin *incubare,* "to lie upon"). (See ***Figure 9.4.***)

interim summary

A Physiological and Behavioral Description of Sleep

Sleep is generally regarded as a state, but it is nevertheless a behavior. The stages of non-REM sleep, stages 1–4, are defined by EEG activity. Slow-wave sleep (stages 3 and 4) includes the two deepest stages. Alertness consists of desynchronized beta activity (13–30 Hz); relaxation and drowsiness consist of alpha activity (8–12 Hz); stage 1 sleep consists of alternating periods of alpha activity, irregular fast activity, and theta activity (3.5–7.5 Hz); the EEG of stage 2 sleep lacks alpha activity but contains sleep spindles (short periods of 12–14 Hz activity) and occasional K complexes; stage 3 sleep consists of 20–50 percent delta activity (less than 3.5 Hz); and stage 4 sleep consists of more than 50 percent delta activity. About 90 minutes after the beginning of sleep, people enter REM sleep. Cycles of REM and slow-wave sleep alternate in periods of approximately 90 minutes.

REM sleep consists of rapid eye movements, a desynchronized EEG, sensitivity to external stimulation, muscular paralysis, genital activity, and dreaming. Mental activity can accompany slow-wave sleep, too, but most narrative dreams occur during REM sleep.

Disorders of Sleep

Because we spend about one-third of our lives sleeping, sleep disorders can have a significant impact on our quality of life. They can also affect the way we feel while we are awake.

Insomnia

Insomnia is a problem that is said to affect approximately 25 percent of the population occasionally and 9 percent regularly (Ancoli-Israel and Roth, 1999). But we need to define *insomnia* carefully. First, there is no single definition of insomnia that can apply to all people. The amount of sleep that individuals require is quite variable. A short sleeper may feel fine with 5 hours; a long sleeper may still feel unrefreshed after 10 hours of sleep. Insomnia must be defined in relation to a person's particular sleep needs. Some short sleepers have sought medical assistance because they thought that they were supposed to get more sleep, even though they felt fine. These people should be reassured that whatever amount of sleep seems to be enough *is* enough.

Ironically, one of the most important causes of insomnia seems to be sleeping medication. Insomnia is not a disease that can be corrected with a medicine in the way that diabetes can be treated with insulin. Insomnia is a symptom. If it is caused by pain or discomfort, the physical ailment that leads to the sleeplessness should be treated. If it is secondary to personal problems or psychological disorders, these problems should be dealt with directly. Patients who receive a sleeping medication develop a tolerance to the drug and suffer rebound symptoms if it is withdrawn (Weitzman, 1981). That is, the drug loses its effectiveness, so the patient requests larger doses from the physician. If the patient attempts to sleep without the accustomed medication or even takes a smaller dose one night, he or she is likely to experience a withdrawal effect: a severe disturbance of sleep. The patient becomes convinced that the insomnia is even worse than before and turns to more medication for relief. This common syndrome is called **drug dependency insomnia.** Kales et al. (1979) found that withdrawal of some sleeping medications produced a rebound insomnia after the drugs were used for as few as three nights.

The second consideration in defining insomnia is the unreliability of self reports. Most patients who receive a prescription for a sleeping medication are given one on the basis of their own description of their symptoms. That is, they tell their physician that they sleep very little at night, and the drug is prescribed on the basis of this testimony. Very few patients are observed during a night's sleep in a sleep laboratory; thus, insomnia is one of the few medical problems that physicians treat without having direct clinical evidence for its existence. But studies on the sleep of people who complain of insomnia show that most of them grossly underestimate the amount of time they actually sleep. In fact, Rosa and Bonnet (2000) evaluated the sleep of people who complained of insomnia and people who did not in a sleep laboratory and found no differences between the two groups. They *did,* however, find personality differences, which could account for the complaints. The U.S. Institute of Medicine (1979) found that most insomniacs, even without sleeping medication, fall asleep in less than 30 minutes and sleep for at least 6 hours. *With* sleeping medication they obtained less than a 15-minute reduction in falling asleep, and their sleep length was increased by only about 30 minutes. Given the unfortunate side effects, sleeping medication does not seem to be worthwhile, except perhaps on a short-term basis.

For many years the goal of sleeping medication was to help people fall asleep, and when drug companies evaluated potential medications, they concentrated on that property. However, if we think about the ultimate goal of sleeping medication, it is to make the person feel more refreshed the next day. If a medication puts people to sleep right away but produces a hangover of grogginess and difficulty concentrating the next day, it is worse than useless. In fact, many drugs that are traditionally used to treat insomnia had just this effect. More recently, researchers have recognized that the true evaluation of a sleeping medication must be made during wakefulness the following day (American Psychiatric Association, 1994), and "hangover-free" drugs are finally being developed (Hajak et al., 1995).

A particular form of insomnia is caused by an inability to sleep and breathe at the same time. Patients with this disorder, called **sleep apnea,** fall asleep and then cease to breathe. (Nearly all people, especially people who snore, have occasional episodes of sleep apnea, but not to the extent that it interferes with sleep.) During a period of sleep apnea the level of carbon dioxide in the blood stimulates chemoreceptors (neurons that detect the presence of certain chemicals), and the person wakes up, gasping for air. The oxygen level of the blood returns to normal, the person falls asleep, and the whole cycle begins again. Fortunately, many cases of sleep apnea are caused by an obstruction of the airway that can be corrected surgically or relieved by a device that attaches to the sleeper's face and provides pressurized air that keeps the airway open (Sher, 1990; Piccirillo, Duntley, and Schotland, 2000).

Narcolepsy

Narcolepsy (*narke* means "numbness," and *lepsis* means "seizure") is a neurological disorder characterized by sleep (or some of its components) at inappropriate

---

drug dependency insomnia An insomnia caused by the side effects of ever-increasing doses of sleeping medications.

sleep apnea (*app nee a*) Cessation of breathing while sleeping.

narcolepsy (*nahr ko lep see*) A sleep disorder characterized by periods of irresistible sleep, attacks of cataplexy, sleep paralysis, and hypnagogic hallucinations.

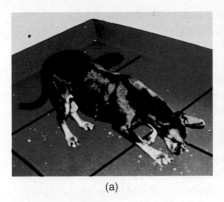
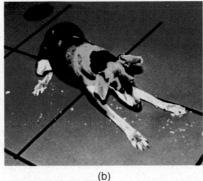
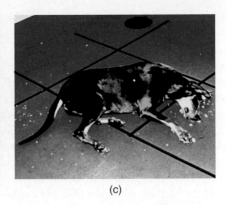

(a)   (b)   (c)

figure 9.5

A dog undergoing a cataplectic attack triggered by its excitement at finding some food on the floor. (a) Sniffing the food. (b) Muscles beginning to relax. (c) The dog is temporarily paralyzed, as it would be during REM sleep.
(Photos courtesy of the Sleep Disorders Foundation, Stanford University.)

times. The symptoms can be described in terms of what we know about the phenomena of sleep. The primary symptom of narcolepsy is the **sleep attack.** The narcoleptic sleep attack is an overwhelming urge to sleep that can happen at any time but occurs most often under monotonous, boring conditions. Sleep (which appears to be entirely normal) generally lasts for 2–5 minutes. The person usually wakes up feeling refreshed.

Another symptom of narcolepsy—in fact, the most striking one—is **cataplexy** (from *kata,* "down," and *plexis,* "stroke"). During a cataplectic attack a person will suddenly wilt and fall like a sack of flour. The person will lie there, *fully conscious,* for a few seconds to several minutes. What apparently happens is that one of the phenomena of REM sleep—muscular paralysis—occurs at an inappropriate time. As we saw, this loss of tonus is caused by massive inhibition of motor neurons in the spinal cord. When this happens during waking, the victim of a cataplectic attack falls as suddenly as if a switch had been thrown.

Cataplexy is quite different from a narcoleptic sleep attack; cataplexy is usually precipitated by strong emotion or by sudden physical effort, especially if the patient is caught unawares. Laughter, anger, or an effort to catch a suddenly thrown object can trigger a cataplectic attack. In fact, as Guilleminault, Wilson, and Dement (1974) noted, even people who do not have cataplexy sometimes lose muscle strength after a bout of intense laughter. (Perhaps that is why we say a person can become "weak from laughter.") Common situations that bring on cataplexy are attempting to discipline one's children and making love (an awkward time to become paralyzed!). Michael, the man described in the opener to this chapter, had his first cataplectic attack when he was addressing the board of directors of the company he worked for.

REM sleep paralysis sometimes intrudes into waking, but at a time that does not present any physical danger—just before or just after normal sleep, when a person is already lying down. This symptom of narcolepsy is referred to as **sleep paralysis,** an inability to move just before the onset of sleep or upon waking in the morning. A person can be snapped out of sleep paralysis by being touched or by hearing someone call his or her name. Sometimes, the mental components of REM sleep intrude into sleep paralysis; that is, the person dreams while lying awake, paralyzed. These episodes, called **hypnagogic hallucinations,** are often alarming or even terrifying. (The term *hypnagogic* comes from the Greek words *hupnos,* "sleep," and *agogos,* "leading.")

Narcolepsy is produced by a brain abnormality that disrupts the neural mechanisms that control various aspects of sleep and arousal. As we saw, narcoleptic patients have difficulty staying awake, and aspects of REM sleep intrude into the waking state. In addition, they generally skip the slow-wave sleep that normally begins a night's sleep; instead, they go directly into REM sleep from waking. Finally, their sleep is often disrupted by periods of wakefulness.

Human narcolepsy is a genetic disorder that is influenced by unknown environmental factors (Mignot, 1998). Years ago, researchers began a program to maintain breeds of dogs that are afflicted with narcolepsy, with the hopes that discovery of the causes of canine narcolepsy would further our understanding of the causes of human narcolepsy. (See *Figure 9.5.*) This research has finally paid off.

sleep attack A symptom of narcolepsy; an irresistible urge to sleep during the day, after which the person awakes feeling refreshed.

cataplexy (*kat a plex ee*) A symptom of narcolepsy; complete paralysis that occurs during waking.

sleep paralysis A symptom of narcolepsy; paralysis occurring just before a person falls asleep.

hypnagogic hallucination (*hip na gah jik*) A symptom of narcolepsy; vivid dreams that occur just before a person falls asleep; accompanied by sleep paralysis.

Lin et al. (1999) discovered that a mutation of a specific gene is responsible for canine narcolepsy. The product of this gene is a receptor for a recently discovered peptide neurotransmitter called **hypocretin** (also known by some researchers as *orexin*). The name "hypocretin" comes from the fact that the lateral *hypo*thalamus contains the cell bodies of all of the neurons that se*crete* this peptide. The name "orexin" comes from the role this peptide plays in the control of eating and metabolism, which are discussed in Chapter 12. (Orexis means "appetite" in Greek.) There are two hypocretin receptors. Lin and his colleagues discovered that the mutation responsible for canine narcolepsy involves the hypocretin 2 receptor.

Chemelli et al. (1999) prepared a targeted mutation in mice against the hypocretin gene and found that the animals showed symptoms of narcolepsy. Like human patients with narcolepsy, they went directly into REM sleep from waking and showed periods of cataplexy while they were awake. (Videos of narcoleptic dogs, mice, and people are shown in *Animation 9.1*.) Hara et al. (2001) created a strain of mice with a genetic mutation that caused the eventual death of hypocretinergic neurons. The mice were born with these neurons, but the neurons degenerated later in life, at which time the mice showed the symptoms of narcolepsy: behavioral arrests (cataplexy), early-onset REM sleep, and fragmented sleep. Geraschchenko et al. (2001) prepared a toxin that attacked hypocretinergic neurons, which they administered to rats. The destruction of the hypocretin system produced the symptoms of narcolepsy.

> See the interactive CD for more information on this topic.

Abnormalities in the hypocretin system appear to be the cause of narcolepsy in humans as well. Nishino et al. (2000) performed an analysis of the cerebrospinal fluid of normal subjects and patients with narcolepsy. They found a complete absence of hypocretin in seven of the nine narcoleptic patients. They hypothesized that the cause of narcolepsy in these seven patients was a hereditary disorder that caused the immune system to attack and destroy hypocretin-secreting neurons. Most patients with narcolepsy are born with hypocretinergic neurons, but during adolescence, the immune system attacks these neurons, and the symptoms of narcolepsy begin. The narcolepsy that was seen in two patients with high levels of hypocretin may have been caused by a mutation of a gene responsible for production of the hypocretin 2 receptor. Peyron et al. (2000) reported the case of a child (See *Animation 9.1*) with a mutation of the gene responsible for the production of hypocretin. Scammell et al. (2001) reported the case of a patient who developed narcolepsy after a stroke that damaged the hypothalamus. An analysis of the patient's cerebrospinal fluid showed a very low level of hypocretin; apparently, the stroke had damaged the patient's hypocretinergic neurons.

The symptoms of narcolepsy can be successfully treated with drugs. Sleep attacks can be diminished by stimulants such a methylphenidate (Ritalin), a catecholamine agonist (Vgontzas and Kales, 1999). The REM sleep phenomena (cataplexy, sleep paralysis, and hypnagogic hallucinations) can be alleviated by antidepressant drugs, which facilitate both serotonergic and noradrenergic activity (Mitler, 1994; Hublin, 1996). More recently, modafinil, a stimulant drug whose precise site of action is still unknown, has been used to treat narcolepsy (Fry, 1998). (Michael, the man introduced in the opener to this chapter, is now taking this drug.) A study by Scammell et al. (2000) suggests that modafinil acts, directly or indirectly, on hypocretinergic neurons. The investigators found that administration of modafinil increased the expression of Fos protein in hypocretinergic neurons, which indicates that the neurons had been activated. As we will see in Chapter 16, abnormalities in patterns of REM sleep are seen in people suffering from depression. The fact that drugs that reduce depression also suppress the phenomena of REM sleep is probably not coincidental.

The connections of hypocretinergic neurons with other regions of the brain is discussed later in this chapter.

REM Sleep Behavior Disorder

Several years ago, Schenck et al. (1986) reported the existence of an interesting disorder: **REM sleep behavior disorder.** As you now know, REM sleep is accompanied by paralysis. Although the motor cortex and subcortical motor systems are extremely active (McCarley and Hobson, 1979), people are unable to move at this time.

> The fact that people are paralyzed while they dream suggests the possibility that but for the paralysis, they would act out their dreams. Indeed, they would. The behavior of people who exhibit REM-sleep behavior disorder corresponds with the contents of their dreams. Consider the following case:
>
> > I was a halfback playing football, and after the quarterback received the ball from the center he lateraled it sideways to me and I'm supposed to go around end and cut back over tackle and—this is very vivid—as I cut back over tackle there is this big 280-pound tackle waiting, so I, according to football rules, was to give him my shoulder and bounce him out of the way . . . when I came to I was standing in front of our dresser and I had [gotten up out of bed and run and] knocked lamps, mirrors and everything off the dresser, hit my head against the wall and my knee against the dresser. (Schenck et al., 1986, p. 294)

hypocretin A peptide, also known as *orexin*, produced by neurons whose cell bodies are located in the hypothalamus; their destruction causes narcolepsy.

REM sleep behavior disorder (*ay tone ee a*) A neurological disorder in which the person does not become paralyzed during REM sleep and thus acts out dreams.

Like narcolepsy, REM sleep behavior disorder appears to be a neurodegenerative disorder with at least some genetic component (Schenck et al., 1996). It is often associated with better known neurodegenerative disorders such as Parkinson's disease and multiple system atrophy (Boeve et al., 2001). These disorders are called *synucleinopathies* because they involve the inclusion of α-synuclein protein in degenerating neurons. In addition, REM sleep behavior disorder can be caused by brain damage—in some cases to the neural circuits in the brain stem that control the phenomena of REM sleep (Culebras and Moore, 1989). The symptoms of REM sleep behavior disorder are the opposite of those of cataplexy; that is, rather than exhibit paralysis outside REM sleep, patients with REM-sleep behavior disorder *fail* to exhibit paralysis *during* REM sleep. As you might expect, the drugs that are used to treat the symptoms of cataplexy will aggravate the symptoms of REM sleep behavior disorder (Schenck and Mahowald, 1992). REM sleep behavior disorder is usually treated by clonazepam, a benzodiazepine (Schenck, Hurwitz, and Mahowald, 1996).

Problems Associated with Slow-Wave Sleep

Some maladaptive behaviors occur during slow-wave sleep, especially during its deepest phase, stage 4. These behaviors include bedwetting *(nocturnal enuresis),* sleepwalking *(somnambulism),* and night terrors *(pavor nocturnus).* All three events occur most frequently in children. Often bedwetting can be cured by training methods, such as having a special electronic circuit ring a bell when the first few drops of urine are detected in the bed sheet (a few drops usually precede the ensuing flood). Night terrors consist of anguished screams, trembling, a rapid pulse, and usually no memory of what caused the terror. Night terrors and somnambulism usually cure themselves as the child gets older. Neither of these phenomena is related to REM sleep; a sleepwalking person is *not* acting out a dream. Most authorities firmly advise that the best treatment for these two disorders is no treatment at all. There is no evidence that they are associated (at least in childhood) with mental disorders or personality variables.

i n t e r i m s u m m a r y

Disorders of Sleep

Although many people believe that they have insomnia—that they do not obtain as much sleep as they would like—insomnia is not a disease. Insomnia can be caused by depression, pain, illness, or even excited anticipation of a pleasurable event. Far too many people receive sleeping medications, which often lead to a condition called drug dependency insomnia. Sometimes, insomnia is caused by sleep apnea,

which can often be corrected surgically or treated by wearing a mask that delivers pressurized air.

Narcolepsy is characterized by four symptoms. *Sleep attacks* consist of overwhelming urges to sleep for a few minutes. *Cataplexy* is sudden paralysis, during which the person remains conscious. *Sleep paralysis* is similar to cataplexy, but it occurs just before sleep or on waking. *Hypnagogic hallucinations* are dreams that occur during periods of sleep paralysis, just before a night's sleep. Sleep attacks are treated with stimulants such as amphetamine, and the other symptoms are treated with serotonin agonists. Studies with narcoleptic dogs and humans indicate that this disorder is caused by pathologies in a system of neurons that secrete a neuropeptide known as hypocretin (also known as orexin). Another disorder associated with REM sleep, REM sleep behavior disorder, is a neurodegenerative disease that damages brain mechanisms that produce paralysis during REM sleep.

During slow-wave sleep, especially during stage 4, some people are afflicted by bedwetting (nocturnal enuresis), sleepwalking (somnambulism), or night terrors (pavor nocturnus). These problems are most common in children, who usually outgrow them. Only if they occur in adults do they suggest the existence of a physical or psychological disorder.

Why Do We Sleep?

We all know how insistent the urge to sleep can be and how uncomfortable we feel when we have to resist it and stay awake. With the exception of the effects of severe pain and the need to breathe, sleepiness is probably the most insistent drive. People can commit suicide by refusing to eat or drink, but even the most stoical person cannot indefinitely defy the urge to sleep. Sleep will come, sooner or later, no matter how hard a person tries to stay awake. Although the issue is not yet settled, most researchers believe that the primary function of slow-wave sleep is to permit the brain to rest. REM sleep appears to promote brain development and learning, but how it might do so is not yet understood.

Functions of Slow-Wave Sleep

Sleep is a universal phenomenon among vertebrates. As far as we know, all mammals and birds sleep (Durie, 1981). Reptiles also sleep, and fish and amphibians enter periods of quiescence that probably can be called sleep. However, only warm-blooded vertebrates (mammals and birds) exhibit unequivocal REM sleep, with muscular paralysis, EEG signs of desynchrony, and rapid eye movements. Obviously, birds such as flamingos, which sleep while perched on one leg, do not lose tone in the muscles they use to remain standing. Also, animals such as moles, which move their eyes very little while awake, show few signs of eye movement while asleep. The functions of REM sleep will be discussed separately, in a later section.

Sleep appears to be essential to survival. Evidence for this assertion comes from the fact that sleep is found in some species of mammals that would seem to be better off without it. For example, the Indus dolphin *(Platanista indi)* lives in the muddy waters of the Indus estuary in Pakistan (Pilleri, 1979). Over the years it has become blind, presumably because vision is not useful in the animal's environment. (It has an excellent sonar system, which it uses to navigate and find prey.) However, despite the dangers caused by sleeping, sleep has not disappeared in this species. The Indus dolphin never stops swimming; doing so would result in injury, because of the dangerous currents and the vast quantities of debris carried by the river during the monsoon season. Pilleri captured two dolphins and studied their habits. He found that they slept a total of 7 hours a day, in brief naps of 4–60 seconds each. If sleep were simply an adaptive response, why was it not eliminated (as vision was) through the process of natural selection?

Some other species of marine mammals have developed an extraordinary pattern of sleep: The cerebral hemispheres take turns sleeping, presumably because that strategy always permits at least one hemisphere to be alert. The bottlenose dolphin *(Tursiops truncatus)* and the porpoise *(Phocoena phocoena)* both sleep this way (Mukhametov, 1984). Figure 9.6 shows the EEG recordings from the two hemispheres; note that slow-wave sleep occurs independently in the left and right hemispheres. (See *Figure 9.6.*)

Effects of Sleep Deprivation

When we are forced to miss a night's sleep, we become very sleepy. The fact that sleepiness is so motivating suggests that sleep is a necessity of life. If so, it should be possible to deprive people or laboratory animals of sleep and see what functions are disrupted. We should then be able to infer the role that sleep plays. However,

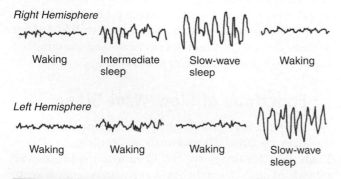

Right Hemisphere

Waking   Intermediate   Slow-wave   Waking
          sleep   sleep

Left Hemisphere

Waking   Waking   Waking   Slow-wave
                              sleep

figure 9.6

Sleep in a dolphin. The two hemispheres sleep independently, presumably so that the animal remains behaviorally alert.

(Adapted from Mukhametov, L. M., in *Sleep Mechanisms,* edited by A. A. Borbély and J. L. Valatx. Munich: Springer-Verlag, 1984.)

the results of sleep deprivation studies have not revealed as much as investigators had originally hoped.

■ **Studies with Humans** Deprivation studies with human subjects have not obtained persuasive evidence that sleep is needed to keep the body functioning normally. Horne (1978) reviewed over fifty experiments in which people had been deprived of sleep. He reported that most of them found that sleep deprivation did not interfere with people's ability to perform physical exercise. In addition, the studies found no evidence of a physiological stress response to sleep deprivation. Thus, the primary role of sleep does not seem to be rest and recuperation of the body. However, people's cognitive abilities were affected; some people reported perceptual distortions or even hallucinations and had trouble concentrating on mental tasks. Perhaps sleep provides the opportunity for the brain to rest.

What happens to sleep-deprived subjects after they are permitted to sleep again? Most of them sleep longer the next night or two, but they never regain all of the sleep they lost. In one remarkable case a seventeen-year-old boy stayed awake for 264 hours so that he could obtain a place in the *Guinness Book of World Records* (Gulevich, Dement, and Johnson, 1966). After his ordeal the boy slept for a little less than 15 hours and awoke feeling fine. He slept slightly more than 10 hours the second night and just under 9 hours the third. Almost 67 hours were never made up. However, percentages of recovery were not equal for all stages of sleep. Only 7 percent of stages 1 and 2 were made up, but 68 percent of stage 4 slow-wave sleep and 53 percent of REM sleep were made up. Other studies (for example, Kales et al., 1970) have found similar results, suggesting that stage 4 sleep and REM sleep are more important than the other stages.

As I mentioned earlier, REM sleep will be discussed later. But what do we know about the possible functions of slow-wave sleep? What happens then that is so important? Both cerebral metabolic rate and cerebral blood flow decline during slow-wave sleep, falling to about 75 percent of the waking level during stage 4 sleep (Sakai et al., 1979; Buchsbaum et al., 1989; Maquet, 1995). In particular, the regions that have the highest levels of activity during waking show the highest levels of delta waves—and the lowest levels of activity—during slow-wave sleep. Thus, the presence of delta activity in a particular region of the brain appears to indicate that that region is resting. As we know from behavioral observation, people are unreactive to all but intense stimuli during slow-wave sleep and, if awakened, act groggy and confused, as if their cerebral cortex has been shut down and has not yet resumed its functioning. In addition, several studies have shown that missing a single night's sleep impairs people's cognitive abilities; presumably, the brain needs sleep to function at peak efficiency (Harrison and Horne, 1998, 1999) These observations suggest that during stage 4 sleep the brain is indeed resting.

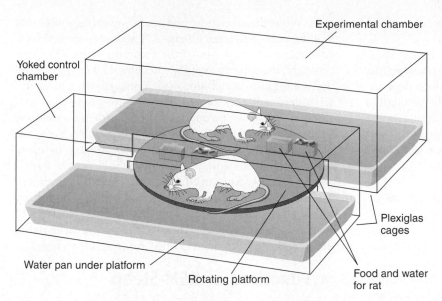

Yoked control chamber

Experimental chamber

Plexiglas cages

Water pan under platform

Rotating platform

Food and water for rat

figure 9.7

The apparatus used to deprive rats of sleep. Whenever one of the pair of rats in the experimental chambers fell asleep, the turntable was rotated until the animal was awake for 6 seconds.

(Redrawn from Rechtschaffen, A., Gilliland, M. A., Bergmann, B. M., and Winter, J. B. *Science,* 1983, *221,* 182–184.)

An inherited neurological disorder called **fatal familial insomnia** results in damage to portions of the thalamus (Sforza et al., 1995; Gallassi et al., 1996). The symptoms of this disease include deficits in attention and memory, followed by a dreamlike, confused state; loss of control of the autonomic nervous system and the endocrine system; and insomnia. The first signs of sleep disturbances are reductions in sleep spindles and K complexes. As the disease progresses, slow-wave sleep completely disappears, and only brief episodes of REM sleep (without the accompanying paralysis) remain. As the name indicates, the disease is fatal. Whether the insomnia, caused by the brain damage, contributes to the other symptoms and to the patient's death is not known. In any case, as we shall see in the next section, when laboratory animals are kept awake indefinitely, they too will die.

■ **Studies with Laboratory Animals** Until recently, sleep deprivation studies with animals have provided us with little insight into the role of sleep. Because animals cannot be "persuaded" to stay awake, it is especially difficult to separate the effects of sleep deprivation from those caused by the method used to keep the animals awake. We can ask a human volunteer to try to stay awake and can expect some cooperation. He or she will say, "I'm getting sleepy—help me to stay awake." However, animals are interested only in getting to sleep and must constantly be stimulated—and hence stressed. Rechtschaffen and his colleagues (Rechtschaffen et al., 1983, 1989; Rechtschaffen and Bergmann, 1995, 2002) devised a procedure to control for the effects of forced exercise that are necessary to keep an animal from sleeping. They constructed a circular platform on which two rats lived, each restrained in a plastic cage. When the platform was rotated by an electrical motor, the rats were forced to walk to avoid falling into a pool of water. (See *Figure 9.7.*)

The investigators employed a *yoked-control* procedure to deprive one rat of sleep but force both members of the pair to exercise an equal amount of time. (The term is used for any experiment in which two animals receive the same treatment at the same time, like two oxen fastened together with a yoke.) A computer recorded the EEGs and EMGs of both rats and detected both slow-wave and REM sleep. One rat served as the experimental (sleep-deprived) animal, and the other served as the yoked control. As soon as the EEG recording indicated that the experimental animal was falling asleep, the computer turned on the motor that rotated the disk, forcing both animals to exercise. Because the platform rotated whenever the experimental animal started to sleep, the procedure reduced the experimental animal's total sleep time by 87 percent. However, the sleep time of the yoked-control rat was reduced by only 31 percent.

Sleep deprivation had serious effects. The control animals remained in perfect health. However, the experimental animals looked sick and stopped grooming their fur. They became weak and uncoordinated and lost their ability to regulate their body temperature. Although they began eating much more food than normal, their metabolic rates became so high that they continued to lose weight. Eventually, the rats died. The cause of death is still not certain. The rats' brains appeared to be normal, and there were no obvious signs of inflammation or damage to other internal organs. The animals' levels of stress hormones were not unusually high, so the deaths could not be attributed to simple stress. If they were given a high-calorie diet to compensate for their increased metabolic

---

fatal familial insomnia A fatal inherited disorder characterized by progressive insomnia.

rate, the rats lived longer, but eventually they succumbed (Everson and Wehr, 1993).

In the previous subsection I described the neurodegenerative disorder called fatal familial insomnia, which, as you can see, resembles the effects of forced sleep deprivation in rats. Budka et al. (1998) reported another similarity. The investigators studied five people with fatal familial insomnia who, along with insomnia, memory loss, and autonomic dysfunction, exhibited prominent weight loss.

Effects of Exercise on Sleep

Sleep deprivation studies with humans suggest that the brain may need slow-wave sleep to recover from the day's activities but that the rest of the body does not. Another way to determine whether sleep is needed for restoration of physiological functioning is to look at the effects of daytime activity on nighttime sleep. If the function of sleep is to repair the effects of activity during waking hours, then we should expect that sleep and exercise are related. That is, we should sleep more after a day of vigorous exercise than after a day spent quietly at an office desk.

However, the relationship between sleep and exercise is not very compelling. For example, Ryback and Lewis (1971) found no changes in slow-wave or REM sleep of healthy subjects who spent six weeks resting in bed. If sleep repairs wear and tear, we would expect these people to sleep less. Adey, Bors, and Porter (1968) studied the sleep of *completely* immobile quadriplegics and paraplegics and found only a small decrease in slow-wave sleep as compared with uninjured people. Thus, although sleep certainly provides the body with rest, its primary function appears to be something else.

Effects of Mental Activity on Sleep

If the primary function of slow-wave sleep is to permit the brain to rest and recover from its daily activity, then we might expect that a person would spend more time in slow-wave sleep after a day of intense cerebral activity. First of all, tasks that demand alertness and mental activity *do* increase glucose metabolism in the brain, as measured by a PET scanner (Roland, 1984). The most significant increases are seen in the frontal lobes, where delta activity is most intense during slow-wave sleep. In an experiment that supports this interpretation, Kattler, Dijk, and Borbély (1994) stimulated a person's hand with a vibrator, which activated the contralateral somatosensory cortex. The next night, a recording of the subject's EEG showed more delta activity in that region of the brain. Presumably, the increased activity of the cortical neurons called for more rest during the following night's sleep.

In an ingenious study Horne and Minard (1985) found a way to increase mental activity without affecting physical activity and without causing stress. The investigators told subjects to show up for an experiment in which they were supposed to take some tests designed to measure reading

skills. When the subjects turned up, however, they were told that the plans had been changed. They were invited for a day out, at the expense of the experimenters. (Not surprisingly, the subjects willingly accepted.) They spent the day visiting an art exhibition, a shopping center, a museum, an amusement park, a zoo, and an interesting mansion. After a scenic drive through the countryside they watched a movie in a local theater. They were driven from place to place and certainly did not become overheated by exercise. After the movie they returned to the sleep laboratory. They said they were tired, and they readily fell asleep. Their sleep duration was normal, and they awoke feeling refreshed. However, their slow-wave sleep—particularly stage 4 sleep—was increased. After all that mental exercise, the brain appears to have needed more rest than usual.

Functions of REM Sleep

Clearly, REM sleep is a time of intense physiological activity. The eyes dart about rapidly, the heart rate shows sudden accelerations and decelerations, breathing becomes irregular, and the brain becomes more active. It would be unreasonable to expect that REM sleep has the same functions as slow-wave sleep. An early report on the effects of REM sleep deprivation (Dement, 1960) observed that as the deprivation progressed, subjects had to be awakened from REM sleep more frequently; the "pressure" to enter REM sleep built up. Furthermore, after several days of REM sleep deprivation, subjects would show a **rebound phenomenon** when permitted to sleep normally; they spent a much greater-than-normal percentage of the recovery night in REM sleep. This rebound suggests that there is a need for a certain amount of REM sleep—that REM sleep is controlled by a regulatory mechanism. If selective deprivation causes a deficiency in REM sleep, the deficiency is made up later, when uninterrupted sleep is permitted.

Researchers have long been struck by the fact that the highest proportion of REM sleep is seen during the most active phase of brain development. Perhaps, then, REM sleep plays a role in this process (Roffwarg, Muzio, and Dement, 1966). The association could go either way; brain development could cause REM sleep (perhaps to tidy up after spurts of neural growth), or REM sleep could be setting the stage for brain growth to occur. The developmental hypothesis is supported by the fact that infant animals born with well-developed brains (such as guinea pigs) spend proportionally less time in REM sleep than infant animals born with less-developed brains (such as rats, cats, or humans). Studies of human fetuses and infants born prematurely indicate that REM sleep begins to appear 30

---

rebound phenomenon The increased frequency or intensity of a phenomenon after it has been temporarily suppressed; for example, the increase in REM sleep seen after a period of REM sleep deprivation.

weeks after conception and peaks at around 40 weeks (Roffwarg, Muzio, and Dement, 1966; Petre-Quadens and De Lee, 1974; Inoue et al., 1986). Approximately 70 percent of a newborn infant's sleep is REM sleep. By six months of age this proportion has declined to approximately 30 percent. By eight years of age it has fallen to approximately 22 percent, and by late adulthood it is less than 15 percent.

But if the function of REM sleep is to promote brain development, why do adults have REM sleep? One possibility is that REM sleep facilitates the massive changes in the brain that occur during development but also the more modest changes responsible for learning that occur later in life. Some investigators have suggested that memories of events of the previous day—especially those dealing with emotionally related information—are consolidated and integrated with existing memories (Greenberg and Pearlman, 1974); others have suggested that this time is utilized to accomplish the opposite function: to flush useless information from memory, to prevent the storage of useless clutter (Crick and Mitchison, 1983, 1995).

Studies with laboratory animals suggest that REM sleep does indeed perform functions that facilitate learning. Investigators have carried out two types of experiments. In the first, they train animals in a learning task and then deprive them of REM sleep for a period of time. If REM sleep facilitates learning—perhaps by promoting changes in the brain that store the information just acquired—then animals that are deprived of the opportunity to engage in REM sleep after the training session should not learn as well as control subjects. In the second type of experiment, investigators train animals in a learning task and then monitor their sleep for several hours. An increase in REM sleep suggests that learning increases the need for this stage of sleep.

Experiments of both types have obtained positive results. For example, when animals are deprived of REM sleep after participating in a training session, they learn the task more slowly; thus, REM sleep deprivation retards memory formation (Smith, 1996). In an example of the second type of experiment, Bloch, Hennevin, and Leconte (1977) gave rats daily training trials in a complex maze. They found that the experience enhanced subsequent REM sleep. Moreover, daily performance was related to subsequent REM sleep. The lower curve in Figure 9.8 shows REM sleep as a percentage of total sleep. The upper curve illustrates the animals' performance in the maze. You can see that the largest increase in running speed (possibly representing the largest increase in learning) was accompanied by the largest amount of REM sleep. Also note that once the task was well learned (after day 6), REM sleep declined to baseline levels. (See *Figure 9.8.*)

In contrast to the studies with laboratory animals, studies with human subjects show that REM sleep deprivation has only a small effect on a person's ability to learn or to remember what was previously learned. But several studies have found that learning can affect the amount of

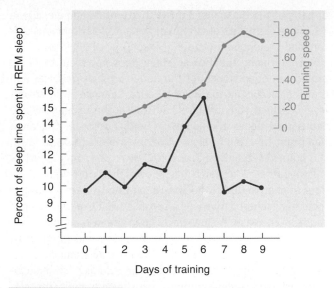

figure **9.8**

Percentage of sleep time spent in REM sleep (*lower curve*) as a function of maze-learning performance (*upper curve*).
(From Bloch, V., Hennevin, E., and Leconte, P., in *Neurobiology of Sleep and Memory,* edited by R. R. Drucker-Colín and J. L. McGaugh. New York: Academic Press, 1978.)

REM sleep a person obtains. For example, several studies found that retarded children engaged in less REM sleep than normal children and that intellectually gifted children engaged in more (Dujardin, Guerrien, and Leconte, 1990). In addition, Smith and Lapp (1991) found that REM sleep of college students increased during exam time, when they presumably were spending more time learning new information.

interim summary

Why Do We Sleep?

The two principal explanations for sleep are that sleep serves as an adaptive response or that it provides a period of restoration. The fact that all vertebrates sleep, including some that would seem to be better off without it, suggests that sleep is more than an adaptive response.

In humans the effects of several days of sleep deprivation include perceptual distortions and (sometimes) mild hallucinations and difficulty performing tasks that require prolonged concentration. These effects suggest that sleep deprivation impairs cerebral functioning. Deep slow-wave sleep appears to be the most important stage, and perhaps its function is to permit the brain to recuperate. Animals that are sleep-deprived eventually die. Their symptoms include increased body temperature and metabolic rate, voracious eating, and weight loss but no obvious signs of a stress response. Fatal familial insomnia is an inherited disease that results in degeneration of parts of the thalamus, deficits in attention and memory, a dreamlike state, loss of control of the autonomic nervous system and the endocrine system, insomnia, and death.

The primary function of sleep does not seem to be to provide an opportunity for the body to repair the wear and tear that occurs during waking hours. Changes in a person's level of exercise do not significantly alter the amount of sleep the person needs the following night. Instead, the most important function of slow-wave sleep seem to be to lower the brain's metabolism and permit it to rest. In support of this hypothesis, research has shown that slow-wave sleep does indeed reduce the brain's metabolic rate and that increased mental activity (the surprise treat experiment) can cause an increase in slow-wave sleep the next night.

The functions of REM sleep are even less understood than those of slow-wave sleep. REM sleep may promote brain development and learning. So far, the evidence is inconclusive, although several studies have shown a moderate relationship between REM sleep and learning.

Physiological Mechanisms of Sleep and Waking

So far, I have discussed the nature of sleep, problems associated with it, and its functions. Now it is time to examine what researchers have discovered about the physiological mechanisms that are responsible for the behavior of sleep and for its counterpart, alert wakefulness. But before doing so, I must emphasize that sleep does not occur simply because neurons get tired and begin to fire more slowly. Like other behaviors, sleep occurs when a particular neural circuit becomes *active*.

Chemical Control of Sleep

As we have seen, sleep is *regulated;* that is, if an organism is deprived of slow-wave sleep or REM sleep, the organism will make up at least part of the missed sleep when permitted to do so. In addition, the amount of slow-wave sleep that a person obtains during a daytime nap is deducted from the amount of slow-wave sleep he or she obtains the next night (Karacan et al., 1970). These facts suggest that some physiological mechanism monitors the amount of sleep that an organism receives. What might this mechanism be?

The most obvious explanation would be that the body produces either *sleep-promoting substances* during wakefulness or *wakefulness-promoting* substances during sleep. For example, a sleep-promoting substance might accumulate during wakefulness and be destroyed during sleep. The longer someone is awake, the longer he or she has to

sleep to deactivate this substance. And because REM sleep deprivation produces an independent REM sleep "debt," there might have to be two substances, one for each stage of sleep. Of course, the opposite could be true; sleep could be regulated by a *wakefulness-promoting* substance. This substance would be used up during wakefulness and be manufactured only during sleep. A *decline* in the level of this substance would cause sleepiness. (See *Figure 9.9.*)

Where might these substances be located? They do not appear to be found in the general circulation of the body. As we saw earlier, the cerebral hemispheres of the bottlenose dolphin sleep at different times (Mukhametov, 1984). If sleep were controlled by *blood-borne* chemicals, the hemispheres should sleep at the same time. This observation suggests that if sleep is controlled by chemicals, these chemicals are produced within the brain and act there. In support of this suggestion, Oleksenko et al. (1992) obtained evidence that indicates that each hemisphere of the brain incurs its own sleep debt. The researchers deprived a bottlenose dolphin of sleep in only one hemisphere. When they allowed the animal to sleep normally, they saw a rebound of slow-wave sleep only in the deprived hemisphere.

What chemical (or chemicals) might be involved in the control of sleep? An important category of drugs, the benzodiazepines, promotes sleep. In fact, they are widely used to treat insomnia. As we saw in Chapter 4, these drugs act on the benzodiazepine-binding site located at the $GABA_A$ receptor. The existence of a special receptor suggests the existence of at least one endogenous ligand for this receptor, and this ligand could be involved in the control of sleep. However, no one has yet discovered a benzodiazepinelike substance whose concentration in the brain varies as a function of sleepiness.

Benington, Kodali, and Heller (1995) suggested that a nucleoside neurotransmitter, *adenosine,* might play a primary role in the control of sleep. They noted that the primary nutrient of the brain is glucose, carried to it by the blood. The blood supply usually delivers an adequate amount of glucose, but if some regions of the brain become especially active, the cells located there consume the glucose faster than it can be supplied. In such cases extra nutrients are supplied by astrocytes (Swanson, 1992; Swanson and Choi, 1993). As we saw in Chapter 2, astrocytes maintain a small stock of nutrients in the form of glycogen, an insoluble carbohydrate that is also stocked by the liver and the muscles. The metabolism of glycogen causes an increase in the levels of adenosine, a chemical that has inhibitory effects. Benington and his colleagues suggested that this accumulation of adenosine produces increased amounts of delta activity during the next night's sleep. The cells in that region rest, and the astrocytes renew their stock of glycogen. If wakefulness is prolonged, even more adenosine accumulates, producing the cognitive and emo-

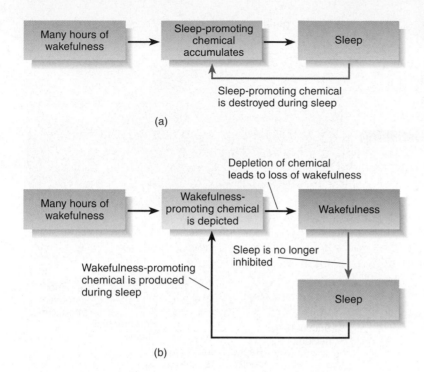

figure **9.9**

Hypothetical roles of chemicals in sleep.
(a) A sleep-promoting chemical accumulates during wakefulness and is destroyed during sleep.
(b) A wakefulness-promoting chemical is depleted during waking and is produced during sleep.

tional effects seen during sleep deprivation. In support of this hypothesis, the investigators found that when they administered a drug that directly stimulates adenosine receptors, they saw increases in delta activity during the animals' slow-wave sleep.

More recent evidence supports the hypothesis that adenosine plays a role in regulating sleep and suggests that it acts on particular neural mechanisms involved in sleep and waking. The adenosine hypothesis is discussed later in this chapter, in a section on the neural control of sleep.

Neural Control of Arousal

As we have seen, sleep is not a unitary condition but consists of several different stages with very different characteristics. The waking state, too, is nonuniform; sometimes we are alert and attentive, and sometimes we fail to notice much about what is happening around us. Of course, sleepiness has an effect on wakefulness; if we are fighting to stay awake, the struggle might impair our ability to concentrate on other things. But everyday observations suggest that even when we are not sleepy, our alertness can vary. For example, when we observe something very interesting (or frightening or simply surprising), we feel ourselves become more alert and aware of our surroundings.

Circuits of neurons that secrete at least five different neurotransmitters play a role in some aspect of an animal's level of alertness and wakefulness—what is commonly called arousal: acetylcholine, norepinephrine, serotonin, histamine,

and hypocretin (Wada et al., 1991; McCormick, 1992; Marrocco, Witte, and Davidson, 1994; Hungs and Mignot, 2001).

Acetylcholine

One of the most important neurotransmitters involved in arousal—especially of the cerebral cortex—is acetylcholine. Two groups of acetylcholinergic neurons, one in the pons and one located in the basal forebrain, produce activation and cortical desynchrony when they are stimulated (Jones, 1990; Steriade, 1996). (A third group of neurons, located in the medial septum, controls the activity of the hippocampus. Because of the importance of the hippocampus in learning, this structure is described later, in Chapters 13 and 14.)

Researchers have long known that acetylcholinergic antagonists decrease EEG signs of cortical arousal and that acetylcholinergic agonists increase them (Vanderwolf, 1992). Day, Damsma, and Fibiger (1991) used microdialysis probes to measure the release of acetylcholine in the striatum, hippocampus, and frontal cortex—three regions whose activity is closely related to an animal's alertness and behavioral arousal. They found that the levels of ACh in these regions were closely related to the animals' level of activity. In addition, Rasmusson, Clow, and Szerb (1994) electrically stimulated a region of the dorsal pons and found that the stimulation activated the cerebral cortex and increased the release of acetylcholine there by 350 percent (as measured by microdialysis probes). A group of acetylcholinergic neurons located in the basal forebrain forms an essential part of the pathway that is responsible for this effect. If these neurons were deactivated by

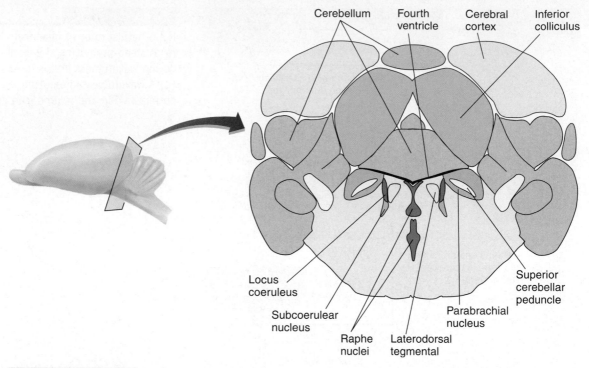

figure 9.10

A section through the pons of a rat, showing the location of the locus coeruleus, which contains the cell bodies of most of the brain's noradrenergic neurons. Also shown are some structures that play a role in REM sleep, which is discussed later.

(Adapted from Paxinos, G., and Watson, C. *The Rat Brain in Stereotaxic Coordinates.* Sydney: Academic Press, 1982. Redrawn with permission.)

infusing a local anesthetic or drugs that blocked synaptic transmission, the activating effects of the pontine stimulation were abolished.

Norepinephrine

Investigators have long known that catecholamine agonists such as amphetamine produce arousal and sleeplessness. These effects appear to be mediated primarily by the noradrenergic system of the **locus coeruleus,** located in the dorsal pons. Neurons of the locus coeruleus give rise to axons that branch widely, releasing norepinephrine (from axonal varicosities) throughout the neocortex, hippocampus, thalamus, cerebellar cortex, pons, and medulla; thus, they potentially affect widespread and important regions of the brain. (See ***Figure 9.10.***)

Aston-Jones and Bloom (1981a) recorded from noradrenergic neurons of the locus coeruleus (LC) across the sleep-waking cycle in unrestrained rats. As Figure 9.11 shows, these neurons exhibited a close relation to behavioral arousal. Note the decline in firing rate before and during sleep and the abrupt increase when the animal wakes. The rate of firing of neurons in the locus coeruleus falls almost to zero during REM sleep and increases dramatically when the animal wakes. As we shall see later in this chapter, these facts suggest that these neurons (along with serotonergic neurons) play a role in controlling REM sleep. (See ***Figure 9.11.***)

Most investigators believe that activity of noradrenergic LC neurons increases an animal's vigilance—its

locus coeruleus (*sa **roo** lee us*) A dark-colored group of noradrenergic cell bodies located in the pons near the rostral end of the floor of the fourth ventricle; involved in arousal and vigilance.

raphe nuclei (*ruh **fay***) A group of nuclei located in the reticular formation of the medulla, pons, and midbrain, situated along the midline; contain serotonergic neurons.

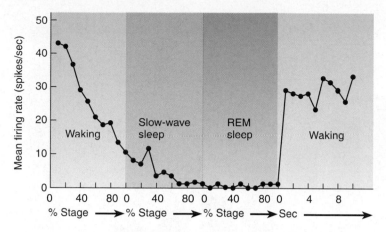

figure 9.11

Activity of noradrenergic neurons in the locus coeruleus of freely moving rats during various stages of sleep and waking.

(From Aston-Jones, G., and Bloom, F. E. *The Journal of Neuroscience,* 1981, *1,* 876–886. Copyright 1981, The Society for Neuroscience.)

ability to pay attention to stimuli in the environment. For example, Aston-Jones et al. (1994) recorded the electrical activity of noradrenergic LC neurons in monkeys performing a task that required them to watch for a particular stimulus that would appear on a video display. The investigators observed that the monkeys performed best when the rate of firing of the LC neurons was high. After the monkeys worked for a long time at the task, the neurons' rate of firing fell, and so did the monkeys' performance. These results support the conclusion that the activation of LC neurons (and their release of norepinephrine) increases vigilance.

Serotonin

A third neurotransmitter, serotonin (5-HT) also appears to play a role in activating behavior. Almost all of the brain's serotonergic neurons are found in the **raphe nuclei,** which are located in the medullary and pontine regions of the reticular formation. (See *Figure 9.12.*) The axons of these neurons project to many parts of the brain, including the thalamus, hypothalamus, basal ganglia, hippocampus, and neocortex. Stimulation of the raphe nuclei causes locomotion and cortical arousal (as measured by the EEG), whereas PCPA, a drug that prevents the synthesis of serotonin, reduces cortical arousal (Peck and Vanderwolf, 1991). Unlike noradrenergic neurons, which increase their rate of firing during stressful situations, serotonergic neurons do not respond to external stimuli that produce pain or induce a stress response (Jacobs, Wilkinson, and Fornal, 1990).

Jacobs and Fornal (1999) suggested that one specific contribution of serotonergic neurons to activation is facilitation of continuous, automatic movements, such as pacing, chewing, and grooming. On the other hand, when animals engage in orienting responses to novel stimuli, the activity of serotonergic neurons decreases. Perhaps serotonergic neurons are involved in facilitating ongoing activities and suppressing the processing of sensory information, preventing reactions that might disrupt the ongoing activities.

Figure 9.13 shows the activity of serotonergic neurons, recorded by Trulson and Jacobs (1979). As you can see, these neurons, like the noradrenergic neurons studied by Aston-Jones and Bloom (1981a), were most active during waking. Their firing rate declined during slow-wave sleep and became virtually zero during REM sleep. However, once the period of REM sleep ended, the neurons temporarily became very active again. (See *Figure 9.13.*)

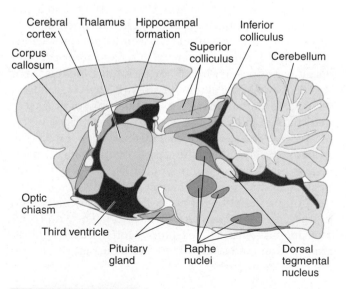

figure 9.12

The raphe nuclei, the location of the cell bodies of most of the brain's serotonergic neurons.

(Adapted from Paxinos, G., and Watson, C. *The Rat Brain in Stereotaxic Coordinates.* Sydney: Academic Press, 1982. Redrawn with permission.)

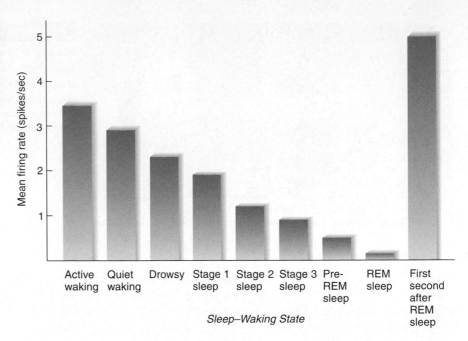

figure 9.13

Activity of serotonergic (5-HT-secreting) neurons in the dorsal raphe nuclei of freely moving cats during various stages of sleep and waking. (Adapted from Trulson, M. E., and Jacobs, B. L. *Brain Research,* 1979, *163,* 135–150. Redrawn with permission.)

Histamine

The fourth neurotransmitter implicated in the control of wakefulness and arousal is histamine, a compound synthesized from histidine, an amino acid. The cell bodies of histaminergic neurons are located in the **tuberomammillary nucleus** of the hypothalamus, located at the base of the brain just rostral to the mammillary bodies. The axons of these neurons project primarily to the cerebral cortex, thalamus, basal ganglia, basal forebrain, and hypothalamus. The projections to the cerebral cortex directly increase cortical activation and arousal, and projections to acetylcholinergic neurons of the basal forebrain and dorsal pons do so indirectly, by increasing the release of acetylcholine in the cerebral cortex (Khateb et al., 1995; Brown, Stevens, and Haas, 2001). Injections of drugs that prevent the synthesis of histamine or block histamine H_1 receptors decrease waking and increase sleep (Lin, Sakai, and Jouvet, 1988). Also, the activity of histaminergic neurons is high during waking but low during slow-wave sleep and REM sleep (Steininger et al., 1996).

You are undoubtedly aware that antihistamines, used to treat allergies, can cause drowsiness. They do so by blocking histamine H_1 receptors. More modern antihistamines cannot cross the blood–brain barrier, so they do not cause drowsiness.

Hypocretin

As we saw in the section on sleep disorders, recent investigations discovered that the cause of narcolepsy is degeneration of hypocretinergic neurons in humans and a hereditary absence of hypocretin-2 receptors in dogs. The cell bodies of neurons that secrete hypocretin (as we saw, also called orexin) are located in the lateral hypo-

thalamus. The axons of these neurons terminate in several regions involved in arousal, including the locus coeruleus, raphe nuclei, tuberomammillary nucleus, acetylcholinergic neurons in the dorsal pons and basal forebrain, and cerebral cortex (Saper, Chou, and Scammel, 2001). Hypocretin has an excitatory, wakefulness-promoting, effect in all of these regions.

Estabrooke et al. (2001) found that hypocretinergic neurons are active (as measured by production of Fos protein) during sleep and inactive during sleep. High levels of hypocretinergic activity were seen during normal waking or through enforced waking produced by injections of methamphetamine or by tapping on the rats' cages whenever they fell asleep.

Neural Control of Slow-Wave Sleep

Although sleep is a behavior that involves most of the brain, one region seems to be particularly important: the **ventrolateral preoptic area (VLPA).** The preoptic area is located just rostral to the hypothalamus. Nauta (1946) found that destruction of the preoptic area produced total insomnia in rats. The animals subsequently fell into a

---

tuberomammillary nucleus A nucleus in the ventral posterior hypothalamus, just rostral to the mammillary bodies; contains histaminergic neurons involved in cortical activation and behavioral arousal.

ventrolateral preoptic area (VLPA) A group of GABAergic neurons in the preoptic area whose activity suppresses alertness and behavioral arousal and promotes sleep.

coma and died; the average survival time was only three days. McGinty and Sterman (1968) found that cats reacted somewhat differently; the animals did not become sleepless until several days after the lesion was made. Two of the cats, whose sleep was totally suppressed, died within ten days.

The effects of these lesion experiments are corroborated by the effects of electrical stimulation of the preoptic area. Sterman and Clemente (1962a, 1962b) found that electrical stimulation of this region produced signs of drowsiness in the behavior and the EEG of unanesthetized, freely moving cats. The average latency period between the stimulation and the changes in the EEG was 30 seconds, but sometimes the effect was immediate. The animals often subsequently fell asleep.

Several recording studies confirm the effects of lesions and stimulation. For example, Sherin et al. (1996) found increased levels of Fos protein during sleep in a cluster of neurons in the ventrolateral preoptic area. Lu et al. (2000) found that excitotoxic lesions of this cluster of neurons suppressed sleep. Szymusiak et al. (1998) found that the activity of single neurons in the VLPA increased during sleep. When the animals were kept awake for 12–14 hours and were then allowed to sleep, neurons in the VLPA showed an especially high rate of firing, as if the drive to sleep were particularly intense.

Anatomical and histochemical studies indicate that the VLPA contains inhibitory GABA-secreting neurons and that these neurons send their axons to the tuberomammillary nucleus, dorsal pons, raphe nuclei, and locus coeruleus (Sherin et al., 1998). As we saw in the previous section, activity of neurons in these regions causes cortical activation and behavioral arousal. The fact that stimulation of the VLPA inhibits these regions is consistent with other evidence indicating that activation of the VLPA induces sleep.

The VLPA receives inhibitory inputs from many of the same regions it inhibits, including the tuberomammillary nucleus, raphe nuclei, and locus coeruleus (Chou et al., 2002). As Saper et al. (2001) suggest, this mutual inhibition may provide the basis for establishing periods of sleep and waking. They note that reciprocal inhibition also characterizes an electronic circuit known as a *flip-flop*. A flip-flop can assume one of two states, usually referred to as on or off—or 0 or 1 in computer applications. Thus, either the VLPA is active and inhibits the wakefulness-promoting regions or the wakefulness-promoting regions are active and inhibit the VLPA. Because these regions are mutually inhibitory, it is impossible for neurons in both sets of regions to be active at the same time. (See *Figure 9.14.*)

A flip-flop has an important advantage: When it switches from one state to another, it does so quickly. Clearly, it is most advantageous to be either asleep or awake; a state that has some of the characteristics of both

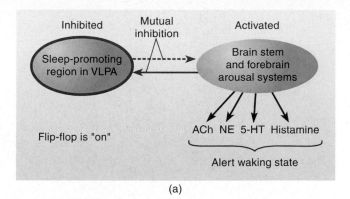

(a)

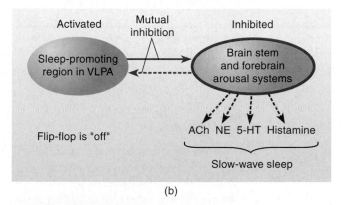

(b)

figure 9.14

A schematic diagram of the sleep/waking flip-flop proposed by Saper et al. (2001). The major sleep-promoting region (the VLPA) and the major wakefulness-promoting regions (the basal forebrain and peribrachial regions, which contain acetylcholinergic neurons; the locus coeruleus, which contains noradrenergic neurons; the raphe nuclei, which contain serotonergic neurons; and the tuberomammillary nucleus of the hypothalamus, which contains histaminergic neurons) are reciprocally connected by inhibitory GABAergic neurons. When the flip-flop is "on," the arousal systems are active and the VLPA is inhibited, and the animal is awake. When the flip-flop is "off," the VLPA is active and the arousal systems are inhibited, and the animal is asleep.

sleep and wakefulness would be maladaptive. However, there is one problem with flip-flops: They can be unstable. In fact, people with narcolepsy and animals with damage to the hypocretinergic system of neurons exhibit just this characteristic. They have great difficulty remaining awake when nothing interesting is happening, and they have trouble remaining asleep for an extended amount of time. (They also show intrusions of the characteristics of REM sleep at inappropriate time. I will discuss this phenomenon in the next section.)

Saper et al. (2001) suggest that an important function of hypocretinergic neurons is to help stabilize the flip-flop.

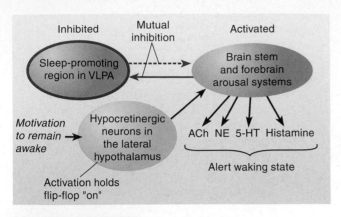

figure 9.15

A schematic diagram of the effect of activation of the hypocretinergic system of neurons of the lateral hypothalamus on the sleep/waking flip-flop. Motivation to remain awake or events that disturb sleep activate the hypocretinergic neurons.

Activity of this system of neurons promotes wakefulness and inhibits sleep. As far as we know, hypocretinergic neurons do not receive inhibitory input from either side of the flip-flop, so activation of either side does not affect them. As we saw in the previous subsection, Estabrooke et al. (2001) found that enforced wakefulness increased the activity of hypocretinergic neurons. Perhaps, then, events that keep an animal awake do so by activating these neurons. Perhaps your success at staying awake in a boring lecture depends on maintaining a high rate of firing of your hypocretinergic neurons. This event would keep the flip-flop in the on (waking) state. Because we know very little about the inputs to hypocretinergic neurons, we cannot yet say how we manage to control the firing of these neurons. (See *Figure 9.15.*)

The evidence I have reviewed so far in this section concerns the brain mechanisms that are responsible for waking and sleep. But as we all know, sleepiness is controlled by two factors: time of day and length of time our brains have been awake and active. As we will see in the final section of this chapter, an internal clock, located in the hypothalamus, controls daily rhythms of sleep. But what is responsible for the sleepiness that accumulates as a result of mental activity?

As we saw earlier in this chapter, adenosine is produced when neurons become especially active, and accumulation of adenosine may be at least one of the chemicals that stimulates drowsiness and sleep. In a review of the literature, Dunwiddie and Masino (2001) concluded that increases in the level of energy consumption of the brain cause an accumulation of adenosine, which acts as an inhibitory neuromodulator. (You will recall that caffeine, used by so many people to keep awake, is an adenosine

antagonist.) Evidence suggests that adenosine exerts an antiwaking effect in the basal forebrain. Porkka-Heiskanen, Strecker, and McCarley (2000) used microdialysis to measure adenosine levels in several regions of the brain. They found that the level of adenosine increased during wakefulness and slowly decreased during sleep, especially in the region of the basal forebrain that contains acetylcholinergic neurons. In addition, infusion of an adenosine agonist into this region inhibited the acetylcholinergic neurons and increased sleep (Strecker et al., 2000).

As we just saw, the VLPA appears to be a critical brain region in the production of sleep. Thus, if the accumulation of adenosine is one of the factors that makes us sleepy, we would expect this chemical to activate the VLPA. As far as we know, the activation of adenosine receptors has an inhibitory effect, which means that any excitatory action this chemical has on the VLPA must be indirect. Scammell et al. (2001) found that an infusion of an adenosine agonist in the subarachnoid space adjacent to the VLPA activated neurons there (as measured by levels of Fos protein), decreased the activity of histaminergic neurons of the tuberomammillary nucleus, and increased slow-wave sleep. The investigators hypothesized that adenosine might increase sleep by inhibiting neurons that normally inhibit VLPA neurons. The release from inhibition would activate these neurons. (See *Figure 9.16.*)

A study by Thakkar, Winston, and McCarley (2002) suggests another possibility. These investigators found that hypocretinergic neurons in the lateral hypothalamus contain adenosine A1 receptors. They suggest that the inhibition of these neurons caused by the accumulation of adenosine during wakefulness may be one of the signals that promotes sleep.

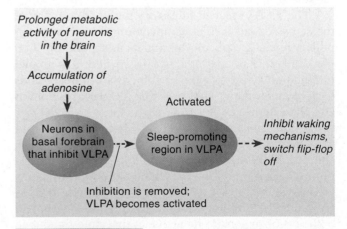

figure 9.16

Role of adenosine on sleep and waking. Prolonged neural activity causes adenosine to accumulate, which disinhibits the sleep-promoting neurons of the VLPA.

Neural Control of REM Sleep

As we saw earlier in this chapter, REM sleep consists of desynchronized EEG activity, muscular paralysis, rapid eye movements, and (in humans, at least) increased genital activity. The rate of cerebral metabolism is as high as it is during waking (Maquet et al., 1990), and were it not for the state of paralysis, the level of *physical* activity would also be high. In laboratory animals REM sleep also includes *PGO waves*. **PGO waves** (for **p**ons, **g**eniculate, and **o**ccipital) are the first manifestation of REM sleep. They consist of brief, phasic bursts of electrical activity that originate in the pons and are propagated to the lateral geniculate nuclei and then to the primary visual (occipital) cortex. They can be seen only when electrodes are placed directly into the brain, so they have not been recorded in humans. It seems likely, however, that they occur in our species, too. Figure 9.17 shows the typical onset of REM sleep, recorded in a cat. The first sign of an impending bout of REM sleep is the presence of PGO waves—in this case recorded from electrodes implanted in the lateral geniculate nucleus. Next, the EEG becomes desynchronized, and then muscular activity ceases and rapid eye movements commence. (See *Figure 9.17.*)

As we shall see, REM sleep is controlled by mechanisms located within the pons. The executive mechanism (that is, the one whose activity turns on the various components of REM sleep) consists of a group of neurons in the dorsal pons that secrete acetylcholine. During waking and slow-wave sleep, REM sleep is inhibited by the serotonergic neurons of the raphe nuclei and the noradrenergic neurons of the locus coeruleus.

The Executive Mechanism

Researchers have long known that acetylcholinergic agonists facilitate REM sleep. Stoyva and Metcalf (1968) found that people who have been exposed to organophosphate insecticides, which act as acetylcholine agonists, spend an increased time in REM sleep. In a controlled experiment with human subjects, Sitaram, Moore, and Gillin (1978) found that an ACh agonist (arecoline) shortened the interval between periods of REM sleep and that an acetylcholinergic antagonist (scopolamine) lengthened it.

Jasper and Tessier (1969) analyzed the levels of acetylcholine that had been released by terminal buttons in the cat cerebral cortex. They found that the levels of ACh were highest during waking and REM sleep and were lowest during slow-wave sleep. Using 2-DG autoradiography in cats, Lydic et al. (1991) found that the rate of glucose metabolism was elevated in the regions of the brain that contain ACh-secreting neurons or that receive input from the axons of these neurons. As we saw earlier in this chapter, acetylcholinergic neurons play an important role in

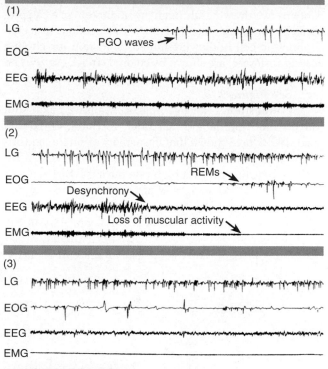

figure 9.17

Onset of REM sleep in a cat. The arrows indicate the onset of PGO waves, EEG desynchrony, loss of muscular activity, and rapid eye movements. LG = lateral geniculate nucleus; EOG = electro-oculogram (eye movements).

(Adapted from Steriade, M., Paré, D., Bouhassira, D., Deschênes, M., and Oakson, G. *Journal of Neuroscience*, 1989, *9*, 2215–2229. Reprinted with permission.)

cerebral activation during alert wakefulness. The findings I just cited suggest that these neurons are also responsible for the cerebral activation seen during REM sleep.

The brain contains several groups of acetylcholinergic neurons. The ones that play the most central role in triggering the onset of REM sleep are found in the dorsolateral pons, primarily in the *pedunculopontine tegmental nucleus* (PPT) and *laterodorsal tegmental nucleus* (LDT) (Jones and Beaudet, 1987). Many investigators now refer to this region as the **peribrachial area,** because it is located in

PGO wave Bursts of phasic electrical activity originating in the pons, followed by activity in the lateral geniculate nucleus and visual cortex; a characteristic of REM sleep.

peribrachial area (*pair ee bray kee ul*) The region around the brachium conjunctivum, located in the dorsolateral pons; contains acetylcholinergic neurons involved in the initiation of REM sleep.

the region of the brachium conjunctivum. Figure 9.18 contains two drawings through the brain stem of a cat, prepared by Jones and Beaudet (1987). The locations of acetylcholinergic cell bodies (identified by a stain for choline acetyltransferase) are shown by colored circles. As you can see, these neurons surround the brachium conjunctivum (bc). (See *Figure 9.18.*)

Several studies (for example, El Mansari, Sakai, and Jouvet, 1989; Steriade et al., 1990; Kayama, Ohta, and Jodo, 1992) have shown that the activity of single neurons in the peribrachial area is related to the sleep cycle. Most of these neurons fire at a high rate during REM sleep or during both REM sleep and active wakefulness. Figure 9.19 shows the activity of a so-called *REM-ON* cell, which fires at a high rate only during REM sleep. As you can see, this neuron increased its activity approximately 80 sec before the onset of REM sleep. The increase in the activ-

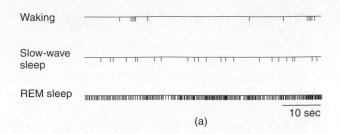

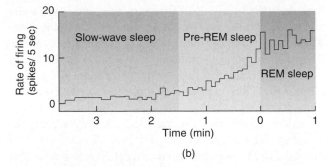

figure 9.19

Firing pattern of an acetylcholinergic REM-ON cell in the peribrachial area of the pons. (a) Action potentials during 60-minute intervals during waking, slow-wave sleep, and REM sleep. (b) Rate of firing just before and after the transition from slow-wave sleep to REM sleep. The increase in activity begins approximately 80 seconds before the onset of REM sleep.

(Adapted from El Mansari, M., Sakai, K., and Jouvet, M. *Experimental Brain Research*, 1989, *76*, 519–529.)

ity of these acetylcholinergic cells may be the event that initiates a bout of REM sleep. (See *Figure 9.19.*)

Webster and Jones (1988) made lesions of the peribrachial area by infusing kainic acid into this region. They found that REM sleep was drastically reduced. The amount of REM sleep that remained was directly related to the number of cholinergic neurons that were spared.

Where do the acetylcholinergic neurons of the peribrachial area exert their effects? The axons of these neurons project to the medial pontine reticular formation; to several regions of the forebrain, including the thalamus, basal ganglia, preoptic area, hippocampus, hypothalamus, and cingulate cortex; and to several brain stem regions that are involved with the control of eye movements (Cornwall, Cooper, and Phillipson, 1990; Bolton, Cornwall, and Phillipson, 1993).

Let us examine the role of these connections. If a small amount of **carbachol,** a drug that stimulates acetyl-

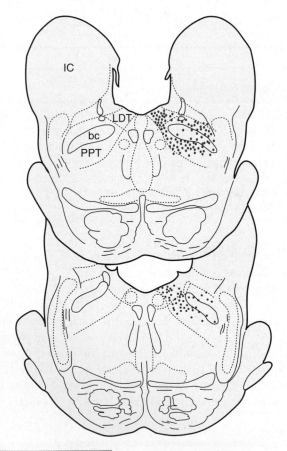

figure 9.18

Acetylcholinergic neurons (colored circles) in the peribrachial area of the cat, as revealed by a stain for choline acetyltransferase. LDT = lateral tegmental nucleus; PPT = pedunculopontine tegmental nucleus; bc = brachium conjunctivum; IC = inferior colliculus.

(Adapted from Jones, B. E., and Beaudet, A. *Journal of Comparative Neurology*, 1987, *261*, 15–32. Reprinted with permission.)

carbachol (*car ba call*) A drug that stimulates acetylcholine receptors.

choline receptors, is infused into the **medial pontine reticular formation (MPRF),** a region of the pons ventral to the locus coeruleus, the animal will display some or all of the components of REM sleep (Katayama et al., 1986; Callaway et al., 1987). Carbachol is effective when infused into the MPRF because it stimulates postsynaptic acetylcholine receptors of neurons that receive projections from the ACh cells of the peribrachial area (Quattrochi et al., 1989). For this reason this region is often referred to as the *cholinoceptive* region of the MPRF because it is *receptive* to ACh. As you might expect, microdialysis studies have found increased levels of acetylcholine in this region during REM sleep (Kodama, Takahashi, and Honda, 1990). In addition, lesions of the MPRF, like those of the peribrachial area, reduce or abolish REM sleep (Siegel, 1989). (See *Figure 9.20.*)

If the acetylcholinergic neurons in the peribrachial area of the pons are responsible for the onset of REM sleep, how do they control each of its components: cortical arousal, PGO waves, rapid eye movements, genital activity, and muscular paralysis? These neurons send axons directly to regions of the thalamus that are involved in the control of cortical arousal. In addition, they send axons to glutamatergic neurons in the mesopontine reticular formation, which, in turn, send axons to the acetyl-

cholinergic neurons of the basal forebrain. Activation of these forebrain neurons produces arousal and cortical desynchrony. PGO waves appear to be controlled by direct connections between the peribrachial area and the lateral geniculate nucleus (Sakai and Jouvet, 1980; Steriade, Paré, Datta, Oakson, and Curró Dossi, 1990). The control of rapid eye movements appears to be achieved by projections from the peribrachial area to the tectum (Webster and Jones, 1988).

Little is known about the function of genital activity that occurs during REM sleep or about the neural mechanisms that are responsible for them. A study by Schmidt et al. (2000) found that excitotoxic lesions of the lateral preoptic area in rats suppressed penile erections during REM sleep but had no effect on erections during waking. Further research will be needed to investigate possible connections between the brain stem regions responsible for REM sleep and the lateral preoptic area.

The last of the REM-related phenomena, muscular paralysis, is particularly interesting. As we saw earlier, patients with REM-sleep behavior disorder fail to become paralyzed during REM sleep and thus act out their dreams. The same thing happens—that is, assuming that cats dream—when a lesion is placed just caudal to the peribrachial area of the pons. Jouvet (1972) described this phenomenon:

> To a naive observer, the cat, which is standing, looks awake since it may attack unknown enemies, play with an absent mouse, or display flight behavior. There are orienting movements of the head or eyes toward imaginary stimuli, although the animal does not respond to visual or auditory stimuli. These extraordinary episodes . . . are a good argument that "dreaming" occurs during [REM sleep] in the cat. (Jouvet, 1972, pp. 236–237)

Jouvet's lesions destroyed a set of neurons responsible for the muscular paralysis that occurs during REM sleep. These neurons are located just ventral to the locus coeruleus—in the subcoerulear region. Their axons travel caudally to the **magnocellular nucleus,** located in the medial medulla (Sakai, 1980). Neurons in the magnocellular nucleus send axons to the spinal cord, where they form inhibitory synapses with motor neurons (Morales, Boxer, and Chase, 1987).

There is good evidence that this pathway is responsible for the paralysis that accompanies REM sleep. Shouse and Siegel (1992) found that lesions of the subcoerulear

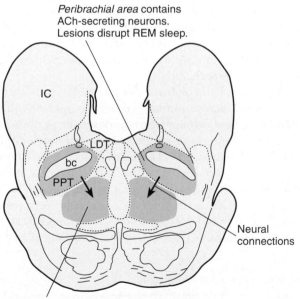

Peribrachial area contains ACh-secreting neurons. Lesions disrupt REM sleep.

IC
LDT
bc
PPT

Neural connections

Medial pontine reticular formation (MPRF) contains cholinoceptive cells. Infusions of carbachol stimulate components of REM sleep. Lesions disrupt REM sleep.

figure 9.20

A cross section through the pons of a cat, showing the locations of the peribrachial area and the medial pontine reticular formation (MPRF), regions involved in the control of REM sleep.

medial pontine reticular formation (MPRF) A region that contains neurons involved in the initiation of REM sleep; activated by acetylcholinergic neurons of the peribrachial area.

magnocellular nucleus A nucleus in the medulla; involved in the muscular paralysis that accompanies REM sleep.

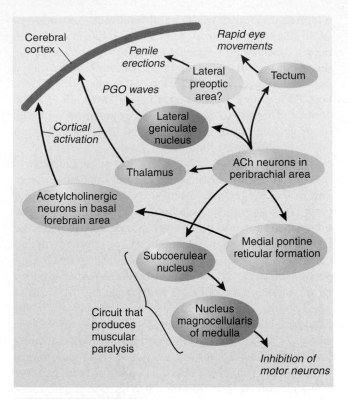

figure 9.21

A summary of the neural circuitry that is thought to be responsible for the components of REM sleep.

region had no effect on REM sleep itself but abolished the paralysis that accompanies it. Kanamori, Sakai, and Jouvet (1980) recorded from single neurons in the magnocellular nucleus in unrestrained cats and found that they became active during REM sleep. Sakai (1980) found that electrical stimulation of this nucleus caused paralysis in awake cats, and Schenkel and Siegel (1989) found that lesions of the magnocellular nucleus produced REM without the accompanying paralysis. Fort et al. (1990) found that the magnocellular nucleus contains glycine-secreting neurons, and this inhibitory neurotransmitter is undoubtedly responsible for the inhibition of the motor neurons located in the spinal cord.

The fact that our brains contain an elaborate mechanism whose sole function is to keep us paralyzed while we dream—that is, to prevent us from acting out our dreams—suggests that the motor components of dreams are as important as the sensory components. Perhaps the practice our motor system gets during REM sleep helps us to improve our performance of behaviors we have learned that day. The inhibition of the motor neurons in the spinal cord prevents the movements being practiced from actually occurring, with the exception of a few harmless twitches of the hands and feet.

Figure 9.21 summarizes the evidence I have reviewed in this subsection. The first event preceding a bout of

REM sleep appears to be activation of acetylcholinergic neurons in the peribrachial area of the dorsolateral pons. These neurons directly activate brain stem mechanisms that are responsible for rapid eye movements and trigger PGO waves through their connections with the lateral geniculate nucleus of the thalamus. They also activate neurons in the subcoerulear area that, through their connections with the nucleus magnocellularis of the medulla, produce muscular paralysis. Presumably, they also activate neurons in the lateral preoptic area that are responsible for penile erections (and perhaps vaginal secretions in females). Finally, these neurons cause cortical activation through connections with the thalamus, medial pontine reticular formation, and acetylcholinergic neurons of the basal forebrain. (See **Figure 9.21.**)

Serotonin and Norepinephrine

As we saw earlier (in Figures 9.11 and 9.13), the rate of activity in the serotonergic neurons of the raphe nuclei and the noradrenergic neurons of the locus coeruleus are at low levels during sleep and at their very lowest levels during REM sleep. Evidence suggests that the activity of neurons in the locus coeruleus and the dorsal raphe nucleus normally inhibits REM sleep and that a reduction in the rate of firing of these neurons may be the event that triggers a bout of REM sleep. For example, Figure 9.22 shows the very close linkage between the activity of a single unit in the dorsal raphe nucleus and the occurrence of PGO waves, the first manifestation of REM sleep (Lydic, McCarley, and Hobson, 1983). Note that the PGO waves occur only when the serotonergic neuron is silent. (See **Figure 9.22.**)

Anatomical and pharmacological studies provide further evidence that serotonin and norepinephrine inhibit REM sleep. Acetylcholinergic neurons in the peribrachial area receive both serotonergic and noradrenergic inputs (Honda and Semba, 1994; Leonard et al., 1995). So does the cholinoceptive region of the MPRF (Semba, 1993). Portas et al. (1996) infused a drug into the dorsal raphe nucleus that inhibits the release of serotonin. As a result, the animals exhibited a threefold increase in REM sleep. Bier and McCarley (1994) found that infusions of a nora-

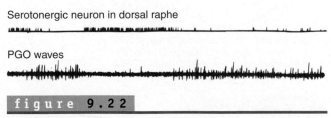

figure 9.22

Activity of a single unit in the dorsal raphe nucleus. Note that the activity is *inversely* related to the occurrence of PGO waves, the first sign of REM sleep.

(Adapted from Lydic, R., McCarley, R. W., and Hobson, J. A. *Brain Research*, 1983, *274*, 365–370. Redrawn with permission.)

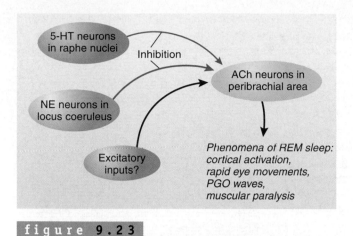

Interactions between serotonergic, noradrenergic, and acetylcholinergic neurons in the control of REM sleep.

drenergic antagonist into the MPRF also causes an increase in REM sleep.

Several unanswered questions await further research. As we saw in an earlier section, neurons in the sleep-promoting region of the VLPA inhibit the wakefulness-promoting regions of the forebrain and pons, which explains why the activity of noradrenergic and serotonergic neurons decreases during sleep. But what is responsible for the further inhibition of these neurons during REM sleep? Is there an excitatory input to the peribrachial area as well as the inhibitory ones whose activity *increases* at the beginning of REM sleep? Where is the pacemaker that controls the regular cycles of REM and slow-wave sleep, and how is this pacemaker connected to the REM sleep mechanisms in the pons? (See *Figure 9.23.*)

interim summary

Physiological Mechanisms of Sleep and Waking

The fact that the amount of sleep is regulated suggests that sleep-promoting substances (produced during wakefulness) or wakefulness-promoting substances (produced during sleep) may exist. The sleeping pattern of the dolphin brain suggests that such substances do not accumulate in the blood. Evidence suggests that adenosine, released when neurons are obliged to utilize the supply of glycogen stored in astrocytes, serves as the link between increased brain metabolism and the necessity of sleep.

Five systems of neurons appear to be important for alert, active wakefulness: the acetylcholinergic system of the peribrachial area of the pons and the basal forebrain, involved in cortical activation; the noradrenergic system of the locus coeruleus, involved in vigilance; the serotonergic system of the raphe nuclei, involved in activation of automatic behaviors such as locomotion and grooming; the histaminergic neurons of the tuberomammillary nucleus, involved in cortical activation, such as the acetylcholinergic systems; and the hypocretinergic system of the lateral hypothalamus, involved in maintaining wakefulness.

Slow-wave sleep occurs when neurons in the ventrolateral preoptic area (VLPA) become active. These neurons inhibit the histaminergic neurons of the tuberomammillary nucleus, the noradrenergic neurons of the locus coeruleus, and the serotonergic neurons of the raphe nuclei. In turn, the VLPA is inhibited by the wakefulness-promoting regions of the brain, forming a kind of flip-flop that keeps us either awake or asleep. The accumulation of adenosine may also promote sleep by inhibiting the acetylcholinergic neurons in the basal forebrain and activating the neurons of the VLPA. Activity of the hypocretinergic neurons of the lateral hypothalamus may keep the flip-flop that controls sleep and waking in the "on" state, thus maintaining wakefulness.

REM sleep occurs when the activity of acetylcholinergic neurons in the peribrachial area increases. These neurons initiate PGO waves and cortical arousal through their connections with the thalamus, and they activate neurons in the MPRF that in turn activate the acetylcholinergic neurons of the basal forebrain. The peribrachial neurons also produce rapid eye movements through their connections with motor neurons in the tectum. Penile erections during REM sleep (but not during waking) are abolished by lesions of the lateral preoptic area. The muscular paralysis that prevents our acting out our dreams is produced by a group of acetylcholinergic neurons located in the subcoerulear nucleus that activate other neurons located in the magnocellular nucleus of the medulla, which in turn produce inhibition of motor neurons in the spinal cord. REM sleep, too, is related to temperature; it normally occurs only after the brain temperature has been lowered by a period of slow-wave sleep.

The noradrenergic neurons of the locus coeruleus and the serotonergic neurons of the raphe nuclei have inhibitory effects on pontine neurons responsible for REM sleep. Bouts of REM sleep begin only after the activity of the noradrenergic and serotonergic neurons ceases; whether this event is the only one to trigger REM sleep or whether direct excitation of acetylcholinergic neurons also occurs is not yet known.

Biological Clocks

Much of our behavior follows regular rhythms. For example, we saw that the stages of sleep are organized around a 90-minute cycle of REM and slow-wave sleep. The same rhythm continues during the day as the basic rest–activity cycle. And, of course, our daily pattern of sleep and waking follows a 24-hour cycle. Finally, many animals display seasonal breeding rhythms in which reproductive

figure 9.24

Wheel-running activity of a rat. Note that the animal's activity occurs at "night" (that is, during the 12 hours the light is off) and that the active period is reset when the light period is changed. When the animal is maintained in constant dim illumination, it displays a free-running activity cycle of approximately 25 hours. (From Groblewski, T. A., Nuñez, A., and Gold, R. M. Paper presented at the meeting of the Eastern Psychological Association, April 1980.)

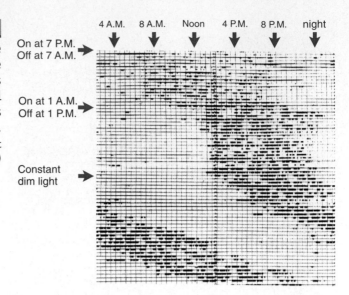

behaviors and hormone levels show yearly fluctuations. In recent years investigators have learned much about the neural mechanisms that are responsible for these rhythms.

Circadian Rhythms and Zeitgebers

Daily rhythms in behavior and physiological processes are found throughout the plant and animal world. These cycles are generally called **circadian rhythms.** (*Circa* means "about," and *dies* means "day"; therefore, a circadian rhythm is one with a cycle of approximately 24 hours.) Some of these rhythms are passive responses to changes in illumination. However, other rhythms are controlled by mechanisms within the organism—by "internal clocks." For example, Figure 9.24 shows the activity of a rat during various conditions of illumination. Each horizontal line represents 24 hours. Vertical tick marks represent the animal's activity in a running wheel. The upper portion of the figure shows the activity of the rat during a normal day—night cycle, with alternating 12-hour periods of light and dark. Notice that the animal is active during the night, which is normal for a rat. (See *Figure 9.24.*)

Next, the dark—light cycle was shifted by 6 hours; the animal's activity cycle quickly followed the change. (See *Figure 9.24.*) Finally, dim lights were left on continuously. The cyclical pattern in the rat's activity remained. Because there were no cycles of light and dark in the rat's environment, the source of rhythmicity must be located within the animal; that is, the animal must possess an internal, biological clock. You can see that the rat's clock was not set precisely to 24 hours; when the illumination was held constant, the clock ran a bit slow. The animal began its bout of activity almost one hour later each day. (See *Figure 9.24.*)

The phenomenon illustrated in Figure 9.24 is typical of the circadian rhythms shown by many species. A free-running clock, with a cycle a little longer than 24 hours, controls some biological functions—in this case, motor activity. Regular daily variation in the level of illumination (that is, sunlight and darkness) normally keeps the clock adjusted to 24 hours. Light serves as a **zeitgeber** (German for "time giver"); it synchronizes the endogenous rhythm. Studies with many species of animals have shown that if they are maintained in constant darkness (or constant dim light), a brief period of bright light will reset their internal clock, advancing or retarding it, depending upon when the light flash occurs (Aschoff, 1979). For example, if an animal is exposed to bright light soon after dusk, the biological clock is set back to an earlier time—as if dusk had not yet arrived. On the other hand, if the light occurs late at night, the biological clock is set ahead to a later time—as if dawn had already come.

Like other animals, humans exhibit circadian rhythms. Our normal period of inactivity begins several hours after the start of the dark portion of the day–night cycle and persists for a variable amount of time into the light portion. Without the benefits of modern civilization we would probably go to sleep earlier and get up earlier than we do; we use artificial lights to delay our bedtime and window shades to extend our time for sleep. Under constant illumination our biological clocks will run free, gaining or los-

circadian rhythm (*sur **kay** dee un* or *sur ka **dee** un*) A daily rhythmical change in behavior or physiological process.

zeitgeber (*tsite gay ber*) A stimulus (usually the light of dawn) that resets the biological clock that is responsible for circadian rhythms.

ing time like a watch that runs too slow or too fast. Different people have different cycle lengths, but most people in that situation will begin to live a "day" that is approximately 25 hours long. This works out quite well, because the morning light, acting as a zeitgeber, simply resets the clock.

The Suprachiasmatic Nucleus

Role in Circadian Rhythms

Researchers working independently in two laboratories (Moore and Eichler, 1972; Stephan and Zucker, 1972) discovered that the primary biological clock of the rat is located in the **suprachiasmatic nucleus (SCN)** of the hypothalamus; they found that lesions disrupted circadian rhythms of wheel running, drinking, and hormonal secretion. The SCN also provides the primary control over the timing of sleep cycles. Rats are nocturnal animals; they sleep during the day and forage and feed at night. Lesions of the SCN abolish this pattern; sleep occurs in bouts randomly dispersed throughout both day and night (Ibuka and Kawamura, 1975; Stephan and Nuñez, 1977). However, rats with SCN lesions still obtain the same amount of sleep that normal animals do. The lesions disrupt the circadian pattern but do not affect the total amount of sleep.

Figure 9.25 shows the suprachiasmatic nuclei in a cross section through the hypothalamus of a mouse; they appear as two clusters of dark-staining neurons at the base of the brain, just above the optic chiasm. (See *Figure 9.25.*) The suprachiasmatic nuclei of the rat consist of approximately ten thousand small neurons, tightly packed into a volume of between 0.1 and 0.3 mm^3 (Meijer and Rietveld, 1989). The dendrites of these neurons form synapses with one another—a phenomenon that is found only in this part of the hypothalamus and that probably relates to the special function of these nuclei. A group of neurons is found clustered around the capillaries that serve the SCN. These neurons contain a large amount of rough endoplasmic reticulum, which suggests that they may be neurosecretory cells (Card, Riley, and Moore, 1980; Moore, Card, and Riley, 1980). Thus, some of the control that the SCN exerts over other parts of the brain may be accomplished by the secretion of neuromodulators.

Because light is the primary zeitgeber for most mammals' activity cycles, we would expect that the SCN receives fibers from the visual system. Indeed, anatomical studies have revealed a direct projection of fibers from the retina to the SCN: the *retinohypothalamic pathway* (Hendrickson, Wagoner, and Cowan, 1972; Aronson et al., 1993). If you look carefully at Figure 9.25, you can see small dark spots within the optic chiasm, just ventral and medial to the base of the SCN; these are cell bodies of oligodendroglia that serve axons that enter the SCN and provide information from the retina. (See *Figure 9.25.*)

The photoreceptors in the retina that provide photic information to the SCN are neither rods nor cones—the cells that provide us with the information used for visual perception. Indeed, Freedman et al. (1999) found that targeted mutations against genes necessary for production of both rods and cones did not disrupt the synchronizing effects of light. However, when they removed the mice's eyes, these effects *were* disrupted. These results suggest that there is a special photoreceptor that is responsible for synchronization of diurnal rhythms. Provencio et al. (2000) found the photochemical responsible for these effects, which they named **melanopsin.**

Unlike the other retinal photopigments, which are found in rods and cones, melanopsin is present in ganglion cells—the neurons whose axons transmit information from the eyes to the rest of the brain. Melanopsin-containing ganglion cells are sensitive to light, and their axons terminate in the SCN, the thalamus, and the olivary pretectal

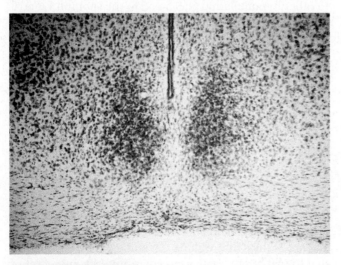

figure 9.25

A cross section through a rat brain, showing the location and appearance of the suprachiasmatic nuclei. Cresyl violet stain.

(Courtesy of Geert DeVries, University of Massachusetts.)

suprachiasmatic nucleus (SCN) (*soo pra ky az **mat** ik*) A nucleus situated atop the optic chiasm. It contains a biological clock that is responsible for organizing many of the body's circadian rhythms.

melanopsin (*mell a **nop** sin*) A photopigment present in ganglion cells in the retina whose axons transmit information to the SCN, the thalamus, and the olivary pretectal nuclei.

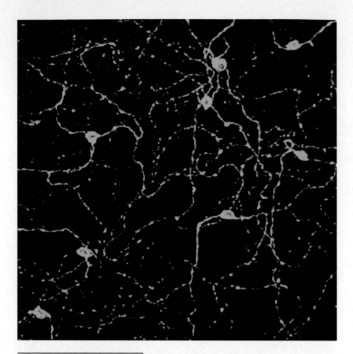

Melanopsin-containing ganglion cells in the retina whose axons form the retinohypothalamic tract. These neurons detect the light of dawn that resets the biological clock in the SCN.

(From Hattar, S., Liao, H.-W., Takao, M., Berson, D. M., and Yau, K.-W. *Science,* 2002, *295,* 1065–1070.

nuclei (Berson, Dunn, and Takao, 2002; Hattar et al., 2002). The pretectal nuclei are involved in the pupillary light response. As you know, our pupils dilate in dim light and constrict in bright light. Apparently, melanopsin-containing ganglion cells, and not rods and cones, are involved in this response. (See *Figure 9.26.*)

Pulses of light that reset an animal's circadian rhythm trigger the production of Fos protein in the SCN, which indicates that the light initiates a period of neural activity in this nucleus (Rusak et al., 1990, 1992). The synaptic connections between the retina and the SCN appear to be glutamatergic; drugs that block glutamate receptors prevent a period of bright light from stimulating Fos production and resetting circadian rhythms (Abe, Rusak, and Robertson, 1991; Vindlacheruvu et al., 1992).

Besides receiving visual information directly from the retina via the retinohypothalamic pathway, the SCN also receives such information indirectly, from the **intergeniculate leaflet (IGL),** a part of the lateral geniculate nucleus (Aronson et al., 1993; Moore and Card, 1994). (You will recall from Chapter 6 that the *dorsal* lateral geniculate nucleus sends visual information to the striate cortex.) The IGL receives photic information from the melanopsin-containing ganglion cells of the retina; in fact, the axons of the retinohypothalamic pathway divide near the optic chiasm and send one collateral to the SCN and another to the IGL. The connection between the IGL and the SCN (the *geniculohypothalamic pathway*) appears to play a role in resetting circadian rhythms; electrical stimulation of the IGL leaflet shifts the timing of circadian rhythms (Albers and Ferris, 1984; Rusak, Meijer, and Harrington, 1989). Damage to the geniculohypothalamic pathways reduces, but does not abolish, the effects of changes in the dark–light cycle on an animal's circadian rhythms (Harrington and Rusak, 1986). Thus, both the direct pathway from the retina to the SCN and the indirect pathway through the thalamus mediate the effects of light as a zeitgeber.

Evidence suggests that the IGL plays a special role in mediating the effects of zeitgebers other than light. Although light is the most potent stimulus for resetting circadian rhythms, other environmental stimuli, such as loud noises or sudden changes in temperature, can do so too. In addition, an animal's own activity can affect its circadian rhythm. For example, if a hamster is suddenly given access to a running wheel, its burst of activity in the wheel will advance or retard the animal's circadian rhythm, according to the time of day during which the access occurs (Reebs and Mrosovsky, 1989; Wickland and Turek, 1991). Wickland and Turek (1994) found that this effect was abolished by lesions of the IGL. Thus, it appears that the geniculohypothalamic tract connecting the IGL with the SCN is the sole pathway for at least one zeitgeber.

How does the SCN control drinking, eating, sleep cycles, and hormone secretion? Neurons of the SCN project caudally to the midbrain and to other hypothalamic nuclei, dorsally to other diencephalic regions, and rostrally to other hypothalamic nuclei and to the septum. Lu et al. (2001) found that excitotoxic lesions of the ventral part of the *subparaventricular zone (SPZ)*—a region just dorsal to the SCN—disrupted circadian rhythms of sleep and waking. Lesions of the dorsal part of the SPZ disrupted circadian rhythms of body temperature. Neurons in the SPZ project to the VLPA which, as we saw, plays a critical role in sleep. They also project to the medial preoptic area, which is involved in control of body temperature. Thus, the link between the circadian clock in the SCN and the brain mechanisms that control sleep and body temperature may be made by means of the SPZ. (See *Figure 9.27.*)

Although neurons in the SCN form synaptic connections, and although the SPZ appears to play a critical role in communication between the SCN and brain mechanisms of sleep and waking, several experiments suggest that the SCN can control circadian rhythms by secretion of chemicals. Lehman et al. (1987) destroyed the SCN and

intergeniculate leaflet (IGL) A part of the lateral geniculate nucleus that receives information from melanopsin-containing retinal ganglion cells and projects to the SCN.

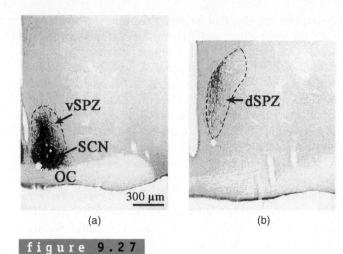

figure 9.27

Brain regions critical to circadian rhythms of sleep and waking (vSPZ) and body temperature (dSPZ). vSPZ = ventral part of the subparaventricular zone; dSPZ = dorsal part of the subparaventricular zone; SCN = suprachiasmatic nucleus; OC = optic chiasm.

(From Lu, J., Zhang, Y.-H., Chou, T. C., Gaus, S. E., Elmquist, J. K., Shiromani, P., and Saper, C. B. *Journal of Neuroscience,* 2001, *21,* 4864–4874.)

then transplanted in its place a new set of suprachiasmatic nuclei obtained from donor animals. The grafts succeeded in reestablishing circadian rhythms, even though very few synaptic connections were observed between the graft and the recipient's brain.

The most convincing evidence for chemical communication between the SCN and other parts of the brain comes from a transplantation study by Silver et al. (1996). Silver and her colleagues first destroyed the SCN in a group of hamsters, abolishing their circadian rhythms. Then, a few weeks later, they removed SCN tissue from donor animals and placed it in tiny semipermeable capsules, which they then implanted in the animals' third ventricles. Nutrients and other chemicals could pass through the walls of the capsules, keeping the SCN tissue alive, but the neurons inside the capsules were not able to establish synaptic connections with the surrounding tissue. Nevertheless, the transplants re-established circadian rhythms in the recipient animals. The identity of the chemical signal is not yet known. The study by Lu et al. (2001) suggests that the chemicals secreted by neurons in the SCN may bind with receptors on neurons in the SPZ.

LeSauter and Silver (1999) discovered that a subregion of the SCN composed of neurons that contain a particular calcium-binding protein (calbindin-D$_{28K}$) is critical for circadian rhythms controlling circadian activity cycles. Neurons in this region receive direct input from the retina, and most of them increase their production of Fos protein when the animal is exposed to light (Bryant et al., 2000). Lesions of the SCN that spare this subregion do not affect

circadian activity cycles, but lesions that destroy it do. In addition, transplants of SCN tissue restore circadian activity cycles in recipient animals with SCN lesions only if the grafts contain neurons from this subregion. These results suggest that the circadian clock may reside in these neurons; what functions are performed by the rest of the SCN is not known. (See *Figure 9.28.*)

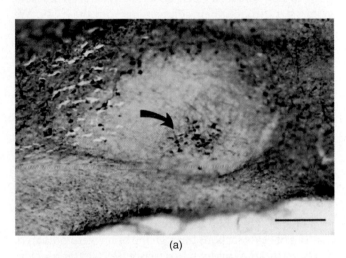

(a)

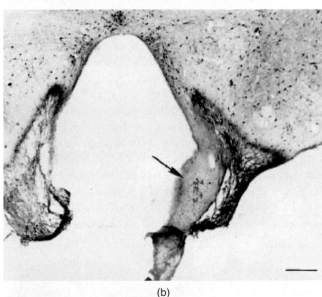

(b)

figure 9.28

A cluster of neurons in the SCN that are responsible for circadian activity rhythms. (a) Photomicrograph of neurons in the SCN stained for the presence of calbindin$_{28K}$. (b) Photomicrograph of transplanted SCN tissue in a rat whose SCN was previously destroyed. The graft, which contains a small group of neurons containing calbindin$_{28K}$, (arrow), restored circadian activity cycles to the recipient animal.

(From LeSauter, J., and Silver, R. *Journal of Neuroscience,* 1999, *19,* 5574–5585.)

The Nature of the Clock

All clocks must have a time base. Mechanical clocks use flywheels or pendulums; electronic clocks use quartz crystals. The SCN, too, must contain a physiological mechanism that parses time into units. After years of research, investigators are finally beginning to discover the nature of the biological clock in the SCN.

First, let us examine some evidence that the SCN does, in fact, contain a clock. So far, we have seen that zeitgebers act through their connections with the SCN. We have also seen that circadian rhythms require that the animal have an intact SCN or a transplant placed in or near the lateral or third ventricles. However, I have not yet described evidence that proves that a clock is located there; the clock could be located elsewhere but fail to run unless it is exposed to chemicals secreted by the SCN.

Several studies have demonstrated daily activity rhythms in the SCN, which indicates that the circadian clock is located there. A study by Schwartz and Gainer (1977) nicely demonstrated day–night fluctuations in the activity of the SCN. The investigators injected some rats with radioactive 2-DG during the day and injected others at night. The animals were then killed, and autoradiographs of cross sections through the brain were prepared. (2-DG autoradiography was described in Chapter 5.) Figure 9.29 shows photographs of two of these cross sections. Note the evidence of radioactivity (and hence a high metabolic rate) in the SCN of the brain that was injected during the day (*left*). (See *Figure 9.29.*)

Schwartz and his colleagues (Schwartz et al., 1983) found a similar pattern of activity in the SCN of squirrel monkeys, which are diurnal animals (active during the day). These results suggest that it is not differences in the SCN that determine whether an animal is nocturnal or diurnal but differences elsewhere in the brain. The SCN keeps track of day and night, but it is up to mechanisms located elsewhere to determine when the animal is to be awake or asleep.

The "ticking" of the biological clock within the SCN could involve interactions of circuits of neurons, or it could be intrinsic to individual neurons themselves. Evidence suggests the latter—that each neuron contains a clock. Several studies have succeeded in keeping individual SCN neurons alive in a culture medium. For example, Welsh et al. (1995) removed tissue from the rat SCN and dissolved the connections between the cells with papain, an enzyme that is sometimes used as a meat tenderizer. The cells were placed on top of an array of microelectrodes so that their electrical activity could be measured. Although these neurons did re-establish synaptic connections with each other, they displayed individual, independent, circadian rhythms in activity. Figure 9.30 shows the activity cycles of four neurons. As you can see, all showed circadian rhythms, but their periods of peak activity occurred at different times of day. Of course, in the intact SCN, their rhythms are synchronized. (See *Figure 9.30.*)

What causes intracellular ticking? For many years investigators have believed that circadian rhythms were

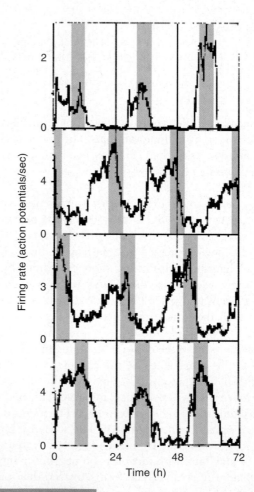

figure 9.30

Firing rate of individual SCN neurons in a tissue culture. Color bars have been added to emphasize the daily peaks. Note that although each neuron has a period of approximately 1 day, their activity cycles are not synchronized.

(From Welsh, D. K., Logothetis, D. E., Meister, M., and Reppert, S. M. *Neuron,* 1995, *14*, 697–706.)

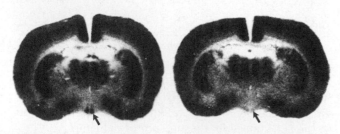

figure 9.29

Autoradiographs of cross sections through the brains of rats that had been injected with carbon 14-labeled 2-deoxyglucose during the day (*left*) and the night (*right*). The dark region at the base of the brain (*arrows*) indicates increased metabolic activity of the suprachiasmatic nuclei.

(From Schwartz, W. J., and Gainer, H. *Science,* 1977, *197*, 1089–1091. Reprinted with permission.)

produced by the production of a protein that, when it reached a certain level in the cell, inhibited its own production. As a result, the levels of the protein would begin to decline, which would remove the inhibition, starting the production cycle again. (See *Figure 9.31*.)

Just such a mechanism was discovered in *Drosophila melanogaster,* the common fruit fly. Subsequent research with mammals discovered a similar system (Shearman et al., 2000; Reppert and Weaver, 2001). The system involves at least seven genes and their proteins and two interlocking feedback loops. When one of the proteins produced by the first loop reaches a sufficient level, it starts the second loop, which eventually inhibits the production of proteins in the first loop, and the cycle begins again. Thus, the intracellular ticking is regulated by the time it takes to produce and degrade a set of proteins.

It appears that the circadian clock in the human brain works the same way as it does in other mammals. A study by Toh et al. (2001) found that a mutation on chromosome 2 of a gene for one of the proteins involved in the feedback loops I mentioned in the previous paragraph (*per2*) is responsible for the **familial advanced sleep phase syndrome.** This syndrome causes a 4-hour advance in rhythms of sleep and temperature cycles. People with this syndrome fall asleep around 7:30 P.M., and awaken around 4:30 A.M. The mutation appears to change the relationship between the zeitgeber of morning light and the phase of the circadian clock that operates in the cells of the SCN.

The protein enters the nucleus, suppressing the gene responsible for its production. No more messenger RNA is made.

The level of the protein falls, so the gene becomes active again.

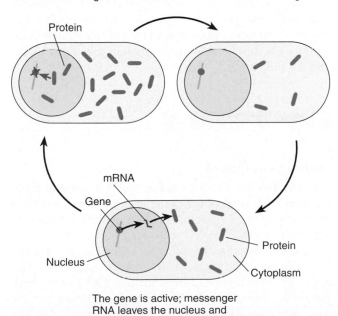

The gene is active; messenger RNA leaves the nucleus and causes the production of the protein.

figure 9.31

A schematic, simplified explanation of the molecular control of the "ticking" of neurons of the SCN.

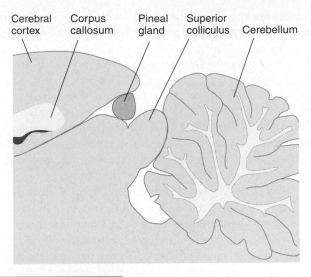

Cerebral cortex | Corpus callosum | Pineal gland | Superior colliculus | Cerebellum

figure 9.32

The pineal gland, located on the dorsal surface of the midbrain.

(Adapted from Paxinos, G., and Watson, C. *The Rat Brain in Stereotaxic Coordinates.* Sydney: Academic Press, 1982. Redrawn with permission.)

Control of Seasonal Rhythms: The Pineal Gland and Melatonin

Although the SCN has an intrinsic rhythm of approximately 24 hours, it plays a role in much longer rhythms. (We could say that it is involved in a biological calendar as well as a biological clock.) Male hamsters show annual rhythms of testosterone secretion, which appear to be based on the amount of light that occurs each day. Their breeding season begins as the day length increases and ends when it decreases. Lesions of the SCN abolish these annual breeding cycles; the animals' testes then secrete testosterone all year (Rusak and Morin, 1976). Possibly, the lesions disrupt these annual cycles because they destroy the 24-hour clock against which the daily light period is measured to determine the season. That is, if the light period is considerably shorter than 12 hours, the season is winter; if it is considerably longer than 12 hours, the season is summer.

The control of seasonal rhythms involves another part of the brain: the **pineal gland** (Bartness et al., 1993; Moore, 1995). This structure sits on top of the midbrain, just in front of the cerebellum. (See *Figure 9.32*.) The pineal gland secretes a hormone called **melatonin,** so

familial advanced sleep phase syndrome A 4-hour advance in rhythms of sleep and temperature cycles, caused by a mutation of a gene involved in the rhythmicity of neurons of the SCN.

pineal gland (*py nee ul*) A gland attached to the dorsal tectum; produces melatonin and plays a role in circadian and seasonal rhythms.

melatonin(*mell a tone in*) A hormone secreted during the night by the pineal body; plays a role in circadian and seasonal rhythms.

named because it has the ability in certain animals (primarily fish, reptiles, and amphibians) to turn the skin temporarily dark. (The dark color is produced by a chemical known as *melanin*.) In mammals melatonin controls seasonal rhythms. Neurons in the SCN make synaptic connections with neurons in the *paraventricular nucleus of the hypothalamus* (the PVN). The axons of these neurons travel all the way to the spinal cord, where they form synapses with preganglionic neurons of the sympathetic nervous system. The postganglionic neurons innervate the pineal gland and control the secretion of melatonin.

In response to input from the SCN, the pineal gland secretes melatonin during the night. This melatonin acts back on various structures in the brain (including the SCN, whose cells contain melatonin receptors) and controls hormones, physiological processes, and behaviors that show seasonal variations. During long nights a large amount of melatonin is secreted, and the animals go into the winter phase of their cycle. Lesions of the SCN, the paraventricular nucleus (PVN), or the pineal gland disrupt seasonal rhythms that are controlled by day length—and so do knife cuts that interrupt the neural connection between the SCN and the PVN, which indicates that this is one function of the SCN that is mediated through its neural connections with another structure. Furthermore, although transplants of fetal suprachiasmatic nuclei will restore circadian rhythms, they will not restore seasonal rhythms, because the transplanted tissue does not establish neural connections with the PVN (Ralph and Lehman, 1991).

Changes in Circadian Rhythms: Shift Work and Jet Lag

When people abruptly change their daily rhythms of activity, their internal circadian rhythms, controlled by the SCN, become desynchronized with those in the external environment. For example, if a person who normally works on the day shift begins working on a night shift or if someone travels east or west across several time zones, his or her SCN will signal the rest of the brain that it is time to sleep during the work shift (or the middle of the day, in the case of jet travel). This disparity between internal rhythms and the external environment results in sleep disturbances and mood changes and interferes with people's ability to function during waking hours.

Jet lag is a temporary phenomenon; after several days, people who have crossed several time zones find it easier to fall asleep at the appropriate time, and their daytime alertness improves. Shift work can present a more enduring problem when people are required to change shifts frequently. Obviously, the solution to jet lag and to the problems caused by shift work is to get the internal clock synchronized with the external environment as quickly as possible. The most obvious way to start is to try to provide strong zeitgebers at the appropriate time. If a person

is exposed to bright light before the low point in the daily rhythm of body temperature (which occurs an hour or two before the person usually awakens), the person's circadian rhythm is delayed. If the exposure to bright light occurs after the low point, the circadian rhythm is advanced (Dijk et al., 1995). In fact, several studies have shown that exposure to bright lights at the appropriate time help to ease the transition (Boulos et al., 1995). Similarly, people adapt to shift work more rapidly if artificial light is kept at a brighter level in the workplace and if the bedroom is kept as dark as possible (Horowitz et al., 2001).

As we saw in the previous subsection, the role of melatonin in seasonal rhythms is well established. Studies in recent years suggest that melatonin may also be involved in circadian rhythms. As we saw, melatonin is secreted during the night, which, for diurnal mammals such as ourselves, is the period during which we sleep. But although our species lacks strong seasonal rhythms, the daily rhythm of melatonin secretion persists. Thus, melatonin must have some functions besides regulation of seasonal rhythms.

Recent studies have found that melatonin, acting on receptors in the SCN, can affect the sensitivity of SCN neurons to zeitgebers and can itself alter circadian rhythms (Gillette and McArthur, 1995; Starkey et al., 1995). Researchers do not yet understand exactly what role melatonin plays in the control of circadian rhythms, but they have already discovered practical applications. Melatonin secretion normally reaches its highest levels early in the night, at around bedtime. Investigators have found that the administration of melatonin at the appropriate time (in most cases, just before going to bed) significantly reduces the adverse effects of both jet lag and shifts in work schedules (Arendt et al., 1995; Deacon and Arendt, 1996). Bedtime melatonin has even helped to synchronize circadian rhythms and has improved the sleep of blind people, for whom light cannot serve as a zeitgeber (Skene, Lockley, and Arendt, 1999).

interim summary

Biological Clocks

Our daily lives are characterized by cycles in physical activity, sleep, body temperature, secretion of hormones, and many other physiological changes. Circadian rhythms—those with a period of approximately 1 day—are controlled by biological clocks in the brain. The principal biological clock appears to be located in the suprachiasmatic nuclei of the hypothalamus; lesions of these nuclei disrupt most circadian rhythms, and the activity of neurons located there correlates with the day–night cycle. Light, detected by special retinal ganglion cells that contain a photopigment called melanopsin, serves as a zeitgeber for most circadian rhythms. That is, the biological clocks tend to run a bit slow, with a period of approximately 25 hours. The sight of sunlight in the morning is conveyed from the retina to the SCN—directly and via the IGL of the lateral geniculate nucleus. The effect of the light is to reset the clock to the start of a new cycle.

Individual neurons, rather than circuits of neurons, are responsible for the "ticking." Each tick, approximately 24 hours long, consists of the production and breakdown of a series of proteins that act back on the genes responsible for their own production.

The SCN and the pineal gland control annual rhythms. During the night the SCN signals the pineal gland to secrete melatonin. Prolonged melatonin secretion, which occurs during winter, causes the animals to enter the winter phase of their annual cycle. Melatonin also appears to be involved in synchronizing circadian rhythms: The hormone can help people to adjust to the effects of shift work or jet lag and even synchronize the daily rhythms of blind people for whom light cannot serve as a zeitgeber.

Suggested Readings

Hastings, J. W., Rusak, B., and Boulos, Z. Circadian rhythms: The physiology of biological timing. In *Neural and Integrative Animal Physiology,* edited by C. L. Prosser. New York: Wiley-Liss, 1991.

Horne, J. *Why We Sleep: The Functions of Sleep in Humans and Other Mammals.* Oxford, England: Oxford University Press, 1988.

Kryger, M. H., Roth, T., and Dement, W. C. *Principles and Practice of Sleep Medicine.* Philadelphia: Saunders, 1994.

Mancia, M., and Marini, G. *The Diencephalon and Sleep.* New York: Raven Press, 1990.

Moorcroft, W. H. *Sleep, Dreaming, and Sleep Disorders: An Introduction.* Lanham, MD: University Press of America, 1993.

Schwartz, W. J. *Sleep Science: Integrating Basic Research and Clinical Practice.* Basel: Karger, 1997.

Webb, W. *Sleep: The Gentle Tyrant,* 2nd ed. Bolton, MA: Anker, 1992.

Suggested Web Sites

The Sleep Well

http://www.stanford.edu/~dement/alphaindex.html

The topic of sleep is the focus of this site. The Sleep Well site provides a number of links to basic research on sleep and to sites that cover sleep disorders.

SleepNet

http://www.sleepnet.com/

SleepNet contains a forum on sleep issues, a set of links to sleep lab sites and to sleep disorders. In addition, the site contains a column written by the sleep scientist Dr. William Dement.

Basics of Sleep Behavior

http://bisleep.medsch.ucla.edu/sleepsyllabus/

This site provides coverage on a number of sleep lecture topics including NREM and REM sleep, chemical and neuronal control of sleep, and sleep functions.

National Centers on Sleep Disorders Research

http://www.nhlbi.nih.gov/about/ncsdr/

This NIH site provides an interactive quiz on sleep, and contains a series of fact sheets and education materials on sleep and sleep disorders.

chapter 10

Reproductive Behavior

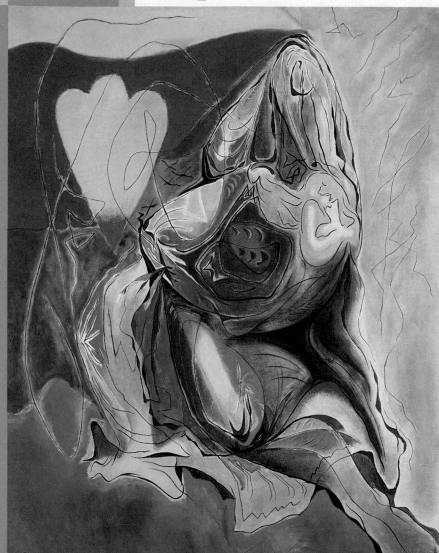

outline

■ **Sexual Development**
Production of Gametes
    and Fertilization
Development of the Sex Organs
Sexual Maturation
Interim Summary

■ **Hormonal Control
of Sexual Behavior**
Hormonal Control of Female
    Reproductive Cycles
Hormonal Control of Sexual
    Behavior of Laboratory Animals
Organizational Effects of Androgens
    on Behavior: Masculinization
    and Defeminization
Effects of Pheromones
Human Sexual Behavior
Sexual Orientation
Interim Summary

■ **Neural Control
of Sexual Behavior**
Males
Females
Interim Summary

■ **Parental Behavior**
Maternal Behavior of Rodents
Hormonal Control of
    Maternal Behavior
Neural Control of Maternal Behavior
Neural Control of Paternal Behavior
Interim Summary

At first, a tragic surgical accident suggested that people's sexual identity and sexual orientation were not under the strong control of biological factors and that these characteristics could be shaped by the way a child was raised (Money and Ehrhardt, 1972). Identical twin boys were raised normally until seven months of age, at which time one of the boys' penis was accidentally removed during circumcision. The cautery (a device that cuts tissue by means of electric current) was adjusted too high, and instead of removing the foreskin, the current burned off the entire penis. After a period of agonized indecision, the parents decided to raise the child as a girl. John became Joan.

Joan's parents started dressing her in girl's clothing and treating her like a little girl. Surgeons performed a sex change operation, removing the testes and creating a vagina. At first, psychologists who studied Joan reported that she was a normal, happy girl and concluded that it was a child's upbringing that determined his or her sexual identity. Many writers saw this case as a triumph of socialization over biology.

Unfortunately, this conclusion was premature (Diamond and Sigmundson, 1997). It turned out that although Joan did not know she had been born as a boy, she was unhappy as a girl. She felt that she really was a boy and even tried to stand to urinate. When, as an unhappy adolescent, she threatened to commit suicide, her family and physicians agreed to a sex change. The estrogen treatment she had been receiving was terminated, she started taking androgens, she had a mastectomy, and surgeons began creating a phallus. Joan became John again. His father finally told him that he was born a boy, a revelation that John received with great relief. John is now happily married and has adopted his wife's children.

We now know this person's real names—actually, Bruce became Brenda, who then chose the name David after deciding to become a boy again. A book has told his story (Colapinto, 2000), and a 2002 television documentary ("Nova, Sex: Unknown") presented interviews with David, his mother, Dr. Diamond, and others involved in this unfortunate case.

R eproductive behaviors constitute the most important category of social behaviors, because without them, most species would not survive. These behaviors—which include courting, mating, parental behavior, and most forms of aggressive behaviors—are the most striking categories of **sexually dimorphic behaviors,** that is, behaviors that differ in males and females (*di + morphous,* "two forms"). As you will see, hormones that are present both before and after birth play a very special role in the development and control of sexually dimorphic behaviors.

This chapter describes male and female sexual development and then discusses the neural and hormonal con-

trol of two sexually dimorphic behaviors that are most important to reproduction: sexual behavior and parental behavior.

Sexual Development

A person's chromosomal sex is determined at the time of fertilization. However, this event is merely the first in a series of steps that culminate in the development of a male or female. This section considers the major features of sexual development.

Production of Gametes and Fertilization

All cells of the human body (other than sperms or ova) contain twenty-three pairs of chromosomes. The genetic information that programs the development of a human is contained in the DNA that constitutes these chromosomes. We pride ourselves on our ability to miniaturize computer circuits on silicon chips, but that accomplishment looks primitive when we consider that the blueprint for a human being is too small to be seen by the naked eye.

The production of **gametes** (ova and sperms; *gamein* means "to marry") entails a special form of cell division. This process produces cells that contain one member of each of the twenty-three pairs of chromosomes. The development of a human begins at the time of fertilization, when a single sperm and ovum join, sharing their twenty-three single chromosomes to reconstitute the twenty-three pairs.

A person's genetic sex is determined at the time of fertilization by the father's sperm. Twenty-two of the twenty-three pairs of chromosomes determine the organism's physical development independent of its sex. The last pair consists of two **sex chromosomes,** which determine whether the offspring will be a boy or a girl.

There are two types of sex chromosomes: X chromosomes and Y chromosomes. Females have two X chromosomes (XX); thus, all the ova that a woman produces will contain an X chromosome. Males have an X and a Y chromosome (XY). When a man's sex chromosomes divide, half the sperms contain an X chromosome and the

---

sexually dimorphic behavior A behavior that has different forms or that occurs with different probabilities or under different circumstances in males and females.

gamete (*gamm eet*) A mature reproductive cell; a sperm or ovum.

sex chromosome The X and Y chromosomes, which determine an organism's gender. Normally, XX individuals are female, and XY individuals are male.

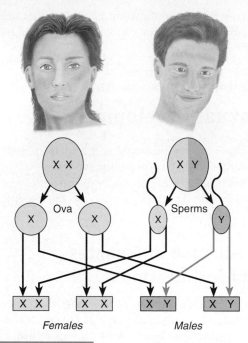

figure 10.1

Determination of gender. The gender of the offspring depends on whether the sperm cell that fertilizes the ovum carries an X or a Y chromosome.

other half contain a Y chromosome. A Y-bearing sperm produces an XY-fertilized ovum and therefore a male. An X-bearing sperm produces an XX-fertilized ovum and therefore a female. (See *Figure 10.1*.)

Development of the Sex Organs

Men and women differ in many ways: Their bodies are different, parts of their brains are different, and their reproductive behaviors are different. Are all these differences encoded on the tiny Y chromosome, the sole piece of genetic material that distinguishes males from females? The answer is no. The X chromosome and the twenty-two nonsex chromosomes that are found in the cells of both males and females contain all the information needed to develop the bodies of either sex. Exposure to sex hormones, both before and after birth, is responsible for our sexual dimorphism. What the Y chromosome does control is the development of the glands that produce the male sex hormones.

Gonads

There are three general categories of sex organs: the gonads, the internal sex organs, and the external genitalia. The **gonads**—testes or ovaries—are the first to develop. Gonads (from the Greek *gonos*, "procreation") have a dual function: They produce ova or sperms, and they secrete hormones. Through the sixth week of prenatal develop-

ment, male and female fetuses are identical. Both sexes have a pair of identical undifferentiated gonads, which have the potential of developing into either testes or ovaries. The factor that controls their development appears to be a single gene on the Y chromosome called *Sry*. This gene produces a protein called *testis-determining factor,* which binds to the DNA of cells in the undifferentiated gonads and causes them to become testes. (Testes are also known as *testicles,* Latin for "little testes." Believe it or not, the words "testis" and "testify" have the same root, meaning "witness." Legend has it that ancient Romans placed their right hand over their testes while swearing that they would tell the truth in court.) If the *Sry* gene is not present, they become ovaries (Sinclair et al., 1990; Smith, 1994; Koopman, 2001). In fact, a few cases of XX males have been reported. This anomaly can occur when the *Sry* gene becomes translocated from the Y chromosome to the X chromosome during production of sperms (Warne and Zajac, 1998).

Once the gonads have developed, a series of events is set into action that determines the individual's gender. These events are directed by hormones, which affect sexual development in two ways. During prenatal development these hormones have **organizational effects,** which influence the development of a person's sex organs and brain. These effects are permanent; once a particular path is followed in the course of development, there is no going back. The second role of sex hormones is their **activational effect.** These effects occur later in life, after the sex organs have developed. For example, hormones activate the production of sperms, make erection and ejaculation possible, and induce ovulation. Because the bodies of adult males and females have been organized differently, sex hormones will have different activational effects in the two sexes.

Internal Sex Organs

Early in embryonic development, the internal sex organs are *bisexual;* that is, all embryos contain the precursors for both female and male sex organs. However, during the third month of gestation, only one of these precursors develops; the other withers away. The precursor of the internal female sex organs, which develops into the *fimbriae* and *Fallopian tubes,* the *uterus,* and the *inner two-thirds of the vagina,* is called the **Müllerian system.** The

gonad (rhymes with *moan ad*) An ovary or testis.

organizational effect (of hormone) The effect of a hormone on tissue differentiation and development.

activational effect (of hormone) The effect of a hormone that occurs in the fully developed organism; may depend on the organism's prior exposure to the organizational effects of hormones.

Müllerian system The embryonic precursors of the female internal sex organs.

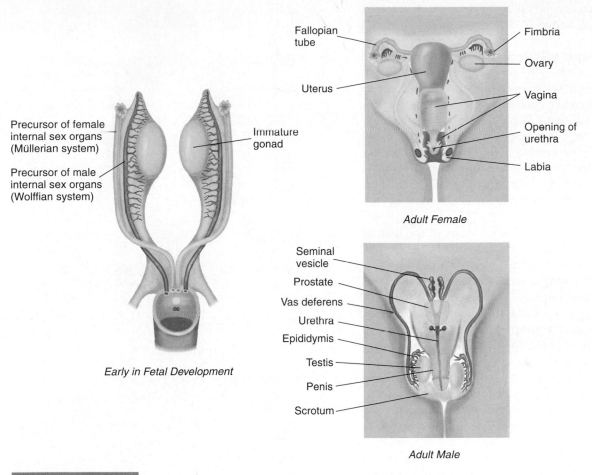

Development of the internal sex organs.

precursor of the internal male sex organs, which develops into the *epididymis, vas deferens,* and *seminal vesicles,* is called the **Wolffian system.** (These systems were named after their discoverers, Müller and Wolff. See *Figure 10.2*.)

The gender of the internal sex organs of a fetus is determined by the presence or absence of hormones secreted by the testes. If these hormones are present, the Wolffian system develops. If they are not, the Müllerian system develops. The Müllerian (female) system needs no hormonal stimulus from the gonads to develop; it just normally does so. In contrast, the cells of the Wolffian (male) system do not develop unless they are stimulated to do so by a hormone. Thus, testes secrete two types of hormones. The first, a peptide hormone called **anti-Müllerian hormone,** does exactly what its name says: It prevents the Müllerian (female) system from developing. It therefore has a **defeminizing effect.** The second, a set of steroid hormones called **androgens,** stimulates the development of the Wolffian system. (This class of hormone is also aptly named: *Andros* means "man," and *gennan* means "to produce.") Androgens have a **masculinizing effect.**

Two different androgens are responsible for masculinization. The first, **testosterone,** is secreted by the testes and gets its name from these glands. An enzyme

Wolffian system   The embryonic precursors of the male internal sex organs.

anti-Müllerian hormone   A peptide secreted by the fetal testes that inhibits the development of the Müllerian system, which would otherwise become the female internal sex organs.

defeminizing effect   An effect of a hormone present early in development that reduces or prevents the later development of anatomical or behavioral characteristics typical of females.

androgen (*an dro jen*)   A male sex steroid hormone. Testosterone is the principal mammalian androgen.

masculinizing effect   An effect of a hormone present early in development that promotes the later development of anatomical or behavioral characteristics typical of males.

testosterone (*tess tahss ter own*)   The principal androgen found in males.

called *5α reductase* converts some of the testosterone into another androgen, known as **dihydrotestosterone.**

As you will recall from Chapter 2, hormones exert their effects on target cells by stimulating the appropriate hormone receptor. Thus, the precursor of the male internal sex organs—the Wolffian system—contains androgen receptors that are coupled to cellular mechanisms that promote growth and division. When molecules of androgens bind with these receptors, the epididymis, vas deferens, and seminal vesicles develop and grow. In contrast, the cells of the Müllerian system contain receptors for anti-Müllerian hormone that *prevent* growth and division. Thus, anti-Müllerian hormone prevents the development of the female internal sex organs.

The fact that the internal sex organs of the human embryo are bisexual and could potentially develop as either male or female is dramatically illustrated by two genetic disorders: *androgen insensitivity syndrome* and *persistent Müllerian duct syndrome*. Some people are insensitive to androgens; they have **androgen insensitivity syndrome,** one of the more aptly named disorders (Money and Ehrhardt, 1972; MacLean, Warne, and Zajac, 1995). The cause of androgen insensitivity syndrome is a genetic mutation that prevents the formation of functioning androgen receptors. (The gene for the androgen receptor is located on the X chromosome.) The primitive gonads of a genetic male fetus with androgen insensitivity syndrome become testes and secrete both anti-Müllerian hormone and androgens. The lack of androgen receptors prevents the androgens from having a masculinizing effect; thus, the epididymis, vas deferens, seminal vesicles, and prostate fail to develop. However, the anti-Müllerian hormone still has its defeminizing effect, preventing the female internal sex organs from developing. The uterus, fimbriae, and Fallopian tubes fail to develop, and the vagina is shallow. Their external genitalia are female, and at puberty they develop a woman's body. Of course, lacking a uterus and ovaries, these people cannot have children. (See *Figure 10.3*.)

The second genetic disorder, **persistent Müllerian duct syndrome,** has two causes: either a failure to produce anti-Müllerian hormone or the absence of receptors for this hormone (Warne and Zajac, 1998). When this syndrome occurs in genetic males, androgens have their masculinizing effect but defeminization does not occur. Thus, the person is born with *both* sets of internal sex organs, male and female. The presence of the additional female sex organs usually interferes with normal functioning of the male sex organs.

So far, I have been discussing only male sex hormones. What about prenatal sexual development in females? A chromosomal anomaly indicates that female sex organs are not needed for development of the Müllerian system. This fact has led to the dictum "Nature's impulse is to create a female." People with **Turner's syndrome**

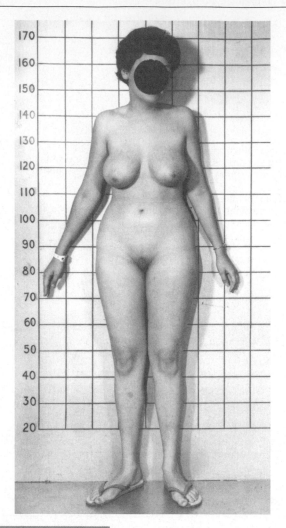

figure 10.3

An XY female displaying androgen insensitivity syndrome. (From Money, J., and Ehrhardt, A. A. *Man & Woman, Boy & Girl.* Copyright 1973 by The Johns Hopkins University Press, Baltimore, Maryland. By permission.)

dihydrotestosterone (*dy hy dro tess **tahss** ter own*) An androgen, produced from testosterone through the action of the enzyme 5α reductase.

androgen insensitivity syndrome A condition caused by a congenital lack of functioning androgen receptors; in a person with XY sex chromosomes, causes the development of a female with testes but no internal sex organs.

persistent Müllerian duct syndrome A condition caused by a congenital lack of anti-Müllerian hormone or receptors for this hormone; in a male, causes development of both male and female internal sex organs.

Turner's syndrome The presence of only one sex chromosome (an X chromosome); characterized by lack of ovaries but otherwise normal female sex organs and genitalia.

have only one sex chromosome: an X chromosome. (Thus, instead of having XX cells, they have X0 cells—0 indicating a missing sex chromosome.) In most cases the existing X chromosome comes from the mother, which means that the cause of the disorder lies with a defective sperm (Knebelmann et al., 1991). Because a Y chromosome is not present, testes do not develop. In addition, because two X chromosomes are needed to produce ovaries, these glands are not produced either. But even though people with Turner's syndrome have no gonads at all, they develop into females, with normal female internal sex organs and external genitalia—which proves that fetuses do not need ovaries or the hormones they produce to develop as females. Of course, they cannot bear children, because without ovaries they cannot produce ova.

External Genitalia

The external genitalia are the visible sex organs, including the penis and scrotum in males and the labia, clitoris, and outer part of the vagina in females. (See *Figure 10.4*.) As we just saw, the external genitalia do not need to be stimulated by female sex hormones to become female; they just naturally develop that way. In the presence of dihydrotestosterone the external genitalia will become male. Thus, the gender of a person's external genitalia is determined by the presence or absence of an androgen, which explains why people with Turner's syndrome have female external genitalia even though they lack ovaries. People with androgen insensitivity syndrome have female external genitalia too, because without androgen receptors, their cells cannot respond to the androgens produced by their testes.

Figure 10.5 summarizes the factors that control the development of the gonads, internal sex organs, and genitalia. (See *Figure 10.5*.)

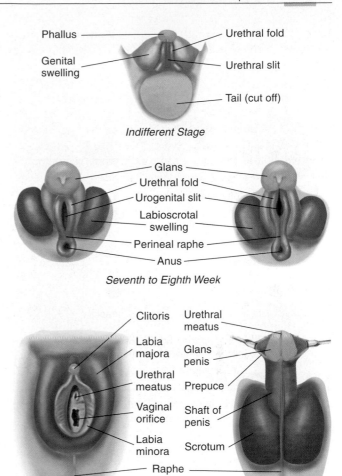

figure 10.4

Development of the external genitalia.

(Adapted from Spaulding, M. H., in *Contributions to Embryology*, Vol. 13. Washington, DC: Carnegie Institute of Washington, 1921.)

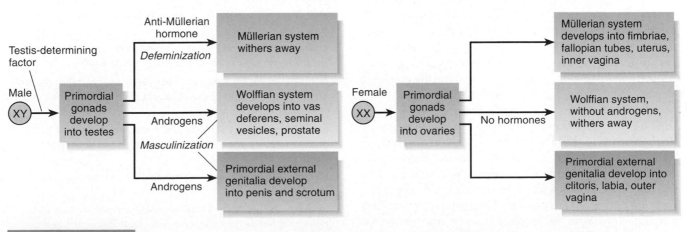

figure 10.5

Hormonal control of development of the internal sex organs.

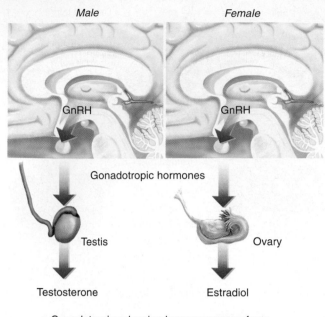

Male   *Female*

GnRH   GnRH

Gonadotropic hormones

Testis   Ovary

Testosterone   Estradiol

Gonadotropin-releasing hormones move from
hypothalamus to anterior pituitary gland

figure 10.6

Sexual maturation. Puberty is initiated when the
hypothalamus secretes gonadotropin-releasing hormones.

Sexual Maturation

The *primary* sex characteristics include the gonads,
internal sex organs, and external genitalia. These organs
are present at birth. The *secondary* sex characteristics, such
as enlarged breasts and widened hips or a beard and deep
voice, do not appear until puberty. Without seeing genitals, we must guess the sex of a prepubescent child from
his or her haircut and clothing; the bodies of young boys
and girls are rather similar. However, at puberty the gonads
are stimulated to produce their hormones, and these hormones cause the person to mature sexually. The onset of
puberty occurs when cells in the hypothalamus secrete
gonadotropin-releasing hormones (GnRH), which stimulate the production and release of two **gonadotropic
hormones** by the anterior pituitary gland. The gonadotropic ("gonad-turning") hormones stimulate the gonads to
produce *their* hormones, which are ultimately responsible
for sexual maturation. (See *Figure 10.6*.)

The two gonadotropic hormones are **follicle-stimulating hormone** (FSH) and **luteinizing hormone** (LH),
named for the effects they produce in the female (production of a *follicle* and its subsequent *luteinization,* to be
described in the next section of this chapter). However,
the same hormones are produced in the male, where they
stimulate the testes to produce sperms and to secrete
testosterone. If male and female pituitary glands are
exchanged in rats, the ovaries and testes respond per-

fectly to the hormones secreted by the new glands (Harris and Jacobsohn, 1951–1952).

For over a century the age at which children (particularly girls) reach puberty has been diminishing in developed countries, presumably because of improved nutrition
(Foster and Nagatani, 1999). Girls who remain unusually
thin through exercise and diet tend to reach puberty later
than normal, while obese girls tend to reach puberty
sooner (Frisch, 1990). As we will see in Chapter 12, *leptin,* a peptide hormone secreted by well-nourished fat
cells, provides an important signal to the brain concerning the amount of fat tissue in the body. If body fat
increases, the level of leptin in the blood increase and signals the brain to suppress appetite. This hormone also
appears to play a role in determining the onset of puberty
in females. Chehab et al. (1997) gave juvenile female mice
daily injections of leptin. Although the appetite-suppressing effects of the injections caused the animals' body
weight to decrease, they nevertheless entered puberty earlier than mice that were given control injections of a
placebo. Thus, a hormone that normally signifies increased
body fat accelerates the onset of sexual maturity, at least
in females.

In response to the gonadotropic hormones (usually
called *gonadotropins*), the gonads secrete steroid sex hormones. The ovaries produce **estradiol,** one of a class of
hormones known as **estrogens.** As we saw, the testes produce testosterone, an androgen. Both types of glands also
produce a small amount of the hormones of the other sex.
The gonadal steroids affect many parts of the body. Both
estradiol and androgens initiate closure of the growing portions of the bones and thus halt skeletal growth. Estradiol
also causes breast development, growth of the lining of the
uterus, changes in the deposition of body fat, and maturation of the female genitalia. Androgens stimulate growth

gonadotropin-releasing hormone (*go nad oh **trow** pin*) A hypothalamic hormone that stimulates the anterior pituitary gland to secrete
gonadotropic hormone.

gonadotropic hormone A hormone of the anterior pituitary gland
that has a stimulating effect on cells of the gonads.

follicle-stimulating hormone (FSH) The hormone of the anterior
pituitary gland that causes development of an ovarian follicle and
the maturation of an ovum.

luteinizing hormone (LH) (*lew tee a nize ing*) A hormone of the
anterior pituitary gland that causes ovulation and development of
the ovarian follicle into a corpus luteum.

estradiol (*ess tra **dye** ahl*) The principal estrogen of many mammals,
including humans.

estrogen (*ess **trow** jen*) A class of sex hormones that cause maturation of the female genitalia, growth of breast tissue, and development of other physical features characteristic of females.

table **10.1**

Classification of Sex Steroid Hormones

CLASS	PRINCIPAL HORMONE IN HUMANS (WHERE PRODUCED)	EXAMPLES OF EFFECTS
Androgens	Testosterone (testes)	Development of Wolffian system; production of sperms; growth of facial, pubic, and axillary hair; muscular development; enlargement of larynx; inhibition of bone growth; sex drive in men (and women?)
	Dihydrotestosterone (produced from testosterone by action of 5α reductase)	Maturation of male external genitalia
	Androstenedione (adrenal glands)	In women, growth of pubic and axillary hair; less important than testosterone and dihydrotestosterone in men
Estrogens	Estradiol (ovaries)	Maturation of female genitalia; growth of breasts; alterations in fat deposits; growth of uterine lining; inhibition of bone growth; sex drive in women (?)
Gestagens	Progesterone (ovaries)	Maintenance of uterine lining
Hypothalamic hormones	Gonadotropin-releasing hormone (hypothalamus)	Secretion of gonadotropins
Gonadotropins	Follicle-stimulating hormone (anterior pituitary)	Development of ovarian follicle
	Luteinizing hormone (anterior pituitary)	Ovulation; development of corpus luteum
Other hormones	Prolactin (posterior pituitary)	Milk production; male refractory period (?)
	Oxytocin (posterior pituitary)	Milk ejection; orgasm

of facial, axillary (underarm), and pubic hair; lower the voice; alter the hairline on the head (often causing baldness later in life); stimulate muscular development; and cause genital growth. This description leaves out two of the female secondary characteristics: axillary and pubic hair. These characteristics are produced not by estradiol but rather by androgens secreted by the cortex of the adrenal glands. Even a male who is castrated before puberty (whose testes are removed) will grow axillary and pubic hair, stimulated by his own adrenal androgens. A list of the principal sex hormones and examples of their effects are presented in Table 10.1. Note that some of these effects are discussed later in this chapter. (See *Table 10.1*.)

The bipotentiality of some of the secondary sex characteristics remains throughout life. If a man is treated with an estrogen (for example, to control an androgen-dependent tumor), he will grow breasts, and his facial hair will become finer and softer. However, his voice will remain low, because the enlargement of the larynx is permanent. Conversely, a woman who receives high levels of an androgen (usually from a tumor that secretes androgens) will grow a beard, and her voice will become lower.

interim summary

Sexual Development

Gender is determined by the sex chromosomes: XX produces a female, and XY produces a male. Males are produced by the action of the *Sry* gene on the Y chromosome, which contains the code for the production of the testis-determining protein, which in turn causes the primitive gonads to become testes. The testes secrete two kinds of hormones that cause a male to develop. Testosterone (an androgen) stimulates the development of the Wolffian system (masculinization), and anti-Müllerian hormone suppresses the development of the Müllerian system (defeminization). Androgen insensitivity syndrome results from a hereditary defect in androgen receptors, and persistent Müllerian duct syndrome results from a hereditary defect in anti-Müllerian hormone receptors.

By default, the body is female ("Nature's impulse is to create a female"); only by the actions of testicular hormones does it become male. Masculinization and defeminization are referred to as *organizational* effects of hormones; *activational* effects occur after development is complete. A person with Turner's syndrome (X0) fails to develop gonads but nevertheless develops female internal sex organs and external genitalia. The external genitalia develop from common precursors. In the absence of gonadal hormones, the precursors develop the female form; in the presence of androgens (primarily dihydrotestosterone, which derives from testosterone through the action of 5α reductase), they develop the male form (masculinization).

Sexual maturity occurs when the hypothalamus begins secreting gonadotropin-releasing hormone, which stimulates the secretion of follicle-stimulating hormone and luteinizing hormone by the anterior pituitary gland. These hormones stimulate the gonads to secrete their hormones, thus causing the genitals to mature and the body to develop the secondary sex characteristics (activational effects). Leptin, a hormone secreted by well-nourished fat tissue, appears to be one of the signals that stimulates the onset of puberty, at least in females.

Hormonal Control of Sexual Behavior

We have seen that hormones are responsible for sexual dimorphism in the structure of the body and its organs. Hormones have organizational and activational effects on the internal sex organs, genitals, and secondary sex characteristics. Naturally, all of these effects influence a person's behavior. Simply having the physique and genitals of a man or a woman exerts a powerful effect. But hormones do more than give us masculine or feminine bodies; they also affect behavior by interacting directly with the nervous system. Androgens that are present during prenatal development affect the development of the nervous system. In addition, both male and female sex hormones have activational effects on the adult nervous system that influence both physiological processes and behavior. This section considers some of these hormonal effects.

Hormonal Control of Female Reproductive Cycles

The reproductive cycle of female primates is called a **menstrual cycle** (from *mensis,* meaning "month"). Females of other species of mammals also have reproductive cycles, called **estrous cycles.** *Estrus* means "gadfly"; when a female rat is in estrus, her hormonal condition goads her to act differently than she does at other times. (For that matter, it goads male rats to act differently, too.) The primary feature that distinguishes menstrual cycles from estrous cycles is the monthly growth and loss of the lining of the uterus. The other features are approximately the

same—except that the estrous cycle of rats takes four days. Also, the sexual behavior of female mammals with estrous cycles is linked with ovulation, whereas most female primates can mate at any time during their menstrual cycle.

Menstrual cycles and estrous cycles consist of a sequence of events that are controlled by hormonal secretions of the pituitary gland and ovaries. These glands interact, the secretions of one affecting those of the other. A cycle begins with the secretion of gonadotropins by the anterior pituitary gland. These hormones (especially FSH) stimulate the growth of **ovarian follicles,** small spheres of epithelial cells surrounding each ovum. Women normally produce one ovarian follicle each month; if two are produced and fertilized, dizygotic (fraternal) twins will develop. As ovarian follicles mature, they secrete estradiol, which causes the growth of the lining of the uterus in

 See the interactive CD for more on the menstrual cycle.

preparation for implantation of the ovum, should it be fertilized by a sperm. Feedback from the increasing level of estradiol eventually triggers the release of a surge of LH by the anterior pituitary gland. (See *Figure 10.7* and *Animation 10.1 The Menstrual Cycle.*)

The LH surge causes *ovulation:* The ovarian follicle ruptures, releasing the ovum. Under the continued influence of LH, the ruptured ovarian follicle becomes a **corpus luteum** ("yellow body"), which produces estradiol and **progesterone.** (See *Figure 10.7.*) The latter hormone promotes pregnancy *(gestation).* It maintains the lining of the uterus, and it inhibits the ovaries from producing another follicle. Meanwhile, the ovum enters one of the Fallopian tubes and begins its progress toward the uterus. If it meets sperm cells during its travel down the Fallopian tube and becomes fertilized, it begins to divide, and several days later it attaches itself to the uterine wall.

If the ovum is not fertilized or if it is fertilized too late to develop sufficiently by the time it gets to the uterus, the

menstrual cycle (*men strew al*) The female reproductive cycle of most primates, including humans; characterized by growth of the lining of the uterus, ovulation, development of a corpus luteum, and (if pregnancy does not occur), menstruation.

estrous cycle The female reproductive cycle of mammals other than primates.

ovarian follicle A cluster of epithelial cells surrounding an oocyte, which develops into an ovum.

corpus luteum (*lew tee um*) A cluster of cells that develops from the ovarian follicle after ovulation; secretes estradiol and progesterone.

progesterone (*pro jess ter own*) A steroid hormone produced by the ovary that maintains the endometrial lining of the uterus during the later part of the menstrual cycle and during pregnancy; along with estradiol, it promotes receptivity in female mammals with estrous cycles.

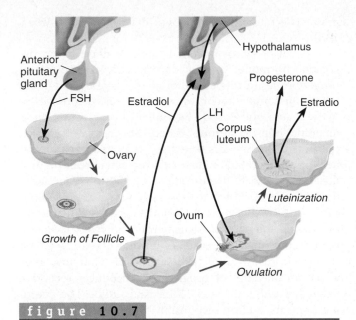

figure 10.7

Neuroendocrine control of the menstrual cycle.

corpus luteum will stop producing estradiol and progesterone, and then the lining of the walls of the uterus will slough off. At this point menstruation will commence.

Hormonal Control of Sexual Behavior of Laboratory Animals

The interactions between sex hormones and the human brain are difficult to study. We must turn to two sources of information: experiments with animals and various developmental disorders in humans, which serve as nature's own "experiments." Let us first consider the evidence gathered from research with laboratory animals.

Males

Male sexual behavior is quite varied, although the essential features of *intromission* (entry of the penis into the female's vagina), *pelvic thrusting* (rhythmic movement of the hindquarters, causing genital friction), and *ejaculation* (discharge of semen) are characteristic of all male mammals. Humans, of course, have invented all kinds of copulatory and noncopulatory sexual behavior. For example, the pelvic movements leading to ejaculation may be performed by the woman, and sex play can lead to orgasm without intromission.

The sexual behavior of rats has been studied more than that of any other laboratory animal. When a male rat encounters a receptive female, he will spend some time nuzzling her and sniffing and licking her genitals, mount her, and engage in pelvic thrusting. He will mount her several times, achieving intromission on most of the mountings. After eight to fifteen intromissions approximately 1

minute apart (each lasting only about one-quarter of a second), the male will ejaculate.

After ejaculating, the male refrains from sexual activity for a period of time (minutes, in the rat). Most mammals will return to copulate again and again, showing a longer pause, called a **refractory period,** after each ejaculation. (The term comes from the Latin *refringere,* "to break off.") An interesting phenomenon occurs in some mammals. If a male, after finally becoming "exhausted" by repeated copulation with the same female, is presented with a new female, he begins to respond quickly—often as fast as he did in his initial contact with the first female. Successive introductions of new females can keep up his performance for prolonged periods of time. This phenomenon is undoubtedly important in species in which a single male inseminates all the females in his harem. Species with approximately equal numbers of reproductively active males and females are less likely to act this way.

In one of the most unusual studies I have read about, Beamer, Bermant, and Clegg (1969) tested the ability of a ram (male sheep) to recognize ewes with which he had mated. A ram that is given a new ewe each time will quickly begin copulating and will ejaculate within 2 minutes. (In one study, a ram kept up this performance with twelve ewes. The experimenters finally got tired of shuffling sheep around; the ram was still ready to go.) Beamer and his colleagues tried to fool rams by putting trench coats and Halloween face masks on females with which the rams had mated. (No, I'm not making this up.) The males were not fooled by the disguise; they apparently recognized their former partners by their odor and were no longer interested in them.

The rejuvenating effect of a new female, also seen in roosters, is usually called the **Coolidge effect.** The following story is reputed to be true, but I cannot vouch for that fact. (If it is not true, it ought to be.) The former U.S. president Calvin Coolidge and his wife were touring a farm, when Mrs. Coolidge asked the farmer whether the continuous and vigorous sexual activity among the flock of hens was the work of just one rooster. The reply was yes. She smiled and said, "You might point that out to Mr. Coolidge." The president looked thoughtfully at the birds and then asked the farmer whether a different hen was involved each time. The answer, again, was yes. "You might point *that* out to Mrs. Coolidge," he said.

refractory period (*ree **frak** to ree*) A period of time after a particular action (for example, an ejaculation by a male) during which that action cannot occur again.

Coolidge effect The restorative effect of introducing a new female sex partner to a male that has apparently become "exhausted" by sexual activity.

Sexual behavior of male rodents depends on testosterone, a fact that has long been recognized (Bermant and Davidson, 1974). If a male rat is castrated (that is, if his testes are removed), his sexual activity eventually ceases. However, the behavior can be reinstated by injections of testosterone. I will describe the neural basis of this activational effect later in this chapter.

Other hormones play a role in male sexual behavior. **Oxytocin** is a hormone produced by the posterior pituitary gland that contracts the milk ducts and thus causes milk ejection in lactating females. It is also produced in males, where it obviously plays no role in lactation. Oxytocin is released at the time of orgasm in both males and females and appears to contribute to the contractions of the smooth muscle in the male ejaculatory system and of the vagina and uterus (Carmichael et al., 1994; Carter, 1992). The effects of this hormonal release can easily be seen in lactating women, who often eject some milk at the time of orgasm.

The refractory period that occurs after an ejaculation may be produced by another hormone, perhaps in conjunction with oxytocin. **Prolactin,** a hormone secreted by the anterior pituitary gland, stimulates milk production by the mammary glands. Like oxytocin, prolactin is released by male rats after ejaculation (Oaknin et al., 1989). In addition, prolactin has an inhibitory effect on male sexual behavior; in fact, one of the symptoms of *hyperprolactinemia* (oversecretion of prolactin) is loss of sexual desire (Foster et al., 1990). Doherty, Baum, and Todd (1986) transplanted a pituitary gland into males rats, which causes their blood level of prolactin to increase dramatically. The investigators found that the hormone severely depressed mounting behavior and intromissions. Mas et al. (1995) observed similar effects when they injected small amounts of prolactin directly into male rats' brains, into a region known to be involved in male sex behavior (the *MPA,* discussed later in this chapter).

Females

The mammalian female has been described as the passive participant in copulation. It is true that in some species the female's role during the act of copulation is merely to assume a posture that exposes her genitals to the male. This behavior is called the **lordosis** response (from the Greek *lordos,* meaning "bent backward"). The female will also move her tail away (if she has one) and stand rigidly enough to support the weight of the male. However, the behavior of a female rodent in *initiating* copulation is often very active. Certainly, if a male attempts to copulate with a nonestrous rodent, the female will either actively flee or rebuff him. But when the female is in a receptive state, she will often approach the male, nuzzle him, sniff his genitals, and show behaviors characteristic of her species. For example, a female rat will exhibit quick, short, hopping movements and rapid ear wiggling, which

most male rats find irresistible (McClintock and Adler, 1978).

Sexual behavior of female rodents depends on the gonadal hormones present during estrus: estradiol and progesterone. In rats estradiol increases about 40 hours before the female becomes receptive; just before receptivity occurs, the corpus luteum begins secreting large quantities of progesterone (Feder, 1981). Ovariectomized rats (rats whose ovaries have been removed) are not sexually receptive. Although sexual receptivity can be produced in ovariectomized rodents by administering large doses of estradiol alone, the most effective treatment duplicates the normal sequence of hormones: a small amount of estradiol, followed by progesterone. Progesterone alone is ineffective; thus, the estradiol "primes" its effectiveness. Priming with estradiol takes about 16–24 hours, after which an injection of progesterone produces receptive behaviors within an hour (Takahashi, 1990). The neural mechanisms that are responsible for these effects will be described later in this chapter.

Studies with targeted mutations confirm the importance of estradiol and progesterone on sexual behavior in female rodents. Rissman et al. (1997) found that female mice without estrogen receptors were unreceptive to males even after treatment with estradiol and progesterone, and Lydon et al. (1995) observed similar effects in female mice without progesterone receptors.

The sequence of estradiol followed by progesterone has three effects on female rats: It increases their receptivity, their proceptivity, and their attractiveness. *Receptivity* refers to their ability and willingness to copulate—to accept the advances of a male by holding still and displaying lordosis when he attempts to mount her. *Proceptivity* refers to a female's eagerness to copulate, as shown by the fact that she seeks out a male and engages in behaviors that tend to arouse his sexual interest. *Attractiveness* refers to physiological and behavioral changes that affect the male. The male rat (along with many other male mammals) is most responsive to females who are in estrus ("in heat"). Males will ignore a female whose ovaries have been removed, but injections of estradiol and progesterone will restore her attractiveness (and also change her behavior toward the male). The stimuli that arouse a male rat's sexual interest

---

oxytocin (*ox ee tow sin*) A hormone secreted by the posterior pituitary gland; causes contraction of the smooth muscle of the milk ducts, the uterus, and the male ejaculatory system; also serves as a neurotransmitter in the brain.

prolactin A hormone of the anterior pituitary gland, necessary for production of milk; has an inhibitory effect on male sexual behavior.

lordosis A spinal sexual reflex seen in many four-legged female mammals; arching of the back in response to approach of a male or to touching the flanks, which elevates the hindquarters.

include her odor and her behavior. In some species visible changes, such as the swollen sex skin in the genital region of a female monkey, also affect sex appeal.

Organizational Effects of Androgens on Behavior: Masculinization and Defeminization

The dictum "Nature's impulse is to create a female" applies to sexual behavior as well as to sex organs. That is, if a rodent's brain is *not* exposed to androgens during a critical period of development, the animal will engage in female sexual behavior as an adult (if then given estradiol and progesterone). Fortunately for experimenters this critical time comes shortly after birth for rats and for several other species of rodents that are born in a rather immature condition. Thus, if a male rat is castrated immediately after birth, permitted to grow to adulthood, and then given injections of estradiol and progesterone, it will respond to the presence of another male by arching its back and presenting its hindquarters. In other words, it will act as if it were a female (Blaustein and Olster, 1989).

In contrast, if a rodent brain is exposed to androgens during development, two phenomena occur: behavioral defeminization and behavioral masculinization. *Behavioral defeminization* refers to the organizational effect of androgens that prevents the animal from displaying female sexual behavior in adulthood. As we shall see later, this effect is accomplished by suppressing the development of neural circuits controlling female sexual behavior. For example, if a female rodent is ovariectomized and given an injection of testosterone immediately after birth, she will *not* respond to a male rat when, as an adult, she is given injections of estradiol and progesterone. *Behavioral masculinization* refers to the organizational effect of androgens that enables animals to engage in male sexual behavior in adulthood. This effect is accomplished by stimulating the development of neural circuits controlling male sexual behavior. For example, if the female rodent in my previous example is given testosterone in adulthood rather than estradiol and progesterone, she will mount and attempt to copulate with a receptive female. (See Breedlove, 1992, and Carter, 1992, for references to specific studies.) (See *Figure 10.8*.)

Research by Moore and her colleagues (reviewed by Moore, 1986) indicates that some of the masculinizing and defeminizing effects of androgens are even more indirect. As we will see in a later section in this chapter, female rats spend a considerable amount of time licking the genital region of their offspring. This behavior is very useful, because it stimulates urination and permits the mother to ingest the water and minerals that are released so they can be recycled in her milk.

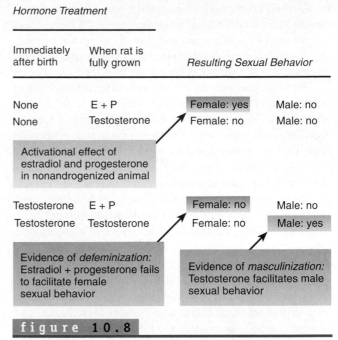

figure 10.8

Organizational effects of testosterone. Around the time of birth, testosterone masculinizes and defeminizes rodents' sexual behavior.

Moore and her colleagues discovered that mothers spent much more time licking their male offspring and wondered whether this licking could have any effects on the sexual behavior of these offspring later in life. Indeed, it did. First, the experimenters found that androgens caused the secretion of an odorous chemical in the male pups' urine, which was attractive to the mothers. Next, they found that if they destroyed the mothers' ability to smell the odor, the mothers failed to give the males special attention—and that these males showed decreases in their sexual behavior in adulthood. But if the experimenters stroked the genitals of the male pups with a small brush each day, the animals showed a greater level sexual behavior when they grew up. Thus, at least some of the organizational effects of androgens are accomplished through an intermediary—the infant's mother.

Effects of Pheromones

Hormones transmit messages from one part of the body (the secreting gland) to another (the target tissue). Another class of chemicals, called **pheromones,** carries messages from one animal to another. Some of these chemicals, like hormones, affect reproductive behavior.

pheromone (*fair oh moan*) A chemical released by one animal that affects the behavior or physiology of another animal; usually smelled or tasted.

Karlson and Luscher (1959) coined the term, from the Greek *pherein*, "to carry," and *horman*, "to excite." Pheromones are released by one animal and directly affect the physiology or behavior of another. In mammalian species most pheromones are detected by means of olfaction.

Pheromones can affect reproductive physiology or behavior. First, let us consider the effects on reproductive physiology. When groups of female mice are housed together, their estrous cycles slow down and eventually stop. This phenomenon is known as the **Lee-Boot effect** (van der Lee and Boot, 1955). If groups of females are exposed to the odor of a male (or of his urine), they begin cycling again, and their cycles tend to be synchronized. This phenomenon is known as the **Whitten effect** (Whitten, 1959). The **Vandenbergh effect** (Vandenbergh, Whitsett, and Lombardi, 1975) is the acceleration of the onset of puberty in a female rodent caused by the odor of a male. Both the Whitten effect and the Vandenbergh effect are caused by a group of compounds that are resent only in the urine of intact adult males (Ma, Miao, and Novotny, 1999; Novotny et al., 1999); the urine of a juvenile or castrated male has no effect. Thus, the production of the pheromone requires the presence of testosterone.

The **Bruce effect** (Bruce, 1960a, 1960b) is a particularly interesting phenomenon: When a recently impregnated female mouse encounters a normal male mouse other than the one with which she mated, the pregnancy is very likely to fail. This effect, too, is caused by a substance secreted in the urine of intact males—but not of males that have been castrated. Thus, a male mouse that encounters a pregnant female is able to prevent the birth of infants carrying another male's genes and subsequently impregnate the female himself. This phenomenon is advantageous even from the female's point of view. The fact that the new male has managed to take over the old male's territory indicates that he is probably healthier and more vigorous, and therefore his genes will contribute to the formation of offspring that are more likely to survive.

As you learned in Chapter 7, detection of odors is accomplished by the olfactory bulbs, which constitute the primary olfactory system. However, the four effects that pheromones have on reproductive cycles appear to be mediated by another organ—the **vomeronasal organ (VNO)**—which consists of a small group of sensory receptors arranged around a pouch connected by a duct to the nasal passage. The vomeronasal organ, which is present in all orders of mammals except for cetaceans (whales and dolphins), projects to the **accessory olfactory bulb,** located immediately behind the olfactory bulb (Wysocki, 1979). (See *Figure 10.9.*) The VNO contains two large multigene families of G-protein-linked receptor molecules (V1R and V2R), which are responsible for detection of chemicals that serve as pheromones (Dulac and Axel, 1995; Ryba and Tirindelli, 1997). These receptor molecules are only distantly related to the ones present in the olfactory epithelium.

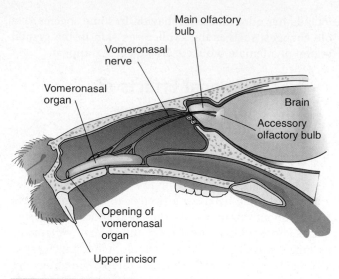

figure 10.9

The rodent accessory olfactory system.
(Adapted from Wysocki, C. J. *Neuroscience & Biobehavioral Reviews,* 1979, *3,* 301–341.)

The vomeronasal organ probably does not detect airborne molecules, as the olfactory bulbs do, but instead is sensitive to nonvolatile compounds found in urine or other substances. In fact, stimulation of a nerve that serves the nasal region of the hamster causes fluid to be pumped into the vomeronasal organ, which exposes the receptors to any substances that may be present (Meredith and O'Connell, 1979). This pump is activated whenever the animal encounters a novel stimulus (Meredith, 1994).

Removal of the accessory olfactory bulb disrupts the Lee-Boot effect, the Whitten effect, the Vandenbergh effect, and the Bruce effect; thus, the vomeronasal system

Lee-Boot effect The slowing and eventual cessation of estrous cycles in groups of female animals that are housed together; caused by a pheromone in the animals' urine; first observed in mice.

Whitten effect The synchronization of the menstrual or estrous cycles of a group of females, which occurs only in the presence of a pheromone in a male's urine.

Vandenbergh effect The earlier onset of puberty seen in female animals that are housed with males; caused by a pheromone in the male's urine; first observed in mice.

Bruce effect Termination of pregnancy caused by the odor of a pheromone in the urine of a male other than the one that impregnated the female; first identified in mice.

vomeronasal organ (VNO) (*voah mer oh nay zul*) A sensory organ that detects the presence of certain chemicals, especially when a liquid is actively sniffed; mediates the effects of some pheromones.

accessory olfactory bulb A neural structure located in the main olfactory bulb that receives information from the vomeronasal organ.

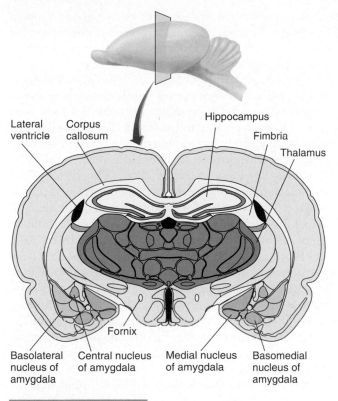

Lateral ventricle Corpus callosum Hippocampus Fimbria Thalamus

Fornix

Basolateral nucleus of amygdala   Central nucleus of amygdala   Medial nucleus of amygdala   Basomedial nucleus of amygdala

figure 10.10

A cross section through the rat brain showing the location of the amygdala.

(Adapted from Swanson, L. W. *Brain Maps: Structure of the Rat Brain.* New York: Elsevier, 1992.)

is essential for these phenomena (Halpern, 1987). The accessory olfactory bulb sends axons to the **medial nucleus of the amygdala,** which in turn projects to the preoptic area and anterior hypothalamus and to the ventromedial nucleus of the hypothalamus. (As you learned in Chapter 7, so does the main olfactory bulb.) Thus, the neural circuit responsible for the effects of these pheromones appears to involve these regions. As we shall see, the preoptic area, the medial amygdala, and the ventromedial nucleus of the hypothalamus all play important roles in reproductive behavior. (See *Figure 10.10.*)

The Bruce effect involves learning; the female obviously learns to recognize the odor of the male with which she mates, because his odor will not cause her to abort if she encounters it later. This learning appears to require the activity of a set of noradrenergic axons that enter the olfactory bulbs and form synapses with neurons in both the main and accessory olfactory bulbs. Keverne and de la Riva (1982) found that after these axons had been destroyed with infusions of 6-hydroxydopamine (6-HD), a female mouse would not learn to recognize the odor of the male that mated with her; even *his* odor would cause her to abort.

It is possible that the stimuli associated with copulation trigger the noradrenergic mechanism and "imprint" the odor of the male on the female, ensuring that she will not abort if she later encounters his odor. Indeed, Rosser and Keverne (1985) found that vaginal stimulation increases the activity in the noradrenergic axons that serve the olfactory bulbs. As other studies have shown (Gray, Freeman, and Skinner, 1986; Leon, 1987), the release of norepinephrine in the olfactory bulbs is necessary for olfactory learning.

Halem, Cherry, and Baum (2001) found that mating changed the response of neurons in the medial amygdala to the odor of the male with which the female had mated. They mated one group of female mice with a male and simply exposed the females in another group to bedding that contained urine from a male mouse. Forty-two hours later, they exposed both groups of mice to two kinds of bedding: bedding that contained "familiar" urine (from the male with which the female had mated or simply smelled) and "unfamiliar" urine, from a male of a different genetic strain. Neurons in the medial amygdala of the females that had not been mated responded the same way to both "familiar" and "unfamiliar" urine, but neurons in the medial amygdala of the females that had been mated showed increased activation only to the "unfamiliar" urine. In other words, the act of mating instructed the vomeronasal system to ignore the pheromone associated with the odor of the stud mouse.

Besides having effects on reproductive physiology, some pheromones directly affect behavior. For example, pheromones present in the vaginal secretions of female hamsters stimulate sexual behavior in males. Males are attracted to the secretions of females, and they sniff and lick the female's genitals before copulating. In fact, there may be two categories of pheromones: one detected by the vomeronasal organ and another detected by the olfactory epithelium; mating behavior of male hamsters is disrupted only if *both* systems are interrupted (Powers and Winans, 1975; Winans and Powers, 1977). As we saw, both the primary and accessory olfactory systems send fibers to the medial nucleus of the amygdala. Lehman and Winans (1982) found that lesions of the medial amygdala abolished the sexual behavior of male hamsters. Thus, the amygdala is part of the system that mediates the effects of pheromones on the sexual behavior of male hamsters.

Singer and his colleagues (Singer et al., 1986; Singer, 1991; Jang, Singer, and O'Connell, 2001) succeeded in

medial nucleus of the amygdala (*a mig da la*) A nucleus that receives olfactory information from the olfactory bulb and accessory olfactory bulb; involved in the effects of odors and pheromones on reproductive behavior.

isolating and analyzing the molecular structure of a sex-attractant pheromone in the vaginal discharge of female hamsters, a protein that they named *aphrodisin*. They tested the effectiveness of this pheromone by swabbing it on the hindquarters of an anesthetized male hamster; test males who sniffed the substance subsequently attempted to mount the animal. In addition, aphrodisin, but not chemically related compounds that do not serve as sex attractants, activated neurons in the accessory olfactory bulb. Magert et al. (1999) found that the gene responsible for the production of aphrodisin is active in cells in the uterus and vagina of the hamster, and Pes et al. (1998) found evidence for an odorant-binding protein similar to aphrodisin in the mouse olfactory epithelium.

Some evidence suggests that males may also produce sex-attractant pheromones that affect the behavior of females. If given a choice, receptive female rats prefer to be close to normal males rather than to males that have been castrated; this preference disappears after the vomeronasal organ is destroyed (Romero et al., 1990). Halem, Baum, and Cherry (2001) found that neurons in the VNO responded differently in male and female mice: Neurons in the basal VNO of female mice were activated by smell of male urine but not female urine, and the reverse was seen in males. (See *Figure 10.11*.)

It appears that at least some pheromone-related phenomena occur in humans. McClintock (1971) studied the menstrual cycles of women attending an all-female college. She found that women who spent a large amount of time together tended to have synchronized cycles—Their men-

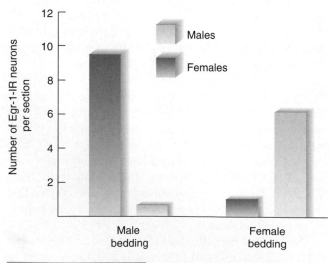

figure 10.11

Activation of neurons in the basal vomeronasal organs of male and female mice exposed to bedding containing urine from male or female mice. Egr-1 is a protein similar to the Fos protein; thus, its presence indicates neural activation.

(Adapted from Halem, H. A., Baum, M. J., and Cherry, J. A. *Journal of Neuroscience*, 2001, *21*, 2474–2480.)

strual periods began within a day or two of one another. In addition, women who regularly spent some time in the presence of men tended to have shorter cycles than those who rarely spent time with (smelled?) men.

Russell, Switz, and Thompson (1980) obtained direct evidence that olfactory stimuli can synchronize women's menstrual cycles. The investigators collected daily samples of a woman's underarm sweat. They dissolved the samples in alcohol and swabbed them on the upper lips of a group of women three times each week, in the order in which they were originally taken. The cycles of the women who received the extract (but not those of control subjects whose lips were swabbed with pure alcohol) began to synchronize with the cycle of the odor donor. These results were confirmed by a similar study by Stern and McClintock (1998), who found that compounds from the armpits of women taken around the time of ovulation lengthened other women's menstrual cycles, and compounds taken late in the cycle shortened them. Shinohara et al. (2001) found that these effects were caused by pheromone-induced changes in the rate of LH secretion.

Several studies have found that two compounds present in human sweat have different effects in men and women. Jacob and McClintock (2000) found that the androgenic chemical *androstadienone* increases alertness and positive mood in women but decreased positive mood in men. A functional imaging study by Savic et al. (2001) found that the androstadienone activated the preoptic area and ventromedial hypothalamus in women, whereas the estrogenic chemical *estratetraene* activated the paraventricular nucleus and dorsomedial hypothalamus in men.

Two recent studies suggest that men and women may possess pheromones that serve to attract potential sex partners. A double-blind study by Cutler, Friedmann, and McCoy (1998) found that men who used an aftershave cologne spiked with a chemical called 10X, sold commercially as a male pheromone, showed an increase in frequency of sexual intercourse and sleeping next to a romantic partner. Approximately 41 percent of men using the pheromone showed an increase in three or more sociosexual behaviors, compared with approximately 9.5 percent of those using a placebo. Another double-blind study, by McCoy and Pitino (2002), followed a similar procedure and found similar results with women who used perfume mixed with 10:13, a chemical that is sold commercially as a female pheromone. This study found that approximately 74 percent of the women showed an increase in three or more sociosexual behaviors, compared with approximately 23 percent of those using a placebo. The authors of these studies concluded that the chemicals made their wearers more attractive to members of the other sex.

A more careful examination of the data suggest that the magnitude of the phenomenon is not as great as it might seem. For example, the study by McCoy and Pitino found that women in the pheromone group were having intercourse once every 11.1 days (on average) before the chemical was mixed with their perfume. After the perfume had been spiked, they had intercourse every 7.3 days. In contrast, women in the placebo group were having intercourse every 5.5 days (more than twice as often as women in the pheromone group), and this number went down to once every 9.1 days after their perfume had been spiked with the placebo. In other words, the decrease in frequency of intercourse of the women in the placebo group was greater than the increase in the women in the pheromone group. Clearly, these results are worthy of further study.

Whether or not pheromones play a role in sexual attraction in humans, the familiar odor of a sex partner probably has a positive effect on sexual arousal—just like the sight of a sex partner or the sound of his or her voice. We are not generally conscious of the fact, but we can identify other people on the basis of olfactory cues. For example, a study by Russell (1976) found that people were able to distinguish by odor between T-shirts that they had worn and those previously worn by other people. They could also tell whether the unknown owner of a T-shirt was male or female. Thus, it is likely that men and women can *learn* to be attracted by their partners' characteristic odors, just as they can learn to be attracted by the sound of their voice. In an instance like this, the odors are serving simply as sensory cues, not as pheromones.

In the past most investigators believed that the human nose did not contain a vomeronasal organ, and therefore they assumed that all effects of pheromones on humans involved the main olfactory system. However, recent studies suggest that we do have such an organ and that this organ contains chemosensitive neurons. Two plastic surgeons, Garcia-Velasco and Mondragon (1991), examining the olfactory mucosae of 1000 patients during surgical reconstructions of their noses, found vomeronasal organs in virtually every case. This organ is 2–10 mm long, 1 mm in diameter, and located along the nasal septum (bridge of tissue between the nostrils) approximately 2 cm from the opening of the nostril. The VNO can even be seen in MRI scans of the nose (Abolmaali et al., 2001). (See *Figure 10.12*.)

Clearly, there is no doubt that a vomeronasal organ exists in humans. However, not all investigators agree that the VNO detects pheromones. The density of neurons in the VNO is very sparse, and investigators have not yet succeeded in tracing neural connections from this organ to the brain (Doty, 2001), which has led some researchers to conclude that the human VNO is a vestigial organ like the human appendix. Evidence clearly shows that human reproductive physiology is affected by pheromones, but it is possible that these chemical signals are detected by the "standard" olfactory system—the receptor cells in the olfactory epithelium—and not by cells in the VNO.

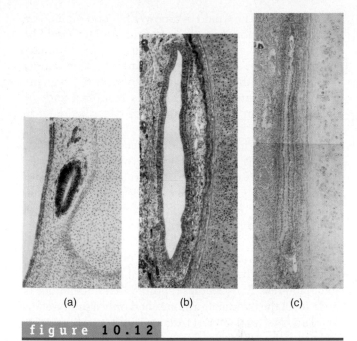

(a)   (b)   (c)

figure 10.12

Photomicrographs of cross sections through the human vomeronasal organ. (a) 10-week fetus. (b) newborn infant. (c) 45-year-old adult.

(From Monti-Bloch, L., Jennings-White, C., and Berliner, D. L. *Annals of the New York Academy of Sciences,* 1998, *855,* 373–389.)

Human Sexual Behavior

Human sexual behavior, like that of other mammals, is influenced by activational effects of gonadal hormones and, almost certainly, organizational effects as well. But as we will see in the following subsections, the effects of these hormones are different in our species—especially in women.

If hormones have organizational effects on human sexual behavior, they must exert these effects by altering the development of the brain. Although there is good evidence that prenatal exposure to androgens affects development of the human brain, we cannot yet be certain that this exposure has long-lasting behavioral effects. The evidence pertaining to these issues is discussed later, in a section on sexual orientation.

Activational Effects of Sex Hormones in Women

As we saw, the sexual behavior of most female mammals other than higher primates is controlled by the ovarian hormones estradiol and progesterone. (In some species, such as cats and rabbits, only estradiol is necessary.) As Wallen (1990) pointed out, the ovarian hormones control not only the *willingness* (or even eagerness) of an estrous female to mate but also her *ability* to mate. That is, a male rat cannot copulate with a female rat that is not in estrus. Even if he would overpower her and mount her, her lordosis response would not occur, and he would be unable to achieve intromission. Thus, the evolutionary process seems to have selected animals that mate only at a time when the female is able to become pregnant. (The neural control of the lordosis response and the effects of ovarian hormones on it are described later in this chapter.)

In higher primates (including our own species), the ability to mate is not controlled by ovarian hormones. There are no physical barriers to sexual intercourse during any part of the menstrual cycle. If a woman or other female primate consents to sexual activity at any time (or is forced to submit by a male), intercourse can certainly take place.

Although ovarian hormones do not *control* women's sexual activity, they may still have an influence on their sexual interest. Early studies reported that fluctuations in the level of the ovarian hormones had only a minor effect on women's sexual interest (Adams, Gold, and Burt, 1978; Morris et al., 1987). However, as Wallen (1990) pointed out, these studies have almost all involved married women who live with their husbands. In stable, monogamous relationships in which the partners are together on a daily basis, sexual activity can be instigated by either of them. Normally, a husband does not force his wife to have intercourse with him, but even if she is not interested in engaging in sexual activity at that moment, she may find that she wants to do so because of her affection for him. Thus, changes in sexual interest and arousability might not always be reflected in changes in sexual behavior. In fact, a study of lesbian couples (whose menstrual cycles are likely to be synchronized) found a significant increase in sexual interest and activity during the middle portions of the women's cycles (Matteo and Rissman, 1984), which suggests that ovarian hormones *do* influence women's sexual interest.

Several studies have found that the sexual behavior of female monkeys, like that of women, is only poorly related to their menstrual cycles. However, most of these studies were carried out with small numbers of monkeys living in small cages. Thus, intercourse was as likely to be instigated by a male as by the female. Wallen et al. (1986) observed female monkeys that were housed in large groups in large cages, in a situation in which a female could seek out a sex partner if she wanted one but could avoid sexual contact if she preferred. Figure 10.13 contrasts the results of these two types of studies; note that the sexual activity of females housed in large-group situations closely corresponded with their cycles of ovarian hormones. (See *Figure 10.13*.)

These results pose an interesting question. If all of a woman's sexual encounters were initiated by her, without regard to her partner's desires, would we find as strong an effect of ovarian hormones as Wallen and his col-

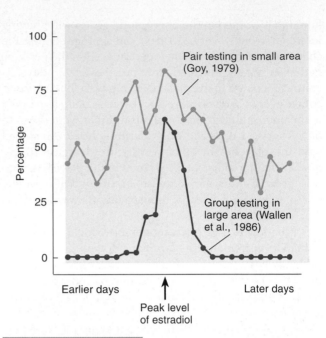

figure 10.13

Percentage of tests in which ejaculations occurred in the course of a female monkey's menstrual cycle.

(Adapted from Wallen, K. *Neuroscience and Biobehavioral Reviews,* 1990, *14,* 233–241; after Goy, 1979 and Wallen et al., 1984.)

leagues found in monkeys? As Alexander et al. (1990) showed, women taking oral contraceptives (which prevent the normal cycles in secretion of ovarian hormones) were less likely to show fluctuations in sexual interest during the menstrual cycle. Van Goozen et al. (1997) found that the sexual activity initiated by men and women showed very different relations to the woman's menstrual cycle (and hence, to her level of ovarian hormones). Men initiated sexual activity at about the same rate throughout the woman's cycle, whereas sexual activity initiated by women showed a distinct peak around the time of ovulation, when estradiol levels are highest. (See *Figure 10.14*.)

Wallen (2001) points out that although ovarian hormones may affect a woman's sexual interest, her behavior can be influenced by other factors as well. For example, if a woman does not want to become pregnant and does not have absolute confidence in her method of birth control, she may avoid sexual intercourse at midcycle, around the time of ovulation—even if her potential sexual interest is at a peak. In fact, Harvey (1987) found that women were more likely to engage in autosexual activity at this time. On the other hand, women who *want* to become pregnant are more likely to initiate sexual intercourse during the time when they are most likely to conceive.

Several studies suggest that women's sexual interest can be stimulated by androgens. There are two primary

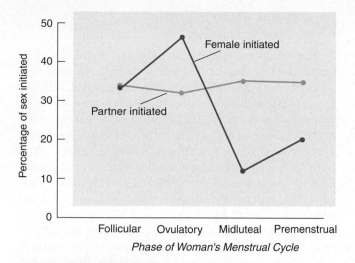

figure 10.14

The distribution of sexual activity of heterosexual couples initiated by the man and by the woman.
(Adapted from Wallen, K. *Hormones and Behavior*, 2001, *40*, 339–357. After data from Van Goozen et al., 1997.)

sources of androgens in the female body: the ovaries and the adrenal glands. The primary ovarian sex steroids are, of course, estradiol and progesterone, but these glands also produce testosterone. The adrenal glands produce another androgen, androstenedione, along with other adrenocortical steroids.

The evidence concerning the role of androgens in women's sexual interest is mixed (Wallen, 2001). Most studies investigating this issue have used two methodologies: establishing correlations between a woman's androgen levels and her sexual interests and behavior and evaluating the effects of hormone administration in women who have passed menopause or whose ovaries have been removed. At the present time, the most likely conclusion seems to be that although androgens by themselves (in the absence of estradiol) do not stimulate women's sexual interest, they appear to amplify the effects of estradiol. For example, Shifren et al. (2000) studied ovariectomized women aged 31–56 years who were receiving estrogen-replacement therapy. The women were given, in addition to the estrogen, either a placebo or one of two different doses of testosterone, delivered through transdermal patches. Although the placebo produced a positive effect, the testosterone further increased sexual activity and rate of orgasm. At the higher dose, the percentage of women who had sex fantasies, masturbated, and had intercourse increased two to three times over baseline levels and reported higher levels of well-being.

Another hormone, oxytocin, may also play a role in a woman's sexual response. As we saw earlier in this chapter, oxytocin appears to stimulate contractions of the uterus and vagina that accompany orgasm. Some investigators have suggested that the presence of oxytocin before sexual activity might enhance a woman's sexual interest (Anderson-Hunt and Dennerstein, 1995).

Activational Effects of Sex Hormones in Men

Although women and mammals with estrous cycles differ in their behavioral responsiveness to sex hormones, men resemble other mammals in their behavioral responsiveness to testosterone. With normal levels they can be potent and fertile; without testosterone sperm production ceases, and sooner or later, so does sexual potency. In a double-blind study, Bagatell et al. (1994) gave a placebo or a gonadotropin-releasing hormone (GnRH) antagonist to young male volunteers to suppress secretion of testicular androgens. Within two weeks, the subjects who received the GnRH antagonist reported a decrease in sexual interest, sexual fantasy, and intercourse. Men who received replacement doses of testosterone along with the antagonist did not show these changes.

The decline of sexual activity after castration is quite variable. As reported by Money and Ehrhardt (1972), some men lose potency immediately, whereas others show a slow, gradual decline over several years. Perhaps at least some of the variability is a function of prior experience; practice not only may "make perfect," but may also forestall a decline in function. Although there is no direct evidence with respect to this possibility in humans, Wallen and his colleagues (Wallen et al., 1991; Wallen, 2001) injected a GnRH antagonist in seven adult male rhesus monkeys that were part of a larger group. The injection suppressed testosterone secretion, and sexual behavior declined after one week. However, the decline was related to the animal's social rank and sexual experience: More sexually experienced, high-ranking males continued to copulate. In fact, the highest-ranking male continued to copulate and ejaculate at the same rate as before, even though his testosterone secretion was suppressed for almost eight weeks. The mounting behavior of the lowest ranking monkey completely ceased and did not resume until testosterone secretion recovered from the anti-GnRH treatment.

Testosterone not only affects sexual activity but also is affected by it—or even by thinking about it. A scientist stationed on a remote island (Anonymous, 1970) removed his beard with an electric shaver each day and weighed the clippings. Just before he left for visits to the mainland (and to the company of a female companion), his beard began growing faster. Because rate of beard growth is related to androgen levels, the effect indicates that his anticipation of sexual activity stimulated testosterone production. Confirming these results, Hellhammer, Hubert, and Schurmeyer (1985) found that watching an erotic film increased men's testosterone level.

As we saw earlier in this chapter, oxytocin and pro-lactin may play a role in male sexual behavior. Both hormones are secreted during orgasm, and both may be at least partly responsible for the refractory period.

Sexual Orientation

What controls a person's sexual orientation: the gender of the preferred sex partner? Some people (especially males) who are essentially heterosexual engage in homosexual episodes at some time during their lives. Although many animals occasionally engage in sexual activity with a member of the same sex, *exclusive* homosexuality appears to occur only in humans (Ehrhardt and Meyer-Bahlburg, 1981). Animals of other species, if they are not exclusively heterosexual, are likely to be bisexual, engaging in sexual activity with members of both sexes. In contrast, the number of men and women who describe themselves as exclusively homosexual exceeds the number who describe themselves as bisexual.

Some investigators believe that homosexuality is a result of childhood experiences, especially interactions between the child and parents. A large-scale study of several hundred male and female homosexuals reported by Bell, Weinberg, and Hammersmith (1981) attempted to assess the effects of these factors. The researchers found no evidence that homosexuals had been raised by domineering mothers or submissive fathers, as some clinicians had suggested. The best predictor of adult homosexuality was a self-report of homosexual feelings, which usually preceded homosexual activity by three years. The investigators concluded that their data did not support social explanations for homosexuality but were consistent with the possibility that homosexuality is at least partly biologically determined.

If homosexuality does have a physiological cause, it certainly is not variations in the levels of sex hormones during adulthood. Many studies have examined the levels of sex steroids in male homosexuals (Meyer-Bahlburg, 1984), and the vast majority of them found these levels to be similar to those of heterosexuals. A few studies suggest that about 30 percent of female homosexuals have elevated levels of testosterone (but still lower than those found in men). Whether these differences are related to a biological cause of lesbianism or whether differences in lifestyles may increase the secretion of testosterone is not yet known.

A more likely biological cause of homosexuality is a subtle difference in brain structure caused by differences in the amount of prenatal exposure to androgens. Perhaps, then, the brains of male homosexuals are neither masculinized nor defeminized, those of female homosexuals are masculinized and defeminized, and those of bisexuals are masculinized but not defeminized. Of course, these are *speculations* that so far cannot be supported by human data; they are not *conclusions*. They should be regarded as suggestions to guide future research.

Prenatal Androgenization of Genetic Females

Evidence suggests that prenatal androgens can affect human social behavior and sexual orientation, as well as anatomy. In a disorder known as **congenital adrenal hyperplasia (CAH),** the adrenal glands secrete abnormal amounts of androgens. (*Hyperplasia* means "excessive formation.") The secretion of androgens begins prenatally; thus, the syndrome causes prenatal masculinization. Boys born with CAH develop normally; the extra androgen does not seem to have significant effects. However, a girl with CAH will be born with an enlarged clitoris, and her labia may be partly fused together. (As Figure 10.4 shows, the scrotum and labia develop from the same tissue in the fetus.) If the masculinization of the genitals is pronounced, surgery will be performed to correct them. In any event, once the syndrome is identified, the person will be given a synthetic hormone that suppresses the abnormal secretion of androgens.

Money, Schwartz, and Lewis (1984) studied thirty young women with a history of CAH. They had all been born with enlarged clitorises and partly fused labia, which led to the diagnosis. (A few mild cases were not diagnosed for several years.) Once the diagnosis was made, they were treated with drugs that suppress the secretion of adrenal androgens, and, if necessary, genital surgery was performed. Money and his colleagues asked the young women to describe their sexual orientation. Thirty-seven percent of the women described themselves as bisexual or homosexual, 40 percent said they were exclusively heterosexual, and 23 percent refused to talk about their sex lives. If the noncommittal women are excluded from the sample, the percentage of homosexuality or bisexuality rises to 48 percent.

The Kinsey report on sexuality in women (Kinsey et al., 1943) reported that approximately 10 percent of American women had had some sexual contact with another woman by the age of 20; in the sample of women who had been exposed prenatally to androgens the percentage was at least four times as high. The results therefore suggest that the exposure of a female fetus to an abnormally high level of androgens does affect sexual orientation.

A study by Iijima et al. (2001) found that prenatal androgenization may be responsible for other sexually dimorphic behaviors besides sexual orientation. The investigators asked young children, including girls with CAH, to draw pictures. Typically, boys are more likely to make drawings that use dark or cold colors and to feature moving objects such as cars, trucks, trains, and airplanes, whereas girls are more likely to use light and warm colors and to include people,

---

congenital adrenal hyperplasia (CAH) (*hy per play zha*) A condition characterized by hypersecretion of androgens by the adrenal cortex; in females, causes masculinization of the external genitalia.

flowers, and butterflies. The investigators found that masculine motifs were much more likely to appear in the drawings of girls with CAH. (See *Figure 10.15.*)

(a)

(b)

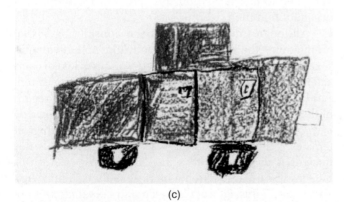

(c)

Prenatal androgens and children's drawings. (a) Drawing by a 5-year-old girl. (b) Drawing by a 5-year-old boy. (c) Drawing by a 5-year-old girl with congenital adrenal hyperplasia.

(From Iijima, M., Arisaka, O., Minamoto, F., and Arai, Y. *Hormones and Behavior*, 2001, *20*, 99–104.)

A plausible explanation for the high prevalence of masculine sexual orientation of women with CAH is that the androgens affect development of the brain. However, we must remember that the androgens also affect the genitals; possibly, the changes in the genitals played a role in shaping the development of the girls' sexual orientation. If the differences seen in sexual orientation *is* caused by effects of prenatal androgens on brain development, then we could reasonably conclude that prenatal androgens are responsible for establishing the sexual orientation of males, too. That is, these results support the hypothesis that male sexual orientation is at least partly determined by masculinizing (and defeminizing) effects of androgens on the human brain.

Because of the masculinizing effects of CAH, some clinicians have suggested that parents of strongly androgenized girls with this disorder raise them as boys and not subject them to surgical procedures that feminize their genitalia. The rationale for this strategy is that the social behavior and sexual orientation of strongly androgenized girls is likely to be masculine anyway, and the enlarged clitoris could serve for sexual intercourse with women. The disadvantages include the fact that the girls' ovaries would have to be removed, which would eliminate the possibility of natural parenthood. (Most women with CAH are able to conceive and bear children.) A review by Meyer-Bahlburg (2001) provides a thoughtful and sensitive discussion of these issues.

Because controlled experiments cannot be performed on humans, some investigators have turned to our close relatives to see whether exposure to prenatal androgens has enduring behavioral effects. Goy, Bercovitch, and McBrair (1988) administered injections of testosterone to pregnant monkeys. The testosterone entered the blood supply of the fetuses and masculinized them. Female infants that had been exposed to androgens during early fetal development were born with masculinized genitals; the genitals of those that had been exposed to androgens later were normal. *Both* groups showed differences in their sociosexual interactions with peers, displaying a higher proportion of malelike behavior than normal females did. For example, even as young adults, the experimental group with normal genitals continued to mount their peers significantly more than normal females did. The results suggest that genital changes cannot account for all the behavioral effects of prenatal exposure to androgens in primates. Whether *human* primates share these characteristics is, of course, another question.

Failure of Androgenization of Genetic Males

As we saw, genetic males with androgen insensitivity syndrome develop as females, with female external genitalia—but also with testes and without uterus or Fallopian tubes. If an individual with this syndrome is raised as a girl, all is well. Normally, the testes are removed because they often become cancerous; but if they are not, the body will mature into that of a woman at the time of puberty through the effects of the small amounts of estradiol produced by the testes. (If the testes are removed, the person will be given estradiol to accomplish the same result.) At adulthood the individual will function sexually as a woman, although surgical lengthening of the vagina may be necessary. Women with this syndrome report average sex drives, including normal frequency of orgasm in intercourse. Most marry and lead normal sex lives.

Studies of the social behavior of people with androgen insensitivity syndrome indicate that they tend to be very "feminine" (Money and Ehrhardt, 1972). There is no indication of sexual orientation toward women. Thus, the lack of androgen receptors appears to prevent both the masculinizing and defeminizing effects of androgens on a person's sexual interest. If the lack of androgen receptors results in a person with a sexual orientation toward men, then perhaps events that interfere with prenatal androgenization in male fetuses could increase the likelihood of homosexuality. Of course, it is also possible that rearing an XY child with androgen insensitivity syndrome as a girl plays an important role in that person's sexual orientation.

The case presented in the opener to this chapter (Bruce/Brenda/David) suggests that people's sexual identity and sexual orientation are strongly influenced by biological factors and cannot easily be changed by the way a child is raised. Presumably, the exposure of Bruce's brain to testosterone prenatally and during the first few months of life affected neural development, favoring the emergence of male sexual identity and an orientation toward women as romantic and sexual partners. Fortunately, cases like this one are rare. The only other case that I could find of penile ablation in infancy followed by a sex reassignment was reported by Bradley et al. (1998). As a child, the girl was described as being a "tomboy" but appears to have been happy with her identity as a female. However, she described herself as bisexual but primarily attracted to women and is currently living with a woman.

Sexual Orientation and the Brain

The human brain is a sexually dimorphic organ. This fact has long been suspected, even before confirmation was received from anatomical studies and studies of regional cerebral metabolism using PET and functional MRI. For example, neurologists discovered that the two hemispheres of a woman's brain appear to share functions more than those of a man's brain do. If a man sustains a stroke that damages the left side of the brain, he is more likely to show impairments in language than a woman with similar damage. Presumably, the woman's right hemisphere shares language functions with the left, so damage to one hemisphere is less devastating than it is in men. Also, men's brains are, on average, somewhat larger—apparently because men's bodies are generally larger than those of women's. In addition, the sizes of some specific regions of the telencephalon and diencephalon are different in males and females, and

the shape of the corpus callosum may also be sexually dimorphic. (See Breedlove, 1994, and Swaab, Gooren, and Hofman, 1995, for specific references.)

Most investigators believe that the sexual dimorphism of the human brain is a result of differential exposure to androgens prenatally and during early postnatal life. Of course, additional changes could occur at the time of puberty, when another surge in androgens occurs. The differences could even be a result of differences in the social environments of males and females. We cannot manipulate the hormone levels of humans before and after birth as we can with laboratory animals, so it might be a long time before enough evidence is gathered to permit us to make definite conclusions.

Several studies have examined the brains of deceased heterosexual and homosexual men and heterosexual women. So far, these studies have found differences in the size of three different subregions of the brain: the suprachiasmatic nucleus, a sexually dimorphic nucleus of the hypothalamus, and the anterior commissure (Swaab and Hofman, 1990; LeVay, 1991; Allen and Gorski, 1992). You are already familiar with the suprachiasmatic nucleus from Chapter 9; the anterior commissure is a fiber bundle that interconnects parts of the left and right temporal lobes. The suprachiasmatic nucleus was found to be larger in homosexual men and smaller in heterosexual men and women; a sexually dimorphic nucleus of the hypothalamus (the *third interstitial nucleus of the anterior hypothalamus, or INAH-3*) was found to be larger in heterosexual men and smaller in homosexual men and heterosexual women; and the anterior commissure was found to be larger in homosexual men and heterosexual women and smaller in heterosexual men. However, a follow-up study failed to replicate this effect. Byne et al. (2002) found that the INAH-3 was larger in heterosexual men than in women but failed to find a relationship between size and sexual orientation in men.

Although this section has been considering sexual orientation—the sex of a person to whom an individual is sexually and romantically attracted—another sexual characteristic is related to structural differences in the brain. Zhou et al. (1995) found that the size of a particular region of the forebrain, the central subdivision of the *bed nucleus of the stria terminalis (BNST),* is larger in males than in females. They also found that in male transsexuals this nucleus is as small as it is in females. The size of this nucleus was as large in male homosexuals as in male heterosexuals. Thus, its size was related to sexual *identity,* not to sexual *orientation.* (See *Figure 10.16*.) Male transsexuals are men who regard themselves as females trapped in male bodies. Some go so far as to seek medical assistance to obtain female sex hormones and sex-change operations. (Most male homosexuals have male sexual identities; although they are romantically and sexually oriented toward other men, they do not regard themselves as women, nor do they wish to be.) Whether the BNST actu-

| Heterosexual man | Heterosexual woman | Homosexual man | Transexual male-to-female |

figure 10.16

Photomicrographs of slices of the human brain containing the central subdivision of the bed nucleus of the stria terminalis (BNST).

(From Zhou, J.-N., Hofman, M. A., Gooren, L. J. G., and Swaab, D. F. *Nature*, 1995, *378*, 68–70. Reprinted with permission.)

ally plays a role in a person's sexual identity will have to be determined by further research.

We cannot necessarily conclude that any of the brain regions I mentioned in this section are directly involved in people's sexual orientation (or sexual identity), but the results do suggest the following: The brains of heterosexual women, heterosexual men, and homosexual men may have been exposed to different patterns of hormones prenatally. The *real* differences—if indeed sexual orientation is determined by prenatal exposure to androgens—may lie elsewhere in the brain, but at least we have an indication that differences do exist and that exposure to prenatal hormones has a profound effect on the nature of a person's sexuality.

Possible Causes of Differences in Brain Development

If sexual orientation is, indeed, affected by differences in exposure of the developing brain to androgens, what factors might cause this exposure to vary? Presumably, something must decrease the prenatal androgen levels to which male homosexuals are exposed and increase the levels to which female homosexuals are exposed. As we saw, congenital adrenal hyperplasia exposes the developing fetus to increased levels of androgens, but most homosexual women do not have CAH. So far, no other plausible sources of high levels of prenatal androgens have been proposed.

Studies performed with laboratory animals suggest an event that could potentially interfere with prenatal androgenization of males: maternal stress. Ward (1972) subjected pregnant rats to periods of stress by confining them and exposing them to a bright light, which suppresses androgen production in male fetuses. The male rats born

to the stressed mothers were less likely than control subjects to display male sexual behavior and were more likely to display female sexual behavior when they were given injections of estradiol and progesterone. Another study (Ward and Stehm, 1991) found that the play behavior of juvenile male rats whose mothers were stressed while pregnant resembled that of females more than that of males—that is, the animals showed less rough-and-tumble play. Thus, the behavioral effects caused by prenatal stress are not restricted to changes in sexual behavior.

Other studies with laboratory animals have shown that besides having behavioral effects, prenatal stress reduces the size of a sexually dimorphic nucleus of the preoptic area, which normally is larger in males than in females and which (as we will see in a later section) plays an important role in male sex behavior (Anderson et al., 1986). Although we cannot assume that prenatal stress in humans and laboratory animals has similar effects on the brain and behavior, the results of these studies are consistent with the hypothesis that male homosexuality may be related to events that reduce exposure to prenatal androgens.

Studies by Blanchard and his colleagues (reviewed in Blanchard, 2001) suggest another factor that can influence sexual differentiation of the brain. The investigators found that homosexual men tend to have more older brothers—but not older sisters or younger brothers or sisters—than heterosexual men. In contrast, the numbers of brothers or sisters (younger or older) of homosexual and heterosexual women did not differ, nor did the age of the mother or father or the interval between births. The presence of older brothers and sisters had no effect on women's sexual orientation. The data obtained by Blanchard and his colleagues suggest that the odds of a boy becoming homosexual increased by approximately 3.3 percent for each older brother. Assuming a 2 percent rate of homosexuality in boys without older brothers, the predicted rate would be 3.6 percent for a boy with two older brothers and 6.3 percent for one with four older brothers. Thus, the odds are still strongly against the incidence of homosexuality even in a family with several boys.

The authors suggest that when mothers are exposed to several male fetuses, their immune system may become sensitized to proteins that only males possess. As a result, the response of the mother's immune system may affect the prenatal brain development of later male fetuses. Of course, most men who have several older brothers are heterosexual, so even if this hypothesis is correct, it appears that only some women become sensitized to a protein produced by their male fetuses.

Heredity and Sexual Orientation

Another factor that may play a role in sexual orientation is heredity. Twin studies take advantage of the fact that identical twins have identical genes, whereas the genetic similarity between fraternal twins is, on the average,

50 percent. Bailey and Pillard (1991) studied pairs of male twins in which at least one member identified himself as homosexual. If both twins are homosexual, they are said to be *concordant* for this trait. If only one is homosexual, the twins are said to be *discordant*. Thus, if homosexuality has a genetic basis, the percentage of monozygotic twins who are concordant for homosexuality should be higher than that for dizygotic twins. This is exactly what Bailey and Pillard found: The concordance rate was 52 percent for identical twins and only 22 percent for fraternal twins.

Genetic factors also appear to affect female homosexuality. Bailey et al. (1993) found that the concordance of female monozygotic twins for homosexuality was 48 percent, while that of dizygotic twins was 16 percent. Another study, by Pattatucci and Hamer (1995), found an increased incidence of homosexuality and bisexuality in sisters, daughters, nieces, and female cousins (through a paternal uncle) of homosexual women.

To summarize, evidence suggests that two biological factors—prenatal hormonal exposure and heredity—may affect a person's sexual orientation. These research findings certainly contradict the suggestion that a person's sexual orientation is a moral issue. It appears that homosexuals are no more responsible for their sexual orientation than heterosexuals are. Ernulf, Innala, and Whitam (1989) found that people who believed that homosexuals were "born that way" expressed more positive attitudes toward them than people who believed that they "chose to be" or "learned to be" that way. Thus, we can hope that research on the origins of homosexuality will reduce prejudice based on a person's sexual orientation. The question "Why does someone become homosexual?" will probably be answered when we find out why someone becomes *heterosexual*.

interim
summary

Hormonal Control of Sexual Behavior

Sexual behaviors are controlled by the organizational and activational effects of hormones. The female reproductive cycle (menstrual cycle or estrous cycle) begins with the maturation of one or more ovarian follicles, which occurs in response to the secretion of FSH by the anterior pituitary gland. As the ovarian follicle matures, it secretes estradiol, which causes the lining of the uterus to develop. When estradiol reaches a critical level, it causes the pituitary gland to secrete a surge of LH, triggering ovulation. The empty ovarian follicle becomes a corpus luteum, under the continued influence of LH, and secretes estradiol and progesterone. If pregnancy does not occur, the corpus luteum dies and stops producing hormones, and menstruation begins.

The sexual behavior of males of all mammalian species appears to depend on the presence of androgens. Oxytocin has a facilitatory effect on erection and ejaculation, whereas prolactin has a generally inhibitory effect—and so does dynorphin, an endogenous opioid. Both prolactin and dynorphin may be involved in the male refractory period. The proceptivity, receptivity, and attractiveness of female mammals other than primates depend primarily on estradiol and progesterone. In particular, estradiol has a priming effect on the subsequent appearance of progesterone.

In most mammals female sexual behavior is the norm, just as the female body and female sex organs are the norm. That is, unless prenatal androgens masculinize and defeminize the animal's brain, its sexual behavior will be feminine. Behavioral masculinization refers to the androgen-stimulated development of neural circuits that respond to testosterone in adulthood, producing male sexual behavior. Behavioral defeminization refers to the inhibitory effects of androgens on the development of neural circuits that respond to estradiol and progesterone in adulthood, producing female sexual behavior. Behavioral defeminization is caused by intracellular estradiol, derived from testosterone through the action of aromatase.

Some organizational effects of androgens are indirect. Androgens cause the secretion of a chemical into the urine of male rat pups that makes it more attractive to their mothers, which spend more time licking the pups' anogenital region. This tactile stimulation contributes to the pups' behavioral masculinization.

Pheromones can affect sexual physiology and behavior. Odorants present in the urine of female mice affect their estrous cycles, lengthening and eventually stopping them (the Lee-Boot effect). Odorants present in the urine of male mice abolish these effects and cause the females' cycles to become synchronized (the Whitten effect). (Phenomena similar to the Lee-Boot effect and the Whitten effect also occur in women.) Odorants can also accelerate the onset of puberty in females (the Vandenbergh effect). In addition, the odor of the urine from a male other than the one that impregnated a female mouse will cause her to abort (Bruce effect). The Bruce effect involves learning the odor of the male that impregnates the female, and the activity of a noradrenergic input to the olfactory bulb (triggered by vaginal stimulation) is involved in this learning.

In the hamster the attractiveness of an estrous female to the male derives in part from chemicals present in her vaginal secretions, detected by the olfactory epithelium and vomeronasal organ. Connections between the olfactory system and the amygdala appear to be important in stimulating male sexual behavior. One sex-attractant chemical, a protein named aphrodisin, has been isolated from the urine of female hamsters.

Males produce pheromones that affect female behavior. Female rats prefer to be near intact adult males rather than those whose testes have been removed, and contact with several males increases the females' level of sexual arousal; both phenomena disappear after removal of the vomeronasal system. The search for sex attractant pheromones in humans has so far been fruitless, although we might well recognize our sex partners by their odors. One study does suggest that exposure to androstenol, a substance that is present in male underarm sweat, may increase a woman's tendency to engage in social interchanges with men.

The behavioral effects of prenatal exposure to androgens in humans, if any, are not well understood. Studies of prenatally androgenized girls suggest that organizational effects might well influence the development of sexual orientation; androgenization appears to increase the incidence of homosexuality. If androgens cannot act (as they cannot in cases of androgen insensitivity syndrome), then the person's anatomy and behavior are feminine. Testosterone has an activational effect on the sexual behavior of men, just as it does on the behavior of other male mammals. Women do not require estradiol or progesterone to experience sexual interest or to engage in sexual behavior. These hormones may affect the quality and intensity of their sex drive, and studies comparing the sexual behavior of female monkeys housed in small groups with that of females housed in large groups in large cages suggest that the sexual proceptivity may be related to ovarian hormones, even in higher primates. Studies with women suggest that variations in levels of ovarian hormones across the menstrual cycle do affect sexual interest but that other factors (such as initiation of sexual activity by partners or a desire to avoid or attain pregnancy) can affect behavior. In addition, the presence of androgens may have a facilitating effect in women's sexual interest.

Sexual orientation (that is, heterosexuality or homosexuality) may be influenced by prenatal exposure to androgens. So far, researchers have obtained evidence that suggests that the sizes of three brain regions are related to a man's sexual orientation. The size of another part of the brain has been found to be related to sexual identity in males. The case of a twin boy whose penis was accidentally destroyed during infancy suggests that the effects of prenatal androgenization are not easily reversed by the way a child is reared. Studies with rats have shown that events that cause stress during pregnancy can interfere with defeminization of the sexual behavior of the male offspring. The fact that male homosexuals tend to have more older brothers than male heterosexuals do has led to the suggestion that a woman's immune system may become sensitized to a protein expressed only in male fetuses. Finally, twin studies suggest that heredity may play a role in sexual orientation in both men and women.

Neural Control of Sexual Behavior

The control of sexual behavior—at least in laboratory animals—involves different brain mechanisms in males and females. This section describes these mechanisms.

Males

Spinal Mechanisms

Some sexual responses are controlled by neural circuits contained within the spinal cord. For example, genital stimulation can elicit sexual movements and postures in female cats and rats even after their spinal cord is transected below the brain (Beach, 1967; Hart, 1969). In male dogs with spinal cord transections, genital stimulation can produce erection and ejaculation (Hart, 1967). Thus, the brain is not required for these reflexes.

In humans, too, erection and ejaculation are controlled by spinal reflexes. Men with spinal damage have become fathers when their wives have been artificially inseminated with semen obtained by mechanical stimulation (Hart, 1978). Because the spinal damage prevents sensory information from reaching the brain, these men do not experience an orgasm; thus, they are unaware of the erection and ejaculation unless they see it happening. However, they do occasionally experience a "phantom erection" along with an orgasm (Money, 1960; Comarr, 1970). Nothing happens to their genitals or internal sex organs, but the spontaneous activity of various brain mechanisms gives rise to feelings of arousal and orgasm.

Breedlove and Arnold (1980, 1983) discovered striking sex differences in the size of a nucleus in the ventral horn of the lumbar region of the spinal cord of rats. This structure, called the **spinal nucleus of the bulbocavernosus (SNB),** contains motor neurons whose axons innervate the bulbocavernosus muscle, which is attached to the base of the penis and is involved in sexual activity. Although the muscle is not present in female rats, it is present in both sexes in humans. (It is usually called the *sphincter vaginae* in women.) The size of this nucleus—which is larger in males than in females—is controlled by the level of androgens present in a newborn rat (Arnold and Jordan, 1988).

As we saw earlier in this chapter, Moore and her colleagues have found that in rats some of the masculinizing and defeminizing effects of androgens on behavior are indirect. That is, androgens make the urine of infant male pups more attractive to the mothers, which spend more time licking the male pups' anogenital region, which affects the males' behavior in adulthood. Moore, Dou, and Juraska (1992) found that this licking also affects the development of the structure of the nervous system. They found that when they destroyed the mothers' sense of smell, so that they spent less time licking their male offspring, the animals showed 11 percent fewer neurons in the SNB. Thus, although androgens have direct effects on the survival of these motor neurons, tactile stimuli delivered by the mother reinforce these effects.

spinal nucleus of the bulbocavernosus (SNB) (*bul bo kav er no sis*) A nucleus located in the lower spinal cord; in some species of rodents, present only in males.

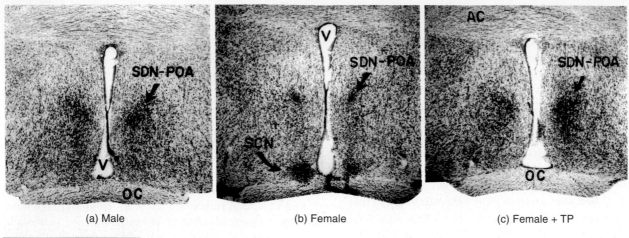

(a) Male (b) Female (c) Female + TP

figure 10.17

Photomicrographs of sections through the preoptic area of the rat brain. (a) Normal male. (b) Normal female. (c) Androgenized female. SDN-POA = sexually dimorphic nucleus of the preoptic area; OC = optic chiasm; V = third ventricle; SCN = suprachiasmatic nucleus; AC = anterior commissure.

(From Gorski, R. A., in *Neuroendocrine Perspectives,* Vol. 2, edited by E. E. Müller and R. M. MacLeod. Amsterdam: Elsevier-North Holland, 1983.)

Brain Mechanisms

As we just saw, erection and ejaculation are controlled by circuits of neurons that reside in the spinal cord. However, brain mechanisms have both excitatory and inhibitory control of these circuits. Although tactile stimulation of a man's genitals can stimulate erection and ejaculation, these responses can be inhibited by the context. For example, the outcomes of tactile stimulation of a man's penis will have different outcomes when his physician is carrying out physical examination or when his partner touches him while they are lying in bed. In addition, a man's penis can become erect when he sees his partner or has erotic thoughts—even when his penis is not being touched. Thus, we should expect to find brain mechanisms that can activate or suppress the spinal mechanisms that control genital reflexes.

The **medial preoptic area (MPA),** located just rostral to the hypothalamus, is the forebrain region most critical for male sexual behavior. (As we will see later in this chapter, it is also critical for other sexually dimorphic behavior, including maternal behavior.) Electrical stimulation of this region elicits male copulatory behavior (Malsbury, 1971), and sexual activity increases the firing rate of single neurons in the MPA (Shimura, Yamamoto, and Shimokochi, 1994; Mas, 1995). In addition, the act of copulation increases the metabolic activity of the MPA and induces the production of Fos protein (Oaknin et al., 1989; Robertson et al., 1991; Wood and Newman, 1993). (The significance of the Fos protein as an indicator of neural activation was discussed in Chapter 5.) Finally, destruction of the MPA abolishes male sexual behavior (Heimer and Larsson, 1966/1967).

The organizational effects of androgens are responsible for sexual dimorphisms in brain structure. Gorski et al. (1978) discovered a nucleus within the MPA of the rat that is three to seven times larger in males than in females. This area is called (appropriately enough) the **sexually dimorphic nucleus (SDN)** of the preoptic area. The size of this nucleus is controlled by the amount of androgens present during fetal development. According to Rhees, Shryne, and Gorski (1990a, 1990b), the critical period for masculinization of the SDN appears to start on the eighteenth day of gestation and end once the animals are five days old. (Normally, rats are born on the twenty-second day of gestation. See *Figure 10.17*.)

In the section on sexual orientation I mentioned that Anderson et al. (1986) found that prenatal stress reduced the size of the SDN in male rats. These investigators also found that volume of the SDN in an individual male rat was directly related to the animal's level of sexual activity. De Jonge et al. (1989) confirmed the importance of these results, observing that lesions of the SDN decrease masculine sexual behavior. In addition, Humm, Lambert, and Kinsley (1995) found that when prenatally stressed male rats were exposed to sexually receptive females, little Fos protein was seen in the MPA.

medial preoptic area (MPA) An area of cell bodies just rostral to the hypothalamus; plays an essential role in male sexual behavior.

sexually dimorphic nucleus (SDN) A nucleus in the preoptic area that is much larger in males than in females; first observed in rats; plays a role in male sexual behavior.

The medial amygdala, like the medial preoptic area, is sexually dimorphic: One region within this structure (which contains an especially high concentration of androgen receptors) is 85 percent larger in male rats than in female rats (Hines, Allen, and Gorski, 1992). In addition, destruction of the medial amygdala disrupts the sexual behavior of male rats. De Jonge et al. (1992) found that the rats with these lesions took longer to mount receptive females and to ejaculate. Wood and Newman (1993) observed that mating increased the production of Fos protein in the medial amygdala.

The MPA receives chemosensory input from the vomeronasal organ through connections with the medial amygdala and the bed nucleus of the stria terminalis (BNST). (You will recall that in humans the BNST is sexually dimorphic and that it is smaller in transsexual males.) The MPA also receives somatosensory information from the genitals through connections with the central tegmental field of the midbrain and the medial amygdala. The act of copulation induces the production of Fos protein in both of these regions (Gréco et al., 1998). (See *Figure 10.18.*)

Communication of sensory information from the medial amygdala to the MPA appears to involve the activ-

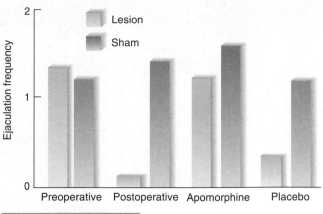

figure 10.19

Effects of lesions of the medial amygdala on male sexual behavior and restorative effects of infusion of apomorphine, a dopamine agonist, into the medial preoptic area.

(Adapted from Dominquez, J., Riolo, J. V., Xu, Zhujian, and Hull, E. M. *Journal of Neuroscience,* 2001, *21,* 349–355.

ity of dopaminergic neurons. For example, the infusion of dopamine agonists into the MPA facilitates sexual behavior, and infusions of dopamine antagonists decrease it. In addition, chemical stimulation of the medial amygdala with a glutamate agonist or exposure to a receptive female increase the levels of dopamine in the MPA, as measured by microdialysis (Hull, 1995; Dominguez and Hull, 2001). Dominguez et al. (2001) found that male sexual behavior, which was suppressed by lesions of the medial amygdala, could be restored by infusing apomorphine, dopamine agonist, into the MPA. (See *Figure 10.19.*)

Androgens exert their activational effects on neurons in the MPA and associated brain regions. If a male rodent is castrated in adulthood, its sexual behavior will cease. However, the behavior can be reinstated by implanting a small amount of testosterone directly into the MPA or in two regions whose axons project to the MPA: the central tegmental field and the medial amygdala (Sipos and Nyby, 1996; Coolen and Wood, 1999). Both of these regions contain a high concentration of androgen receptors in the male rat brain (Cottingham and Pfaff, 1986).

The motor neurons that innervate the pelvic organs involved in copulation are located in the dorsomedial and dorsolateral nuclei of the lumbar and sacral regions of the spinal cord. Anatomical tracing studies suggest that the most important connections between the MPA and the motor neurons of the spinal cord are accomplished through the **periaqueductal gray matter (PAG)** of the

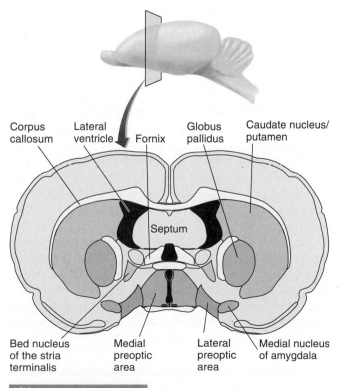

Corpus callosum   Lateral ventricle   Fornix   Globus pallidus   Caudate nucleus/ putamen

Septum

Bed nucleus of the stria terminalis   Medial preoptic area   Lateral preoptic area   Medial nucleus of amygdala

figure 10.18

Cross sections through the rat brain showing the location of the medial preoptic area, the medial amygdala, the bed nucleus of the stria terminalis, and the central tegmental field of the midbrain.

(Adapted from Swanson, L. W. *Brain Maps: Structure of the Rat Brain.* New York: Elsevier, 1992.)

periaqueductal gray matter (PAG) The region of the midbrain that surrounds the cerebral aqueduct; plays an essential role in various species-typical behaviors, including female sexual behavior.

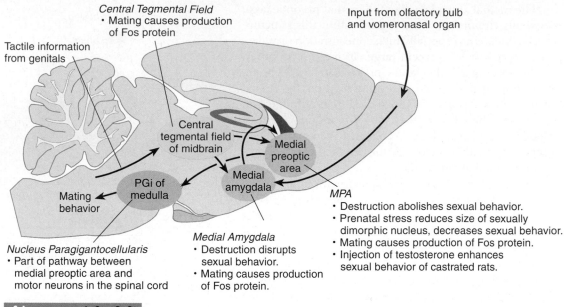

Tactile information from genitals

Central Tegmental Field
• Mating causes production of Fos protein

Input from olfactory bulb and vomeronasal organ

Central tegmental field of midbrain

Medial preoptic area

Medial amygdala

PGi of medulla

Mating behavior

MPA
• Destruction abolishes sexual behavior.
• Prenatal stress reduces size of sexually dimorphic nucleus, decreases sexual behavior.
• Mating causes production of Fos protein.
• Injection of testosterone enhances sexual behavior of castrated rats.

Nucleus Paragigantocellularis
• Part of pathway between medial preoptic area and motor neurons in the spinal cord

Medial Amygdala
• Destruction disrupts sexual behavior.
• Mating causes production of Fos protein.

figure 10.20

A possible explanation of the interacting excitatory effects of pheromones, genital stimulation, and testosterone on male sexual behavior.

midbrain and the **nucleus paragigantocellularis (PGi)** of the medulla. (See Murphy and Hoffman, 2001, for particular references.) The PGi has inhibitory effects on spinal cord sexual reflexes, so one of the tasks of the pathway originating in the MPA is to suppress this inhibition (Marson and McKenna, 1996). Excitatory input to the spinal mechanisms from the MPA appear to be conveyed via the PAG.

Figure 10.20 summarizes the evidence I have presented in this section. (See *Figure 10.20.*)

Females

Just as the MPA plays an essential role in male sex behavior, another region in the ventral forebrain plays a similar role in female sexual behavior: the **ventromedial nucleus of the hypothalamus (VMH).** A female rat with bilateral lesions of the ventromedial nuclei will not display lordosis, even if she is treated with estradiol and progesterone. Conversely, electrical stimulation of the ventromedial nucleus facilitates female sexual behavior (Pfaff and Sakuma, 1979). (See *Figure 10.21.*)

As we saw in the previous section, the medial amygdala of males receives chemosensory information from the vomeronasal system and somatosensory information from the genitals, and it sends efferent axons to the medial preoptic area. These connections are found in females as well. In addition, neurons in the medial amygdala also send efferent axons to the VMH. In fact, copulation or mechanical stimulation of the genitals or flanks increases the production of Fos protein in both the medial amygdala and the VMH (Pfaus et al., 1993; Tetel, Getzinger, and Blaustein, 1993).

As we saw earlier, sexual behavior of female rats is activated by a priming dose of estradiol, followed by progesterone. The estrogen sets the stage, so to speak, and the progesterone stimulates the sexual behavior. Injections of these hormones directly into the VMH will stimulate sexual behavior even in females whose ovaries have been removed (Rubin and Barfield, 1980; Pleim and Barfield, 1988). And if a chemical that blocks the production of progesterone receptors is injected into the VMH, the animal's sexual behavior is disrupted (Ogawa et al., 1994). Thus, estradiol and progesterone exert their effects on female sexual behavior by activating neurons in this nucleus.

Rose (1990) recorded from single neurons in the ventromedial hypothalamus of freely moving female hamsters and found that injections of progesterone (following estradiol pretreatment) increased the activity level of these neurons, particularly when the animals were displaying lordosis. In a double-labeling study Tetel, Celentano, and Blaustein (1994) found that neurons in both the VMH and the medial amygdala that showed increased Fos production when the animal's genitals were stimulated also contained estrogen receptors. Thus, the stimulating effects of estradiol and genital stimulation converge on the same neurons.

nucleus paragigantocellularis (PGi) A nucleus of the medulla that receives input from the medial preoptic area and contains neurons whose axons form synapses with motor neurons in the spinal cord that participate in sexual reflexes in males.

ventromedial nucleus of the hypothalamus (VMH) A large nucleus of the hypothalamus located near the walls of the third ventricle; plays an essential role in female sexual behavior.

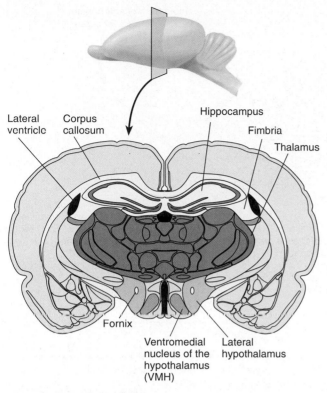

figure   10.21

A cross section through the rat brain showing the location of the ventromedial nucleus of the hypothalamus.
(Adapted from Swanson, L. W. *Brain Maps: Structure of the Rat Brain.* New York: Elsevier, 1992.)

The mechanism by which estradiol primes a female's sensitivity to progesterone appears to be simple: Estradiol increases the production of progesterone receptors, which greatly increases the effectiveness of progesterone. Blaustein

and Feder (1979) administered estradiol to ovariectomized guinea pigs and found a 150 percent increase in the number of progesterone receptors in the hypothalamus. Presumably, the estradiol activates genetic mechanisms in the nucleus that are responsible for the production of progesterone receptors.

Figure 10.22 shows two slices through the hypothalamus of ovariectomized guinea pigs, stained for progesterone receptors. One of the animals had previously received a priming dose of estradiol; the other had not. As this figure shows, the estradiol dramatically increased the number of cells containing progesterone receptors. See *Figure 10.22*.)

The neurons of the ventromedial nucleus send axons to the periaqueductal gray matter (PAG) of the midbrain, which surrounds the cerebral aqueduct. This region, too, has been implicated in female sexual behavior; Sakuma and Pfaff (1979a, 1979b) found that electrical stimulation of the PAG facilitates lordosis in female rats and that lesions there disrupt it. In addition, Hennessey et al. (1990) found that lesions that disconnect the VMH from the PAG abolish female sexual behavior. Finally, Sakuma and Pfaff (1980a, 1980b) found that estradiol treatment or electrical stimulation of the ventromedial nuclei increased the firing rate of neurons in the PAG. (The PAG contains both estrogen and progesterone receptors.)

Daniels, Miselis, and Flanagan-Cato (1999) injected a transneuronal retrograde tracer, pseudorabies virus, in the muscles responsible for the lordosis response in female rats. They found that the pathway innervating these muscles was as previous studies predicted: VMH → PAG → medullary reticular formation → motor neurons in the ventral horn of the lumbar region of the spinal cord.

As we saw in the previous subsection, the brain regions that control male genital reflexes include the MPA,

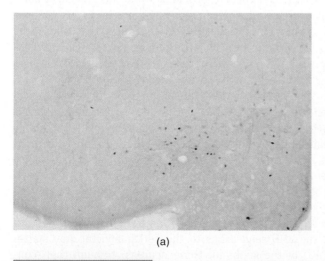

(a)

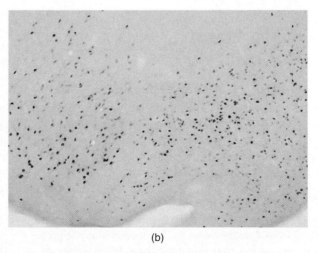

(b)

figure   10.22

Photomicrographs of sections through the hypothalamus of ovariectomized guinea pigs, stained for progesterone receptors. (a) No priming. (b) After receiving a priming dose of estradiol.
(Courtesy of Joanne Turcotte and Jeffrey Blaustein, University of Massachusetts.)

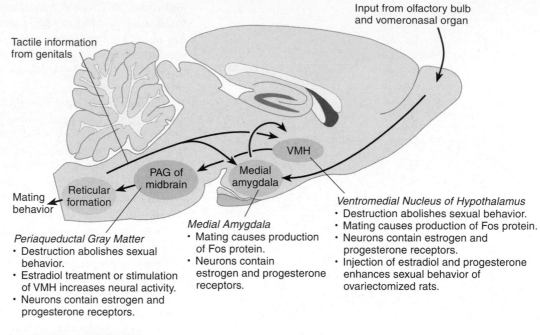

Tactile information
from genitals

Input from olfactory bulb
and vomeronasal organ

VMH

PAG of
midbrain

Medial
amygdala

Reticular
formation

Mating
behavior

Periaqueductal Gray Matter
• Destruction abolishes sexual
  behavior.
• Estradiol treatment or stimulation
  of VMH increases neural activity.
• Neurons contain estrogen and
  progesterone receptors.

Medial Amygdala
• Mating causes production
  of Fos protein.
• Neurons contain
  estrogen and progesterone
  receptors.

Ventromedial Nucleus of Hypothalamus
• Destruction abolishes sexual behavior.
• Mating causes production of Fos protein.
• Neurons contain estrogen and
  progesterone receptors.
• Injection of estradiol and progesterone
  enhances sexual behavior of
  ovariectomized rats.

figure 10.23

A possible explanation of the interacting excitatory effects of pheromones, genital
stimulation, and estradiol and progesterone on female sexual behavior.

PAG, and PGi. Marson (1995) injected pseudorabies virus into the clitorises of female rats and found retrograde labeling in these three brain structures (and some others, as well). Thus, it seems likely that erections of the penis and clitoris are controlled by similar brain mechanisms. This finding is not surprising, because these organs derive from the same embryonic tissue.

Figure 10.23 summarizes the evidence I have presented in this section. (See *Figure 10.23*.)

interim summary

Neural Control of Sexual Behavior

Sexual reflexes such as sexual posturing, erection, and ejaculation are organized in the spinal cord. The spinal cord contains at least one sexually dimorphic region, the spinal nucleus of the bulbocavernosus (SNB), whose size is controlled by prenatal androgens. In rats at least part of the masculinization of this nucleus is a result of tactile stimulation delivered by the animal's mother.

In laboratory animals different brain mechanisms control male and female sexual behavior. The medial preoptic area is the forebrain region that is most critical for male sexual behavior. Stimulating this area produces copulatory behavior; destroying it permanently abolishes the behavior. The sex-

ually dimorphic nucleus, located in the medial preoptic area, develops only if an animal is exposed to androgens early in life. This nucleus is found in humans as well. The size of the SDN (part of the MPA) is reduced by prenatal stress and correlates with an animal's level of sexual behavior; its destruction impairs such behavior.

Neurons in the MPA contain testosterone receptors. Copulatory activity causes an increase in the activity of neurons in this region. Implantation of testosterone directly into the MPA reinstates copulatory behavior that was previously abolished by castration in adulthood. Neurons in the MPA are part of a circuit that includes the periaqueductal gray matter, the nucleus paragigantocellularis of the medulla, and motor neurons controlling genital reflexes in the spinal cord. Connections of the PGi with the spinal cord are inhibitory.

The most important forebrain region for female sexual behavior is the ventromedial nucleus of the hypothalamus (VMH). Its destruction abolishes copulatory behavior, and its stimulation facilitates this behavior. Both estradiol and progesterone exert their facilitating effects on female sexual behavior in this region, and studies have confirmed the existence of progesterone and estrogen receptors there. The priming effect of estradiol is caused by an increase in progesterone receptors in the VMH. The steroid-sensitive neurons of the VMH send axons to the periaqueductal gray matter (PAG) of the midbrain; these neurons, through their connections with the medullary reticular formation, control the particular responses that constitute female sexual behavior.

Parental Behavior

In most mammalian species reproductive behavior takes place after the offspring are born as well as at the time they are conceived. This section examines the role of hormones in the initiation and maintenance of maternal behavior and the role of the neural circuits that are responsible for their expression. Most of the research has involved rodents; less is known about the neural and endocrine bases of maternal behavior in primates.

Although most research on the physiology of parental behavior has focused on maternal behavior, some researchers are now studying paternal behavior shown by the males of some species of rodents. It goes without saying that the human paternal behavior is very important for the offspring of our species, but the physiological basis of this behavior has not yet been studied.

Maternal Behavior of Rodents

The final test of the fitness of an animal's genes is the number of offspring that survive to a reproductive age. Just as the process of natural selection favors reproductively competent animals, it favors those that care adequately for their young, if their young in fact require care. Rat and mouse pups certainly do; they cannot survive without a mother to attend to their needs.

At birth rats and mice resemble fetuses. The infants are blind (their eyes are still shut), and they can only wriggle helplessly. They are poikilothermous ("cold-blooded"); their brain is not yet developed enough to regulate body temperature. They even lack the ability to release their own urine and feces spontaneously and must be helped to do so by their mother. As we will see shortly, this phenomenon actually serves a useful function.

During gestation female rats and mice build nests. The form this structure takes depends on the material available for its construction. In the laboratory the animals are usually given strips of paper or lengths of rope or twine. A good *brood nest,* as it is called, is shown in Figure 10.24. This nest is made of hemp rope; a piece of the rope is shown below the nest. The mouse laboriously shredded the rope and then wove an enclosed nest, with a small hole for access to the interior. (See *Figure 10.24*.)

At the time of **parturition** (delivery of offspring) the female begins to groom and lick the area around her vagina. As a pup begins to emerge, she assists the uterine contractions by pulling the pup out with her teeth. She then eats the placenta and umbilical cord and cleans off the fetal membranes—a quite delicate operation. (A newborn pup looks as though it is sealed in very thin plastic wrap.) After all the pups are born and cleaned up, the

figure 10.24

A mouse's brood nest. Beside it is a length of the kind of rope the mouse used to construct it.

mother will probably nurse them. Milk is usually present in the mammary glands very near the time of birth.

Periodically, the mother licks the pups' anogenital region, stimulating reflexive urination and defecation. Friedman and Bruno (1976) have shown the utility of this mechanism. They noted that a lactating female rat produces approximately 48 grams (g) of milk on the tenth day of lactation. This milk contains approximately 35 milliliters (ml) of water. The experimenters injected some of the pups with tritiated (radioactive) water and later found radioactivity in the mother and in the littermates. They calculated that a lactating rat normally consumes 21 ml of water in the urine of her young, thus recycling approximately two-thirds of the water she gives to the pups in the form of milk. The water, traded back and forth between mother and young, serves as a vehicle for the nutrients—fats, protein, and sugar—contained in milk. Because each day the milk production of a lactating rat is approximately 14 percent of her body weight (for a human weighing 120 pounds, that would be around 2 gallons), the recycling is extremely useful, especially when the availability of water is a problem.

Besides cleaning, nursing, and purging her offspring, a female rodent will retrieve pups if they leave or are removed from the nest. The mother will even construct

parturition (*par tew **ri** shun*) The act of giving birth.

another nest in a new location and move her litter there, should the conditions at the old site become unfavorable (for example, when an inconsiderate experimenter puts a heat lamp over it). The way a female rodent picks up her pup is quite consistent: She gingerly grasps the animal by the back, managing not to injure it with her very sharp teeth. (I can personally attest to the ease with which these teeth can penetrate skin.) She then carries the pup with a characteristic prancing walk, her head held high. (See *Figure 10.25*.) The pup is brought back to the nest and is left there. The female then leaves the nest again to search for another pup. She continues to retrieve pups until she finds no more; she does not count her pups and stop retrieving when they are all back. A mouse or rat will usually accept all the pups she is offered, if they are young enough. I once observed two lactating female mice with nests in corners of the same cage, diagonally opposite each other. I disturbed their nests, which triggered a long bout of retrieving, during which each mother stole youngsters from the other's nest. The mothers kept up their exchange for a long time, passing each other in the middle of the cage.

Maternal behavior begins to wane as the pups become more active and begin to look more like adults. At around sixteen to eighteen days of age they are able to get about easily by themselves, and they begin to obtain their own food. The mother ceases to retrieve them when they leave the nest and will eventually run away from them if they attempt to nurse.

Under normal conditions, one of the stimuli that induce a female rat to begin taking care of pups is the act of par-

turition. Female rodents normally begin taking care of their pups as soon as they are born. Some of this effect is caused by prenatal hormones, but the passage of the pups through the birth canal also stimulates maternal behavior: Artificially distending the birth canal in nonpregnant females stimulates maternal behavior, whereas deafferenting the birth canal retards the appearance of maternal behavior (Graber and Kristal, 1977; Yeo and Keverne, 1986).

Audition plays a role in the control of maternal behavior. For example, mouse, rat, and hamster pups emit at least two different kinds of ultrasonic calls (Noirot, 1972; Hofer and Shair, 1993; Ihnat, White, and Barfield, 1995). These sounds cannot be heard by humans; they have to be translated into lower frequencies by a special device (a "bat detector") to be perceived by the experimenter. Of course, the mother can hear these calls. When a pup gets cold (as it would if it were removed from the nest), it emits a characteristic call that brings the mother out of her nest. The sound is so effective that female mice have been observed to chew the cover off a loudspeaker that is transmitting a recording of this call. Once out of the nest, the female uses olfactory cues as well as auditory ones to find the pups; she can find a buried, anesthetized baby mouse that is unable to make any noise. The second call is made in response to rough handling. When a mother hears this sound, she stops what she is doing. Typically, it is she that is administering the rough handling, and the distress call makes her stop. This mechanism undoubtedly plays an important role in training mother mice to handle pups properly.

Hormonal Control of Maternal Behavior

As we saw earlier in this chapter, most sexually dimorphic behaviors are controlled by the organizational and activational effects of sex hormones. Maternal behavior is somewhat different in this respect. First, there is no evidence that organizational effects of hormones play a role; as we will see, under the proper conditions even males will take care of infants. (Obviously, they cannot provide them with milk.) Second, although maternal behavior is affected by hormones, it is not *controlled* by them. Most virgin female rats will begin to retrieve and care for young pups after having infants placed with them for several days (Wiesner and Sheard, 1933). And once the rats are sensitized, they will thereafter take care of pups as soon as they encounter them; sensitization lasts for a lifetime.

Although hormones are not essential for the activation of maternal behavior, many aspects of maternal behavior are facilitated by hormones. Nest-building behavior is facilitated by progesterone, the principal hormone of pregnancy (Lisk, Pretlow, and Friedman, 1969). After parturition, mothers continue to maintain their nests, and they construct new nests if necessary, even

figure 10.25

A female mouse carrying one of her pups.

though their blood level of progesterone is very low then. Voci and Carlson (1973) found that hypothalamic implants of prolactin as well as progesterone facilitated nest building in virgin female mice. Presumably, nest building can be facilitated by either hormone: progesterone during pregnancy and prolactin after parturition. Prolactin, produced by the anterior pituitary gland, is responsible for milk production. Unlike many other peptides, special mechanisms transport this hormone from the blood into the brain (Grattan et al., 2001).

Although pregnant female rats will not immediately care for foster pups that are given to them during pregnancy, they will do so as soon as their pups are born. The hormones that influence a female rodent's responsiveness to her offspring are the ones that are present shortly before parturition. Figure 10.26 shows the levels of the three hormones that have been implicated in maternal behavior: progesterone, estradiol, and prolactin. Note that just before parturition the level of estradiol begins rising, then the level of progesterone falls dramatically, followed by a sharp increase in prolactin. (See *Figure 10.26*.) If ovariectomized virgin female rats are given estradiol and progesterone in a pattern that duplicates this sequence, the time it takes to sensitize their maternal behavior is drastically reduced (Moltz, Lubin, Leon, and Numan, 1970; Bridges, 1984). Prolactin is not necessary.

Another hormone that is present during lactation—prolactin—may also have stimulating effects on maternal behavior; and its effects, like those of estradiol, may be exerted in the medial preoptic area. Bridges et al. (1990) infused minute quantities of prolactin into the lateral ventricles or directly into the MPA of virgin female rats. They found that the animals quickly began taking care of pups. The effect occurred only if the animals were first given a series of injections of progesterone and estradiol; thus, the maternal behavior of normal females may depend on an interaction between several hormones. Lucas et al. (1998) found that mice with a targeted mutation against the gene for the prolactin receptor showed deficient maternal behavior, which supports the importance of prolactin in this behavior.

Prolactin is not the only lactogenic hormone (that is, hormone that stimulates the production of milk). Lactogenic hormones are also produced by the placenta, and evidence suggests that these hormones, too, may stimulate maternal behavior. Bridges et al. (1996) analyzed the cerebrospinal fluid of freely moving pregnant rats and discovered the presence of placental lactogenic hormones after day 12 of pregnancy. The fact that these hormones were present in the CSF indicates that they were transported into the brain, where they could potentially affect behavior. The investigators found that an infusion of placental lactogenic hormones into the medial preoptic area shortened the time it took to sensitize maternal behavior in virgin female mice. (The role of the medial preoptic area in maternal behavior is described below.)

Neural Control of Maternal Behavior

The medial preoptic area, the region of the forebrain that plays the most critical role in male sexual behavior, appears to play a similar role in maternal behavior. Numan (1974) found that lesions of the MPA disrupted both nest building and pup care. The mothers simply ignored their offspring. However, female sexual behavior was unaffected by these lesions.

As we saw earlier, distension of the birth canal, normally caused by passage of a pup, provides an important stimulating effect on maternal behavior. Del Cerro et al. (1995) found that the act of parturition increased the

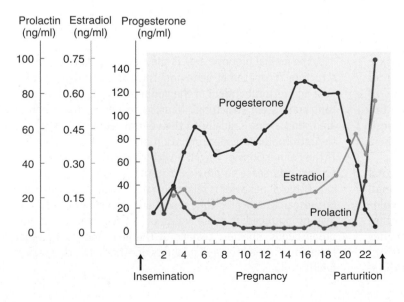

figure 10.26

Blood levels of progesterone, estradiol, and prolactin in pregnant rats.
(From Rosenblatt, J. S., Siegel, H. I., and Mayer, A. D. *Advances in the Study of Behavior,* 1979, *10,* 225–310.)

metabolic activity of the MPA, measured by 2-DG autoradiography. They also found that virgin females whose maternal behavior had been sensitized by exposure to pups showed a similar increase. Thus, stimuli associated with pup care activate the MPA.

As you learned earlier, in the discussion of the neural basis of male sexual behavior, the MPA sends axons to the midbrain and lower brain stem. Numan and Numan (1997) found that neurons of the MPA that were activated by the performance of maternal behavior (as indicated by the production of Fos protein) sent their axons to two regions of the midbrain: the ventral tegmental area (VTA) and retrorubral field. The retrorubral field of the midbrain sends axons to regions of the brain stem reticular formation that may be involved in the expression of maternal behavior. Cutting the connections of the MPA with the brain stem abolishes maternal behavior (Numan and Smith, 1984).

The medial preoptic area appears to be the place where estradiol affects maternal behavior. The MPA contains estrogen receptors (Pfaff and Keiner, 1973). Giordano et al. (1989) found that the concentration of estrogen receptors in the MPA increases during pregnancy and appears to reflect the priming effect produced by the sequence of hormones that occurs during pregnancy. In addition, direct implants of estradiol in the MPA facilitate maternal behavior (Numan, Rosenblatt, and Komisaruk, 1977), and injections of an antiestrogen into the MPA block it (Adieh, Mayer, and Rosenblatt, 1987).

Prolactin also appears to affect maternal behavior by acting on neurons in the MPA. Bridges et al. (1990) found that an infusion of prolactin into the MPA of virgin female rats that had been primed with estradiol and progesterone stimulated maternal behavior. And as we saw a few paragraphs ago, infusion of placental lactogenic hormones into this region has the same effect (Bridges et al., 1996).

Neural Control of Paternal Behavior

Newborn infants of most species of mammals are cared for by their mother, and it is, of course, their mother that feeds them. However, males of a few species of rodents share the task of infant care with the mothers, and the brains of these nurturing fathers show some interesting differences compared with those of nonpaternal fathers of other species.

Several laboratories have been investigating parental behavior in some closely related species of voles (small rodents that are often mistaken for mice). Prairie voles *(Microtus ochrogaster)* and pine voles *(Microtus pinetorum)* are monogamous; males and females form pair bonds after mating, and the fathers help to care for the pups. Montane voles *(Microtus montanus)* and meadow voles *(Micro-*

tus pennsylvanicus) are promiscuous; after mating, the male leaves, and the mother cares for the pups by herself. The size of the MPA, which plays an essential role in maternal behavior, shows less sexual dimorphism in monogamous prairie voles than in promiscuous montane voles (Shapiro et al., 1991).

Kirkpatrick, Kim, and Insel (1994) found that when male prairie voles were exposed to a pup, Fos production increased in the MPA (and also several other regions of the forebrain). In addition, electrolytic or excitotoxic lesions of the MPA produce severe deficits in paternal behavior of male rats (Rosenblatt, Hazelwood, and Poole, 1996; Sturgis and Bridges, 1997). Finally, implants of estradiol in the MPA of male rats shortened the time it took to stimulate paternal behavior by exposure to pups. Thus, the MPA appears to play a similar roles in parental behavior of both males and females.

interim summary

Parental Behavior

Many species must care for their offspring. Among most rodents this duty falls to the mother, which must build a nest, deliver her own pups, clean them, keep them warm, nurse them, and retrieve them if they are moved out of the nest. They must even induce their pups' urination and defecation, and the mother's ingestion of the urine recycles water, which is often a scarce commodity.

Exposure of virgin females to young pups stimulates maternal behavior within a few days. The stimuli that normally induce maternal behavior are those produced by the act of parturition and the hormones present around the end of pregnancy. Nest building appears to be facilitated by progesterone during pregnancy and by prolactin during the lactation period. Injections of progesterone and estradiol that duplicate the sequence that occurs during pregnancy facilitate of maternal behavior, as does injection of prolactin directly into the brain.

The medial preoptic area is the most important forebrain structure for maternal behavior, and the ventral tegmental area and retrorubal field of the midbrain are the most important brain stem structures. Neurons in the medial preoptic area send axons caudally to the ventral tegmental area and the retrorubral reticular formation of the pons and medulla. If the connections of the MPA with the brain stem are interrupted, rats cease to provide maternal care.

Paternal behavior is relatively rare in mammalian species, but research indicates that sexual dimorphism of the MPA is less pronounced in male voles of monogamous, but not promiscuous, species. Lesions of the MPA abolish paternal behavior of male rats, and implants of estradiol in this region facilitate it.

Suggested Readings

Becker, J. B., Breedlove, S. M., and Crews, D. *Behavioral Endocrinology,* 2nd ed. Cambridge, MA: MIT Press, 2002.

Bornstein, M. H. *Handbook of Parenting. Vol. 2: Biology and Ecology of Parenting.* Mahwah, NJ: Lawrence Erlbaum Associates, 1995.

Gerall, A. A., Moltz, H., and Ward, I. I. *Handbook of Behavioral Neurobiology. Vol. 11: Sexual Differentiation.* New York: Plenum Press, 1992.

Kandeel, F. R., Koussa, V. K. T., and Swerdloff, R. S. Male sexual function and its disorders: Physiology, pathophysiology, clinical investigation, and treatment. *Endocrine Reviews,* 2001, *22,* 342–388.

Krasnegor, N. A., and Bridges, R. S. *Mammalian Parenting: Biochemical, Neurobiological, and Behavioral Determinants.* New York: Oxford University Press, 1990.

Suggested Web Sites

Archive for Sexology

http://www.rki.de/GESUND/ARCHIV/FIRST.HTM

This German Web site contains a series of links on the history of sexology, various WHO reports on sexology, and links to scientific sites dealing with sexology.

Neurobiology of Sexual Behavior

http://salmon.psy.plym.ac.uk/year2/sexbehav.htm

The focus of this site is an online course in the neurobiology of sexual behavior. Topics include gender identity, the genetics of homosexuality, and the impact of hormones on sexual behavior.

Scientific Study of Human Sexuality: Academia

http://www.byz.org/~sexuality/html/body_academia.html

The focus of this site is advisory material on the academic study of human sexuality.

Hormones and Sexual Behavior

http://salmon.psy.plym.ac.uk/year1/sexbehav.htm

The impact of hormones on sexual behavior and function is the focus of this online course.

chapter 11

Emotion

outline

- **Emotions as Response Patterns**
  Fear
  Anger and Aggression
  Hormonal Control of
    Aggressive Behavior
  Interim Summary

- **Communication of Emotions**
  Facial Expression of Emotions:
    Innate Responses
  Neural Basis of the Communication
    of Emotions: Recognition
  Neural Basis of the Communication
    of Emotions: Expression
  Interim Summary

- **Feelings of Emotions**
  The James-Lange Theory
  Feedback From Simulated Emotions
  Interim Summary

Stanton MacDonald-Wright, *The Prophecy–Sleep Suite 2,* 1955. © CNAC/MNAM/Dist. Réunion des Musées Nationaux/Art Resoure, NY.

Several years ago, while I was on a sabbatical leave, a colleague stopped by my office and asked whether I would like to see an interesting patient. The patient, a 72-year-old man, had suffered a massive stroke in his right hemisphere that had paralyzed the left side of his body.

Mr. V. was seated in a wheelchair equipped with a large tray on which his right arm was resting; his left arm was immobilized in a sling, to keep it out of the way. He greeted us politely, almost formally, articulating his words carefully with a slight European accent.

Mr. V. seemed intelligent, and this impression was confirmed when we gave him some of the subtests of the Wechsler Adult Intelligence Test. His verbal intelligence appeared to be in the upper 5 percent of the population. The fact that English was not his native language made his performance even more remarkable.

The most interesting aspect of Mr. V.'s behavior after his stroke was his lack of reaction to his symptoms. After we had finished with the testing, we asked him to tell us a little about himself and his lifestyle. What, for example, was his favorite pastime?

"I like to walk," he said. "I walk at least two hours each day around the city, but mostly I like to walk in the woods. I have maps of most of the national forests in the state on the walls of my study, and I mark all of the trails I've taken. I figure that in about six months I will have walked all of the trails that are short enough to do in a day."

"You're going to finish up those trails in the next six months?" asked Dr. W.

"Yes, and then I'll start over again!" he replied.

"Mr. V., are you having any trouble?" asked Dr. W.

"Trouble? What do you mean?"

"I mean physical difficulty."

"No." Mr. V. gave him a slightly puzzled look.

"Well, what are you sitting in?"

Mr. V. gave him a look that indicated he thought that the question was rather stupid—or perhaps insulting. "A wheelchair, of course," he answered.

"Why are you in a wheelchair?"

Now Mr. V. looked frankly exasperated; he obviously did not like to answer foolish questions. "Because my left leg is paralyzed!" he snapped.

Mr. V. clearly knew what his problem was, but he failed to understand its implications. He could verbally recognize his disability, but he was unable to grasp its significance. Thus, he blandly accepted the fact that he was confined to a wheelchair. The implications of his disability did not affect him emotionally or figure into his plans.

T he word *emotion* can mean several things. Most of the time, it refers to positive or negative feelings that are produced by particular situations. For example, being treated unfairly makes us angry, seeing someone suffer makes us sad, and being close to a loved one makes us feel happy. Emotions consist of patterns of physiological responses and species-typical behaviors. In humans these responses are accompanied by feelings. In fact, most of us use the word *emotion* to refer to the feelings, not to the behaviors. But it is behavior, and not private experience, that has consequences for survival and reproduction. Thus, the useful purposes served by emotional behaviors are what guided the evolution of our brain. The feelings that accompany these behaviors came rather late in the game.

This chapter is divided into three major sections. The first considers the patterns of behavioral and physiological responses that constitute the negative emotions of fear and anger. It describes the nature of these response patterns and their neural and hormonal control. The second section describes the communication of emotions—their expression and recognition. The third section examines the nature of the feelings that accompany emotions.

Emotions as Response Patterns

An emotional response consists of three types of components: behavioral, autonomic, and hormonal. The *behavioral* component consists of muscular movements that are appropriate to the situation that elicits them. For example, a dog defending its territory against an intruder first adopts an aggressive posture, growls, and shows its teeth. If the intruder does not leave, the defender runs toward it and attacks. *Autonomic* responses facilitate the behaviors and provide quick mobilization of energy for vigorous movement. In this example the activity of the sympathetic branch increases while that of the parasympathetic branch decreases. As a consequence, the dog's heart rate increases, and changes in the size of blood vessels shunt the circulation of blood away from the digestive organs toward the muscles. *Hormonal* responses reinforce the autonomic responses. The hormones secreted by the adrenal medulla—epinephrine and norepinephrine—further increase blood flow to the muscles and cause nutrients stored in the muscles to be converted into glucose.

In addition, the adrenal cortex secretes steroid hormones, which also help to make glucose available to the muscles.

This section discusses research on the control of overt emotional behaviors and the autonomic and hormonal responses that accompany them. Special behaviors that serve to communicate emotional states to other animals, such as the threat gestures that precede an actual attack and the smiles and frowns used by humans, are discussed in the second section of the chapter. As you will see, negative emotions receive much more attention than positive ones. Most of the research on the physiology of emotions has been confined to fear and anger—emotions associated with situations in which we must defend ourselves or our loved ones. The physiology of behaviors associated with positive emotions—such as those associated with lovemaking, caring for one's offspring, or enjoying a good meal or a cool drink of water (or an alcoholic beverage)—is described in other chapters but not in the specific context of emotions. And Chapter 17 discusses the consequences of situations that evoke negative emotions: stress.

Fear

As we saw, emotional responses involve behavioral, autonomic, and hormonal components. These components are controlled by separate neural systems. The *integration* of the components of fear appears to be controlled by the amygdala.

Research with Laboratory Animals

The amygdala plays a special role in physiological and behavioral reactions to objects and situations that have special biological significance, such as those that warn of pain or other unpleasant consequences or signify the presence of food, water, salt, potential mates or rivals, or infants in need of care. Researchers in several different laboratories have shown that single neurons in various nuclei of the amygdala become active when emotionally relevant stimuli are presented. For example, these neurons are excited by such stimuli as the sight of a device that has been used to squirt either a bad-tasting solution or a sweet solution into the animal's mouth, the sound of another animal's vocalization, the sound of the opening of the laboratory door, the smell of smoke, or the sight of another animal's face (O'Keefe and Bouma, 1969; Jacobs and McGinty, 1972; Rolls, 1982; Leonard et al., 1985). And as we have already seen in Chapter 10, the amygdala is involved in the effects of pheromones on reproductive physiology and behavior (including maternal behavior). This section describes research on the role of the amygdala in organizing emotional responses produced by aversive stimuli.

The amygdala (or more precisely, the *amygdaloid complex*) is located within the temporal lobes. It consists of sev-

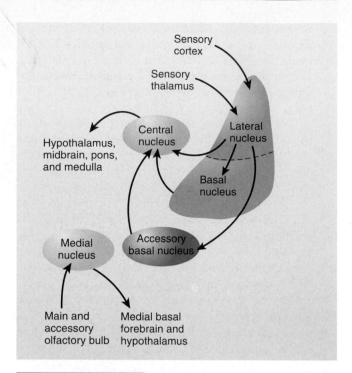

figure 11.1

A much-simplified diagram of the major divisions and connections of the amygdala that play a role in emotions.

eral groups of nuclei, each with different inputs and outputs—and with different functions (Amaral et al., 1992; Pitkaenen et al., 1997). The amygdala has been subdivided into approximately twelve regions, each containing several subregions. However, we need concern ourselves with just five major regions: the *medial nucleus*, the *lateral nucleus*, the *basal nucleus*, the *accessory basal nucleus*, and the *central nucleus*. The **medial nucleus** consists of several subnuclei that receive sensory input (including information about the presence of odors and pheromones) and relay the information to the medial basal forebrain and to the hypothalamus. Reproductive functions of the medial

medial nucleus A group of subnuclei of the amygdala that receives sensory input, including information about the presence of odors and pheromones, and relays it to the medial basal forebrain and hypothalamus.

lateral nucleus (LA) A nucleus of the amygdala that receives sensory information from the neocortex, thalamus, and hippocampus and send projections to the basal, accessory basal, and central nucleus of the amygdala.

central nucleus (CE) The region of the amygdala that receives information from the basal, lateral, and accessory basal nuclei and sends projections to a wide variety of regions in the brain; involved in emotional responses.

nucleus were discussed in Chapter 10. The **lateral nucleus (LA)** receives sensory information from the primary sensory cortex, association cortex, thalamus, and hippocampal formation. The lateral nucleus sends information to other parts of the brain, including the ventral striatum (a region involved in the effects of reinforcing stimuli on learning) and the dorsomedial nucleus of the thalamus, whose projection region is the prefrontal cortex. The lateral nucleus also sends information to the basal (B) and accessory basal (AB) nuclei. The LA, B, and AB nuclei all send information to the **central nucleus (CE),** which is the part of the amygdala that will most concern us in this chapter. The central nucleus projects to regions of the hypothalamus, midbrain, pons, and medulla that are responsible for the expression of the various components of emotional responses. As we will see, activation of the central nucleus elicits a variety of emotional responses: behavioral, autonomic, and hormonal. (See *Figure 11.1.*)

The central nucleus of the amygdala is the single most important part of the brain for the expression of emotional responses provoked by aversive stimuli. When threatening stimuli are presented, both the neural activity of the central nucleus and the production of Fos protein increase (Pascoe and Kapp, 1985; Campeau et al., 1991). Damage to the central nucleus (or to the nuclei that provide it with sensory information) reduces or abolishes a wide range of emotional behaviors and physiological responses. After the central nucleus has been destroyed, animals no longer show signs of fear when confronted with stimuli that have been paired with aversive events. They also act more tamely when handled by humans, their blood levels of stress hormones are lower, and they are less likely to develop ulcers or other forms of stress-induced illnesses (Coover, Murison, and Jellestad, 1992; Davis, 1992b; LeDoux, 1992). In contrast, when the central amygdala is stimulated by means of electricity or by an injection of an excitatory amino acid, the animal shows physiological and behavioral signs of fear and agitation (Davis, 1992b), and long-term stimulation of the central nucleus produces stress-induced illnesses such as gastric ulcers (Henke, 1982). These observations suggest that the autonomic and endocrine responses controlled by the central nucleus are among those responsible for the harmful effects of long-term stress, which are discussed in Chapter 17.

As we saw earlier, neurons in the central nucleus of the amygdala send axons to regions of the brain that are responsible for the expression of the various components of emotional responses. Rather than describe each of these regions and the responses they control, I will refer you to Figure 11.2, which summarizes them. (See *Figure 11.2.*)

The central nucleus of the amygdala is particularly important for aversive emotional learning. A few stimuli automatically produce fear reactions—for example, loud

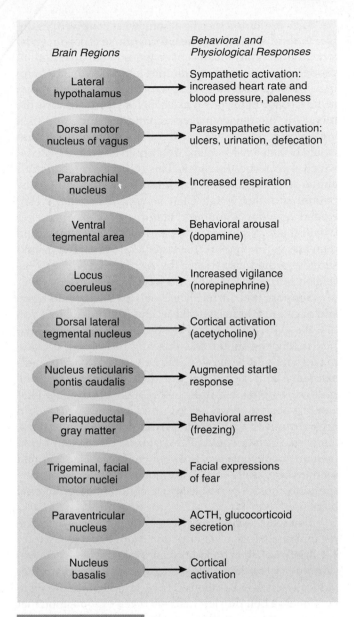

Brain Regions	Behavioral and Physiological Responses
Lateral hypothalamus	Sympathetic activation: increased heart rate and blood pressure, paleness
Dorsal motor nucleus of vagus	Parasympathetic activation: ulcers, urination, defecation
Parabrachial nucleus	Increased respiration
Ventral tegmental area	Behavioral arousal (dopamine)
Locus coeruleus	Increased vigilance (norepinephrine)
Dorsal lateral tegmental nucleus	Cortical activation (acetycholine)
Nucleus reticularis pontis caudalis	Augmented startle response
Periaqueductal gray matter	Behavioral arrest (freezing)
Trigeminal, facial motor nuclei	Facial expressions of fear
Paraventricular nucleus	ACTH, glucocorticoid secretion
Nucleus basalis	Cortical activation

figure 11.2

Some important brain regions that receive input from the central nucleus of the amygdala and the emotional responses controlled by these regions.

(Adapted from Davis, M., *Trends in Pharmacological Sciences*, 1992, *13*, 35–41.)

unexpected noises, the approach of large animals, heights, or (for some species) specific sounds or odors. Even more important, however, is the fact that we can *learn* that a particular situation is dangerous or threatening. Once the learning has taken place, we will become frightened when we encounter that situation. Our heart rate and blood pressure will increase, our muscles will become more tense, our adrenal glands will secrete epinephrine, and we will proceed cautiously, alert and ready to respond.

Let's examine a specific (if somewhat contrived) example. A **conditioned emotional response** is produced by a neutral stimulus that has been paired with an emotion-producing stimulus. For example, suppose you are helping a friend prepare a meal. You pick up an electric mixer to mix some batter for a cake. Before you can turn the mixer on, the device makes a sputtering noise and then gives you a painful electrical shock. Your first response would be a defensive reflex: You would let go of the mixer, which would end the shock. This response is *specific;* it is aimed at terminating the painful stimulus. In addition, the painful stimulus would elicit *nonspecific* responses controlled by your autonomic nervous system: Your eyes would dilate, your heart rate and blood pressure would increase, you would breathe faster, and so on. The painful stimulus would also trigger the secretion of some stress-related hormones, another nonspecific response.

Suppose that a while later you visit your friend again and once more agree to make a cake. Your friend tells you that the electric mixer is perfectly safe. It has been fixed. Just seeing the mixer and thinking of holding it again makes you a little nervous, but you accept your friend's assurance and pick it up. Just then, it makes the same sputtering noise that it did when it shocked you. What would your response be? Almost certainly, you would drop the mixer again, even if it did not give you a shock. And your pupils would dilate, your heart rate and blood pressure would increase, and your endocrine glands would secrete some stress-related hormones. In other words, the sputtering sound would trigger a conditioned emotional response.

The word *conditioned* refers to the process of *classical conditioning,* which is described in more detail in Chapter 13. Briefly, classical conditioning occurs when a neutral stimulus is regularly followed by a stimulus that automatically evokes a response. For example, if a dog regularly hears a bell ring just before it receives some food that makes it salivate, it will begin salivating as soon as it hears the sound of the bell. (You probably already know that this phenomenon was discovered by Ivan Pavlov.)

If an organism learns to make a specific response that avoids contact with the aversive stimulus (or at least minimizes its painful effect), most of the nonspecific "emotional" responses will eventually disappear. That is, if the organism learns a successful **coping response**—a response that terminates, avoids, or minimizes an aversive stimulus—the emotional responses will no longer occur. For example, suppose you suspect that your friend's electric mixer is still defective but you are determined to make the cake anyway. You get your gloves from the pocket of your overcoat and put them on. Now you can safely handle the mixer; the gloves provide electrical insulation for your hands. This time the sputtering noise does not bother you because you are protected from electrical shocks. The noise does not activate your autonomic nervous system

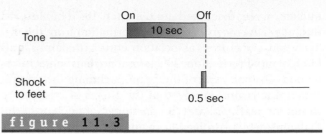

The procedure used to produce conditioned emotional responses.

(at least, not very much), nor does it cause your glands to secrete stress-related hormones.

Several laboratories have investigated the role of the central nucleus of the amygdala in the development of classically conditioned emotional responses. For example, LeDoux and his colleagues have studied these responses in rats by pairing an auditory stimulus with a brief electrical shock delivered to the feet (reviewed by LeDoux, 1995). In their studies they presented an 800-Hz tone for 10 sec, and then they delivered a brief (0.5-sec) shock to the floor on which the animals were standing. (See *Figure 11.3.*) By itself the shock produces an *unconditional* emotional response: The animal jumps into the air, its heart rate and blood pressure increase, its breathing becomes more rapid, and its adrenal glands secrete catecholamines and steroid stress hormones. The experimenters presented several pairings of the two stimuli, which established classical conditioning.

The investigators tested conditioned emotional responses the next day by presenting the 800-Hz tone several times and measuring the animals' blood pressure and heart rate and observing their behavior. (This time, they did not present the shock.) Upon hearing the tone, the rats showed the same type of physiological responses as they had when they were shocked the previous day. In addition, they showed behavioral arrest—a species-typical defensive response called *freezing.* That is, the animals acted as if they were expecting to receive a shock.

LeDoux and his colleagues have shown that the central nucleus is necessary for the development of a conditioned emotional response (LeDoux, 1995). If this nucleus is destroyed, conditioning does not take place. In addition, LeDoux et al. (1988) destroyed two regions that receive projections from the central nucleus: the lateral hypothalamus

conditioned emotional response A classically conditioned response that occurs when a neutral stimulus is followed by an aversive stimulus; usually includes autonomic, behavioral, and endocrine components such as changes in heart rate, freezing, and secretion of stress-related hormones.

coping response A response through which an organism can avoid, escape from, or minimize an aversive stimulus; reduces the stressful effects of an aversive stimulus.

and the caudal periaqueductal gray matter. They found that lesions of the lateral hypothalamus interfered with the change in blood pressure, whereas lesions of the periaqueductal gray matter interfered with the freezing response. Thus, two different mechanisms, both under the control of the central nucleus of the amygdala, are responsible for the autonomic and behavioral components of conditioned emotional responses. (As you saw in Figure 11.2, activation of the central nucleus produces many other responses, but not all of them have been studied in this situation.)

Although most of the experiments investigating the role of the central nucleus of the amygdala in conditioned emotional responses have used auditory stimuli, results from studies using stimuli of other sensory modalities are consistent with the ones I have reviewed. For example, lesions of the central nucleus disrupt conditioned responses evoked by visual or olfactory stimuli that have been paired with a foot shock, and they make an animal act less timid in a strange environment (Hitchcock and Davis, 1986; Sananes and Campbell, 1989; Grijalva et al., 1990). By the way, timidity in a strange environment is a useful trait; animals that enter an unfamiliar place boldly and heedlessly might find something awaiting them that will end their opportunity to contribute to the gene pool.

Research on the details of the physical changes responsible for classical conditioning—including the role of the central nucleus of the amygdala—has provided some interesting information about the physiology of learning and memory. This research will be discussed in more detail in Chapter 13.

Some of the effects of anxiolytic (anxiety-reducing) drugs appear to be produced through the central nucleus. The amygdala contains a high concentration of benzodiazepine receptors, especially the regions that project to the central nucleus, and the central nucleus itself contains a high concentration of opiate receptors. The infusion of either opiates or benzodiazepine tranquilizers into the amygdala decreases both the learning and the expression of conditioned emotional responses (Kapp et al., 1982; Davis, 1992a). In addition, Sanders and Shekhar (1995) found that an injection of a benzodiazepine antagonist into the amygdala blocked the anxiolytic effects of an intraperitoneal injection of chlordiazepoxide (*Librium*). Thus, tranquilizers and opiates appear to exert their anxiolytic effect in the amygdala. It is possible that some other regions of the brain are also involved in the effects of these drugs; Yadin et al. (1991) found that even after the amygdala is destroyed, benzodiazepines still have some anxiolytic effect.

As we will see in Chapter 17, some evidence suggests that increased activity of the neural mechanisms described in this section are associated with a fairly common category of psychological disorders: the *anxiety disorders*. Some investigators have suggested that anxiety disorders are caused by hyperactivity of the central nucleus of the amygdala, perhaps as a result of increased secretion of endogenous anxiety-producing ligands for the $GABA_A$ receptor, of which the benzodiazepine receptor is a part. Whether the primary cause of the increased anxiety lies within these circuits or elsewhere in the brain (or in people's environments and past histories) has yet to be determined.

Research with Humans

A considerable amount of evidence indicates that the amygdala is involved in emotional responses in humans. One of the earliest studies observed the reactions of people who were being evaluated for surgical removal of parts of the brain to treat severe seizure disorders. These studies found that stimulation of parts of the brain (for example, the hypothalamus) produced autonomic responses that are often associated with fear and anxiety but that only when the amygdala was stimulated did people also report that they actually felt afraid (White, 1940; Halgren et al., 1978; Gloor et al., 1982).

Lesions of the amygdala decrease people's emotional responses. Two studies (LaBar et al., 1995; Bechara et al., 1995) found that people with lesions of the amygdala showed impaired acquisition of a conditioned emotional response, just as rats do. Angrilli et al. (1996) found that the startle response of a man with a localized lesion of the right amygdala was not augmented by an unpleasant emotion. Normally, a person's startle response, elicited by a sudden noise, is larger when the person looks at unpleasant photos than when he or she looks at neutral ones. Presumably, the augmentation is produced by the negative emotion elicited by the unpleasant scene. Angrilli and his colleagues did not observe this effect in their patient—The man showed the same startle response regardless of the nature of the photographs.

Damage to the amygdala interferes with the effects of emotions on memory. Normally, when people encounter events that produce a strong emotional response, they are more likely to remember these events. Cahill et al. (1995) studied a patient with bilateral degeneration of the amygdala. The investigators narrated a story about a young boy walking with his mother on his way to visit his father at work. To accompany the story, they showed a series of slides. During one part of the story, the boy was injured in a traffic accident, and gruesome slides illustrated his injuries. When this slide show is presented to normal subjects, they remember more details from the emotion-laden part of the story. However, a patient with amygdala damage showed no such increase in memory. Another study (Mori et al., 1999) questioned patients with Alzheimer's disease who had witnessed the devastating earthquake that struck Kobe, Japan, in 1955. They found that memory of this frightening event was inversely correlated with amygdala damage: The more a patient's amygdala was degenerated, the less likely it was that the patient remembered the earthquake.

Several imaging studies have shown that the human amygdala participates in emotional responses. For example, Cahill et al. (1996) had people watch both neutral and

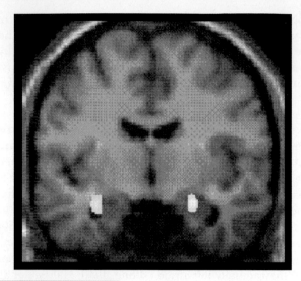

figure 11.4

An averaged PET scan from a group of people while looking at threatening words. The scan shows increased activity in the amygdala.

(From Isenberg, N., Silbersweig, D., Engelien, A., Emmerich, S., Malavade, K., Beattie, B., Leon, A. C., and Stern, E. *Proceedings of the National Academy of Sciences, USA,* 1999, *96,* 10456–10459.)

emotionally arousing films (such as scenes of violent crimes). Later, the experimenters placed the subjects in a PET scanner and asked them to recall the films. The activity of the right amygdala increased while the subjects recalled the emotionally arousing films but not when they recalled the neutral ones. In addition, the subjects were most likely to recall the emotionally arousing films that produced the highest level of activity in the right amygdala when they were originally viewed. Schneider et al. (1996) had people attempt to solve anagrams (rearrangements of scrambled words into sentences). Some of the anagrams could be solved relatively easily, but others were actually impossible to solve. When well-motivated people work on such tasks, they tend to become tense and unhappy and usually report feelings of frustration. A PET scanner showed that the blood flow in the amygdala increased while the subjects were working on the unsolvable anagrams but not while they worked on the solvable ones.

In another PET study, Isenberg et al. (1999) found that seeing words that denote threatening situations increases the activity of the amygdala. The investigators had people look at words presented in various colors on a computer screen. Some of the words were neutral (e. g., list, dial, wheel, label, bookcase, spin, cups, repeat), and some were threatening (e. g., slaughter, prisoner, evil, rape, knife, suffer, mutilate, danger). The subjects were not asked to read the words, but simply to name the color of the letters. Seeing the threatening words (but not the neutral ones) caused a bilateral increase in the activity of the amygdala. (See *Figure 11.4.*)

Anger and Aggression

Almost all species of animals engage in aggressive behaviors, which involve threatening gestures or actual attack directed toward another animal. Aggressive behaviors are species-typical; that is, the patterns of movements (for example, posturing, biting, striking, and hissing) are organized by neural circuits whose development is largely programmed by an animal's genes. Many aggressive behaviors are related to reproduction. For example, aggressive behaviors that gain access to mates, defend territory needed to attract mates or to provide a site for building a nest, or defend offspring against intruders can all be regarded as reproductive behaviors. Other aggressive behaviors are related to self-defense, such as that of an animal threatened by a predator.

Aggressive behavior can consist of actual attacks, or they may simply involve **threat behaviors,** which consist of postures or gestures that warn the adversary to leave or it will become the target of an attack. The threatened animal might show **defensive behaviors**—threat behaviors or an actual attack against the animal that is threatening it—or it might show **submissive behaviors**—behaviors that indicate that it accepts defeat and will not challenge the other animal. In the natural environment most animals display far more threats than actual attacks. Threat behaviors are useful in reinforcing social hierarchies in organized groups of animals or in warning intruders away from an animal's territory. They have the advantage of not involving actual fighting, which can harm one or both of the combatants.

Predation is the attack of a member of one species on that of another, usually because the latter serves as food for the former. While engaged in attacking a member of the same species or defending oneself against the attack, an animal appears to be extremely aroused and excited, and the activity of the sympathetic branch of its autonomic nervous system is high. In contrast, the attack of a predator is much more "cold-blooded"; it is generally efficient and not accompanied by a high level of sympathetic activation.

threat behavior A stereotypical species-typical behavior that warns another animal that it may be attacked if it does not flee or show a submissive behavior.

defensive behavior A species-typical behavior by which an animal defends itself against the threat of another animal.

submissive behavior A stereotyped behavior shown by an animal in response to threat behavior by another animal; serves to prevent an attack.

predation Attack of one animal directed at an individual of another species on which the attacking animal normally preys.

Research with Laboratory Animals

■ **Neural Control of Aggressive Behavior** The neural control of aggressive behavior is hierarchical. That is, the particular muscular movements an animal makes in attacking or defending itself are programmed by neural circuits in the brain stem. Whether an animal attacks depends on many factors, including the nature of the eliciting stimuli in the environment and the animal's previous experience. The activity of the brain stem circuits appears to be controlled by the hypothalamus and the amygdala, which also influence many other species-typical behaviors. And, of course, the activity of the limbic system is controlled by perceptual systems that detect the status of the environment, including the presence of other animals.

Both defensive behavior and predation can be elicited by stimulating the periaqueductal gray matter (PAG) of a cat's midbrain. It might seem surprising that a cat should need any special treatment to induce it to attack a rat, but most laboratory cats do *not* spontaneously attack rats. During a defensive display, a cat turns sideways and arches its back, and its fur stands on end, making the animal look larger. It also flattens its ears, unsheathes its claws, and growls and hisses. A predatory attack is directed against a small animal such as a rat. Predation is not accompanied by a strong display of rage. A cat stalks a rat and suddenly pounces on it, directing powerful bites to the head and neck region. The cat does not growl or scream, and it stops attacking once the rat ceases to move. Although a cat looks excited when it pounces on a rat and bites it, it does not show signs of "rage." The attack appears cold-blooded and ruthless.

A series of studies by Shaikh, Siegel, and their colleagues (reviewed by Siegel et al., 1999) investigated the neural circuitry involved in defensive behavior and predation in cats. The investigators placed electrodes in various regions of the brain and observed the effects of electrical stimulation of these regions on the animals' behavior. In some cases the electrode was actually a stainless-steel cannula, coated with an insulating material except for the tip. These devices (called *cannula electrodes*) could be used to infuse chemicals into the brain as well as to stimulate it. The investigators found that defensive behavior and predation can be elicited by stimulation of different parts of the PAG and that the hypothalamus and the amygdala influence these behaviors through excitatory and inhibitory connections with the PAG. They found that the three principal regions of the amygdala and two regions of the hypothalamus affect defensive rage and predation, both of which appear to be organized by the PAG. (They assessed predation by presenting the cats with an anesthetized rat, so no pain was inflicted.) A possible connection between the lateral hypothalamus and the ventral PAG has not yet been verified. Rather than list the connections and their effects, I will direct you to *Figure 11.5*.

■ **Role of Serotonin** An overwhelming amount of evidence suggests that the activity of serotonergic synapses inhibits aggression. In contrast, destruction of serotonergic axons in the forebrain facilitates aggressive attack, presumably by removing an inhibitory effect (Vergnes et al., 1988).

A group of researchers has studied the relationship between serotonergic activity and aggressiveness in a free-ranging colony of rhesus monkeys (Mehlman et al., 1995; Higley et al., 1996a, 1996b). They assessed serotonergic activity by capturing the monkeys, removing a sample of cerebrospinal fluid, and analyzing it for 5-HIAA, a metabolite of serotonin (5-HT). When 5-HT is released, most of the neurotransmitter is taken back into the terminal buttons by means of reuptake, but some escapes and is

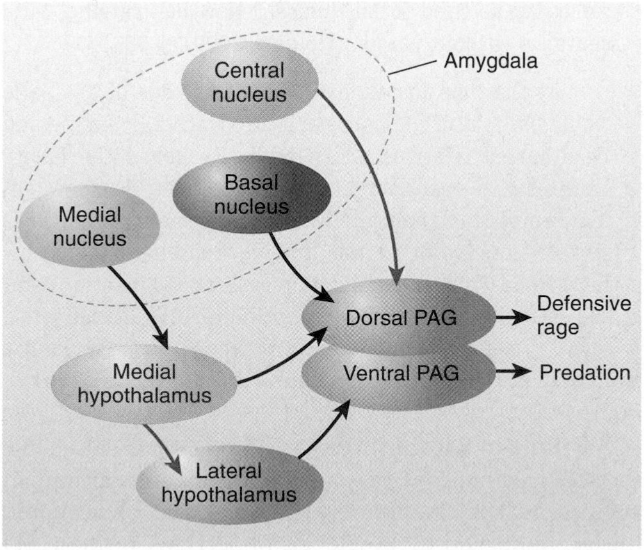

figure 11.5

Results of the studies by Shaikh, Siegel, and their colleagues. The diagram shows interconnections of parts of the amygdala, hypothalamus, and periaqueductal gray matter and their effects on defensive rage and predation in cats. Black arrows indicate excitation; red arrows indicate inhibition.

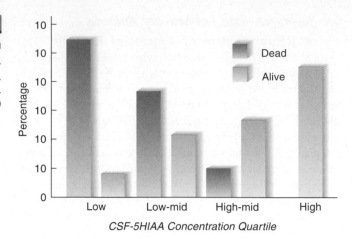

figure   11.6

Percentage of young male monkeys alive or dead as a function of 5-HIAA level in the CSF, measured four years previously.
(Adapted from Higley, J. D., Mehlman, P. T., Higley, S. B., Fernald, B., Vickers, J., Lindell, S. G., Taub, D. M., Suomi, S. J., and Linnoila, M., *Archives of General Psychiatry*, 1996, *53*, 537–543.)

broken down to 5-HIAA, which finds its way into the cerebrospinal fluid. Thus, high levels of 5-HIAA in the CSF indicates an elevated level of serotonergic activity. The investigators found that young male monkeys with the lowest levels of 5-HIAA showed a pattern of risk-taking behavior, including high levels of aggression directed toward animals that were older and much larger than themselves. They were much more likely to take dangerous unprovoked long leaps from tree to tree at a height of more than 7 m (27.6 ft). They were also more likely to pick fights that they could not possibly win. Of 49 preadolescent male monkeys that the investigators followed for four years, 46 percent of those with the lowest 5-HIAA levels died, while all of the monkeys with the highest levels survived. (See *Figure 11.6.*) Most of the monkeys were killed by other monkeys. In fact, the first monkey to be killed had the lowest level of 5-HIAA and was seen attacking two mature males the night before his death.

It is clear that serotonin does not simply inhibit aggression; rather, it exerts a controlling influence on risky behavior, which includes aggression. A study by Raleigh et al. (1991) removed the dominant male from each of several groups of vervet monkeys and treated the top two remaining males with serotonergic drugs: One received an agonist, and the other received an antagonist. The monkeys that received the serotonin agonist became dominant, while the status of those that received the antagonist declined. You might think that removing some inhibitory control over aggressiveness would increase a monkey's dominance. However, dominance and aggression are not synonymous. Certainly, a dominant animal will use aggression if it is overtly challenged by a rival. However, becoming the dominant animal in a group of monkeys requires good social skills. As Mehlman et al. (1995) noted in their naturalistic study, the monkeys with low levels of serotonergic activity showed the lowest levels of social competency.

Several studies with targeted mutations in mice confirm the conclusion that serotonin has an inhibitory role

in aggression. For example, Saudou et al. (1994) and Bouwknecht et al. (2001) found that mice lacking 5-HT$_{1B}$ receptors attacked an intruder more quickly and intensely than normal mice, but otherwise, their behavior appeared normal.

Research with Humans

Human violence and aggression are serious social problems. Consider the following case histories:

Born to an alcoholic teen mother who raised him with an abusive alcoholic stepfather, Steve was hyperactive, irritable, and disobedient as a toddler. . . . After dropping out of school at age 14, Steve spent his teen years fighting, stealing, taking drugs, and beating up girlfriends. . . . School counseling, a probation officer, and meetings with child protective service failed to forestall disaster: At 19, several weeks after his last interview with researchers, Steve visited a girlfriend who had recently dumped him, found her with another man, and shot him to death. The same day he tried to kill himself. Now he's serving a life sentence without parole. (Holden, 2000, p. 580)

By the time Joshua had reached the age of 2, . . . he would bolt out of the house and into traffic. He kicked and head-butted relatives and friends. He poked the family hamster with a pencil and tried to strangle it. He threw regular temper tantrums and would stage toy-throwing frenzies. "At one point he was hurting himself—banging his head against a wall, pinching himself, not to mention leaping off the refrigerator. . . . Showering Joshua with love . . . made little difference: By age 3, his behavior got him kicked out of his preschool. (Holden, 2000, p. 581)

■ **Role of Serotonin**   Several studies have found that serotonergic neurons play an inhibitory role in human aggression. For example, a depressed rate of serotonin release (indicated by low levels of 5-HIAA in the CSF) are associated with aggression and other forms of antisocial behavior, including assault, arson, murder, and child beating (Lidberg et al., 1984, 1985; Virkkunen et al, 1989). Coccaro et al. (1994) studied a group of men with personality disorders (including a history of impulsive aggression). They found that the men with the lowest serotonergic activity were most likely to have close relatives with a history of similar behavior problems.

If low levels of serotonin release contribute to aggression, perhaps drugs that act as serotonin agonists might help to reduce antisocial behavior. In fact, a study by Coccaro and Kavoussi (1997) found that fluoxetine (Prozac), a serotonin agonist, decreased irritability and aggressiveness, as measured by a psychological test. Joshua, the little boy described in the introduction to this subsection came under the care of a psychiatrist who prescribed monoaminergic agonists and began a course of behavior therapy that managed to stem Joshua's violent outbursts and risk-taking behaviors.

A functional imaging study by Hariri et al. (2002) found an association between differences in the genes responsible for production of serotonin transporters and the reaction of people's amygdala to the viewing of facial expressions of negative emotions. The serotonin transporter gene has two common alleles, one long and one short. People who carry at least one short allele are slightly more likely to show higher levels of anxiety or develop an affective disorder such as depression (Lesch and Mossner, 1998). Hariri and his colleagues had people look at sets of three faces expressing fear or anger. Their task was to decide which of the two faces at the left and right of the display matched the expression of the face in the middle. (See *Figure 11.7a.*) The investigators found that the right amygdala of people carrying the short form of the serotonin transporter gene showed a higher rate of activity during this task. (See *Figure 11.7b.*) Just why the different alleles influence the reactivity of the amygdala to emotional stimuli is not yet known.

■ **Role of the Prefrontal Cortex** Many investigators believe that impulsive violence is a consequence of faulty emotional regulation. For most of us, frustrations may elicit an urge to respond emotionally, but we manage to calm ourselves and suppress these urges. As we shall see, the prefrontal cortex plays an important role in recognizing the emotional significance of complex social situations and in regulating our responses to such situations. The analysis of social situations involves much more than sensory analysis; it involves experiences and memories, inferences and judgments. In fact, the skills involved include some of the most complex ones we possess. These skills are not localized in any one part of the cerebral cortex, although research does suggest that the right hemisphere is more important than the left. But one region of

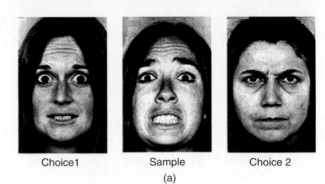

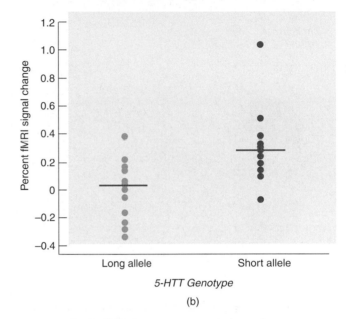

figure 11.7

Procedure and results of the study by Hariri et al. (2002). (a) The matching task. Subjects chose the face at the left or right of the display that had the same expression (anger or fear) as the one in the middle. (b) Relative activity of the right amygdala during performance of the task, of people with the short and long alleles of the serotonin transporter gene, as measured by fMRI.
(Adapted from Hariri, A. R., Mattay, V. S., Tessitore, A., Kolachana, B., Fera, F., Goldman, D., Egan, M. F., and Weinberger, D. R. *Science*, 2002, *297*, 400–403.)

the prefrontal cortex—the orbitofrontal cortex—plays a special role.

The **orbitofrontal cortex** is located at the base of the frontal lobes. It covers the part of the brain just above the *orbits*—the bones that form the eye sockets—hence the term

orbitofrontal cortex The region of the prefrontal cortex at the base of the anterior frontal lobes.

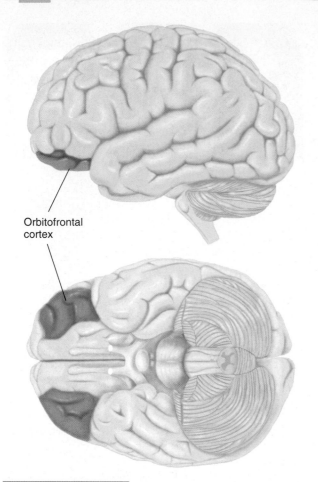

Orbitofrontal
cortex

The orbitofrontal cortex.

orbitofrontal. (See ***Figure 11.8***.) The orbitofrontal cortex receives direct inputs from the dorsomedial thalamus, temporal cortex, ventral tegmental area, olfactory system, and amygdala. Its outputs go to several brain regions, including the cingulate cortex, hippocampal formation, temporal cortex, lateral hypothalamus, and amygdala. Finally, it communicates with other regions of the frontal cortex. Thus, its inputs provide it with information about what is happening in the environment and what plans are being made by the rest of the frontal lobes, and its outputs permit it to affect a variety of behaviors and physiological responses, including emotional responses organized by the amygdala.

The fact that the orbitofrontal cortex plays an important role in control of emotional behavior is shown by the effects of damage to this region. The first—and most famous—case comes from the mid-1800s. Phineas Gage, the foreman of a railway construction crew, was using a steel rod to ram a charge of blasting powder into a hole drilled in solid rock. Suddenly, the charge exploded and sent the rod into his cheek, through his brain, and out the top of his head.

(See ***Figure 11.9***.) He survived, but he was a different man. Before his injury he was serious, industrious, and energetic. Afterward, he became childish, irresponsible, and thoughtless of others. His outbursts of temper led some people to remark that it looked as if Dr. Jekyll had become Mr. Hyde. He was unable to make or carry out plans, and his actions appeared to be capricious and whimsical. His accident largely destroyed the orbitofrontal cortex (Damasio et al., 1994).

What, exactly, does the orbitofrontal cortex do? Evidence suggests that it serves as in interface between brain mechanisms involved in automatic emotional responses (both learned and unlearned) and those involved in the control of complex behaviors. This role includes using our emotional reactions to guide our behavior and in controlling the occurrence of emotional reactions in various social situations.

People whose orbitofrontal cortex has been damaged by disease or accident are still able to accurately assess the significance of particular situations, but only in a *theoretical* sense. For example, Eslinger and Damasio (1985) found that a patient with bilateral damage of the orbitofrontal cortex (produced by a benign tumor, which was successfully removed) displayed excellent social judgment. When he was given hypothetical situations that required him to make decisions about what the people involved should do—situations involving moral, ethical, or practical dilemmas—he always gave sensible answers and justified them with carefully reasoned logic. However, his own life was a different matter. He frittered away his life's savings on investments that his family and friends pointed out were bound to fail. He lost one job after another because of his irresponsibility. He became unable to distinguish between trivial decisions and important ones, spending hours trying to decide where to have dinner but failing to use good judgment in situations that concerned his occupation and family life. (His wife finally left him and sued for divorce.) As the authors noted, "He had learned and used normal patterns of social behavior before his brain lesion, and although he could recall such patterns when he was questioned about their applicability, *real-life situations failed to evoke them*" (p. 1737). Thus, it appears that the orbitofrontal cortex is not directly involved in making judgments and conclusions about events (these occur elsewhere in the brain); rather, it is involved in translating these judgments into appropriate feelings and behaviors.

Mr. V., described in the opener to this chapter, had brain damage that impaired his judgment without affecting traditional measures of verbal intelligence. This damage included the right frontal and parietal lobes, so we cannot attribute his symptoms to any single region.

A series of experiments by Bechara et al. (1997, 1999) explored the poor judgment shown by patients with ven-

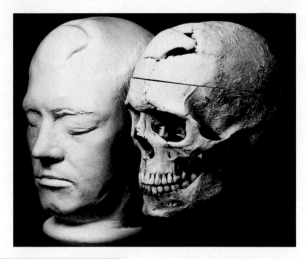

A bust and skull of Phineas Gage. The steel rod entered his left cheek and exited through his left forehead.
(From Warren Museum, Harvard Medical School. Reprinted with permission.)

tromedial prefrontal lesions (including the orbitofrontal cortex). The investigators had subjects play a gambling card game. The subjects received a stake of $2000 (in play money) and were instructed to try to win as much as possible. They were to draw cards, one at a time, from four decks. Two of the decks were "bad"; they contained many cards that awarded the players with $100 dollars, but they also contained several that took much larger amounts from them. The other two decks were "good"; although most of the cards they contained gave the players only $50, their penalty cards demanded relatively small sums. If the players chose cards from only the "good" decks, they would gain money in the long run, but if they chose them from the "bad" decks, they would lose.

Several interesting results emerged. After playing for a while, normal subjects showed changes in skin conductance (a measure of emotional stress) just before they chose a card from a "bad" deck. Once this response began to occur, the subjects started shifting their strategy, choosing from the "good" decks more often. At this point some of them said that they got a bad feeling just before they chose a card from one of the "bad" decks. In other words, they let their emotional response guide their choice behavior. However, subjects with prefrontal lesions did not show signs of stress before choosing cards from the "bad" decks, although they did show these autonomic changes *after* choosing a card that cost them money. A group of subjects with amygdala lesions failed to show emotional changes either before or after choosing a card from one of the "bad" decks.

The investigators suggest that emotional responses often provide an important element in making decisions.

When we contemplate a choice that has previously resulted in a bad outcome, an unpleasant emotional response is evoked, and this response warns us away from that choice. In fact, the normal subjects in these experiments started following this emotional warning before they were conscious of the fact that two of the decks should be avoided. Prefrontal lesions (and lesions of the amygdala, too), seem to prevent this anticipatory emotional response, and subjects blunder on despite the fact that their choices are producing bad results.

Two functional imaging studies (Rogers et al., 1999; Ernst et al., 2002) found that the prefrontal cortex (including the orbitofrontal cortex) became active while the subjects were participating in decision making during gambling games. Another gambling study, by Gehring and Willoughby (2002), found that the medial prefrontal cortex was activated when subjects lost money and not when they simply made an error. For example, if they made the correct choice and lost only 5 cents instead of 25 cents, the medial prefrontal cortex was activated. On the other hand, if they made the wrong choice and won only 5 cents instead of 25 cents, this region was *not* activated. Thus, the region appeared to monitor whether something good or bad happened and not whether the person made the correct choice.

Blair, Colledge, and Mitchell (2001) demonstrated an interesting association between tendencies for antisocial behavior and decisions involving risks and rewards. They found that boys with psychopathic tendencies performed poorly on the card gambling card game used by Bechara et al. Perhaps a decreased sensitivity to unpleasant outcomes are responsible for both the poor gambling behavior and the failure to avoid behaviors with adverse outcomes. A possible cause of this decreased sensitivity could be damage to or inadequate development of the prefrontal cortex. In fact, Raine et al. (2000) found that people with antisocial personality disorder showed an 11 percent reduction in volume of the gray matter of the prefrontal cortex.

Evidence suggests that emotional reactions guide moral judgments as well as decisions involving personal risks and rewards and that the prefrontal cortex plays a role in these judgments as well. Consider the following moral dilemma: You see a runaway trolley with five people aboard hurtling down a track leading to a cliff. Without your intervention, these people will soon die. However, you are standing near a switch that will shunt the trolley off to another track, where the vehicle will stop safely. But a worker is standing on that track, and he will be killed if you throw the switch to save the five helpless passengers. Should you stand by and watch the trolley go off the cliff, or should you save them—and kill the man on the track?

Most people conclude that the better choice would be to throw the switch; saving five people justifies the sacrifice of one man. But consider a variation of this dilemma.

As before, the trolley is hurtling toward doom, but there is no switch at hand to shunt it to another track. Instead, you are standing on a bridge over the track. An obese man is standing there too, and if you give him a push, his body will fall on the track and stop the trolley. (You are too small to stop the trolley, so you cannot save the five people by sacrificing yourself.) What should you do?

Most people balk at pushing the man off the bridge, even though the result would be the same as the first dilemma: one person lost, five people saved. Whether we kill someone by sending a trolley his way or by pushing him off a bridge into the path of an oncoming trolley, he dies when the trolley strikes him. But somehow pushing a person's body and causing his death seems more emotionally wrenching than throwing a switch that changes the course of a runaway trolley. Thus, moral judgments appear to be guided by emotional reactions and are not simply the products of rational, logical decision-making processes.

In a functional imaging study, Greene et al. (2001) presented people with the moral dilemmas such as the one I just described and found that thinking about them activated several brain regions involved in emotional reactions, including the medial prefrontal cortex. (Making innocuous decisions, such as whether to take a bus or train to some destination, did not activate these regions.) Perhaps, then, our reluctance to push someone to his death is guided by the emotional reaction we feel when we contemplate this action.

If the prefrontal cortex helps to mediate the role of emotions in moral judgments, then damage to this area should impair such judgments. As we saw, tendencies toward antisocial behavior are apparently associated with decreased volume of the prefrontal cortex. Anderson et al. (1999) found that two adults who had sustained damage to the prefrontal cortex during infancy showed the insensitivity to the probable consequences of their behavior, as many other studies have shown. However, in addition, they showed defective social and moral reasoning—which is generally not seen in people who sustain prefrontal damage later in life. The authors suggest that people learn to make social and moral judgments early in life and that these judgments are based in part on their own emotional reactions. If prefrontal damage occurs early in life, people never learn to incorporate their emotional reactions in their decision-making process.

It might seem that I have been getting away from the topic of this section: anger and aggression. However, recall that many investigators believe that impulsive violence is a consequence of faulty emotional regulation. The amygdala plays an important role in provoking anger and violent emotional reactions, and the prefrontal cortex plays an important role in suppressing such behavior by making us see its negative consequences. Let's look at some evidence. A functional imaging study by Dougherty et al. (1999) found that when subjects read and thought about stories from their own lives that had made them angry, they became angry again, and their orbitofrontal cortex and medial prefrontal cortex became activated. As we saw earlier, antisocial behavior may be associated with decreased volume of the prefrontal cortex; thus, activation of the prefrontal cortex may reflect its role in inhibiting aggressive behavior. Another functional imaging study (Amen et al., 1996) found evidence of decreased activity in the prefrontal cortex of adolescents and adults with a history of physical attacks on other people or destruction of property. Raine et al. (1998) found evidence of decreased prefrontal activity and increased subcortical activity (including the amygdala) in the brains of convicted murderers. These changes were primarily seen in impulsive, emotional murderers. Cold-blooded, calculating, predatory murderers—whose crimes were not accompanied by anger and rage—showed more normal prefrontal activity. Presumably, increased activation of the amygdala reflected an increased tendency for display of negative emotions, and the decreased activation of the prefrontal cortex reflected a decreased ability to control one's emotions.

There is some evidence that the prefrontal cortex is involved in control of emotions other than anger. For example, in a functional imaging study, Beauregard, Lévesque, and Bourgouin (2001) showed erotic films to normal, healthy men. Under one condition, the subjects were told to react normally—to allow themselves to become sexually aroused in response to the films. Under this condition, the films did indeed produce sexual arousal, which was accompanied by activation of various regions of the limbic system, including the amygdala and the hypothalamus. Under another condition, the subjects were told to inhibit their emotional reaction—to distance themselves from the films and act like detached observers. Under this condition, the subjects did not become sexually aroused, and the limbic system did *not* become activated. However, the prefrontal cortex became activated. Presumably, this activation reflected the successful attempts of the subjects to inhibit their emotional reaction to the erotic films.

In an earlier section of this chapter we saw that decreased activity of serotonergic neurons is associated with aggression, violence, and risk taking. As we saw in this subsection, decreased activity of the prefrontal cortex is also associated with antisocial behavior. These two fact appear to be linked. The prefrontal cortex receives a major projection of serotonergic axons. Research indicates that serotonergic input to the prefrontal cortex activates this region; thus, an abnormally low level of serotonin release can result in decreased activity of the prefrontal cortex.

A functional imaging study by Mann et al. (1996) showed that fenfluramine, a drug that stimulates the release of 5-HT, increases the activity of the prefrontal cortex. A study by New et al. (2002) found that a serotonin-releasing drug increased the activity of the orbitofrontal cortex in normal, nonviolent subjects but failed to do so in subjects with a history of impulsive aggression.

In summary, the prefrontal cortex appears to provide information about our ongoing emotional states and the predicted consequences of our actions to regions of the brain involved in rational, logical cognitive processes. This information plays a critical role our ability to regulate and control our emotional responses, including those that would result in anger and violence. The inhibitory role that serotonin plays in aggression and risk-taking behavior may reflect the fact that serotonin activates the prefrontal cortex and hence enhances the ability of this brain region to control these behaviors.

Hormonal Control of Aggressive Behavior

As we saw, many instances of aggressive behavior are in some way related to reproduction. For example, males of some species establish territories that attract females during the breeding season. To do so, they must defend the territories against the intrusion of other males. Even in species in which breeding does not depend on the establishment of a territory, males may compete for access to females, which also involves aggressive behavior. Females, too, often compete with other females for space in which to build nests or dens in which to rear their offspring, and they will defend their offspring against the intrusion of other animals. As you learned in Chapter 10, most reproductive behaviors are controlled by the organizational and activational effects of hormones; thus, we should not be surprised that many forms of aggressive behavior are, like mating, affected by hormones.

Aggression in Males

Adult males of many species fight for territory or access to females. In laboratory rodents androgen secretion occurs prenatally, decreases, and then increases again at the time of puberty. Intermale aggressiveness also begins around the time of puberty, which suggests that the behavior is controlled by neural circuits that are stimulated by androgens. Indeed, many years ago Beeman (1947) found that castration reduced aggressiveness and that injections of testosterone reinstated it.

In Chapter 10 we saw that early androgenization has an *organizational effect*. The secretion of androgens early in development modifies the developing brain, making neural circuits that control male sexual behavior become more responsive to testosterone. Similarly, early androgenization has an organizational effect that stimulates the development of testosterone-sensitive neural circuits that facilitate intermale aggression. (See *Figure 11.10*.)

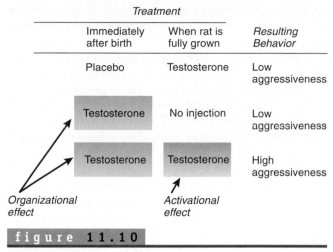

Treatment		Resulting Behavior
Immediately after birth	When rat is fully grown	
Placebo	Testosterone	Low aggressiveness
Testosterone	No injection	Low aggressiveness
Testosterone	Testosterone	High aggressiveness

Organizational effect   Activational effect

figure 11.10

Organizational and activational effects of testosterone on social aggression.

The organizational effect of androgens on intermale aggression (aggressive displays or actual fights between two males of the same species) is important, but it is not an all-or-none phenomenon. Prolonged administration of testosterone will eventually induce intermale aggression even in rodents that were castrated immediately after birth. Data reviewed by vom Saal (1983) show that exposure to androgens early in life decreases the amount of exposure that is necessary to activate aggressive behavior later in life. Thus, early androgenization *sensitizes* the neural circuits—The earlier the androgenization, the more effective the sensitization.

As we saw in Chapter 10, when a pregnant female is subjected to stress, her male offspring show less male sexual behavior, presumably because the stress interferes with the prenatal secretion of androgens. Kinsley and Svare (1986) found that prenatal stress also reduces intermale aggression. They subjected pregnant female mice to stress by restraining them several times in a plastic tube that was placed under bright lights. The male offspring were tested as adults for intermale aggression by placing them in a cage with an unfamiliar male. The prenatally stressed animals were much less likely than the control animals to attack the intruder. Thus, a treatment that interferes with prenatal masculinization of sexual behavior also interferes with the masculinization of aggressive behavior.

We also saw in Chapter 10 that androgens stimulate male sexual behavior by interacting with androgen receptors in neurons located in the medial preoptic area (MPA). This region also appears to be important in mediating the effects of androgens on intermale aggression. Bean and Conner (1978) found that implanting testosterone in the MPA reinstated intermale aggression in castrated male rats. Presumably, the testosterone directly activated the behavior by stimulating the androgen-sensitive neurons located there. The medial preoptic area, then, appears to be involved in several behaviors related to reproduction: male sexual behavior, maternal behavior, and intermale aggression.

Males readily attack other males but usually do not attack females. Their ability to discriminate the sex of the intruder appears to be based on the presence of particular pheromones. Bean (1982) found that intermale aggression was abolished in mice by cutting the vomeronasal nerve, which deprives the brain of input from the vomeronasal organ. And if the urine of female mice is painted on a male mouse, it will not be attacked if it is introduced into another male's cage (Dixon and Mackintosh, 1971; Dixon, 1973). In fact, a targeted mutation against a protein that is essential for the detection of pheromones by the vomeronasal organ abolishes a male mouse's ability to discriminate between males and females. The authors of this study (Stowers et al., 2002) also found that the mutation abolished intermale aggression. Because male intruders were not recognized as rival males, they were not attacked. (See *Animation 11.1, Role of Pheromones in Intermale Aggression.*)

> See the interactive CD for more on pheromones and aggression.

Aggression in Females

Two adult female rodents that meet in a neutral territory are less likely than males to fight. But aggression between females, like aggression between males, appears to be facilitated by testosterone. Van de Poll et al. (1988) ovariectomized female rats and then give them daily injections of testosterone, estradiol, or a placebo for 14 days. The animals were then placed in a test cage, and an unfamiliar female was introduced. As Figure 11.11 shows, testosterone increased aggressiveness, whereas estradiol had no effect. (See *Figure 11.11.*)

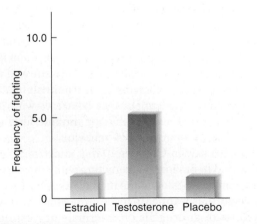

figure 11.11

Effects of estradiol and testosterone on interfemale aggression in rats.
(Adapted from van de Poll, N. E., Taminiau, M. S., Endert, E., and Louwerse, A. L., *International Journal of Neuroscience,* 1988, *41,* 271–286.)

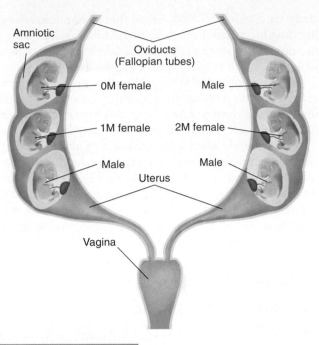

figure 11.12

0M, 1M, and 2M female mouse fetuses.
(Adapted from vom Saal, F. S., in *Hormones and Aggressive Behavior,* edited by B. B. Svare. New York: Plenum Press, 1983.)

Androgens have an organizational effect on the aggressiveness of females, and a certain amount of prenatal androgenization appears to occur naturally. Most rodent fetuses share their mother's uterus with brothers and sisters, arranged in a row like peas in a pod. A female mouse may have zero, one, or two brothers adjacent to her. Researchers refer to these females as 0M, 1M, or 2M, respectively. (See *Figure 11.12.*) Being next to a male fetus has an effect on a female's blood levels of androgens prenatally. Vom Saal and Bronson (1980) found that females located between two males had significantly higher levels of testosterone in their blood than females located between two females (or between a female and the end of the uterus). When they are tested as adults, 2M females are more likely to exhibit interfemale aggressiveness.

Females of some primate species (for example, rhesus monkeys and baboons) are more likely to engage in fights around the time of ovulation (Carpenter, 1942; Saayman, 1971). This phenomenon is probably caused by their increased sexual interest and consequent proximity to males. Another period of fighting occurs just before menstruation (Sassenrath, Powell, and Hendrickx, 1973; Mallow, 1979). During this time females tend to attack other females.

Maternal Aggression

Most parents who actively raise their offspring will vigorously defend them against intruders. In laboratory rodents the responsible parent is the female, so the most commonly studied form of parental defense is maternal aggression. Female mice very effectively defend their young, driving away intruding adults of either sex. Counterattacks by the intruder are rare (Svare, Betteridge, Katz, and Samuels, 1981). Whereas strange males who encounter each other engage in mutual investigation for a minute or two before fighting begins, the attack of a lactating female on an intruder is immediate (Svare, 1983).

Maternal aggressiveness actually begins during pregnancy. Like maternal nest building, it appears to be stimulated by progesterone. The onset of aggressiveness in pregnant mice occurs when progesterone levels begin to rise significantly (Mann, Konen, and Svare, 1984). Immediately after birth, for a period of approximately 48 hours, female mice become completely docile; they do not attack intruders (Ghiraldi and Svare, 1989). As Svare (1989) noted, it is at this time that female mice typically mate again; thus, the fact that they do not attack a male is biologically significant. This phenomenon is probably caused by the high level of estradiol that is present at that time. Ghiraldi and Svare found that removing a female mouse's ovaries just before parturition shortened the period of docility by 24 hours, and administering estradiol restored it.

The tendency for a lactating female mouse to attack a stranger is induced by stimuli provided by her offspring. If the newborn mice are removed, the mother fails to become aggressive. Two activating stimuli appear to be important: suckling and odors. First, let us consider the tactile stimulation produced by suckling. Normally, maternal aggressiveness begins after the mother has suckled her young for 48 hours. If the mother's nipples are surgically removed, she does not become aggressive, even if pups are present (Svare and Gandelman, 1976; Gandelman and Simon, 1980). These effects do not depend on the presence of ovarian or pituitary hormones (Svare et al., 1982.)

Prenatal exposure to androgens appears to have an organizational effect on maternal aggression. As we saw in the previous section, female mice who were located between two males in the uterus (2M females) are more likely to attack other females and are more responsive to the activating effects of androgens in adulthood. Vom Saal and Bronson (1980a) also found that 2M females are more maternally aggressive than 0M females. Kinsley, Konen, Miele, Ghiraldi, and Svare (1986) found that they were also more likely to exhibit aggressiveness during pregnancy.

Effects of Androgens on Human Aggressive Behavior

Boys are generally more aggressive than girls. Clearly, Western society tolerates assertiveness and aggressive behavior from boys more than from girls. Without doubt the way we treat boys and girls and the models to which we expose them play important roles in sex differences in aggressiveness in our species. The question is not whether socialization has an effect (certainly, it does) but whether biological influences, such as exposure to androgens, have an effect too.

Prenatal androgenization increases aggressive behavior in all species that have been studied, including primates. Therefore, if androgens did not affect aggressive behavior in humans, our species would be exceptional. After puberty androgens also begin to have activational effects. Boys' testosterone levels begin to increase during the early teens, at which time aggressive behavior and intermale fighting also increase (Mazur, 1983). Of course, boys' social status changes during puberty, and their testosterone affects their muscles as well as their brains, so we cannot be sure that the effect is hormonally produced or, if it is, that it is mediated by the brain.

Scientifically rigorous evidence that androgens increase aggression in humans is difficult to obtain. Obviously, we cannot randomly castrate some men to find out whether their aggressiveness declines. In the past authorities attempted to suppress sex-related aggression by castrating convicted male sex offenders. Investigators have reported that both heterosexual and homosexual aggressive attacks disappear, along with the offender's sex drive (Hawke, 1951; Sturup, 1961; Laschet, 1973). However, the studies typically lack appropriate control groups and usually do not measure aggressive behavior directly.

Some cases of aggressiveness, especially sexual assault, have been treated with synthetic steroids that inhibit the production of androgens by the testes. Clearly, treatment with drugs is preferable to castration, because the effects are not irreversible. However, the efficacy of treatment with antiandrogens has yet to be established conclusively. According to Walker and Meyer (1981), these drugs decrease sex-related aggression but have no effect on other forms of aggression. In fact, Zumpe et al. (1991) found that one of these drugs decreased sexual activity and aggression toward females when administered to male monkeys but that it actually *increased* intermale aggression.

Another way to determine whether androgens affect aggressiveness in humans is to examine the testosterone levels of people who exhibit varying levels of aggressive behavior. However, even though this approach poses fewer ethical problems, it presents methodological ones. First, let me review some evidence. In a review of the literature Archer (1994) found that most studies found a positive relation between men's testosterone levels and their level of aggressiveness. For example, Dabbs and Morris (1990) studied 4462 U.S. military veterans. The men with the highest testosterone levels had records of more antisocial activities, including assaults of other adults and histories of more trouble with parents, teachers, and classmates during adolescence. The largest effects were seen in men of lower socioeconomic status. Dabbs et al. (1987) measured the testosterone levels of male prison inmates and found a significant correlation with several measures of violence, including the nature of the crime for which they were convicted, infractions of prison rules, and ratings of "toughness" by their peers. These relationships are also seen in female prison inmates; Dabbs et al. (1988) found that women prisoners who showed unprovoked violence and had several prior convictions also showed higher levels of testosterone than the other female inmates. (As we saw earlier, testosterone increases interfemale aggression in laboratory animals as well.)

In a review of the literature Mazur and Booth (1998) suggest that the primary social effect of androgens may be not on aggression but on dominance. If androgens enhance motivation to dominate others, that motivation may sometimes lead to aggression, but not in all situations. For example, a person might strive to defeat others symbolically (through athletic competition or acquisition of symbols of status) rather than through direct aggression.

In any event we must remember that *correlation* does not necessarily indicate *causation*. A person's environment can affect his or her testosterone level. For example, losing a tennis match or a wrestling competition causes a fall in blood levels of testosterone (Mazur and Lamb, 1980; Elias, 1981). Even winning or losing a simple game of chance carried out in a psychology laboratory can affect participants' testosterone levels: Winners feel better afterward and have a higher level of testosterone (McCaul, Gladue, and Joppa, 1992). Bernhardt et al. (1998) found that basketball and soccer fans showed an increase in testosterone levels if their team won and a decrease if it lost. Thus, we cannot be sure in any correlational study that high testosterone levels *cause* people to become dominant or aggressive; perhaps their success in establishing a position of dominance increases their testosterone levels relative to those of the people they dominate.

A few studies have looked at the behavioral effects of administering androgens. Because of ethical concerns, people cannot be given androgen supplements for any length of time merely to find out whether they become more aggressive; excessive amounts of androgens have deleterious effects on a person's health. Thus, the only evidence we have of the effects of long-term administration comes from case studies in which people with abnormally low levels of testosterone (the *hypogonadal syndrome*) are given an androgen to replace what would normally be present. In general, such people feel happier and their sexual activity increases, but they do not usually show more aggressiveness (Skakkebaek et al., 1981; O'Carroll, Shapiro, and Bancroft, 1985). One double-blind study (Su et al., 1993) did administer testosterone for several days to a group of normal volunteers, men aged 18 to 42 years. Those receiving the highest doses reported more euphoria and sexual arousal but also more irritability and feelings of hostility. However, the effects were small, and the investigators did not observe behaviors, only self-reports of feelings.

As everyone knows, some athletes take anabolic steroids to increase their muscle mass and strength and, supposedly, to increase their competitiveness. Anabolic steroids include natural androgens and synthetic hormones with androgenic effects. Thus, we might expect that these hormones would increase aggressiveness. Indeed, several studies have found exactly that. For example, Yates, Perry, and Murray (1992) found male weight lifters who were taking anabolic steroids to be more aggressive and hostile than those who were not. But as the authors note, we cannot be certain that the steroid is responsible for the increased aggressiveness; it could simply be that the men who were already more competitive and aggressive were the ones who chose to take the steroids.

An interesting set of experiments with another species of primates might have some relevance to human aggression. As we saw earlier, alcohol intake is often associated with aggression in humans, and its effects may interact with those of serotonin. Evidence suggests that its effects may also interact with those of androgens. Winslow and Miczek (1985, 1988) found that alcohol increases intermale aggression in dominant male squirrel monkeys, but only during the mating season, when their blood level of testosterone is two to three times higher than that during the nonmating season. These studies suggest that the effects of alcohol interact both with social status and with testosterone. (See *Figure 11.13*.) This suggestion was confirmed by Winslow, Ellingoe, and Miczek (1988), who tested monkeys during the nonmating season. They found that alcohol increased the aggressive behavior of dominant monkeys if they were also given injections of testosterone.

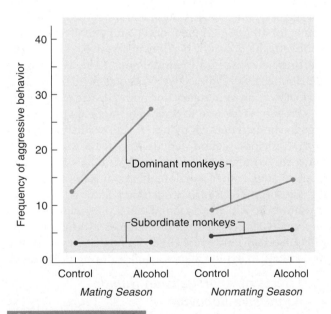

figure 11.13

Effect of alcohol intake on frequency of aggressive behavior of dominant and subordinate male squirrel monkeys during the mating season and the nonmating season.

(Based on data from Winslow, J. T., and Miczek, J. A., *Psychopharmacologia*, 1988, *95*, 92–98.)

However, these treatments were ineffective in subordinate monkeys, which had presumably learned not to be aggressive. The next step will be to find the neural mechanisms that are responsible for these interactions.

interim summary

Emotions as Response Patterns

The word *emotion* refers to behaviors, physiological responses, and feelings. This section has discussed emotional response patterns, which consist of behaviors that deal with particular situations and physiological responses (both autonomic and hormonal) that support the behaviors. The amygdala organizes behavioral, autonomic, and hormonal responses to a variety of situations, including those that produce fear, anger, or disgust. In addition, it is involved in the effects of odors and pheromones on sexual and maternal behavior. It receives inputs from the olfactory system, the association cortex of the temporal lobe, the frontal cortex, and the rest of the limbic system. Its outputs go to the frontal cortex, hypothalamus, hippocampal formation, and brain stem nuclei that control autonomic functions and some species-typical behaviors. Damage to specific brain regions that receive these outputs will abolish particular components of emotional response patterns. Electrical recordings of single neurons in the amygdala indicate that some of them respond when the animal perceives particular stimuli with emotional significance. Stimulation of the amygdala leads to emotional responses, and its destruction disrupts them. Receptors in the amygdala are largely responsible for the anxiolytic effects of the benzodiazepine tranquilizers and the opiates, whereas CCK, a neuropeptide, exerts its anxiety-producing effects there. Studies of people with amygdala lesions and PET and functional MRI studies with humans indicate that the amygdala is involved in emotional reactions in our species, too.

Aggressive behaviors are species-typical and serve useful functions most of the time. In addition, animals may exhibit threat or submissive behaviors, which may avoid an actual fight. The periaqueductal gray matter appears to be involved in defensive behavior and predation. These mechanisms are modulated by the hypothalamus and amygdala.

The activity of serotonergic neurons appears to inhibit risk-taking behaviors, including aggression. Destruction of serotonergic axons in the forebrain enhances aggression, and administration of drugs that facilitate serotonergic transmission reduces it. Low CSF levels of 5-HIAA (a metabolite of serotonin) are correlated with increased risk-taking and aggressive behavior in monkeys and humans. A mutation of the gene responsible for monoamine oxidase type A results in aggression and other antisocial behaviors. Alcohol increases aggression in some people, and research with laboratory animals suggests that the effects of this drug can be opposed by those of serotonin.

The ventromedial prefrontal cortex (which includes the orbitofrontal cortex) plays an important role in emotional reactions. This region communicates with other regions of the frontal lobes, the temporal pole, and the amygdala and other parts of the limbic system. People with orbitofrontal lesions show impulsive behavior and often display outbursts of inappropriate anger. They are able to explain the implications of complex situations but are often unable to respond appropriately when these situations concern *them*. Their lack of an emotional response in a situation that has important consequences for them often leads to poor decision making. Evidence suggests that the prefrontal cortex is involved in making moral judgments.

The prefrontal cortex plays an important role in regulation of emotional expression, including anger and aggression. In a laboratory setting, anger activates this region, perhaps reflecting inhibitory control on behavior. Violent criminals generally show a low level of activity of this region, and the volume of gray matter in this region was lower than normal in a group of people with antisocial personality disorder. The release of serotonin in the prefrontal cortex activates this region, and some investigators believe that the serotonergic input to this region is responsible for the ability of serotonin to inhibit aggression and risky behavior.

Because many aggressive behaviors are related to reproduction, they are influenced by hormones, especially sex steroid hormones. Androgens primarily affect offensive attack; they are not necessary for defensive behaviors, which are shown by females as well as males. In males androgens have organizational and activational effects on offensive attack, just as they have on male sexual behavior. The effects of androgens on intermale aggression appear to be mediated by the medial preoptic area.

Females rodents will fight when they meet in neutral territory but less often than males. Female rodents that have been slightly androgenized (2M females) are more likely to attack other females. Female primates are most likely to fight around the time of ovulation, perhaps because their increased sexual interest brings them closer to males. Although some women report irritability just before menstruation, the phenomenon is not universal.

Maternal aggression is a very swift and effective behavior. It begins during pregnancy, apparently triggered by the secretion of progesterone. After parturition maternal aggression is stimulated by the tactile feedback from suckling. The odor of pups is also necessary. Prenatal androgens have an organizational effect on maternal aggression; 2M females are more likely than 0M females to display maternal aggression.

Androgens apparently promote aggressive behavior in humans, but this topic is more difficult to study in our species than in laboratory animals. Differences in testosterone levels have been observed in criminals with a history of violence. Research suggests that the primary effect of androgens may be to increase motivation to achieve dominance and that increased aggression may be secondary to this effect. In any case we cannot be sure whether higher androgen levels promote dominance or whether successful dominance increases androgen levels. Studies with monkeys suggest that testosterone and alcohol have synergistic effects, particularly in dominant animals. (*Synergy,* from a Greek word meaning "working together," refers to combinations of factors that are more effective than the sum of their individual actions.) Perhaps these effects are related to our observations that some men with a history of violent behavior become more aggressive when they drink.

Communication of Emotions

The previous section described emotions as organized responses (behavioral, autonomic, and hormonal) that prepare an animal to deal with existing situations in the environment, such as events that pose a threat to the organism. For our earliest premammalian ancestors that is undoubtedly all there was to emotions. But over time other responses, with new functions, evolved. Many species of animals (including our own) communicate their emotions to others by means of postural changes, facial expressions, and nonverbal sounds (such as sighs, moans, and growls). These expressions serve useful social functions; they tell other individuals how we feel and—more to the point—what we are likely to do. For example, they warn a rival that we are angry or tell friends that we are sad and would like some comfort and reassurance. In many species they indicate that a danger might be present or that something interesting seems to be happening. This section examines such expression and communication of emotions.

Facial Expression of Emotions: Innate Responses

Charles Darwin (1872/1965) suggested that human expressions of emotion have evolved from similar expressions in other animals. He said that emotional expressions are innate, unlearned responses consisting of a complex set of movements, principally of the facial muscles. Thus, a man's sneer and a wolf's snarl are biologically determined response patterns, both controlled by innate brain mechanisms, just as coughing and sneezing are. (Of course, men can sneer and wolves can snarl for quite different reasons.) Some of these movements resemble the behaviors themselves and may have evolved from them. For example, a snarl shows one's teeth and can be seen as an anticipation of biting.

Darwin obtained evidence for his conclusion that emotional expressions were innate by observing his own children and by corresponding with people living in various isolated cultures around the world. He reasoned that if people all over the world, no matter how isolated, show the same facial expressions of emotion, then these expressions must be inherited instead of learned. The logical argument goes like this: When groups of people are isolated for many years, they develop different languages. Thus, we can say that the words people use are arbitrary; there is no biological basis for using particular words to represent particular concepts. However, if facial expressions are inherited, then they should take approximately the same form in people from all cultures, despite their isolation from one another. And Darwin did, indeed, find that people in different cultures used the same patterns of movement of facial muscles to express a particular emotional state.

Research by Ekman and his colleagues (Ekman and Friesen, 1971; Ekman, 1980) tends to confirm Darwin's hypothesis that facial expression of emotion uses an innate, species-typical repertoire of movements of facial muscles (Darwin, 1872/1965). For example, Ekman and Friesen (1971) studied the ability of members of an isolated tribe in New Guinea to recognize facial expressions of emotion produced by Westerners. They had no trouble doing so and themselves produced facial expressions that Westerners readily recognized. Figure 11.14 shows four photographs taken from videotapes of a man from this tribe reacting to stories designed to evoke facial expressions of happiness, sadness, angers, and disgust. I am sure that you will have no trouble recognizing which is which. (See *Figure 11.14*.)

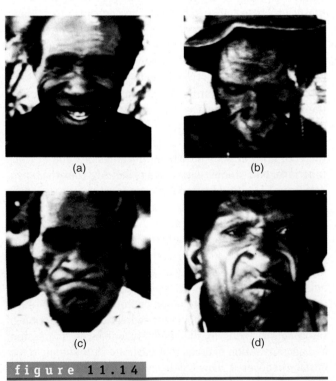

(a) (b)

(c) (d)

figure 11.14

A member of an isolated New Guinea tribe, studied by Ekman and Friesen, making faces when told stories. (a) "Your friend has come and you are happy." (b) "Your child had died." (c) "You are angry and about to fight." (d) "You see a dead pig that has been lying there a long time."
(From Ekman, P., *The Face of Man: Expressions of Universal Emotions in a New Guinea Village.* New York: Garland STPM Press, 1980. Reprinted with permission.)

Because the same facial expressions were used by people who had not previously been exposed to each other, Ekman and Friesen concluded that the expressions were unlearned behavior patterns. In contrast, different cultures use different words to express particular concepts; production of these words does not involve innate responses but must be learned.

Other researchers have compared the facial expressions of blind and normally sighted children. They reasoned that if the facial expressions of the two groups are similar, then the expressions are natural for our species and do not require learning by imitation. (Studies of blind adults would not be conclusive, because adults would probably have heard enough descriptions of facial expressions to be able to pose them.) In fact, the facial expressions of young blind and sighted children are very similar (Woodworth and Schlosberg, 1954; Izard, 1971). Thus, both the cross-cultural studies and the investigations with blind children confirm the naturalness of these expressions.

Although facial expressions of emotion seems to be innate, we all realize that other people can perceive our expressions of emotions. Consequently, we sometimes try to hide our true feelings, attempting to appear impassive or even to display an emotion that is different from what we feel. At other times we might exaggerate our emotional response to ensure that others see how we feel. For example, if a friend tells us about a devastating experience, we make sure that our facial expression conveys sadness and sympathy. Although the patterns of muscular movements that accompany particular feelings are biologically determined, these movements can, to a certain extent, be modulated.

Cultures, as well as situations, influence our expressions of emotions. According to Ekman and Friesen (1975), the expression of emotions often follows culturally determined **display rules**—rules that prescribe under what situations we should or should not display signs of particular emotions. For example, in Western society it is impolite for a winner to show too much pleasure and for a loser to show too much disappointment. The expression of these emotions is supposed to be modulated downward. Also, in many societies it is considered unmanly to cry or show fear and unfeminine to show anger. Ekman and his colleagues (Ekman, Friesen, and Ellsworth, 1972; Friesen, 1972) attempted to assess a different kind of culturally determined display rule. They showed a distressing film to Japanese and American college students, singly and in the presence of a visitor, who was described to the subjects as a scientist. Because the Japanese culture discourages public display of emotion, the researchers expected that the Japanese students would show fewer facial expressions of emotion when in public than when alone.

The researchers recorded the facial expressions of their subjects with hidden cameras while the subjects viewed a film showing a gruesome and bloody coming-of-age rite in a primitive tribe. The results were as predicted. When the subjects were alone, American and Japanese subjects showed the same facial expressions. When they were with another person, the Japanese students were less likely to express negative emotions and more likely to mask these expressions with polite smiles. Thus, people from both societies used the same facial expressions of emotion but were subject to different social display rules.

Investigators have not yet determined whether other means of communicating emotions, such as tone of voice or changes in body posture, are learned or are at least partly innate. However, as we will see, some progress has been made in studying the neuroanatomical basis of expressing and recognizing emotions.

Neural Basis of the Communication of Emotions: Recognition

Effective communication is a two-way process. That is, the ability to display one's emotional state by changes in expression is useful only if other people are able to recognize them. In fact, Kraut and Johnston (1979) unobtrusively observed people in circumstances that would be likely to make them happy. They found that happy situations (such as making a strike while bowling, seeing the home team score, or experiencing a beautiful day) produced only small signs of happiness when the people were alone. However, when the people were interacting socially with other people, they were much more likely to smile. For example, bowlers who made a strike usually did not smile when the ball hit the pins, but when they turned around to face their companions, they often smiled. Jones et al. (1991) found that even 10-month-old children showed this tendency.

We recognize other people's feelings by means of vision and audition—seeing their facial expressions and hearing their tone of voice and choice of words. Many studies have found that the right hemisphere plays a more important role than the left hemisphere in comprehension of emotion. For example, many investigators have found a left-ear and a left-visual field advantage in recognition of emotionally related stimuli. The rationale for these studies is that each hemisphere directly receives information from the contralateral part of the environment. When a person looks directly ahead, visual stimuli to the left of the fixation point (seen with *both* eyes) are transmitted to the right hemisphere, and stimuli to the right are transmitted to the left hemisphere. Of course, the hemispheres exchange information by means of the corpus callosum, but it appears that this transcommissural information is not as precise and detailed as information that

---

display rule A culturally determined rule that modifies the expression of emotion in a particular situation.

is directly received. Similarly, although each hemisphere receives auditory information from both ears, the contralateral projections are richer than the ipsilateral ones. Thus, when stimuli are presented to the left visual field or left ear, the right hemisphere receives more specific information than the left hemisphere does.

In studies of hemispherical differences in visual recognition, stimuli are usually presented to the left or right visual field so rapidly that the subject does not have time to move his or her eyes. Many studies (reviewed by Bryden and Ley, 1983) have shown that the left hemisphere is better than the right at recognizing words or letter strings but that the right hemisphere is better at detecting differences in facial expressions of emotion. Similarly, subjects can more easily understand the verbal content of a message that is presented to the left hemisphere but can more accurately detect the emotional tone of the voice presented to the right hemisphere. These results suggest that when a message is heard, the right hemisphere assesses the emotional expression of the voice while the left hemisphere assesses the meaning of the words.

Blonder, Bowers, and Heilman (1991) found that patients with right hemisphere lesions had no difficulty making emotional judgments about particular situations but were severely impaired in judging the emotions conveyed by facial expressions or hand gestures. For example, they had no difficulty deciding what emotion would be evoked by the situations described in sentences such as *After you drink the water, you see the sign* (fear) or *Your house seems empty without her* (sadness). However, these patients had difficulty recognizing the emotions depicted by sentences such as *He scowled, Tears fell from her eyes,* or *He shook his fist.* In addition, Bowers et al. (1991) found that patients with right hemisphere damage had difficulty producing or describing mental images of facial expressions of emotions. Subjects were asked to imagine the face of someone who was very happy (or very sad, angry, or afraid). Then they were asked questions about the facial expression—for example, *Do the eyes look twinkly? Is the brow raised? Are the corners of the lips raised up?* People with right hemisphere damage had trouble answering these questions but could easily answer questions about nonemotional images, such as *What's higher off the ground: a horse's knee or the top of its tail?* or *What number from one to ten does a peanut look like?* or *What's bigger: a thimble or a pencil eraser?*

Several PET studies have confirmed these results. For example, George et al. (1996) measured subjects' regional cerebral blood flow with a PET scanner while the subjects listened to some sentences and identified their emotional content. In one condition the subjects listened to the meaning of the words and said whether they described a situation in which someone would be happy, sad, angry, or neutral. In another condition they judged the emotional state from the tone of the voice. In a control condition they simply repeated the second word they heard from each sentence. The investigators found that comprehension of emotion from word meaning increased the activity of both frontal lobes, the left more than the right. Comprehension of emotion from tone of voice increased the activity of only the right prefrontal cortex. (See *Figure 11.15*.)

Chimpanzees, too, show increased involvement of the right hemisphere in emotional recognition. Parr and Hopkins (2000) showed videos to chimpanzees that depicted positive, negative, and neutral scenes. For example, the positive scenes showed other chimpanzees playing, while negative scenes showed other chimpanzees making threat gestures. The investigators measured the temperature of the animals' eardrums with miniature thermosensors and found that viewing the negative videos increased the temperature of the right eardrum. Because of the circulation pattern in the head, this change in temperature indicated that the blood flow (and presumably, the activation) of the right hemisphere had increased.

Observations of people with brain damage are consistent with the studies with normal subjects. Heilman, Scholes, and Watson (1975) had patients with unilateral lesions of the temporal-parietal region listen to sentences with neutral content (such as *The boy went to the store*) said

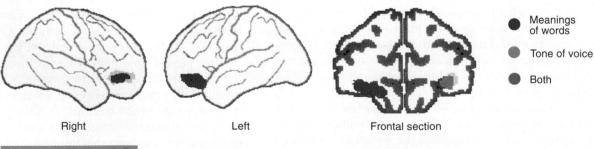

Right   Left   Frontal section

● Meanings of words
● Tone of voice
● Both

figure 11.15

PET scans indicating brain regions activated by listening to emotions expressed by tone of voice (green) or meanings of words (red).
(From George, M. S., Parekh, P. I., Rosinsky, N., Ketter, T. A., Kimbrell, T. A., Heilman, K. M., Herscovitch, P., and Post, R. M., *Archives of Neurology,* 1996, *53,* 665–670.)

in a happy, sad, angry, or indifferent tone of voice. Patients with right hemisphere damage judged the emotion being expressed less accurately. Heilman, Watson, and Bowers (1983) recorded a particularly interesting case of a man with a disorder called *pure word deafness* (described in Chapter 15). The man could not comprehend the meaning of speech but had no difficulty identifying the emotion being expressed by its intonation. This case, like the study by George et al. (1996), indicates that comprehension of words and recognition of tone of voice are independent functions.

Adolphs et al. (2000) compiled computerized information about the locations of brain damage in 108 patients with localized brain lesions. They correlated this information with the patients' ability to recognize and identify facial expressions of emotions. They found that the most severe damage to this ability was caused by damage to the somatosensory cortex of the right hemisphere. (See *Figure 11.16*.)

Adolphs and his colleagues propose a possible explanation for the apparent relationship between somatosensation and emotional recognition. They suggest that when we see a facial expression of an emotion, we unconsciously imagine ourselves making that expression. (In fact, as we will see in the final section of this chapter, we often do more than imagine—we often actually imitate other people's expressions.) The somatosensory representation of what it feels like to make the perceived expression provide the cues we use to recognize the emotion being expressed in the face we are viewing. In support of this hypothesis, Aldophs and his colleagues report that the ability of patients with right-hemisphere lesions to recognize facial expressions of emotions is correlated with their ability to perceive somatosensory stimuli. That is, patients with somatosensory impairments (caused by right-hemisphere lesions) also had impairments in recognition of emotions.

Right hemisphere   Left hemisphere

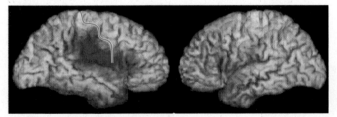

figure 11.16

A computer-generated representation of performance of subjects with localized brain damage on recognition of facial expressions of emotion. The colored areas outline the site of the lesions. Good performance is shown in shades of blue; poor performance is shown in red and yellow. The green line marks the central sulcus.

(From Adolphs, R., Damasio, H., Tranel, D., Cooper, G., and Damasio, A. R. *The Journal of Neuroscience*, 2000, *20*, 2683–2690.)

Obviously, we need visual information to recognize facial expressions of emotion, but this information does not appear to come from regions of the visual association cortex that are devoted to the recognition of individual faces. As we saw in Chapter 6, damage to a region of the visual association cortex can cause *prosopagnosia*—inability to recognize particular faces. However, if the lesions do not involve other parts of the brain, they do not impair recognition of facial expressions of emotions. Just as recognition of the meaning of words and the emotion expressed by tone of voice are accomplished by different brain functions, so are recognition of particular faces and facial expressions of emotions. Some patients can recognize faces but not the emotions they express, and others can recognize the emotions but not the faces (Bowers and Heilman, 1981; Humphreys, Donnelly, and Riddoch, 1993).

As we saw in the previous section, the amygdala plays a special role in emotional responses. It might play a role in emotional recognition as well. For example, several studies have found that lesions of the amygdala (the result of degenerative diseases or surgery for severe seizure disorders) impair people's ability to recognize facial expressions of emotion, especially expressions of fear (Adolphs et al., 1994, 1995; Young et al., 1995; Calder et al., 1996; Adolphs et al., 1999). In addition, functional imaging studies (Morris et al., 1996; Whalen et al., 1998) have found large increases in the activity of the amygdala when people view photographs of faces expressing fear but only small increases (or even decreases) when they look at photographs of happy faces.

Although amygdala lesions impair visual recognition of facial expressions of emotion, several studies have found that they do not appear to affect people's ability to recognize emotions in tone of voice (Anderson and Phelps, 1998; Adolphs and Tranel, 1999). Adolphs, Tranel, and Damasio (1998) found that people with bilateral amygdala lesions were unable to make accurate judgments of another kind from pictures of a person's face. The investigators had normal subjects make judgments about the approachability and trustworthiness of people who were unfamiliar to them by examining their photographs. These subjects showed good agreement about which people they would prefer not to approach. The patients with amygdala lesions judged even the most suspicious-looking individuals as being approachable and trustworthy. In other words, they failed to recognize features and expressions that put normal people on their guard. Adolphs et al. (1999) suggest that the role of the amygdala in the recognition of facial expressions of negative emotions (and of untrustworthiness) is related to the involvement of this structure in recognition of dangerous and threatening situations. After all, if someone in your vicinity looks fearful, there might be something nearby that could harm you, too. And if the person looks at you with an angry expression, that person might be a threat to your safety.

Several studies suggest that the amygdala receives visual information we use to recognize facial expressions of emotion directly from the thalamus and not from the visual association cortex. Adolphs (2002) notes that the amygdala receives visual input from two sources, subcortical and cortical. The subcortical input (from the superior colliculus and the *pulvinar,* a large nucleus in the posterior thalamus) appears to provide the most important information for this task. In fact, some people with blindness caused by damage to the visual cortex can recognize facial expressions of emotion *even though they have no conscious awareness of looking at a person's face* (de Gelder et al., 1999). Morris et al. (2001) performed a functional imaging study with one such patient and discovered that when he viewed faces with fearful expressions (of which he had no conscious perception), the superior colliculus, posterior thalamus, and amygdala became active. Presumably, this subcortical pathway provides the visual information to the amygdala and other brain regions involved in emotional perception.

Perrett and his colleagues (see Perrett et al., 1992) have discovered an interesting brain function that may be related to recognition of emotional expression. They found that neurons in the monkey's superior temporal sulcus are involved in recognition of the direction of another monkey's gaze—or even that of a human. They found that some neurons in this region responded when the monkey looked at photographs of a monkey's face or a human face, but only when the gaze of the face in the photograph was oriented in a particular direction. For example, Figure 11.17

shows the activity level of a neuron that responded when a human face was looking up. (See *Figure 11.17.*)

Why is gaze important in recognition of emotions? First, it is important to know whether an emotional expression is directed toward you or toward someone else. For example, an angry expression directed toward you means something very different from a similar expression directed toward someone else. And if someone else shows signs of fear, the expression can serve as a useful warning to us, but only if we can figure out what he or she is looking at. The neocortex that lines the superior temporal sulcus seems to provide such information. Lesions there disrupt monkeys' ability to discriminate the direction of another animal's gaze, but they do not impair their ability to recognize other animals' faces (Campbell et al., 1990; Heywood and Cowey, 1992). As we saw in Chapter 6, the parietal lobe—the endpoint of the dorsal stream of visual analysis—is concerned with perceiving the location of objects in space. Presumably, the connections that exist between the superior temporal sulcus and the parietal cortex enable the orientation of another animal's gaze to direct one's attention to a particular location in space (Harries and Perrett, 1991).

Damage to a particular part of the brain—the basal ganglia—disrupts a person's ability to recognize a particular emotion: disgust. Disgust (literally, "bad taste") is an emotion provoked by something that tastes or smells bad—or by an action that we consider to be in bad taste (figuratively, not literally). Disgust has a very characteristic facial expression. (If you want to see a good example, refer to Figure 11.14 or 11.20.) Several studies have found that

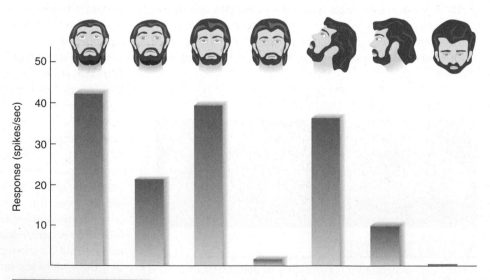

figure 11.17

Responses of a single neuron in the cortex lining the superior temporal sulcus of a monkey's brain. The cell fired most vigorously when the monkey was presented a photograph of a face looking up.

(From Perrett, D. I., Harries, M. H., Mistlin, A. J., Hietanen, J. K., Benson, P. J., Bevan, R., Thomas, S., Oram, M. W., Ortega, J., and Brierley, K., *International Journal of Comparative Psychology,* 1990, 4, 25–55.)

figure 11.18

A photograph of Dr. Duchenne electrically stimulating muscles in the face of a volunteer, causing contraction of muscles around the mouth that become active during a smile. As Duchenne discovered, however, a true smile also involves muscles around the eyes.

Corbis

people with Huntington's disease or obsessive-compulsive disorder have lost the ability to recognize facial expressions of disgust (Sprengelmeyer et al., 1996, 1997). Huntington's disease (described in Chapter 8) is a progressive, fatal, genetic disorder that involves the degeneration of the putamen and caudate nucleus, two components of the basal ganglia. Obsessive-compulsive disorder (described in Chapter 17) is a mental disorder that appears to be caused by abnormalities in the basal ganglia. Results of functional imaging studies by Sprengelmeyer et al. (1998) and Phillips et al. (1998) support these findings. These investigators found that subjects who viewed pictures of faces showing expressions of disgust showed increased activity in the basal ganglia and also in the anterior insular region (a portion of the frontal lobe that is normally hidden behind the temporal lobe). As we saw in Chapter 7, the insular region contains the primary gustatory cortex, so perhaps it is not a coincidence that this region is also involved in recognition of "bad taste."

Neural Basis of the Communication of Emotions: Expression

Facial expressions of emotion are automatic and involuntary (although, as we saw, they can be modified by display rules). It is not easy to produce a realistic facial expression of emotion when we do not really feel that way. In fact, Ekman and Davidson have confirmed an early observation by a nineteenth-century neurologist, Guil-laume-Benjamin Duchenne de Boulogne, that genuinely happy smiles, as opposed to false smiles or social smiles people make when they greet someone else, involve contraction of a muscle near the eyes, the lateral part of the orbicularis oculi—now sometimes referred to as Duchenne's muscle (Ekman, 1992; Ekman and Davidson, 1993). As Duchenne put it, "The first [zygomatic major muscle] obeys the will but the second [orbicularis oculi] is only put in play by the sweet emotions of the soul; the . . . fake joy, the deceitful laugh, cannot provoke the contraction of this latter muscle" (Duchenne, 1862/1990, p. 72). (See *Figure 11.18.*) The difficulty actors have in voluntarily producing a convincing facial expression of emotion is one of the reasons that led Konstantin Stanislavsky to develop his system of *method acting,* in which actors attempt to imagine themselves in a situation that would lead to the desired emotion. Once the emotion is evoked, the facial expressions follow naturally.

This observation is confirmed by two neurological disorders with complementary symptoms (Hopf et al., 1992; Topper et al., 1995; Urban et al., 1998). The first, **volitional facial paresis,** is caused by damage to the face region of the primary motor cortex or to the fibers connecting this region with the motor nucleus of the facial

---

volitional facial paresis Difficulty in moving the facial muscles voluntarily; caused by damage to the face region of the primary motor cortex or its subcortical connections.

nerve, which controls the muscles responsible for movement of the facial muscles. (*Paresis,* from the Greek "to let go," refers to a partial paralysis.) The interesting thing about volitional facial paresis is that the patient cannot voluntarily move the facial muscles but will express a genuine emotion with those muscles. For example, Figure 11.19(a) shows a woman trying to pull her lips apart and show her teeth. Because of the lesion in the face region of her right primary motor cortex, she could not move the left side of her face. However, when she laughed (Figure 11.19b), both sides of her face moved normally. (See *Figure 11.19a* and *11.19b*.) In contrast, **emotional facial paresis** is caused by damage to the insular region of the prefrontal cortex, to the white matter of the frontal lobe,

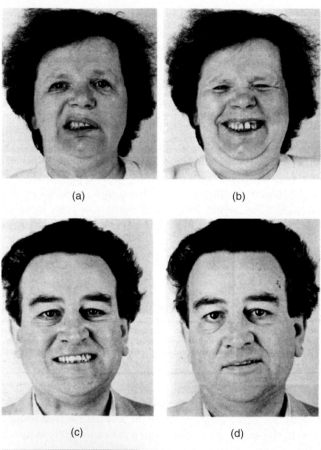

(a) (b)

(c) (d)

figure 11.19

Emotional and volitional paresis. (a) A woman with volitional facial paresis caused by a right-hemisphere lesion trying to pull her lips apart and show her teeth. Only the right side of her face responds. (b) The same woman showing a genuine smile. (c) A man with emotional facial paresis caused by a left-hemisphere lesion showing his teeth. (d) The same man smiling. Only the left side of his face responds.

(From Hopf, H. C., Mueller-Forell, W., and Hopf, N. J., *Neurology,* 1992, *42*, 1918–1923.)

or to parts of the thalamus. This system joins the system responsible for voluntary movements of the facial muscles in the medulla or caudal pons. People with this disorder can move their face muscles voluntarily but do not express emotions on the affected side of the face. Figure 11.19(c) shows a man pulling his lips apart to show his teeth, which he had no trouble doing. Figure 11.19(d) shows him smiling; as you can see, only the left side of his mouth is raised. He had a stroke that damaged the white matter of the left frontal lobe. (See *Figure 11.19c* and *11.19d*.) These two syndromes clearly indicate that different brain mechanisms are responsible for voluntary movements of the facial muscles and automatic, involuntary expression of emotions involving the same muscles.

Several studies have investigated the brain mechanisms involved in laughter, an expression of emotion more intense than smiling. Arroyo et al. (1993) reported the case of a patient who had seizures that were accompanied by mirthless laughter—that is, the patient laughed but was neither happy nor amused. Recordings made with depth electrodes indicated that the seizure began in the left anterior cingulate gyrus. Removal of a noncancerous tumor located nearby ended both the seizures and the mirthless laughter. The authors suggest that anterior cingulate cortex may be involved in the muscular movements that produce laughter. Shammi and Stuss (1999) found that damage to the right ventromedial prefrontal cortex impaired people's ability to understand—and be amused by—jokes. For example, consider the following joke:

> Mr. Smith's neighbor approaches him and asks, "Say, are you using your lawnmower this afternoon?" "Yes, I am," replies Mr. Smith.
> Which alternative below finishes the joke?
> a. "Oops!" as he steps on a rake that barely misses his face.
> b. "Fine, then you won't be wanting your golf clubs—I'll just borrow them."
> c. "Oh well, can I borrow it when you're done, then?"
> d. "The birds are always eating my grass seed."

The funny alternative is, of course, (b). But people with ventromedial prefrontal damage usually chose (a), presumably because it's slapstick aspect reminded them of humor that they had seen in the past. Clearly, they did not get the point of the joke.

A functional imaging study provides further evidence that the right ventromedial prefrontal cortex is involved in the appreciation of humor. Goel and Dolan (2001) had

emotional facial paresis Lack of movement of facial muscles in response to emotions in people who have no difficulty moving these muscles voluntarily; caused by damage to the insular prefrontal cortex, subcortical white matter of the frontal lobe, or parts of the thalamus.

subjects listen to jokes while their brains were being scanned. Different types of jokes activated different regions of the brain, but all of them activated one region: the ventromedial prefrontal cortex.

As we saw in the previous subsection, the right hemisphere plays a more significant role in recognizing emotions in the voice or facial expressions of other people—especially negative emotions. The same hemispheric specialization appears to be true for expressing emotions. When people show emotions with their facial muscles, the left side of the face usually makes a more intense expression. For example, Sackheim and Gur (1978) cut photographs of people who were espressing emotions into right and left halves, prepared mirror images of each of them, and pasted them together, producing so-called *chimerical faces* (from the mythical Chimera, a fire-breathing monster, part goat, part lion, and part serpent). They found that the left halves were more expressive than the right ones. (See *Figure 11.20*.) Because motor control is contralateral, the results suggest that the right hemisphere is more expressive than the left.

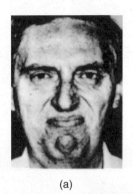

(a)

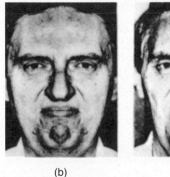 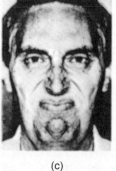

(b)   (c)

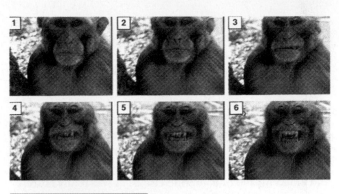

figure 11.21

Successive frames from a videotape of a rhesus monkey showing a fear grimace in response to an interaction with a more dominant monkey.
(From Hauser, M. D., *Science*, 1993, *261*, 475–477.)

Moscovitch and Olds (1982) made more natural observations of people in restaurants and parks and found that the left side of their faces appeared to make stronger expressions of emotions. They confirmed these results in the laboratory by analyzing videotapes of people telling sad or humorous stories. A review of the literature by Borod et al. (1998) found 48 other studies that obtained similar results.

Using the chimerical faces technique, Hauser (1993) found that rhesus monkeys, like humans, express emotions more strongly in the left sides of their faces. Analysis of videotapes further showed that emotional expressions also begin sooner in the left side of the face. These findings suggest that hemispherical specialization for emotional expression appeared before the emergence of our own species. Figure 11.21 shows six videotape frames of a monkey's fear grimace expressed during the course of an interaction with a more dominant monkey. (See *Figure 11.21*.)

Left hemisphere lesions do not usually impair vocal expressions of emotion. For example, people with Wernicke's aphasia (described in Chapter 15) usually modulate their voice according to mood, even though the words they say make no sense. In contrast, right-hemisphere lesions do impair expression of emotion, both facially and by tone of voice.

Interesting information about hemispherical specialization in the expression of emotion has been obtained during the Wada test. The **Wada test** (named after its developer) is performed before a person receives surgery for removal of a seizure focus. Ross, Homan, and Buck (1994) asked people who were about to be evaluated for

figure 11.20

An example of a stimulus used by Sackheim and Gur (1978). (a) Original photo. (b) Composite of the right side of the man's face. (c) Composite of the left side of the man's face.
(Reprinted with permission from *Neuropsychologia, 16,* H. A. Sackheim and R. C. Gur, Lateral asymmetry in intensity of emotional expression. Copyright 1978, Pergamon Press.)

Wada test A test that is often performed before brain surgery; verifies the functions of one hemisphere by testing patients while the other hemisphere is anesthetized.

seizure surgery about experiences they had had that caused an intense emotion. The subjects narrated their experiences and described their feelings at the time. Then, while the right hemisphere was anesthetized with a fast-acting barbiturate injected into the right carotid artery, the subjects were asked about these experiences again. This time, most of the subjects described less intense emotions. For example, one subject described an accident in which he had wrecked his car. Before the injection, he said, "I was scared, scared to death. I could have run off the road and killed myself or someone else. . . . I was really scared." During the right-hemisphere anesthesia he said that after the accident he felt "silly . . . silly." Another patient described an accident with a truck as the scariest situation he had ever experienced. While his right hemisphere was anesthetized, he said he was "sort of scared" but denied that the accident was the scariest event in his life. Another patient said he was very angry when he learned that his wife was having an affair and threw a phone across the room. During the anesthesia he said that he had become "a little angry" and "kinda tossed the phone."

Ross and his colleagues suggest that the right hemisphere plays a role in what they call *primary* emotions, most of which are negative. The left hemisphere, they believe, is involved in modulating emotional displays controlled by the right hemisphere and organizing social displays of positive emotions, such as the quick smile we flash when we meet someone we know. These social displays are different from the expressions of genuine emotions; for example, the social smile does not involve the contraction of Duchenne's muscle. Unfortunately, it is not possible to query people about their emotional responses while the left hemisphere is anesthetized, because the anesthesia of the speech mechanisms in the left hemisphere prevents them from speaking or understanding the speech of other people.

We saw in the previous subsection that the amygdala is involved in the recognition of facial expression of emotions. Research indicates that it is *not* involved in emotional expression. Anderson and Phelps (2000) reported the case of S. P., a 54-year-old woman whose right amygdala was removed to treat a serious seizure disorder. Because of a preexisting lesion of the left amygdala, the surgery resulted in a bilateral amygdalectomy. After the surgery, S. P. lost the ability to recognize facial expressions of emotion, but she had no difficulty recognizing individual faces, and she could easily identify male and female faces and accurately judge their ages. What is particularly interesting is that the amygdala lesions did not impair S. P.'s ability to produce her own facial expressions of emotions. Figure 11.22 shows S. P. displaying a neutral expression (1) and six emotional expressions: fear, anger, happiness, sadness, disgust, and surprise. By the way, when she saw these pictures of herself, she could not tell what emotions her face had been expressing. (See *Figure 11.22.*)

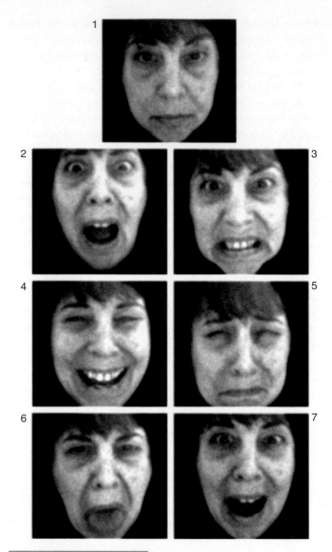

figure 11.22

Photographs of posed facial expressions of emotions (from a videotape) by Patient S. P., a woman with bilateral amygdala lesions who was unable to recognize such expressions—even her own. (1) Neutral expression, (2) fear, (3) anger, (4) happiness, (5) sadness, (6) disgust, (7) surprise.
(From Anderson, A. K., and Phelps, E. A. *Psychological Science,* 2000, *11,* 106–111.)

interim
summary

Communication of Emotions

We (and members of other species) communicate our emotions primarily through facial gestures. Darwin believed that such expressions of emotion were innate—that these muscular movements were inherited behavioral patterns. Ekman and his colleagues performed cross-cultural studies with members of an isolated tribe in New Guinea. Their results supported Darwin's hypothesis. But although expressions of genuine emotions are automatic and innate, research has shown that people can follow culturally determined display rules and exert a certain amount of control over their emotional expressions.

Recognition of other people's emotional expressions involves the right hemisphere more than the left. Studies with normal people have shown that people can judge facial expressions or tone of voice better when the information is presented to the right hemisphere than when it is presented to the left hemisphere. PET scans made while people judge the emotions of voices activate the right hemisphere more than the left. Studies of people with left- or right-hemisphere brain damage corroborate these findings. In addition, they show that recognition of particular faces involves neural circuits different from those needed to recognize facial expressions of emotions. Finally, the amygdala plays a role in recognition of facial expressions of emotions; lesions of the amygdala disrupt this ability, and PET scans show increased activity of the amygdala while the subject is engaging in this task. The ability to judge emotions by a person's tone of voice is not affected. Damage to the caudate nucleus and putamen (components of the basal ganglia) disrupts recognition of facial expressions of disgust, and functional imaging studies suggest that the insular cortex (which contains the primary gustatory cortex) is also involved in this emotion.

Facial expression of emotions (and other stereotypical behaviors such as laughing and crying) are almost impossible to simulate. For example, only a genuine smile of pleasure causes the contraction of the lateral part of the orbicularis oculi (Duchenne's muscle). The anterior cingulate gyrus appears to play a role in the motor aspects of laughter, while the appreciation of humor appears to involve the right ventromedial prefrontal cortex. Genuine expressions of emotion are controlled by special neural circuits. The best evidence for this assertion comes from the complementary syndromes of emotional and volitional facial paresis. People with emotional facial paresis can move their facial muscles voluntarily but not in response to an emotion, whereas people with volitional facial paresis show the opposite symptoms. In addition, the left halves of people's faces—and the faces of monkeys—tend to be more expressive than the right halves. While the right hemisphere is anesthetized during the Wada test, the emotional feelings that accompany people's recollection of memories generally become less intense.

Feelings of Emotions

So far, we have examined two aspects of emotions: the organization of patterns of responses that deal with the situation that provokes the emotion and the communication of emotional states with other members of the species. The final aspect of emotion to be examined in this chapter is the subjective component: feelings of emotion.

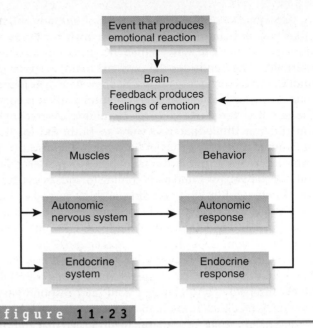

figure 11.23

A diagrammatic representation of the James-Lange theory of emotion. An event in the environment triggers behavioral, autonomic, and endocrine responses. Feedback from these responses produces feelings of emotions.

The James-Lange Theory

William James (1842–1910), an American psychologist, and Carl Lange (1834–1900), a Danish physiologist, independently suggested similar explanations for emotion, which most people refer to collectively as the **James-Lange theory** (James, 1884; Lange, 1887). Basically, the theory states that emotion-producing situations elicit an appropriate set of physiological responses, such as trembling, sweating, and increased heart rate. The situations also elicit behaviors, such as clenching of the fists or fighting. The brain receives sensory feedback from the muscles and from the organs that produce these responses, and it is this feedback that constitutes our feeling of emotion.

James says that our own emotional feelings are based on what we find ourselves doing and on the sensory feedback we receive from the activity of our muscles and internal organs. Thus, when we find ourselves trembling and feel queasy, we experience fear. Where feelings of emotions are concerned, we are self-observers. Thus, the two aspects of emotions reported in the first two sections of this chapter (patterns of emotional responses and expressions of emotions) give rise to the third: feelings. (See *Figure 11.23.*)

James-Lange theory A theory of emotion that suggests that behaviors and physiological responses are directly elicited by situations and that feelings of emotions are produced by feedback from these behaviors and responses.

James's description of the process of emotion might strike you as being at odds with your own experience. Many people think that they experience emotions directly, internally. They consider the outward manifestations of emotions to be secondary events. But have you ever found yourself in an unpleasant confrontation with someone else and discovered that you were trembling, even though you did not think that you were so bothered by the encounter? Or did you ever find yourself blushing in response to some public remark that was made about you? Or did you ever find tears coming to your eyes while you watched a film that you did not think was affecting you? What would you conclude about your emotional states in situations like these? Would you ignore the evidence from your own physiological reactions?

A well-known physiologist, Walter Cannon, criticized James's theory. He said that the internal organs were relatively insensitive and that they could not respond very quickly, so feedback from them could not account for our feelings of emotions. In addition, he observed that cutting the nerves that provide feedback from the internal organs to the brain did not alter emotional behavior (Cannon, 1927). However, subsequent research indicated that Cannon's criticisms are not relevant. For example, although the viscera are not sensitive to some kinds of stimuli, such as cutting and burning, they provide much better feedback than Cannon suspected. Moreover, many changes in the viscera can occur rapidly enough that they could be the causes of feelings of emotion.

Cannon cited the fact that cutting the sensory nerves between the internal organs and the central nervous system does not abolish emotional behavior in laboratory animals. However, this observation misses the point. It does not prove that feelings of emotion survive this surgical disruption—only that emotional *behaviors* do. We do not know how the animals feel; we know only that they will snarl and attempt to bite if threatened. In any case James did not attribute all feelings of emotion to the internal organs; he also said that feedback from muscles was important. The threat might make the animal snarl and bite, and the feedback from the facial and neck muscles might constitute a "feeling" of anger, even if feedback from the internal organs was cut off. But we have no way to ask the animal how it felt.

James's theory is difficult to verify experimentally, because it attempts to explain *feelings* of emotion, not the causes of emotional responses, and feelings are private events. Some anecdotal evidence supports the theory. For example, Sweet (1966) reported the case of a man in whom some sympathetic nerves were severed on one side of the body to treat a cardiovascular disorder. The man—a music lover—reported that the shivering sensation he felt while listening to music now occurred only on the unoperated side of his body. He still enjoyed listening to music, but the surgery altered his emotional reaction.

In one of the few tests of James's theory, Hohman (1966) collected data from people with spinal cord damage. He asked these people about the intensity of their emotional feelings. If feedback is important, one would expect that emotional feelings would be less intense if the injury were high (that is, close to the brain) than if it were low, because a high spinal cord injury would make the person become insensitive to a larger part of the body. In fact, this result is precisely what Hohman found: The higher the injury, the less intense the feeling was. As one of Hohman's subjects said:

> I sit around and build things up in my mind, and I worry a lot, but it's not much but the power of thought. I was at home alone in bed one day and dropped a cigarette where I couldn't reach it. I finally managed to scrounge around and put it out. I could have burned up right there, but the funny thing is, I didn't get all shook up about it. I just didn't feel afraid at all, like you would suppose. (Hohman, 1966, p. 150)

Another subject showed that angry behavior (an emotional response) does not appear to depend on *feelings* of emotion. Instead, the behavior is evoked by the situation (and by the person's evaluation of it) even if the spinal cord damage has reduced the intensity of the person's emotional feelings.

> Now, I don't get a feeling of physical animation, it's sort of cold anger. Sometimes I act angry when I see some injustice. I yell and cuss and raise hell, because if you don't do it sometimes, I've learned people will take advantage of you, but it doesn't have the heat to it that it used to. It's a mental kind of anger. (Hohman, 1966, p. 150)

Feedback From Simulated Emotions

James stressed the importance of two aspects of emotional responses: emotional behaviors and autonomic responses. As we saw earlier in this chapter, a particular set of muscles—those of the face—helps us to communicate our emotional state to other people. Several experiments suggest that feedback from the contraction of facial muscles can affect people's moods and even alter the activity of the autonomic nervous system.

Ekman and his colleagues (Ekman, Levenson, and Friesen, 1983; Levenson, Ekman, and Friesen, 1990) asked subjects to move particular facial muscles to simulate the emotional expressions of fear, anger, surprise, disgust, sadness, and happiness. They did not tell the subjects what emotion they were trying to make them produce, but only what movements they should make. For example, to simulate fear, they told the subjects, "Raise your brows. While holding them raised, pull your brows together. Now raise your upper eyelids and tighten the lower eyelids. Now stretch your lips horizontally." (These movements produce a facial expression of fear.) While the subjects made the expressions, the investigators monitored several physiological responses controlled by the autonomic nervous system.

The simulated expressions *did* alter the activity of the autonomic nervous system. In fact, different facial expressions produced somewhat different patterns of activity. For example, anger increased heart rate and skin temperature, fear increased heart rate but decreased skin temperature, and happiness decreased heart rate without affecting skin temperature.

Why should a particular pattern of movements of the facial muscles cause changes in mood or in the activity of the autonomic nervous system? Perhaps the connection is a result of experience; in other words, perhaps the occurrence of particular facial movements along with changes in the autonomic nervous system leads to classical conditioning, so feedback from the facial movements becomes capable of eliciting the autonomic response—and a change in perceived emotion. Or perhaps the connection is innate. As we saw earlier, the adaptive value of emotional expressions is that they communicate feelings and intentions to others. One of the ways we communicate feelings may be through imitation.

When people see someone expressing an emotion, they tend to imitate the expression. This tendency to imitate appears to be innate. Field et al. (1982) had adults make facial expressions in front of infants. The infants' own facial expressions were videotaped and were subsequently rated by people who did not know what expressions the adults were displaying. Field and her colleagues found that even newborn babies (with an average age of 36 hours) tended to imitate the expressions they saw. Clearly, the effect occurs too early in life to be a result of learning. Figure 11.24 shows three photographs of the adult expressions and the expressions they elicited in a baby. Can you look at them yourself without changing your own expression, at least a little? (See *Figure 11.24*.)

Perhaps imitation provides one of the channels by which organisms communicate their emotions. For example, if we see someone looking sad, we tend to assume a sad expression ourselves. The feedback from our own expression helps to put us in the other person's place and makes us more likely to respond with solace or assistance. And perhaps one of the reasons we derive pleasure from making someone else smile is that their smile makes *us* smile and feel happy.

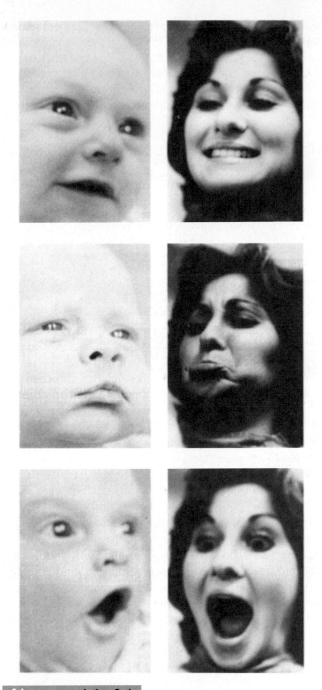

figure 11.24

Photographs of happy, sad, and surprised faces posed by an adult and the responses made by the infant.

(From Field, T., in *Development of Nonverbal Behavior in Children,* edited by R. S. Feldman. New York: Springer-Verlag, 1982. Reprinted with permission.)

interim summary

Feeling of Emotions

From the earliest times people recognized that emotions were accompanied by feelings that seemed to come from inside the body, which probably provided the impetus for developing physiological theories of emotion. James and Lange suggested that emotions were primarily responses to situations. Feedback from the physiological and behavioral reactions to emotion-producing situations gave rise to the feelings of emotion; thus, feelings are the *results,* not the *causes,* of emotional reactions. Hohman's study of people with spinal cord damage supported the James-Lange theory; people who could no longer feel the reactions from most of their body reported that they no longer experienced intense emotional states.

Ekman and his colleagues have shown that even simulating an emotional expression causes changes in the activity of the autonomic nervous system. Perhaps feedback from these changes explains why an emotion can be "contagious": We see someone smile with pleasure, we ourselves imitate the smile, and the internal feedback makes us feel at least somewhat happier.

Suggested Readings

Aggleton, J. (ed.). *The Amygdala: Neurobiological Aspects of Emotion, Memory, and Mental Dysfunction.* New York: Wiley-Liss, 1992.

Damasio, A. R. *Decartes' Error: Emotion, Reason, and the Human Brain.* New York: G. P. Putnam, 1994.

Damasio, A. R. *The Feeling of What Happens: Body and Emotion in the Making of Consciousness.* New York: Harcourt Brace, 1999.

LeDoux, J. E. *The Emotional Brain: The Mysterious Underpinnings of the Emotional Life.* New York: Simon and Schuster, 1996.

Stoff, D. M., and Cairns, R. B. (eds.) *Aggression and Violence: Genetic, Neurobiological, and Biosocial Perspectives.* Mahwah, NJ: Lawrence Erlbaum Associates, 1996.

Suggested Web Sites

The Emotion Home Page

http://emotion.salk.edu/Emotion/History/
Hgeneral.html

The Emotion Page provides a series of lecture outlines on the history of emotion theories, ranging from Plato through the 20th century.

What is an Emotion? by William James

http://www.yorku.ca/dept/psych/classics/James/
emotion.htm

The Classics in the History of Psychology site provides the original text of an article on emotions published by William James in 1884.

Dr. Ivan's Depression Central

http://www.psycom.net/depression.central.html

Depression is the focus of this site by Dr. Ivan Goldberg. The site provides fact sheets on the genetics of depression, treatments for depression, and a host of links to other depression Web sites.

Research on Human Emotion

http://www-white.media.mit.edu/vismod/demos/affect/
AC_research/emotions.html

This site contains an overview of three theories of emotion and provides links to various research projects on the topic of emotion.

Emotions and Emotional Intelligence

http://trochim.human.cornell.edu/gallery/young/emotion.htm

The focus of this site is on theories of emotion and of emotional intelligence.

chapter

12

Ingestive Behavior

outline

- **Physiological Regulatory Mechanisms**
- **Drinking**
Some Facts About Fluid Balance
Two Types of Thirst
Neural Mechanisms of Thirst
Interim Summary
- **Eating: Some Facts About Metabolism**
Absorption, Fasting, and the Two
    Nutrient Reservoirs
Interim Summary
- **What Starts a Meal?**
Social and Environmental Factors
Physiological Hunger Signals
Interim Summary
- **What Stops a Meal?**
Head Factors
Gastric Factors
Intestinal Factors
Liver Factors
Metabolic Factors Present in
    the Blood
Long-Term Satiety: Signals from
    Adipose Tissue
Interim Summary
- **Brain Mechanisms**
Brain Stem
Hypothalamus
Interim Summary
- **Eating Disorders**
Obesity
Anorexia Nervosa/Bulimia Nervosa
Interim Summary

Carrie was a frail little baby. She nursed poorly, apparently because she was so weak. For several years, she was underweight. Her motor and cognitive development was much slower than normal, she often seemed to have trouble breathing, and her hands and feet were especially small. Finally, her appetite seemed to improve. She began gaining weight and soon surpassed other children of her age. Previously, she was passive and well behaved, but she became difficult and demanding. She also showed compulsive behavior—picking at her skin, collecting and lining up objects, and protesting violently when her parents tried to put things away.

The worst problem, though, was her appetite. She ate everything she could and never seemed satisfied. At first her parents were so pleased to see her finally gain weight that they gave her food whenever she asked for it. But after a while it was clear that she was becoming obese. A specialist diagnosed her condition and told her parents that they would have to strictly limit Carrie's food intake. Because of her weak muscles and low metabolic rate, she needed only 1200 calories per day to maintain a normal weight. But Carrie was constantly looking for food. She would raid the refrigerator until her parents installed a lock on it and on the cabinets where they put food. They had to be careful of how they disposed of leftover food, vegetable peels, or meat trimmings because Carrie would raid the garbage can and eat them.

When Carrie went to school, she began gaining weight once more. She would quickly eat everything on her tray and would then eat everything her classmates did not finish. If anyone dropped food on the floor near her, she would pick that up and eat it too. Because of Carrie's special needs, the school appointed an aide to monitor her food intake to be sure that she ate only the low-calorie meal that she was served.

Carrie has Prader-Willi syndrome, caused by deletion of several genes in a segment of chromosome 15. This region appears to be involved in production of proteins that are critical to normal functioning of the hypothalamus. Most cases of Prader-Willi syndrome are apparently caused by random accidents that occur during the production of the father's sperm cells. As you will learn in this chapter, much progress has been made in our understanding of the neural and hormonal mechanisms that control appetite and regulate body weight. Undoubtedly, we will soon learn which of these mechanisms are disrupted in Prader-Willi syndrome.

A
s the French physiologist Claude Bernard (1813–1878) said, "The constancy of the internal milieu is a necessary condition for a free life." This famous quotation says succinctly what organisms must do to be able to exist in environments that are hostile to the living cells that compose them (that is, to live a "free life"): They must provide a barrier between their cells and the external environment—in the case of mammals this barrier consists of skin and mucous membrane. Within the barrier they must regulate the nature of the internal fluid that bathes the cells.

The physiological characteristics of the cells that constitute our bodies evolved long ago, when these cells floated freely in the ocean. In essence, what the evolutionary process has accomplished is the ability to make our own seawater for bathing our cells, to add to this seawater the oxygen and nutrients that our cells need, and to remove from it waste products that would otherwise poison them. To perform these functions, we have digestive, respiratory, circulatory, and excretory systems. We also have the behaviors necessary for finding and ingesting food and water.

Regulation of the fluid that bathes our cells is part of a process called **homeostasis** ("similar standing"). This chapter discusses the means by which we mammals achieve homeostatic control of the vital characteristics of our extracellular fluid through our **ingestive behavior:** intake of food, water, and minerals such as sodium. First, we will examine the general nature of regulatory mechanisms; then we will consider drinking and eating and the neural mechanisms that are responsible for these behaviors. Finally, we will look at some research on the eating disorders.

homeostasis (*home ee oh stay sis*) The process by which the body's substances and characteristics (such as temperature and glucose level) are maintained at their optimal level.

ingestive behavior (*in jess tiv*) Eating or drinking.

system variable A variable that is controlled by a regulatory mechanism; for example, temperature in a heating system.

set point The optimal value of the system variable in a regulatory mechanism.

detector In a regulatory process, a mechanism that signals when the system variable deviates from its set point.

correctional mechanism In a regulatory process, the mechanism that is capable of changing the value of the system variable.

negative feedback A process whereby the effect produced by an action serves to diminish or terminate that action; a characteristic of regulatory systems.

satiety mechanism A brain mechanism that causes cessation of hunger or thirst, produced by adequate and available supplies of nutrients or water.

Physiological Regulatory Mechanisms

A physiological regulatory mechanism is one that maintains the constancy of some internal characteristic of the organism in the face of external variability—for example, keeping body temperature constant despite changes in the ambient temperature. A regulatory mechanism contains four essential features: the **system variable** (the characteristic to be regulated), a **set point** (the optimal value of the system variable), a **detector** that monitors the value of the system variable, and a **correctional mechanism** that restores the system variable to the set point.

An example of a regulatory system is a room whose temperature is regulated by a thermostatically controlled heater. The system variable is the air temperature of the room, and the detector for this variable is a thermostat. This device can be adjusted so that contacts of a switch will be closed when the temperature falls below a preset value (the set point). Closure of the contacts turns on the correctional mechanism—the coils of the heater. (See *Figure 12.1.*) If the room cools below the set point of the thermostat, the thermostat turns the heater on, and the heater warms the room. The rise in room temperature causes the thermostat to turn the heater off. Because the activity of the correctional mechanism (heat production) feeds back to the thermostat and causes it to turn the heater off, this process is called **negative feedback.** Negative feedback is an essential characteristic of all regulatory systems.

This chapter considers regulatory systems that involve ingestive behaviors: drinking and eating. These behaviors are correctional mechanisms that replenish the body's depleted stores of water or nutrients. Because of the delay between ingestion and replenishment of the depleted

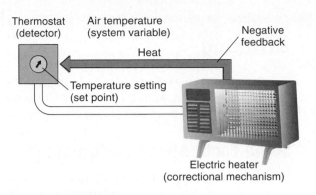

figure 12.1

An example of a regulatory system.

stores, ingestive behaviors are controlled by **satiety mechanisms** as well as by detectors that monitor the system variables. Satiety mechanisms are required because of the physiology of our digestive system. For example, suppose you spend some time in a hot, dry environment and lose body water. The loss of water causes internal detectors to initiate the correctional mechanism—drinking. You quickly drink a glass or two of water and then stop. What stops your ingestive behavior? The water is still in your digestive system, not yet in the fluid surrounding your cells, where it is needed. Therefore, although drinking was initiated by detectors that measure your body's need for water, *it was stopped by other means.* There must be a satiety mechanism that says, in effect, "Stop—this water, when absorbed by the digestive system into the blood, will eventually replenish the body's need." Satiety mechanisms monitor the activity of the correctional mechanism (in this case, drinking), not the system variables themselves. When a sufficient amount of drinking occurs, the satiety mechanisms stop further drinking *in anticipation* of the replenishment that will occur later. (See *Figure 12.2.*)

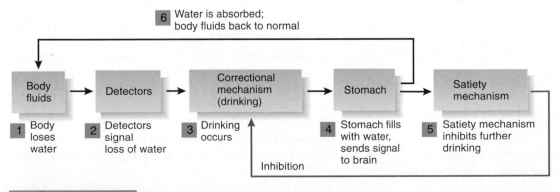

figure 12.2

An outline of the system that controls drinking.

Drinking

To maintain our internal milieu at its optimal state, we have to drink some water from time to time. This section describes the control of this form of ingestive behavior.

Some Facts About Fluid Balance

Before you can understand the physiological control of drinking, you must know something about the fluid compartments of the body and their relationships with each other. The body contains four major fluid compartments: one compartment of intracellular fluid and three compartments of extracellular fluid. Approximately two-thirds of the body's water is contained in the **intracellular fluid,** the fluid portion of the cytoplasm of cells. The rest is **extracellular fluid,** which includes the **intravascular fluid** (the blood plasma), the cerebrospinal fluid, and the **interstitial fluid.** *Interstitial* means "standing between"; indeed, the interstitial fluid stands between our cells—it is the "seawater" that bathes them. For the purposes of this chapter we will ignore the cerebrospinal fluid and concentrate on the other three compartments. (See *Figure 12.3.*)

Two of the fluid compartments of the body must be kept within precise limits: the intracellular fluid and the intravascular fluid. The intracellular fluid is controlled by the concentration of solutes in the interstitial fluid. (*Solutes* are the substances dissolved in a solution.) Normally, the interstitial fluid is **isotonic** (from *isos,* "equal," and *tonos,* "tension") with the intracellular fluid. That is, the concentration of solutes in the cells and in the interstitial fluid

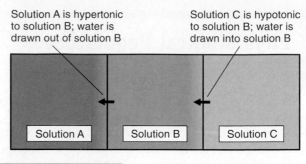

figure 12.4

Effects of differences in solute concentration on the movement of water molecules.

that bathes them is balanced, so that water does not tend to move into or out of the cells. If the interstitial fluid loses water (becomes more concentrated, or **hypertonic**), water will be pulled out of the cells. On the other hand, if the interstitial fluid gains water (becomes more dilute, or **hypotonic**), water will move into the cells. Either condition endangers cells; a loss of water deprives them of the ability to perform many chemical reactions, and a gain of water can cause their membranes to rupture. Therefore, the concentration of the interstitial fluid must be closely regulated. (See *Figure 12.4.*)

The volume of the blood plasma must be closely regulated because of the mechanics of the operation of the heart. If the blood volume falls too low, the heart can no longer pump the blood effectively; if the volume is not restored, heart failure will result. This condition is called **hypovolemia,** literally "low volume of the blood" (-*emia* comes from the Greek *haima,* "blood"). The vascular system of the body can make some adjustments for loss of blood volume by contracting the muscles in smaller

intracellular fluid The fluid contained within cells.

extracellular fluid All body fluids outside cells: interstitial fluid, blood plasma, and cerebrospinal fluid.

intravascular fluid The fluid found within the blood vessels.

interstitial fluid The fluid that bathes the cells, filling the space between the cells of the body (the "interstices").

isotonic Equal in osmotic pressure to the contents of a cell. A cell placed in an isotonic solution neither gains nor loses water.

hypertonic The characteristic of a solution that contains enough solute that it will draw water out of a cell placed in it, through the process of osmosis.

hypotonic The characteristic of a solution that contains so little solute that a cell placed in it will absorb water, through the process of osmosis.

hypovolemia (*hy poh voh lee mee a*) Reduction in the volume of the intravascular fluid.

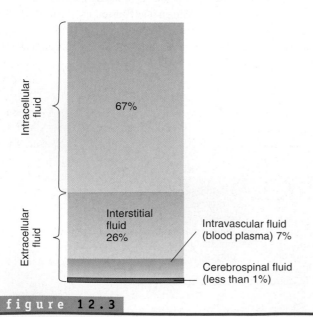

figure 12.3

The relative size of the body's fluid compartments.

veins and arteries, thereby presenting a smaller space for the blood to fill, but this correctional mechanism has definite limits.

The two important characteristics of the body fluids—the solute concentration of the intracellular fluid and the volume of the blood—are monitored by two different sets of receptors. A single set of receptors would not work, because it is possible for one of these fluid compartments to be changed without affecting the other. For example, a loss of blood obviously reduces the volume of the intravascular fluid, but it has no effect on the volume of the intracellular fluid. On the other hand, a salty meal will increase the solute concentration of the interstitial fluid, drawing water out of the cells, but it will not cause hypovolemia. Thus, the body needs two sets of receptors, one measuring blood volume and another measuring cell volume.

Two Types of Thirst

As we just saw, for our bodies to function properly, the volume of two fluid compartments—intracellular and intravascular—must be regulated. Most of the time, we ingest more water and sodium than we need and the kidneys excrete the excess. However, if the levels of water or sodium fall too low, correctional mechanisms—drinking water or ingesting sodium—are activated. Everyone is familiar with the sensation of thirst, which occurs when we need to ingest water. However, a salt appetite is much more rare, because it is difficult for people *not* to get enough sodium in their diet, even if they do not put extra salt on their food. Nevertheless, the mechanisms to increase sodium intake exist, even though they are seldom called upon in members of our species.

Because loss of water from either the intracellular or intravascular fluid compartments stimulates drinking, researchers have adopted the terms *osmometric thirst* and *volumetric thirst* to describe them. The term *volumetric* is clear; it refers to the metering (measuring) of the volume of the blood plasma. The term *osmometric* requires more explanation, which will be provided in the next section. The term *thirst* means different things in different circumstances. Its original definition referred to a sensation that people say they have when they are dehydrated. Here I use it in a descriptive sense. Because we do not know how other animals feel, *thirst* simply means a tendency to seek water and to ingest it.

Our bodies lose water continuously, primarily through evaporation. Each breath exposes the moist inner surfaces of the respiratory system to the air; thus, each breath causes the loss of a small amount of water. In addition, our skin is not completely waterproof; some water finds its way through the layers of the skin and evaporates from the surface. The moisture that is lost through evaporation is, of course, pure distilled water. (Sweating

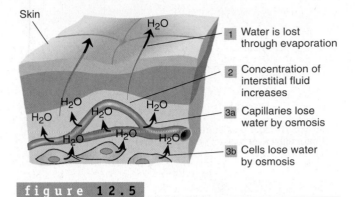

Skin
1 Water is lost through evaporation
2 Concentration of interstitial fluid increases
3a Capillaries lose water by osmosis
3b Cells lose water by osmosis

figure 12.5

The loss of water through evaporation.

loses water, too; but because it loses salt along with the water, it produces a need for sodium as well as for water.) Figure 12.5 illustrates how the loss of water through evaporation depletes both the intracellular fluid and intravascular fluid compartments. For the sake of simplicity only a few cells are shown, and the volume of the interstitial fluid is greatly exaggerated. Water is lost directly from the interstitial fluid, which becomes slightly more concentrated than either the intracellular or the intravascular fluid. Thus, water is drawn from both the cells and the blood plasma. Eventually, the loss of water from the cells and the blood plasma will be great enough that both osmometric thirst and volumetric thirst will be produced. (See *Figure 12.5.*)

Osmometric Thirst

Osmometric thirst occurs when the tonicity (solute concentration) of the interstitial fluid increases. This increase draws water out of the cells, and they shrink in volume. The term *osmometric* refers to the fact that the detectors are actually responding to (metering) changes in the concentration of the interstitial fluid that surrounds them. *Osmosis* is the movement of water through a semipermeable membrane from a region of low solute concentration to one of high solute concentration.

The existence of neurons that respond to changes in the solute concentration of the interstitial fluid was first hypothesized by Verney (1947). Verney suggested that these detectors, which he called **osmoreceptors,** were neurons whose firing rate was affected by their level of hydration. That is, if the interstitial fluid surrounding them became more concentrated, they would lose water through

osmometric thirst Thirst produced by an increase in the osmotic pressure of the interstitial fluid relative to the intracellular fluid, thus producing cellular dehydration.

osmoreceptor A neuron that detects changes in the solute concentration of the interstitial fluid that surrounds it.

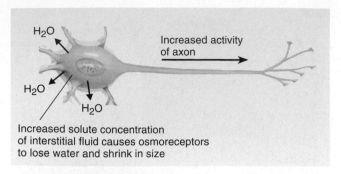

H₂O

Increased activity
of axon

H₂O

H₂O

Increased solute concentration
of interstitial fluid causes osmoreceptors
to lose water and shrink in size

figure 12.6

A hypothetical explanation of the workings of an
osmoreceptor.

osmosis. The shrinkage would cause them to alter their firing rate, which would send signals to other parts of the
brain. (See *Figure 12.6*.)

When we eat a salty meal, we incur a pure osmometric
thirst. The salt is absorbed from the digestive system into
the blood plasma; hence, the blood plasma becomes
hypertonic. This condition draws water from the intersti-

tial fluid, which makes this compartment become hypertonic too and thus causes water to leave the cells. As the
blood plasma increases in volume, the kidneys begin
excreting large amounts of both sodium and water. Eventually, the excess sodium is excreted, along with the water
that was taken from the interstitial and intracellular fluid.
The net result is a loss of water from the cells. *At no time
does the volume of the blood plasma fall.*

Most researchers now believe that osmoreceptors
responsible for osmometric thirst are located in the region
of the anterior hypothalamus that borders the anteroventral tip of the third ventricle (the *AV3V*). Buggy et al. (1979)
found that injections of hypertonic saline directly into the
AV3V produced drinking, whereas injections into the lateral preoptic area did not. In some species (such as the dog)
the osmoreceptors may be located in the OVCI, a specialized *circumventricular organ* located just rostral to the
AV3V. The brain contains several circumventricular
organs, specialized regions with rich blood supplies located
along the ventricular system. You are already familiar
with one of these: the area postrema, discussed in Chapter 2. You will learn about two more in this chapter: the
OVLT and the SFO. (See *Figure 12.7*.)

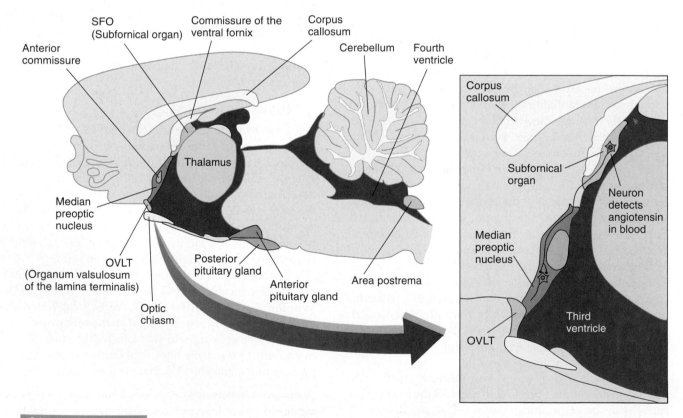

figure 12.7

A sagittal section of the rat brain, showing the location of the circumventricular
organs. *Inset:* A hypothetical circuit connecting the subfornical organ with the
median preoptic nucleus.

The **OVLT** (if you really want to know, that stands for the *organum vasculosum of the lamina terminalis*), like the other circumventricular organs, is located on the *blood* side of the blood–brain barrier. That means that substances dissolved in the blood pass easily into the interstitial fluid within this organ. Thrasher and Keil (1987) found that after the OVLT was destroyed, dogs no longer drank when they were given injections of hypertonic saline.

Volumetric Thirst

Volumetric thirst occurs when the volume of the blood plasma—the intravascular volume—decreases. As we saw earlier, when we lose water through evaporation, we lose it from all three fluid compartments: intracellular, interstitial, and intravascular. Thus, evaporation produces both volumetric thirst and osmometric thirst. In addition, loss of blood, vomiting, and diarrhea all cause loss of blood volume (hypovolemia) without depleting the intracellular fluid.

Loss of blood is the most obvious cause of pure volumetric thirst. From the earliest recorded history, reports of battles note that the wounded survivors called out for water. In addition, because hypovolemia involves a loss of sodium as well as water (that is, the sodium that was contained in the isotonic fluid that was lost), volumetric thirst leads to a salt appetite.

What detectors are responsible for initiating volumetric thirst and a salt appetite? There are two sets of receptors that accomplish this dual function: one set in the kidneys, which controls the production of angiotensin, and one set in the heart and large blood vessels (atrial baroreceptors).

■ **The Role of Angiotensin** The kidneys contain cells that are able to detect decreases in the flow of blood to the kidneys. The usual cause of a reduced flow of blood is a loss of blood volume; thus, these cells detect the presence of hypovolemia. When the flow of blood to the kidneys decreases, these cells secrete an enzyme called **renin.** Renin enters the blood, where it catalyzes the conversion of a protein called *angiotensinogen* into a hormone called **angiotensin.** In fact, there are two forms of angiotensin.

OVLT (organum vasculosum of the lamina terminalis) A circumventricular organ located anterior to the anteroventral portion of the third ventricle; served by fenestrated capillaries and thus lacks a blood–brain barrier.

volumetric thirst Thirst produced by hypovolemia.

renin (*ree nin*) A hormone secreted by the kidneys that causes the conversion of angiotensinogen in the blood into angiotensin.

angiotensin (*ann gee oh ten sin*) A peptide hormone that constricts blood vessels, causes the retention of sodium and water, and produces thirst and a salt appetite.

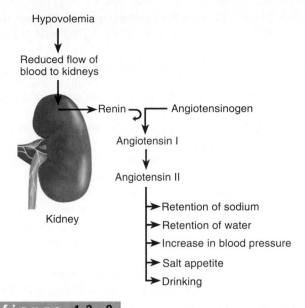

figure 12.8

Detection of hypovolemia by the kidney and the renin–angiotensin system.

Angiotensinogen becomes angiotensin I, which is quickly converted by an enzyme to angiotensin II. The active form is angiotensin II, which I shall abbreviate as *AII*.

Angiotensin II has several physiological effects: It stimulates the secretion of hormones by the posterior pituitary gland and the adrenal cortex that cause the kidneys to conserve water and sodium, and it increases blood pressure by causing muscles in the small arteries to contract. In addition, AII has two behavioral effects: It initiates both drinking and a salt appetite. Therefore, a reduction in the flow of blood to the kidneys causes water and sodium to be retained by the body, helps to compensate for their loss by reducing the size of the blood vessels, and encourages the animal to find and ingest both water and salt. (See *Figure 12.8.*)

Hypertension (high blood pressure) is sometimes caused by oversecretion of renin—or, more precisely, by the increased blood levels of AII that follows. Captopril, a drug that blocks the enzyme that converts AI to AII, is often used to treat such forms of hypertension.

Little Billy started eating salt. He always liked plenty of salt on his food, but his craving had finally gotten out of hand. His mother noticed that a carton of salt lasted only a few days, and one afternoon she caught Billy in the kitchen with the container of salt on the counter next to him, eating something out of his hand. It was salt, pure salt! She grabbed his hand and shook the salt out of it into the sink and then put the container on a shelf where Billy couldn't reach it. Billy started crying and said, "Mommy, don't take it away—I need that!"

The next morning she heard a crash in the kitchen and found Billy on the floor, an overturned chair next to him. Clearly, he was trying to get at the salt. "What's wrong with you?" she cried. "Billy sobbed and said, "Please, Mommy, I need some salt! I need it!" Bewildered but moved by his distress, she reached down the container and poured some salt in his hand, which he ate eagerly.

After consulting with the family physician, Billy's parents decided to have him admitted to the hospital, where his bizarre craving could be investigated. Although Billy cried piteously that he needed salt, the hospital staff made sure that he received no more than a child normally needed. He tried several times to leave his room, presumably to try to find some salt, but he was brought back, and the door to his room was finally locked. Unfortunately, before definitive testing could be begun, Billy died.

The diagnosis of Billy's craving came too late to help him. A disease process had caused his adrenal glands to stop secreting aldosterone, a steroid hormone that stimulates the kidneys to retain sodium. Without this hormone, excessive amounts of sodium are excreted by the kidneys, which causes the volume of the blood to fall. In Billy's case the fall in blood volume that occurred when his access to salt was blocked led to a fatal loss of blood pressure. This unhappy story occurred several decades ago, and we can hope that physicians today would recognize an intense salt craving as a cardinal symptom of adrenal insufficiency.

■ **Atrial Baroreceptors** The second set of receptors for volumetric thirst lies within the heart. Physiologists had long known that the *atria* of the heart (the parts that receive blood from the veins) contain sensory neurons that detect stretch. (The term *baro-* comes from the Greek *baros*, "heavy," and refers to weight or pressure.) The atria are passively filled with blood being returned from the body by the veins. The more blood in the veins, the fuller the atria become just before each contraction of the heart. Thus, when the volume of the blood plasma falls, the atria become less full, and the stretch receptors within them will detect this change.

Fitzsimons and Moore-Gillon (1980) showed that information from these receptors can stimulate thirst. They operated on dogs and placed a small balloon in the inferior vena cava, the vein that brings blood from most of the body (excluding the head and arms) to the heart. When the balloon was inflated, it reduced the flow of blood to the heart and thus lowered the amount of blood that entered the right atrium. Within thirty minutes the dogs began to drink. Quillen, Keil, and Reid (1990) confirmed these results. They also found that when the nerves connecting the atrial baroreceptors with the brain were cut,

animals drank much less water when the blood flow to their heart was temporarily reduced.

Neural Mechanisms of Thirst

As you have already learned, the osmoreceptors that initiate drinking are located in the brain tissue around the AV3V—in some species, in the OVLT. The entire region around the anterior third ventricle—dorsal as well as ventral—seems to be the part of the brain where osmometric and volumetric signals are integrated to control drinking. The AV3V also appears to receive information that can stimulate volumetric thirst. Sensory information from the baroreceptors located in the atria of the heart is sent to a nucleus in the medulla: the **nucleus of the solitary tract.** This nucleus sends efferent axons to many parts of the brain, including the region around the AV3V (see Johnson and Edwards, 1990).

The second signal for volumetric thirst is provided by angiotensin II. Because this peptide does not cross the blood–brain barrier, it cannot directly affect neurons in the brain except for those located in one of the circumventricular organs. In fact, research indicates that one of these organs, the **subfornical organ (SFO),** is the site at which blood angiotensin acts to produce thirst. This structure gets its name from its location, just below the commissure of the ventral fornix. (See *Figure 12.7*.)

Simpson, Epstein, and Camardo (1978) found that very low doses of angiotensin injected directly into the SFO caused drinking and that destruction of the SFO or injection of a drug that blocks angiotensin receptors abolished the drinking that normally occurs when angiotensin is injected into the blood. In addition, Phillips and Felix (1976) found that injections of minute quantities of angiotensin into the SFO increased the firing rate of single neurons located there; evidently, these neurons contain angiotensin receptors.

Neurons in the subfornical organ send their axons to the **median preoptic nucleus** (not to be confused with the *medial* preoptic nucleus), a small nucleus wrapped around the front of the anterior commissure, a fiber bun-

---

nucleus of the solitary tract A nucleus of the medulla that receives information from visceral organs and from the gustatory system.

subfornical organ (SFO) A small organ located in the confluence of the lateral ventricles, attached to the underside of the fornix; contains neurons that detect the presence of angiotensin in the blood and excite neural circuits that initiate drinking.

median preoptic nucleus A small nucleus situated around the decussation of the anterior commissure; plays a role in thirst stimulated by angiotensin.

dle that connects the amygdala and anterior temporal lobe. (See the inset in *Figure 12.7.*)

On the basis of these findings, Thrasher and his colleagues (see Thrasher, 1989) suggested that the region in front of the third ventricle acts as an integrating system for most or all of the stimuli for osmometric and volumetric thirst. As you just saw, the median preoptic nucleus receives information from angiotensin-sensitive neurons in the SFO. In addition, this nucleus receives information from the OVLT (which contains osmoreceptors) and from the nucleus of the solitary tract (which receives information from the atrial baroreceptors). According to Thrasher and his colleagues, the median preoptic nucleus integrates the information it receives and, through its efferent connections with other parts of the brain, controls drinking. (See *Figure 12.9.*)

The region of the AV3V seems to play a critical role in fluid regulation in humans as well. For example, McIver et al. (1991) report that brain damage that includes this region can cause *adipsia*—lack of drinking. The patients report no sensation of thirst even after they are given an injection of hypertonic saline. To survive, they must deliberately drink water at regular intervals each day, even though they feel no need to do so.

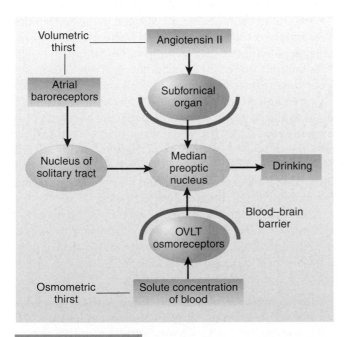

figure   12.9

Neural circuitry concerned with the control of drinking. Not all connections are shown, and some connections may be indirect. OVLT = organum vasculosum of the lamina terminalis.

(Adapted from Thrasher, T. N. *Acta Physiologica Scandanivica*, 1989, *136*, 141–150.)

interim summary

Drinking

A regulatory system contains four features: a system variable (the variable that is regulated), a set point (the optimal value of the system variable), a detector to measure the system variable, and a correctional mechanism to change it. Physiological regulatory systems, such as control of body fluids and nutrients, require a satiety mechanism to anticipate the effects of the correctional mechanism, because the changes brought about by eating and drinking occur only after a considerable period of time.

The body contains three major fluid compartments: intracellular, interstitial, and intravascular. Sodium and water can easily pass between the intravascular fluid and the interstitial fluid, but sodium cannot penetrate the cell membrane. The solute concentration of the interstitial fluid must be closely regulated. If it becomes hypertonic, cells lose water; if it becomes hypotonic, they gain water. The volume of the intravascular fluid (blood plasma) must also be kept within bounds.

Osmometric thirst occurs when the interstitial fluid becomes hypertonic, drawing water out of cells. This event, which can be caused by evaporation of water from the body or by ingestion of a salty meal, is detected by osmoreceptors in the region of the anteroventral third ventricle (the AV3V). The receptors are located both in the OVLT, a circumventricular organ, and in adjacent regions of the brain. Activation of the osmoreceptors stimulates drinking.

Volumetric thirst occurs along with osmometric thirst when the body loses fluid through evaporation. Pure volumetric thirst is caused by blood loss, vomiting, and diarrhea. One stimulus for volumetric thirst is provided by a fall in blood flow to the kidneys. This event triggers the secretion of renin, which converts plasma angiotensinogen to angiotensin I. Angiotensin I is subsequently converted to its active form, Angiotensin II. Angiotensin II acts on neurons in the brain and stimulates thirst. The hormone also increases blood pressure and stimulates the secretion of pituitary and adrenal hormones that inhibit the secretion of water and sodium by the kidneys and induce a sodium appetite. (Sodium is needed to help restore the plasma volume.) Volumetric drinking can also be stimulated by a set of baroreceptors in the atria of the heart that detect decreased blood volume and send this information to the brain.

The region of the AV3V detects and integrates signals that produce both osmometric and volumetric thirst. Volumetric thirst stimulated by angiotensin involves another circumventricular organ: the subfornical organ. Volumetric thirst stimulated by the atrial stretch receptor system reaches the AV3V region via a relay in the nucleus of the solitary tract.

Neurons in the SFO, the AV3V region, and the OVLT (which, you will remember, contains osmoreceptors) all send axons to the median preoptic nucleus. Neurons in this nucleus stimulate drinking through their connections with other parts of the brain.

Eating: Some Facts About Metabolism

Clearly, eating is one of the most important things we do, and it can also be one of the most pleasurable. Much of what an animal learns to do is motivated by the constant struggle to obtain food; thus, the need to ingest undoubtedly shaped the evolutionary development of our own species. After having read the first part of this chapter, in which you saw that the signals that cause thirst are well understood, you might be surprised to learn that researchers are only now discovering what the system variables for hunger are. Control of ingestive behavior is even more complicated than the control of drinking and sodium intake. We can achieve water balance by the intake of two ingredients: water and sodium chloride. When we eat, we must obtain adequate amounts of carbohydrates, fats, amino acids, vitamins, and minerals other than sodium. Thus, our food-ingestive behaviors are more complex, as are the physiological mechanisms that control them.

The rest of this chapter describes research on the control of eating: metabolism, regulation of body weight, the environmental and physiological factors that begin and stop a meal, and the neural mechanisms that monitor the nutritional state of our bodies and control our ingestive behavior. It also describes the most serious eating disorders: obesity and anorexia nervosa. Despite all the effort that has gone into understanding the physiology of ingestive behavior, these disorders are still difficult to treat. Our best hope of finding effective treatments is to achieve a better understanding of the physiology of metabolism and ingestive behavior.

As you saw in the discussion of the physiology of drinking, you must know something about the fluid compartments of the body and the functions of the kidney to understand the physiology of drinking. Thus, you will not be surprised that this chapter begins with a discussion of metabolism. Your first inclination might be to skip over this section; but if you do so, you will find that you will not understand experiments that are described later. For example, the system variables that cause an animal to seek food and eat it are obviously related to the animal's metab-

olism. This section will discuss only as much about this subject as you will need to understand these experiments.

Absorption, Fasting, and the Two Nutrient Reservoirs

When we eat, we incorporate into our own bodies molecules that were once part of other living organisms, plant and animal. We ingest these molecules for two reasons: to construct and maintain our own organs and to obtain energy for muscular movements and for keeping our bodies warm. In other words, we need both building blocks and fuel. Although food used for building blocks is essential, I will discuss only the food used for fuel, because most of the molecules we eat get "burned" to provide energy for movement and heating.

To stay alive, our cells must be supplied with fuel and oxygen. Obviously, fuel comes from the digestive tract, and its presence there is a result of eating. But the digestive tract is sometimes empty; in fact, most of us wake up in the morning in that condition. So there has to be a reservoir that stores nutrients to keep the cells of the body nourished when the gut is empty. Indeed, there are two reservoirs: one short-term and the other long-term. The short-term reservoir stores carbohydrates, and the long-term reservoir stores fats.

The short-term reservoir is located in the cells of the liver and the muscles, and it is filled with a complex, insoluble carbohydrate called **glycogen.** For simplicity I will consider only one of these locations: the liver. Cells in the liver convert glucose (a simple, soluble carbohydrate) into glycogen and store the glycogen. They are stimulated to do so by the presence of **insulin,** a peptide hormone produced by the pancreas. Thus, when glucose and insulin are present in the blood, some of the glucose is used as a fuel, and some of it is stored as glycogen. Later, when all of the food has been absorbed from the digestive tract, the level of glucose in the blood begins to fall.

The fall in glucose is detected by cells in the pancreas and in the brain. The pancreas responds by stopping its secretion of insulin and starting to secrete a different peptide hormone: **glucagon.** The effect of glucagon is oppo-

---

glycogen (*gly ko jen*) A polysaccharide often referred to as *animal starch;* stored in liver and muscle; constitutes the short-term store of nutrients.

insulin A pancreatic hormone that facilitates entry of glucose and amino acids into the cell, conversion of glucose into glycogen, and transport of fats into adipose tissue.

glucagon (*gloo ka gahn*) A pancreatic hormone that promotes the conversion of liver glycogen into glucose.

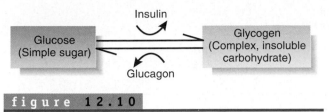

figure 12.10

Effects of insulin and glucagon on glucose
and glycogen.

site that of insulin: It stimulates the conversion of glyco-gen into glucose. (Unfortunately, the terms *glucose, glyco-gen,* and *glucagon* are similar enough that it is easy to confuse them. Even worse, you will soon encounter another one: *glycerol.*) (See *Figure 12.10.*) Thus, the liver soaks up excess glucose and stores it as glycogen when plenty of glucose is available, and it releases glucose from its reservoir when the digestive tract becomes empty and the level of glucose in the blood begins to fall.

The carbohydrate reservoir in the liver is primarily reserved for the central nervous system. When you wake in the morning, your brain is being fed by your liver, which is in the process of converting glycogen to glucose and releasing it into the blood. The glucose reaches the CNS, where it is absorbed and metabolized by the neu-rons and the glia. This process can continue for a few hours, until all of the carbohydrate reservoir in the liver is used up. (The average liver holds approximately 300 calories of carbohydrate.) Usually, we eat some food before this reservoir gets depleted, which permits us to refill it. But if we do not eat, the CNS has to start living on the products of the long-term reservoir.

Our long-term reservoir consists of adipose tissue (fat tissue). This reservoir is filled with fats, or, more precisely, with **triglycerides.** Triglycerides are complex molecules that contain **glycerol** (a soluble carbohydrate, also called *glycerine*) combined with three **fatty acids** (stearic acid, oleic acid, and palmitic acid). Adipose tissue is found beneath the skin and in various loca-tions in the abdominal cavity. It consists of cells that are capable of absorbing nutrients from the blood, convert-ing them to triglycerides, and storing them. These cells can expand enormously in size; in fact, the primary physical difference between an obese person and a per-son of normal weight is the size of their fat cells, which is determined by the amount of triglycerides that these cells contain.

The long-term fat reservoir is obviously what keeps us alive when we are fasting. As we begin to use the con-tents of our short-term carbohydrate reservoir, fat cells start converting triglycerides into fuels that the cells can use and

releasing these fuels into the bloodstream. As we just saw, when we wake in the morning with an empty digestive tract, our brain (in fact, all of the central nervous system) is living on glucose released by the liver. But what about the other cells of the body? They are living on fatty acids, sparing the glucose for the brain. As you will recall from Chapter 3, the sympathetic nervous system is primarily involved in the breakdown and utilization of stored nutri-ents. When the digestive system is empty, there is an increase in the activity of the sympathetic axons that inner-vate adipose tissue, the pancreas, and the adrenal medulla. All three effects (direct neural stimulation, secretion of glucagon, and secretion of catecholamines) cause triglyc-erides in the long-term fat reservoir to be broken down into glycerol and fatty acids. The fatty acids can be directly metabolized by cells in all of the body *except the brain,* which needs glucose. That leaves glycerol. The liver takes up glycerol and converts it to glucose. That glucose, too, is available to the brain.

You may be asking why the cells of the rest of the body treat the brain so kindly, letting it consume almost all the glucose that the liver releases from its carbohydrate reservoir and constructs from glycerol. The answer is simple: Insulin has several other functions besides caus-ing glucose to be converted to glycogen. One of these functions is controlling the entry of glucose into cells. Glucose easily dissolves in water, but it will not dissolve in fats. Cell membranes are made of lipids (fatlike sub-stances); thus, glucose cannot directly pass through them. To be taken into a cell, glucose must be trans-ported there by *glucose transporters*—protein molecules that are situated in the membrane and are similar to those responsible for the reuptake of transmitter substances. Glucose transporters contain insulin receptors, which control their activity; only when insulin binds with these receptors can glucose be transported into the cell. But the cells of the nervous system are an exception to this rule. Their glucose transporters do not contain insulin recep-tors; thus, these cells can absorb glucose *even when insulin is not present.*

---

triglyceride (*try **gliss** er ide*) The form of fat storage in adipose cells; consists of a molecule of glycerol joined with three fatty acids.

glycerol (***gliss** er all*) A substance (also called glycerine) derived from the breakdown of triglycerides, along with fatty acids; can be converted by the liver into glucose.

fatty acid A substance derived from the breakdown of triglycerides, along with glycerol; can be metabolized by most cells of the body except for the brain.

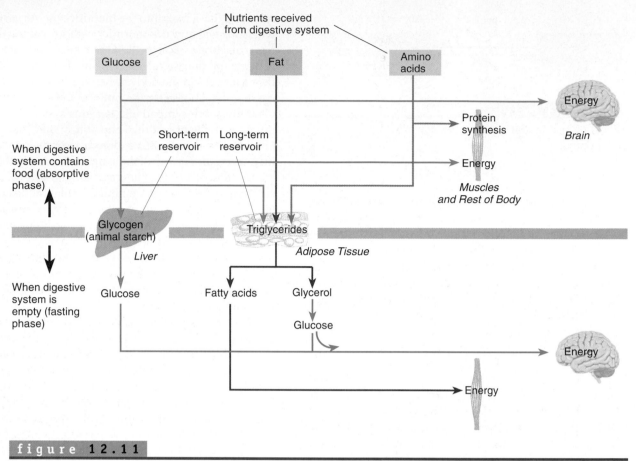

figure **12.11**

Metabolic pathways during the fasting phase and absorptive phase of metabolism.

Figure 12.11 reviews what I have said so far about the metabolism that takes place while the digestive tract is empty, which physiologists refer to as the **fasting phase** of metabolism. A fall in the blood glucose level causes the pancreas to stop secreting insulin and to start secreting glucagon. The absence of insulin means that most of the cells of the body can no longer use glucose; thus, all the glucose present in the blood is reserved for the central nervous system. The presence of glucagon and the absence of insulin instructs the liver to start drawing on the short-term carbohydrate reservoir—to start converting its glycogen into glucose. The presence of glucagon and the absence of insulin, along with increased activity of the sympathetic nervous system, also instruct fat cells to start drawing on the long-term fat reservoir—to start breaking down triglycerides into fatty acids and glycerol. Most of the body lives on the fatty acids, and the glycerol, which is converted into glucose by the liver, gets used by the brain. If fasting is prolonged, proteins (especially protein found in muscle) will be broken down to amino acids, which can be metabolized by all of the body except the central nervous system. (See *Figure 12.11* and *Animation 12.1, Metabolism.*)

The phase of metabolism that occurs when food is present in the digestive tract is called the **absorptive phase.** Now that you understand the fasting phase, this one is simple. Suppose that we eat a balanced meal of carbohydrates, proteins, and fats. The carbohydrates are broken down into glucose, and the proteins are broken down

fasting phase The phase of metabolism during which nutrients are not available from the digestive system; glucose, amino acids, and fatty acids are derived from glycogen, protein, and adipose tissue during this phase.

absorptive phase The phase of metabolism during which nutrients are absorbed from the digestive system; glucose and amino acids constitute the principal source of energy for cells during this phase, and excess nutrients are stored in adipose tissue in the form of triglycerides.

into amino acids. The fats basically remain as fats. Let us consider each of these three nutrients.

1. As we start absorbing the nutrients, the level of glucose in the blood rises. This rise is detected by cells in the brain, which causes the activity of the sympathetic nervous system to decrease and the activity of the parasympathetic nervous system to increase. This change tells the pancreas to stop secreting glucagon and to begin secreting insulin. The insulin permits all the cells of the body to use glucose as a fuel. Extra glucose is converted into glycogen, which fills the short-term carbohydrate reservoir. If some glucose is left over, it is converted into fat and absorbed by fat cells.

2. A small proportion of the amino acids received from the digestive tract are used as building blocks to construct proteins and peptides; the rest are converted to fats and stored in adipose tissue.

3. Fats are not used at this time; they are simply stored in adipose tissue. (See *Figure 12.11.*)

interim
summary

Eating: Some Facts About Metabolism

Metabolism consists of two phases. During the absorptive phase we receive glucose, amino acids, and fats from the intestines. The blood level of insulin is high, which permits all cells to metabolize glucose. In addition, the liver and the muscles convert glucose to glycogen, which replenishes the short-term reservoir. Excess carbohydrates and amino acids are converted to fats, and fats are placed into the long-term reservoir in the adipose tissue.

During the fasting phase the activity of the parasympathetic nervous system falls, and the activity of the sympathetic nervous system increases. In response, the level of insulin falls, and the level of glucagon and the adrenal catecholamines rises. These events cause liver glycogen to be converted to glucose and triglycerides to be broken down into glycerol and fatty acids. In the absence of insulin only the central nervous system can use the glucose available in the blood; the rest of the body lives on fatty acids. Glycerol is converted to glucose by the liver, and the glucose is metabolized by the brain.

What Starts a Meal?

The heading to this section is a very simple question, but the answer is complex. The short answer, I suppose, is that we still are not sure, but that will not stop me from continuing to write. In fact, many factors start a meal,

including the presence of appetizing food, the company of people who are eating, or the words "It's time to eat!" More fundamentally, there must be some sort of signal that tells the brain that the supply of nutrients has gotten low and that it is time to begin looking for, and ingesting, some food. This section considers all of these factors.

Before I begin, I will point out that the physiological signals that cause a meal to begin are different from the ones that cause it to end. As I said in the discussion of regulatory systems at the beginning of this chapter, there is a considerable delay between the act of eating (the correctional mechanism) and a change in the system variable. We may start eating because the supply of nutrients has fallen below a certain level, but we certainly do not stop eating because the level of those nutrients has been restored to normal. In fact, we stop eating long before that happens, because digestion takes several hours. Thus, the signals for hunger and satiety are sure to be different.

Social and Environmental Factors

Most people, if they were asked why they eat, would say that they do so because they get hungry. By that they probably mean that something happens inside their body that provides a sensation that makes them want to eat. In other words, we tend to think of eating as something provoked by physiological factors. But often we eat because of habit or because of some stimuli present in our environment. These stimuli may include a clock indicating that it is time to eat, the sight of a plate of food, the smell of food cooking in the kitchen, or the presence of other people sitting around the table.

One of the most important variables affecting appetite is the meal schedule. We tend to take our meals at fixed times: soon after waking, at midday, and in the evening. This custom makes it difficult for us to adjust the timing of our meals, as other animals can do. What we do instead is adjust the *size* of our meals. If we have eaten recently or if the previous meal was large, we tend to eat a smaller meal (Jiang and Hunt, 1983; de Castro et al., 1986). However, if someone else prepares and serves us our meal (for example, at a restaurant), we are more likely to ignore internal satiety signals and finish what is on our plate.

The presence of other people is yet another factor that strongly affects our eating behavior. De Castro and de Castro (1989) asked people to keep diaries that listed all the food they ate during a seven-day period and the number of other people who were present while they were eating. The investigators found that the amount of food eaten was directly related to the number of other people who were present—The more people present, the more the subjects ate. In addition, the correlation that is normally seen between the time since the previous meal and the size of the present meal was observed only when the subjects ate alone; when other people were present, the correlation was abolished. Thus, social factors can overcome the effects of metabolic factors.

Physiological Hunger Signals

Most of the time, we begin a meal because it is time to eat. The amount of food we eat during that meal depends on several factors, including the amount and variety of food available to us, how good the food tastes to us, and (as we saw earlier) the presence of other people. But the amount of food we eat also depends on metabolic factors. If we skip several meals, we get hungrier and hungrier, presumably because of physiological signals indicating that we have been withdrawing nutrients from our long-term reservoir. And all other things being equal, the hungrier we are, the more we will eat. In addition, if clocks and dinner bells are not present, we eat soon after a small meal but wait longer after a large one. These facts suggest that the amount of food we eat is inversely related to the amount of nutrients left over from previous meals (De Castro, 1999).

What happens to the level of nutrients in our body as time passes after a meal? As you learned earlier in this chapter, during the absorptive phase of metabolism we live on food that is being absorbed from the digestive tract. After that we start drawing on our nutrient reservoirs: The brain lives on glucose, and the rest of the body lives on fatty acids. Although the metabolic needs of the cells of the body are being met, we are taking fuel out of our long-term reservoir—making withdrawals rather than deposits. Clearly, this is the time to start thinking about our next meal.

A fall in blood glucose level (a condition known as *hypoglycemia*) is a potent stimulus for hunger. Hypoglycemia can be produced experimentally by giving an animal a large injection of insulin, which causes liver cells and fat cells to take up glucose and store it away. We can also deprive cells of glucose by injecting an animal with 2-deoxyglucose (2-DG). You are already familiar with this chemical, because I described several experiments in previous chapters that used radioactive 2-DG in conjunction with PET scanners or autoradiography to study the metabolic rate of different parts of the brain. When (nonradioactive) 2-DG is given in large doses, it interferes with glucose metabolism by competing with glucose for access to the mechanism that transports glucose through the cell membrane and for access to the enzymes that metabolize glucose. (A similar chemical, *5-TG,* has the same effect.) Both hypoglycemia and 2-DG cause **glucoprivation;** that is, they deprive cells of glucose. And glucoprivation, whatever its cause, stimulates eating.

Hunger can also be produced by causing **lipoprivation**—depriving cells of lipids. More precisely, they are deprived of the ability to metabolize fatty acids through

injection of one of two drugs, **methyl palmoxirate** (**MP**) or **mercaptoacetate** (**MA**).

What is the nature of the detectors that monitor the level of metabolic fuels, and where are they located? The evidence that has been gathered so far indicates that there are two sets of detectors: one set located in the brain and the other set located in the liver. The detectors in the brain monitor the nutrients that are available on their side of the blood–brain barrier, and the detectors in the liver monitor the nutrients that are available to the rest of the body. Because the brain can use only glucose, its detectors are sensitive to glucoprivation, and because the rest of the body can use both glucose and fatty acids, the detectors in the liver are sensitive to both glucoprivation and lipoprivation.

Let's first review the evidence for the detectors in the liver. A study by Novin, VanderWeele, and Rezek (1973) suggested that receptors in the liver can stimulate glucoprivic hunger; when these neurons are deprived of nutrients, they cause eating. The investigators infused 2-DG into the **hepatic portal vein.** This vein brings blood from the intestines to the liver; thus, an injection of a drug into this vein delivers it directly to the liver. (See *Figure 12.12.*) The investigators found that the intraportal infusions of 2-DG caused immediate eating. When they cut the vagus nerve, which connects the liver with the brain, the infusions no longer stimulated eating. Thus, the brain receives the hunger signal through this connection.

What about liproprivic hunger? Ritter and Taylor (1990) induced lipoprivic hunger with an injection of MA and found that cutting the vagus nerve abolished this hunger. Furthermore, Lutz, Diener, and Scharrer (1997) found that infusion of MA into the hepatic portal vein increased the activity of afferent axons in the hepatic branch of the vagus nerve. Thus, the liver appears to contain receptors that detect low availability of glucose or fatty acids (glucoprivation or lipoprivation) and send this information to the brain through the vagus nerve.

Now let's look at some of the evidence that indicates that the brain has its own nutrient detectors. Because the

---

glucoprivation A dramatic fall in the level of glucose available to cells; can be caused by a fall in the blood level of glucose or by drugs that inhibit glucose metabolism.

lipoprivation A dramatic fall in the level of fatty acids available to cells; usually caused by drugs that inhibit fatty acid metabolism.

methyl palmoxirate (MP) A drug that inhibits fatty acid metabolism and produces lipoprivic hunger.

mercaptoacetate (MA) A drug that inhibits fatty acid metabolism and produces lipoprivic hunger.

hepatic portal vein The vein that transports blood from the digestive system to the liver.

brain can use only glucose, it would make sense that these detectors respond to glucoprivation—and, indeed, they do. Ritter, Slusser, and Stone (1981) injected some silicone grease into the cerebral aqueduct, which blocked communication between the third and fourth ventricles. Next, they injected 5-TG into either the third ventricle or the fourth ventricle. (5-TG, like 2-DG, produces glucoprivation.) Injections into the fourth ventricle stimulated eating, but injections into the third ventricle (located in the middle of the diencephalon) had no effect. Presumably, the 5-TG diffused out of the fourth ventricle into the surrounding brain tissue and inhibited glucose metabolism in neurons in the hindbrain.

The location of the hindbrain nutrient receptors is not yet known, but one possible location is the area postrema or the adjacent nucleus of the solitary tract, located in the medulla. Bird, Cardone, and Contreras (1983) found that after the area postrema had been destroyed, an injection of 5-TG into the ventricular system no longer stimulated food intake. Also, Yettefti, Orsini, and Perrin (1997) found that the firing rate of some neurons in the nucleus of the solitary tract changed when the investigators infused glucose into that region by means of iontophoresis or injected glucose intravenously. Finally, Singer and Ritter (1996) found that infusion of glucose into the ventricular system suppressed glucoprivic feeding stimulated by an intraperitoneal injection of 2-DG. Presumably, the glucose infused

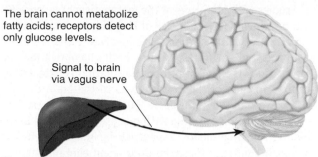

The brain cannot metabolize fatty acids; receptors detect only glucose levels.

Signal to brain via vagus nerve

The liver can metabolize glucose and fatty acids; receptors detect levels of both nutrients.

figure 12.13

Probable location of nutrient receptors responsible for hunger signals.

into the ventricular system "fooled" the nutrient receptors in the brain and inhibited the glucoprivic hunger.

To summarize: The brain contains detectors that monitor the availability of glucose (its only fuel) inside the blood–brain barrier, and the liver contains detectors that monitor the availability of nutrients (glucose and fatty acids) outside the blood–brain barrier. (See *Figure 12.13*.)

Before closing this section, I should note that no single set of receptors is solely responsible for the information the brain uses to control eating. For example, Tordoff, Hopfenbeck, and Novin (1982) found that cutting the hepatic branch of the vagus nerve, which prevents hunger signals originating in the liver from reaching the brain, had little effect on an animal's day-to-day eating. In addition, lesions of the area postrema and the nucleus of the solitary tract, which abolish both glucoprivic and lipoprivic signals, do not lead to long-term disturbances in the control of feeding (Ritter et al., 1992). Apparently, the control of metabolism and ingestive behavior is just too important to entrust to one mechanism.

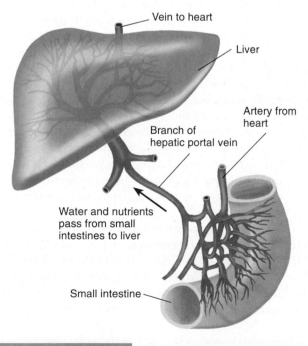

Vein to heart

Liver

Artery from heart

Branch of hepatic portal vein

Water and nutrients pass from small intestines to liver

Small intestine

figure 12.12

The hepatic portal blood supply. The liver receives water, minerals, and nutrients from the digestive system through this blood supply.

interim summary

What Starts a Meal?

Many stimuli, environmental and physiological, can initiate a meal. Stimuli associated with eating—such as clocks pointing to lunchtime or dinnertime, the smell or sight of food, or (especially) the taste of food—increase appetite. The size of a meal taken by a rat (or a person living in isolation) determines the interval until the next one. In contrast, most people eat at relatively fixed times but vary their intake according to how much (or when) they ate the previous meal. The presence of other people tends to increase the size of our meal and removes the controlling effect of the previous meal.

Studies with inhibitors of the metabolism of glucose (2-DG or 5-TG) and fatty acids (MP or MA) indicate that low levels of both of these nutrients are involved in hunger; that is, animals will eat in response to both glucoprivation and lipoprivation. The signal for lipoprivic eating is detected by receptors in the liver and transmitted to the brain through sensory axons of the vagus nerve. Glucoprivic eating can also be stimulated by interfering with glucose metabolism in the region surrounding the fourth ventricle by injecting 5-TG into the fourth ventricle; thus, the brain stem contains its own glucose-sensitive detectors. Although the evidence is not yet conclusive, these detectors may lie in the area postrema/nucleus of the solitary tract, which also receives information from the detectors in the liver.

What Stops a Meal?

As we saw, the signals that stop a meal are different from those that start it. However, these two types of signals interact. If a meal is started when there is not much physiological need for nutrients (that is, when the nutrient reservoirs are well stocked), the meal will be a small one. However, is a meal is started after a long fast, when the nutrient reservoirs are somewhat depleted, the meal will be a large one. In other words, if the hunger signal is moderate, a moderate satiety signal will stop the meal. If the hunger signal is strong, only a strong satiety signal will stop it.

There are two primary sources of satiety signals—the signals that stop a meal. Short-term satiety signals come from the immediate consequence of eating a particular meal. To search for these signals, we follow the pathway traveled by ingested food: the eyes, nose, and mouth; the stomach; the small intestine; and the liver. Each of these locations can potentially provide a signal to the brain that indicates that food has been ingested and is progressing on the way toward absorption. In addition, metabolic signals present in the blood inform the brain that the body is in the absorptive phase. Long-term satiety signals arise in the adipose tissue, which contains the long-term nutrient reservoir. These signals do not control the beginning and end of a particular meal, but they do, in the long run, control the intake of calories by modulating the sensitivity of brain mechanisms involved in hunger.

Head Factors

The term *head factors* refers to several sets of receptors located in the head: the eyes, the nose, the tongue, and the throat. Information about the appearance, odor, taste, texture, and temperature of food has some automatic effects on food intake, but most of the effects involve learning. The mere act of eating does not produce long-lasting satiety; an animal with a **gastric fistula** (a tube that drains food out of the stomach before it can be digested) will eat indefinitely.

Undoubtedly, the most important role of head factors in satiety is the fact that taste and odor of food can serve as stimuli that permit animals to learn about the caloric contents of different foods. Thus, animals can learn to adjust their intake according to the caloric value of what they are eating. For example, Mather, Nicolaïdis, and Booth (1978) found that rats learned to eat less of a food with a particular flavor when the eating of that food was accompanied by intravenous infusions of glucose, which supplied extra calories.

Head factors operate in humans, too. For example, Cecil, Francis, and Read (1998) found that people became more satiated when they ate a bowl of high-fat soup than when the experimenters infused an equal amount of soup into their stomachs with a flexible tube. Apparently, the act of tasting and swallowing the soup contributed to the feeling of fullness caused by the presence of the soup in the stomach.

Gastric Factors

Although most people associate feelings of hunger with "hunger pangs" in the stomach and feelings of satiety with an impression of gastric fullness, the stomach is not necessary for feelings of hunger. Humans whose stomachs have been removed because of cancer or the presence of large ulcers still periodically get hungry (Ingelfinger, 1944). Of necessity, these people eat frequent, small meals; in fact, a large meal causes nausea and discomfort, apparently because the duodenum quickly fills up. The **duodenum** is the part of the small intestine that attaches to the stomach. (The original Greek name for this part of the gut was *dodekadaktulon,* or "twelve fingers long." In fact, the duodenum is twelve finger *widths* long.) However, although the stomach might not be especially important in producing hunger, it does appear to play an important role in satiety.

The stomach apparently contains receptors that can detect the presence of nutrients. Davis and Campbell (1973) allowed rats to eat their fill, and shortly thereafter, they removed food from the rats' stomachs through an implanted tube. When the rats were permitted to eat again, they ate almost exactly the same amount of food

gastric fistula A tube that drains out the contents of the stomach.

duodenum The first portion of the small intestine, attached directly to the stomach.

that had been taken out. This finding suggests that animals are able to monitor the amount of food in their stomachs.

Deutsch and Gonzalez (1980) confirmed and extended these findings. They found that when they removed food from the stomach of a rat that had just eaten all it wanted, the animal would immediately eat just enough food to replace what had been removed—even if the experimenters replaced the food with a nonnutritive saline solution. Obviously, the rats did not do so simply by measuring the volume of the food in their stomachs, because they were not fooled by the infusion of a saline solution. Of course, this study proves only that the stomach contains nutrient receptors; it does not prove that there are not detectors in the intestines as well.

Intestinal Factors

Indeed, the intestines do contain nutrient detectors. Studies have shown that afferent axons arising from the duodenum are sensitive to the presence of glucose, amino acids, and fatty acids (Ritter et al., 1992). These axons may transmit a satiety signal to the brain.

Greenberg, Smith, and Gibbs (1990) showed that the entry of food into the duodenum suppresses food intake. They attached gastric fistulas to a group of rats so that when the animals drank a liquid diet, it would drain out of their stomachs. Under these conditions animals will eat for a long time, because food does not accumulate in the digestive system. (This behavior is referred to as **sham feeding** because it is an imitation of the real thing.) The researchers infused *Intralipid,* a commercial mixture of lipids and fatty acids, into the rats' duodenums. The infusion inhibited the sham feeding, which indicates the presence of a duodenal satiety signal. When the researchers added a local anesthetic to the liquid diet, the infusion was much less effective in reducing sham feeding. Thus, the signal seems to arise from nutrient detectors located inside the duodenum; the local anesthetic prevented these detectors from sending a signal to the brain, and the animals continued to eat. In support of this conclusion Greenberg et al. (1991) found that the satiating effect of an injection of radioactively labeled *Intralipid* into the duodenum occurred before radioactivity was seen in the blood of the hepatic portal vein. Thus, the satiating effect occurred before digestion had taken place.

Studies with humans have also found evidence for intestinal satiety factors. Feinle, Grundy, and Read (1997) placed an inflatable bag in people's stomachs. When the stomach and duodenum were empty, the subjects reported that they simply felt bloated when the bag was inflated, filling the stomach. However, when fats or carbohydrates were infused into the duodenum while the bag was being inflated, the people reported sensations of fullness like those experienced after eating a meal. Thus, stomach and

intestinal satiety factors can interact. That's not surprising, given the fact that by the time we finish a normal meal, our stomachs are full and a small amount of nutrients have been received by the duodenum.

After food reaches the stomach, it is mixed with hydrochloric acid and pepsin, an enzyme that breaks proteins into their constituent amino acids. As digestion proceeds, food is gradually introduced into the duodenum. There, the food is mixed with bile and pancreatic enzymes, which continue the digestive process. The duodenum controls the rate of stomach emptying by secreting a peptide hormone called **cholecystokinin (CCK).** This hormone receives its name from the fact that it causes the gallbladder (cholecyst) to contract, injecting bile into the duodenum. (Bile breaks fats down into small particles so that they can be absorbed from the intestines.) CCK is secreted in response to the presence of fats, which are detected by receptors in the walls of the duodenum. In addition to stimulating contraction of the gallbladder, CCK causes the pylorus to constrict and inhibits gastric contractions, thus keeping the stomach from giving it more food.

Obviously, the blood level of CCK must be related to the amount of nutrients (particularly fats) that the duodenum receives from the stomach. Thus, this hormone could potentially provide a satiety signal to the brain, telling it that the duodenum was receiving food from the stomach. Many studies have indeed found that injections of CCK suppress eating (Gibbs, Young, and Smith, 1973; Smith, Gibbs, and Kulkosky, 1982). In addition, a strain of rats with a genetic mutation that prevents the production of CCK receptors become obese, apparently because of a disruption in normal satiety (Moran et al., 1998). The suppressive effects are only temporary; if CCK is administered with each meal, the animal eats less but then compensates for the decreased food intake by taking more frequent meals (West, Fey, and Woods, 1984). CCK cannot cross the blood–brain barrier, so its site of action is outside the central nervous system or in one of the circumventricular organs (like that of angiotensin). In fact, it acts on receptors located in the junction between the stomach and the duodenum. Signals from these receptors are transmitted to the brain via the vagus nerve (Smith, Gibbs, and Kulkosky, 1982; Moran et al., 1989).

Recently, investigators have discovered a chemical produced by cells in the gastrointestinal tract that may

---

sham feeding Feeding behavior of an animal with an open gastric or esophageal fistula that prevents food from remaining in the stomach.

cholecystokinin (CCK) (*coal i sis toe ky nin*) A hormone secreted by the duodenum that regulates gastric motility and causes the gallbladder (cholecyst) to contract; appears to provide a satiety signal transmitted to the brain through the vagus nerve.

serve as a satiety signal. This chemical, **peptide YY$_{3-36}$** (let's just call it **PYY**), is released after a meal in amounts proportional to the calories that were just ingested (Pedersen-Bjergaard et al., 1996. Only nutrients caused PYY to be secreted; a large drink of water had no effect. Batterham et al. (2002) found that injections of PYY significantly decreased the amount of food that hungry rats would eat. Because PYY interacts with peptide receptors in the hypothalamus that are involved with hunger and satiety, I will discuss the actions of this chemical later in this chapter, in a section dealing with brain mechanisms of ingestive behavior.

Liver Factors

Satiety produced by gastric factors or duodenal factors is anticipatory; that is, these factors predict that the food in the digestive system will, when absorbed, eventually restore the system variables that cause hunger. Food in the mouth or stomach does not restore the body's store of nutrients. Not until nutrients are absorbed from the intestines are the internal system variables that cause hunger returned to normal. The last stage of satiety appears to occur in the liver, which is the first organ to learn that food is finally being received by the intestines.

Evidence that nutrient detectors in the liver play a role in satiety comes from several sources. For example, Tordoff and Friedman (1988) infused small amounts of two nutrients, glucose and fructose, into the hepatic portal vein. The amounts they used were similar to those that are produced when a meal is being digested. The infusions "fooled" the liver; both nutrients reduced the amount of food that the rats ate. Fructose cannot cross the blood–brain barrier and is metabolized very poorly by cells in the rest of the body, but it can readily be metabolized by the liver. Therefore, the signal from this nutrient must have originated in the liver. These results strongly suggest that when the liver receives nutrients from the intestines, it sends a signal to the brain that produces satiety. (More accurately, the signal *continues* the satiety that was already started by signals arising from the stomach and duodenum.)

Metabolic Factors Present in the Blood

Satiety begins with the eating of a meal, which is detected by factors in the head, stomach, duodenum, and liver. The liver absorbs some nutrients—particularly glucose, which it converts into glycogen and stores in the short-term reservoir. But soon, the level of nutrients in the blood begins to rise. When this happens, physiological changes occur, and the body enters the absorptive phase of metabolism. Perhaps some signals that arise from these changes provide a satiety signal to the brain.

As you will recall, the absorptive phase of metabolism is accompanied by an increased level of insulin in the blood. Insulin permits organs other than the brain to metabolize glucose, and it promotes the entry of nutrients into fat cells where they are converted into triglycerides. You will also recall that cells in the brain do not need insulin to metabolize glucose. Nevertheless, the brain contains insulin receptors (Unger et al., 1989). What purpose do these insulin receptors serve? The answer is that they appear to detect insulin present in the blood, which tells the brain that the body is probably in the fasting phase of metabolism. Thus, insulin may serve as a satiety signal.

Insulin is a peptide and would not normally be admitted to the brain. However, a transport mechanism delivers it through the blood–brain barrier, and it reaches neurons in the hypothalamus that are involved in regulation of hunger and satiety. Infusion of insulin into the third ventricle inhibits eating and causes a loss of body weight (Woods et al., 1979). In addition, Brüning et al. (2000) prepared a mutation in mice that prevented the synthesis of insulin receptors in the brain without affecting their production elsewhere in the body. The mice became obese, especially when they were fed a tasty, high-fat diet, which would be expected if one of the factors that promotes satiety was absent.

Long-Term Satiety: Signals from Adipose Tissue

So far, I have discussed satiety factors arising from a meal. But as we saw in the first section of this chapter, total body fat appears to be regulated over a long-term basis. If an animal is force-fed so that it becomes fatter than normal, it will reduce its food intake once it is permitted to choose how much to eat (Wilson et al., 1990). (See *Figure 12.14.*) Similar studies have shown that an animal will adjust its food intake appropriately if it is given a high-calorie or low-calorie diet. And if an animal is put on a diet that reduces its body weight, gastric satiety factors become much less effective (Cabanac and Lafrance, 1991). Thus, signals arising from the long-term nutrient reservoir may either suppress hunger signals or augment short-term satiety signals.

What exactly is the system variable that permits the body weight of most organisms to remain relatively stable? It seems highly unlikely that body *weight* itself is regulated; this variable would have to be measured by detectors in the soles of our feet or (for those of us who are sedentary) in the skin of our buttocks. What is more

peptide YY$_{3-36}$ (PYY) A peptide released by the gastrointestinal system after a meal in amounts proportional to the size of the meal.

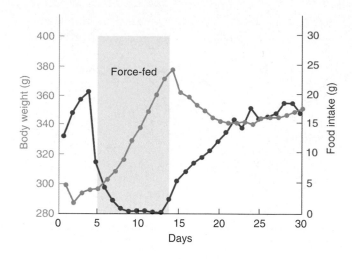

figure 12.14

Food intake and body weight of rats that received an excess of their normal food intake through force feeding. Their food intake fell during the period of force feeding and recovered only when their body weight returned to normal.

(Adapted from Wilson, B. E., Meyer, G. E., Cleveland, J. C., and Weigle, D. S. *American Journal of Physiology*, 1990, *259*, R1148–R1155.)

likely is that some variable related to body fat is regulated. The basic difference between obese and nonobese people is the amount of fat stored in their adipose tissue. Perhaps fat tissue provides a signal to the brain that indicates how much of it there is. If so, the signal is almost certainly some sort of chemical, because cutting the nerves that serve the fat tissue in an animal's body does not affect its total body fat.

For years, researchers have been trying to identify a signal from fat tissue that could tell the brain how well stocked the long-term reservoir was. Finally, they succeeded. The discovery came after years of study with a strain of genetically obese mice. The **ob mouse** (as this strain is called) has a low metabolism, overeats, and gets exceedingly fat. It also develops diabetes in adulthood, just as many obese people do. Researchers in several laboratories have discovered the cause of the obesity (Campfield et al., 1995; Halaas et al., 1995; Pelleymounter et al., 1995). A particular gene, called OB, normally produces a protein that has been given the name **leptin** (from the Greek word *leptos,* "thin"). Leptin is normally secreted by fat cells that contain a large amount of triglycerides. Because of a genetic mutation, the fat cells of ob mice are unable to produce leptin.

Leptin has profound effects on metabolism and eating, acting as an antiobesity hormone. If ob mice are given daily injections of leptin, their metabolic rate increases, their body temperature rises, they become more active, and they eat less. As a result, their weight returns to normal. Figure 12.15 shows a picture of an untreated

ob mouse and an ob mouse that has received injections of leptin. (See *Figure 12.15.*)

Leptin affects the metabolism and food intake of normal animals. If leptin is given to rats each day, the animals eat smaller meals and lose weight (Eckel et al., 1998; Kahler et al., 1998). The leptin affected only meal size; the animals ate the same number of meals each day. These results suggest that leptin sensitizes the brain to the satiety signals it receives from the stomach and duodenum, causing meals to stop earlier than they otherwise would. (See *Figure 12.16.*)

The most recently discovered candidate for the role of satiety factor is an intermediate product of the synthesis of triglycerides, *malonyl-CoA*. When an animal's metabolism is in the absorptive phase, blood levels of malonyl-CoA rise. When the animal is fasting, blood levels of malonyl-CoA fall. Perhaps, reasoned some researchers, malonyl-CoA

figure 12.15

The effects of leptin on obesity in mice of the ob (obese) strain. The ob mouse on the left is untreated; the one on the right received daily injections of leptin.

(Photo courtesy of Dr. J. Sholtis, The Rockefeller University. Copyright © 1995 Amgen, Inc.)

ob mouse A strain of mice whose obesity and low metabolic rate is caused by a mutation that prevents the production of leptin.

leptin A hormone secreted by adipose tissue; decreases food intake and increases metabolic rate, primarily by inhibiting NPY-secreting neurons in the arcuate nucleus.

figure 12.16

Body weight and meal size of rats
given daily injections of leptin.
(Adapted from Kahler, A., Geary, N., Eckel, L. A., Campfield, L. A., Smith, F. J., and Langhans, W. *American
Journal of Physiology,* 1998, *275,* R180-R185.)

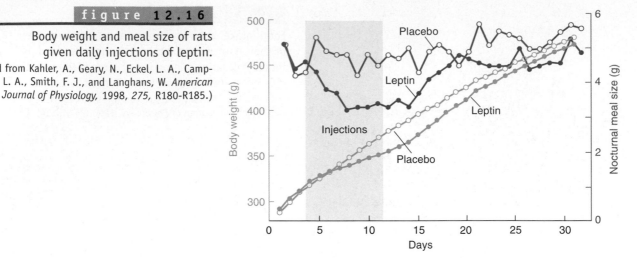

might provide a signal to the brain, telling it that the body contains plenty of nutrients and that they were being stored away in adipose tissue. Loftus et al. (2000) developed a drug that inactivates the enzyme *fatty acid synthase,* which catalyzes an essential step in fatty-acid synthesis. When this enzyme is inhibited, blood levels of malonyl-CoA rise. Loftus and his colleagues found that a single injection of this drug, which they named *C75,* caused an immediate cessation of eating and a dramatic loss of body weight.

Several other laboratories have confirmed these results. For example, Kumar et al. (2002) found that daily injections of a moderate dose of C75 reduced food intake in both normal and obese mice. (See ***Figure 12.17****.*) The drug eventually lost its potency in the normal mice, but it continued to suppress eating of the obese mice until they lost a substantial amount of weight. These results suggest that malonyl-CoA may provide the brain with a long-term satiety signal, just as leptin does. I will discuss the effects of malonyl-CoA on the brain later in this chapter. I will also discuss the possible use of C75 as a drug to treat obesity.

The discovery of leptin has stimulated much interest among researchers who are interested in finding ways to treat human obesity. Because it is a natural hormone, it might provide a way to help people to lose weight without the use of drugs that have potentially harmful effects. The fatty acid synthase inhibitor C75 is provoking excitement too, and studies are underway to determine whether this drug can safely be administered to humans.

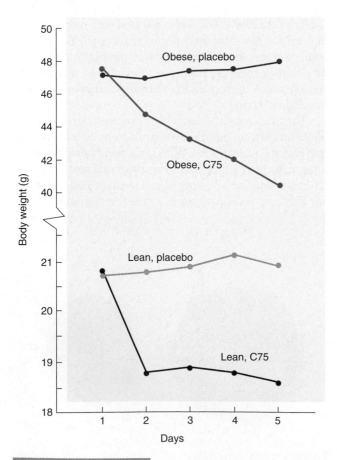

figure 12.17

Feeding behavior of rats who received daily injections
of C75 or a placebo. The drug inhibited the action of the
enzyme fatty acid synthase and raised the blood levels
of malonyl-CoA.

(Adapted from Kumar, M. V., Shimokawa, T., Nagy, T. R., and Lane,
M. D. *Proceedings of the National Academy of Science, USA,* 2002, *99,*
1921–1925.)

interim
summary

What Stops a Meal?

Because of the long delay between swallowing food and digesting it, the regulation of food intake requires a satiety mechanism; without it we would overeat and damage our stomachs. The feedback produced by tasting, smelling, and swallowing food provides the first satiety signal, but unless this signal is followed by feedback from the stomach indicating that food has arrived there, the animal will eat again. The stomach contains nutrient detectors that tell the brain how much food has been received. If some food is removed from the stomach, the animal eats enough to replace it, and if the experimenter tries to fool the animal by injecting a saline solution into the stomach, food intake is not reduced.

Signals originating in the intestines may also produce satiety. Several investigators have suggested that cholecystokinin, released by the duodenum when it receives fat-rich food from the stomach, provides a satiety signal. The inhibitory effect of CCK on eating appears to be mediated by receptors in the pylorus and transmitted to the brain via the vagus nerve. The duodenum also appears to contain nutrient detectors that send a satiety signal to the brain without the intermediate of a hormone; infusion of a mixture of lipids and fatty acids suppresses sham feeding. PYY, a peptide secreted after a meal by the gastrointestinal system, appears to act as a satiety signal.

Another satiety signal comes from the liver, which detects nutrients being received from the intestines. Infusion of glucose or fructose (which does not cross the blood–brain barrier) directly into the hepatic portal vein suppresses food intake of hungry animals. Insulin, which is present in high levels during the absorptive phase of metabolism, enters the brain and activates insulin receptors there, providing another satiety signal.

Signals arising from nutrient reservoirs affect food intake on a long-term basis. Force-feeding facilitates satiety, and starvation inhibits it. Studies of the ob mouse led to the discovery of leptin, a peptide hormone secreted by well-nourished adipose tissue that increases an animal's metabolic rate and decreases food intake. Leptin decreases meal size, apparently by increasing the brain's sensitivity to short-term satiety signals. An intermediate product of fatty acid metabolism, malonyl-CoA, also appears to suppress eating. The drug C75, which increases levels of malonyl-CoA in the blood, causes a dramatic suppression of eating and a decrease in body weight.

Brain Mechanisms

Although hunger and satiety signals originate in the digestive system and in the body's nutrient reservoirs, the target of these signals is the brain. This section looks at some of the research on brain mechanisms of food intake and metabolism.

Brain Stem

Ingestive behaviors are phylogenetically ancient; obviously, all our ancestors ate and drank or died. Therefore, we should expect that the basic ingestive behaviors of chewing and swallowing are programmed by phylogenetically ancient brain circuits. Indeed, studies have shown that these behaviors can be performed by decerebrate rats, whose brains were transected between the diencephalon and the midbrain (Norgren and Grill, 1982;

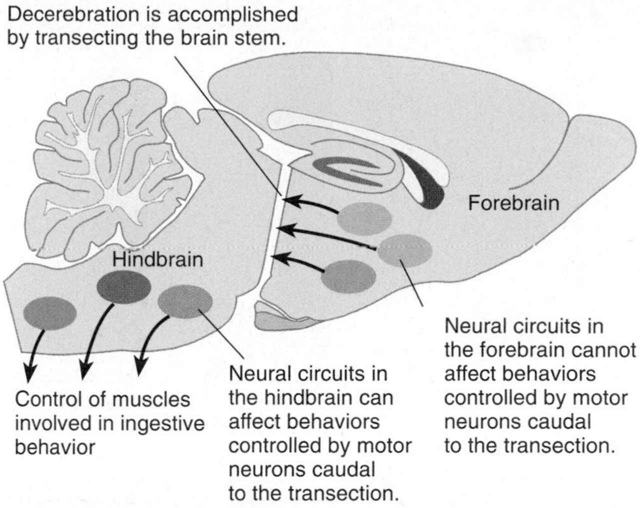

Decerebration is accomplished by transecting the brain stem.

Forebrain

Hindbrain

Control of muscles involved in ingestive behavior

Neural circuits in the hindbrain can affect behaviors controlled by motor neurons caudal to the transection.

Neural circuits in the forebrain cannot affect behaviors controlled by motor neurons caudal to the transection.

figure 12.18

Decerebration. The operation disconnects the forebrain from the hindbrain so that the muscles involved in ingestive behavior are controlled solely by hindbrain mechanisms.

Grill and Kaplan, 1990). **Decerebration** disconnects the motor neurons of the brain stem and spinal cord from the neural circuits of the cerebral hemispheres (such as the cerebral cortex and basal ganglia) that normally control them. The only behaviors that decerebrate animals can display are those that are directly controlled by neural circuits located within the brain stem. (See *Figure 12.18.*)

Decerebrate rats cannot approach and eat food; the experimenters must place food, in liquid form, into their mouths. Decerebrate rats can distinguish between different tastes; they drink and swallow sweet or slightly salty liquids and spit out bitter ones. They even respond to hunger and satiety signals. They drink more sucrose after having been deprived of food for 24 hours, and they drink less of it if some sucrose is first injected directly into their stomachs. These studies indicate that the brain stem contains neural circuits that can control at least some aspects of food intake.

The area postrema and the nucleus of the solitary tract (henceforth referred to as the AP/NST) receive taste information from the tongue and a variety of sensory information from the internal organs, including signals from detectors in the stomach, duodenum, and liver. In addition, we saw that this region appears to contain a set of detectors that are sensitive to the brain's own fuel: glucose. All this information is transmitted to regions of the forebrain that are more directly involved in control of eating and metabolism. Evidence indicates that events that produce hunger increase the activity of neurons in the AP/NST. In

decerebration A surgical procedure that severs the brain stem, disconnecting the hindbrain from the forebrain.

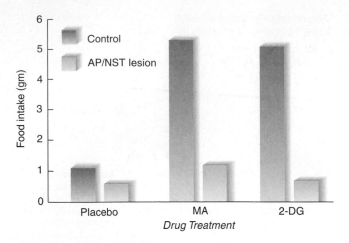

Effects of lesions of the nucleus of the solitary tract and adjacent area postrema on lipoprivic hunger (MA treatment) and glucoprivic hunger (2-DG treatment).

(Based on data from Ritter, S., and Taylor, J. S. *American Journal of Physiology,* 1990, *258,* R1395–R1401.)

addition, lesions of this region abolish both glucoprivic and lipoprivic feeding (Ritter and Taylor, 1990; Ritter, Dinh, and Friedman, 1994). (See ***Figure 12.19***.)

Hypothalamus

Discoveries made in the 1940s and 1950s focused the attention of researchers interested in ingestive behavior on two regions of the hypothalamus: the lateral area and the ventromedial area. For many years investigators believed that these two regions controlled hunger and satiety, respectively; one was the accelerator, and the other was the brake. The basic findings were these: After the lateral hypothalamus was destroyed, animals stopped eating or drinking (Anand and Brobeck, 1951; Teitelbaum and Stellar, 1954). Electrical stimulation of the same region would produce eating, drinking, or both behaviors. Conversely, lesions of the ventromedial hypothalamus produced overeating that led to gross obesity, whereas electrical stimulation suppressed eating (Hetherington and Ranson, 1942). (See ***Figure 12.20***.)

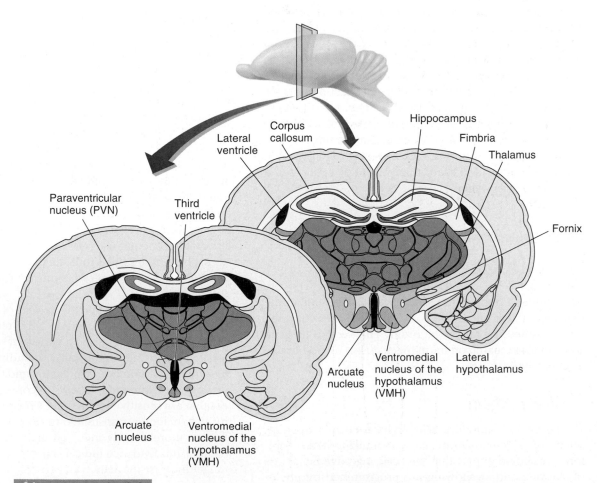

Cross sections through the rat brain, showing the location of regions of the hypothalamus that play a role in the control of eating and metabolism.

(Adapted from Swanson, L. W. *Brain Maps: Structure of the Rat Brain.* New York: Elsevier, 1992.)

Role in Hunger

Research in the latter half of the twentieth century has shown that the lateral hypothalamus does indeed play a role in eating. Neurotoxic lesions of the lateral hypothalamus made with ibotenic acid, which kills cells while sparing axons passing through the region, produce a long-lasting decrease in food intake and body weight (Stricker, Swerdloff, and Zigmond, 1978; Dunnett, Lane, and Winn, 1985). In addition, stimulation of the lateral hypothalamus with direct injections of excitatory amino acids produces eating (Stanley et al., 1993a; Duva et al., 2001), and injections of a glutamate antagonist in this region decrease food intake (Stanley et al., 1996). (See *Figure 12.21*.)

We now know that these injections activate two populations of neurons located in the lateral hypothalamus that stimulate hunger and decrease metabolic rate, thus preserving the body's energy stores. The neurons secrete two different peptide neurotransmitters: **melanin-concentrating hormone (MCH)** and **orexin**. (See *Figure 12.22*.)

Melanin-concentrating hormone received its name from its role in regulating changes in skin pigmentation in fish and other nonmammalian vertebrates (Kawauchi et al., 1983). In mammals it serves as a neurotransmitter. Orexin (from the Greek word *orexis*, "appetite") was discovered by Sakurai et al. (1998), who were searching for a ligand for an "orphan" receptor—a protein that appeared to be a membrane-bound receptor found in the brain. In

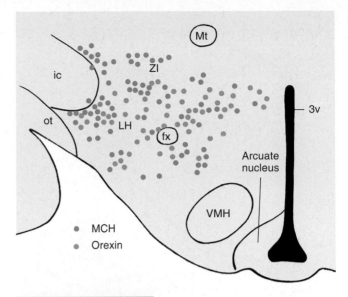

figure 12.22

Melanin-concentrating hormone (MCH) neurons and orexin neurons of the lateral hypothalamus. Abbreviations: ic = internal capsule, ot = optic tract, ZI = zona incerta, LH = lateral hypothalamus, fx = fornix, 3v = third ventricle, Mt = mammillothalamic tract.

(Adapted from Elias, C. F., Saper, C. B., Maratos-Flier, E., Tritos, N. A., Lee, C., Kelly, J., Tatro, J. B., Hoffman, G. E., Ollmann, M. M., Barsh, G. S., Sakurai, T., Yanagisawa, M., and Elmquist, J. K. *Journal of Comparative Neurology*, 1998, *402*, 442–459.)

fact, they discovered two slightly different ligands, orexin A and orexin B, that bound two slightly different receptors. These peptides are also known as *hypocretins*—particularly by researchers studying sleep. As we saw in Chapter 9, degeneration of neurons that secrete hypocretin-2 (also known as orexin B) is responsible for narcolepsy. Evidence reviewed there suggests that it plays a role in keeping the brain's sleep–waking switch in the "waking" position. I used the term *hypocretin* in Chapter 9 because most researchers interested in sleep use this term. I use the term *orexin* in this chapter because most researchers interested in the control of food intake do so too.

Injections of either MCH or orexin into the lateral ventricles or various regions of the brain induce eating. In addition, if rats are deprived of food, messenger RNA levels for MCH and orexin in the lateral hypothalamus increase (Qu et al., 1996; Sakurai et al., 1998; Dube, Kalra, and Kalra, 1999). Researchers refer to these peptides as *orexigens*, "appetite-inducing chemicals."

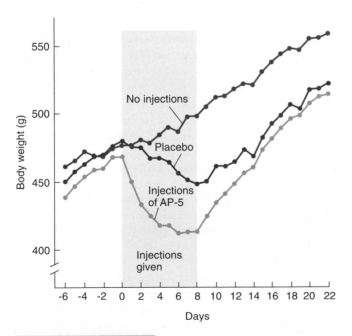

figure 12.21

Body weight of rats that received twice-daily injections of a glutamate antagonist into the lateral hypothalamus.

(Adapted from Stanley, B. G., Willett, V. L., Donias, H. W., Dee, M. G., and Duva, M. A. *American Journal of Physiology: Regulatory, Integrative and Comparative Physiology*, 1996, *270*, R443–R449.)

melanin-concentrating hormone (MCH) A peptide neurotransmitter found in a system of lateral hypothalamic neurons that stimulate appetite and reduce metabolic rate.

orexin A peptide neurotransmitter found in a system of lateral hypothalamic neurons that stimulate appetite and reduce metabolic rate.

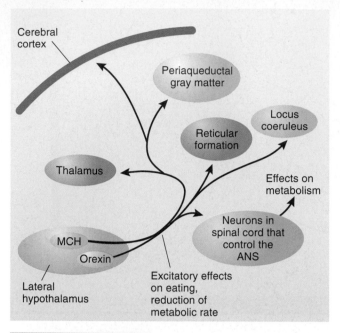

figure 12.23

Connections of the MCH neurons and orexin neurons of the lateral hypothalamus.

The axons of MCH and orexin neurons travel to a variety of brain structures that are known to be involved in motivation and movement, including the neocortex, periaqueductal gray matter, reticular formation, thalamus, and locus coeruleus. These neurons also have connections with neurons in the spinal cord that control the autonomic nervous system, which explains how they can affect the body's metabolic rate (Sawchenko, 1998; Nambu et al., 1999). These connections are shown in *Figure 12.23.*

Of these two orexigenic hypothalamic peptides, MCH appears to play the more important role. Mice with a targeted mutation against the MCH gene eat less than normal mice and are consequently underweight (Shimada et al., 1998). Although mice with a targeted mutation against orexin eat somewhat less than normal mice, they become obese in late adulthood (Hara et al., 2001).

As we saw earlier, metabolic hunger signals caused by glucoprivation or lipoprivation arise from detectors in the liver and medulla. How do these signals activate the MCH and orexin neurons of the lateral hypothalamus? Part of the pathway involves a system of neurons that secrete a neurotransmitter called **neuropeptide Y (NPY)**, an extremely potent stimulator of food intake (Clark et al., 1984). Infusion of NPY into the hypothalamus produces ravenous, almost frantic eating. Rats who receive an infusion of this peptide will work very hard, pressing a lever many times for each morsel of food; they will eat food made bitter with quinine; and they will continue to drink milk even when doing so means that they receive an electric shock to their tongue (Flood and Morley, 1991; Jewett et al., 1992).

Neuropeptide Y appears to have at least two sites of action in the hypothalamus. When infused into the lateral

hypothalamus, it produces eating (Stanley et al., 1993b). When infused into the **paraventricular nucleus (PVN),** located in the medial hypothalamus around the dorsal part of the third ventricle, it produces metabolic effects, including insulin and glucocorticoid secretion, decreased breakdown of triglycerides in adipose tissue, and a decrease in body temperature (Wahlestedt et al., 1987; Abe, Saito, and Shimazu, 1989; Currie and Coscina, 1996). These effects complement the increased appetite by preserving the body's energy supplies. (Refer to *Figure 12.20.*)

Levels of neuropeptide Y are affected by hunger and satiety signals; Sahu, Kalra, and Kalra (1988) found that hypothalamic levels of NPY are increased by food deprivation and lowered by eating. In addition, Myers et al. (1995) found that hypothalamic injections of a drug that blocks neuropeptide Y receptors suppress eating caused by food deprivation. This last finding, in particular, provides strong evidence that normal food intake is at least partially stimulated by neuropeptide Y.

The neurons that secrete NPY are found in the **arcuate nucleus,** located in the hypothalamus at the base of the third ventricle. The arcuate nucleus also contains neurosecretory cells whose hormones control the secretions of the anterior pituitary gland. (Refer to *Figure 12.20.*) The NPY neurons send a dense projection of axons to the paraventricular nucleus—the region where infusions of NPY affect metabolic functions (Bai et al., 1985). They also send a projection directly to MCH and orexin neurons in the lateral hypothalamus (Broberger et al., 1998; Elias et al., 1998a). Presumably, these connections are responsible for the feeding elicited by activation of NPY neurons.

The terminals of NPY neurons release another orexigenic peptide in addition to neuropeptide Y: **agouti-related peptide,** otherwise known as **AGRP** (Hahn et al., 1998). I will describe the story behind the discovery of this oddly named peptide in the next subsection and say more about the receptors for which it serves as a ligand. Suffice it to say that AGRP is a potent and extremely long-lasting orexigen. Infusion of a very small amount of this peptide into the third ventricle of rats produced an increase in food intake that lasted for six days (Lu et al., 2001).

neuropeptide Y (NPY) A peptide neurotransmitter found in a system of neurons of the arcuate nucleus that stimulate feeding, insulin and glucocorticoid secretion, decrease the breakdown of triglycerides, and decrease body temperature.

paraventricular nucleus (PVN) A nucleus of the hypothalamus located adjacent to the dorsal third ventricle; contains neurons involved in control of the autonomic nervous system and the posterior pituitary gland.

arcuate nucleus A nucleus in the base of the hypothalamus that controls secretions of the anterior pituitary gland; contains NPY-secreting neurons involved in feeding and control of metabolism.

agouti-related protein (AGRP) A neuropeptide that acts as an antagonist at MC-4 receptors and increases eating.

Researchers have not yet determined by what pathways NPY neurons in the arcuate nucleus receive information concerning the animal's nutritional status. These neurons receive input from a variety of forebrain and hindbrain structures, so it is possible that these connections convey information from detectors that are sensitive to glucoprivation and lipoprivation (Li, Chen, and Smith, 1999).

Recently, researchers discovered that the gastrointestinal system (especially the stomach) releases a peptide hormone called **ghrelin** (Kojima et al., 1999). The name *ghrelin* is a contraction of *GH releasin,* which reflects the fact that this peptide is involved in controlling the release of growth hormone, usually abbreviated as *GH.* Although the physiological signal that triggers ghrelin release by the stomach is not yet known, researchers have discovered that blood levels of this peptide increase with fasting and are reduced when the animal eats. Cummings et al. (2001) discovered that in humans, blood levels of ghrelin increase shortly before each meal, a finding that suggests that this peptide may be involved in the initiation of a meal. (See *Figure 12.24.*)

Just to confuse matters even more, ghrelin is also produced by neurons in the brain. The relative importance of ghrelin produced by the stomach and by neurons in the brain is not known (Murakami et al., 2002). Subcutaneous injections or infusions of ghrelin into the cerebral ventricles cause weight gain by increasing food intake and decreasing the metabolism of fats (Tschöp, Smiley, and Heiman, 2000; Nakazato et al., 2001). In addition, Shuto et al. (2002) found that rats with a genetic alteration that prevents ghrelin receptors from being produced in the hypothalamus eat less and gain weight more slowly than normal rats do. These studies provide strong evidence that ghrelin acts as an orexigen. Ghrelin appears to exert its effects on appetite and metabolism by stimulating receptors located on neurons that release NPY and AGRP; Willesen, Kristensen, and Romer (1999) found that over 90

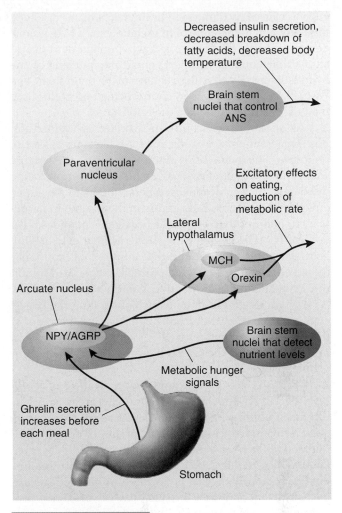

Connections of the NPY neurons of the arcuate nucleus.

percent of NPY/AGRP neurons in the arcuate nucleus of the hypothalamus contain ghrelin receptors, and Nakazato et al. (2001) found that drugs that blocked the action of NPY and AGRP abolished the feeding produced by ghrelin.

In summary, activity of MCH and orexin neurons of the lateral hypothalamus increases food intake and decreases metabolic rate. These neurons are activated by NPY-secreting neurons of the arcuate nucleus. The NPY neurons also project to the paraventricular nucleus, which plays a role in control of insulin secretion and metabolism. One of the signals that activates NPY/AGRP neurons is ghrelin, an orexigenic peptide released by the stomach. (See *Figure 12.25.*)

Role in Satiety

One of the most striking effects of a localized brain lesion is the overeating and obesity that are produced by a lesion of the ventromedial hypothalamus (VMH). This

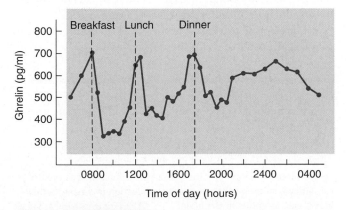

Levels of ghrelin in human blood plasma. A rise in the level of this peptide preceded each meal.

(Adapted from Cummings, D. E., Purnell, J. Q., Frayo, R. S., Schmidova, K., Wisse, B. E., and Weigle, D. S. *Diabetes,* 2001, *50,* 1714–1719.)

ghrelin A peptide hormone released by the stomach that increases eating; also produced by neurons in the brain.

effect is caused by damage to brain mechanisms involved in satiety and in the control of metabolism. VMH lesions destroy not only the ventromedial hypothalamus but also axons that connect the paraventricular nucleus of the hypothalamus (PVN) with structures in the brain stem. The PVN plays a critical role in coordinating and controlling many aspects of the body's metabolism.

As we saw, leptin, a hormone secreted by well-fed adipose tissue, suppresses eating and raises the animal's metabolic rate. The interactions of this long-term satiety signal with neural circuits involved in hunger are now being discovered. Leptin produces its behavioral and metabolic effects by binding with receptors in the brain—in particular, on neurons that secrete the orexigenic peptides NPY and AGRP (Hakansson et al., 1996; Mercer et al., 1996). Schwartz et al. (1996) found that infusions of leptin into the cerebral ventricles, which inhibit eating, also inhibit the production of neuropeptide Y in the arcuate nucleus. As you will recall, the arcuate nucleus contains the largest concentration of NPY-secreting neurons, and the axons of these neurons project to the PVN and to the MCH and orexin neurons in the lateral hypothalamus, which stimulate appetite.

Glaum et al. (1996) found that activation of leptin receptors on NPY-secreting neurons in the arcuate nucleus has an inhibitory effect on these neurons. As a consequence, leptin reduces the amount of the NPY and AGRP released in the hypothalamus (Wang et al., 1997; Li et al., 2000). Lopez et al. (2000) found that leptin also inhibits the release of orexin that is normally stimulated by fasting. Thus, leptin inhibits the release of the orexigens produced in the hypothalamus.

The arcuate nucleus contains two other systems of peptide-secreting neurons, both of which serve as *anorexigens* "appetite-suppressing chemicals." Douglass, McKinzie, and Couceyro (1995) discovered a peptide that is now called **CART** (for *cocaine- and amphetamine-regulated transcript*). When cocaine or amphetamine is administered to an animal, levels of this peptide increase, which may have something to do with the fact that these drugs suppress appetite. CART neurons appear to play an important role in satiety. If animals are deprived of food, levels of CART decrease. CART is almost totally absent in ob mice, which lack leptin, but injections of leptin in their cerebral ventricles will stimulate the production of CART. Injections of CART into their cerebral ventricles inhibit feeding, including the feeding stimulated by NPY. Finally, infusion of a CART antibody increases feeding (Kristensen et al., 1998).

CART neurons are located in the arcuate nucleus and send their axons to a variety of locations, including several other hypothalamic nuclei, the periaqueductal gray matter, and regions of the spinal cord that control the autonomic nervous system (Koylu et al., 1998). In the context of the present topic the most important connections are probably those with the paraventricular nucleus and those with the MCH and orexin neurons of the lat-

eral hypothalamus. Activity of CART neurons increases metabolic rate through its connections with the paraventricular nucleus, and it appears to inhibit MCH and orexin neurons, thus suppressing eating. CART neurons contain leptin receptors that have an *excitatory* effect; thus, CART-secreting neurons appear to be responsible for at least part of the satiating effect of leptin (Elias et al., 1998b).

The second anorexigen, **α-melanocyte-stimulating hormone (α-MSH),** has an interesting history. The **agouti mouse** has a genetic defect that causes bright yellow fur and obesity that shows up later in life, as it often does in humans (the obesity, that is, not the bright yellow fur). The mutation does not interfere with the production of a protein; it causes a protein that is normally produced only in hair follicles to be produced all over the body. This protein is an antagonist of the **melanocortin-4 receptor (MC4-R);** it binds with and blocks the receptor, causing overeating and obesity (Lu et al., 1994). Another natural ligand for the MC4 receptor is melanocortin, a hormone that causes the production of melanin, a black pigment found in skin and hair.

Until recently, researchers had no reason to suspect that MC4 receptors were found in the brain or that they had anything to do with eating or metabolism. But Mountjoy et al. (1994) found that these receptors can be found in locations throughout the brain, including the arcuate nucleus. They also found two natural ligands for the MC4 receptor produced in the brain: α-MSH and agouti-related protein (ARGP). These peptides have opposing effects on MC4 receptors: α-MSH acts as an agonist and inhibits feeding, whereas AGRP acts as an antagonist and causes feeding (as we saw in the previous subsection). Just to confuse matters even more (sorry!), α-MSH is found in CART neurons of the arcuate nucleus, just as AGRP is found in NPY neurons of the arcuate nucleus, and these pairs of peptides appear to be released together. This means that CART/α-MSH neurons are activated by leptin and that NPY/AGRP neurons are inhibited by leptin. (See Elmquist, Elias, and Saper, 1999, for specific references.) So leptin stimulates the production of the anorexigens CART, and α-MSH and inhibits the production of the orexigens NPY and AGRP.

The peptide α-MSH and the MC4 receptor appear to play an important role in the control of eating. Although

---

CART Cocaine- and amphetamine-regulated transcript; a peptide neurotransmitter found in a system of neurons of the arcuate nucleus that inhibit feeding.

α-melanocyte-stimulating hormone (α-MSH) A neuropeptide that acts as an agonist at MC4 receptors and inhibits eating.

agouti mouse A strain of mice whose yellow fur and obesity are caused by a mutation that causes the production of a peptide that blocks MC4 receptors in the brain.

melanocortin-4 receptor (MC4-R) A receptor found in the brain that binds with α-MSH and agouti-related protein; plays a role in control of appetite.

the MC4 receptor has two natural ligands, one with an orexigenic effect and the other with an anorexigenic effect, its primary function seems to be to suppress appetite: Huszar et al. (1997) found that mice with a targeted mutation against the gene for the MC4 receptor became obese. Agonists for the MC4 receptor increase metabolic rate as well as suppress eating; thus, this activation of this receptor reduces body weight by its effects on metabolism as well as on behavior (Hwa et al., 2001).

Earlier in this chapter, I mentioned an anorexigenic peptide, PYY, which is produced by cells in the gastrointestinal tract in amounts proportional to the calories that were just ingested. PYY binds with the Y2 receptor, an inhibitory autoreceptor found on NPY neurons in the arcuate nucleus of the hypothalamus. When PYY binds with the Y2 receptor, it suppressed the release of NPY (and AGRP, the other orexigenic peptide released by these neurons). Both peripheral injection of PYY and infusion directly into the arcuate nucleus of the hypothalamus suppress food intake. A single injection of PYY suppresses eating for up to 12 hours in both humans and rats (Batterham et al., 2002). Yes, PYY has been tested in humans, as we will see later in this chapter in the section on obesity. It might turn out that PYY is a very important short-term satiety signal; I am sure that several laboratories, including those supported by drug companies, are actively studying this peptide.

In summary, leptin appears to exert at least some of its satiating effects by stimulating receptors on neurons in the arcuate nucleus. Leptin inhibits NPY/AGRP neurons, which suppresses the feeding that these peptides stimulate and prevents the decrease in metabolic rate. Leptin activates CART/α-MSH neurons, which inhibit MCH and orexin neurons in the lateral hypothalamus and prevent their stimulatory effect on appetite. PYY, released by the gastrointestinal tract just after a meal, inhibits NPY/AGRP neurons. (See *Figure 12.26*.)

You will recall that the drug C75, which blocks fatty acid synthesis, raises blood levels of malonyl-CoA and inhibits eating. Shimokawa, Kumar, and Lane (2002) found that C75 blocks the increase in NPY and AGRP produced by fasting, and prevents levels of CART and α-MSH from falling. Thus, the presence of malonyl-CoA acts as an anorexigen by interacting with the release of hypothalamic peptides involved in the control of eating and metabolism.

Infusions of serotonin (5-HT) into various parts of the brain, including the PVN and ventromedial hypothalamus, suppress eating (Leibowitz, Weiss, and Suh, 1990). In addition, administration of serotonin agonists suppress eating (Blundell and Halford, 1998). In fact, such drugs have been used to treat people with obesity. In contrast, drugs that destroy serotonergic neurons, inhibit the synthesis of 5-HT, or block 5-HT receptors have an effect opposite that of 5-HT: They *increase* food intake, especially carbohydrates (Breisch, Zemlan, and Hoebel, 1976; Saller and Stricker, 1976; Stallone and Nicolaïdis, 1989). Dryden

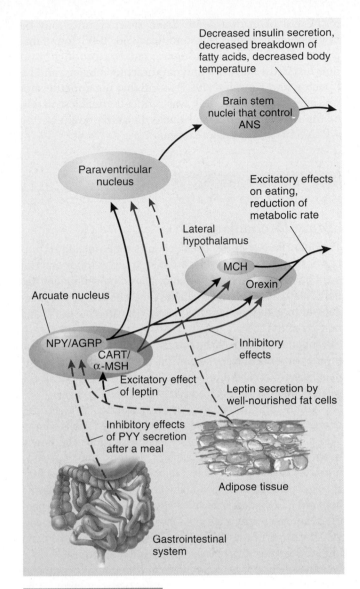

figure 12.26

Connections of CART neurons of the arcuate nucleus and effects of leptin on hypothalamic neurons involved in control of hunger, satiety, and metabolic rate.

et al. (1995) found that an IP injection of methysergide, a 5-HT antagonist, increased the secretion of NPY in the hypothalamus and (as you might expect) increased food intake. This finding suggests that serotonergic neurons somehow inhibit the activity of NPY neurons. In addition, mice with a targeted mutation against the 5-HT$_{2C}$ receptor eat more food and develop obesity in middle age (Nonogaki et al., 1998).

The neural circuits that are responsible for the suppressive effect of 5-HT on feeding are not yet understood. Although, as we saw, infusions of serotonin or serotonin agonists into the PVN suppress eating, Fletcher et al. (1993) found that IP injections of fenfluramine, a potent serotonin agonist, still decreased food intake after the

PVN had been destroyed. Brain stem circuits may be involved in these effects; Li and Rowland (1995) found that injections of fenfluramine increased Fos production in neurons in the AP/NST and parabrachial nucleus, and Li, Spector, and Rowland (1994) found that the appetite-suppressing effect of the drug was reduced after destruction of the lateral parabrachial nucleus, which connects the AP/NST with the hypothalamus.

interim summary

Brain Mechanisms

The brain stem contains neural circuits that are able to control acceptance or rejection of sweet or bitter foods and can even be modulated by satiation or physiological hunger signals, such as a decrease in glucose metabolism or the presence of food in the digestive system. The area postrema and nucleus of the solitary tract and (AP/NST) receive signals from the tongue, stomach, small intestine, and liver and send the information on to many regions of the forebrain. These signals interact and help to control food intake. Lesions of the AP/NST disrupt both glucoprivic and lipoprivic eating.

Stimulation of the lateral hypothalamus with electricity or excitatory amino acids produces eating, while lesions or infusion of glutamate antagonists decreases eating. The lateral hypothalamus contains two sets of neurons whose activity increases eating and decreases metabolic rate. These neurons secrete the peptides orexin and MCH (melanin-concentrating hormone). Food deprivation increases the level of these peptides, and mice with a targeted mutation against MCH undereat. The axons of these neurons project to regions of the brain involved in motivation, movement, and metabolism.

The release of neuropeptide Y in the lateral hypothalamus induces ravenous eating, an effect that appears to be produced by the connection of NPY-secreting neurons with the orexin and MCH neurons. When NPY is infused in the paraventricular nucleus, it decreases metabolic rate. Levels of NPY increase when an animal is deprived of food and fall again when the animal eats. A drug that blocks NPY receptors suppresses eating. NPY neurons also release a peptide called AGRP. This peptide serves as an antagonist at MC4 receptors and stimulates eating.

Although lesions of the ventromedial hypothalamus produce overeating and obesity, they apparently do so by damaging the arcuate nucleus or disrupting its connections with other regions of the brain. Leptin, the long-term satiety hormone secreted by well-stocked adipose tissue, desensitizes the brain to hunger signals. It binds with receptors in the arcuate nucleus of the hypothalamus, where it inhibits NPY-secreting neurons, increasing metabolic rate and suppressing eating. The arcuate nucleus also contains neurons that secrete CART (cocaine- and amphetamine-regulated transcript), a peptide that suppresses eating. These neurons,

which are *activated* by leptin, have inhibitory connections with MCH and orexin neurons in the lateral hypothalamus. CART neurons also secrete a peptide called α-MSH, which serves as an agonist at MC4 receptors and inhibits eating. Malonyl-CoA, an intermediate product of fatty acid synthesis present in high levels during the absorptive state of metabolism, also suppresses eating, apparently by reducing levels of hypothalamic orexigenic peptides.

A monoaminergic transmitter substance, 5-HT, has an inhibitory effect on eating in the PVN. Serotonin agonists have been used to treat obesity in humans. The site of action of such drugs may be in the brain stem as well as in the hypothalamus.

Eating Disorders

Unfortunately, some people are susceptible to the development of eating disorders. Some people grow obese, even though our society regards this condition as unattractive and even though obese people generally have more health problems than people of normal weight and die sooner. Other people (especially young women) can become obsessed with losing weight, eating little and increasing their activity level until their body weight becomes extremely low—sometimes fatally so. Others manage to keep from losing or gaining weight but often lose control of intake, eating enormous amounts of food and then taking strong laxatives or forcing themselves to vomit. Has what we have learned about the physiology of appetite helped us to understand these conditions?

Obesity

Obesity is a widespread problem that can have serious medical consequences. In the United States approximately 63 percent of men and 55 percent of women are overweight, defined as a body mass index (BMI) of over 25. The incidence of obesity, defined as a BMI of over 30, has increased by 50 percent in the past 20 years and stood at approximately 18 percent in 1998. In addition, the number of overweight children has doubled (Must et al., 1999; Yanovski and Yanovski, 1999; Hirsch, 2002). The known health hazards of obesity include cardiovascular disease, diabetes, strokes, arthritis, and some forms of cancer.

Possible Causes

Obesity undoubtedly has many causes, including learning and innate or acquired differences in metabolism. The behavior of eating, like most other behaviors, is subject to modification through learning. Unfortunately, many aspects of modern, industrialized societies tend to weaken physiological controls over eating. For example, as children we learn to eat what is put on our plates; indeed, many children are praised for eating all they have been given and punished for failing to do so. As Birch et al. (1987) showed, the effect of this kind of training can be to make children less sensitive to the nutrient content of their diet. As we get older, our metabolic requirements decrease; and if we continue to eat as we did when we were younger, we tend to accumulate fat. The inhibitory signals associated with food consumption are certainly not absolute; they can be overridden by habit or by the simple pleasure of ingesting good-tasting food.

As we will see, genetic differences—and their effects on development of the brain and organs involved in metabolism—appear to be responsible for the overwhelming proportion of people with extreme obesity. But as we saw, the problem of obesity has been growing over recent years. Clearly, changes in the gene pool cannot account for this increase; instead, we must look to environmental causes that have produced changes in people's behavior.

Body weight is the result of the difference between two factors: calories consumed and energy expended. If we consume more calories than we expend as heat and work, we gain weight. If we expend more than we consume, we lose weight. In modern industrialized societies inexpensive, convenient, good-tasting, high-fat food is readily available, which promotes an increase in intake. Fast-food restaurants are close at hand, parking is convenient (or even unnecessary at restaurants with drive-up windows), and the size of the portions they serve has increased in recent years. In recent years people have begun to eat out more often, and most often they do so at inexpensive fast-food restaurants.

Of course, fast-food restaurants are not the only environmental factor responsible for the increased incidence of obesity. Snack foods are available in convenience stores and vending machines, and even school cafeterias make high-calorie, high-fat foods and sweetened beverages available to their young students. In fact, school administrators often welcome the installation of vending machines because of the income they provide. In addition, changes in the workplace affect people's expenditure of energy. The proportion of people employed in jobs that require a high level of physical activity has decreased considerably, which means that on the average we need less food than we did previously.

One reason that many people have so much difficulty losing weight is that metabolic factors appear to play an important role in obesity. In fact, most cases of extreme obesity are caused not by *eating disorders* (despite the title of this section) but rather by *metabolic disorders.*

Just as cars differ in their fuel efficiency, so do living organisms, and hereditary factors can affect the level of efficiency. For example, farmers have bred cattle, pigs, and chickens for their efficiency in converting feed into muscle tissue, and researchers have done the same with rats (Pomp and Nielsen, 1999). People differ in this form of efficiency too. Those with an efficient metabolism have

calories left over to deposit in the long-term nutrient reservoir; thus, they have difficulty keeping this reservoir from growing. Researchers have referred to this condition as a "thrifty phenotype." In contrast, people with an inefficient metabolism (a "spendthrift phenotype") can eat large meals without getting fat. A fuel-efficient automobile is desirable, but a fuel-efficient body runs the risk of becoming obese—at least in an environment where food is cheap and plentiful.

One of the problems in studying the role of metabolism in overweight and obesity is the difficulty in obtaining accurate measurements of food intake. Of course, if people are kept in a laboratory or clinic where their food intake can be monitored, the investigators can know precisely what the subjects eat. But a procedure like this is expensive, and long-term studies are virtually impossible. Few people are willing to spend weeks or months in an environment away from their homes and jobs, where their food intake can be monitored. We could, one might think, simply ask people to write down everything they eat, which would tell us how many calories of carbohydrate, fat, and protein they consumed, and many studies have done just that. However, it has long been apparent that people—especially obese people—do not accurately record all they eat.

Two factors affect the accuracy of self-reported food intake. Researchers have discovered that when obese people enroll in a study that is obviously related to factors involved in being overweight, they begin eating less—at least, for the duration of the study. For example, Goris, Westerterp-Plantenga, and Westerterp (2000) found that obese men ate 26 percent less while they were participating in a study of obesity than they did during the previous week. They also underreported their actual food intake during the study by 12 percent. They particularly underreported their intake of fat. Previous studies showed that such underreporting was correlated with BMI: People who were overweight were most likely to underreport. As Blundell (2000) put it, "The more we tell people that they should reduce the amount of fat in their diets, the more they tell us how little of it they eat; however, actual intakes do not appear to change or even increase. Individuals may not wish to admit . . . , even to themselves, exactly what they put in their mouths" (p. 4).

Almost all excess body weight is carried in the form of fat. Normally, we carry a certain amount of fat in our long-term nutrient reservoir, making deposits and withdrawals each day during the absorptive and fasting phases of metabolism but keeping the total amount stable. Obesity occurs when deposits exceed withdrawals. We expend energy in two basic ways: through physical exercise and through the production of heat. A study by Levine, Eberhardt, and Jensen (1999) fed nonobese people a diet that contained 1000 calories more than they needed to sustain their weight. Approximately 39 percent of the calories were converted into fat tissue, and approximately 26 percent went into lean tissue, increased resting metabolic rate, and the energy required to digest the extra food. The rest, approximately 33 percent, went into an increase in involuntary activity: muscle tone, postural changes, and fidgeting. Levine and his colleagues referred to this phenomenon as "nonexercise activity thermogenesis," or NEAT. A follow-up study by Levine, Schleusner, and Jensen (2000) found large individual differences in people's levels of NEAT. This variability may constitute one of the ways in which people differ in the efficiency of their metabolisms.

Differences in body weight (perhaps reflecting physiological differences in metabolism or appetite) appear to have a hereditary basis. Twin studies suggest that between 40 percent and 85 percent of the variability in body fat is due to genetic differences (Price and Gottesman, 1991; Allison et al., 1996; Comuzzie and Allison, 1998). And the family environment in which people are raised apparently has no significant effect on their body weight as adults; Stunkard et al. (1986) found that the body weight of a sample of people who had been adopted as infants was highly correlated with their *biological* parents but not with their *adoptive* parents. Sørensen et al. (1989) came to similar conclusions in a study comparing adopted people with their full and half siblings with whom they had not been raised.

Why are there genetic differences in metabolic efficiency? James and Trayhurn (1981) suggested that under some environmental conditions metabolic efficiency is advantageous. That is, in places where food is only intermittently available in sufficient quantities, being able to stay alive on small amounts of food and to store up extra nutrients in the form of fat when food becomes available for a while is a highly adaptive trait. When the famine comes, it is the people with efficient metabolisms and adequate supplies of fat—and their genes—who survive. Therefore, people's metabolic rates may reflect the nature of the environment experienced by their ancestors.

James and Trayhurn's hypothesis has received support from epidemiological studies. The tiny island of Nauru, containing only eight square miles of territory, contains a stock of seabird guano, which is now mined for its rich source of phosphate by companies that sell fertilizer. The average per capita income of Nauru suddenly went from very low to one of the highest in the world (Gibbs, 1996). With this wealth came a much less active lifestyle and the ability to buy expensive, imported foods. In the course of a generation the Nauru islanders became some of the most obese people on earth.

Ravussin et al. (1994) studied two groups of Pima Indians, who live in the southwestern United States and northwestern Mexico. Members of the two groups appear to have the same genetic background; they speak the same language and have common historical traditions. The two groups separated 700–1000 years ago and now live under very different environmental conditions. The Pima Indians in the southwestern United States eat a high-fat American diet and weigh an average of 90 kg (198 lb), men and women combined. In contrast, the lifestyle of the Mexican Pimas is probably similar to that of their ancestors. They spend long hours working at subsistence farming and eat a low-fat diet—and weigh an average of 64 kg (141 lb). The cholesterol level of the American Pimas is much higher than that of the Mexican Pimas, and the American Pimas' rate of diabetes is more than five times higher. These findings show that genes that promote an efficient metabolism are of benefit to people who must work hard for their calories but that these same genes turn into a liability when people live in an environment where the physical demands are low and high-calorie food is cheap and plentiful.

Nongenetic factors can also affect metabolic efficiency. Studies of humans and laboratory animals suggest that early overnourishment or undernourishment can promote obesity later in life. First, let's consider the effects of overnourishment. Davidowa and Plagemann (2001) compared adult rats that had been overnourished early in life with those that had been normally nourished. They produced overnourishment by the simple expedient of removing some pups from some of the litters, which meant that the remaining pups received more milk from their mothers. The rats that had been overnourished as pups showed persistent overweight in adulthood. In addition, leptin no longer had a suppressive effect on the firing rate of neurons in the arcuate nucleus of the hypothalamus. As we saw, leptin normally decreases appetite and increases metabolic activity. Overnutrition early in life appears to desensitize the brain to the antiobesity effects of leptin.

Undernutrition can also promote obesity. Children whose growth is stunted by malnourishment during childhood show a higher incidence of obesity in adulthood. Hoffman et al. (2000) found that this effect may be caused by an increased metabolic efficiency. They found that poor, undernourished children living in the shantytowns of São Paulo, Brazil, showed a lower level of fat breakdown during fasting. The investigators suggest that this increased metabolic efficiency may put the children at risk for developing obesity in adulthood (assuming, of course, that they are able to obtain sufficient quantities of food).

As we saw earlier, study of the ob mouse led to the discovery of leptin, the hormone secreted by well-nourished adipose tissue. The explanation of obesity in the ob mouse was simple: The animals could not produce leptin. Following this discovery, researchers have been trying to determine whether understanding the role of leptin can help us understand at least some of the causes of obesity in humans.

So far, researchers have found several cases of familial obesity caused by the absence of leptin produced by the mutation of the gene responsible for its production (Montague et al., 1997; Strobel et al., 1998; Ozata, Ozdemir, and Licinio, 1999), and more will undoubtedly be discovered. Farooqi et al. (2001) found three unrelated families with mutations that caused slightly lower levels of leptin to be produced. These mutations, too, caused obesity. However, such mutations are rare, so they do not explain the vast majority of cases of obesity. Schwartz et al. (1996) found that plasma levels of leptin were related to total body fat in both lean and obese people. Therefore, most investigators believe that if leptin plays a role in human obesity, the likely mechanism is reduced *sensitivity* to the hormone and not decreased secretion.

How could people differ in sensitivity to leptin? One possible mechanism could be a mutation of the gene responsible for production of the leptin receptor. In fact, three strains of obese rodents—the *db mouse,* the *corpulent rat,* and the *Zucker rat*—all have mutations of the leptin receptor gene (Gura, 1997). But familial obesity in humans caused by a defective leptin receptor gene appears to be a very rare event (Clément et al., 1998).

Leptin is a peptide, and peptides normally cannot cross the blood–brain barrier. However, an active mechanism transports molecules of leptin across this barrier so that it can exert its behavioral and metabolic effects (Banks et al., 1996; Golden, MacCagnan, and Pardridge, 1997). Caro et al. (1996) suggested that differences in the effectiveness of this transport system may be one cause of obesity. If not much leptin gets across the blood–brain barrier, the leptin signal in the brain will be weaker than it should be. Caro and his colleagues found that although the level of leptin in the blood was 318 percent higher in obese people, it was only 30 percent higher in the cerebrospinal fluid (which is presumably related to the concentration of the hormone in the brain). Thus, differences in sensitivity to leptin could be caused by differences in the transport of leptin molecules into the brain.

Evidence suggests that sensitivity to leptin can be affected by environmental factors. As you undoubtedly know, a high-fat diet encourages weight gain. This effect is partly caused by the fact that a gram of fat contains approximately nine calories, whereas a gram of carbohydrate or protein contain approximately five calories. But there appear to be other reasons as well. In a study with humans, Havel et al. (1999) found that high-fat meals produce less of an increase in plasma leptin levels than low-fat meals equated for caloric content. This finding suggests that a high-fat diet decreases the strength of the primary long-term satiety factor. (See *Figure 12.27.*)

As you have undoubtedly noticed, many people gain weight as they grow older. There are undoubtedly several causes for this tendency, including a decrease in levels of physical activity. But some evidence suggests that there can be age-related changes in sensitivity to leptin. Scarpace, Matheny, and Tümer (2001) found that hypothalamic neurons in aged obese rats showed a smaller response to leptin than those in rats of normal weight. They also observed a 50 percent reduction in the number of leptin receptors, which may account for this difference.

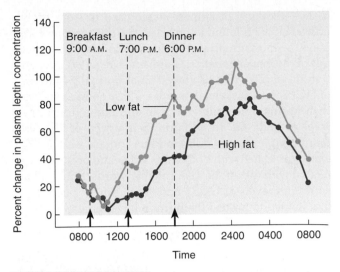

figure 12.27

Percent change in plasma leptin concentration in response to high-fat or low-fat meals of equal caloric value.
(Adapted from Havel, P. J., Townsend, R., Chaump, L., and Teff, K. *Diabetes,* 1999, *48,* 334–341.)

As we saw earlier in this chapter, the MC4 receptor plays a role in the control of eating and metabolism. Several groups of researchers (Vaisse et al., 1998; Yeo et al., 1998; Farooqi et al., 2000) have found families with severe obesity caused by mutations of the MC4 receptor. It appears that mutation of the MC4 receptor is the most common simple genetic cause of severe obesity. Approximately 4 percent of such people have a mutation of these receptors (Barsh, Farooqi, and O'Rahilly, 2000).

The final physiological factor that I will mention in this section is a chemical known as **uncoupling protein (UCP).** This protein is found in mitochondria and may be one of the factors that determine the rate at which an animal burns off its calories. In other words, it may be a factor in metabolic efficiency. Uncoupling protein was first discovered by Nicholls and Wenner (1972) in brown adipose tissue. This special form of fat tissue is specially adapted for heat production and is found in many species of animals, especially those that need to raise their body temperature after hibernation. (It disappears in humans shortly after birth.) Uncoupling protein affects the membranes of mitochondria, so instead of producing molecules of ATP that can be used as a source of energy in the cell, the energy derived from metabolizing fuels is "wasted" as heat.

More recently, researchers discovered two other forms of uncoupling protein. UCP2 is found in white adipose

---

uncoupling protein (UCP) A mitochondrial protein that facilitates the conversion of nutrients into heat.

tissue—the kind of adipose tissue used to store triglycerides. UCP3 is found in muscles, and this form probably plays the most important role in metabolism. Using methods of molecular genetics, Clapham et al. (2000) prepared a strain of mice that produced an abnormally high level of UCP3 in their skeletal muscles. These animals ate more than normal mice but were lean and had a much lower level of body fat. In addition, Schrauwen et al. (1999) found that levels of UCP3 in Pima Indians were a negatively correlated with body mass index and positively correlated with metabolic rate. In other words, Pima Indians with high levels of UCP3 had "spendthrift" phenotypes that helped to protect them from developing obesity.

Treatment of Obesity

Obesity is extremely difficult to treat; the enormous financial success of diet books, health spas, and weight reduction programs attests to the trouble people have losing weight. More precisely, many programs help people to lose weight initially, but then the weight is quickly regained. Kramer et al. (1989) reported that four to five years after participating in a fifteen-week behavioral weight loss program, fewer than 3 percent of the participants managed to maintain the weight loss they had achieved during the program. Some experts have suggested that given the extremely low long-term success rate, perhaps we should stop treating people for obesity until our treatments are more successful. As Wooley and Garner (1994) said,

> We should stop offering ineffective treatments aimed at weight loss. Researchers who think they have invented a better mousetrap should test it in controlled research before setting out their bait for the entire population. Only by admitting that our treatments do not work—and showing that we mean it by refraining from offering them—can we begin to undo a century of recruiting fat people for failure. (p. 656)

Whatever the cause of obesity, the metabolic fact of life is this: If calories in exceed calories out, then body fat will increase. Because it is difficult to increase the "calories out" side of the equation enough to bring an obese person's weight back to normal, most treatments for obesity attempt to reduce the "calories in." The extraordinary difficulty that obese people have in reducing caloric intake for a sustained period of time (that is, for the rest of their lives) has led to the development of some extraordinary means. In this section I shall describe mechanical, surgical, and pharmacological methods that have been devised to make obese people eat less.

Eating requires that we open our mouths. This obvious fact led to the development of jaw wiring, a procedure in which wires are attached to a person's teeth to keep the jaw from opening. The patient is not left to starve; he or she is given a liquid diet to sip through a straw. Of course, there is no guarantee that a person will ingest fewer calories each day simply because he or she is deprived of the opportunity to chew. In fact, Munro et al. (1987) reported that some of their patients managed to *gain* weight on a liquid diet. However, many patients do manage to lose weight. Unfortunately, almost all of them regain it once the wires are removed, and many become even more obese than they were when they started out.

To reduce the recidivism rate, some therapists have fastened a nylon cord around the waist of their patients after they had lost weight through a jaw-wiring procedure. The ends of the cord were fused together so that the cord could not be removed without cutting it. Unfortunately, about half of the patients did just that.

Surgeons have also become involved in trying to help obese people lose weight. The procedures they have developed either reduce the amount of food that can be eaten during a meal or interfere with absorption of calories from the intestines. Surgery has been aimed at the stomach, the small intestine, or both.

The most common surgical procedure for reducing food intake has been to make the person's stomach smaller. Early procedures actually removed some of the stomach, but more recent methods have stapled part of it shut or have put bands around it so that it can expand only a limited amount—a procedure known as *gastroplasty* (literally, "a reshaping of the stomach"). Ideally, gastroplasty should result in a feeling of satiety after the ingestion of a small amount of food. But in fact, the surgery often produces *nimiety,* or an aversive feeling of overfullness (from the Latin *nimius,* "excessive"). The meal stops not because the patients feel satisfied but because they feel so uncomfortable that they cannot go on eating.

Surgeons have developed several procedures that reduce the absorption of food from the intestines. All of these procedures rearrange the intestines so that food takes a shorter path to the large intestine, leaving less time for nutrients to be absorbed. The unabsorbed nutrients are evacuated from the body, of course, so it should come as no surprise that diarrhea and flatulence (excessive intestinal gas) are commonly associated with these procedures. Many types of intestinal bypass operations do not simply interfere with absorption; they also reduce food intake by producing nimiety. After some surgical procedures relatively undigested food is dumped into regions of the intestines that normally receive only well-digested food, and the result is a feeling of discomfort.

Besides producing diarrhea and flatulence, intestinal bypass surgery can produce undesirable side effects such as bacterial overgrowth and production of toxins in a bypassed segment of intestine; deficiencies of iron, vitamin B_{12}, vitamin B_1, or protein; and abnormalities in calcium metabolism. A severe vitamin B_1 (thiamine) deficiency can damage the nervous system; as you will learn in Chapter 14, the result can be a permanent memory loss. Of course, if a patient's condition is carefully monitored by a physician after the surgery, these complications can be avoided or corrected; but not all patients cooperate with their physicians for postsurgical care.

A less drastic form of therapy for obesity—exercise—has significant benefits. Exercise burns off calories, of course, but it also appears to have beneficial effects on metabolic rate. Bunyard et al. (1998) found that when middle-aged men participated in an aerobic exercise program for six months, their body fat decreased and their daily energy requirement increased—by 5 percent for obese men and by 8 percent for lean men. (Remember, a less efficient metabolism means that it is easier to avoid gaining weight.) Gurin et al. (1999) found that an exercise program helped obese children to lose fat and had the additional benefit of increasing bone density. Of course, a regular program of exercise requires a commitment of time and effort that not everyone is able—or willing—to make.

King et al. (2001) studied the relationship between occupational and leisure-time activity and people's body weight. They found that both factors were important. People with jobs that required more physical activity weighed less than those with sedentary jobs, and people who reported that they regularly got moderate or vigorous exercise weighed less than people who were physically inactive during their leisure time. Of the two factors, leisure-time activity level was more important.

Another type of therapy for obesity—drug treatment—shows some promise. There are three possible ways that drugs could help people lose weight: reduce the amount of food they eat, prevent some of the food they eat from being digested, and increase their metabolic rate (that is, provide them with a "spendthrift phenotype."

As we saw earlier in this chapter, serotonergic agonists suppress eating. A review by Bray (1992) concluded that serotonin agonists can be of benefit in weight-loss programs. However, one of the drugs most commonly used for this purpose, fenfluramine, was found to have hazardous side effects, including pulmonary hypertension and damage to the valves of the heart, so the drug was withdrawn from the market in the United States (Blundell and Halford, 1998). Fenfluramine acts by stimulating the release of 5-HT. Fortunately, another drug, sibutramine, has similar therapeutic effects and has not yet been associated with serious side effects.

Another drug, orlistat, interferes with the absorption of fats by the small intestine. As a result, some of the fat in the person's diet passes through the digestive system and is excreted with the feces. A double-blind, placebo-controlled study by Hiel et al. (1999) found that orlistat helped people maintain weight loss they had achieved by participating in a conventional weight-loss program. People who received the placebo were much more likely to regain the weight they had lost.

As we have seen, appetite can be stimulated by activation of NPY, MCH, orexin, and ghrelin receptors, and it can be suppressed by the activation of leptin, CCK, CART, and MC4 receptors. Appetite can also be suppressed by activation of inhibitory presynaptic Y2 autoreceptors by PYY. C75, a drug that interferes with fatty acid metabolism, dramatically suppresses eating and body weight. Most of these orexigenic and anorexigenic chemicals also affect metabolism: Orexigenic chemicals tend to decrease metabolic rate, and anorexigenic chemicals tend to increase it. In addition, uncoupling protein causes nutrients to be "burned"—converted into heat instead of adipose tissue. Do these discoveries hold any promise for the treatment of obesity? Is there any possibility that researchers will find drugs that will stimulate or block these receptors, thus decreasing people's appetite and increasing the rate at which they burn rather than store their calories? Drug companies certainly hope so, and they are working hard on developing medications that will do so, because they know that there will be a very large number of people willing to pay for them.

The variety of methods—surgical, mechanical, behavioral, and pharmacological—that therapists and surgeons have developed to treat obesity attests to the tenacity of the problem. The basic difficulty, beyond that caused by having an efficient metabolism, is that eating is pleasurable and satiety signals are easy to ignore or override. Despite the fact that relatively little success has been seen until now, I am personally optimistic about what the future may hold. I think that if we learn more about the physiology of hunger signals, satiety signals, and the reinforcement provided by eating, we will be able to develop safe and effective drugs that attenuate the signals that encourage us to eat and strengthen those that encourage us to stop eating.

Anorexia Nervosa/Bulimia Nervosa

Most people, if they have an eating problem, tend to overeat. However, some people, especially adolescent women, have the opposite problem: They eat too little, even to the point of starvation. This disorder is called **anorexia nervosa.** Another eating disorder, **bulimia nervosa,** is characterized by a loss of control of food intake. (The term *bulimia* comes from the Greek *bous,* "ox," and *limos,* "hunger.") People with bulimia nervosa periodically gorge themselves with food, especially dessert or snack food and especially in the afternoon or evening. These binges are usually followed by self-induced vomiting or the use

anorexia nervosa A disorder that most frequently afflicts young women; exaggerated concern with overweight that leads to excessive dieting and often compulsive exercising; can lead to starvation.

bulimia nervosa Bouts of excessive hunger and eating, often followed by forced vomiting or purging with laxatives; sometimes seen in people with anorexia nervosa.

of laxatives, along with feelings of depression and guilt (Mawson, 1974; Halmi, 1978). With this combination of binging and purging, the net nutrient intake (and consequently, the body weight) of bulimics can vary; Weltzin et al. (1991) reported that 19 percent of bulimics undereat, 37 percent eat a normal amount, and 44 percent overeat. Episodes of bulimia are seen in some patients with anorexia nervosa. Bulimia nervosa is more common than anorexia nervosa, and its incidence seems to be increasing (Walsh and Devlin, 1998).

The literal meaning of the word *anorexia* suggests a loss of appetite, but people with this disorder are usually interested in—even preoccupied with—food. They may enjoy preparing meals for others to consume, collect recipes, and even hoard food that they do not eat. Broberg and Bernstein (1989) presented anorexic and lean (but nonanorexic) young women with a warm, appetizing cinnamon roll. They cut the roll and said that the women could eat it if they wanted. For the next 10 minutes the experimenters withdrew blood samples and analyzed the insulin content. They found that both groups of subjects showed an increase in insulin level; surprisingly, the increase was even higher in the anorexic subjects. Thus, we cannot conclude that anorexics are simply unresponsive to food. (See *Figure 12.28*.) Incidentally, as you might expect, the normal subjects ate the roll, but the anorexics did not, saying that they were not hungry.

Although anorexics might not be oblivious to the effects of food, they express an intense fear of becoming obese, which continues even if they become dangerously thin. Many exercise by cycling, running, or almost constant walking and pacing. Studies with animals suggest that the increased activity may be a result of the fasting. When

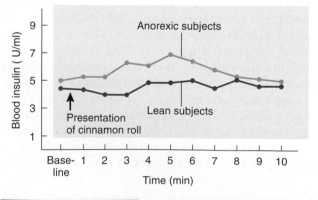

figure 12.28

Effects of the sight and smell of a warm cinnamon roll on insulin secretion in anorexic women and thin, nonanorexic women.

(Adapted from Broberg, D. J., and Bernstein, I. L. *Physiology and Behavior*, 1989, *45*, 871–874.)

rats are deprived of food, they will spend more and more time running in a wheel if one is available, even though doing so means that the animals will lose weight faster (Routtenberg, 1968). Some investigators believe that the exercise stimulates the breakdown of lipids into fatty acids and glycerol and thus actually reduces feelings of hunger. Wilckens, Schweiger, and Pirke (1992) found that deprivation-induced wheel running can be inhibited by drugs that stimulate 5-HT_{1C} receptors.

The fact that anorexia nervosa is seen primarily in young women has prompted both biological and social explanations. Most psychologists favor the latter, concluding that the emphasis our society places on slimness—especially in women—is responsible for this disorder. However, the success of therapy is not especially encouraging; Ratnasuriya et al. (1991) reported that twenty years later, only 29 percent of a group of patients treated for anorexia nervosa showed a good recovery. Almost 15 percent of the patients had died of suicide or complications of the disease. Many anorexics suffer from osteoporosis, and bone fractures are common. When the weight loss becomes severe enough, the anorexics cease menstruating. Some disturbing reports (Artmann et al., 1985; Herholz, 1996; Kingston et al., 1996) indicate that CT scans revealed enlarged ventricles and widened sulci, which indicates shrinkage of brain tissue. The widened sulci, but not the enlarged ventricles, apparently return to normal after recovery.

There is good evidence, primarily from twin studies, that hereditary factors play an important role in the development of anorexia (Russell and Treasure, 1989; Walters and Kendler, 1995; Kortegaard et al., 2001). The existence of hereditary factors suggests that abnormalities in physiological mechanisms may be involved. As you might suspect, many investigators have suggested that anorexia and bulimia may be caused by biochemical or structural abnormalities in the brain mechanisms that control metabolism or eating. In a review of the literature Fava et al. (1989) reported that studies have found evidence for changes in NE, 5-HT, and opioids in people with anorexia nervosa and changes in NE and 5-HT in people with bulimia nervosa. Many studies have reported changes in endocrine levels of anorexic patients, but these changes are probably effects of the disorder, not causes. In most cases when a patient recovers, the endocrine system returns to normal.

Some investigators have suggested that neuropeptide Y may play a role in anorexia (Kaye et al., 1990; Kaye, 1996). Kaye and his colleagues found elevated levels of NPY in the cerebrospinal fluid of severely underweight anorexics. However, once the patients regained their normal weights, the levels of the peptide returned to normal. The investigators suggested that the increased level of NPY is a response to the loss of weight and at least partly accounts for the obsession with food that is typical in anorexia. In addition, the high level of NPY is probably responsible for the absence of menstruation in these patients. (You will recall that neuropeptide Y suppresses ovulation in laboratory animals.) CSF levels of leptin are, as one would expect, low in underweight anorexics. However, if the patients begin eating again, their leptin levels reach normal values even before their weight returns to normal, which may make it difficult for them to maintain their weight gain (Mantzoros et al., 1997).

We cannot rule out the possibility that some biochemical disturbance in brain functions related to metabolism or food intake underlie anorexia nervosa. Measurement of neurotransmitters, neuromodulators, and their metabolites in the cerebrospinal fluid is a crude and indirect indication of the release and activity of these substances in the brain. Unfortunately, we do not have a good animal model of anorexia to study in the laboratory.

Researchers have tried to treat anorexia nervosa with many drugs that increase appetite in nonanorexics or in laboratory animals—for example, antipsychotic medications, drugs that stimulate adrenergic α_2 receptors, L-DOPA, and THC (the active ingredient in marijuana). Unfortunately, none of these drugs have shown themselves to be helpful (Mitchell, 1989). One study (Halmi et al., 1986) found that cyproheptadine, an antihistaminergic drug that also has an antiserotonergic effect, may speed the recovery of anorexics. The drug aided only patients who did not exhibit bulimia; the drug actually interfered with the recovery of those who did exhibit bulimia. These results have not yet been confirmed by other investigators. In any event the fact that anorexics are usually obsessed with food (and show high levels of neuropeptide Y in their CSF) suggests that the disorder is not caused by the absence of hunger. Researchers have had better luck with bulimia nervosa; several studies suggest that serotonin agonists such as fluoxetine (an antidepressant drug that is best known as Prozac) may aid in the treatment of this disorder (Advokat and Kutlesic, 1995; Kaye et al., 2001). However, fluoxetine does not help anorexic patients (Attia et al., 1998).

Anorexia nervosa is a serious condition; understanding its causes is more than an academic matter. We can hope that research on the biological and social control of feeding and metabolism will help us to understand this puzzling and dangerous disorder.

interim summary

Eating Disorders

Two sets of eating disorders—obesity and anorexia/bulimia nervosa—present serious health problems. Although environmental effects, such as learning to eat everything on the plate and arranging food in appetizing courses, may contribute to overeating, the most important cause appears to be an efficient metabolism, which permits fat to accumulate easily. Metabolic rates are controlled by hereditary and environmental factors. Adoption studies find no evidence that a person's early family environment has a significant effect on his or her body weight in adulthood. But other environmental factors do play an important role in the development of obesity. A high percentage of Pima Indians who live in the United States and consume a high-fat diet become obese and, as a consequence, develop diabetes. In contrast, Mexican Pima Indians, who work hard at subsistence farming and eat a low-fat diet, remain thin and have a low incidence of obesity.

So far, there is little evidence that obesity in humans is related to a deficient secretion of leptin, as it is in ob mice; in general, obese people have very high levels of leptin in their blood. Nor is there good evidence that obese people have faulty leptin receptors, as do db mice and Zucker rats. One possible reason for insensitivity to leptin in obese people might be inefficient transport of leptin through the blood–brain barrier. In addition, a high-fat meal produces a smaller increase in leptin levels than a low-fat meal, and obesity produced by a high-fat diet leads to decreased sensitivity to leptin. The most significant simple genetic cause of severe obesity is mutation of the MC4 receptor, which responds to the orexigen AGRP and the anorexigen α-MSH.

Researchers have tried many mechanical, surgical, and pharmacological treatments for obesity, but no panacea has yet been found. The best hope probably comes from drugs; specific serotonin agonists suppress eating and decrease body weight. At present many pharmaceutical companies are trying to apply the results of the discoveries of orexigens and anorexigens described in this chapter to the development of antiobesity drugs.

Anorexia nervosa is a serious—even life-threatening—disorder. Although anorexic patients avoid eating, they often remain preoccupied with food, and their insulin level rises when they are presented with an appetizing stimulus. Bulimia nervosa (sometimes associated with anorexia) consists of periodic binging and purging.

Researchers are beginning to study possible abnormalities in the regulation of transmitter substances and neuropeptides that seem to play a role in normal control of feeding to determine whether medical treatments for anorexia and bulimia can be discovered. So far, no useful drugs have been found to treat anorexia nervosa; but fluoxetine, a serotonin agonist used to treat depression, may help to suppress episodes of bulimia.

This section and the previous one introduced several neuropeptides and peripheral peptides that play a role in control of eating and metabolism. Table 12.1 summarizes information about these compounds. (See **Table 12.1**.)

Neuropeptides and Peripheral Peptides Involved in Control of Food Intake and Metabolism

NEUROPEPTIDES

Name	Location of Cell Bodies	Location of Terminals	Interaction with Other Peptides	Physiological or Behavioral Effects
Melanin-concentrating hormone (MCH)	Perifornical region of lateral hypothalamus	Neocortex, periaqueductal gray matter, reticular formation, thalamus, locus coeruleus, neurons in spinal cord that control the sympathetic nervous system	Inhibited by leptin and CART/α-MSH; activated by NPY/AGRP	Eating, decreased metabolic rate
Orexin	Perifornical region of lateral hypothalamus	Similar to those of MCH neurons	Inhibited by leptin and CART/α-MSH; activated by NPY/AGRP	Eating, decreased metabolic rate
Neuropeptide Y (NPY)	Arcuate nucleus of hypothalamus	Paraventricular nucleus, MCH and orexin neurons of the perifornical region	Inhibited by leptin	Eating, decreased metabolic rate
Agouti-related protein (AGRP)	Arcuate nucleus of hypothalamus (colocalized with NPY)	Same regions as NPY neurons	Inhibited by leptin	Eating, decreased metabolic rate; acts as agonist at MC4 receptors
Cocaine- and amphetamine-regulated transcript (CART)	Arcuate nucleus of hypothalamus	Paraventricular nucleus, lateral hypothalamus, periaqueductal gray matter, neurons in spinal cord that control the sympathetic nervous system	Activated by leptin	Suppression of eating, increased metabolic rate
α-melanocyte stimulating hormone (α-MSH)	Arcuate nucleus of hypothalamus (colocalized with CART)	Same regions as CART neurons	Activated by leptin	Suppression of eating, increased metabolic rate; acts as antagonist at MC4 receptors

PERIPHERAL PEPTIDE

Name	Where Produced	Site of Actions	Physiological or Behavioral Effects
Leptin	Fat tissue	Inhibits NPY/AGRP neurons; excites CART/α-MSH neurons	Suppression of eating, increased metabolic rate
Insulin	Pancreas	Similar to leptin	Similar to leptin
Ghrelin	Gastrointestinal system	Excites NPY/AGRP neurons	Eating
Cholecystokinin (CCK)	Duodenum	Neurons in pylorus	Suppression of eating
Peptide YY$_{3-36}$ (PYY)	Gastrointestinal system	Inhibits NPY/AGRP neurons	Suppression of eating

Suggested Readings

Barsh, G. S., and Schwartz, M. W. Genetic approaches to studying energy balance: Perception and integration. *Nature Reviews: Genetics*, 2002, *3*, 589–600.

Bouchard, C., and Bray, G. A. *Regulation of Body Weight: Biological and Behavioral Mechanisms.* New York: John Wiley & Sons, 1996.

Bourque, C. W., Oliet, S. H., and Richard, D. Osmoreceptors, osmoreception, and osmoregulation. *Frontiers in Neuroendocrinology*, 1994, *15*, 231–274.

Brownell, K. D., and Fairburn, C. G. *Eating Disorders and Obesity: A Comprehensive Handbook.* New York: Guilford Press, 1995.

Chiesi, M., Huppertz, C., and Hofbauer, K. G. Pharmacotherapy of obesity: Targets and perspectives. *Trends in Pharmacological Sciences*, 2001, *22*, 247–254.

Havel, P. J. Peripheral signals conveying metabolic information to the brain: Short-term and long-term regulation of food intake and energy homeostasis. *Proceedings of the Society for Experimental Biology and Medicine*, 2001, *226*, 963–977.

Johnson, A. K., and Thunhorst, R. L. The neuroendocrinology of thirst and salt appetite: Visceral sensory signals and mechanisms of central integration. *Frontiers in Neuroendocrinology*, 1997, *18*, 292–353.

Kreipe, R. E., and Mou, S. M. Eating disorders in adolescents and young adults. *Obstetrics and Gynecology Clinics of North America*, 2000, *27*, 101–124.

Suggested Web Sites

The Society for the Study of Ingestive Behavior
http://lshome.utsa.edu/SSIB/
Eating and drinking are the research topics of scientists within this society. The site contains links to journals, a newsletter, and links relating to ingestive behavior.

Endocrine-Related Sites
http://www.endo-society.org/coolsite.htm
This site provides a comprehensive set of links to sites relating to the topic of endocrinology.

Eating Disorders
http://eatingdisorders.mentalhelp.net/
This site contains facts about eating disorders as well as links to sites dealing with treatments for eating disorders.

Nutrition and Obesity
http://www.niddk.nih.gov/health/nutrit/nutrit.htm
Nutrition and obesity issues and facts are contained within this site provided by the National Institutes of Health (NIH).

Obesity Links
http://www.dimensionsmagazine.com/links/scientific.html
This site provides a series of interesting and informative sites relating to obesity, weight loss, and surgical treatments for obesity.

North American Association for the Study of Obesity (NAASO)
http://www.naaso.org/calendar/
This is the Web site of the North American Association for the Study of Obesity, a group dedicated to understanding and treating obesity. The site provides access to online abstracts of the journal Obesity Research *and to an obesity discussion group.*

Eating Disorders Tutorials
http://psy71.dur.ac.uk/Education/index.html
The site contains a comprehensive set of links to documents and tutorials on eating disorders.

chapter

13

Learning and Memory: Basic Mechanisms

outline

■ **The Nature of Learning**
Interim Summary

■ **Learning and Synaptic Plasticity**
Induction of Long-Term Potentiation
Role of NMDA Receptors
Mechanisms of Synaptic Plasticity
Long-Term Depression
Other Forms of Long-Term Potentiation
Role of Long-Term Potentiation in Learning
Interim Summary

■ **Perceptual Learning**
Learning to Recognize Visual Stimuli
Perceptual Short-Term Memory
Interim Summary

■ **Classical Conditioning**
Interim Summary

■ **Instrumental Conditioning and Motor Learning**
Basal Ganglia
Premotor Cortex
Reinforcement
Interim Summary

Gerhard Richter, *Abstract Painting (726),* 1990.
© Gerhard Richter. © Tate Gallery, London/Art Resource, NY.

In 1954 James Olds, a young assistant professor, designed an experiment to determine whether the reticular formation might play a role in learning. Recent studies had suggested that the reticular formation was involved in arousal; when it was active, it would apparently increase an animal's attention and vigilance. Olds decided to place an electrode in the brains of rats to electrically stimulate the reticular formation. Perhaps the stimulation would increase the rats' attention to their environment and facilitate their learning a maze. If the stimulated animals learned the task faster than those that were not stimulated, his hypothesis would have strong support.

Olds enlisted the aid of Peter Milner, a graduate student who had experience with the surgical procedure needed to implant the electrodes in the brain. Because the procedure had only recently been developed and was not very accurate, one of the electrodes wound up in the wrong place—near the opposite end of the brain, in fact. This accident was a lucky one for the investigators, because they discovered a phenomenon that they would not have seen if the electrode had been located where they had intended it to be.

Olds and Milner had heard a talk by another physiological psychologist, Neal Miller, who reported that he had discovered that electrical stimulation of some parts of the brain could be aversive; the animals would work to avoid having the current turned on. The investigators decided that before they began their study, they would make sure that aversive stimulation was not occurring, because it might interfere with the animals' performance in the maze. The behavior of most of the animals was unremarkable, but here is Olds's report of what happened when he tested the rat with the misplaced electrode:

> I applied a brief train of 60-cycle sine-wave electrical current whenever the animal entered one corner of the enclosure. The animal did not stay away from that corner, but rather came back quickly after a brief sortie

which followed the first stimulation and came back even more quickly after a briefer sortie which followed the second stimulation. By the time the third electrical stimulus had been applied the animal seemed indubitably to be "coming back for more." (Olds, 1973, p. 81)

Realizing that they had just seen something very important, Olds and Milner put more electrodes in rats' brains and allowed the rats to press a switch that controlled the current to the brain. The rats quickly learned to press the switch at a rate of over seven hundred times per hour. Subsequent studies obtained response rates of several thousand presses per hour. It turned out that the reinforcing effect of the electrical brain stimulation was very potent; when given a choice between pressing the lever and eating, drinking, or copulating, animals would choose the lever.

Olds and Milner's discovery probably had more impact on psychology than any other experiment performed by physiological psychologists. Articles in the popular press speculated on the nature of the "pleasure centers" in the brain. Some writers warned that a totalitarian society might one day control its population by putting electrodes in their brains and providing rewarding stimulation when they did what they were supposed to and withholding it when they did not. Such speculations prompted Eliot Valenstein to write a book demystifying the phenomenon, putting it in perspective (Valenstein, 1973).

The interest in reinforcing brain stimulation has peaked, but because the circuits discovered by Olds and Milner are responsible for the powerful addictive potential of drugs such as cocaine, the research they began is still continuing. Many investigators are trying to understand the function these circuits play and how they relate to the effects of addictive drugs and the effectiveness of natural reinforcers. (By the way, it turns out that electrical stimulation of the reticular formation does *not* facilitate learning, but that is another story.)

Experiences change us; encounters with our environment alter our behavior by modifying our nervous system. As many investigators have said, an understanding of the physiology of memory is the ultimate challenge to neuroscience research. The brain is complex, and so are learning and remembering. Although the individual changes that occur within the cells of the brain may be relatively simple, the brain consists of many billions of neurons. Therefore, isolating and identifying the particular changes that are responsible for a particular memory are exceedingly difficult. Similarly, although the elements of a particular learning task may be simple, its implications for an organism may be complex. The behavior that the investigator observes and measures may be only one of many that change as a result of an experience.

However, despite the difficulties, the long years of work finally seem to be paying off. New approaches and new methods have evolved from old ones, and real progress has been made in understanding the anatomy and physiology of learning and remembering.

The Nature of Learning

Learning refers to the process by which experiences change our nervous system and hence our behavior. We refer to these changes as *memories*. Although it is convenient to describe memories as if they were notes placed in filing cabinets, this is certainly not the way experiences are reflected within the brain. Experiences are not "stored"; rather, they change the way we perceive, perform, think, and plan. They do so by physically changing the structure of the nervous system, altering neural circuits that participate in perceiving, performing, thinking, and planning.

The primary function of the ability to learn is to develop behaviors that are adapted to an ever-changing environment. The ability to learn permits us to find food when we are hungry, warmth when we are cold, companions when we are lonely. It also permits us to avoid objects or situations that might harm us. However, the fact that the ultimate function of learning is a useful change in behavior does not mean that learning takes place only in the parts of the brain that control movement. Learning can take at least four basic forms: perceptual learning, stimulus-response learning, motor learning, and relational learning. This chapter discusses the first three forms, and Chapter 14 discusses relational learning.

Perceptual learning is the ability to learn to recognize stimuli that have been perceived before. The primary function of this type of learning is the ability to identify and categorize objects (including other members of our own species) and situations. Unless we have learned to recognize something, we cannot learn how we should behave with respect to it—We will not profit from our experiences with it, and profiting from experience is what learning is all about.

Each of our sensory systems is capable of perceptual learning. We can learn to recognize objects by their visual appearance, the sounds they make, how they feel, or how they smell. We can recognize people by the shape of their faces, the movements they make when they walk, or the sound of their voices. When we hear people talk, we can recognize the words they are saying and, perhaps, their emotional state. As we shall see, perceptual learning appears to be accomplished primarily by changes in the sensory association cortex. That is, learning to recognize complex visual stimuli involves changes in the visual association cortex, learning to recognize complex auditory stimuli involves changes in the auditory association cortex, and so on.

Stimulus-response learning is the ability to learn to perform a particular behavior when a particular stimulus is present. Thus, it involves the establishment of connections between circuits involved in perception and those involved in movement. The behavior could be an automatic response such as a defensive reflex, or it could be a complicated sequence of movements that was learned previously. Stimulus-response learning includes two major categories of learning that psychologists have studied extensively: *classical conditioning* and *instrumental conditioning*.

Classical conditioning is a form of learning in which an unimportant stimulus acquires the properties of an important one. It involves an *association between two stimuli*. A stimulus that previously had little effect on behavior becomes able to evoke a reflexive, species-typical behav-

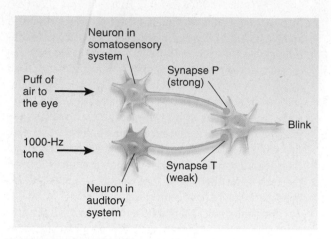

figure   13.1

A simple neural model of classical conditioning. When the 1000-Hz tone is presented just before the puff of air to the eye, synapse T is strengthened.

ior. For example, a defensive eyeblink response can be conditioned to a tone. If we direct a brief puff of air toward a rabbit's eye, the eye will automatically blink. The response is called an **unconditional response (UR)** because it occurs unconditionally, without any special training. The stimulus that produces it (the puff of air) is called an **unconditional stimulus (US).** Now we begin the training. We present a series of brief 1000-Hz tones, each followed 500 ms later by a puff of air. After several trials the rabbit's eye begins to close even before the puff of air occurs. Classical conditioning has occurred; the **conditional stimulus (CS**—the 1000-Hz tone) now elicits the **conditional response (CR**—the eye blink). (See *Figure 13.1*.)

When classical conditioning takes place, what kinds of changes occur in the brain? Figure 13.1 shows a simplified neural circuit that could account for this type of learning. For the sake of simplicity we will assume that the US (the puff of air) is detected by a single neuron in the somatosensory system and that the CS (the 1000-Hz tone) is detected by a single neuron in the auditory system. We will also assume that the response—the eyeblink—is controlled by a single neuron in the motor system. (See *Figure 13.1*.)

---

perceptual learning Learning to recognize a particular stimulus.

stimulus-response learning Learning to automatically make a particular response in the presence of a particular stimulus; includes classical and instrumental conditioning.

classical conditioning A learning procedure; when a stimulus that initially produces no particular response is followed several times by an **unconditional stimulus** that produces a defensive or appetitive response (the **unconditional response**), the first stimulus (now called a **conditional stimulus**) itself evokes the response (now called a **conditional response**).

Now let us see how the circuits work. If we present a 1000-Hz tone, we find that the animal makes no reaction, because the synapse connecting the tone-sensitive neuron with the neuron in the motor system is weak. That is, when an action potential reaches the terminal button of synapse T (tone), the EPSP it produces in the dendrite of the motor neuron is too small to make that neuron fire. However, if we present a puff of air to the eye, the eye blinks. This reaction occurs because nature has provided the animal with a strong synapse between the somatosensory neuron and the motor neuron that causes a blink (synapse P, for "puff"). To establish classical conditioning, we first present the 1000-Hz tone and then almost immediately follow it with a puff of air. After we repeat these pairs of stimuli several times, we find that we can dispense with the air puff; the 1000-Hz tone produces the blink all by itself.

Over fifty years ago, Donald Hebb proposed a rule that might explain how neurons are changed by experience in a way that would cause changes in behavior (Hebb, 1949). The **Hebb rule** says that if a synapse repeatedly becomes active at about the same time that the postsynaptic neuron fires, changes will take place in the structure or chemistry of the synapse that will strengthen it. How would the Hebb rule apply to our circuit? If the 1000-Hz tone is presented first, then weak synapse T (for "tone") becomes active. If the puff is presented immediately afterward, then strong synapse P becomes active and makes the motor neuron fire. The act of firing then strengthens any synapse with the motor neuron *that has just been active*. Of course, this means synapse T. After several pairings of the two stimuli, and after several increments of strengthening, synapse T becomes strong enough to cause the motor neuron to fire by itself. Learning has occurred. (See *Figure 13.1*.)

Obviously, the rabbit's auditory system contains more than one neuron, and so does its motor system. Neurons in the auditory system have connections with all kinds of neurons in the motor system—with neurons that control ear wiggling, nose twitching, running, sniffing, chewing, and other things rabbits can do. But before learning takes place, all of these connections are weak; hearing a 1000-Hz tone produces so little activation of the neurons in the motor system that the animal does not make an overt response. (Of course, the noise might startle the animal, but this response usually disappears after the tone is presented a few times.) Of all the thousands of synapses in the motor system that become activated by the 1000-Hz tone, only those located on neurons that have just fired will become strengthened. If the US has just been presented and the animal has just blinked, most of the recently activated cells will be those controlling eyeblinks, and only synapses on these cells will be strengthened.

When Hebb formulated his rule, he was unable to determine whether it was true or false. Now, finally, enough progress has been made in laboratory techniques that the strength of individual synapses can be determined, and investigators are studying the physiological bases of learning. We will see the results of some of these approaches in the next section of this chapter.

The second major class of stimulus-response learning is **instrumental conditioning** (also called *operant conditioning*). Whereas classical conditioning involves automatic, species-typical responses, instrumental conditioning involves behaviors that have been learned. And whereas classical conditioning involves an association between two stimuli, instrumental conditioning involves an *association between a response and a stimulus*. Instrumental conditioning is a more flexible form of learning. It permits an organism to adjust its behavior according to the consequences of that behavior. That is, when a behavior is followed by favorable consequences, the behavior tends to occur more frequently; when it is followed by unfavorable consequences, it tends to occur less frequently. Collectively, "favorable consequences" are referred to as **reinforcing stimuli,** and "unfavorable consequences" are referred to as **punishing stimuli.** For example, a response that enables a hungry organism to find food will be reinforced, and a response that causes pain will be punished. (Psychologists often refer to these terms as *reinforcers* and *punishers.*)

Let's consider the process of reinforcement. Briefly stated, reinforcement causes changes in an animal's nervous system that increase the likelihood that a particular stimulus will elicit a particular response. For example, when a hungry rat is first put in an operant chamber (a "Skinner box"), it is not very likely to press the lever mounted on a wall. However, if it does press the lever and if it receives a piece of food immediately afterward, the likelihood of its making another response increases. Put another way, reinforcement causes the sight of the lever to serve as the stimulus that elicits the lever-pressing response. It is not accurate to say simply that a particular behavior becomes more frequent. If no lever is present, a rat that has learned to press one will not wave its paw around in the air. The *sight of a lever* is needed to produce the response. Thus, the process of reinforcement strengthens a connection between neural circuits involved in perception (the sight of the lever) and those involved in movement (the act of lever pressing). As we will see later

---

Hebb rule The hypothesis proposed by Donald Hebb that the cellular basis of learning involves strengthening of a synapse that is repeatedly active when the postsynaptic neuron fires.

instrumental conditioning A learning procedure whereby the effects of a particular behavior in a particular situation increase (reinforce) or decrease (punish) the probability of the behavior; also called *operant conditioning*.

reinforcing stimulus An appetitive stimulus that follows a particular behavior and thus makes the behavior become more frequent.

punishing stimulus An aversive stimulus that follows a particular behavior and thus makes the behavior become less frequent.

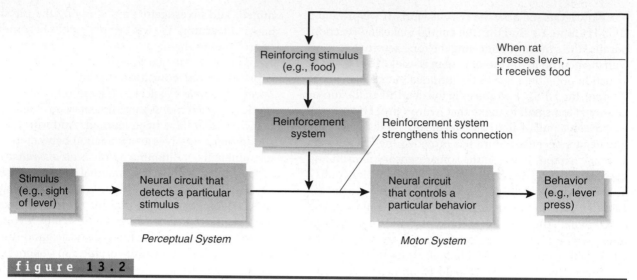

figure 13.2

A simple neural model of instrumental conditioning.

in this chapter, the brain contains reinforcement mechanisms that control this process. (See ***Figure 13.2***.)

The third major category of learning, **motor learning**, is actually a component of stimulus-response learning. For simplicity's sake we can think of perceptual learning as the establishment of changes within the sensory systems of the brain, stimulus-response learning as the establishment of connections between sensory systems and motor systems, and motor learning as the establishment of changes within motor systems. But, in fact, motor learning cannot occur without sensory guidance from the environment. For example, most skilled movements involve interactions with objects: bicycles, pinball machines, tennis racquets, knitting needles, and so on. Even skilled movements that we make by ourselves, such as solitary dance steps, involve feedback from the joints, muscles, vestibular apparatus, eyes, and contact between the feet and the floor. Motor learning differs from other forms of learning primarily in the degree to which new forms of behavior are learned; the more novel the behavior, the more the neural circuits in the motor systems of the brain must be modified. (See ***Figure 13.3***.)

A particular learning situation can involve varying amounts of all three types of learning that I have described so far: perceptual, stimulus-response, and motor. For example, if we teach an animal to make a new response whenever we present a stimulus it has never seen before, it must learn to recognize the stimulus (perceptual learning) and make the response (motor learning), and a connection must be established between these two new memories (stimulus-response learning). If we teach it to make a response it has already learned whenever we present a new stimulus, only perceptual learning and stimulus-response learning will take place.

The three forms of learning I have described so far consist primarily of changes in one sensory system, between one sensory system and the motor system, or in the motor system. But obviously, learning is usually more complex than that. The fourth form of learning involves learning the *relationships* among individual stimuli. For example, a somewhat more complex form of perceptual learning involves connections between different areas of the association cortex. When we hear the sound of a cat meowing in the dark, we can imagine what a cat looks like and what it would feel like if we stroked its fur. Thus, the neural circuits in the auditory association cortex that recognize the meow are somehow connected to the appropriate circuits in the visual association cortex and the somatosensory association cortex. These interconnections, too, are accomplished as a result of learning.

Perception of spatial location—*spatial learning*—also involves learning about the relations among many stimuli. For example, consider what we must learn to become familiar with the contents of a room. First, we must learn to recognize each of the objects. In addition, we must learn the relative locations of the objects with respect to each other. As a result, when we find ourselves located in a particular place in the room, our perceptions of these objects and their locations relative to us tell us exactly where we are.

Other types of relational learning are even more complex. *Episodic learning*—remembering sequences of events (episodes) that we witness—requires us to keep track not only of individual stimuli but also of the order

motor learning Learning to make a new response.

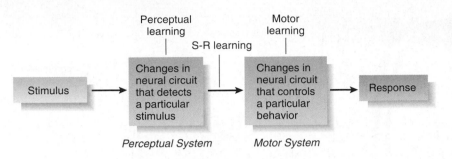

figure 13.3

An overview of perceptual, stimulus-response (S-R), and motor learning.

in which they occur. *Observational learning*—learning by watching and imitating other people—requires us to remember what someone else does, the situation in which the behavior is performed, and the relationship between the other person's movements and our own. As we will see in Chapter 14, a special system that involves the hippocampus and associated structures appears to perform coordinating functions that are necessary for many types of learning that go beyond simple perceptual, stimulus-response, or motor learning.

interim
summary

The Nature of Learning

Learning produces changes in the way we perceive, act, think, and feel. It does so by producing changes in the nervous system in the circuits responsible for perception, in those responsible for the control of movement, and in connections between the two.

Perceptual learning consists primarily of changes in perceptual systems that make it possible for us to recognize stimuli so that we can respond to them appropriately. Stimulus-response learning consists of connections between perceptual and motor systems. The most important forms are classical and instrumental conditioning. Classical conditioning occurs when a neutral stimulus is followed by an unconditional stimulus (US) that naturally elicits an unconditional response (UR). After this pairing, the neutral stimulus becomes a conditional stimulus (CS); it now elicits the response by itself, which we refer to as the conditional response (CR).

Instrumental conditioning occurs when a response is followed by a reinforcing stimulus, such as a drink of water for a thirsty animal. The reinforcing stimulus increases the likelihood that the other stimuli that were present when the response was made will evoke the response. Both forms of stimulus-response learning may occur as a result of strengthened synaptic connections, as described by the Hebb rule.

Motor learning, although it may primarily involve changes within neural circuits that control movement, is

guided by sensory stimuli; thus, it is actually a form of stimulus-response learning. Relational learning, the most complex form of learning, is described in Chapter 14. It includes the ability to recognize objects through more than one sensory modality, to recognize the relative location of objects in the environment, and to remember the sequence in which events occurred during particular episodes.

Learning and Synaptic Plasticity

On theoretical considerations alone, it would appear that learning must involve synaptic plasticity: changes in the structure or biochemistry of synapses that alter their effects on postsynaptic neurons. Recent years have seen an explosion of research on this topic, largely stimulated by the development of methods that permit researchers to observe structural and biochemical changes in microscopically small structures: the presynaptic and postsynaptic components of synapses.

Induction of Long-Term Potentiation

As we saw in the first section of this chapter, the Hebb rule states that if a synapse is active at about the same time that the postsynaptic neuron is active, that synapse will be strengthened. As we will see in this section, research on a phenomenon that was originally discovered in the hippocampal formation has confirmed the Hebb rule and has discovered at least one way in which it operates.

Electrical stimulation of circuits within the hippocampal formation can lead to long-term synaptic changes that seem to be among those responsible for learning. Lømo (1966) discovered that intense electrical stimulation of axons leading from the entorhinal cortex to the dentate gyrus caused a long-term increase in the magnitude of excitatory postsynaptic potentials in the postsynaptic neurons; this increase has come to be called

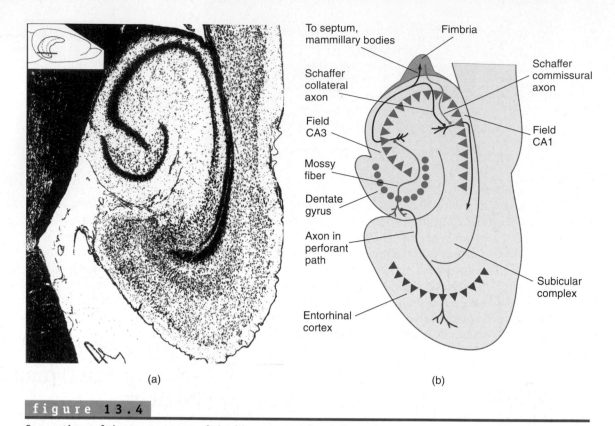

(a)   (b)

figure 13.4

Connections of the components of the hippocampal formation.
(Photograph from Swanson, L. W., Köhler, C., and Björklund, A., in *Handbook of Chemical Neuroanatomy.*
Vol. 5: Integrated Systems of the CNS, Part I. Amsterdam: Elsevier Science Publishers, 1987.)

long-term potentiation. (The word *potentiate* means "to strengthen, to make more potent.")

First, let's review some anatomy. The **hippocampal formation** is a specialized region of the limbic cortex located in the temporal lobe. (Its location in a human brain is shown in Figure 3.17.) Because the hippocampal formation is folded in one dimension and then curved in another, it has a complex, three-dimensional shape. Therefore, it is difficult to show what it looks like with a diagram on a two-dimensional sheet of paper. Fortunately, the structure of the hippocampal formation is orderly; a slice taken anywhere perpendicular to its curving long axis contains the same set of circuits.

The hippocampal formation includes the subicular complex, the hippocampus itself, and the dentate gyrus. Figure 13.4(a) shows a photomicrograph of a horizontal section through the hippocampal formation of a rat brain, and part (b) shows its intrinsic connections. The major neocortical inputs and outputs of the hippocampal formation are channeled through the **entorhinal cortex.** Neurons in the entorhinal cortex relay incoming information to the **granule cells** of the **dentate gyrus** through a bundle of axons known as the **perforant path.** These neurons then send axons into **field CA3** of the hippocampus itself. The hippocampus is also called "Ammon's horn" or, in Latin, *cornu ammonis.* That fact

might seem like a piece of trivia, but it explains why its two major divisions are called CA1 and CA3. (CA2 and CA4 exist, too, but we will not need to talk about them.) The terminals of the fibers from the dentate gyrus form synapses with dendritic spines of the **pyramidal cells** of

long-term potentiation A long-term increase in the excitability of a neuron to a particular synaptic input caused by repeated high-frequency activity of that input.

hippocampal formation A forebrain structure of the temporal lobe, constituting an important part of the limbic system; includes the hippocampus proper (Ammon's horn), dentate gyrus, and subiculum.

entorhinal cortex A region of the limbic cortex that provides the major source of input to the hippocampal formation.

granule cell A small, granular cell; those found in the dentate gyrus send axons to the field CA3 of the hippocampus.

dentate gyrus Part of the hippocampal formation; receives inputs from the entorhinal cortex and projects to the field CA3 of the hippocampus.

perforant path The system of axons that travel from cells in the entorhinal cortex to the dentate gyrus of the hippocampal formation.

field CA3 Part of the hippocampus; receives inputs from the dentate gyrus and projects to field CA1.

pyramidal cell A category of large neurons with a pyramid shape; found in the cerebral cortex and Ammon's horn of the hippocampal formation.

field CA3. The cell bodies of pyramidal cells are shaped just as their name suggests. An axon grows downward, out of the base of the pyramid, while a long, thick dendritic trunk grows out of the top. This dendrite and its branches are studded with approximately 30,000 dendritic spines. As we will see, these spines are the site of the structural and biochemical changes that are responsible for long-term potentiation.

The axons of CA3 pyramidal cells branch in two directions. One branch terminates in the adjacent **field CA1,** where it forms synapses with the dendritic spines of other pyramidal cells. The other branch travels through the fornix to structures in the basal forebrain, including the septum and the mammillary bodies. Another system of axons connects CA1 pyramidal cells with their counterparts on the opposite side of the brain. CA1 pyramidal cells provide the primary output of the hippocampus: They send axons to neurons in the subicular complex, whose axons then project out of the hippocampal formation to the entorhinal cortex and also through the fimbria to the basal forebrain. (See *Figure 13.4*.)

Figure 13.5 shows a typical procedure for producing long-term potentiation. A stimulating electrode is placed among the axons in the perforant path, and a recording electrode is placed in the dentate gyrus, near the granule cells that receive input from these axons. (See *Figure 13.5*.) First, a single pulse of electrical stimulation is delivered to the perforant path, and the resulting population EPSP is recorded in the dentate gyrus. The **population EPSP** is an extracellular measurement of the excitatory postsynaptic potentials (EPSPs) produced by the synapses of the perforant path axons with the dentate granule cells.

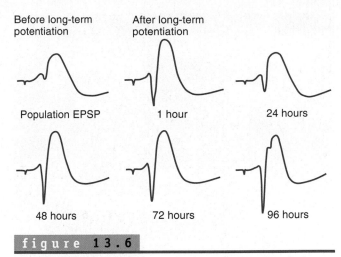

Before long-term potentiation   After long-term potentiation

Population EPSP   1 hour   24 hours

48 hours   72 hours   96 hours

figure   13.6

Population EPSPs recorded from the dentate gyrus before and after electrical stimulation that led to long-term potentiation.

(From Berger, T. W. *Science*, 1984, *224*, 627–630. Copyright 1984 by the American Association for the Advancement of Science.)

The size of the first population EPSP indicates the strength of the synaptic connections *before* long-term potentiation has taken place. Long-term potentiation can be induced by stimulating the axons in the perforant path with a burst of approximately one hundred pulses of electrical stimulation, delivered within a few seconds. Evidence for long-term potentiation is obtained by periodically delivering single pulses to the perforant path and recording the response in the dentate gyrus. If the response is greater than it was before the burst of pulses was delivered, long-term potentiation has occurred. (See *Figure 13.6*.)

Long-term potentiation can be produced in other regions of the hippocampal formation and, as we shall see, in other places in the brain. It can last for several months (Bliss and Lømo, 1973). It can be produced in isolated slices of the hippocampal formation as well as in the brains of living animals, which allows researchers to stimulate and record from individual neurons and to analyze biochemical changes. The brain is removed from the skull, the hippocampal complex is dissected, and slices are placed in a temperature-controlled chamber filled with liquid that resembles interstitial fluid. Figure 13.7 shows a 400-micrometer slice of the hippocampal formation being maintained in a tissue chamber. Under optimal conditions a slice remains alive for up to several days. (See *Figure 13.7*.)

field CA1 Part of the hippocampus; receives inputs from field CA3 and projects out of the hippocampal formation via the subiculum.

population EPSP An evoked potential that represents the EPSPs of a population of neurons.

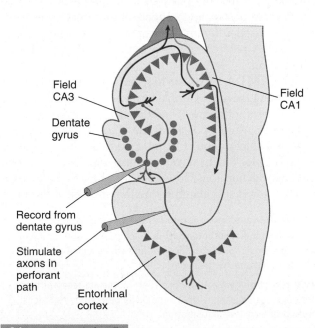

Field CA3

Dentate gyrus

Field CA1

Record from dentate gyrus

Stimulate axons in perforant path

Entorhinal cortex

figure   13.5

The procedure for producing long-term potentiation.

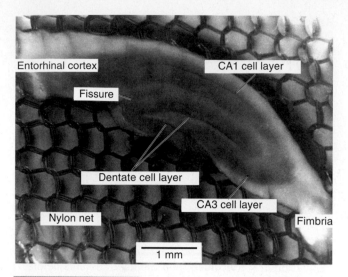

figure 13.7

A photograph of a hippocampal slice in a tissue chamber.
(From Teyler, T. J. *Brain Research Bulletin*, 1980, *5*, 391–403.
Reprinted with permission.)

Many experiments have demonstrated that long-term potentiation in hippocampal slices can follow the Hebb rule. That is, when weak and strong synapses on a single neuron are stimulated at approximately the same time, the weak synapse becomes strengthened. This phenomenon is called **associative long-term potentiation,** because it is produced by the association (in time) between the activity of the two sets of synapses. (See *Figure 13.8*.)

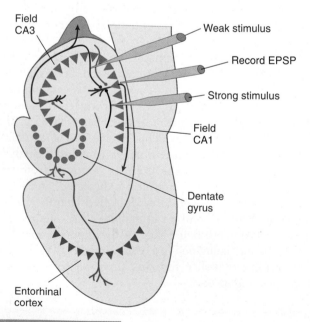

figure 13.8

A procedure used to establish associative long-term potentiation.

Role of NMDA Receptors

Nonassociative long-term potentiation requires some sort of additive effect. That is, a series of pulses delivered at a high rate all in one burst will produce long-term potentiation, but the same number of pulses given at a slow rate will not. (In fact, as we shall see, low-frequency stimulation can lead to the opposite phenomenon: long-term *depression.*) The reason for this phenomenon is now clear. A rapid rate of stimulation causes the excitatory postsynaptic potentials to summate, because each successive EPSP occurs before the previous one has dissipated. This means that rapid stimulation depolarizes the postsynaptic membrane much more than slow stimulation does. (See *Figure 13.9*.)

Several experiments have shown that synaptic strengthening occurs when molecules of the neurotransmitter bind with postsynaptic receptors located in a dendritic spine that is already depolarized. Kelso, Ganong, and Brown (1986) found that if they used a microelectrode to artificially depolarize CA1 neurons and then stimulated the axons that formed synapses with them, the synapses became stronger. However, if the stimulation of the synapses and the depolarization of the neuron occurred at different times, no effect was seen; thus, the two events had to occur together. (See *Figure 13.10*.)

Experiments such as the ones I just described indicate that long-term potentiation requires two events: activation of synapses and depolarization of the postsynaptic neuron. The explanation for this phenomenon, at least in some parts of the brain, lies in the characteristics of a very special receptor. As we saw in Chapter 4, the most important excitatory neurotransmitter in the brain is glutamic acid (usually referred to as *glutamate*). We also saw that the postsynaptic effects of glutamate are mediated by several different types of receptors. One of them, the NMDA receptor plays a critical role in long-term potentiation.

The **NMDA receptor** has some unusual properties. It is found in the hippocampal formation, especially in field CA1. It gets its name from the drug that specifically activates it: *N*-methyl-D-aspartate. The NMDA receptor controls a calcium ion channel. However, this channel is normally blocked by a magnesium ion (Mg^{2+}), which prevents calcium ions from entering the cell even when the receptor is stimulated by glutamate. But if the post-

associative long-term potentiation A long-term potentiation in which concurrent stimulation of weak and strong synapses to a given neuron strengthens the weak ones.

NMDA receptor A specialized ionotropic glutamate receptor that controls a calcium channel that is normally blocked by Mg^{2+} ions; involved in long-term potentiation.

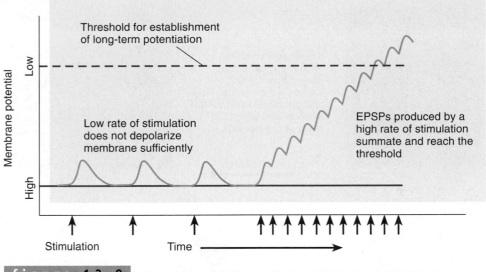

figure 13.9

The role of summation in long-term potentiation. If axons are stimulated rapidly, the EPSPs produced by the terminal buttons will summate, and the postsynaptic membrane will depolarize enough for long-term potentiation to occur. If axons are stimulated slowly, the EPSPs will not summate, and long-term potentiation will not occur.

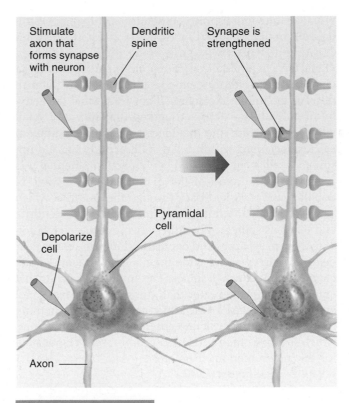

figure 13.10

Long-term potentiation. Synaptic strengthening occurs when synapses are active while the membrane of the postsynaptic cell is depolarized.

synaptic membrane is depolarized, the Mg^{2+} is ejected from the ion channel, and the channel is free to admit Ca^{2+} ions. Thus, calcium ions enter the cells through the channels controlled by NMDA receptors only when glutamate is present *and* when the postsynaptic membrane is depolarized. This means that the ion channel controlled by the NMDA receptor is a neurotransmitter *and* voltage-dependent ion channel. (See *Figure 13.11* and *Animation 13.1, The NMDA receptor.*)

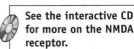

See the interactive CD for more on the NMDA receptor.

The strongest evidence implicating NMDA receptors in long-term potentiation comes from research with drugs that block NMDA receptors, such as **AP5** (2-amino-5-phosphonopentanoate). AP5 prevents the establishment of long-term potentiation in field CA1 and the dentate gyrus. However, it has no effect on long-term potentiation that has already been established (Brown et al., 1989). Thus, although the activation of NMDA receptors is necessary for long-term potentiation, transmission in the potentiated synapses involves *non*-NMDA receptors—primarily **AMPA receptors.**

AP5 2-Amino-5-phosphonopentanoate; a drug that blocks NMDA receptors.

AMPA receptor An ionotropic glutamate receptor that controls a sodium channel; when open, it produces EPSPs.

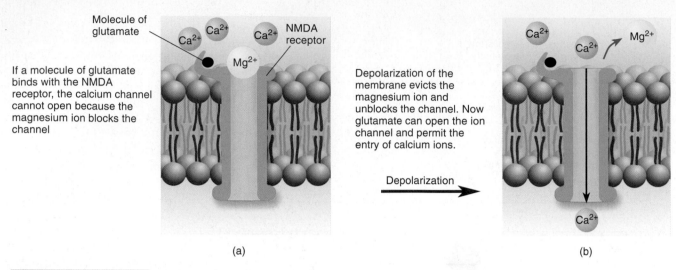

If a molecule of glutamate binds with the NMDA receptor, the calcium channel cannot open because the magnesium ion blocks the channel

Molecule of glutamate

NMDA receptor

Depolarization of the membrane evicts the magnesium ion and unblocks the channel. Now glutamate can open the ion channel and permit the entry of calcium ions.

Depolarization

(a)

(b)

figure 13.11

The NMDA receptor, a neurotransmitter- and voltage-dependent ion channel. (a) When the postsynaptic membrane is at the resting potential, Mg^{2+} blocks the ion channel, preventing Ca^{2+} from entering. (b) When the membrane is depolarized, the magnesium ion is evicted. Thus, the attachment of glutamate to the binding site causes the ion channel to open, allowing calcium ions to enter the dendritic spine.

Cell biologists have discovered that the calcium ion is used by many cells as a second messenger. The entry of calcium ions through the ion channels controlled by NMDA receptors is an essential step in long-term potentiation. Lynch et al. (1984) demonstrated this fact by injecting EGTA directly into hippocampal pyramidal cells. This chemical binds with calcium and makes it insoluble, destroying its biological activity. The EGTA blocked the establishment of long-term potentiation in the injected cells; their excitability was not increased by high-frequency stimulation of axons that formed synapses with them. However, neighboring cells, which were not injected with EGTA, showed long-term potentiation.

In Chapter 2 you learned that only axons are capable of producing action potentials. Actually, they can also occur in dendrites of some types of pyramidal cells, including those in field CA1 of the hippocampal formation. The threshold of excitation for **dendritic spikes** (as these action potentials are called) is rather high. As far as we know, they occur only when an action potential is triggered in the axon of the pyramidal cell. The backwash of depolarization across the cell body triggers a dendritic spike, which is propagated up the trunk of the dendrite. This means that whenever the axon of a pyramidal cell fires, all of its dendritic spines become depolarized for a brief time.

The development of a special technique, two-photon laser scanning microscopy, now enables researchers to visualize individual spines on dendrites of living pyramidal cells in hippocampal slices. Yuste and her colleagues (Yuste and Denk, 1995; Yuste et al., 1999) injected individual CA1 pyramidal cells in hippocampal slices with calcium-green-1, a fluorescent dye that permitted them to observe the influx of calcium. They found that the activity of individual synapses triggered the entry of a small amount of calcium into the dendritic spine. The influx of calcium occurred within a few milliseconds and did not spread to adjacent spines. When an action potential was triggered in the axon of the pyramidal cell, a wave of depolarization washed back through the dendrite, which caused a small amount of calcium to enter the dendrite and all of its spines. When these two events—activation of individual synapses and depolarization of the entire dendrite—occurred at the same time, a large amount of calcium entered the active spines. The amount of calcium that entered was much greater than the sum of the two small amounts. When AP5 was added to the solution bathing the slices, very little calcium entered the dendritic spines, which indicates that NMDA receptors were responsible for this phenomenon. (Remember, AP5 blocks NMDA receptors. See *Figure 13.12.*)

dendritic spike An action potential that occurs in the dendrite of some types of pyramidal cells.

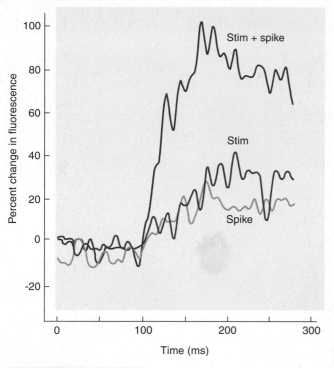

figure 13.12

The results of the experiment by Yuste and Denk (1995). Changes in calcium concentration in single dendritic spines, measured as percentage change in fluorescence. *Stim* = stimulate axon alone, *Spike* = trigger action potential alone, *Stim + spike* = stimulate axon and trigger action potential simultaneously.

(Adapted from Yuste, R., and Denk, W. *Nature,* 1995, *375,* 682–684.)

A study by Magee and Johnston (1997) proved that the simultaneous occurrence of synaptic activation and a dendritic spike strengthens the active synapse. The investigators measured both calcium influx into individual dendrites of CA1 pyramidal cells and the excitatory post-synaptic potentials produced by activation of terminals that formed synapses with these dendrites. Like Yuste and her colleagues, they found that when synapses became active at the same time a dendritic spike had been triggered, calcium "hotspots" occurred near the activated synapses. Moreover, the size of the excitatory postsynaptic potential produced by these activated synapses became larger. In other words, these synapses became strengthened. To confirm that the dendritic spikes were necessary for the synaptic potentiation to take place, the investigators infused a small amount of TTX (tetrodotoxin) onto the base of the dendrite just before triggering an action potential. (The TTX prevented the formation of dendritic spikes by blocking voltage-dependent sodium channels.) Under these conditions potentiation did not occur. (See *Figure 13.13.*)

I think that considering what you already know about associative long-term potentiation, you can anticipate the role that NMDA receptors play in this phenomenon. If weak synapses are active by themselves, nothing happens, because the membrane of the dendritic spine does not depolarize sufficiently for the calcium channels controlled by the NMDA receptors to open. (Remember that for these channels to open, the postsynaptic membrane must depolarize and displace the Mg^{2+} ions that normally block them.) However, if the activity of strong synapses

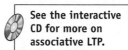

See the interactive CD for more on associative LTP.

located elsewhere on the postsynaptic cell have caused the cell to fire, then a dendritic spike will depolarize the postsynaptic membrane enough for calcium to enter the ion channels controlled by the NMDA receptors. Thus, the special properties of NMDA receptors account not only for the existence of long-term potentiation, but also for its associative nature. (See *Figure 13.14* and *Animation 13.2, Associative LTP.*)

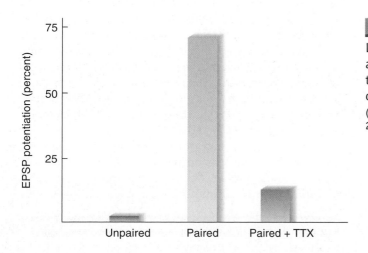

figure 13.13

Long-term potentiation caused by pairing of synaptic activation with dendritic spikes triggered by stimulation of the pyramidal cells. The effect was abolished by the infusion of TTX, which blocks the formation of dendritic spikes.

(Adapted from Magee, J. C., and Johnston, D. *Science,* 1997, *275,* 209–213.)

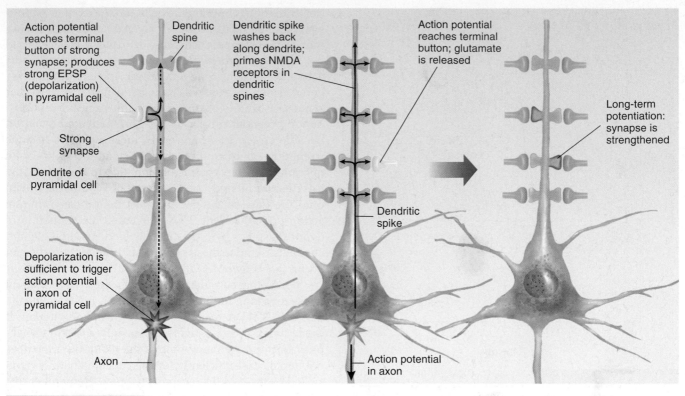

figure 13.14

Associative long-term potentiation. If the activity of strong synapses is sufficient to trigger an action potential in the neuron, the dendritic spike will depolarize the membrane of dendritic spines, priming NMDA receptors so that any weak synapses active at that time will become strengthened.

Mechanisms of Synaptic Plasticity

What is responsible for the increases in synaptic strength that occur during long-term potentiation? Research indicates that at least two types of modifications occur when a synapse becomes strengthened: Individual synapses are strengthened, and new synapses are produced. Strengthening of an individual synapse appears to be accomplished by an increase in the number of postsynaptic AMPA receptors—that is, *non*-NMDA glutamate receptors—present in that synapse. For example, Liao, Hessler, and Malinow (1995) recorded postsynaptic potentials produced by the activity of single synapses on dendritic spines of CA1 pyramidal cells. By either depolarizing the postsynaptic membrane or holding it at the resting potential, they could control whether NMDA receptors were blocked by Mg^{2+}. Initially, they found evidence that the spines of many of the synapses contained only NMDA receptors. But after inducing long-term potentiation in the inputs to the cells, they found evidence that the spines now contained AMPA receptors as well. Thus, one of the effects of long-term potentiation appears to be insertion of new AMPA receptors in the postsynaptic membrane. With more AMPA receptors present, the release of glutamate by the terminal button causes a larger postsynaptic potential.

Where do these new AMPA receptors come from? Shi et al. (1999) prepared a gene for a subunit of the AMPA receptor that had a fluorescent dye molecule attached to it. They used a harmless virus to insert this gene into neurons in hippocampal slices. This procedure permitted the investigators to use a two-photon laser scanning microscope to see the exact location of AMPA receptors in dendritic spines of CA1 neurons. The investigators induced long-term potentiation by stimulating axons that form synapses with these dendrites. Before long-term potentiation was induced, they saw AMPA receptors clustered at the base of the dendritic spines. Fifteen minutes after the induction of long-term potentiation, the AMPA receptors flooded into the spines and moved to their tips—the location of the postsynaptic membrane. This movement of AMPA receptors was prevented by AP5, the drug that blocks NMDA receptors. (See *Figures 13.15* and *13.16*.)

As we saw, the entry of calcium ions into dendritic spines is the event that begins the process that leads to long-term potentiation. The next step appears to involve **CaM-KII** (type II calcium-calmodulin kinase), an enzyme

CaM-KII Type II calcium-calmodulin kinase, an enzyme that must be activated by calcium; may play a role in the establishment of long-term potentiation.

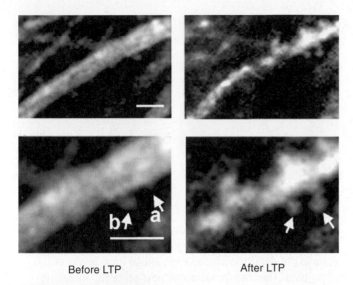

Before LTP   After LTP

figure 13.15

Two-photon laser scanning microscopy of the CA1 region of living hippocampal slices showing delivery of AMPA receptors into dendritic spines after long-term potentiation. The AMPA receptors were tagged with a fluorescent dye molecule. The two photographs at the bottom are higher magnifications of the ones above. The arrows labeled *a* and *b* point to dendritic spines that became filled with AMPA receptors after the induction of long-term potentiation.

(From Shi, S.-H., Hayashi, Y., Petralia, R. S., Zaman, S. H., Wenthold, R. J., Svoboda, K., and Malinow, R. *Science*, 1999, *284*, 1811–1816.)

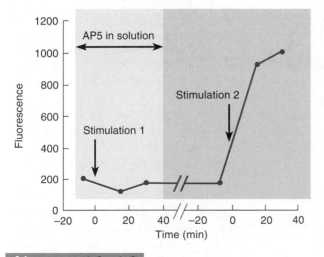

figure 13.16

Changes in fluorescence in dendritic spines of CA1 neurons (indicating the presence of AMPA receptors) after electrical stimulation with or without the presence of AP5 in the fluid bathing the hippocampal slices. AP5 blocked NMDA receptors and prevented the movement of AMPA receptors into the spines.

(Adapted from Shi, S.-H., Hayashi, Y., Petralia, R. S., Zaman, S. H., Wenthold, R. J., Svoboda, K., and Malinow, R. *Science*, 1999, *284*, 1811–1816.)

that is present in dendritic spines. CaM-KII is a *calcium-dependent* enzyme, which is inactive until a calcium ion binds with it and activates it. Many studies have shown that CaM-KII plays a critical role in long-term potentiation. For example, Silva et al. (1992a) produced a targeted mutation of the gene responsible for the production of CaM-KII in mice. The mice had no obvious neuroanatomical defects, and the responses of their NMDA receptors were normal. However, the investigators were unable to produce long-term potentiation in field CA1 of hippocampal slices taken from these animals. Lledo et al. (1995) found that injection of activated CaM-KII directly into CA1 pyramidal cells mimicked the effects of long-term potentiation: It strengthened synaptic transmission in those cells.

Shen and Meyer (1999) used a virus to insert a fluorescent dye molecule attached to CaM-KII in cultured hippocampal neurons. They found that after long-term potentiation was induced, CaM-KII molecules became concentrated in the postsynaptic densities of dendritic spines, where the postsynaptic receptors are located. (See *Figure 13.17*.)

As we saw in Chapter 3, when synapses are examined under an electron microscope, a dark band is seen just inside the postsynaptic membrane. This band, known as

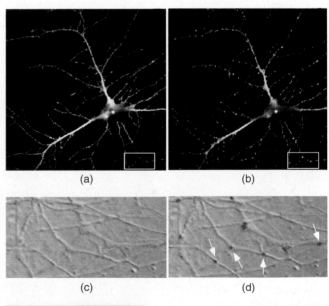

(a)   (b)

(c)   (d)

figure 13.17

Migration of CaM-KII molecules into the postsynaptic densities of dendritic spines after long-term potentiation. (a) A single hippocampal pyramidal neuron, stained for the presence of CaM-KII, before NMDA receptor stimulation. (b) The same neuron after NMDA receptor stimulation. (c) An enlargement of the area in (a) marked by a white rectangle. The presence of CaM-KII is shown in green. (d) An enlargement of the area in (b) marked by a white rectangle. The presence of CaM-KII that has moved into dendritic spines is shown in red.

(From Shen, K., and Meyer, T. *Science*, 1999, *284*, 162–166.)

the *postsynaptic density*, contains a variety of proteins: receptors, enzymes, messenger proteins, and scaffolding proteins—structural proteins that anchor the receptors, enzymes, and messengers in place (Allison et al., 2000). Dosemeci et al. (2001) found that when hippocampal neurons in a cell culture were exposed to high levels of glutamate, the postsynaptic density became thicker as new proteins, including CaM-KII, migrated there. (See *Figure 13.18.*)

Lisman and Zhabotinsky (2001) present a hypothetical model to explain the role that activated CaM-KII play in the insertion of new AMPA receptors into the postsynaptic membrane. NMDA receptors are normally anchored to a scaffolding protein known as PSD95, located inside the postsynaptic membrane. Research has shown that activated CaM-KII can bind with an intracellular component of the NMDA receptor—and also with a set of linking proteins that can attach to AMPA receptors. AMPA receptors are brought in vesicles to the postsynaptic membrane of dendritic spines. They attach to the NMDA receptors, linking proteins attach to them, and then AMPA receptors attach to the linking proteins. (See *Figure 13.19.*)

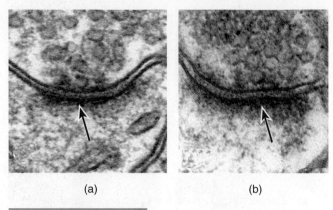

(a)   (b)

figure 13.18

Increased thickness of the postsynaptic density (arrows) of dendritic spines exposed to high levels of glutamate. The incorporation of new proteins, including CaM-KII, increased the density. (a) Unstimulated synapse. (b) Synapse stimulated by high levels of glutamate.

(From Dosemeci, A., Tao-Cheng, J.-H., Vinade, L., Winters, C. A., Pozzo-Miller, L., and Reese, T. S. *Proceedings of the National Academy of Science, USA,* 2001, *98,* 10428–10432.)

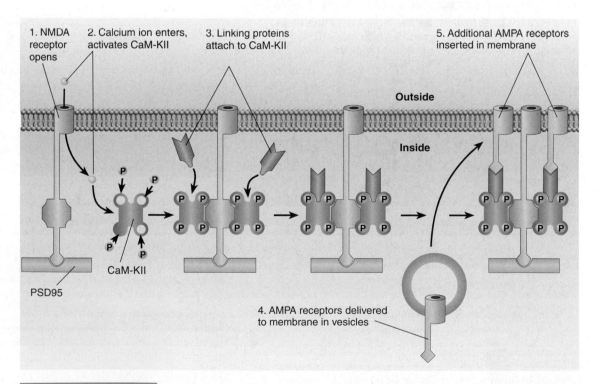

figure 13.19

A hypothetical model that describes the insertion of new AMPA receptors into the postsynaptic membrane of dendritic spines after long-term potentiation. The presence of glutamate and membrane depolarization open NMDA receptors. Calcium ions enter and activate molecules of CaM-KII by attaching phosphate groups (P), a process known as *phosphorylation*. Linking proteins attach to the activated CaM-KII, and AMPA receptors, brought to the postsynaptic membrane in vesicles, attach to the linking proteins. The addition of new AMPA receptors results in larger postsynaptic potentials when the terminal button releases glutamate.

(Adapted from Lisman, J., Schulman, H., and Cline, H. *Nature Reviews: Neuroscience,* 2002, *3,* 175–190.)

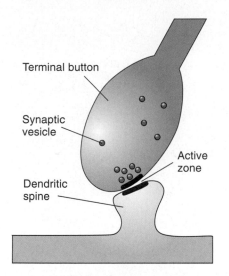

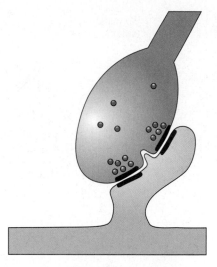

Before long-term potentiation   After long-term potentiation:
                                                   Generation of a perforated synapse

(a)   (b)

figure 13.20

Hypothetical changes in the structure of synapses on dendritic spines produced by long-term potentiation. (a) Before long-term potentiation. (b) After long-term potentiation. The dendritic spine develops a fingerlike projection that pushes into the terminal button, dividing the active zone into two parts. Each active zone grows, and in the terminal button more machinery necessary for the release of the neurotransmitter is inserted into the presynaptic membrane.

(Adapted from Hosokawa, T., Rusakov, D. A., Bliss, T. V. P., and Fine, A. *Journal of Neuroscience*, 1995, *15*, 5560–5573.)

A second change that appears to accompany long-term potentiation is growth of new synaptic connections. Buchs and Muller (1996) used a special stain that labeled calcium in order to identify dendritic spines that were part of synapses that had undergone long-term potentiation. They found that most of the postsynaptic densities of the labeled spines appeared to be "perforated." Edwards (1995) suggested that the dendritic spine develops a fingerlike projection that projects into the terminal button, dividing the active zone into two parts. Each active zone then grows. In the terminal button more machinery necessary for the release of the neurotransmitter is inserted into the presynaptic membrane. More AMPA receptors are then inserted into the postsynaptic membrane of the dendritic spine. (See *Figure 13.20* and *Animation 13.3, Long-lasting LTP.*)

> See the interactive CD for more on long-lasting LTP.

Toni et al. (1999) found evidence that supported the suggestion that perforated synapses are a waypoint on the path to production of new synapses. These investigators produced long-term potentiation in hippocampal slices and then treated the slices with a chemical that precipitates calcium. They sliced the tissue into very fine sections and prepared electron micrographs that showed the location of the intracellular calcium. They scanned the electron micrographs and used a computer program to prepare three-dimensional reconstructions of synapses that had undergone long-term potentiation, as indicated by the presence of large amounts of calcium. By examining different hippocampal slices at different times after the induction of long-term potentiation, they could follow the time course of structural changes. At first they saw perforated synapses, but these soon disappeared, to be replaced by a threefold increase in the number of terminal buttons forming synapses with two or more spines. They did not see multiple spine synapses when they pretreated the hippocampal slice with a chemical that prevents the formation of long-term potentiation. (See *Figures 13.21* and *13.22.*)

Terminal   Dendritic
button   spine

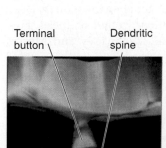

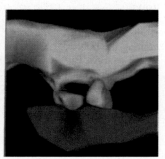

Before induction of LTP   After induction of LTP

figure 13.21

Results of the study by Toni et al. (1999). Three-dimensional reconstructions of synapses in hippocampal slices before and after long-term potentiation. Long-term potentiation increased the number of synapses with multiple dendritic spines.

(Courtesy of Dominique Muller, University of Geneva, Switzerland.)

figure 13.22

A hypothetical series of changes that synapses undergo following long-term potentiation.

(Adapted from Sorra, K. E., Fiala, J. C., and Harris, K. M. Critical assessment of the involvement of perforations, spinules, and spine branching in hippocampal synapse formation. *Journal of Comparative Neurology*, 1998, *398*, 225–240.)

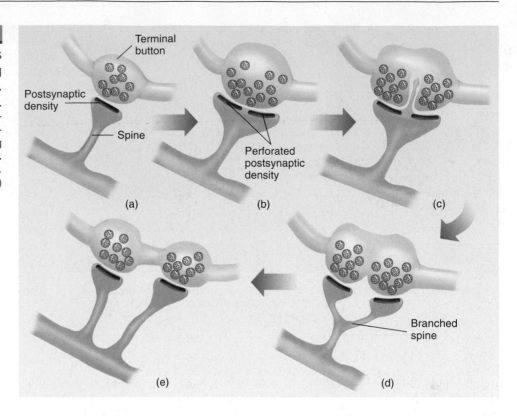

Researchers believe that long-term potentiation may also involve a third type of synaptic modifications: *presynaptic* changes, such as an increase in the amount of glutamate that is released by the terminal button. But how could a process that occurs postsynaptically, in the dendritic spines, cause presynaptic changes? A possible answer comes from the discovery that a simple molecule, nitric oxide, can communicate messages from one cell to another. As we saw in Chapter 4, nitric oxide is a soluble gas produced from the amino acid arginine by the activity of an enzyme known as **nitric oxide synthase.** Researchers have found that nitric oxide (NO) is used as a messenger in many parts of the body; for example, it is involved in the control of the muscles in the wall of the intestines, it dilates blood vessels in regions of the brain that become metabolically active, and it stimulates the changes in blood vessels that produce penile erections (Culotta and Koshland, 1992). Once produced, NO lasts only a short time before it is destroyed. Thus, if it were produced in dendritic spines in the hippocampal formation, it could diffuse only as far as the nearby terminal buttons, where it might produce changes related to the induction of long-term potentiation.

Several experiments suggest that NO may indeed be a retrograde messenger involved in long-term potentiation. (*Retrograde* means "moving backward"; in this context it refers to messages sent from the dendritic spine back to the terminal button.) Almost simultaneously, four laboratories reported that drugs that block nitric oxide synthase prevented the establishment of long-term potentiation in hippocampal slices (O'Dell et al., 1991; Schuman and Madison, 1991; Bon et al., 1992; Haley, Wilcox, and Chapman, 1992). In addition, Endoh, Maiese, and Wagner (1994) found that a calcium-activated NO synthase is found in several regions of the brain, including the dentate gyrus and fields CA1 and CA3 of the hippocampus. Finally, Zhang and Wong-Riley (1996) found that most cells that contain NO synthase also contain NMDA receptors. Although there is good evidence that NO is one of the signals the dendritic spine uses to communicate with the terminal button, most investigators believe that there must be other signals as well. After all, alterations in synapses require coordinated changes in both presynaptic and postsynaptic elements.

For several years after its discovery, researchers believed that long-term potentiation involved a single process. Since then it has become clear that long-term potentiation consists of several stages. *Long-lasting* long-term potentiation—that is, long-term potentiation that lasts more than a few hours—requires protein synthesis. Frey and his colleagues (Frey et al., 1988; Frey and Morris, 1997) found that drugs that blocks protein synthesis could block the establishment of long-lasting long-term potentiation in field CA1. If the drug was administered before, during, or immediately after a prolonged burst of stimu-

nitric oxide synthase An enzyme responsible for the production of nitric oxide.

lation was delivered, long-term potentiation occurred, but it disappeared a few hours later. However, if the drug was administered one hour after the synapses had been stimulated, the long-term potentiation persisted. Apparently, the protein synthesis necessary for establishing the later phase of long-lasting, long-term potentiation is accomplished within an hour of stimulation.

Where does the protein synthesis take place? As we saw, long-term potentiation involves individual synapses. Only the synapses that are activated when the postsynaptic membrane is depolarized are strengthened. But protein synthesis normally takes place in the cell body. If the long-lasting phase of long-term potentiation requires protein synthesis, then it would seem that the proteins synthesized in the cell body would have to be delivered only to the appropriate dendritic spines. But how could this targeted delivery process be accomplished?

The answer is that the protein synthesis takes place where the proteins are needed: in the dendrites themselves. Studies have shown that dendrites contain all they need to synthesize proteins: ribosomes, messenger RNAs, transfer RNAs, and various enzymes that participate in the process (Tiedge and Brosius, 1996; Steward and Schuman, 2001). Analysis of the messenger RNAs present in dendrites indicates that they code for the production of components of the postsynaptic density: scaffolding proteins, protein kinases, and receptors. Clearly, these products could be involved in establishing the structural changes needed for long-lasting, long-term potentiation.

Figure 13.23 summarizes the biochemistry discussed in this subsection. I suspect that you might feel overwhelmed by all the new terms I have introduced here, and I hope that the figure will help to clarify things. The evidence we have seen so far indicates that the entry of calcium ions through channels controlled by NMDA receptors activates CaM-KII, a calcium-dependent protein kinase. Activated CaM-KII travels to the postsynaptic density of dendritic spines, where it enables AMPA receptors, sent to the spines in vesicles, to bind with NMDA receptors, which themselves are anchored on strands of PSD95, the scaffolding protein that holds molecules in place in the postsynaptic density. In addition, long-term potentiation initiates rapid changes in synaptic structure such as development of perforated synaptic density. (See *Figure 13.23*.) The entry of calcium also activates a calcium-dependent NO synthase, and the newly produced NO then presumably diffuses out of the dendritic spine, back to the terminal button. There, it may trigger unknown chemical reactions that increase the release of glutamate. (See *Figure 13.23*.) Finally, long-lasting long-term potentiation requires the synthesis of new proteins, which may include components of the cytoskeleton, protein kinases, and receptors. (See *Animation 13.4, Chemistry of LTP.*)

> **See the interactive CD for more on the chemistry of LTP.**

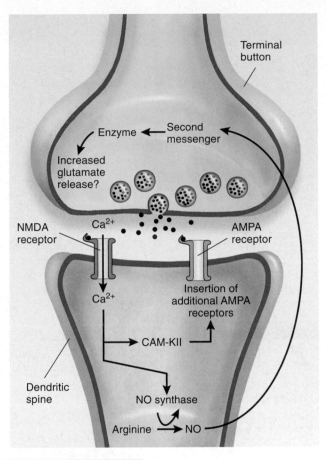

Long-term potentiation. A summary of the chemical reactions that appear to be triggered by the entry of an adequate amount of calcium into the dendritic spine.

Long-Term Depression

I mentioned earlier that low-frequency stimulation of the synaptic inputs to a cell can *decrease* rather than increase their strength. This phenomenon, known as **long-term depression,** also plays a role in learning. After all, even though the number of synapses in the brain is very large, it is still finite, and animals can continue to learn throughout their lives. Thus, it seems unlikely that once a synapse is strengthened, it must remain that way forever. Dudek and Bear (1992) stimulated Schaffer collateral inputs to CA1 neurons in hippocampal slices with 900 pulses of electrical current, delivered at rates ranging from 1 to 50 Hz. They found that frequencies above 10 Hz

long-term depression (LTD) A long-term decrease in the excitability of a neuron to a particular synaptic input caused by stimulation of the terminal button while the postsynaptic membrane is hyperpolarized or only slightly depolarized.

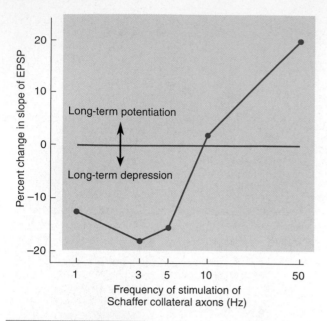

figure 13.24

Long-term potentiation and long-term depression. Changes in the sensitivity of synapses of Schaffer collateral axons with CA1 pyramidal cells after electrical stimulation at various frequencies.

(Adapted from Dudek, S. M., and Bear, M. F. *Proceedings of the National Academy of Sciences*, 1992, *89*, 4363–4367.)

caused long-term potentiation, whereas those below 10 Hz caused long-term depression. Both of these effects were blocked by application of AP5, the NMDA receptor blocker; thus, both effects require the activation of NMDA receptors. (See *Figure 13.24*.)

Stanton and Sejnowski (1989) demonstrated associative long-term depression in field CA1. They found that when a weak input was paired with a strong input, long-term potentiation was produced. However, when the two inputs were stimulated at different times, long-term *depression* was produced. Other studies have shown that long-term depression is produced when synaptic inputs are activated at the same time that the postsynaptic membrane is either weakly depolarized or hyperpolarized (Debanne, Gähwiler, and Thompson, 1994; Thiels et al., 1996).

As we saw, long-term potentiation involves an increase in the number of AMPA receptors in the postsynaptic membrane of dendritic spines. Long-term depression appears to involve the opposite: a *decrease* in the number of AMPA receptors (Carroll et al., 1999). And just as AMPA receptors are brought into dendritic spines by vesicles during long-term potentiation, they are taken away from the spines in vesicles during long-term depression (Lüscher et al., 1999).

Thus, at least at some synapses the Hebb rule appears to work in both directions: Inputs that are correlated with strong inputs (or with activation of the postsynaptic neuron) are strengthened, whereas inputs that are *not* correlated with strong inputs (or correlated with *nonactivation* of the postsynaptic neuron) are weakened. This mechanism could conceivably allow for the reversal of previously established synaptic changes when the contingencies in the environment change.

Other Forms of Long-Term Potentiation

Long-term potentiation was discovered in the hippocampal formation and has been studied more in this region than in others, but it also occurs elsewhere in the brain. So far, it has been demonstrated in the prefrontal cortex, piriform cortex, entorhinal cortex, motor cortex, visual cortex, thalamus, and amygdala (Gerren and Weinberger, 1983; Clugnet and LeDoux, 1990; Aroniadou and Teyler, 1991; Baranyi, Szente, and Woody, 1991; Lynch et al., 1991). It has even been demonstrated in slices of human neocortex that was removed during surgery to treat seizure disorders (Chen et al., 1996). NMDA receptors are probably involved in the potentiation that takes place in the piriform and entorhinal cortex and in the amygdala, but research on the role of these receptors in the other regions has not yet been reported. At least one form of long-term potentiation that takes place in the visual cortex does not involve NMDA receptors (Aroniadou and Teyler, 1991).

In the hippocampal formation NMDA receptors are present in highest concentrations in field CA1 and in the dentate gyrus. However, very few NMDA receptors are found in the region of field CA3 that receives mossy fiber input from the dentate gyrus (Monaghan and Cotman, 1985). High-frequency stimulation of the mossy fibers produces long-term potentiation that gradually decays over a period of several hours (Lynch et al., 1991). AP5, the drug that blocks NMDA receptors and prevents the establishment of long-term potentiation in CA1 neurons, has no effect on long-term potentiation in field CA3. The mechanism responsible for long-term potentiation in field CA3 is not yet known.

In recent years the phenomenon of long-term potentiation has received a considerable amount of attention from scientists who are interested in the cellular basis of learning, and their interest appears to be justified. The fact that long-term potentiation can be produced in several regions besides the hippocampal formation suggests that the mechanisms that underlie this phenomenon may be widespread in the brain. The discovery of the functions of the NMDA receptor provides solid evidence for at least one mechanism that produces the type of synapse that Hebb predicted a half-century ago. However, other mechanisms of synaptic plasticity also exist, and little is known about them. The progress that has been made during the last few years in research on the cellular basis of learning suggests that someday we really may come to understand it.

Role of Long-Term Potentiation in Learning

If the synaptic changes that constitute learning are accomplished by long-term potentiation, then we should suspect that disruption of long-term potentiation should also disrupt learning, and it does. The injection of AP5 into the hippocampal formation, which disrupts NMDA-mediated long-term potentiation, interferes with learning. In addition, certain learning experiences produce synaptic changes in the hippocampal formation. Because the role of the hippocampus in learning is complex, research on this topic is discussed in Chapter 14, which deals with relational learning.

Several studies have shown that long-term potentiation plays a role in classical and instrumental conditioning; these studies are discussed later in this chapter.

interim summary

Learning and Synaptic Plasticity

The study of long-term potentiation in the hippocampal formation has suggested a mechanism that might be responsible for at least some of the synaptic changes that occur during learning. A circuit of neurons passes through the hippocampal formation, from the entorhinal cortex to the dentate gyrus, to field CA3, to field CA1, to the subiculum. High-frequency stimulation of the axons in this circuit strengthens synapses; it leads to an increase in the size of the EPSPs in the dendritic spines of the postsynaptic neurons. Associative long-term potentiation can also occur, in which weak synapses are strengthened by the action of strong ones. In fact, the only requirement for long-term potentiation is that the postsynaptic membrane be depolarized at the same time that the synapses are active.

In field CA1 and in the dentate gyrus, NMDA receptors play a special role in long-term potentiation. These receptors, sensitive to glutamate, control calcium channels but can open them only if the membrane is already depolarized. Thus, the combination of membrane depolarization (for example, from a dendritic spike produced by the activity of strong synapses) and activation of a NMDA receptor causes the entry of calcium ions. The increase in calcium activates several calcium-dependent enzymes, including CaM-KII. Inhibition of CaM-KII disrupts long-term potentiation; presumably, this enzyme causes the insertion of AMPA receptors into the membrane of the dendritic spine, increasing their sensitivity to glutamate released by the terminal button. This change

is accompanied by structural alterations in the shape of the dendritic spine, including the appearance of synapse perforated by "fingers" inserted into the terminal button, which may be the first step toward producing additional synapses. Long-term potentiation may also involve presynaptic changes, through the activation of NO synthase, an enzyme responsible for the production of nitric oxide. This soluble gas may diffuse into nearby terminal buttons, where it facilitates the release of glutamate. Long-lasting, long-term potentiation requires protein synthesis, which appears to take place in the dendrite adjacent to the dendritic spines.

Long-term depression occurs when a synapse is activated at the time that the postsynaptic membrane is hyperpolarized or only slightly depolarized. If long-term potentiation and long-term depression occurred only in the hippocampal formation, their discovery would still be an interesting finding, but the fact that they also occur in several other regions of the brain suggests that they may play an important role in many forms of learning.

Perceptual Learning

Learning enables us to adapt to our environment and to respond to changes in it. In particular, it provides us with the ability to perform an appropriate behavior in an appropriate situation. Situations can be as simple as the sound of a buzzer or as complex as the social interactions of a group of people. The first part of learning involves learning to perceive particular stimuli.

Perceptual learning involves learning *about* things, not *what to do* when they are present. (Learning what to do is discussed in the subsequent sections of this chapter.) Perceptual learning can involve learning to recognize entirely new stimuli, or it can involve learning to recognize changes or variations in familiar stimuli. For example, if a friend gets a new hairstyle or replaces glasses with contact lenses, our visual memory of that person changes. We also learn that particular stimuli are found in particular locations or contexts or in the presence of other stimuli. We can even learn and remember particular *episodes:* sequences of events taking place at a particular time and place. The more complex forms of perceptual learning will be discussed in Chapter 14, which is devoted to relational learning.

Simple perceptual learning—learning to recognize particular stimuli or categories of stimuli—appears to take place in appropriate regions of sensory association cortex. That is, learning to recognize particular sounds takes place in the auditory association cortex; learning to recognize particular objects by sight takes place in the visual association cortex; and so on. This section describes research on perceptual learning that illustrates some of the progress that has been made in understanding this topic.

Learning to Recognize Particular Stimuli

In mammals with large and complex brains, objects are recognized visually by circuits of neurons in the visual association cortex. Visual learning can take place very rapidly, and the number of items that can be remembered is enormous. In fact, Standing (1973) showed people 10,000 color slides and found that they could recognize most of them weeks later. Other primates are capable of remembering items that they have seen for just a few seconds, and the experience changes the responses of neurons in their visual association cortex (Rolls, 1995b).

As we saw in Chapter 6, the primary visual cortex receives information from the lateral geniculate nucleus of the thalamus. Within the primary visual cortex individual modules of neurons analyze information from restricted regions of the visual scene that pertain to movement, orientation, color, binocular disparity, and spatial frequency. Information about each of these attributes is collected in subregions of the extrastriate cortex, which surrounds the primary visual cortex (striate cortex). For example, specific regions are devoted to the analysis of form, color, and movement. After analyzing particular attributes of the visual scene, the subregions of the extrastriate cortex send the results of their analysis to the next level of the visual association cortex. As we saw in Chapter 6, the second level of the visual association cortex is divided into two "streams." The *ventral stream,* which is involved with object recognition, begins in the extrastriate cortex and continues ventrally into the inferior temporal cortex. The *dorsal stream,* which is involved with perception of the location of objects, also begins in the extrastriate cortex of the occipital lobe, but it continues dorsally into the posterior parietal cortex. As some investigators have said, the ventral stream is involved with the *what* of visual perception; the dorsal stream is involved with the *where.* (See *Figure 13.25.*)

Many studies have shown that lesions that damage the inferior temporal cortex—part of the ventral stream—disrupt the ability to discriminate between different visual stimuli. Mishkin (1966) showed that if visual information were prevented from reaching the inferior temporal cortex, monkeys lost the ability to distinguish between different visual patterns. First, he removed the striate cortex on one side of the brain and tested the animals' ability to discriminate between visual patterns. They performed well. Next, he removed the contralateral inferior temporal cortex; again, no deficit. Finally, he cut the corpus callosum, which isolated the remaining inferior temporal cortex from the remaining primary visual cortex. This time, the animals could no longer perform the visual discrimination task. Therefore, we can conclude that the inferior temporal cortex is necessary for visual pattern discrimination and that it must receive information from the primary visual cortex. (See *Figure 13.26.*)

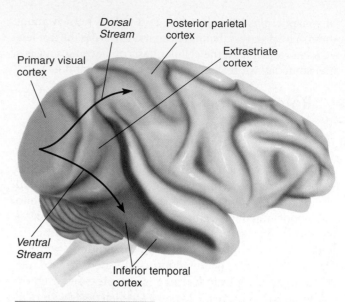

figure 13.25

The major divisions of the visual cortex of the rhesus monkey. The arrows indicate the primary direction of the flow of information in the dorsal and ventral streams.

People with damage to the visual association cortex show deficits similar to those seen in monkeys. These lesions impair their ability to perceive (and thus, to learn to recognize) particular kinds of visual information. As we saw in Chapter 6, people with damage to the inferior temporal cortex may have excellent vision but be unable to recognize familiar, everyday objects such as scissors, clothespins, or light bulbs—and faces of friends and relatives.

Presumably, learning to recognize a particular visual stimulus is accomplished by changes in synaptic connections in the inferior temporal cortex that establish new neural circuits—changes such as the ones described in the previous section of this chapter. At a later time, when the animal sees the same stimulus again and the same pattern of activity is transmitted to the inferior temporal cortex, these circuits become active again. This activity constitutes the recognition of the stimulus—the readout of the visual memory, so to speak.

As we saw in Chapter 6, some neurons in the inferior temporal cortex show remarkable specificity in their response characteristics, which suggests that they are part of circuits that detect the presence of specific stimuli. For example, neurons located near the superior temporal sulcus become active when the animal is shown pictures of faces. Baylis, Rolls, and Leonard (1985) found that most of these neurons are sensitive to *particular* faces. Rolls and Baylis (1986) found that the responses of some of these neurons remain constant even if the picture is blurred or changed in color, size, or distance. Thus, these neurons belong to circuits of neurons that recognize the *identities* of particular faces, not simply a specific view.

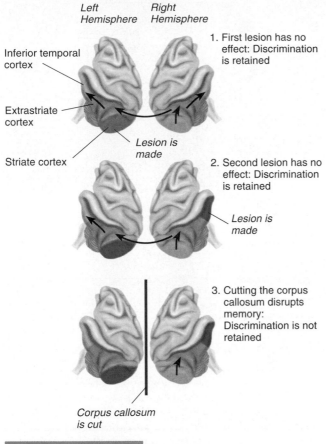

Left Hemisphere   Right Hemisphere

Inferior temporal cortex

Extrastriate cortex

Striate cortex

Lesion is made

1. First lesion has no effect: Discrimination is retained

2. Second lesion has no effect: Discrimination is retained

Lesion is made

3. Cutting the corpus callosum disrupts memory: Discrimination is not retained

Corpus callosum is cut

figure 13.26

The procedure used by Mishkin (1966). Arrows show the flow of information from the striate cortex to the extrastriate cortex to the inferior temporal cortex. Not all of the control groups used in the experiment are shown here.

(Adapted from Mishkin, M., in *Frontiers in Physiological Psychology*, edited by R. W. Russell. New York: Academic Press, 1966.)

Let's look at some evidence from studies with humans that supports the conclusion that activation of neural circuits in sensory association cortex constitutes the "readout" of a perceptual memory. Many years ago, Penfield and Perot (1963) discovered that when they stimulated the visual and auditory association cortex as patients were undergoing seizure surgery, the patients reported memories of images or sounds—for example, images of a familiar street or the sound of the patient's mother's voice. (You will recall from Chapter 3 that seizure surgery is performed under a local anesthetic so that the surgeons can test the effects of brain stimulation on the patients' cognitive functions.)

More recently, functional imaging studies have found that tasks that entail the recall of visual or auditory information activate the appropriate regions of sensory association cortex. Wheeler et al. (2000) presented subjects with forty printed words followed by either pictures or sounds.

For example, the word DOG was followed by either a picture of a dog or the sound of a dog barking. Once the subjects had learned the pairs of stimuli, their brain activation was measured with fMRI while they looked at each word. They did *not* see any pictures or hear any sounds while their brains were being scanned. The results indicated that the printed words served as stimuli to elicit the visual or auditory memories previously associated with them. Words paired with pictures primarily activated visual association cortex, and words paired with sounds primarily activated auditory association cortex. (See *Figure 13.27*.)

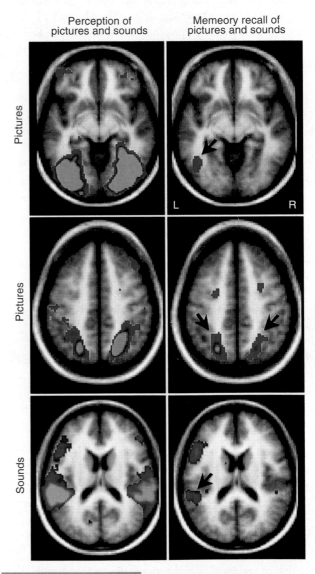

Perception of pictures and sounds

Memeory recall of pictures and sounds

Pictures

Pictures

Sounds

figure 13.27

Activation caused by retrieval of auditory (red/orange) and visual (green/blue) memories, as shown by fMRI. The subjects read words that had previously been accompanied with sounds or pictures.

(From Wheeler, M. E., Petersen, S. E., and Buckner, R. L. *Proceedings of the National Academy of Science, USA*, 2000, *97*, 11125–11129.)

Kourtzi and Kanwisher (2000) found that specific kinds of visual information can activate very specific regions of visual association cortex. As we saw in Chapter 6, two adjacent regions of the visual association cortex, MT and MST, play an essential role in perception of movement. (That chapter contains a description of a woman with lesions to this area who could no longer detect movement but had otherwise normal vision. We also saw that transcranial magnetic stimulation of this region interferes with detection of motion in normal subjects.) Kourtzi and Kanwisher presented subjects with photographs that implied motion—for example, an athlete getting ready to throw a discus. They found that photographs like these, but not photographs of people remaining still, activated area MT/MST. Obviously, the photographs did not move, but presumably the subjects' memories contained information about movements they had previously seen. (See *Figure 13.28*.)

Moscovitch et al. (1995) found that the recall of perceptual memories of the identities and locations of objects in the human brain involve activity in the ventral and dorsal streams, respectively. These investigators measured the activity of the human brain during the recall of the identity and location of visual stimuli—in other words, the

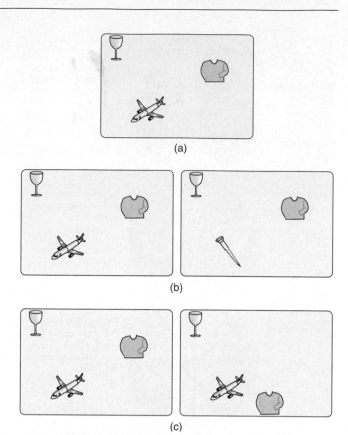

figure 13.29

Examples of the types of stimuli used in the PET scanning study by Moscovitch et al. (1995). (a) One of the stimuli to be memorized. (b) The object-memory retrieval task. One of the objects in the right-hand figure is incorrect. (c) The spatial-memory retrieval task. One of the objects in the right-hand figure is located in the wrong place.

(Adapted from Moscovitch, M., Kapur, S., Koehler, S., and Houle, S. *Proceedings of the National Academy of Sciences,* 1995, *92,* 3721–3725.)

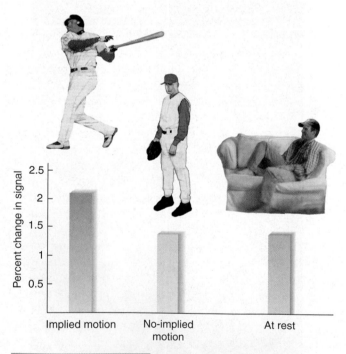

figure 13.28

Evidence of retrieval of visual memories of movement. The bars represent the level of activation, measured by fMRI, of MT/MST, regions of the visual association cortex that respond to movement. Subjects looked at photographs of static scenes or scenes that implied motion similar to those shown here.

(Adapted from Kourtzi, A., and Kanwisher, N. *Journal of Cognitive Neuroscience,* 2000, *12,* 48–55.)

retrieval of perceptual memories of objects and their locations. First, they had people study and memorize twenty-eight different visual displays such as the ones illustrated in Figure 13.29. Each display contained a set of three objects placed in specific locations on the screen. Later, the subjects were shown a pair of displays, one that they had seen before and one that they had never seen, and were asked to indicate which was which. The displays differed in one of two ways. During the *object-memory retrieval task,* one of the objects from the familiar display was replaced with a new object. During the *spatial-memory retrieval task* all three objects were the same, but one of them was shown in a new location. A PET scanner recorded the subjects' regional cerebral blood flow while they were performing these tasks. (See *Figure 13.29*.)

The results of the experiment are shown in Figure 13.30. Both tasks produced activity in the visual association cortex of the occipital, temporal, and parietal lobes,

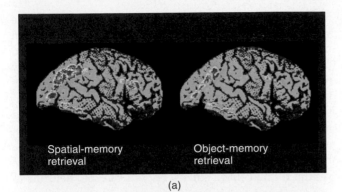

Spatial-memory retrieval   Object-memory retrieval

(a)

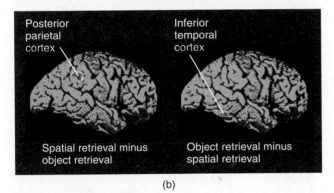

Posterior parietal cortex   Inferior temporal cortex

Spatial retrieval minus object retrieval   Object retrieval minus spatial retrieval

(b)

figure 13.30

The results of PET scans from the task shown in
Figure 13.29.

(From Moscovitch, M., Kapur, S., Koehler, S., and Houle, S. *Proceedings of the National Academy of Sciences*, 1995, *92*, 3721–3725.)

as well as a region of the frontal cortex. (See *Figure 13.30a*.)
The two scans at the bottom show the differences between
the upper two scans. As you can see, the object-memory
retrieval task activated the ventral stream in the inferior
temporal cortex, while the spatial-memory retrieval task
activated the dorsal stream in the posterior parietal cortex. (See *Figure 13.30b*.)

Perceptual Short-Term Memory

So far, all the studies I have mentioned involved recognition of stimuli, either particular objects or their locations.
Often, recognition is all that is necessary: We see a stimulus and immediately make the appropriate response. But
sometimes the situation demands that we make the appropriate response after a delay, even after the stimulus is no
longer visible. For example, suppose that we have driven
into a large parking lot, and because we will have to carry
a heavy package, we want to park as near as possible to
the entrance of a store located just in front of us. We look
to the left and see a space about 100 feet away. We then
look to the right and see a space about 50 feet away. Mentally comparing the distances, we turn to the right. Because

we could not look in both directions simultaneously, we
had to compare the distance to the second space with our
memory of the distance to first one. In other words, we had
to compare a perception with a short-term memory of something else we had just perceived. A **short-term memory** is
the memory for a stimulus or an event that lasts for a short
while—usually on the order of a few seconds.

As we saw in the previous subsection, *learning* to recognize a stimulus involves synaptic changes in the appropriate regions of sensory association cortex that establish
new circuits of neurons. *Recognition* of a stimulus occurs
when sensory input activates these established sets of
neural circuits. *Short-term memory* of a stimulus involves
activity of these circuits—or other circuits that are activated by them—that continues even after the stimulus
disappears. For example, learning to recognize a friend's
face involves changes in synaptic strength in our visual
association cortex, recognizing that she is present involves
activation of the circuits that are established by these
changes, and remembering that she is still in the room
even when we look elsewhere involves continued activity of these circuits (or related ones).

Many studies of short-term memory employ a
delayed matching-to-sample task, which requires an
animal to remember a particular stimulus for a period of
time. A subject is shown a stimulus (the sample) and then,
after a delay, must indicate which of several alternatives
is the same as the sample. These studies have shown that
neurons in the inferior temporal cortex that are activated
by the sight of a particular stimulus will continue to fire
during the delay interval—after the stimulus has been
turned off (Fuster and Jervey, 1981). Presumably, these
neurons belong to circuits that recognize particular stimuli, and their continued activity during the delay interval
represents short-term memory for those stimuli. Experiments have also shown that neurons in the posterior parietal lobe—in the dorsal stream—retain information about
the location of a visual stimulus that has just been perceived (Constantinidis and Steinmetz, 1996).

As we saw in Chapter 6, transcranial magnetic stimulation (TMS) of the visual association cortex interferes with
visual perception. TMS induces a weak electrical current in
the brain that disrupts neural activity and thus interferes with
the normal functions of the stimulated region. Oliveri et al.
(2001) trained people on a delayed matching-to-sample
task that required them to remember either abstract figures
or the locations of a white square on a video screen. On
some trials the investigators applied TMS to the association

---

short-term memory   Memory for a stimulus that has just been
perceived.

delayed matching-to-sample task   A task that requires the subject
to indicate which of several stimuli has just been perceived.

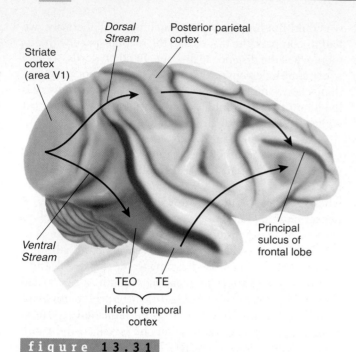

figure 13.31

Connections of the dorsal and ventral streams of the visual association cortex with the prefrontal cortex.

cortex of either the ventral stream or the dorsal stream during the delay interval, after the sample stimuli had been turned off. They found that, as expected, stimulating the ventral stream interfered with short-term memory for visual patterns and stimulating the dorsal stream interfered with short memory for location. In a similar study using a different sensory modality, Harris et al. (2002) found that TMS applied to the somatosensory cortex disrupted somatosensory short-term memory (remembering the frequency of a vibrating stimulus applied to a fingertip).

Although the neural circuits responsible for learning to recognize particular stimuli appear to reside in the sensory association cortex, perceptual short-term memories involve other brain regions, as well—especially the prefrontal cortex. For example, both major regions of the visual association cortex—the ventral stream of the inferior temporal cortex and the dorsal stream of the posterior parietal cortex—have direct, reciprocal connections with the prefrontal cortex. In the monkey brain the dorsal stream has connections with the region inside and just dorsal to the *principal sulcus,* and the ventral stream has connections with the region ventral to this sulcus. (Wilson, Ó Scalaidhe, and Goldman-Rakic, 1993). (See *Figure 13.31.*) In fact, the prefrontal cortex is involved in short-term memory for all sense modalities. Damage to this region or temporary deactivation by cooling the cortex disrupts performance on a variety of delayed matching-to-sample tasks using visual, tactile, or auditory stimuli (Passingham, 1975; Bauer and Fuster, 1976; Shindy, Posley, and Fuster, 1994; Bodner, Kroger, and Fuster, 1996).

As we saw, researchers have found that neurons in the visual association cortex appear to encode short-term memory for visual stimuli. Several studies have found that neurons in the prefrontal cortex do so as well. Many neurons in this region that respond selectively to particular visual stimuli (patterns or spatial locations) and maintain their activity during the delay period of a delayed matching-to-sample task (Wilson, Ó Scalaidhe, and Goldman-Rakic, 1993; Miller, Erickson, and Desimone, 1996). Figure 13.32 shows the responses of neurons dorsal and ventral to the central sulcus. As you can see, neurons in

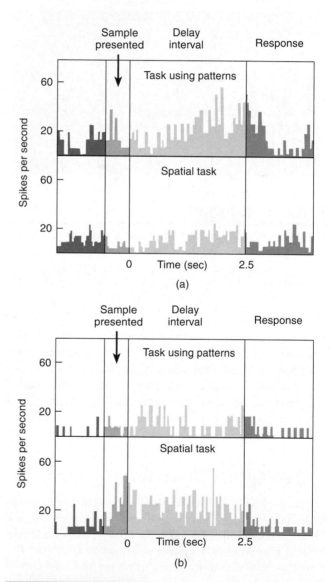

figure 13.32

Responses of neurons in the prefrontal cortex during visual matching-to-sample tasks. (a) Responses of a neuron ventral to the principal sulcus. (b) Responses of a neuron in the principal sulcus.

(Adapted from Wilson, F. A. W., Ó Scalaidhe, S. P. O., and Goldman-Rakic, P. S. *Science,* 1993, *260,* 1955–1958.)

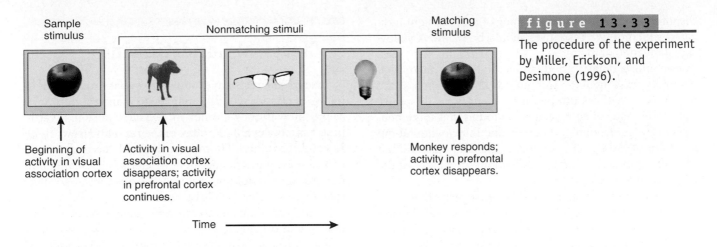

figure 13.33

The procedure of the experiment by Miller, Erickson, and Desimone (1996).

the dorsal region became active during the delay interval of a spatial task, while neurons in the ventral region became active during the delay interval of a task that used patterns. (See *Figure 13.32*.)

A functional imaging study by Courtney et al. (1998) found that two regions of human prefrontal cortex also become active during a delayed matching-to-sample task. The dorsolateral prefrontal cortex becomes active during the delay interval when the stimuli are different patterns, and the inferior prefrontal cortex becomes active when the stimuli were specific spatial locations. Thus, the pattern of connections in the human brain resembles that found in the monkey brain.

But why should there be neural activity encoding sensory information in the frontal lobes? It would be wasteful if identical information about just-perceived stimuli were maintained in two different locations in the brain. In fact, the activity in the visual association cortex and that in the prefrontal cortex appear to play different roles. Miller, Erickson, and Desimone (1996) trained monkeys on a delayed matching-to-sample task in which the test stimuli were presented serially, one at a time, after the delay interval. As soon as the animal saw a test stimulus that matched the sample stimulus, it made a response. If it was correct, the animal was rewarded with some fruit juice.

Miller and his colleagues found that stimulus-specific activity continued during the delay interval in both the visual association cortex and the prefrontal cortex—until they presented a test stimulus that did not match the sample stimulus. At this point the activity in the visual association cortex representing the sample stimulus disappeared, but the activity in the prefrontal cortex continued. The activity in the prefrontal cortex continued until the experimenters presented a test stimulus that matched the sample stimulus, at which time the animal responded. Thus, perhaps, the activity in the prefrontal cortex is able to retain the short-term memory of the sample stimulus, leaving the visual association cortex free to

go about the business of visual perception. After all, an animal must be able to perceive new information even while it is holding onto a visual short-term memory. (See *Figure 13.33*.)

Another possible role of the prefrontal cortex in short-term memory is representation of newly perceived information in terms of previously learned associations. For example, suppose an animal learns a **paired-associate task.** It learns that if it sees stimulus A, then it will receive a reward if it chooses stimulus B. If it sees stimulus C, then it will be rewarded for choosing stimulus D, and so on. Consider the role that the prefrontal cortex may play in a delayed paired-associate task. It sees stimulus A on a video screen, and then the screen goes blank. It has already learned that stimulus B is the correct choice, and it waits for this stimulus to be presented on the screen. What information would we expect to be represented in the prefrontal cortex? Rainer, Rao, and Miller (1999) found that early in the delay interval, neurons in the prefrontal cortex encoded information about stimulus A, the sample, but then they shifted to stimulus B, the correct choice. This shift makes sense. Perhaps the representation of the stimulus that the monkey was watching for tells the visual association cortex to be watching out for stimulus B. As Rainer and his colleagues note, if you are looking for a key, you can use your visual long-term memory to imagine what the key looks like. Then if the information being received from the visual system matches this image, you have just seen what you are looking for.

Quintana and Fuster (1992) found that under some conditions neurons in the prefrontal cortex also encode information about the *response* that the animal is about to make, not simply the stimulus it has seen (or is watching for). The investigators trained monkeys on a delayed

paired-associate task A task that requires the subject to learn to recognize pairs of stimuli.

responding task in which the color of a signal light indicated which of two responses should be made. A yellow signal meant that the monkey should press the right-hand button after a delay period, and a blue signal meant that it should press the left-hand button. Thus, as soon as the monkeys saw the stimulus, they knew what response should be made. The investigators found that some neurons in the prefrontal cortex encoded information about the color of the signal light during the delay interval but that others encoded information about the nature of the response that was to be made.

The study by Quintana and Fuster suggests that some tasks permit the subject to remember a *response,* not simply the stimulus that was presented. For example, if someone shows you a written word, you can remember what the word looks like, what it sounds like, or what movements you would make to pronounce it. We might predict, then, that seeing a word would first activate neurons in the visual association cortex, but after that, neurons in the auditory association cortex or motor association cortex would become active. As we shall see in a discussion of verbal abilities in Chapter 15, this appears to be exactly what happens.

interim
summary

Perceptual Learning

Perceptual learning occurs as a result of changes in synaptic connections within the sensory association cortex. Damage to a monkey's inferior temporal cortex—the highest level of visual association cortex—disrupts visual discriminations. Electrical recording studies have shown that some neurons respond preferentially to particular complex stimuli, including faces. Functional imaging studies with humans have shown that retrieval of memories of pictures, sounds, movements, or spatial locations activate the appropriate regions of sensory association cortex.

Perceptual short-term memory involves sustained activity of neurons in sensory association cortex. Electrical-recording studies have shown that some neurons in the inferior temporal cortex encode the information presented during the sample period of a delayed matching-to-sample task and continue to fire during the delay interval. In humans transcranial magnetic stimulation of various regions of sensory association cortex disrupt short-term perceptual memories. The dorsolateral prefrontal cortex is also involved in short-term memory. Lesions or temporary deactivation of this brain region disrupts performance on delayed matching-to-sample tasks using a variety of different sense modalities. Neurons in this region encode information pertaining to the stimulus that must be remembered or, in some tasks, to the response to be made.

Classical Conditioning

Neuroscientists have studied the anatomy and physiology of classical conditioning using many models, such as the gill withdrawal reflex in *Aplysia* (a marine invertebrate) and the eyeblink reflex in the rabbit (Carew, 1989; Lavond, Kim, and Thompson, 1993). I have chosen to describe a simple mammalian model of classical conditioning—the conditioned emotional response—to illustrate the results of such investigations.

The central nucleus of the amygdala plays an important role in organizing a pattern of emotional responses that are provoked by aversive stimuli, both learned and unlearned. As we saw in Chapter 11, when this nucleus is activated, its efferent connections with other regions of the brain trigger several behavioral, autonomic, and endocrine responses that are elicited by aversive stimuli. Most stimuli that cause an aversive emotional response are not intrinsically aversive; we have to *learn* to fear them. The central nucleus of the amygdala is part of an important system involved in a particular form of stimulus-response (S-R) learning: classically conditioned emotional responses.

An aversive stimulus such as a painful foot shock produces a variety of behavioral, autonomic, and hormonal responses: freezing, increased blood pressure, secretion of adrenal stress hormones, and so on. A classically conditioned emotional response is established by pairing a neutral stimulus (such as a tone of a particular frequency) with an aversive stimulus (such as a brief foot shock). As we saw in Chapter 11, after these stimuli are paired, the tone becomes a CS; when it is presented by itself, it elicits the same type of responses as the unconditional stimulus does.

A conditioned emotional response can occur in the absence of the auditory cortex (LeDoux et al., 1984); thus, I will confine my discussion to the subcortical components of this process. Information about the CS (the tone) reaches the lateral nucleus of the amygdala. This nucleus also receives information about the US (the foot shock) from the somatosensory system. Thus, these two sources of information converge in the lateral nucleus, which means that synaptic changes responsible for learning could take place in this location.

A hypothetical neural circuit is shown in Figure 13.34. The lateral nucleus of the amygdala contains pyramidal cells whose axons project to the central nucleus. Terminal buttons from neurons that transmit auditory and somatosensory information to the lateral nucleus form synapses with dendritic spines on these pyramidal cells. When a rat encounters a painful stimulus, strong synapses in the lateral nucleus are activated; as a result, the pyramidal neurons in this nucleus begin firing, which acti-

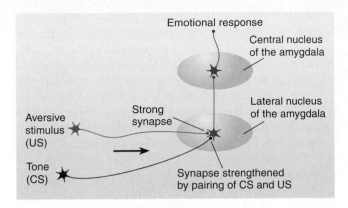

figure 13.34

The probable location of the changes in synaptic strength produced by the classically conditioned emotional response that results from pairing a tone with a foot shock.

vates neurons in the central nucleus, evoking an unlearned (unconditional) emotional response. If a tone is paired with the painful stimulus, the weak synapses in the lateral amygdala are strengthened through the action of the Hebb rule. (See *Figure 13.34*.)

This hypothesis has a considerable amount of support. Lesions of the lateral or central nucleus of the amygdala (but not other regions of the amygdala) disrupt conditioned emotional responses that involve a simple auditory stimulus as a CS and a shock to the feet as a US (Kapp et al., 1979; Nader et al., 2001). Thus, the synaptic changes responsible for this learning may take place within this circuit.

Wilensky, Schafe, and LeDoux (1999) temporarily inactivated the lateral amygdala by infusing muscimol, a drug that activates inhibitory GABA receptors, and hence suppresses neural firing. They found that if the lateral amygdala was inactivated during training, when the CS and US pairing were taking place, the animals did not acquire a conditioned emotional response.

Quirk, Repa, and LeDoux (1995) found evidence for synaptic changes in the lateral nucleus of the amygdala. They recorded the activity of neurons in this nucleus in freely moving rats before, during, and after pairing of a

tone with a foot shock. Within a few trials the neurons became more responsive to the tone, and many neurons that had not previously responded to the tone began doing so. (See *Figure 13.35*.) The greatest augmentation was seen in short-latency responses, which are received directly from the thalamus; thus, the synaptic changes must have been occurring in the circuit shown in Figure 13.34, not elsewhere in the brain. Maren (2000) confirmed these results and also found that the magnitude of the increased firing rate in neurons in the lateral nucleus correlated with the magnitude of the conditioned emotional response.

Collins and Paré (2000) trained animals on a *differential* conditioned emotional response task. They presented two tones of different frequencies. One of them (the CS+) was followed by a brief foot shock. The other one (the CS−) was always presented by itself. After several trials the animals showed a conditioned emotional response when the CS+ was presented but not when the CS− was presented. Electrical recordings of the activity of single neurons in the lateral amygdala showed that after learning had taken place, the CS+ elicited a larger response, while the CS− elicited a *smaller* response. Thus, the differential conditioning may have produced both

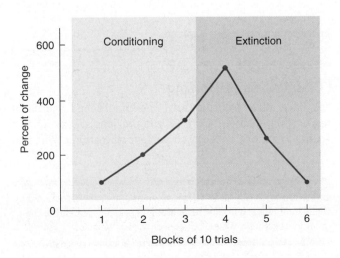

figure 13.35

Change in rate of firing of neurons in the lateral amygdala in response to the tone, relative to baseline levels.

(Adapted from Quirk, G. J., Repa, J. C., and LeDoux, J. E. *Neuron*, 1995, *15*, 1029–1039.)

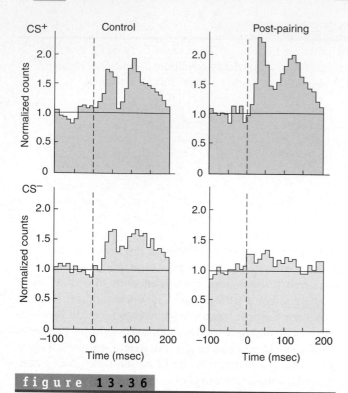

figure 13.36

figure 13.36

Effects of differential classical conditioning on neural activity in the lateral amygdala. The CS+ was paired with a brief foot shock; the CS− was not. After the training had taken place, the response to the CS+ was larger than before, and the response to the CS− was smaller.

(Adapted from Collins, D. R., and Paré, D. *Learning and Memory,* 2000, *7,* 97–103.)

long-term potentiation and long-term depression in the lateral amygdala. (See *Figure 13.36.*)

The evidence from several studies supports the hypothesis that the changes in the lateral amygdala responsible for acquisition of a conditioned emotional response involve long-term potentiation. Experiments have shown that long-term potentiation can take place in the synaptic connections in the lateral nucleus of the amygdala. For example, Clugnet and LeDoux (1990) found that electrically stimulating the medial geniculate nucleus produced long-term potentiation in the lateral amygdala. Even more significantly, Rogan and LeDoux (1995) found that when long-term potentiation was produced in the lateral nucleus of the amygdala, neurons there became more responsive to auditory stimuli.

As we saw, long-term potentiation in at least some parts of the brain is accomplished through the activation of NMDA receptors. Research suggests that these receptors also participate in the synaptic plasticity that occurs in the amygdala. Rodrigues, Schafe, and LeDoux (2001) used a drug called *ifenprodil* to block the NR2B subunit of the NMDA receptor. The investigators found that infusion of this drug into the lateral amygdala blocks the acquisition of a conditioned emotional response, but not its

expression. That is, if ifenprodil is infused just before training, the animals do not acquire the conditional emotional response, but if the drug is infused in animals who have already acquired the conditioned emotional response, they continue to make the response when the CS is presented. In addition, as we will see in Chapter 14, a genetic manipulation that increases the amount of NR2B receptors in the mouse forebrain facilitates both long-term potentiation and acquisition of a conditioned emotional response (Tang et al., 1999). These studies strongly suggest that long-term potentiation in the lateral amygdala, mediated by NMDA receptors, plays a critical role in the establishment of conditioned emotional responses.

Some experimental evidence suggests that synaptic plasticity controlled by the activation of NMDA receptors may also play a role in the *extinction* of a classically conditioned emotional response. Classical conditioning is not always forever. If, after classical conditioning has been established by pairing a CS and a US, the CS is presented repeatedly by itself, the conditioned response will eventually disappear—a process known as **extinction.** Falls, Miserendino, and Davis (1992) found that thirty presentations of the CS alone were sufficient to extinguish a classically conditioned emotional response. However, if they injected AP5 into the amygdala just before beginning these thirty extinction trials, the response did *not* extinguish. Santini, Muller, and Quirk (2001) confirmed these results using a different drug to block NMDA receptors. Thus, NMDA-mediated synaptic plasticity seems to be necessary for both learning and extinction.

As we saw earlier in this chapter, protein synthesis is necessary for long-lasting long-term potentiation. Schafe and LeDoux (2000) found that anisomycin, a drug that prevents long-lasting long-term potentiation by disrupting protein synthesis, also blocks long-term retention of a conditioned emotional response when it is injected into the lateral amygdala. Thus, long-lasting long-term potentiation appears to be essential for this form of stimulus-response learning.

interim summary

Classical Conditioning

You have already encountered the conditioned emotional response in Chapter 11 and in the previous section of this chapter, in which I discussed perceptual learning. When an

---

extinction With respect to classical conditioning, the reduction or elimination of a conditional response by repeatedly presenting the conditional stimulus without the unconditional stimulus.

auditory stimulus (CS) is paired with a foot shock (US), the two types of information converge in the lateral nucleus of the amygdala. This nucleus is connected, directly and via the basal nucleus and accessory basal nucleus, with the central nucleus, which is responsible for the various components of the emotional response. Lesions anywhere in this circuit disrupt the response.

Recordings of single neurons in the lateral nucleus of the amygdala indicate that classical conditioning changes the response of neurons to the CS. The mechanism of synaptic plasticity in this system appears to be NMDA-mediated long-term potentiation. High-frequency electrical stimulation of the inputs to the lateral amygdala produces long-term potentiation, and long-term potentiation in the lateral nucleus increases the responses of neurons there to auditory stimuli. In addition, the infusion of an NMDA receptor blocker into the lateral amygdala prevents classical conditioning from taking place but has no effect on conditioning that was established earlier. Drugs that block NMDA receptors also prevent the *extinction* of a conditioned emotional response.

Instrumental Conditioning and Motor Learning

Instrumental (operant) conditioning is the means by which we (and other animals) profit from experience. If, in a particular situation, we make a response that has favorable outcomes, we will tend to make the response again. Sometimes the response is one that we already know how to perform, which means that all that needs to occur is a strengthening of connections between neural circuits that detect the relevant stimuli and those that control the relevant response. However, if the response is one that we have not made before, our performance is likely to be slow and awkward. As we continue to practice the response, our behavior becomes faster, smoother, and more automatic. In other words, motor learning takes place as well. This section first describes the neural pathways involved in instrumental conditioning and its close relative, motor learning, and then discusses the neural basis of reinforcement.

Basal Ganglia

As we saw earlier in this chapter, instrumental conditioning entails the strengthening of connections between neural circuits that detect a particular stimulus and neural circuits that produce a particular response. Clearly, the circuits responsible for instrumental conditioning begin in various regions of the sensory association cortex, where perception takes place, and end in the motor association

cortex of the frontal lobe, which controls movements. But what pathways are responsible for these connections, and where do the synaptic changes responsible for the learning take place?

There are two major pathways between the sensory association cortex and the motor association cortex: direct transcortical connections and connections via the basal ganglia and thalamus. (A third pathway, involving the cerebellum and thalamus, also exists, but the role of this pathway in instrumental conditioning has until very recently received little attention from neuroscientists.) Both of these pathways appear to be involved in instrumental conditioning, but they play different roles.

The direct connections between the sensory association cortex and the motor association cortex are, as we saw earlier, involved in short-term memory. In conjunction with the hippocampal formation they are also involved in the acquisition of episodic memories—complex perceptual memories of sequences of events that we witness or are described to us. (The acquisition of these types of memories is discussed in Chapter 14.) The transcortical connections are also involved in the acquisition of complex behaviors that involve deliberation or instruction. For example, a person learning to drive a car with a manual transmission might say, "Let's see, push in the clutch, move the shift lever to the left and then away from me—there, it's in gear—now let the clutch come up—oh! It died—I should have given it more gas. Let's see, clutch down, turn the key. . . ." A memorized set of rules (or an instructor sitting next to us) provides a script for us to follow. Of course, this process does not have to be audible or even involve actual movements of the speech muscles; a person can think in words with neural activity that does not result in overt behavior. (Animals that cannot communicate by means of language can acquire complex responses by observing and imitating the behavior of other animals.)

At first, performing a behavior through observation or by following a set of rules is slow and awkward. And because so much of the brain's resources are involved with recalling the rules and applying them to our behavior, we cannot respond to other stimuli in the environment—we must ignore events that might distract us. But then, with practice, the behavior becomes much more fluid. Eventually, we perform it without thinking and can easily do other things at the same time, such as carrying on a conversation with passengers as we drive our car.

Evidence suggests that as learned behaviors become automatic and routine, they are "transferred" to the basal ganglia. The process seems to work like this. As we deliberately perform a complex behavior, the basal ganglia receive information about the stimuli that are present and the responses we are making. At first the basal ganglia are passive "observers" of the situation, but as the behaviors are repeated again and again, they begin to learn what to do. Eventually, they take over most of the details of the process, leaving the transcortical circuits free to do something else. We need no longer think about what we are doing.

Before I discuss some evidence that supports the assertion that the basal ganglia are involved in instrumental conditioning, let me review the anatomy of the basal ganglia, first described in Chapter 8. The neostriatum—the caudate nucleus and the putamen—receives sensory information from all regions of the cerebral cortex. It also receives information from the frontal lobes about movements that are planned or are actually in progress. (So as you can see, the basal ganglia have all the information they need to monitor the progress of someone learning to drive a car.) The outputs of the caudate nucleus and the putamen are sent to another part of the basal ganglia: the globus pallidus. The outputs of this structure are sent to the frontal cortex: to the premotor and supplementary motor cortex, where plans for movements are made, and to the primary motor cortex, where they are executed. (See *Figure 13.37*.)

Now let's review some evidence that supports the assertion that the basal ganglia are involved in learning. Studies with laboratory animals have found that lesions of the basal ganglia disrupt instrumental condi-

tioning but do not affect other forms of learning. Divac, Rosvold, and Szcwarcbart (1967) found that lesions of the caudate nucleus in monkeys disrupted acquisition of a simple instrumental conditioning task—a visual discrimination task. Gaffan and his colleagues (Gaffan and Harrison, 1987; Gaffan and Eacott, 1995) found that cutting all the connections between the visual association cortex and the frontal cortex *except* for the connections via the basal ganglia had no effect on a visual discrimination task. By a process of elimination, they said, acquisition of this task must involve the connections through the basal ganglia.

Several studies have obtained similar results in rats. In a follow-up to a study by Packard, Hirsh, and White (1989), McDonald and White (1993) tested three groups of animals, with lesions of three different parts of the brain, on three different learning tasks. One task involved episodic learning (remembering what places the rat had visited that day), another involved learning that a particular stimulus was associated with reinforcement, and the other involved an instrumental task: a simple brightness discrimination. Damage to the hippocampal formation disrupted only the episodic learning, damage to the amygdala disrupted only the ability to learn the association of a stimulus with reinforcement, and damage to the caudate

figure 13.37

A schematic diagram of the basal ganglia and their connections.

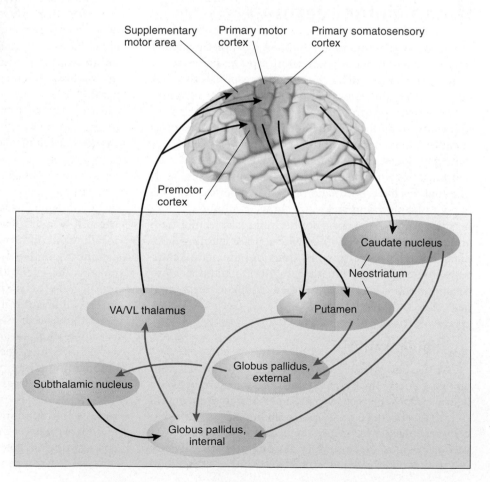

nucleus and putamen disrupted the ability to learn the instrumental task. Clearly, different neural pathways are involved in different types of learning.

Levy et al. (1997) had monkeys perform a task that required them to retain information in short-term memory about either the location or the identity of visual stimuli. They used the 2-DG autoradiography procedure to analyze whether the caudate nucleus became activated during these tasks. They found that remembering spatial information increased the activity of neurons in the head of the caudate nucleus, which receives input from the dorsal stream of visual information (via the dorsolateral prefrontal cortex), and that remembering information about the identity of an object increased the activity of neurons in the body of the caudate nucleus, which receives input directly from the ventral stream.

Fernandez-Ruiz et al. (2001) confirmed that the basal ganglia play a role in an operant discrimination task. The investigators destroyed the portions of the caudate nucleus and putamen that receive visual information from the ventral stream. They found that although the lesions did not disrupt visual perceptual learning, the monkeys' ability to learn to make a visually guided operant response was impaired.

As we saw in the previous section, long-term potentiation appears to play a critical role in classical conditioning. This form of neural plasticity appears to be involved in instrumental conditioning, as well. Packard and Teather (1997) found that blocking NMDA receptors in the basal ganglia with an injection of AP5 disrupted learning guided by a simple visual cue.

Studies with humans also indicate that the basal ganglia play an important role in automatic, nondeliberate learning. Investigators have studied people with Parkinson's disease, a neurological disorder that affects the basal ganglia. As we saw in Chapters 4 and 8, Parkinson's disease is caused by degeneration of the dopaminergic neurons of the nigrostriatal system. The cell bodies of these neurons are located in the substantia nigra of the midbrain, and their axons terminate in the neostriatum: the caudate nucleus and the putamen. When the degeneration causes the release of dopamine in the neostriatum to fall to a sufficiently low level, the basal ganglia cease to function normally.

In the past the symptoms of Parkinson's disease have been described as "motor deficits." However, some of them can be seen as failures of automated memories. For example, although people with Parkinson's disease have sufficient muscular strength, they have difficulty performing many everyday tasks, such as getting out of a chair. Also, if someone bumps into them while they are standing, they are likely to fall, and they will not put their hands out in front of them to catch themselves. These symptoms can, of course, be viewed as motor deficits. But we can also regard them as failure to remember how to do something. We do not think of rising from a chair as a learned behavior, but it surely must be. It involves leaning forward to bring our center of gravity over our feet before beginning to contract the extensor muscles of our legs. Unless the disease is well advanced, people with Parkinson's disease can eventually stand up from a chair, but it takes them some time, as if they have to think about how to do it. Similarly, we do not think of putting our hands out in front of us to break a fall as a learned response, but perhaps it is.

Several experiments have shown that people with diseases of the basal ganglia have deficits that can definitely be attributed to difficulty in learning automatic responses. For example, Owen et al. (1992) found that patients with Parkinson's disease were impaired on learning a visual discrimination task. The patients performed normally on a test of visual recognition, which indicates that their impairment was not caused by a perceptual deficit. Partiot et al. (1996) found that patients with Parkinson's disease showed a deficit in tasks that required them to retain information in short-term memory. Paulsen et al. (1993) found that patients with Huntington's disease (a degenerative disease of the basal ganglia) failed to learn a sequence of button presses.

Knowlton, Mangels, and Squire (1996) found that patients with Parkinson's disease did poorly on a probability learning task. The task required them to predict the weather. On each trial the subjects were shown one to three cards, each of which contained a particular pattern. Each pattern predicted either sunshine or rain, with a probability ranging from 25 percent to 75 percent. (See *Figure 13.38*.) Normal subjects gradually get better and better at this task, but most of them remain unaware of what they have learned: They are unable to state explicitly the rules they use to predict the weather.

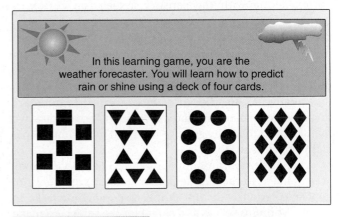

In this learning game, you are the weather forecaster. You will learn how to predict rain or shine using a deck of four cards.

figure 13.38

The probability learning task used by Knowlton, Mangels, and Squire.

(Adapted from Knowlton, B. J., Mangels, J. A., and Squire, L. R. *Science*, 1996, *273*, 1399–1402.)

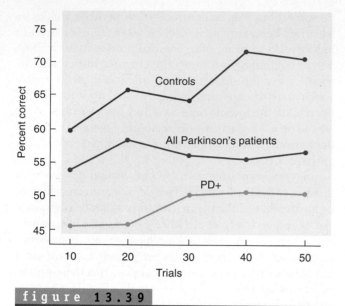

figure 13.39

Results of subjects on the task illustrated in Figure 13.38. The curve labeled PD+ refers to the patients with Parkinson's disease who exhibited the worst motor symptoms.

(Adapted from Knowlton, B. J., Mangels, J. A., and Squire, L. R. *Science*, 1996, *273*, 1399–1402.)

Knowlton and her colleagues found that the patients with severe Parkinson's disease failed to learn this task. Clearly, the results cannot be attributed to a motor deficit. (See *Figure 13.39*.)

Premotor Cortex

The evidence I have reviewed indicates that the basal ganglia are involved in learning. And as we saw in the previous section of this chapter, the dorsolateral prefrontal cortex, along with the sensory association cortex, is involved in remembering stimuli that have just been perceived and, in some cases, the response that is about to be made. As we saw in Chapter 8, most of the output from the basal ganglia is directed, via the thalamus, to the premotor cortex and the adjacent supplementary motor area. (See *Figure 13.40*.) Because these cortical regions are involved in the planning and execution of movements, we might expect that they are also involved in learning, especially motor learning.

A considerable amount of research indicates that they are. Damage to the supplementary motor area does not appear to seriously disrupt simple discrimination tasks, in which a stimulus serves as a signal for the subject to make a response. However, it does disrupt the ability to learn sequences of responses in which the performance of one response serves as the signal that the next response must be made. Chen et al. (1995) found that lesions of the supplementary motor area severely impaired monkeys' ability to perform a simple sequence of two responses. The task

required them to push a lever in and then turn it to the left, receiving a peanut after each response. (See *Figure 13.41*.)

A single-unit recording study came to similar conclusions. Mushiake, Inase, and Tanji (1991) trained monkeys to perform a memorized series of responses, pressing each of three buttons in a specific sequence. While the monkeys were performing this task, more than half of the neurons in the supplementary motor area became activated. However, when the sequence was cued by visual stimuli—the monkeys simply had to press the button that was illuminated—these neurons showed little activity.

Shima and Tanji (2000) taught monkeys six sequences of three motor responses. For example, one of the sequences was push, then pull, then turn. They recorded from neurons in the supplementary motor area and found neurons whose activity appeared to encode elements of these sequences. For example, some neurons responded just before a particular sequence of three movements occurred; some neurons responded between two particular responses; and some neurons responded as the monkey was preparing to make the last response of the sequence. Presumably, these neurons were members of circuits that encoded the information necessary to perform the six sequences.

Shima and Tanji (1998) temporarily inactivated the supplementary motor area in monkeys with injections of muscimol. They found that after inactivation of this region, monkeys could still reach for objects or make particular movements in response to visual cues, but they could no longer make a sequence of three movements they had previously learned.

A PET study with human subjects obtained similar results. Hikosaka et al. (1996) had people learn a sequence

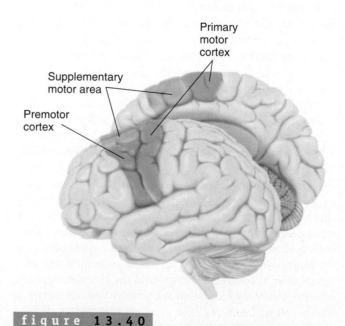

figure 13.40

The premotor cortex: lateral premotor cortex and supplementary motor area.

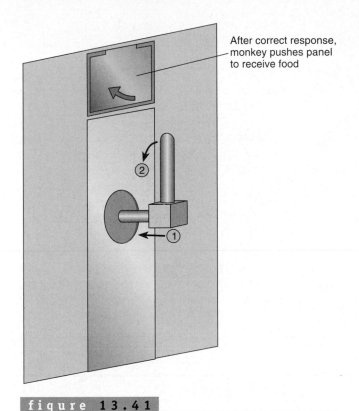

After correct response, monkey pushes panel to receive food

figure 13.41

The handle used in the experiment by Chen et al. (1995). The monkey was required to (1) push the handle in and then (2) turn it to the left, receiving a piece of food in the door above the lever after each component of the sequence. (Adapted from Chen, Y.-C., Thaler, D., Nixon, P. D., Stern, C. E., and Passingham, R. E. *Experimental Brain Research,* 1995, *102,* 461–473.)

of button presses while their heads were placed in the scanner. During learning, the anterior supplementary motor area became activated, and then during performance of the learned sequence the posterior supplementary motor area—the part immediately adjacent to the primary motor cortex—became activated. As anatomical studies have shown, the anterior and posterior supplementary motor areas have different inputs and outputs. The posterior region appears to be "downstream" from the anterior region—that is, it receives information from the anterior region. Only the posterior region has direct connections with the primary motor cortex (Luppino et al., 1993).

The other major region of motor association cortex, the premotor cortex, appears to play a role in the programming of complex movements and in using sensory information to select a particular movement. For example, Kakei, Hoffman, and Strick (2001) recorded the electrical activity of single neurons in the premotor cortex of monkeys while the animals were making movements in different directions while their wrists were in different positions. They found that different neurons were active when different movements were made and that most of the neurons appeared to encode the direction of the move-

ment in space, no matter what the posture of the arm was. These results indicate that the premotor cortex appears to be concerned with where in space a movement is to be made, not what particular muscular contractions must be made to produce that movement. That is, these neurons are involved with goals of movements, not the details of the muscular contractions needed to achieve these goals.

The results of several studies suggest that the premotor cortex is involved in using arbitrary stimuli to indicate what movement should be made. For example, reaching for an object that we see in a particular location involves *nonarbitrary* spatial information—that is, the visual information provided by the location of the object specifies just where we should target our reaching movement. However, we have the ability to learn to make movements based on *arbitrary* information—information that is not directly related to the movement that it signals. For example, a person can point to a particular object when someone says its name, or a dancer can make a particular movement when asked to do so by a choreographer. Different languages use different sounds to indicate the names of objects, and different choreographers could invent different names for movements used in their dances. Or a person could be told to "wave your left hand when you hear the buzz and touch your nose when you hear the bell." The associations between these stimuli and the movements they designate are arbitrary and must be learned.

Kurata and Hoffman (1994) trained monkeys to move their hand toward the right or left in response to either a spatial or nonspatial signal. The spatial signal required the animals to move in the direction indicated by signal lights located to the right and left of its hand. The nonspatial signal consisted of a pair of lights, one red and one green, located in the middle of the display. The red light signaled a movement to the left, and the green light signaled a movement to the right. The investigators temporarily inactivated the premotor cortex with injections of muscimol. When this region was inactivated, the monkeys could still move their hand toward a signal light located to the left or right (a nonarbitrary signal), but they could no longer make the appropriate movements when the red or green signal lights were illuminated.

Similar results are seen in people with damage to the premotor cortex. Halsband and Freund (1990) found that patients with these lesions could learn to make six different movements in response to spatial cues but not to arbitrary visual cues. That is, they could learn to point to one of six locations in which they had just seen a visual stimulus, but they could not learn to use a set of visual, auditory, and tactile cues to make particular movements.

In a functional imaging study, Grafton, Fagg, and Arbib (1998) trained people to use spatial signals to reach for one of three targets and then to grip the target in one of two different ways. They found that when the type of grip they were to use was signaled by arbitrary visual signals (the color of a light), the parietal cortex and the

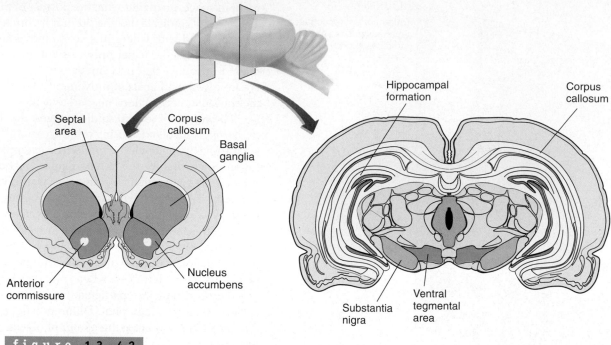

Sections through a rat brain showing the location of the ventral tegmental area and the nucleus accumbens.
(Adapted from Swanson, L. W. *Brain Maps: Structure of the Rat Brain.* New York: Elsevier, 1992.)

dorsal premotor cortex became activated. As we saw in Chapter 6, the parietal cortex, part of the dorsal stream of visual processing, is involved in guiding movements signaled by visual stimuli. For example, damage to this region impairs people's ability to adjust the shape of their hand in anticipation of the size and shape of an object they are reaching for and planning to pick up (Jakobson et al., 1991). In fact, the parietal cortex is one of the most important sources of inputs to the dorsal premotor cortex (Tanne et al., 1995).

Reinforcement

Learning provides a means for us to profit from experience—to make responses that provide favorable outcomes. When good things happen (that is, when reinforcing stimuli occur), reinforcement mechanisms in the brain become active, and the establishment of synaptic changes is facilitated. The discovery of the existence of such reinforcement mechanisms occurred by accident.

Neural Circuits Involved in Reinforcement

As you read in this chapter's opening case, an animal's behavior can be reinforced by electrical stimulation of the brain. Subsequent research has found that stimulation of many parts of the brain is reinforcing (Olds and Fobes, 1981). The best and most reliable location is the **medial forebrain bundle (MFB),** a bundle of axons that travel in a rostral–caudal axis from the midbrain to the rostral basal forebrain. The MFB passes through the lateral hypo-

thalamus, and it is in this region that most investigators place the tips of their electrodes.

Although there may well be more than one reinforcement mechanism, the activity of dopaminergic neurons plays a particularly important role in this phenomenon. As we saw in Chapter 4, there are three major systems of dopaminergic neurons: the *nigrostriatal system,* the *mesolimbic system,* and the *mesocortical system.* The mesolimbic system begins in the **ventral tegmental area (VTA)** of the midbrain and projects rostrally to several forebrain regions, including the amygdala, the hippocampus, and the **nucleus accumbens (NAC).** This nucleus is located in the basal forebrain rostral to the preoptic area and immediately adjacent to the septum. (In fact, the full name of this region is the *nucleus accumbens septi,* or "nucleus leaning against the septum.") (See *Figure 13.42.*) The

medial forebrain bundle (MFB) A fiber bundle that runs in a rostral–caudal direction through the basal forebrain and lateral hypothalamus; electrical stimulation of these axons is reinforcing.

ventral tegmental area (VTA) A group of dopaminergic neurons in the ventral midbrain whose axons form the mesolimbic and mesocortical systems; plays a critical role in reinforcement.

nucleus accumbens A nucleus of the basal forebrain near the septum; receives dopamine-secreting terminal buttons from neurons of the ventral tegmental area and is thought to be involved in reinforcement and attention.

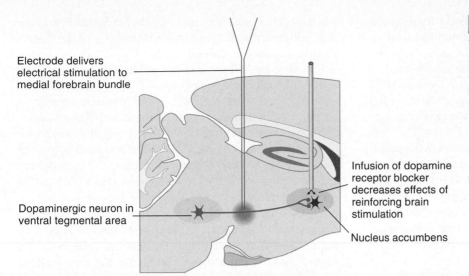

figure 1 3 . 4 3

The experiment by Stellar, Kelley, and Corbett (1983). Blocking dopamine receptors in the nucleus accumbens reduces the reinforcing effects of electrical stimulation of the medial forebrain bundle.

Electrode delivers electrical stimulation to medial forebrain bundle

Dopaminergic neuron in ventral tegmental area

Infusion of dopamine receptor blocker decreases effects of reinforcing brain stimulation

Nucleus accumbens

mesocortical system also plays a role in reinforcement. This system also begins in the ventral tegmental area but projects to the prefrontal cortex, the limbic cortex, and the hippocampus.

A large body of experimental evidence indicates that the projections of the mesolimbic pathway that terminate in the nucleus accumbens are at least partly responsible for the reinforcing effects of electrical brain stimulation. These neurons also play an important role in the reinforcing effects of amphetamine and cocaine and other addictive drugs. (This role is discussed in more detail in Chapter 16.) Treatments that stimulate dopamine receptors in the nucleus accumbens will reinforce behaviors; thus, animals will press a lever that causes electrical stimulation of the ventral tegmental area, the medial forebrain bundle, or the nucleus accumbens itself (Routtenberg and Malsbury, 1969; Crow, 1972; Olds and Fobes, 1981). They will also press a lever that delivers injections of very small amounts of dopamine or amphetamine directly into the nucleus accumbens (Hoebel et al., 1983; Guerin et al., 1984). And if a drug that blocks dopamine receptors is injected directly into the nucleus accumbens, then electrical stimulation of the mesolimbic pathway becomes less reinforcing (Stellar, Kelley, and Corbett, 1983). (See *Figure 13.43*.)

Chapter 5 described a research technique called *microdialysis,* which enables an investigator to analyze the contents of the interstitial fluid within a specific region of the brain. Researchers using this method have shown that reinforcing electrical stimulation of the medial forebrain bundle or the ventral tegmental area, or the administration of cocaine or amphetamine, causes the release of dopamine in the nucleus accumbens (Moghaddam and Bunney, 1989; Nakahara et al., 1989; Phillips et al., 1992). (See *Figure 13.44*.) Microdialysis studies have also found that the presence of natural reinforcers, such as water, food, or a sex partner, stimulates the release of dopamine in the nucleus accumbens. Thus, the effects of reinforcing brain

stimulation seem to be similar in many ways to those of natural reinforcers.

Although microdialysis probes are not placed in the brain of humans for experimental purposes, functional imaging studies have shown that reinforcing events activate the human nucleus accumbens. For example, Knutson et al. (2001) found that the nucleus accumbens became more active (and, presumably, dopamine was being released there) when people were presented with stimuli that indicated that they would be receiving money. Aharon

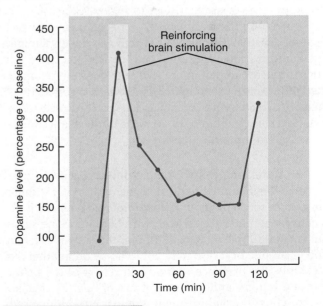

figure 1 3 . 4 4

Release of dopamine in the nucleus accumbens, measured by microdialysis, produced when a rat pressed a lever that delivered electrical stimulation to the ventral tegmental area.

(Adapted from Phillips, A. G., Coury, A., Fiorino, D., LePiane, F. G., Brown, E., and Fibiger, H. C. *Annals of the New York Academy of Sciences*, 1992, *654*, 199–206.)

et al. (2001) found that young heterosexual men would press a lever that presented pictures of beautiful women (but not handsome men) and that when they saw these pictures, the activity of the nucleus accumbens increased.

I should note that microdialysis studies have found that aversive stimuli, as well as reinforcing stimuli, can cause the release of dopamine in various parts of the brain, including the nucleus accumbens (Salamone, 1992). Thus, it is clear that reinforcement is not the sole function of dopaminergic neurons; these neurons appear to be involved in stress as well. Also, because the stimulation of so many regions of the brain is reinforcing, the mesolimbic system is only one of several reinforcement systems. The mesolimbic system is by far the one that has received the most attention; little is known about other possible mechanisms.

Functions of the Reinforcement System

What does reinforcing brain stimulation tell us about the brain mechanisms that are involved in instrumental conditioning? Almost all investigators believe that electrical stimulation of some parts of the brain is reinforcing because it activates the same systems that are activated by natural reinforcers, such as food, water, or sexual contact. A reinforcement system must perform two functions: detect the presence of a reinforcing stimulus (that is, recognize that something good has just happened) and strengthen the connections between the neurons that detect the discriminative stimulus (such as the sight of a lever) and the neurons that produce the instrumental response (a lever press). (Refer to *Figure 13.2.*)

Assuming that this proposed mechanism is correct, several questions remain: What activates the dopaminergic neurons in the midbrain, causing their terminal buttons to release dopamine? What role does the release of dopamine play in strengthening synaptic connections? Where do these synaptic changes take place? Research that suggests some preliminary answers to these questions is discussed in the rest of this section.

■ **Detecting Reinforcing Stimuli** Reinforcement occurs when neural circuits detect a reinforcing stimulus and cause the activation of dopaminergic neurons in the ventral tegmental area. Detection of a reinforcing stimulus is not a simple matter; a stimulus that serves as a reinforcer on one occasion may fail to do so on another. For example, the presence of food will reinforce the behavior of a hungry animal but not that of one that has just eaten. Thus, the reinforcement system is not automatically activated when particular stimuli are present; its activation also depends on the state of the animal.

In general, if a stimulus causes the animal to engage in an appetitive behavior (that is, if it approaches the stimulus rather than runs away from it), that stimulus can reinforce the animal's behavior. When that stimulus occurs,

it activates the brain's reinforcement mechanism, and the link between the discriminative stimulus and the instrumental response is strengthened.

Studies by Schultz and his colleagues, recording the activity of dopaminergic neurons in the nucleus accumbens, have discovered that the reinforcement system appears to be activated by *unexpected* reinforcing stimuli. For example, Mirenowicz and Schultz (1994, 1996) taught monkeys an operant task that required them to make a response when they heard an auditory stimulus. During training, dopaminergic neurons in the VTA responded rapidly when the reinforcing stimulus (a tasty liquid) was delivered. However, once the animals learned the task, the VTA neurons became active when the auditory stimulus was presented but not when the reinforcing stimulus was delivered. The animals did not know exactly when the auditory stimulus would be presented, so in that sense, the sound surprised them. However, they knew that if they then made the response, they would receive a reward. A functional imaging study by Berns et al. (2001) found similar results with humans. Figure 13.45 shows that when a small amount of tasty fruit juice was squirted in people's mouths unpredictably, the nucleus accumbens was activated, but when the delivery of fruit juice was predictable, no such activity occurred. (See *Figure 13.45.*) Schultz and his colleagues suggest that activation of the dopaminergic neurons of the VTA tell other circuits in the brain that an event that has informational value with respect to a potentially reinforcing stimulus has just occurred. In other words, the activity of these neurons sends a signal that there is something to be learned. If the delivery of the reinforcer is already expected, then there is nothing that needs to be learned.

The studies by Schultz and his colleagues indicate that dopaminergic neurons in the ventral tegmental area are activated not only by primary reinforcing stimuli such as food but also by conditioned reinforcers—in this case the sound that told the monkey that if it made a response, it would be rewarded. When a neutral stimulus is paired several times with a reinforcing stimulus, it acquires the ability to serve as a reinforcing stimulus itself—it becomes a **conditioned reinforcer.** The process of classical conditioning is responsible for this phenomenon: The response an animal makes to the primary reinforcer becomes attached to the conditioned reinforcer. Similarly, when a neutral stimulus is paired with an aversive stimulus, it becomes a **conditioned punisher.** Our behavior

---

conditioned reinforcer A previously neutral stimulus that has been paired with an appetitive stimulus, which then itself becomes capable of reinforcing a response.

conditioned punisher A previously neutral stimulus that has been followed by an aversive stimulus, which then itself becomes capable of punishing a response.

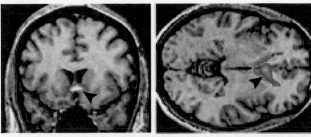
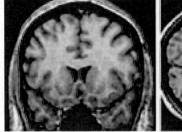
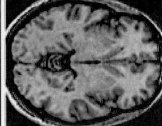

Unexpected reward

Expected reward

figure 13.45

Effects of expected and unexpected reinforcers (sips of fruit juice) on activity of the nucleus accumbens (arrows) in humans as shown by functional MRI.

(From Berns, G. S., McClure, S. M., Pagnoni, G., and Montague, P. R. *Journal of neuroscience,* 2001, *21,* 2793–2798.)

can be reinforced by an enormous variety of conditioned reinforcers, including money, good grades, and words of praise. It can also be punished by conditioned punishers such as fines, bad grades, and signs of disapproval.

What neural circuits are responsible for detecting the presence of a reinforcing stimulus (primary or conditioned) and then activating dopaminergic neurons in this region? The ventral tegmental area receives inputs from many regions of the brain. Although we still know very little about how reinforcing stimuli are detected, the three inputs that probably play the most important role in reinforcement are the amygdala, the lateral hypothalamus, and the prefrontal cortex.

As we saw in Chapter 11 and again in this chapter, the amygdala is involved in classically conditioned emotional responses. Several studies have shown that the basolateral amygdala (consisting of the lateral, basal, and accessory basal nuclei) are essential for learning about associations between neutral stimuli and reinforcing stimuli, which includes the establishment of conditioned reinforcers. For example, destruction of the amygdala or its disconnection from the visual system has no effect on monkeys' ability to recognize particular visual stimuli by sight, but it does disrupt their ability to remember which of them had previously been paired with food (Spiegler and Mishkin, 1981; Gaffan, Gaffan, and Harrison, 1988).

Hatfield et al. (1996) trained normal rats and rats with neurotoxic lesions of the basolateral amygdala to approach a food cup and eat a piece of food each time a light was illuminated. All rats learned to do so. Then the rats received four sessions designed to establish an auditory stimulus as a conditioned reinforcer. During these sessions the experimenters paired a 1500-Hz tone with the light. The results are presented in Figure 13.46. As you can see, all rats learned to put their heads into the food cup when the light was illuminated, but the rats with basolateral amygdala lesions did not investigate the food cup when the tone was presented. (See *Figure 13.46.*) Similar results were seen in a study with monkeys (Parkinson et al., 2001).

The basolateral amygdala has direct connections with both the VTA and the nucleus accumbens. Howland, Taepavarapruk, and Phillips (2002) found that stimulation of the basolateral amygdala produced a long-lasting increase in dopamine release in the nucleus accumbens, as measured by microdialysis. Presumably, these connections are activated when a neutral stimulus is paired with a reinforcing stimulus, resulting in the establishment of a conditioned reinforcer.

The inputs to the ventral tegmental area from the lateral hypothalamus may also play a role in the detection of reinforcing stimuli. For example, Burton, Rolls, and Mora (1976) studied the response characteristics of single neurons in the lateral hypothalamus and substantia

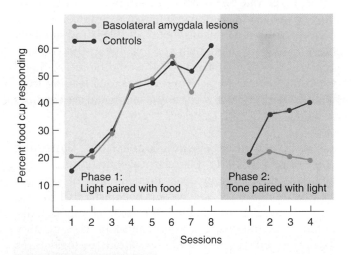

figure 13.46

Effects of lesions of the basolateral amygdala on conditioned reinforcement. During the first phase all animals learned to approach the food cup and eat the food that was delivered each time the light was illuminated. During the second phase a tone was paired with the light. Normal rats, but not rats with basolateral amygdala lesions, learned to approach the food cup when the tone was presented.

(Adapted from Holland, P. C., and Gallagher, M. *Trends in Cognitive Sciences,* 1999, *3,* 65–73. After data from Hatfield et al., 1996.)

innominata (a nearby region in the basal forebrain). They found that some neurons located there responded to either the sight or taste of food, but they did so *only if the animal was hungry*. Rolls et al. (1986) found that the firing rate of these neurons was related to an animal's willingness to eat a particular type of food. Once the animal had eaten all it wanted of a particular food, the rate of firing of these neurons fell. Then, if the experimenters presented a new food that the monkey wanted to eat, the firing rate increased again. Connections between the neurons like these and neurons in the ventral tegmental area could potentially convey information about the presence of reinforcing stimuli.

The prefrontal cortex also provides an important input to the ventral tegmental area. The terminal buttons of the axons connecting these two areas secrete glutamate, an excitatory neurotransmitter, and the activity of these synapses makes dopaminergic neurons in the ventral tegmental area fire in a bursting pattern, which greatly increases the amount of dopamine they secrete in the nucleus accumbens (Gariano and Groves, 1988). The prefrontal cortex is generally involved in devising strategies, making plans, evaluating progress made toward goals, judging the appropriateness of one's own behavior, and so on (Mesulam, 1986). Perhaps the prefrontal cortex turns on the reinforcement mechanism when it determines that the ongoing behavior is bringing the organism nearer to its goals—that the present strategy is working.

Even private behaviors such as thinking and planning may be subject to reinforcement. For example, recall the last time you were thinking about a problem and suddenly had an idea that might help you to solve it. Did you suddenly feel excited and happy? It would be interesting if we could record the activity of the axons leading from your frontal cortex to your ventral tegmental area at times like that.

■ Strengthening Neural Connections: Dopamine and Neural Plasticity

Like classical conditioning, instrumental conditioning involves strengthening of synapses located on neurons that have just been active. However, instrumental conditioning involves three elements: a discriminative stimulus, a response, and a reinforcing stimulus. How are the neural manifestations of these three elements combined?

Let's consider a hungry rat learning to press a lever and obtain food. As in classical conditioning, one element (the discriminative stimulus—in this case the lever) activates weak synapses on motor neurons responsible for a movement that causes a lever press. The second element—the particular circumstance that happened to induce the animal to press the lever—activates strong synapses, making the neurons fire. The third element comes into play only if the response is followed by a reinforcing stimulus. If it is, the reinforcement mechanism triggers the

secretion of a neurotransmitter or neuromodulator throughout the region in which the synaptic changes take place. This chemical is the third element; only if it is present can weak synapses be strengthened. Dopamine appears to serve such a role. Several studies suggest that long-term potentiation is essential for instrumental conditioning and that dopamine enhances long-term potentiation. Thus, dopamine may serve as the third element that I described in the previous paragraph.

Kelley, Smith-Roe, and Holahan (1997) found that the infusion of AP5 into the nucleus accumbens prevented rats from learning to press a lever to receive a food pellet. However, an infusion of AP5 had no effect on the behavior of animals that had already learned to press the lever. These results indicate that blocking NMDA receptors in the nucleus accumbens (and hence suppressing the establishment of long-term potentiation there) interferes with learning but not with performance of a task that has already been learned. (See *Figure 13.47*.) A subsequent study by Baldwin et al. (2000) found that instrumental conditioning could be disrupted by the infusion of AP5 into two other parts of the brain that, as we have just seen, play a role in this form of learning: the amygdala and the prefrontal cortex.

Smith-Roe and Kelley (2000) found that the presence of dopamine and the activation of NMDA receptors in the nucleus accumbens both appear to be necessary for instrumental conditioning to take place. They found that a low dose of a dopamine D1 receptor antagonist or a low dose of AP5 into the nucleus accumbens had no effect on rats' ability to learn a lever-press task. However, simultaneous infusion of the same doses of the two drugs severely impaired the ability of the animals to learn this task.

As I mentioned earlier, the prefrontal cortex may activate the reinforcement system when it detects that the animal's behavior is resulting in progress toward a goal. But the prefrontal cortex is a *target* of dopaminergic neurons as well as a source of their control. For example, Stein and Belluzzi (1989) found that rats will press a lever that produces an injection of a dopamine agonist into this region. Duvauchelle and Ettenberg (1991) found that if a rat's prefrontal cortex is electrically stimulated while the animal is in a particular location, it will learn to prefer that location to others where the stimulation did not take place. This learning appears to involve the release of dopamine, because it is prevented by injections of a drug that blocks dopamine receptors. And in a microdialysis study, Hernandez and Hoebel (1990) found that when rats were performing a food-reinforced lever-pressing task, the levels of dopamine in the prefrontal cortex increased.

Dopamine modulates long-term potentiation in the prefrontal cortex as well as in the nucleus accumbens. Gurden, Tassin, and Jay (1999) found that stimulation of the VTA enhanced long-term potentiation in the prefrontal cortex produced by electrical stimulation of the hip-

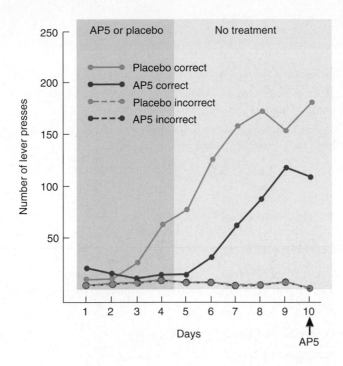

figure 13.47

Effects of AP-5, an NMDA blocker, or instrumental conditioning. Two levers were present in the apparatus, and only responses on the "correct" lever were reinforced with food. During the first four sessions the animals received infusions of AP5 or a placebo in the nucleus accumbens. During this time the placebo-treated animals began to press the "correct" lever. The drug-treated animals did not; thus, AP5 impaired acquisition of this task. However, AP5 treatment on day 10 had no effect on the behavior of animals that had already learned the task.

(Adapted from Kelley, A. E., Smith-Roe, S. L., and Holahan, M. R. *Proceedings of the National Academy of Science, USA*, 1997, *94*, 12174–12179.)

pocampus. Gurden, Takita, and Jay (2000) found that infusion of D1 receptor agonists into the prefrontal cortex did so as well, but that D1 antagonists impaired long-term potentiation. A study by Rosenkranz and Grace (1999) suggests that dopamine may facilitate long-term potentiation in the basolateral amygdala as well. These findings provide further evidence that dopamine plays a modulating role in synaptic plasticity in parts of the brain that are involved in reinforcement.

interim summary

Instrumental Conditioning and Motor Learning

Instrumental conditioning entails the strengthening of connections between neural circuits that detect stimuli and neural circuits that produce responses. One of the locations of these changes appears to be the basal ganglia, especially the changes responsible for learning of automated and routine behaviors. The basal ganglia receive sensory information and information about plans for movement from the neocortex. Damage to the basal ganglia disrupts instrumental conditioning in laboratory animals, and Parkinson's disease disrupts automatic motor responses (as opposed to deliberate ones) and even impairs learning of some tasks that do not involve learning particular movements. Electrical recording, lesion, and functional imaging studies indicate that the supplementary motor area is involved in learning sequences of movements and that the premotor cortex is involved in selecting particular movements to make in response to arbitrary stimuli.

Olds and Milner discovered that rats would perform a response that caused electrical current to be delivered through an electrode placed in their brain; thus, the stimulation was reinforcing. Subsequent studies found that stimulation of many locations had reinforcing effects but that the medial forebrain bundle produced the strongest and most reliable ones.

Although several neurotransmitters may play a role in reinforcement, one is particularly important: dopamine. The cell bodies of the most important system of dopaminergic neurons are located in the ventral tegmental area, and their axons project to the nucleus accumbens, prefrontal cortex, and amygdala.

Infusions of dopamine agonists directly into the nucleus accumbens will reinforce an animal's behavior. Both laboratory animals and humans will self-administer dopamine agonists such as amphetamine or cocaine; laboratory animals will press a lever to have amphetamine injected directly into the nucleus accumbens. Microdialysis studies have also shown that natural and artificial reinforcers stimulate the release of dopamine in the nucleus accumbens. The system of neurons that detect reinforcing stimuli and activate the dopaminergic neurons in the mesolimbic and mesocortical systems probably involves the amygdala, lateral hypothalamus, and prefrontal cortex; these neurons fire in response to various categories of stimuli that are capable of reinforcing an animal's behavior. Damage to the amygdala disrupts conditioned reinforcement. The frontal cortex may play a role in reinforcement that occurs when our own behavior brings us nearer to a goal.

Dopamine induces synaptic plasticity by facilitating associative long-term potentiation. Evidence indicates that dopamine can facilitate long-term potentiation in the nucleus accumbens, amygdala, and prefrontal cortex.

Suggested Readings

Gazzaniga, M. S. *The Mind's Past.* Berkeley, CA: University of California Press, 1998.

Lisman, J., Schulman, H., and Cline, H. The molecular basis of CaMKII function in synaptic and behavioural memory. *Nature Reviews: Neuroscience*, 2002, *3*, 175–190.

McGaugh, J. L., Weinberger, N. M., and Lynch, G. *Brain and Memory: Modulation and Mediation of Neuroplasticity.* New York: Oxford University Press, 1995.

Squire, L. R., and Kandel, E. R. *Memory: From Mind to Molecules.* New York: Scientific American Library, 1999.

Suggested Web Sites

Neural Plasticity and LTP Page

http://hallux.medschool.hscbklyn.edu/~eric/#Plastica

The site contains tutorials relating to neural plasticity and to long-term potentiation.

Medial Temporal Lobe and Memory

http://thalamus.wustl.edu/course/limbic.html

The site contains an overview of the limbic system anatomy supplemented by several line-art diagrams illustrating the anatomy of the amygdala and hippocampus.

Learning and Memory

http://brembs.net/

This site provides a basic tutorial on mechanisms of learning and of memory.

Tutorials on Learning and Memory

http://psy71.dur.ac.uk/Education/memory/index.html

The site contains a link to a tutorial on learning and memory.

Relational Learning and Amnesia

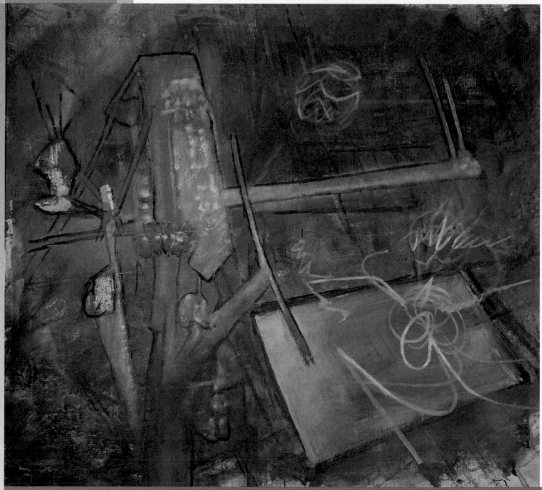

Roberto Matta-Echaurren, *L'Inconnear (the "Unknower"), 1951.* © 2003 Artists Rights Society (ARS) New York/ADAGP, Paris.
© Erich Lessing/Art Resource, NY.

outline

■ **Human Anterograde Amnesia**
Basic Description
Spared Learning Abilities
Declarative and Nondeclarative Memories
Anterograde Amnesia: Failure
    of Relational Learning
Anatomy of Anterograde Amnesia
Role of the Medial Temporal Lobe
    in Spatial Memory
Role of the Medial Temporal Lobe
    in Memory Retrieval

Confabulation: Role of the Prefrontal
    Cortex in Evaluating the Accuracy
    of Memories
Interim Summary
■ **Relational Learning in
    Laboratory Animals**
Remembering Places Visited
Spatial Perception and Learning
Role of the Hippocampal Formation
    in Memory Consolidation

Place Cells in the Hippocampal
    Formation
Role of Long-Term Potentiation
    in Relational Learning
Modulation of Hippocampal Functions
    by Monoaminergic and
    Acetylcholinergic Inputs
Theoretical Explanations of
    Hippocampal Functioning
Interim Summary

Patient H. M. has a relatively pure amnesia. His intellectual ability and his immediate verbal memory appear to be normal. He can repeat seven numbers forward and five numbers backward, and he can carry on conversations, rephrase sentences, and perform mental arithmetic. He is unable to remember events that occurred during several years preceding his brain surgery, but he can recall older memories very well. He showed no personality change after the operation, and he appears to be generally polite and good-natured.

However, since the operation, H. M. has been unable to learn anything new. He cannot identify by name people he has met since the operation (performed in 1953, when he was twenty-seven years old). His family moved to a new house after his operation, and he never learned how to get around in the new neighborhood. (He now lives in a nursing home, where he can be cared for.) He is aware of his disorder and often says something like this:

> Every day is alone in itself, whatever enjoyment I've had, and whatever sorrow I've had. . . . Right now, I'm wondering. Have I done or said anything amiss? You see, at this moment everything looks clear to me, but what happened just before? That's what worries me. It's like waking from a dream; I just don't remember. (Milner, 1970, p. 37)

H. M. is capable of remembering a small amount of verbal information as long as he is not distracted; constant rehearsal can keep information in his immediate memory for a long time. However, rehearsal does not appear to have any long-term effects; if he is distracted for a moment, he will completely forget whatever he had been rehearsing. He works very well at repetitive tasks. Indeed, because he so quickly forgets what previously happened, he does not easily become bored. He can endlessly reread the same magazine or laugh at the same jokes, finding them fresh and new each time. His time is typically spent solving crossword puzzles and watching television.

Chapter 13 discussed relatively simple forms of learning, which can be understood as changes in circuits of neurons that detect the presence of particular stimuli or as strengthened connections between neurons that analyze sensory information and those that produce responses. But most forms of learning are more complex; most memories of real objects and events are related to other memories. Seeing a photograph of an old friend may remind you of the sound of the person's name and of the movements you have to make to pronounce it. You may also be reminded of things you have done with your friend: places you have visited, conversations you have had, experiences you have shared. Each of these memories can contain a series of events, complete with sights and sounds, that you will be able to recall in the proper sequence. Obviously, the neural circuits in the visual association cortex that recognize your friend's face are connected to circuits in many other parts of the brain, and these circuits are connected to many others. This chapter discusses research on relational learning, which includes the establishment and retrieval of memories of events and episodes.

Human Anterograde Amnesia

One of the most dramatic and intriguing phenomena caused by brain damage is *anterograde amnesia*, which, at first glance, appears to be the inability to learn new information. However, when we examine the phenomenon more carefully, we find that the basic abilities of perceptual learning, stimulus-response learning, and motor learning are intact but that complex relational learning, of the type I just described, is gone. This section discusses the nature of anterograde amnesia in humans and its anatomical basis. The section that follows discusses related research with laboratory animals.

The term **anterograde amnesia** refers to difficulty in learning new information. A person with pure anterograde amnesia can remember events that occurred in the past, during the time before the brain damage occurred, but cannot retain information he or she encounters *after* the damage. In contrast, **retrograde amnesia** refers to the inability to remember events that happened *before* the brain damage occurred. (See *Figure 14.1.*) As we will see, pure anterograde amnesia is rare; usually, there is also a retrograde amnesia for events that occurred for a period of time before the brain damage occurred.

In 1889 Sergei Korsakoff, a Russian physician, first described a severe memory impairment caused by brain damage, and the disorder was given his name. The most profound symptom of **Korsakoff's syndrome** is a severe anterograde amnesia: The patients appear to be unable to form new memories, although they can still remember old ones. They can converse normally and can remember events that happened long before their brain damage occurred, but they cannot remember events that happened afterward.

Korsakoff's syndrome is usually (but not always) a result of chronic alcoholism. The disorder actually results

---

anterograde amnesia Amnesia for events that occur after some disturbance to the brain, such as head injury or certain degenerative brain diseases.

retrograde amnesia Amnesia for events that preceded some disturbance to the brain, such as a head injury or electroconvulsive shock.

Korsakoff's syndrome Permanent anterograde amnesia caused by brain damage resulting from chronic alcoholism or malnutrition.

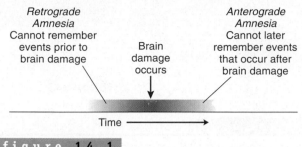

figure 14.1

A schematic definition of retrograde amnesia and anterograde amnesia.

from a thiamine (vitamin B_1) deficiency caused by the alcoholism (Adams, 1969; Haas, 1988). Because alcoholics receive a substantial number of calories from the alcohol they ingest, they usually eat a poor diet, so their vitamin intake is consequently low. Furthermore, alcohol interferes with intestinal absorption of thiamine. The ensuing deficiency produces brain damage. Thiamine is essential for a step in metabolism: the carboxylation of pyruvate, an intermediate product in the breakdown of carbohydrates, fats, and amino acids. Korsakoff's syndrome sometimes occurs in people who have been severely malnourished and have then received intravenous infusions of glucose; the sudden availability of glucose to the cells of the brain without adequate thiamine with which to metabolize it damages the cells, probably because they accumulate pyruvate. Hence, standard medical practice is to administer thiamine along with intravenous glucose to severely malnourished patients. I will discuss the location of the brain damage that causes Korsakoff's syndrome later in this chapter.

Another symptom of Korsakoff's syndrome is **confabulation.** When people with this disorder are asked about events that occurred recently, they often describe a fictitious event rather than simply saying, "I don't remember." (Notice that *confabulate* has the same root as *fable.*) Confabulations can contain mixtures of things that really occurred, or they can be completely imaginary. People who confabulate are not deliberately trying to deceive; they appear to believe that what they are saying really occurred. I will describe some research on confabulation later in this chapter.

Anterograde amnesia can also be caused by damage to the temporal lobes. Scoville and Milner (1957) reported that bilateral removal of the medial temporal lobe produced a memory impairment in humans that was apparently identical to that seen in Korsakoff's syndrome. Thirty operations had been performed on psychotic patients in an attempt to alleviate their mental disorder, but it was not until this operation was performed on patient H. M. that the anterograde amnesia was discovered. The psychotic patients' behavior was already so disturbed that their amnesia was not detected. However, patient H. M. was reasonably intelligent and was not psychotic; therefore, his

postoperative deficit was discovered immediately. He had received the surgery in an attempt to treat his very severe epilepsy, which could not be controlled even by high doses of anticonvulsant medication. The epilepsy appears to have been caused by a head injury he received when he was struck by a bicycle at age nine (Corkin et al., 1997).

The surgery successfully treated H. M.'s seizure disorder, but it became apparent that the operation had produced a serious memory impairment. Subsequently, Scoville and Milner (1957) examined eight of the psychotic patients who were coherent enough to cooperate with them. Careful testing revealed that some of these patients also had anterograde amnesia; the deficit appeared to occur only when the hippocampus was removed. They concluded that the hippocampus was the critical structure destroyed by the surgery. Once it was discovered that bilateral medial temporal lobectomy causes anterograde amnesia, neurosurgeons stopped performing them and are now careful to operate on only one temporal lobe.

Basic Description

H. M.'s history and memory deficits were described in the introduction to this chapter (Milner, Corkin, and Teuber, 1968; Milner, 1970; Corkin et al., 1981). Because of his relatively pure amnesia, he has been extensively studied. Milner and her colleagues based the following conclusions on his pattern of deficits:

1. *The hippocampus is not the location of long-term memories; nor is it necessary for the retrieval of long-term memories.* If it were, H. M. would not have been able to remember events from early in his life, he would not know how to talk, he would not know how to dress himself, and so on.

2. *The hippocampus is not the location of immediate (short-term) memories.* If it were, H. M. would not be able to carry on a conversation, because he would not remember what the other person said long enough to think of a reply.

3. *The hippocampus is involved in converting immediate (short-term) memories into long-term memories.* This conclusion is based on a particular hypothesis of memory function: that our immediate memory of an event is retained by neural activity and that long-term memories consist of relatively permanent biochemical or structural changes in neurons. The conclusion seems a reasonable explanation for the fact that when presented with new information, H. M. seems to understand it and remember it as long as he thinks about it but that a permanent record of the information is just never made.

confabulation The reporting of memories of events that did not take place without the intention to deceive; seen in people with Korsakoff's syndrome.

As we will see, these three conclusions are too simple. Subsequent research on patients with anterograde amnesia indicates that the facts are more complicated—and more interesting—than they first appeared to be. But to appreciate the significance of the findings of more recent research, we must understand these three conclusions and remember the facts that led to them.

Many psychologists believe that learning consists of at least two stages: short-term memory and long-term memory. They conceive of short-term memory as a means of storing a limited amount of information temporarily and long-term memory as a means of storing an unlimited amount (or at least an enormously large amount) of information permanently. **Short-term memory** is an immediate memory for stimuli that have just been perceived. We can remember a new item of information (such as a telephone number) for as long as we want to by engaging in a particular behavior: rehearsal. However, once we stop rehearsing the information, we might or might not be able to remember it later; that is, the information might or might not get stored in **long-term memory.**

Short-term memory can hold only a limited amount of information. To demonstrate this fact, read the following numbers to yourself just once, and then close your eyes and recite them back.

1 4 9 2 3 0 7

You probably had no trouble remembering them. Now try the following set of numbers, and go through them *only once* before you close your eyes.

7 2 5 2 3 9 1 6 5 8 4

Very few people can repeat eleven numbers; in fact, you might not have even bothered to try, once you saw how many numbers there were. Therefore, short-term memory has definite limits. But of course, if you wanted to, you could recite the numbers again and again until you had memorized them; that is, you could rehearse the information in short-term memory until it was eventually stored in long-term memory. Long-term memory has no known limits; and as its name suggests, it is relatively durable. Presumably, it is a result of changes in synaptic strength, such as the ones responsible for long-term potentiation. If we stop thinking about something we have just perceived (that is, something contained in short-term memory), we might or might not remember the information later. However, information in long-term memory need not be continuously rehearsed; once we have learned something, we can stop thinking about it until we need the information at a future time.

The simplest model of the memory process says that sensory information enters short-term memory, rehearsal keeps it there, and eventually, the information makes its way into long-term memory, where it is permanently

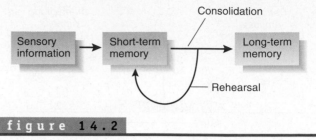

figure 14.2

A simple model of the learning process.

stored. The conversion of short-term memories into long-term memories has been called **consolidation,** because the memories are "made solid," so to speak. (See *Figure 14.2.*)

Now you can understand the original conclusions of Milner and her colleagues: If H. M.'s short-term memory is intact and if he can remember events from before his operation, then the problem must be that consolidation does not take place. Thus, the role of the hippocampal formation in memory is consolidation—converting short-term memories to long-term memories.

Spared Learning Abilities

H. M.'s memory deficit is striking and dramatic. However, when he and other patients with anterograde amnesia are studied more carefully, it becomes apparent that the amnesia does not represent a total failure in learning ability. When the patients are appropriately trained and tested, we find that they are capable of three of the four major types of learning described in Chapter 13: perceptual learning, sensory-response learning, and motor learning. A review by Spiers, Maguire, and Burgess (2001) summarized 147 cases of anterograde amnesia that are consistent with the description that follow.

First, let us consider perceptual learning. Figure 14.3 shows two sample items from a test of the ability to recognize broken drawings; note how the drawings are successively more complete. (See *Figure 14.3.*) Subjects are first shown the least complete set (set I) of each of twenty different drawings. If they do not recognize a figure (and most people do not recognize set I), they are shown more complete sets until they identify it. One hour later, the subjects are tested again for retention, starting with set I. H. M. was given this test and, when retested an hour later, showed

short-term memory Immediate memory for events, which may or may not be consolidated into long-term memory.

long-term memory Relatively stable memory of events that occurred in the more distant past, as opposed to short-term memory.

consolidation The process by which short-term memories are converted into long-term memories.

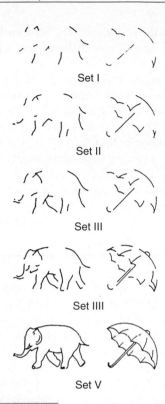

Set I

Set II

Set III

Set IIII

Set V

figure 14.3

Examples of broken drawings.

(Reprinted with permission of author and publisher from Gollin, E. S. Developmental studies of visual recognition of incomplete objects. *Perceptual and Motor Skills*, 1960, *11*, 289–298.)

acquire a classically conditioned eyeblink response. H. M. even showed retention of the task two years later: He acquired the response again in one-tenth the number of trials that were needed previously. Sidman, Stoddard, and Mohr (1968) successfully trained patient H. M. on an instrumental conditioning task—a visual discrimination task in which pennies were given for correct responses.

Finally, several studies have demonstrated motor learning in patients with anterograde amnesia. Milner and her colleagues presented H. M. with a mirror-drawing task (Milner, 1965). This procedure requires the subject to trace the outline of a figure (in this case, a star) with a pencil while looking at the figure in a mirror. (See *Figure 14.4*.) The task might seem simple, but it is actually rather difficult and requires some practice to perform well. With practice, H. M. became proficient at mirror drawing; his errors were reduced considerably during the first session, and his improvement was retained on subsequent days of testing. (I have prepared a computerized version of this task on *Animation 14.1, Implicit Memory Tasks: Mirror Drawing*.)

> See the interactive CD for more on mirror drawings.

Reber and Squire (1998) found that subjects with anterograde amnesia could learn a sequence of button presses. They sat in front of a computer screen and watched an asterisk appear—apparently randomly—in one of four locations. Their task was to press the one of four buttons that corresponded to the location of the asterisk. As soon as they did so, the asterisk moved to a new

considerable improvement (Milner, 1970). When he was retested four months later, he *still* showed this improvement. His performance was not as good as that of normal control subjects, but he showed unmistakable evidence of long-term retention. (You can try this task yourself by running *Animation 14.1, Implicit Memory Tasks: Broken Drawings*.)

> See the interactive CD for more on broken drawings.

Johnson, Kim, and Risse (1985) found that patients with anterograde amnesia could learn to recognize faces and melodies. They played unfamiliar melodies from Korean songs to amnesic patients and found that when they were tested later, the patients preferred these melodies to ones they had not heard before. The experimenters also presented photographs of two men along with stories of their lives: One man was dishonest, mean, and vicious, and the other was nice enough to invite home to dinner. Twenty days later, the amnesic patients said they liked the picture of the "nice" man better than that of the "nasty" one.

Investigators have also succeeded in demonstrating stimulus-response learning by H. M. and other amnesic subjects. For example, Woodruff-Pak (1993) found that H. M. and another patient with anterograde amnesia could

figure 14.4

The mirror-drawing task.

DBCACBDCBA

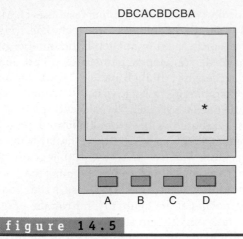

figure 14.5

The procedure of the study by Reber and Squire (1998). Subjects pressed the button in a sequence indicated by movement of the asterisk on the computer screen.

location, and they pressed the corresponding button. (See *Figure 14.5.*)

Although experimenters did not say so, the sequence of button presses specified by the moving asterisk was not random. For example, it might be DBCACBDCBA, a ten-item sequence that is repeated continuously. With practice subjects become faster and faster at this task. It is clear that their rate increases because they have learned the sequence, because if the sequence is changed, their performance decreases. The amnesic subjects learned this task just as well as normal subjects did.

As you can see, patients with anterograde amnesia are capable of a variety of forms of perceptual learning, stimulus-response learning, and motor learning.

Declarative and Nondeclarative Memories

If amnesic patients can learn tasks like these, you might ask, why do we call them *amnesic?* The answer is this: Although the patients can learn to perform these tasks, they do not remember anything about having learned them. They do not remember the experimenters, the room in which the training took place, the apparatus that was used, or any events that occurred during the training. Although H. M. learned to recognize the broken drawings, he denied that he had ever seen them before. Although the amnesic patients in the study by Johnson, Kim, and Risse learned to like some of the Korean melodies better, they did not recognize that they had heard them before; nor did they remember having seen the pictures of the two young men. Although H. M. successfully acquired a classically conditioned eyeblink response, he did not remember the experimenter, the apparatus, or the headband he wore that held the device that delivered a puff of air to his eye.

In the experiment by Sidman, Stoddard, and Mohr, although H. M. learned to make the correct response (press a panel with a picture of a circle on it), he was unable to recall having done so. In fact, once H. M. had learned the task, the experimenters interrupted him, had him count his pennies (to distract him for a little while), and then asked him to say what he was supposed to do. He seemed puzzled by the question; he had absolutely no idea. But when they turned on the stimuli again, he immediately made the correct response. Finally, although the amnesic subjects in Reber and Squire's study obviously learned the sequence of finger movements, they were completely unaware that there was, in fact, a sequence; they thought that the movement of the asterisk was random.

It should be clear by now that the words *learning* and *memory* refer to a variety of different processes. For example, as we saw in Chapters 11 and 13, the amygdala is involved in emotional learning—in particular, in the establishment of conditioned emotional responses. A study by Bechara et al. (1995) showed that the hippocampus and the amygdala play very different roles in the development of emotional and episodic memories. The investigators studied patients with different brain lesions. Patient S. M. had bilateral amygdala damage, and patient W. C. had bilateral hippocampal damage. The patients were shown a random series of red, green, yellow, and blue lights. Each time the blue light was presented, the experimenters sounded a boat horn that made a very loud—and very unpleasant—noise. The noise elicited an emotional reaction in all subjects: a change in the electrical resistance of the skin that is caused by increased activity of the sympathetic nervous system. Patient W. C., who had hippocampal damage, showed a conditioned emotional response: a change in skin resistance when the blue light was presented. As we would predict, patient S. M., whose amygdala was damaged, did not show such a response. Thus, amygdala lesions disrupt the establishment of simple conditioned emotional responses but hippocampal lesions do not.

The opposite pattern was seen when the patients were asked about what had happened. Patient S. M., with amygdala damage, said that the boat horn was sounded every time the blue light was presented. Patient W. C., who had hippocampal damage, could not remember anything about what had occurred during the experimental procedure. (A third patient, R. H., had bilateral damage to both the hippocampus and amygdala. Both kinds of learning were disrupted in this patient.) Clearly, episodic memories and conditioned emotional memories involve different neural circuits, and knowing that a stimulus is associated with the occurrence of a noxious event is not the same as having a conditioned fear response to that stimulus.

The distinction between what people with anterograde amnesia can and cannot learn is obviously important, because it reflects the basic organization of the learning process. Clearly, there are at least two major categories of memories. Psychologists have given them several different names. For example, some investigators (Eichenbaum, Otto, and Cohen, 1992; Squire, 1992) suggest that patients with anterograde amnesia are unable to form **declarative memories,** which have been defined as those that are "explicitly available to conscious recollection as facts, events, or specific stimuli" (Squire, Shimamura, and Amaral, 1989, p. 218). The term *declarative* obviously comes from *declare,* which means "to proclaim; to announce." The term reflects the fact that patients with anterograde amnesia cannot talk about experiences that they have had since the time of their brain damage. Thus, according to Squire and his colleagues, declarative memory is memory of events and facts that we can think and talk about.

The other category of memories, often called **nondeclarative memories,** includes instances of perceptual, stimulus-response, and motor learning that we are not necessarily conscious of. (Some psychologists refer to these two categories as *explicit* and *implicit* memories, respectively.) Nondeclarative memories appear to operate automatically. They do not require deliberate attempts on the part of the learner to memorize something. They do not seem to include facts or experiences; instead, they control behaviors. If someone asks us a question about a fact that we have learned or something that we have experienced, the question evokes images in the declarative (or explicit) memory system that we can then describe in words. For example, suppose that someone asks you how many windows your house has. If you have never answered that question before, you will probably do so by taking a mental tour of your house, going from room to room and counting the windows you see there. The question evokes the image (that is, gets you to call up a memory), which you then examine.

In contrast, nondeclarative (implicit) memories are not something we answer questions about. Suppose we learn to ride a bicycle. We do so quite consciously and develop declarative memories about our attempts: who helped us learn, where we rode, how we felt, how many times we fell, and so on. But we also form nondeclarative stimulus-response and motor memories; *we learn to ride.* We learn to make automatic adjustments with our hands and bodies that keep our center of gravity above the wheels. Most of us cannot describe the rules that govern our behavior. For example, what do you think you must do if you start falling to the right while riding a bicycle? Many cyclists would say that they compensate by leaning to the left. But they are wrong; what they really do is turn the handlebars

declarative memory Memory that can be verbally expressed, such as memory for events in a person's past.

nondeclarative memory Memory whose formation does not depend on the hippocampal formation; a collective term for perceptual, stimulus-response, and motor memory.

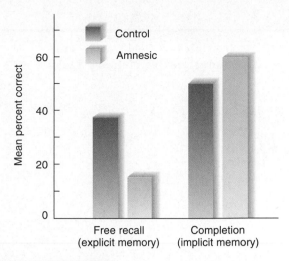

figure 14.6

Explicit and implicit memory of amnesic patients and control subjects. The performance of amnesic patients was impaired when they were instructed to try to recall the words they had previously seen but not when they were asked to say the first word that came into their minds.
(Based on data from Graf, Squire, and Mandler, 1984.)

to the right. Leaning to the left would actually make them fall faster, because it would force the bicycle even farther to the right. The point is that although they have learned to make the appropriate movements (which involve stimulus-response and motor learning), they cannot necessarily describe in words what these movements are.

Graf, Squire, and Mandler (1984) demonstrated perceptual learning for verbal stimuli in subjects with anterograde amnesia. They showed lists of six-letter words to amnesic and nonamnesic subjects and asked them to study each one carefully and rate how much they liked them. The purpose of the rating was to make sure that the subjects spent some time thinking about each word. The investigators then administered two types of memory tests. In the *explicit memory* (declarative memory) condition they asked the subjects to recall the words they had seen. In the *implicit memory* (nondeclarative memory) condition they presented cards containing the first three letters of the words. For example, if one of the words had been DEFINE, they would have been shown a card on which DEF was printed. Several different six-letter words besides *define* begin with the letters DEF, such as *deface, defame, defeat, defect, defend, defied,* and *deform,* so there are several possible responses. The investigators asked the subjects simply to say the first word that started with those letters that came into their minds. As Figure 14.6 shows, the amnesic subjects explicitly remembered fewer than half as many words as the control subjects, but the two groups performed equally well on the implicit memory task. (See *Figure 14.6.*)

table 14.1

Examples of Declarative and Nondeclarative Memory Tasks	
DECLARATIVE MEMORY TASKS	
Remembering past experiences	
Learning new words	
Recalling words (DEF___)	
NONDECLARATIVE MEMORY TASKS	**TYPE OF LEARNING**
Broken drawings	Perceptual
Faster recognition of words and pictures	Perceptual
Recognizing faces	Perceptual (and stimulus-response?)
Recognizing melodies	Perceptual
Classical conditioning (eyeblink)	Stimulus-Response
Instrumental conditioning (choose circle)	Stimulus-Response
Mirror drawing	Motor
Sequence of button presses	Motor
Conditioned emotional response (blue light + boat horn)	Stimulus-Response
Word completion (DEF___)	Stimulus-Response

Table 14.1 lists the declarative and nondeclarative memory tasks that I have described so far. (See **Table 14.1**.)

Anterograde Amnesia: Failure of Relational Learning

As we have seen, anterograde amnesia appears to be a loss of the ability to establish new declarative memories; the ability to establish new nondeclarative memories (perceptual, stimulus-response, or motor learning) is intact. What, exactly, are declarative memories? Are they *verbal* memories? Is it simply that people with anterograde amnesia cannot learn new verbal information?

Clearly, verbal learning *is* disrupted in anterograde amnesia. Gabrieli, Cohen, and Corkin (1988) found that patient H. M. does not seem to have learned any words that have been introduced into the English language since his surgery. For example, he defined *biodegradable* as "two grades," *flower child* as "a young person who grows flowers," and *soul food* as "forgiveness." As the authors noted, for H. M., modern-day English is partly a foreign language. But declarative memories are not necessarily *verbal* memories; they are retelling of things or events we have previously experienced.

Anterograde amnesia includes more than a verbal memory deficit. Let us consider the most complex forms of declarative memories: memories of particular episodes. **Episodic memories** consist of collections of perceptions of events organized in time and identified by a particular context. For example, consider my memory of this morning's breakfast. I put on my robe and slippers, walked downstairs, made coffee, drank some orange juice, made waffle batter, baked a waffle, and ate it at the table next to the window. If I wanted to (and if I thought you were interested), I could give you many more details. The point is that the memory contains many events, organized in time. But would we say that my memory is a *verbal* memory? Clearly not; what I remember about my experience this morning is perceptions of a series of *events,* not a series of *words.* I remember not words but perceptions: the sight of the snow falling outside, the feel of the cold floor replaced by the comfortable warmth of my slippers, the smell of the coffee beans as I opened the container, the rasping sound made by the coffee grinder, and so on.

What started my reminiscence about this morning's breakfast? In this case it was prompted by my thinking about how to explain a particular concept to you. But suppose that you had asked me to tell you about this morning's breakfast. Your words would bring to mind memories of what happened, and I would then describe these memories to you. That sounds simple enough, but in fact, what happens must be extraordinarily complex. The phrase *this morning's breakfast* makes me think of a particular episode. My memory contains many details about many breakfasts, and if I wanted to, I could describe a good number of them. The distinguishing feature among them is the context: today's breakfast, yesterday's breakfast, the first breakfast in a hotel room in Paris, and so on. How do I keep them straight and tell you about the right one?

Obviously, memories must be organized. When you ask me about this morning's breakfast, your words bring to mind a *set* of perceptual memories—memories of events that occurred at a particular time and place. What does the hippocampal formation have to do with that ability? The most likely explanation is that during the original experience, it somehow ties together a series of perceptions in such a way that their memories, too, are linked. The hippocampal formation enables us to learn the *relationship* between the stimuli that were present at the time—the *context* in which the episode occurred—and the events themselves. As we saw, people with anterograde amnesia can form perceptual memories. As the perceptual learning studies have shown, once they see something, they are more likely to recognize it later. But their perceptual memories are isolated; the memories of individual objects and events are not tied together or to the context in which they occurred. Thus, see-

episodic memory Memory of a collection of perceptions of events organized in time and identified by a particular context.

ing a particular person does not remind them of other times they have seen that person or of the things they have done together. In fact, they do not even say that they have a feeling of familiarity when they see someone they have met many times after they became amnesic. Anterograde amnesia appears to be a loss of the ability to learn about the relationships among stimuli, including the time and place in which they occurred and the order of their occurrence.

Why have I introduced the term *relational learning?* Why not simply use the term *declarative?* If we consider only humans, there would probably be no reason to introduce a new term. But as we will see later in this chapter, nonverbal animals can have anterograde amnesia, too. And obviously, the term *declarative* cannot apply to animals that cannot talk. Therefore, we must look beyond a verbal–nonverbal distinction to understand what functions have been disrupted. And that is exactly what we will do when we consider research with laboratory animals later in this chapter. I will develop the idea of relational learning more fully there, in the section devoted to theoretical explanations of hippocampal functioning.

Anatomy of Anterograde Amnesia

The phenomenon of anterograde amnesia—and its implications for the nature of relational learning—has led investigators to study this phenomenon in laboratory animals. But before I review this research (which has provided some very interesting results), we should examine the brain damage that produces anterograde amnesia. One fact is clear: Damage to the hippocampus or to regions that supply its inputs and receive its outputs causes anterograde amnesia.

Connections of the Hippocampal Formation with the Rest of the Brain

As we saw in Chapter 13, the hippocampal formation consists of the dentate gyrus, the CA fields of the hippocampus itself, and the subiculum (and its subregions). The most important input to the hippocampal formation is the entorhinal cortex; neurons there have axons that terminate in the dentate gyrus, CA3, and CA1. The entorhinal cortex receives its inputs from the amygdala, various regions of the limbic cortex, and all association regions of the neocortex, either directly or via two adjacent regions of limbic cortex: the **perirhinal cortex** and the **parahippocampal cortex.** Collectively, these three regions constitute the limbic cortex of the medial temporal lobe. (See *Figure 14.7*.)

The outputs of the hippocampal system come primarily from field CA1 and the subiculum. Most of these outputs are relayed back through the entorhinal, perirhinal, and parahippocampal cortex to the same regions of association cortex that provide inputs.

As we saw earlier in this chapter, the hippocampus is not the location of either short-term or long-term memories;

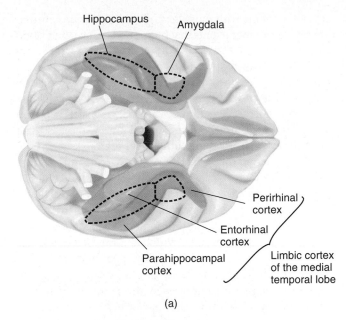

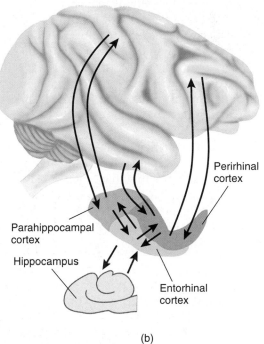

figure 14.7

Cortical connections of the hippocampal formation. (a) A view of the base of a monkey's brain. (b) Connections with the cerebral cortex.

perirhinal cortex A region of limbic cortex adjacent to the hippocampal formation that, along with the parahippocampal cortex, relays information between the entorhinal cortex and other regions of the brain.

parahippocampal cortex A region of limbic cortex adjacent to the hippocampal formation that, along with the perirhinal cortex, relays information between the entorhinal cortex and other regions of the brain.

after all, patients with damage to the hippocampal formation can remember events that happened before their brain became damaged, and their short-term memory is relatively normal. But the hippocampal formation clearly plays a role in the process through which declarative memories are formed. Most researchers believe that the process works something like this: The hippocampus receives information about what is going on from sensory and motor association cortex and from some subcortical regions, such as the basal ganglia and amygdala. It processes this information and then, through its *efferent* connections with these regions, modifies the memories that are being consolidated there, linking them together in ways that will permit us to remember the relationships among the elements of the memories—for example, the order in which events occurred, the context in which we perceived a particular item, and so on. Without the hippocampal formation we would be left with individual, isolated memories without the linkage that makes it possible to remember episodes and contexts.

If the hippocampus does modify memories as they are being formed, then experiences that lead to declarative memories should activate the hippocampal formation. In fact, several studies have found this prediction to be true. In general, pictorial or spatial information activates the right hippocampal formation, and verbal information activates the left hippocampal formation. For example, Brewer et al. (1998) had normal subjects look at a series of complex color photos and later tested their ability to say whether they remembered them. (As we saw, people with anterograde amnesia are capable of perceptual learning, but they cannot *say* whether they have seen a particular item.) While the subjects were studying the pictures the first time, the experimenters recorded regional brain activity by functional MRI. Brewer and his colleagues found that the pictures that the subjects were most likely to

remember later were those that caused the most activation of the right hippocampal region, suggesting that this region was involved in the encoding phase of memory formation. A study by Alkire et al. (1998) found that activation of the left hippocampal formation was related to a person's ability to remember a list of words: Those subjects with the greatest amount of activation showed the best memory for the words. (See *Figure 14.8.*)

The hippocampal formation also receives input from subcortical regions via the fornix. As far as we know, these inputs select and modulate the functions of the hippocampal formation but do not supply it with specific information. (An analogy might make this distinction clearer. An antenna supplies a radio with information that is being broadcast, whereas the on–off switch, the volume control, and the station selector control the radio's functions.) The hippocampal formation receives dopaminergic input from the ventral tegmental area, noradrenergic input from the locus coeruleus, serotonergic input from the raphe nuclei, and acetylcholinergic input from the medial septum. The release of these neurotransmitters modulates hippocampal functions. The hippocampal formation also sends a set of efferent fibers through the fornix to nuclei contained in the mammillary bodies, located at the caudal end of the hypothalamus. These fibers *do* seem to contain information that has been processed by the hippocampal formation. The mammillary bodies send axons to the anterior thalamus, which in turn sends axons to the cingulate cortex. (See *Figure 14.9.*)

Evidence That Hippocampal Damage Causes Anterograde Amnesia

The clearest evidence that damage to the hippocampal formation produces anterograde amnesia came from a case studied by Zola-Morgan, Squire, and Amaral (1986).

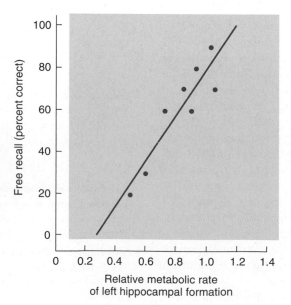

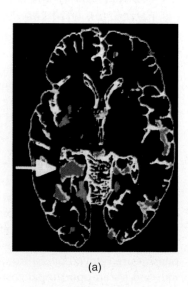

figure 14.8

Involvement of the hippocampal formation in encoding of declarative memories. (a) Regions whose metabolic activity during learning correlated with likelihood of recall later. "Hot" colors reflect positive correlations; "cool" colors reflect negative correlations. The arrow points to the hippocampal formation. (b) Percentage correct during free recall as a function of relative metabolic rate of the left hippocampal formation of the nine subjects in the study.
(Adapted from Alkire, M. T., Haier, R. J., Fallon, J. H., and Cahill, L. *Proceedings of the National Academy of Sciences, USA*, 1998, *95*, 14506–14510.)

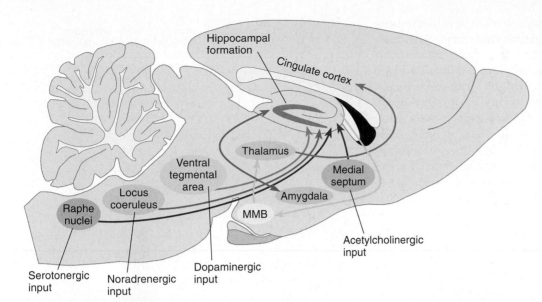

figure 14.9

A midsagittal view of a rat brain showing the major subcortical connections of the hippocampal formation.

Patient R. B., a 52-year-old man with a history of heart trouble, sustained a cardiac arrest. Although his heart was successfully restarted, the period of anoxia caused by the temporary halt in blood flow resulted in brain damage. The primary symptom of this brain damage was a permanent anterograde amnesia, which Zola-Morgan and his colleagues carefully documented. Five years after the onset of the amnesia, R. B. died of heart failure. His family gave permission for histological examination of his brain.

The investigators discovered that field CA1 of the hippocampal formation was gone; its neurons had completely degenerated. Subsequent studies reported other patients with anterograde amnesia caused by CA1 damage (Victor and Agamonolis, 1990; Kartsounis, Rudge, and Stevens, 1995; Rempel-Clower et al., 1996). (See *Figure 14.10.*) In addition, several studies have found that a period of anoxia causes damage to field CA1 in monkeys and in rats and that the damage causes anterograde amnesia in these species, too (Auer, Jensen, and Whishaw, 1989; Zola-Morgan et al., 1992).

Why is field CA1 of the hippocampus so sensitive to anoxia? The answer appears to lie in the fact that this region is especially rich in NMDA receptors. For some reason metabolic disturbances of various kinds, including seizures, anoxia, or hypoglycemia, cause glutamatergic terminal buttons to release glutamate at abnormally high

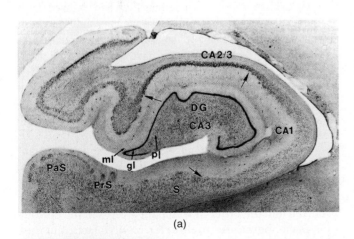

(a)

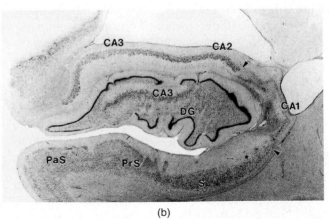

(b)

figure 14.10

Damage to field CA1 caused by anoxia. (a) Section through a normal hippocampus. (b) Section through the hippocampus of patient G. D. The pyramidal cells of field CA1 (between the two arrowheads) have degenerated. (DG = dentate gyrus, gl, ml, pl = layers of the dentate gyrus, PaS = parasubiculum, PrS = presubiculum, S = subiculum).

(From Rempel-Clower, N. L., Zola, S. M., Squire, L. R., and Amaral, D. G. *Journal of Neuroscience,* 1996, *16,* 5233–5255. Reprinted with permission.)

levels. The effect of this glutamate release is to stimulate NMDA receptors, which permit the entry of calcium. Within a few minutes excessive amounts of intracellular calcium begins to destroy the neurons. If animals are pre-treated with drugs that block NMDA receptors, a period of anoxia is much less likely to produce brain damage (Rothman and Olney, 1987). CA1 neurons contain many NMDA receptors, so long-term potentiation can quickly become established there. This flexibility undoubtedly contributes to our ability to learn as quickly as we do. But it also renders these neurons particularly susceptible to damage by metabolic disturbances.

Evidence for Involvement of Other Brain Structures

Although the evidence I have discussed so far indicates that hippocampal damage can cause anterograde amnesia, it does not rule out the possibility that other structures are also involved. In fact, the amnesia produced by damage limited to CA1 is not as severe as that caused by medial temporal lobectomy, which destroys other parts of the hippocampal formation, the amygdala, and the surrounding cortex. In addition, there is evidence that damage to some subcortical regions that communicate with the hippocampus can cause memory impairments.

■ **Limbic Cortex of the Medial Temporal Lobe** As we saw in Figure 14.7, the hippocampus seems to be located at the top of a pyramid. Information is received by the limbic cortex of the medial temporal lobe and funneled into the hippocampus. The hippocampus processes this information and then, again through the limbic cortex, exerts some control over the nature of the memories that are being stored elsewhere in the brain. The question is this: Does the limbic cortex of the medial temporal lobe perform some functions on their own, independently of the hippocampus, or is the hippocampus in charge of all the memory functions of this region? (See *Figure 14.11*.)

Vargha-Khadem et al. (1997) reported three interesting cases of anterograde amnesia that suggests that people with damage limited to the hippocampus can acquire memories of factual information even though they show a severe anterograde amnesia for episodic information.

The patients received hippocampal damage early in life: at birth in two cases and at the age of nine years in the third case. The damage was restricted to the hippocampus itself; no damage was apparent in the limbic cortex of the medial temporal lobe.

The patients, like other patients with anterograde amnesia, had severe deficits in spatial, temporal, and episodic memory. They could not find their way in surroundings that should have been familiar to them, they could not remember where objects were normally kept,

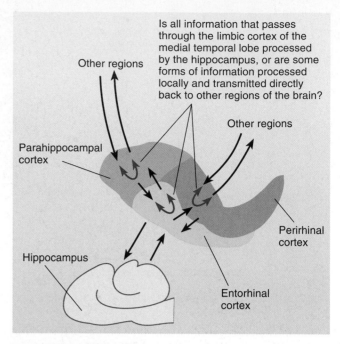

Is all information that passes through the limbic cortex of the medial temporal lobe processed by the hippocampus, or are some forms of information processed locally and transmitted directly back to other regions of the brain?

Other regions

Other regions

Parahippocampal cortex

Perirhinal cortex

Hippocampus

Entorhinal cortex

figure 14.11

Does the limbic cortex of the medial temporal lobe perform some functions independently of the hippocampus, or is the hippocampus in charge of all the memory functions of this region?

and they could not remember where they placed things. They were unaware of the time and date, and they could not remember appointments or dates of events. They could not describe what happened to them at the end of a day, which meant that they could not remember conversations they had had, television programs they had watched, trips they had made, and so on. These memory deficits meant that they could not be left alone. What is remarkable about these patients is that they did have good semantic memories—memories of facts and general information. They attended school, where they did relatively well. They had good vocabularies, and they had learned a considerable amount of information, as you can see in *Table 14.2*.

These cases suggest that semantic and episodic memories are distinct forms of declarative memory. Episodic memories involve context; they include information about when and under what conditions a particular episode occurred and the order in which the events in the episode took place. **Semantic memories** involve facts, but they do not include information about the context in which the facts were learned. In other words, semantic memories are less specific than episodic memories. For example, know-

semantic memory A memory of facts and general information.

table 14.2

Responses of Amnesic Patients That Indicate the Presence of Semantic Memories

Information

Question:
Which country in the world has the largest population?
Answer:
China.

Question:
Who was Martin Luther King?
Answer:
An American; fought for black rights; black rights leader in the 1970s; got assassinated.

Question:
What is the Koran?
Answer:
Holy Book of Moslems.

Vocabulary

Question:
What does "boast" mean?
Answer:
If someone has done something, they boast about it; they show off.

Question:
What is a "sanctuary"?
Answer:
Safe haven; place of safety everyone can go to.

Question:
What does "encumber" mean?
Answer:
When you try and burden them with lots of things.

Comprehension

Question:
Why it is important for the government to make sure that meat is inspected before it is sold?
Answer:
Because it could be not clean and people could get a disease and die.

Question:
What does this saying mean? "One swallow does not make a summer."
Answer:
Just because you see a little bit of evidence toward something, unless you've got more evidence it's not really proof that you're right.

Question:
Why do some people prefer to borrow money from a bank rather than from a friend?
Answer:
Because they can pay back the money in their own time; a friend may pester them.

ing that the sun is a star involves a less specific memory than being able to remember when, where, and from whom you learned this fact.

Vargha-Khadem et al. (1997) suggest that destruction of the hippocampus alone disrupts only the ability to incorporate contextual information into memory and thus impairs only episodic memory. Destruction of both the hippocampal formation and the limbic cortex of the medial temporal lobe prevents the consolidation of all types of declarative memory. Of course, it is possible that hippocampal lesions have different effects when they occur early in life. Zola et al. (2000) suggest that the abilities of such patients may reflect some compensatory behavioral strategies that are not seen in patients whose brains are damaged during adulthood.

■ **Fornix and Mammillary Bodies** We can conclude that bilateral lesions of the medial temporal lobes cause anterograde amnesia because they damage the hippocampal formation and the region of cortex that surrounds it, but what about Korsakoff's syndrome? You will recall that I promised earlier to discuss the anatomy of this disorder. Postmortem examination of the brains of patients with Korsakoff's syndrome almost always reveal severe degeneration of the mammillary bodies (Kopelman, 1995). Sullivan et al. (1999) used MRI scanning to measure the volume of the mammillary bodies of alcoholics with mild to severe anterograde amnesia, and found that shrinkage of this region was positively correlated with memory deficits. As we saw, most of the efferent axons of the fornix, which originates in the subiculum, terminate in the mammillary bodies. Thus, it would appear that this pathway plays a role in relational learning. (See *Figure 14.12.*)

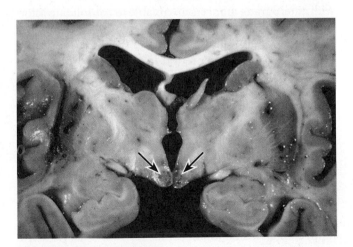

figure 14.12

Degeneration of the mammillary bodies in a patient with Korsakoff's syndrome.

(Courtesy of A. D'Agostino, Good Samaritan Hospital, Portland, Oregon.)

Patients with Korsakoff's syndrome almost always have damage to several regions of the brain, so it is not possible to make definitive conclusions about the anatomy of anterograde amnesia by studying these people. However, study of the symptoms of people with brain damage produced by other means does support the conclusion that damage to any part of the neural circuit that includes the hippocampus, fornix, mammillary bodies, and anterior thalamus causes memory impairments. Several studies (for example, Calabrese et al., 1995; D'Esposito et al., 1995; McMackin et al., 1995) have reported that damage to the fornix caused by head injury or surgery to remove tumors or cysts causes anterograde amnesia. In fact, McMackin et al. (1995) and Aggleton et al. (2000) found that the amount of damage to the fornix was correlated to the severity of the patients' symptoms. Malamut et al. (1992) found that a patient with a bilateral thalamic lesion that severed the mammillothalamic tract (the fiber bundle that connects the mammillary bodies with the anterior thalamus) had anterograde amnesia. Most investigators believe that the amnesia in cases such as these is caused by interrupting the outflow of information from the hippocampal formation to the diencephalon through the fornix. However, the fornix also carries axons *into* the hippocampus, so it is possible that damage to these fibers is responsible for the memory deficits.

Role of the Medial Temporal Lobe in Spatial Memory

I mentioned earlier in this chapter that patient H. M. has not been able to find his way around his present environment. Although spatial information need not be declared (we can demonstrate our topographical memories by successfully getting from place to place), people with anterograde amnesia are unable to consolidate information about the location of rooms, corridors, buildings, roads, and other important items in their environment.

Bilateral medial temporal lobe lesions produce the most profound impairment in spatial memory, but significant deficits can be produced by damage that is limited to the right hemisphere. For example, Luzzi et al. (2001) reported the case of a man with a lesion of the right parahippocampal gyrus who lost his ability to find his way around a new environment. The only way he could find his room was by counting doorways from the end of the hall or by seeing a red napkin that was located on top of his bedside table.

Functional imaging studies have shown that the right hippocampal formation becomes active when a person is remembering or performing a navigational task. For example Maguire, Frackowiak, and Frith (1997) had London taxi drivers describe the routes they would take in driving from one location to another. A PET scan taken during their description of the route showed activation of the right hippocampal formation. Maguire et al. (1998) had subjects play a virtual reality computer game that permitted them

to navigate around a town. The subjects played the game long enough that its streets, buildings, open spaces, and other features became familiar. The experimenters could close doors or put up barricades that required the subjects to follow alternative routes to get to a particular location. Then they arranged for the subjects to play the game while their heads were in a PET scanner that measured regional brain activation. The images they obtained indicated that the right hippocampal formation became active when the subjects were navigating. In fact, the amount of activity in this region was correlated with the subjects' accuracy in navigation. (See *Figure 14.13.*)

(a)

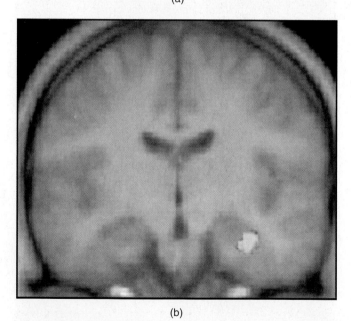

(b)

figure 14.13

The experiment by Maguire et al. (1991). (a) A scene from the virtual reality game. (b) A PET scan showing activation of the right hippocampal formation from subjects navigating through the "town."

(From Maguire, E. A., Burgess, N., Donnett, J. G., Frackowiak, R. S. J., Frith, C. D., and O'Keefe, J. *Science,* 1998, *280,* 921–924.)

Memory for configurations of objects. Subjects examined the toy objects on the table and later were asked to place them on the paper in their original locations.

(From Nunn, J. A., Graydon, F. J. X., Polkey, C. E., and Morris, R. G. *Brain*, 1999, *122*, 47–59.)

Spiers et al. (2001) had patients with medial temporal lobectomies play the same virtual reality computer game. The investigators found that people with right hemisphere damage were poor at navigating through the town and were poor at drawing a map of the town.

Besides interfering with the ability to navigate through space, damage to the right medial temporal lobe also interferes with the ability to learn spatial arrangements of objects. For example, Nunn et al. (1999) had patients with lesions of the medial temporal lobe study a group of sixteen toy objects placed on a table top and estimate the prices of the real objects they represented. This procedure ensured that the subjects looked carefully at the objects without being encouraged to try to memorize their names in the order of their location. (See *Figure 14.14*.) Later, the experimenters presented the subjects with the objects and asked them to place them on the table where they had seen them. Subjects with lesions of the right medial temporal lobe performed much more poorly than subjects with left-sided lesions or normal controls. In fact, the subjects' performance was inversely correlated with the amount of damage to the right medial temporal lobe.

Role of the Medial Temporal Lobe in Memory Retrieval

So far, I have been discussing the effects of lesions of the hippocampal formation and medial temporal cortex on the consolidation of declarative memories: episodic, semantic, and spatial. Do the hippocampal formation and related structures also play a role in retrieval of these memories? The functional imaging studies that I have described suggests that they do.

As we saw, anterograde amnesia is usually accompanied by retrograde amnesia—the inability to remember events that occurred for a period of time before the brain damage occurred. There are two possible explanations for

retrograde amnesia: loss of the neural circuits that contain the memories or damage to neural circuits that play a role in retrieving these memories. That is, the brain damage can cause the loss of memories or loss of the access to them.

I said that anterograde amnesia is *usually* accompanied by retrograde amnesia because in some rare instances, patients will display only anterograde amnesia. Rempel-Clower et al. (1996) studied three patients with anterograde amnesia caused by hippocampal degeneration. They found that if the damage was limited to field CA1, the patient did not show retrograde amnesia. Reed and Squire (1998) studied four patients with damage to the medial temporal lobe. Patients with lesions limited to the hippocampal formation had a minor retrograde amnesia that was limited to the decade before the damage occurred. However, patients whose lesions included the limbic cortex of the medial temporal lobe as well as the hippocampal formation showed a profound retrograde amnesia that extended for several decades. But even these patients were able to recall episodic memories from childhood, which means that the structures of the medial temporal lobe are not required for the recollection of remote memories. For example, patient E. P. made the following response when he was asked to describe an incident from the period before he attended school.

> When I was 5 years old, we moved from Oakland to the country. I was very excited and looked forward to the change. I remember the truck that dad rented. It was hardly full because we didn't have much furniture. When it was time to leave, mom got in the car and followed behind the truck. I rode in the truck with dad. (Reed and Squire, 1998, p. 3951)

Not all autobiographical memories are episodic in nature. As we saw, we can remember facts without being able to recall the circumstances under which we learned these facts. These facts can be autobiographical.

Patient R. S., reported by Kitchener, Hodges, and McCarthy (1998), sustained a severe deficit in episodic memory, both anterograde and retrograde, after a stroke that damaged much of the left medial temporal lobe and some of the right hippocampus. However, R. S. could remember semantic information from earlier in his life, including autobiographical information. He knew that he and his wife had gotten married and that his wife had borne two children, but he remembered nothing about his wedding or the birth of his children. He often asked his wife where their daughter was, not remembering that she was grown up and had left home several years previously. He knew that his son had accidentally been shot in the eye but did not know how or where it happened or who had taken him to the hospital. He did not know the year or his own age. His autobiographical memories were those of isolated facts, lacking any contextual information that would categorize them as episodic memories. Although he seemed to be unaware of his memory deficit, he never displayed any confabulation.

What about damage to structures outside the medial temporal lobe? Korsakoff's syndrome is invariably accompanied by retrograde amnesia, but as we saw, it is also invariably accompanied by degeneration of many parts of the brain. Several studies have reported that lesions restricted to the fornix or mammillary bodies can produce anterograde amnesia without retrograde amnesia (Calabrese et al., 1995; Kapur et al., 1996).

As we saw in Chapter 13, perceptual memories appear to be located in sensory association cortex, the regions where the perceptions take place. What about semantic memories—memories for factual information? Knowing that the sun is a star certainly involves memories different from knowing what the sun looks like. Thus, semantic memories are not simply perceptual memories. A degenerative neurological disorder knows as **semantic dementia** suggests that the lateral temporal lobe plays an important role in storing semantic information. Semantic dementia is caused by degeneration of the neocortex of the lateral temporal lobe. At least in the early stages of the disease the hippocampal formation and the rest of the medial temporal lobe are not affected. Murre, Graham, and Hodges (2001) describe the case of patient A. M., born in 1930 and studied by the investigators between 1994 and 1997.

A. M. was active, intelligent man who received an undergraduate degree in engineering and a master's degree in science. He worked for an internationally renowned company, where he was responsible for managing over 450 employees. His neurological symptoms began with progressive difficulty in understanding the speech of others and finding appropriate words of his own. By the time Murre and his colleagues met A. M., his speech was fluent and grammatical but contained little meaning.

Examiner: Can you tell me about a time you were in a hospital?
A. M.: Well one of the best places was in April last year here (ha ha) and then April, May, June, July, August, September and then October, and then April today.
Examiner: Can you remember April last year?
A. M.: April last year, that was the first time, and eh, on the Monday, for example, they were checking all my whatsit, and that was the first time, when my brain was, eh, shown, you know, you know that bar of the brain (indicates left), not the, the other one was okay, but that was lousy, so they did that and then doing everything like that, like this and probably a bit better than I am just now (indicates scanning by moving his hands over his head). (Murre, Graham, and Hodges, 2001, p. 651)

Patient A. M.'s loss of semantic information had a profound effect on his everyday activities. He seemed not to understand functions of commonplace objects. For example, he held a closed umbrella horizontally over his head during a rainstorm and brought his wife a lawnmower when she had asked for a stepladder. He put sugar into a

glass of wine and put yoghurt on a raw defrosting salmon steak and ate it. He nevertheless showed some surprisingly complex behaviors. Because he could not be trusted to drive a car, his wife surreptitiously removed the car keys from his key ring. He noticed their absence, and rather than complain to her (presumably he realized that would be fruitless), he surreptitiously removed the car keys from *her* key ring, went to a locksmith, and had a duplicate set made.

Although his semantic memory was severely damaged, his episodic memory was surprisingly good. The investigators reported that even when his dementia had progressed to the point at which he was scoring at chance levels on a test of semantic information, he answered a phone call that was meant for his wife, who was out of the house. When she returned later, he remembered to tell her about the call.

As you can see, the symptoms of semantic dementia are quite different from those of anterograde amnesia. Semantic information is lost, but episodic memory for recent events is spared. The hippocampal formation and the limbic cortex of the medial temporal lobe appear to be involved in the consolidation and retrieval of declarative memories, both episodic and semantic, but the semantic memories themselves appear to be stored in the neocortex of the lateral temporal lobe.

Retrograde amnesia is still something of a puzzle. Patients with retrograde amnesia are unable to remember events for several years before the time of their brain damage but can remember events from the remote past. This finding means that we need the structures of our medial temporal lobes to retrieve relatively young declarative memories but do not need it to retrieve very old ones. What happens over the course of years that makes declarative memories accessible without the use of the hippocampus? Is it simply a matter of practice? Does the act of remembering something again and again, over a period of years, somehow reinforce that memory so that it can be more easily retrieved later, or is there a long, slow consolidation process that takes place automatically?

Confabulation: Role of the Prefrontal Cortex in Evaluating the Accuracy of Memories

Recollecting a memory is a creative process. We do not simply retrieve stored information the way we might check a fact in a book; instead, we take fragmentary information and *interpret* what that information means. Suppose that you are waiting for a bus on a cold, rainy day. As you stand there, musing, you realize that you forgot to pay your rent, which was due several days ago. You resolve to do

semantic dementia Loss of semantic memories caused by progressive degeneration of the neocortex of the lateral temporal lobes.

so as soon as you get home. In fact, you imagine yourself sitting down and writing a check, putting it in an envelope, and carrying it to the mailbox on the corner. However, you meet a friend on the bus, and the interesting conversation you have wipes the thought of paying the rent from your mind. That night, just as you are falling asleep, you suddenly think about the rent. You have a vague memory of writing a check and posting it, but as you think about it more, you realize that you must not have done so, because you remember thinking how glad you were not to have to go out again as you put your wet raincoat away. On further reflection you realize that the memory of writing the check and posting it is simply a memory of your having *thought about* doing so.

You will recall that one of the symptoms of Korsakoff's syndrome is confabulation—the reporting of memories of events that did not really occur. Some of these events are plausible, but some of them are contradicted by other information and cannot possibly be true. Direct damage to the fornix, mammillary bodies, or thalamus does not cause confabulation, so damage elsewhere must be responsible for this phenomenon. A study by Benson et al. (1996) suggests that confabulation may be a result of disruption of the normal functions of the prefrontal cortex. The investigators reported the case of a man who developed Korsakoff's syndrome, complete with confabulation. Neuropsychological testing found symptoms that indicated frontal lobe dysfunction, and a PET scan revealed hypoactivity of the medial and orbital prefrontal cortex. Four months later, the confabulation was gone, the neuropsychological tests did not show frontal lobe symptoms, and another PET scan revealed that the activity of the prefrontal cortex was back to normal. O'Connor et al. (1996) reported a case with complementary findings: A patient who had been amnesic for years had a close-head injury and suddenly began confabulating. Neuropsychological testing found evidence for frontal lobe dysfunction.

Another study supports the suggestion that the frontal lobes may be involved in distinguishing between real and imaginary memories. Schacter et al. (1996) reported the case of a man with damage to the right frontal lobe who showed an unusually high rate of false alarms in a test of memory for written and spoken words, sounds, and pictures. The experimenters presented sets of items and later tested the patient by presenting him with items he had seen or heard, along with some that had never been presented before. The patient correctly recognized items he had seen or heard but also claimed to recognize many of the new items. (In this context a *false alarm* is the incorrect identification of a novel item as one that has been perceived before.) The patient made false alarms only when an item bore some similarity to the items that were previously presented. For example, if he studied items that fell into particular categories, he made many false alarms to novel items that also belonged to these categories but very seldom made false alarms to items that belong to categories he had *not* studied. Schacter and his colleagues suggested

that the frontal lobes may help us to distinguish items with general familiarity from specific items we have encountered before. Johnson and Raye (1998) suggest that one of the functions of the frontal lobes is to help evaluate the plausibility of a proposition or an ambiguous perception. When information is uncertain, the frontal lobes become involved in retrieving memories that might help us evaluate whether a given interpretation makes sense. For example, the patient reported by O'Connor et al. (1996) thought that her husband was her father. She knew that her father had died some time ago and realized that her husband did not resemble her father, but this additional information somehow did not banish her erroneous belief.

interim
summary
Human Anterograde Amnesia

Brain damage can produce anterograde amnesia, which consists of the inability to remember events that happen after the damage occurs, even though short-term memory (such as that needed to carry on a conversation) is largely intact. The patients also have a retrograde amnesia of several years' duration but can remember information from the distant past. Anterograde amnesia can be caused by the thiamine deficiency that sometimes accompanies chronic alcoholism (Korsakoff's syndrome), or it can be produced by bilateral damage to the medial temporal lobes. Most patients with Korsakoff's syndrome show confabulation. This symptom may be caused by disruption of the frontal lobes, which are involved in hypothesis testing and evaluating the plausibility of a recollection.

The first explanation for anterograde amnesia was that the ability of the brain to consolidate short-term memories into long-term memories was damaged. However, ordinary perceptual, stimulus-response, and motor learning do not appear to be impaired; people can learn to recognize new stimuli, they are capable of instrumental and classical conditioning, and they can acquire motor memories. But they are not capable of *declarative learning*—of describing events that happen to them. The amnesia has also been called a deficit in explicit memory. An even more descriptive term—one that applies to laboratory animals as well as to humans—is *relational learning*. People with anterograde amnesia caused by damage to the hippocampal formation are also unable to learn the meanings of words they did not know before the brain damage took place.

Although other structures may be involved, researchers are now confident that the primary cause of anterograde amnesia is damage to the hippocampal formation or to its inputs and outputs. Temporary anoxia damages field CA1 because of the high concentration of NMDA receptors there and produces anterograde amnesia (but not retrograde amnesia). The entorhinal cortex receives information from all regions of the association cortex, directly and through its connections with the perirhinal and parahippocampal cortex that surrounds it. The outputs of the hippocampal formation are relayed through these same regions. Some evidence suggests that damage limited to the hippocampus may disrupt the establishment of episodic memories but not semantic memories and that only damage to both the hippocampal formation and the limbic cortex of the medial temporal lobes will produce anterograde amnesia for both forms of declarative memory. Subcortical inputs and outputs to the hippocampal formation pass through the fornix.

Korsakoff's syndrome is apparently caused by damage to the mammillary bodies, which receive input from the hippocampal formation via the fornix and relay it to the anterior thalamus. Traumatic or surgical damage to the fornix, mammillary bodies, or the connection between the mammillary bodies and the anterior thalamus also produce anterograde amnesia.

Damage to the medial temporal lobe disrupts spatial memory. The most profound deficits are caused by bilateral damage, but damage to the right hemisphere also impairs performance. Functional imaging studies have shown that performance of spatial tasks increase activity in the right hippocampal formation.

If damage is limited to field CA1, the anterograde amnesia this destruction causes will not be accompanied by retrograde amnesia. Hippocampal damage that includes the limbic cortex of the medial temporal lobe produces a profound retrograde amnesia that extends several decades, but patients are able to recall episodic information from their childhood. Korsakoff's syndrome invariably includes retrograde amnesia, but this symptom may be caused by damage to structures besides the mammillary bodies.

Damage to the neocortex of the lateral temporal lobes causes semantic dementia, loss of memories of factual information. If the damage is limited to this region, people do not sustain an anterograde amnesia and retain the ability to recall episodic information.

An unresolved puzzle is why damage to the hippocampal formation does not disrupt recall of memories that occurred early in a person's life but do disrupt recall of more recent memories. The period of retrograde amnesia of a person with severe anterograde amnesia can be as long as several decades.

Relational Learning in Laboratory Animals

The discovery that hippocampal lesions produced anterograde amnesia in humans stimulated interest in the exact role that this structure plays in the learning process. To pursue this interest, experimenters began making lesions of the hippocampal formation in animals and testing their learning ability. They quickly found that the animals remained capable of learning most tasks. At the time they were surprised, and some even thought that the hippocampal formation had different functions in humans than it had in other animals. We now realize that most of the learning tasks that the animals were given tested simple stimulus-response learning, and as we saw in the previous section, even humans with anterograde amnesia can do well on such tasks. People's anterograde amnesia becomes apparent only when we talk with them, which is something we cannot do with other animals. However, researchers have developed other tasks that require relational learning, and on such tasks laboratory animals with hippocampal lesions show memory deficits, just as humans do.

Remembering Places Visited

Olton and Samuelson (1976) devised a task that requires rats to remember where they have just been. The investigators placed the rats on a circular platform located at the junction of eight arms, which radiated away from the center like the spokes of a wheel. (See *Figure 14.15*.) The entire maze was elevated high enough above the ground that the rats would not jump to the floor. Before placing the rats on the platform in the center, the experimenters put a piece of food at the end of each of the arms. The rats (who were hungry, of course) were permitted to explore the maze and eat the food. The animals soon learned to retrieve the food efficiently, entering each arm once. After twenty trials most animals did not enter an arm from which they had already obtained food during that session. A later study (Olton, Collison, and Werz, 1977) showed that rats could perform well even when they were prevented from following a fixed sequence of visits to the arms; thus, they had to remember where they had been, not simply follow the same pattern of responses each time. Control procedures in several studies ruled out the possi-

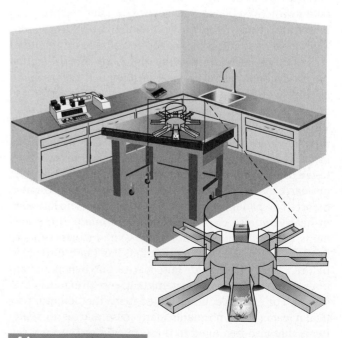

figure 14.15

An eight-arm radial maze.

bility that the rats simply smelled their own odor in arms they had previously visited.

The radial-arm-maze task uses a behavioral capacity that is well developed in rats. Rats are scavengers and often find food in different locations each day. Thus, they must be able to find their way around the environment efficiently, not getting lost and not revisiting too soon a place where they previously found food. Of course, they must also learn which places in the environment are likely to contain food and visit them occasionally. Although these two abilities might appear to require the same brain functions, they do not. Let us consider the ability to avoid revisiting a place where food was just found. Olton and his colleagues (reviewed by Olton, 1983) found that lesions of the hippocampus, fornix, or entorhinal cortex severely disrupted the ability of rats to visit the arms of a radial maze efficiently. In fact, their postoperative performance reached chance levels; they acted as if they had no memory of which arms they had previously entered. They eventually obtained all the food, but only after entering many of the arms repeatedly.

The problem was not that the rats could not distinguish among the eight arms of the maze; indeed, they could. Rats with fornix lesions (which disrupt the functioning of the hippocampus) can remember that particular locations sometimes contain food or never do. This type of memory is acquired through stimulus-response learning; thus, it is analogous to nondeclarative (implicit) memory. Olton and Papas (1979) demonstrated the distinction between explicit and implicit memory in a single experiment. They trained rats in a seventeen-arm radial maze. Before each session eight of the arms were baited with food; the other nine *never* were. Although rats with lesions of the fornix visited the baited arms randomly, failing to avoid visiting the ones in which they had just eaten, they remembered to stay away from the nine arms that never contained food. They apparently could not remember where they had just been, but they could remember which locations regularly contained food. (See *Figure 14.16.*)

These results can be explained in terms of relational memory. Each set of trials can be seen as a separate episode during which the animal enters the arms in a particular order. The study with the seventeen-arm maze proves that rats with fornix lesions have no trouble remembering the association between a particular arm and the presence or absence of food. But the task in the eight-arm maze is more complicated than that: The animal must remember where it has been *that day.* Somehow, the memory of today's explorations must be kept separate from the memory of yesterday's explorations, those of the day before, and so on. If we think of each day's trials as separate episodes, we can see the similarity to the ability of humans to remember today's breakfast without confusing it with yesterday's or that of the day before. Of course, the rats are not talking to us about what they remember, but their performance suggests that without a functioning hippocampal system they cannot keep the episodes straight.

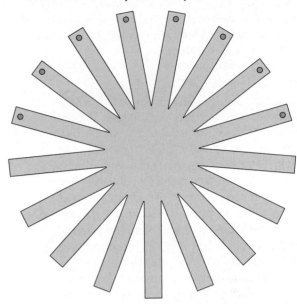

Eight arms always contained food; rats with hippocampal lesions entered them aimlessly, visiting ones from which they had already received food.

Nine arms never contained food; rats with hippocampal lesions learned not to enter them.

figure 14.16

An explanation of the experiment by Olton and Papas (1979).

In this case all episodes take place in the same location, so the nature of the contextual stimulus is *time.*

Spatial Perception and Learning

Hippocampal lesions disrupt the ability to keep track of and remember spatial locations. As we saw, H. M. never learned to find his way home when his parents moved after his surgery. Laboratory animals show similar problems in navigation. Morris et al. (1982) developed a task that has been adopted by other researchers as a standard test of rodents' spatial abilities. The task requires rats to find a particular location in space solely by means of visual cues external to the apparatus. The "maze" consists of a circular pool, 1.3 meters in diameter, filled with a mixture of water and something to increase the opacity of the water, such as powdered milk. The water hides the location of a small platform, situated just beneath the surface of the liquid. The experimenters put the rats into the water and let them swim until they encountered the hidden platform and climbed onto it. They released the rats from a new position on each trial. After a few trials normal rats learned to swim directly to the hidden platform from wherever they were released.

The Morris water maze requires relational learning; to navigate around the maze, the animals get their bearings from the relative locations of stimuli located outside the maze—furniture, windows, doors, and so on. But the maze can be used for nonrelational, stimulus-response learning too. If the animals are always released at the same place, they learn to head in a particular direction—say, toward a particular landmark they can see above the wall of the maze (Eichenbaum, Stewart, and Morris, 1990). I will say more later about why spatial learning is an example of relational learning.

If rats with hippocampal lesions are always released from the same place, they learn this nonrelational, stimulus-response task about as well as normal rats do. However, if they are released from a new position on each trial, they swim in what appears to be an aimless fashion until they finally encounter the platform. (See *Figure 14.17*.)

figure 14.17

The Morris water maze. (a) Environmental cues present in the room provide information that permits the animals to orient themselves in space. (b) Variable and fixed starting positions. Normally, rats are released from a different position on each trial. If they are released from the same position every time, the rats can learn to find the hidden platform through stimulus-response learning. (c) Performance of normal rats and rats with hippocampal lesions using variable or fixed starting positions. Hippocampal lesions impair acquisition of the relational task. (d) Representative samples of the paths followed by normal rats and rats with hippocampal lesions on the relational task.

(Adapted from Eichenbaum, H. *Nature Reviews: Neuroscience,* 2000, *1,* 41–50. Data from Eichenbaum et al., 1990.)

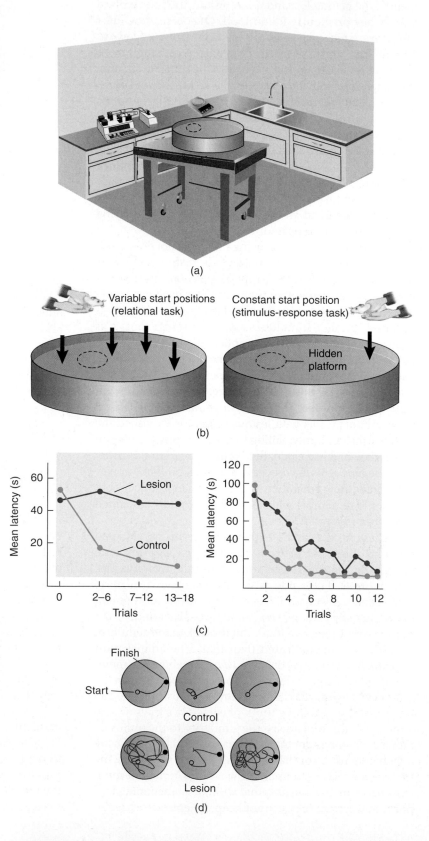

Many different types of studies have confirmed the importance of the hippocampus in spatial learning. For example, Gagliardo, Ioalé, and Bingman (1999) found that hippocampal lesions disrupted navigation in homing pigeons. The lesions did not disrupt the birds' ability to use the position of the sun at a particular time of day as a compass pointing toward their home roost. Instead, the lesions disrupted their ability to keep track of where they were when they got near the end of their flight—at a time when the birds begin to use familiar landmarks to determine where they are. In addition, Rehkämper, Haase, and Frahm (1988) found that homing pigeons have larger hippocampal formations than breeds of pigeons that do not have such good navigational ability. In a review of the literature Sherry, Jacobs, and Gaulin (1992) reported that the hippocampal formation of species of birds and rodents that normally store seeds in hidden caches and later retrieve them (and that have excellent memories for spatial locations) is larger than that of animals without this ability. Smulders, Sasson, and DeVoogd (1995) even found that the size of the hippocampal formation of the black-capped chickadee increased during late fall, a time when the birds spend a lot of time hoarding food. These changes do not take place in birds that do not cache food (Lee et al., 2001).

You may recall from a discussion earlier in this chapter that the left hippocampal formation of London taxi drivers become activated when the drivers describe a complicated route they would take to get between two points in the city. London taxi drivers undergo extensive training to learn how to navigate efficiently in that city; in fact, this training takes about two years, and the drivers receive their license only after passing a rigorous set of tests. We would expect that this topographical learning would produce some changes in various parts of their brains, including their hippocampal formation. Using MRI scans, Maguire et al. (2000) found that the volume of the posterior hippocampus of London taxi drivers was larger than that of control subjects. On the other hand, the volume of the anterior hippocampus was smaller. Furthermore, the longer an individual taxi driver had spent in this occupation, the larger was the volume of the posterior hippocampus—and the smaller was the volume of the anterior hippocampus. As we will see later in this chapter, the dorsal hippocampus of rats (which corresponds to the posterior hippocampus of humans) contains *place cells*—neurons that are directly involved in navigation in space.

Role of the Hippocampal Formation in Memory Consolidation

Several experiments indicate that the hippocampal formation plays a role in consolidation of relational memories. For example, Bontempi et al. (1999) trained mice in a spatial learning task. Five days later, they used a 2-DG imaging procedure to measure regional brain activation while they tested the animals' memory for the task. The activity of the hippocampus 5 was elevated and was positively correlated with the animal's performance—the higher the activity, the better the performance. At twenty-five days, hippocampal activity was down by 15–20 percent, and the correlation between activity and performance was gone. However, the activity of several regions of the cerebral cortex was elevated while the animals were being tested. The investigators suggest that these findings support the hypothesis that the hippocampus is involved in consolidation of spatial memories for a limited time, and the result of this activity is to help establish the memories in the cerebral cortex.

Riedel et al. (1999) temporarily deactivated the dorsal hippocampus by infusing a glutamatergic AMPA-receptor antagonist directly into that brain region. The rats were trained in a Morris water maze and tested later for their memory of the location of the platform. Not surprisingly, if the hippocampus was deactivated during training, the rats failed to learn the task. However, if the hippocampus was deactivated for seven days just after training, their performance was impaired when the animals were tested sixteen days later. This finding suggests that hippocampal activity for several days after spatial learning is required for consolidation to take place. The authors also found that hippocampal inactivation disrupted animals' performance on a task that they had successfully learned, which indicates that the hippocampus is required for retrieval of spatial memories as well as their consolidation.

Place Cells in the Hippocampal Formation

One of the most intriguing discoveries about the hippocampal formation was made by O'Keefe and Dostrovsky (1971), who recorded the activity of individual pyramidal cells in the hippocampus as an animal moved around the environment. The experimenters found that some neurons fired at a high rate only when the rat was in a particular location. Different neurons had different *spatial receptive fields;* that is, they responded when the animals were in different locations. A particular neuron might fire twenty times per second when the animal was in a particular location but only a few times per hour when it was located elsewhere. For obvious reasons these neurons were named **place cells.** When, for example, a rat is exploring a radial-arm maze, place cells in its hippocampus respond in places defined in relation to objects in the environment outside the maze (for example, lighting fixtures, cabinets, and racks of cages). If a particular place

place cell A neuron that becomes active when the animal is in a particular location in the environment; most typically found in the hippocampal formation.

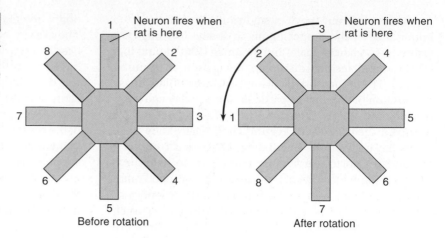

figure 14.18

Response of place cells to environmental cues. If the maze is rotated 90 degrees, place cells maintain their locations relative to objects located outside the maze.

cell is active when the rat is at the end of the arm that points north, it will continue to fire in the end of the northern arm, even after the maze is rotated so that a different arm points north. (See *Figure 14.18*.)

When a rat is placed in a symmetrical chamber, where there are few cues to distinguish one part of the apparatus from another, the animal must keep track of its location from objects it sees (or hears) in the environment outside the maze. Changes in these items affect the firing of the rats' place cells as well as their navigational ability. When experimenters move the stimuli as a group, maintaining their relative positions, the animals simply reorient their responses accordingly. However, when the experimenters interchange the stimuli so that they are arranged in a new order, the animals' performance (and the firing of their place cells) is disrupted. (Imagine how disoriented you might be if you entered a familiar room and found that the windows, doors, and furniture were in new positions.)

In many situations an animal can perceive both local and distal cues. Local cues are those located nearby—for example, within an experimental chamber. Distal cues are those located farther away—for example, in the room outside the experimental chamber. If an animal is placed in a symmetrical chamber without strong local cues (such as a Morris water maze or a radial arm maze), they will orient themselves by means of the distal cues, and the receptive fields of their hippocampal place cells will be defined in relation to these cues. An experiment by Jeffery and O'Keefe (1999) showed that rats can learn whether or not distal cues are trustworthy. The investigators placed rats on a circular platter located in a square box surrounded by a circular black curtain. A white card located against the curtain was the only distal cue that the rats could see.

The circular platter on which the rats stood could be rotated very slowly—so slowly that the rats were not able to detect its movement. When this was done for one group of rats, the animals' place cells ignored the local cues (which were minimal) and continued to orient themselves to the card. Another group of rats saw the experimenters move the white card from time to time. The place cells of

these rats, now that the animals had learned that the card did not remain in a constant location, began orienting themselves to the local cues present in the box. When the experimenters then slowly rotated the circular platter, the rats' place cells ignored the card and maintained their orientation to the local cues. (See *Figure 14.19*.)

The fact that neurons in the hippocampal formation have spatial receptive fields does not mean that each neuron encodes a particular location. Instead, this information is undoubtedly represented by particular *patterns* of activity in circuits of neurons within the hippocampal for-

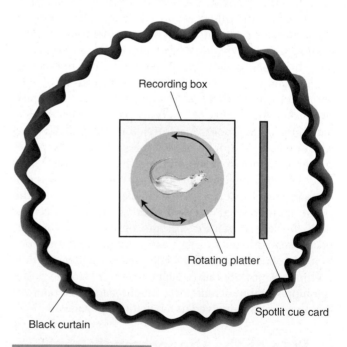

figure 14.19

The apparatus used in the study by Jeffery and O'Keefe (1999). The chamber was surrounded by a black curtain. An illuminated white card served as a distal cue. A circular platter in the chamber could be turned so slowly that the rat could not detect the movement.

(Adapted from Jeffery, K. J., and O'Keefe, J. M. *Experimental Brain Research*, 1999, *127*, 151–161.

mation. In rodents most hippocampal place cells are found in the dorsal hippocampus, which corresponds to the posterior hippocampus is humans (Best, White, and Minai, 2001).

When animals encounter new environments, they learn their layout, and "maps" become established in their hippocampus. (As we will see, evidence suggests that these maps are formed through the process of synaptic strengthening that is responsible for long-term potentiation.) An animal's location within each environment (the animal's place on the map) is encoded by the pattern of firing of these neurons. Obviously, a useful map must remain stable over time. Indeed, Thompson and Best (1990) obtained evidence that the hippocampal maps *are* stable; they found that the receptive fields of hippocampal neurons remained unchanged for as long as they were able to record from them—up to 153 days in one case.

The acquisition of spatial receptive fields by hippocampal neurons was demonstrated by an experiment by Hollup et al. (2001). The investigators constructed an annular water maze—a doughnut-shaped trough around which rats could swim continuously. A platform located in the water could be lowered by remote control to the bottom of the maze where rats could not reach it or left just under the surface. On test trials the platform was lowered, and the rat continued to swim around the maze. During these trials Hollup and his colleagues recorded from neurons in the dorsal hippocampus and found that place fields gradually accumulated near the location of the platform. It appeared as if the hippocampus was paying special attention to that particular place because of its importance.

Hippocampal place cells are obviously guided by visual stimuli, because their receptive fields change when objects outside an environment are moved. They also receive internally generated stimuli. Hill and Best (1981) deafened and blindfolded rats and found that the spatial receptive fields of most of their place cells remained constant, even when the experimenters rotated the maze. At first the experimenters were surprised and puzzled by the results, but then it occurred to them that the animals might have been keeping track of where they were by feedback from proprioceptive cues. The rats might have been keeping track of their starting point, left and right turns, and so on, which kept resetting their "mental map." To test this hypothesis, Hill and Best wrapped their deafened and blindfolded rats in a towel, spun them around, and then placed them in the maze. (If you have ever played blindman's buff or pin-the-tail-on-the-donkey, you will understand how disorienting this treatment is.) The experimenters' hypothesis was correct; after the rats had been spun, the receptive fields of their place cells were disrupted.

Evidence indicates that firing of hippocampal place cells appears to reflect the location where an animal "thinks" it is. Skaggs and McNaughton (1998) constructed an apparatus that contained two nearly identical chambers connected by a corridor. Each day, rats were placed in one

of the chambers, and a cluster of electrodes in the animals' brains recorded the activity of hippocampal place cells. Each rat was always placed in the same chamber each day. Some of the place cells showed similar patterns of activity in each of the chambers, and some showed different patterns, which suggests that the hippocampus "realized" that there were two different compartments but also "recognized" the similarities between them. Then, on the last day of the experiment, the investigators placed the rats in the other chamber of the apparatus. For example, if a rat was usually placed in the north chamber, it was placed in the south chamber. The firing pattern of the place cells in at least half of the rats indicated that the hippocampus "thought" it was in the usual chamber—the one to the north. However, once the rat left the chamber and entered the corridor, it saw that it had to turn to the left to get to the other chamber and not to the right. The animal apparently realized its mistake, because for the rest of that session the neurons fired appropriately. They displayed the "north" pattern in the north chamber and the "south" pattern in the south chamber. (See *Figure 14.20*.)

The hippocampus appears to receive its spatial information through the entorhinal cortex. Quirk et al. (1992)

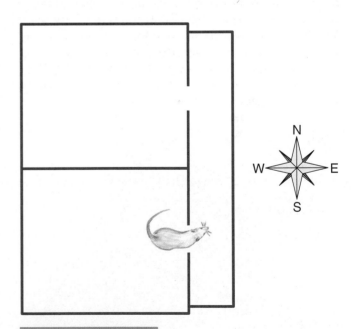

figure   14.20

The apparatus used in the study by Skaggs and McNaughton (1998). Place cells reflect the location where the animal "thinks" it is. Because the rat was normally placed in the north chamber, its hippocampal place cells responded as if it were there when it was placed in the south chamber one day. However, once it stuck its head into the corridor, it saw that the other chamber was located to its right, so it "realized" that it had just been in the south chamber. From then on, the pattern of firing of the hippocampal place cells accurately reflected the chamber in which the animal was located.

found that neurons in the entorhinal cortex have spatial receptive fields, although these fields are not nearly as clear-cut as those of hippocampal pyramidal cells. Damage to the entorhinal cortex alone impairs animals' ability to navigate in spatial tasks; it also disrupts the spatial receptive fields of place cells in the hippocampus (Miller and Best, 1980). Critical spatial information appears to enter the hippocampus by means of direct connections between the entorhinal cortex and field CA1. Pyramidal cells in field CA1 still exhibit spatial receptive fields after the dentate gyrus or the pyramidal cells of field CA3 have been damaged (McNaughton et al., 1989; Brun et al., 2002).

The activity of circuits of hippocampal place cells provide information about more than space. Wood et al. (2000) trained rats on a spatial alternation task in a T-maze. The task required the rats to enter the left and the right arms on alternate trials; when they did so, they received a piece of food in goal boxes located at the ends of the arms of the T. Corridors connected to the goal boxes led back to the stem of the T-maze, where the next trial began. (See *Figure 14.21*.) Wood and her colleagues recorded from field CA1 pyramidal cells and, as expected, found that different cells fired when the rat was in different parts of the maze. However, two-thirds of the neurons fired differentially in the stem of the T on left-turn and right-turn trials. In other words, the cells not only encoded the rat's location in the maze, but also signaled whether the rat was going to turn right or turn left after it got to the choice point. Thus, besides encoding spatial information, CA1 pyramidal cells encode other forms of contextual information.

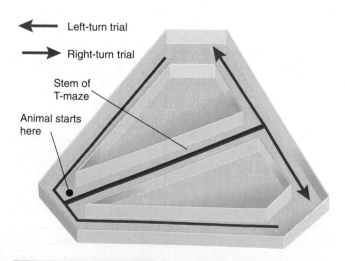

figure 14.21

The apparatus used in the study by Wood et al. (2000). The rats were trained to turn right and turn left at the end of the stem of the T-maze on alternate trials. The firing patterns of hippocampal place cells with spatial receptive fields in the stem of the maze were different on trials during which the animals turned left or right.

(Adapted from Wood, E. R., Dudchenko, P. A., Robitsek, R. J., and Eichenbaum, H. *Neuron,* 2000, *27,* 623–633.)

The hippocampal formations of monkeys, like those of rodents, also contain neurons that respond to location, but most of them encode information about what part of the environment the animal is *looking at* rather than where the animal is located. The firing of these cells is not affected by the position of the eye, the orientation of its head, or the position in which the monkey is located. Thus, the neurons seem to represent locations "out there" (Rolls, 1996; Georges-François, Rolls, and Robertson, 1999). Rolls and his colleagues refer to these neurons as *spatial view cells* and suggests that their presence in the hippocampus of the monkey reflects the fact that vision is such an important sense modality for primates. The hippocampus of the monkey also contains place cells that respond the way they do in the hippocampus of the rat, but there are many fewer of these cells (O'Mara et al., 1994).

Role of Long-Term Potentiation in Relational Learning

In Chapter 13 we saw how synaptic connections could be quickly modified in the hippocampal formation, leading to long-term potentiation or long-term depression. How are these changes in synaptic strength related to the role the hippocampus plays in learning?

As you just learned, place cells in the hippocampal formation become active when the animal is present in particular locations. The sensory information reaches the dentate gyrus from the entorhinal cortex. Does this increased activity cause changes in the excitability of neurons in the hippocampal formation? The answer is clearly yes. Green and Greenough (1986) raised rats in a complex environment or in small, rather sterile cages. The experimenters removed hippocampal slices from these animals and found that the synaptic connections between the entorhinal cortex and dentate gyrus appeared to be stronger in the rats that were raised in the complex environment. Mitsuno et al. (1994) found that as rats learned a radial-arm maze, the strength of the population EPSP in field CA3 increased. Thus, when animals learn tasks that involve the hippocampal formation, the experience appears to induce the same types of changes that are produced by long-term potentiation.

More recently, researchers have developed targeted mutations of the gene responsible for the production of NMDA receptors which, as we saw in Chapter 13, are responsible for long-term potentiation in several parts of the hippocampal formation. Two studies from the same laboratory (McHugh et al., 1996; Tsien, Huerta, and Tonegawa, 1996) produced a targeted mutation of the NMDA receptor gene that affected only the CA1 pyramidal cells. NMDA receptors in these neurons failed to develop; in all other parts of the brain these receptors were normal. Figure 14.22 shows photomicrographs of slices through the hippocampus of a normal mouse and a knock-out mouse,

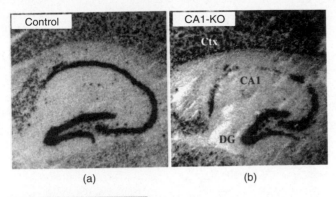

figure 14.22

Effects of a targeted mutation (knockout) of the NMDA receptor gene expressed only in field CA1 of the hippocampus. Photomicrographs of sections through the hippocampus showing in situ hybridization of messenger RNA responsible for the production of NMDA receptors. (a) Normal mouse. (b) Mouse with the targeted mutation (CA1 knockout). Ctx = neocortex, CA1 = hippocampal field CA1, DG = dentate gyrus.

(From Tsien, J. Z., Huerta, P. T., and Tonegawa, S. *Cell*, 1996, *87*, 1327–1338. Reprinted by permission.)

showing in situ hybridization of the messenger RNA for the NMDA receptor. As you can see, this chemical is missing in the CA1 field of the mouse with the targeted mutation. (See *Figure 14.22*.)

As you might expect, the experimenters found that the lack of NMDA receptors prevented the establishment of long-term potentiation in field CA1 in the mice with the targeted mutation. In addition, although the pyramidal cells of CA1 did show spatial receptive fields, these fields were larger and less focused than those shown by cells in normal animals. Finally, the knockout mice learned a Morris water maze much more slowly than mice whose CA1 neurons contained NMDA receptors.

An extraordinary experiment from Tsien's laboratory (Tang et al., 1999) performed a genetic manipulation in mice that caused the increased production of a particular subunit of the NMDA receptor—NMDA-R2B—in the forebrain. The calcium channel of an NMDA receptor that contains this subunit produces a slightly larger excitatory postsynaptic potential than an NMDA receptor that contains the other subunit—NMDA-R2A. Thus, EPSPs produced by NMDA receptors in the hippocampus, amygdala, cortex, and basal ganglia were slightly longer in the genetically modified mice. As a consequence, long-term potentiation was enhanced in hippocampal slices taken from the genetically modified mice. The animals also learned to find the platform in a Morris water maze faster than animals with normal NMDA receptors, which strongly suggests that hippocampal long-term potentiation plays an important role in relational learning. Some commentators have suggested that this genetic manipulation

might enable us to produce smarter animals—or even smarter people. However, if we would really be better off with more NMDA-R2B subunits in our brains, natural selection would probably have bequeathed them to us. Considering the fact that the large concentration of NMDA receptors already makes the hippocampus susceptible to seizure activity and to damage from anoxia, we are probably better off the way we are.

Kentros et al. (1998) found that NMDA-mediated long-term potentiation appears to be required for the consolidation of spatial receptive fields in field CA1 pyramidal cells but not their short-term establishment. The experimenters injected rats with a drug that blocked NMDA receptors and placed the animals in a novel environment. CA1 pyramidal cells rapidly acquired spatial receptive fields, so obviously, NMDA receptors were not necessary for the establishment of these fields. However, when the animals were tested the next day, the receptive fields had disappeared.

Learning experiences that involve the hippocampal formation also induce biochemical changes that have been implicated in long-term potentiation. As we saw in Chapter 13, when NMDA receptors admit calcium ions into the cell, the ions activate the enzyme CaM-KII, which plays an important role in synaptic plasticity. Indeed, when animals participate in spatial learning tasks, the levels of CaM-KII in the hippocampal formation increases (Tan and Liang, 1996). We also saw in Chapter 13 that researchers have produced targeted mutations in mice against the gene responsible for the production of CaM-KII. These mutations suppressed long-term potentiation. They also produced impairments in the animals' ability to learn the Morris water maze (Grant et al., 1992; Silva et al., 1992b).

In summary, an overwhelming amount of information indicates that the participation of the hippocampal formation in learning involves long-term potentiation.

Modulation of Hippocampal Functions by Monoaminergic and Acetylcholinergic Inputs

I mentioned earlier that the hippocampal formation receives input from acetylcholinergic, noradrenergic, dopaminergic, and serotonergic neurons. These neurons, which innervate widespread regions of the brain, do not appear to convey specific information that becomes part of memories. Instead, they appear to control the information-processing functions of the hippocampal formation, which affects what is learned.

Serotonin appears to have a suppressive effect on the establishment of long-term potentiation in the hippocampal formation. Sandler and Ross (1999) found that serotonin decreased the size of dendritic spikes in hippocampal pyramidal cells, which would interfere with associative long-term potentiation. Conversely, norepinephrine has a facilitatory effect, particularly on synapses of terminals of entorhinal neurons with granule cells of the dentate gyrus (Dahl and Sarvey, 1989; Klukowski and Harley, 1994; Bramham, Bacher-Svendsen, and Sarvey, 1997). In fact, long-term potentiation at these synapses does not require activation of NMDA receptors but does require activation of noradrenergic β receptors.

Dopamine also has excitatory effects on long-term potentiation and, apparently, memory-related functions of the hippocampal formation. Presumably, synaptic plasticity is induced by simultaneous depolarization of hippocampal neurons and activation of dopamine receptors on these neurons. Gasbarri et al. (1996) infused 6-HD, a chemical toxic to dopaminergic neurons, into the hippocampal formation. The infusions, which destroyed dopaminergic axons in field CA1 and the subiculum, disrupted the animals' performance on the Morris water maze.

One of the most important modulatory inputs to the hippocampus comes from the medial septum, whose acetylcholinergic axons enter the hippocampal formation via the fornix. Activity of these neurons is responsible for hippocampal **theta rhythms**—medium-amplitude, medium-frequency (5–8 hertz) waves (Stewart and Fox, 1990). These waves influence the establishment of long-term potentiation in the hippocampus. Pavlides et al. (1988) found that when bursts of electrical stimulation coincided with the peaks of the theta waves, long-term potentiation was more easily established. Subsequent studies showed that depolarizing stimulation that coincided with the peaks of the theta waves produced long-term potentiation, while stimulation that coincided with the troughs produced long-term *depression* (Huerta and Lisman, 1996). In other words, theta activity consists of waxing and waning excitability of the hippocampal formation that alternately facilitate or inhibit synaptic strengthening. (See *Figure 14.23*.)

If hippocampal theta activity is disrupted, animals show deficits in learning tasks that are affected by hippocampal lesions. For example, Givens and Olton (1990) found that injections of scopolamine, a drug that blocks muscarinic acetylcholine receptors, suppressed hippocampal theta rhythms and impaired learning of a spatial alternation task that required rats to remember in which arm of a T-maze they had most recently entered. Givens (1995) found that low doses of alcohol, which interfere with short-term spatial memory, also disrupted hippocampal theta rhythms. Presumably, at least some of the memory deficits caused by alcohol are produced by its effects on hippocampal theta rhythms.

Several studies have shown that transplantation of acetylcholine-secreting cells from the medial septum into the hippocampus can partially reverse the effects of damage to its cholinergic input. For example, such transplants can restore theta activity and spatial receptive fields that are lost by cutting the fornix in rats (Buzsáki, Gage, and Czopf, 1987; Shapiro et al., 1989). These transplants can also reduce deficits in performance in the Morris water

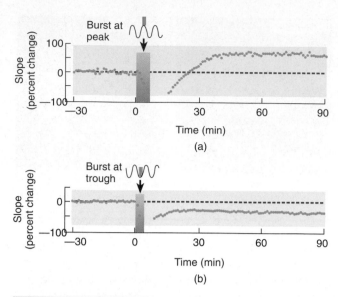

Long-term potentiation or long-term depression produced by stimulation of CA1 neurons at (a) the peak or (b) the trough of hippocampal theta waves.

(Adapted from Huerta, P. T., and Lisman, J. E. *Hippocampus,* 1996, *6*, 58–61.)

maze caused by fornix lesions (Nilsson et al., 1987). Similar results were obtained in monkeys (Ridley et al., 1991). In all cases histological examination of the tissue after the experiment was over showed that the transplants took and that they began secreting acetylcholine.

Vanderwolf and his colleagues (Vanderwolf, 1969; Vanderwolf et al., 1975) observed that hippocampal theta activity is closely related to the type of behavior the animal is performing. In rats *theta behaviors* are associated with exploration or investigation; they include such behaviors as walking, running, rearing up on the hind legs, sniffing, and manipulating objects with the forepaws. They also occur during REM sleep (when the animal is dreaming?). *Nontheta behaviors* are not involved with exploration; they include alert immobility ("freezing"), drinking, and various self-directed behaviors.

Many investigators believe that the presence of theta rhythms is correlated with the acquisition of sensory information by the hippocampal formation. When a rat investigates odors in the environment, its rate of sniffing is synchronized with the waves of its hippocampal theta rhythm (Wiener, Paul, and Eichenbaum, 1989). And as we saw, when pulses of electrical stimulation are delivered to the perforant pathway in synchrony with the peaks of the theta waves, long-term potentiation can be established

theta rhythm EEG activity of 5–8 Hz; an important indication of the physiological state of the hippocampus.

more easily. Buzsáki (1989, 1996) suggests that during theta rhythms information is sampled by the dentate gyrus and CA3 field. Then after the bout of exploration is over, the cessation of the theta rhythms permits the information to be transferred to the CA1 field. During slow-wave sleep, information is transferred in bursts from the hippocampal formation to the neocortex, where the long-term memories are stored. Hippocampal theta waves are somewhat reminiscent of the cycles of a computer; whether they actually function this way will have to be resolved by future research.

Theoretical Explanations of Hippocampal Functioning

As we saw earlier, people with anterograde amnesia can learn to recognize new stimuli, can learn new responses, and can learn to make a particular response when a particular stimulus is presented. What they cannot do is talk about what they have learned. Anterograde amnesia appears to be a loss of the ability to learn about complex relationships between many stimuli, including the order of their occurrence in time.

I think it is likely that the original function of the hippocampus was to help the animal learn to navigate in the environment. Later, the process of evolution gave the hippocampus the ability to detect other types of contexts, also. Let's first consider the spatial functions. Suppose you are standing in an environment similar to the circular water maze I described earlier: a large field covered with grass and surrounded by distinctive objects such as trees and buildings. You are familiar with the environment, having walked across it and played games on it many times. If someone blindfolds you and then picks you up and drops you somewhere on the field, you will recognize your location as soon as you remove the blindfold. Your location is defined by the *configuration* of objects you see—the *relationship* they have with respect to each other. You will get a different view of these objects from each position on the field. Of course, if there are distinctive objects present on the field itself (trees, garbage cans, lampposts), the task will be even easier, because you can judge your position relative to nearby objects as well as distant ones. Learning to find a drinking fountain located near a large tree does not involve learning the relationships among several landmarks—If you are thirsty, you can simply head toward the tree.

Spatial location obviously involves contextual stimuli. Another contextual stimulus is *time*. As we saw earlier, rats in a radial-arm maze are able to visit each arm only once, which means that they can remember where they had been *that day*. Disruption of the hippocampal formation makes it impossible for the animals to remember what happened in the context of time.

How can we put all the information about the hippocampal complex together? As you will recall, the hippocampal complex receives information from all regions of the sensory association cortex and from the motor association cortex of the frontal lobe. It also receives information from the amygdala concerning odors and dangerous stimuli. Thus, the hippocampal complex knows what is going on in the environment, where the animal is located, and what responses it has just made. It also knows about the animal's emotional state: whether the animal is hungry, sexually aroused, frightened, and so on. Thus, when something happens, the hippocampal system has all the information necessary to put that event into the proper context.

What does context have to do with declarative memory deficits in humans? Let's go back to a study involving a human with hippocampal damage and consider why the person can learn a nondeclarative task but cannot recall anything about the experience later. Consider a normal person learning to press a panel with a picture of a circle on it, as patient H. M. did in the experiment by Sidman, Stoddard, and Mohr (1968). While the person is seated in front of the apparatus, his or her hippocampal formation receives information about the context in which the learning is taking place: the room, the other people present, the person's mood, and so on. These pieces of information are collected and are somehow attached to the patterns of activity in the association cortex in several different regions of the brain. Later, when the person is asked about the task, the question reactivates the pattern of activity in the hippocampus, which causes the retrieval of the memory of the episode, pieces of which are stored all over the brain. Patient H. M., lacking a functioning hippocampal system, is unable to accomplish this act.

How might the hippocampus recognize a particular context? Rolls (1989, 1996) presents a hypothetical model of the role of the hippocampal formation in learning and memory that may prove to be useful. Like other researchers who study the physiology of learning and memory, he believes that perceptual learning takes place in the neocortex. The neocortex then sends information about events and episodes to the hippocampal formation, where it is further analyzed. The information reaches the entorhinal cortex and is then relayed to the dentate gyrus, fields CA3 and CA1, and finally to the subiculum, which conveys the results of the hippocampal information processing back to the neocortex, both directly and indirectly, through the entorhinal cortex. Field CA3 contains a large number of **recurrent collaterals**—branches of axons leaving the region that turn back and form synapses with other neurons in field CA3. Rolls suggests that this field contains a network of neurons that functions as an *autoassociator*. An autoassociative network quickly and efficiently learns to

---

recurrent collateral A branch of an axon leaving a particular region of the brain that turns back and forms synapses with neurons near the one that gives rise to it.

recognize particular pattern of inputs and produces a unique output for each pattern. Then if a similar pattern is presented later—or if parts of the pattern are presented—the network produces the appropriate output, which it sends on to field CA1.

Neural networks such as the one that Rolls proposes are capable of *pattern completion:* When they are presented with a fuzzy version of the original pattern or simply a fragment of it, they supply the complete pattern in their output. Let's go back to an example I described earlier: this morning's breakfast. When I got up, put on my slippers and robe, and went downstairs to have breakfast, my hippocampus received information from multiple sites in the neocortex about where I was, what time it was, how I was feeling, and so on. That is, it registered the context of that situation. As I went about preparing my breakfast, the memories of what was happening were being recorded in the form of synaptic changes in various regions of my sensory association cortex. The hippocampus communicated with these regions, somehow tying together these memories as they were being formed.

When you asked me about what I had for breakfast this morning, the words were recognized and understood by language mechanisms in my left temporal and parietal lobes (more about that in Chapter 15). Information about this recognition was sufficient for my hippocampal formation to recognize the context—to *complete the pattern.* The pattern was broadcast through outputs of the hippocampal formation to the locations in my neocortex that contain the individual components of the memory of the episode, and I told you about my breakfast.

This analysis is certainly speculative, but I think it is consistent with the experimental data I have presented in this chapter. Of course, it is vague about many parts of the process. For example, just how does asking someone a question activate the pattern of activity in the hippocampus? And how, exactly, are memories "tied together"? How are pieces of information collected and attached to sets of neural circuits? Obviously, we need to think about these questions, design clever experiments to obtain useful information, think about the questions in light of the new information, design more clever experiments, and so on.

interim summary

Relational Learning in Laboratory Animals

Studies with laboratory animals indicate that damage to the hippocampal formation disrupts the ability to learn spatial relations and to distinguish events that have just occurred from those that have occurred at another time. For example, rats with hippocampal damage cannot remember which arms of a radial maze they have just visited, but they can remember to visit only those arms that contain food. Also, they can-

not learn the Morris water maze unless they are always released from the same place in the maze, which turns the task into one of stimulus-response learning. The basic deficit appears to be an inability to distinguish among different contexts, which includes locations in space and in time.

Research has shown that the hippocampal formation plays a role in memory consolidation. A 2-DG imaging study found that the hippocampal activity correlates with animals' ability to remember a spatial learning task a few days after the original learning, but that the correlation disappears after a few weeks. Similarly, deactivation of the dorsal hippocampus prevents consolidation if it occurs shortly after learning a Morris water maze task.

The hippocampal formation contains place cells—neurons that respond when the animal is in a particular location, which implies that the hippocampus contains neural networks that keep track of the relationships among stimuli in the environment that define the animal's location. These networks also receive information concerning the animal's own locomotion, even when the animal moves about in the darkness. Disruption of hippocampal functioning impaired the ability of animals to keep track of their location while moving around a familiar environment. Neurons in the hippocampal formation reflect where an animal "thinks" it is. If a prominent cue outside the apparatus is seen to move, the animals will no longer trust it, and the spatial receptive fields of their place cells will begin to use local cues as their reference points. When rats learn an annular water maze, place cells gradually accumulate near the location of the hidden platform. Topographical information reaches field CA1 of hippocampus directly from the entorhinal cortex. Place cells encode more than space; they can include information about the response that the animal should perform next. Place cells in primates tend to respond according to the particular location the animal is looking at.

Long-term potentiation appears to be related to learning. When rats are raised in complex environments, the synaptic connections between the entorhinal cortex and the dentate gyrus are strengthened. A unique targeted mutation against the NMDA receptor gene only in field CA1 disrupts long-term potentiation and the ability to learn the Morris water maze. A mutation that increases the number of NMDA receptors in the forebrain that contain the NMDA-R2B subunit also increases long-term potentiation and the ability to learn tasks that involve the participation of the hippocampal formation. Spatial learning tasks increase the levels of an enzyme involved in long-term potentiation—CaM-KII—in the hippocampal formation, and a targeted mutation against CaM-KII disrupts both long-term potentiation and spatial learning. A mutation that increased the effectiveness of NMDA receptors facilitates both long-term potentiation and the speed at which the animals learn a Morris water maze. Inactivation of NMDA receptors shortly after exposure to a novel environment does not prevent the formation of spatial receptive fields, but it prevents their consolidation.

Hippocampal theta activity, controlled by acetylcholinergic neurons in the medial septum, appears to be a time during which the hippocampus receives and stores sensory input. In addition, the establishment of long-term potentiation is modulated by the presence of theta waves: Bursts of hippocampal stimulation delivered during the peaks of the waves produce long-term potentiation, and stimulation delivered during the troughs produces long-term depression. Drugs that block muscarinic acetylcholine receptors disrupt hippocampal theta rhythms and impair short-term spatial memory. The memory deficits produced by fornix lesions, which appear to be caused by loss of acetylcholinergic neurons that send axons to the hippocampal formation, can be ameliorated by hippocampal transplants of fetal brain tissue that is rich in ACh-secreting neurons.

The original role of the hippocampal formation may well have been to provide animals with the ability to orient in space, keeping track of the multiple stimuli that define spatial location; but it is clear that its role has expanded to learning relations among nonspatial stimuli and situations, as well. One of the functions of the hippocampal formation may be to take a "snapshot" of what is currently happening and modify memories that are being stored in a variety of locations in the brain. Later, if a fragment of this "snapshot" is perceived, the hippocampal formation completes the pattern and facilitates the retrieval of the associated memories.

Suggested Readings

Best, P. J., White, A. M., and Minai, A. Spatial processing in the brain: The activity of hippocampal place cells. *Annual Review of Neuroscience*, 2001, *24*, 459–486.

McGaugh, J. L., Weinberger, N. M., and Lynch, G. *Brain and Memory: Modulation and Mediation of Neuroplasticity.* New York: Oxford University Press, 1995.

Redish, A. D. *Beyond the Cognitive Map: From Place Cells to Episodic Memory.* Cambridge, MA: MIT Press, 1999.

Schacter, D. L. *Searching for Memory: The Brain, the Mind, and the Past.* New York: Basic Books, 1996.

Squire, L. R., and Kandel, E. R. *Memory: From Mind to Molecules.* New York: Scientific American Library, 1999.

Suggested Web Sites

NIH Consensus Statement on Electroconvulsive Therapy

http://text.nlm.nih.gov/nih/cdc/www/51txt.html

This site contains a document describing the history of ECT as a treatment for various forms of mental illness and provides an assessment of the action of ECT on memory.

Working Memory

http://www.nimh.nih.gov/events/prfmri.htm

This site provides a series of MRI images collected from human subjects during a study of working memory.

Amnesia Information

http://www.diseases.nu/amnesia.htm

This site from the Disease Information Center provides links to fact sheets, lecture notes, PowerPoint slides, and related links on the topic of amnesia.

Human Communication

Wassily Kandinsky, *Landscape with a Green House*, 1908. © 2003 Artists Rights Society (ARS) New York/ADAGP, Paris. © SCALA/Art Resource, NY.

outline

■ **Speech Production and Comprehension: Brain Mechanisms**
Lateralization
Speech Production
Speech Comprehension
Aphasia in Deaf People

The Bilingual Brain
Prosody: Rhythm, Tone, and Emphasis in Speech
Interim Summary
■ **Disorders of Reading and Writing**
Relation to Aphasia

Pure Alexia
Toward an Understanding of Reading
Toward an Understanding of Writing
Developmental Dyslexias
Interim Summary

While driving her car to visit some friends, R. F., a 39-year-old woman, was broadsided by an intoxicated driver who ignored (or was too drunk to see) a stop sign. The left side of R. F.'s head was fractured, and the bone fragments caused considerable damage to her brain. A neurosurgeon repaired the damage as best he could, but R. F. remained in a coma for several weeks. By the time my colleagues and I met her, she had shown considerable recovery. However, she had difficulty remembering the names of even the most common objects, and she could no longer read.

Although R. F. could not read, she could match words with pictures, which indicated that she could still *perceive* words. This fact was made especially apparent one day when she was trying (without success) to read some words that I had typed. Suddenly, she said, "Hey! You spelled this one wrong." I looked at the word and realized that she was right; I had. But although she saw that the word was misspelled, she still could not say what it was, even when she tried very hard to sound it out. That evening I made up a list of eighty pairs of words, one spelled correctly and the other incorrectly. The next day I gave her a pencil and asked her to cross out the misspelled words. She was able to go through the list quickly and easily, correctly identifying 95 percent of the misspelled words. She was able to *read* only five of them.

V erbal behaviors constitute one of the most important classes of human social behavior. Our cultural evolution has been possible because we can talk and listen, write and read. Language enables our discoveries to be cumulative; knowledge gained by one generation can be passed on to the next.

The basic function of verbal communication is seen in its effects on other people. When we talk to someone, we almost always expect our speech to induce the person to engage in some sort of behavior. Sometimes, the behavior is of obvious advantage to us, as when we ask for an object or for help in performing a task. At other times we are simply asking for a social exchange: some attention and perhaps some conversation. Even "idle" conversation is not idle, because it causes another person to look at us and say something in return.

This chapter discusses the neural basis of verbal behavior: talking, understanding speech, reading, and writing.

Speech Production and Comprehension: Brain Mechanisms

Our knowledge of the physiology of language has been obtained primarily by observing the effects of brain lesions on people's verbal behavior. Although investiga-

tors have studied people who have undergone brain surgery or who have sustained head injuries, brain tumors, or infections, most of the observations have been made on people who have suffered strokes, or **cerebrovascular accidents.** The most common type of cerebrovascular accident is caused by obstruction of a blood vessel. The interruption in blood flow deprives a region of the brain of its blood supply, which causes cells in that region to die.

Another source of information about the brain mechanisms of verbal communication has been studies of patients with seizure disorders that are severe enough to require brain surgery. As we saw in Chapter 3, seizure surgery usually entails removal of a seizure focus—a region of the brain that includes scar tissue or other abnormalities that irritates neurons in the vicinity and periodically triggers a seizure. Sometimes, before the surgery is performed, a set of electrodes will be temporarily implanted in the patient's brain. Electrical recordings can be made through these electrodes to try to find the location of the seizure focus, and the patient's reactions can be studied while electrical stimulation is delivered through the electrodes. Then, if the patient is operated on, the surgeon can stimulate various regions of the brain and observe the effects of the stimulation on the patient's verbal behavior. (As we saw in Chapter 3, such surgery is performed under local anesthesia so that the patient can remain conscious.) Finally, if part of the brain is removed, the patient's behavior before the surgery can be compared with his or her behavior after removal of the brain tissue.

Although one might think that patients like these would be ideal subjects for studies of the brain mechanisms of language, we must remember that their brains contain abnormalities. If they did not, they would not be candidates for surgery. Many of these abnormalities occurred early in life—for example, as a consequence of obstetric difficulties. We know that when damage occurs in the immature brain, the course of development is altered. Thus, the brain of an adult with a long-standing seizure disorder is likely to be different from that of a person without such a disorder. In fact, Devinsky et al. (1993) used cortical stimulation to map the location of speech areas of the temporal lobe of seizure patients and found a more widespread or atypical distribution of these areas in patients with a history of early onset of seizures. Thus, we must be careful in drawing conclusions about the location of brain regions that are involved in specific functions from patients undergoing seizure surgery.

A third source of information about the physiology of language comes from studies using functional imaging devices. In recent years, researchers have used PET and functional MRI to gather information about language processes from normal subjects. In general, these studies have confirmed or complemented what we have learned by studying patients with brain damage.

---

cerebrovascular accident A "stroke"; brain damage caused by occlusion or rupture of a blood vessel in the brain.

The most important category of speech disorders is **aphasia,** a primary disturbance in the comprehension or production of speech, caused by brain damage. Not all speech disturbances are aphasias; a patient must have difficulty comprehending, repeating, or producing meaningful speech, and this difficulty must not be caused by simple sensory or motor deficits or by lack of motivation. For example, inability to speak caused by deafness or paralysis of the speech muscles is not considered to be aphasia. In addition, the deficit must be relatively isolated; that is, the patient must appear to be aware of what is happening in his or her environment and to comprehend that others are attempting to communicate.

Lateralization

Verbal behavior is a *lateralized* function; most language disturbances occur after damage to the left side of the brain, whether people are left-handed or right-handed. Using an ultrasonic procedure to measure changes in cerebral blood flow while people performed a verbal task, Knecht et al. (2000) assessed the relationship between handedness and lateralization of speech mechanisms in people without any known brain damage. They found that left-hemisphere speech dominance was seen in only 4 percent of right-handed people, in 15 percent of ambidextrous people, and in 27 percent of left-handed people. If the left hemisphere is malformed or damaged early in life, then language dominance is very likely to pass to the right hemisphere (Vikingstad et al., 2000). Because the left hemisphere of approximately 90 percent of the total population is dominant for speech, you can assume that the brain damage described in this chapter is located in the left (speech-dominant) hemisphere unless I say otherwise.

Why is one hemisphere specialized for speech? The perceptual functions of the left hemisphere are more specialized for the analysis of sequences of stimuli, occurring one after the other. The perceptual functions of the right hemisphere are more specialized for the analysis of space and geometrical shapes and forms, the elements of which are all present at the same time. Speech is certainly sequential; it consists of sequences of words, which are composed of sequences of sounds. Therefore, it makes sense for the left hemisphere to have become specialized at perceiving speech. In addition, as we saw in Chapter 8, the left hemisphere is involved in the control of sequences of voluntary movements. Perhaps this fact accounts for the localization of neural circuits involved in speech production, as well as speech perception, in the left hemisphere.

The brain is asymmetrical in structure as well as in function. For example, the size of speech areas in the frontal and temporal lobes is larger in the speech-dominant hemisphere, and there are differences in the size of some populations of neurons in these regions (Galaburda, Rosen, and Sherman, 1991; Foundas et al., 1996). Galuske et al. (2000) studied the composition of clusters of neurons in the posterior part of Wernicke's area, a region of the superior temporal lobe known to play a role in speech. These clusters are similar to the modules seen in visual cortex and, in the left hemisphere, appear to perform elementary computations required for language. The investigators found that although the number of clusters in this region was the same in the left and right hemisphere, the spacing between the clusters in the left hemisphere was 20 percent greater, and their interconnecting axons were longer, too. (Obviously, the size of this region is larger in the left hemisphere.) Galuske and his colleagues suggest that the increased interconnectivity of the cell clusters in the left hemisphere may permit the fine-grained analyses necessary for speech recognition.

Although the circuits that are *primarily* involved in speech comprehension and production are located in one hemisphere (almost always, the left hemisphere), it would be a mistake to conclude that the other hemisphere plays no role in speech. Speech is not simply a matter of talking; it is also having something to say. Similarly, listening is not simply hearing and recognizing words; it is understanding the meaning of what has been said. When we hear and understand words and when we talk about or think about our own perceptions or memories, we are using neural circuits besides those directly involved in speech. Thus, these circuits, too, play a role in verbal behavior. For example, damage to the right hemisphere makes it difficult for a person to read maps, perceive spatial relations, and recognize complex geometrical forms. People with such damage also have trouble talking about things like maps and complex geometrical forms or understanding what other people have to say about them. The right hemisphere also appears to be involved in organizing a narrative—selecting and assembling the elements of what we want to say (Gardner et al., 1983). As we saw in Chapter 11, the right hemisphere is involved in the expression and recognition of emotion in the tone of voice. And as we shall see in this chapter, it is also involved in control of *prosody*—the normal rhythm and stress found in speech. Therefore, both hemispheres of the brain have a contribution to make to our language abilities.

Speech Production

Being able to talk—that is, to produce meaningful speech—requires several abilities. First, the person must have something to talk about. Let us consider what this means. We can talk about something that is currently happening or something that happened in the past. In the first case we are talking about our perceptions: things we are seeing, hearing, feeling, smelling, and so on. In the second case we are talking about our memories of what happened in the past. Both perceptions of current events and memories of events that occurred in the past involve brain mechanisms in the posterior part of the cerebral hemispheres (the occipital, temporal, and parietal lobes). Thus, this region is largely responsible for our having something to say.

aphasia Difficulty in producing or comprehending speech not produced by deafness or a simple motor deficit; caused by brain damage.

Of course, we can also talk about something that *did not happen.* That is, we can use our imagination to make up a story (or to tell a lie). We know very little about the neural mechanisms that are responsible for imagination, but it seems likely that they involve the mechanisms responsible for perceptions and memories; after all, when we make up a story, we must base it on knowledge that we originally acquired through perception and have retained in our memory.

Given that a person has something to say, actually doing so requires some additional brain functions. As we shall see in this section, the conversion of perceptions, memories, and thoughts into speech makes use of neural mechanisms located in the frontal lobes.

Damage to a region of the inferior left frontal lobe (Broca's area) disrupts the ability to speak: It causes **Broca's aphasia.** This disorder is characterized by slow, laborious, and nonfluent speech. When trying to talk with patients who have Broca's aphasia, most people find it hard to resist supplying the words the patients are obviously groping for. But although they often mispronounce words, the ones they manage to come out with are usually meaningful. The posterior part of the cerebral hemispheres has something to say, but the damage to the frontal lobe makes it difficult for the patients to express these thoughts.

People with Broca's aphasia find it easier to say some types of words than others. They have great difficulty saying the little words with grammatical meaning, such as *a, the, some, in,* or *about.* These words are called **function words,** because they have important grammatical functions. The words that they do manage to say are almost entirely **content words**—words that convey meaning, including nouns, verbs, adjectives, and adverbs, such as *apple, house, throw,* or *heavy.* Here is a sample of speech from a man with Broca's aphasia, who is trying to describe the scene shown in ***Figure 15.1***. As you will see, his words are

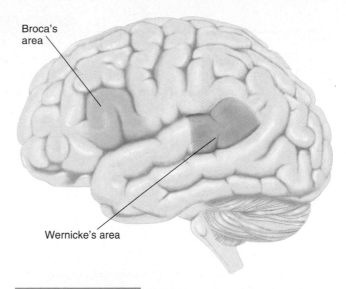

Broca's area

Wernicke's area

figure   **15.2**

The location of the primary speech areas of the brain. (Wernicke's area will be described later.)

meaningful, but what he says is certainly not grammatical. The dots indicate long pauses.

> kid . . . kk . . . can . . . candy . . . cookie . . . candy . . . well I don't know but it's writ . . . easy does it . . . slam . . . early . . . fall . . . men . . . many no . . . girl. Dishes . . . soap . . . soap . . . water . . . water . . . falling pah that's all . . . dish . . . that's all.
>
> Cookies . . . can . . . candy . . . cookies cookies . . . he . . . down . . . That's all. Girl . . . slipping water . . . water . . . and it hurts . . . much to do . . . Her . . . clean up . . . Dishes . . . up there . . . I think that's doing it. (Obler and Gjerlow, 1999, p. 41)

People with Broca's aphasia can comprehend speech much better than they can produce it. In fact, some observers have said that their comprehension is unimpaired, but as we will see, this is not quite true. Broca (1861) suggested that this form of aphasia is produced by a lesion of the frontal association cortex, just anterior to the face region of the primary motor cortex. Subsequent research proved him to be essentially correct, and we now call the region **Broca's area.** (See ***Figure 15.2***.)

Lesions that produce Broca's aphasia are certainly centered in the vicinity of Broca's area. However, dam-

figure   **15.1**

The drawing of the kitchen story, part of the Boston Diagnostic Aphasia Test.

(From Goodglass, H., and Kaplan, E. *The Assessment of Aphasia and Related Disorders,* 2nd ed. Philadelphia: Lea & Febiger, 1983. Reprinted with permission.)

Broca's aphasia A form of aphasia characterized by agrammatism, anomia, and extreme difficulty in speech articulation.

function word A preposition, article, or other word that conveys little of the meaning of a sentence but is important in specifying its grammatical structure.

content word A noun, verb, adjective, or adverb that conveys meaning.

Broca's area A region of frontal cortex, located just rostral to the base of the left primary motor cortex, that is necessary for normal speech production.

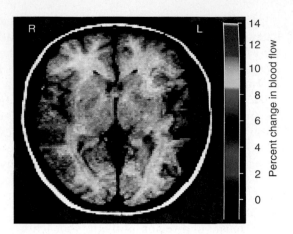

figure 15.3

An averaged plot of PET scans of regional cerebral blood flow, superimposed on an MRI scan, taken while the subjects were reading words aloud. Note that the region of activation includes subcortical regions as well as the cerebral cortex of Broca's area. Also note that left and right are reversed. (From Leblanc, R., Meyer, E., Bub, D., Zatorre, R. J., and Evans, A. C. *Neurosurgery*, 1992, *31*, 369–373. Reprinted with permission.)

age that is restricted to the cortex of Broca's area does not appear to produce Broca's aphasia; the damage must extend to surrounding regions of the frontal lobe and to the underlying subcortical white matter (H. Damasio, 1989; Naeser et al., 1989). In addition, there is evidence that lesions of the basal ganglia—especially the head of the caudate nucleus—can also produce a Broca-like aphasia (Damasio, Eslinger, and Adams, 1984). Figure 15.3 shows the averaged plot of PET scans of regional blood flow from a group of subjects who were reading words aloud (Leblanc et al., 1992). As you can see, the task activated subcortical regions under Broca's area (including the head of the caudate nucleus) as well as the neocortex. (See *Figure 15.3*.)

Watkins et al. (2002a, 2002b) studied three generations of the KE family, half of whose members are affected by a severe speech and language disorder caused by the mutation of a single gene found on chromosome 7. The primary deficit appears to involve the ability to perform the sequential movements necessary for speech, but the people also have difficulty repeating sounds they hear and forming the past tense of verbs. The mutation causes abnormal development of the caudate nucleus and the left inferior frontal cortex, including Broca's area.

What do the neural circuits in and around Broca's area do? Wernicke (1874) suggested that Broca's area contains motor memories—in particular, *memories of the sequences of muscular movements that are needed to articulate words.* Talking involves rapid movements of the tongue, lips, and jaw, and these movements must be coordinated with each other and with those of the vocal cords; thus, talking requires some very sophisticated motor control mechanisms. Obviously, circuits of neurons somewhere in our brain will, when properly activated, cause these sequences of movements to be executed. Because damage to the inferior caudal left frontal lobe (including Broca's area) disrupts the ability to articulate words, this region is the most likely candidate for the location of these "programs." The fact that this region is directly connected to the part of the primary motor cortex that controls the muscles used for speech certainly supports this conclusion.

But the speech functions of the left frontal lobe include more than programming the movements used to speak. Broca's aphasia is much more than a deficit in pronouncing words. In general, three major speech deficits are produced by lesions in and around Broca's area: *agrammatism, anomia,* and *articulation difficulties.* Although most patients with Broca's aphasia will have all of these deficits to some degree, their severity can vary considerably from person to person—presumably, because their brain lesions differ. You can also hear the voice of an agrammatic patient and one with articulation difficulties in *Animation 15.1, Voices of Aphasia: Broca's Aphasia.*

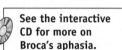

See the interactive CD for more on Broca's aphasia.

Agrammatism refers to a patient's difficulty in using grammatical constructions. This disorder can appear all by itself, without any difficulty in pronouncing words (Nadeau, 1988). As we saw, people with Broca's aphasia rarely use function words. In addition, they rarely use grammatical markers such as -*ed* or auxiliaries such as *have* (as in *I have gone*). For some reason, they *do* often use -*ing*, perhaps because this ending converts a verb into a noun. A study by Saffran, Schwartz, and Marin (1980) illustrates this difficulty. The following quotations are from agrammatic patients attempting to describe pictures:

> Picture of a boy being hit in the head by a baseball
>
> The boy is catch . . . the boy is hitch . . . the boy is hit the ball. (Saffran, Schwartz, and Marin, 1980, p. 229)
>
> Picture of a girl giving flowers to her teacher
>
> Girl . . . wants to . . . flowers . . . flowers and wants to. . . . The woman . . . wants to. . . . The girl wants to . . . the flowers and the woman. (Saffran, Schwartz, and Marin, 1980, p. 234)

---

agrammatism One of the usual symptoms of Broca's aphasia; a difficulty in comprehending or properly employing grammatical devices, such as verb endings and word order.

So far, I have described Broca's aphasia as a disorder in speech *production*. In an ordinary conversation Broca's aphasics seem to understand everything that is said to them. They appear to be irritated and annoyed by their inability to express their thoughts well, and they often make gestures to supplement their scanty speech. The striking disparity between their speech and their comprehension often leads people to assume that their comprehension is normal. But it is not. Schwartz, Saffran, and Marin (1980) showed Broca's aphasics pairs of pictures in which agents and objects of the action were reversed: for example, a horse kicking a cow and a cow kicking a horse, a truck pulling a car and a car pulling a truck, and a dancer applauding a clown and a clown applauding a dancer. As they showed each pair of pictures, they read the subject a sentence, for example, *The horse kicks the cow.* The subjects' task was to point to the appropriate picture, indicating whether they understood the grammatical construction of the sentence. (See *Figure 15.4*.) They performed very poorly.

The correct picture in the study by Schwartz and her colleagues was specified by a particular aspect of grammar: word order. The agrammatism that accompanies Broca's aphasia appears to disrupt patients' ability to use grammatical information, including word order, to decode the meaning of a sentence. Thus, their deficit in comprehension parallels their deficit in production. If they heard a sentence such as *The man swats the mosquito,* they would understand that it concerns a man and a mosquito and the action of swatting. They would have no trouble figuring out who is doing what to whom. But a sentence such as *The horse kicks the cow* does not provide any extra cues; if

the grammar is not understood, neither is the meaning of the sentence.

The second major speech deficit seen in Broca's aphasia is **anomia** ("without name"). Anomia refers to a word-finding difficulty; and because all aphasics omit words or use inappropriate ones, anomia is actually a primary symptom of *all* forms of aphasia. However, because the speech of Broca's aphasics lacks fluency, their anomia is especially apparent; their facial expression and frequent use of sounds like "uh" make it obvious that they are groping for the correct words.

The third major characteristic of Broca's aphasia is *difficulty with articulation*. Patients mispronounce words, often altering the sequence of sounds. For example, *lipstick* might be pronounced "likstip." People with Broca's aphasia recognize that their pronunciation is erroneous, and they usually try to correct it.

These three deficits are seen in various combinations in different patients, depending on the exact location of the lesion and, to a certain extent, on their stage of recovery. We can think of these deficits as constituting a hierarchy. On the lowest, most elementary level is control of the sequence of movements of the muscles of speech; damage to this ability leads to articulation difficulties. The next higher level is selection of the particular "programs" for individual words; damage to this ability leads to anomia. Finally, the highest level is selection of grammatical structure, including word order, use of function words, and word endings; damage to this ability leads to agrammatism.

We might expect that the direct control of articulation would involve the face area of the primary motor cortex and portions of the basal ganglia, while the selection of words, word order, and grammatical markers would involve Broca's area and adjacent regions of the frontal association cortex. Some recent studies indicate that different categories of symptoms of Broca's aphasia do, indeed, involve different brain regions. Dronkers (1996) appears to have found a critical location for control of speech articulation: the left precentral gyrus of the insula. The insular cortex is located on the lateral wall of the cerebral hemisphere behind the anterior temporal lobe. Normally, this region is hidden and can be seen only when the temporal lobe is dissected away. (See *Figure 15.5*.) Dronkers discovered the apparent role of this region by plotting the lesions of patients with and without apraxia of speech who had strokes that damaged the same general area of the brain. (**Apraxia of speech** is an impairment

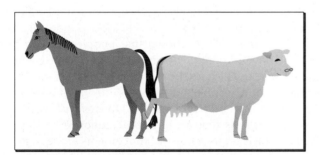

figure 15.4

An example of the stimuli used in the experiment by Schwartz, Saffran, and Marin (1980).

anomia Difficulty in finding (remembering) the appropriate word to describe an object, action, or attribute; one of the symptoms of aphasia.

apraxia of speech Impairment in the ability to program movements of the tongue, lips, and throat required to produce the proper sequence of speech sounds.

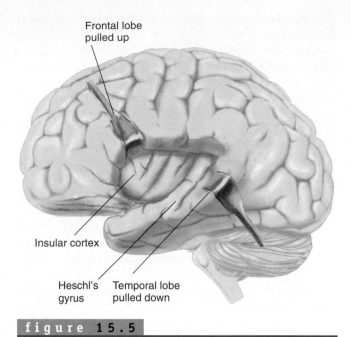

Frontal lobe
pulled up

Insular cortex

Heschl's
gyrus

Temporal lobe
pulled down

figure 15.5

The insular cortex, normally hidden behind the rostral temporal lobe.

in the ability to program movements of the tongue, lips, and throat that are required to produce the proper sequence of speech sounds.) Figure 15.6(a) shows the overlap of the lesions of twenty-five patients with apraxia of speech. As you can see, a region of 100 percent overlap, shown in yellow, falls on the left precentral gyrus of the insula. (See *Figure 15.6a*.) In contrast, *none* of the lesions of nineteen patients who did not show apraxia of speech included damage to this region. (See *Figure 15.6b*.)

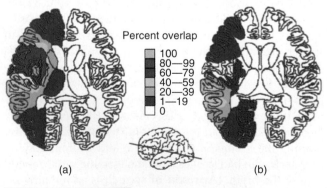

Percent overlap

100
80—99
60—79
40—59
20—39
1—19
0

(a)   (b)

figure 15.6

Evidence for involvement of the insular cortex in speech articulation. Percentage overlap in the lesions of twenty-five patients (a) with apraxia of speech and (b) without apraxia of speech. The only region common to all lesions that produced apraxia of speech was the precentral gyrus of the insular cortex.

(From Dronkers, N. F. *Nature*, 1996, *384*, 159–161.)

At least two functional imaging studies support Dronkers's conclusion. Kuriki, Mori, and Hirata (1999) and Wise et al. (1999) found that pronunciation of words caused activation of the left anterior insula.

Another region of the brain seems to be involved in speech production. Studies have found that damage to the periaqueductal gray matter (PAG) of the midbrain disrupts vocalization in a variety of species, including frogs, cats, dogs, monkeys, and apes. In addition, electrical or chemical stimulation of the PAG elicits vocalization, and the firing rate of single neurons in this region increases when an animal vocalizes (Jürgens, 1998). Lesions of the PAG also cause mutism in humans. For example, Esposito et al. (1999) described the case of a woman with a PAG lesions who could understand speech and respond to it nonverbally but could not make any speech sounds herself—even in response to pain. However, she could move her lips as if she were speaking. For example, when an examiner asked her if she were thirsty, she moved her lips as if to say, "Oui." (The patient spoke French.)

The agrammatism and anomia of Broca's aphasia are normally caused by subcortical damage or damage to the neocortex of the inferior frontal lobe. These findings are supported by a PET study by Stromswold et al. (1996). Subjects listened to syntactically complex sentences and had to decide whether they made sense. For example, "The dog that the cat scratched chased the mouse" makes sense, but "The mouse that the cat scratched chased the dog" does not. Listening to such sentences and judging their plausibility certainly exercises neural circuits involved in comprehension of grammar—and the investigators found that doing so increased the activity of Broca's area, especially the part closest to the lateral fissure. A functional MRI study with Japanese subjects obtained similar results (Inui et al., 1998).

Experiments have shown that people with Broca's aphasia have difficulty carrying out a sequence of commands such as "Pick up the red circle and touch the green square with it" (Boller and Dennis, 1979). This finding, along with the other symptoms I have described in this section, suggests that an important function of the left frontal lobe is sequencing—of movements of the muscles of speech (producing words) and of words (comprehending and producing grammatical speech).

Speech Comprehension

Comprehension of speech obviously begins in the auditory system, which detects and analyzes sounds. But *recognizing* words is one thing; *comprehending* them—understanding their meaning—is another. Recognizing a spoken word is a complex perceptual task that relies on memories of sequences of sounds. This task appears to be accomplished by neural circuits in the middle and posterior portion of the superior temporal gyrus of the left hemisphere, a region that has come to be known as **Wernicke's area.** (Refer to *Figure 15.2*.)

Wernicke's Aphasia: Description

The primary characteristics of **Wernicke's aphasia** are poor speech comprehension and production of meaningless speech. Unlike Broca's aphasia, Wernicke's aphasia is fluent and unlabored; the person does not strain to articulate words and does not appear to be searching for them. The patient maintains a melodic line, with the voice rising and falling normally. When you listen to the speech of a person with Wernicke's aphasia, it appears to be grammatical. That is, the person uses function words such as *the* and *but* and employs complex verb tenses and subordinate clauses. However, the person uses few content words, and the words that he or she strings together just do not make sense. In the extreme, speech deteriorates into a meaningless jumble, illustrated by the following quotation:

> *Examiner:* What kind of work did you do before you came into the hospital?
>
> *Patient:* Never, now mista oyge I wanna tell you this happened when happened when he rent. His—his kell come down here and is—he got ren something. It happened. In thesse ropiers were with him for hi—is friend—like was. And it just happened so I don't know, he did not bring around anything. And he did not pay it. And he roden all o these arranjen from the pedis on from iss pescid. In these floors now and so. He hadn't had em round here. (Kertesz, 1981, p. 73)

Because of the speech deficit of people with Wernicke's aphasia, when we try to assess their ability to comprehend speech, we must ask them to use nonverbal responses. That is, we cannot assume that they do not understand what other people say to them just because they do not give the proper answer. A commonly used test of comprehension assesses their ability to understand questions by pointing to objects on a table in front of them. For example, they are asked to "Point to the one with ink." If they point to an object other than the pen, they have not understood the request. When tested this way, people with severe Wernicke's aphasia do indeed show poor comprehension.

A remarkable fact about people with Wernicke's aphasia is that they often seem unaware of their deficit. That is, they do not appear to recognize that their speech is faulty, nor do they recognize they cannot understand the speech of others. They do not look puzzled when someone tells them something, even though they obviously cannot understand what they hear. Perhaps their comprehension deficit prevents them from realizing that what they say and hear makes no sense. They still follow social conventions, taking turns in conversation with the examiner, even though they do not understand what the examiner says and what they say in return makes little sense. They remain sensitive to the other person's facial expression and tone of voice and begin talking when he or she asks a question and pauses for an answer. One patient with Wernicke's aphasia made the following responses when asked to name ten common objects.

> *toothbrush* → "stoktery"
> *cigarette* → "cigarette"
> *pen* → "tankt"
> *knife* → "nike"
> *fork* → "fahk"
> *quarter* → "minkt"
> *pen* → "spentee"
> *matches* → "senktr"
> *key* → "seek"
> *comb* → "sahk"

He acted sure of himself and gave no indication that he recognized that most of his responses were meaningless. The responses he made were not simply new words that 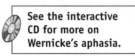 he had invented; he was asked several times to name the objects and gave different responses each time (except for *cigarette*, which he always named correctly). You can hear the speech of people with Wernicke's aphasia in *Animation 15.1, Voices of Aphasia: Wernicke's Aphasia.*

See the interactive CD for more on Wernicke's aphasia.

Wernicke's Aphasia: Analysis

Because the superior temporal gyrus is a region of auditory association cortex, and because a comprehension deficit is so prominent in Wernicke's aphasia, this disorder has been characterized as a *receptive* aphasia. Wernicke suggested that the region that now bears his name is the location of *memories of the sequences of sounds that constitute words*. This hypothesis is reasonable; it suggests that the auditory association cortex of the superior temporal gyrus recognizes the sounds of words, just as the visual association cortex of the inferior temporal gyrus recognizes the sight of objects.

There seems little doubt that Wernicke's area is involved in learning. In fact, Jacobs, Schall, and Scheibel (1993) found that the average length of apical dendrites of pyramidal cells in Wernicke's area was positively related to a person's educational level.

But why should damage to an area that is responsible for the ability to recognize spoken words disrupt people's

---

Wernicke's area A region of auditory association cortex on the left temporal lobe of humans, which is important in the comprehension of words and the production of meaningful speech.

Wernicke's aphasia A form of aphasia characterized by poor speech comprehension and fluent but meaningless speech.

Speech sounds

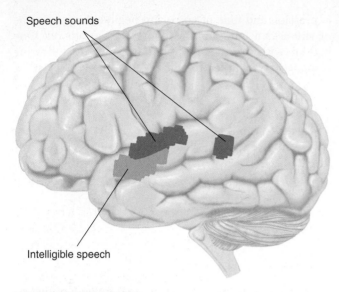

Intelligible speech

figure 15.7

Results of PET scans indicating regions of the superior temporal lobe that respond to speech sounds. *Red:* Regions that responded to phonetic information (normal speech sounds or a computerized transformation speech that preserved the complexity of the speech sounds but rendered it unintelligible). *Yellow:* Region that responded only to intelligible speech (normal speech sounds or a computerized transformation that removed most normal frequencies but preserved intelligibility).

(Adapted from Scott, S. K., Blank, E. C., Rosen, S., and Wise, R. J. S. *Brain*, 2000, *123*, 2400–2406.)

ability to speak? In fact, it does not; Wernicke's aphasia, like Broca's aphasia, actually appears to consist of several deficits. The abilities that are disrupted include *recognition of spoken words, comprehension of the meaning of words,* and the *ability to convert thoughts into words.* Let us consider each of these abilities in turn.

■ **Recognition: Pure Word Deafness** As I said in the introduction to this section, *recognizing* a word is not the same as *comprehending* it. If you hear a foreign word several times, you will learn to recognize it; but unless someone tells you what it means, you will not comprehend it. Recognition is a perceptual task; comprehension involves retrieval of additional information from memory.

Damage to the left temporal lobe can produce a disorder of auditory word recognition, uncontaminated by other problems. This syndrome is called **pure word deafness.** Although people with pure word deafness are not deaf, they cannot understand speech. As one patient put it, "I can hear you talking, I just can't understand what you're saying." Another said, "It's as if there were a bypass somewhere, and my ears were not connected to my voice" (Saffran, Marin, and Yeni-Komshian, 1976, p. 211). These

patients can recognize nonspeech sounds such as the barking of a dog, the sound of a doorbell, and the chirping of a bird. Often, they can recognize the emotion expressed by the intonation of speech even though they cannot understand what is being said. More significantly, their own speech is excellent. They can often understand what other people are saying by reading their lips. They can also read and write, and they sometimes ask people to communicate with them in writing. Clearly, pure word deafness is not an inability to comprehend the meaning of words; if it were, people with this disorder would not be able to read people's lips or read words written on paper.

Functional imaging studies confirm that perception of speech sounds activates neurons in the auditory association cortex of the superior temporal gyrus. Belin et al. (2000) found that as they presented more and more distorted speech, they saw parallel decreases in the subjects' ability to recognize words and the level of activation of the superior temporal gyrus. They also found regions that were sensitive to nonspeech vocal sounds, such as laughs, coughs, and sighs.

Although several studies have found that speech sounds activate regions of the superior temporal cortex, Scott et al. (2000) prepared a computerized transformation of normal speech that preserved the complexity of the speech sounds but rendered it unintelligible. They also prepared a transformation that removed most of the complexity of speech but could nevertheless be understood. Scott and her colleagues found that three regions of the superior temporal lobe were activated by phonetic information—that is, speech sounds, regardless of intelligibility. One of these regions was activated only by intelligibility—speech that could be understood, regardless of complexity. Presumably, damage to this region (or to its inputs) is responsible for pure word deafness. (See *Figure 15.7* and listen to the transformations in *Animation 15.2: Speech Perception.*)

> **See the interactive CD for more on speech perception.**

What is involved in the analysis of speech sounds? Just what tasks does the auditory system have to accomplish? And what are the differences in the functions of the auditory association cortex of the left and right hemispheres? Most researchers believe that the left hemisphere is primarily involved in judging the timing of the components of rapidly changing complex sounds, whereas the right hemisphere is primarily involved in judging more slowly changing components, including melody. Evidence suggests that the most crucial aspect of

pure word deafness The ability to hear, to speak, and (usually) to read and write without being able to comprehend the meaning of speech; caused by damage to Wernicke's area or disruption of auditory input to this region.

speech sounds is timing, not pitch. We can recognize words whether they are conveyed by the low pitch of a man or the high pitch of a woman or child. In fact, as you heard in Animation 15.2, we can understand speech from which almost all tonal information has been removed, leaving only some noise modulated by the rapid stops and starts that characterize human speech sounds. On the other hand, emphasis or the emotional state of the speaker is conveyed by the pitch and melody of speech and by much slower changes in rhythm. In other words, the sounds that convey the identity of words are very brief, whereas those that convey *prosody* (emphasis and emotion) are of longer duration. (As we will see later, the right hemisphere is specialized for recognition of prosody.) Perhaps the auditory system of the left hemisphere is particularly specialized for the recognition of acoustical events of short duration.

In a review of the literature, Phillips and Farmer (1990) suggest precisely this hypothesis. They note that careful studies of patients with pure word deafness have shown that the patients can distinguish between different vowels but not between different consonants, especially between different stop consonants, such as /t/, /d/, /k/, or /p/. (Linguists represent speech sounds by putting letters or special phonetic symbols between pairs of slashes.) Patients with pure word deafness *can* generally recognize consonants with a long duration, such as /s/, /z/, or /f/. (Say these consonants to yourself, and you will see how different they sound from the first four examples.)

Phillips and Farmer note that the important acoustical events in speech sounds fall within a time range of a few milliseconds to a few tens of milliseconds. Speech sounds are made by rapidly moving the lips, tongue, and soft palate, which produce acoustical events that can be distinguished only by a fine-grained analysis. In contrast, most environmental sounds do not contain such a fine temporal structure. The authors also note that "pure" word deafness is not absolutely pure. That is, when people with this disorder are tested carefully with recordings of a variety of environmental sounds, they have difficulty recognizing at least some of them. Although *most* environmental sounds do not contain a fine temporal structure, some do, and patients have difficulty recognizing them. For example, one patient with pure word deafness could no longer understand messages in Morse code but could still *send* messages that way.

Apparently, two types of brain injury can cause pure word deafness: disruption of auditory input to Wernicke's area or damage to Wernicke's area itself. Disruption of auditory input can be produced by bilateral damage to the primary auditory cortex, or it can be caused by damage to the white matter in the left temporal lobes that cuts axons bringing auditory information from the primary auditory cortex to Wernicke's area (Digiovanni et al., 1992; Takahashi et al., 1992). Either type of damage—disruption of auditory input or damage to Wernicke's area—disturbs the analysis of the sounds of words and hence prevents people from recognizing other people's speech. (See *Figure 15.8*.)

■ **Comprehension: Transcortical Sensory Aphasia**

The other symptoms of Wernicke's aphasia—failure to comprehend the meaning of words and inability to express thoughts in meaningful speech—appear to be produced by damage that extends beyond Wernicke's area into the region that surrounds the posterior part of the lateral fissure, near the junction of the temporal, occipital, and parietal lobes. For want of a better term, I will refer to this

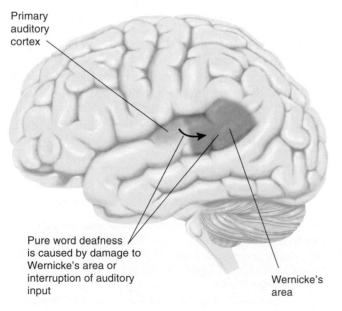

Primary auditory cortex

Pure word deafness is caused by damage to Wernicke's area or interruption of auditory input

Wernicke's area

figure 15.8

The brain damage that causes pure word deafness.

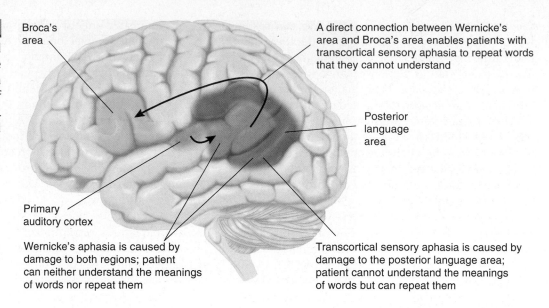

figure 15.9

The location and interconnections of the posterior language area and an explanation of its role in transcortical sensory aphasia and Wernicke's aphasia.

Broca's area

A direct connection between Wernicke's area and Broca's area enables patients with transcortical sensory aphasia to repeat words that they cannot understand

Posterior language area

Primary auditory cortex

Wernicke's aphasia is caused by damage to both regions; patient can neither understand the meanings of words nor repeat them

Transcortical sensory aphasia is caused by damage to the posterior language area; patient cannot understand the meanings of words but can repeat them

region as the *posterior language area*. (See *Figure 15.9*.) The posterior language area appears to serve as a place for interchanging information between the auditory representation of words and the meanings of these words, stored as memories in the rest of the sensory association cortex.

Damage to the posterior language area alone, which isolates Wernicke's area from the rest of the posterior language area, produces a disorder known as **transcortical sensory aphasia.** (See *Figure 15.9*.) The difference between transcortical sensory aphasia and Wernicke's aphasia is that patients with this disorder *can repeat what other people say to them;* therefore, they can recognize words. However, *they cannot comprehend the meaning of what they hear and repeat; nor can they produce meaningful speech of their own.* How can these people repeat what they hear? Because the posterior language area is damaged, repetition does not involve this part of the brain. Obviously, there must be a direct connection between Wernicke's area and Broca's area that bypasses the posterior language area. (See *Figure 15.9*.)

Boatman et al. (2000) stimulated various language-related areas of the brains of people who were being evaluated for seizure surgery. They found that in most cases, electrical stimulation of the lateral temporal lobe, ventral or anteroventral to Wernicke's area, produced the symptoms of transcortical sensory aphasia: The patients could not comprehend what was said to them when the stimulation was turned on, but they could repeat what they heard. (See *Figure 15.10*.) These findings suggest that perhaps my representation of the posterior language area should extend more rostrally than I have depicted it in Figure 15.9.

A woman sustained extensive brain damage from carbon monoxide produced by a faulty water heater. She spent several years in the hospital before she died, without ever saying anything meaningful on her own. She did not follow verbal commands or otherwise give signs of understanding them. However, she often repeated what was said to her. For example, if an examiner said "Please raise your right hand," she would reply "Please raise your right hand" The repetition was not parrotlike; she did not imitate accents different from her own, and if someone made a grammatical error while saying something to her, she sometimes repeated the sentence correctly, without the error. She could also recite poems if someone started them. For example, when an examiner said "Roses are red, violets are blue," she continued with "Sugar is sweet and so are you." She could sing and would do so when someone started singing a song she knew. She even learned new songs from the radio while in the hospital. Remember, though, that she gave *no signs of understanding anything she heard or said.* This disorder, along with pure word deafness, clearly confirms the conclusion that *recognizing* spoken words and *comprehending* them are different processes and involve different brain mechanisms (Geschwind, Quadfasel, and Segarra, 1968).

In conclusion, transcortical sensory aphasia can be seen as Wernicke's aphasia without a repetition deficit. To put it another way, the symptoms of Wernicke's aphasia consist of those of pure word deafness plus those of transcortical sensory aphasia. As I tell my students, WA = TSA + PWD. By simple algebra, TSA = WA – PWD, and so on. (Refer to *Figure 15.9*.)

■ **What Is Meaning?** As we have seen, Wernicke's area is involved in the analysis of speech sounds and thus in the recognition of words. Damage to the posterior lan-

transcortical sensory aphasia A speech disorder in which a person has difficulty comprehending speech and producing meaningful spontaneous speech but can repeat speech; caused by damage to the region of the brain posterior to Wernicke's area.

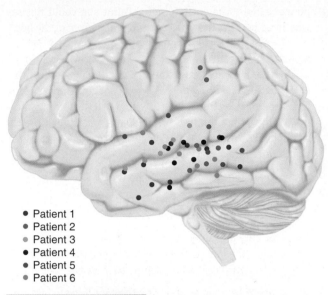

- Patient 1
- Patient 2
- Patient 3
- Patient 4
- Patient 5
- Patient 6

figure 15.10

Location of sites where electrical stimulation interfered with normal cortical activity and produced the symptoms of transcortical sensory aphasia: loss of speech comprehension but preservation of the ability to repeat speech.

(Adapted from Boatman, D., Gordon, B., Hart, J., Selnes, O., Miglioretti, D., and Lenz, F. *Brain,* 2000, *123,* 1634–1642.)

guage area does not disrupt people's ability to recognize words, but it does disrupt their ability to understand them or to produce meaningful speech of their own. But what, exactly, do we mean by the word *meaning?* And what types of brain mechanisms are involved?

Words refer to objects, actions, or relationships in the world. Thus, the meaning of a word is defined by particular memories associated with it. For example, knowing the meaning of the word *tree* means being able to imag-

ine the physical characteristics of trees: what they look like, what the wind sounds like blowing through their leaves, what the bark feels like, and so on. It also means knowing facts about trees: about their roots, buds, flowers, nuts, and wood and the chlorophyll in their leaves. These memories are stored not in the primary speech areas but in other parts of the brain, especially regions of the association cortex. Different categories of memories may be stored in particular regions of the brain, but they are somehow tied together, so hearing the word *tree* activates all of them. (As we saw in Chapter 14, the hippocampal formation is involved in this process of tying related memories together.)

In thinking about the brain's verbal mechanisms involved in recognizing words and comprehending their meaning, I find that the concept of a dictionary serves as a useful analogy. Dictionaries contain entries (the words) and definitions (the meanings of the words). In the brain we have at least two types of entries: auditory and visual. That is, we can look up a word according to how it sounds or how it looks (in writing). Let us just consider just one type of entry: the sound of a word. (I will discuss reading and writing later in this chapter.) We hear a familiar word and understand its meaning. How do we do so?

First, we must recognize the sequence of sounds that constitute the word—We find the auditory entry for the word in our "dictionary." As we saw, this entry appears in Wernicke's area. Next, the memories that constitute the meaning of the word must be activated. Presumably, Wernicke's area is connected—through the posterior language area—with the neural circuits that contain these memories. (See *Figure 15.11*.)

The Hebb rule, which we encountered in Chapter 13, can be invoked to explain the acquisition of words and their meanings. Recall that the Hebb rule says that when interconnected neurons are repeatedly active at the same

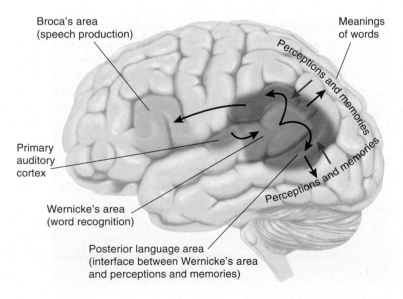

Broca's area
(speech production)

Meanings
of words

Perceptions and memories

Primary
auditory
cortex

Wernicke's area
(word recognition)

Perceptions and memories

Posterior language area
(interface between Wernicke's area
and perceptions and memories)

figure 15.11

The "dictionary" in the brain. Wernicke's area contains the auditory entries of words; the meanings are contained as memories in the sensory association areas. Black arrows represent comprehension of words—the activation of memories that correspond to a word's meaning. Red arrows represent translation of thoughts or perceptions into words.

time, the synaptic connections between them are strengthened. Thus, when we hear a word several times, a particular set of neurons in the superior temporal lobe become active, and their interconnections eventually become strengthened. (We could also hear the word once and repeat it to ourselves, thus activating these neurons enough to strengthen their interconnections.) As Hebb put it, the coactivated neurons became a *cell assembly*—an assembly of interconnected neurons.

Suppose the word is "ball" and a child hears the word several times while she is playing with a ball or simply looking at one. Cell assemblies in Wernicke's area would constitute the memory of the sound of the word, while cell assemblies in the visual association cortex would constitute the memory of the child's ball. And because these two cell assemblies, which we can think of as the auditory entry of the word in the brain's dictionary and its definition, are active at the same time, they become linked through axons that interconnect these two regions. The Hebb rule predicts that other interconnections will also occur. For example, if the child successfully repeats the word "ball," a third cell assembly will develop in Broca's area that is responsible for the word's pronunciation. Eventually, interconnections will develop between all three areas, so the child will be able to say "ball" when she sees the ball or wants to play with it, and she will look for the ball when someone else says the word. Eventually, the child will learn that other round objects of different colors and sizes are also balls, and so on. Pulvermüller (1999) develops this explanation of the "dictionary in the brain," (my words, not his) in more detail.

The process works in reverse when we describe our thoughts or perceptions in words. Suppose we want to tell someone about a tree that we just planted in our yard. Thoughts about the tree (for example, a visual image of it) occur in our association cortex—the visual association cortex, in this example. Information about the activity of these circuits first activates circuits of neurons in the posterior language area and then circuits of neurons in Broca's area, which cause the words to be set into a grammatical sentence and be pronounced. (See *Figure 15.11*.)

What evidence do we have that meanings of words are represented by cell assemblies located in various regions of the association cortex? The best evidence comes from the fact that damage to particular regions of the sensory association cortex can damage particular kinds of information and thus abolish particular kinds of meanings.

I met a patient who had recently had a stroke that damaged a part of her right parietal lobe that played a role in spatial perception. She was alert and intelligent and showed no signs of aphasia. However, she was confused about directions and other spatial relationships. When asked to, she could point to the ceiling and the floor, but she could not say which was *over* the other. Her perception of other people appeared to be entirely normal, but she could not say whether a person's head was at the *top* or *bottom* of the body.

I wrote a set of multiple-choice questions to test her ability to use words denoting spatial relations. The results of the test indicated that she did not know the meaning of words such as *up, down,* and *under* when they referred to spatial relationships, but she could use these words normally when they referred to nonspatial relationships. For example, here are some of her incorrect responses when the words referred to spatial relations:

> A tree's branches are *under* its roots.
> The sky is *down.*
> The ceiling is *under* the floor.

She made only ten correct responses on the sixteen-item test. In contrast, she got all eight items correct when the words referred to nonspatial relationships such as the following:

> After exchanging pleasantries, they got *down* to business.
> He got sick and threw *up.*

Damage to part of the association cortex of the *left* parietal lobe can produce an inability to name the body parts. The disorder is called **autotopagnosia,** or "poor knowledge of one's own topography." (A better name would have been *autotopanomia,* "poor naming of one's own topography.") People who can otherwise converse normally cannot reliably point to their elbow, knee, or cheek when asked to do so and cannot name body parts when the examiner points to them. However, they have no difficulty understanding the meaning of other words.

Other investigators have reported verbal deficits that include disruption of particular categories of meaning. McCarthy and Warrington (1988) reported the case of a man with left temporal lobe damage (patient T. B.) who was unable to explain the meaning of words that denoted living things. For example, when he was asked to define the word *rhinoceros,* he said, "Animal, can't give you any functions." However, when he was shown a *picture* of a rhinoceros, he said, "Enormous, weighs over one ton, lives in Africa." Similarly, when asked what a *dolphin* was, he said, "a fish or a bird"; but he responded to a *picture* of a dolphin by saying, "Dolphin lives in water . . . they are trained to jump up and come out . . . In America during the war years they started to get this particular animal to go through to look into ships." Clearly, patient T. B. has not lost his knowledge of specific animals but only the ability to name them. Presumably, the damage to his brain disconnected circuits involved in the recognition of words from those involved in his memories of animals. When

---

autotopagnosia Inability to name body parts or to identify body parts that another person names.

T. B. was asked to define the meanings of words that denoted inanimate objects (such as *lighthouse* or *wheelbarrow*), he had no trouble at all.

Functional imaging studies of people without brain damage confirm these findings. Several experiments have found that perception of words and concepts from different categories activate different parts of the brain. For example, Spitzer et al. (1995) had people name pictures of items that belonged to four different categories: animals, furniture, fruit, and tools. Functional MRI scans revealed some category-specific sites of activation in the frontal and temporal lobes.

Some patients have even more specific deficits; Semenza and Zettin (1989) described patient P. C., who had great difficulty with proper nouns (names of people and places). Damasio et al. (1991) studied several patients with similar deficits and concluded that anomia for proper nouns is caused by damage to the temporal pole (the rostral end of the temporal lobe), whereas anomia for common nouns is caused by damage to the inferior temporal cortex. An electrical recording study also found activation of different regions by common and proper nouns (Proverbio et al., 2001). Damasio and his colleagues suggest that the important distinction between the two types of words is that proper nouns are specific to particular individuals (people or places), whereas common nouns apply to *categories*. Presumably, the cortex of the temporal pole is specifically involved with recognition of individuals. This suggestion was supported by a functional imaging study from Damasio's laboratory (Grabowski et al., 2001). The investigators found that when people tried to name pictures of either famous landmarks or famous faces, their left temporal pole was activated.

Hamberger et al. (2001) asked patients who were being assessed for possible seizure surgery to try to name common objects. The items were presented visually or acoustically; the patients were shown drawings of objects or heard oral descriptions, such as "What a king wears on his head." While the patients were performing this task, the experimenters stimulated different regions of the temporal lobe and parietal lobe just dorsal to the lateral fissure. As you can see in Figure 15.12, stimulation of different regions disrupted naming elicited by visual and auditory cues. (See *Figure 15.12*.)

So far, most of the studies I have described have dealt with comprehension of simple concepts: spatial direction and orientation, body parts, animals, and other concrete objects. But speech also conveys abstract concepts, some of them quite subtle. What parts of the brain are responsible for comprehending the meaning behind proverbs such as "People who live in glass houses shouldn't throw stones" or the moral of stories such as the one about the race between the tortoise and the hare?

Studies of brain-damaged patients suggest that comprehension of the more subtle, figurative aspects of speech

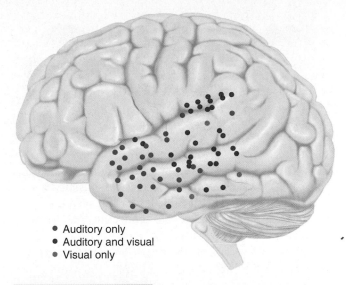

- ● Auditory only
- ● Auditory and visual
- ● Visual only

figure 15.12

Location of sites in and near the lateral temporal cortex where electrical stimulation interfered with visual naming (drawings of common objects) or auditory naming (spoken definitions of common items).

(Adapted from Hamberger, M. J., Goodman, R. R., Perrine, K., and Tamny, T. *Neurology,* 2001, *56,* 56–61.)

involves the right hemisphere in particular (Brownell et al., 1983, 1990). Functional imaging studies confirm these observations. Bottini et al. (1994) had people listen to sentences and judge their plausibility. Some sentences were straightforward and factual. For example, "The old man has a branch as a walking stick" is plausible, whereas "The lady has a bucket as a walking stick" is not. Other sentences presented metaphors, the comprehension of which goes beyond the literal meaning of the words. For example, "The old man had a head full of dead leaves" is plausible, whereas "The old man had a head full of barn doors" is not. The investigators found that judging the metaphors activated parts of the right hemisphere, while judging factual sentences did not. Nichelli et al. (1995) found that judging the moral of Aesop's fables (as opposed to judging more superficial aspects of the stories) also activated additional regions of the right hemisphere.

■ **Repetition: Conduction Aphasia** As we saw earlier in this section, the fact that people with transcortical sensory aphasia can repeat what they hear suggests that there is a direct connection between Wernicke's area and Broca's area—and there is, the **arcuate fasciculus** ("arch-shaped

arcuate fasciculus A bundle of axons that connects Wernicke's area with Broca's area; damage causes conduction aphasia.

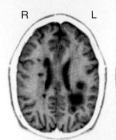
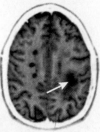
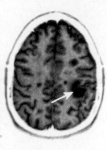

R   L

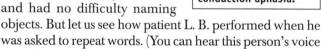

figure 15.13

MRI scans showing subcortical damage responsible for a case of conduction aphasia. This lesion damaged the arcuate fasciculus, a fiber bundle connecting Wernicke's area and Broca's area.

(From Arnett, P. A., Rao, S. M., Hussain, M., Swanson, S. J., and Hammeke, T. A. *Neurology*, 1996, *47*, 576-578.)

bundle"). This bundle of axons appears to convey information about the *sounds* of words but not their *meanings*. The best evidence for this conclusion comes from a syndrome known as conduction aphasia, which is produced by damage to the inferior parietal lobe that extends into the subcortical white matter and damages the arcuate fasciculus (Damasio and Damasio, 1980). (See *Figure 15.13*.)

Conduction aphasia is characterized by meaningful, fluent speech; relatively good comprehension; but very poor repetition. For example, the spontaneous speech of patient L. B. (observed by Margolin and Walker, 1981) was excellent; he made very few errors and had no difficulty naming objects. But let us see how patient L. B. performed when he was asked to repeat words. (You can hear this person's voice on *Animation 5.1, Voices of Aphasia: Conduction Aphasia*.)

> See the interactive CD for more on conduction aphasia.

Examiner: bicycle
Patient: bicycle
Examiner: hippopotamus
Patient: hippopotamus
Examiner: blaynge
Patient: I didn't get it.
Examiner: Okay, some of these won't be real words, they'll just be sounds. Blaynge.
Patient: I'm not . . .
Examiner: blanch
Patient: blanch
Examiner: north
Patient: north
Examiner: rilld
Patient: Nope, I can't say.

You will notice that the patient can repeat individual words (all nouns, in this case) but utterly fails to repeat nonwords. And as you can hear in the animation, he can repeat a meaningful three-word phrase but not three unrelated words. People with conduction aphasia

can repeat speech sounds that they hear *only if these sounds have meaning*.

Sometimes, when a person with conduction aphasia is asked to repeat a word, he or she says a word with the same meaning—or at least one that is related. For example, if the examiner says *house*, the patient may say *home*. If the examiner says *chair*, the patient may say *sit*. One patient made the following response when asked to repeat an entire sentence:

Examiner: The auto's leaking gas tank soiled the roadway.
Patient: The car's tank leaked and made a mess on the street.

The symptoms that are seen in transcortical sensory aphasia and conduction aphasia lead to the conclusion that there are pathways connecting the speech mechanisms of the temporal lobe with those of the frontal lobe. The direct pathway through the arcuate fasciculus simply conveys speech sounds from Wernicke's area to Broca's area. We use this pathway to repeat unfamiliar words—for example, when we are learning a foreign language or a new word in our own language or when we are trying to repeat a nonword such as *blaynge*. The second pathway, between the posterior language area and Broca's area, is indirect and is based on the *meaning* of words, not the sounds they make. When patients with conduction aphasia hear a word or a sentence, the meaning of what they hear evokes some sort of image related to that meaning. (The patient in the second example presumably imagined the sight of an automobile leaking fuel onto the pavement.) They are then able to describe that image, just as they would put their own thoughts into words. Of course, the words they choose might not be the same as the ones used by the person who spoke to them. (See *Figure 15.14*.)

The symptoms of conduction aphasia indicate that the connection between Wernicke's area and Broca's area appears to play an important role in short-term memory of words and speech sounds that have just been heard. Presumably, rehearsal of such information can be accomplished by "talking to ourselves" inside our head without actually having to say anything aloud. Imagining ourselves saying the word activates the region of Broca's area, whereas imagining that we are hearing it activates the auditory association area of the temporal lobe. These two regions, connected by means of the arcuate fasciculus (which contains axons traveling in *both* directions) circulate information back and forth, keeping the short-term memory alive. Baddeley (1993) refers to this circuit as the *phonological loop*.

Functional imaging studies support this hypothesis. For example, Paulesu, Frith, and Frackowiak (1993) observed activation of Broca's area and a region within the posterior language area while subjects were remembering sets of six consonants. (See *Figure 15.15*.) Fiez et al. (1996) obtained

conduction aphasia An aphasia characterized by inability to repeat words that are heard but the ability to speak normally and comprehend the speech of others.

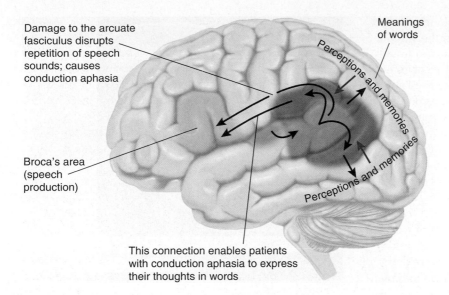

Damage to the arcuate fasciculus disrupts repetition of speech sounds; causes conduction aphasia

Meanings of words

Perceptions and memories

Broca's area (speech production)

Perceptions and memories

This connection enables patients with conduction aphasia to express their thoughts in words

figure 15.14

A hypothetical explanation of conduction aphasia. A lesion that damages the arcuate fasciculus disrupts transmission of auditory information, but not information related to meaning, to the frontal lobe.

---

similar results in a task that required subjects to remember pronounceable pseudowords. They found that the subjects who performed best at this task showed the greatest activation of Broca's area, while subjects who did poorly showed greater activation of the occipital lobe. The subjects read the pseudowords on a screen before the PET scan and then remembered them during the 40 seconds that the machine was performing a scan. Perhaps, reasoned Fiez and her colleagues, the subjects who did poorly were trying to remember what the pseudowords looked like rather than how they sounded, a less effective strategy in such a task.

Memory of Words: Anomic Aphasia

As I have already noted, anomia, in one form or other, is a hallmark of aphasia. However, one category of aphasia consists of almost pure anomia, the other symp-

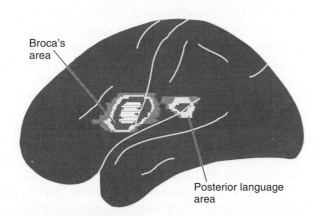

Broca's area

Posterior language area

figure 15.15

The phonological loop. A PET scan showing activation of Broca's area and the auditory association cortex during rehearsal of six consonants.

(Adapted from Baddeley, A. D. *Current Biology,* 1993, *3,* 563–565; after data from Paulesu, E., Frith, C. D., and Frackowiak, R. S. J. *Nature,* 1993, *362,* 342–344.)

toms being inconsequential. Speech of patients with anomic aphasia is fluent and grammatical, and their comprehension is excellent, but they have difficulty finding the appropriate words. They often employ **circumlocutions** (literally, "speaking in a roundabout way") to get around missing words. Anomic aphasia is different from Wernicke's aphasia. People with anomic aphasia can understand what other people say, and what they say makes perfect sense, even if they often choose roundabout ways to say it.

The following quotation is from a patient that some colleagues and I studied (Margolin, Marcel, and Carlson, 1985). We asked her to describe the kitchen picture shown earlier, in *Figure 15.1.* Her pauses, which are marked with

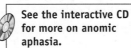

See the interactive CD for more on anomic aphasia.

three dots, indicate word-finding difficulties. In some cases, when she could not find a word, she supplied a definition instead (a form of circumlocution) or went off on a new track. I have added the words in brackets that I think she intended to use. (You can hear this person's voice on *Animation 5.1, Voices of Aphasia: Anomic Aphasia.*)

Examiner: Tell us about that picture.

Patient: It's a woman who has two children, a son and a daughter, and her son is to get into the . . . cupboard in the kitchen to get out [*take*] some . . . cookies out of the [*cookie jar*] . . . that she possibly had made, and consequently he's slipping [*falling*] . . . the wrong direction [*backward*] . . . on the . . . what he's standing on [*stool*], heading to the . . . the cupboard [*floor*] and if he falls backwards he could have some problems [*get hurt*], because that [*the stool*] is off balance.

---

circumlocution A strategy by which people with anomia find alternative ways to say something when they are unable to think of the most appropriate word.

Anomia has been described as a partial amnesia for words. It can be produced by lesions in either the anterior or posterior regions of the brain, but only posterior lesions produce a *fluent* anomia. The most likely location of lesions that produce anomia without the other symptoms of aphasia, such as comprehension deficits, agrammatism, or difficulties in articulation, is the left temporal or parietal lobe, usually sparing Wernicke's area. In the case of the woman described above, the damage included the middle and inferior temporal gyri, which includes an important region of the visual association cortex. Wernicke's area was not damaged.

When my colleagues and I were studying the anomic patient, I was struck by the fact that she seemed to have more difficulty finding nouns than other types of words. I informally tested her ability to name actions by asking her what people shown in a series of pictures were doing. She made almost no errors in finding verbs. For example, although she could not say what a boy was holding in his hand, she had no trouble saying that he was *throwing* it. Similarly, she knew that a girl was *climbing* something but could not tell me the name of what she was climbing (a fence). In addition, she had no trouble finding nonvisual adjectives; for example, she could say that lemons tasted *sour,* that ice was *cold,* and that a cat's fur felt *soft.*

For several years I thought that our patient was unique. But other researchers have reported similar patterns of deficits. For example, Semenza and Zettin (1989) and Manning and Campbell (1992) described patients who had difficulty naming objects but not actions. Several studies have found that anomia for verbs (more correctly called *averbia*) is caused by damage to the frontal cortex, in and around Broca's area (Damasio and Tranel, 1993; Daniele et al., 1994; Bak et al., 2001). If you think about it, that makes sense. The frontal lobes are devoted to planning, organizing, and executing actions, so it should not surprise us that they are involved in the task of remembering the names of actions.

Several functional imaging studies have confirmed the importance of Broca's area and the region surrounding it in the production of verbs (Petersen et al., 1988; Wise et al., 1991; McCarthy et al., 1993; Fiez et al., 1996). In these studies, subjects either read or heard nouns and then had to say (or think to themselves) verbs describing actions appropriate to these nouns. For example, on reading or hearing the noun *hammer,* they might think of the verb *pound.* Figure 15.16 shows a PET scan from people who generated verbs in response to written nouns. The activity produced by simply reading nouns aloud has been subtracted out, leaving only the activity associated with the verb generation process. Presumably, the activity in the temporal lobe represents neural processes involved with comprehension of the nouns, while the activity in the frontal lobe represents the neural processes directly involved with thinking of appropriate actions and the associated verbs. (See *Figure 15.16.*)

A study by Pulvermüller, Harle, and Hummel (2000) lends considerable support to this suggestion. These investigators recorded electrical activity evoked in the brain when people distinguished between verbs that referred to

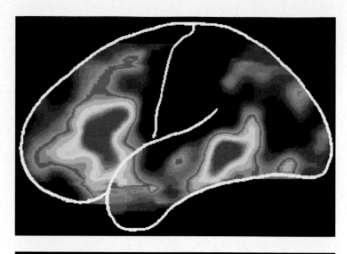

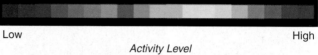

Low　　　　　　　　　　　　　　　　　　　　　　High

Activity Level

figure　15.16

A PET scan showing the regions of activation while people thought of verbs that depicted actions appropriate to nouns supplied by the experimenters.

(From Fiez, J. A., Raichle, M. E., Balota, D. A., Tallal, P., and Petersen, S. E. *Cerebral Cortex,* 1996, *6,* 1–10.)

different actions. They found that verbs pertaining to the legs (for example, *to kick*) activated the region of the motor cortex controlling leg movements, while verbs pertaining to the face (for example, *to speak*) activated the face region of the motor cortex. Presumably, thinking about particular actions activated regions that control these actions.

A PET study by Martin et al. (1996) investigated the brain regions activated by naming pictures of animals and tools. They found that naming both categories activated the inferior temporal cortex (the ventral stream of visual processing) and Broca's area. However, animal naming selectively activated the visual association cortex of the medial occipital lobe. Naming tools selectively activated the left middle temporal gyrus and the left premotor cortex—the same region that is activated when people imagine they are making hand movements. (See *Figure 15.17.*)

The picture I have drawn so far suggests that comprehension of speech includes a flow of information from Wernicke's area to the posterior language area to various regions of sensory and motor association cortex, which contain memories that provide meanings to words. Production of spontaneous speech involves the flow of information concerning perceptions and memories from the sensory and motor association cortex to the posterior language area to Broca's area. This model is certainly an oversimplification, but it is a useful starting point in conceptualizing basic mental processes. For example, thinking in words probably involves two-way communication between the speech areas and surrounding association cortex (and subcortical regions such as the hippocampus, of course).

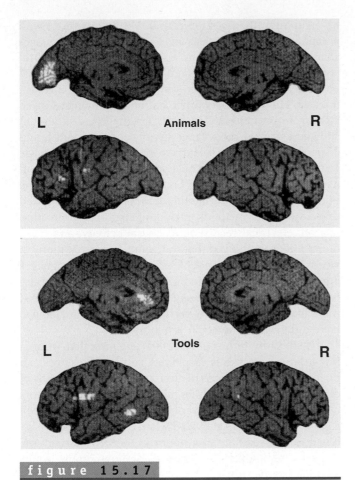

figure 15.17

PET scans showing the regions of activation when people named pictures of animals (top) or tools (bottom).

(From Martin, A., Wiggs, C. L., Ungerleider, L. G., and Haxby, J. V. *Nature*, 1996, *379*, 649–652.)

Aphasia in Deaf People

So far, I have restricted my discussion to brain mechanisms of spoken and written language. But communication among members of the Deaf community involves another medium: sign language. Sign language is expressed manually, by movements of the hands. Sign language is *not* English; nor is it French, Spanish, or Chinese. The most common sign language in North America is ASL—American Sign Language. ASL is a full-fledged language, having signs for nouns, verbs, adjectives, adverbs, and all the other parts of speech contained in oral languages. People can converse rapidly and efficiently by means of sign language, can tell jokes, and can even make puns based on the similarity between signs. They can also use their language ability to think in words.

Some researchers believe that in the history of our species, sign language preceded spoken language—that our ancestors began using gestures to communicate before they switched to speech. You may recall (from Chapter 6) that Rizzolatti and his colleagues (Gallese et al., 1996; Rizzolatti et al. 1996) found an area of the rostral part of

the ventral premotor cortex in the monkey brain (the equivalent of Broca's area in humans) that became active whenever the monkeys either *saw* or *performed* various grasping, holding, or manipulating movements. Presumably, these *mirror neurons* would play an important role in learning to mimic another animal's hand movements. Indeed, they might have been involved in the development of hand gestures used for communication, and they undoubtedly are used by deaf people when they communicate by sign language. A functional imaging study by Iacoboni et al. (1999) found that Broca's area was activated when people observed and imitated finger movements. (See *Figure 15.18*.)

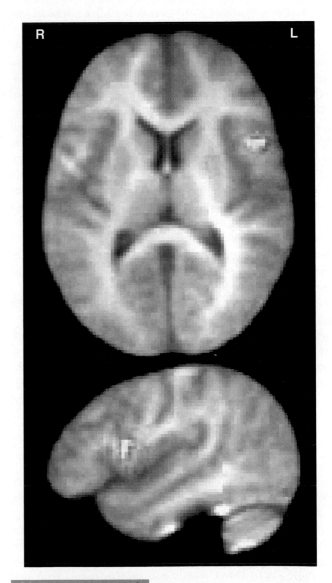

figure 15.18

PET scans showing a region of the inferior left frontal lobe that was activated when a person saw a finger movement or imitated it. *Top:* Horizontal section. *Bottom:* Lateral view of left hemisphere.

(From Iacoboni, M., Woods, R. P., Brass, M., Bekkering, H., Mazziotta, J. C., and Rizzolatti, G. *Science*, 1999, *286*, 2526–2528.)

The grammar of ASL is based on its visual, spatial nature. For example, if a person makes the sign for *John* in one place and later makes the sign for *Mary* in another place, she can place her hand in the *John* location and move it toward the *Mary* location while making the sign for *love*. As you undoubtedly figured out for yourself, she is saying, "John loves Mary." Signers can also modify the meaning of signs through facial expressions or the speed and vigor with which they make a sign. Thus, many of the prepositions, adjectives, and adverbs found in spoken languages do not require specific words in ASL. The fact that signed languages are based on three-dimensional hand and arm movements accompanied by facial expressions means that their grammars are very different from those of spoken languages. Therefore, a word-for-word translation from a spoken language to a signed language (or vice versa) is impossible.

The fact that the grammar of ASL is spatial suggests that aphasic disorders in deaf people who use sign language might be caused by lesions of the right hemisphere, which is primarily involved in spatial perception and memory. However, all the cases of deaf people with aphasia for signs reported in the literature so far have involved lesions of the left hemisphere (Hickok, Bellugi, and Klima, 1996). Functional imaging studies confirm these findings. For example, Pettito et al. (2000) found that when deaf signers produced meaningful signs, increased activity was seen in the left inferior frontal cortex—the region of Broca's area. When these subjects viewed signs made by others, they showed increased activity in the left superior temporal cortex. Therefore, sign language, like auditory and written language, appears to rely primarily on the left hemisphere for comprehension and expression.

We saw earlier that the right hemisphere contributes to the more subtle, figurative aspects of speech in hearing people. The same seems to be true for deaf signers. Hickok et al. (1999) described the case of two deaf signers who had damage to the right hemisphere. Both showed problems with discourse using sign language: One had trouble maintaining a coherent topic, and the other had difficulty with subtle uses of spatial features.

The Bilingual Brain

One question has long puzzled scientists who are interested in brain mechanisms of language: How does the brain handle two or more different languages? Obviously, we can learn new words in our native languages all our lives. (In fact, I hope you are doing so as you read this book.) Presumably, the cell assemblies that contain information about these words are intermingled with cell assemblies that contain information about words we already know. But when a second language is learned, are the cell assemblies that represent the newly learned words and grammatical conventions intermingled with the previously established ones, or are they stored in locations somewhat apart from those used for our native language?

Although the question cannot yet be answered with certainty, evidence suggests that first and second languages share the same brain regions. For example, Fabbro (2001a) studied the recovery of language functions in bilingual patients after they sustained a stroke that caused a severe aphasia. He found that 65 percent of the patients showed similar improvements in both languages, 20 percent showed a greater recovery in their second language, and 15 percent showed a greater recovery in their first language. In other words, there was no evidence that the brain damage was more likely to affect one language more than the other. In a review of the literature, Fabbro (2001b) reported that a variety of methods, including electrical brain stimulation, electrical recording of neural activity, and functional imaging, showed that the neural representations of words that belonged to people's first and second languages appeared to be intermingled. However, the cell assemblies required for storage of different grammatical rules appeared more likely to be separate, perhaps because languages can have different grammatical structures.

A study by Simos et al. (2001) suggests that when a fine-grained analysis is employed, subtle differences can be found in the locations of circuits activated by words of different languages in a bilingual brain. The investigators used magnetoencephalography to find the location of cell assemblies that were activated when bilingual subjects listened to and read abstract nouns in their two languages, English and Spanish. As Figure 15.19 shows, in the brains of at least some subjects, English and Spanish words activated different regions of the left temporal lobe. (See *Figure 15.19*.)

What about information that is learned through one or another language in a bilingual person? Does the original source of the language matter, or is semantic memory represented in a language-free manner? A study by Dehaene et al. (1999) suggests that the answer is, "It depends." In particular, it depends on the nature of the information that has been learned. The investigators taught bilingual speakers of English and Russian methods to solve mathematical problems. One method required a specific set of rules to solve one type of problem, and the other method provided a way to estimate an approximate value for another type of problem. Half of the subjects learned the first method in English and the second in Russian, and the other half learned the first in Russian and the second in English. Later, the subjects were tested in both languages on their ability to solve both kinds of problems. For the approximate method, the language of training and testing did not matter; the subjects did equally well on both. Thus, it appears that these rules were stored in a way that was independent of a particular language. However, for the exact method, which required precise rules, subjects did best when they were trained and tested in the same language. If, for example, they were trained in English and tested in Russian, their performance was slower—as if they had to translate the problem presented in Russian

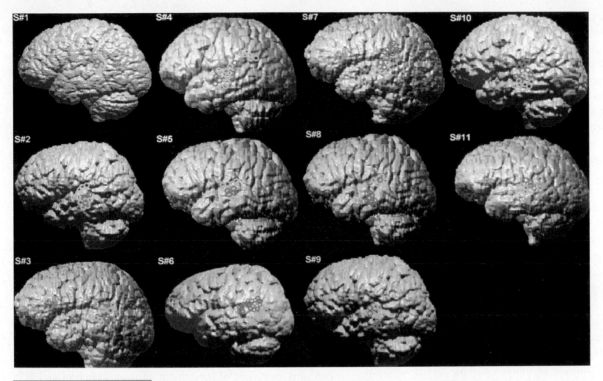

figure 15.19

Depictions of the results of magnetoencephalographic scans showing regions in the lateral temporal cortex that were activated when bilingual subjects listened to and read abstract nouns in English (green circles) or Spanish (yellow circles).
(From Simos, P. G., Castillo, E. M., Fletcher, J. M., Francis, D. J., Maestu, F., Breier, J. I., Maggio, W. W., and Papanicolaou, A. C. *Journal of Neurosurgery,* 2001, *95,* 76–81.)

into English so that they could use the rules they had learned in that language. Furthermore, functional MRI scans and recording of electrical brain activity indicated that solving problems with the approximate method produced the greatest activation in both the left and right parietal lobes, while solving problems with the exact method produced the greatest activation in a region of the left frontal lobe that included Broca's area.

Prosody: Rhythm, Tone, and Emphasis in Speech

When we speak, we do not merely utter words. Our speech has a regular rhythm and cadence; we give some words stress (that is, we pronounce them louder), and we vary the pitch of our voice to indicate phrasing and to distinguish between assertions and questions. In addition, we can impart information about our emotional state through the rhythm, emphasis, and tone of our speech. These rhythmic, emphatic, and melodic aspects of speech are referred to as **prosody.** The importance of these aspects of speech is illustrated by our use of punctuation symbols to indicate some elements of prosody when we write. For example, a comma indicates a short pause; a period indicates a longer one with an accompanying fall in the pitch of the voice; a question mark indicates a pause and a rise in the pitch of the voice; an exclamation mark indicates that the words are articulated with special emphasis; and so on.

The prosody of people with fluent aphasias, caused by posterior lesions, sounds normal. Their speech is rhythmical, with pauses after phrases and sentences, and has a melodic line. Even when the speech of a person with severe Wernicke's aphasia makes no sense, the prosody sounds normal. As Goodglass and Kaplan (1972) note, a person with Wernicke's aphasia may "sound like a normal speaker at a distance, because of his fluency and normal melodic contour of his speech." (Up close, of course, we hear the speech clearly enough to realize that it is meaningless.) In contrast, just as the lesions that produce Broca's aphasia destroy grammar, they also severely disrupt prosody. In patients with Broca's aphasia, articulation is so labored and words are uttered so slowly that there is

prosody The use of changes in intonation and emphasis to convey meaning in speech besides that specified by the particular words; an important means of communication of emotion.

little opportunity for the patient to demonstrate any rhythmic elements; and because of the relative lack of function words, there is little variation in stress or pitch of voice.

Evidence from studies of normal people and patients with brain lesions suggests that prosody is a special function of the right hemisphere. This function is undoubtedly related to the more general role of this hemisphere in musical skills and the expression and recognition of emotions: Production of prosody is rather like singing, and prosody often serves as a vehicle for conveying emotion.

Weintraub, Mesulam, and Kramer (1981) tested the ability of patients with right-hemisphere damage to recognize and express prosodic elements of speech. In one experiment they showed their subjects two pictures, named one of them, and asked the subjects to point to the appropriate one. For example, they showed them a picture of a greenhouse and a house that was painted green. In speech we distinguish between *greenhouse* and *green house* by stress: *GREEN house* means the former, and *GREEN HOUSE* (syllables equally stressed) means the latter. In a second experiment, Weintraub and her colleagues tested the subjects' ability simply to detect differences in prosody. They presented pairs of sentences and asked the subjects whether they were the same or different. The pairs of sentences either were identical or differed in terms of intonation (for example, *Margo plays the piano?* and *Margo plays the piano*) or location of stress (for example, *STEVE drives the car* and *Steve drives the CAR*). The patients with right-hemisphere lesions (but not control subjects) performed poorly on both of these tasks. Thus, they showed a deficit in prosodic comprehension.

To test production, the investigators presented two written sentences and asked a question about them. For example, they presented the following pair:

The man walked to the grocery store.
The woman rode to the shoe store.

The subjects were instructed to answer questions by reading one of the sentences. Try this one yourself. Read the question below and then read aloud the sentence (above) that answers it.

Who walked to the grocery store, the man or the woman?

The question asserts that someone walked to the grocery store but asks who that person was. When answering a question like this, people normally stress the requested item of information; in this case they say, "The *man* walked to the grocery store." However, Weintraub and her colleagues found that although patients with right-hemisphere brain damage chose the correct sentence, they either failed to stress a word or stressed the wrong one. Thus, the right hemisphere plays a role in production as well as perception of prosody.

interim summary

Speech Production and Comprehension: Brain Mechanims

Two regions of the brain are especially important in understanding and producing speech. Broca's area, in the left frontal lobe just rostral to the region of the primary motor cortex that controls the muscles of speech, is involved with speech production. This region contains memories of the sequences of muscular movements that produce words, each of which is connected with its auditory counterpart in the posterior part of the brain. Broca's aphasia—which is caused by damage to Broca's area, adjacent regions of the frontal cortex, and underlying white matter—consists of varying degrees of agrammatism, anomia, and articulation difficulties.

Wernicke's area, in the posterior superior temporal lobe, is involved with speech perception. The region just adjacent to Wernicke's area, which I have called the posterior language area, is necessary for speech comprehension and the translation of thoughts into words. Presumably, Wernicke's area contains memories of the sounds of words, each of which is connected through the posterior language area with circuits that contain memories about the properties of the things the words denote and with circuits that are responsible for pronouncing the words. Damage restricted to Wernicke's area causes pure word deafness—loss of the ability to understand speech but intact speech production, reading, and writing. Wernicke's aphasia, caused by damage to Wernicke's area and the posterior language area, consists of poor speech comprehension, poor repetition, and production of fluent, meaningless speech. Transcortical sensory aphasia, caused by damage to the posterior speech area, consists of poor speech comprehension and production, but the patients can repeat what they hear. Thus, the symptoms of Wernicke's aphasia consist of those of transcortical sensory aphasia plus those of pure word deafness. (WA = TSA + PWD) The fact that people with transcortical sensory aphasia can repeat words they cannot understand suggests that there is a direct connection between Wernicke's area and Broca's area. Indeed, there is: the arcuate fasciculus. Damage to this bundle of axons produces conduction aphasia: disruption of the ability to repeat exactly what was heard without disruption of the ability to comprehend or produce meaningful speech.

The meanings of words are our memories of objects, actions, and other concepts associated with them. These meanings are memories and are stored in the association cortex, not in the speech areas themselves. Pure anomia, caused by damage to the temporal or parietal lobes, consists of difficulty in word finding, particularly in naming objects. Some patients have a specific difficulty with proper nouns, while others have difficulty with common nouns; most patients have little difficulty with verbs. Damage to Broca's

Aphasic Syndromes Produced by Brain Damage

DISORDER	AREAS OF LESION	SPONTANEOUS SPEECH	COMPREHENSION	REPETITION	NAMING
Wernicke's aphasia	Posterior portion of superior temporal gyrus (Wernicke's area) and posterior language areas	Fluent	Poor	Poor	Poor
Pure word deafness	Wernicke's area or its connection with primary auditory cortex	Fluent	Poor	Poor	Good
Broca's aphasia	Frontal cortex rostral to base of primary motor cortex (Broca's area)	Nonfluent	Good	Poor*	Poor
Conduction aphasia	White matter beneath parietal lobe superior to lateral fissure (arcuate fasciculus)	Fluent	Good	Poor	Good
Anomic aphasia	Various parts of parietal and temporal lobes	Fluent	Good	Good	Poor
Transcortical sensory aphasia	Posterior language area	Fluent	Poor	Good	Poor

*May be better than spontaneous speech.

area and surrounding regions disrupts the ability to name actions—to think of appropriate verbs. Brain damage can also disrupt the "definitions" as well as the "entries" in the mental dictionary; damage to specific regions of the association cortex effectively erases some categories of the meanings of words.

The left hemisphere plays the more important role in the language abilities of deaf people who use sign language, just as it is in people who communicate acoustically. However, the right hemisphere plays a role in the more subtle, figurative aspects of speech in both deaf and hearing people.

The location of cell assemblies that encode words in different languages in the brains of bilingual people appear to be located in approximately the same places, although one study suggests that there may be some subtle segregation. The separation of cell assemblies that represent the grammatical rules of different languages can be more substantial.

Prosody includes changes in intonation, rhythm, and stress that add meaning, especially emotional meaning, to the sentences that we speak. The neural mechanisms that control the prosodic elements of speech appear to be in the right hemisphere.

Because so many terms and symptoms were described in this section, I have provided a table that summarizes them. (See *Table 15.1*.)

Disorders of Reading and Writing

Reading and writing are closely related to listening and talking; thus, oral and written language abilities have many brain mechanisms in common. This section discusses the neural basis of reading and writing disorders. As you will see, the study of these disorders has provided us with some useful and interesting information.

Relation to Aphasia

The reading and writing skills of people with aphasia almost always resemble their speaking and comprehending abilities. For example, patients with Wernicke's aphasia have as much difficulty reading and writing as they do speaking and understanding speech. Patients with Broca's aphasia comprehend what they read about as well as they can understand speech, but their reading aloud is poor, of course. If their speech is agrammatical, so is their writing; and to the extent that they fail to comprehend grammar when listening to speech, they fail to do so when reading. Patients with conduction aphasia generally have some difficulty reading; and when they read aloud, they often make semantic paraphasias (saying synonyms for some of the words they read), just as they do when attempting to repeat what they hear. Depending on the location of the lesion, some patients with transcortical sensory aphasia may read aloud accurately but fail to comprehend what they read.

There are a few exceptions to this general rule. For example, Semenza, Cipolotti, and Denes (1992) studied a patient with a severe fluent aphasia. Although she could not understand the speech of others, she could read. She clearly understood what she was reading, because she could follow written instructions. And although her spontaneous speech was meaningless and she could not say the names of objects, she could write their names, and she could read aloud. Clearly, her comprehension and production of oral language was very different from that of written language. Although cases like this one are rare, they do indicate that our verbal abilities make use of a large number of individual neural modules. Reading and writing undoubtedly share many modules with oral comprehension and production, but some modules are devoted to particular methods of communication.

Pure Alexia

Dejerine (1892) described a remarkable syndrome, which we now call **pure alexia,** or sometimes *pure word blindness* or *alexia without agraphia.* His patient had a lesion in the visual cortex of the left occipital lobe and the posterior end of the corpus callosum. The patient could still write, although he had lost the ability to read. In fact, if he was shown some of his own writing, he could not read it.

Several years ago, some colleagues and I studied a man with pure alexia who discovered his ability to write in an interesting way. A few months after he sustained a head injury that caused his brain damage, he and his wife were watching a service person repair their washing machine. The patient wanted to say something privately to his wife, so he picked up a pad of paper and jotted a note. As he was handing it to her, they suddenly realized with amazement that although he could not read, he was able to write! His wife brought the note to their neurologist, who asked the patient to read it. Although he remembered the gist of the message, he could not read the words. Unfortunately, I do not have that note, but Figure 15.20 shows the writing of another person with pure alexia. (See *Figure 15.20.*)

Although patients with pure alexia cannot read, they can recognize words that are spelled aloud to them; therefore, they have not lost their memories of the spellings of words. Pure alexia is obviously a perceptual disorder; it is similar to pure word deafness, except that the patient has difficulty with visual input, not auditory input. The dis-

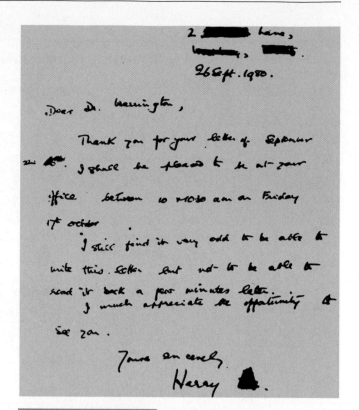

figure   15.20

A letter written to Dr. Elizabeth Warrington by a patient with pure alexia. The letter reads as follows: "Dear Dr. Warrington, Thank you for your letter of September 16th. I shall be pleased to be at your office between 10–10:30 am on Friday 17th october. I still find it very odd to be able to write this letter but not to be able to read it back a few minutes later. I much appreciate the opportunity to see you. Yours sincerely, Harry X.

(From McCarthy, R. A., and Warrington, E. K. *Cognitive Neuropsychology: A Clinical Introduction.* San Diego: Academic Press, 1990. Reprinted with permission.)

order is caused by lesions that prevent visual information from reaching the extrastriate cortex of the left hemisphere (Damasio and Damasio, 1983, 1986). Figure 15.21 explains why Dejerine's original patient could not read. (*Animation 15.3, Pure Alexia,* also illustrates the brain damage responsible for this disorder.) The first diagram shows the pathway that visual information would take if a person had damage *only to the left primary visual cortex.* In this case the person's right visual field would be blind; he or she would see

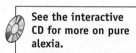 **See the interactive CD for more on pure alexia.**

pure alexia Loss of the ability to read without loss of the ability to write; produced by brain damage.

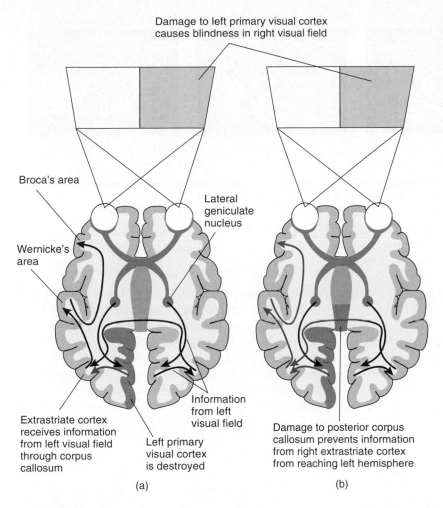

Damage to left primary visual cortex
causes blindness in right visual field

Broca's area

Wernicke's
area

Lateral
geniculate
nucleus

Extrastriate cortex
receives information
from left visual field
through corpus
callosum

Left primary
visual cortex
is destroyed

Information
from left
visual field

Damage to posterior corpus
callosum prevents information
from right extrastriate cortex
from reaching left hemisphere

(a)   (b)

figure 15.21

Pure alexia. Red arrows indicate the flow of information that has been interrupted by brain damage. (a) The route followed by information as a person with damage to the left primary visual cortex reads aloud. (b) Additional damage to the posterior corpus callosum interrupts the flow of information and produces pure alexia.

nothing to the right of the fixation point. But people with this disorder can read. Their only problem is that they must look to the right of each word so that they can see all of it, which means that they read somewhat more slowly than someone with full vision.

Let us trace the flow of visual information for a person with this brain damage. Information from the left side of the visual field is transmitted to the right striate cortex (primary visual cortex) and then to the lingual and fusiform gyri—a region of extrastriate cortex involved in the recognition of written text. From there, the information crosses the posterior corpus callosum and is transmitted to the left extrastriate cortex and then to speech mechanisms located in the left frontal lobe. Thus, the person can read the words aloud. (See *Figure 15.21a*.)

The second diagram shows Dejerine's patient. Notice how the additional lesion of the corpus callosum prevents visual information concerning written text from reaching the posterior left hemisphere. Without this information, the patient cannot read. (See *Figure 15.21b*.)

I must note that the diagrams shown in Figure 15.21 are as simple and schematic as possible. They illustrate

only the pathway involved in seeing a word and pronouncing it, and they ignore neural structures that would be involved in understanding its meaning. As we will see later in this chapter, evidence from patients with brain lesions indicates that seeing and pronouncing words can take place independently of understanding them. Thus, although the diagrams are simplified, they are not unreasonable, given what we know about the neural components of the reading process.

Presumably, some parts of the visual association cortex are involved in perceiving written words. The fact that damage to the posterior end of the corpus callosum disrupts the exchange of information concerning the shape of words suggests that the extrastriate cortex may be responsible for this analysis. Petersen et al. (1990) obtained results that support this suggestion. The investigators used a PET scanner to measure regional cerebral blood flow while presenting subjects with four types of visual stimuli: unfamiliar letterlike forms, strings of consonants, pronounceable nonwords, and real words. They found that one region of the medial extrastriate cortex was activated only when a person viewed pronounceable nonwords or

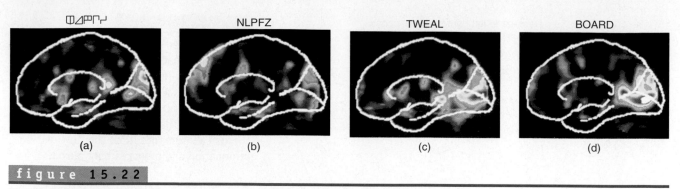

figure 15.22

PET scans of the medial surface of the brains of subjects who read (a) letterlike forms,
(b) strings of consonants, (c) pronounceable nonwords, or (d) real words.
(From Petersen, S. E., Fox, P. T., Snyder, A. Z., and Raichle, M. E. *Science*, 1990, *249*, 1041–1044.
Reprinted with permission.)

real words. Their finding suggests that this region plays a role in recognition of familiar combinations of letters. (See *Figure 15.22*.)

You will recall that writing is not the only form of visible language; deaf people can communicate by means of sign language just as well as hearing people can communicate by means of spoken language. Hickok et al. (1995) reported on a case of "sign blindness" caused by damage similar to that which causes pure alexia. The patient, a right handed deaf woman, sustained a stroke that damaged her left occipital lobe and the posterior corpus callosum. The lesion did not impair her ability to sign in coherent sentences, so she did not have a Wernicke-like aphasia. However, she could no longer understand other people's sign language, and she lost her ability to read. She had some ability to comprehend single signs (corresponding to single words), but she could not comprehend signed sentences.

You will recall from Chapter 6 that visual agnosia is a perceptual deficit in which people with bilateral damage to the visual association cortex cannot recognize objects by sight. Patients with pure alexia do *not* have visual agnosia; they can recognize objects and supply their names. Similarly, people with visual agnosia can still read. Thus, the perceptual analysis of objects and words requires different brain mechanisms. This fact is both interesting and puzzling. Certainly, the ability to read cannot have shaped the evolution of the human brain, because the invention of writing is only a few thousand years old, and until very recently, the vast majority of the world's population was illiterate. Thus, reading and object recognition use brain mechanisms that undoubtedly existed long before the invention of writing. As Patterson and Ralph (1999) conclude, natural selection has provided us with brain mechanisms for visual perception, speaking, and comprehending spoken language. Our ability to recognize words and understand them undoubtedly utilizes these mechanisms. Although the argument can be made

that we have inherited brain mechanisms that play a special role in *language,* the same cannot be said for the brain mechanisms we use to read and write.

At least two written languages were invented by specific individuals. Hangul, the written form of the Korean language, was invented by King Sejong (and his scholars) in the fourteenth century. The characters of the Hangul alphabet are designed to look like the shapes the mouth makes when they are pronounced. In the early nineteenth century, Sequoyah, a Cherokee living in what is now the state of North Carolina, recognized the value of the "talking leaves" that European settlers used to record information and send messages to each other. He spent twelve years developing a written version of his language. At first, he tried to develop pictograms to represent individual words, but he abandoned that attempt when its complexity became obvious. He then analyzed the sounds of his language and selected eighty-five symbols—from English and Greek letters he found in books and some additional ones that he invented. He did not know the sounds that English and Greek letters represented, so the sounds he assigned to them bore no relationship to those of the languages they came from. Within a few months of the introduction of Sequoyah's alphabet, thousands of Cherokees learned to read and write.

For people who can hear, comprehension of written language depends on prior knowledge of spoken language. (Learning to read is a more difficult process for deaf people, because signed languages cannot be translated word for word into the spoken languages that written languages depict.) Presumably, once we perceive and identify a written word, we can understand its meaning (and the meaning of sentences composed of groups of words) by using the same brain mechanisms used to understand speech. The question is, what is the nature of the perceptual mechanisms used to identify written words? Why can a person with damage to one part of the brain recognize objects but not words, while a person with damage to

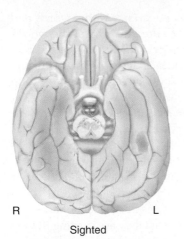 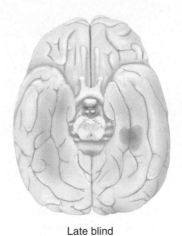 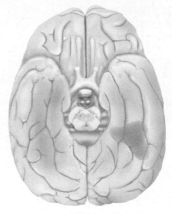

R   L
Sighted   Late blind   Blind from birth

figure 15.23

Averaged PET scans of the ventral surface of brains of sighted people, people who were blind since birth, and people who became blind late in life as the subjects read words or meaningless strings of letters visually or by means of Braille letters. In all cases, the reading task activated area BA37, located in the left basal posterior temporal lobe.
(Adapted from Büchel, C., Price, C., and Friston, K. *Nature,* 1998, *394,* 274–277.)

another part of the brain can recognize words but not objects? Behrmann, Nelson, and Sekuler (1998) suggest that recognition of real objects involves several different types of cues: depth, color, luminance, shadow, surface texture, and so on. On the other hand, recognition of written words involves detection of a few specific features—primarily edges, line lengths, and angles, which are analyzed by the extrastriate cortex. In other words, there is more redundancy in the perception of objects, and loss of some of the information will still permit a person to recognize them reasonably well.

Careful study of the perceptual abilities of people with pure alexia has found evidence for other perceptual deficits beside word blindness. For example, two studies found that musicians with pure alexia also lost the ability to read music (Horikoshi et al., 1997; Beversdorf and Heilman, 1998). The patient studied by Horikoshi and his colleagues was also unable to recognize visual symbols such as road signs. Visual recognition of words, musical notes, and other symbols presumably involves similar types of perceptual analysis.

A functional imaging study by Büchel, Price, and Friston (1998) found evidence for a region of the brain that appears to be involved in word recognition in both sighted people and blind people. The investigators presented the subjects—sighted, blind since birth, and blind late in life—with words or meaningless strings of letters visually or by means of Braille letters. In all three groups of subjects, the reading of words activated the left basal posterior temporal lobe—a region known as BA37. (See *Figure 15.23.*)

Toward an Understanding of Reading

Most investigators believe that reading involves at least two different processes: direct recognition of the word as a whole and sounding it out letter by letter. When we see a familiar word, we normally recognize it by its shape and pronounce it—a process known as **whole-word reading.** (With very long words we might instead perceive segments of several letters each.) The second method, which we use for unfamiliar words, requires recognition of individual letters and knowledge of the sounds they make. This process is known as **phonetic reading.**

Evidence for our ability to sound out words is easy to obtain. In fact, you can prove to yourself that phonetic reading exists by trying to read the following words:

glab   trisk   chint

Well, as you could see, they are not really words, but I doubt that you had trouble pronouncing them. Obviously, you did not *recognize* them, because you probably never saw them before. Therefore, you had to use what you know about the sounds that are represented by particular

whole-word reading Reading by recognizing a word as a whole; "sight reading."

phonetic reading Reading by decoding the phonetic significance of letter strings; "sound reading."

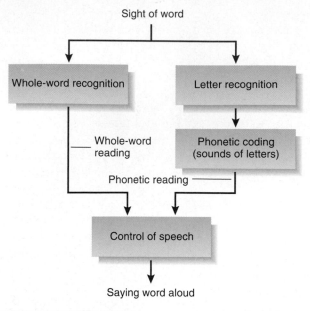

Sight of word

Whole-word recognition

Letter recognition

Whole-word reading

Phonetic coding (sounds of letters)

Phonetic reading

Control of speech

Saying word aloud

figure 15.24

A simplified model of the reading process, showing whole-word and phonetic reading. Whole-word reading is used for most familiar words; phonetic reading is used for unfamiliar words and for nonwords such as *glab, trisk,* or *chint.*

letters (or groups of letters, such as *ch*) to figure out how to pronounce the words.

The best evidence that proves that people can read words without sounding them out, using the whole-word method, comes from studies of patients with acquired dyslexias. *Dyslexia* means "faulty reading." *Acquired* dyslexias are those caused by damage to the brains of people who already know how to read. In contrast, *developmental* dyslexias refer to reading difficulties that become apparent when children are learning to read. Developmental dyslexias, which may involve anomalies in brain circuitry, are discussed in a later section.

Figure 15.24 illustrates some elements of the reading processes. The diagram is an oversimplification of a very complex process, but it helps to organize some of the facts that investigators have obtained. It considers only reading and pronouncing single words, not understanding the meaning of text. When we see a familiar word, we normally recognize it as a whole and pronounce it. If we see an unfamiliar word or a pronounceable nonword, we must try to read it phonetically. (See *Figure 15.24.*)

Although investigators have reported several types of acquired dyslexias, I will mention five of them here. **Surface dyslexia** is a deficit in whole-word reading, usually caused by a lesion of the left lateral temporal lobe (Marshall and Newcombe, 1973; McCarthy and Warrington, 1990; Patterson and Ralph, 1999). The term *surface* reflects the fact that people with this disorder make

errors related to the visual appearance of the words and to pronunciation rules, not to the meaning of the words, which is metaphorically "deeper" than the appearance.

Because patients with surface dyslexia have difficulty recognizing words as a whole, they are obliged to sound them out. Thus, they can easily read words with regular spelling, such as *hand, table,* or *chin.* However, they have difficulty reading words with irregular spelling, such as *sew, pint,* and *yacht.* In fact, they may read these words as *sue, pinnt,* and *yatchet.* They have no difficulty reading pronounceable nonwords, such as *glab, trisk,* and *chint.* Because people with surface dyslexia cannot recognize whole words by their appearance, they must, in effect, listen to their own pronunciation to understand what they are reading. If they read the word *pint* and pronounce it *pinnt,* they will say that it is not an English word (which it is not, pronounced that way). If the word is one member of a homophone, it will be impossible to understand it unless it is read in the context of a sentence. For example, if you hear the single word "pair" without additional information, you cannot know whether the speaker is referring to *pair, pear,* or *pare.* Thus, a patient with surface dyslexia who reads the word *pair* might say, " . . . it could be two of a kind, apples and . . . or what you do with your fingernails" (Gurd and Marshall, 1993, p. 594). (See *Figure 15.25.*)

Patients with **phonological dyslexia** have the opposite problem; they can read by the whole-word method but cannot sound words out. Thus, they can read words that they are already familiar with but have great difficulty figuring out how to read unfamiliar words or pronounceable nonwords (Beauvois and Dérouesné, 1979; Dérouesné and Beauvois, 1979). (In this context, *phonology*—loosely translated as "laws of sound"—refers to the relation between letters and the sounds they represent.) People with phonological dyslexia may be excellent readers if they had already acquired a good reading vocabulary before their brain damage occurred.

Phonological dyslexia provides further evidence that whole-word reading and phonological reading involve different brain mechanisms. Phonological reading, which is the only way we can read nonwords or words we have not yet learned, entails some sort of letter-to-sound decoding. Obviously, phonological reading of English requires more than decoding of the sounds produced by single letters, because, for example, some sounds are transcribed as two-letter sequences (such as *th* or *sh*) and the addition

surface dyslexia A reading disorder in which a person can read words phonetically but has difficulty reading irregularly spelled words by the whole-word method.

phonological dyslexia A reading disorder in which a person can read familiar words but has difficulty reading unfamiliar words or pronounceable nonwords.

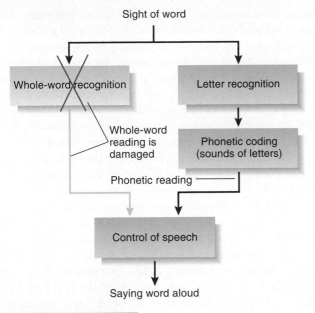

Sight of word

figure **15.25**

A hypothetical explanation of surface dyslexia. Whole-word reading is damaged; only phonetic reading remains.

of the letter *e* to the end of a word lengthens an internal vowel (*can* becomes *cane*). (See ***Figure 15.26.***)

Phonological dyslexia is usually caused by damage to the left frontal lobe (Price, 1998; Fiez and Petersen, 1998). A PET study by Fiez et al. (1999) found that phonological reading activated Broca's area and the left insular

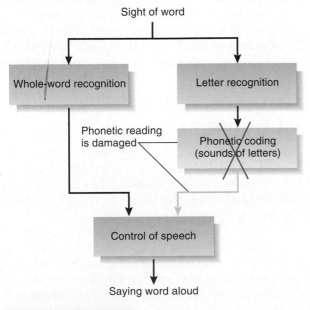

Sight of word

figure **15.26**

A hypothetical explanation of phonological dyslexia. Phonetic reading is damaged; only whole-word reading remains.

region. They suggest that "phonological" reading may actually involve articulation—that we sound out words not so much by "hearing" them in our heads as by feeling ourselves pronounce them silently to ourselves. Of course, both processes could be taking place simultaneously.

The Japanese language provides a particularly interesting distinction between phonetic and whole-word reading. The Japanese language makes use of two kinds of written symbols. *Kanji* symbols are pictographs, adopted from the Chinese language (although they are pronounced as Japanese words). Thus, they represent concepts by means of visual symbols but do not provide a guide to their pronunciation. Reading words expressed in kanji symbols is analogous, then, to whole-word reading. *Kana* symbols are phonetic representations of syllables; thus, they encode acoustical information. These symbols are used primarily to represent foreign words or Japanese words that the average reader would be unlikely to recognize if they were represented by their kanji symbols. Reading words expressed in kana symbols is obviously phonetic.

Studies of Japanese people with localized brain damage have shown that the reading of kana and kanji symbols involves different brain mechanisms (Iwata, 1984; Sakurai et al., 1994; Sakurai Ichikawa, and Mannen, 2001). Difficulty reading kanji symbols is analogous to surface dyslexia, whereas difficulty reading kana symbols is analogous to phonological dyslexia. A functional imaging study suggests that the left basal posterior temporal lobe (area BA37) is involved in reading of kanji symbols, while the extrastriate cortex and temporoparietal region is involved in reading of kana symbols (Sakurai et al., 2000).

What would happen if individuals sustained brain damage that did not make them blind but destroyed their ability to read words by either the whole-word or phonetic methods? Would they be *completely* unable to read? The answer is no—not quite. They would have a disorder known as **word-form dyslexia** or **spelling dyslexia** (Warrington and Shallice, 1980). Although patients with word-form dyslexia cannot either recognize words as a whole or sound them out phonetically, they can still recognize individual letters and can read the words if they are permitted to name the letters, one at a time. Thus, they read very slowly, taking more time with longer words. As you might expect, patients with word-form dyslexia can identify words that someone else spells aloud, just as they can recognize their own oral spelling. Sometimes, the deficit is so severe that patients have difficulty identifying individual letters, in which case they make mistakes in spelling that prevent them from reading test words. For example, a

word-form dyslexia A disorder in which a person can read a word only after spelling out the individual letters.

spelling dyslexia An alternative name for word-form dyslexia.

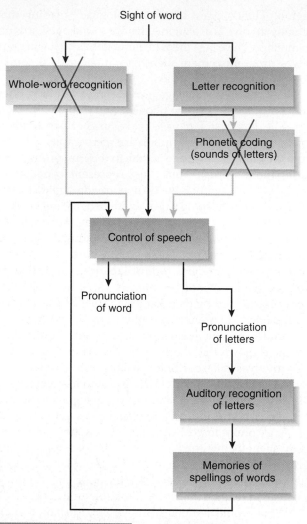

Sight of word

Whole-word recognition

Letter recognition

Phonetic coding (sounds of letters)

Control of speech

Pronunciation of word

Pronunciation of letters

Auditory recognition of letters

Memories of spellings of words

figure   15.27

A hypothetical explanation of spelling dyslexia. The patient pronounces the letters, recognizes the words, and then says them.

patient studied by Patterson and Kay (1980) was shown the word *men* and said, "h, e, n, hen." (See *Figure 15.27*.)

As we saw earlier in this chapter, recognizing a spoken word is different from understanding it. For example, patients with transcortical sensory aphasia can repeat what is said to them even though they show no signs of understanding what they hear or say. The same is true for reading. **Direct dyslexia** resembles transcortical sensory aphasia, except that the words in question are written, not spoken (Schwartz, Marin, and Saffran, 1979; Lytton and Brust, 1989; Gerhand, 2001). Patients with direct dyslexia are able to read aloud *even though they cannot understand the words they are saying.* After sustaining a stroke that damaged his left frontal and temporal lobes, Lytton and Brust's patient lost the ability to communicate verbally; his speech was meaningless, and he was unable to comprehend what other people said to him. However, he could read words with

which he was already familiar. He could *not* read pronounceable nonwords; therefore, he had lost the ability to read phonetically. His comprehension deficit seemed complete; when the investigators presented him with a word and several pictures, one of which corresponded to the word, he read the word correctly but had no idea what picture went with it. Gerhand's patient showed a similar pattern of deficits, except that she was able to read phonetically: She could sound out pronounceable nonwords. These findings indicate that the brain regions responsible for phonetic reading and whole-word reading are each directly connected with brain regions responsible for speech.

Several investigators have reported a deficit opposite to that of direct dyslexia. People with this unnamed disorder (we could call it *comprehension without reading*) show some comprehension of words that they cannot read (Margolin, Marcel, and Carlson, 1985). Our patient, R. F., sustained a head injury in an automobile accident that destroyed much of her left temporal lobe and part of the anterior occipital lobe. She had a classic case of anomic aphasia, in fact, I quoted her in the section on that topic earlier in this chapter. Although her speech was fluent and she could repeat whatever we said to her, she could not name most common objects, nor could she read most words. Nevertheless, she could match pictures of *objects she could not name* with *words she could not read.* For example, when we showed her the picture and words that appear in Figure 15.28, she immediately pointed to the correct word, *flag,* even though she could not name the object or read any of the words. (See *Figure 15.28*.)

Patient R. F. was utterly unable to read words phonetically. However, the fact that she could match words with pictures indicates that she could still *perceive* them by the whole-word method. As I mentioned in the case study at the beginning of this chapter, she was able to recognize misspelled words, even though she could not read them.

Toward an Understanding of Writing

Writing depends on knowledge of the words that are to be used, along with the proper grammatical structure of the sentences they are to form. Thus, if a patient is unable to express himself or herself by speech, we should not be surprised to see a writing disturbance as well.

One type of writing disorder involves difficulties in motor control—in directing the movements of a pen or pencil to form letters and words. Investigators have reported surprisingly specific types of writing disorders that fall under this category. For example, some patients can write

direct dyslexia A language disorder caused by brain damage in which the person can read words aloud without understanding them.

 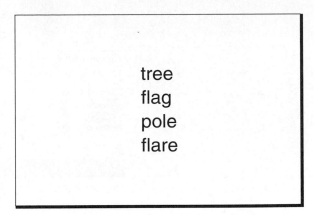

tree
flag
pole
flare

figure 15.28

An item from a task given to patient R. F. Although she could not read, she could choose the word that went with the picture.

numbers but not letters, some can write uppercase letters but not lowercase letters, some can write consonants but not vowels, some can write cursively but not print uppercase letters, and others can write letters normally but have difficulty placing them in an orderly fashion on the page (Cubelli, 1991; Alexander et al., 1992; Margolin and Goodman-Schulman, 1992; Silveri, 1996).

The second type of writing disorder involves problems in the ability to spell words, as opposed to problems with making accurate movements of the fingers. I will devote the rest of this section to this type of disorder. Like reading, writing (or more specifically, spelling) involves more than one method. The first is related to audition. When children acquire language skills, they first learn the sounds of words, then learn to say them, then learn to read, and then learn to write. Undoubtedly, reading and writing depend heavily on the skills that are learned earlier. For example, to write most words, we must be able to "sound them out in our heads," that is, to hear them and to articulate them subvocally. If you want to demonstrate this to yourself, try to write a long word such as *antidisestablishmentarianism* from memory and see whether you can do it without saying the word to yourself. If you recite a poem or sing a song to yourself under your breath at the same time, you will see that the writing comes to a halt.

A second way of writing involves transcribing an image of what a particular word looks like—copying a visual mental image. Have you ever looked off into the distance to picture a word so that you can remember how to spell it? Some people are not very good at phonological spelling and have to write some words down to see whether they look correct. This method obviously involves *visual* memories, not acoustical ones.

A third way of writing involves memorization of letter sequences. We learn these sequences the way we learn poems or the lyrics to a song. For example, many Americans learned to spell *Mississippi* with a singsong chant

that goes like this: **M**-i-s-s-**i**-s-s-**i**-p-p-**i,** emphasizing the boldfaced letters. (Similarly, most speakers of English say the alphabet with the rhythm of a nursery song that is commonly used to teach it.) This method involves memorizing sequences of letter names, not translating sounds into the corresponding letters. As you will recognize, it is exactly this method that permits people with word-form dyslexia to recognize words as they spell out their letters, one by one.

Finally, the fourth way of writing involves motor memories. We undoubtedly memorize motor sequences for very familiar words, such as our own names. Most of us need not sound out our names to ourselves when we write our signature, nor need we say the sequence of letters to ourselves, nor need we imagine what our signature looks like.

Writing normally involves holding a pen or pencil and moving its point across a piece of paper. But we can create visual records with the keyboard of a typewriter or a computer. The first three methods of writing (sounding out the letters of a word, visualizing it, or reciting a memorized sequence of letters) apply as well to typing as they do to writing. However, the movements we make with our hands and fingers are different when we write or type. Skilled typists learn automatic sequences of movements that produce frequently used words, but these are different from the movements we would make when we write these words. Otsuki et al. (2002) reported the case of a man who lost the ability to type after a stroke that damaged the ventral left frontal lobe. His ability to speak and understand speech, his ability to read, and his ability to write were not affected, and he showed no other obvious motor impairments besides his *dystypia,* as the investigators named it.

Neurological evidence supports at least the first three of these speculations. Brain damage can impair the first of these methods: phonetic writing. This deficit is called

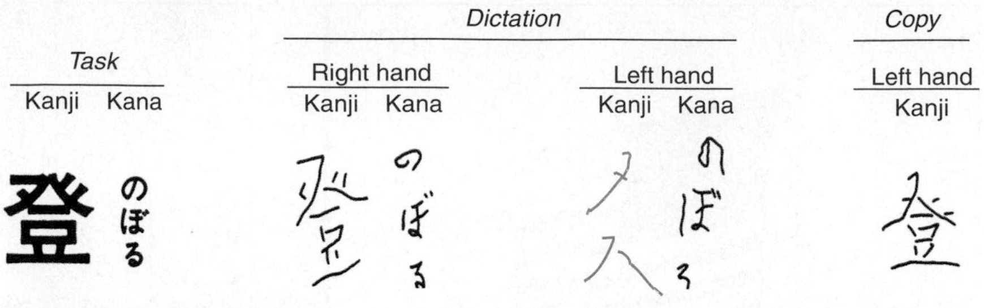

	Task	Dictation				Copy
		Right hand		Left hand		Left hand
	Kanji Kana	Kanji Kana		Kanji Kana		Kanji

figure 15.29

The writing of a Japanese patient with damage to the middle part of the corpus callosum. He could write both kanji and kana characters with his right hand, but he could not write kanji characters with his left hand (color). He could, however, *copy* kanji characters with his left hand if he was given a model to look at.

(From Kawamura, M., Hirayama, K., and Yamamoto, H. *Brain*, 1989, *112*, 1011–1018. Reprinted by permission of Oxford University Press.)

phonological dysgraphia (Shallice, 1981). (*Dysgraphia* refers to a writing deficit just as *dyslexia* refers to a reading deficit.) People with this disorder are unable to sound out words and write them phonetically. Thus, they cannot write unfamiliar words or pronounceable nonwords, such as the ones I presented in the section on reading. They can, however, visually imagine familiar words and then write them.

Orthographic dysgraphia is just the opposite of phonological dysgraphia: it is a disorder of visually based writing. People with orthographic dysgraphia can *only* sound words out; thus, they can spell regular words such as *care* or *tree,* and they can write pronounceable nonsense words. However, they have difficulty spelling irregular words such as *half* or *busy* (Beauvois and Dérouesné, 1981); they may write *haff* or *bizzy.* According to Benson and Geschwind (1985), phonological dysgraphia (impaired phonological writing) is caused by damage to the superior temporal lobe, whereas orthographic dysgraphia (impaired visual, whole-word writing) is usually caused by damage to the inferior parietal lobe.

The third method of spelling depends on a person's having memorized sequences of letters that spell particular words. Cipolotti and Warrington (1996) reported the case of a patient who lacked this ability. The patient sustained a left hemisphere stroke that severely disrupted his ability to spell words orally and impaired his ability to recognize words that the examiners would spell aloud. Presumably, his ability to spell written words depended on the first two methods of writing: auditory and visual. The examiners noted that when they spelled out words to him, he would make writing movements with his hand on top of his knee. When they asked him to clasp his hands together so that he could not make these writing movements, his ability to recognize four-letter words being spelled aloud

dropped from 66 percent to 14 percent. It appears that he was using feedback from hand movements to recognize the words he was "writing" on his knee.

Japanese patients show writing deficits similar to those of patients whose languages use the Roman alphabet; some patients have difficulty writing kana symbols, whereas others have difficulty with kanji symbols (Iwata, 1984; Yokota et al., 1990). Kawamura, Hirayama, and Yamamoto (1989) reported a particularly interesting case of a man with damage to the middle part of the corpus callosum who could write kana symbols with both hands and could write kanji symbols with the right hand but not the left. He could *copy* kanji symbols with his left hand; he just could not write them down when the investigators dictated them to him. (See *Figure 15.29.*) Another patient, reported by Tei, Soma, and Maruyama (1994), had the opposite symptoms: very bad kana writing with the nondominant hand but better kanji writing.

These results have interesting implications. Writing appears to be organized in the speech-dominant hemisphere (normally, the left hemisphere). That is, the information needed to specify the shape of the symbols is provided by circuits in this hemisphere. When a person uses his or her left hand to write these symbols, the information must be sent across the corpus callosum to the motor cortex of the right hemisphere, which controls the left hand. Apparently, information about the two forms of Japanese symbols is transmitted through

phonological dysgraphia A writing disorder in which the person cannot sound out words and write them phonetically.

orthographic dysgraphia A writing disorder in which the person can spell regularly spelled words but not irregularly spelled ones.

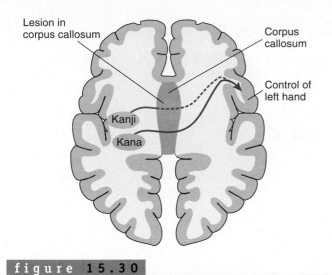

figure 15.30

The role of the corpus callosum in Japanese writing. Information about kana and kanji characters apparently crosses different parts of the corpus callosum.

different parts of the corpus callosum; the brain damage of the patient studied by Kawamura and his colleagues disrupted one of these pathways but not the other. (See *Figure 15.30*.)

As we saw in the section on reading, some patients (those with direct dyslexia) can read aloud without being able to understand what they are reading. Similarly, some patients can write words that are dictated to them even though they cannot understand these words (Roeltgen, Rothi, and Heilman, 1986; Lesser, 1989). Of course, they cannot communicate by means of writing, because they cannot translate their thoughts into words. (In fact, because most of these patients have sustained extensive brain damage, their thought processes themselves are severely disturbed.) Some of these patients can even spell pronounceable nonwords, which indicates that their ability to spell phonetically is intact. Roeltgen et al. (1986) referred to this disorder as *semantic agraphia,* but perhaps the term *direct dysgraphia* would be more appropriate, because of the parallel with direct dyslexia.

Developmental Dyslexias

Some children have great difficulty learning to read and never become fluent readers, even though they are otherwise intelligent. Specific language learning disorders, called **developmental dyslexias,** tend to occur in families, a finding that suggests a genetic (and hence biological) component (Pennington et al., 1991; Wolff and Melngailis, 1994). Linkage studies suggest that chromosomes 6 and 15 may contain genes responsible for different components of this disorder (Grigorenko et al., 1997; Fisher et al., 1999; Gayán et al., 1999; Petryshen et al.,

2001). A study of fifty-six dyslexic boys in Sydney, Australia, found that two-thirds of them showed impairments in both phonological and word-form reading. Among the other third, 64 percent had difficulty only with phonological reading, and 46 percent had difficulty only with word-form reading (Castles and Coltheart, 1993). (You will recall that phonological difficulty is the primary symptom of phonological dyslexia, while word-form difficulty is the primary symptom of surface dyslexia.)

As we saw earlier, the fact that written language is a recent invention means that natural selection could not have given us brain mechanisms whose only role is to interpret written language. Thus, we should not expect that developmental dyslexia involves only deficits in reading. Indeed, researchers have found a variety of language deficits that do *not* involve reading. One common deficit is deficient phonological awareness. That is, people with developmental dyslexia have difficulty blending or rearranging the sounds of words that they hear (Eden and Zeffiro, 1998). For example, they have difficulty recognizing that if we remove the first sound from "cat," we are left with the word "at." They also have difficulty distinguishing the order of sequences of sounds (Helenius, Uutela, and Hari, 1999). Problems such as these might be expected to impair the ability to read phonetically. Dyslexic children also tend to have great difficulty in writing: They make spelling errors, they show poor spatial arrangements of letters, they omit letters, and their writing tends to have weak grammatical development (Habib, 2000).

Several studies have suggested that abnormal development of specific regions of the brain may be responsible for developmental dyslexia. However, in a review of the literature, Filipek (1995) concluded that imaging studies have failed to find a "marker" for developmental dyslexia—that is, a reliable abnormality that is universally found in a particular location in the brains of dyslexics. A more recent MRI study (Brown et al., 2001) found evidence for decreases in gray matter in the left temporal lobe and bilateral decreases in the junction of the temporal, parietal, and occipital lobes; the frontal lobe; the caudate nucleus; the thalamus; and the cerebellum. Clearly, results like this do not point to a simple neurological explanation for developmental dyslexia. Given the fact that the symptoms can vary from person to person, perhaps we would not expect a simple explanation.

Some evidence has been obtained from functional imaging that suggests that the brains of dyslexics process written information differently than do proficient readers.

developmental dyslexia A reading difficulty in a person of normal intelligence and perceptual ability; of genetic origin or caused by prenatal or perinatal factors.

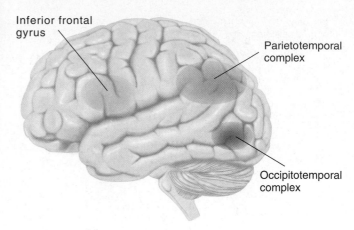

figure 15.31

Three regions of the brain activated in the brains of children as they read words and pronounceable nonwords. Proficient readers showed activation of all three areas: the left occipitotemporal and parietotemporal regions, and the left and right inferior frontal cortex. Reading ability was positively correlated to the level of activation of the occipitotemporal region; activation of this area was lower in dyslexic children.

(Adapted from Shaywitz, B. A., Shaywitz, S. E., Pugh, K. R., Mencl, W. E., Fulbright, R. K., Skudlarski P., Constable, R. T., Marchione, K. E., Fletcher, J. M., Lyon, G. R., and Gore, J. C. *Biological Psychiatry*, 2002, *52*, 101–110.)

For example, Shaywitz et al. (2002) had seventy dyslexic and seventy-four nondyslexic children read words and pronounceable nonwords. They found significantly different patterns of brain activation in the two groups. The proficient readers showed activation of the left occipitotemporal and parietotemporal regions and of the left and right inferior frontal cortex (which included Broca's area). A child's reading skill was positively correlated with activation of the left occipitotemporal cortex. (See *Figure 15.31*.)

One neurological finding received a considerable amount of attention. Galaburda and Livingstone (1993) found evidence for a deficit in the magnocellular layers of the lateral geniculate nucleus. As we saw in Chapter 6, the visual system has two major components, named after two types of layers in the lateral geniculate nucleus, which relays information from the retina to the visual cortex. The *magnocellular system* is more ancient. It consists of two layers of neurons with large cell bodies that transmit information about movement, depth, and small differences in contrast. The *parvocellular system,* which evolved more recently, consists of four layers of neurons that transmit information about color and fine details. Galaburda and Livingstone studied the brains of deceased patients with developmental dyslexia and discovered that the magnocellular layers of these people were disorganized. The cell bodies in these layers were 27 percent smaller, and they were more variable in their size and shape. The parvocellular layers were normal.

Why should abnormalities in the magnocellular system impair people's ability to read? Stein and Walsh (1997) note that the primary target of the magnocellular system is the posterior parietal lobe, the endpoint of the dorsal stream of the visual system. As we saw in Chapter 6, this system is concerned with the "where" of vision, while the ventral stream, which terminates in the inferior temporal lobe, is concerned with the "what" of vision. Indeed, some dyslexics have trouble with spatial perception and per-

ception of movements in space. For example, they may transpose letters (reading *saw* as *was*), they are often clumsy and have difficulties with balance, their handwriting tends to be very poor, they learn to walk later than most other children and have trouble learning to ride a bike, they are slower to learn to tell time or learn the days of the week and months of the year, they have difficulty reading maps and distinguishing between left and right, and they tend not to establish strong handedness. However, these problems do not explain the difficulty most dyslexic children have with phonetic reading and processing of sequences of sounds. In recent years, the magnocellular hypothesis has failed to receive much experimental support (Wright, Bowen, and Zecker, 2000).

Most languages—including English—contain many irregular words. For example, consider *cough, rough, bough,* and *through*. Because there is no phonetic rule that describes how these words are to be pronounced, readers of English are obliged to memorize them. In fact, the forty sounds that distinguish English words can be spelled in up to 1120 different ways. In contrast, Italian is much more regular; this language contains twenty-five different sounds that can be spelled in only thirty-three combinations of letters (Helmuth, 2001). Paulesu et al. (2001) found that developmental dyslexia is rare among people who speak Italian and is much more common among speakers of English and French (another language with many irregular words). Paulesu and his colleagues identified college students with a history of dyslexia from Italy, France, and Great Britain. The Italian dyslexics were much harder to find, and their disorders were much less severe than those of their English-speaking and French-speaking counterparts. However, when all three groups were asked to read while their heads were in a PET scanner, their scans all showed the same pattern: a decrease in the activity of the left occipitotemporal region—the same general region that Shaywitz et al. (2002) identified. (See the green region of *Figure 15.31*.)

Paulesu and his colleagues concluded that the brain anomalies that cause dyslexia are similar in the three countries they studied but that the regularity of Italian spelling made it much easier for potential dyslexics in Italy to learn to read. By the way, other "dyslexia-friendly" languages include Spanish, Finnish, Czech, and Japanese. One of the authors of this study, Chris D. Frith, cites the case of an Australian boy who lived in Japan. He learned to read Japanese normally but was dyslexic in English (Recer, 2001).

Geschwind and Behan (1984) noted that investigators have long recognized that a disproportionate number of people with developmental dyslexias are also left-handed. Furthermore, clinical observations suggested a relation between left-handedness and various immune disorders. Therefore, Geschwind and Behan studied a group of left-handed and right-handed people to see whether the relationships were statistically significant. They found that they were: The left-handed subjects were ten times more likely to have specific learning disorders (10 percent versus 1 percent) and two and one-half times more likely to have immune disorders (8 percent versus 3 percent). The immune disorders included various thyroid and bowel diseases, diabetes, and rheumatoid arthritis. Of course, although the relationship was statistically significant, it was not perfect. After all, most left-handed people are healthy and are good readers.

interim summary

Disorders of Reading and Writing

Brain damage can produce reading and writing disorders. With few exceptions, aphasias are accompanied by writing deficits that parallel the speech production deficits and by reading deficits that parallel the speech comprehension deficits. Pure alexia is caused by lesions that produce blindness in the right visual field and that destroy fibers of the posterior corpus callosum.

Research in the past few decades has discovered that acquired reading disorders (dyslexias) can fall into one of several categories, and the study of these disorders has provided neuropsychologists and cognitive psychologists with thought-provoking information that has helped them understand the brain mechanisms involved in reading. A region of the left basal posterior temporal lobe known as BA37 appears to play a role in the visual and tactual recognition (through Braille) of words. Surface dyslexia, usually caused by damage to the left lateral temporal lobe, is a loss of whole-word reading ability. Phonological dyslexia, usually caused by damage to the left frontal lobe, is loss of the ability to read phonetically. Reading of kana (phonetic) and kanji (pictographic) symbols by Japanese people are equivalent to pho-

netic and whole-word reading, and damage to different parts of the brain interfere with these two forms of reading. Functional imaging suggests that area BA37 is involved in reading of kanji symbols.

Word-form (spelling) dyslexia is caused by a deficit in both phonetic and whole-word reading; patients can still recognize individual letters and can read slowly by pronouncing each letter. Direct dyslexia is analogous to transcortical sensory aphasia; the patients can read words aloud but cannot understand what they are reading. Some can read both real words and pronounceable nonwords, so both phonetic and whole-word reading can be preserved. Some dyslexia patients can at least partially comprehend written words without being able to pronounce them; they can match corresponding words and pictures and recognize misspelled words that they cannot read.

Brain damage can disrupt writing ability by impairing people's ability to form letters—or even specific types of letters, such as uppercase or lowercase letters or vowels. Other deficits involve the ability to spell words. We normally use at least four different strategies to spell words: phonetic (sounding the word out), visual (remembering how it looks on paper), sequential (recalling memorized sequences of letters), and motor (recalling memorized hand movements in writing very familiar words). Two types of dysgraphia—phonological and orthographic—represent difficulties implementing phonetic and visual strategies, respectively. The existence of these two disorders indicates that several different brain mechanisms are involved in the process of writing. One case of dystypia— a specific deficit in the ability to type without other reading or writing disorders—has been reported. In addition, some patients have a deficit parallel to direct dyslexia; they can write words they cannot understand.

Developmental dyslexia is a hereditary condition that may involve abnormal development of parts of the brain that play a role in language. Most developmental dyslexics have difficulty with phonological processing—of spoken words as well as written ones. Some investigators suggest that abnormal development of the magnocellular system of the lateral geniculate nucleus, seen in some people with developmental dyslexia, may impair normal development of the posterior parietal lobe. Functional imaging studies report decreased activation of a region of the left occipitotemporal cortex may be involved in reading deficits. Children who learn to read languages that have writing with regular correspondence between spelling and pronunciation (such as Italian) are much less likely to become dyslexic than those who learn to read languages with irregular spelling (such as English or French). A better understanding of the components of reading and writing may help us to develop effective teaching methods that will permit people with dyslexia to take advantage of the abilities that they do have.

Table 15.2 summarizes the disorders that were described in this section.

table **15.2**

Reading and Writing Disorder Produced by Brain Damage			
READING DISORDER	**WHOLE-WORD READING**	**PHONETIC READING**	**REMARKS**
Pure alexia	Poor	Poor	Can write
Surface dyslexia	Poor	Good	
Phonological dyslexia	Good	Poor	
Spelling dyslexia	Poor	Poor	Can read words letter by letter
Direct dyslexia	Good	Good	Cannot comprehend words
WRITING DISORDER	**WHOLE-WORD READING**	**PHONETIC WRITING**	
Phonological dysgraphia	Good	Poor	
Orthographic dysgraphia	Poor	Good	

Suggested Readings

Davis, G. A. *Aphasiology: Disorders and Clinical Practice*. Boston: Allyn and Bacon, 2000.

Obler, L. K., and Gjerlow, K. *Language and the Brain*. Cambridge, England: Cambridge: University Press, 1999.

Parkin, A. J. *Explorations in Cognitive Neuropsychology*. Oxford, England: Blackwell Publishers, 1996.

Posner, M. I., and Raichle, M. E. *Images of Mind*. New York: Scientific American Library, 1994.

Sarno, M. T. *Acquired Aphasia* (3rd ed.). New York: Academic Press, 1998.

Suggested Web Sites

Sleep and Language
http://thalamus.wustl.edu/course/sleep.html
This Web site provides an overview of sleep phenomena and of language.

Dyslexia Web Resources
http://www.krgraphics.co.uk/texthelp/d_web.htm
The focus of the collection of Web links is on the topic of dyslexia.

Aphasia: Treatment, Prevention, and Cure
http://www.healthlinkusa.com/A.html
This page contain a series of links that will take you to a page devoted to the topic of aphasia.

Schizophrenia and the Affective Disorders

Frank Stella, *Yooloomooloo 4*, 1994. © Frank Stella/Artists Rights Society (ARS), New York. © Steven Sloman/Art Resource, NY.

outline

■ **Schizophrenia**
Description
Heritability
Pharmacology of Schizophrenia:
    The Dopamine Hypothesis
Schizophrenia as a Neurological Disorder
Interim Summary

■ **Major Affective Disorders**
Description
Heritability
Physiological Treatments
Role of Monoamines

A Role for Substance P?
Evidence for Brain
    Abnormalities
Role of Circadian Rhythms
Interim Summary

Larry had become a permanent resident of the state hospital. His parents had originally hoped that treatment would help him enough that he could live in a halfway house with a small group of other young men, but his condition was so serious that he required constant supervision. Larry had severe schizophrenia. The medication he was taking helped, but he still exhibited severe psychotic symptoms. In addition, he had begun showing signs of a neurological disorder that seemed to be getting worse.

Larry had always been a difficult child, shy and socially awkward. He had no real friends. During adolescence he became even more withdrawn and insisted that his parents and older sister keep out of his room. He stopped taking meals with the family, and he even bought a small refrigerator of his own for his room so that he could keep his own food, which he said he preferred to that "pesticide-contaminated" food his parents ate. His grades in school, which were never outstanding, got progressively worse, and when he was seventeen years old, he dropped out of high school.

Larry's parents recognized that something was seriously wrong with him. Their family physician suggested that he see a psychiatrist and gave them the name of a colleague that he respected, but Larry flatly refused to go. Within a year after he had quit high school, he became frankly psychotic. He heard voices talking to him, and sometimes his parents could hear him shouting for the voices to go away. He was convinced that his parents were trying to poison him, and he would eat only factory-sealed food that he had opened himself. Although he kept his body clean—sometimes he would stand in the shower for an hour "purifying" himself—his room became frightfully messy. He insisted on keeping old cans and food packages because, he said, he needed to compare them with items his parents brought from the store to be sure they were not counterfeit.

One day, while Larry was in the shower purifying himself, his mother cleaned his room. She filled several large plastic garbage bags with the cans and packages and put them out for the trash collector. As she reentered the house, she heard a howling noise from upstairs. Larry had emerged from the shower and discovered that his room had been cleaned. When he saw his mother coming up the stairs, he screamed at her, cursed her savagely, and rushed down the stairs toward her. He hit her so hard that she flew through the air, landing heavily on the floor below. He wheeled around, ran up the stairs, and went into his room, slamming the door behind him.

An hour later, Larry's father discovered his wife unconscious at the foot of the stairs. She soon recovered from the mild concussion she had sustained, but Larry's parents realized that it was time for him to be put in custody. Because he had attacked his mother, a judge ordered that he be temporarily detained and, as a result of a psychiatric evaluation, had him committed to the state hospital. The diagnosis was "schizophrenia, paranoid type."

In the state hospital, Larry was given Thorazine (chlorpromazine), which helped considerably. For the first few weeks, he showed some symptoms that are commonly seen in Parkinson's disease—tremors, rigidity, a shuffling gait, and lack of facial expression—but these symptoms cleared up spontaneously, as his physician had predicted. The voices still talked to him occasionally, but less often than before, and even then he could ignore them most of the time. His suspiciousness decreased, and he was willing to eat with the residents in the dining room. But he still obviously had paranoid delusions, and the psychiatric staff was unwilling to let him leave the hospital. For one thing, he refused to take his medication voluntarily. Once, after he had suffered a serious relapse, the staff discovered that he had only been pretending to swallow his pills and was later throwing them away. After that, they made sure that he swallowed them.

After several years, Larry began developing more serious neurological symptoms. He began pursing his lips and making puffing sounds; later, he started grimacing, sticking his tongue out, and turning his head sharply to the left. The symptoms became so severe that they interfered with his ability to eat. His physician prescribed an additional drug, which reduced the symptoms considerably but did not eliminate them. As he explained to Larry's parents, "His neurological problems are caused by the medication that we are using to help with his psychiatric symptoms. These problems usually do not develop until a patient has taken the medication for many years, but Larry appears to be one of the unfortunate exceptions. If we take him off the medication, the neurological symptoms will get even worse. We could reduce the symptoms by giving him a higher dose of the medication, but then the problem would come back later, and it would be even worse. All we can do is try to treat the symptoms with another drug, as we have been doing. We really need a medication that helps treat schizophrenia without producing these tragic side effects."

Most of the discussion in this book has concentrated on the physiology of normal, adaptive behavior. The last three chapters summarize research on the nature and physiology of syndromes characterized by maladaptive behavior: mental disorders and drug abuse. The symptoms of mental disorders include deficient or inappropriate social behaviors; illogical, incoherent, or obsessional thoughts; inappropriate emotional responses, including depression, mania, or anxiety; and delusions and hallucinations. Research in recent years indicates that many of these symptoms are caused by abnormalities in the brain, both structural and biochemical.

This chapter discusses two serious mental disorders: schizophrenia and the major affective disorders. Chapter 17 discusses anxiety disorders, autism, attention deficit disorder, and disorders caused by stress. Chapter 18 discusses drug abuse.

Schizophrenia

Description

Schizophrenia is a serious mental disorder that afflicts approximately 1 percent of the world's population. Its monetary cost to society is enormous; in the United States this figure exceeds that of that cost of all cancers (Thaker and Carpenter, 2001). Descriptions of symptoms in ancient writings indicate that the disorder has been around for thousands of years (Jeste et al., 1985). The major symptoms of schizophrenia are universal, and clinicians have developed criteria for reliably diagnosing the disorder in people of a wide variety of cultures (Flaum and Andreasen, 1990). *Schizophrenia* is probably the most misused psychological term in existence. The word literally means "split mind," but it does *not* imply a split or multiple personality. People often say that they "feel schizophrenic" about an issue when they really mean that they have mixed feelings about it. A person who sometimes wants to build a cabin in Alaska and live off the land and at other times wants to take over the family insurance agency might be undecided, but he or she is not schizophrenic. The man who invented the term, Eugen Bleuler (1911/1950), intended it to refer to a break with reality caused by disorganization of the various functions of the mind, such that thoughts and feelings no longer worked together normally.

Schizophrenia is characterized by two categories of symptoms: positive and negative (Crow, 1980; Andreasen, 1995). **Positive symptoms** make themselves known by their presence. They include thought disorders, hallucinations, and delusions. A **thought disorder**—disorganized, irrational thinking—is probably the most important symptom of schizophrenia. Schizophrenics have great difficulty arranging their thoughts logically and sorting out plausible conclusions from absurd ones. In conversation they jump from one topic to another as new associations come up. Sometimes, they utter meaningless words or choose words for rhyme rather than for meaning. **Delusions** are beliefs that are obviously contrary to fact. Delusions of *persecution* are false beliefs that others are plotting and conspiring against oneself. Delusions of *grandeur* are false beliefs in one's power and importance, such as a conviction that one has godlike powers or has special knowledge that no one else possesses. Delusions of *control* are related to delusions of persecution; the person believes (for example) that he or she is being controlled by others through

table 16.1

Positive and Negative Symptoms of Schizophrenia

SCHIZOPHRENIC SYMPTOM
Positive
Hallucinations
Thought disorders
Delusions
Presecution
Grandeur
Control
Negative
Flattened emotional response
Poverty of speech
Lack of initiative and persistence
Anhedonia (inability to experience pleasure)
Social withdrawal

such means as radar or tiny radio receivers implanted in his or her brain.

The third positive symptom of schizophrenia is **hallucinations,** perceptions of stimuli that are not actually present. The most common schizophrenic hallucinations are auditory, but they can also involve any of the other senses. The typical schizophrenic hallucination consists of voices talking to the person. Sometimes, the voices order the person to do something; sometimes, they scold the person for his or her unworthiness; sometimes, they just utter meaningless phrases. Olfactory hallucinations are also fairly common; often they contribute to the delusion that others are trying to kill the person with poison gas. (See *Table 16.1*.)

In contrast to the positive symptoms, the **negative symptoms** of schizophrenia are known by the absence of normal behaviors: flattened emotional response, poverty of speech, lack of initiative and persistence, inability to

---

schizophrenia A serious mental disorder characterized by disordered thoughts, delusions, hallucinations, and often bizarre behaviors.

positive symptom A symptom of schizophrenia evident by its presence: delusions, hallucinations, or thought disorders.

thought disorder Disorganized, irrational thinking.

delusion A belief that is clearly in contradiction to reality.

hallucination Perception of a nonexistent object or event.

negative symptom A symptom of schizophrenia characterized by the absence of behaviors that are normally present: social withdrawal, lack of affect, and reduced motivation.

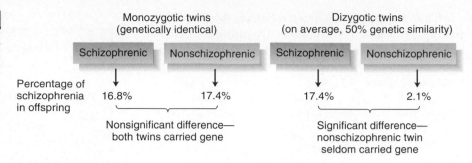

figure 16.1

An explanation for evidence that people can have an unexpressed "schizophrenia gene."

experience pleasure, and social withdrawal. Negative symptoms are not specific to schizophrenia; they are seen in many neurological disorders that involve brain damage, especially to the frontal lobes. As we will see later in this chapter, research suggests that these two sets of symptoms are caused by different abnormalities in the brain: Positive symptoms appear to involve excessive activity in some neural circuits that include dopamine as a neurotransmitter, and negative symptoms appear to be caused by developmental or degenerative processes that impair the normal functions of some regions of the brain. Recent evidence suggests that these two sets of symptoms may involve a common set of underlying causes. (See *Table 16.1*.)

Heritability

One of the strongest pieces of evidence that schizophrenia is a biological disorder is that it appears to be heritable. Both adoption studies (Kety et al., 1968, 1994) and twin studies (Gottesman and Shields, 1982; Tsuang, Gilbertson, and Faraone, 1991) indicate that schizophrenia is a heritable trait.

If schizophrenia were a simple trait produced by a single gene, we would expect to see this disorder in at least 75 percent of the children of two schizophrenic parents if the gene were dominant. If it were recessive, *all* children of two schizophrenic parents should become schizophrenic. However, the actual incidence is less than 50 percent, which means either that several genes are involved or that having a "schizophrenia gene" imparts a *susceptibility* to develop schizophrenia, the disease itself being triggered by other factors.

If the susceptibility hypothesis is true, then we would expect that some people carry a "schizophrenia gene" but do not express it; that is, their environment is such that schizophrenia is never triggered. One such person would be the nonschizophrenic member of a pair of monozygotic twins who are discordant for schizophrenia. The logical way to test this hypothesis is to examine the children of both members of discordant pairs. Gottesman and Bertelsen (1989) found that the percentage of schizophrenic children was identical for both members of such pairs: 16.8 percent for the schizophrenic parents and 17.4 percent for the nonschizophrenic parents. For the dizygotic

twins the percentages were 17.4 percent and 2.1 percent, respectively. These results provide strong evidence for the heritability of schizophrenia and also support the conclusion that carrying a "schizophrenia gene" does not mean that a person will necessarily become schizophrenic. (See *Figure 16.1*.)

Another recently discovered genetic factor is paternal age. Malaspina et al. (2001) looked at records of 87,907 people born in Jerusalem between 1964 and 1976. Of these people, 658 were diagnosed with schizophrenia or related disorders (such as schizoaffective disorder, a mixture of the symptoms of schizophrenia and affective disorders). After controlling for maternal age, sex, ethnicity, education, and so on, they found a significant relationship between the probability of schizophrenia and age of the father at the time of the patient's birth. Only 1 of 121 of the children of men who became fathers during their late twenties became schizophrenic, compared with 1 of 47 of the children with fathers aged fifty to fifty-four years—an increase of over 250 percent. A sample of schizophrenic patients in California found similar results (Brown et al., 2002). Most investigators believe that the increased incidence of schizophrenia is caused by mutations in the spermatocytes—the cells that produce sperms. These cells divide every sixteen days after puberty, which means that they have divided approximately 540 times by age thirty-five. In contrast, women's oocytes divide twenty-three times before the time of birth and only once after that. The likelihood of a copying error in DNA replication when a cell divides increases with the number of cell divisions, and an increase in copying errors may be responsible for the increased incidence of schizophrenia.

So far, researchers have not yet located a "schizophrenia gene," although many candidates have been found. A review by Shastry (2002) notes that evidence for linkage to susceptibility for schizophrenia has been reported for chromosomes 1, 2, 4, 5, 6, 7, 8, 9, 10, 11, 13, 15, 18, 22, and X. (That includes all but 3, 12, 14, 16, 17, 19, 20, 21, and Y—at least, so far.) If susceptibility to schizophrenia is caused by a small number of genes, geneticists will undoubtedly succeed in finding them some day. Once they are found, other researchers will try to determine what role these genes play, which should provide useful information about the causes of schizophrenia.

Pharmacology of Schizophrenia: The Dopamine Hypothesis

Pharmacological evidence suggests that the positive symptoms of schizophrenia are caused by a biochemical disorder. The explanation that has received the most attention from researchers is the *dopamine hypothesis,* which suggests that schizophrenia is caused by overactivity of dopaminergic synapses, probably those in the mesolimbic pathway, which projects from the ventral tegmental area to the nucleus accumbens and amygdala.

Effects of Dopamine Agonists and Antagonists

Almost fifty years ago, a French surgeon named Henri Laborit discovered that a drug used to prevent surgical shock seemed also to reduce anxiety (Snyder, 1974). A French drug company developed a related compound called **chlorpromazine,** which seemed to be even more effective. Chlorpromazine was tried on patients with a variety of mental disorders: mania, depression, anxiety, neuroses, and schizophrenia (Delay and Deniker, 1952a, 1952b). The drug was not very effective in treating neuroses or affective psychoses, but it had dramatic effects on schizophrenia.

The discovery of the antipsychotic effects of chlorpromazine profoundly altered the way in which physicians treated schizophrenic patients and made prolonged hospital stays unnecessary for many of them (the patients, that is). The efficacy of antipsychotic drugs has been established in many double-blind studies (Baldessarini, 1977). The drugs actually eliminate, or at least diminish, the patients' symptoms. The beneficial effects are not just a change in the patient's attitudes; the hallucinations and delusions go away or at least become less severe. A review that analyzed sixty-six studies found that within ten months, 53 percent of patients who stopped taking antischizophrenic drugs had a relapse, compared with only 16 percent of those who continued taking the drugs (Gilbert et al., 1955).

Since the discovery of chlorpromazine, many other drugs have been developed that relieve the positive symptoms of schizophrenia. These drugs were found to have one property in common: They block dopamine receptors (Creese, Burt, and Snyder, 1976). Other drugs that interfere with dopaminergic transmission, such as reserpine (which prevents the storage of monoamines in synaptic vesicles) or α-methyl *p*-tyrosine (which blocks the synthesis of dopamine), either facilitate the antipsychotic action of drugs such as chlorpromazine or themselves exert antipsychotic effects (Tamminga et al., 1988). Thus, the positive symptoms of schizophrenia are reduced by a variety of drugs with one common effect: antagonism of dopaminergic transmission.

Another category of drugs has the opposite effect, namely, *production* of the positive symptoms of schizophrenia. The drugs that can produce these symptoms have one known pharmacological effect in common: They act as dopamine agonists. These drugs include amphetamine, cocaine, and methylphenidate (which block the reuptake of dopamine) and L-DOPA (which stimulates the synthesis of dopamine). The symptoms that these drugs produce can be alleviated with antipsychotic drugs, a result that further strengthens the argument that the antipsychotic drugs exert their therapeutic effects by blocking dopamine receptors.

How might we explain the apparent link between overactivity of dopaminergic synapses and the positive symptoms of schizophrenia? As we saw in Chapters 4 and 13, the most important systems of dopaminergic neurons begin in two midbrain nuclei: the substantia nigra and the ventral tegmental area. Most researchers believe that the mesolimbic pathway, which begins in the ventral tegmental area and ends in the nucleus accumbens and amygdala, is more likely to be involved in the symptoms of schizophrenia. As we saw in Chapter 13, the activity of dopaminergic synapses in the nucleus accumbens appears to be a vital link in the process of reinforcement. Drugs that act as agonists at these synapses (such as cocaine and amphetamine) strongly reinforce behavior; if taken in large doses, they also produce the positive symptoms of schizophrenia. Perhaps the two effects of the drugs are related. If reinforcement mechanisms were activated at inappropriate times, then inappropriate behaviors—including delusional thoughts—might be reinforced. At one time or another, all of us have had some irrational thoughts, which we normally brush aside and forget. But if neural mechanisms of reinforcement became active while these thoughts were occurring, we would tend to take them more seriously. In time, full-fledged delusions might develop.

As Snyder (1974) notes, schizophrenics often report feelings of elation and euphoria at the beginning of a schizophrenic episode, when their symptoms flare up. Presumably, this euphoria is caused by hyperactivity of dopaminergic neurons involved in reinforcement. But the positive symptoms of schizophrenia also include disordered thinking and unpleasant, often terrifying delusions. The disordered thinking may be caused by disorganized attentional processes; the indiscriminate activity of the dopaminergic synapses in the nucleus accumbens makes it difficult for the patients to follow an orderly, rational thought sequence. Fibiger (1991) suggests that paranoid delusions may be caused by increased activity of the dopaminergic input to the amygdala. As we saw in Chapter 11, the central nucleus of the amygdala is involved with conditioned emotional responses elicited by aversive stimuli. The central nucleus receives a strong projection from the mesolimbic dopaminergic system, so Fibiger's suggestion is certainly plausible.

chlorpromazine A dopamine receptor blocker; a commonly prescribed antischizophrenic drug.

t a b l e   1 6 . 2

Possible Causes of Increased Dopaminergic Transmission in the Brains of Schizophrenic Patients
Increased dopamine release 　　More excitatory input to dopaminergic neurons 　　Less inhibitory input to dopaminergic neurons 　　Fewer or defective autoreceptors on dopaminergic neurons
Increased postsynaptic response to dopamine release 　　More postsynaptic dopamine receptors 　　More response in postsynaptic neuron to activation of dopamine receptors
Prolonged activation of postsynaptic receptors 　　Decreased reuptake of dopamine by dopaminergic terminal button

The Search for Abnormalities in Dopamine Transmission in the Brains of Schizophrenic Patients

Is there any evidence that dopaminergic activity in the brains of schizophrenic patients is indeed abnormal? Before I discuss the search for abnormalities, let's consider the possibilities. (These possibilities are based on what you learned about the pharmacology of neurons in Chapter 4.) Too much dopamine might be released, neurons that receive dopaminergic input could be excessively sensitive to this input, or a slow reuptake process in dopaminergic terminals could keep molecules of dopamine in the synaptic cleft for an unusually long time, resulting in prolonged activation of the postsynaptic dopamine receptors. (See *Table 16.2.*)

Let's look at some of the evidence. Studies have found evidence that dopaminergic neurons may indeed release more dopamine (Laruelle et al., 1996; Breier et al., 1997). Laruelle and colleagues used a device similar to a PET scanner to estimate the release of dopamine caused by an intravenous injection of amphetamine. As we saw in Chapter 4, amphetamine stimulates the release of dopamine, apparently by causing the dopamine transporters that are present in the terminal buttons to run backward, pumping dopamine out rather than retrieving it after it has been released. Of course, this effect inhibits the reuptake of dopamine as well. Laruelle and his colleagues found that the amphetamine caused the release of more dopamine in the striatum of schizophrenic patients. They also found that subjects with greater amounts of dopamine release showed greater increases in positive symptoms. (See *Figure 16.2.*)

Another possibility—that the brains of schizophrenic patients contain a greater number of dopamine receptors—received much attention for several years. Because the earliest antipsychotic drugs appeared to work by blocking D_2 receptors, the earliest studies looked for increases in the numbers of these receptors in the brains of schizo-

phrenics. Researchers have performed two types of analyses: postmortem measurements in the brains of deceased schizophrenic patients and PET scans after treatment with radioactive ligands for dopamine receptors. The results have been mixed. Although some studies have found evidence for increased numbers of dopamine receptors, others have not; and some researchers suggest that the positive results may be caused by antipsychotic medication that the patients received A review by Kestler, Walker, and Vega (2001) concludes that there might be moderate increases in the numbers of D_2 receptors in the brains of schizophrenics. However, it seems unlikely that these increases are the primary cause of the disorder.

The older antipsychotic drugs certainly act as D_2 receptor antagonists, and they have a strong effect in the neostriatum. This action undoubtedly accounts for the motor side effects that these drugs produce. (I will discuss this matter in the next subsection.) But the affinity for D_2 receptors does not necessarily account for the ability of these drugs to relieve the symptoms of schizophrenia. **Clozapine,** a more recently developed drug, is a very effective antipsychotic medication, and its site of action is primarily in the nucleus accumbens, not the neostriatum (Kinon and Lieberman, 1996). In addition, it has little effect on D_2 receptors (Pickar, 1995), a feature that has earned it the label of *atypical* antischizophrenic medication. Clozapine serves as a potent blocker of D_4 dopamine receptor; in fact, it has ten times more affinity for D_4 receptors than for D_2 receptors (Van Tol et al., 1991). Consequently, researchers are beginning to turn their attention to these receptors. They are also beginning to examine the possible role of another dopamine receptor: the D_3 receptor, which is found in especially high concentrations in the human nucleus accumbens (Murray et al., 1994).

---

clozapine An atypical antipsychotic drug; blocks D_4 receptors in the nucleus accumbens.

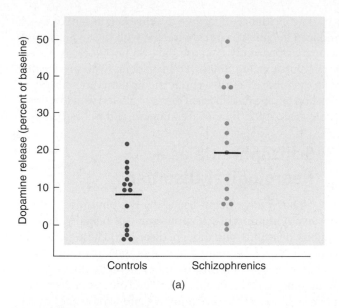

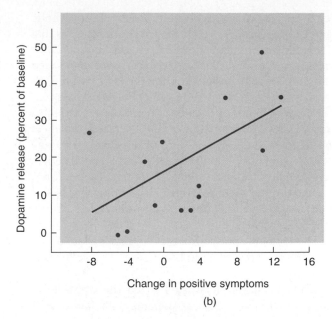

figure 16.2

Results of the study by Laruelle et al. (1996). (a) Relative amount of dopamine released in response to amphetamine. (b) Relation between dopamine release and changes in positive symptoms of schizophrenic patients.

(Adapted from Laruelle, M., Abi-Dargham, A., Van Dyck, C. H., Gil, R., D'Souza, C. D., Erdos, J., McCance, E., Rosenblatt, W., Fingado, C., Zoghbi, S. S., Baldwin, R. M., Seibyl, J. P., Krystal, J. H., Charney, D. S., and Innis, R. B. *Proceedings of the National Academy of Sciences, USA*, 1996, *93*, 9235–9240.)

Two studies have found evidence for increased amounts of D_3 and D_4 dopamine receptors in the brains of deceased schizophrenics. Murray et al. (1995) found a twofold increase in the concentration of D_4 receptors in the nucleus accumbens. Gurevich et al. (1997) found a twofold increase in D_3 receptors in both the neostriatum and the nucleus accumbens of schizophrenic patients. The patients had been drug free for at least one month before their deaths, so the increased concentration of D_3 receptors is unlikely to have been caused by medication. (See *Figure 16.3*.)

Consequences of Long-Term Drug Treatment of Schizophrenia

The discovery of drugs that reduce or eliminate the symptoms of schizophrenia has had a revolutionary effect on the treatment of this disorder. Before this discovery many schizophrenics spent much of their lives in psychiatric hospitals. Now many of these people receive antipsychotic medication on an outpatient basis and are able to live relatively normal lives. But not everyone is helped; the symptoms of up to one-third of all schizophrenic

Receptor Density

High   Low

Pt

Cd

NA

(a)   (b)   (c)

figure 16.3

Pseudocolor images of concentrations of D_3-receptor binding in the human striatum. (a) Control subject. (b) Unmedicated schizophrenic patient. (c) Schizophrenic patient receiving antipsychotic medication. Cd = caudate nucleus, Pt = putamen, NA = nucleus accumbens.

(From Gurevich, E. V., Bordelon, Y., Shapiro, R. M., Arnold, S. E., Gur, R. E., and Joyce, J. N. *Archives of General Psychiatry*, 1997, *54*, 225–232.)

patients are not substantially reduced by antipsychotic drugs. Another problem with antipsychotic drugs is that they sometimes produce serious side effects. Until recently, all the drugs commonly used to treat schizophrenia caused at least some symptoms resembling those of Parkinson's disease: slowness in movement, lack of facial expression, and general weakness. For most patients these symptoms are temporary. Unfortunately, a more serious side effect occurs in approximately one-third of all patients who take the "classic" antischizophrenic drugs for an extended period.

As a result of taking an antipsychotic medication, Larry, the schizophrenic man described in the opening of this chapter, developed a neurological disorder called **tardive dyskinesia.** *Tardus* means "slow," and *dyskinesia* means "faulty movement"; thus, tardive dyskinesia is a late-developing movement disorder. (In Larry's case it actually came rather early.)

Tardive dyskinesia appears to be the opposite of Parkinson's disease. Whereas patients with Parkinson's disease have difficulty moving, patients with tardive dyskinesia are unable to stop moving. Indeed, dyskinesia commonly occurs when patients with Parkinson's disease receive too much L-DOPA. In schizophrenic patients, once tardive dyskinesia occurs, it is made *worse* by discontinuing the antipsychotic drug and is improved by increasing the dose. The symptoms are also intensified by dopamine agonists such as L-DOPA or amphetamine. Therefore, the disorder appears to be produced by an overstimulation of dopamine D_2 receptors. But if it is, why should it be originally caused by antipsychotic drugs, which are dopamine *antagonists?*

The most common explanation for tardive dyskinesia has been a phenomenon known as **supersensitivity,** a compensatory mechanism in which some types of receptors become more sensitive if they are inhibited for a period of time by a drug that blocks them. Studies indicate that tardive dyskinesia is associated with chronic administration of drugs that block D_2 receptors in the basal ganglia (Adler et al., 2002; Tarsy, Baldessarini, and Tarazi, 2002). Presumably, when D_2 receptors in the caudate nucleus and putamen are chronically blocked by an antipsychotic drug, they become supersensitive, which in some cases overcompensates for the effects of the drug, causing the neurological symptoms to occur.

Fortunately, the wish expressed by Larry's physician has come true. Researchers *have* discovered medications that treat the symptoms of schizophrenia without producing neurological side effects, and early indications suggest that tardive dyskinesia may become a thing of the past. Better yet, these drugs, the *atypical antipsychotic medications,* reduce the psychotic symptoms of many patients who are not significantly helped by the older antipsychotic drugs. Clozapine, the first of the atypical antipsychotic medications, has been joined by several others, including risperidone, olanzapine, and amisulpride.

The incidence of tardive dyskinesia is absent or much reduced in patients who are treated with the atypical medications, apparently because they do not block D_2 receptors (Llorca et al., 2002). Even patients who are treated with the "classic" antipsychotic medications are unlikely to develop tardive dyskinesia if they are treated with low doses (Lohr et al., 2002; Turrone, Remington, and Nobrega, 2002).

Schizophrenia as a Neurological Disorder

So far, I have been discussing the physiology of the positive symptoms of schizophrenia—principally, hallucinations, delusions, and thought disorders. These symptoms could very well be related to one of the known functions of dopaminergic neurons: reinforcement. But the negative symptoms of schizophrenia—flattened emotional response, poverty of speech, lack of initiative and persistence, inability to experience pleasure, and social withdrawal—are very different. Whereas the positive symptoms are unique to schizophrenia (and to amphetamine or cocaine psychosis), the negative symptoms are similar to those produced by brain damage caused by several different means. Many pieces of evidence suggest that the negative symptoms of schizophrenia are indeed a result of brain abnormalities.

Evidence for Brain Abnormalities in Schizophrenia

Although schizophrenia has traditionally been labeled a psychiatric disorder, most patients with schizophrenia exhibit neurological symptoms that suggest the presence of brain damage—in particular, poor control of eye movements and unusual facial expressions (Stevens, 1982). Although these symptoms can be caused by a variety of neuropathological conditions and hence are not unique to schizophrenia, their presence suggests that schizophrenia may be associated with brain damage (or perhaps abnormal brain development) of some kind.

Many studies have found evidence of loss of brain tissue in CT and MRI scans of schizophrenic patients. In one of the earliest studies, Weinberger and Wyatt (1982) obtained CT scans of eighty chronic schizophrenics and sixty-six normal controls of the same mean age (twenty-nine years). Without knowledge of the patients' diagnoses they measured the area of the lateral ventricles in the scan

tardive dyskinesia A movement disorder that can occur after prolonged treatment with antipsychotic medication, characterized by involuntary movements of the face and neck.

supersensitivity The increased sensitivity of neurotransmitter receptors; caused by damage to the afferent axons or long-term blockage of neurotransmitter release.

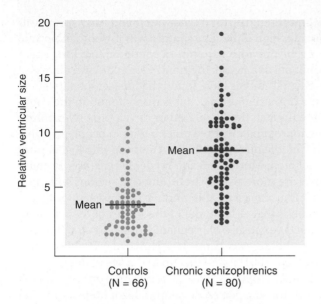

figure 16.4

Relative ventricular size in chronic schizophrenics and controls.
(From Weinberger, D. R., and Wyatt, R. J., in *Schizophrenia as a Brain Disease,*
edited by F. A. Henn and H. A. Nasrallah. New York: Oxford University Press,
1982. Reprinted with permission.)

that cut through them at their largest extent, and they expressed this area relative to the area of brain tissue in the same scan. The relative ventricle size of the schizophrenic patients was more than twice as great as that of normal control subjects. (See *Figure 16.4.*) The most likely cause of the enlarged ventricles is loss of brain tissue; thus, the CT scans provide evidence that chronic schizophrenia is associated with brain abnormalities. In fact, Hulshoff-Pol et al. (2002) found that although everyone loses some cerebral gray matter as they age, the rate of tissue loss is greater in schizophrenic patients. (See *Figure 16.5.*)

Many studies have investigated the specific locations of abnormalities in the brain of schizophrenics; these studies are described in a later section of this chapter.

Possible Causes of the Brain Abnormalities

As we saw earlier, schizophrenia is a heritable disease, but its heritability is less than perfect. Why do fewer than half the children of parents with chronic schizophrenia become schizophrenic? Perhaps what is inherited is a defect that renders people susceptible to some environmental factors that adversely affect brain development or cause brain damage later in life. According to this hypothesis, having a "schizophrenia gene" makes a person more likely to develop schizophrenia if he or she is exposed to these factors. In other words, schizophrenia is caused by an interaction between genetic and environmental factors. But as we shall see, the absence of a "schizophrenia gene" does not guarantee that a person will not develop schizophrenia; some cases of schizophrenia occur even in families with no history of schizophrenia or related mental illnesses. Let's look at the evidence concerning environmental factors that increase the risk of schizophrenia.

■ **Epidemiological Studies** Epidemiology is the study of the distribution and causes of diseases in populations. Thus, epidemiological studies examine the relative frequency of diseases in groups of people in different environments and try to correlate the disease frequencies with factors that are present in these environments. Evidence from these studies indicates that the incidence of

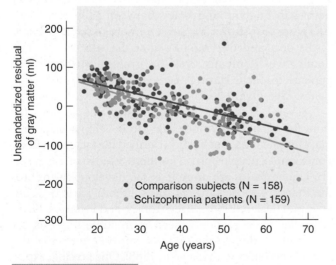

figure 16.5

Changes in volume of cerebral gray matter with age in normal subjects and people with schizophrenia.

(Adapted from Hulshoff-Pol, H. E., Schnack, H. G., Bertens, M. G. B. C., van Haren, N. E. M., Staal, W. G., Baaré, W. F. C., and Kahn, R. S. *American Journal of Psychiatry,* 2002, *159,* 244–250.)

epidemiology The study of the distribution and causes of diseases in populations.

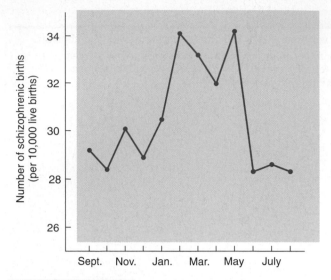

figure 16.6

The seasonality effect. The graph shows the number of schizophrenic births per 10,000 live births.

(Based on data from Kendell, R. E., and Adams, W. *British Journal of Psychiatry*, 1991, *158*, 758–763.)

schizophrenia is related to several environmental factors: season of birth, viral epidemics, population density, latitude, prenatal malnutrition, Rh incompatibility, and maternal stress. Let's examine each of these factors in turn.

Many studies have shown that people born during the late winter and early spring are more likely to develop schizophrenia—a phenomenon known as the **seasonality effect.** For example, Kendell and Adams (1991) studied the month of birth of over 13,000 schizophrenic patients born in Scotland between 1914 and 1960. They found that disproportionately more patients were born in February, March, April, and May. (See ***Figure 16.6.***) These results have been confirmed by studies in several parts of the world, including Japan (Takei et al., 1995) and Taiwan (Tam and Sewell, 1995). In the southern hemisphere some studies have reported that a disproportionate number of schizophrenic births also take place during late winter and early spring—during the months of August through December—while others have found no effect (McGrath and Welham, 1999).

What factors might be responsible for the seasonality effect? One possibility is that pregnant women may be more likely to contract a viral illness during a critical phase of their infants' development. The brain development of their fetuses may be adversely affected either by a toxin produced by the virus or by the mother's antibodies against the virus. As Pallast et al. (1994) note, the winter flu season coincides with the second trimester of pregnancy of babies born in late winter and early spring. (As we shall see later, evidence suggests that critical aspects of brain development occur during the second trimester.) In fact, Kendell and Adams (1991) found that the relative number

of schizophrenic births in late winter and early spring was especially high if the temperature was lower than normal during the previous autumn—a condition that keeps people indoors and favors the transmission of viral illnesses.

Several studies have found that the seasonality effect occurs primarily in cities but is rarely found in the countryside. In fact, the likelihood of developing schizophrenia is approximately three times higher in people who live in the middle of large cities than in those who live in rural areas (Eaton, Mortensen, and Frydenberg, 2000). Because viruses are more readily transmitted in regions with high population densities, this finding is consistent with the hypothesis that at least one of the causes of the seasonality effect is exposure of pregnant women to viral illnesses during the second trimester. However, Pedersen and Mortensen (2001) found that up to the age of fifteen years, the longer a person lives in a city, the more likely it becomes that the person develops schizophrenia. Thus, an urban environment may also affect people's susceptibility to schizophrenia postnatally.

If the viral hypothesis is true, then an increased incidence of schizophrenia should be seen in babies born a few months after an influenza epidemic, whatever the season. Several studies have observed just that. For example, a study of the offspring of women who were pregnant during an epidemic of type A2 influenza in Finland during 1957 showed an elevated incidence of schizophrenia (Mednick, Machon, and Huttunen, 1990). The increased incidence was seen only in the children of women who were in the second trimester of their pregnancy when the epidemic occurred. Another study (Sham et al., 1992) confirmed these findings in a study of infants born to mothers who were pregnant during several influenza epidemics in England and Wales between 1939 and 1960. As Figure 16.7 shows, the peak number of schizophrenic births occurred five months after the start of the epidemic, which means that the greatest susceptibility appears to occur during the second trimester of pregnancy. (See ***Figure 16.7.***)

Several studies have reported that people born far from the equator are more likely to develop schizophrenia. This phenomenon has been termed the **latitude effect.** For example, people born in northern Sweden or the northern United States are more likely to develop schizophrenia than are those born in the southern parts of these countries (Dalen, 1968; Torrey, Torrey, and Peterson, 1979). A similar phenomenon is seen in multiple sclerosis, an autoimmune disease that attacks the white matter of the central nervous system (Stevens, 1988). One possible expla-

seasonality effect The increased incidence of schizophrenia in people born during late winter and early spring.

latitude effect The increased incidence of schizophrenia in people born far from the equator.

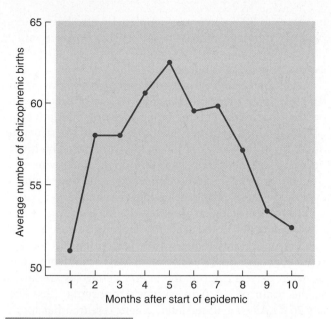

figure 16.7

Average number of schizophrenic births in each of the ten months following an influenza epidemic in England and Wales between 1939 and 1960.

(Adapted from Sham, P. C., O'Callaghan, E., Takei, N., Murray, G. K., Hare, E. H., and Murray, R. M. *British Journal of Psychiatry,* 1992, *160,* 461–466. Reprinted with permission.)

nation for the latitude effect is that the climate is colder in higher latitudes, and the decreased winter temperature might simply magnify the seasonality effect.

Another prenatal effect was discovered by Susser and his colleagues (Susser and Lin, 1992; Susser et al, 1996), who studied the offspring of women who were pregnant during the *Hunger Winter,* a severe food shortage that occurred in the Netherlands when Germany blockaded the country during World War II. The investigators found that the offspring of these women were twice as likely to become schizophrenic. Davis and Bracha (1996) suggest that the specific cause of the famine-related schizophrenia may have been a thiamine deficiency—or, more precisely, a sudden buildup of toxins in the brains of the developing fetuses when their mothers suddenly began eating a normal diet when the blockade ended in May 1945. As we saw in Chapter 14, sudden refeeding after a thiamine deficiency can cause brain damage in an adult, so it is certainly plausible that it could interfere with the brain development of a fetus. As Davis and Bracha note, the end of the fast occurred during the second trimester of the babies born during the time that an increased incidence of schizophrenia was seen. Other studies have shown that underweight women are more likely to give birth to babies who later develop schizophrenia and that low-birth-weight babies have a higher incidence of schizophrenia (Kunugi, Nanko, and Murray, 2001; Wahlbeck et al., 2001).

Another possible nutritional factor in the development of schizophrenia—a vitamin D deficiency—was proposed by McGrath (1999). Vitamin D, essential for development of bones and possibly involved in brain development, is produced by the action of ultraviolet light from the sun on a chemical present in the skin. Most evolutionary biologists believe that this chemical reaction is responsible for the differences in skin pigmentation that are seen in people whose ancestors lived in various parts of the world. Populations that evolved in the tropics have dark skin to protect them from the damaging effects of sunlight, and populations that evolved in temperate regions have light skin so that the weaker sunlight can more easily penetrate the skin and increase blood levels of vitamin D. (People whose ancestors lived in the arctic have dark skins, but they received sufficient doses of vitamin D from their diet of fish and seals.) McGrath noted that the latitude effect might be caused by differential exposure of pregnant women to the sunlight in regions near or far from the equator. He also noted that children of second-generation Afro-Caribbean immigrants to Great Britain had a higher incidence of rickets (a sign of vitamin D deficiency) and of schizophrenia. He suggests that these effects were caused by dark-skinned people moving to a colder, less sunny climate, where they presumably spent more time indoors and wore clothes that cover their skin more completely than those they wore when they lived in the tropics.

Rh incompatibility may be yet another prenatal condition that increases the risk of schizophrenia. The red blood cells of an Rh-positive person contain a protein—the Rh factor—while those of an Rh-negative person do not. If an RH-negative woman is pregnant with an Rh-positive fetus, her immune system will begin to produce antibodies against the protein. If the woman carries another Rh-positive fetus during a subsequent pregnancy, her Rh antibodies will attach the fetus's red blood cells, causing anemia. Hollister, Laing, and Mednick (1996) found that Rh incompatibility increased the likelihood of schizophrenia. The first Rh-positive child born to an Rh-negative mother did not have an increased risk of schizophrenia, but subsequent Rh-positive children did.

The final prenatal effect that I will mention may be independent of the ones I have described so far, or it may also involve viral infections. Huttunen and Niskanen (1978) reported a higher incidence of schizophrenia in the children born to women who learned that their husbands had been killed in combat during World War II. The stress of this news may have had direct effects on the development of the women's fetuses, or it may have suppressed their immune systems, increasing the likelihood of their contracting a viral illness. As we will see in Chapter 17, stress has an inhibitory effect on the immune system.

■ **Evidence for Abnormal Brain Development** So far, the evidence that I have cited concerning developmental factors in schizophrenia is epidemiological, having

table   16.3

Examples of Minor Physical Abnormalities Associated with Schizophrenia

LOCATION	DESCRIPTION
Head	Two or more hair whorls Head circumference outside normal range
Eyes	Shin fold at inner corner of eye Wide-set eyes
Ears	Low-set ears Asymmetrical ears
Mouth	High-steepled palate Furrowed tongue
Hands	Curved fifth finger Single transverse crease in palm
Feet	Third toe longer than second toe Partial webbing of two middle toes

Source: Adapted from Schiffman, J., Ekstrom, M., LaBrie, J., Schulsinger, F., Sorensen, H., and Mednick, S. *American Journal of Psychiatry,* 2002, *159,* 238–243.

come from studies of populations, not individuals. Is there any direct evidence that abnormal prenatal development is associated with schizophrenia? The answer is yes; studies have reported both behavioral and anatomical evidence for developmental abnormalities. Walker and her colleagues (Walker, Savoie, and Davis, 1994; Walker, Lewine, and Neumann, 1996) obtained home movies from families with a schizophrenic child. They had independent observers examine the behavior of the children. In comparison with their normal siblings the children who subsequently became schizophrenic displayed more negative affect in their facial expressions and were more likely to show abnormal movements. (The ratings were done blind; the observers did not know which children subsequently became schizophrenic.) In addition, a study by Cannon et al. (1997) found that children who later became schizophrenic had poorer social adjustment and did more poorly in school. The results of these studies are consistent with the hypothesis that the prenatal brain development of the children who became schizophrenic was not entirely normal.

Minor physical anomalies, such as a high-steepled palate or especially wide-set or narrow-set eyes, have also been shown to be associated with the incidence of schizophrenia (Schiffman et al., 2002). (See *Table 16.3.*) These differences were first reported in the late nineteenth century by Kraepelin, one of the pioneers in schizophrenia research. As Schiffman and his colleagues note, these anomalies provide evidence of factors that have adverse effects on development. They found that people with schizophrenic relatives normally have an 11.9 percent likelihood of developing schizophrenia. This likelihood

increases to 30.8 percent in people who also have minor physical anomalies; thus, the factors that produce minor physical anomalies are independent of the genetic factors associated with schizophrenia.

As I mentioned earlier, some monozygotic twins are discordant for schizophrenia; that is, one of them develops schizophrenia, and the other does not. Suddath et al. (1990) obtained evidence that differences in the structure of the brain may account for the discordance. The investigators examined MRI scans of monozygotic twins who were discordant for schizophrenia and found that in almost every case the twin with schizophrenia had larger lateral and third ventricles. In addition, the anterior hippocampus was smaller in the schizophrenic twin, and the total volume of the gray matter in the left temporal lobe was reduced. Figure 16.8 shows a set of MRI scans from a pair of twins; as you can see, the lateral ventricles are larger in the brain of the twin with schizophrenia. (See *Figure 16.8.*) As we will see later, recent research has found that schizophrenic twins also show signs of degeneration in specific regions of their cerebral cortex.

In the past, most researchers assumed that discordance for schizophrenia in monozygotic twins must be caused by differential exposure to some environmental factors after birth. Not only are monozygotic twins genetically identical, but they also share the same intrauterine environment. Thus, because all prenatal factors should be identical, any differences must be a result of factors in the postnatal environment. However, some investigators have pointed out that the prenatal environment of monozygotic twins is *not* identical. In fact, there are two types of monozygotic twins: monochorionic and dichorionic. The formation of monozygotic twins occurs when the blastocyst (the developing organism) splits in two—when it clones

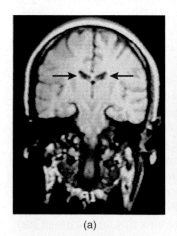
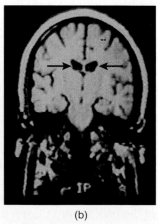

(a)   (b)

figure   16.8

MRI scans of the brains of twins who are discordant for schizophrenia. The arrows point to the lateral ventricles. (a) Normal twin. (b) Twin with schizophrenia.
(Courtesy of D. R. Weinberger, National Institute of Mental Health, Saint Elizabeth's Hospital, Washington, D.C.)

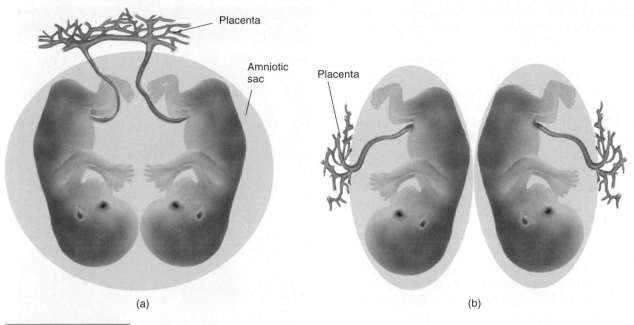

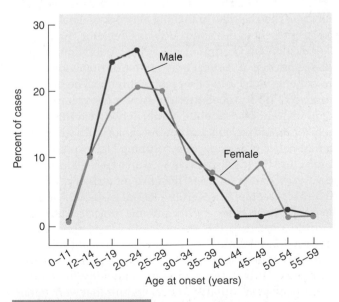

figure 16.9

Monozygotic twins. (a) Monochorionic twins, sharing a single placenta. (b) Dichorionic twins, each with its own placenta.

itself. If twinning occurs before day 4, the two organisms develop independently, each forming its own placenta. (That is, the twins are *dichorionic*. The *chorion* is the outer layer of the blastocyst, which gives rise to the placenta.) If twinning occurs after day 4, the two organisms become *monochorionic,* sharing a single placenta. (See *Figure 16.9*.)

The placenta plays an extremely important role in prenatal development. It transports nutrients to the developing organism from the mother's circulation and transports waste products to her, which she metabolizes in her liver or excretes in her urine. It also constitutes the barrier through which toxins or infectious agents must pass if they are to affect fetal development. The prenatal environments of monochorionic twins, who share a single placenta, are obviously more similar than those of dichorionic twins. Thus, we might expect that the concordance rates for schizophrenia of *monochorionic* monozygotic twins should be higher than those of *dichorionic* monozygotic twins—and, as Davis, Phelps, and Bracha (1995) reported, they are. Davis and his colleagues examined sets of monozygotic twins who were concordant and discordant for schizophrenia. They used several indices to estimate whether a given pair was monochorionic or dichorionic. (For example, twins with mirror images of physical features such as fingerprints, handedness, birthmarks, or hair swirls are more likely to be monochorionic.) The investigators estimated that the concordance rate for schizophrenia was 10.7 percent in the dichorionic twins and 60 percent in the monochorionic twins. These results provide strong evidence for an interaction between heredity and environment during prenatal development.

Although studies have found that people who develop schizophrenia show some abnormalities even during child-

hood, the symptoms of schizophrenia itself rarely occur before late adolescence or early adulthood. (They also rarely first occur later in life.) Figure 16.10 shows a graph of the ages of first signs of mental disorder in males and females diagnosed with schizophrenia. (See *Figure 16.10*.) Even if most cases of schizophrenia involve abnormalities in prenatal

figure 16.10

Age at first sign of psychotic symptoms in schizophrenic patients.

(Adapted from Häfner H., Riecher-Rössler A., an der Heiden W., Maurer K., Fätkenheuer B., and Löffler W. *Psychological Medicine,* 1993, *23,* 925–940.)

brain development, something else must happen later in life to cause the onset of schizophrenic symptoms. Researchers have proposed various hypotheses to account for this phenomenon. For example, Squires (1977) notes that the total number of synapses in the brain reaches a peak at five years of age and then declines until the age of fifteen to twenty years. Perhaps, he suggests, a prenatal viral infection kills some neurons in the developing brain, and it is not until more synapses are lost during the period of "synaptic pruning" that the loss of these neurons manifests itself.

In a review of the literature, Woods (1998) notes that MRI studies suggest that schizophrenia is not caused by a degenerative process, as are Parkinson's disease, Huntington's disease, or Alzheimer's disease, in which neurons continue to die over a period of years. Instead, a sudden, rapid loss of brain volume occurs during young adulthood, with little evidence for continuing degeneration. Woods suggests that the disease process of schizophrenia begins prenatally and then lies dormant until puberty, when some unknown mechanism triggers degeneration of some population of neurons. The brain abnormalities that develop prenatally account for the deficits in social behavior and poor academic performance seen in people who later become schizophrenic. Then, sometime after puberty, when many developmental changes occur in the brain, more serious degeneration occurs, and the symptoms of schizophrenia begin to appear.

The most recent evidence suggests that the degenerative process that occurs during adolescence and early adulthood does not involve death of neurons. A review by Lewis and Levitt (2002) finds no evidence of *gliosis*—the replacement of dead neurons by glial cells—in the brains of schizophrenic patients. Instead, what is lost is the volume of the *neuropil*—the hairlike branching network of dendrites and axons present in the brain. (*Pilos* is Greek for "hair.")

A study by Thompson et al. (2001) found dramatic evidence for loss of cortical gray matter during adolescence in patients with early-onset schizophrenia. The investigators used MRI procedures to measure the volume of the gray matter of the cerebral cortex at two-year intervals in schizophrenic patients and control subjects. As we just saw, adolescence is a time when "pruning" takes place in the brain, and the MRI scans showed an expected loss of cortical gray matter in nonschizophrenic subjects of about 0.5–1.0 percent. However, the loss of tissue was approximately twice as large in schizophrenic subjects. The degeneration started in the parietal lobes, and the wave of destruction continued rostrally, including the temporal lobes, somatosensory and motor cortex, and dorsolateral prefrontal cortex. The symptoms shown by the patients were associated with the cortical regions that were undergoing tissue loss. For example, auditory hallucinations occurred with changes in the temporal lobes, and their severity was correlated with the amount of tissue that was lost. Figure 16.11 shows the regions of the brain that underwent the greatest amount of tissue loss. (See *Figure 16.11*.)

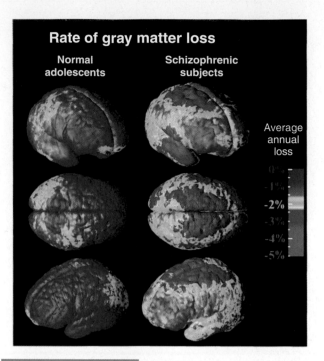

figure 16.11

Average annual rate of loss of cortical gray matter in normal and schizophrenic adolescents.
(From Thompson, P. M., Vidal, C., Giedd, J. N., Gochman, P., Blumenthal, J., Nicolson, R., Toga, A. W., and Rapoport, J. L. *Proceedings of the National Academy of Science, USA*, 2001, *98*, 11650–11655.)

A subsequent study from the same laboratory (Cannon et al., 2002) compared members of twins who were discordant for schizophrenia and confirmed that these changes were much greater in the twins with schizophrenia. They also found evidence that the dorsolateral prefrontal cortex was the region of the brain most strongly affected by genetic influences. (I'll say more about this part of the brain in the next subsection.)

The evidence I have cited so far suggests that the most important cause of schizophrenia is disturbance of normal prenatal brain development. Presumably, genetic factors make some fetuses more sensitive to events that can disturb development. There is good evidence that obstetric complications can also cause schizophrenia. In fact, several studies have found that if a schizophrenic person does *not* have relatives with a schizophrenic disorder, that person is more likely to have had a history of complications at or around the time of childbirth, and the person is more likely to develop the schizophrenic symptoms at an earlier age (Schwarzkopf et al., 1989; O'Callaghan et al., 1992; Cannon, Jones, and Murray, 2002.) In other words, if the schizophrenia is not a result of genetic factors, then nongenetic factors such as obstetric complications are the most likely cause. Thus, brain damage that is *not related to heredity* may also be a cause of schizophrenia.

Relationship between Positive and Negative Symptoms: Role of the Prefrontal Cortex

As we saw, schizophrenia has both positive and negative symptoms. The positive symptoms may be caused by hyperactivity of dopaminergic synapses, and the negative symptoms may be caused by brain abnormalities. Is there a relationship between the two categories of schizophrenic symptoms? An accumulating amount of evidence suggests that the causes of positive and negative symptoms may indeed be related.

A very large number of studies have shown evidence from MRI scans and postmortem examination of brain tissue that schizophrenia is associated with abnormalities in the frontal lobes, medial temporal lobes, lateral temporal lobes, parietal lobe, basal ganglia, corpus callosum, and thalamus and perhaps the cerebellum (Shenton et al., 2001). In recent years the prefrontal cortex has received a great deal of attention. Weinberger (1988) suggested that the negative symptoms of schizophrenia are caused primarily by **hypofrontality,** decreased activity of the frontal lobes—in particular, of the dorsolateral prefrontal cortex. Many studies have shown that schizophrenic patients do poorly on neuropsychological tests that are sensitive to prefrontal damage. In a review of the literature, Taylor (1996) found that most functional imaging studies of the prefrontal cortex of schizophrenic patients found evidence for decreased activity, particularly when the patients were being challenged by tasks that require the use of the prefrontal cortex.

What might produce the hypofrontality that so many studies have observed? Ironically, the cause might be a *decrease* in the release of dopamine in the prefrontal cortex. Dopamine does indeed play an important role in the normal functioning of the prefrontal cortex; studies with monkeys indicate that destruction of the dopaminergic input to the prefrontal cortex lowers its metabolic rate and leads to cognitive dysfunctions (Brozowski et al., 1979). The activating effect of dopamine in the prefrontal cortex appears to be mediated by D_1 dopamine receptors; Sawaguchi and Goldman-Rakic (1994) found that injection of D_1 antagonists into the prefrontal cortex caused behavioral deficits like those produced by prefrontal lesions. Dopamine appears to have similar effects in the human prefrontal cortex: Daniel et al. (1991) found that when they administered amphetamine to schizophrenic patients, the blood flow in the patients' dorsolateral prefrontal cortex increased, and their performance on a test sensitive to prefrontal damage improved.

As we saw, dopamine agonists such as cocaine and amphetamine can cause positive symptoms of schizo-

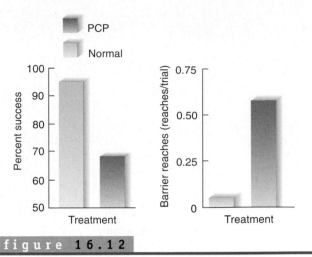

figure 16.12

Effects of two weeks of PCP treatment on the performance of monkeys on the object retrieval with a detour task. An increased number of reaches toward the barrier is an indication of perseveration of an incorrect response.
(Adapted from Jentsch, J. D., Redmond, D. E., Elsworth, J. D., Taylor, J. R., Youngren, K. D., and Roth, R. H. *Science*, 1997, *277*, 953–955.)

phrenia. Two other drugs, PCP (phencyclidine, also known as "angel dust") and ketamine ("Special K"), can cause both positive and negative symptoms of schizophrenia (Adler et al., 2000; Lahti et al., 2001; Avila et al., 2002). Chronic abuse of PCP impairs a person's working memory; causes deficits in attention; decreases drive; interferes with planning; and causes thought disorders, hallucinations, and delusions (Javitt and Zukin, 1991). Because PCP and ketamine elicit both positive and negative symptoms, many researchers believe that studying the physiological and behavioral effects of these drugs will help to solve the puzzle of schizophrenia.

Chronic abuse of PCP causes negative symptoms. This effect is apparently caused by a decrease in the metabolic activity of the frontal lobes (Hertzmann, Reba, and Kotlyarov, 1990; Wu, Buchsbaum, and Bunney, 1991). Jentsch et al. (1997) administered PCP to monkeys twice a day for two weeks. Then, one week later, they tested the animals on a task known as "object retrieval with a detour." Previous studies had shown that performance on this task is disrupted by lesions of the prefrontal cortex (see Jentsch, Roth, and Taylor, 2000). The experimenters put a slice of banana in a clear plastic box with one open side and placed it on a table in front of the each monkey's home cage. The monkeys quickly learned to reach into the front of the box and retrieve the food. Then the experimenters began presenting the box with the open side turned to the right or the left. Normal monkeys quickly learned to reach around to the side to obtain the banana slice, but monkeys that had been treated with PCP continued to try to reach through the front of the box. (See *Figure 16.12*.)

---

hypofrontality Decreased activity of the prefrontal cortex; believed to be responsible for the negative symptoms of schizophrenia.

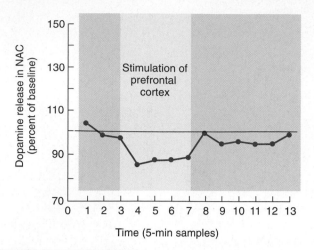

figure 16.13

Effects of electrical stimulation of the prefrontal cortex on the release of dopamine in the nucleus accumbens (NAC), as measured by microdialysis.

(Adapted from Jackson, M. E., Frost, A. D.,and Moghaddam, B. *Journal of Neurochemistry*, 2001, *78*, 920–923.)

Jentsch and his colleagues found that chronic PCP treatment decreased the level of dopamine utilization in the dorsolateral prefrontal cortex. They also found that clozapine, which reduces both positive and negative symptoms of schizophrenia, improved the performance of the PCP-treated monkeys on the object retrieval task. In a subsequent study, Jentsch et al. (1999) found that the degree of behavioral impairment caused by PCP was positively correlated with the decrease in dopaminergic transmission in the prefrontal cortex. In other words, chronic PCP treatment reduces dopaminergic activity in the prefrontal cortex, which in turn produces the hypofrontality that appears to be responsible for the negative symptoms of schizophrenia.

What is the relationship between hypoactivity of the prefrontal cortex and the positive symptoms of schizophrenia, which appear to be produced by *hyperactivity* of dopaminergic synapses in the nucleus accumbens? Several investigators have suggested that the events are linked—that prefrontal hypoactivity causes mesolimbic dopamine hyperactivity (Weinberger, 1988; Grace, 1991; Deutch, 1992). Neurons of the prefrontal cortex send axons to the ventral tegmental area, where they form synapses with GABA-secreting neurons that project to the nucleus accumbens (Carr and Sesack, 2000). Jackson, Frost, and Moghaddam (2001) found that electrical stimulation of the prefrontal cortex inhibited the release of dopamine in the nucleus accumbens, as measured by microdialysis. It makes sense, then, that decreased activation of the prefrontal cortex causes an increase in the release of dopamine in the nucleus accumbens. (See *Figure 16.13.*)

As we saw, PCP decreases dopaminergic activity in the prefrontal cortex and increases it in the nucleus accumbens. The primary effects of this drug appear to take place in the prefrontal cortex; Jentsch et al. (1998) found that

infusing PCP directly into the prefrontal cortex increased the level of dopamine utilization in the nucleus accumbens.

We also saw that the atypical antipsychotic drug clozapine alleviates both the positive and negative symptoms of schizophrenia. It also reduces the psychotic symptoms that are triggered by ketamine (Malhotia et al., 1997). (Because PCP has toxic effects, it is not used in studies with human subjects.) In a study with rats, Youngren et al. (1999) found that injections of clozapine, which cause an *increase* in the release of dopamine in the prefrontal cortex, also caused a *decrease* in the release of dopamine in the nucleus accumbens.

The studies I have cited suggest that schizophrenia may begin with the loss of neurons somewhere in the brain that causes hypofrontality, perhaps by reducing the volume of the gray matter in the dorsolateral prefrontal cortex, perhaps by disrupting the release of dopamine in this region. The hypofrontality produces the negative symptoms of schizophrenia. It also causes an increase in the activity of the dopaminergic neurons in the mesolimbic system, which produces positive symptoms. (See *Figure 16.14.*)

If this hypothesis is true, then we might expect to see structural or biochemical abnormalities in the prefrontal cortex of schizophrenic patients. In fact, there are. As we saw earlier, the volume of gray matter in several regions of the cerebral cortex of schizophrenic patients significantly declines during adolescence. In addition, Akil et al. (1999) found a 34 percent reduction in the length of dopaminergic axons in layer 6 of the prefrontal cortex of deceased schizophrenic patients.

Although we do not yet understand how PCP decreases dopamine release in the prefrontal cortex, the PCP model of schizophrenia has stimulated research that could lead to the development of more drugs that can be used to treat this disorder. First, let's look at the site of action of PCP. PCP acts as an indirect (noncompetitive) antagonist for

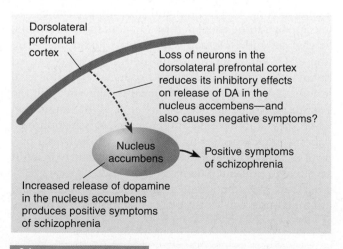

figure 16.14

A hypothetical explanation for the role of the dorsolateral prefrontal cortex in positive and negative symptoms of schizophrenia.

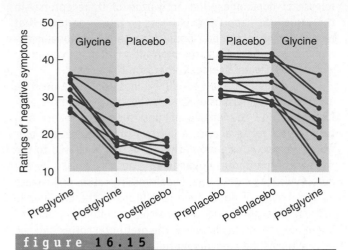

Effects of large doses of oral glycine on the negative symptoms of schizophrenia. Individual curves represent individual patients.

(Adapted from Heresco-Levy, U., Javitt, D.C., Ermilov, M., Mordel, C., Silipo, G., and Lichtenstein, M. *Archives of General Psychiatry*, 1999, *56*, 29–36.)

NMDA receptors. It binds with a site on the NMDA receptor and prevents the ion channel from opening, even if glutamate—the neurotransmitter that binds with this receptor—is present. (As we saw in Chapter 13, NMDA receptors are involved in synaptic plasticity. Whether this special property of the NMDA receptor is relevant in this context is not known.)

If disrupting the activity of NMDA receptors causes the symptoms of schizophrenia, then we might expect drugs that act as NMDA agonists to reduce these symptoms. Unfortunately, direct NMDA agonists (such as NMDA itself) cannot be used, because they increase the risk of seizures and might even cause brain abnormalities. But you might remember from Chapter 4 that NMDA receptors have several other sites to which ligands can bind besides the glutamate site and the PCP site. Glycine binds to one of these sites, where it acts as an indirect agonist. In fact, without the presence of glycine, the ion channel of an NMDA receptor will not open, even if glutamate is present and the postsynaptic membrane is depolarized. Normally, adequate amounts of glycine are present, but it is possible that increasing the level of glycine or administering a glycine agonist might facilitate NMDA activity and reduce schizophrenic symptoms. Several studies have found exactly that. (See Trai and Coyle, 2002, for a review.) In a double-blind, randomized clinical trial, Goff et al. (1999) found that D-cycloserine, a glycine agonist, improved negative symptoms of schizophrenic patients. In another double-blind study—this one with a crossover between drug and placebo—Heresco-Levy et al. (1999) found that very large doses of oral glycine reduced patients' negative (but not positive) symptoms. The large doses were necessary because only a small percentage of the glycine crossed the blood–brain barrier. (See *Figure 16.15*.)

Before I conclude this section, I want to mention an interesting sidelight that might have some relevance to the causes of schizophrenia. As we saw, ketamine and PCP have similar effects. Ketamine is used as an anesthetic for children and animals. It is not often used as an anesthetic in adult humans because it produces episodes of psychosis when the person awakens after the surgery. Ketamine does not have this effect in prepubertal children (Marshall and Longnecker, 1990). (You might recall that THC, the active ingredient of marijuana, does not have a psychotropic effect in children, either.) No one knows why ketamine (and probably PCP) produces psychotic behavior only in adults; perhaps the explanation is related to the fact that the symptoms of schizophrenia also emerge after puberty. Whatever developmental changes occur after puberty that make the brain susceptible to the psychotic effects of NMDA antagonists may also be related to the emergence of symptoms of schizophrenia at this time.

Farber et al. (1995) found that large doses of another noncompetitive NMDA antagonist, MK 801, produced brain abnormalities in adult rats but not prepubertal rats. Between the age of puberty and full adulthood, the animals' brains became more and more sensitive to the effects of the drug. These findings support the hypothesis that developmental changes that begin around the time of puberty may play a role in the development of schizophrenia.

In the interest of clarity and brevity I have been selective in my review of research on schizophrenia. This puzzling and serious disorder has stimulated many ingenious hypotheses and much research. Some hypotheses have been proved wrong; others have not yet been adequately tested. Possibly, future research will find that all of these hypotheses (including the ones I have discussed) are incorrect or that one that I have not mentioned is correct. However, I am impressed with recent research, and I believe that we have real hope of finding the causes of schizophrenia in the near future. With the discovery of the causes we can hope for the discovery of methods of prevention.

interim
summary

Researchers have made considerable progress in the past few years in their study of the physiology of mental disorders, but many puzzles still remain. Schizophrenia consists of positive and negative symptoms, the former involving the presence of unusual behavior and the latter involving the absence of normal behavior. Because schizophrenia is at least somewhat heritable, it appears to have a biological basis. But evidence indicates that not all cases are caused by heredity, and some people who appear to carry a "schizophrenia gene" do not become schizophrenic. Recent evidence suggests that paternal age is a factor in schizophrenia, presumably because of the increased likelihood of mutations in the chromosomes of cells that produce sperms.

The dopamine hypothesis—inspired by the findings that dopamine antagonists alleviate the positive symptoms of schizophrenia and that dopamine agonists increase or even produce them—is still dominant. This hypothesis states that the positive symptoms of schizophrenia are caused by hyperactivity of dopaminergic synapses. The involvement of dopamine in reinforcement could plausibly explain the positive effects of schizophrenia; inappropriately reinforced thoughts could persist and become delusions. Paranoid thoughts may be caused by dopaminergic activation of the central nucleus of the amygdala, a region involved in negative emotional responses. There is no evidence that an abnormally large amount of dopamine is released under resting conditions, but PET studies indicate that the administration of amphetamine causes a larger release of dopamine in the brains of schizophrenics. Evidence that the brains of schizophrenic patients contain increased numbers of D_2 dopamine receptors is mixed. It is still possible that an abnormality exists in the dopaminergic systems that project to the nucleus accumbens. Studies suggest that the nucleus accumbens in the brains of schizophrenic patients may contain increased numbers of D_3 or D_4 dopamine receptors.

That some patients are not helped by antipsychotic drugs poses an unsolved problem for the dopamine hypothesis. In addition, these drugs cause parkinsonian side effects (usually temporary) and, in some cases, tardive dyskinesia. Atypical antipsychotic drugs, including clozapine, risperidone, olanzapine, and amisulpride, are much less likely to produce parkinsonian side effects and apparently do not produce tardive dyskinesia. In addition, most of these drugs reduce positive symptoms as well as negative ones, and they reduce the symptoms of some patients who are not helped by traditional antipsychotic medication.

MRI scans and the presence of signs of neurological impairments indicate the presence of brain abnormalities in schizophrenic patients. Studies of the epidemiology of schizophrenia indicate that season of birth, viral epidemics during pregnancy, population density, latitude, prenatal malnutrition, Rh incompatibility, and prenatal stress all contribute to the occurrence of schizophrenia. In addition, home movies of very young children who became schizophrenic indicate the early presence of abnormalities in movements and facial expressions. All these factors provide evidence for problems with prenatal development. Further evidence is provided by the presence of an increased size of the third and lateral ventricles and a decreased size of the hippocampus in the schizophrenic member of monozygotic twins who are discordant for schizophrenia. The increased concordance rate of monochorionic monozygotic twins provides further evidence that hereditary and prenatal environmental factors may interact.

The symptoms of schizophrenia usually emerge soon after puberty, when the brain is undergoing important maturational changes. Some investigators believe that the disease process of schizophrenia begins prenatally, lies dormant until puberty, and then causes a period of neural degeneration that causes the symptoms to appear. Obstetric complications can also produce the symptoms of schizophrenia.

The negative symptoms of schizophrenia appear to be a result of hypofrontality (decreased activity of the dorsolateral prefrontal cortex), which may be caused by a decreased release of dopamine—and activation of D_1 receptors—in this region. Schizophrenic patients do poorly on tasks that require activity of the prefrontal cortex, and functional imaging studies indicate that the prefrontal cortex is hypoactive when the patients attempt to perform these tasks.

The drugs PCP and ketamine mimics both the positive and negative symptoms of schizophrenia. Long-term administration of PCP to monkeys disrupts their performance of a task (object retrieval with a detour) that requires the prefrontal cortex. Furthermore, the disruption is related to the decrease in prefrontal dopaminergic activity caused by the drug. Evidence suggests that hypofrontality causes an increase in the activity of dopaminergic neurons in the mesolimbic system, thus producing the positive symptoms of schizophrenia. Connections between the prefrontal cortex and the ventral tegmental area appear to be responsible for this phenomenon. Clozapine reduces hypofrontality, increases the performance of monkeys on the object retrieval task, and decreases the release of dopamine in the ventral tegmental area—and decreases both the positive and negative symptoms of schizophrenia.

PCP and ketamine act as indirect antagonists for NMDA receptors. Glycine and D-cycloserine, which serve as NMDA receptor agonists, produce modest reductions in negative symptoms of schizophrenia, providing further support for the PCP model of this disorder. Ketamine causes psychotic reactions in adults but not children. Another indirect NMDA antagonist causes brain abnormalities in adult, but not juvenile, rats. These disparities may be related to the apparent changes in the brain that are responsible for the emergence of the symptoms of schizophrenia after puberty.

Major Affective Disorders

Affect, as a noun, refers to feelings or emotions. Just as the primary symptom of schizophrenia is disordered thoughts, the **major affective disorders** (also called *mood disorders*) are characterized by disordered feelings.

Description

Feelings and emotions are essential parts of human existence; they represent our evaluation of the events in our lives. In a very real sense, feelings and emotions are what human life is all about. The emotional state of most of us reflects what is happening to us: Our feelings are tied to events in the real world, and they are usually the result of reasonable assessments of the importance these events have for our lives. But for some people, affect becomes

---

major affective disorder A serious mood disorder; includes unipolar depression and bipolar disorder.

divorced from reality. These people have feelings of extreme elation (*mania*) or despair (*depression*) that are not justified by events in their lives. For example, depression that accompanies the loss of a loved one is normal, but depression that becomes a way of life—and will not respond to the sympathetic effort of friends and relatives or even to psychotherapy—is pathological.

There are two principal types of major affective disorders. The first type is characterized by alternating periods of mania and depression—a condition called **bipolar disorder.** This disorder afflicts men and women in approximately equal numbers. Episodes of mania can last a few days or several months, but they usually take a few weeks to run their course. The episodes of depression that follow generally last three times as long as the mania. The second type is **unipolar depression,** or depression without mania. This depression may be continuous and unremitting or, more typically, may come in episodes. Unipolar depression strikes women two to three times more often than men. Mania without periods of depression sometimes occurs, but it is rare.

Severely depressed people usually feel extremely unworthy and have strong feelings of guilt. The affective disorders are dangerous; a person who suffers from a major affective disorder runs a considerable risk of death by suicide. According to Chen and Dilsaver (1996), 15.9 percent of people with unipolar depression and 29.2 percent of people with bipolar disorder attempt to commit suicide. Schneider, Muller, and Philipp (2001) found that the rate of death by unnatural causes (not all suicides are diagnosed as such) for people with affective disorders was 28.8 times higher than expected for people of the same age in the general population. Depressed people have very little energy, and they move and talk slowly, sometimes becoming almost torpid. At other times, they may pace around restlessly and aimlessly. They may cry a lot. They are unable to experience pleasure; they lose their appetite for food and sex. Their sleep is disturbed; they usually have difficulty falling asleep and awaken early and find it difficult to get to sleep again. Even their body functions become depressed; they often become constipated, and secretion of saliva decreases.

> [A psychiatrist] asked me if I was suicidal, and I reluctantly told him yes. I did not particularize—since there seemed no need to—did not tell him that in truth many of the artifacts of my house had become potential devices for my own destruction: the attic rafters (and an outside maple or two) a means to hang myself, the garage a place to inhale carbon monoxide, the bathtub a vessel to receive the flow from my opened arteries. The kitchen knives in their drawers had but one purpose for me. Death by heart attack seemed particularly inviting, absolving me as it would of active responsibility, and I had toyed with the idea of self-induced pneumonia—a long frigid, shirt-sleeved hike through the rainy woods. Nor had I overlooked an ostensible acci-

> dent . . . by walking in front of a truck on the highway nearby . . . Such hideous fantasies, which cause well people to shudder, are to the deeply depressed mind what lascivious daydreams are to persons of robust sexuality. (Styron, 1990)

Episodes of mania are characterized by a sense of euphoria that does not seem to be justified by circumstances. The diagnosis of mania is partly a matter of degree; one would not call exuberance and a zest for life pathological. People with mania usually exhibit nonstop speech and motor activity. They flit from topic to topic and often have delusions, but they lack the severe disorganization that is seen in schizophrenia. They are usually full of their own importance and often become angry or defensive if they are contradicted. Frequently, they go for long periods without sleep, working furiously on projects that are often unrealistic. (Sometimes, their work is fruitful; George Frideric Handel wrote *Messiah*, one of the masterpieces of choral music, during one of his periods of mania.)

Heritability

The tendency to develop an affective disorder appears to be heritable. (See Moldin, Reich, and Rice, 1991, for a review.) For example, Rosenthal (1971) found that close relatives of people who suffer from affective psychoses are ten times more likely to develop these disorders than are people without afflicted relatives. Gershon et al. (1976) found that if one member of a set of monozygotic twins was afflicted with an affective disorder, the likelihood that the other twin was similarly afflicted was 69 percent. In contrast, the concordance rate for dizygotic twins was only 13 percent. Furthermore, the concordance rate for monozygotic twins appears to be the same whether the twins were raised together or apart (Price, 1968). The heritability of the affective disorders implies that they have a physiological basis.

Evidence suggests that a single dominant gene is responsible for susceptibility to developing bipolar disorder (Spence et al., 1995). For years, several groups of researchers have been trying to find the location of this gene. Early studies suggested that it might be located on chromosome 11, but follow-up studies found that it was not (Egeland et al., 1987; Kelsoe et al., 1989). More recent studies suggest that the "bipolar gene" might be located on chromosome 4, 5, 18, or 21 or the X chromosome

bipolar disorder A serious mood disorder characterized by cyclical periods of mania and depression.

unipolar depression A serious mood disorder that consists of unremitting depression or periods of depression that do not alternate with periods of mania.

(MacKinnon, Jamison, and DePaulo, 1997; Berrettini, 1998; Garner et al., 2001).

Physiological Treatments

There are four effective biological treatments for unipolar depression: monoamine oxidase (MAO) inhibitors, drugs that inhibit the reuptake of norepinephrine or serotonin, electroconvulsive therapy (ECT), and sleep deprivation. (Sleep deprivation is discussed in a later section.) Bipolar disorder can be effectively treated by lithium and some anticonvulsant drugs. The fact that these disorders respond to medical treatment provides additional evidence that they have a physiological basis. Furthermore, the fact that lithium is very effective in treating bipolar affective disorders but not unipolar depression suggests that there is a fundamental difference between these two illnesses (Soares and Gershon, 1998).

Before the 1950s there was no effective drug treatment for depression. In the late 1940s clinicians noticed that some drugs used for treating tuberculosis seemed to elevate the patient's mood. Researchers subsequently found that a derivative of these drugs, iproniazid, reduced symptoms of psychotic depression (Crane, 1957). Iproniazid inhibits the activity of MAO, which destroys excess monoamine transmitter substances within terminal buttons. Thus, the drug increases the release of dopamine, norepinephrine, and serotonin. Other MAO inhibitors were soon discovered. Unfortunately, MAO inhibitors can have harmful side effects. The most common problem is the *cheese effect.* Many foods (for example, cheese, yogurt, wine, yeast breads, chocolate, and various fruits and nuts) contain *pressor amines*—substances similar to catecholamines. Normally, these amines are deactivated by MAO, which is present in the blood and in other tissues of the body. But a person who is being treated with an MAO inhibitor may suffer a serious sympathetic reaction after eating food containing pressor amines. The pressor amines simulate the effects of increased activity of the sympathetic nervous system, increasing blood pressure and heart rate. The reaction can raise blood pressure enough to produce intracranial bleeding or cardiovascular collapse.

Fortunately, another class of antidepressant drugs was soon discovered that did not produce a cheese effect: the **tricyclic antidepressants.** These drugs were found to inhibit the reuptake of 5-HT and norepinephrine by terminal buttons. By retarding reuptake, the drugs keep the neurotransmitter in contact with the postsynaptic receptors, thus prolonging the postsynaptic potentials. Thus, both the MAO inhibitors and the tricyclic antidepressant drugs are monoaminergic agonists.

Since the discovery of the tricyclic antidepressants, other drugs have been discovered that have similar effects. The most important of these are the **specific serotonin reuptake inhibitors,** whose action is described by their name. One of them, fluoxetine (Prozac) is widely prescribed for its antidepressant properties and for its ability to reduce the symptoms of obsessive-compulsive disorder and social phobia (described in Chapter 17).

For many years, attempts were made to treat mental disorders with various sorts of shock treatments, such as dunking the patient in cold water, exposing the patient to snakes, producing a fever—doing something to shake the patient up and initiate some change, hopefully for the better (Valenstein, 1973). Particular popular types of shock treatment were the induction of comas by injection of insulin or of seizures by injections of *metrazol* (the active ingredient in camphor). The rationale for the therapeutic application derived partly from the fact that schizophrenia and epilepsy appeared to occur infrequently in the same person and from the observation that a seizure appeared to produce a remission from the psychotic symptoms (von Meduna, 1938). Unfortunately, the effects of large doses of insulin or metrazol were unpredictable and dangerous.

The production of electrically elicited seizures was first performed by Ugo Cerletti, an Italian psychiatrist (Cerletti and Bini, 1938). He noted that pigs in the local slaughterhouse were first made unconscious by electric shock across the temples and were then killed with a knife. He tried the same treatment (the electric shock, that is, not the stabbing) on dogs and observed that seizures could be produced by application of current to the head for a few tenths of a second. The dogs did not appear to suffer any long-term ill effects.

Cerletti then went on to try the procedure on a schizophrenic patient, who apparently experienced hallucinations and whose speech was full of meaningless babbling. He applied a low-current shock to the head, which was insufficient to produce unconsciousness. When the patient heard Cerletti say that he would try it again the next day with higher current, the patient cried, "Not another one! It's deadly!" Encouraged by this sudden display of rational speech, Cerletti did not wait but immediately tried a more intense shock. Here are his observations:

> We observed the same instantaneous, brief, generalized spasm, and soon after, the onset of the classic epileptic convulsion. We were all breathless during the tonic phase of the attack, and really overwhelmed during the apnea as we watched the cadaverous cyanosis of the patient's face; the apnea of the spontaneous epileptic convulsion is always impressive, but at that moment it seemed to all

---

tricyclic antidepressant A class of drugs used to treat depression; inhibits the reuptake of norepinephrine and serotonin; named for the molecular structure.

specific serotonin reuptake inhibitor A drug that inhibits the reuptake of serotonin without affecting the reuptake of other neurotransmitters.

of us painfully endless. Finally, with the first stertorous breathing and the first clonic spasm, the blood flowed better not only in the patient's vessels but also in our own. Thereupon we observed with the most intensely gratifying sensation the characteristic gradual awakening of the patient "by steps." He rose to sitting position and looked at us, calm and smiling, as though to inquire what we wanted of him. We asked: "What happened to you?" He answered: "I don't know. Maybe I was asleep." Thus occurred the first electrically produced convulsion in man, which I at once named "electroshock." (Cerletti, 1956)

As a result of Cerletti's experiments, **electroconvulsive therapy (ECT)** became a common treatment for mental illness. Before a person receives ECT, he or she is anesthetized and is given a drug similar to curare, which paralyzes the muscles, preventing injuries that might be produced by a convulsion. (Of course, the patient is attached to a respirator until the effects of this drug wear off.) Electrodes are placed on the patient's scalp (most often to the nonspeech-dominant hemisphere, to avoid damaging verbal memories), and a jolt of electricity triggers a seizure. Usually, a patient receives three treatments per week until maximum improvement is seen, which usually involves six to twelve treatments. The effectiveness of ECT has been established by placebo studies, in which some patients are anesthetized but not given shocks (Weiner and Krystal, 1994). Although ECT was originally used for a variety of disorders, including schizophrenia, we now know that its usefulness is limited to treatment of mania and depression. (See *Figure 16.16.*)

A depressed patient does not respond immediately to treatment with antidepressant drugs; improvement in symptoms is not usually seen before two to three weeks of drug treatment. In contrast, the effects of ECT are more rapid. A few seizures induced by ECT can often snap a

person out of a deep depression within a few days. Although prolonged and excessive use of ECT causes brain damage, resulting in long-lasting impairments in memory (Squire, 1974), the judicious use of ECT during the interim period before antidepressant drugs become effective has undoubtedly saved the lives of some suicidal patients (Baldessarini, 1977). A study by Ende et al. (2000) found no evidence of hippocampal damage after a typical course of ECT. In addition, some severely depressed people are not helped by drug therapy; for them occasional ECT is the only effective treatment.

Another procedure may provide at least some of the benefits of ECT without introducing the risk of cognitive impairments or memory loss. As we saw in Chapter 5, transcranial magnetic stimulation (TMS) is accomplished by applying a strong localized magnetic field into the brain by passing an electrical current through a coil of wire placed on the scalp. The magnetic field induces a weak electrical current in the brain. Several studies have found that TMS applied to the prefrontal cortex reduces the symptoms of depression without producing any apparent negative side effects (George et al., 1995; Klein et al., 1999; Szuba et al., 2001). Further investigations will have to determine whether this procedure produces long-term beneficial effects.

The therapeutic effect of **lithium,** the drug used to treat bipolar affective disorders, is very rapid. This drug, which is administered in the form of lithium carbonate, is most effective in treating the manic phase of a bipolar affective disorder; once the mania is eliminated, depression usually does not follow (Gerbino, Oleshansky, and Gershon, 1978; Soares and Gershon, 1998). Many clinicians and investigators have referred to lithium as psychiatry's wonder drug: It does not suppress normal feelings of emotions, but it leaves patients able to feel and express joy and sadness in response to events in their lives. Similarly, it does not impair intellectual processes; many patients have received the drug continuously for years without any apparent ill effects (Fieve, 1979). Between 70 and 80 percent of patients with bipolar disorder show a positive response to lithium within a week or two (Price and Heninger, 1994).

Lithium does have adverse side effects. The therapeutic index (the difference between an effective dose and an overdose) is low. Side effects include hand tremors, weight gain, excessive urine production, and thirst. Toxic doses produce nausea, diarrhea, motor incoordination, confusion, and coma. Because of the low therapeutic

figure 16.16

A patient being prepared for electroconvulsive therapy. (Photo Researchers, Inc.)

electroconvulsive therapy (ECT) A brief electrical shock, applied to the head, that results in an electrical seizure; used therapeutically to alleviate severe depression.

lithium A chemical element; lithium carbonate is used to treat bipolar disorder.

index, patients' blood levels of lithium must be tested regularly to be certain that they do not receive an overdose. Unfortunately, some patients are not able to tolerate the side effects of lithium.

One of the most serious difficulties in treating bipolar disorder is compliance with the prescribed treatment. After taking lithium for a while, some patients find that they miss the intense pleasure they felt during their manic periods. Some of them apparently tell themselves that now that they are "cured," they can stop taking their medication—and when they do, their cycling begins again. Then the pain of the depression usually motivates them to start taking the drug again. Several studies suggest that strong efforts should be made to convince patients with bipolar disorder not to discontinue their medication, because occasionally, the drug is no longer effective after a relapse (Suppes et al., 1991; Post et al., 1992).

Researchers have found that lithium has many physiological effects, but they have not yet discovered the pharmacological effects of lithium that are responsible for its ability to eliminate mania (Phiel and Klein, 2001). Some suggest that the drug stabilizes the population of certain classes of neurotransmitter receptors in the brain (especially serotonin receptors), thus preventing wide shifts in neural sensitivity. This effect may involve interference with the production of a class of second messengers, the *phosphoinositide system* (Atack, Broughton, and Pollack, 1995; Jope et al., 1996; Manji and Lenox, 1999). Others have shown that lithium may increase the production of neuroprotective proteins—proteins that help to prevent cell death (Manji, Moore, and Chen, 2001). In fact, Moore et al. (2000) found that four weeks of lithium treatment for bipolar disorder increased the volume of cerebral gray matter in the patients' brains, a finding that suggests that lithium facilitates neural or glial growth. As we will see later in this chapter, many studies have found decreased cerebral gray matter in patients suffering from depression.

Because some patients cannot tolerate the side effects of lithium, and because of the potential danger of overdose, researchers have been searching for alternative medications for bipolar disorder. One medication that has shown considerable promise is **carbamazepine** (Tegretol), a drug used to treat seizures that originate in the medial temporal lobes. Although carbamazepine is effective in treating the depressed phase of bipolar disorder, its effects on mania are more impressive (Post et al., 1984). (See *Figure 16.17*.) In addition, it appears to help some bipolar patients who do not respond to treatment with lithium (Post, Weiss, and Chuang, 1992). Other anticonvulsive drugs also appear to alleviate the symptoms of bipolar disorder, and trials with these drugs are under way (Marcotte, 1998; Calabrese et al., 1998). You might wonder why anyone ever thought of testing antiseizure medications as a treatment for affective disorders. The answer

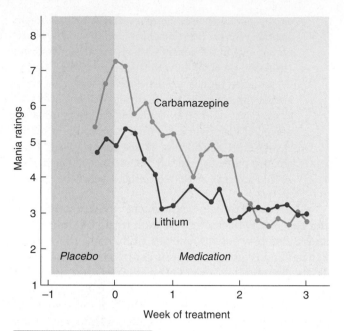

figure 16.17

The effects of lithium carbonate and carbamazepine on symptoms of mania in patients with bipolar disorder. (Adapted from Feldman, R. S., Meyer, J. S., and Quenzer, L. F. *Principles of Neuropsychopharmacology*. Sunderland, MA: Sinauer Associates, 1997. After Post et al., 1984.)

is that seizures themselves have anticonvulsant effects: ECT decreases brain activity and reduces the seizure threshold of the brain (Sackeim et al., 1983). This fact suggested to researchers that the anticonvulsant effects of ECT, and not the seizure they produce, might be responsible for the therapeutic effect. If this was the case, then anticonvulsant medications might also be useful in treating affective disorders—as indeed they were found to be (Post et al., 1998).

Role of Monoamines

The fact that depression can be treated effectively with MAO inhibitors and drugs that inhibit the reuptake of norepinephrine suggested the **monoamine hypothesis:** Depression is caused by insufficient activity of monoaminergic neurons. Because the symptoms of depression do not respond to potent dopamine agonists such as amphetamine or cocaine, most investigators have focused their

carbamazepine A drug (trade name: Tegretol) that is used to treat seizures originating from a focus, generally in the medial temporal lobe.

monoamine hypothesis A hypothesis that states that depression is caused by a low level of activity of one or more monoaminergic synapses.

research efforts on the other two monoamines: norepinephrine and serotonin.

As we saw earlier in this chapter, the dopamine hypothesis of schizophrenia receives support from the fact that dopamine agonists can produce the symptoms of schizophrenia. Similarly, the monoamine hypothesis of depression receives support from the fact that depression can be caused by monoamine antagonists. Many hundreds of years ago, an alkaloid extract from *Rauwolfia serpentina,* a shrub of Southeast Asia, was found to be useful for treating snakebite, circulatory disorders, and insanity. Modern research has confirmed that the alkaloid, now called reserpine, has both an antipsychotic effect and a hypotensive effect (that is, it lowers blood pressure). The effect on blood pressure precludes its use in treating schizophrenia, but the drug is still occasionally used to treat patients with high blood pressure.

Reserpine has a serious side effect: It can cause depression. In fact, in the early years of its use as a hypotensive agent, up to 15 percent of the people who received it became depressed (Sachar and Baron, 1979). Reserpine interferes with the storage of monoamines in synaptic vesicles, reducing the amount of neurotransmitter released by the terminal buttons. Thus, the drug serves as a potent norepinephrine, dopamine, and serotonin antagonist. The pharmacological and behavioral effects of reserpine complement the pharmacological and behavioral effects of the drugs that are used to treat depression—MAO inhibitors and drugs that block the reuptake of norepinephrine and serotonin. That is, a monoamine antagonist produces depression, whereas monoamine agonists alleviate it.

Several studies have found that suicidal depression is related to decreased CSF levels of **5-HIAA** (5-hydroxyindoleacetic acid), a metabolite of serotonin that is produced when serotonin is destroyed by MAO. A decreased level of 5-HIAA implies that less 5-HT (serotonin) is being produced and released in the brain. Träskmann et al. (1981) found that CSF levels of 5-HIAA in people who had attempted suicide were significantly lower than those in controls. In a follow-up study of depressed and potentially suicidal patients, 20 percent of those with levels of 5-HIAA below the median subsequently killed themselves, whereas none of those with levels above the median committed suicide. More recent studies have confirmed these results (Roy, De Jong, and Linnoila, 1989).

Sedvall et al. (1980) analyzed the CSF of healthy, nondepressed volunteers. The families of subjects with unusually low levels of 5-HIAA were more likely to include people with depression. The results suggest that serotonin metabolism or release is genetically controlled and is linked to depression. Yatham et al. (2000) found a lower level of 5-HT_2 receptors in the neocortex of depressed patients. These findings clearly support the monoamine hypothesis.

As we saw in Chapter 11, the activity of serotonergic neurons appears to inhibit aggression, perhaps by activating the prefrontal cortex. Some investigators have suggested that this role is consistent with the findings of Sedvall et al. Suicide can be seen as a form of aggression—self-directed aggression (Siever et al., 1991); thus, the decreased CSF levels of 5-HIAA may simply indicate a lower level of impulse control. Of course, the fact that serotonin is involved in aggression does not rule out the possibility that low levels of serotonin are responsible for depressed mood as well.

Delgado et al. (1990) used a different approach to study the role of serotonin in depression—the **tryptophan depletion procedure.** They studied depressed patients who were receiving antidepressant medication and were currently feeling well. For one day they had the patients follow a low-tryptophan diet (for example, salad, corn, cream cheese, and a gelatin dessert). Then the next day, the patients drank an amino acid "cocktail" that contained no tryptophan. The uptake of amino acids through the blood–brain barrier is accomplished by amino acid transporters. Because the patients' blood level of tryptophan was very low and that of the other amino acids was high, very little tryptophan found its way into the brain, and the level of tryptophan in the brain fell drastically. As you will recall, tryptophan is the precursor of 5-HT, or serotonin. Thus, the treatment lowered the level of serotonin in the brain.

Delgado and his colleagues found that the tryptophan depletion caused most of the patients to relapse back into depression. Then when they began eating a normal diet again, they recovered. These results strongly suggest that the therapeutic effect of at least some antidepressant drugs depends on the availability of serotonin in the brain.

Subsequent studies have confirmed these results. These studies also indicate that tryptophan depletion has little or no effect on the mood of healthy subjects, but it does lower the mood of people with a family history of affective disorders (Van der Does, 2001; Young and Leyton, 2002). Also, tryptophan depletion (which affects brain serotonin levels) causes relapses in patients who are successfully being treated with serotonin reuptake inhibitors but not in those who are being treated with norepinephrine reuptake inhibitors. In contrast, administration of AMPT, a drug that inhibits the synthesis of dopamine and norepinephrine, causes relapses only in patients who are being successfully

---

5-HIAA A breakdown product of the neurotransmitter serotonin (5-HT).

tryptophan depletion procedure A procedure involving a low-tryptophan diet and a tryptophan-free amino acid "cocktail" that lowers brain tryptophan and consequently decreases the synthesis of 5-HT.

treated with norepinephrine reuptake inhibitors (Heninger, Delgado, and Charney, 1996). (See *Figure 16.18*.)

Two PET studies attempted to determine the brain regions involved in the relapse of depression caused by tryptophan depletion (Bremner et al., 1997; Smith et al., 1999). The investigators measured patients' regional cerebral metabolic rate before and after the patients drank a placebo or the amino acid "cocktail." Both studies found that patients whose depression returned showed a decrease in brain metabolism in the prefrontal cortex. Patients who did not relapse did not show these changes. These results are consistent with the general finding (discussed in Chapter 11) that the prefrontal cortex is involved in emotions.

A Role for Substance P?

Recent research indicates that yet another neurotransmitter may be involved in depression: **substance P.** This peptide exerts its effects by binding with the NK_1 receptor. (NK stands for *neurokinin,* a chemical category of neuropeptides.) The NK_1 receptor is found in brain regions that are known to play a role in emotional behavior and the response to stress, including the medial and central nuclei of the amygdala, the hypothalamus, the ventral tegmental area, the locus coeruleus, and the cerebral cortex (Mantyh, Hunt, and Maggio, 1984; Stout, Owens, and Nemeroff, 2001). In addition, long-term administration of antidepressant drugs causes a reduction of substance P levels in several regions of the brain (Shirayama et al., 1996). These and other observations suggested that a drug that blocked NK_1 receptors might reduce the symptoms of depression.

In a randomized double-blind study, Kramer et al. (1998) tried such a drug, MK-869, on patients with major depression. For six weeks they administered MK-869 to sixty-six patients, paroxetine (a selective serotonin reuptake inhibitor) to sixty-eight patients, and a placebo to sixty-four patients. They found that MK-869 reduced depressive

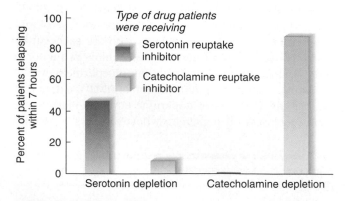

figure **16.18**

Effects of tryptophan depletion and catecholamine depletion on the symptoms of depressed patients receiving a serotonin reuptake inhibitor or a norepinephrine reuptake inhibitor.
(Adapted from Heninger, G. R., Delgado, P. L., and Charney, D. S. *Pharmacopsychiatry,* 1996, *29,* 2–11.)

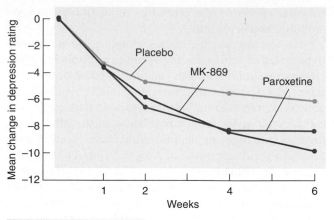

figure **16.19**

Effects of MK-869 (NK_1 receptor antagonist), paroxetine (specific serotonin reuptake inhibitor) and placebo on the symptoms of depression.
(Adapted from Kramer, M. S., Cutler, N., Feighner, J., Shrivastava, R., Carman, J., Sramek, J. J., Reines, S. A., Liu, G., Snavely, D., Wyatt-Knowles, E., Hale, J. J., Mills, S. G, MacCoss, M., Swain, C. J., Harrison, T., Hill, R. G., Hefti, F., Scolnick, E. M., Cascieri, M. A., Chicchi, G. G., Sadowski, S., Williams, A. R., Hewson, L., Smith, D., Carlson, E. J., Hargreaves, R. J., and Rupniak, N. M. *Science,* 1998, *281,* 1640–1645.)

symptoms as well as paroxetine did and that it did not produce serious side effects. In fact, sexual dysfunction (a common side effect of antidepressant drugs) was seen in only 3 percent of patients receiving MK-869, compared with 4 percent of patients receiving the placebo and 26 percent of patients receiving paroxetine. (See *Figure 16.19*.)

Kramer and his colleagues also performed some studies with laboratory animals that indicated that MK-869 does not affect serotonergic or noradrenergic neurons, nor do standard antidepressant drugs interact with NK_1 receptors. Thus, substance P antagonists appear to act independently of drugs that reduce depression by blocking the reuptake of serotonin and norepinephrine. Lejeune, Gobert, and Millan (2002) found that an NK_1 antagonist enhanced the activity of dopaminergic neurons in the ventral tegmental area and increased the release of dopamine in the frontal cortex. Now that researchers have another potential mechanism to investigate, we may see a new line of research on the physiology of depression.

Evidence for Brain Abnormalities

As we saw earlier in this chapter, many studies have found structural and biochemical abnormalities in the brains of schizophrenic patients. Studies have also reported abnormalities in patients with affective disorders. A review

substance P A peptide secreted as a neurotransmitter and neuromodulator in several regions of the brain; may be involved in emotional behavior, the response to stress, and the symptoms of depression.

by Soares and Mann (1997) noted that investigators have reported abnormalities in the prefrontal cortex, basal ganglia, hippocampus, thalamus, cerebellum, and temporal lobe. The most reliable findings were abnormalities in the prefrontal cortex, basal ganglia, and cerebellum of patients with unipolar depression and abnormalities of the cerebellum (and perhaps the temporal lobe) in those with bipolar disorder. For example, Elkis et al. (1996) found evidence for a decreased amount of tissue in the prefrontal cortex of young patients with unipolar depression, which suggests the presence of a developmental abnormality or a degenerative process that occurs early in life. A structural MRI study by Strakowski et al. (2002) found evidence that repeated episodes of depression and mania caused an increase in the size of the lateral ventricles, which implies a loss of brain tissue. They found that the relative size of the lateral ventricles was the same in healthy subjects and patients who had just had their first episode of bipolar disorder but was increased in patients who had several episodes. (See *Figure 16.20*.)

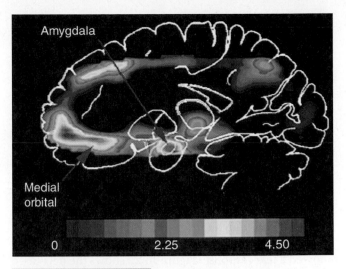

figure 16.21

Composite fMRI image showing increased metabolic rate in the amygdala and medial orbitofrontal cortex of patients with unipolar depression.

(From Drevets, W. C., *Current Opinion in Neurobiology*, 2001, *11*, 240–249.)

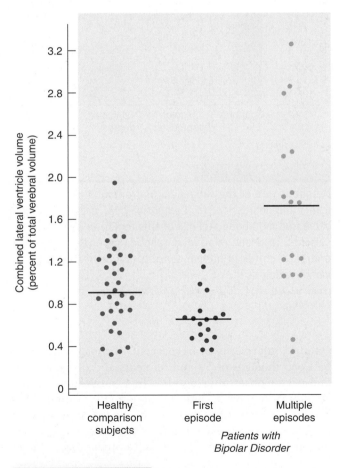

figure 16.20

Relative volume of lateral ventricles of normal subjects and patients with a single episode or multiple episodes of bipolar disorder.

(Adapted from Strakowski, S. M., DelBello, M. P., Zimmerman, M. E., Getz, G. E., Mills, N. P., Ret, J., Shear, P., and Adler, C. M. *American Journal of Psychiatry*, 2002, *11*, 1841–1847.)

In a review of the relevant literature, Drevets (2001) suggests that the amygdala and several regions of the prefrontal cortex play special roles in the development of depression. As we saw in Chapter 11, the amygdala is critically involved in the expression of negative emotions. As Drevets notes, functional imaging studies of depressed patients indicate an increase in blood flow and metabolism of 50–75 percent (Drevets et al., 1992; Links et al., 1996). A study by Abercrombie et al. (1998) found that the activity of the amygdala of depressed patients was correlated with the severity of their depression. In addition, the metabolic activity of the amygdala increases in normal subjects when they look at pictures of faces with expressions of sadness, and it also increases when depressed subjects remember episodes in their lives that made them sad (Drevets, 2000b; Liotti et al., 2002).

Several areas of the prefrontal cortex are involved in modulating emotional behavior. Like the amygdala, the orbitofrontal cortex is generally more activated in depressed patients than in healthy subjects (Drevets, 2000a). Damage to the orbitofrontal cortex disrupts the ability to abandon previously reinforced behaviors that are no longer fruitful (Bechara et al., 1998). Drevets (2001) suggests that the activation of this region in depressed patients may reflect their attempt to suppress unreinforced, unpleasant thoughts and emotions. Figure 16.21 illustrates the increased activity of the amygdala and orbitofrontal cortex in depressed patients. (See *Figure 16.21*.)

Another region of the medial prefrontal cortex—the *subgenual prefrontal cortex*—shows a *lower* level of activation in depressed patients (Drevets et al., 1997). If you look at a sagittal view of the corpus callosum, you will notice that the front of this structure looks like a bent knee—*genu*, in

Latin. The subgenual prefrontal cortex is located below the "knee" at the front of the corpus callosum. This region plays an inhibitory role in emotions and emotional memories. For example, damage to the subgenual prefrontal cortex in laboratory animals interferes with extinction of conditioned emotional responses. As we saw in Chapters 11 and 13, emotional responses can be conditioned to neutral stimuli if these stimuli are paired with aversive events. However, if the neutral stimulus is then presented repeatedly by itself, it ceases to produce an emotional response. The response becomes *extinguished*. As Quirk et al. (2000) showed in a study with rats, damage to the medial prefrontal cortex disrupts the process of extinction. Even after an auditory stimulus no longer signaled that the rats would receive a shock to their feet, they showed a fear response. Figure 16.22 shows the decreased activity of the subgenual prefrontal cortex in depressed patients. As the bar graph shows, the activity of this region is *increased* during a manic episode in patients with bipolar disorder (Drevets et al., 1997). Thus the activity of this region decreases during times of negative mood and increases during times of positive mood. (See *Figure 16.22.*)

An anatomical study by Öngür, Drevets, and Price (1998) found evidence that supports these results. The investigators examined the brains of deceased patients with affective disorders. They found a 24 percent decrease in the number of glial cells in the subgenual prefrontal cortex of patients with major depression and a 41 percent decrease in patients with bipolar disorder. Öngür and his colleagues suggest that the decreased number of glial cells may be responsible for the decreased activity seen in this region.

As we saw earlier in this chapter, evidence indicates that schizophrenia can be produced by brain damage resulting from obstetric complications. Kinney et al. (1993) found that patients with bipolar disorder were more likely than their normal siblings to have a record of obstetric complications. The complications were mostly minor, so the authors suggest that they probably served as a contributing factor to the development of the disorder rather than the sole cause. A subsequent study with a larger sample of subjects confirmed these results (Kinney et al., 1998).

As people age, the likelihood of cardiovascular disease and strokes increases. Some cerebrovascular accidents produce brain damage, as seen on MRI or CT scans, but do not produce obvious neurological symptoms. These events, known as **silent cerebral infarctions (SCI),** appear to be a major cause of depression that first occurs later in life—the so-called *late-onset depression*. The risk factors for silent cerebral infarctions are similar to those for strokes: primarily, cigarette smoking and hypertension (Howard et al., 1998). Fujikawa, Yamawaki, and Touhouda (1993) performed MRI scans on patients with late-onset depression and found evidence of silent

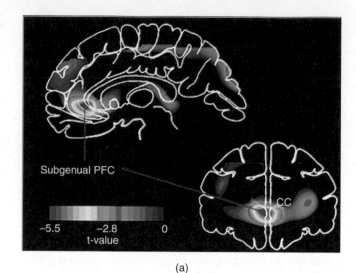

(a)

(b)

figure 16.22

Metabolic rate of the subgenual prefrontal cortex in mania and depression. (a) Composite fMRI image showing decreased metabolic activity of this region in depressed patients. (b) Mean relative metabolic rate of the subgenual prefrontal cortex in normal controls and depressed and manic patients.

(From Drevets, W. C., *Current Opinion in Neurobiology*, 2001, *11*, 240–249.)

cerebral infarctions in 51 percent of those with onset between the ages of 50 and 65 years and 66 percent of those with onset after age 65. In a subsequent study, Fujikawa, Yamawaki, and Touhouda (1994) found that patients with late-onset depression who did *not* have SCIs were more likely to have relatives with affective disorder than patients who did have SCIs. In other words, if late-

silent cerebral infarction (SCI) A small cerebrovascular accident (stroke) that causes minor brain damage without producing obvious neurological symptoms.

onset depression was not caused by cerebrovascular accidents, it was likely to be caused by hereditary factors. In support of this conclusion Yamashita et al. (2001) found that depressed patients with SCIs were less likely to respond well to antidepressant medication and consequently required a longer hospital treatment than those without SCIs.

Role of Circadian Rhythms

One of the most prominent symptoms of depression is disordered sleep. The sleep of people with depression tends to be shallow; slow-wave delta sleep (stages 3 and 4) is reduced, and stage 1 is increased. Sleep is fragmented; people tend to waken frequently, especially toward the morning. In addition, REM sleep occurs earlier, the first half of the night contains a higher proportion of REM periods, and REM sleep contains an increased number of rapid eye movements (Kupfer, 1976; Vogel et al., 1980). (See *Figure 16.23.*)

REM Sleep Deprivation

One of the most effective antidepressant treatments is sleep deprivation, either total or selective. Selective deprivation of REM sleep, accomplished by monitoring people's EEG and awakening them whenever they show signs of REM sleep, alleviates depression (Vogel et al., 1975; Vogel et al., 1990). The therapeutic effect, like that of the antidepressant medications, occurs slowly, over the course of several weeks. Some patients show long-term

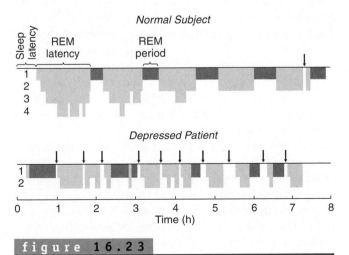

figure 16.23

Patterns of the stages of sleep of a normal subject and of a patient with major depression. Note the reduced sleep latency, reduced REM latency, reduction in slow-wave sleep (stages 3 and 4), and general fragmentation of sleep (arrows) in the depressed patient.

(From Gillin, J. C., and Borbély, A. A. *Trends in Neurosciences,* 1985, 8, 537–542. Reprinted with permission.)

improvement even after the deprivation is discontinued; thus, it is a practical as well as an effective treatment. In addition, regardless of their specific pharmacological effects, other treatments for depression suppress REM sleep, delaying its onset and decreasing its duration. These facts suggest that REM sleep and mood might somehow be causally related.

Scherschlicht et al. (1982) examined the effects of twenty antidepressant drugs on the sleep cycles of cats and found that all of them profoundly reduced REM sleep and most of them increased slow-wave sleep. In an extensive review of the literature, Vogel et al. (1990) found that all drugs that suppressed REM sleep (and produced a rebound effect when their administration was discontinued) acted as antidepressants. As a consequence, an increased amount of delta sleep occurs during the first pre-REM period. Kupfer et al. (1994) found that the effects of antidepressant drugs on sleep persisted throughout long-term treatment. (They observed patients for as long as three years.) In addition, Grunhaus et al. (1997) found that successful ECT treatment also suppressed REM sleep in depressed patients. In fact, the symptoms of those patients who continued to show an early onset of REM sleep were less likely to improve after receiving ECT treatments. These results suggest that the primary effect of successful antidepressant treatment may be to suppress REM sleep, and the changes in mood may be a result of this suppression. However, at least one antidepressant drug has been shown in a double-blind, placebo-controlled study *not* to suppress REM sleep (Vogel et al., 1998). Thus, suppression of REM sleep cannot be the *only* way that antidepressant drugs work. (So far, it does appear that all drugs that suppress REM sleep without interfering with normal sleep do act as antidepressants.)

Studies of families with a history of major depression also suggest a link between this disorder and abnormalities in REM sleep. For example, Giles, Roffwarg, and Rush (1987) found that first-degree relatives of people with depression are likely to show a short REM sleep latency, even if they have not yet had an episode of depression. Giles et al. (1988) found that the members of these families who had the lowest REM latency had the highest risk of subsequently becoming depressed. Abnormalities in REM sleep are seen early in life; Coble et al. (1988) found that newborn infants of mothers with a history of major depression showed patterns of REM sleep that were different from those of the infants of mothers without such a history.

Total Sleep Deprivation

Total sleep deprivation also has an antidepressant effect. Unlike specific deprivation of REM sleep, which takes several weeks to reduce depression, total sleep deprivation produces immediate effects (Wu and Bunney,

1990). Figure 16.24 shows the mood rating of a patient who stayed awake one night; as you can see, the depression was lifted by the sleep deprivation but returned the next day, after a normal night's sleep. (See *Figure 16.24.*)

Wu and Bunney suggest that during sleep a substance is produced that has a *depressogenic* effect. That is, the substance produces depression in a susceptible person. Presumably, this substance is produced in the brain and acts as a neuromodulator. During waking, this substance is gradually metabolized and hence inactivated. Some of the evidence for this hypothesis is presented in Figure 16.25. The data are taken from eight different studies (cited by Wu and Bunney, 1990) and show self-ratings of depression of people who did and did not respond to sleep deprivation. (Total sleep deprivation improves the mood of patients with major depression approximately two-thirds of the time.) (See *Figure 16.25.*)

Why do only some people profit from sleep deprivation? This question has not yet been answered, but several studies have shown that it is possible to predict who will profit and who will not (Riemann, Wiegand, and Berger, 1991; Haug, 1992; Wirz-Justice and Van den Hoofdakker, 1999). In general, depressed patients whose mood remains stable will probably not benefit from sleep depression, whereas those whose mood fluctuates probably will. The patients who are most likely to respond are those who feel depressed in the morning but then gradually feel better as the day progresses. In these people sleep deprivation appears to prevent the depressogenic effects of sleep from taking place and simply permits the trend to continue. If you examine Figure 16.25, you can see that the responders were already feeling better by the end of the day. This improvement continued through the sleepless night and during the following day. The next night they were permitted to sleep normally, and their depression was

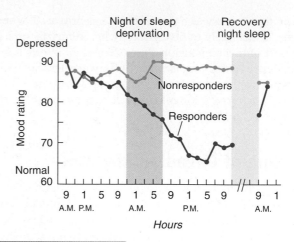

figure 16.25

Mean mood rating of responding and nonresponding patients deprived of one night's sleep as a function of the time of day.

(From Wu, J. C., and Bunney, W. E. *American Journal of Psychiatry,* Vol. 147, pp. 14–21, 1990. Copyright 1990, the American Psychiatric Association. Reprinted by permission.)

back the following morning. As Wu and Bunney note, these data are consistent with the hypothesis that sleep produces a substance with a depressogenic effect. (See *Figure 16.25.*)

An alternative interpretation of the results we just saw is that waking might produce a substance with *antidepressant* effects, which is destroyed during sleep. However, Wu and Bunney point out that several studies have found that for some subjects a short nap reinstates the depression that had been reduced by sleep deprivation. In some cases a nap as short as 90 seconds (timed by EEG monitoring) can eliminate the beneficial effects of sleep depression. They conclude that the simplest hypothesis is that a nap produces a sudden secretion of a substance that causes depression. It seems less likely that a nap could be responsible for the sudden *destruction* of a substance with an antidepressant effect.

The antidepressant effect of REM sleep deprivation and that of total sleep deprivation appear to be different; one is slow and long-lasting, whereas the other is fast and short-lived. In addition, total sleep deprivation can even trigger an episode of mania in patients with bipolar disorder (Wehr, 1992). (Even nondepressed people often report feeling "high" after spending a night without sleep.) The fact that a person's mood can be altered so quickly suggests that it would be worthwhile to look for physiological changes before and after sleep deprivation to try to identify those that may play a role in the control of mood.

Although total sleep deprivation is not a practical method for treating depression (it is impossible to keep people awake indefinitely), several studies suggest that *partial* sleep deprivation can hasten the beneficial effects

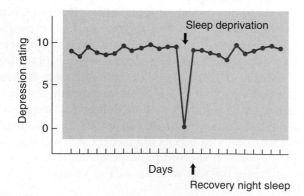

figure 16.24

Changes in the depression rating of a depressed patient produced by a single night's total sleep deprivation.

(From Wu, J. C., and Bunney, W. E. *American Journal of Psychiatry,* Vol. 147, pp. 14–21, 1990. Copyright 1990, the American Psychiatric Association. Reprinted by permission.)

of antidepressant drugs (Szuba, Baxter, and Fairbanks, 1991; Leibenluft and Wehr, 1992). Some investigators have found that *intermittent* total sleep deprivation (say, twice a week for four weeks) can have beneficial results (Papadimitriou et al., 1993).

Riemann et al. (1999) found that advancing the time of day that depressed patients sleep can prolong the beneficial effects of total sleep deprivation. They deprived patients of sleep for one night and continued to study those who showed a good response to the deprivation. The next night, the experimenters had some of the patients go to bed six hours earlier than usual, while the others went to bed three hours *later* than normal. Gradually, over several days, the subjects' bedtimes were returned to normal. Seventy-five percent of the early sleepers showed a continued remission of their depression, compared with only 40 percent of the late sleepers. As Riemann, Berger, and Voderholzer (2001) note, only sleep in the morning seems to be able to produce depression; thus, the best advice to depressed patients may be to get out of bed early in the morning and go to bed early at night.

Role of Zeitgebers

Yet another phenomenon relates depression to sleep and waking—or, more specifically, to the mechanisms that are responsible for circadian rhythms. Some people become depressed during the winter season, when days are short and nights are long (Rosenthal et al., 1984). The symptoms of this form of depression, called **seasonal affective disorder,** are somewhat different from those of major depression; both forms include lethargy and sleep disturbances, but seasonal depression includes a craving for carbohydrate and an accompanying weight gain. (As you will recall, people with major depression tend to lose their appetite.) A much smaller percentage of the population becomes depressed during the summer (Wehr, Sack, and Rosenthal, 1987). People with **summer depression** are more likely to sleep less, lose their appetite, and lose weight (Wehr et al., 1991).

Seasonal affective disorder, like unipolar depression and bipolar disorder, appears to have a genetic basis. In a study of 6439 adult twins, Madden et al. (1996) found that seasonal affective disorder ran in families, and they estimated that at least 29 percent of the variance in seasonal mood disorders could be attributed to genetic factors. Molecular genetic studies suggest that seasonal affective disorder may be linked to genes involved in production of the 5-HT transporter and the 5-HT$_{2A}$ receptor (Sher et al., 1999).

Seasonal affective disorder can be treated by **phototherapy:** exposing people to bright light for several hours a day (Rosenthal et al., 1985; Stinson and Thompson, 1990). As you will recall, circadian rhythms of sleep and wakefulness are controlled by the activity of the suprachiasmatic nucleus of the hypothalamus. Light serves as a *zeit-*

geber; that is, it synchronizes the activity of the biological clock to the day–night cycle. One possibility is that people with seasonal affective disorder require a stronger-than-normal zeitgeber to reset their biological clock. The evidence on this issue is mixed: Two studies found that light therapy had an antidepressant effect no matter what time of day it occurred (Wirz-Justice et al., 1993; Meesters et al., 1995), and two studies found that morning light exposure was effective but evening exposure was not (Lewy et al., 1998; Terman, Terman, and Ross, 1998). If the light serves as a zeitgeber, we would expect different effects depending on the time of day the phototherapy occurred, so it is important to resolve the conflicting evidence.

One interesting procedure has been shown to successfully treat seasonal affective disorder: *dawn simulation.* The brain mechanisms that control our circadian rhythms evolved long before the advent of artificial light. Morning light came on gradually, as the sun arose. Several studies have shown that arranging for a light in the bedroom to slowly increase in intensity around the time the sleeper wants to awaken can reduce depressive symptoms. For example, Avery et al. (2001) arranged for a white light next to sleepers' beds to gradually increase from 4:30 A.M. to 6:00 A.M., peaking at 250 lux, which is the average indoors light level. Control groups were exposed to a dim red light between 4:30 A.M. and 6:00 A.M. or a sudden very bright (10,000 lux) light between 6:00 A.M. and 6:30 A.M. Patients who were exposed to dawn simulation showed the best response. At the end of the six-week period, 83 percent of those patients showed a significant decrease in their symptoms, compared with 67 percent of the control groups.

Phototherapy has even been found to help patients with unipolar depression. Neumeister et al. (1996) found that patients with unipolar depression who responded to total sleep depression were less likely to relapse later if they received phototherapy in the early morning and late afternoon. Patients who sat in front of a dim light (the placebo treatment) quickly relapsed.

Many people are sensitive to seasonal changes in the hours of sunlight and darkness. Ninety-two percent of the respondents to a survey by Kasper et al. (1989a) said that they noticed seasonal changes in their mood, 27 percent reported that these changes caused problems, and 4 percent reported problems severe enough to qualify as a seasonal

---

seasonal affective disorder A mood disorder characterized by depression, lethargy, sleep disturbances, and craving for carbohydrates during the winter season when days are short.

summer depression A mood disorder characterized by depression, sleep disturbances, and loss of appetite.

phototherapy Treatment of seasonal affective disorder by daily exposure to bright light.

affective disorder. Kasper et al. (1989b) recruited people with "winter blahs" through newspaper advertisements. They excluded people with evidence of a true seasonal affective disorder and exposed the others to bright light each day. They found that the exposure to bright light improved the mood of the subjects with the "blahs," whereas the mood of normal subjects was not changed. The study suggests that we should consider increasing the level of illumination in the home or workplace. The only negative aspect of the change would seem to be a higher electric bill.

According to a study by Wirz-Justice et al. (1996), even a high electric bill can be avoided. They found that a one-hour walk outside each morning reduced the symptoms of seasonal affective disorder. The investigators note that even on an overcast winter day, the early morning sky provides considerably more illumination than normal indoor artificial lighting, so a walk outside increases a person's exposure to light. The exercise probably doesn't hurt, either.

In fact, exercise appears to have a beneficial effect on depression. Singh, Clements, and Fiatarone (1997) enrolled depressed patients (aged 60–84 years) in a supervised weight-training program. The exercise program improved both their depression and their sleep.

interim summary

The major affective disorders include bipolar affective disorder, with its cyclical episodes of mania and depression, and unipolar depression. Heritability studies suggest that genetic anomalies are at least partly responsible for these disorders. Unipolar depression can be successfully treated by for biological treatments: MAO inhibitors, drugs that block the reuptake of norepinephrine and serotonin, electroconvulsive therapy, and sleep deprivation. Bipolar disorder can be successfully treated by lithium salts. Lithium appears to stabilize neural transmission, especially in serotonin-secreting neurons. It may do so by interfering with the phosphoinosi-

tide system, which is responsible for the production of several categories of second messengers. It also appears to protect neurons from damage and perhaps facilitate their repair.

The therapeutic effect of noradrenergic and serotonergic agonists and the depressant effect of reserpine, a monoaminergic antagonist, suggested the monoamine hypothesis of depression. Several other lines of evidence support this hypothesis. Low levels of 5-HIAA (a serotonin metabolite) in the cerebrospinal fluid correlate with attempts at suicide. It is possible that these results are related to the effects of serotonin on (self-directed) aggression. Depletion of tryptophan (the precursor of 5-HT) in the brain reverses the therapeutic effects of antidepressant medication in depressed patients, which lends further support to the conclusion that 5-HT plays a role in mood. Some evidence also suggests that drugs that block NK_1 receptors, which normally respond to a peptide known as substance P, reduce the symptoms of depression.

Several studies have looked for abnormalities in the brains of depressed patients. In general, patients with unipolar depression show abnormalities in the prefrontal cortex, basal ganglia, and cerebellum, while patients with bipolar disorder show abnormalities in the cerebellum and (perhaps) temporal lobe. One hypothesis suggests that depression results from hyperactivity of the amygdala and orbitofrontal cortex and hypoactivity of the subgenual prefrontal cortex. Depression can also be caused by the accumulating effect of silent cerebral infarctions—small cerebrovascular accidents (strokes) that cause progressive damage to the brain.

Sleep disturbances are characteristic of affective disorders. In fact, total sleep deprivation rapidly (but temporarily) reduces depression in many people, and selective deprivation of REM sleep does so slowly (but more lastingly). In addition, almost all effective antidepressant treatments suppress REM sleep. Finally, a specific form of depression, seasonal affective disorder, can be treated by exposure to bright light or to a simulation of dawn. Clearly, the mood disorders are somehow linked to biological rhythms.

Suggested Readings

Breier, A. *The New Pharmacotherapy of Schizophrenia*. Washington, DC: American Psychiatric Press, 1996.

Coleman, M., and Gillberg, C. *The Schizophrenias: A Biological Approach to the Schizophrenia Spectrum Disorders*. New York: Springer, 1996.

Goodwin, D. W., and Guze, S. B. *Psychiatric Diagnosis,* 6th ed. New York: Oxford University Press, 1996.

Mann, J. J., and Kupfer, D. J. *Biology of Depressive Disorders*. New York: Plenum Press, 1993.

Strange, P. G. *Brain Biochemistry and Brain Disorders*. Oxford, England: Oxford University Press, 1992.

Tsai, G., and Coyle, J. T. Glutamatergic mechanisms in schizophrenia. *Annual Review of Pharmacology and Toxicology*, 2002, *42*, 165–179.

Waddington, J. L., and Buckley, P. F. *The Neurodevelopmental Basis of Schizophrenia*. New York: Chapman & Hall, 1996.

Suggested Web Sites

Schizophrenia

http://www.schizophrenia.com/

This comprehensive site contains discussion areas devoted to schizophrenia as well as fact sheets about schizophrenia.

Dana Brain Web

http://www.dana.org/brainweb/

The focus of the Dana Brain Web is on sites relating to brain diseases and disorders.

All About Depression

http://depression.mentalhelp.net/

This site from the Mental Health Network contains links on depression diagnosis, therapy, and organizations.

The Search for Novel Antipsychotic Drugs

http://salmon.psy.plym.ac.uk/year2/schizo1.htm

This site provides student access to a comprehensive set of materials relating to the pharmacology of schizophrenia.

Anxiety Disorders, Autistic Disorder, Attention-Deficit/ Hyperactivity Disorder, and Stress Disorders

o u t l i n e

■ **Anxiety Disorders**
Panic Disorder
Obsessive-Compulsive Disorder
Interim Summary

■ **Autistic Disorder**
Description
Possible Causes
Interim Summary

■ **Attention-Deficit/**
 Hyperactivity Disorder
Description
Possible Causes
Interim Summary

■ **Stress Disorders**
Physiology of the Stress Response
Health Effects of Long-Term Stress
Posttraumatic Stress Disorder
Stress and Cardiovascular Disease
The Coping Response
Psychoneuroimmunology
Interim Summary

In 1935 the report of an experiment with a chimpanzee triggered events whose repercussions are still felt today. Jacobsen, Wolf, and Jackson (1935) tested some chimpanzees on a behavioral task that requires the animal to remain quiet and remember the location of food that the experimenter has placed behind a screen. One animal, Becky, displayed a violent emotional reaction whenever she made an error while performing this task. "[When] the experimenter lowered . . . the opaque door to exclude the animal's view of the cups, she immediately flew into a temper tantrum, rolled on the floor, defecated, and urinated. After a few such reactions during the training period, the animal would make no further responses." After the chimpanzee's frontal lobes were removed, it became a model of good comportment. It "offered its usual friendly greeting, and eagerly ran from its living quarters to the transfer cage, and in turn went properly to the experimental cage. . . .If the animal made a mistake, it showed no evidence of emotional disturbance but quietly awaited the loading of the cups for the next trial" (Jacobsen, Wolf, and Jackson, 1935, pp. 9–10).

These findings were reported at a scientific meeting in 1935, which was attended by Egas Moniz, a Portuguese neuropsychiatrist. He heard the report by Jacobsen and his colleagues and also one by Brickner (1936), which indicated that radical removal of the frontal lobes in a human patient (performed because of a tumor) did not appear to produce intellectual impairment; therefore, people could presumably get along without their frontal lobes. These two reports suggested to Moniz that "if frontal-lobe removal . . . eliminates frustrational behavior, why would it not be feasible to relieve anxiety states in man by surgical means?" (Fulton, 1949, pp. 63–64). In fact, Moniz persuaded a neurosurgeon to do so, and approximately one hundred operations were eventually performed under his supervision. (In 1949 Moniz received the Nobel Prize for the development of this procedure.)

I wrote that the repercussions of the 1935 meeting are still felt today. Since that time tens of thousands of people have received prefrontal lobotomies, primarily to reduce symptoms of emotional distress, and many of these people are still alive. At first, the medical community welcomed the procedure because it provided their patients with relief from emotional anguish. Only after many years were careful studies performed on the side effects of the procedure. These studies showed that although patients did perform well on standard tests of intellectual ability, they showed serious changes in personality, becoming irresponsible and childish. They also lost the ability to carry out plans, and most were unemployable. And although pathological emotional reactions were eliminated, so were normal ones. Because of these findings, and because of the discovery of drugs and therapeutic methods that relieve the patients' symptoms without producing such drastic side effects, neurosurgeons eventually abandoned the prefrontal lobotomy procedure (Valenstein, 1986).

I should point out that the prefrontal lobotomies that were performed under Moniz's supervision, and by the neurosurgeons who followed, were not as drastic as the surgery performed by Jacobsen and his colleagues on Becky, the chimpanzee. In fact, no brain tissue was removed. Instead, the surgeons introduced various kinds of cutting devices into the frontal lobes and severed white matter (bundles of axons). One rather gruesome procedure did not even require an operating room; it could be performed in a physician's office. A *transorbital leucotome,* shaped like an ice pick, was introduced into the brain by passing it beneath the upper eyelid until the point reached the orbital bone above the eye. The instrument was hit with a mallet, driving it through the bone into the brain. The end was then swept back and forth so that it cut through the white matter. The patient often left the office within an hour.

Many physicians objected to the "ice pick" procedure because it was done blind (that is, the surgeon could not see just where the blade of the leucotome was located) and because it produced more damage than was necessary. Also, the fact that it was so easy and left no external signs other than a pair of black eyes may have tempted its practitioners to perform it too casually. In fact, at least twenty-five hundred patients received this form of surgery (Valenstein, 1986).

What we know today about the effects of prefrontal lobotomy—whether done transorbitally or by more conventional means—tells us that such radical surgery should never have been performed. For too long the harmful side effects were ignored. (As we will see later in this chapter, neurosurgeons have developed a much restricted version of this surgery to treat intractable obsessive-compulsive disorder, which reduces the symptoms without producing the harmful side effects.)

Not too many years ago, the first three topics discussed in this chapter—the anxiety disorders, autism, and attention-deficit/hyperactivity disorder—would not have been covered in a book concerned with the physiology of behavior. (The importance of physiology to the fourth topic, stress, has long been recognized.) The anxiety disorders, autism, and attention-deficit/hyperactivity disorder were believed to be learned, primarily from parents who did a bad job raising their children. Although there was always at least some support for the suggestion that serious psychoses such as schizophrenia had a biological basis, other mental disorders were almost universally believed to be psychogenic in origin—that is, produced by "psychological" factors.

The tide has turned (or the pendulum has swung back, if you prefer that metaphor). Certainly, a person's family environment, social class, economic status, and similar factors affect the likelihood that he or she will develop a mental disorder and may help or hinder recovery. But physiological factors, including inherited ones and those that adversely affect development or damage the brain, play an important role too. The first three sections of this chapter are devoted to research on these physiological factors. The final section of this chapter considers the physiology of stress—the harmful aspects of negative emotional reactions.

Anxiety Disorders

As we saw in Chapter 16, the affective disorders are characterized by unrealistic extremes of emotion: depression or elation (mania). The **anxiety disorders** are characterized by unrealistic, unfounded fear and anxiety. This section describes two of the anxiety disorders that appear to have biological causes: panic disorder and obsessive-compulsive disorder. The causes of other anxiety disorders, such as generalized anxiety disorder and phobic disorders, seem to be similar to those of panic disorder, so they will not be discussed separately here.

Panic Disorder

Description

People with **panic disorder** suffer from episodic attacks of acute anxiety—periods of acute and unremitting terror that grip them for variable lengths of time, from a few seconds to a few hours. The disorder usually has its onset in young adulthood. Women appear to be about 2.5 times more likely than men to suffer from panic disorder (Eaton et al., 1994. See *Figure 17.1*.)

The basic symptoms of panic attack appear to be universal. For example, these symptoms are similar in residents of the United States, Puerto Rico, Germany, Lebanon, Korea, and New Zealand (Weissman et al., 1995). Panic attacks include many physical symptoms, such as shortness of breath, clammy sweat, irregularities in heartbeat, dizziness, faintness, and feelings of unreality. The victim of a panic attack often feels that he or she is going to die. Anxiety is a normal reaction to many stresses of life, and none of us is completely free from it. In fact, anxiety is undoubtedly useful in causing us to be more alert and to take important things seriously. However, the anxiety that we all feel from time to time is obviously different from the intense fear and terror experienced by a person gripped by a panic attack.

Between panic attacks many people with panic disorder suffer from **anticipatory anxiety**—the fear that

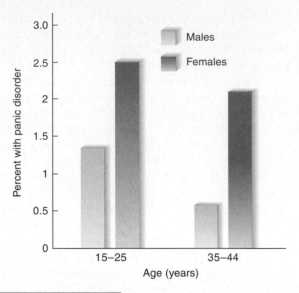

figure 17.1

Percentage of men and women who receive a diagnosis of panic disorder earlier and later in life.

(Based on data from Eaton, W. W., Kessler, R. C., Wittchen, H. U., and Magee, W. J. *American Journal of Psychiatry,* 1994, *151,* 413–420.)

another panic attack will strike them. This anticipatory anxiety often leads to the development of a serious phobic disorder: **agoraphobia** (*agora* means "open space"). According to the American Psychiatric Association's official *Diagnostic and Statistical Manual IV (DSM-IV),* agoraphobia associated with panic attacks is a fear of "being in places or situations from which escape might be difficult (or embarrassing) or in which help might not be available in the event of . . . a Panic Attack" (American Psychiatric Association, 1994, p. 200). Agoraphobia can be severely disabling; some people with this disorder have stayed inside their houses or apartments for years, afraid to venture outside.

Possible Causes

Because the physical symptoms of panic attacks are so overwhelming, many patients reject the suggestion that they have a mental disorder, insisting that their problem

anxiety disorder A psychological disorder characterized by tension, overactivity of the autonomic nervous system, expectation of an impending disaster, and continuous vigilance for danger.

panic disorder A disorder characterized by episodic periods of symptoms such as shortness of breath, irregularities in heartbeat, and other autonomic symptoms, accompanied by intense fear.

anticipatory anxiety A fear of having a panic attack; may lead to the development of agoraphobia.

agoraphobia A fear of being away from home or other protected places.

is medical. In fact, a considerable amount of evidence suggests that panic disorder may have biological origins. First, the disorder appears to be hereditary. In a review of the literature, Hettema, Neale, and Kendler (2001) found five family studies and three twin studies that indicate a significant genetic factor in panic disorder.

Several studies have shown a peculiar and puzzling genetic association between loose joints (*joint hypermobility syndrome,* or "double-jointedness") and panic disorder. Martin-Santos et al. (1998) reported that joint hypermobility syndrome was seen in 68 percent of patients with panic disorder but only 12.5 percent of control subjects. Gratacos et al. (2001) found that both joint hypermobility syndrome and panic and phobic disorders appear to be associated with a duplicated region of chromosome 15.

Susceptibility to lactate-induced panic attacks appears to be at least partly heritable. Balon et al. (1989) infused forty-five normal subjects with sodium lactate and found that ten of them had panic attacks. The investigators obtained the family history of their subjects, using an interviewer who did not know which subjects had had panic attacks. They found that over 24 percent of the relatives of the subjects with the panic attacks themselves had a history of anxiety disorders, compared with fewer than 8 percent in the nonresponders.

Anxiety disorders were previously treated by a combination of behavior therapy and a benzodiazepine. As we saw in Chapter 4, benzodiazepines have strong anxiolytic ("anxiety-dissolving") effects. The brain possesses benzodiazepine receptors, which are part of the $GABA_A$ receptor complex. When a benzodiazepine agonist binds with its receptor, it increases the sensitivity of the GABA binding site and produces an anxiolytic effect. On the other hand, when a benzodiazepine antagonist occupies the receptor site, it *reduces* the sensitivity of the GABA binding site and *increases* anxiety. Anxiety disorders, then, might be caused by a diminished number of benzodiazepine receptors or by the secretion of a neuromodulator that blocks the benzodiazepine binding site at the $GABA_A$ receptor. Nutt et al. (1990) found that administration of flumazenil, a benzodiazepine antagonist (having an action opposite that of the benzodiazepine tranquilizers), produced panic in patients with panic disorder but not in control subjects. In addition, a functional imaging study by Malizia et al. (1998) found evidence for a reduction in $GABA_A$ receptors in the brains of patients with panic disorder.

As we saw in Chapter 16, serotonin appears to play a role in depression. Much evidence suggests that serotonin may play a role in anxiety disorders too. Even though the symptoms of panic disorder and obsessive-compulsive disorder (described in the next section) are very different, specific serotonin reuptake inhibitors, which serve as potent serotonin agonists (such as fluoxetine), have become the first-line medications for treating both of these disorders (American Psychiatric Association, 1998; Asnis et al., 2001). Figure 17.2 shows the effect of

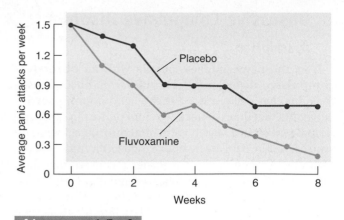

Effects of fluvoxamine (a specific serotonin reuptake inhibitor) on the severity of panic disorder.
(Adapted from Asnis, G. M., Hameedi, F. A., Goddard, A. W., Potkin, S. G., Black, D., Jameel, M., Desagani, K., and Woods, S. W. *Psychiatry Research,* 2001, *103,* 1–14.)

fluvoxamine, a serotonin reuptake inhibitor, on the number of panic attacks in patients with panic disorder. (See *Figure 17.2.*)

You will recall from Chapter 16 that short-term tryptophan depletion, caused by a low-tryptophan diet followed by the drinking of an amino acid "cocktail" that is deficient in tryptophan, rapidly increases the symptoms of depression in people with a history of unipolar depression. (The tryptophan depletion interferes with the synthesis of 5-HT.) Goddard et al. (1994) found that tryptophan depletion had no effects in people with a history of panic disorder. These results have yet to be reconciled with the fact that serotonin agonists such as fluoxetine reduce the symptoms of panic disorder.

Functional imaging studies suggest that the cingulate, prefrontal, and anterior temporal cortices are involved in panic attack. Fischer et al. (1998) witnessed an unexpected panic attack in a subject while her regional cerebral blood flow was being measured by a PET scanner. They observed decreased activity in the right orbitofrontal cortex, anterior cingulate cortex, and anterior temporal cortex. Johanson et al. (1998) measured regional cerebral blood flow in women with severe spider phobias. He showed the women videos of spiders, which provoked panic attacks in half of the subjects. Those who panicked showed a decrease in the frontal cortex. Those who did not panic showed an *increase* in the frontal cortex. Johanson and his colleagues suggest that the increased frontal activity in those who managed to suppress their panic reflected brain mechanisms involved in control of fear. (All the subjects reported intense fear when they viewed the spider videos.) Bystritsky et al. (2001) found that when patients with panic disorder imagined situations that caused them anxiety, fMRI revealed increased activity in the inferior frontal cortex, cingulate cortex, and hippocampus.

Obsessive-Compulsive Disorder

Description

As the name implies, people with an **obsessive-compulsive disorder (OCD)** suffer from **obsessions**—thoughts that will not leave them—and **compulsions**—behaviors that they cannot keep from performing. Obsessions are seen in a variety of mental disorders, including schizophrenia. However, unlike schizophrenics, people with obsessive-compulsive disorder recognize that their thoughts and behaviors are senseless and desperately wish that they would go away. Compulsions often become more and more demanding until they interfere with people's careers and daily lives.

The incidence of obsessive-compulsive disorder is 1–2 percent. Females are slightly more likely than males to have this diagnosis. Like panic disorder, OCD most commonly begins in young adulthood (Robbins et al., 1984). Cross-cultural studies find that the symptoms of this disorder are similar in various racial and ethnic groups (Akhtar et al., 1975; Khanna and Channabasavanna, 1987; Hinjo et al., 1989). People with this disorder are unlikely to marry, perhaps because of the common obsessional fear of dirt and contamination or because of the shame associated with the rituals they are compelled to perform, which causes them to avoid social contacts (Turner, Beidel, and Nathan, 1985).

Most compulsions fall into one of four categories: *counting, checking, cleaning,* and *avoidance.* For example, people might repeatedly check burners on the stove to see that they are off and windows and locks to be sure that they are locked. Davison and Neale (1974) reported the case of a woman who washed her hands more than five hundred times a day because she feared being contaminated by germs. The hand washing persisted even when her hands became covered with painful sores. Other people meticulously clean their apartment or endlessly wash, dry, and fold their clothes. Some become afraid to leave home because they fear contamination, and they refuse to touch other members of their family. If they do accidentally become "contaminated," they usually have lengthy purification rituals. (See *Table 17.1.*)

Some investigators believe that the compulsive behaviors seen in OCD are forms of species-typical behaviors—for example, grooming, cleaning, and attention to sources of potential danger—that are released from normal control mechanisms by a brain dysfunction (Wise and Rapoport, 1988). Fiske and Haslam (1997) suggest that the behaviors seen in obsessive-compulsive disorder are simply pathological examples of a natural behavioral tendency to develop and practice social rituals. For example, people perform cultural rituals to mark transitions or changes in social status, to diagnose or treat illnesses, to restore relationships with deities, or to ensure the success of hunting or planting. These rituals define the status of individuals and their relationships with other members of the society, and they provide comfort in knowing that the structure of the society approves the transition or change in status or is doing all it can to avert misfortune. Consider the following scenario (from Fiske and Haslam, 1997):

> Imagine that you are traveling in an unfamiliar country. Going out for a walk, you observe a man dressed in red, standing on a red mat in a red-painted gateway. . . . He utters the same prayer six times. He brings out six basins of water and meticulously arranges them in a symmetrical configuration in front of the gateway. Then he washes his hands six times in each of the six basins, using precisely the same motions each time. As he does this, he repeats the same phrase, occasionally tapping his right finger on his earlobe. Through your interpreter, you ask him what he is doing. He replies that there are dangerous polluting substances in the ground, . . . [and that] he must purify himself or something terrible will happen. He seems eager to tell you about his concerns. (p. 211)

Why is the man acting this way? Is he a priest following a sacred ritual or does he have obsessive-compulsive disorder? Without knowing more about the spiritual rituals followed by the man's culture, we cannot say. Fiske and Haslam compared the features of OCD and other psychological disorders in descriptions of rituals, work, or other activities in fifty-two cultures. They found that the features of OCD (for example, observing lucky or unlucky numbers or colors with special significance, repeating activities, ordering or arranging things in specific configurations, or paying special attention to thresholds or entrances) were found in rituals in these cultures. The features of other psychological disorders were much less common. On the whole, the evidence suggests that the symptoms of obsessive-compulsive disorder represent an exaggeration of natural human tendencies.

Possible Causes

Evidence is beginning to accumulate suggesting that obsessive-compulsive disorder might have a genetic origin. So far, no properly controlled twin studies have studied people with a diagnosis of OCD, but several studies have found a greater concordance for obsessions and compulsions in monozygotic twins than in dizygotic twins (Hettema, Neale, and Kendler, 2001).

Family studies have found that OCD is associated with a neurological disorder that appears during childhood (Pauls and Leckman, 1986; Pauls et al., 1986). This dis-

---

obsessive-compulsive disorder (OCD) A mental disorder characterized by obsessions and compulsions.

obsession An unwanted thought or idea with which a person is preoccupied.

compulsion The feeling that one is obliged to perform a behavior, even if one prefers not to do so.

table **17.1**

Reported Obsessions and Compulsions of Child and Adolescent Patients

MAJOR PRESENTING SYMPTOMS	PERCENT REPORTING SYMPTOM AT INITIAL INTERVIEW
Obsession	
Concern or disgust with bodily wastes or secretions (urine, stool, saliva), dirt, germs, environmental toxins, etc.	43
Fear something terrible might happen (fire, death/illness of loved one, self, or others)	24
Concern or need for symmetry, order, or exactness	17
Scrupulosity (excessive praying or religious concerns out of keeping with patient's background)	13
Lucky/unlucky numbers	18
Forbidden or perverse sexual thoughts, images, or impulses	14
Intrusive nonsense sounds, words, or music	11
Compulsion	
Excessive or ritualized hand washing, showering, bathing, toothbrushing, or grooming	85
Repeating rituals (going in/out of door, up/down from chair, etc.)	51
Checking doors, locks, stove, appliances, car brakes, etc.	46
Cleaning and other rituals to remove contact with contaminants	23
Touching	20
Ordering/arranging	17
Measures to prevent harm to self or others (e.g., hanging clothes a certain way)	16
Counting	18
Hoarding/collecting	11
Miscellaneous rituals (e.g., licking, spitting, special dress pattern)	26

Source: Rapoport, J. L. *Journal of the American Medical Association,* 1988, *260,* 2888–2890.

order, **Tourette's syndrome,** is characterized by muscular and vocal tics: facial grimaces, squatting, pacing, twirling, barking, sniffing, coughing, grunting, or repeating specific words (especially vulgarities). Treatment for Tourette's syndrome includes antischizophrenic medications that block dopamine D2 receptors, such as haloperidol or pimozide; risperidone (an atypical antipsychotic medication); or clonidine, an α_2 agonist (Swerdlow, 2001).

Leonard et al. (1992b, 1992c) found that many patients with obsessive-compulsive disorder had tics and that many patients with Tourette's syndrome showed obsessions and compulsions. Grados et al. (2001) found a family association between OCD and tic disorders (a broad category that includes Tourette's syndrome). Both groups of investigators believe that the two disorders are produced by the same underlying genotype. It is not clear why some peo-

ple with this genotype gene develop Tourette's syndrome and others develop obsessive-compulsive disorder.

As with schizophrenia, not all cases of OCD have a genetic origin; the disorder sometimes occurs after brain damage caused by various means, such as birth trauma, encephalitis, and head trauma (Berthier et al., 1966; Hollander et al., 1990). In particular, the symptoms appear to be associated with damage to or dysfunction of the basal ganglia, cingulate gyrus, and prefrontal cortex (Giedd et al., 1995; Robinson et al., 1995).

Tourette's syndrome A neurological disorder characterized by tics and involuntary vocalizations and sometimes by compulsive uttering of obscenities and repetition of the utterances of others.

Frances, a 5½ year-old girl, was brought to at the outpatient psychiatric clinic at the U.S. National Institute of Mental Health after a sudden onset of tics and symptoms of obsessions and compulsions. Two months previously, she had developed a hypersensitivity to her clothing. Within a month, she would change her clothing five or more times each morning until it "felt right." Soon thereafter, she started exhibiting eye-rolling tics, followed by blinking, head-jerking, and nose-rubbing. Next, she showed obsessions and compulsions: she insisted on arranging her crayons in a particular order, became fearful of insects (which previously had fascinated her), and worried about contamination, especially with urine and feces. She developed compulsive counting, turning in circles while she counted to four, and would touch objects "until it felt right." She began saving uneaten food and food wrappers. Her eating rituals prolonged meals; more seriously, they interfered with eating so much that her weight decreased from 47 to 45 pounds over the course of a month—during a time when she should have been gaining weight. She also developed motor symptom: general clumsiness and uncoordinated running, jumping, and climbing.

Before her symptoms began, Frances had been intermittently ill for several months with what was diagnosed as a chronic viral infection. When a throat culture was finally taken, it was apparent that she had a group A β-hemolytic streptococcal infection and was immediately treated with the antibiotic amoxicillin. Within a few days her tics subsided, but her obsessions and compulsions continued. She developed another fever after finishing her course of amoxicillin, and her tics returned and became even more intense and frequent. Another course of amoxicillin reduced the tics but not the symptoms of OCD.

Frances was eventually given a course of treatment with intravenous immunoglobulin (antibody) to counteract the effects of the streptoccus bacterium and its toxic products. Within two months, her OCD symptoms were gone, and her tics were mild. Over the next year or so, she had recurrent infections and exacerbations of her OCD symptoms, which were treated with antibiotics and immunoglobulin. Each time her symptoms decreased but did not disappear. At the time her case was written for publication, her tics were improved by 90 percent, and her OCD symptoms were reduced by 70 percent (Perlmutter et al., 1998).

As the case of Frances illustrates, tic disorders (including OCD) can be caused by a group A β-hemolytic streptococcal infection. This infection can trigger several autoimmune diseases, in which the patient's immune system attacks and damages certain tissues of the body, including the valves of the heart, the kidneys, and—in this case—parts of the brain. Figure 17.3 shows the parallel course of Frances's symptoms and the level of antistreptococcal DNA-B in her blood (indicating the presence of

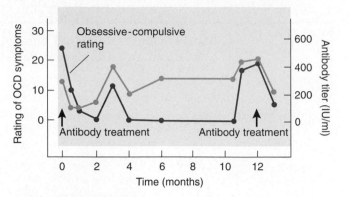

figure 17.3

The parallel course of Frances's symptoms and the level of antistreptococcal DNA-B in her blood, which indicates the presence of an active infection. This relation provides evidence that a group A β-hemolytic streptococcal infection can produce tics and the symptoms of OCD, presumably by affecting the basal ganglia.

(Adapted from Perlmutter, S. J., Garvey, M. A., Castellanos, X., Mittleman, B. B., Giedd, J., Rapoport, J. L., and Swedo, S. E. *American Journal of Psychiatry*, 1998, *155*, 1592–1598.)

an active infection). (See ***Figure 17.3***.) The symptoms of OCD appear to be produced by damage to the basal ganglia. Bodner, Morshed, and Peterson (2001) report the case of a 25-year-old man whose untreated sore throat (he lived in a religious group that prohibited antibiotics) developed into an autoimmune disease that produced obsessions and compulsions. The investigators found antibodies to type A β-hemolytic streptococcus, and MRI scans indicated abnormalities in the basal ganglia.

Several studies using PET scans have found evidence of increased activity in the frontal lobes and caudate nucleus in patients with OCD. A review by Saxena et al. (1998) reported on six PET studies. Five studies found increased activity in the orbitofrontal cortex, two studies found increased activity in the cingulate cortex, and two studies found increased activity in the caudate nucleus. Saxena and his colleagues also reported on several studies that measured regional brain activity of OCD patients before and after successful treatment with drugs or behavior therapy. In general, the improvement in a patient's symptoms was correlated with a reduction in the activity of the caudate nucleus and orbitofrontal cortex. The fact that behavior therapy and drug therapy produced similar results is especially remarkable: It indicates that very different procedures may be bringing about physiological changes that alleviate a serious mental disorder.

Breiter et al. (1996) performed a particularly intriguing study with a group of patients with obsessive-compulsive disorder. They used functional MRI to measure their subjects' regional cerebral metabolism before and after having them hold some "contaminated" items. These items included tissue soaked in toilet water, plastic bags from contaminated waste barrels, and tissues into which someone had blown his nose. They also gave them some innocuous stimuli, including tissue soaked in clean water and new plastic bags. In fact, *all* the items the experimenters actually put in the subjects' hands were clean, but the switch was made out of the subjects' sight, so they believed that they were handling some items that were contaminated. Apparently, the act was convincing, because the subjects were quite disturbed by the "contaminated" objects. When the subjects were holding the "contaminated" items, the anterior cingulate cortex, the basal ganglia, the amygdala, and several regions of the prefrontal cortex (including the orbitofrontal cortex) showed increased activity. (You might be wondering how the experimenters induced the subjects to hold the "contaminated" items. I did, too, but the authors did not explain their methods of persuasion.)

As we saw in Chapter 11, the prefrontal cortex (particularly the orbitofrontal cortex) and the cingulate cortex are involved in emotional reactions, so it is not surprising to learn that they might be implicated in OCD. In fact, some patients with severe OCD have been successfully treated with **cingulotomy**—surgical destruction of specific fiber bundles in the subcortical frontal lobe, including the cingulum bundle (which connects the prefrontal and cingulate cortex with the limbic cortex of the temporal lobe) and a region that contains fibers that connect the basal ganglia with the prefrontal cortex (Ballantine et al., 1987; Mindus, Rasmussen, and Lindquist, 1994). These operations, which are performed only when a patient has serious obsessive and compulsive symptoms that do not respond to behavior therapy or drugs, have a reasonably good success rate. Baer et al. (1995) studied patients whose cingulum bundles were destroyed through MRI-guided stereotaxic surgery destruction and found that 27 percent showed definite improvement, 27 percent showed probably improvement, and 46 percent showed no improvement. Dougherty et al. (2002) reported similar statistics: 32 percent definite improvement, 14 percent partial improvement, and 54 percent unchanged. Sachdev and Hay (1995) found that patients who received neurosurgery for OCD using modern methods were very unlikely to show negative personality changes. Of course, neurosurgery cannot be undone, so such procedures must be considered only as a last resort.

In one extraordinary case a patient performed his own psychosurgery. Solyom, Turnbull, and Wilensky (1987) reported the case of a young man with a serious obsessive-compulsive disorder whose ritual hand washing and other behaviors made it impossible for him to continue his schooling or lead a normal life. Finding that his life was no longer worthwhile, he decided to end it. He placed the muzzle of a .22-caliber rifle in his mouth and pulled the trigger. The bullet entered the base of the brain and damaged the frontal lobes. He survived, and he was amazed to find that his compulsions were gone. Fortunately, the damage did not disrupt his ability to make or execute plans; he went back to school and completed his education and now has a job. His IQ was unchanged. Ordinary surgery would have been less hazardous and messy, but it could hardly have been more successful.

As we saw in Chapters 8 and 14, the caudate nucleus and putamen receive information from the cerebral cortex. As this information is processed by the basal ganglia, it flows through two pathways before it passes to the thalamus and is sent back to the cortex. The *direct pathway* is excitatory, and the *indirect pathway* is inhibitory. (Refer to *Figure 8.17*.) Saxena et al. (1998) suggest that the symptoms of OCD may be a result of overactivity of the direct pathway. They propose that one of the functions of this pathway is control of previously learned behavior sequences that have become automatic so that they can be executed rapidly. The orbitofrontal cortex, which is involved in recognizing situations that have personal significance, can activate this pathway and the behaviors that it controls. The inhibitory indirect pathway is involved in suppressing these automatic behaviors, permitting the person to switch to other, more adaptive behaviors. Thus, obsessive-compulsive behavior could be a result of an imbalance between the direct and indirect pathways.

By far the most effective treatment of OCD is drug therapy. To date, three effective drugs have been found: clomipramine, fluoxetine, and fluvoxamine. Although these drugs are also effective antidepressants, their antidepressant action does not seem to be related to their ability to relieve the symptoms of OCD. For example, Leonard et al. (1989) compared the effects of clomipramine and desipramine (an antidepressant drug that inhibits the reuptake of norepinephrine but not serotonin) on the symptoms of children and adolescents with severe obsessive-compulsive disorder. For three weeks, all patients received a placebo. Then for five weeks half of them received clomipramine (CMI) and the other half received desipramine (DMI), on a double-blind basis. At the end of that time the drugs were switched. As Figure 17.4 shows, CMI was a much more effective drug; in fact, when the patients were switched from CMI to DMI, their symptoms got worse. (See *Figure 17.4*.)

---

cingulotomy The surgical destruction of the cingulum bundle, which connects the prefrontal cortex with the limbic system; helps to reduce intense anxiety and the symptoms of obsessive-compulsive disorder.

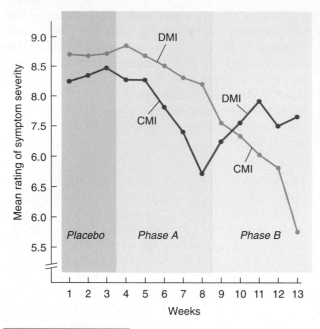

figure 17.4

Mean rating of symptom severity of patients with obsessive-compulsive disorder treated with desipramine (DMI) or clomipramine (CMI).

(From Leonard, H. L., Swedo, S. E., Rapoport, J. L., Koby, E. V., Lenane, M. C., Cheslow, D. L., and Hamburger, S. D. *Archives of General Psychiatry,* 1989, *46,* 1088–1092. Copyright 1989, American Medical Association.)

All of the effective antiobsessional drugs are specific blockers of 5-HT reuptake; thus, they are specific serotonergic agonists. When patients are given a serotonin *antagonist,* their symptoms get worse (Hollander et al., 1992). However, Barr et al. (1994) found that tryptophan depletion did not increase the symptoms of OCD, even though the treatment reduced the level of plasma tryptophan by 84 percent. In general, serotonin has an inhibitory effect on species-typical behaviors, which has tempted several investigators to speculate that these drugs alleviate the symptoms of obsessive-compulsive disorder by reducing the strength of the washing, cleaning, and danger avoidance behaviors that may underlie this disorder. Brain regions that have been implicated in OCD, including the orbitofrontal cortex and the basal ganglia, receive input from serotonergic terminals (Lavoie and Parent, 1990; El Mansari and Blier, 1997).

The importance of serotonergic activity in inhibiting compulsive behaviors is underscored by three interesting compulsions: trichotillomania, onychophagia, and acral lick dermatitis. *Trichotillomania* is compulsive hair pulling. People with this disorder (almost always females) often spend hours each night pulling hairs out one by one, sometimes eating them (Rapoport, 1991). *Onychophagia* is compulsive nail biting, which in its extreme can cause severe

damage to the ends of the fingers. (For those who are sufficiently agile, toenail biting is not uncommon.) Double-blind studies have shown that both of these disorders can be treated successfully by clomipramine, the drug of choice for obsessive-compulsive disorder (Leonard et al., 1992a).

Acral lick dermatitis is a disease of dogs, not humans. Some dogs will continuously lick at a part of their body, especially their wrist or ankle (called the *carpus* and the *hock*). The licking removes the hair and often erodes away the skin as well. The disorder seems to be genetic; it is seen almost exclusively in large breeds such as Great Danes, Labrador retrievers, and German shepherds, and it runs in families. A double-blind study found that clomipramine reduces this compulsive behavior (Rapoport, Ryland, and Kriete, 1992). At first, when I read the term "double-blind" in the report by Rapoport and her colleagues, I was amused to think that the investigators were careful not to let the dogs learn whether they were receiving clomipramine or a placebo. Then I realized that, of course, it was the dogs' owners who had to be kept in the dark.

Anxiety Disorders

The anxiety disorders severely disrupt some people's lives. Panic disorder is approximately 2.5 times more frequent in females than in males. People with panic disorder periodically have panic attacks, during which they experience intense symptoms of autonomic activity and often feel as if they are going to die. Frequently, panic attacks lead to the development of agoraphobia, an avoidance of being away from a safe place, such as home. Family and twin studies have shown that panic disorder is at least partly heritable, which suggests that it has biological causes. An association between joint hypermobility syndrome ("double-jointedness") and panic disorder and panic disorder may involve a region of chromosome 15.

Panic attacks can be triggered in many susceptible people by conditions that activate the autonomic nervous system, such as an caffeine, yohimbine, injection of lactate, or inhalation of air containing an elevated amount of carbon dioxide. Panic attacks can be alleviated by the administration of a benzodiazepine, a finding that suggests that the disorder may involve decreased numbers of benzodiazepine receptors or an inadequate secretion of an endogenous benzodiazepine agonist. A benzodiazepine antagonist can trigger a panic attack, and a study found evidence for a reduction of $GABA_A$ receptors in the brains of people with panic disorder. Nowadays, the first choice of medical treatment for panic attacks is a serotonergic agonist such as Prozac. Functional imaging studies suggest that the prefrontal, cingulate, and anterior temporal cortices are involved in panic attacks.

Obsessive-compulsive disorder (OCD) is characterized by obsessions—unwanted thoughts—and compulsions—uncontrollable behaviors, especially those involving cleanliness and attention to danger. Some investigators believe that these behaviors represent overactivity of species-typical behavioral tendencies.

OCD has a heritable basis and is related to Tourette's syndrome, a neurological disorder characterized by tics and strange verbalizations. It can also be caused by brain damage at birth, encephalitis, and head injuries, especially when the basal ganglia are involved. A type A β-hemolytic streptococcus infection can stimulate an autoimmune attack—presumably on the basal ganglia—that produces the symptoms of OCD. Birth trauma, as well, can cause this disorder.

PET scans indicate that people with obsessive-compulsive disorder tend to show increased activity in the orbitofrontal cortex, cingulate cortex, and caudate nucleus. Drug treatment or behavior therapy that successfully reduces the symptoms of OCD generally reduces the activity of the orbitofrontal cortex and caudate nucleus. Cingulotomy, the destruction of the cingulum bundle, which links the prefrontal cortex and cingulate cortex with the anterior temporal lobe, reduces the symptoms of OCD, as do drugs such as clomipramine, which specifically block the reuptake of serotonin. Some investigators believe that clomipramine and related drugs alleviate the symptoms of OCD by increasing the activity of serotonergic pathways that play an inhibitory role on species-typical behaviors. Three other compulsions, hair pulling, nail biting, and (in dogs) acral lick syndrome, are also suppressed by clomipramine.

Autistic Disorder

Description

When a baby is born, the parents normally expect to love and cherish the child and to be loved and cherished in return. Unfortunately, approximately 4 in every 10,000 infants are born with a disorder that impairs their ability to return their parents' affection. The symptoms of **autistic disorder** include a failure to develop normal social relations with other people, impaired development of communicative ability, and lack of imaginative ability. The syndrome was named and characterized by Kanner (1943), who chose the term (*auto*, "self," *-ism*, "condition") to refer to the child's apparent self-absorption. The disorder afflicts boys three times more often than girls.

Infants with autistic disorder do not seem to care whether they are held, or they may arch their backs when picked up, as if they do not want to be held. They do not look or smile at their caregivers. If they are ill, hurt, or tired, they will not look to someone else for comfort. As they get older, they do not enter into social relationships with other children and avoid eye contact with them. Their language development is abnormal or even nonexistent. They often echo what is said to them, and they may refer to themselves

as others do—in the second or third person. For example, they may say, "You want some milk?" to mean "I want some milk." They may learn words and phrases by rote, but they fail to use them productively and creatively. Those who do acquire reasonably good language skills talk about their own preoccupations without regard for other people's interests. They usually interpret other people's speech literally. For example, when an autistic person is asked, "Can you pass the salt?," he might simply say "Yes"—and not because he is trying to be funny or sarcastic.

Autistic people generally show abnormal interests and behaviors. For example, they may show stereotyped movements, such as flapping their hand back and forth or rocking back and forth. They may become obsessed with investigating objects, sniffing them, feeling their texture, or moving them back and forth. They may become attached to a particular object and insist on carrying it around with them. They may become preoccupied in lining up objects or in forming patterns with them, oblivious to everything else that is going on around them. They often insist on following precise routines and may become violently upset when they are hindered from doing so. They show no make-believe play and are uninterested in stories that involve fantasy. Although most autistic people are mentally retarded, not all are; and unlike most retarded people, they may be physically adept and graceful. Some have isolated skills, such as the ability to multiply two four-digit numbers very quickly, without apparent effort.

Autistic disorder is one of several pervasive developmental disorders that have similar symptoms (Rapin, 1999). *Asperger's disorder* is generally less severe, and its symptoms do not include a delay in language development or the presence of important cognitive deficits. The primary symptoms are deficient or absent social interactions and repetitive and stereotyped behaviors and obsessional interest in narrow subjects. *Rett's disorder* is a genetic neurological syndrome seen in girls that accompanies an arrest of normal brain development that occurs during infancy. Children with *childhood disintegrative disorder* show normal intellectual and social development and then, sometime between the ages of 2 and 10 years, show a severe regression into autism. When autistic children with mental retardation reach puberty, many of them develop epileptic seizures, an occurrence that suggests that abnormal changes take place in the brain at this stage of development (Rapin, 1995). The prevalence of all forms of pervasive developmental disorders is 18.7 in 10,000 (Fombonne, 1999).

autistic disorder A chronic disorder whose symptoms include failure to develop normal social relations with other people, impaired development of communicative ability, lack of imaginative ability, and repetitive, stereotyped movements.

As you can see, autistic disorder includes affective, cognitive, and behavioral abnormalities. Frith, Morton, and Leslie (1991) suggest that the impaired socialization, communicative ability, and imagination that characterize autism stem from abnormalities in the brain that prevent the person from forming a "theory of mind." That is, the person is unable "to predict and explain the behavior of other humans in terms of their mental states" (p. 434). He or she just cannot see things from another person's point of view. As one autistic man complained, "Other people seem to have a special sense by which they can read other people's thoughts" (Rutter, 1983).

The lack of interest in or understanding of other people is reflected in the response of the autistic brain to the sight of the human face. As we saw in Chapter 6, the *fusiform face area,* located on the fusiform gyrus, a region of visual association cortex on the base of the brain, is involved in the recognition of individual faces. A functional imaging study by Pierce et al. (2001) found little or no activity in the fusiform face area of autistic adults looking at pictures of human faces. In contrast, this region showed the greatest increase of all brain regions of control subjects performing the same task. (See *Figure 17.5.*) As Pierce and her colleagues note, autistics are poor at recognizing facial expressions of emotion or the direction of another person's gaze and have low rates of eye contact with other people. It seems likely that the fusiform face area of autistics fails to respond to the sight of the human face because these people spend very little time studying other people's faces and hence do not develop the expertise the rest of us acquire through normal interpersonal interactions.

Of course, a lack of interest in other people or an understanding of what they are thinking does not account for all the symptoms of autism. For example, it does not explain why autistic children engage in stereotyped behaviors and seem to have a need for sameness in their environment. Nor does it explain the high rate of mental retardation. But it does suggest that a careful analysis of the syndrome may yield some hints about the underlying brain functions that are disrupted.

Possible Causes

When Kanner first described autism, he suggested that it was of biological origin; but not long afterward, influential clinicians argued that autism was learned. More precisely, it was taught—by cold, insensitive, distant, demanding, introverted parents. Bettelheim (1967) believed that autism was similar to the apathetic, withdrawn, and hopeless behavior seen in some of the survivors of the German concentration camps of World War II. You can imagine the guilt felt by parents who were told by a mental health professional that they were to blame for their child's pitiful condition. Some professionals saw the existence of autism as evidence for child abuse and advocated that autistic children be removed from their families and placed with foster parents.

Nowadays, researchers and mental health professionals are convinced that autism is caused by biological factors and that parents should be given help and sympathy, not blame. Careful studies have shown that the parents of autistic children are just as warm, sociable, and responsive as other parents (Cox et al., 1975). In addition, parents with one autistic child often raise one or more normal children. If the parents were at fault, we should expect *all* of their offspring to be autistic.

Heritability

Like all the mental disorders I have described so far, at least some forms of autism appear to be heritable. As we shall see, there appear to be *several* hereditary causes, as well as some nonhereditary ones. Between 2 and 3 percent of the siblings of people with autism are themselves autistic (Folstein and Piven, 1991; Bailey, 1993). That figure might seem low, but it is between 50 and 100 times the expected frequency of autism in the general population (4 cases per 10,000 people). As Jones and Szatmari (1988) note, many parents stop having children after an autistic child is born for fear of having another one with the same disorder; if they did not, the percentage of autistic siblings would be even larger.

The best evidence for genetic factors in autism comes from twin studies. These studies indicate that the concordance rate for monozygotic twins is approximately 70 percent, while the rate for dizygotic twins studied so far

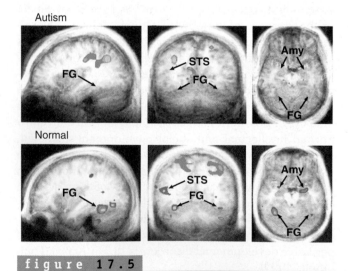

figure   1 7 . 5

Responses of the fusiform face area in normal and autistic adults looking at pictures of human faces. This region received very little activation in the autistic subjects, but in every normal subject this region was the most active one in the brain. FG = fusiform gyrus, STS = superior temporal sulcus, Amy = amygdala.

(From Pierce, K., Müller, R.-A., Ambrose, J., Allen, G., and Courchesne, E. *Brain,* 2001, *124,* 2059–2073.)

is 0 percent (Folstein and Rosen-Scheidley, 2001). In addition, most of the nonautistic members of discordant monozygotic twins exhibited deficient language development and showed signs of social withdrawal (Bailey et al., 1995). These results indicate that autism is highly heritable. Genetic investigations have suggested that genes involved in autistic disorder may be located on chromosomes 2, 7, 15, and X (Folstein and Rosen-Scheidley, 2001). Evidence obtained by Wassink et al. (2001) suggests that the *WNT2* gene, located on chromosome 7 and involved in development, may play a role in autism.

Investigators have suggested that autism is associated with some specific genetic disorders, such as phenylketonuria. **Phenylketonuria** (PKU) is caused by an inherited lack of an enzyme that converts phenylalanine (an amino acid) into tyrosine (another amino acid). Excessive amounts of phenylalanine in the blood interfere with the myelinization of neurons in the central nervous system, much of which takes place after birth. When PKU is diagnosed soon after birth, it can be treated by putting the infant on a low-phenylalanine diet. The diet keeps the blood level of phenylalanine low, and myelinization of the central nervous system takes place normally. However, if PKU is not diagnosed and an infant born with this disorder receives foods containing phenylalanine, the amino acid accumulates, and the brain fails to develop normally. The result is severe mental retardation—and in some cases autism (Lowe et al., 1980; Folstein and Rutter, 1988).

Brain Pathology

The fact that autism is highly heritable is presumptive evidence that the disorder is a result of structural or biochemical abnormalities in the brain. In addition, a variety of nongenetic pathological conditions—especially those that occur during prenatal development—can produce the symptoms of autism. Evidence suggests that approximately 20 percent of all cases of autism have definable biological causes, such as rubella (German measles) during pregnancy; prenatal thalidomide; encephalitis caused by the herpes virus; and tuberous sclerosis, a genetic disorder that causes the formation of benign tumors in many organs, including the brain (De Long, 1999; Rapin, 1999). Hollander et al. (1999) found evidence for an autoimmune process in some cases of autism. As we saw earlier in this chapter, tic disorders and obsessive-compulsive disorder can be produced by an autoimmune reaction provoked by a group A β-hemolytic streptococcal infection. Hollander and his colleagues found streptococcal antibodies in blood samples from 78 percent of the autistic patients but only

21 percent of the normal subjects. All these findings suggest that autistic disorder can result from a wide variety of factors that damage the brain or impair its development.

Studies by Miller and Strömland (1993) and Strömland et al. (1994) identified a drug that can increase the likelihood of autism. Thalidomide, a drug that was given to pregnant women in some countries during the 1960s to treat the symptoms of morning sickness, was later found to cause serious birth defects. Miller, Strömland, and their colleagues studied eighty-six people whose mothers had taken thalidomide during pregnancy and found that five of them were autistic. (This rate is 145 times higher than the rate of autism in the population as a whole.) All of the autistic people had been exposed to thalidomide between prenatal days 20 and 24. As Rodier et al. (1996) note, the only part of the central nervous system that forms at this time is the brain stem. They suggest that either genetic abnormalities or exposure of a developing embryo to toxic chemicals just after closure of the neural tube may be responsible for anomalies in brain development that are responsible for autism. By the way, studies have failed to find evidence that autism is linked to childhood immunization (Farrington, Miller, and Taylor, 2001; Andrews et al., 2002; Taylor et al., 2002).

Researchers have found evidence for structural abnormalities in the brains of autistics, but so far we cannot point to any single abnormality as the cause of the disorder. Courchesne et al. (2001) use structural MRI to study the brain development of autistic and normal boys. They found that although the average head size (and presumably the brain size) of the two groups was identical at birth, by ages 2–4 years the brains of children who became autistic were larger than normal. MRI scans showed increased growth of white matter in the cerebellum and gray and white matter in the cerebral hemispheres. The cerebellar gray matter grew more slowly than normal. One region of the cerebellum—the vermis, a structure located on the midline—was much smaller than normal. Bailey et al. (1998) studied the brains of six deceased autistics and found enlarged brain size in most cases, along with developmental abnormalities in the cortex, brain stem, and cerebellum. They found a 31 percent decrease in the number of Purkinje cells, the largest neurons found in the cerebellar cortex. The relationship between these abnormalities and the symptoms of autism is not yet understood.

---

phenylketonuria A hereditary disorder caused by the absence of an enzyme that converts the amino acid phenylalanine to tyrosine; causes brain damage unless a special diet is implemented soon after birth.

---

i n t e r i m
s u m m a r y

Autistic Disorder

Autistic disorder occurs in approximately 4 of 10,000 infants. It is characterized by poor or absent social relations, communicative abilities, and imaginative abilities and the presence of repetitive, purposeless movements. Although autistics are usually, but not always, retarded, they may have a particular, isolated talent. Autistic people tend not to pay attention to other people's faces, which is reflected in the lack of activation of the fusiform face area when they do so. Some investigators believe that the most important cognitive deficit is the inability to imagine what others know or think about something and how they feel.

In the past, clinicians blamed parents for autism, but now it is generally accepted as a disorder with biological roots. Twin studies have shown that autism is highly heritable but that several genes are responsible for its development. It can be caused by untreated phenylketonuria. Autism can also be caused by events that interfere with prenatal development, such as prenatal thalidomide or maternal infection with rubella. Evidence suggests that the most critical period occurs between the 20th and 24th days of gestation. Autism does not appear to be associated with childhood vaccinations. MRI studies indicate that although the brain size of babies who become autistic is normal at birth, their brains are larger than normal by ages 2–4 years. Parts of the brain, such as the vermis of the cerebellum, are much smaller than normal. Studies of the brains of deceased autistics have found abnormalities in the cortex, brain stem, and cerebellum.

Attention-Deficit/ Hyperactivity Disorder

Description

Some children have difficulty concentrating, remaining still, and working on a task. At one time or other, *most* children exhibit these characteristics. But children with **attention-deficit/hyperactivity disorder (ADHD)** display these symptoms so often that they interfere with the children's ability to learn. ADHD is the most common behavior disorder that shows itself in childhood. It is usually first discovered in the classroom, where children are expected to sit quietly and pay attention to the teacher or work steadily on a project. Some children's inability to meet these expectations then becomes evident. They have difficulty withholding a response, act without reflecting, often show reckless and impetuous behavior, and let interfering activities intrude into ongoing tasks.

According to the DSM-IV, the diagnosis of ADHD requires the presence of six or more of nine symptoms of inattention and six or more of nine symptoms of hyperactivity and impulsivity that have persisted for at least six months. Symptoms of inattention include such things as "often had difficulty sustaining attention in tasks of play activities" or "is often easily distracted by extraneous stimuli"; and symptoms of hyperactivity and impulsivity include such things as "often runs about or climbs excessively in situations in which it is inappropriate" or "often

interrupts or intrudes on others (e.g., butts into conversations or games)" (American Psychiatric Association, 1994, pp. 64–65).

ADHD can be very disruptive of a child's education and that of other children in the same classroom. (See Wilens, Biederman, and Spencer, 2002, for a review.) It is seen in 4–5 percent of grade school children. Boys are about ten times more likely than girls to receive a diagnosis of ADHD, but in adulthood the ratio is approximately 2 to 1, which suggests that many girls with this disorder fail to be diagnosed. Because the symptoms can vary—some children's symptoms are primarily those of inattention, some are those of hyperactivity, and some show mixed symptoms—most investigators believe that this disorder has more than one cause. Diagnosis is often difficult, because the symptoms are not well defined. ADHD is often associated with aggression, conduct disorder, learning disabilities, depression, anxiety, and low self-esteem. Approximately 60 percent of children with ADHD continue to display symptoms of this disorder into adulthood, at which time a disproportionate number develop antisocial personality disorder and substance abuse disorder (Ernst et al., 1998). Adults with ADHD are also more likely to show cognitive impairments and lower occupational attainment than would be predicted by their education (Seidman et al., 1998). The most common treatment for ADHD is administration of methylphenidate (Ritalin), a drug that inhibits the reuptake of dopamine. Amphetamine, another dopamine agonist, also reduces the symptoms of ADHD, but this drug is used much less often.

Possible Causes

There is strong evidence from both family studies and twin studies for hereditary factors in a person's likelihood of developing ADHD (Faraone and Biederman, 1994; Levy et al., 1997). In their twin study, Levy and her colleagues conclude that "ADHD is best viewed as the extreme of a behavior that varies genetically throughout the entire population rather than as a disorder with discrete determinants" (p. 737).

According to Sagvolden and Sergeant (1998), the impulsive and hyperactive behaviors that are seen in children with ADHD are the result of a *delay of reinforcement gradient* that is steeper than normal. As we saw in Chapter 13, the occurrence of an appetitive stimulus can reinforce the behavior that just preceded it. For example, a piece of food can reinforce the lever press that a rat just

---

attention-deficit/hyperactivity disorder (ADHD) A disorder characterized by uninhibited responses, lack of sustained attention, and hyperactivity; first shows itself in childhood.

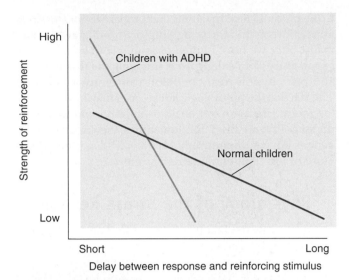

figure 17.6

Different delay of reinforcement gradients, hypothesized by Sagvolden and Sergeant (1998) to be responsible for the impulsive behavior of children with ADHD.

made, and a smile can reinforce a person's attempts at conversation. Reinforcing stimuli are most effective if they immediately follow a behavior: The longer the delay, the less effective the reinforcement. Sagvolden and Sergeant suggest that some physiological differences in the brains of children with ADHD increase the steepness of their delay of reinforcement gradient, which means that immediate reinforcement is even more effective in these children, but even slightly delayed reinforcement loses its potency. (See *Figure 17.6*.)

Why would a steeper delay of reinforcement gradient produce the symptoms of ADHD? According to Sagvolden and Sergeant, for people with a steep gradient, reinforcement with a short delay will be even more effective, thus producing overactivity. On the other hand, these people will be less likely to engage in behaviors that are followed by delayed reinforcement, as many of our behaviors (especially classroom activities) are. In support of this hypothesis, Sagvolden et al. (1998) trained normal boys and boys with ADHD on an instrumental conditioning task. When a signal was present, responses would be reinforced every 30 seconds with coins or trinkets. When the signal was not present, responses were never reinforced. The normal boys learned to respond only when the signal was present. When the signal was off, they waited patiently until it came on again. In contrast, the boys with ADHD showed impulsive behavior—intermittent bursts of rapid responses whether the signal was present or not. According to the investigators, this pattern of responding was what would be expected by a steep delay of reinforcement gradient.

As we saw in Chapter 16, the fact that dopamine antagonists were discovered to reduce the positive symptoms of schizophrenia suggested the hypothesis that schizophrenia is caused by overactivity of dopaminergic transmission. Similarly, the fact that methylphenidate, a dopamine *agonist,* alleviates the symptoms of ADHD has suggested the hypothesis that this disorder is caused by *underactivity* of dopaminergic transmission. As we saw in Chapter 13, the mesolimbic dopaminergic pathway plays a critical role in reinforcement, so the suggestion that abnormalities in dopaminergic transmission play a role in ADHD seem reasonable.

Some researchers (including Sagvolden and his colleagues) suggest that the abnormality is exactly at the location where methylphenidate works: the dopamine transporters. Dopamine transporters are located in the presynaptic membrane of dopaminergic terminals and are responsible for the reuptake of dopamine that terminates transmission at these synapses. Methylphenidate decreases reuptake at dopaminergic synapses by blocking dopamine transporters.

PET studies of dopamine transporters in the brains of children and adults with ADHD have been mixed. Some studies (Doherty et al., 1999; Dresel et al., 2000; Krause et al., 2000) found evidence for increased numbers of dopamine transporters and a reduction in their number after the administration of methylphenidate. However, a study by van Dyck et al. (2002) found no differences in the numbers of dopamine transporters in the brain of people with ADHD.

If an increase in numbers of dopamine transporters is responsible for ADHD, we would expect animals with a decreased number of these transporters to be hypoactive. However, Zhuang et al. (2001) created genetically modified mice with a *knock-down* of the gene for the dopamine transporter. Rather than abolishing dopamine transporters, the knock-down reduced their number by 90 percent. As far as the investigators could tell, the mice developed normally, and their activity level was normal in their home environment. However, when they were put into a novel environment, they became hyperactive, and their ability to inhibit responses was impaired. Administration of dopamine agonists such as amphetamine brought their activity levels back to normal. These results seem to contradict the hypothesis that an excessive number of dopamine transporters is responsible for the symptoms of ADHD.

Studies of brain structure of people with ADHD do not reveal any localized abnormalities, though the total volume of their brains is approximately 4 percent smaller than normal (Castellanos et al., 2002). However, a special functional imaging method that estimates the blood volume in various regions of the brain revealed decreased blood volumes in the basal ganglia and cerebellar vermis of boys with ADHD (Teicher et al., 2000; Anderson et al., 2002).

i n t e r i m
s u m m a r y

Attention-Deficit/Hyperactivity Disorder

Attention-deficit/hyperactivity disorder is the most common behavior disorder that first appears in childhood. Children with ADHD show symptoms of inattention, hyperactivity, and impulsivity. This disorder is seen in 4–5 percent of grade school children and is more frequent in boys. The symptoms of about 60 percent of children with ADHD continue into adulthood, and the disorder is associated with antisocial personality disorder and substance abuse disorder. The most common medical treatment is methylphenidate, a dopamine agonist.

Family and twin studies indicate a heritable component in this disorder. Evidence suggests that a steeper delay of reinforcement gradient, perhaps caused by an increased number of dopamine transporters, may account for impulsiveness and hyperactivity. Some PET studies of dopamine transporters have found increased numbers of dopamine transporters, but one study found no differences. This explanation must be reconciled with the finding that a genetic manipulation that results in decreased numbers of dopamine transporters in mice causes hyperactivity, which is reduced by administration of dopamine agonists.

The brains of people with ADHD are approximately 4 percent smaller than normal, and functional imaging indicates a decreased blood volume in the basal ganglia and cerebellar vermis.

Stress Disorders

Aversive stimuli can harm people's health. Many of these harmful effects are produced not by the stimuli themselves but by our reactions to them. Walter Cannon, the physiologist who criticized the James-Lange theory described in Chapter 11, introduced the term **stress** to refer to the physiological reaction caused by the perception of aversive or threatening situations.

The word *stress* was borrowed from engineering, in which it refers to the action of physical forces of mechanical structures. The word can be a noun or a verb; and the noun can refer to situations or the individual's response to them. Because of this potential confusion, I will refer to "stressful" stimuli and situations as **stressors** and to the individual's reaction as a **stress response.** The word *stress* will refer to the general process (as in the title to this section).

The physiological responses that accompany the negative emotions prepare us to threaten rivals or fight them or to run away from dangerous situations. Walter Cannon introduced the phrase **fight-or-flight response** to refer to the physiological reactions that prepare us for the strenuous efforts required by fighting or running away. Normally, once we have bluffed or fought with an adversary or run away from a dangerous situation, the threat is over and our physiological condition can return to normal. The fact that the physiological responses may have adverse long-term effects on our health is unimportant as long as the responses are brief. But sometimes, the threatening situations are continuous rather than episodic, producing a more or less continuous stress response.

Physiology of the Stress Response

As we saw in Chapter 11, emotions consist of behavioral, autonomic, and endocrine responses. The latter two components, the autonomic and endocrine responses, are the ones that can have adverse effects on health. (Well, I guess the behavioral components can too, if a person rashly gets into a fight with someone who is much bigger and stronger.) Because threatening situations generally call for vigorous activity, the autonomic and endocrine responses that accompany them are catabolic; that is, they help to mobilize the body's energy resources. The sympathetic branch of the autonomic nervous system is active, and the adrenal glands secrete epinephrine, norepinephrine, and steroid stress hormones. Because the effects of sympathetic activity are similar to those of the adrenal hormones, I will limit my discussion to the hormonal responses.

Epinephrine affects glucose metabolism, causing the nutrients stored in muscles to become available to provide energy for strenuous exercise. Along with norepinephrine, the hormone also increases blood flow to the muscles by increasing the output of the heart. In doing so, it also increases blood pressure, which, over the long term, contributes to cardiovascular disease.

Besides serving as a stress hormone, norepinephrine is (as you know) secreted in the brain as a neurotransmitter. Some of the behavioral and physiological responses produced by aversive stimuli appear to be mediated by noradrenergic neurons. For example, microdialysis studies have found that stressful situations increase the release

stress A general, imprecise term that can refer either to a stress response or to a stressor (stressful situation).

stressor A stimulus (or situation) that produces a stress response.

stress response A physiological reaction caused by the perception of aversive or threatening situations.

fight-or-flight response A species-typical response preparatory to fighting or fleeing; thought to be responsible for some of the deleterious effects of stressful situations on health.

of norepinephrine in the hypothalamus, frontal cortex, and lateral basal forebrain (Yokoo, et al. 1990; Cenci et al., 1992). Montero, Fuentes, and Fernandez-Tome (1990) found that destruction of the noradrenergic axons that ascend from the brain stem to the forebrain prevented the rise in blood pressure that is normally produced by social isolation stress. Presumably, the release of norepinephrine in the brain is produced by a pathway from the central nucleus of the amygdala to the norepinephrine-secreting regions of the brain stem (Van Bockstaele et al., 2001).

The other stress-related hormone is *cortisol,* a steroid secreted by the adrenal cortex. Cortisol is called a **glucocorticoid** because it has profound effects on glucose metabolism. In addition, glucocorticoids help to break down protein and convert it to glucose, help to make fats available for energy, increase blood flow, and stimulate behavioral responsiveness, presumably by affecting the brain. They decrease the sensitivity of the gonads to luteinizing hormone (LH), which suppresses the secretion of the sex steroid hormones. In fact, Singer and Zumoff (1992) found that the blood level of testosterone in male hospital residents (doctors, not patients) was severely depressed, presumably because of the stressful work schedule they were obliged to follow. Glucocorticoids have other physiological effects, too, some of which are only poorly understood. Almost every cell in the body contains glucocorticoid receptors, which means that few of them are unaffected by these hormones.

The secretion of glucocorticoids is controlled by neurons in the paraventricular nucleus of the hypothalamus (PVN), whose axons terminate in the median eminence, where the hypothalamic capillaries of the portal blood supply to the anterior pituitary gland are located. (The pituitary portal blood supply was described in Chapter 3.) The neurons of the PVN secrete a peptide called **corticotropin-releasing hormone (CRH),** which stimulates the anterior pituitary gland to secrete **adrenocorticotropic hormone (ACTH).** ACTH enters the general circulation and stimulates the adrenal cortex to secrete glucocorticoids. (See *Figure 17.7.*)

CRH is also secreted within the brain, where it serves as a neuromodulator/neurotransmitter, especially in regions of the limbic system that are involved in emotional responses, such as the periaqueductal gray matter, the locus coeruleus, and the central nucleus of the amygdala. The behavioral effects produced by an injection of CRH into the brain are similar to those produced by aversive situations; thus, some elements of the stress response appear to be produced by the release of CRH by neurons in the brain. For example, intracerebroventricular injection of CRH decreases the amount of time a rat spends in the center of a large open chamber (Britton et al., 1982), enhances the acquisition of a classically conditioned fear response (Cole and Koob, 1988), and increases

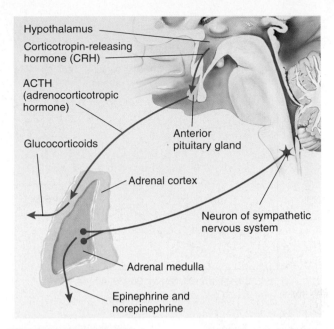

Hypothalamus

Corticotropin-releasing hormone (CRH)

ACTH (adrenocorticotropic hormone)

Glucocorticoids

Anterior pituitary gland

Adrenal cortex

Neuron of sympathetic nervous system

Adrenal medulla

Epinephrine and norepinephrine

figure   17.7

Control of the secretion of glucocorticoids by the adrenal cortex and of catecholamines by the adrenal medulla.

the startle response elicited by a sudden loud noise (Swerdlow et al., 1986). On the other hand, intracerebroventricular injection of a CRH antagonist *reduces* the anxiety caused by a variety of stressful situations (Kalin, Sherman, and Takahaski, 1988; Heinrichs, et al., 1994; Skutella et al., 1994).

The secretion of glucocorticoids does more than help an animal react to a stressful situation: It helps the animal to survive. If a rat's adrenal glands are removed, the rat becomes much more susceptible to the effects of stress. In fact, a stressful situation that a normal rat would take in its stride might kill one whose adrenal glands have been removed. And physicians know that if an adrenalectomized human is subjected to stressors, he or she must be given additional amounts of glucocorticoid (Tyrell and Baxter, 1981).

glucocorticoid One of a group of hormones of the adrenal cortex that are important in protein and carbohydrate metabolism, secreted especially in times of stress.

corticotropin-releasing hormone (CRH) A hypothalamic hormone that stimulates the anterior pituitary gland to secrete ACTH (adrenocorticotropic hormone).

adrenocorticotropic hormone (ACTH) A hormone released by the anterior pituitary gland in response to CRH; stimulates the adrenal cortex to produce glucocorticoids.

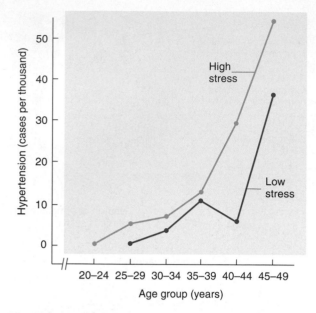

figure 17.8

Incidence of hypertension in various age groups of air traffic controllers at high-stress and low-stress airports. (Based on data from Cobb and Rose, 1973.)

Health Effects of Long-Term Stress

Many studies of humans who have been subjected to stressful situations have found evidence of ill health. For example, survivors of concentration camps, who were obviously subjected to long-term stress, have generally poorer health later in life than other people of the same age (Cohen, 1953). Drivers of subway trains that injure or kill people are more likely to suffer from illnesses several months later (Theorell et al., 1992). Air traffic controllers, especially those who work at busy airports where the danger of collisions is greatest, show a greater incidence of high blood pressure, which gets worse as they grow older (Cobb and Rose, 1973). (See *Figure 17.8.*) They also are more likely to suffer from ulcers or diabetes.

A pioneer in the study of stress, Hans Selye, suggested that most of the harmful effects of stress were produced by the prolonged secretion of glucocorticoids (Selye, 1976). Although the short-term effects of glucocorticoids are essential, the long-term effects are damaging. These effects include increased blood pressure, damage to muscle tissue, steroid diabetes, infertility, inhibition of growth, inhibition of the inflammatory responses, and suppression of the immune system. High blood pressure can lead to heart attacks and stroke. Inhibition of growth in children who are subjected to prolonged stress prevents them from attaining their full height. Inhibition of the inflammatory response makes it more difficult for the body to heal itself after an injury, and suppression of the immune system makes an individual vulnerable to infections. Long-term administration of steroids to treat inflammatory diseases

often produces cognitive deficits and can even lead to *steroid psychosis,* whose symptoms include profound distractibility, anxiety, insomnia, depression, hallucinations, and delusions (Lewis and Smith, 1983).

The adverse effects of stress on healing were demonstrated in a study by Kiecolt-Glaser et al. (1995), who performed punch biopsy wounds in the subjects' forearms, a harmless procedure that is used often in medical research. The subjects were people who were providing long-term care for relatives with Alzheimer's disease—a situation that is known to cause stress—and control subjects of the same approximate age and family income. The investigators found that healing of the wounds took significantly longer in the caregivers (48.7 days versus 39.3 days). (See *Figure 17.9.*)

Sapolsky and his colleagues have investigated one rather serious long-term effect of stress: brain damage. As you learned in Chapter 14, the hippocampal formation plays a crucial role in learning and memory, and evidence suggests that one of the causes of memory loss that occurs with aging is degeneration of this brain structure. Research with animals has shown that long-term exposure to glucocorticoids destroys neurons located in field CA1 of the hippocampal formation. The hormone appears to destroy the neurons by decreasing the entry of glucose and decreasing the reuptake of glutamate (Sapolsky, 1992, 1995; McEwen and Sapolsky, 1995). Both of these effects make neurons more susceptible to potentially harmful events, such as decreased blood flow, which often occurs as a result of the aging process. The increased amounts of extra-

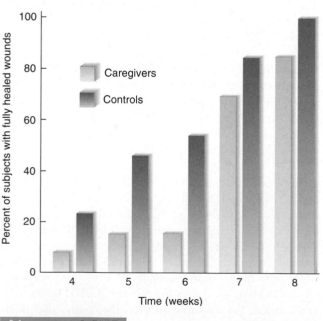

figure 17.9

Percentage of caregivers and control subjects whose wounds had healed as a function of time after the biopsy was performed.

(Adapted from Kiecolt-Glaser, J. K., Marucha, P. T., Malarkey, W. B., Mercado, A. M., and Glaser, R. *Lancet,* 1995, *346,* 1194–1196.)

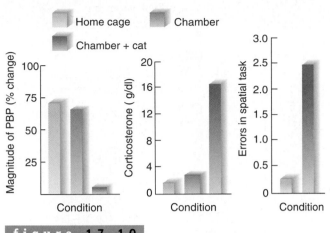

figure   17.10

Effects of acute stress caused by exposing a rat to the sight and smell of a cat. The stress raised the glucocorticoid level (corticosterone, in the case of a rat), impaired the development of primed-burst potentiation (a form of long-term potentiation) in slices taken from these animals, and interfered with learning of a spatial task that requires the hippocampus.

(Adapted from Diamond, D. M., Park, C. R., Heman, K. L., and Rose, G. M. *Hippocampus,* 1999, *9,* 542–552, and Mesches, M. H., Fleshner, M., Heman, K. L., Rose, G. M., and Diamond, D. M. *Journal of Neuroscience,* 1999, *19,* RC18(1–5).)

cellular glutamate permit calcium to enter through NMDA receptors. (You will recall that the entry of excessive amounts of calcium can kill neurons.) Perhaps, then, the stressors to which people are subjected throughout their lives increase the likelihood of memory problems as they grow older. In fact, Lupien et al. (1996) found that elderly people with elevated blood levels of glucocorticoids learned a maze more slowly than did those with normal levels.

Even acute exposure to stress can have adverse effects on normal brain functioning. Diamond and his colleagues (Diamond et al., 1999; Mesches et al., 1999) placed rats individually in a Plexiglas box and then placed the box in a cage with a cat for 75 minutes. Although the cat could not harm the rats, the cat's presence (and odor) clearly alarmed the rats and elicited a stress response; the stressed rats' blood glucocorticoid increased to approximately five times its normal level. The investigators found that this short-term stress affected the functioning of the animals' hippocampus. The stressed rats' ability to learn a spatial task (which requires the hippocampus) was impaired, and primed-burst potentiation (a form of long-term potentiation) was impaired in hippocampal slices taken from stressed rats. (See *Figure 17.10.*)

Not all of the effects of short-term stress on hippocampal memory functions are mediated by increased glucocorticoid secretion. Kim et al. (2001) found that lesions of the amygdala abolished the effects of stress on rats' performance in the Morris water maze. (As we saw in Chapter 14, animals with impaired hippocampal func-

tion do poorly on this task.) Kim and his colleagues found that rats that were exposed to restraint and tail shock stress showed deficits in learning the Morris task unless their amygdalas were damaged, in which case they did as well as unstressed rats. The lesions did not prevent stress from raising the animals' glucocorticoid level, so presumably the effects of stress are mediated through neural connections between the amygdala and the hippocampus.

Uno et al. (1989) found that if long-term stress is intense enough, it can even cause brain damage in young primates. The investigators studied a colony of vervet monkeys housed in a primate center in Kenya. They found that some monkeys died, apparently from stress. Vervet monkeys have a hierarchical society, and monkeys near the bottom of the hierarchy are picked on by the others; thus, they are almost continuously subjected to stress. (Ours is not the only species with social structures that cause a stress reaction in some of its members.) The deceased monkeys had gastric ulcers and enlarged adrenal glands, which are signs of chronic stress. And as Figure 17.11 shows, neurons in the CA1 field of the hippocampal formation were completely destroyed. (See *Figure 17.11.*)

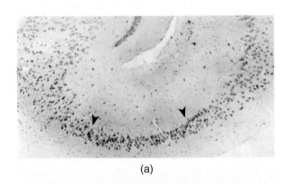

(a)

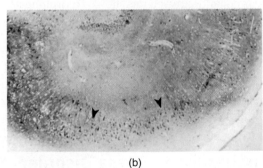

(b)

figure   17.11

Photomicrographs showing brain damage caused by stress. (a) Section through the hippocampus of a normal monkey. (b) Section through the hippocampus of a monkey of low social status subjected to stress. Compare the regions between the arrowheads, which are normally filled with large pyramidal cells.

(From Uno, H., Tarara, R., Else, J. G., Suleman, M. A., and Sapolsky, R. M. *Journal of Neuroscience,* 1989, *9,* 1706–1711. Reprinted by permission of the *Journal of Neuroscience.*)

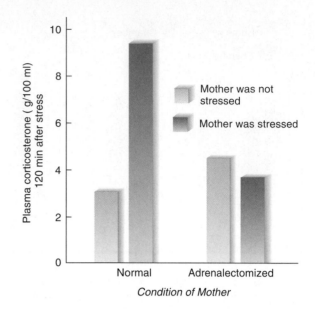

figure 17.12

Effects of prenatal stress and glucocorticoid level on the stress response of adult rats. Adrenalectomy of the mother before she was subjected to stress prevented the development of an elevated stress response in the offspring during adulthood.
(Adapted from Barbazanges, A., Piazza, P. V., Le Moal, M., and Maccari, S. *Journal of Neuroscience,* 1996, *16,* 3943–3949.)

Severe stress appears to cause brain damage in humans as well; Jensen, Genefke, and Hyldebrandt (1982) found evidence of brain degeneration in CT scans of people who had been subjected to torture.

As we saw in Chapter 10, prenatal stress tends to inhibit androgenization of the fetuses. That is, when a pregnant female is exposed to stressors, the behavior and brain structure of her male offspring appear less masculinized and defeminized than those of control animals. Prenatal stress also appears to produce long-term effects on animals' stress reactions. At least some of the effects of prenatal stress on the fetus appear to be mediated by the secretion of glucocorticoids. Barbazanges et al. (1996) subjected pregnant female rats to stress and later observed the effects of this treatment on their offspring once they grew up. They found that the prenatally stressed rats showed a prolonged secretion of glucocorticoids when they were subjected to restraint stress. However, if the mothers' adrenal glands had been removed so that glucocorticoid levels could not increase during the stressful situation, their offspring reacted normally in adulthood. (The experimenters gave the adrenalectomized mothers controlled amounts of glucocorticoids to maintain them in good health.) (See *Figure 17.12.*)

Posttraumatic Stress Disorder

The aftermath of tragic and traumatic events such as those that accompany wars and natural disasters often includes psychological symptoms that persist long after the stressful events are over. According to the DSM IV, **posttraumatic stress disorder (PTSD)** is caused by a situation in which a person "experienced, witnessed, or was confronted with an event or events that involved actual or threatened death or serious injury, or a threat to the physical integrity of self or others" that provoked a response that "involved intense fear, helplessness, or horror." The symptoms produced by such exposure include recurrent dreams or recollections of the event, feelings that the traumatic event is recurring ("flashback" episodes), and intense psychological distress. These dreams, recollections, or flashback episodes can lead the person to avoid thinking about the traumatic event, which often results in diminished interest in social activities, feelings of detachment from others, suppressed emotional feelings, and a sense that the future is bleak and empty. Particular psychological symptoms include difficulty falling or staying asleep, irritability, outbursts of anger, difficulty in concentrating, and heightened reactions to sudden noises or movements. As this description indicates, people with PTSD have impaired mental health functioning. They also tend to have generally poor physical health (Zayfert et al, 2002). Although men are exposed to traumatic events more often than women are, women are approximately four times more likely to develop PTSD after being exposed to such events (Fullerton et al., 2001).

Posttraumatic stress disorder can strike people at any age. Children may show particular symptoms that are not usually seen in adulthood, such as loss of recently acquired language skills or toilet training, and somatic complaints such as stomachaches and headaches. Usually, the symptoms begin immediately after the traumatic event, but they are sometimes delayed for several months or years.

Evidence from twin studies suggest that genetic factors play a role in a person's susceptibility to develop PTSD. In fact, genetic factors influence not only the likelihood of developing PTSD after being exposed to traumatic events, but also the likelihood that the person will be involved in such an event (Stein et al., 2002). For example, people with a genetic predisposition toward irritabil-

posttraumatic stress disorder (PTSD) A psychological disorder caused by exposure to a situation of extreme danger and stress; symptoms include recurrent dreams or recollections; can interfere with social activities and cause a feeling of hopelessness.

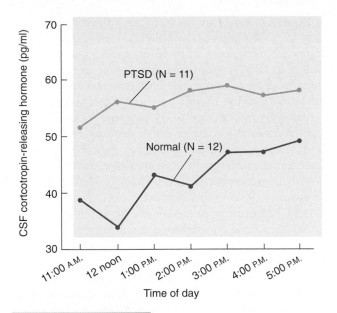

figure 1 7 . 1 3

Concentrations of CRH in the cerebrospinal fluid of normal subjects and subjects with PTSD.

(Adapted from Baker, D. G., West, S. A., Nicholson, W. E., Ekhator, N. N., Kasckow, J. W., Hill, K. K., Bruce, A. B., Orth, D. N., and Geracioti, T. D. *American Journal of Psychiatry,* 1999, *156,* 585–588.)

ity and anger are more likely to be assaulted, and those with a predisposition toward risky behavior are more likely to be involved in accidents. In a review of the Vietnam Era Twin Registry, Koenen et al (2002) reported that the following demographic and personality factors predict an increased risk for being exposed to traumatic events: military service in Southeast Asia during the Vietnam war, a preexisting conduct disorder or substance dependence, and a family history of mood disorders. The following factors predict the risk of developing PTSD after exposure: earlier age at the time of the traumatic event, exposure to more than one traumatic event, a father with a depressive disorder, a low educational level, and a preexisting conduct disorder, panic disorder, generalized anxiety disorder, or depressive disorder.

As we saw earlier in this chapter, prolonged exposure to stress can cause brain damage, particularly in the hippocampus. At least two MRI studies have found evidence of hippocampal damage in veterans with combat-related posttraumatic stress disorder (Bremner et al., 1995; Gurvits et al., 1996). In the study by Gurvits et al., the volume of the hippocampal formation was reduced by over 20 percent, and the loss was proportional to the amount of combat exposure the veteran had experienced. Other studies have found similar effects in adult patients with posttraumatic stress disorder who had been subjected to severe childhood abuse (Bremner, 1999).

Although many investigators have assumed that the reduction in hippocampal volume in posttraumatic stress disorder is caused by hypersecretion of cortisol, evidence indicates that people with PTSD actually have *lower* levels

of cortisol, and evidence suggests that trauma victims who develop PTSD show smaller increases in cortisol secretion at the time of the trauma. Resnick et al. (1995) analyzed blood samples from female rape victims that were obtained in the emergency room soon after the rape. They found that women who had been previously assaulted had the highest likelihood of developing PTSD—and the lowest levels of cortisol. McFarlane, Atchison, and Yehuda (1997) found similar effects in people involved in motor vehicle accidents.

Why should people who have been exposed to traumatic events show *decreased* cortisol secretion when they are exposed to stressful situations? Yehuda (2001) suggests that exposure to severe stress increases the number and sensitivity of glucocorticoid receptors in the hypothalamus and anterior pituitary gland. These receptors regulate cortisol secretion: If cortisol levels rise, stimulation of these receptors inhibits the secretion of ACTH. However, other factors (perhaps including the amygdala) continue to stimulate the release of CRH. Baker et al. (1999) placed a catheter in the subarachnoid space of the lumbar spine of combat veterans with PTSD and normal volunteers and withdrew samples of cerebrospinal fluid over a six-hour period. They found significantly elevated CRH levels in the men with PTSD. However, the levels of cortisol were not elevated, and in fact, the patients with the lowest cortisol levels had the highest levels of PTSD symptoms. As we saw earlier in this chapter, CRH has anxiety-producing effects on the brain. Thus, high levels of CRH, rather than high levels of cortisol, may play a role in the development of the symptoms of PTSD. (See *Figures 17.13 and 17.14*.)

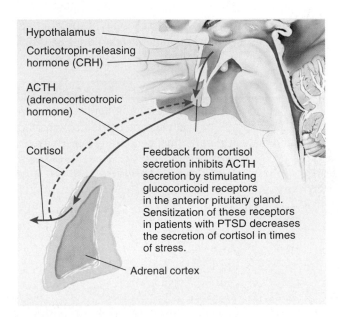

Feedback from cortisol secretion inhibits ACTH secretion by stimulating glucocorticoid receptors in the anterior pituitary gland. Sensitization of these receptors in patients with PTSD decreases the secretion of cortisol in times of stress.

figure 1 7 . 1 4

A hypothetical explanation by Yehuda (2001) of the pattern of cortisol secretion in response to stress seen in patients with PTSD.

Stress and Cardiovascular Disease

One of the most important causes of death is cardiovascular diseases—diseases of the heart and the blood vessels. Cardiovascular diseases can cause heart attacks and strokes; heart attacks occur when the blood vessels that serve the heart become blocked, while strokes involve the blood vessels in the brain. The two most important risk factors in cardiovascular disease are high blood pressure and a high level of cholesterol in the blood.

The degree to which people react to potential stressors may affect the likelihood that they will suffer from cardiovascular disease. For example, Wood et al. (1984) examined the blood pressure of people who had been subjected to a *cold pressor test* in 1934, when they were children. The cold pressor test reveals how people's blood pressure reacts to the stress caused by their hand being placed in a container of ice water for 1 minute. Wood and his colleagues found that 70 percent of the subjects who hyperreacted to cold pressor test when they were children had high blood pressure, compared with 19 percent of those who showed little reaction to the test.

A study with monkeys showed that individual differences in emotional reactivity are a risk factor for cardiovascular disease. Manuck et al. (1983, 1986) fed a high-cholesterol diet to a group of monkeys, which increases the likelihood of their developing coronary artery disease. They measured the animals' emotional reactivity by threatening to capture the animals. (Monkeys avoid contact with humans, and they perceive being captured as a stressful situation.) The animals who showed the strongest negative reactions eventually developed the highest rates of coronary artery disease. Presumably, these animals reacted more strongly to all types of stressors, and their reactions had detrimental effects on their health.

Apparently, at least some of the differences in emotional reactivity displayed by individual animals are caused by genetic differences in brain chemistry and function. Eilam et al. (1991) transplanted some tissue from the hypothalamus of genetically hypertensive rats into normal rats and found that the blood pressure of the recipient rats increased by an average of 31 percent. (Transplants of hypothalamic tissue from normotensive rats did not increase recipients' blood pressure.) (See *Figure 17.15*.) These genetic differences may involve alterations in the control of the secretion of CRH. Krukoff, MacTavish, and Jhamandas (1999) found that stress caused more activation of CRH neurons in genetically hypertensive rats.

So far, I have concentrated on chronic stress. However, acute stress can also aggravate cardiovascular disease. As Rozanski, Blumenthal, and Kaplan (1999) note, acute stress can cause constriction of the coronary arteries, arrhythmias in the heartbeat, stimulation of platelet function (which promotes the formation of clots), and increased viscosity of the blood, and these effects can provoke fatal crises. The effects of acute stress were demonstrated by the results of the Los Angeles earthquake of 1994. During the week before the earthquake, the mean rate of sudden cardiac deaths was 4.6 per day. On the day of the earthquake, 24 people died of these causes (Leor, Poole, and Kloner, 1996).

The Coping Response

As we have seen, many of the harmful effects of long-term stress are caused by our own reactions—primarily the secretion of stress hormones. Some events that cause stress responses, such as prolonged exertion or extreme cold, cause damage directly. These stressors will affect everyone; their severity will depend on each person's physical capac-

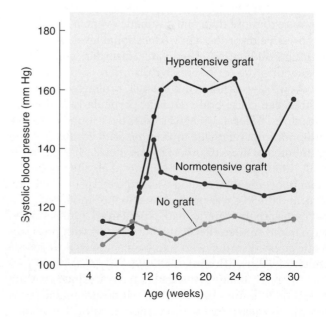

figure 17.15

Systolic blood pressure in normal rats, rats with grafts of hypothalamic tissue from normal rats, and rats with grafts from genetically hypertensive rats.

(Adapted from Eilam, R., Malach, R., Bergmann, F., and Segal, M. *Journal of Neuroscience,* 1991, *11,* 401–411.)

ity. The effects of other stressors, such as situations that cause fear or anxiety, depend on people's perceptions and emotional reactivity. That is, because of individual differences in temperament or experience with a particular situation, some people may find a situation stressful and others may not. In these cases it is the perception that counts.

One of the most important variables that determines whether an aversive stimulus will cause a stress reaction is the degree to which the situation can be controlled. As we saw in Chapter 11, when an animal can learn a *coping response* that avoids contact with an aversive stimulus or decreases its severity, the animal's emotional response will diminish or disappear. Weiss (1968) found that rats who learned to minimize (but not completely avoid) shocks by making a response whenever they heard a warning tone developed fewer stomach ulcers than did rats who had no control over the shocks. The effect was not caused by the pain itself, because both groups of animals received exactly the same number of shocks. Thus, being able to exert some control over an aversive situation reduces an animal's stress response. Humans react similarly. Situations that permit some control are less likely to produce signs of stress than are those in which other people (or machines) control the situation (Gatchel, Baum, and Krantz, 1989). Perhaps this phenomenon explains why some people like to have a magic charm or other "security blanket" with them in stressful situations. Perhaps even the *illusion* of control can be reassuring.

Foy et al. (1987) found that restraint stress or tail shock impaired the establishment of long-term potentiation in hippocampal slices taken from the stressed animals. A subsequent study from the same laboratory (Shors et al., 1989) found that this effect did not occur if the rats were given a chance to escape from the shock. (The study used a yoked control group so that rats that could escape the shock received just as many as those that could not.) Thus, the opportunity to make a coping response decreases the negative impact of stress on the hippocampus. The neural or hormonal mechanisms that are responsible for the beneficial effects of coping responses are not yet understood.

Psychoneuroimmunology

As we have seen, long-term stress can be harmful to one's health and can even result in brain damage. The most important cause of these effects is elevated levels of glucocorticoids, but the high blood pressure caused by epinephrine and norepinephrine also plays a contributing role. In addition, the stress response can impair the functions of the immune system, which protects us from assault from viruses, microbes, fungi, and other types of parasites. Study of the interactions between the immune system and behavior (mediated by the nervous system, of course) is called **psychoneuroimmunology.** This relatively new field is described in the following subsection.

The Immune System

The immune system is one of the most complex systems of the body. Its function is to protect us from infection; and because infectious organisms have developed devious tricks through the process of evolution, our immune system has evolved devious tricks of its own. The description I provide here is abbreviated and simplified, but it presents some of the important elements of the system.

The immune system derives from white blood cells that develop in the bone marrow and in the thymus gland. Some of the cells roam through the blood or lymphatic system; others reside permanently in one place. Two types of specific immune reaction occur when the body is invaded by foreign organisms, including bacteria, fungi, and viruses: *chemically mediated* and *cell-mediated.* Chemically mediated immune reactions involve antibodies. Infectious microorganisms have unique proteins on their surfaces, called **antigens.** These proteins serve as the invaders' calling cards, identifying them to the immune system. Through exposure to the microorganisms, the immune system learns to recognize these proteins. (I will not try to explain the mechanism by which this learning takes place.) The result of this learning is the development of special lines of cells that produce specific **antibodies—** proteins that recognize antigens and help to kill the invading microorganism.

One type of antibody is released into the circulation by **B-lymphocytes,** which receive their name from the fact that they develop in bone marrow. These antibodies, called **immunoglobulins,** are chains of protein. Each type of immunoglobulin (there are five of them) is identical except for one end, which contains a unique receptor. A particular receptor binds with a particular antigen, just as a molecule of a hormone or neurotransmitter binds with its receptor. When the appropriate line of B-lymphocytes detects the presence of an invading bacterium, the cells release their antibodies, which bind with the antigens present on the surface of the invading microorganisms. The antigens either kill the invaders directly or

psychoneuroimmunology The branch of neuroscience involved with interactions between environmental stimuli, the nervous system, and the immune system.

antigen A protein present on a microorganism that permits the immune system to recognize the microorganism as an invader.

antibody A protein produced by a cell of the immune system that recognizes antigens present on invading microorganisms.

B-lymphocyte A white blood cell that originates in the bone marrow; part of the immune system.

immunoglobulin An antibody released by B-lymphocytes that bind with antigens and help to destroy invading microorganisms.

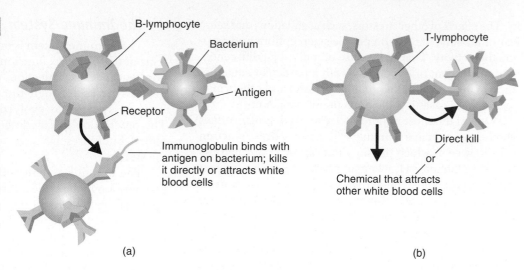

figure 17.16

Immune reactions. (a) Chemically mediated reaction. The B-lymphocyte detects an antigen on a bacterium and releases a specific immunoglobulin. (b) Cell-mediated reaction. The T-lymphocyte detects an antigen on a bacterium and kills it directly or releases a chemical that attracts other white blood cells.

attract other white blood cells, which then destroy them. (See *Figure 17.16a.*)

The other type of defense by the immune system, cell-mediated immune reactions, is produced by **T-lympho-cytes,** which originally develop in the thymus gland. These cells also produce antibodies, but the antibodies remain attached to the outside of their membrane. T-lympho-cytes primarily defend the body against fungi, viruses, and multicellular parasites. When antigens bind with their surface antibodies, the cells either directly kill the invaders or signal other white blood cells to come and kill them. (See *Figure 17.16b.*)

The reactions illustrated in Figure 17.16 are much simplified; actually, both chemically mediated and cell-mediated immune reactions involve several different types of cells. The communication between these cells is accomplished by **cytokines,** chemicals that stimulate cell division. The cytokines that are released by certain white blood cells when an invading microorganism is detected (principally *interleukin-1* and *interleukin-2*) cause other white blood cells to proliferate and direct an attack against the invader. The primary way in which glucocorticoids suppress specific immune responses is by interfering with the messages conveyed by the cytokines (Sapolsky, 1992).

Neural Control of the Immune System

As we will see in the next subsection, the stress response can increase the likelihood of infectious diseases. What is the physiological explanation for these effects? One answer, probably the most important one, is that stress increases the

T-lymphocyte A white blood cell that originates in the thymus gland; part of the immune system.

cytokine A category of chemicals released by certain white blood cells when they detect the presence of an invading microorganism; causes other white blood cells to proliferate and mount an attack against the invader.

secretion of glucocorticoids, and as we saw, these hormones directly suppress the activity of the immune system.

A direct relationship between stress and the immune system was demonstrated by Kiecolt-Glaser et al. (1987). Using several different laboratory tests, these investigators found that caregivers of family members with Alzheimer's disease, who certainly underwent considerable stress, showed weaker immune systems. One measure of the quality of a person's immune response is measurement of antibodies produced in response to a vaccination. Glaser et al. (2000) found that people taking care of spouses with Alzheimer's disease maintained lower levels of IgG antibodies after receiving a pneumococcal bacterial vaccine. (See *Figure 17.17.*) Bereavement, another source of stress, also suppresses the immune system. Schleifer et al. (1983) tested the husbands of women with breast cancer and found that their immune response was lower after their wives died. Knapp et al. (1992) even found that when healthy subjects imagined themselves reliving unpleasant emotional experiences, the immune response measured in samples of their blood was decreased.

Several studies indicate that the suppression of the immune response by stress is largely (but not entirely) mediated by glucocorticoids (Keller et al., 1983). Because the secretion of glucocorticoids is controlled by the brain (through its secretion of CRH), the brain is obviously responsible for the suppressing effect of these hormones on the immune system. Neurons in the central nucleus of the amygdala send axons to CRH-secreting neurons in the paraventricular nucleus of the hypothalamus; thus, we can reasonably expect that the mechanism that is responsible for negative emotional responses is also responsible for the stress response and the immunosuppression that accompanies it. Several studies have shown that stress increases the activity of neurons in brain regions that have been shown to play a role in emotional responses, including the central nucleus of the amygdala and the paraventricular nucleus (Sharp et al., 1991; Imaki et al., 1992).

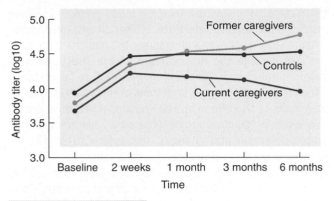

figure 17.17

Effect of stress on immune function. Levels of antibodies produced in response to a pneumococcal bacterial vaccine in the blood of controls and former and current caregivers of spouses with Alzheimer's disease.

(Adapted from Glaser, R., Sheridan, J., Malarkey, W. B., MacCallum, R. C., and Kiecolt-Glaser, J. K. *Psychosomatic Medicine*, 2000, *62*, 804–807.)

Some stress-induced immunosuppression may be under direct neural control. The bone marrow, the thymus gland, and the lymph nodes all receive neural input. Although researchers have not yet obtained direct proof that this input modulates immune function, it would be surprising if it did not. In addition, the immune system appears to be sensitive to chemicals produced by the nervous system. The best evidence comes from studies with the opioids produced by the brain. Shavit et al. (1984) found that inescapable intermittent shock produced both analgesia (decreased sensitivity to pain) and suppression of the production of natural killer cells. These effects both seem to have been mediated by endogenous opioids, because both effects were abolished when the experimenters administered a drug that blocks opiate receptors.

Stress and Infectious Diseases

Often when a married person dies, his or her spouse dies soon afterward, frequently of an infection. In fact, a wide variety of stress-producing events in a person's life can increase the susceptibility to illness. For example, Glaser et al. (1987) found that medical students were more likely to contract acute infections and to show evidence of suppression of the immune system during the time that final examinations were given. In addition, autoimmune diseases often get worse when a person is subjected to stress, as Feigenbaum, Masi, and Kaplan (1979) found for rheumatoid arthritis. In a laboratory study, Rogers et al. (1980) found that when rats were stressed by being handled or being exposed to a cat, they developed a more severe case of an artificially induced autoimmune disease. Lehman et al. (1991) found that the incidence of diabetes in a strain of rats that are susceptible to this autoimmune disease was considerably higher when the animals were subjected to moderate chronic stress.

Stone, Reed, and Neale (1987) attempted to determine whether stressful events in people's daily lives might predispose them to upper respiratory infection. If a person is exposed to a microorganism that might cause such a disease, the symptoms do not occur for several days; that is, there is an incubation period between exposure and signs of the actual illness. Thus, the authors reasoned that if stressful events suppressed the immune system, one might expect to see a higher likelihood of respiratory infections several days after such stress. To test their hypothesis, they asked volunteers to keep a daily record of desirable and undesirable events in their lives over a twelve-week period. The volunteers also kept a daily record of any discomfort or symptoms of illness.

The results were as predicted: During the three-to-five-day period just before showing symptoms of an upper respiratory infection, people experienced an increased number of undesirable events and a decreased number of desirable events in their lives. (See *Figure 17.18*.) Stone et al. (1987) suggest that the effect is caused by decreased production of a particular immunoglobulin that is present in the secretions of mucous membranes, including those in the nose, mouth, throat, and lungs. This immunoglobulin, IgA, serves as the first defense against infectious microorganisms that enter the nose or mouth. They found that IgA is associated with mood; when a subject is unhappy or depressed, IgA levels are lower than normal. The results suggest that the stress caused by undesirable events may, by suppressing the production of IgA, lead to a rise in the likelihood of upper respiratory infections.

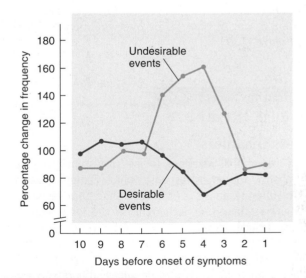

figure 17.18

Mean percentage change in frequency of undesirable and desirable events during the ten-day period preceding the onset of symptoms of upper respiratory infections.

(Based on data from Stone, A. A., Reed, B. R., and Neale, J. M. *Journal of Human Stress*, 1987, *13*, 70–74.)

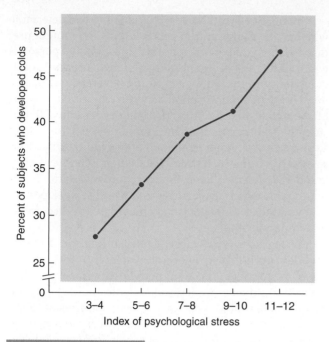

figure 17.19

Percent of subjects with colds as a function of an index of psychological stress.

(Adapted from Cohen, S., Tyrrell, D. A. J., and Smith, A. P. *New England Journal of Medicine,* 1991, *325,* 606–612.)

The results of the study by Stone and his colleagues were confirmed by an experiment by Cohen, Tyrrell, and Smith (1991). The investigators found that subjects who were given nasal drops containing cold viruses were much more likely to develop colds if they reported stressful experiences during the past year and if they said they felt threatened, out of control, or overwhelmed by events. (See *Figure 17.19*.)

interim summary

Stress Disorders

People's emotional reactions to aversive stimuli can harm their health. The stress response, which Cannon called the fight-or-flight response, is useful as a short-term response to threatening stimuli but is harmful in the long term. This response includes increased activity of the sympathetic branch of the autonomic nervous system and increased secretion of hormones by the adrenal gland: epinephrine, norepinephrine, and glucocorticoids. Corticotropin-releasing hormone, which stimulates the secretion of ACTH by the anterior pituitary gland, is also secreted in the brain, where it elicits some of the emotional responses to stressful situations.

Although increased levels of epinephrine and norepinephrine can raise blood pressure, most of the harm to health comes from glucocorticoids. Prolonged exposure to high lev-els of these hormones can increase blood pressure, damage muscle tissue, lead to infertility, inhibit growth, inhibit the inflammatory response, and suppress the immune system. It can also damage the hippocampus. Acute stress can also impair hippocampal functioning. At least some of these effects involve the amygdala; lesions of this structure reduce the effects of short-term stress. Prenatal exposure to excessive levels of glucocorticoids (caused by maternal stress) causes developmental changes that appear to predispose animals to react more to stressful situations.

Exposure to extreme stress can also have long-lasting effects; it can lead to the development of posttraumatic stress disorder. This disorder, to which women appear to be more susceptible than men, is associated with memory deficits, poorer health, and a decrease in the size of the hippocampus. Twin studies indicate a hereditary component to susceptibility to PTSD. Functional imaging studies have found an increase in the activity of the prefrontal cortex and amygdala when patients think about the situations that led to their disorder. People with PTSD generally show a smaller cortisol response to a traumatic experience; however, they secrete large amounts of CRH. This pattern of secretion suggests that glucocorticoid receptors in the hypothalamus and anterior pituitary that inhibit ACTH secretion have become hypersensitive.

Because the harm of most forms of stress comes from our own response to it, individual differences in personality variables can alter the effects of stressful situations. Research with twin studies indicates that heredity is one of the factors that determines an individual's response to stress. Another important variable is the ability to perform a coping response; being able to do so considerably reduces the aversive effects of stressful situations. One study suggests that performance of a coping response causes the release of endogenous benzodiazepines by neurons in the brain.

Psychoneuroimmunology is a relatively new field of study that investigates interactions between behavior and the immune system, mediated by the nervous system. The immune system consists of several types of white blood cells that produce both nonspecific and specific responses to invading microorganisms. The nonspecific responses include the inflammatory response, the antiviral effect of interferon, and the action of natural killer cells against viruses and cancer cells. The specific responses include chemically mediated and cell-mediated responses. Chemically mediated responses are carried out by B-lymphocytes, which release antibodies that bind with the antigens on microorganisms and kill them directly or target them for attack by other white blood cells. Cell-mediated responses are carried out by T-lymphocytes, whose antibodies remain attached to their membranes.

A wide variety of stressful situations have been shown to increase people's susceptibility to infectious diseases. The most important mechanism by which stress impairs immune function is the increased blood levels of glucocorticoids. In addition, the neural input to the bone marrow, lymph nodes, and thymus gland may also play a role; and the endogenous opioids appear to suppress the activity of natural killer cells.

Suggested Readings

Ader, R., Felten, D. L., and Cohen, N. (eds.). *Psychoneuroimmunology,* 2nd ed. San Diego: Academic Press, 1991.

Bauman, M. L., and Kemper, T. L. *The Neurobiology of Autism.* Baltimore: Johns Hopkins University Press, 1994.

Brown, M. R., Koob, G. F., and Rivier, C. (eds.). *Stress: Neurobiology and Neuroendocrinology.* New York: Dekker, 1990.

Gershon, E. S., and Cloninger, C. R. *New Genetic Approaches to Mental Disorders.* Washington, DC: American Psychiatric Press, 1994.

Goodwin, D. W., and Guze, S. B. *Psychiatric Diagnosis,* 5th ed. New York: Oxford University Press, 1996.

Hollander, E. *Obsessive-Compulsive Related Disorders.* Washington, DC: American Psychiatric Press, 1993.

Yudofsky, S. C., and Hales, R. E. *The American Psychiatric Press Textbook of Neuropsychiatry.* Washington, DC: American Psychiatric Press, 1997.

Suggested Web Sites

Facts on Post-Traumatic Stress Disorder (PTSD)

http://www.nimh.nih.gov/events/ptsdfact.htm

This NIH site discusses the causes and symptoms of PTSD and provides links to key sites on PTSD.

On-Line Anxiety Course

http://salmon.psy.plym.ac.uk/year2/anxiety.htm

This site provides access to a comprehensive set of materials relating to the pharmacology of anxiety.

The Emotional Brain

http://www.nimh.nih.gov/events/ledoux.htm

This site details the research of Dr. Joseph LeDoux relating the emotion of fear to mechanisms within the amygdala.

Anxiety Disorder Education Program

http://www.nimh.nih.gov/anxiety/news/index.htm

This NIMH site provides links to articles and fact sheets on anxiety disorders.

Generalized Anxiety Disorder

http://www.mentalhealth.com/dis/p20-an07.html

This site contains descriptions of diagnosis and treatment issues for generalized anxiety disorder.

Drug Abuse

Gerhard Richter, *Cloud*, 1982. © Gerhard Richter. © Digital Image. © The Museum of Modern Art/Licensed by SCALA/Art Resource, NY.

outline

■ **Common Features of Addiction**
A Little Background
Physical Versus Psychological Addiction
Positive Reinforcement
Negative Reinforcement
Tolerance and Withdrawal
Craving and Relapse
Interim Summary

■ **Commonly Abused Drugs**
Opiates
Cocaine and Amphetamine
Nicotine
Alcohol and Barbiturates
Cannabis
Interim Summary

■ **Heredity and Drug Abuse**
Heritability Studies
of Humans
Animal Models of Drug Abuse
Interim Summary
■ **Therapy for Drug Abuse**
Interim Summary

John was beginning to feel that perhaps he would be able to get his life back together. It looked as though his drug habit was going to be licked. He had started taking drugs several years ago. At first, he had used them only on special occasions—mostly on weekends with his friends—but heroin proved to be his undoing. One of his acquaintances had introduced him to the needle, and John had found the rush so blissful that he couldn't wait a whole week for his next fix. Soon he was shooting up daily. Shortly after that, he lost his job and, to support his habit, began earning money through car theft and small-time drug dealing. As time went on, he needed more and more heroin at shorter and shorter intervals, which necessitated even more money. Eventually, he was arrested and convicted of selling heroin to an undercover agent.

The judge gave John the choice of prison or a drug rehabilitation program, and he chose the latter. Soon after starting the program, he realized that he was relieved to have been caught. Now that he was clean and could reflect on his life, he realized what would have become of him had he continued to take drugs. Withdrawal from heroin was not an experience he would want to live through again, but it turned out not to be as bad as he had feared. The counselors in his program told him to avoid his old neighborhood and to break contact with his old acquaintances, and he followed their advice. He had been clean for eight weeks, he had a job, and he had met a woman who really seemed sympathetic. He knew that he hadn't completely kicked his habit, because every now and then, despite his best intentions, he found himself thinking about the wonderful glow that heroin provided him. But things were definitely looking up.

Then one day, while walking home from work, he turned a corner and saw a new poster plastered on the wall of a building. The poster, produced by an antidrug agency, showed all sorts of drug paraphernalia in full color: glassine envelopes with white powder spilling out of them, syringes, needles, a spoon and candle used to heat and dissolve the drug. John was seized with a sudden, intense compulsion to take some heroin. He closed his eyes, trying to will the feeling away, but all he could feel were his churning stomach and his trembling limbs, and all he could think about was getting a fix. He hopped on a bus and went back to his old neighborhood.

Drug addiction poses a serious problem to our species. Consider the disastrous effects caused by the abuse of one of our oldest drugs, alcohol: automobile accidents, fetal alcohol syndrome, cirrhosis of the liver, Korsakoff's syndrome, increased rate of heart disease, and increased rate of intracerebral hemorrhage. Smoking (addiction to nicotine) greatly increases the chances of dying of lung cancer, heart attack, and stroke; and women who smoke give birth to smaller, less healthy babies. Cocaine addiction can cause psychotic behavior, brain damage, and death from overdose; and competition for lucrative illegal drug markets terrorizes neighborhoods, subverts political and judicial systems, and causes many violent deaths. The use of "designer drugs" exposes users to unknown dangers of untested and often contaminated products, as several people discovered when they acquired Parkinson's disease after taking a synthetic opiate that was tainted with a neurotoxin. Addicts who take their drugs intravenously run a serious risk of contracting AIDS, hepatitis, or other infectious diseases. What makes these drugs so attractive to so many people?

The answer, as you might have predicted from what you learned about the physiology of reinforcement in Chapter 13, is that all of these substances stimulate brain mechanisms responsible for positive reinforcement. In addition, some of them reduce or eliminate unpleasant feelings, some of which are produced by the drugs themselves. The immediate consequences of these drugs are more powerful than the realization that in the long term, bad things will happen.

Common Features of Addiction

The term *addiction* derives from the Latin word *addicere*, "to sentence." Someone who is addicted to a drug is, in a way, sentenced to a term of involuntary servitude, being obliged to fulfill the demands of his or her drug dependency.

A Little Background

Long ago, people discovered that many substances found in nature—primarily leaves, seeds, and roots of plants but also some animal products—had medicinal qualities. They discovered herbs that helped to prevent infections, that promoted healing, that calmed an upset stomach, that reduced pain, or that helped to provide a night's sleep. They also discovered "recreational drugs"—drugs that produced pleasurable effects when eaten, drunk, or smoked. The most universal recreational drug, and perhaps the first one that our ancestors discovered, is ethyl alcohol. Yeast spores are present everywhere, and these microorganisms can feed on sugar solutions and produce alcohol as a by-product. Undoubtedly, people in many different parts of the world discovered the pleasurable effects of drinking liquids that had been left alone for a while, such as the juice that had accumulated in the bottom of a container of fruit. The juice may have become sour and bad-tasting because of the action of bacteria, but the effects of the alcohol encouraged people to experiment, which led to the development of a wide variety of fermented beverages.

table 18.1	
Addictive Drugs	
DRUG	**SITES OF ACTION**
Ethyl alcohol	NMDA receptor (indirect antagonist); GABA$_A$ receptor (indirect antagonist)
Barbiturates	GABA$_A$ receptor (indirect agonist)
Benzodiazepines (tranquilizers)	GABA$_A$ receptor (indirect agonist)
Cannabis (marijuana)	CB1 cannabinoid receptor (agonist)
Nicotine	Nicotinic ACh receptor (agonist)
Opiates (heroin, morphine, etc.)	μ and δ opioid receptor agonist
Phencyclidine (PCP) and ketamine	NMDA receptor (indirect antagonist)
Cocaine	Blocks reuptake of dopamine (and serotonin and norepinephrine)
Amphetamine	Causes release of dopamine (by running dopamine transporters in reverse)

Source: Adapted from Hyman, S. E., and Malenka, R. C. *Nature Reviews: Neuroscience,* 2001, *2,* 695–703.

Our ancestors also discovered other recreational drugs. Some of them were consumed only locally; others became so popular that their cultivation as commercial crops spread throughout the world. For example, Asians discovered the effects of the sap of the opium poppy and the beverage made from the leaves of the tea plant, Indians discovered the effects of the smoke of cannabis, South Americans discovered the effects of chewing coca leaves and making a drink from coffee beans, and North Americans discovered the effects of the smoke of the tobacco plant. Many of the drugs they discovered served to protect the plants from animals (primarily insects) that ate them. Although the drugs were toxic in sufficient quantities, our ancestors learned how to take these drugs in quantities that would not make them ill—at least, not right away. The effects of these drugs on their brains kept them coming back for more.

Table 18.1 lists the most important addictive drugs and indicates their sites of action.

Physical Versus Psychological Addiction

Some drugs have very potent reinforcing effects, which lead some people to abuse them or even to become addicted to them. Many people (psychologists, health professionals, and laypeople) believe that "true" addiction is caused by the unpleasant physiological effects that occur when an addict tries to stop taking the drug. For example, Eddy et al. (1965) defined *physical dependence* as "an adaptive state that manifests itself by intense physical disturbances when the administration of a drug is suspended" (p. 723). In contrast, they defined *psychic dependence* as a condition in which

a drug produces "a feeling of satisfaction and a psychic drive that requires periodic or continuous administration of the drug to produce pleasure or to avoid discomfort" (p. 723). Most people regard the latter as less important than the former, but as we shall see, the *reverse* is true.

For many years, heroin addiction was considered the prototype for all drug addictions. People who habitually take heroin become physically dependent on the drug; that is, they show *tolerance* and *withdrawal symptoms.* As we saw in Chapter 4, **tolerance** is the decreased sensitivity to a drug that comes from its continued use; the drug user must take larger and larger amounts of the drug for it to be effective. Once a person has taken an opiate regularly enough to develop tolerance, that person will suffer *withdrawal symptoms* if he or she stops taking the drug. **Withdrawal symptoms** are primarily the opposite of the effects of the drug itself. The effects of heroin—euphoria, constipation, and relaxation—lead to the withdrawal effects of dysphoria, cramping and diarrhea, and agitation.

Most investigators believe that tolerance is produced by the body's attempt to compensate for the unusual condition of heroin intoxication. The drug disturbs normal homeostatic mechanisms in the brain, and in reaction these mechanisms begin to produce effects opposite to

tolerance The fact that increasingly large doses of drugs must be taken to achieve a particular effect; caused by compensatory mechanisms that oppose the effect of the drug.

withdrawal symptoms The appearance of symptoms opposite to those produced by a drug when the drug is suddenly no longer taken; caused by the presence of compensatory mechanisms.

those of the drug, partially compensating for the disturbance. Because of these compensatory mechanisms, the user must take increasing amounts of heroin to achieve the effects that were produced when he or she first started taking the drug. These mechanisms also account for the symptoms of withdrawal: When the person stops taking the drug, the compensatory mechanisms make themselves felt, unopposed by the action of the drug.

Heroin addiction has provided such a striking example of drug dependence that some authorities have concluded that "real" addiction does not occur unless a drug causes tolerance and withdrawal. Without doubt, withdrawal symptoms make it difficult for a person to stop taking heroin: They help to keep the person hooked. But withdrawal symptoms do not explain why a person becomes a heroin addict in the first place; that fact is explained by the drug's reinforcing effect. Certainly, people do not start taking heroin so that they will become physically dependent on it and feel miserable when they go without it. Instead, they begin taking it because it makes them feel good.

Perhaps the best evidence that the tolerance and withdrawal are not the causes of addiction is the fact that prolonged use of some drugs—in particular, β-adrenergic agonists inhalers used to treat asthma, α-adrenergic agonists used as nasal decongestants, and several drugs used to treat hypertension and the pain of angina pectoris—leads to tolerance and withdrawal, but the drugs are not themselves addictive (Hyman and Malenka, 2001).

In the past, the preoccupation with "physical" drug dependence has led to the neglect of the addictive properties of some drugs. For example, some very potent drugs, including cocaine, do not produce physical dependency. That is, people who take the drug do not show tolerance; and if they stop, they do not show significant physical symptoms of withdrawal. As a result, experts believed for many years that cocaine was a relatively innocuous drug, not in the same league as heroin. Obviously, they were wrong; cocaine is even more addictive than heroin.

The most important lesson that we can learn from the misguided distinction between "physiological" and "psychological" addiction is that we should never underestimate the importance of "psychological" factors. After all, given that behavior is controlled by circuits of neurons in the brain, even "psychological" factors involve physiological mechanisms. People often pay more attention to physiological symptoms than to psychological ones because they consider them more "real." But behavioral research indicates that a preoccupation with physiological symptoms can hinder our understanding of the causes of addiction.

Positive Reinforcement

Drugs that lead to dependency must first reinforce people's behavior. As we saw in Chapter 13, positive reinforcement refers to the effect that certain stimuli have on the behaviors that preceded them. If, in a particular situation, a behavior is regularly followed by an appetitive stimulus (one that the organism will tend to approach), then that behavior will become more frequent in that situation. For example, if a hungry rat accidentally bumps into a lever and receives some food, it will eventually learn to press the lever. What actually seems to happen is that the occurrence of an appetitive stimulus activates a reinforcement mechanism in the brain that increases the likelihood of the most recent response (the lever press) in the present situation (the chamber that contains the lever).

Addictive drugs have reinforcing effects. That is, their effects include activation of the reinforcement mechanism. This activation strengthens the response that was just made. If the drug was taken by a fast-acting route such as injection or inhalation, the last response will be the act of taking the drug, so that response will be reinforced. This form of reinforcement is powerful and immediate and works with a wide variety of species. For example, a rat or a monkey will quickly learn to press a lever that controls a device that injects cocaine through a plastic tube inserted into a vein.

Role in Drug Abuse

When appetitive stimuli occur, they usually do so because we just did something to make them happen—and not because an experimenter was controlling the situation. The effectiveness of a reinforcing stimulus is greatest if it occurs immediately after a response occurs. If the reinforcing stimulus is delayed, it becomes considerably less effective. The reason for this fact is found by examining the function of instrumental conditioning: learning about the consequences of our own behavior. Normally, causes and effects are closely related in time; we do something, and something happens, good or bad. The consequences of the actions teach us whether to repeat that action, and events that follow a response by more than a few seconds were probably not caused by that response.

An experiment by Logan (1965) illustrates the importance of the immediacy of reinforcement. Logan trained hungry rats to run through a simple maze in which a single passage led to two corridors. At the end of one corridor the rats would find a small piece of food. At the end of the other corridor they would receive much more food, but it would be delivered only after a delay. Although the most intelligent strategy would be to enter the second corridor and wait for the larger amount of food, the rats chose to take the small amount of food that was delivered right away. Immediacy of reinforcement took precedence over quantity.

This phenomenon explains why the most addictive drugs are those that have immediate effects. As we saw in Chapter 4, drug users prefer heroin to morphine not because heroin has a *different* effect, but because it has a more *rapid* effect. In fact, heroin is converted to morphine as soon as it reaches the brain. But because heroin is more lipid soluble, it passes through the blood–brain barrier more rapidly, and its effects on the brain are felt sooner than those of morphine. The most potent reinforcement occurs when drugs produce sudden changes in the activity of the reinforcement mechanism; slow changes are much less reinforcing. A person taking an addictive drug seeks a sudden "rush" produced by a fast-acting drug. (As we will see later, the use of methadone for opiate addiction and nicotine patches for tobacco addiction are based on this phenomenon.)

Earlier, I posed the question of why people would ever expose themselves to the risks associated with dangerous addictive drugs. Who would rationally chose to become addicted to a drug that produced pleasurable effects in the short term but also produced even more powerful aversive effects in the long term: loss of employment and social status, legal problems and possible imprisonment, damage to health, and even premature death? The answer is that, as we saw, our reinforcement mechanism evolved to deal with the *immediate* effects of our behavior. The immediate reinforcing effects of an addictive drug can, for some individuals, overpower the recognition of the long-term aversive effects. Fortunately, most people are able to resist the short-term effects; only a minority of people who try addictive drugs go on to become dependent on them.

If an addictive drug is taken by a slow-acting route, reinforcement can also occur, but the process is somewhat more complicated. If a person takes a pill and several minutes later experiences a feeling of euphoria, he or she will certainly remember swallowing the pill. The recollection of this behavior will activate some of the same neural circuits involved in actually swallowing the pill, and the reinforcement mechanism, now active because of the effects of the drug, will reinforce the behavior. In other words, people's ability to remember having performed a behavior makes it possible to reinforce their behavior vicariously. The immediacy is between an imagined act and a reinforcing stimulus—the euphoria produced by the drug. Other cognitive processes contribute to the reinforcement, too, such as the expectation that euphoric effects will occur. Perhaps someone said, "Take one of these pills; you'll get a great high!" But if a nonhuman animal is fed one of these pills, its behavior is unlikely to be reinforced. By the time the euphoric effect occurs, the animal will be doing something other than ingesting the drug. Without the ability to recall an earlier behavior and thus activate circuits involved in the performance of that behavior, the delay between the behavior and the reinforcing effect of the drug prevent the animal from learning to take the drug. As we will see later in this chapter, researchers have developed ways to teach animals to become addicted to drugs that have delayed effects, such as alcohol.

Neural Mechanisms

As we saw in Chapter 13, all natural reinforcers that have been studied so far (such as food for a hungry animal, water for a thirsty one, or sexual contact) have one physiological effect in common: They cause the release of dopamine in the nucleus accumbens (White, 1996). This effect is undoubtedly not the *only* effect of reinforcing stimuli, and even aversive stimuli can trigger the release of dopamine (Salamone, 1992). But even though there is much that we do not yet understand about the neural basis of reinforcement, the release of dopamine appears to be a *necessary* (but not *sufficient*) condition for positive reinforcement to take place.

Addictive drugs—including amphetamine, cocaine, opiates, nicotine, alcohol, PCP, and cannabis—trigger the release of dopamine in the nucleus accumbens, as measured by microdialysis (Di Chiara, 1995). Some drugs do so by increasing the activity of the dopaminergic neurons of the mesolimbic system, which originates in the ventral tegmental area and terminates in the nucleus accumbens (and some other forebrain regions). Other drugs inhibit the reuptake of dopamine by terminal buttons and hence facilitate the postsynaptic effects of dopamine. If the release of dopamine in the nucleus accumbens is prevented by damaging the mesolimbic neurons, most addictive drugs lose their reinforcing effects. The details of the ways in which particular drugs interact with the mesolimbic dopaminergic system are described later.

Negative Reinforcement

You have probably heard the old joke in which someone says that the reason he bangs his head against the wall is that "it feels so good when I stop." Of course, that joke is funny (well, mildly amusing) because we know that although no one would act that way, ceasing to bang our head against the wall is certainly better than continuing to do so. If someone else started hitting us on the head and we were able to do something to get them to stop, whatever it was that we did would certainly be reinforced.

A behavior that turns off (or reduces) an aversive stimulus will be reinforced. This phenomenon is known as **negative reinforcement,** and its usefulness is obvious. For example, consider the following scenario: A woman staying in a rented house cannot get to sleep because of the unpleasant screeching noise that the furnace makes. She goes to the basement to discover the source of the noise and finally kicks the side of the oil burner. The noise ceases. The next time the furnace screeches, she immediately goes to the basement and kicks the side of the oil burner. The unpleasant noise (the aversive stimulus) is terminated when the woman kicks the side of the oil burner (the response), so the response is reinforced.

It is worth pointing out that *negative reinforcement* should not be confused with *punishment*. Both phenomena involve aversive stimuli, but one makes a response more likely, while the other makes it less likely. For negative reinforcement to occur, the response must make the unpleasant stimulus end (or at least decrease). For punishment to occur,

---

negative reinforcement The removal or reduction of an aversive stimulus that is contingent on a particular response, with an attendant increase in the frequency of that response.

the response must *make the unpleasant stimulus occur.* For example, if a little boy touches a mousetrap and hurts his finger, he is unlikely to touch a mousetrap again. The painful stimulus *punishes* the behavior of touching the mousetrap.

As we saw earlier in this chapter, the withdrawal effects, which occur when a habitual user of a drug stops taking the drug, are unpleasant. Although positive reinforcement seems to be what provokes drug taking in the first place, reduction of withdrawal effects could certainly play a role in maintaining someone's drug addiction. The withdrawal effects are unpleasant, but as soon as the person takes some of the drug, these effects go away, producing negative reinforcement.

Negative reinforcement could also explain the acquisition of drug addictions under some conditions. If a person is suffering from some unpleasant feelings and then takes a drug that eliminates these feelings, the person's drug-taking behavior is likely to be reinforced. For example, alcohol can relieve feelings of anxiety. If a person finds himself in a situation that arouses anxiety, he might find that having a drink or two makes him feel much better. In fact, people often anticipate this effect and begin drinking before the situation actually occurs.

Craving and Relapse

Why do drug addicts crave drugs? Why does this craving occur even after a long period of abstinence? Even after going for months or years without taking an addictive drug, a former drug addict might sometimes experience intense craving that leads to relapse. Clearly, taking a drug over an extended period of time must produce some long-lasting changes in the brain that increase a person's likelihood of relapsing. Understanding this process might help clinicians to devise therapies that will assist people in breaking their drug dependence once and for all.

Robinson and Berridge (1993) suggest that when an addictive drug activates the mesolimbic dopaminergic system, it gives *incentive salience* to stimuli present at that time. By this they mean that the stimuli associated with drug taking become exciting and motivating—a provocation to act. When a person with a history of drug abuse sees or thinks about these stimuli, he or she experiences craving—an impulsion to take the drug. Note that this hypothesis does not imply that the craving is caused solely by an unpleasant feeling, as described in the previous subsection. Koob and Le Moal (2000) propose that drug addiction involves "a cycle of spiraling dysregulation of brain reward systems that progressively increases, resulting in the compulsive use and loss of control over drug-taking" (p. 97). They refer to these changes in the brain's reinforcement mechanisms as *allostasis,* a long-term change in the set point around which these mechanisms are regulated. (The term is related to *homeostasis,* which, as we saw in Chapter 11, refers to a process of physiological regulation. *Allos-* is Greek for "other" and is at the origin of the English word "else.")

As everyone knows, a taste of food can provoke hunger, which is why we refer to tidbits we eat before a meal as "appetizers." For a person with a history of drug abuse, a small dose of the drug has similar effects: It increases craving, or "appetite," for the drug. The same phenomenon is seen in laboratory animals. If a rat that has been trained to self-administer cocaine is given a small dose of the drug, the animal will immediately seek to perform the behaviors it had previously learned to perform to obtain the drug.

Through the process of classical conditioning, stimuli that have been associated with drugs in the past can also elicit craving. For example, an alcoholic who sees a liquor bottle is likely to feel the urge to take a drink. In the past, agencies that sponsored antiaddiction programs sometimes prepared posters illustrating the dangers of drug abuse that featured drug paraphernalia—syringes, needles, spoons, piles of white powder, and so on. Possibly, these posters did succeed in reminding people who did not use drugs that they should avoid them. But we do know that their effect on people who were trying to break a drug habit was exactly the opposite of what was intended. As we saw in the opener to this chapter, a former drug addict would see the poster, and the sight of the drug paraphernalia would intensify the urge to take the drug again. For this reason, such posters are no longer used in campaigns against drug addiction.

One of the ways in which craving has been investigated in laboratory animals is through the *reinstatement model* of drug seeking. Animals are first trained to make a response (for example, press a lever) that is reinforced by intravenous injections of a drug such as cocaine. Next, the response is extinguished by providing injections of a saline solution rather than the drug. Once the animal has stopped responding, a "free" injection of the drug is administered or a stimulus that has been associated with the drug is presented. In response to these stimuli, the animals begin responding at the lever once more (Shalev, Grimm, and Shaham, 2002). Presumably, this kind of relapse (reinstatement of a previously extinguished response) is a good model for the craving that motivates drug-seeking behavior in a former addict.

Not surprisingly, relapses involve activation of the mesolimbic system of dopaminergic neurons. If a drug that prevents action potentials is injected directly into the nucleus accumbens, a "free" shot of cocaine fails to reinstate responding in rats (Grimm and See, 2000). In addition, deactivation of the ventral tegmental area or prefrontal cortex with a drug that stimulates inhibitory GABA receptors prevents a shot of cocaine from causing relapse (McFarland and Kalivas, 2001). Cocaine appears to directly activate a circuit from the prefrontal cortex to the nucleus accumbens via the ventral tegmental area; infusion of this drug into the prefrontal cortex or the nucleus accumbens reinstates cocaine seeking in rats (Park et al., 2002).

Relapse caused by stimuli previously associated with cocaine appears to involve the amygdala as well as the mesolimbic dopamine system. Several studies have found that lesions or temporary inactivation of the basolateral amygdala abolishes the reinstatement of responding when rats are presented with stimuli previously associated with cocaine (Everitt and Wolf, 2002). As we saw in Chapter 13, the amygdala plays an essential role in conditioned reinforcement. Presumably, this structure is also involved in conditioned drug craving, as well.

Evidence obtained from both humans and laboratory animals indicates that long-term drug abuse does indeed produce long-term changes in the brain. Lets consider humans first. A review by Goldstein and Volkow (2002) reported that most functional imaging studies show activation of the orbitofrontal cortex and the anterior cingulate cortex when taking or craving an addictive drug. During withdrawal these regions generally show a decreased level of activation in drug abusers. For example, Wang et al. (1999) induced craving in cocaine abusers by having them describe their own method of preparing cocaine. As a control condition, they asked them to discuss their family tree. PET scanning revealed that the orbitofrontal cortex was activated while the subjects were craving cocaine. (See *Figure 18.1*.)

In another PET study, Volkow et al. (1992) examined regional cerebral blood flow of cocaine abusers and control subjects during resting conditions. As Figure 18.2 shows, the activity of the prefrontal cortex and the anterior cin-

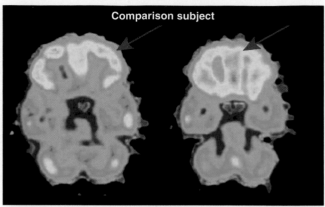
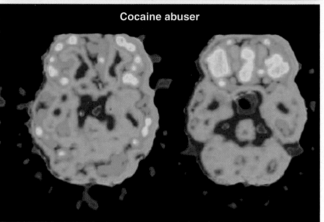

figure 18.2

Effects of prior cocaine abuse on resting cerebral blood flow. PET scans show higher activity of the prefrontal cortex and the anterior cingulate cortex in a normal subject than in an abstinent cocaine abuser.
(From Volkow, N. D., Hitzemann, R., Wang, G.-J., Fowler, J. S., Wolf, A. P., Dewey, S. L., and Handlesman, L. *Synapse,* 1992, *11,* 184–190.)

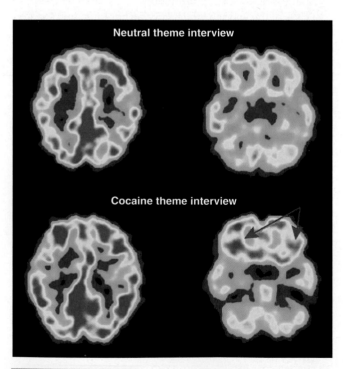

figure 18.1

Cocaine craving. PET scans show activation of the orbitofrontal cortex (arrows) in abstinent cocaine abusers describing their own method of preparing cocaine.
(From Wang, Wang, G.-J., Volkow, N. D., Fowler, J. S., Cervany, P., Hitzemann, R. J., Pappas, N. R., Wong, C. T., and Felder, C. *Life Sciences,* 1999, *64,* 775–784.)

gulate cortex of cocaine abusers was less active than that of normal subjects during abstinence. (See *Figure 18.2*.)

Studies with laboratory animals have also shown changes in brain function after administration of addictive drugs. Some of these changes involve long-term potentiation or long-term depression—changes in synaptic strength that play a role in learning and memory. First, several studies have shown that NMDA-receptor-dependent long-term potentiation and long-term depression can take place in the nucleus accumbens and ventral tegmental area. (See Hyman and Malenka, 2001, for a review.) Ungless et al. (2001) found that cocaine administration induces long-term potentiation in the ventral tegmental area by increasing the strength of synaptic transmission between glutamatergic synapses on dopaminergic neurons located there. Robinson et al. (2001) found increased dendritic branching and increased numbers of dendritic spines on neurons in the nucleus accumbens and the prefrontal cortex in rats that had previously self-administered cocaine one hour each day for one month. Finally, Vorel et al.

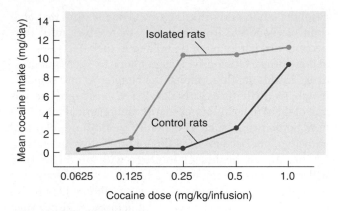

figure 18.3

Effects of social stress on cocaine intake. Mean cocaine intake of control rats and rats that had been subjected to isolation stress early in life.

(Adapted from Kosten, T. A., Miserendino, M. J. D., and Kehoe, P. *Brain Research*, 2000, *875*, 44–50.)

(2001) stimulated glutamatergic axons in a portion of the hippocampal formation that projects to the ventral tegmental area. The stimulation produced long-lasting activation of neurons in the ventral tegmental area, increased the release of dopamine in the nucleus accumbens, and reinstated cocaine-seeking behavior.

Other stimuli can also trigger drug-seeking behavior. For example, clinicians have long observed that stressful situations can cause former drug addicts to relapse. Presumably, the intense, pleasurable effects of the drug help them to forget about their current difficulties. These effects have been observed in rats that had previously learned to self-administer cocaine or heroin. Covington and Miczek (2001) paired naïve rats with rats that had been trained to become dominant. After being defeated by the dominant rats, the socially stressed rats became more sensitive to the effects of cocaine and showed bingeing—self-administration of larger amounts of the drug. Kosten, Miserendino, and Kehoe (2000) showed that stress that occurs early in life can have long-lasting effects. They stressed infant rats by isolating them from their mother and littermates for one hour per day for eight days. When these rats were given the opportunity to inject themselves with cocaine, they readily acquired the habit and took more of the drugs than control rats that had not been stressed. (See *Figure 18.3*.)

If stress (social and otherwise) increases susceptibility to the addictive potential of stimulant drugs, then perhaps the opposite of social stress—let's call it social satisfaction—can provide some protection against addiction. A recent study showed just this effect. Morgan et al. (2002) put rhesus monkeys together in small groups. Once each group of animals established its order of social dominance, the investigators performed PET scans that measured the level of dopamine D_2 receptors in the monkeys' brains and also permitted them to inject themselves with cocaine. The

investigators found that levels of D_2 receptors increased in the dominant monkeys' brains and that only the subordinate monkeys became addicted to the drug. These results suggest that animals receiving satisfaction from their social situation have less need of artificial reward than those who have a subordinate relationship to them.

Several studies have found that the drug craving elicited by stress depends on the secretion of corticotropin-releasing hormone (CRH). As we saw in Chapter 17, CRH is a neuropeptide released in several regions of the brain that plays an important role in the stress response. Erb and Stewart (1999) permitted rats to self-administer cocaine for 9–10 days and then extinguished the response by giving the animals injections of a saline solution when they pressed the lever. Next, they gave the rats a brief shock to their feet, which caused the animals to resume pressing the lever. This relapse did not occur if the experimenters had previously infused a CRH-receptor antagonist into the *bed nucleus of the stria terminalis (BNST)*, a region of the brain just rostral to the amygdala that contains a large number of CRH receptors. In a subsequent study, Erb et al. (2001) found that activity of CRH-secreting neurons in the central nucleus of the amygdala that project to the BNST are responsible for this priming effect. As we saw in Chapter 11, the central nucleus of the amygdala plays a key role in organizing a variety of aversive emotional responses, and stress-induced reinstatement of self-administration of cocaine appears to be yet another of the responses controlled by this nucleus.

interim
summary

Common Features of Addiction

Addictive drugs are those whose reinforcing effects are so potent that some people who are exposed to them are unable to go for very long without taking the drugs and whose lives become organized around taking them. Originally, addictive drugs came from plants, which used them as a defense against insects or other animals that otherwise would eat them, but chemists have synthesized many other drugs that have even more potent effects. If a person regularly takes some addictive drugs (most notably, the opiates), the effects of the drug show tolerance, and the person must take increasing doses to achieve the same effect. If the person then stops taking the drug, withdrawal effects, opposite to the primary effects of the drug, will occur. However, withdrawal effects are not the cause of addiction—the abuse potential of a drug is related to its ability to reinforce drug-taking behavior.

Positive reinforcement occurs when a behavior is regularly followed by an appetitive stimulus—one that an organism will approach. Most addictive drugs produce positive reinforcement; they reinforce drug-taking behavior. Laboratory animals will learn to make responses that result in the delivery of these drugs. The faster a drug produces its effects, the more quickly dependence will be established. All addictive drugs that produce positive reinforcement stimulate the release of dopamine in the nucleus accumbens, a structure that plays an important role in reinforcement.

Negative reinforcement occurs when a behavior is followed by the reduction or termination of an aversive stimulus. If, because of a person's social situation or personality characteristics, he or she feels unhappy or anxious, a drug that reduces these feelings can reinforce drug-taking behavior by means of negative reinforcement. Also, the reduction of unpleasant withdrawal symptoms by a dose of the drug undoubtedly plays a role in maintaining drug addictions, but it is not the sole cause of craving.

Tolerance of the effects of a drug is part of a compensatory mechanism by which the brain resists long-term disruption of normal balances in its activity. Tolerance is caused by a decrease in the sensitivity of the receptors for that drug or the intracellular mechanism that is responsible for the drug's effects. In addition, compensatory activity of neural circuits can be classically conditioned to stimuli associated with taking the drug or the place in which it is regularly taken. These stimuli can intensify an addict's craving for the drug.

Craving—the urge to take a drug to which one has become addicted—cannot be completely explained by withdrawal symptoms, because it can occur even after an addict has refrained from taking the drug for a long time. In laboratory animals inactivation of the prefrontal cortex, ventral tegmental area, or nucleus accumbens prevents a "free" shot of cocaine from reinstating drug-seeking behavior; conversely, injection of cocaine into the prefrontal cortex or the nucleus accumbens causes reinstatement. Presentation of stimuli previously associated with cocaine also causes reinstatement but not if the basolateral amygdala is destroyed or inactivated. Functional imaging studies find that craving for cocaine increases the activity of the orbitofrontal prefrontal cortex and the anterior cingulate cortex. Chronic cocaine intake produces long-term potentiation in the ventral tegmental area, which increases the sensitivity of dopamine-secreting neurons to excitatory glutamatergic input; it also causes increased dendritic branching and increased numbers of dendritic spines in the nucleus accumbens and prefrontal cortex. Stressful stimuli—even those that occur early in life—increase an animal's susceptibility to drug addiction. This phenomenon is associated with the release of CRH in the brain, particularly by cells in the central nucleus of the amygdala whose terminals release this peptide in the bed nucleus of the stria terminalis.

Commonly Abused Drugs

People have been known to abuse an enormous variety of drugs, including alcohol, barbiturates, opiates, tobacco, amphetamine, cocaine, cannabis, hallucinogens such as LSD, PCP, volatile solvents such as glues or even gasoline, ether, and nitrous oxide. The pleasure that children often derive from spinning themselves until they become dizzy may even be related to the effects of some of these drugs. Obviously, I cannot hope to discuss all these drugs in any depth and keep the chapter to a reasonable length, so I will restrict my discussion to the most important of them in terms of popularity and potential for addiction. Some drugs, such as caffeine, are both popular and addictive, but because they do not normally cause intoxication, impair health, or interfere with productivity, I will not discuss them here. (Chapter 4 did discuss the behavioral effects and site of action of caffeine.) I will also not discuss the wide variety of hallucinogenic drugs such as LSD or PCP. Although some people enjoy the mind-altering effects of LSD, many people simply find them frightening; and in any event, LSD use does not normally lead to addiction. PCP (phencyclidine) acts as an indirect antagonist at the NMDA receptor, which means that its effects overlap with those of alcohol. Rather than devoting space to this drug, I have chosen to say more about alcohol, which is abused far more than any of the hallucinogenic drugs. If you would like to learn more about drugs other than the ones I discuss here, I suggest you consult the books listed among the suggested readings at the end of this chapter.

Opiates

Opium, derived from a sticky resin produced by the opium poppy, has been eaten and smoked for centuries. Opiate addiction has several high personal and social costs. First, because heroin, the most commonly abused opiate, is an illegal drug in most countries, an addict becomes, by definition, a criminal. Second, because of tolerance, a person must take increasing amounts of the drug to achieve a "high." The habit thus becomes more and more expensive, and the person often turns to crime to obtain enough money to support his or her habit. Third, an opiate addict often uses unsanitary needles; at present, a substantial percentage of people who inject illicit drugs have been exposed in this way to hepatitis or the AIDS virus. Fourth, if the addict is a pregnant woman, her infant will also become dependent on the drug, which easily crosses the placental barrier. The infant must be given opiates right after being born and then weaned off the drug with gradually decreasing doses. Fifth, the uncertainty about the strength of a given batch of heroin makes it possible for a user to receive an unusually large dose of the drug, with possibly fatal consequences.

As we saw in Chapters 4 and 7, opiates are secreted when an animal is performing behaviors that are important to its survival or the survival of its species. For example, when an animal fights with another animal, the outcome of the battle is usually very important for that animal. The animal may be fighting with a rival in a dispute over territory or access to a mate, defending its offspring, attacking prey, or defending itself against a predator. Fighting usually produces pain, and if an animal were too easily inhibited by pain, it would be less likely to thrive and reproduce—or it might even die. For this reason, the evolutionary process has equipped mammals with circuits of neurons that release endogenous opioids when the animal is fighting or mating. These chemicals stimulate receptors that produce analgesia that reduces the inhibitory effects of pain and positive reinforcement that encourages the animal to continue what it is doing. The problem is, of course, that when a person takes an artificial opiate, the effects of the drug encourage the person to continue taking that drug.

Neural Basis of Reinforcing Effects

As we saw earlier, laboratory animals will self-administer opiates. When an opiate is administered systemically, it stimulates opiate receptors located on neurons in various parts of the brain and produces a variety of effects, including analgesia, hypothermia (lowering of body temperature), sedation, and reinforcement. Opiate receptors in the periaqueductal gray matter are primarily responsible for the analgesia, those in the preoptic area are responsible for the hypothermia, and those in the mesencephalic reticular formation are responsible for the sedation. As we shall see, opiate receptors in the ventral tegmental area and the nucleus accumbens may play a role in the reinforcing effects of opiates, but other regions appear to be important too.

As we saw in Chapter 4, there are three major types of opiate receptors: μ (mu), δ (delta), and κ (kappa). Evidence suggests that μ receptors and δ receptors are responsible for reinforcement and analgesia and that stimulation of κ receptors produces aversive effects. The best evidence for the role of μ receptors comes from a study by Matthes et al. (1996), who performed a targeted mutation ("knockout") of the gene responsible for production of the μ opiate receptor in mice. These animals, when they grew up, were completely insensitive to the reinforcing or analgesic effects of morphine, and they showed no signs of withdrawal symptoms after having been given increasing doses of morphine for six days. (See *Figure 18.4*.)

Chemicals that stimulate κ opiate receptors, including **dynorphin** (an endogenous opioid) and various artificial κ-receptor agonists, produce aversive effects (Mucha and Herz, 1985; Suzuki et al., 1993). Infusion of κ-receptor agonists into several brain regions, including the periaqueductal gray matter, ventral tegmental area, and nucleus accumbens, has aversive effects (Balskubik et al., 1993; Motta, Penha, and Brandao, 1995). Kappa receptor

dynorphin An endogenous opioid; the natural ligand for κ opiate receptors.

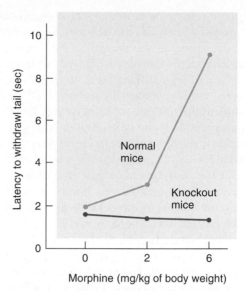

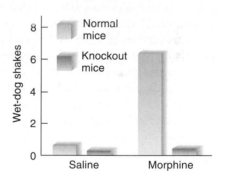

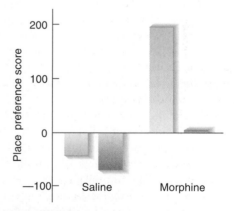

figure 18.4

Lack of responses to morphine in mice with targeted mutations of the μ opiate receptor. (Top) Latency to tail withdrawal from a hot object (a measure of analgesia). (Middle) Wet-dog shakes after being withdrawn from long-term morphine administration (a prominent withdrawal symptom in rodents). (Bottom) Conditioned place preference for a chamber associated with an injection of morphine (a measure of reinforcement).

(Adapted from Matthes, H. W. D., Maldonado, R., Simonin, F., Valverde, O., Slowe, S., Kitchen, I., Befort, K., Dierich, A., Le Meur, M., Dolle, P., Tzavara, E., Hanoune, J., Roques, B. P., and Kieffer, B. L. *Nature,* 1996, *383,* 819–823.)

agonists, acting on neurons in the ventral tegmental area and the nucleus accumbens, dramatically reduce the release of dopamine in the nucleus accumbens—a phenomenon that occurs during withdrawal from long-term administration of opiates (Devine et al., 1993).

As we saw earlier, reinforcing stimuli cause the release of dopamine in the nucleus accumbens. Injections of opiates are no exception to this general rule; Wise et al. (1995) found that the level of dopamine in the nucleus accumbens increased by 150 to 300 percent while a rat was pressing a lever that delivered intravenous injections of heroin. Rats will also press a lever that delivers injections of an opiate directly into the ventral tegmental area (Devine and Wise, 1994) or the nucleus accumbens Goeders, Lane, and Smith (1984). In other words, injections of opiates into both ends of the mesolimbic dopaminergic system are reinforcing. Injection of an opiate into the ventral tegmental area activates the dopaminergic neurons located there by decreasing the activity of GABA-secreting neurons that normally inhibit the DA neurons (Johnson and North, 1992). All these findings suggest that the reinforcing effects of opiates are produced by activation of neurons of the mesolimbic system and release of dopamine in the nucleus accumbens.

However, other experimental findings indicate that opiates can reinforce behavior independent of their effects on the mesolimbic dopamine system. Several studies have found that lesions of the nucleus accumbens do not prevent opiates from reinforcing behavior. For example, Gerrits and Vanree (1996) found that 6-HD lesions of the nucleus accumbens, which destroys dopaminergic axons and terminals, disrupted lever pressing of rats for intravenous injections of cocaine but had no effect on lever pressing for IV injections of heroin. Olmstead and Franklin (1996) found that destruction of all the cells of the nucleus accumbens with kainic acid had similar effects. They trained rats on a **conditioned place preference.** A conditioned place preference task is often used in studies investigating the reinforcing or punishing properties of drugs. The apparatus consists of two distinctly different chambers, which the animal can easily distinguish. Photocells automatically keep track of the animal's location. An animal that receives an addictive drug just before being placed in one chamber and an injection of a placebo before being placed in another will learn to prefer the "drug" chamber and will go there if given a choice. If a drug produces an unpleasant aversive effect, the animal will avoid the drug chamber and will show a conditioned place *aversion*. (See *Figure 18.5*.) Olmstead and Franklin found that destruction of the nucleus accumbens blocked development of a conditioned place preference to amphetamine but not to morphine. These studies indicate that unlike other addictive drugs, opiates need not trigger the release of dopamine by neurons of the mesolimbic system to reinforce behavior.

As I mentioned earlier, a considerable amount of evidence suggests that endogenous opioids are involved in the behavioral effects of natural reinforcers. Let's look at

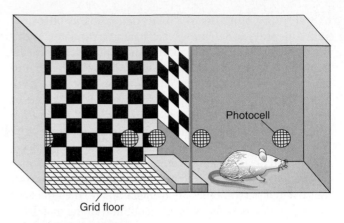

figure 18.5

The conditioned place preference procedure.
(Adapted from Feldman, R. S., Meyer, J. S., and Quenzer, L. F. *Principles of Neuropsychopharmacology*. Sunderland, MA: Sinauer Associates, 1997.)

some of this evidence. Agmo et al. (1993) used a conditioned place preference task to measure the reinforcing effects of a drink of water for thirsty rats. Rats in the control group, previously given an injection of a placebo, showed a clear preference for the chamber in which they were placed after drinking the water. Rats that were given an injection of **naloxone** (a drug that blocks opiate receptors) or **pimozide** (a drug that blocks dopamine receptors) showed no preference. Thus, the release of both dopamine and the endogenous opioids are essential for the reinforcing effects of a drink of water.

The release of endogenous opioids may even play a role in the reinforcing effects of some addictive drugs. Many studies have shown that naloxone and other drugs that block opiate receptors reduce the reinforcing effects of alcohol in both humans and laboratory animals. Because the use of opiate blockers has recently been approved as a treatment for alcoholism, I will discuss relevant research later in this chapter.

Neural Basis of Withdrawal Effects

Several studies have investigated the neural systems that are responsible for the withdrawal effects of opiates. Several regions of the brain have been implicated, including the periaqueductal gray matter (PAG), the locus coeruleus, and the amygdala. As we saw in Chapter 7, the

---

conditioned place preference The learned preference for a location in which an organism encountered a reinforcing stimulus, such as food or a reinforcing drug.

naloxone A drug that blocks μ opiate receptors; antagonizes the reinforcing and sedative effects of opiates.

pimozide A drug that blocks dopamine receptors.

PAG contains a high concentration of opiate receptors and is involved in the analgesic effects of opiates. As we saw in Chapters 4 and 9, the locus coeruleus contains noradrenergic neurons whose terminals innervate most regions of the brain. This nucleus plays an excitatory role in vigilance and an inhibitory role in REM sleep. And as we saw in Chapter 11, the amygdala is involved in emotional responses to aversive stimuli.

Maldonado et al. (1992) made rats physically dependent on morphine and then injected naloxone into various regions of the brain to see whether the sudden blocking of opiate receptors would stimulate symptoms of withdrawal. (This technique—administering an opiate for a prolonged interval and then blocking its effects with an antagonist—is referred to as **antagonist-precipitated withdrawal.**) The investigators found that the most sensitive site was the locus coeruleus, followed by the periaqueductal gray matter. Injection of naloxone into the amygdala produced a weak withdrawal syndrome. Using a similar technique (first infusing morphine into various regions of the brain and then precipitating withdrawal by giving the animals an intraperitoneal injection of naloxone), Bozarth (1994) found that injections into the locus coeruleus and the PAG produced withdrawal symptoms.

These studies suggest that opiate receptors in the locus coeruleus and periaqueductal gray matter are involved in withdrawal symptoms. So far, most of the research effort has been directed toward study of the locus coeruleus. A single dose of an opiate decreases the firing rate of these neurons, but if the drug is administered chronically, the firing rate will return to normal. Then, if an opiate antagonist is administered (to precipitate withdrawal symptoms), the firing rate of neurons in the locus coeruleus increases dramatically, which increases the release of norepinephrine in the projection of this nucleus (Hyman, 1996b; Koob, 1996; Nestler, 1996). In addition, lesions of the locus coeruleus reduce the severity of antagonist-precipitated withdrawal symptoms (Maldonado and Koob, 1993). A microdialysis study by Aghajanian, Kogan, and Moghaddam (1994) found that antagonist-precipitated withdrawal caused an increase in the level of glutamate and aspartate, two excitatory amino acid neurotransmitters, in the locus coeruleus.

The intracellular processes involved in the development of withdrawal symptoms to opiates appear to involve a protein known as **CREB** (cyclic AMP-responsive element-binding protein). As we saw, long-term exposure to opiates causes tolerance—a decreased sensitivity of neurons to opiates. This decreased sensitivity (also known as *down-regulation*) occurs even though the number of opiate receptors does not change, which implies that the alteration must be intracellular, in the biochemical steps that link activation of the opiate receptor (a metabotropic receptor) to production of second messengers and the effects they produce (Hyman, 1996a). When μ receptors are activated by an opiate, they cause the production of cyclic AMP within the cell. This second messenger travels to the nucleus, where it

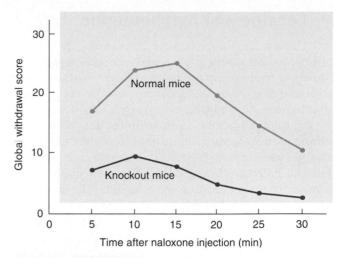

figure 18.6

Withdrawal symptoms of normal mice and mice with a targeted mutation (knockout) of the gene responsible for the production of CREB.

(Adapted from Maldonado, R., Blendy, J. A., Tzavara, E., Gass, P., Roques, B. P., Hanoune, J., and Schütz, G. *Science,* 1996, *273,* 657–659.)

binds with CREB. CREB itself plays a role in regulating the activity of some genes. Just what occurs in the nucleus when CREB is activated by cyclic AMP is not yet known.

Maldonado et al. (1996) produced a targeted mutation of the gene responsible for the production of CREB in mice. The animals appeared behaviorally normal, and injections of morphine produced analgesia and increased the animals' activity. (The investigators did not assess morphine's reinforcing effects.) However, the animals' response to antagonist-precipitated withdrawal from morphine was drastically reduced. (See *Figure 18.6.*) This study strongly suggests that CREB plays a critical role in the intracellular events responsible for the withdrawal effects of opioids. It will be interesting to learn whether other drugs that produce withdrawal effects, such as alcohol, also involve this mechanism.

Earlier in this chapter, we saw that the neuropeptide CRH is involved in the stimulation of drug craving caused by stress. Several studies suggest that it is also involved in the aversive effects of withdrawal from cocaine, opiates, alcohol, and marijuana (Rodriguez de Fonseca et al., 1997; Koob, 1999; Richter and Weiss, 1999; Service, 1999).

antagonist-precipitated withdrawal Sudden withdrawal from long-term administration of a drug caused by cessation of the drug and administration of an antagonistic drug.

CREB Cyclic AMP-responsive element-binding protein; a nuclear protein to which cyclic AMP can bind and affect the activity of a gene or set of genes.

Cocaine and Amphetamine

Cocaine and amphetamine have similar behavioral effects, because both act as potent dopamine agonists. However, their sites of action are different. Cocaine binds with and deactivates the dopamine transporter proteins, thus blocking the reuptake of dopamine after it is released by the terminal buttons. Amphetamine also inhibits the reuptake of dopamine, but its most important effect is to directly stimulate the release of dopamine from terminal buttons. Freebase cocaine ("crack"), a particularly potent form of the drug, is smoked and thus enters the blood supply of the lungs and reaches the brain very quickly. Because its effects are so potent and so rapid, it is probably the most effective reinforcer of all available drugs.

When people take cocaine, they become euphoric, active, and talkative. They say that they feel powerful and alert. Some of them become addicted to the drug, and obtaining it becomes an obsession to which they devote more and more time and money. Laboratory animals, which will quickly learn to self-administer cocaine intravenously, also act excited and show intense exploratory activity. After receiving the drug for a day or two, rats start showing stereotyped movements, such as grooming, head bobbing, and persistent locomotion (Geary, 1987). If rats or monkeys are given continuous access to a lever that permits them to self-administer cocaine, they often self-inject so much cocaine that they die. In fact, Bozarth and Wise (1985) found that rats that self-administered cocaine were almost three times more likely to die than rats that self-administered heroin. (See *Figure 18.7*.)

One of the alarming effects of cocaine and amphetamine seen in people who abuse these drugs regularly is psychotic behavior: hallucinations, delusions of persecu-

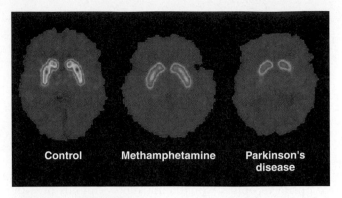

Control   Methamphetamine   Parkinson's disease

figure 18.8

PET scans of the brain showing concentrations of dopamine transporters from a control subject, a subject who had previously abused methamphetamine, and a subject with Parkinson's disease. Decreased concentrations of dopamine transporters indicate loss of dopaminergic terminals.
(From McCann, U. D., Wong, D. F., Yokoi, F., Villemagne, V., Dannls, R. F., and Ricaurte, G. A. *Journal of Neuroscience*, 1998, *18*, 8417–8422.)

tion, mood disturbances, and repetitive behaviors. These symptoms so closely resemble those of paranoid schizophrenia that even a trained mental health professional cannot distinguish them unless he or she knows about the person's history of drug abuse. As we saw in Chapter 16, the fact that these symptoms are provoked by dopamine agonists and reduced by drugs that block dopamine receptors suggests that overactivity of dopaminergic synapses is one of the causes of schizophrenia.

Some evidence suggests that the use of stimulants such as cocaine and amphetamine may have adverse long-term effects on the brain. For example, a PET study by McCann et al. (1998) discovered that prior abusers of methamphetamine showed a decrease in the numbers of dopamine transporters in the caudate nucleus and putamen, despite the fact that they had abstained from the drug for approximately three years. The decreased number of dopamine transporters suggests that the number of dopaminergic terminals in these regions is diminished. As the authors note, these people might have an increased risk of Parkinson's disease as they get older. (See *Figure 18.8*.)

As we have seen, the mesolimbic dopamine system plays an essential role in all forms of reinforcement, except perhaps for reinforcement mediated by opiate receptors. Because cocaine and amphetamine are potent dopamine agonists, these drugs activate the mesolimbic system and reinforce drug-taking behavior. Because cocaine is currently the stimulant drug of choice, more research effort has been devoted to cocaine than to amphetamine.

Several studies have shown that intravenous injections of cocaine and amphetamine increase the concentration of dopamine in the nucleus accumbens, as measured by microdialysis (Petit and Justice, 1989; Di Ciano et al., 1995;

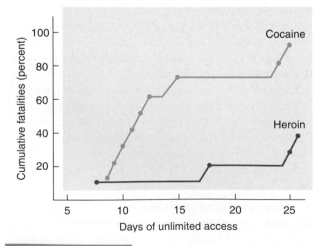

figure 18.7

Cumulative fatalities in groups of rats self-administering cocaine or heroin.
(Adapted from Bozarth, M. A., and Wise, R. A. *Journal of the American Medical Association*, 1985, *254*, 81–83. Reprinted with permission.)

Wise et al., 1995). For example, Figure 18.9 shows data collected from rats that learned to press a lever that delivered intravenous injections of cocaine or amphetamine. The colored bars at the base of the graphs indicate the animals' responses, and the line graphs indicate the level of dopamine in the nucleus accumbens. (See *Figure 18.9*.)

Several other lines of research also indicate that the nucleus accumbens is a critical site for the reinforcing effects of cocaine and amphetamine. For example, if drugs that block dopamine receptors are injected into the nucleus

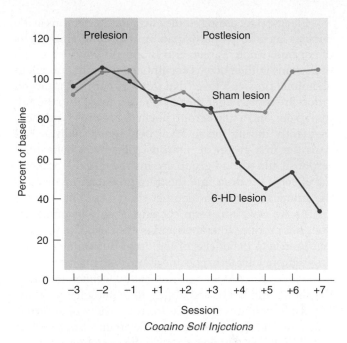

Cocaine Self-Injections

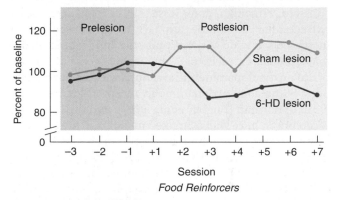

Food Reinforcers

figure 18.10

Changes in rate of responding for cocaine or food reinforcement by rats with sham lesions or 6-HD lesions of the nucleus accumbens, expressed as percentage of baseline rate.

(Adapted from Caine, S. B., and Koob, G. F. *Journal of the Experimental Analysis of Behavior,* 1994, *61*, 213–221.)

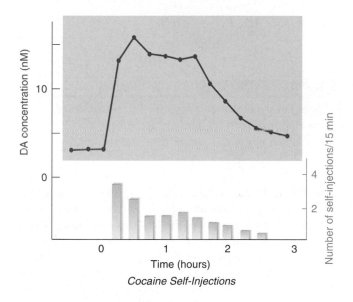

Cocaine Self-Injections

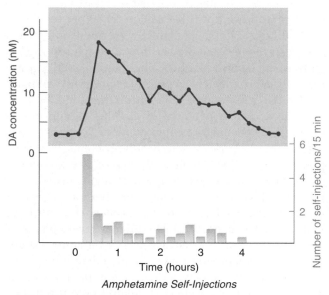

Amphetamine Self-Injections

figure 18.9

Dopamine concentration in the nucleus accumbens, measured by microdialysis, during self-administration of intravenous cocaine or amphetamine by rats.

(Adapted from Di Ciano, P., Coury, A., Depoortere, R. Y., Egilmez, Y., Lane, J. D., Emmett-Oglesby, M. W., Lepiane, F. G., Phillips, A. G., and Blaha, C. D. *Behavioural Pharmacology,* 1995, *6*, 311–322.)

accumbens, cocaine loses much of its reinforcing effect (McGregor and Roberts, 1993; Caine et al., 1995). In addition, lesions of the nucleus accumbens or destruction of dopaminergic terminals there with a local injection of 6-HD interferes with the reinforcing effects of both cocaine and amphetamine. Caine and Koob (1994) found that after they injected 6-HD into the nucleus accumbens, rats stopped pressing a lever that produced intravenous injections of cocaine. They did, however, continue pressing the lever when doing so caused the delivery of a small pellet of food. Thus, the damage caused by the 6-HD did not simply interfere with the animals' ability to press the lever. (See *Figure 18.10*.)

Electrical recording studies suggest that neurons in the nucleus accumbens participate in the reinforcing effects of cocaine (Koob, Sanna, and Bloom, 1998). One group of neurons in the nucleus accumbens respond just before an animal presses a lever that delivers cocaine, a second group fire shortly after the cocaine is infused into the animal's vein, and a third group begin to fire more and more frequently during the interval between responses. Perhaps the first group of neurons trigger the behavioral response, the second group are involved in the reinforcing effect of the drug, and the third group are involved in the animals' craving for another shot of cocaine.

As we saw, long-term cocaine or amphetamine use does not produce tolerance and is even likely to produce *sensitization* to the effects of the drug. But although withdrawal from long-term cocaine abuse does not cause physical symptoms, it does cause unpleasant feelings, including dysphoria and decreased ability to experience pleasure. We also saw that withdrawal from a variety of addictive drugs—including cocaine and amphetamine—causes a drastic fall in the level of dopamine in the nucleus accumbens (Rossetti, Hmaidan, and Gessa, 1992). This decrease in extracellular dopamine appears to be caused by an increased secretion of dynorphin, the endogenous opioid that stimulates κ receptors. Dynorphin seems to act as a brake on the dopaminergic system of the nucleus accumbens. Stimulation of dopamine D_1 receptors increases levels of dynorphin (Engber et al., 1992), and the lack of D_1 receptors (in mice with a targeted mutation in the gene that produces this receptor) dramatically decreases the production of dynorphin (Xu et al., 1994). Kappa receptors serve as heteroreceptors on dopaminergic terminal buttons, where they produce presynaptic inhibition; thus, dynorphin has an inhibitory effect on the release of dopamine and reverses the effects of cocaine (Steiner and Gerfen, 1995).

Hyman (1996a) proposes that chronic, long-term cocaine or amphetamine use sensitizes dynorphin-secreting neurons in the nucleus accumbens. The increased release of dynorphin stimulates presynaptic κ opiate receptors on dopaminergic terminal buttons, which decreases the release of dopamine. Then, if cocaine or amphetamine is suddenly withdrawn, the continuing activity of the dynorphin-secreting neurons reduces the levels of dopamine in the nucleus accumbens, causing the unpleasant symptoms that accompany discontinuation of these drugs. (See *Figure 18.11*.)

Nicotine

Nicotine might seem rather tame in comparison to opiates, cocaine, and amphetamine. Nevertheless, nicotine is an addictive drug, and it accounts for more deaths than the so-called "hard" drugs. The combination of nicotine and other substances in tobacco smoke is carcinogenic and leads to cancer of the lungs, mouth, throat, and esophagus.

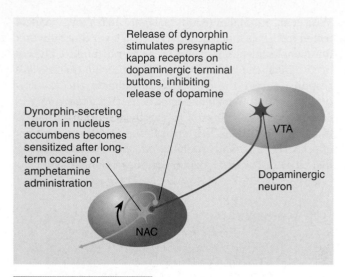

Release of dynorphin stimulates presynaptic kappa receptors on dopaminergic terminal buttons, inhibiting release of dopamine

Dynorphin-secreting neuron in nucleus accumbens becomes sensitized after long-term cocaine or amphetamine administration

VTA

Dopaminergic neuron

NAC

figure 18.11

The role of dynorphin secretion in the regulation of dopamine release in the nucleus accumbens.
(Adapted from Hyman, S. E. *Neuron,* 1996, *16,* 901–904.)

The World Health Organization (WHO, 1997) reported that one-third of the adult population of the world smokes and that smoking is one of the few causes of death that is rising in developing countries. The WHO estimates that 50 percent of the people who begin to smoke as adolescents and continue smoking throughout their lives will die from smoking-related diseases. Investigators estimate that by the year 2020, tobacco will be the largest single health problem worldwide, with 8.4 million deaths per year (Murray and Lopez, 1997). Smoking by pregnant women also has negative effects on the health of their fetuses—apparently worse than those of cocaine (Slotkin 1998). Unfortunately, approximately 25 percent of pregnant women in the United States expose their fetuses to nicotine.

The addictive potential of nicotine should not be underestimated; many people continue to smoke even when doing so causes serious health problems. For example, Sigmund Freud, whose theory of psychoanalysis stressed the importance of insight in changing one's behavior, was unable to stop smoking even after most of his jaw had been removed because of the cancer that this habit had caused (Brecher, 1972). He suffered severe pain and, as a physician, realized that he should have stopped smoking. He did not, and his cancer finally killed him.

Although executives of tobacco companies and others whose economic welfare is linked to the production and sale of tobacco products have argued that smoking is a "habit" rather than an "addiction," evidence suggests that the behavior of people who regularly use tobacco is that of compulsive drug users. In a review of the literature, Stolerman and Jarvis (1995) note that smokers tend to smoke regularly or not at all; few can smoke just a little. Males smoke an average of seventeen cigarettes per day, while

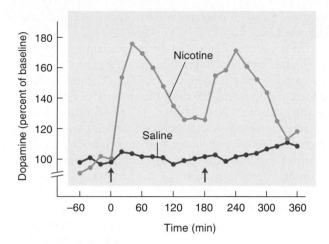

figure 18.12

Changes in dopamine concentration in the nucleus accumbens, measured by microdialysis, in response to injections of nicotine or saline. The arrows indicate the time of the injections.

(Adapted from Damsma, G., Day, J., and Fibiger, H. C. *European Journal of Pharmacology,* 1989, *168,* 363–368. Reprinted with permission.)

females smoke an average of fourteen. Nineteen out of twenty smokers smoke every day, and only 60 out of 3500 smokers questioned smoke fewer than five cigarettes per day. Forty percent of people continue to smoke after having had a laryngectomy (which is usually performed to treat throat cancer). Indeed, physicians have reported that patients with tubes inserted into their tracheas so that they can breathe will sometimes press a cigarette against the opening of these tubes and try to smoke (Hyman and Malenka, 2001). More than 50 percent of heart attack survivors continue to smoke, and about 50 percent of people continue to smoke after submitting to surgery for lung cancer. Of those who attempt to quit smoking by enrolling in a special program, 20 percent manage to abstain for one year. The record is much poorer for those who try to quit on their own: One-third manage to stop for one day, one-fourth for one week, but only 4 percent manage to abstain for six months. It is difficult to reconcile these figures with the assertion that smoking is merely a "habit" that is pursued for the "pleasure" that it produces.

Ours is not the only species willing to self-administer nicotine; so will laboratory animals (Donny et al., 1995). Nicotine stimulates acetylcholine receptors, of course. It also increases the activity of dopaminergic neurons of the mesolimbic system, which contain these receptors (Mereu et al., 1987), and causes dopamine to be released in the nucleus accumbens (Damsma, Day, and Fibiger, 1989). Figure 18.12 shows the effects of two injections of nicotine or saline on the extracellular dopamine level of the nucleus accumbens, measured by microdialysis. (See *Figure 18.12.*)

Injection of a nicotinic agonist directly into the ventral tegmental area will reinforce a conditioned place pref-

erence (Museo and Wise, 1994). Conversely, injection of a nicotinic antagonist into the VTA will reduce the reinforcing effect of intravenous injections of nicotine (Corrigall, Coen, and Adamson, 1994). But although nicotinic receptors are found in both the ventral tegmental area and the nucleus accumbens (Swanson et al., 1987), Corrigall and his colleagues found that injections of a nicotinic antagonist in the nucleus accumbens has no effect on reinforcement. Corroborating these findings, Nisell, Nomikos, and Svensson (1994) found that infusion of a nicotinic antagonist into the VTA—but not into the nucleus accumbens—will prevent an intravenous injection of nicotine from triggering the release of dopamine in the nucleus accumbens. (See *Figure 18.13.*) Thus, the reinforcing effect of nicotine appears to occur in the ventral tegmental area.

A study by Rose et al. (1998) suggests that some of the reinforcing effects of tobacco smoke may be mediated by nicotinic acetylcholine receptors located outside the central nervous system. The investigators administered a placebo or a drug that blocks nicotinic receptors but does not cross the blood–brain barrier. The drug reduced the sensations produced by cigarette smoke as it passed through the airways into the lungs and decreased the satisfaction the smokers normally received from their cigarettes.

The nicotinic ACh receptor, which is of course the target of nicotine, exists in three states. When a burst of ACh is released by an acetylcholinergic terminal button, the receptors open briefly, permitting the entry of calcium.

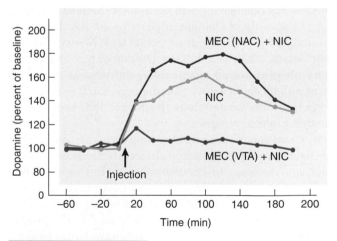

figure 18.13

Changes in dopamine concentration in the nucleus accumbens, measured by microdialysis, in response to injections of intravenous nicotine (NIC) alone or in conjunction with an infusion of a nicotinic antagonist (MEC) in the ventral tegmental area of the nucleus accumbens. Only the injection of MEC in the ventral tegmental area blocked the secretion of dopamine in the nucleus accumbens.

(Adapted from Nisell, M., Nomikos, G. G., and Svensson, T. H. *Synapse,* 1994, *16,* 36–44.)

(Most nicotinic receptors serve as heteroreceptors on terminal buttons that release another neurotransmitter. The entry of calcium stimulates the release of that neurotransmitter.) Within a few milliseconds the enzyme AChE has destroyed the acetylcholine, and the receptors either close again or enter a desensitized state, during which they bind with, but do not react to, ACh. Normally, few nicotinic receptors enter the desensitized state. However, when a person smokes, the level of nicotine in the brain rises slowly and stays steady for a prolonged period because it is not destroyed by AChE. At first, nicotinic receptors are activated, but the sustained low levels of the drug convert many nicotinic receptors to the desensitized state. Thus, nicotine has dual effects on nicotinic receptors: activation and then desensitization. In addition, probably in response to desensitization, the number of nicotinic receptors increases (Dani and De Biasi, 2001).

Most smokers report that their first cigarette in the morning brings the most pleasure, presumably because the period of abstinence during the night has allowed many of their nicotinic receptors to enter the closed state and become sensitized again. The first dose of nicotine in the morning activates these receptors and has a reinforcing effect. After that, a large proportion of the smoker's nicotinic receptors become desensitized again; as a consequence, most smokers say that they smoke less for pleasure than to relax and gain relief from nervousness and craving. If smokers abstain for a few weeks, the number of nicotinic receptors in their brains returns to normal. However, as the high rate of relapse indicates, craving continues, which means that other changes in the brain must have occurred.

One of these changes appears to involve long-term potentiation in the ventral tegmental area. Mansvelder and McGehee (2000) found that activation of nicotinic receptors on presynaptic terminals in the ventral tegmental area enhances excitatory glutamatergic input to dopaminergic neurons located there, leading to long-term potentiation of these synapses.

Cessation of smoking after long-term use causes withdrawal symptoms, including anxiety, restlessness, insomnia, and inability to concentrate (Hughes et al., 1989). Like the withdrawal symptoms of other drugs, these symptoms may increase the likelihood of relapse, but they do not explain why people become addicted to the drug in the first place. As we saw earlier, withdrawal from cocaine, amphetamine, or the opiates causes a dramatic decrease in the level of dopamine in the nucleus accumbens. The same phenomenon accompanies withdrawal from nicotine (Fung et al., 1996).

A functional imaging study by Due et al. (2002) showed color photographs of neutral scenes (pictures of animals) or smoking-related scenes (people smoking and hands holding cigarettes) to smokers and nonsmokers. The smoking-related images, but not the neutral images, activated several regions in the brains of smokers, including the prefrontal cortex, amygdala, and ventral tegmen-

tal area. These differences were not seen in the brains of nonsmokers.

Wise (1988) notes that because nicotine stimulates the tegmentostriatal dopaminergic system, smoking could potentially make it more difficult for a cocaine or heroin addict to stop taking the drug. As several studies with laboratory animals have shown, if self-administration of cocaine or heroin is extinguished through nonreinforcement, an injection of drugs that stimulate dopaminergic neurons can reinstate the responding. A similar cross-priming effect from cigarette smoking could potentially contribute to a relapse in people who are trying to abstain. In fact, Reid et al. (1999) found that a nicotine antagonist reduced cocaine craving in cocaine-dependent smokers.

Alcohol and Barbiturates

Alcohol has greater costs to society than any other drug. A large percentage of deaths and injuries caused by motor vehicle accidents are related to alcohol use, and alcohol contributes to violence and aggression. Chronic alcoholics often lose their jobs, their homes, and their families; and many die of cirrhosis of the liver, exposure, or diseases caused by poor living conditions and abuse of their bodies. Women who drink during pregnancy run the risk of giving birth to babies with fetal alcohol syndrome, which includes malformation of the head and the brain. Figure 18.14 compares a child and a rat fetus with fetal alcohol syndrome; as you can see, similar malformations are seen in the face and head in both species. More serious, of course, are the malformations in the brain. (See *Figure 18.14*.) The leading cause of mental retardation in the Western world today is alcohol consumption by pregnant women (Abel and Sokol, 1986). Therefore, understanding the physiological and behavioral effects of this drug is an important issue.

Alcohol has the most serious effects on fetal development during the brain growth spurt period, which occurs during the last trimester of pregnancy and for several years after birth. Ikonomidou et al. (2000) found that exposure of the immature rat brain triggered widespread apoptosis, the death of cells caused by chemical signals that activate a genetic mechanism inside the cell. The investigators exposed immature rats to alcohol at different times during the period of brain growth and found that different regions were vulnerable to the effects of the alcohol at different times. Alcohol has two primary sites of action: It serves as an indirect agonist at $GABA_A$ receptors and as an indirect antagonist at NMDA receptors. Apparently, both of these actions trigger apoptosis. Ikonomidou and her colleagues found that administration of a $GABA_A$ agonist (a barbiturate) or an NMDA antagonist (MK-801) to seven-day-old rats caused brain damage by means of apoptosis. (See **Figure 18.15**.)

Exposure to alcohol somewhat later in life may also produce long-lasting changes in susceptibility to addiction.

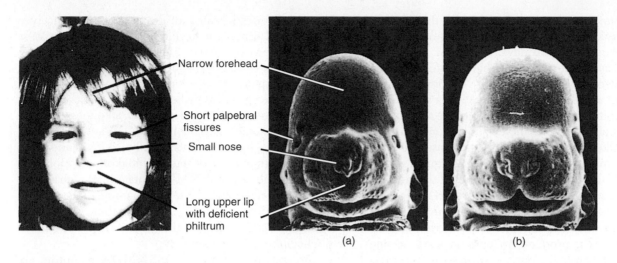

Narrow forehead

Short palpebral fissures

Small nose

Long upper lip with deficient philtrum

(a)

(b)

figure 18.14

A child with fetal alcohol syndrome, along with magnified views of rat fetuses. (a) Fetus whose mother received alcohol during pregnancy. (b) Normal rat fetus.

(Photograph courtesy of Katherine K. Sulik.)

Siciliano and Smith (2001) found that rats that had been given only a 10 percent solution alcohol to drink during adolescence drank 68 percent more alcohol than control rats in late adulthood.

At low doses, alcohol produces mild euphoria and has an *anxiolytic* effect—that is, it reduces the discomfort of anxiety. At higher doses, it produces incoordination and sedation. In studies with laboratory animals the anxiolytic effects manifest themselves as a release from the punish-

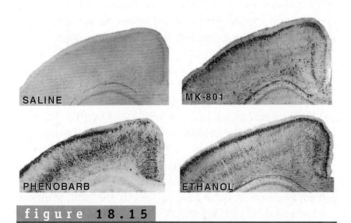

SALINE

MK-801

PHENOBARB

ETHANOL

figure 18.15

Sections of rat brain showing degenerating neurons (black spots). Exposure to alcohol during the period of rapid brain growth causes cell death by inducing apoptosis. These effects are mediated by the actions of alcohol as an NMDA antagonist and a GABA$_A$ agonist. MK-901, an NMDA antagonist, and phenobarbital, a GABA$_A$ agonist, also induce apoptosis.

(From Ikonomidou, C., Bittigau, P., Ishimaru, M. J., Wozniak, D. F., Koch, C., Genz, K., Price, M. T., Stefovska, V., Hörster, F., Tenkova, T., Dikranian, K., and Olney, J. W. *Science,* 2000, *287,* 1056–1060.)

ing effects of aversive stimuli. For example, if an animal is given electric shocks whenever it makes a particular response (say, one that obtains food or water), it will stop doing so. However, if it is then given some alcohol, it will begin making the response again (Koob et al., 1984). This phenomenon explains why people often do things they normally would not when they have had too much to drink; the alcohol removes the inhibitory effect of social controls on their behavior.

Alcohol produces both positive and negative reinforcement. The positive reinforcement manifests itself as mild euphoria. As we saw earlier, *negative* reinforcement is caused by the termination of an aversive stimulus. If a person feels anxious and uncomfortable, then an anxiolytic drug that relieves this discomfort provides at least a temporary escape from an unpleasant situation.

The negative reinforcement provided by the anxiolytic effect of alcohol is probably not enough to explain the drug's addictive potential. Other drugs, such as the benzodiazepines (tranquilizers such as Valium), are even more potent anxiolytics than alcohol, yet such drugs are abused much less often. It is probably the unique combination of stimulating and anxiolytic effects—of positive and negative reinforcement—that makes alcohol so difficult for some people to resist.

Laboratory animals can be induced to become dependent on alcohol. As I mentioned earlier, the drugs with the strongest abuse potential are those that produce the most rapid effects, such as heroin, cocaine, and nicotine. Because alcohol is ingested orally, its reinforcing effects do not occur for several minutes. Most animals find the flavor of alcohol to be aversive. For example, if rats are offered a 10 percent alcohol solution, they tend not to drink it and hence do not experience its reinforcing effects.

However, if some saccharine is mixed with the solution, they begin drinking it. At first, they drink a small amount each day, but after several days, they drink enough to become intoxicated (Reid, 1996). What appears to happen is that they begin to experience the reinforcing effects while drinking, and these effects increase their intake. The sweet taste gets them to sample enough of the alcohol and its reinforcing effects to become dependent on the drug.

Alcohol, like other addictive drugs, increases the activity of the dopaminergic neurons of the mesolimbic system and increases the release of dopamine in the nucleus accumbens as measured by microdialysis (Gessa et al., 1985; Imperato and Di Chiara, 1986). The release of dopamine appears to be related to the positive reinforcement that alcohol can produce. An injection of a dopamine antagonist directly into the nucleus accumbens decreases alcohol intake (Samson et al., 1993), as does the injection of a drug into the ventral tegmental area that decreases the activity of the dopaminergic neurons there (Hodge et al., 1993). In a double-blind study, Enggasser and de Wit (2001) found that haloperidol, an antischizophrenic drug that blocks dopamine D2 receptors, decreased the amount of alcohol that nonalcoholic subjects subsequently drank. Presumably, the drug reduced the reinforcing effect of the alcohol. In addition, those subjects who normally feel stimulated and euphoric after having a drink reported a reduction in these effects after taking haloperidol.

As we saw, alcohol has two major sites of action in the nervous system, acting as an indirect antagonist at NMDA receptors and an indirect agonist at GABA$_A$ receptors (Chandler, Harris, and Crews, 1998). That is, alcohol enhances the action of GABA at GABA$_A$ receptors and interferes with the transmission of glutamate at NMDA receptors. A study by Shelton and Balster (1994) indicated that the perceptual effects of alcohol are mimicked by both GABA agonists and NMDA antagonists. To do this, they employed the **drug discrimination procedure.** This procedure uses the physiological effects of drugs as discriminative stimuli to learn something about the nature of these effects (Schuster and Balster, 1977). An animal is given a drug and then is trained to press one of two levers to receive food. The next day, it receives an injection of saline (or another placebo) and is trained to press the other lever. Each day thereafter, it is injected with either the drug or the saline, and it receives food only if it presses the appropriate lever. Obviously, the presence or absence of feedback from the effects of the drug tells the animal which lever to press. Then on test days the animal is given another drug. If the animal presses the "drug" lever, we can conclude that the feedback feels similar to that of the first drug; if it presses the "saline" lever, we can conclude that it does not.

Shelton and Balster (1994) trained rats to discriminate between the effects of injections of alcohol and saline and then injected the animals with various drugs on test days.

The rats pressed the "alcohol" lever when they received injections of drugs that facilitated GABA transmission (including a benzodiazepine tranquilizer and a barbiturate) or those that interfered with glutamate transmission at NMDA receptors. Thus, the perceptual effects of alcohol include those produced by both of these classes of drugs.

Let's consider the evidence that alcohol acts as an NMDA antagonist. Like alcohol, NMDA antagonists produce sedative, hypnotic, and anxiolytic effects and interfere with cognitive performance (Tabakoff and Hoffman, 1996). Also like alcohol, NMDA antagonists such as PCP or ketamine cause the release of dopamine in the nucleus accumbens (Imperato et al., 1990; Loscher, Annies, and Honack, 1991). (I described these effects in the discussion of schizophrenia in Chapter 16.)

As we saw in Chapter 13, NMDA receptors are involved in long-term potentiation, a phenomenon that plays an important role in learning. Therefore, it will not surprise you to learn that alcohol, which antagonizes the action of glutamate at NMDA receptors, disrupts long-term potentiation and interferes with the spatial receptive fields of place cells in the hippocampus (Givens and McMahon, 1995; Matthews, Simson, and Best, 1996). Presumably, this effect at least partly accounts for the deleterious effects of alcohol on memory and other cognitive functions.

Withdrawal from long-term alcohol intake (like that of heroin, cocaine, amphetamine, and nicotine) decreases the activity of mesolimbic neurons and their release of dopamine in the nucleus accumbens (Diana et al., 1993). If an indirect antagonist for NMDA receptors is then administered, dopamine secretion in the nucleus accumbens recovers. The evidence suggests the following sequence of events: Some of the acute effects of a single dose of alcohol are caused by the antagonistic effect of the drug on NMDA receptors. Long-term suppression of NMDA receptors causes upregulation—a compensatory increase in the sensitivity of the receptors. Then, when alcohol intake suddenly ceases, the increased activity of NMDA receptors inhibits the activity of ventral tegmental neurons and the release of dopamine in the nucleus accumbens.

Although the effects of heroin withdrawal have been exaggerated, those produced by barbiturate or alcohol withdrawal are serious and can even be fatal. Convulsions caused by alcohol withdrawal are considered to be a medical emergency and are usually treated with benzodiazepines. Evidence suggests that activation of NMDA receptors may be responsible for the seizures caused by

drug discrimination procedure An experimental procedure in which an animal shows, through instrumental conditioning, whether the perceived effects of two drugs are similar.

alcohol withdrawal. For example, Valverius et al. (1990) studied two strains of mice that had been bred for their sensitivity to the effects of alcohol withdrawal (Crabbe et al., 1990). Like humans, mice will develop seizures if they are given large doses of alcohol for several days and are then abruptly withdrawn from the drug. Under these conditions animals from the withdrawal-seizure-prone (WSP) strain are much more likely than those from the withdrawal-seizure-resistant (WSR) strain to develop seizures. (Incidentally, the WSP mice do not voluntarily drink alcohol any more than do the WSR mice; thus, the neural mechanisms of seizure susceptibility are different from those of alcohol preference. The genetics of alcohol addiction are discussed later in this chapter.) Valverius and his colleagues found that the WSP mice had a greater number of NMDA receptors in the hippocampus than the WSR mice. Confirming these results, Liljequist (1991) found that seizures caused by alcohol withdrawal could be prevented by giving mice a drug that blocks NMDA receptors. These observations strongly suggest that NMDA receptors are responsible for seizures produced by alcohol withdrawal.

The second site of action of alcohol is the $GABA_A$ receptor. Alcohol binds with one of the many binding sites on this receptor and increases the effectiveness of GABA in opening the chloride channel and producing inhibitory postsynaptic potentials. Proctor et al. (1992) used the microiontophoresis technique to record the activity of single neurons in the cerebral cortex of slices of rat brains. They found that the presence of alcohol significantly increased the postsynaptic response produced by the action of GABA at the $GABA_A$ receptor. As we saw in Chapter 4, the anxiolytic effects of the benzodiazepine tranquilizers is caused by their action as indirect agonists at the $GABA_A$ receptor. Because alcohol has this effect also, we can surmise that the anxiolytic effect of alcohol is a result of this action of the drug.

The sedative effect of alcohol also appears to be exerted at the $GABA_A$ receptor. Suzdak et al. (1986) discovered a drug (Ro15-4513) that reverses alcohol intoxication by blocking the alcohol binding site on this receptor. Figure 18.16 shows two rats who received injections of enough alcohol to make them pass out. The one facing us also received an injection of the alcohol antagonist and appears completely sober. (See *Figure 18.16*.)

This wonder drug is not likely to reach the market soon, if ever. Although the behavioral effects of alcohol are mediated by their action on $GABA_A$ receptors and NMDA receptors, high doses of alcohol have other, potentially fatal effects on all cells of the body, including destabilization of cell membranes. Thus, people taking some of the alcohol antagonist could then go on to drink themselves to death without becoming drunk in the process. Drug companies naturally fear possible liability suits stemming from such occurrences.

figure 18.16

Effects of Ro15–4513, an alcohol antagonist. Both rats received an injection of alcohol, but the one facing us also received an injection of the alcohol antagonist.

(Photograph courtesy of Steven M. Paul, National Institute of Mental Health, Bethesda, MD.)

Barbiturates have effects very similar to those of alcohol. In fact, both drugs act as indirect agonists on the $GABA_A$ receptor (Maksay and Ticku, 1985). However, the binding sites for alcohol and barbiturates appear to be different; Ro15-4513, the alcohol antagonist, does not reverse the intoxicating effects of barbiturates (Suzdak et al., 1986). But because both drugs act on the same receptor, their effects are additive; if a person takes a moderate dose of alcohol and a moderate dose of a barbiturate, the effect can be fatal.

I mentioned earlier that opiate receptors appear to be involved in a reinforcement mechanism that does not directly involve dopaminergic neurons. The reinforcing effects of alcohol is at least partly caused by its ability to trigger the release of the endogenous opioids. Several studies have shown that opiate receptor blockers such as naloxone or naltrexone block the reinforcing effects of alcohol in a variety of species, including rats, monkeys, and humans (Altschuler, Phillips, and Feinhandler, 1980; Davidson, Swift, and Fitz, 1996; Reid, 1996). Because naltrexone has become a useful adjunct to treatment of alcoholism, I will discuss this topic further in the last section of this chapter.

Cannabis

Another drug that people regularly self-administer—almost exclusively by smoking—is THC, the active ingredient in marijuana. As you learned in Chapter 4, the site of action of the endogenous cannabinoid receptor in the brain, the CB1 receptor, has been discovered, and the distribution of this receptor has been mapped. The endogenous ligands for the CB1 receptor, anandamide and 2-AG, are lipids. Administration of a drug that blocks CB1 receptors abolishes the "high" produced by smoking marijuana (Huestis et al., 2001).

THC, like other drugs with abuse potential, has a stimulating effect on dopaminergic neurons. Chen et al.

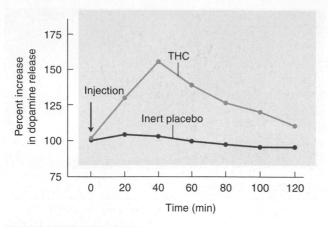

figure 18.17

Changes in dopamine concentration in the nucleus accumbens, measured by microdialysis, in response to injections of THC or an inert placebo.

(Adapted from Chen, J., Paredes, W., Li, J., Smith, D., Lowinson, J., and Gardner, E. L. *Psychopharmacology,* 1990, *102,* 156–162. Reprinted with permission.)

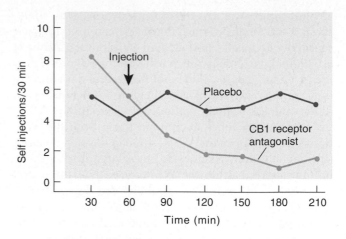

figure 18.18

Role of cannabinoid receptors in the reinforcing effects of opiates in rats. Effects of injection of a CB1 cannabinoid receptor antagonist on self-injection for heroin.

(From Navarro, M., Carrera, M. R. A., Fratta, W., Valverde, O., Cossu, G., Fattore, L., Chowen, J. A., Gómez, R., del Arco, I., Vallanúa, M. A., Maldonado, R., Koob, G. F., and Rodriguez de Fonseca, F. *Journal of Neuroscience,* 2001, *21,* 5344–5350.)

(1990) injected rats with low doses of THC and measured the release of dopamine in the nucleus accumbens by means of microdialysis. Sure enough, they found that the injections caused the release of dopamine. (See *Figure 18.17.*) Chen et al. (1993) found that local injections of small amounts of THC into the ventral tegmental area had no effect on the release of dopamine in the nucleus accumbens. However, injection of THC into the nucleus accumbens *did* cause dopamine release there. Thus, the drug appears to act directly on dopaminergic terminal buttons—presumably on presynaptic heteroreceptors.

A variety of laboratory animals, including mice, rats, and monkeys, will self-administer drugs that stimulate CB1 receptors (Maldonado and Rodriguez de Fonseca, 2002). A targeted mutation that blocks the production of CB1 receptors abolishes the reinforcing effect not only of cannabinoids, but also of morphine and heroin (Cossu et al., 2001). However, the mutation does not suppress the reinforcing effects of cocaine, amphetamine, or nicotine. Navarro et al. (2001) demonstrated the interdependence of opioid and cannabinoid reinforcement mechanisms. They found that administration of a CB1-receptor antagonist suppressed self-administration of heroin in rats. (See *Figure 18.18.*) They also found that rats that had developed tolerance to morphine showed withdrawal symptoms when they were given a CB1-receptor antagonist and that rats that had developed tolerance to a cannabinoid showed withdrawal symptoms when they were given naloxone, an opiate antagonist. The precise nature of the interactions between cannabinoid and opioid systems is not yet known.

As we saw in Chapter 4, the hippocampus contains a large concentration of THC receptors. Marijuana is known to affect people's memory. Specifically, it impairs their abil-

ity to keep track of a particular topic; they frequently lose the thread of a conversation if they are momentarily distracted. Evidence indicates that the drug does so by disrupting the normal functions of the hippocampus, which plays such an important role in memory. Pyramidal cells in the CA1 region of the hippocampus release endogenous cannabinoids, which provide a retrograde signal that inhibits GABAergic neurons that normally inhibit them. In this way the release of endogenous cannabinoids facilitates the activity of CA1 pyramidal cells and facilitates long-term potentiation (Kunos and Batkai, 2001).

We might expect that facilitating long-term potentiation in the hippocampus would enhance its memory functions. However, the reverse is true; Hampson and Deadwyler (2000) found that the effects of cannabinoids on a spatial memory task were similar to those produced by hippocampal lesions. Thus, excessive activation of CB1 receptors in field CA1 appears to interfere with normal functioning of the hippocampal formation.

Students often ask me whether researchers have discovered any damaging effects of long-term marijuana use. Reviews of the literature by (Hall and Solowij, 1998; Rogers and Robbins, 2001) concluded that the long-term effects of chronic marijuana smoking included bronchitis, a possibility of increased risk for lung cancer, development of an inability to control the use of the drug, minor impairments of attention and memory, and slower choices in decision-making tasks. It is unclear whether these deficits disappear after prolonged abstinence.

So far, the cognitive impairments demonstrated by carefully controlled studies appear to be subtle. For example, Fletcher et al. (1996) examined Costa Rican men with

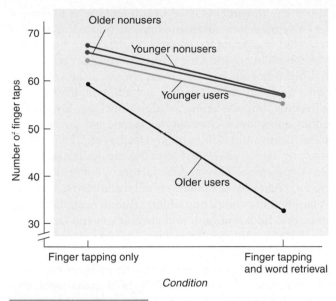

figure 18.19

Speed of finger tapping alone or while naming words in a particular category of younger and older users and nonusers of cannabis.

(Adapted from Fletcher, J. M., Page, J. B., Francis, D. J., Copeland, K., Naus, M. J., Davis, C. M., Morris, R., Krauskopf, D., and Satz, P. *Archives of General Psychiatry,* 1996, *53,* 1051–1057.)

long histories of cannabis use. The users were compared with nonusers who were matched on age, occupational status, education, marital status, and use of alcohol and tobacco. Several measures of cognitive abilities showed small but statistically significant impairments in the cannabis users. A test of the ability to perform two different tasks simultaneously (tapping a finger rapidly while trying to think of words that fit a particular category) was especially sensitive to long-term cannabis use. Men who had used cannabis for eight years showed no deficit on this task, while those who had used it for about 25 years showed a substantial decline. (See *Figure 18.19*.)

By the way, di Tomaso, Beltramo, and Piomelli (1996) discovered that chocolate contains three anandamidelike chemicals. Whether the existence of these chemicals is related to the great appeal that chocolate has for many people is not yet known. (I suppose that this is the place for a chocoholic joke.)

interim
summary

Commonly Abused Drugs

Opiates produce analgesia, hypothermia, sedation, and reinforcement. Opiate receptors in the periaqueductal gray matter are responsible for the analgesia, those in the preoptic area for the hypothermia, those in the mesencephalic reticular formation for the sedation, and those in the ventral tegmental area and nucleus accumbens at least partly for the reinforcement. A targeted mutation in mice indicates that μ receptors are responsible for analgesia, reinforcement, and withdrawal symptoms. K receptors, which are normally stimulated by dynorphin, have an inhibitory effect on the release of dopamine in the nucleus accumbens and have an aversive effect. A study using the conditioned place preference procedure found that morphine will reinforce behavior even after the destruction of the nucleus accumbens, so the release of dopamine there is not the only cause of the reinforcing effects of opiates. The release of the endogenous opioids may play a role in the reinforcing effects of natural stimuli such as water or even other addictive drugs such as alcohol.

The symptoms that are produced by antagonist-precipitated withdrawal from opiates can be elicited by injecting naloxone into the periaqueductal gray matter and the locus coeruleus, which implicate these structures in these symptoms. A targeted mutation of the gene that is responsible for the production of CREB (cyclic AMP-responsive element-binding protein) drastically reduces the magnitude of withdrawal effects.

Cocaine inhibits the reuptake of dopamine by terminal buttons, and amphetamine causes the dopamine transporters in terminal buttons to run in reverse, releasing dopamine from terminal buttons. Besides producing alertness, activation, and positive reinforcement, cocaine and amphetamine can produce psychotic symptoms that resemble those of paranoid schizophrenia. Long-term use of these drugs leads to sensitization rather than tolerance. The reinforcing effects of cocaine and amphetamine are mediated by an increase in dopamine in the nucleus accumbens. Unpleasant symptoms that accompany withdrawal from these drugs may be mediated by the activity of dynorphin-secreting neurons.

The status of nicotine as a strongly addictive drug (for both humans and laboratory animals) was long ignored, primarily because it does not cause intoxication and because the ready availability of cigarettes and other tobacco products does not make it necessary for addicts to engage in illegal activities. However, the craving for nicotine is extremely motivating. Nicotine stimulates the release of mesolimbic dopaminergic neurons, and injection of nicotine into the ventral tegmental area is reinforcing. Nicotine from smoking excites nicotinic acetylcholine receptors but also desensitizes them, which leads to unpleasant withdrawal effects. The activation of nicotinic receptors on presynaptic terminal buttons in the ventral tegmental area also produced long-term potentiation. Functional imaging indicates that nicotine craving activates the prefrontal cortex, amygdala, and ventral tegmental area.

Exposure to alcohol during the period of rapid brain development has devastating effects and is the leading cause of mental retardation. This exposure causes neural destruction through apoptosis. Drinking during adolescence can predispose rats to high alcohol intake later in life. Alcohol and barbiturates have similar (but not identical) effects. Alcohol has positively reinforcing effects and, through its anxiolytic action, has negatively reinforcing effects as well. It serves as an indirect antagonist at NMDA receptors and an indirect agonist at $GABA_A$ receptors. It stimulates the release of dopamine in the nucleus accumbens. Withdrawal from long-term alcohol abuse can lead to seizures, an effect that seems to be caused by compensatory upregulation of NMDA receptors. Release of the endogenous opioids also plays a role in the reinforcing effects of alcohol.

The active ingredient in cannabis, THC, stimulates receptors whose natural ligand is anandamide. THC, like other addictive drugs, stimulates the release of dopamine in the nucleus accumbens. The CB1 receptor is responsible for the physiological and behavioral effects of THC and the endogenous cannabinoids. Symptoms of opiate withdrawal can be induced by a drug that blocks CB1 receptors, and symptoms of cannabinoid withdrawal can be induced by a drug that blocks opiate receptors. Cannabinoids produce memory deficits by acting on inhibitory GABAergic neurons in the CA1 field of the hippocampus.

Heredity and Drug Abuse

Not everyone is equally likely to become addicted to a drug. Many people manage to drink alcohol moderately, and even many users of potent drugs such as cocaine and heroin use them "recreationally" without becoming dependent on them. There are only two possible sources of individual differences in any characteristic: heredity and environment. Because this book considers the *physiology* of behavior, I will not discuss the role that environment plays in a person's susceptibility to the addicting effects of drugs. Obviously, environmental effects are important; people who are raised in a squalid environment without any real hope for a better life are more likely than other people to turn to drugs for some temporary euphoria and removal from the unpleasant world that surrounds them. But even in a given environment, poor or privileged, some people become addicts and some do not—and some of these behavioral differences are a result of genetic differences, as we will see in the following subsections.

Heritability Studies of Humans

Most of the research on the effects of heredity on addiction have been devoted to alcoholism. One of the reasons for this focus—aside from the importance of the problems caused by alcohol—is that almost everyone is exposed to alcohol. Most people drink alcohol sometime in their lives and thus have firsthand experience with its reinforcing effects. The same is not true for cocaine, heroin, and other drugs that have even more potent effects. In most countries alcohol is freely and legally available in local shops, whereas in purchasing cocaine and heroin, one runs the risk of being arrested, perhaps even imprisoned.

A few researchers have begun looking at the genetics of dependence on other drugs, such as cocaine, nicotine, and marijuana. In general, studies have found that the heritability of smoking is just as strong as that of alcoholism. Smoking has also been shown to be related to some personal characteristics, including neurosis, social alienation, impulsiveness, sensation seeking, low conscientiousness, low socioeconomic status, and low achievement (Gilbert and Gilbert, 1995; Heath et al., 1995). A twin study by True et al. (1999) found that alcoholism and nicotine dependence have genetic factors in common, which may explain why alcoholics are often addicted to nicotine. A family study comparing siblings (Bierut et al., 1998) suggests that both common and specific genetic factors are involved in addiction to alcohol, cocaine, nicotine, and marijuana. In other words, there appears to be a genetic trait that increases vulnerability to dependence on addictive substances in general and genetic traits associated with vulnerability to dependence on each of the particular drugs.

The Evidence

Alcohol consumption is not distributed equally across the population; in the United States, 10 percent of the people drink 50 percent of the alcohol (Heckler, 1983). As we saw in Chapter 5, the best evidence for an effect of heredity on susceptibility to alcoholism comes from twin studies and adoption studies.

The advantage of adoption studies, which study people who were adopted at a young age, is that the investigator can estimate the effects of family environment as well as genetics. That is, one can examine the effects of being raised by an alcoholic parent or having a biological parent who is an alcoholic or both on the probability of becoming alcoholic. Such a study was carried out in Stockholm by Cloninger et al. (1981, 1985) and was replicated in Gothenburg, another Swedish city (Sigvardsson, Bohman, and Cloninger, 1996). Briefly, the studies found that heredity was much more important than family environment. But the story is not quite that simple.

In a review of the literature on alcohol abuse, Cloninger (1987) notes that many investigators have concluded that there are two principal types of alcoholics: those who cannot abstain but drink consistently and those who are able to go without drinking for long periods of time but are unable to control themselves once they start. (For convenience I will refer to these two groups as "steady drinkers" and "bingers.") Steady drinking is associated with antisocial personality disorder, which includes a lifelong history of impulsiveness, fighting, lying, and lack of remorse for antisocial acts. Binge drinking is associated with emotional dependence, behavioral rigidity, perfectionism, introversion, and guilt feelings about one's drinking behavior. Steady drinkers usually begin their alcohol consumption early in life, whereas binge drinkers begin much later. (See *Table 18.2*.)

Characteristic Features of Two Types of Alcoholism

	TYPE OF ALCOHOLISM	
Feature	*Steady*	*Binge*
Usual age of onset (years)	Before 25	After 25
Spontaneous alcohol seeking (inability to abstain)	Frequent	Infrequent
Fighting and arrests while drinking	Frequent	Infrequent
Psychological dependence (loss of control)	Infrequent	Frequent
Guilt and fear about alcohol dependence	Infrequent	Frequent
Novelty seeking	High	Low
Harm avoidance	Low	High
Reward dependence	Low	High

Source: From Cloninger, C. R. *Science,* 1987, *236,* 410–416. Copyright 1987 by the American Association for the Advancement of Science.

Steady drinking is strongly influenced by heredity. The Stockholm adoption study found that men with fathers who were steady drinkers were almost seven times more likely to become steady drinkers themselves than were men whose fathers did not abuse alcohol. Family environment had no measurable effect; the boys began drinking whether or not the members of their adoptive family themselves drank heavily. Very few women become steady drinkers; the daughters of steady-drinking fathers instead tend to develop *somatization disorder.* People with this disorder chronically complain of symptoms for which no physiological cause can be found, leading them to seek medical care almost continuously. Thus, the genes that predispose a man to become a steady-drinking alcoholic (antisocial type) predispose a woman to develop somatization disorder. The reason for this interaction with gender is not known.

Binge drinking is influenced both by heredity and by environment. The Stockholm adoption study found that having a biological parent who was a binge drinker had little effect on the development of binge drinking unless the child was exposed to a family environment in which there was heavy drinking. The effect was seen in both males and females.

Possible Mechanisms

When we find an effect of heredity on behavior, we have good reason to suspect the existence of a biological difference. That is, genes affect behavior only by affecting the body. A susceptibility to alcoholism could conceivably be caused by differences in the ability to digest or metabolize alcohol or by differences in the structure or biochemistry of the brain. Most investigators believe that differences in brain physiology are more likely to play a role. Cloninger (1987) notes that many studies have shown that people with antisocial tendencies, which includes the group of steady drinkers, show a strong tendency to seek novelty and excitement. These people are disorderly and distractible (many have a history of hyperactivity as children) and show little restraint in their behavior. They tend not to fear dangerous situations or social disapproval. They are easily bored. On the other hand, binge drinkers tend to be anxious, emotionally dependent, sentimental, sensitive to social cues, cautious and apprehensive, fearful of novelty or change, rigid, and attentive to details. Their EEGs show little slow alpha activity, which is characteristic of a relaxed state (Propping, Kruger, and Mark, 1981). When they take alcohol, they report a pleasant relief of tension (Propping, Kruger, and Janah, 1980). Perhaps, as Cloninger suggests, these personality differences are a result of differences in the sensitivity of neural mechanisms involved in reinforcement, exploration, and punishment.

For example, steady drinkers may have an undersensitive punishment mechanism, which makes them unresponsive to danger and to social disapproval. They may also have an undersensitive reinforcement system, which leads them to seek more intense thrills (including those provided by alcohol) to experience pleasurable sensations. Thus, they seek the excitatory (dopamine-stimulating) effect of alcohol. In fact, a twin study by Heath et al. (1999) found that men (but not women) who had a genetic susceptibility to development of alcoholism were less sensitive to the effects of alcohol.

Binge drinkers may have oversensitive punishment systems. Normally, they avoid drinking because of the guilt they experience afterward; but once they begin, and once the sedative effect begins, the alcohol-induced suppression of the punishment system makes it impossible for them to stop.

Recently, investigators have focused on the possibility that susceptibility to addiction may involve differences in dopaminergic mechanisms—for reasons you will understand, having read this chapter. Blum et al. (1990) reported that severe alcoholism was related to the presence of the A1 allele of the gene responsible for the production of the D_2 dopamine receptor, which is found on chromosome 11. (An *allele* is a particular form of a gene.) The idea that susceptibility to addiction is related to genetic differences in receptors that are known to be involved in the physiology of reinforcement is an intriguing one, and the report of the research was greeted with considerable interest from clinicians and other researchers. Unfortunately, these findings have not been replicated by other research groups. A large family-based study concluded that there was no association between the D_2 receptor gene and alcohol dependence (Endenberg et al., 1998).

Animal Models of Drug Abuse

Another approach to the study of the physiology of addiction is through the use of animal models. Several different strains of alcohol-preferring rats have been developed through selective breeding, and studies have shown that these animals differ from normal rats in interesting ways. Alcohol-preferring rats do just what their name implies: If they are given a drinking tube containing a solution of alcohol along with their water and food, they become heavy drinkers. The alcohol-nonpreferring rats abstain (Li, Lumeng, and Doolittle, 1993). Figure 18.20 shows the amount of alcohol consumed by subsequent generations of rats selected for high and low preference for alcohol. (See *Figure 18.20*.)

Alcohol-preferring rats (*P rats*) and alcohol-nonpreferring rats (*NP rats*) show interesting behavioral and physiological differences. If they are given small doses of alcohol, the P rats show more behavioral activation. They also are more tolerant of the aversive effects of high doses, and they have lower brain levels of serotonin and dopamine (Gongwer et al., 1989; McBride et al., 1991). Li, Lumeng, and Doolittle (1993) suggest that the mesolimbic dopaminergic system in P rats may be more sensitive to the effects of alcohol, but so far the evidence is inconclusive. P rats may also be more sensitive to the hedonic value of tastes; they drink more of a tasty sucrose solution and less of an aversive sodium chloride solution than NP rats do (Stewart et al., 1994).

Several studies (for example, Murphy et al., 1987) have found a lower level of dopamine in the nucleus accumbens of P rats. Zhou et al. (1995) found a smaller number of dopaminergic neurons projecting from the ventral tegmental area to the nucleus accumbens. McBride

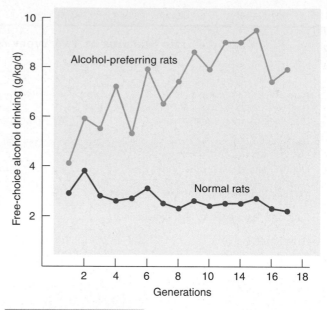

figure 18.20

Alcohol intake of successive generations of rats selected for alcohol preference and nonpreference.
(Adapted from Li, T.-K., Lumeng, L., and Doolittle, D. P. *Behavioral Genetics*, 1993, *23*, 163–170.)

et al. (1995) studied the offspring of rats of mixed P and NP parentage. They found that heavier drinkers had a lower level of dopamine in the nucleus accumbens, as measured by microdialysis. As we saw, a low level of dopamine in the nucleus accumbens correlates with anhedonia and dysphoria, and Cloninger suggests that at least some forms of alcoholism may be caused by a decreased sensitivity to reinforcement. Perhaps the P rats drink more to make up for this insensitivity.

As we saw earlier in this chapter, the reinforcing effects of alcohol are mediated, at least in part, by neurons that release opioids. And as we will see in the next section, drugs that block opiate receptors are often used to help treat alcoholism. The success of these drugs has led researchers to investigate the possibility that genetic factors that affect opioid release may also affect susceptibility to alcohol dependence. There are some indications that there may indeed be a link between opioid mechanisms and alcohol preference. For example, Li, Li, and Froelich (1998) found that the administration of alcohol to P rats, but not to NP rats, caused an increase in the production of an opioid precursor protein in the nucleus accumbens. Myers and Robinson (1999) found that infusion of a compound that interferes with the production of μ opioid receptors directly into the nucleus accumbens decreased alcohol intake in an alcohol-preferring strain of rats. Infusion of a compound that interferes with the production of dopamine D_2 receptors caused an even larger decline.

Not all laboratory research on the role of heredity in drug abuse has involved rodents. Higley, Suomi, and Linnoila (1996) report the results of a long-term study with rhesus monkeys. They found that the cerebrospinal fluid levels of 5-HIAA in monkeys was stable from infancy to adulthood; thus, the levels were probably under the control of genetic factors. The level of 5-HIAA, a metabolite of serotonin (5-HT), is an indirect measure of the activity of serotonergic neurons. (As we saw in Chapter 16, the level of 5-HIAA in the CSF of humans is related to depression and suicide.) Higley and his colleagues made an alcoholic beverage available to the monkeys and found that those with the lowest levels of 5-HIAA had the highest rates of alcohol intake. They also found evidence for environmental effects: Monkeys that had been deprived of contact with their mothers early in life also tended to drink more.

interim summary

Heredity and Drug Abuse

Most people who are exposed to addictive drugs—even drugs with a high abuse potential—do not become addicts. Evidence suggests that the likelihood of addiction, especially to alcohol and nicotine, is strongly affected by heredity. There may be two types of alcoholism: one related to an antisocial, pleasure-seeking personality (steady drinkers) and another related to a repressed, anxiety-ridden personality (binge drinkers). Alcoholism may be related to the presence of the A1 allele of the D2 dopamine receptor gene. Some investigators believe that a better understanding of the physiological basis of reinforcement and punishment will help us to understand the effects of heredity on susceptibility to addiction. In fact, animal studies have shown that it is possible to selectively breed animals that do or do not prefer alcohol, and physiological studies have found that the level of dopamine release is lower in alcohol-preferring rats. The low level of serotonin may play an important role in alcoholism; a long-term study with monkeys showed that CSF levels of the serotonin metabolite 5-HIAA were stable throughout life and that low levels were associated with higher levels of alcohol intake.

Therapy for Drug Abuse

There are many reasons for engaging in research on the physiology of drug abuse, including an academic interest in the nature of reinforcement and the pharmacology of psychoactive drugs. But most researchers entertain the hope that the results of their research will contribute to the development of ways to treat and (better yet) prevent drug abuse in members of our own species. As you well know, the incidence of drug abuse is far too high, so obviously, research has not yet solved the problem. However, real progress has been made.

The most common treatment for opiate addiction is methadone maintenance. Methadone is a potent opiate, just like morphine or heroin. If it were available in a form suitable for injection, it would be abused. (In fact, methadone clinics must control their stock of methadone carefully to prevent it from being stolen and sold to opiate abusers.) Methadone maintenance programs administer the drug to their patients in the form of a liquid, which they must drink in the presence of the personnel supervising this procedure. Because the oral route of administration increases the opiate level in the brain slowly, the drug does not produce a high, the way an injection of heroin will. In addition, because methadone is long-lasting, the patient's opiate receptors remain occupied for a long time, which means that an injection of heroin has little effect. Of course, a very large dose of heroin will displace methadone from opiate receptors and produce a "rush," so the method is not foolproof.

As we saw, opiate receptor blockers such as naloxone and naltrexone interfere with the action of opiates. Emergency rooms always have one of these drugs available to rescue patients who have taken an overdose of heroin, and many lives have been saved by these means. But although an opiate antagonist will block the effects of heroin, the research reviewed earlier in this chapter suggests that it should *increase* the craving for heroin.

As we saw earlier, the reinforcing effects of cocaine and amphetamine are primarily a result of the sharply increased levels of dopamine these drugs produce in the nucleus accumbens. Drugs that block dopamine receptors certainly block the reinforcing effects of cocaine and amphetamine, but they also produce dysphoria and anhedonia. People will not tolerate the unpleasant feelings these drugs produce, so they are not useful treatments for cocaine and amphetamine abuse. Drugs that *stimulate* dopamine receptors can reduce a person's dependence on cocaine or amphetamine, but these drugs are just as addictive as the drugs they replace and have the same deleterious effects on health.

You might recall that several studies have found that the increased sensitivity of D_3 dopamine receptors produced by chronic exposure to cocaine may be involved in the craving for cocaine experienced by people who are trying to break their dependency on cocaine and that Pilla et al. (1999) found that a partial agonist for the D_3 receptor decreased cocaine craving in rats. Researchers hope that drugs that interact with D_3 receptors may someday be a useful adjunct to treatment of cocaine dependency.

An interesting approach to cocaine addiction is suggested by a study by Carrera et al. (1995), who conjugated cocaine to a foreign protein and managed to stimulate rats' immune systems to develop antibodies to cocaine. These "cocaine-immunized" rats were less sensitive to the activating effects of cocaine, and brain levels of cocaine in these animals were lower after an injection of the drug. As Leshner (1996) suggests, it might someday be possible to vaccinate cocaine abusers (or perhaps inject them with an antibody developed by genetic engineering) so that an injection of cocaine will not produce reinforcing effects. This treatment would have many advantages because (theoretically, at least) it would interfere only with the action of cocaine and not with the normal operations of people's reinforcement mechanisms. Thus, the treatment should not decrease their ability to experience normal pleasure.

Yet another approach to cocaine addiction is being investigated. Dewey et al. (1997) discovered that a GABA agonist, gamma-vinyl GABA (GVG), decreased the amount of dopamine released in the nucleus accumbens after injecting a rat with cocaine. This finding suggested that GVG might reduce the reinforcing effects of cocaine as well. Dewey et al. (1998) found that it did. They pretreated baboons with GVG and found that the animals no longer learned a conditioned place preference for cocaine. GVG is not an addictive drug, and it has been used for treatment of seizure disorders in both adults and children, so it appears to be a safe medication. It will be interesting to see whether GVG finds a place in the treatment of cocaine addiction. Incidentally, in a study with rats, Dewey et al. (1999) found that GVG also suppresses the reinforcing effects of nicotine.

A treatment similar to methadone maintenance has been used as an adjunct to treatment for nicotine addiction. For several years, chewing gum containing nicotine has been available by prescription, and more recently, transdermal patches that release nicotine through the skin have been marketed. Both methods maintain a sufficiently high level of nicotine in the brain to decrease a person's craving for nicotine. Once the habit of smoking has subsided, the dose of nicotine can be decreased to wean the person from the drug. Carefully controlled studies have shown that nicotine maintenance therapy, and not administration of a placebo, is useful in treatment for nicotine dependence (Stolerman and Jarvis, 1995). However, nicotine maintenance therapy is most effective if it is part of a counseling program. (See *Figure 18.21*.)

As we saw in Chapter 17, serotonin agonists have proved useful in treatment of panic disorder and obsessive-compulsive disorder (and related disorders such as hair pulling and nail biting). These drugs also appear to be useful in treating alcoholism; several double-blind studies have found that 5-HT reuptake blockers make it easier for alcoholics to abstain. For example, Naranjo et al. (1992) found that citalopram (a serotonin agonist) "decreased interest, desire, craving, and liking for alcohol" in alcoholics who were receiving treatment for their addiction. It appeared to do so by decreasing the reinforcing effects of alcohol.

As I mentioned earlier, several studies have shown that opiate antagonists decrease the reinforcing value of alcohol in a variety of species, including our own. This find-

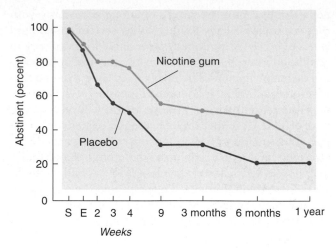

Groups Receiving Counseling and Gum

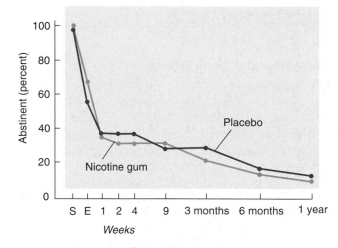

Groups Receiving Gum Only

figure 18.21

Percentage of smokers chewing nicotine gum alone or in conjunction with counseling who abstained from smoking. S = start of treatment; E = end of treatment.

(Adapted from Schneider, N. G., and Jarvik, M. E. *NIDA Research Monographs,* 1985, *53,* 83–101.)

ing suggests that the reinforcing effect of alcohol—at least in part—is produced by the secretion of endogenous opioids and the activation of opiate receptors in the brain. A study by Davidson, Swift, and Fitz (1996) clearly illustrates this effect. The investigators arranged a double-blind, placebo-controlled study with sixteen college-age men and women to investigate the effects of naltrexone on social drinkers. None of the participants were alcohol abusers, and pregnancy tests ensured that the women were not pregnant. They gathered around a table in a local restaurant/bar for three two-hour drinking sessions, two weeks apart. For several days before the meeting, they swallowed capsules that contained either naltrexone or an inert placebo. The results showed that naltrexone increased the latency to take the first sip and to take a second drink and that the blood alcohol levels of the naltrexone-treated participants were lower at the end of the session. In general, the people who had taken naltrexone found that their drinks did not taste very good—and in fact, some of them asked for a different drink after taking the first sip.

These results are consistent with reports of the effectiveness of naltrexone as an adjunct to programs designed to treat alcohol abuse. For example, O'Brien, Volpicelli, and Volpicelli (1996) reported the results of two long-term programs using naltrexone along with more traditional behavioral treatments. Both programs found that administration of naltrexone significantly increased the likelihood of success. As Figure 18.22 shows, naltrexone decreased the participants' craving for alcohol and increased the number of participants who managed to abstain from alcohol. (See *Figure 18.22.*) Currently, many treatment programs are using a sustained-release form of naltrexone to help treat alcoholism, and results with the drug have been encouraging (Kranzler, Modesto-Lowe, and Nuwayser, 1998). Naltrexone may even reduce craving for cigarettes (Vewers, Dhatt, and Tejwani, 1998).

One more drug has shown promise for treatment of alcoholism. As we saw earlier in this chapter, alcohol serves as an indirect agonist at the $GABA_A$ receptor and an indirect antagonist at the NMDA receptor. Acamprosate, an NMDA-receptor antagonist that has been used in Europe to treat seizure disorders, was tested for its ability to stop seizure induced by withdrawal from alcohol. The researchers discovered that the drug had an unexpected benefit: Alcoholic patients who received the drug were less likely to start drinking again (Wickelgren, 1998). According to Johnson and Ait-Daoud (2000), ongoing studies are investigating the potential benefits of combining acamprosate with naltrexone.

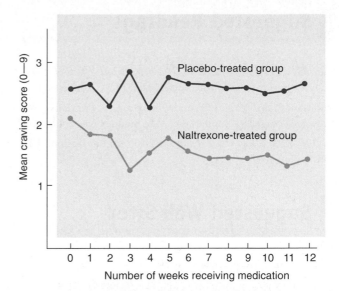

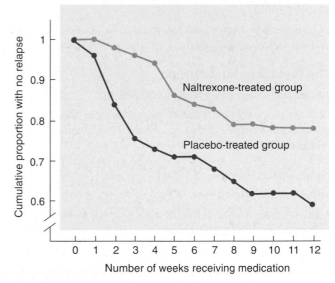

---

figure 18.22

Mean craving score and proportion of patients who abstained from drinking while receiving naltrexone or a placebo.

(Adapted from O'Brien, C. P., Volpicelli, L. A., and Volpicelli, J. R. *Alcohol,* 1996, *13,* 35–39.)

---

interim summary

Therapy for Drug Abuse

Although drug abuse is difficult to treat, researchers have developed several useful therapies. Methadone maintenance replaces addiction to heroin by addiction to an opiate that does not produce euphoric effects when administered orally. Similarly, nicotine-containing gum and transdermal patches help smokers to combat their addiction. Naloxone and naltrexone block opiate receptors, but because they produce unpleasant effects, they are useful only for addicts who are strongly motivated to break their habit. D_3 receptor antagonists show promise of helping people to break an addiction to cocaine. The development of antibodies to cocaine in rats holds out the possibility that people may some day be immunized against the drug. Serotonin agonists and a GABA agonist show promise in decreasing craving for alcohol. However, the most effective pharmacological adjunct to treatment for alcoholism appears to be naltrexone, an opiate receptor blocker that reduces the drug's reinforcing effects.

A personal note: You are now at the end of the book (as you well know), and you have spent a considerable amount of time reading my words. While working on this book, I have tried to imagine myself talking to someone who is interested in learning something about the physiology of behavior. As I mentioned in the preface, writing is often a lonely activity, and the imaginary audience helped keep me company. If you would like to turn this communication into a two-way conversation, write to me. My address is given at the end of the preface.

Suggested Readings

Dietrich, R., and Erwin, V. G. *Pharmacological Effects of Ethanol on the Central Nervous System.* Boca Raton, FL: CRC Press, 1996.

Feldman, R. S., Meyer, J. S., and Quenzer, L. F. *Principles of Neuropsychopharmacology.* Sunderland, MA: Sinauer Associates, 1997.

Grilly, D. M. *Drugs and Human Behavior,* 3rd ed. Boston: Allyn and Bacon, 1998.

Winger, G., Hofmann, F. G., and Woods, J. H. *A Handbook on Drug and Alcohol Abuse: The Biomedical Aspects.* New York: Oxford University Press, 1992.

Suggested Web Sites

Animations: How Drugs Work

http://www.pbs.org/wnet/closetohome/science/html/animations.html

This site provides a series of color animations that illustrate the action of drugs such as alcohol, opiates, and cocaine on synaptic function.

The Psychology of Addiction

http://orion.it.luc.edu/~pcrowe/psyc375.htm

This site is devoted to a course on the psychology of addiction. The site contains a course syllabus as well as links to substance abuse/addiction web sites.

Drug Test

http://www.drugtest.org/

Fact sheet links relating to specific illicit drugs such as alcohol and cocaine are provided within this site.

Fact Sheets on Drug Addiction

http://www.well.com/user/woa/facts.htm

This portion of the Web of Addictions site contains links to fact sheets on addiction.

Addictions as a Disease

http://www.pbs.org/wnet/closetohome/science/index.html

This PBS site provides facts and information relating to addiction. It also contains a series of links to animations of the effects of addictive drugs within the synapse.

Addiction Lecture Notes

http://www.nyu.edu/classes/azmitia/lectures/lecture18/index.html

A lecture note outline relating to addictive drugs including cocaine and other stimulants are the focus of this Web site.

References

Abe, H., Rusak, B., and Robertson, H. A. Photic induction of Fos protein in the suprachiasmatic nucleus is inhibited by the NMDA receptor antagonist MK-801. *Neuroscience Letters*, 1991, *127*, 9–12.

Abe, M., Saito, M., and Shimazu, T. Neuropeptide Y and norepinephrine injected into the paraventricular nucleus of the hypothalamus activate endocrine pancreas. *Biomedical Research*, 1989, *10*, 431–436.

Abel, E. L., and Sokol, R. J. Fetal alcohol syndrome is now a leading cause of mental retardation. *Lancet*, 1986, *2*, 1222.

Abercrombie, H. C., Schaefer, S. M., Larson, C. L., Oakes, T. R., Lindgren, K. A., Holden, J. E., Perlman, S. B., Turski, P. A., Krahn, D. D., Benca, R. M., and Davidson, R. J. Metabolic rate in the right amygdala predicts negative affect in depressed patients. *Neuroreport*, 1998, *9*, 3301–3307.

Abolmaali, N. D., Kühnau, D., Knecht, M., Köhler, K., Hüttenbrink, K.-M., and Hummel, T. Imaging of the human vomeronasal duct. *Chemical Senses*, 2001, *25*, 35–39.

Abrahamov, A., Abrahamov, A., and Mechoulam, R. An efficient new cannabinoid antiemetic in pediatric oncology. *Life Sciences*, 1995, *56*, 2097–2102.

Adams, D. B., Gold, A. R., and Burt, A. D. Rise in female-initiated sexual activity at ovulation and its suppression by oral contraceptives. *New England Journal of Medicine*, 1978, *299*, 1145–1150.

Adams, R. D. The anatomy of memory mechanisms in the human brain. In *The Pathology of Memory*, edited by G. A. Talland and N. C. Waugh. New York: Academic Press, 1969.

Adey, W. R., Bors, E., and Porter, R. W. EEG sleep patterns after high cervical lesions in man. *Archives of Neurology*, 1968, *19*, 377–383.

Adieh, H. B., Mayer, A. D., and Rosenblatt, J. S. Effects of brain antiestrogen implants on maternal behavior and on postpartum estrus in pregnant rats. *Neuroendocrinology*, 1987, *46*, 522–531.

Adler, C. M., Malhotra, A. K., Elman, I., Goldberg, T., Egan, M., Pickar, D., and Breier, A. Comparison of ketamine-induced thought disorder in healthy volunteers and thought disorder in schizophrenia. *American Journal of Psychiatry*, 1999, *156*, 1646–1649.

Adler, C. M., Malhotra, A. K., Elman, I., Pickar, D., and Breier, A. Amphetamine-induced dopamine release and post-synaptic specific binding in patients with mild tardive dyskinesia. *Neuropsychopharmacology*, 2002, *26*, 295–300.

Adolphs, R. Neural systems for recognizing emotion. *Current Opinion in Neurobioloty*, 2002, *12*, 169–177.

Adolphs, R., and Tranel, D. Intact recognition of emotional prosody following amygdala damage. *Neuropsychologia*, 1999, *37*, 1285–1292.

Adolphs, R., Damasio, H., Tranel, D., Cooper, G., and Damasio, A. R. A Role for somatosensory cortices in the visual recognition of emotion as revealed by three-dimensional lesion mapping. *Journal of Neuroscience*, 2000, *20*, 2683–2690.

Adolphs, R., Tranel, D., and Damasio, A. R. The human amygdala in social judgment. *Nature*, 1998, *393*, 470–474.

Adolphs, R., Tranel, D., Damasio, H., and Damasio, A. Impaired recognition of emotion in facial expressions following bilateral damage to the human amygdala. *Nature*, 1994, *372*, 669–672.

Adolphs, R., Tranel, D., Damasio, H., and Damasio, A. Fear and the human amygdala. *Journal of Neuroscience*, 1995, *15*, 5879–5891.

Adolphs, R., Tranel, D., Hamann, S., Young, A. W., Calder, A. J., Phelps, E. A., Anderson, A., Lee, G. P., and Damasio, A. R. Recognition of facila emotion in nine individuals with bilateral amygdala damage. *Neuropsychologia*, 1999, *37*, 1111–1117.

Advokat, C., and Kutlesic, V. Pharmacotherapy of the eating disorders: A commentary. *Neuroscience and Biobehavioral Reviews*, 1995, *19*, 59–66.

Aggleton, J. P., McMackin, D., Carpenter, K., Hornak, J., Kapur, N., Salpin, S., Wiles, C. M., Kamel, H., Brennan, P., Carton, S., and Gaffan, D. Differential cognitive effects of colloid cysts in the third ventricle that spare or compromise the fornix. *Brain*, 2000, *123*, 800–815.

Aghajanian, G. K., Kogan, J. H., and Moghaddam, B. Opiate withdrawal increases glutamate and aspartate efflux in the locus coeruleus: An in vivo microdialysis study. *Brain Research*, 1994, *636*, 126–130.

Agmo, A., Federman, I., Navarro, V., Padua, M., and Velasquez, G. Reward and reinforcement produced by drinking water: Role of opioids and dopamine-receptor subtypes. *Pharmacology, Biochemistry and Behavior*, 1993, *46*, 183–194.

Aharon, Etcoff, N., Ariely, D., Chabris, C. F., O'Connor, E., and Breiter, H. C. Beautiful faces have variable reward value: fMRI and behavioral evidence. *Neuron*, 2001, *32*, 537–551.

Akhtar, S., Wig, N., Pershad, D., and Varma, S. A phenomenological analysis of symptoms in obsessive compulsive disorder. *British Journal of Psychiatry*, 1975, *127*, 342–348.

Akil, M., Pierri, J. N., Whitehead, R. E., Edgar, C. L., Mohila, C., Sampson, A. R., and Lewis, D. A. Lamina-specific alterations in the dopamine innervation of the prefrontal cortex in schizophrenic subjects. *American Journal of Psychiatry*, 1999, *156*, 1580–1589.

Alain, C., Arnott, S. R., Hevenor, S., Graham, S., and Grady, C. L. "What" and "where" in the human auditory system. *Proceedings of the National Academy of Science, USA*, 2001, *98*, 12301–12306.

Albers, H. E., and Ferris, C. F. Neuropeptide Y: Role in light-dark cycle entrainment of hamster circadian rhythms. *Neuroscience Letters*, 1984, *50*, 163–168.

Albrecht, D. G. Analysis of visual form. Doctoral dissertation, University of California, Berkeley, 1978.

Albright, T. D., Desimone, R., and Gross, C. G. Columnar organization of directionally selective cells in visual area MT of the macaque. *Journal of Neurophysiology*, 1984, *51*, 16–31.

Alexander, G. M., Sherwin, B. B., Bancroft, J., and Davidson, D. W. Testosterone and sexual behavior in oral contraceptive users and nonusers: A prospective study. *Hormones and Behavior*, 1990, *24*, 388–402.

Alexander, M. P., Fischer, R. S., and Friedman, R. Lesion localization in apractic agraphia. *Archives of Neurology*, 1992, *49*, 246–251.

Alkire, M. T., Haier, R. J., Fallon, J. H., and Cahill, L. Hippocampal, but not amygdala, activity at encoding correlates with long-term, free recall of nonemotional information. *Proceedings of the National Academy of Sciences, USA*, 1998, *95*, 14506–14510.

Allen, L. S., and Gorski, R. A. Sexual orientation and the size of the anterior commissure in the human brain. *Proceedings of the National Academy of Sciences*, 1992, *89*, 7199–7202.

Allison, D. B., Kaprio, J., Korkeila, M., Koskenvuo, M., Neale, M. C., and Hayakawa, K. The heritability of body mass index among an international sample of monozygotic twins reared apart. *International Journal of Obesity*, 1996, *20*, 501–506.

Allison, D. W., Chervin, A. S., Gelfand, V. I., and Crain, A. M. Postsynaptic scaffolds of excitatory and inhibitory synapses in hippocampal neurons: Maintenance of core components independent of actin filaments and microtubules. *Journal of Neuroscience*, 2000, *20*, 4645–4654.

Allison, T., McCarthy, G., Nobre, A., Puce, A., and Belger, A. Human extrastriate visual cortex and the perception of faces, words, numbers, and colors. *Cerebral Cortex*, 1994, *4*, 544–554.

Allman, J. M. *Evolving Brains*. New York: Scientific American Library, 1999.

Almers, W. Exocytosis. *Annual Review of Physiology*, 1990, *52*, 607–624.

Altschuler, H. L., Phillips, P. E., and Feinhandler, D. A. Alterations of ethanol self-administration by naltrexone. *Life Sciences*, 1980, *26*, 679–688.

Amaral, D. G., Price, J. L., Pitkänen, A., and Carmichael, S. T. Anatomical organization of the primate amygdalid complex. In *The Amygdala: Neurobiological Aspects of Emotion, Memory, and Mental Dysfunction*. New York: Wiley-Liss, 1992.

Amen, D. G., Stubblefield, M., Carmichael, B., and Thisted, R. Brain SPECT findings and aggressiveness. *Annals of Clinical Psychiatry*, 1996, *8*, 129–137.

American Psychiatric Association. Practice guidline for the treatment of patients with panic disorder. *American Journal of Psychiatry*, 1998, *155(Suppl.)*, 1–34.

Anand, B. K., and Brobeck, J. R. Hypothalamic control of food intake in rats and cats. *Yale Journal of Biology and Medicine*, 1951, *24*, 123–140.

Ancoli-Israel, S., and Roth, T. Characteristics of insomnia in the United States: Results of the 1991 National Sleep Foundation survey. *Sleep*, 1999, *22*, S347–S353.

Anderson, A. K., and Phelps, E. K. Intact recognition of vocal expressions of fear following bilateral lesions of the human amygdala. *Neuroreport*, 1998, *9*, 3607–3613.

Anderson, A. K., and Phelps, E. A. Expression without recognition: Contributions of the human amygdala to emotional communication. *Psychological Science*, 2000, *11*, 106–111.

Anderson, C. M., Polcari, A., Lowen, S. B., Renshaw, P. F., and Teicher, M. H. Effects of methylphenidate on functional magnetic resonance relaxometry of the cerebellar vermis in boys with ADHD. *American Journal of Psychiatry*, 2002, *159*, 1322–1328.

Anderson, R. H., Fleming, D. E., Rhees, R. W., and Kinghorn, E. Relationships between sexual activity, plasma testosterone, and the volume of the sexually dimorphic nucleus of the preoptic area in prenatally stressed and non-stressed rats. *Brain Research*, 1986, *370*, 1–10.

Anderson, S. W., Bechara, A., Damasio, H., Tranel, D., and Damasio, A. R. Impairment of social and moral behavior related to early damage in human prefrontal cortex. *Nature Neuroscience*, 1999, *2*, 1032–1037.

Anderson-Hunt, M., and Dennerstein, L. Oxytocin and female sexuality. *Gynecological and Obstetrical Investigations*, 1995, *40*, 217–221.

Andreasen, N. C. Symptoms, signs, and diagnosis of schizophrenia. *Lancet*, 1995, *346*, 477–481.

Andrews, N., Miller, E., Taylor, B., Lingam, R., Simmons, A., Stowe, J., and Waight, P. Recall bias, MMR, and autism. *Archives of Disease in Childhood*, 2002, *87*, 493–494.

Angrilli, A., Mauri, A., Palomba, D., Flor, H., Birbaumer, N., Sartori, G., and Dipaola, F. Startle reflex and emotion modulation impairment after a right amygdala lesion. *Brain*, 1996, *119*, 1991–2000.

Anonymous. Effects of sexual activity on beard growth in man. *Nature*, 1970, *226*, 867–870.

Archer, J. Testosterone and aggression. *Journal of Offender Rehabilitation*, 1994, *5*, 3–25.

Arendt, J., Deacon, S., English, J., Hampton, S., and Morgan, L. Melatonin and adjustment to phase-shift. *Journal of Sleep Research*, 1995, *4*, 74–79.

Arnold, A. P., and Jordan, C. L. Hormonal organization of neural circuits. In *Frontiers in Neuroendocrinology, Vol. 10*, edited by L. Martini and W. F. Ganong. New York: Raven Press, 1988.

Aroniadou, V. A., and Teyler, T. J. The role of NMDA receptors in long-term potentiation (LTP) and depression (LTD) in rat visual cortex. *Brain Research*, 1991, *562*, 136–143.

Aronson, B. D., Bell-Pedersen, D., Block, G. D., Bos, N. P. A., Dunlap, J. C., Eskin, A., Garceau, N. Y., Geusz, M. E., Johnson, K. A., Khalsa, S. B. S., Koster-Van Hoffen, G. C., Koumenis, C., Lee, T. M., LeSauter, J., Lindgren, K. M., Liu, Q., Loros, J. J., Michel, S. H., Mirmiran, M., Moore, R. Y., Ruby, N. F., Silver, R., Turek, F. W., and Zatz, M. Circadian rhythms. *Brain Research Reviews*, 1993, *18*, 315–333.

Arroyo, S., Lesser, R. P., Gordon, B., Uematsu, S., Hart, J., Scherdt, P., Andreasson, K., and Fisher, R. S. Mirth, laughter and gelastic seizures. *Brain*, 1993, *116*, 757–780.

Artmann, H., Grau, H., Adelman, M., and Schleiffer, R. Reversible and non-reversible enlargement of cerebrospinal fluid spaces in anorexia nervosa. *Neuroradiology*, 1985, *27*, 103–112.

Asanuma, H., and Rosén, I. Topographical organization of cortical efferent zones projecting to distal forelimb muscles in monkey. *Experimental Brain Research*, 1972, *13*, 243–256.

Aschoff, J. Circadian rhythms: General features and endocrinological aspects. In *Endocrine Rhythms,* edited by D. T. Krieger. New York: Raven Press, 1979.

Asnis, G. M., Hameedi, F. A., Goddard, A. W., Potkin, S. G., Black, D., Jameel, M., Desagani, K., and Woods, S. W. Fluvoxamine in the treatment of panic disorder: A multi-center, double-blind, placebo-controlled study in outpatients. *Psychiatry Research,* 2001, *103,* 1–14.

Aston-Jones, G., and Bloom, F. E. Activity of norepinephrine-containing locus coeruleus neurons in behaving rats anticipates fluctuations in the sleep-waking cycle. *Journal of Neuroscience,* 1981a, *1,* 876–886.

Aston-Jones, G., Rajkowski, J., Kubiak, P., and Alexinsky, T. Locus coeruleus neurons in monkey are selectively activated by attended cues in a vigilance task. *Journal of Neuroscience,* 1994, *14,* 4467–4480.

Atack, J. R., Broughton, H. B., and Pollack, S. J. Inositol monophosphatase: A putative target for Li⁺ in the treatment of bipolar disorder. *Trends in Neurosciences,* 1995, *18,* 343–349.

Attia, E., Haiman, C., Walsh, T., and Flater, S. T. Does fluoxetine augment the inpatient treatment of anorexia nervosa? *American Journal of Psychiatry,* 1998, *155,* 548–551.

Auer, R. N., Jensen, M. L., and Whishaw, I. Q. Neurobehavioral deficit due to ischemic brain damage limited to half of the CA1 section of the hippocampus. *Journal of Neuroscience,* 1989, *9,* 1641–1647.

Avenet, P., and Lindemann, B. Perspectives of taste reception. *Journal of Membrane Biology,* 1989, *112,* 1–8.

Avery, D. H., Eder, D. N., Bolte, M. A., Hellekson, C. J., Dunner, D. L., Vitiello, M. V., and Prinz, P. N. Dawn stimulation and bright light in the treatment of SAD: A controlled study. *Biological Psychiatry,* 2001, *50,* 205–216.

Avila, M. T., Weiler, M. A., Lahti, A. C., Tamminga, C. A., and Thaker, G. K. Effects of ketamine on leading saccades during smooth-pursuit eye movements may implicate cerebellar dysfunction in schizophrenia. *American Journal of Psychiatry,* 2002, *159,* 1490–1496.

Baddeley, A. D. Memory: Verbal and visual subsystems of working memory. *Current Biology,* 1993, *3,* 563–565.

Baer, L., Rauch, S. L., Ballantine, H. T., Martuza, R., Cosgrove, R., Cassem, E., Giriunas, I., Manzo, P. A., Dimino, C., and Jenike, M. A. Cingulotomy for intractable obsessive-compulsive disorder: Prospective long-term follow-up of 18 patients. *Archives of General Psychiatry,* 1995, *52,* 384–392.

Bagatell, C. J., Heiman, J. R., Rivier, J. E., and Bremner, W. J. Effects of endogenous testosterone and estradiol on sexual behavior in normal young men. *Journal of Clinical Endocrinology and Metabolism,* 1994, *7,* 211–216.

Bai, F. L., Yamano, M., Shiotani, Y., Emson, P. C., Smith, A. D., Powell, J. F., and Tohyama, M. An arcuato-paraventricular and-dorsomedial hypothalamic neuropeptide Y-containing system which lacks noradrenaline in the rat. *Brain Research,* 1985, *331,* 172–175.

Bailey, A., Le Couteur, A., Gottesman, I., Bolton, P., Simonoff, E., Yuzda, E., and Rutter, M. Autism as a strongly genetic disorder: Evidence from a British twin study. *Psychological Medicine,* 1995, *25,* 63–77.

Bailey, A., Luthert, P., Dean, A., Harding, B., Janota, I., Montgomery, M., Rutter, M., and Lantos, P. A clinicopathological study of autism. *Brain,* 1998, *121,* 889–905.

Bailey, A. J. The biology of autism. *Psychological Medicine,* 1993, *23,* 7–11.

Bailey, J. M., and Pillard, R. C. A genetic study of male sexual orientation. *Archives of General Psychiatry,* 1991, *48,* 1089–1096.

Bailey, J. M., Pillard, R. C., Neale, M. C., and Agyei, Y. Heritable factors influence sexual orientation in women. *Archives of General Psychiatry,* 1993, *50,* 217–223.

Baizer, J. S., Ungerleider, L. G., and Desimone, R. Organization of visual inputs to the inferior temporal and posterior parietal cortex in macaques. *Journal of Neuroscience,* 1991, *11,* 168–190.

Bak, T. H., O'Donovan, D. G., Xuereb, J. H., Boniface, S., and Hodges, J. R. Selective impairment of verb processing associated with pathological changes in Brodman areas 44 and 45 in the motor neurone disease-dementia-aphasia syndrome. *Brain,* 2001, *124,* 103–120.

Baker, D. G., West, S. A., Nicholson, W. E., Ekhator, N. N., Kasckow, J. W., Hill, K. K., Bruce, A. B., Orth, D. N., and Geracioti, T. D. Serial CSF corticotropin-releasing hormone levels and adrenocortical activity in combat veterans with posttraumatic stress disorder. *American Journal of Psychiatry,* 1999, *156,* 585–588.

Baldessarini, R. J. *Chemotherapy in Psychiatry.* Cambridge, Mass.: Harvard University Press, 1977.

Baldwin, A. E., Holahan, M. R. Sadeghian, K., and Kelley, A. E. *N*-methyl-D-aspartate receptor-dependent plasticity within a distributed corticostriatal network mediates appetitive instrumental learning. *Behavioral Neuroscience,* 2000, *114,* 84–98.

Balint, R. Seelenlahmung des "Schauens," optische Ataxie, raumliche Storung der Aufmerksamkeit. *Monatschrift für Psychiatrie und Neurologie,* 1909, *25,* 51–81.

Ballantine, H. T., Bouckoms, A. J., Thomas, E. K., and Giriunas, I. E. Treatment of psychiatric illness by stereotactic cingulotomy. *Biological Psychiatry,* 1987, *22,* 807–819.

Balon, R., Jordan, M., Pohl, R., and Yeragani, V. K. Family history of anxiety disorders in control subjects with lactate-induced panic attacks. *American Journal of Psychiatry,* 1989, *146,* 1304–1306.

Balskubik, R., Ableitner, A., Herz, A., and Shippenberg, T. S. Neuroanatomical sites mediating the motivational effects of opioids as mapped by the conditioned place preference paradigm in rats. *Journal of Pharmacology and Experimental Therapeutics,* 1993, *264,* 489–495.

Banks, M. S., Aslin, R. N., and Letson, R. D. Sensitive period for the development of human binocular vision. *Science,* 1975, *190,* 675–677.

Banks, W. A., Kastin, A. J., Huang, W. T., Jaspan, J. B., and Maness, L. M. Leptin enters the brain by a saturable system independent of insulin. *Peptides,* 1996, *17,* 305–311.

Baranaga, M. How cannabinoids work in the brain. *Science,* 2001, *291,* 2530.

Baranyi, A., Szente, M. B., and Woody, C. D. Properties of associative long-lasting potentiation induced by cellular conditioning in the motor cortex of conscious cats. *Neuroscience,* 1991, *42,* 321–334.

Barbazanges, A., Piazza, P. V., Le Moal, M., and Maccari, S. Maternal glucocorticoid secretion mediates long-term effects of prenatal stress. *Journal of Neuroscience,* 1996, *16,* 3943–3949.

Barclay, C. D., Cutting, J. E., and Kozlowski, L. T. Temporal and spatial factors in gait perception that influence gender recognition. *Perception and Psychophysics,* 1978, *23,* 145–152.

Barr, L. C., Goodman, W. K., McDougle, C. J., Delgado, P. L., Heninger, G. R., Charney, D. S., and Price, L. H. Tryptophan depletion in patients with obsessive-compulsive disorder who respond to serotonin reuptake inhibitors. *Archives of General Psychiatry,* 1994, *51,* 309–317.

Barsh, G. S., Farooqi, I. S., and O'Rahilly, S. Genetics of body-weight regulation. *Nature,* 2000, *404,* 644–651.

Bartness, T. J., Powers, J. B., Hastings, M. H., Bittman, E. L., and Goldman, B. D. The timed infusion paradigm for melatonin delivery: What has it taught us about the melatonin signal, its reception, and the photoperiodic control of seasonal responses? *Journal of Pineal Research,* 1993, *15,* 161–190.

Basbaum, A. I., and Fields, H. L. Endogenous pain control mechanisms: Review and hypothesis. *Annals of Neurology,* 1978, *4,* 451–462.

Basbaum, A. I., and Fields, H. L. Endogenous pain control systems: Brainstem spinal pathways and endorphin circuitry. *Annual Review of Neuroscience,* 1984, *7,* 309–338.

Basbaum, A. I., and Woolf, C. J. Pain. *Current Biology,* 1999, *9,* R429–R431.

Batterham, R. L., Cowley, M. A., Small, C. J., Herzog, H., Cohen, M. A., Dakin, C. L., Wren, A. M., Brynes, A. E., Low, M. J., Ghatei, M. A., Cone, R. D., and Bloom, S. R. Gut hormone PYY$_{3-36}$ physiologically inhibits food intake. *Nature,* 2002, *418,* 650–654.

Bauer, R. H., and Fuster, J. M. Delayed-matching and delayed-response deficit from cooling dorsolateral prefrontal cortex in monkeys. *Journal of Comparative and Physiological Psychology,* 1976, *90,* 293–302.

Baylis, G. C., Rolls, E. T., and Leonard, C. M. Selectivity between faces in the responses of a population of neurons in the cortex in the superior temporal sulcus of the monkey. *Brain Research,* 1985, *342,* 91–102.

Baylor, D. How photons start vision. *Proceedings of the National Academy of Sciences, USA,* 1996, *93,* 560–565.

Bazett, H. C., McGlone, B., Williams, R. G., and Lufkin, H. M. Sensation. I. Depth, distribution, and probable identification in the prepuce of sensory end-organs concerned in sensations of temperature and touch: Thermometric conductivity. *Archives of Neurology and Psychiatry (Chicago),* 1932, *27,* 489–517.

Beach, F. A. Cerebral and hormonal control of reflexive mechanisms involved in copulatory behavior. *Physiological Review,* 1967, *47,* 289–316.

Beamer, W., Bermant, G., and Clegg, M. T. Copulatory behaviour of the ram, Ovis aries. II. Factors affecting copulatory satiation. *Animal Behavior,* 1969, *17,* 706–711.

Bean, N. J. Modulation of agonistic behavior by the dual olfactory system in male mice. *Physiology and Behavior,* 1982, *29,* 433–437.

Bean, N. J., and Conner, R. Central hormonal replacement and home-cage dominance in castrated rats. *Hormones and Behavior,* 1978, *11,* 100–109.

Beauregard, M., Lévesque, J., and Bourgouin, P. Neural correlates of conscious self-regulation of emotion. *Journal of Neuroscience,* 2001, *21,* RC165(1–6).

Beauvois, M. F., and Dérouesné, J. Phonological alexia: Three dissociations. *Journal of Neurology, Neurosurgery and Psychiatry,* 1979, *42,* 1115–1124.

Beauvois, M. F., and Dérouesné, J. Lexical or orthographic dysgraphia. *Brain,* 1981, *104,* 21–45.

Bechara, A., Damasio, H., Damasio, A. R., and Lee, G. P. Different contributions of the human amygdala and ventromedial prefrontal cortex to decision-making. *Journal of Neuroscience,* 1999, *19,* 5473–5481.

Bechara, A., Damasio, H., Tranel, D., and Anderson, S. W. Dissociation of working memory from decision making within the human prefrontal cortex. *Journal of Neuroscience,* 1998, *18,* 428–437.

Bechara, A., Damasio, H., Tranel, D., and Damasio, A. R. Deciding advantageously before knowing the advantageous strategy. *Science,* 1997, *275,* 1293–1295.

Bechara, A., Tranel, D., Damasio, H., Adolphs, R., Rockland, C., and Damasio, A. R. Double dissociation of conditioning and declarative knowledge relative to the amygdala and hippocampus in humans. *Science,* 1995, *269,* 1115–1118.

Beckstead, R. M., Morse, J. R., and Norgren, R. The nucleus of the solitary tract in the monkey: Projections to the thalamus and brainstem nuclei. *Journal of Comparative Neurology,* 1980, *190,* 259–282.

Beecher, H. K. *Measurement of Subjective Responses: Quantitative Effects of Drugs.* New York: Oxford University Press, 1959.

Beeman, E. A. The effect of male hormone on aggressive behavior in mice. *Physiological Zoology,* 1947, *20,* 373–405.

Behrmann, M., Nelson, J., and Sekuler, E. B. Visual complexity in letter-by-letter reading: "Pure" alexia is not pure. *Neuropsychologia,* 1998, *36,* 1115–1132.

Beidler, L. M. Physiological properties of mammalian taste receptors. In *Taste and Smell in Vertebrates,* edited by G. E. W. Wolstenholme. London: J. & A. Churchill, 1970.

Beitz, A. J. The organization of afferent projections to the midbrain periaqueductal gray of the rat. *Neuroscience,* 1982, *7,* 133–159.

Belin, P., Zatorre, R. J., Lafaille, P., Ahad, P., and Pike, B. Voice-selective areas in human auditory cortex. *Nature,* 2000, *403,* 309–312.

Bell, A. P., Weinberg, M. S., and Hammersmith, S. K. *Sexual Preference: Its Development in Men and Women.* Bloomington: Indiana University Press, 1981.

Benington, J. H., Koldali, S. K., and Heller, H. C. Monoaminergic and cholinergic modulation of REM-sleep timing in rats. *Brain Research,* 1995, *681,* 141–146.

Benson, D. F., and Geschwind, N. Aphasia and related disorders: A clinical approach. In *Principles of Behavioral Neurology,* edited by M.-M. Mesulam. Philadelphia: F. A. Davis, 1985.

Benson, D. F., Djenderedjian, A., Miller, B. L., Pachana, N. A., Chang, L., Itti, L., and Mena, I. Neural basis of confabulation. *Neurology,* 1996, *46,* 1239–1243.

Benson, D. L., Colman, D. R., and Huntley, G. W. Molecules, maps and synapse specificity. *Nature Reviews: Neuroscience,* 2001, *2,* 899–909.

Bermant, G., and Davidson, J. M. *Biological Bases of Sexual Behavior.* New York: Harper & Row, 1974.

Bernhardt, P. C., Dabbs, J. M., Fielden, J. A., and Lutter, C. D. Testosterone changes during vicarious experiences of winning and losing among fans at sporting events. *Physiology and Behavior,* 1998, *65,* 59–62.

Berns, G. S., McClure, S. M., Pagnoni, G., and Montague, P. R. Predictability modulates human brain response to reward. *Journal of Neuroscience,* 2001, *21,* 2793–2798.

Berrettini, W. Progress and pitfalls: Bipolar molecular linkange studies. *Journal of Affective Disorders,* 1998, *50,* 287–297.

Berson, D. M., Dunn, F. A., and Takao, M. Phototransduction by retinal ganglion cells that set the circadian clock. *Science,* 2002, *295,* 1070–1073.

Berthier, M., Kulisevsky, J., Gironell, A., and Heras, J. A. Obsessive-compulsive disorder associated with brain lesions: Clinical phenomenology, cognitive function, and anatomic correlates. *Neurology,* 1996, *47,* 353–361.

Berthier, M., Starkstein, S., and Leiguarda, R. Asymbolia for pain: A sensory-limbic disconnection syndrome. *Annals of Neurology,* 1988, *24,* 41–49.

Best, P. J., White, A. M., and Minai, A. Spatial processing in the brain: The activity of hippocampal place cells. *Annual Review of Neuroscience,* 2001, *24,* 459–486.

Bettelheim, B. *The Empty Fortress.* New York: Free Press, 1967.

Betz, W. J., and Berwick, G. S. Optical analysis of synaptic vesicle recycling at the frog neuromuscular junction. *Science,* 1992, *244,* 200–203.

Beversdorf, D. Q., and Heilman, K. M. Progressive ventral posterior cortical degeneration presenting as alexia for music and words. *Neurology,* 1998, *50,* 657–659.

Bier, M. J., and McCarley, R. W. REM-enhancing effects of the adrenergic antagonist idazoxan infused into the medial pontine reticular formation of the freely moving cat. *Brain Research,* 1994, *634,* 333–338.

Bierut, L. J., Dinwiddie, S. H., Begliter, H., Crowe, R. R., Hesselbrock, V., Nurnberger, J. I., Porjexz, B., Schukit, M. A., and Reich, T. Familial transmission of substance dependence: Alcohol, marijuana, cocaine, and habitual smoking. *Archives of General Psychiatry,* 1998, *55,* 982–988.

Bigiani, A., Delay, R. J., Chaudhair, N., Kinnamon, S. C., and Roper, S. D. Responses to glutamate in rat taste cells. *Journal of Neurophysiology,* 1997, *77,* 3048–3059.

Birch, L. L., McPhee, L., Shoba, B. C., Steinberg, L., and Krehbiel, R. "Clean up your plate": Effects of child feeding practices on the conditioning of meal size. *Learning and Motivation,* 1987, *18,* 301–317.

Bird, E., Cardone, C. C., and Contreras, R. J. Area postrema lesions disrupt food intake induced by cerebroventricular infusions of 5-thioglucose in the rat. *Brain Research,* 1983, *270,* 193–196.

Bisiach, E., and Luzzatti, C. Unilateral neglect of representational space. *Cortex,* 1978, *14,* 129–133.

Blair, R. J., Colledge, E., and Mitchell, D. G. Somatic markers and response reversal: Is there orbitofrontal cortex dysfunction in boys with psychopathic tendencies? *Journal of Abnormal Child Psychology,* 2001, *29,* 499–511.

Blanchard, R. Fraternal birth order and the maternal immune hypothesis of male homosexuality. *Hormones and Behavior,* 2001, *40,* 105–114.

Blaustein, J. D., and Feder, H. H. Cytoplasmic progestin receptors in guinea pig brain: Characteristics and relationship to the induction of sexual behavior. *Brain Research,* 1979, *169,* 481–497.

Blaustein, J. D., and Olster, D. H. Gonadal steroid hormone receptors and social behaviors. In *Advances in Comparative and Environmental Physiology, Vol. 3,* edited by J. Balthazart. Berlin: Springer-Verlag, 1989.

Blest, A. D. The function of eyespot patterns in insects. *Behaviour,* 1957, *11,* 209–256.

Bleuler, E. *Dementia Praecox of the Group of Schizophrenia, 1911.* Translated by J. Zinkin. New York: International Universities Press, 1911/1950.

Bliss, T. V. P., and Lømo, T. Long-lasting potentiation of synaptic transmission in the dentate area of the anaesthetized rabbit following stimulation of the perforant path. *Journal of Physiology (London),* 1973, *232,* 331–356.

Bloch, V., Hennevin, E., and Leconte, P. Interaction between post-trial reticular stimulation and subsequent paradoxical sleep in memory consolidation processes. In *Neurobiology of Sleep and Memory,* edited by R. R. Drucker-Colín and J. L. McGaugh. New York: Academic Press, 1977.

Blonder, L. X., Bowers, D., and Heilman, K. M. The role of the right hemisphere in emotional communication. *Brain,* 1991, *114,* 1115–1127.

Blum, K., Noble, E. P., Sheridan, P. J., Montgomery, A., Ritchie, T., Jagadeeswaran, P., Nogami, H., Briggs, A. H., and Cohn, J. B. Allelic association of human dopamine D_2 receptor gene in alcoholism. *Journal of the American Medical Association,* 1990, *263,* 2055–2060.

Blundell, J. E. What foods do people habitually eat? A dilemma for nutrition, an enigma for psychology. *American Journal of Clinical Nutrition,* 2000, *71,* 3–5.

Blundell, J. E., and Halford, J. C. G. Serotonin and appetite regulation: Implications for the pharmacological treatment of obesity. *CNS Drugs,* 1998, *9,* 473–495.

Boatman, D., Gordon, B., Hart, J., Selnes, O., Miglioretti, D., and Lenz, F. Transcortical sensory aphasia: Revisited and revised. *Brain,* 2000, *123,* 1634–1642.

Bodner, M., Kroger, J., and Fuster, J. M. Auditory memory cells in dorsolateral prefrontal cortex. *NeuroReport,* 1996, *7,* 1905–1908.

Bodner, S. M., Morshed, S. A., and Peterson, B. S. The question of PANDAS in adults. *Biological Psychiatry,* 2001, *49,* 807–810.

Boeve, B. F., Silber, M. H., Ferman, T. J., Lucas, J. A., and Parisi, J. E. Association of REM sleep behavior disorder and neurodegenerative disease may reflect an underlying synucleinopathy. *Movement Disorders,* 2001, *16,* 622–630.

Boller, F., and Dennis, M. *Auditory Comprehension: Clinical and Experimental Studies with the Token Test.* New York: Academic Press, 1979.

Bolton, R. F., Cornwall, J., and Phillipson, O. R. Collateral axons of cholinergic pontine neurones projecting to midline, mediodorsal and parafascicular thalamic nuclei in the rat. *Journal of Chemical Neuroanatomy,* 1993, *6,* 101–114.

Bon, C., Böhme, G. A., Doble, A., Stutzmann, J.-M., and Blanchard, J.-C. A role for nitric oxide in long-term potentiation. *European Journal of Neuroscience,* 1992, *4,* 420–424.

Bontempi, B., Laurent-Demir, C., Destrade, C., and Jaffard, R. Time-dependent reorganization of brain circuitry underlying long-term memory storage. *Nature,* 1999, *400,* 671–675.

Born, R. T. Center-surround interactions in the middle temporal visual area of the owl monkey. *Journal of Neurophysiology,* 2000, *84,* 2658–2669.

Born, R. T., and Tootell, R. B. H. Spatial frequency tuning of single units in macaque supragranular striate cortex. *Proceedings of the National Academy of Sciences,* 1991, *88,* 7066–7070.

Bornstein, B., Stroka, H., and Munitz, H. Prosopagnosia with animal face agnosia. *Cortex,* 1969, *5,* 164–169.

Borod, J. C., Koff, E., Yecker, S., Santschi, C., and Schmidt, J. M. Facial asymmetry during emotional expression: Gender, falence, and measurement technique. *Neuropsychologia,* 1998, *36,* 1209–1215.

Bottini, G., Corcoran, R., Sterzi, R., Paulesu, E., Schenone, P., Scarpa, P., Frackowiak, R. S. J., and Frith, C. D. The role of the right hemisphere in the interpretation of figurative aspects of language. A positron emission tomography activation study. *Brain,* 1994, *117,* 1241–1253.

Boulos, Z., Campbell, S. S., Lewy, A. J., Terman, M., Dijk, D. J., and Eastman, C. I. Light treatment for sleep disorders: Consensus report. 7: Jet-lag. *Journal of Biological Rhythms,* 1995, *10,* 167–176.

Boussaoud, D., Desimone, R., and Ungerleider, L. G. Visual topography of area TEO in the macaque. *Journal of Comparative Neurology,* 1991, *306,* 554–575.

Bouwknecht, J. A., Hijzen, T. H., van der Gugten, J., Maes, R. A. A., Hen, R., and Olivier, B. Absence of 5-HT$_{1B}$ receptors is associated with impaired impulse control in Male 5-HT$_{1B}$ knockout mice. *Biological Psychiatry,* 2001, *49,* 557–568.

Bowers, D., and Heilman, K. M. A dissociation between the processing of affective and nonaffective faces. Paper presented at the meeting of the International Neuropsychological Society, Atlanta, 1981.

Bowers, D., Blonder, L. X., Feinberg, T., and Heilman, K. M. Differential impact of right and left hemisphere lesions on facial emotion and object imagery. *Brain,* 1991, *114,* 2593–2609.

Bowersox, S. S., Kaitin, K. I., and Dement, W. C. EEG spindle activity as a function of age: Relationship to sleep continuity. *Brain Research,* 1985, *63,* 526–539.

Boynton, R. M. *Human Color Vision.* New York: Holt, Rinehart and Winston, 1979.

Boynton, R. M., and Olson, C. X. Locating basic colors in the OSA space. *Color Research and Application,* 1987, *12,* 94–105.

Bozarth, M. A. Physical dependence produced by central morphine infusions: An anatomical mapping study *Neuroscience and Biobehavioral Reviews,* 1994, *18,* 373–383.

Bozarth, M. A., and Wise, R. A. Toxicity associated with long-term intravenous heroin and cocaine self-administration in the rat. *Journal of the American Medical Association,* 1985, *254,* 81–83.

Bradbury, M. W. B. *The Concept of a Blood-Brain Barrier.* New York: John Wiley & Sons, 1979.

Bradley, D. C., Maxwell, M., Andersen, R. A., Banks, M. S., and Shenoy, K. V. Mechanisms of heading perception in primate visual cortex. *Science,* 1996, *273,* 1544–1547.

Bradley, S. J., Oliver, G. D., Chernick, A. B., and Zucker, K. H. Experiment of nurture: Ablatio penis at 2 months, sex reas-

signment at 7 months, and a psychosexual follow-up in young adulthood. *Pediatrics,* 1998, *102,* E91–E95.

Bramham, C. R., Bacher-Svendsen, K., and Sarvey, J. M. LTP in the lateral perforant path is β-adrenergic receptor-dependent. *Neuroreport,* 1997, *8,* 719–724.

Bray, G. A. Drug treatment of obesity. *American Journal of Clinical Nutrition,* 1992, *55,* 538S–544S.

Brecher, E. M. *Licit and Illicit Drugs.* Boston: Little, Brown & Co., 1972.

Breedlove, S. M. Sexual differentiation of the brain and behavior. In *Behavioral Endocrinology,* edited by J. B. Becker, S. M. Breedlove, and D. Crews. Cambridge, Mass.: MIT Press, 1992.

Breedlove, S. M. Sexual differentiation of the human nervous system. *Annual Review of Psychology,* 1994, *45,* 389–418.

Breedlove, S. M., and Arnold, A. Hormone accumulation in a sexually dimorphic motor nucleus of the rat spinal cord. *Science,* 1980, *210,* 564–566.

Breedlove, S. M., and Arnold, A. Sex differences in the pattern of steroid accumulation by motoneurons of the rat lumbar spinal cord. *Journal of Comparative Neurology,* 1983, *215,* 211–216.

Breier, A., Su, T.-P., Saunders, R., Carson, R. E., Kolachana, B. S., de Bartolemeis, A., Weinberger, D. R., Weisenfeld, N., Malhotra, A. K., Eckelman, W. C., and Pickar, D. Schizophrenia is associated with elevated amphetamine-induced synaptic dopamine concentrations: evidence from a novel positron emission tomography method. *Proceedings of the National Academy of Science, USA,* 1997, *94,* 2569–2574.

Breisch, S. T., Zemlan, F. P., and Hoebel, B. G. Hyperphagia and obesity following serotonin depletion by intraventricular *p*-chlorphenylalanine. *Science,* 1976, *192,* 382–384.

Breiter, H. C., Rauch, S. L., Kwong, K. K., Baker, J. R., Weisskoff, R. M., Kennedy, D. N., Kendrick, A. D., Davis, T. L., Jiang, A. P., Cohen, M. S., Stern, C. E., Belliveau, J. W., Baer, L., O'Sullivan, R. L., Savage, C. R., Jenike, M. A., and Rosen, B. R. Functional magnetic resonance imaging of symptom provocation in obsessive-compulsive disorder. *Archives of General Psychiatry,* 1996, *53,* 595–606.

Bremner, J. D. Does stress damage the brain? *Biological Psychiatry,* 1999, *45,* 797–805.

Bremner, J. D., Innis, R. B., Salomon, R. M., Staib, L. H., Ng, C. K., Miller, H. L., Bronen, R. A., Krystal, J. H., Duncan, J., Rich, D., Price, L. H., Malison, R., Dey, H., Soufer, R., and Charney, D. S. Positron emission tomography measurement of cerebral metabolic correlates of tryptophan depletion-induced depressive relapse. *Archives of General Psychiatry,* 1997, *54,* 364–374.

Bremner, J. D., Randall, P., Scott, T. M., Bronen, R. A., Seibyl, J. P., Southwick, S. M., Delaney, R. C., McCarthy, G., Charney, D. S., and Innis, R. B. MRI-based measurement of hippocampal volume in patients with combat-related posttraumatic stress disorder. *American Journal of Psychiatry,* 1995, *152,* 973–981.

Brewer, J. B., Zhao, Z., Desmond, J. E., Glover, G. H., and Gabrieli, J. D. E. Making memories: Brain activity that predicts how well visual experience will be remembered. *Science,* 1998, *281,* 1185–1187.

Brickner, R. M. *The Intellectual Functions of the Frontal Lobe: A Study Based Upon Observations of a Man After Partial Frontal Lobectomy.* New York: Macmillan, 1936.

Bridges, R. S. A quantitative analysis of the roles of dosage, sequence and duration of estradiol and progesterone exposure in the regulation of maternal behavior in the rat. *Endocrinology,* 1984, *114,* 930–940.

Bridges, R. S., Numan, M., Ronsheim, P. M., Mann, P. E., and Lupini, C. E. Central prolactin infusions stimulate maternal behavior in steroid-treated, nulliparous female rats. *Proceedings of the National Academy of Sciences, USA,* 1990, *87,* 8003–8007.

Bridges, R. S., Robertson, M. C., Shiu, R. P. C., Friesen, H. G., Stuer, A. M., and Mann, P. E. Endocrine communication between conceptus and mother: Placental lactogen stimulation of maternal behavior. *Neuroendocrinology,* 1996, *64,* 57–64.

Britten, K. H., and van Wezel, R. J. Electrical microstimulation of cortical area MST biases heading perception in monkeys. *Nature Neuroscience,* 1998, *1,* 59–63.

Britton, D. R., Koob, G. F., Rivier, J., and Vale, W. Intraventricular corticotropin-releasing factor enhances behavioral effects of novelty. *Life Sciences,* 1982, *31,* 363–367.

Broberg, D. J., and Bernstein, I. L. Cephalic insulin release in anorexic women. *Physiology and Behavior,* 1989, *45,* 871–874.

Broberger, C., de Lecea, L., Sutcliffe, J. G., and Hökfelt, T. Hypocretin/orexin- and melanin concentrating hormone-expressing cells form distinct populations in the rodent lateral hypothalamus: Relationship to the neuropeptide Y and agouti gene-related protein systems. *Journal of Comparative Neurology,* 1998, *402,* 460–474.

Broca, P. Remarques sur le siège de la faculté du langage articulé, suivies d'une observation d'aphemie (perte de la parole). *Bulletin de la Société Anatomique (Paris),* 1861, *36,* 330–357.

Broussaud, D., di Pellegrino, G., and Wise, S. P. Frontal lobe mechanisms subserving vision-for-action versus vision-for-perception. *Behavioural Brain Research,* 1996, *72,* 1–15.

Brown, A. S., Schaefer, C. A., Wyatt, R. J., Begg, M. D., Goetz, R., Bresnahan, M. A., Harkavy-Friedman, J., Gorman, J. M., Malaspina, D., and Susser, E. S. Paternal age and risk of schizophrenia in adult offspring. *American Journal of Psychiatry,* 2002, *159,* 1528–1533.

Brown, R. E., Stevens, D. R., and Haas, H. L. The physiology of brain histamine. *Progress in Neurobiology,* 2001, *63,* 637–672.

Brown, T. H., Ganong, A. H., Kairiss, E. W., Keenan, C. L., and Kelso, S. R. Long-term potentiation in two synaptic systems of the hippocampal brain slice. In *Neural Models of Plasticity: Experimental and Theoretical Approaches,* edited by J. H. Byrne and W. O. Berry. San Diego: Academic Press, 1989.

Brown, W. E., Eliez, S., Menon, V., Rumsey, J. M., White, C. D., and Reiss, A. L. Preliminary evidence of widespread morphological variations of the brain in dyslexia. *Neurology,* 2001, *56,* 781–783.

Brownell, H. H., Michel, D., Powelson, J., and Gardner, H. Surprise but not coherence: Sensitivity to verbal humor in right-hemisphere patients. *Brain and Language,* 1983, *18,* 20–27.

Brownell, H. H., Simpson, T. L., Bihrle, A. M., Potter, H. H., and Gardner, H. Appreciation of metaphoric alternative word meanings by left and right brain-damaged patients. *Neuropsychologia,* 1990, *28,* 173–184.

Brownell, W. E., Bader, C. R., Bertrand, D., and de-Ribaupierre, Y. Evoked mechanical responses of isolated cochlear outer hair cells. *Science,* 1985, *227,* 194–196.

Brozowski, T. J., Brown, R. M., Rosvold, H. E., and Goldman, P. S. Cognitive deficit caused by regional depletion of dopamine in prefrontal cortex of rhesus monkey. *Science,* 1979, *205,* 929–932.

Bruce, H. M. A block to pregnancy in the mouse caused by proximity of strange males. *Journal of Reproduction and Fertility,* 1960a, *1,* 96–103.

Bruce, H. M. Further observations of pregnancy block in mice caused by proximity of strange males. *Journal of Reproduction and Fertility,* 1960b, *2,* 311–312.

Brun, V. J., Otnæss, M. K., Molden, S., Steffenach, H.-A., Witter, M. P., Moser, M.-B., and Moser, E. I. Place cells and place recognition maintained by direct entorhinal-hippocampal circuitry. *Science,* 2002, *296,* 2243–2246.

Brüning, J. C., Gautam, D., Burks, D. J., Gillette, J., Schubert, M., Orban, P. C., Klein, R., Krone, W., Muller-Wieland, D., and Kahn, C. R. Role of brain insulin receptor in control of body weight and reproduction. *Science,* 2000, *289,* 2122–2125.

Bryant, D. N., LeSauter, J., Silver, R., and Romero, M. T. Retinal innervation of calbindin-D28K cells in the hamster suprachiasmatic nucleus: Ultrastructural characterization. *Journal of Biological Rhythms,* 2000, *2,* 103–111.

Bryden, M. P., and Ley, R. G. Right-hemispheric involvement in the perception and expression of emotion in normal humans. In *Neuropsychology of Human Emotion,* edited by K. M. Heilman and P. Satz. New York: Guilford Press, 1983.

Büchel, C., Price, C., and Friston, K. A multimodal language region in the ventral visual pathway. *Nature,* 1998, *394,* 274–277.

Buchs, P. A., and Muller, D. Induction of long-term potentiation is associated with major ultrastructural changes of activated synapses. *Proceedings of the National Academy of Sciences of the United States of America,* 1996, *93,* 8040–8045.

Buchsbaum, M. S., Gillin, J. C., Wu, J., Hazlett, E., Sicotte, N., Dupont, R. M., and Bunney, W. E. Regional cerebral glucose metabolic rate in human sleep assessed by positron emission tomography. *Life Sciences,* 1989, *45,* 1349–1356.

Buck, L., and Axel, R. A novel multigene family may encode odorant receptors: A molecular basis for odor recognition. *Cell,* 1991, *65,* 175–187.

Buck, L. B. Information coding in the vertebrate olfactory system. *Annual Review of Neuroscience,* 1996, *19,* 517–544.

Budka, H., Almer, G., Hainfellner, J. A., Brücke, T., and Jellinger, K. The Austrian FFI cases. *Brain Pathology,* 1998, *8,* 554.

Buggy, J., Hoffman, W. E., Phillips, M. I., Fisher, A. E., and Johnson, A. K. Osmosensitivity of rat third ventricle and interactions with angiotensin. *American Journal of Physiology,* 1979, *236,* R75–R82.

Bunyard, L. B., Katzel, L. I., Busby-Whitehead, M. J., Wu, Zhong, and Goldberg, A. P. Energy requirements of middle-aged men are modifiable by physical activity. *American Journal of Clinical Nutrition,* 1998, *68,* 1136–1142.

Burke, J. R., Enghild, J. J., Martin, M. E., Jou, Y. S., Myers, R. M., Roses, A. D., Vance, J. M., and Strittmatter, W. J. Huntingtin and DRPLA proteins selectively interact with the enzyme GAPDH. *Nature Medicine,* 1996, *2,* 347–350.

Burnstock, G., and Wood, J. N. Purinergic receptors: Their role in nociception and primary afferent neurotransmission. *Current Opinion in Neurobiology,* 1996, *6,* 526–532.

Burton, M. J., Rolls, E. T., and Mora, F. Effects of hunger on the responses of neurons in the lateral hypothalamus to the sight and taste of food. *Experimental Neurology,* 1976, *51,* 668–677.

Buxbaum, L. J., Glosser, G., and Coslett, H. B. Impaired face and word recognition without object agnosia. *Neuropsychologia,* 1999, *37,* 41–50.

Buzsáki, G. Two-stage model of memory trace formation: A role for "noisy" brain states. *Neuroscience,* 1989, *31,* 551–570.

Buzsáki, G. The hippocampo-neocortical dialogue. *Cerebral Cortex,* 1996, *6,* 81–92.

Buzsáki, G., Gage, F. H., Czopf, J., and Björklund, A. Restoration of rhythmic slow activity (theta) in the subcortically denervated hippocampus by fetal CNS transplants. *Brain Research,* 1987, *400,* 334–347.

Byne, W., Tobet, S., Mattiace, L. A., Lasco, M. S., Kemether, E., Edgar, M. A., Morgello, S., Buchsbaum, M. S., and Jones, L. B. The interstitial nucleus of the human anterior hypothalamus: An investigation of variation with sex, sexual orientation, and HIV status. *Hormones and Behavior,* 2001, *40,* 86–92.

Bystritsky, A., Pontillo, D., Powers, M., Sabb, F. W., Craske, M. G., and Bookheimer, S. Y. Functional MRI changes during panic anticipation and imagery exposure. *Neuroreport,* 2001, *12,* 3953–3957.

Cabanac, M., and Lafrance, L. Facial consummatory responses in rats support the ponderostat hypothesis. *Physiology and Behavior,* 1991, *50,* 179–183.

Cahill, L., Babinsky, R., Markowitsch, H. J., and McGaugh, J. L. The amygdala and emotional memory. *Nature,* 1995, *377,* 295–296.

Cahill, L., Haier, R. J., Fallon, J., Alkire, M. T., Tang, C., Keator, D., Wu, J., and McGaugh, J. L. Amygdala activity at encoding correlated with long-term, free recall of emotional information. *Proceedings of the National Academy of Sciences of the United States of America,* 1996, *93,* 8016–8021.

Cain, W. S. Olfaction. In *Stevens' Handbook of Experimental Psychology. Vol. 1: Perception and Motivation,* edited by R. C. Atkinson, R. J. Herrnstein, G. Lindzey, and R. D. Luce. New York: John Wiley & Sons, 1988.

Caine, S. B., and Koob, G. F. Effects of mesolimbic dopamine depletion on responding maintained by cocaine and food. *Journal of the Experimental Analysis of Behavior,* 1994, *61,* 213–221.

Caine, S. B., Heinrichs, S. C., Coffin, V. L., and Koob, G. F. Effects of the dopamine D-1 antagonist SCH 23390 microinjected into the accumbens, amygdala or striatum on cocaine self-administration in the ra. *Brain Res,* 1995, *692,* 47–56.

Calabrese, J. R., Rapport, D. J., Shelton, M. D., and Kimmel, S. E. Clinical studies on the use of lamatrigine in bipolar disorder. *Neuropsychobiology,* 1998, *38,* 185–191.

Calabrese, P., Markowitsch, H. J., Harders, A. G., Scholz, M., and Gehlen, W. Fornix damage and memory: A case report. *Cortex,* 1995, *31,* 555–564.

Calder, A. J., Young, A. W., Rowland, D., Perrett, D. I., Hodges, J. R., and Etcoff, N. L. Facial emotion recognition after bilateral amygdala damage: Differentially severe impairment of fear. *Cognitive Neuropsychology,* 1996, *13,* 699–745.

Callaway, C. W., Lydic, R., Baghdoyan, H. A., and Hobson, J. A. Pontogeniculooccipital waves: Spontaneous visual system activity during rapid eye movement sleep. *Cellular and Molecular Neurobiology,* 1987, *2,* 105–149.

Cameron, H. A., and McKay, R. D. G. Adult neurogenesis produces a large pool of new granule cells in the dentate gyrus. *Journal of Comparative Neurology,* 2001, *435,* 406–417.

Campbell, R., Heywood, C. A., Cower, A., Regard, M., and Landis, T. Sensitivity to eye gaze in prosopagnosic patients and monkeys with superior temporal sulcus ablation. *Neuropsychologia,* 1990, *28,* 1123–1142.

Campeau, S., Hayward, M. D., Hope, B. T., Rosen, J. B., Nestler, E. J., and Davis, M. Induction of the c-fos proto-oncogene in rat amygdala during unconditioned and conditioned fear. *Brain Research,* 1991, *565,* 349–352.

Campfield, L. A., Smith, F. J., Guisez, Y., Devos, R., and Burn, P. Recombinant mouse ob protein: Evidence for a peripheral signal linking adiposity and central neural networks. *Science,* 1995, *269,* 546–549.

Cannon, M., Jones, P., Gilvarry, C., Rifkin, L., McKenzie, K., Foerster, A., and Murray, R. M. Premorbid social functioning in schizophrenia and bipolar disorder: Similarities and differences. *American Journal of Psychiatry,* 1997, *154,* 1544–1550.

Cannon, M., Jones, P. B., and Murray, R. M. Obstetric complications and schizophrenia: Historical and meta-analytic review. *American Journal of Psychiatry,* 2002, *159,* 1080–1092.

Cannon, T. D., Thompson, P. M., van Erp, T. G., Toga, A. W., Poutanen, V. P., Huttunen, M., Lonnqvist, J., Standerskjold-Nordenstam, C. G., Narr, K. L., Khaledy, M., Aoumalan, C. I., Dail, R., and Kaprio, J. Cortex mapping reveals regionally specific patterns of genetic and disease-specific gray-matter deficits in twins discordant for schizophrenia. *Proceedings of the National Academy of Sciences, USA,* 2002, *99,* 3228–3233.

Cannon, W. B. The James-Lange theory of emotions: A critical examination and an alternative. *American Journal of Psychology,* 1927, *39,* 106–124.

Card, J. P., Riley, J. N., and Moore, R. Y. The suprachiasmatic hypothalamic nucleus: Ultrastructure of relations to optic chiasm. *Neuroscience Abstracts,* 1980, *6,* 758.

Carew, T. J. Development assembly of learning in Aplysia. *Trends in Neuroscience,* 1989, *12,* 389–394.

Carmichael, M. S., Humbert, R., Dixen, J., Palmisano, G., Greenleaf, W., and Davidson, J. M. Plasma oxytocin increases in the human sexual response. *Journal of Clinical Endocrinology and Metabolism,* 1987, *64,* 27–31.

Caro, J. F., Kolaczynski, J. W., Nyce, M. R., Ohannesian, J. P., Opentanova, I., Goldman, W. H., Lynn, R. B., Zhang, P. L., Sinha, M. K., and Considine, R. V. Decreased cerebrospinal fluid/serum leptin ration in obesity: A possible mechanism for leptin resistance. *Lancet,* 1996, *348,* 159–161.

Carpenter, C. R. Sexual behavior of free ranging rhesus monkeys (*Macaca mulatta*). I. Specimens, procedures and behavioral characteristics of estrus. *Journal of Comparative Psychology,* 1942, *33,* 113–142.

Carr, C. E., and Konishi, M. Axonal delay lines for time measurement in the owl's brainstem. *Proceedings of the National Academy of Sciences, USA,* 1989, *85,* 8311–8315.

Carr, C. E., and Konishi, M. A circuit for detection of interaural time differences in the brain stem of the barn owl. *Journal of Neuroscience,* 1990, *10,* 3227–3246.

Carr, D. B., and Sesack, S. R. Projections from the rat prefrontal cortex to the ventral tegmental area: Target specificity in the synaptic associations with mesoaccumbens and mesocortical neurons. *Journal of Neuroscience,* 2000, *20,* 3864–3873.

Carrera, M. R., Ashley, J. A., Parsons, L. H., Wirsching, P., Koob, G. F., and Janda, K. D. Suppression of psychoactive effects of cocaine by active immunization. *Nature,* 1995, *378,* 727–730.

Carroll, R. C., Lissin, D. V., von Zastrow, M., Nicolol, R. A., and Malenka, R. C. Rapid redistribution of glutamate receptors contributes to long-term depression in hippocampal cultures. *Nature Neuroscience,* 1999, *2,* 454–460.

Carter, C. S. Hormonal influences on human sexual behavior. In *Behavioral Endocrinology,* edited by J. B. Becker, S. M. Breedlove, and D. Crews. Cambridge, Mass.: MIT Press, 1992.

Castellanos, F. X., Lee, P. P., Sharp, W., Jeffries, N. O., Greenstein, D. K., Clasen, L. S., Blumenthal, J. D., James, R. S., Ebens, C. L., Walter, J. M., Zijdenbos, A., Evans, A. C., Giedd, J. N., Rappoport, J. L. Developmental trajectories of brain volume abnormalities in children and adolescents with attention-deficit/hyperactivity disorder. *Journal of the American Medical Association,* 2002, *288,* 1740–1748.

Castles, A., and Coltheart, M. Varieties of developmental dyslexia. *Cognition,* 1993, *47,* 149–180.

Caterina, M. J., Leffler, A., Malmberg, A. B., Martin, W. J., Trafton, J., Petersen-Zeitz, K. R., Koltzenburg, M., Basbaum, A. I., and Julius, D. Impaired nociception and pain sensation in mice lacking the capsaicin receptor. *Science,* 2000, *288,* 306–313.

Cavada, C., and Goldman-Rakic, P. S. Posterior parietal cortex in rhesus monkey. II. Evidence for segregated corticocortical networks linking sensory and limbic areas with the frontal lobe. *Journal of Comparative Neurology,* 1989, *287,* 422–445.

Cecil, J. E., Francis, J., and Read, N. W. Relative contributions of intestinal, gastric, oro-sensory influences and information to changes in appetite induced by the same liquid meal. *Appetite,* 1998, *31,* 377–390.

Cenci, M. A., Kalen, P., Mandel, R. J., and Bjoerklund, A. Regional differences in the regulation of dopamine and noradrenaline release in medial frontal cortex, nucleus accumbens and caudate-putamen: A microdialysis study in the rat. *Brain Research,* 1992, *581,* 217–228.

Cerletti, U. Electroshock therapy. In *The Great Psychodynamic Therapies in Psychiatry,* edited by F. Marti-Ibanez, A. M. Sackler, M. D. Sackler, and R. R. Sackler. New York: Hoeber-Harper, 1956.

Cerletti, U., and Bini, L. Electric shock treatment. *Bollettino ed Atti della Accademia Medica di Roma,* 1938, *64,* 36.

Chandler, L. J., Harris, R. A., and Crews, F. T. Ethanol tolerance and synaptic plasticity. *Trends in Pharmacological Science,* 1998, *19,* 491–495.

Chaudhari, N., Yang, H., Lamp, C., Delay, E., Cartford, C., Than, T., and Roper, S. The taste of monosodium glutamate: Membrane receptors in taste buds. *Journal of Neuroscience,* 1996, *16,* 3817–3826.

Chehab, F. F., Mounzih, K., Lu, R., and Lim, M. E. Early onset of reproductive function in normal female mice treated with leptin. *Science,* 1997, *275,* 88–90.

Chemelli, R. M., Willie, J. T., Sinton, C. M., Elmquist, J. K., Scammell, T., Lee, C., Richardson, J. A., Williams, S. C., Xiong, Y.,

Kisanuki, Y., Fitch, T. E., Nakazato, M., Hammer, R. E., Saper, C. B., and Yanagisawa, M. Narcolepsy in orexin knockout mice: molecular genetics of sleep regulation. *Cell,* 1999, *98,* 437–451.

Chen, J., Marmer, R., Pulles, A., Paredes, W., and Gardner, E. L. Ventral tegmental microinjection of delta^9-tetrahydrocannabinol enhances ventral tegmental somatodendritic dopamine levels but not forebrain dopamine levels: Evidence for local neural action by marijuana's psychoactive ingredient. *Brain Research,* 1993, *621,* 65–70.

Chen, J., Paredes, W., Li, J., Smith, D., Lowinson, J., and Gardner, E. L. Delta^9-tetrahydrocannabinol produces naloxone-blockable enhancement of presynaptic basal dopamine efflux in nucleus accumbens of conscious, freely-moving rats as measured by intracerebral microdialysis. *Psychopharmacology,* 1990, *102,* 156–162.

Chen, W. R., Lee, S. H., Kato, K., Spencer, D. D., Shepherd, G. M., and Williamson, A. Long-term modifications of synaptic efficacy in the human inferior and middle temporal cortex. *Proceedings of the National Academy of Sciences of the United States of America,* 1996, *93,* 8011–8015.

Chen, Y.-C., Thaler, D., Nixon, P. D., Stern, C. E., and Passingham, R. E. The functions of the medial premotor cortex. II. The timing and selection of learned movements. *Experimental Brain Research,* 1995, *102,* 461–473.

Chen, Y. W., and Dilsaver, S. C. Lifetime rates of suicide attempts among subjects with bipolar and unipolar disorders relative to subjects with other axis I disorders. *Biological Psychiatry,* 1996, *39,* 896–899.

Chou, T. C., Bjorkum, A. A., Gaus, S. E., Lu, J., Scammell, T. E., and Saper, C. B. Afferents to the ventrolateral preoptic nucleus. *Journal of Neuroscience,* 2002, *22,* 977–990.

Cipolotti, L., and Warrington, E. K. Does recognizing orally spelled words depend on reading? An investigation into a case of better written than oral spelling. *Neuropsychologia,* 1996, *34,* 427–440.

Clapham, J. C., Arch, J. R., Chapman, H., Haynes, A., Lister, C., Moore, G. B., Piercy, V., Carter, S. A., Lehner, I., Smith, S. A., Beeley, L. J., Godden, R. J., Herrity, N., Skehel, M., Changani, K. K., Hockings, P. D., Reid, D. G., Squires, S. M., Hatcher, J., Trail, B., Latcham, J., Rastan, S., Harper, A. J., Cadenas, S., Buckingham, J. A., Brand, M. D., Abuin, A. Mice overexpressing human uncoupling protein-3 in skeletal muscle are hyperphagic and lean. *Nature,* 2000, *406,* 415–418.

Clark, J. T., Kalra, P. S., Crowley, W. R., and Kalra, S. P. Neuropeptide Y and human pancreatic polypeptide stimulates feeding behavior in rats. *Endocrinology,* 1984, *115,* 427–429.

Clément, K., Vaisse, C., Lahlou, N., Cabrol, S., Pelloux, V., Cassuto, D., Gourmelen, M., Dina, C., Chambaz, J., Lacorte, J. M., Basdevant, A., Bougnères, P., Lebouc, Y., Froguel, P., Guy-Grand, B. A mutation in the human leptin receptor gene causes obesity and pituitary dysfunction. *Nature,* 1998, *392,* 398–401.

Cloninger, C. R. Neurogenetic adaptive mechanisms in alcoholism. *Science,* 1987, *236,* 410–416.

Cloninger, C. R., Bohman, M., and Sigvardsson, S. Inheritance of alcohol abuse: Cross-fostering analysis of adopted men. *Archives of General Psychiatry,* 1981, *38,* 861–868.

Cloninger, C. R., Bohman, M., Sigvardsson, S., and von Knorring, A.-L. Psychopathology in adopted-out children of alcoholics: The

Stockholm Adoption Study. *Recent Developments in Alcoholism,* 1985, *3,* 37–51.

Clugnet, M.-C., and LeDoux, J. E. Synaptic plasticity in fear conditioning circuits: Induction of LTP in the lateral nucleus of the amygdala by stimulation of the medial geniculate body. *Journal of Neuroscience,* 1990, *10,* 2818–2824.

Cobb, S., and Rose, R. M. Hypertension, peptic ulcer, and diabetes in air traffic controllers. *Journal of the American Medical Association,* 1973, *224,* 489–492.

Coble, P. A., Scher, M. S., Reynolds, C. F., Day, N. L., and Kupfer, D. J. Preliminary findings on the neonatal sleep of offspring of women with and without a prior history of affective disorder. *Sleep Research,* 1988, *16,* 120.

Coccaro, E. F., and Kavoussi, R. J. Fluoxetine and impulsive aggressive behavior in personality-disordered subjects. *Archives of General Psychiatry,* 1997, *54,* 1081–1088.

Coccaro, E. F., Silverman, J. M., Klar, H. M., Horvath, T. B., and Siever, L. J. Familial correlates of reduced central serotonergic system function in patients with personality disorders. *Archives of General Psychiatry,* 1994, *51,* 318–324.

Cohen, E. A. *Human Behavior in the Concentration Camp.* New York: W. W. Norton, 1953.

Cohen, S., Tyrrell, D. A. J., and Smith, A. P. Psychological stress and susceptibility to the common cold. *New England Journal of Medicine,* 1991, *325,* 606–612.

Colapinto, J. *As Nature Made Him: The Boy Who Was Raised as a Girl.* New York: Harper-Collins, 2000.

Cole, B. J., and Koob, G. F. Propranolol antagonizes the enhanced conditioned fear produced by corticotropin releasing factor. *Journal of Pharmacology and Experimental Therapeutics,* 1988, *247,* 901–910.

Collaborative Research Group. A novel gene containing a trinucleotide repeat that is expanded and unstable on Huntington's disease chromosomes. *Cell,* 1993, *72,* 971–983.

Collins, D. R., and Paré, D. Differential fear conditioning induces reciprocal changes in the sensory responses of lateral amygdala neurons to the CS+ and CS−. *Learning and Memory,* 2000, *7,* 97–103.

Comarr, A. E. Sexual function among patients with spinal cord injury. *Urologia Internationalis,* 1970, *25,* 134–168.

Comuzzie, A. G., and Allison, D. B. The search for human obesity genes. *Science,* 1998, *280,* 1374–1377.

Constantinidis, C., and Steinmetz, M. A. Neuronal activity in posterior parietal area 7a during the delay periods of a spatial memory task. *Journal of Neurophysiology,* 1996, *76,* 1352–1355.

Coolen, L. M., and Wood, R. I. Testosterone stimulation of the medial preoptic area and medial amygdala in the control of male hamster sexual behavior: Redundancy without amplification. *Behavioural Brain Research,* 1999, *98,* 143–153.

Coover, G. D., Murison, R., and Jellestad, F. K. Subtotal lesions of the amygdala: The rostral central nucleus in passive avoidance and ulceration. *Physiology and Behavior,* 1992, *51,* 795–803.

Corkin, S., Amaral, D. G., González, R. G., Johnson, K. A., and Hyman, B. R. H. M.'s medial temporal lobe lesion: Findings from magnetic resonance imaging. *Journal of Neuroscience,* 1997, *17,* 3964–3979.

Corkin, S., Sullivan, E. V., Twitchell, T. E., and Grove, E. The amnesic patient H. M.: Clinical observations and test performance 28 years after operation. *Society for Neuroscience Abstracts,* 1981, *7,* 235.

Cornwall, J., Cooper, J. D., and Phillipson, O. T. Afferent and efferent connections of the laterodorsal tegmental nucleus in the rat. *Brain Research Bulletin,* 1990, *27,* 1–84.

Corrigall, W. A., Coen, K. M., and Adamson, K. L. Self-administered nicotine activates the mesolimbic dopamine system through the ventral tegmental area. *Brain Research,* 1994, *653,* 278–284.

Corwin, J. T., and Warchol, M. E. Auditory hair cells: Structure, function, development, and regeneration. *Annual Review of Neuroscience,* 1991, *14,* 301–333.

Cossu, G., Ledent, C., Fattore, L., Imperato, A., Böhme, G. A., Parmentier, M., and Fratta, W. Cannabinoid CB$_1$ receptor knockout mice fail to self-administer morphine but not other drugs of abuse. *Behavioural Brain Research,* 2001, *118,* 61–65.

Cottingham, S. L., and Pfaff, D. Interconnectedness of steroid hormone-binding neurons: Existence and implications. *Current Topics in Neuroendocrinology,* 1986, *7,* 223–249.

Courchesne, E., Karns, C. M., Davis, H. R., Ziccardi, R., Carper, R. A., Tigue, Z. D., Chisum, H. J., Moses, P., Pierce, K., Lord, C., Lincoln, A. J., Pizzo, S., Schreibman, L., Hass, R. H., Akshoomoff, N. A., and Courchesne, R. Y. Unusual brain growth patterns in early life in patients with autistic disorder: an MRI study. *Neurology,* 2001, *57,* 245–254.

Courtney, S. M., Petit, L., Maisog, J. M., Ungerleider, L. G., and Haxby, J. V. An area specialized for spatial working memory in human frontal cortex. *Science,* 1998, *279,* 1347–1351.

Covington, H. E., and Miczek, K. A. Repeated social-defeat stress, cocaine or morphine: Effects on behavioral sensitization and intravenous cocaine self-administration "binges." *Psychopharmacology,* 2001, *158,* 388–398.

Cowey, A., and Stoerig, P. The neurobiology of blindsight. *Trends in Neuroscience,* 1991, *14,* 140–145.

Cowey, A., and Stoerig, P. Blindsight in monkeys. *Nature,* 1995, *373,* 247–249.

Cox, A., Rutter, M., Newman, S., and Bartak, L. A comparative study of infantile autism and specific developmental language disorders. I. Parental characteristics. *British Journal of Psychiatry,* 1975, *126,* 146–159.

Crabbe, J. C., Merrill, C. M., Kim, D., and Belknap, J. K. Alcohol dependence and withdrawal: A genetic animal model. *Annals of Medicine,* 1990, *22,* 259–263.

Crane, G. E. Iproniazid (Marsilid) phosphate, a therapeutic agent for mental disorders and debilitating diseases. *Psychiatry Research Reports,* 1957, *8,* 142–152.

Creese, I., Burt, D. R., and Snyder, S. H. Dopamine receptor binding predicts clinical and pharmacological potencies of antischizophrenic drugs. *Science,* 1976, *192,* 481–483.

Crick, F., and Mitchison, G. The function of dream sleep. *Nature,* 1983, *304,* 111–114.

Crick, F., and Mitchison, G. REM sleep and neural nets. *Behavioural Brain Research,* 1995, *69,* 147–155.

Crow, T. J. A map of the rat mesencephalon for electrical self-stimulation. *Brain Research,* 1972, *36,* 265–273.

Crow, T. J. Positive and negative schizophrenic symptoms and the role of dopamine. *British Journal of Psychiatry,* 1980, *137,* 383–386.

Cubelli, R. A selective deficit for writing vowels in acquired dysgraphia. *Nature,* 1991, *353,* 258–260.

Culebras, A., and Moore, J. T. Magnetic resonance findings in REM sleep behavior disorder. *Neurology,* 1989, *39,* 1519–1523.

Culotta, E., and Koshland, D. E. NO news is good news. *Science,* 1992, *258,* 1862–1865.

Cummings, D. E., Purnell, J. Q., Frayo, R. S., Schmidova, K., Wisse, B. E., and Weigle, D. S. A preprandial rise in plasma ghrelin levels suggests a role in meal initiation in humans. *Diabetes,* 2001, *50,* 1714–1719.

Currie, P. J., and Coscina, D. V. Regional hypothalamic differences in neuropeptide Y-induced feeding and energy substrate utilization. *Brain Research,* 1996, *737,* 238–242.

Cutler, W. B., Friedmann, E., and McCoy, N. L. Pheromonal influences on sociosexual behavior of men. *Archives of Sexual Behavior,* 1998, *27,* 1–13.

Dabbs, J. M., and Morris, R. Testosterone, social class, and antisocial behavior in a sample of 4,462 men. *Psychological Science,* 1990, *1,* 209–211.

Dabbs, J. M., Frady, R. L., Carr, T. S., and Besch, N. F. Saliva testosterone and criminal violence in young adult prison inmates. *Psychosomatic Medicine,* 1987, *49,* 174–182.

Dahl, D., and Sarvey, J. M. Norepinephrine induces pathway-specific long-lasting potentiation and depression in the hippocampal dentate gyrus. *Proceedings of the National Academy of Science, USA,* 1989, *86,* 4775–4780.

Dalen, P. Month of birth and schizophrenia. *Acta Psychiatrica Scandanivica,* 1968, *44* (Suppl.), 55–60.

Dallos, P. The active cochlea. *Journal of Neuroscience,* 1992, *12,* 4575–4585.

Damasio, A. R. Disorders of complex visual processing: Agnosias, achromatopsia, Balint's syndrome, and related difficulties of orientation and construction. In *Principles of Behavioral Neurology,* edited by M.-M. Mesulam. Philadelphia: F. A. Davis, 1985.

Damasio, A. R., and Damasio, H. The anatomic basis of pure alexia. *Neurology,* 1983, *33,* 1573–1583.

Damasio, A. R., and Damasio, H. Hemianopia, hemiachromatopsia, and the mechanisms of alexia. *Cortex,* 1986, *22,* 161–169.

Damasio, A. R., and Tranel, D. Nouns and verbs are retrieved with differentially distributed neural systems. *Proceedings of the National Academy of Sciences, USA,* 1993, *90,* 4957–4960.

Damasio, A. R., Brandt, J. P., Tranel, D., and Damasio, H. Name dropping: Retrieval of proper or common nouns depends on different systems in left temporal cortex. *Society for Neuroscience Abstracts,* 1991, *17,* 4.

Damasio, A. R., Damasio, H., and Van Hoesen, G. W. Prosopagnosia: Anatomic basis and behavioral mechanisms. *Neurology,* 1982, *32,* 331–341.

Damasio, A. R., Yamada, T., Damasio, H., Corbett, J., and McKee, J. Central achromatopsia: Behavioral, anatomic, and physiologic aspects. *Neurology,* 1980, *30,* 1064–1071.

Damasio, H. Neuroimaging contributions to the understanding of aphasia. In *Handbook of Neuropsychology, Vol. 2,* edited by F. Boller and J. Grafman. Amsterdam: Elsevier, 1989.

Damasio, H., and Damasio, A. R. The anatomical basis of conduction aphasia. *Brain,* 1980, *103,* 337–350.

Damasio, H., Eslinger, P., and Adams, H. P. Aphasia following basal ganglia lesions: New evidence. *Seminars in Neurology,* 1984, *4,* 151–161.

Damasio, H., Grabowski, T., Frank, R., Galaburda, A. M., and Damasio, A. R. The return of Phineas Gage: Clues about the brain from the skull of a famous patient. *Science,* 1994, *264,* 1102–1105.

Damsma, G., Day, J., and Fibiger, H. C. Lack of tolerance to nicotine-induced dopamine release in the nucleus accumbens. *European Journal of Pharmacology,* 1989, *168,* 363–368.

Dani, J. A., and De Biasi, M. Cellular mechanisms of nicotine addiction. *Pharmacology, Biochemistry, and Behavior,* 2001, *70,* 439–446.

Daniel, D. G., Weinberger, D. R., Jones, D. W., Zigon, J. R., Cippola, R., Handel, S., Bigelow, L. B., Goldberg, T. E., Berman, K. F., and Kleinman, J. E. The effect of amphetamine on regional cerebral blood flow during cognitive activation in schizophrenia. *Journal of Neuroscience,* 1991, *11,* 1907–1917.

Daniele, A., Giustolisi, L., Silveri, M. C., Colosimo, C., and Gainotti, G. Evidence for a possible neuroanatomical basis for lexical processing of nouns and verbs. *Neuropsychologia,* 1994, *32,* 1325–1341.

Daniels, D., Miselis, R. R., and Flanagan-Cato, L. M. Central neuronal circuit innervating the lordosis-producing muscles defined by transneuronal transport of pseudorabies virus. *Journal of Neuroscience,* 1999, *19,* 2823–2833.

Darwin, C. *The Expression of the Emotions in Man and Animals.* Chicago: University of Chicago Press, 1872/1965.

Davidowa, H., and Plagemann, A. Decreased inhibition by leptin of hypothalamic arcuate neurons in neonatally overfed young rats. *Neuroreport,* 2000, *11,* 1795–1798.

Davidson, D., Swift, R., and Fitz, E. Naltrexone increases the latency to drink alcohol in social drinkers. *Alcoholism: Clinical and Experimental Research,* 1996, *20,* 732–739.

Davis, J. D., and Campbell, C. S. Peripheral control of meal size in the rat: Effect of sham feeding on meal size and drinking rate. *Journal of Comparative and Physiological Psychology,* 1973, *83,* 379–387.

Davis, J. O., and Bracha, H. S. Famine and schizophrenia: First-trimester malnutrition or second-trimester beriberi? *Biological Psychiatry,* 1996, *40,* 1–3.

Davis, J. O., Phelps, J. A., and Bracha, H. S. Prenatal development of monozygotic twins and concordance for schizophrenia. *Schizophrenia Bulletin,* 1995, *21,* 357–366.

Davis, M. The role of the amygdala in fear and anxiety. *Annual Review of Neuroscience,* 1992a, *15,* 353–375.

Davis, M. The role of the amygdala in fear-potentiated startle: Implications for animal models of anxiety. *Trends in Pharmacological Sciences,* 1992b, *13,* 35–41.

Davison, G. C., and Neale, J. M. *Abnormal Psychology: An Experimental Clinical Approach.* New York: John Wiley & Sons, 1974.

Daw, N. W. Colour-coded ganglion cells in the goldfish retina: Extension of their receptive fields by means of new stimuli. *Journal of Physiology (London)*, 1968, *197*, 567–592.

Day, J., Damsma, G., and Fibiger, H. C. Cholinergic activity in the rat hippocampus, cortex and striatum correlates with locomotor activity: An in vivo microdialysis study. *Pharmacology, Biochemistry, and Behavior*, 1991, *38*, 723–729.

de Castro, J. M. What are the major correlates of macronutrient selection in Western populations? *Proceedings of the Nutrition Society*, 1999, *58*, 755–763.

de Castro, J. M., and de Castro, E. S. Spontaneous meal patterns of humans: Influence of the presence of other people. *American Journal of Clinical Nutrition*, 1989, *50*, 237–247.

de Castro, J. M., McCormick, J., Pedersen, M., and Kreitzman, S. N. Spontaneous human meal patterns are related to preprandial factors regardless of natural environmental constraints. *Physiology and Behavior*, 1986, *38*, 25–29.

de Gelder, B., Vroomen, J., Pourtois, G., and Weiskrantz, L. Non-conscious recognition of affect in the absence of striate cortex. *Neuroreport*, 1999, *10*, 3759–3763.

De Gennaro, L., Ferrara, M., and Bertini, M. The spontaneous K-complex during stage 2 sleep: Is it the "forerunner" of delta waves? *Neuroscience Letters*, 2000, *291*, 41–43.

De Jonge, F. H., Louwerse, A. L., Ooms, M. P., Evers, P., Endert, E., and van de Poll, N. E. Lesions of the SDN-POA inhibit sexual behavior of male Wistar rats. *Brain Research Bulletin*, 1989, *23*, 483–492.

De Jonge, F. H., Oldenburger, W. P., Louwerse, A. L., and van de Poll, N. E. Changes in male copulatory behavior after sexual exciting stimuli: Effects of medial amygdala lesions. *Physiology and Behavior*, 1992, *52*, 327–332.

De Valois, R. L., and De Valois, K. K. *Spatial Vision*. New York: Oxford University Press, 1988.

De Valois, R. L., Albrecht, D. G., and Thorell, L. Cortical cells: Bar detectors or spatial frequency filters? In *Frontiers in Visual Science*, edited by S. J. Cool and E. L. Smith. Berlin: Springer-Verlag, 1978.

De Valois, R. L., Thorell, L. G., and Albrecht, D. G. Periodicity of striate-cortex-cell receptive fields. *Journal of the Optical Society of America*, 1985 *2*, 1115–1123.

De Vries, G. J., Rissman, E. F., Simerly, R. B., Yang, L.-Y., Scordalakes, E. M., Auger, C. J., Swain, A., Lovell-Badge, R., Burgoyne, P. S., and Arnold, A. P. A Model System for Study of Sex Chromosome Effects on Sexually Dimorphic Neural and Behavioral Traits. *Journal of Neuroscience*, 2002, *22*, 9005–9014.

Deacon, S., and Arendt, J. Adapting to phase shifts. I. An experimental model for jet lag and shift work. *Physiology and Behavior*, 1996, *59*, 665–673.

Dean, P. Effects of inferotemporal lesions on the behavior of monkeys. *Psychological Bulletin*, 1976, *83*, 41–71.

Dean, P. Visual behavior in monkeys with inferotemporal lesions. In *Analysis of Visual Behavior*, edited by D. J. Ingle, M. A. Goodale, and R. J. W. Mansfield. Cambridge, Mass.: MIT Press, 1982.

Debanne, D., Gähwiler, B. H., and Thompson, S. M. Asynchronous pre- and postsynaptic activity induces associative long-term depression in area CA1 of the rat hippocampus in vitro. *Proceedings of the National Academy of Sciences*, 1994, *91*, 1148–1152.

Dehaene, S., Spelke, E., Pinel, P., Stanescu, R., and Tsivkin, S. Sources of mathematical thinking: Behavioral and brain-imaging evidence. *Science*, 1999, *284*, 970–974.

Dejerine, J. Contribution à l'étude anatomo-pathologique et clinique des différentes variétés de cécité verbale. *Comptes Rendus des Séances de la Société de Biologie et de Ses Filiales*, 1892, *4*, 61–90.

Del Cerro, M. C. R., Izquierdo, M. A. P., Rosenblatt, J. S., Johnson, B. M., Pacheco, P., and Komisaruk, B. R. Brain 2-deoxyglucose levels related to maternal behavior-inducing stimuli in the rat. *Brain Research*, 1995, *696*, 213–220.

Delay, J., and Deniker, P. Le traitement des psychoses par une methode neurolytique derivée d'hibernothéraphie: Le 4560 RP utilisée seul une cure prolongée et continuée. *Comptes Rendus Congrès des Médecins Aliénistes et Neurologistes de France et des Pays de Langue Française*, 1952a, *50*, 497–502.

Delay, J., and Deniker, P. 38 cas des psychoses traitées par la cure prolongée et continuée de 4560 RP. *Comptes Rendus du Congrès des Médecins Aliénistes et Neurologistes de France et des Pays de Langue Française*, 1952b, *50*, 503–513.

Delgado, P. L., Charney, D. S., Price, L. H., Aghajanian, G. K., Landis, H., and Heninger, G. R. Serotonin function and the mechanism of antidepressant action: Reversal of antidepressant induced remission by rapid depletion of plasma tryptophan. *Archives of General Psychiatry*, 1990, *47*, 411–418.

DeLong, G. R. Autism: New data suggest a new hypothesis. *Neurology*, 1999, *52*, 911–916.

Dement, W. C. The effect of dream deprivation. *Science*, 1960, *131*, 1705–1707.

Deol, M. S., and Gluecksohn-Waelsch, S. The role of inner hair cells in hearing. *Nature*, 1979, *278*, 250–252.

Dérousné, J., and Beauvois, M.-F. Phonological processing in reading: Data from alexia. *Journal of Neurology, Neurosurgery, and Psychiatry*, 1979, *42*, 1125–1132.

Desimone, R., Albright, T. D., Gross, C. G., and Bruce, D. Stimulus-selective properties of inferior temporal neurons in the macaque. *Journal of Neuroscience*, 1984, *8*, 2051–2062.

D'Esposito, M., Verfaellie, M., Alexander, M. P., and Katz, D. I. Amnesia following traumatic bilateral fornix transection. *Neurology*, 1995, *45*, 1546–1550.

Deutch, A. Y. The regulation of subcortical dopamine systems by the prefrontal cortex: Interactions of central dopamine systems and the pathogenesis of schizophrenia. *Journal of Neural Transmission*, 1992, *36*, 61–89.

Deutsch, J. A., and Gonzalez, M. F. Gastric nutrient content signals satiety. *Behavioral and Neural Biology*, 1980, *30*, 113–116.

Devane, W. A., Hanus, L., Breuer, A., Pertwee, R. G., Stevenson, L. A., Griffin, G., Gibson, D., Mandelbaum, A., Etinger, A., and Mechoulam, R. Isolation and structure of a brain constituent that binds to the cannabinoid receptor. *Science*, 1992, *258*, 1946–1949.

Devine, D. P., and Wise, R. A. Self-administration of morphine, DAMGO, and DPDPE into the ventral tegmental area of rats. *Journal of Neuroscience*, 1994, *14*, 1978–1984.

Devine, D. P., Leone, P., Pocock, D., and Wise, R. A. Differential involvement of ventral tegmental mu, delta, and kappa opioid receptors in modulation of basal mesolimbic dopamine release: *In vivo* microdialysis studies. *Journal of Pharmacology and Experimental Therapeutics*, 1993, *266*, 1236–1246.

Devinsky, O., Perrine, K., Llinas, R., Luciano, D. J., and Dogali, M. Anterior temporal language areas in patients with early onset of temporal lobe epilepsy. *Annals of Neurology,* 1993, *34,* 727–732.

Dewey, S. L., Brodie, J. D. Gerasimov, M., Horan, B., Gardner, E. L., and Ashby, C. R. A pharmacologic strategy for the treatment of nicotine addiction. *Synapse,* 1999, *31,* 76–86.

Dewey, S. L., Chaurasia, C. S., Chen, C., Volkow, N. D., Clarkson, F. A., Porter, S. P., Straughter-Moore, R. M., Axeloff, D. L., Tedeschi, D., Russo, N. B., Fowler, J. S., and Brodie, J. D. GABAergic attenuation of cocaine-induced dopamine release and locomotor activity. *Synapse,* 1997, *25,* 393–398.

Dewey, S. L., Chaurasia, C. S., Chen, C., Volkow, N. D., Fowler, J. S., Gardner, E. L., and Brodie, J. D. A novel strategy for the treatment of cocaine addiction. *Synapse,* 1998, *30,* 119–129.

Di Chiara, G. The role of dopamine in drug abuse viewed from the perspective of its role in motivation. *Drug and Alcohol Dependency,* 1995, *38,* 95–137.

Di Ciano, P., Coury, A., Depoortere, R. Y., Egilmez, Y., Lane, J. D., Emmett-Oglesby, M. W., Lepiane, F. G., Phillips, A. G., and Blaha, C. D. Comparison of changes in extracellular dopamine concentrations in the nucleus accumbens during intravenous self-administration of cocaine or d-amphetamine. *Behavioural Pharmacology,* 1995, *6,* 311–322.

Di Monte, D. A., Lavasani, M., and Manning-Bog, A. B. Environmental factors in Parkinson's disease. *Neurotoxicology,* 2002, *23,* 487–502.

di Tomaso, E., Beltramo, M., and Piomelli, D. Brain cannabinoids in chocolate. *Nature,* 1996, *382,* 677–678.

Diamond, D. M., Park, C. R., Heman, K. L., and Rose, G. M. Exposing rats to a predator impairs spatial working memory in the radial arm water maze. *Hippocampus,* 1999, *9,* 542–552.

Diamond, M., and Sigmundson, H. K. Sex reassignment at birth: Long-term review and clinical implications. *Archives of Pediatric and Adolescent Medicine,* 1997, *151,* 298–304.

Diana, M., Pistis, M., Carboni, S., Gessa, G. L., and Rossetti, Z. L. Profound decrement of mesolimbic dopaminergic neuronal activity during ethanol withdrawal syndrome in rats: Electrophysiological and biochemical evidence. *Proceedings of the National Academy of Sciences, USA,* 1993, *90,* 7966–7969.

Digiovanni, M., Dalessandro, G., Baldini, S., Cantalupi, D., and Bottacchi, E. Clinical and neuroradiological findings in a case of pure word deafness. *Italian Journal of Neurological Sciences,* 1992, *13,* 507–510.

Dijk, D. J., Boulos, Z., Eastman, C. I., Lewy, A. J., Campbell, S. S., and Terman, M. Light treatment for sleep disorders: Consensus report. 2. Basic properties of circadian physiology and sleep regulation. *Journal of Biological Rhythms,* 1995, *10,* 113–125.

Divac, I., Rosvold, H. E., and Szcwarcbart, M. K. Behavioral effects of selective ablation of the caudate nucleus. *Journal of Comparative and Physiological Psychology,* 1967, *63,* 184–190.

Dixon, A. K. The effect of olfactory stimuli upon the social behaviour of laboratory mice (*Mus musculus L*). Doctoral dissertation, Birmingham University, Birmingham, England, 1973.

Dixon, A. K., and Mackintosh, J. H. Effects of female urine upon the social behaviour of adult male mice. *Animal Behaviour,* 1971, *19,* 138–140.

Doherty, P. C., Baum, M. J., and Todd, R. B. Effects of chronic hyperprolactinemia on sexual arousal and erectile function in male rats. *Neuroendocrinology,* 1986, *42,* 368–375.

Dolan, R. P., and Schiller, P. H. Evidence for only depolarizing rod bipolar cells in the primate retina. *Visual Neuroscience,* 1989, *2,* 421–424.

Dominguez, J., and Hull, E. M. Stimulation of the medial amygdala enhances medial preoptic dopamine release: Implications for male rat sexual behavior. *Brain Research,* 2001, *917,* 225–229.

Dominguez, J., Riolo, J. V., Xu, Zhujian, and Hull, E. M. Regulation by the medial amygdala of copulation and medial preoptic dopamine release. *Journal of Neuroscience,* 2001, *21,* 349–355.

Donny, E. C., Caggiula, A. R., Knopf, S., and Brown, C. Nicotine self-administration in rats. *Psychopharmacology,* 1995, *122,* 390–394.

Dosemeci, A., Tao-Cheng, J.-H., Vinade, L., Winters, C. A., Pozzo-Miller, L., and Reese, T. S. Glutamate-induced transient modification of the postsynaptic density. *Proceedings of the National Academy of Science, USA,* 2001, *98,* 10428–10432.

Doty, R. L. Olfaction. *Annual Review of Psychology,* 2001, *52,* 423–452.

Dougherty, D. D., Baie, L., Gosgrove, G. R., Cassem, E. H., Price, B. H., Nierenberg, A. A., Jenike, M. A., and Rauch, S. L. Prospective long-term follow-up of 44 patients who received cingulotomy for treatment-refractory obsessive-compulsive disorder. *American Journal of Psychiatry,* 2002, *159,* 269–275.

Dougherty, D. D., Bonab, A. A., Spencer, T. J., Rauch, S. L., Madras, B. K., and Fischman, A. J. Dopamine transporter density in patients with attention deficit hyperactivity disorder. *Lancet,* 1999, *354,* 2132–2133.

Dougherty, D. D., Shin, L. M., Alpert, N. M., Pitman, R. K., Orr, S. P., Lasko, M., Macklin, L. M., Fischman, A. J., and Rauch, S. L. Anger in healthy men: A PET study using script-driven imagery. *Biological Psychiatry,* 1999, *46,* 466–472.

Douglass, J., McKinzie, A. A., and Couceyro, P. PCR differential display identifies a rat brain mRNA that is transcriptionally regulated by cocaine and amphetamine. *Journal of Neuroscience,* 1995, *15,* 2471–2481.

Dresel, S., Krause, J., Krause, K. H., LaFougere, C., Brinkbaumer, K., Kung, H. F., Hahn, K., and Tatsch, K. Attention deficit hyperactivity disorder: Binding of [^{99}mTc]TRODAT-1 to the dopamine transporter before and after methylphenidate treatment. *European Journal of Nuclear Medicine,* 2000, *27,* 1518–1524.

Drevets, W. C. Neuroimaging studies of mood disorders. *Biological Psychiatry,* 2000a, *48,* 813–829.

Drevets, W. C. Functional anatomical abnormalities in limbic and prefrontal cortical structures in major depression. *Progress in Brain Research,* 2000b, *126,* 413–431.

Drevets, W. C. Neuroimaging and neuropathological studies of depression: Implications for the cognitive-emotional features of mood disorders. *Current Opinions in Neurobiology,* 2001, *11,* 240–249.

Drevets, W. C., Price, J. L., Simpson, J. R., Todd, R. D., Reich, T., Vannier, M., and Raichle, M. E. Subgenual prefrontal cortex abnormalities in mood disorders. *Nature,* 1997, *386,* 824–827.

Drevets, W. C., Videen, T. O., Price, J. L., Preskorn, S. H., Carmichael, S. T., and Raichle, M. E. A functional anatomical study of unipolar depression. *Journal of Neuroscience,* 1992, *12,* 3628–3641.

Dronkers, N. F. A new brain region for coordinating speech articulation. *Nature,* 1996, *384,* 159–161.

Dryden, S., Wang, Q., Frankish, H. M., Pickavance, L., and Williams, G. The serotonin (5-HT) antagonist methysergide increases neuropeptide-Y (NPY) synthesis and secretion in the hypothalamus of the rat. *Brain Research,* 1995, *699,* 12–18.

Dube, M. G., Kalra, S. P., and Kalra, P. S. Food intake elecited by central administration of orexins/hypocretins: Identification of hypothalamic sites of action. *Brain Research,* 1999, *842,* 473–477.

Duchenne, G.-B. *The Mechanism of Human Facial Expression* (translated by R. A. Cuthbertson). Cambridge, England: Cambridge University Press, 1990. (Original work published 1862.)

Dudek, S. M., and Bear, M. F. Homosynaptic long-term depression in area CA1 of hippocampus and effects of N-methyl-D-aspartate receptor blockade. *Proceedings of the National Academy of Sciences,* 1992, *89,* 4363–4367.

Due, D. L., Huettel, S. A., Hall, W. G., and Rubin, D. C. Activation in mesolimbic and visuospatial neural circuits elicited by smoking cues: Evidence from functional magnetic resonance imaging. *American Journal of Psychiatry,* 2002, *159,* 954–960.

Dujardin, K., Guerrien, A., and Leconte, P. Sleep, brain activation and cognition. *Physiology and Behavior,* 1990, *47,* 1271–1278.

Dulac, C., and Axel, R. A novel family of genes encoding putative pheromone receptors in mammals. *Cell,* 1995, *83,* 195–206.

Dunnett, S. B., Lane, D. M., and Winn, P. Ibotenic acid lesions of the lateral hypothalamus: Comparison with 6-hydroxy-dopamine-induced sensorimotor deficits. *Neuroscience,* 1985, *14,* 509–518.

Dunwiddie, T. V., and Masino, S. A. The role and regulation of adenosine in the central nervous system. *Annual Review of Neuroscience,* 2001, *24,* 31–55.

Durie, D. J. Sleep in animals. In *Psychopharmacology of Sleep,* edited by D. Wheatley. New York: Raven Press, 1981.

Duva, M. A., Tomkins, E. M., Moranda, L. M., Kaplan, R., Sukhaseum, A., Jimenez, A., and Stanley, B. G. Reverse microdialysis of N-methyl-D-aspartic acid into the lateral hypothalamus of rats: Effects on feeding and other behaviors. *Brain Research,* 2001, *921,* 122–132.

Duvauchelle, C. L., and Ettenberg, A. Haloperidol attenuates conditioned place preferences produced by electrical stimulation of the medial prefrontal cortex. *Pharmacology, Biochemistry, and Behavior,* 1991, *38,* 645–650.

Dykes, R. W. Parallel processing of somatosensory information: A theory. *Brain Research Reviews,* 1983, *6,* 47–115.

Eaton, W. W., Kessler, R. C., Wittchen, H. U., and Magee, W. J. Panic and panic disorder in the United States. *American Journal of Psychiatry,* 1994, *151,* 413–420.

Eaton, W. W., Mortensen, P. B., and Frydenberg, M. Obstetric factors, urbanization and psychosis. *Schizophrenia Research,* 2000, *43,* 117–123.

Eckel, L. S., Langhans, W., Kahler, A., Campfield, L. A., Smith, F. J., and Geary, N. Chronic administration of OB protein decreases food intake by selectively reducing meal size in female rats. *American Journal of Physiology,* 1998, *275,* R186–R193.

Eddy, N. B., Halbach, H., Isbell, H., and Seevers, M. H. Drug dependence: Its significance and characteristics. *Bulletin of the World Health Organization,* 1965, *32,* 721–733.

Eden, G. F., and Zeffiro, T. A. Neural systems affected in developmental dyslexia revealed by functional neuroimaging. *Neuron,* 1998, *21,* 279–282.

Edwards, D. P., Purpura, K. P., and Kaplan, E. Contrast sensitivity and spatial-frequency response of primate cortical neurons in and around the cytochrome oxidase blobs. *Vision Research,* 1995, *35,* 1501–1523.

Edwards, F. A. LTP-a structural model to explain the inconsistencies. *Trends in Neuroscience,* 1995, *18,* 250–255.

Egeland, J. A., Gerhard, D. S., Pauls, D. L., Sussex, J. N., Kidd, K. K., Allen, C. R., Hostetter, A. M., and Housman, D. E. Bipolar affective disorders linked to DNA markers on chromosome 11. *Nature,* 1987, *325,* 783–787.

Ehrhardt, A. A., and Meyer-Bahlburg, H. F. L. Effects of prenatal sex hormones on gender-related behavior. *Science,* 1981, *211,* 1312–1318.

Eichenbaum, H., Otto, T., and Cohen, N. J. The hippocampus: What does it do? *Behavioral and Neural Biology,* 1992, *57,* 2–36.

Eichenbaum, H., Stewart, C., and Morris, R. G. M. Hippocampal representation in spatial learning. *Journal of Neuroscience,* 1990, *10,* 331–339.

Eilam, R., Malach, R., Bergmann, F., and Segal, M. Hypertension induced by hypothalamic transplantation from genetically hypertensive to normotensive rats. *Journal of Neuroscience,* 1991, *11,* 401–411.

Ekman, P. *The Face of Man: Expressions of Universal Emotions in a New Guinea Village.* New York: Garland STPM Press, 1980.

Ekman, P. Facial expressions of emotion: An old controversy and new findings. *Philosophical Transactions of the Royal Society of London [B],* 1992, *335,* 63–69.

Ekman, P., and Davidson, R. J. Voluntary smiling changes regional brain activity. *Psychological Science,* 1993, *4,* 342–345.

Ekman, P., and Friesen, W. V. Constants across cultures in the face and emotion. *Journal of Personality and Social Psychology,* 1971, *17,* 124–129.

Ekman, P., and Friesen, W. V. *Unmasking the Face.* Englewood Cliffs, NJ: Prentice-Hall, 1975.

Ekman, P., Friesen, W. V., and Ellsworth, P. *Emotion in the Human Face: Guidelines for Research and a Review of Findings.* New York: Pergamon Press, 1972.

Ekman, P., Levenson, R. W., and Friesen, W. V. Autonomic nervous system activity distinguished between emotions. *Science,* 1983, *221,* 1208–1210.

El Mansari, M., and Blier, P. In vivo electrophysiological characterization of 5-HT receptors in the guinea pig head of caudate nucleus and orbitofrontal cortex. *Neuropharmacology,* 1997, *36,* 577–588.

El Mansari, M., Sakai, K., and Jouvet, M. Unitary characteristics of presumptive cholinergic tegmental neurons during the sleep-waking cycle in freely moving cats. *Experimental Brain Research,* 1989, *76,* 519–529.

Elbert, T., Flor, H., Birbaumer, N., Knecht, S., Hampson, S., Larbig, W., and Taub, E. Extensive reorganization of the somatosensory cortex in adult humans after nervous system injury. *Neuroreport,* 1994, *5,* 2593–2507.

Elbert, T., Pantev, C., Wienbruch, C., Rockstroh, B., and Taub, E. Increased cortical representation of the fingers of the left hand in string players. *Science,* 1995, *270,* 305–307.

Elias, C. F., Lee, C., Kelly, J., Aschkenasi, C., Ahima, R. S., Couceyro, P., Kuhar, M. J., Saper, C. B., and Elmquist, J. K. Leptin activates hypothalamic CART neurons projecting to the spinal cord. *Neuron,* 1998b, *21,* 1375–1385.

Elias, C. F., Saper, C. B., Maratos-Flier, E., Tritos, N. A., Lee, C., Kelly, J., Tatro, J. B., Hoffman, G. E., Ollmann, M. M., Barsh, G. S., Sakurai, T., Yanagisawa, M., and Elmquist, J. K. Chemically defined projections linking the mediobasal hypothalamus and the lateral hypothalamic area. *Journal of Comparative Neurology,* 1998a, *402,* 442–459.

Elias, M. Serum cortisol, testosterone and testosterone binding globulin responses to competitive fighting in human males. *Aggressive Behavior,* 1981, *7,* 215–224.

Elkis, H., Friedman, L., Buckley, P. F., Lee, H. S., Lys, C., Kaufman, B., and Meltzer, H. Y. Increased prefrontal sulcal prominence in relatively young patients with unipolar major depression. *Psychiatry Research: Neuroimaging,* 1996, *67,* 123–134.

Elmquist, J. K., Elias, C. F., and Saper, C. B. From lesions to leptin: Hypothalamic control of food intake and body weight. *Neuron,* 1999, *22,* 221–232.

Ende, G., Braus, D. F., Walter, S., Weber-Fahr, W., and Henn, F. A. The hippocampus in patients treated with electroconvulsive therapy. *Archives of General Psychiatry,* 2000, *57,* 937–943.

Endenberg, H. J., Foroud, T., Koller, D. L., Goate, A., Rice, J., Van Eerdewegh, P., Reich, T., Cloninger, C. R., Nurnberger, J. I., Kowalczuk, M., Wu, B., Li, T. K., Conneally, P. M., Tischfield, J. A., Wu, W., Shears, S., Crowe, R., Hesselbrock, V., Schuckit, M., Porjesz, B., and Begleiter, H. A family-based analysis of the association of the dopamine D2 receptor (DRD2) with alcoholism. *Alcohol: Clinical and Experimental Research,* 1998, *22,* 505–512.

Endoh, M., Maiese, K., and Wagner, J. A. Expression of the neural form of nitric oxide synthase by CA1 hippocampal neurons and other central nervous system neurons. *Neuroscience,* 1994, *63,* 679–689.

Engber, T. M., Boldry, R. C., Kuo, S., and Chase, T. N. Dopaminergic modulation of striatal neuropeptides: Differential effects of D_1 and D_2 receptor stimulation on somatostatin, neuropeptide Y, neurotensin, dynorphin and enkephalin. *Brain Research,* 1992, *581,* 261–268.

Enggasser, J. L., and de Wit, H. Haloperidol reduces stimulant and reinforcing effects of ethanol in social drinkers. *Alcoholism: Clinical and Experimental Research,* 2001, *25,* 1448–1456.

Erb, S., and Stewart, J. A role for the bed nucleus of the stria terminalis, but not the amygdala, in the effects of corticotropin-releasing factor on stress-induced reinstatement of cocaine seeking. *Journal of Neuroscience,* 1999, *19,* RC35(1–6).

Erb, S., Salmaso, N., Rodaros, D., and Stewart, J. A role for the CRF-containing pathway from central nucleus of the amygdala to bed nucleus of the stria terminalis in the stress-induced reinstatement of cocaine seeking in rats. *Psychopharmacology,* 2001, *158,* 360–365.

Ernst, M., Bolla, K., Mouratidis, M., Contoreggi, C., Matochik, J. A., Kurian, V., Cadet, J.-L., Kimes, A. S., and London, E. D. Decision-making in a risk-taking task. *Neuropsychopharmacology,* 2002, *26,* 682–691.

Ernst, M., Zametkin, A. J., Matochik, J. A., Jons, P. H., and Cohen, R. M. DOPA decarboxylase activity in attention deficit hyperactivity disorder adults: A [fluorine[18]]flurodopa positron emission tomographic study. *Journal of Neuroscience,* 1998, *18,* 5901–5907.

Ernulf, K. E., Innala, S. M., and Whitam, F. L. Biological explanation, psychological explanation, and tolerance of homosexuals: A cross-national analysis of beliefs and attitudes. *Psychological Reports,* 1989, *248,* 183–188.

Eslinger, P. J., and Damasio, A. R. Severe disturbance of higher cognition after bilateral frontal lobe ablation: Patient EVR. *Neurology,* 1985, *35,* 1731–1741.

Esposito, A., Demeurisse, G., Alberti, B., and Fabbro, F. Complete mutism after midbrain periaqueductal gray lesion. *Neuroreport,* 1999, *10,* 681–685.

Estabrooke, I. V., McCarthy, M. T., Ko, E., Chou, T. C., Chemelli, R. M., Yanagisawa, M, Saper, C. B., and Scammell, T. E. Fos expression in orexin neurons varies with behavioral state. *Journal of Neuroscience,* 2001, *21,* 1656–1662.

Evans, E. F. Auditory processing of complex sounds: An overview. *Philosophical Transactions of the Royal Society of London [B],* 1992, *336,* 295–306.

Evarts, E. V. Sensorimotor cortex activity associated with movements triggered by visual as compared to somesthetic inputs. In *The Neurosciences: Third Study Program,* edited by F. O. Schmitt and F. G. Worden. Cambridge, Mass.: MIT Press, 1974.

Everitt, B. J., and Wolf, M. E. Psychomotor stimulant addiction: A neural systems perspective. *Journal of Neuroscience,* 2002, *22,* 3312–3320.

Everson, C. A., and Wehr, T. A. Nutritional and metabolic adaptations to prolonged sleep deprivation in the rat. *American Journal of Physiology,* 1993, *264,* R376–R387.

Fabbro, F. The bilingual brain: Bilingual aphasia. *Brain and Language,* 2001a, *79,* 201–210.

Fabbro, F. The bilingual brain: Cerebral representation of languages. *Brain and Language,* 2001b, *79,* 211–222.

Falls, W. A., Miserendino, M. J. D., and Davis, M. Extinction of fear-potentiated startle: Blockade by infusion of an NMDA antagonist into the amygdala. *Journal of Neuroscience,* 1992, *12,* 854–863.

Faraone, S., and Biederman, J. Genetics of attention-deficit hyperactivity disorder. *Child and Adolescent Psychiatric Clinics of North America,* 1994, *3,* 285–302.

Farber, N. B., Wozniak, D. F., Price, M. T., Labruyere, J., Huss, J., St. Peter, H., and Olney, J. W. Age-specific neurotoxicity in the rat associated with NMDA receptor blockade: Potential relevance to schizophrenia? *Biological Psychiatry,* 1995, *38,* 788–796.

Farooqi, I. S., Keogh, J. M., Kamath, S., Jones, S., Gibson, W. T., Trussell, R., Jebb, S. A., Lip, G. Y. H., and O'Rahilly, S. Partial leptin deficiency and human adiposity. *Nature,* 2001, *414,* 34–35.

Farooqi, I. S., Yeo, G. S., Keogh, J. M., Aminian, S., Jebb, S. A., Burler, G., Cheetham, T., and O'Rahilly, S. Dominant and recessive inheritance of morbid obesity associated with melanocortin

4 receptor deficiency. *Journal of Clinical Investigation,* 2000, *106,* 271–279.

Farrington, C. P., Miller, E., and Taylor, B. MMR and autism: Further evidence against a causal association. *Vaccine,* 2001, *27,* 3632–3635.

Fava, M., Copeland, P. M., Schweiger, U., and Herzog, M. D. Neurochemical abnormalities of anorexia nervosa and bulimia nervosa. *American Journal of Psychiatry,* 1989, *146,* 963–971.

Feder, H. H. Estrous cyclicity in mammals. In *Neuroendocrinology of Reproduction,* edited by N. T. Adler. New York: Plenum Press, 1981.

Feigenbaum, S. L., Masi, A. T., and Kaplan, S. B. Prognosis in rheumatoid arthritis: A longitudinal study of newly diagnosed younger adult patients. *American Journal of Medicine,* 1979, *66,* 377–384.

Feinle, C., Grundy, D., and Read, N. W. Effects of duodenal nutrients on sensory and motor responses of the human stomach to distension. *American Journal of Physiology,* 1997, *273,* G721–G726.

Fernandez-Ruiz, J., Wang, J., Aigner, T. G., and Mishkin, M. Visual habit formation in monkeys with neurotoxic lesions of the ventrocaudal neostriatum. *Proceedings of the National Academy of Sciences, USA,* 2001, *98,* 4196–4201.

Fibiger, H. C. The dopamine hypothesis of schizophrenia and mood disorders: Contradictions and speculations. In *The Mesolimbic Dopamine System: From Motivation to Action,* edited by P. Willner and J. Scheel-Krüger. Chichester, England: John Wiley & Sons, 1991.

Field, T., Woodson, R., Greenberg, R., and Cohen, D. Discrimination and imitation of facial expressions in neonates. *Science,* 1982, *218,* 179–181.

Fieve, R. R. The clinical effects of lithium treatment. *Trends in Neurosciences,* 1979, *2,* 66–68.

Fiez, J. A. Cerebellar contributions to cognition. *Neuron,* 1996, *16,* 13–15.

Fiez, J. A., and Petersen, S. E. Neuroimaging studies of word reading. *Proceedings of the National Academy of Science, USA,* 1998, *94,* 914–921.

Fiez, J. A., Balota, D. A., Raichle, M. E., and Petersen, S. E. Effects of lexicality, frequency, and spelling-to-sound consistency on the functional anatomy of reading. *Neuron,* 1999, *24,* 205–218.

Filipek, P. A. Neurobiologic correlates of developmental dyslexia: How do dyslexics' brains differ from those of normal readers?. *Journal of Child Neurology,* 1995, *10,* S62–S69.

Finger, S. *Origins of Neuroscience: A History of Explorations into Brain Function.* New York: Oxford University Press, 1994.

Firestein, S., Zufall, F., and Shepherd, G. M. Single odor-sensitive channels in olfactory receptor neurons are also gated by cyclic nucleotides. *Journal of Neuroscience,* 1991, *11,* 3565–3572.

Fischer, H., Andersson, J. L. R., Furmark, T., and Fredrikson, M. Brain correlates of an unexpected panic attack: A human positron emission tomographic study. *Neuroscience Letters,* 1998, *251,* 137–140.

Fisher, C., Byrne, J., Edwards, A., and Kahn, E. A psychophysiological study of nightmares. *Journal of the American Psychoanalytic Association,* 1970, *18,* 747–782.

Fisher, C., Gross, J., and Zuch, J. Cycle of penile erection synchronous with dreaming (REM) sleep: Preliminary report. *Archives of General Psychiatry,* 1965, *12,* 29–45.

Fisher, S. E., Marlow, A. J., Lamb, J., Maestrini, E., Williams, D. F., Richardson, A. J., Weeks, D. E., Stein, J. F. and Monaco, A. P. A quantitative-trait locus on chromosome 6p influences different aspects of developmental dyslexia. *American Journal of Human Genetics,* 1999, *4,* 146–156.

Fishman, P. S., and Oyler, G. A. Significance of the parkin gene and protein in understanding Parkinson's disease. *Current Neurology and Neuroscience Reports,* 2002, *2,* 296–302.

Fiske, A. P., and Haslam, N. Is obsessive-compulsive disorder a pathology of the human disposition to perform socially meaningful Rituals? Evidence of similar content. *Journal of Nervous and Mental Disease,* 1997, *185,* 211–222.

Fitzpatrick, D., Itoh, K., and Diamond, I. T. The laminar organization of the lateral geniculate body and the striate cortex in the squirrel monkey (*Saimiri sciureus*). *Journal of Neuroscience,* 1983, *3,* 673–702.

Fitzsimons, J. T., and Moore-Gillon, M. J. Drinking and antidiuresis in response to reductions in venous return in the dog: Neural and endocrine mechanisms. *Journal of Physiology (London),* 1980, *308,* 403–416.

Flaum, M., and Andreasen, N. C. Diagnostic criteria for schizophrenia and related disorders: Options for DNS-IV. *Schizophrenia Bulletin,* 1990, *17,* 27–49.

Fletcher, J. M., Page, J. B., Francis, D. J., Copeland, K., Naus, M. J., Davis, C. M., Morris, R., Krauskopf, D., and Satz, P. Cognitive correlates of long-term cannabis use in Costa Rican men. *Archives of General Psychiatry,* 1996, *53,* 1051–1057.

Fletcher, P. J., Currie, P. J., Chambers, J. W., and Coscina, D. V. Radiofrequency lesions of the PVN fail to modify the effects of serotonergic drugs on food intake. *Brain Research,* 1993, *630,* 1–9.

Flock, A. Physiological properties of sensory hairs in the ear. In *Psychophysics and Physiology of Hearing,* edited by E. F. Evans and J. P. Wilson. London: Academic Press, 1977.

Flood, J. F., and Morley, J. E. Increased food intake by neuropeptide Y is due to an increased motivation to eat. *Peptides,* 1991, *12,* 1329–1332.

Folstein, S. E., and Rosen-Sheidley, B. Genetics of autism: Complex aetiology for a heterogeneous disorder. *Nature Reviews: Genetics,* 2001, *2,* 943–955.

Folstein, S. E., and Piven, J. Etiology of autism: Genetic influences. *Pediatrics,* 1991, *87,* 767–773.

Folstein, S. E., and Rutter, M. L. Autism: Familiar aggregation and genetic implications. *Journal of Autism and Developmental Disorders,* 1988, *18,* 3–30.

Fombonne, E. The epidemiology of autism: A review. *Psychological Medicine,* 1999, *29,* 769–786.

Fort, P., Luppi, P.-H., Wenthold, R., and Jouvet, M. Neurones immunoréactifs à la glycine dans le bulbe rachidien du chat. *Comptes Rendus de l'Académie des Sciences (Paris),* 1990, *311,* 205–212.

Foster, D. L., and Nagatani, S. Physiological perspectives on leptin as a regulator of reproduction: Role in timing puberty. *Biology of Reproduction,* 1999, *60,* 205–215.

Foster, R. S., Mulcahy, J. J., Callaghan, J. T., Crabtree, R., and Brashear, D. Role of serum prolactin determination in evaluation of impotent patient. *Urology,* 1990, *36,* 499–501.

Foundas, A. L., Leonard, C. M., Gilmore, R. L., Fennell, E. B., and Heilman, K. M. Pars triangularis asymmetry and language dominance. *Proceedings of the National Academy of Sciences, USA,* 1996, *93,* 719–722.

Foy, M. R., Stanton, M. E., Levine, S., and Thompson, R. F. Behavioral stress impairs long-term potentiation in rodent hippocampus. *Behavioral and Neural Biology,* 1987, *48,* 138–149.

Frank, G., Hemmert, W., and Gummer, A. W. Limiting dynamics of high-frequency electromechanical transduction of outer hair cells. *Proceedings of the National Academy of Science (USA),* 1999, *96,* 4420–4425.

Freed, C. R. Will embryonic stem cells be a useful source of dopamine neurons for transplant into patients with Parkinson's disease? *Proceedings of the National Academy of Science, USA.* 2002, *99,* 1755–1757.

Freed, C. R., Breeze, R. E., DeMasters, B. K., Galvin, J., Trojanowski, J. Q., Greene, P., Eidelberg, D., Fahn, S. Transplants of embryonic dopamine cells show progressive histologic maturation for at least 8 years and improve signs of Parkinsons up to the maximum benefit of L-DOPA preoperatively. *Annual Meeting, American Academy of Neurology,* Denver, CO, April 2002.

Freedman, M. S., Lucas, R. J., Soni, B., von Schantz, M., Muñoz, M., David-Gray, Z., and Foster, R. Regulation of mammalian circadian behavior by non-rod, non-cone, ocular photoreceptors. *Science,* 1999, *284,* 502–504.

Frey, U., and Morris, R. G. Synaptic tagging and long-term potentiation. *Nature,* 1997, *385,* 533–536.

Frey, U., Krug, M., Reymann, K. G., and Matthies, H. Anisomycin, an inhibitor of protein synthesis, blocks late phases of LTP phenomena in the hippocampal CA1 region in vitro. *Brain Research,* 1988, *452,* 57–65.

Fride, E., and Mechoulam, R. Ontogenetic development of the response to anandamide and Δ^9-tetrahydrocannabinol in mice. *Developmental Brain Research,* 1996, *95,* 131–134.

Friedman, M. I., and Bruno, J. P. Exchange of water during lactation. *Science,* 1976, *191,* 409–410.

Friesen, W. V. Cultural differences in facial expression in a social situation: An experimental test of the concept of display rules. Doctoral dissertation, University of California, San Francisco, 1972.

Frisch, R. E. Body fat, menarche, fitness and fertility. In *Adipose Tissue and Reproduction,* edited by R. E. Frisch. Basel, Switzerland: S. Karger, 1990.

Frith, U., Morton, J., and Leslie, A. M. The cognitive basis of a biological disorder: Autism. *Trends in Neuroscience,* 1991, *14,* 433–438.

Fry, J. M. Treatment modalities for narcolepsy. *Neurology,* 1998, *50,* S43–S48.

Fujikawa, T., Yamawaki, S., and Touhouda, Y. Incidence of silent cerebral infarction in patients with major depression. *Stroke,* 1993, *24,* 1631–1634.

Fujikawa, T., Yamawaki, S., and Touhouda, Y. Background factors and clinical symptoms of major depression with silent cerebral infarction. *Stroke,* 1994, *25,* 789–801.

Fukuwatari, T., Kawada, T., Tsuruta, M., Hiraoka, T., Iwanaga, T., Sugimoto, E., and Fushiki, T. Expression of the putative membrane fatty acid transporter (FAT) in taste buds of the circumvallate papillae in rats. *FEBS Letters,* 1997, *414,* 461–464.

Fullerton, C. S., Ursano, R. J., Epstein, R. S., Crowley, B., Vance, K., Kao, T. C., Dougall, A., and Baum, A. Gender differences in posttraumatic stress disorder after motor vehicle accidents. *American Journal of Psychiatry,* 2001, *158,* 1485–1491.

Fulton, J. F. *Functional Localization in Relation to Frontal Lobotomy.* New York: Oxford University Press, 1949.

Fung, Y. K., Schmid, M. J., Anderson, T. M., and Lau, Y. S. Effects of nicotine withdrawal on central dopaminergic systems. *Pharmacology, Biochemistry and Behavior,* 1996, *53,* 635–640.

Fuster, J. M., and Jervey, J. P. Inferotemporal neurons distinguish and retain behaviorally relevant features of visual stimuli. *Science,* 1981, *212,* 952–955.

Gabrieli, J. D. E., Cohen, N. J., and Corkin, S. The impaired learning of semantic knowledge following bilateral medial temporal-lobe resection. *Brain and Cognition,* 1988, *7,* 157–177.

Gaffan, D., and Eacott, M. J. Visual learning for an auditory secondary reinforcer by macaques is intact after uncinate fascicle section: Indirect evidence for the involvement of the corpus striatum. *European Journal of Neuroscience,* 1995, *7,* 1866–1871.

Gaffan, D., and Harrison, S. Amygdalectomy and disconnection in visual learning for auditory secondary reinforcement by monkeys. *Journal of Neuroscience,* 1987, *7,* 2285–2292.

Gaffan, D., Gaffan, E. A., and Harrison, S. Disconnection of the amygdala from visual association cortex impairs visual reward-association learning in monkeys. *Journal of Neuroscience,* 1988, *9,* 3144–3150.

Gagliardo, A., Ioalé, P., and Bingman, V. P. Homing in pigeons: The role of the hippocampal formation in the representation of landmarks used for navigation. *Journal of Neuroscience,* 1999, *19,* 311–315.

Galaburda, A. M., and Livingstone, M. Evidence for a magnocellular defect in developmental dyslexia. *Annals of the New York Academy of Science,* 1993, *682,* 70–82.

Galaburda, A. M., Rosen, G. D., and Sherman, G. F. Cerebrocortical asymmetry. In *Cerebral Cortex,* edited by A. Peters and E. G. Jones. New York: Plenum Press, 1991.

Galen. *De Usu Partium,* translated by M. T. May. Ithaca, N.Y.: Cornell University Press, 1968.

Gallassi, R., Morreale, A., Montagna, P., Cortelli, P., Avoni, P., Castellani, R., Gambetti, P., and Lugaresi, E. Fatal familial insomnia: Behavioral and Cognitive Features. *Neurology,* 1996, *46,* 935–939.

Gallese, V., Fadiga, L., Fogassi, L., and Rizzolatti, G. Action recognition in the premotor cortex. *Brain,* 1996, *119,* 593–609.

Galuske, R. A. W., Schlote, W., Bratzke, H., and Singer, W. Interhemispheric asymmetries of the modular structure in human temporal cortex. *Science,* 2000, *289,* 1946–1949.

Gandelman, R., and Simon, N. G. Postpartum fighting in the rat: Nipple development and the presence of young. *Behavioral and Neural Biology,* 1980, *28,* 350–360.

Garcia-Velasco, J., and Mondragon, M. The incidence of the vomeronasal organ in 1000 human subjects and its possible clinical significance. *Journal of Steroid Biochemistry and Molecular Biololgy,* 1991, *39,* 561–563.

Gardner, H., Brownell, H. H., Wapner, W., and Michelow, D. Missing the point: The role of the right hemisphere in the processing of complex linguistic materials. In *Cognitive Processing in the Right Hemisphere,* edited by E. Pericman. New York: Academic Press, 1983.

Gariano, R. F., and Groves, P. M. Burst firing induced in midbrain dopamine neurons by stimulation of the medial prefrontal and anterior cingulate cortices. *Brain Research,* 1988, *462,* 194–198.

Garner, C., McInnes, L. A., Service, S. K., Spesny, M., Fournier, E., Leon, P., and Freimer, N. B. Linkage analysis of a complex pedigree with severe bipolar disorder, using a Markov chain Monte Carlo method. *American Journal of Human Genetics,* 2001, *68,* 1061–1064.

Gasbarri, A., Sulli, A., Innocenzi, R., Pacitti, C., and Brioni, J. D. Spatial memory impairment induced by lesion of the mesohippocampal dopaminergic system in the rat. *Neuroscience,* 1996, *74,* 1037–1044.

Gatchel, R. J., Baum, A., and Krantz, D. S. *An Introduction to Health Psychology,* 2nd ed. New York: Newbery Award Records, 1989.

Gauthier, I., Skudlarski, P., Gore, J. C., and Anderson, A. W. Expertise for cars and birds recruits brain areas involved in face recognition. *Nature Neuroscience,* 2000, *3,* 191–197.

Gauthier, I., Tarr, M. J., Anderson, A. W., Skudlarski, P., and Gore, J. C. Activation of the middle fusiform "face area" increases with expertise in recognizing novel objects. *Nature Neuroscience,* 1999, *2,* 568–573.

Gayán, J., Smith, S. D., Cherny, S. S., Cardon, L. R., Fulker, D. W., Brower, A. M., Olson, R. K., Pennington, B. F., and DeFries, J. C. Quantative-trait locus for specific language and reading deficits on chromosome 6p. *American Journal of Human Genetics,* 1999, *4,* 157–164.

Gazzaniga, M. S. *The Bisected Brain.* New York: Appleton-Century-Crofts, 1970.

Gazzaniga, M. S., and LeDoux, J. E. *The Integrated Mind.* New York: Plenum Press, 1978.

Geary, N. Cocaine: Animal research studies. In *Cocaine Abuse: New Directions in Treatment and Research,* edited by H. I. Spitz and J. S. Rosecan. New York: Brunner-Mazel, 1987.

Gehring, W. J., and Willoughby, A. R. The medial frontal ortex and the rapid processing of monetary gains and losses. *Science,* 2002, *295,* 2279–2282.

Gentilucci, M., and Rizzolatti, G. In *Vision and Action: The Control of Grasping,* edited by M. A. Goodale. Norwood, N.J.: Ablex, 1990.

George, M. S., Ketter, T. A., Parekh, P. I., Horwitz, B., Herscovitch, P., and Post, R. M. Brain activity during transient sadness and happiness in healthy women. *American Journal of Psychiatry,* 1995, *152,* 341–351.

George, M. S., Parekh, P. I., Rosinsky, N., Ketter, T. A., Kimbrell, T. A., Heilman, K. M., Herscovitch, P., and Post, R. M. Understanding emotional prosody activates right hemisphere regions. *Archives of Neurology,* 1996, *53,* 665–670.

Georges-François, P., Rolls, E. T., and Robertson, R. G. Spatial view cells in the primate hippocampus: Allocentric view not head direction or eye position or place. *Cerebral Cortex,* 1999, *9,* 197–212.

Gerashchenko, D., Kohls, M. D., Greco, M., Waleh, N. S., Salin-Pascual, R., Kilduff, T. S., Lappi, D. A., and Shiromani, P. J. Hypocretin-2-saporin lesions of the lateral hypothalamus produce narcoleptic-like sleep behavior in the rat. *Journal of Neuroscience,* 2001, *21,* 7273–7283.

Gerbino, L., Oleshansky, M., and Gershon, S. Clinical use and mode of action of lithium. In *Psychopharmacology: A Generation of Progress,* edited by M. A. Lipton, A. DiMascio, and K. F. Killam. New York: Raven Press, 1978.

Gerhand, S. Routes to reading: A report of a non-semantic reader with equivalent performance on regular and exception words. *Neuropsychologia,* 2001, *39,* 1473–1484.

Gerren, R., and Weinberger, N. M. Long term potentiation in the magnocellular medial geniculate nucleus of the anesthetized cat. *Brain Research,* 1983, *265,* 138–142.

Gerrits, M. A. F. M., and Vanree, J. M. Effects of nucleus accumbens dopamine depletion on motivational aspects involved in initiation of cocaine and heroin self-administration in rats. *Brain Research,* 1996, *713,* 114–124.

Gershon, E. S., Bunney, W. E., Leckman, J., Van Eerdewegh, M., and DeBauche, B. The inheritance of affective disorders: A review of data and hypotheses. *Behavior Genetics,* 1976, *6,* 227–261.

Geschwind, N., Quadfasel, F. A., and Segarra, J. M. Isolation of the speech area. *Neuropsychologia,* 1968, *6,* 327–340.

Geschwind, N. A., and Behan, P. O. Laterality, hormones, and immunity. In *Cerebral Dominance: The Biological Foundations,* edited by N. Geschwind and A. M. Galaburda. Cambridge, Mass.: Harvard University Press, 1984.

Gessa, G. L., Muntoni, F., Collu, M., Vargiu, L., and Mereu, G. Low doses of ethanol activate dopaminergic neurons in the ventral tegmental area. *Brain Research,* 1985, *348,* 201–204.

Ghiraldi, L., and Svare, B. Unpublished observations cited in Svare, B. Recent advances in the study of female aggressive behavior in mice. In *House Mouse Aggression: A Model for Understanding the Evolution of Social Behavior,* edited by S. Parmigiani, D. Mainardi, and P. Brain. London: Gordon and Breach, 1989.

Gibbs, J., Young, R. C., and Smith, G. P. Cholecystokinin decreases food intake in rats. *Journal of Comparative and Physiological Psychology,* 1973, *84,* 488–495.

Gibbs, W. W. Gaining on fat. *Scientific American,* 1996, *275,* 88–94.

Giedd, J. N., Rapoport, J. L., Kruesi, M. J. P., Parker, C., Schapiro, M. B., Allen, A. J., Leonard, H. L., Kaysen, D., Dickstein, D. P., Marsh, W. L., Kozuch, P. L., Vaituzis, A. C., Hamburger, S. D., and Swedo, S. E. Sydenham's chorea: Magnetic resonance imaging of the basal ganglia. *Neurology,* 1995, *45,* 2199–2202.

Gilbert, D. G., and Gilbert, B. O. Personality, psychopathology, and nicotine response as mediators of the genetics of smoking. *Behavioral Genetics,* 1995, *25,* 133–148.

Gilbert, P. L., Harris, M. J., McAdams, L. A., and Jeste, D. V. Neuroleptic withdrawal in schizophrenic patients. *Archives of General Psychiatry,* 1995, *52,* 173–188.

Gilbertson, T. A., Fontenot, D. T., Liu, L., Zhang, H., and Monroe, W. T. Fatty acid modulation of K^+ channels in taste receptor cells: Gustatory cues for dietary fat. *American Journal of Physiology,* 1997, *272,* C1203–C1210.

Giles, D. E., Biggs, M. M., Rush, A. J., and Roffwarg, H. P. Risk factors in families of unipolar depression. I. Psychiatric illness and reduced REM latency. *Journal of Affective Disorders*, 1988, *14*, 51–59.

Giles, D. E., Roffwarg, H. P., and Rush, A. J. REM latency concordance in depressed family members. *Biological Psychiatry*, 1987, *22*, 910–924.

Gillespie, P. G. Molecular machinery of auditory and vestibular transduction. *Current Opinion in Neurobiology*, 1995, *5*, 449–455.

Gillette, M. U., and McArthur, A. J. Circadian actions of melatonin at the suprachiasmatic nucleus. *Behavioural Brain Research*, 1995, *73*, 135–139.

Giordano, A. L., Siegel, H. I., and Rosenblatt, J. S. Nuclear estrogen receptor binding in the preoptic area and hypothalamus of pregnancy-terminated rats: Correlation with the onset of maternal behavior. *Neuroendocrinology*, 1989, *50*, 248–258.

Givens, B. Low doses of ethanol impair spatial working memory and reduce hippocampal theta activity. *Alcohol: Clinical and Experimental Research*, 1995, *19*, 763–767.

Givens, B., and McMahon, K. Ethanol suppresses the induction of long-term potentiation in vivo. *Brain Research*, 1995, *688*, 27–33.

Givens, B. S., and Olton, D. S. Cholinergic and GABAergic modulation of medial septal area: Effect on working memory. *Behavioral Neuroscience*, 1990, *104*, 849–855.

Glaser, R., Rice, J., Sheridan, J., Post, A., Fertel, R., Stout, J., Speicher, C. E., Kotur, M., and Kiecolt-Glaser, J. K. Stress-related immune suppression: Health implications. *Brain, Behavior, and Immunity*, 1987, *1*, 7–20.

Glaser, R., Sheridan, J., Malarkey, W. B., MacCallum, R. C., and Kiecolt-Glaser, J. K. Chronic stress modulates the immune response to a pneumococcal pneumonia vaccine. *Psychosomatic Medicine*, 2000, *62*, 804–807.

Glaum, S. R., Hara, M., Bindokas, V. P., Lee, C. C., Polonsky, K. S., Bell, G. I., and Miller, R. J. Leptin, the obese gene product, rapidly modulates synaptic transmission in the hypothalamus. *Molecular Pharmacology*, 1996, *50*, 230–235.

Gloor, P., Olivier, A., Quesney, L. F., Andermann, F., and Horowitz, S. The role of the limbic system in experiential phenomena of temporal lobe epilepsy. *Annals of Neurology*, 1982, *12*, 129–144.

Goddard, A. W., Sholomskas, D. E., Walton, K. E., Augeri, F. M., Charney, D. S., Heninger, G. R., Goodman, W. K., and Price, L. H. Effects of tryptophan depletion in panic disorder. *Biological Psychiatry*, 1994, *36*, 775–777.

Goeders, N. E., Lane, J. D., and Smith, J. E. Self-administration of methionine enkephalin into the nucleus accumbens. *Pharmacology, Biochemistry, and Behavior*, 1984, *20*, 451–455.

Goel, V., and Dolan, R. J. The functional anatomy of humor: Segregating cognitive and affective components. *Nature Neuroscience*, 2001, *4*, 237–238.

Goff, D. C., Tsai, G., Levitt, J., Amico, E., Manoach, D., Schoenfeld, D. A., Hayden, D. L., McCarley, R., and Coyle, J. T. A placebo-controlled trial of D-cycloserine added to conventional neuroleptics in patients with schizophrenia. *Archives of General Psychiatry*, 1999, *56*, 21–27.

Golby, A. J., Gabrieli, J. D., Chiao, J. Y., and Eberhardt, J. L. Differential responses in the fusiform region to same-race and other-race faces. *Nature Neuroscience*, 2001, *4*, 845–850.

Golden, P. L., MacCagnan, T. J., and Pardridge, W. M. Human blood–brain barrier leptin receptor: Binding and endocytosis in isolated human brain microvessels. *Journal of Clinical Investigation*, 1997, *99*, 14–18.

Goldstein, R. Z., and Volkow, N. F. Drug addiction and its underlying neurological basis: Neuroimaging evidence for the involvement of the frontal cortex. *American Journal of Psychiatry*, 2002, *159*, 1642–1652.

Golgi, C. *Opera Omnia, Vols. I and II*. Milan: Hoepli, 1903.

Gongwer, M. A., Murphy, J. M., McBride, W. J., Lumeng, L., and Li, R.-K. Regional brain contents of serotonin, dopamine and their metabolites in the selectively bred high- and low-alcohol drinking lines of rats. *Alcohol*, 1989, *6*, 317–320.

Goodale, M. A., and Milner, A. D. Separate visual pathways for perception and action. *Trends in Neuroscience*, 1992, *15*, 20–25.

Goodale, M. A., Meenan, J. P., Bülthoff, H. H., Nicolle, D. A., Murphy, K. H., and Racicot, C. I. Separate neural pathways for the visual analysis of object shape in perception and prehension. *Current Biology*, 1994, *4*, 604–610.

Goodglass, H., and Kaplan, E. *Assessment of Aphasia and Related Disorders*. Philadelphia: Lea & Febiger, 1972.

Goris, A. H. C., Westerterp-Plantenga, M. S., and Westerterp, K. R. Undereating and underrecording of habitual food intake in obese men: Selective underreporting of fat intake. *American Journal of Clinical Nutrition*, 2000, *71*, 130–134.

Gorski, R. A., Gordon, J. H., Shryne, J. E., and Southam, A. M. Evidence for a morphological sex difference within the medial preoptic area of the rat brain. *Brain Research*, 1978, *148*, 333–346.

Gottesman, I. I., and Bertelsen, A. Confirming unexpressed genotypes for schizophrenia. *Archives of General Psychiatry*, 1989, *46*, 867–872.

Gottesman, I. I., and Shields, J. *Schizophrenia: The Epigenetic Puzzle*. New York: Cambridge University Press, 1982.

Gouras, P. Identification of cone mechanisms in monkey ganglion cells. *Journal of Physiology (London)*, 1968, *199*, 533–538.

Goy, R. W., Bercovitch, F. B., and McBrair, M. C. Behavioral masculinization is independent of genital masculinization in prenatally androgenized female rhesus macaques. *Hormones and Behavior*, 1988, *22*, 552–571.

Graber, G. C., and Kristal, M. B. Uterine distention facilitates the onset of maternal beahvior in pseudopregnant but not in cycling rats. *Physiology and Behavior*, 1977, *19*, 133–137.

Grabowski, T. J., Damasio, H., Tranel, D., Ponto, L. L., Hichwa, R. D., and Damasio, A. R. A role for left temporal pole in the retrieval of words for unique entities. *Human Brain Mapping*, 2001, *13*, 199–212.

Grace, A. A. Phasic versus tonic dopamine release and the modulation of dopamine system responsivity: A hypothesis for the etiology of schizophrenia. *Neuroscience*, 1991, *41*, 1–24.

Grados, M. A., Riddle, M. A., Samuels, J. F., Liang, K.-Y., Hoehn-Saric, R., Bienvenu, O. J., Walkup, J. T., Song, D., and Nestadt, G. The familial phenotype of obsessive-compulsive disorder in relation to tic disorders: The Hopkins OCD Family Study. *Biological Psychiatry*, 2001, *50*, 559–565.

Graf, P., Squire, L. R., and Mandler, G. The information that amnesic patients do not forget. *Journal of Experimental Psychology: Learning, Memory, and Cognition*, 1984, *10*, 164–178.

Grafton, S. T., Fagg, A. H., and Arbib, M. A. Dorsal premotor cortex and conditional movement selection: A PET functional mapping study. *Journal of Neurophysiology,* 1998, *79,* 1092–1097.

Grafton, S. T., Waters, C., Sutton, J., Lew, M. F., and Couldwell, W. Pallidotomy increases activity of motor association cortex in Parkinson's disease: A positron emission tomographic study. *Annals of Neurology,* 1995, *37,* 776–783.

Grant, S. G. N., O'Dell, T. J., Karl, K. A., Stein, P. L., Soriano, P., and Kandel, E. R. Impaired long-term potentiation, spatial learning, and hippocampal development in *fyn* mutant mice. *Science,* 1992, *258,* 1903–1910.

Gratacos, M., Nadal, M., Martin-Santos, R., Pijana, M. A., Gago, J., Peral, B., Armengol, L., Ponsa, I., Miro, R., Bulbena, A., and Estivill, X. A polymorphic genomic duplication on human chromosome 15 is a susceptivility factor for panic and phobic disorders. *Cell,* 2001, *106,* 367–379.

Grattan, D. R., Pi, X. J., Andrews, Z. B., Augustine, R. A., Kokay, I. C., Summerfield, M. R., Todd, B., and Bunn, S. J. Prolactin receptors in the brain during pregnancy and lactation: Implications for behavior. *Hormones and Behavior,* 2001, *40,* 115–124.

Gray, C., Freeman, W. J., and Skinner, J. E. Chemical dependencies of learning in the rabbit olfactory bulb: Acquisition of the transient and spatial pattern change depends on norepinephrine. *Behavioral Neuroscience,* 1986, *100,* 585–596.

Graybiel, A. M. Basal ganglia: New therapeutic approaches to Parkinson's disease. *Current Biology,* 1996, *6,* 368–371.

Gréco, B., Edwards, D. A., Zumpe, D., and Clancy, A. N. Androgen receptor and mating-induced Fos immunoreactivity are co-localized in limbic and midbrain neurons that project to the male rat medial preoptic area. *Brain Research,* 1998, *781,* 15–24.

Green, E. J., and Greenough, W. T. Altered synaptic transmission in dentate gyrus of rats reared in complex environments: Evidence from hippocampal slices maintained in vitro. *Journal of Neurophysiology,* 1986, *55,* 739–750.

Greenberg, D., Kava, R., Lewis, D. R., and Greenwood, M. R. C. Satiation following intraduodenal Intralipid preceded appearance of [^{14}C]-Intralipid in hepatic portal blood. *FASEB Journal,* 1991, *5,* A1451.

Greenberg, D., Smith, G. P., and Gibbs, J. Intraduodenal infusions of fats elicit satiety in the sham feeding rat. *American Journal of Physiology,* 1990, *259,* R110–R118.

Greenberg, R., and Pearlman, C. A. Cutting the REM nerve: An approach to the adaptive role of REM sleep. *Perspectives in Biology and Medicine,* 1974, *17,* 513–521.

Greene, J. D., Sommerville, R. B., Nystrom, L. E., Darley, J. M., and Cohen, J. D. An fMRI investigation of emotional engagement in moral judgment. *Science,* 2001, *293,* 2105–2108.

Grelotti, D. J., Gauthier, I., and Schultz, R. T. Social interest and the development of cortical face specialization: What autism teaches us about face processing. *Developmental Psychobiology,* 2002, *40,* 213–225.

Grigorenko, E. L., Wood, F. B., Meyer, M. S., Hart, L. A., Speed, W. C., Shuster, A., and Pauls, D. L. Susceptibility loci for distinct components of developmental dyslexia on chromosomes 6 and 15. *American Journal of Human Genetics,* 1997, *60,* 27–39.

Grijalva, C. V., Levin, E. D., Morgan, M., Roland, B., and Martin, F. C. Contrasting effects of centromedial and basolateral amygdaloid lesions on stress-related responses in the rat. *Physiology and Behavior,* 1990, *48,* 495–500.

Grill, H. J., and Kaplan, J. M. Caudal brainstem participates in the distributed neural control of feeding. In *Handbook of Behavioral Neurobiology. Vol. 10: Neurobiology of Food and Fluid Intake,* edited by E. Stricker. New York: Plenum Press, 1990.

Grimm, J. W., and See, R. E. Dissociation of primary and secondary reward-relevant limbic nuclei in an animal model of relapse. *Neuropsychopharmacology,* 2000, *22,* 473–479.

Gross, C. G. Visual functions of inferotemporal cortex. In *Handbook of Sensory Physiology, Vol. 7: Central Processing of Visual Information,* edited by R. Jung. Berlin: Springer-Verlag, 1973.

Grossman, E. D., and Blake, R. Brain activity evoked by inverted and imagined biological motion. *Vision Research,* 2001, *41,* 1475–1482.

Grossman, E. D., Donnelly, M., Price, R., Pickens, D., Morgan, V., Neighbor, G., and Blake R. Brain areas involved in perception of biological motion. *Journal of Cognitive Neuroscience,* 2000, *12,* 711–720.

Grunhaus, L., Shipley, J. E., Eiser, A., Pande, A. C., Tandon, R., Krahn, D. D., Demitrack, M. A., Remen, A., Hirshmann, S., and Greden, J. F. Sleep-onset rapid eye movement after electroconvulsive therapy is more frequent in patients who respond less well to electroconvulsive therapy. *Biological Psychiatry,* 1997, *42,* 191–200.

Guerin, G. F., Goeders, N. E., Dworkin, S. I., and Smith, J. E. Intracranial self-administration of dopamine into the nucleus accumbens. *Society for Neuroscience Abstracts,* 1984, *10,* 1072.

Guilleminault, C., Wilson, R. A., and Dement, W. C. A study on cataplexy. *Archives of Neurology,* 1974, *31,* 255–261.

Gulevich, G., Dement, W. C., and Johnson, L. Psychiatric and EEG observations on a case of prolonged (264 hours) wakefulness. *Archives of General Psychiatry,* 1966, *15,* 29–35.

Gura, T. Obesity sheds its secrets. *Science,* 1997, *275,* 751–753.

Gurd, J. M., and Marshall, J. C. Cognition: Righting reading. *Current Biology,* 1993, *3,* 593–595.

Gurden, H., Takita, M., and Jay, T. M. Essential role of D1 but not D2 receptors in the NMDA receptor-dependent long-term potentiation at hippocampal-prefrontal cortex synapses in vivo. *Journal of Neuroscience,* 2000, *20,* RC106.

Gurden, H., Tassin, J. P., and Jay, T. M. Integrity of the mesocortical dopaminergic system is necessary for complete expression of in vivo hippocampal-prefrontal cortex long-term potentiation. *Neuroscience,* 1999, *94,* 1019–1027.

Gurevich, E. V., Bordelon, Y., Shapiro, R. M., Arnold, S. E., Gur, R. E., and Joyce, J. N. Mesolimbic dopamine D$_3$ receptors and use of antipsychotics in patients with schizophrenia: A postmortem study. *Archives of General Psychiatry,* 1997, *54,* 225–232.

Guridi, J., and Obeso, J. A. The subthalamic nucleus, hemiballismus and Parkinson's disease: Reappraisal of a neurosurgical dogma. *Brain,* 2001, *124,* 5–19.

Gurin, B., Owens, S., Okuyama, T., Riggs, S. Ferguson, M., and Litaker, M. Effect of physical training and its cessation on percent fat and bone density of children with obesity. *Obesity Research,* 1999, *7,* 208–214.

Gurvits, T. V., Shenton, M. E., Hokama, H., Ohta, H., Lasko, N. B., Gilbertson, M. W., Orr, S. P., Kikinis, R., Jolesz, F. A., McCarley, R. W., and Pitman, R. K. Magnetic resonance imaging study of hippocampal volume in chronic, combat-related posttraumatic stress disorder. *Biological Psychiatry,* 1996, *40,* 1091–1099.

Haarmeier, T., Their, P., Repnow, M., and Petersen, D. False perception of motion in a patient who cannot compensate for eye movements. *Nature,* 1997, *389,* 849–852.

Haas, R. H. Thiamin and the brain. *Annual Review of Nutrition,* 1988, *8,* 483–515.

Habib, M. The neurological basis of developmental dyslexia: An overview and working hypothesis. *Brain,* 2000, *123,* 2373–2399.

Hackett, R. A., Preuss, T. M., and Kaas, J. H. Architectonic identification of the core region in auditory cortex of macaques, chimpanzees, and humans. *Journal of Comparative Neurology,* 2001, *441,* 197–222.

Hadjikhani, N., Liu, A. K., Dale, A. M., Cavanagh, P., and Tootell, R. B. H. Retinotopy and color sensitivity in human visual cortical area V8. *Nature Neuroscience,* 1998, *1,* 235–241.

Hahn, T. M., Breininger, J. F., Baskin, D. G., and Schwartz, M. W. Coexpression of Agrp and NPY in fasting-activated hypothalamic neurons. *Nature Neuroscience,* 1998, *1,* 271–272.

Hajak, G., Clarenbach, P., Fischer, W., Haase, W., Bandelow, B., Adler, L., and Ruther, E. Effects of hypnotics on sleep quality and daytime well-being: Data from a comparative multicentre study in outpatients with insomnia. *European Psychiatry,* 1995, *10* (Suppl. 3), 173S–179S.

Hakansson, M. L., Hulting, A. L., and Meister, B. Expression of leptin receptor messenger RNA in the hypothalamic arcuate nucleus: Relationship with NPY neurons. *Neuroreport,* 1996, *7,* 3087–3092.

Halaas, J. L., Gajiwala, K. D., Maffei, M., Cohen, S. L., Chait, B. T., Rabinowitz, D., Lallone, R. L., Burley, S. K., and Friedman, J. M. Weight-reducing effects of the plasma protein encoded by the obese gene. *Science,* 1995, *269,* 543–546.

Halem, H. A., Baum, M. J., and Cherry, J. A. Sex difference and steroid modulation of pheromone-induced immediate early genes in the two zones of the mouse accessory olfactory system. *Journal of Neuroscience,* 2001, *21,* 2474–2480.

Halem, H. A., Cherry, J. A., and Baum, M. J. Central forebrain Fos responses to familiar male odours are attenuated in recently mated female mice. *European Journal of Neuroscience,* 2001, *13,* 389–399.

Haley, J. E., Wilcox, G. L., and Chapman, P. F. The role of nitric oxide in hippocampal long-term potentiation. *Neuron,* 1992, *8,* 211–216.

Halgren, E. Walter, R. D., Cherlow, D. G., and Crandall, P. E. Mental phenomena evoked by electrical stimultion of the human hippocampal formation and amygdala. *Brain,* 1978, *101,* 83–117.

Hall, W., and Solowij, N. Adverse effects of cannabis. *Lancet,* 1998, *352,* 1611–1616.

Halmi, K. A. Anorexia nervosa: Recent investigations. *Annual Review of Medicine,* 1978, *29,* 137–148.

Halmi, K. A., Eckert, E., LaDu, T. J., and Cohen, J. Anorexia nervose: Treatment efficacy of cyproheptadine and amitriptyline. *Archives of General Psychiatry,* 1986, *43,* 177–181.

Halpern, M. The organization and function of the vomeronasal system. *Annual Review of Neuroscience,* 1987, *10,* 325–362.

Halsband, U., and Freund, H. J. Premotor cortex and conditional motor learning in man. *Brain,* 1990, *113,* 207–222.

Hamberger, M. J., Goodman, R. R., Perrine, K., and Tamny, T. Anatomic dissociation of auditory and visual naming in the lateral temporal cortex. *Neurology,* 2001, *56,* 56–61.

Hampson, R. E., and Deadwyler, S. A. Cannabinoids reveal the necessity of hippocampal neural encoding for short-term memory in rats. *Journal of Neuroscience,* 2000, *20,* 8932–8942.

Hara, J., Beuckmann, C. T., Nambu, T., Willie, J. T., Chemelli, R. M., Sinton, C. M., Sugiyama, F., Yagami, K., Goto, K., Yanagisawa, M., and Sakurai, T. Genetic ablation of orexin neurons in mice results in narcolepsy, hypophagia, and obesity. *Neuron,* 2001, *30,* 345–354.

Hariri, A. R., Mattay, V. S., Tessitore, A., Kolachana, B., Fera, F., Goldman, D., Egan, M. F., and Weinberger, D. R. Serotonin transporter genetic variation and the response of the human amygdala. *Science,* 2002, *297,* 400–403.

Harmon, L. D., and Julesz, B. Masking in visual recognition: Effects of two-dimensional filtered noise. *Science,* 1973, *180,* 1194–1197.

Harries, M. H., and Perrett, D. I. Visual processing of faces in the temporal cortex: Physiological evidence for a modular organization and possible anatomical correlates. *Journal of Cognitive Science,* 1991, *3,* 9–24.

Harrington, M. E., and Rusak, B. Lesions of the thalamic intergeniculate leaflet alter hamster circadian rhythms. *Journal of Biological Rhythms,* 1986, *1,* 309–325.

Harris, G. W., and Jacobsohn, D. Functional grafts of the anterior pituitary gland. *Proceedings of the Royal Society of London [B],* 1951–1952, *139,* 263–267.

Harris, J. A., Miniussi, C., Harris, I. M., and Diamond, M. E. Transient storage of a tactile memory trace in primary somatosensory cortex. *Journal of Neuroscience,* 2002, *22,* 8720–8725.

Harrison, Y., and Horne, J. A. Sleep loss impairs short and novel language tasks having a prefrontal focus. *Journal of Sleep Research,* 1998, *7,* 95–100.

Harrison, Y., and Horne, J. A. One night of sleep loss impairs innovative thinking and flexible decision-making. *Organizational Behavior and Human Decision Processes,* 1999, *78,* 128–145.

Hart, B. Sexual reflexes and mating behavior in the male dog. *Journal of Comparative and Physiological Psychology,* 1967, *66,* 388–399.

Hart, B. Gonadal hormones and sexual reflexes in the female rat. *Hormones and Behavior,* 1969, *1,* 65–71.

Hart, B. L. Hormones, spinal reflexes, and sexual behaviour. In *Determinants of Sexual Behaviour,* edited by J. B. Hutchinson. Chichester, England: John Wiley & Sons, 1978.

Hartline, H. K. The response of single optic nerve fibers of the vertebrate eye to illumination of the retina. *American Journal of Physiology,* 1938, *121,* 400–415.

Harvey, S. M. Female sexual behavior: Fluctuations during the menstrual cycle. *Journal of Psychosomatic Research,* 1987, *31,* 101–110.

Hatfield, T., Han, J.-S., Conley, M., Gallagher, M., and Holland, P. Neurotoxic lesions of basolateral, but not central, amygdala interfere with pavlovian second-order conditioning and reinforcer devaluation effects. *Journal of Neuroscience,* 1966, *16,* 5256–5265.

Hattar, S., Liao, H.-W., Takao, M., Berson, D. M., and Yau, K.-W. Melanopsin-containing retinal ganglion cells: Architecture, projections, and intrinsic photosensitivity. *Science*, 2002, *295*, 1065–1070.

Haug, H.-J. Prediction of sleep deprivation outcome by diurnal variation of mood. *Biological Psychiatry*, 1992, *31*, 271–278.

Hauser, M. D. Right hemisphere dominance for the production of facial expression in monkeys. *Science*, 1993, *261*, 475–477.

Havel, P. J., Townsend, R., Chaump, L., and Teff, K. High-fat meals reduce 24-h circulating leptin concentrations in women. *Diabetes*, 1999, *48*, 334–341.

Hawke, C. Castration and sex crimes. *American Journal of Mental Deficiency*, 1951, *55*, 220–226.

Haxby, J. V., Horwitz, B., Ungerleider, L. G., Maisog, J. M., Pietrini, P., and Grady, C. L. The functional organization of human extrastriate cortex: A PET-rCBF study of selective attention to faces and locations. *Journal of Neuroscience*, 1994, *14*, 6336–6353.

Heath, A. C., Madden, P. A. F., Bucholz, K. K., Dinwiddie, S. H., Slutske, W. S., Bierut, L. J., Rohrbaugh, J. W., Statham, D. J., Dunne, M. P., Whitfield, J. B., and Martin, N. G. Genetic differences in alcohol sensitivity and the inheritance of alcoholism risk. *Psychological Medicine*, 1999, *29*, 1069–1081.

Heath, A. C., Madden, P. A. F., Slutske, W. S., and Martin, N. G. Personality and the inheritance of smoking behavior: A genetic perspective. *Behavioral Genetics*, 1995, *25*, 103–118.

Hebb, D. O. *The Organization of Behaviour*. New York: Wiley-Interscience, 1949.

Heckler, M. M. *Fifth Special Report to the U.S. Congress on Alcohol and Health*. Washington, DC: U.S. Government Printing Office, 1983.

Heffner, H. E., and Heffner, R. S. Role of primate auditory cortex in hearing. In *Comparative Perception. Vol. II: Complex Signals*, edited by W. C. Stebbins and M. A. Berkley. New York: John Wiley & Sons, 1990.

Heilman, K. M., Rothi, L., and Kertesz, A. Localization of apraxia-producing lesions. In *Localization in Neuropsychology*, edited by A. Kertesz. New York: Academic Press, 1983.

Heilman, K. M., Scholes, R., and Watson, R. T. Auditory affective agnosia: Disturbed comprehension of affective speech. *Journal of Neurology, Neurosurgery, and Psychiatry*, 1975, *38*, 69–72.

Heilman, K. M., Watson, R. T., and Bowers, D. Affective disorders associated with hemispheric disease. In *Neuropsychology of Human Emotion*, edited by K. M. Heilman and P. Satz. New York: Guilford Press, 1983.

Heimer, L., and Larsson, K. Impairment of mating behavior in male rats following lesions in the preoptic-anterior hypothalamic continuum. *Brain Research*, 1966/1967, *3*, 248–263.

Heinrichs, S. C., Menzaghi, F., Pich, E. M., Baldwin, H. A., Rassnick, S., Britton, K. T., and Koob, G. F. Anti-stress action of a corticotropin-releasing factor antagonist on behavioral reactivity to stressors of varying type and intensity. *Neuropsychopharmacology*, 1994, *11*, 179–186.

Helenius, P., Uutela, K., and Hari, R. Auditory stream segregation in dyslexic adults. *Brain*, 1999, *122*, 907–913.

Hellhammer, D. H., Hubert, W., and Schurmeyer, T. Changes in saliva testosterone after psychological stimulation in men. *Psychoneuroendocrinology*, 1985, *10*, 77–81.

Helmuth, L. Dyslexia: Same brains, different languages. *Science*, 2001, *291*, 2064–2065.

Hendrickson, A. E., Wagoner, N., and Cowan, W. M. Autoradiographic and electron microscopic study of retino-hypothalamic connections. *Zeitschrift für Zellforschung und Mikroskopische Anatomie*, 1972, *125*, 1–26.

Hendrie, C. A. The calls of murine predators activate endogenous analgesia mechanisms in laboratory mice. *Physiology and Behavior*, 1991, *49*, 569–573.

Hendry, S. H. C., and Yoshioka, T. A neurochemically distinct third channel in the cacaque dorsal lateral geniculare nucleus. *Science*, 1994, *264*, 575–577.

Heninger, G. R., Delgado, P. L., and Charney, D. S. The revised monoamine theory of depression: A modulatory role for monoamines, based on new findings from monoamine depletion experiments in humans. *Pharmacopsychiatry*, 1996, *29*, 2–11.

Henke, P. G. The telencephalic limbic system and experimental gastric pathology: A review. *Neuroscience and Biobehavioral Reviews*, 1982, *6*, 381–390.

Hennessey, A. C., Camak, L., Gordon, F., and Edwards, D. A. Connections between the pontine central gray and the ventromedial hypothalamus are essential for lordosis in female rats. *Behavioral Neuroscience*, 1990, *104*, 477–488.

Heresco-Levy, U., Javitt, D. C., Ermilov, M., Mordel, C., Silipo, G., and Lichtenstein, M. Efficacy of high-dose glycine in the treatment of enduring negative symptoms of schizophrenia. *Archives of General Psychiatry*, 1999, *56*, 29–36.

Herholz, K. Neuroimaging in anorexia nervosa. *Psychiatry Research*, 1996, *62*, 105–110.

Hering, E. *Outlines of a Theory of the Light Sense*, 1905. Translated by L. M. Hurvich and D. Jameson. Cambridge, Mass.: Harvard University Press, 1965.

Hernan, M. S., Takkouche, B., Caamano-Isorna, F., and Gestal-Otero, J. J. A meta-analysis of coffee drinking, cigarette smoking, and the risk of Parkinson's disease. *Annals of Neurology*, 2002, *52*, 276–284.

Hernandez, L., and Hoebel, B. G. Feeding can enhance dopamine turnover in the prefrontal cortex. *Brain Research Bulletin*, 1990, *25*, 975–979.

Hertzmann, M., Reba, R. C., and Kotlyarov, E. V. Single photon emission computed tomography in phencyclidine and related drug abuse. *American Journal of Psychiatry*, 1990, *147*, 255–256.

Hetherington, A. W., and Ranson, S. W. Hypothalamic lesions and adiposity in the rat. *Anatomical Record*, 1942, *78*, 149–172.

Hettema, J. M., Neale, M. C., and Kendler, K. S. A review and meta-analysis of the genetic epidemiology of anxiety disorders. *American Journal of Psychiatry*, 2001, *158*, 1568–1578.

Heuser, J. E. Synaptic vesicle exocytosis revealed in quick-frozen frog neuromuscular junctions treated with 4-aminopyridine and given a single electrical shock. In *Society for Neuroscience Symposia, Vol. II*, edited by W. M. Cowan and J. A. Ferrendelli. Bethesda, Md.: Society for Neuroscience, 1977.

Heuser, J. E., and Reese, T. S. Evidence for recycling of synaptic vesicle membrane during transmitter release at the frog neuromuscular function. *Journal of Cell Biology*, 1973, *57*, 315–344.

Heuser, J. E., Reese, T. S., Dennis, M. J., Jan, Y., Jan, L., and Evans, L. Synaptic vesicle exocytosis captured by quick freezing and correlated with quantal transmitter release. *Journal of Cell Biology*, 1979, *81*, 275–300.

Heywood, C. A., and Cowey, A. The role of the "face-cell" area in the discrimination and recognition of faces by monkeys. *Philosophical Transactions of the Royal Society of London [B]*, 1992, *335*, 31–38.

Heywood, C. A., Gaffan, D., and Cowey, A. Cerebral achromatopsia in monkeys. *European Journal of Neuroscience*, 1995, *7*, 1064–1073.

Hickok, G., Bellugi, U., and Klima, E. S. The neurobiology of sign language and its implications for the neural basis of language. *Nature*, 1996, *381*, 699–702.

Hickok, G., Klima, E., Kritchevsky, M., and Bellugi, U. A case of 'sign blindness' following left occipital damage in a deaf signer. *Neuropsychologia*, 1995, *33*, 1597–1601.

Hickok, G., Wilson, M., Clark, K., Klima, E. S., Kritchevsky, M., and Bellugi, U. Discourse deficits following right hemisphere damage in deaf signers. *Brain and Language*, 1999, *66*, 233–248.

Higley, J., Hasert, M., Suomi, S., and Linnoila, M. The serotonin reuptake inhibitor sertraline reduces excessive alsohol consumption in nonhuman primates: Effect of stress. *Neuropsychopharmacology*, 1998, *18*, 431–443.

Higley, J. D., Mehlman, P. T., Higley, S. B., Fernald, B., Vickers, J., Lindell, S. G., Taub, D. M., Suomi, S. J., and Linnoila, M. Excessive mortaility in young free-ranging male nonhuman primates with low cerebrospinal fluid 5-hydroxyindoleacetic acid concentrations. *Archives of General Psychiatry*, 1996a, *53*, 537–543.

Higley, J. D., Mehlman, P. T., Poland, R. E., Taub, D. M., Vickers, J., Suomi, S. J., and Linnoila, M. CSF testosterone and 5-HIAA correlate with different types of aggressive behaviors. *Biological Psychiatry*, 1996b, *40*, 1067–1082.

Hikosaka, O., Sakai, K., Miyauchi, S., Takino, R., Sasaki, Y., and Puetz, B. Activation of human presupplementary motor area in learning of sequential procedures: A functional MRI study. *Journal of Neurophysiology*, 1996, *76*, 617–621.

Hilditch-Maguire, P., Trettel, F., Passani, L. A., Auerbach, A., Persichetti, F., and MacDonald, M. E. Huntingtin: An iron-regulated protein essential for normal nuclear and perinuclear organelles. *Human Molecular Genetics*, 2000, *9*, 2789–2797.

Hill, A. J., and Best, P. J. Effects of deafness and blindness on the spatial correlates of hippocampal unit activity in the rat. *Experimental Neurology*, 1981, *74*, 204–217.

Hill, J. P., Hauptman, J., Anderson, J., Fujioka, K., O'Neil, P. M., Smith, D. K., Zavoral, J. H., and Aronne, L. J. Orlistat, a lipase inhibitor, for weight maintenance after conventional dieting: A 1-y study. *American Journal of Clinical Nutrition*, 1999, *69*, 1108–1116.

Hines, M., Allen, L. S., and Gorski, R. A. Sex differences in subregions of the medial nucleus of the amygdala and the bed nucleus of the stria terminalis of the rat. *Brain Research*, 1992, *579*, 321–326.

Hinjo, S., Hirano, C., Murase, S., Kaneko, T., Sugiyama, T., Ohtaka, K., Aoyama, T., Takei, Y., Inoko, K., and Wakbayshai, S. Obsessive-compulsive symptoms in childhood and adolescence. *Acta Psychiatrica Scandanivica*, 1989, *80*, 83–91.

Hippocrates. *On the Sacred Disease*. In *Hippocrates and Galen: Great Books of the Western World, Vol. 10*. Chicago: William Benton, 1952.

Hirsch, J. The search for new ways to treat obesity. *Proceedings of the National Academy of Science, USA*, 2002, *99*, 9096–9097.

Hitchcock, J., and Davis, M. Lesions of the amygdala, but not of the cerebellum or red nucleus, block conditioned fear as measured with the potentiated startle paradigm. *Behavioral Neuroscience*, 1986, *100*, 11–22.

Hobson, J. A. *The Dreaming Brain*. New York: Basic Books, 1988.

Hodge, C. W., Haraguchi, M., Erickson, H., and Samson, H. H. Ventral tegmental microinjections of quinpirole decrease ethanol and sucrose-reinforced responding. *Alcohol: Clinical and Experimental Research*, 1993, *17*, 370–375.

Hoebel, B. G., Monaco, A. P., Hernandez, L., Aulisi, E. F., Stanley, B. G., and Lenard, L. Self-injection of amphetamine directly into the brain. *Psychopharmacology*, 1983, *81*, 158–163.

Hofbauer, R. K., Rainville, P., Duncan, G. H., and Bushnell, M. C. Cortical representation of the sensory dimension of pain. *Journal of Neurophysiology*, 2001, *86*, 402–411.

Hofer, M. A., and Shair, H. N. Ultrasonic vocalization, laryngeal braking, and thermogenesis in rat pups: A reappraisal. *Behavioral Neuroscience*, 1993, *107*, 354–362.

Hoffman, D. J., Sawaya, A. L., Verreschi, I., Tucker, K. L., and Roberts, S. B. Why are nutritionally stunted children at increased risk of obesity? Studies of metabolic rate and fat oxidation in shantytown children from Sao Paulo, Brazil. *American Journal of Clinical Nutrition*, 2000, *72*, 702–707.

Hohman, G. W. Some effects of spinal cord lesions on experienced emotional feelings. *Psychophysiology*, 1966, *3*, 143–156.

Holden, C. The violence of the lambs. *Science*, 2000, *289*, 580–581.

Hollander, E., DeCaria, C. M., Nitescu, A., Gully, R., Suckow, R. F., Cooper, T. B., Gorman, J. M., Klein, D. F., and Liebowitz, M. R. Serotonergic function in obsessive-compulsive disorder: Behavioral and neuroendocrine responses to oral m-chlorophenylpiperazine and fenfluramine in patients and healthy volunteers. *Archives of General Psychiatry*, 1992, *49*, 21–28.

Hollander, E., DelGiudice-Asch, G., Simon, L., Schmeidler, J., Cartwright, C., DeCarla, C. M., Kwon, J., Cunningham-Rundles, C., Chapman, F., and Zabriskie, J. B. B lymphocyte antigen D8/17 and repetitive behaviors in autism. *American Journal of Psychiatry*, 1999, *156*, 317–320.

Hollander, E., Schiffman, E., Cohen, B., Rivera-Stein, M. A., Rosen, W., Gorman, J. M., Fyer, A. J., Papp, L., and Liebowitz, M. R. Signs of central nervous system dysfunction in obsessive-compulsive disorder. *Archives of General Psychiatry*, 1990, *47*, 27–32.

Hollister, J. M., Laing, P., and Mednick, S. A. Rhesus incompatibility as a risk factor for schizophrenia in male adults. *Archives of General Psychiatry*, 1996, *53*, 19–24.

Hollup, S. A., Molden, S., Donnett, J. G., Moser, M. B., and Moser, E. I. Place fields of rat hippocampal pyramidal cells and spatial learning in the watermaze. *European Journal of Neuroscience*, 2001, *13*, 1197–1208.

Holmes, G. The cerebellum of man. *Brain*, 1939, *62*, 21–30.

Honda, T., and Semba, K. Serotonergic synaptic input to cholinergic neurons in the rat mesopontine tegmentum. *Brain Research*, 1994, *647*, 299–306.

Hong, C. C. H., Jin, Y., Potkin, S. G., Buchsbaum, M. S., Wu, J., Callaghan, G. M., Nudelman, K. L., and Gillin, J. C. Language in dreaming and regional EEG alpha-power. *Sleep,* 1996, *19,* 232–235.

Hopf, H. C., Mueller-Forell, W., and Hopf, N. J. Localization of emotional and volitional facial paresis. *Neurology,* 1992, *42,* 1918–1923.

Horikoshi, T., Asari, Y., Watanabe, A., Nagaseki, Y., Nukui, H., Sasaki, H., and Komiya, K. Music alexia in a patient with mild pure alexia: Disturbed visual perception of nonverbal meaningful figures. *Cortex,* 1997, *33,* 187–194.

Horne, J. A. A review of the biological effects of total sleep deprivation in man. *Biological Psychology,* 1978, *7,* 55–102.

Horne, J. A., and Minard, A. Sleep and sleepiness following a behaviourally "active" day. *Ergonomics,* 1985, *28,* 567–575.

Horner, P. H., and Gage, F. H. Regenerating the damaged central nervous system. *Nature,* 2000, *407,* 963–970.

Horowitz, R. M., and Gentili, B. Dihydrochalcone sweeteners. In *Symposium: Sweeteners,* edited by G. E. Inglett. Westport, Conn.: Avi Publishing, 1974.

Horowitz, T. S., Cade, B. E., Wolfe, J. M., and Czeisler, C. A. Efficacy of bright light and sleep/darkness scheduling in alleviating circadian maladaptation to night work. *American Journal of Physiology,* 2001, *281,* E384–E391.

Horton, J. C., and Hubel, D. H. Cytochrome oxidase stain preferentially labels intersection of ocular dominance and vertical orientation columns in macaque striate cortex. *Society for Neuroscience Abstracts,* 1980, *6,* 315.

Howard, G., Wagenknecht, L. E., Cai, J., Cooper, L., Kraut, M. A., and Toole, J. F. Cigarette smoking and other risk factors for silent cerebral infarction in the general population. *Stroke,* 1998, *29,* 913–917.

Howland, J. G., Taepavarapruk, P., and Phillips, A. G. Glutamate receptor-dependent modulation of dopamine efflux in the nucleus accumbens by basolateral, but not central, nucleus of the amygdala in ras. *Journal of Neuroscience,* 2002, *22,* 1137–1145.

Hubel, D. H., and Wiesel, T. N. Functional architecture of macaque monkey visual cortex. *Proceedings of the Royal Society of London,* 1977, *198,* 1–59.

Hubel, D. H., and Wiesel, T. N. Brain mechanisms of vision. *Scientific American,* 1979, *241,* 150–162.

Hublin, C. Narcolepsy: Current drug-treatment options. *CNS Drugs,* 1996, *5,* 426–436.

Hudspeth, A. J. Mechanoelectrical transduction by hair cells in the acousticolateralis sensory system. *Annual Review of Neuroscience,* 1983, *6,* 187–215.

Hudspeth, A. J., and Gillespie, P. G. Pulling springs to tune transduction: Adaptation by hair cells. *Neuron,* 1994, *12,* 1–9.

Huerta, P. T., and Lisman, J. E. Synaptic plasticity during the cholinergic theta-frequency oscillation in vitro. *Hippocampus,* 1996, *6,* 58–61.

Huestis, M. A., Gorelick, D. A., Heishman, S. J., Preston, K. L., Nelson, R. A., Moolchan, E. T., and Frank, R. A. Blockade of effects of smoked marijuana by the CB1-selective cannabinoid receptor antagonist SR131716. *Archives of General Psychiatry,* 2001, *58,* 322–328.

Hughes, J., Smith, T. W., Kosterlitz, H. W., Fothergill, L. A., Morgan, B. A., and Moris, H. R. Identification of two related pentapeptides from the brain with potent opiate agonist activity. *Nature,* 1975, *258,* 577–579.

Hughes, J. R., Gust, S. W., Skoog, K., Keenan, R. M., and Fenwick, J. W. Symptoms of tobacco withdrawal: A replication and extension. *Archives of General Psychiatry,* 1989, *14,* 577–580.

Hull, E. M. Dopaminergic influences on male rat sexual behavior. In *Neurobiological Effects of Sex Steroid Hormones,* edited by P. E. Micevych and R. P. Hammer. Cambridge, England: Cambridge University Press, 1995.

Hulshoff Pol, H. E., Schnack, H. G., Bertens, M. G. B. C., van Haren, N. E. M., Staal, W. G., Baaré, W. F. C., and Kahn, R. S. Volume changes in gray matter in patients with schizophrenia. *American Journal of Psychiatry,* 2002, *159,* 244–250.

Humm, J. L., Lambert, K. G., and Kinsley, C. H. Paucity of c-fos expression in the medial preoptic area of prenatally stressed male rats following exposure to sexually receptive females. *Brain Research Bulletin,* 1995, *37,* 363–368.

Humphrey, A. L., and Hendrickson, A. E. Radial zones of high metabolic activity in squirrel monkey striate cortex. *Society for Neuroscience Abstracts,* 1980, *6,* 315.

Humphreys, G. W., Donnelly, N., and Riddoch, M. J. Expression is computed separately from facial identity, and it is computed separately for moving and static faces: Neuropsychological evidence. *Neuropsychologia,* 1993, *31,* 173–181.

Hungs, M., and Mignot, E. Hypocretin/orexin, sleep and narcolepsy. *Bioessays,* 2001, *23,* 397–408.

Hunt, D. M., Dulai, K. S., Cowing, J. A., Julliot, C., Mollon, J. D., Bowmaker, J. K., Li, W.-H., and Hewett-Emmett, D. Molecular evolution of trichromacy in primates. *Vision Research,* 1998, *38,* 3299–3306.

Huszar, D., Lynch, C. A., Fairchild-Huntress, V., Dunmore, J. H., Fang, Q., Berkemeier, L. R., Gu, W., Kesterson, R. A., Boston, B. A., Cone, R. D., Smith, F. J., Campfield, L. A., Burn, P., and Lee, F. *Cell,* 1997, *88,* 131–141.

Huttunen, M. O., and Niskanen, P. Prenatal loss of father and psychiatric disorders. *Archives of General Psychiatry,* 1978, *35,* 429–431.

Hwa, J. J., Ghibaudi, L., Gao, J., and Parker, E. M. Central melanocortin system modulates energy intake and expenditure of obese and lean Zucker rats. *American Journal of Physiology,* 2001, *281,* R444–R451.

Hyman, S. E. Addiction to cocaine and amphetamine. *Neuron,* 1996a, *16,* 901–904.

Hyman, S. E. Shaking out the cause of addiction. *Science,* 1996b, *273,* 611–612.

Hyman, S. E., and Malenka, R. C. Addiction and the brain: The neurobiology of compulsion and its persistence. *Nature Reviews: Neuroscience,* 2001, *2,* 695–703.

Iacoboni, M., Woods, R. P., Brass, M., Bekkering, H., Mazziotta, J. C., and Rizzolatti, G. Cortical mechanisms of human imitation. *Science,* 1999, *286,* 2526–2528.

Ibuka, N., and Kawamura, H. Loss of circadian rhythm in sleep-wakefulness cycle in the rat by suprachiasmatic nucleus lesions. *Brain Research,* 1975, *96,* 76–81.

Iggo, A., and Andres, K. H. Morphology of cutaneous receptors. *Annual Review of Neuroscience,* 1982, *5,* 1–32.

Ihnat, R., White, N. R., and Barfield, R. J. Pup's broadband vocalizations and maternal behavior in the rat. *Behavioral Processes,* 1995, *33,* 257–272.

Iijima, M., Arisaka, O., Minamoto, F., and Arai, Y. Sex differences in children's free drawings: A study on girls with congenital adrenal hyperplasia. *Hormones and Behavior,* 2001, *20,* 99–104.

Ikonomidou, C., Bittigau, P., Ishimaru, M. J., Wozniak, D. F., Koch, C., Genz, K., Price, M. T., Stefovska, V., Hörster, F., Tenkova, T., Dikranian, K., and Olney, J. W. Ethanol-induced apoptotic neurodegeneration and fetal alcohol syndrome. *Science,* 2000, *287,* 1056–1060.

Imaki, T., Shibasaki, T., Hotta, M., and Demura, H. Early induction of c-fos precedes increased expression of corticotropin-releasing factor messenger ribonucleic acid in the paraventricular nucleus after immobilization stress. *Endocrinology,* 1992, *131,* 240–246.

Imperato, A., and Di Chiara, G. Preferential stimulation of dopamine-release in the accumbens of freely moving rats by ethanol. *Journal of Pharmacology and Experimental Therapeutics,* 1986, *239,* 219–228.

Imperato, A., Scrocco, M. G., Bacchi, S., and Angelucci, L. NMDA receptors and in vivo dopamine release in the nucleus accumbens and caudatus. *European Journal of Pharmacology,* 1990, *187,* 555–556.

Ingelfinger, F. J. The late effects of total and subtotal gastrectomy. *New England Journal of Medicine,* 1944, *231,* 321–327.

Inoue, M., Koyanagi, T., Nakahara, H., Hara, K., Hori, E., and Nakano, H. Functional development of human eye movement in utero assessed quantitatively with real time ultrasound. *American Journal of Obstetrics and Gynecology,* 1986, *155,* 170–174.

Institute of Medicine (U.S.). *Sleeping Pills, Insomnia, and Medical Practice.* Washington, D.C.: National Academy of Sciences, 1979.

Inui, T., Otsu, Y., Tanaka, S., Okada, T., Nishizawa, S., and Konishi, J. A functional MRI analysis of comprehension processes of Japanese sentences. *Neuroreport,* 1998, *9,* 3325–3328.

Isenberg, N., Silbersweig, D., Engelien, A., Emmerich, S., Malavade, K., Beattie, B., Leon, A. C., and Stern, E. Linguistic threat activates the human amygdala. *Proceedings of the National Academy of Sciences, USA.,* 1999, *96,* 10456–10459.

Iwai, E., and Mishkin, M. Further evidence of the locus of the visual area in the temporal lobe of the monkey. *Experimental Neurology,* 1969, *25,* 585–594.

Iwata, M. Kanji versus Kana: Neuropsychological correlates of the Japanese writing system. *Trends in Neurosciences,* 1984, *7,* 290–293.

Izard, C. E. *The Face of Emotion.* New York: Appleton-Century-Crofts, 1971.

Jackson, M. E., Frost, A. S., and Moghaddam, B. Stimulation of prefrontal cortex at physiologically relevant frequencies inhibits dopamine release in the nucleus accumbens. *Journal of Neurochemistry,* 2001, *78,* 920–923.

Jacob, S., and McClintock, M. K. Psychological state and mood effects of steroidal chemosignals in women and men. *Hormones and Behavior,* 2000, *37,* 57–78.

Jacobs, B., Schall, M., and Scheibel, A. B. A quantitative dendritic analysis of Wernicke's area in humans. II. Gender, hemispheric, and environmental factors. *Journal of Comparative Neurology,* 1993, *327,* 97–111.

Jacobs, B. L., and Fornal, C. A. Activity of serotonergic neurons in behaving animals. *Neuropsychopharmacology,* 1999, *21,* 9S–15S.

Jacobs, B. L., and McGinty, D. J. Participation of the amygdala in complex stimulus recognition and behavioral inhibition: Evidence from unit studies. *Brain Research,* 1972, *36,* 431–436.

Jacobs, B. L., Wilkinson, L. O., and Fornal, C. A. The role of brain serotonin: A neurophysiologic perspective. *Neuropsychopharmacology,* 1990, *3,* 473–479.

Jacobs, G. H. Primate photopigments and primate color vision. *Proceedings of the National Academy of Sciences, USA,* 1996, *93,* 577–581.

Jacobsen, C. F., Wolfe, J. B., and Jackson, T. A. An experimental analysis of the functions of the frontal association areas in primates. *Journal of Nervous and Mental Disorders,* 1935, *82,* 1–14.

Jakobson, L. S., Archibald, Y. M., Carey, D., and Goodale, M. A. A kinematic analysis of reaching and grasping movements in a patient recovering from optic ataxia. *Neuropsychologia,* 1991, *29,* 803–809.

James, W. What is an emotion? *Mind,* 1884, *9,* 188–205.

James, W. P. T., and Trayhurn, P. Thermogenesis and obesity. *British Medical Bulletin,* 1981, *27,* 43–48.

Jang, T., Singer, A. G., and O'Connell, R. J. Induction of c-*fos* in hamster accessory olfactory bulbs by natural and cloned aphrodisin. *Neuroreport,* 2001, *12,* 449–452.

Jaramillo, F. Signal transduction in hair cells and its regulation by calcium. *Neuron,* 1995, *15,* 1227–1230.

Jasper, J. H., and Tessier, J. Acetylcholine liberation from cerebral cortex during paradoxical (REM) sleep. *Science,* 1969, *172,* 601–602.

Javitt, D. C., and Zukin, S. R. Recent advances in the phencyclidine model of schizophrenia. *American Journal of Psychiatry,* 1991, *148,* 1301–1308.

Jaynes, J. The problem of animate motion in the seventeenth century. *Journal of the History of Ideas,* 1970, *6,* 219–234.

Jeffery, K. J., and O'Keefe, J. M. Learned interaction of visual and idiothetic cues in the control of place field orientation. *Experimental Brain Research,* 1999, *127,* 151–161.

Jeffress, L. A. A place theory of sound localization. *Journal of Comparative and Physiological Psychology,* 1948, *41,* 35–39.

Jensen, T., Genefke, I., and Hyldebrandt, N. Cerebral atrophy in young torture victims. *New England Journal of Medicine,* 1982, *307,* 1341.

Jentsch, J. D., Redmond, D. E., Elsworth, J. D., Taylor, J. R., Youngren, K. D., and Roth, R. H. Enduring cognitive deficits and cortical dopamine dysfunction in monkeys after long-term administration of phencyclidine. *Science,* 1997, *277,* 953–955.

Jentsch, J. D., Roth, R. H., and Taylor, J. R. Object retrieval/detour deficits in monkeys produced by prior subchronic phencyclidine administration: Evidence for cognitive impulsivity. *Biological Psychiatry,* 2000, *48,* 415–424.

Jentsch, J. D., Taylor, J. R., Elsworth, J. D., Redmond, D. E., and Roth, R. H. Altered frontal cortical dopaminergic transmission in monkeys after subchronic phencyclidine exposure: Involvement in frontostriatal cognitive deficits. *Neuroscience,* 1999, *90,* 823–832.

Jentsch, J. D., Tran, A., Taylor, J. R., and Roth, R. H. Prefrontal cortical involvement in phencyclidine-induced activation of the mesolimbic dopamine system: Behavioral and neurochemical evidence. *Psychopharmacology*, 1998, *138*, 89–95.

Jeste, D. V., Del Carmen, R., Lohr, J. B., and Wyatt, R. J. Did schizophrenia exist before the eighteenth century? *Comprehensive Psychiatry*, 1985, *26*, 493–503.

Jewett, D. C., Cleary, J., Levine, A. S., Schaal, D. W., and Thompson, T. Effects of neuropeptide Y on food-reinforced behavior in satiated rats. *Pharmacology, Biochemistry, and Behavior*, 1992, *42*, 207–212.

Jiang, C. L., and Hunt, J. N. The relation between freely chosen meals and body habitus. *American Journal of Clinical Nutrition*, 1983, *38*, 32–40.

Johanson, A., Gustafson, L., Passant, U., Risberg, J., Smith, G., Warkentin, S., and Tucker, D. Brain function in spider phobia. *Psychiatry Research: Neuroimaging Section*, 1998, *84*, 101–111.

Johansson, G. Visual perception of biological motion and a model for its analysis. *Perception and Psychophysics*, 1973, *14*, 201–211.

Johnson, A. K., and Edwards, G. L. The neuroendocrinology of thirst: Afferent signaling and mechanisms of central integration. *Current Topics in Neuroendocrinology*, 1990, *10*, 149–190.

Johnson, B. A., and Ait-Daoud, N. Neuropharmacological treatments for alcoholism: Scientific basis and clinical findings. *Psychopharmacology (Berlin)*, 2000, *149*, 327–344.

Johnson, M. K., and Raye, C. L. False memories and confabulation. *Trends in Cognitive Sciences*, 1998, *2*, 137–145.

Johnson, M. K., Kim, J. K., and Risse, G. Do alcoholic Korsakoff's syndrome patients acquire affective reactions? *Journal of Experimental Psychology: Learning, Memory, and Cognition*, 1985, *11*, 22–36.

Johnson, S. W., and North, R. A. Opioids excite dopamine neurons by hyperpolarization of local interneurons. *Journal of Neuroscience*, 1992, *12*, 483–488.

Jonas, P., Bischofberger, J., and Sandkühler, J. Corelease of two fast neurotransmitters at a central synapse. *Science*, 1998, *281*, 419–523.

Jones, B. E. Influence of the brainstem reticular formation, including intrinsic monoaminergic and cholinergic neurons, on forebrain mechanisms of sleep and waking. In *The Diencephalon and Sleep*, edited by M. Mancia and G. Marini. New York: Raven Press, 1990.

Jones, B. E., and Beaudet, A. Distribution of acetylcholine and catecholamine neurons in the cat brain stem studied by choline acetyltransferase and tyrosine hydroxylase immunohistochemistry. *Journal of Comparative Neurology*, 1987, *261*, 15–32.

Jones, D. T., and Reed, R. R. G$_{olf}$: An olfactory neuron specific-G protein involved in odorant signal transduction. *Science*, 1989, *244*, 790–795.

Jones, M. B., and Szatmari, P. Stoppage rules and genetic studies of autism. *Journal of Autism and Developmental Disorders*, 1988, *18*, 31–40.

Jones, S. S., Collins, K., and Hong, H.-W. An audience effect on smile production in 10-month-old infants. *Psychological Science*, 1991, *2*, 45–49.

Jope, R. S., Song, L., Li, P. P., Young, L. T., Kish, S. J., Pacheco, M. A., and Warsh, J. J. The phosphoinositide signal transduction system is impaired in bipolar affective disorder brain. *Journal of Neurochemistry*, 1996, *66*, 2402–2409.

Jornales, V. E., Jakob, M., Zamani, A., and Vaina, L. M. Deficits on complex motion perception, spatial discrimination and eye-movements in a patient with bilateral occipital-parietal lesions. *Investigative Opthalamolgy and Visual Science*, 1997, *38*, S72.

Jouvet, M. The role of monoamines and acetylcholine-containing neurons in the regulation of the sleep-waking cycle. *Ergebnisse der Physiologie*, 1972, *64*, 166–307.

Jürgens, U. Neuronal control of mammalian vocalization, with special reference to the squirrel monkey. *Naturwissenschaften*, 1998, *85*, 376–388.

Kaas, J. H., and Collins, C. E. The organization of sensory cortex. *Current Opinion in Neurobiology*, 2001, *11*, 498–504.

Kaas, J. H., Hackett, T. A., and Tramo, M. J. Auditory processing in primate cerebral cortex. *Current Opinion in Neurobiology*, 1999, *9*, 164–170.

Kahler, A., Geary, N., Eckel, L. A., Campfield, L. A., Smith, F. J., and Langhans, W. Chronic administration of OB protein decreases food intake by selectively reducing meal size in male rats. *American Journal of Physiology*, 1998, *275*, R180–R185.

Kakei, S., Hoffman, D. S., and Strick, P. L. Direction of action is represented in the ventral premotor cortex. *Nature Neuroscience*, 2001, *4*, 1020–1025.

Kales, A., Scharf, M. B., Kales, J. D., and Soldatos, C. R. Rebound insomnia: A potential hazard following withdrawal of certain benzodiazepines. *Journal of the American Medical Association*, 1979, *241*, 1692–1695.

Kales, A., Tan, T.-L., Kollar, E. J., Naitoh, P., Preston, T. A., and Malmstrom, E. J. Sleep patterns following 205 hours of sleep deprivation. *Psychosomatic Medicine*, 1970, *32*, 189–200.

Kalin, N. H., Sherman, J. E., and Takahashi, L. K. Antagonism of endogenous CRG systems attenuates stress-induced freezing behavior in rats. *Brain Research*, 1988, *457*, 130–135.

Kanamori, N., Sakai, K., and Jouvet, M. Neuronal activity specific to paradoxical sleep in the ventromedial medullary reticular formation of unrestrained cats. *Brain Research*, 1980, *189*, 251–255.

Kanner, L. Autistic disturbances of affective contact. *The Nervous Child*, 1943, *2*, 217–250.

Kanwisher, N., McDermott, J., and Chun, M. M. The fusiform face area: A module in human extrastriate cortex specialized for face perception. *Journal of Neuroscience*, 1997, *17*, 4302–4311.

Kapp, B. S., Frysinger, R. C., Gallagher, M., and Haselton, J. R. Amygdala central nucleus lesions: Effect on heart rate conditioning in the rabbit. *Physiology and Behavior*, 1979, *23*, 1109–1117.

Kapp, B. S., Gallagher, M., Applegate, C. D., and Frysinger, R. C. The amygdala central nucleus: Contributions to conditioned cardiovascular responding during aversive Pavlovian conditioning in the rabbit. In *Conditioning: Representation of Involved Neural Functions*, edited by C. D. Woody. New York: Plenum Press, 1982.

Kaptchuk, T. J. Acupuncture: Theory, efficacy, and practice. *Annals of Internal Medicine*, 2002, *136*, 374–383.

Kapur, N., Thompson, S., Cook, P., Lang, D., and Brice, J. Anterograde but not retrograde memory loss following combined mammillary body and medial thalamic lesions. *Neuropsychologia*, 1996, *34*, 1–8.

Karacan, I., Salis, P. J., and Williams, R. L. The role of the sleep laboratory in diagnosis and treatment of impotence. In *Sleep*

Disorders: Diagnosis and Treatment, edited by R. J. Williams and I. Karacan. New York: John Wiley & Sons, 1978.

Karacan, I., Williams, R. L., Finley, W. W., and Hursch, C. J. The effects of naps on nocturnal sleep: Influence on the need for stage 1 REM and stage 4 sleep. *Biological Psychiatry,* 1970, *2,* 391–399.

Karlson, P., and Luscher, M. "Pheromones": A new term for a class of biologically active substances. *Nature,* 1959, *183,* 55–56.

Kartsounis, L. D., Rudge, P., and Stevens, J. M. Bilateral lesions of CA1 and CA2 fields of the hippocampus are sufficient to cause a severe amnesic syndrome in humans. *Journal of Neurology, Neurosurgery and Psychiatry,* 1995, *59,* 95–98.

Kasper, S., Rogers, S. L. B., Yancey, A., Schulz, P. M., Skwerer, R. G., and Rosenthal, N. E. Phototherapy in individuals with and without subsyndromal seasonal affective disorder. *Archives of General Psychiatry,* 1989a, *46,* 837–844.

Kasper, S., Wehr, T. A., Bartko, J. J., Gaist, P. A., and Rosenthal, N. E. Epidemiological findings of seasonal changes in mood and behavior: A telephone survey of Montgomery County, Maryland. *Archives of General Psychiatry,* 1989b, *46,* 823–833.

Katayama, Y., DeWitt, D. S., Becker, D. P., and Hayes, R. L. Behavioral evidence for cholinoceptive pontine inhibitory area: Descending control of spinal motor output and sensory input. *Brain Research,* 1986, *296,* 241–262.

Kattler, H., Dijk, D. J., and Borbély, A. A. Effect of unilateral somatosensory stimulation prior to sleep on the sleep EEG in humans. *Journal of Sleep Research,* 1994, *3,* 159–164.

Kavaliers, M. Brief exposure to a natural predator, the short-tailed weasel, induces benzodiazepine-sensitive analgesia in white-footed mice. *Physiology and Behavior,* 1985, *43,* 187–193.

Kawamura, M., Hirayama, K., and Yamamoto, H. Different interhemispheric transfer of kanji and kana writing evidenced by a case with left unilateral agraphia without apraxia. *Brain,* 1989, *112,* 1011–1018.

Kawauchi, H., Kawazoe, I., Tsubokawa, M., Kishida, M., and Baker, B. I. Charracterization of melanin-concentrating hormone in chum salmon pituitaries. *Nature,* 1983, *305,* 321–323.

Kayama, Y., Ohta, M., and Jodo, E. Firing of "possibly" cholinergic neurons in the rat laterodorsal tegmental nucleus during sleep and wakefulness. *Brain Research,* 1992, *569,* 210–220.

Kaye, W. H., Nagata, T., Weltzin, T. E., Hsu, G., Sokol, M. S., McConaha, C., Plotnicov, K. H., Weise, J., and Deep, D. Double-blind placebo-controlled administration of fluoxetine in restricting- and restricting-purging-type anorexia nervosa. *Biological Psychiatry,* 2001, *49,* 644–652.

Kaye, W. H. Neuropeptide abnormalities in anorexia nervosa. *Psychiatry Research,* 1996, *62,* 65–74.

Kaye, W. H., Berrettini, W., Gwirtsman, H., and George, D. T. Altered cerebrospinal fluid neuropeptide Y and peptide YY immunoreactivity in anorexia and bulimia nervosa. *Archives of General Psychiatry,* 1990, *47,* 548–556.

Keller, S. E., Weiss, J. M., Schleifer, S. J., Miller, N. E., and Stein, M. Stress-induced suppression of immunity in adrenalectomized rats. *Science,* 1983, *221,* 1301–1304.

Kelley, A. E., Smith-Roe, S. L., and Holahan, M. R. Response-reinforcement learning is dependent on N-methyl-D-aspartate receptor activation in the nucleus accumbens core. *Proceedings of the National Academy of Science, USA,* 1997, *94,* 12174–12179.

Kelso, S. R., Ganong, A. H., and Brown, T. H. Hebbian synapses in hippocampus. *Proceedings of the National Academy of Sciences, USA,* 1986, *83,* 5326–5330.

Kelsoe, J. R., Ginns, E. I., Egeland, J. A., Gerhard, D. S., Goldstein, A. M., Bale, S. J., Pauls, D. L., Long, R. T., Kidd, K. K., Conte, G., Housman, D. E., and Paul, S. M. Re-evaluation of the linkage relationship between chromosome 11p loci and the gene for bipolar affective disorder in the Old Order Amish. *Nature,* 1989, *342,* 238–243.

Kendell, R. E., and Adams, W. Unexplained fluctuations in the risk for schizophrenia by month and year of birth. *British Journal of Psychiatry,* 1991, *158,* 758–763.

Kennard, C., Lawden, M., Morland, A. B., and Ruddock, K. H. Colour identification and colour constancy are impaired in a patient with incomplete achromatopsia associated with prestriate cortical lesions. *Proceedings of the Royal Society of London (B),* 1995, *260,* 169–175.

Kentros, C., Hargreaves, E., Hawkins, R. D., Kandel, E. T., Shapiro, M., and Muller, R. V. Abolition of long-term stability of new hippocampal place cell maps by NMDA receptor blockade. *Science,* 1998, *280,* 2121–2126.

Kertesz, A. Anatomy of jargon. In *Jargonaphasia,* edited by J. Brown. New York: Academic Press, 1981.

Kestler, L. P., Walker, E., and Vega, E. M. Dopamine receptors in the brains of schizophrenia patients: A meta-analysis of the findings. *Behavioral Pharmacology,* 2001, *12,* 355–371.

Kety, S. S., Rosenthal, D., Wender, P. H., and Schulsinger, K. F. The types and prevalence of mental illness in the biological and adoptive families of adopted schizophrenics. In *The Transmission of Schizophrenia,* edited by D. Rosenthal and S. S. Kety. New York: Pergamon Press, 1968.

Kety, S. S., Wender, P. H., Jacobsen, B., Ingraham, L. J., Jansson, L., Faber, B., and Kinney, D. K. Mental illness in the biological and adoptive relatives of schizophrenic adoptees: Replication of the Copenhagen Study in the rest of Denmark. *Archives of General Psychiatry,* 1994, *51,* 442–455.

Keverne, E. B., and de la Riva, C. Pheromones in mice: Reciprocal interactions between the nose and brain. *Nature,* 1982, *296,* 148–150.

Kew, J. J. M., Ridding, M. C., Rothwell, J. C., Passingham, R. E., Leigh, P. N., Sooriakumaran, S., Frackowiak, R. S. G., and Brooks, D. J. Reorganization of cortical blood flow and transcranial magnetic stimulation maps in human subjects after upper limb amputation. *Journal of Neurophysiology,* 1994, *72,* 2517–2524.

Khanna, S., and Channabasavanna, S. Toward a classification of compulsions in obsessive compulsive neurosis. *Psychopathology,* 1987, *20,* 23–28.

Khateb, A., Fort, P., Pegna, A., Jones, B. E., and Muhlethaler, M. Cholinergic nucleus basalis neurons are excited by histamine in vitro. *Neuroscience,* 1995, *69,* 495–506.

Kiang, N. Y.-S. *Discharge Patterns of Single Fibers in the Cat's Auditory Nerve.* Cambridge, Mass.: MIT Press, 1965.

Kiecolt-Glaser, J. K., Glaser, R., Shuttleworth, E. C., Dyer, C. S., Ogrocki, P., and Speicher, C. E. Chronic stress and immunity in family caregivers of Alzheimer's disease victims. *Psychosomatic Medicine,* 1987, *49,* 523–535.

Kiecolt-Glaser, J. K., Marucha, P. T., Malarkey, W. B., Mercado, A. M., and Glaser, R. Slowing of wound healing by psychological stress. *Lancet*, 1995, *346*, 1194–1196.

Kim, J. J., Lee, H. J., Han, J. S., and Packard, M. G. Amygdala is critical for stress-induced modulation of hippocampal long-term potentiation and learning. *Journal of Neuroscience*, 2001, *21*, 5222–5228.

King, G. A., Fitzhugh, E. C., Bassett, D. R., McLaughlin, J. E., Strath, S. J., Swartz, A. M., and Thompson, D. L. Relationship of leisure-time physical activity and occupational activity to the prevalence of obesity. *International Journal of Obesity*, 2001, *25*, 606–612.

Kingston, K., Szmukler, G., Andrewes, D., Tress, B., and Desmond, P. Neuropsychological and structural brain changes in anorexia nervosa before and after refeeding. *Psychological Medicine*, 1996, *26*, 15–28.

Kinnamon, S. C., and Cummings, T. A. Chemosensory transduction mechanisms in taste. *Annual Review of Physiology*, 1992, *54*, 715–731.

Kinnamon, S. C., Dionne, V. E., and Beam, K. G. Apical localization of K$^+$ channels in taste cells provides the basis for sour taste transduction. *Proceedings of the National Academy of Sciences, USA*, 1988, *85*, 7023–7027.

Kinney, D. K., Yurgelun-Todd, D. A., Levy, D. L., Medoff, D., Lajonchere, C. M., and Radford-Paregol, M. Obstetrical complications in patients with bipolar disorder and their siblings. *Psychiatry Research*, 1993, *48*, 47–56.

Kinney, D. K., Yurgelun-Todd, D. A., Tohen, M., and Tramer, S. Pre- and perinatal complications and risk for bipolar disorder: A retrospective study. *Journal of Affective Disorders*, 1998, *50*, 117–124.

Kinon, B. J., and Lieberman, J. A. Mechanisms of action of atypical antipsychotic drugs: A critical analysis. *Psychopharmacology*, 1996, *124*, 2–34.

Kinsey, A. C., Pomeroy, W. B., Martin, C. E., and Gebhard, P. H. *Sexual Behavior in the Human Female*. Philadelphia: Saunders, 1943.

Kinsley, C., and Svare, B. Prenatal stress reduces intermale aggression in mice. *Physiology and Behavior*, 1986, *36*, 783–785.

Kinsley, C. H., Konen, C. M., Miele, L., Ghiraldi, L., and Svare, B. Intrauterine position modulates maternal behaviors in female mice. *Physiology and Behavior*, 1986, *36*, 793–799.

Kirkpatrick, B., Kim, J. W., and Insel, T. R. Limbic system fos expression associated with paternal behavior. *Brain Research*, 1994, *658*, 112–118.

Kitada, T., Asakawa, S., Hattori, N., Matsumine, H., Yamamura, Y., Minoshima, S., Yokochi, M., Mizuno, Y., and Shimizu, N. Mutations in the parkin gene cause autosomal recessive juvenile parkinsonism. *Nature*, 1998, *392*, 605–608.

Kitchener, E. G., Hodges, J. R., and McCarthy, R. Acquisition of post-morbid vocabulary and semantic facts in the absence of episodic memory. *Brain*, 1998, *121*, 1313–1327.

Klein, E., Kreinin, I., Chistyakov, A., Koren, D., Mecz, L., Marmur, S., Ben-Shachar, D., and Feinsod, M. Therapeutic efficacy of right prefrontal slow repetitive transcranial magnetic stimulation in major depression: A double-blind controlled study. *Archives of General Psychiatry*, 1999, *56*, 315–320.

Kleitman, N. The nature of dreaming. In *The Nature of Sleep*, edited by G. E. W. Wolstenholme and M. O'Connor. London: J. & A. Churchill, 1961.

Kleitman, N. Basic rest-activity cycle—22 years later. *Sleep*, 1982, *4*, 311–317.

Klukowski, G., and Harley, C. W. Locus coeruleus activation induces perforant path-evoked population spike potentiation in the dentate gyrus of awake rat. *Experimental Brain Research*, 1994, *102*, 165–170.

Knapp, P. H., Levy, E. M., Giorgi, R. G., Black, P. H., Fox, B. H., and Heeren, T. C. Short-term immunological effects of induced emotion. *Psychosomatic Medicine*, 1992, *54*, 133–148.

Knebelmann, B., Boussin, L., Guerrier, D., Legeai, L., Kahn, A., Josso, N., and Picard, J.-Y. Anti-Muellerian hormone Bruxelles: A nonsense mutation associated with the persistent Muellerian duct syndrome. *Proceedings of the National Academy of Sciences, USA*, 1991, *88*, 3767–3771.

Knecht, S., Drager, B., Deppe, M., Bobe, L., Lohmann, H. Floel, A., Ringelstein, R. B., and Henningsen, H. Handedness and hemispheric language dominance in healthy humans. *Brain*, 2000, *123*, 2512–2518.

Knowlton, B. J., Mangels, J. A., and Squire, L. R. A neostriatal habit learning system in humans. *Science*, 1996, *273*, 1399–1402.

Knutson, B., Adams, C. M., Fong, G. W., and Hommer, D. Anticipation of increasing monetary reward selectively recruits nucleus accumbens. *Journal of Neuroscience*, 2001, *21*, RC159 (1–5).

Kobatake, E., Tanaka, K., and Tamori, Y. Long-term learning changes the stimulus selectivity of cells in the inferotemporal cortex of adult monkeys. *Neuroscience Research*, 1992, *S17*, S237.

Kodama, T., Takahashi, Y., and Honda, Y. Enhancement of acetylcholine release during paradoxical sleep in the dorsal tegmental field of the cat brain stem. *Neuroscience Letters*, 1990, *114*, 277–282.

Koenen, K. C., Harley, R., Lyons, M. J., Wolfe, J., Simpson, J. C., Goldberg, J., Eisen, S. A., and Tsuang, M. A twin registry study of familial and individual risk factors for trauma exposure and posttraumatic stress disorder. *Journal of Nervous and Mental Disease*, 2002, *190*, 209–218.

Kojima, M., Hosoda, H., Date, Y., Nakazato, M., Matsuo, H., and Kangawa, K. Ghrelin is a growth-hormone–releasing acylated peptide from stomach. *Nature*, 1999, *402*, 656–660.

Komatsu, H. Neural representation of color in the inferior temporal cortex of the macaque monkey. In *The Association Cortex*, edited by H. Sakata, A. Mikami, and J. M. Fuster. Amsterdam: Harwood Academic Publishers, 1997.

Komatsu, H. Mechanisms of central color vision. *Current Opinion in Neurobiology*, 1998, *8*, 503–508.

Komisaruk, B. R., and Larsson, K. Suppression of a spinal and a cranial nerve reflex by vaginal or rectal probing in rats. *Brain Research*, 1971, *35*, 231–235.

Komisaruk, B. R., and Steinman, J. L. Genital stimulation as a trigger for neuroendocrine and behavioral control of reproduction. *Annals of the New York Academy of Sciences*, 1987, *474*, 64–75.

Koob, G. F. Drug addiction: The yin and yang of hedonic homeostasis. *Neuron*, 1996, *16*, 893–896.

Koob, G. F. Stress, corticotropin-releasing factor, and drug addiction. *Annals of the New York Academy of Science*, 1999, *897*, 27–45.

Koob, G. F., and Le Moal, M. Drug addiction, dysregulation of reward, and allostasis. *Neuropsychopharmacology,* 2001, *24,* 97–124.

Koob, G. F., Sanna, P. P., and Bloom, F. E. Neuroscience of addiction, *Neuron,* 1998, *21,* 467–476.

Koob, G. F., Thatcher-Britton, K., Britton, D., Roberts, D. C. S., and Bloom, F. E. Destruction of the locus coeruleus or the dorsal NE bundle does not alter the release of punished responding by ethanol and chlordiazepoxide. *Physiology and Behavior,* 1984, *33,* 479–485.

Koopman, P. Gonad development: Signals for sex. *Current Biology,* 2001, *11,* R481–R483.

Kopelman, M. D. The Korsakoff syndrome. *British Journal of Psychiatry,* 1995, *166,* 154–173.

Kornhuber, H. H. Cerebral cortex, cerebellum, and basal ganglia: An introduction to their motor functions. In *The Neurosciences: Third Study Program,* edited by F. O. Schmitt and F. G. Worden. Cambridge, Mass.: MIT Press, 1974.

Kortegaard, L. S., Hoerder, K., Joergensen, J., Gillberg, C., and Kyvik, K. O. A preliminary population-based twin study of self-reported eating disorder. *Psychological Medicine,* 2001, *31,* 361–365.

Kosten, T. A., Miserendino, M. J. D., and Kehoe, P. Enhanced acquisition of cocaine self-administration in adult rats with neonatal isolation stress experience. *Brain Research,* 2000, *875,* 44–50.

Kourtzi, A., and Kanwisher, N. Activation in human MT/MST by static images with implied motion. *Journal of Cognitive Neuroscience,* 2000, *12,* 48–55.

Kovács, G., Vogels, R., and Orban, G. A. Selectivity of macaque inferior temporal neurons for partially occluded shapes. *Journal of Neuroscience,* 1995, *15,* 1984–1997.

Koylu, E. O., Couceyro, P. R., Lambert, P. D., and Kuhar, M. J. Cocaine- and amphetamine-regulated transcript peptide immunohistochemical localization in the rat brain. *Journal of Comparative Neurology,* 1998, *391,* 115–132.

Kozlowski, L. T., and Cutting, J. E. Recognizing the sex of a walker from a dynamic point-light display. *Perception and Psychophysics,* 1977, *21,* 575–580.

Kramer, F. M., Jeffery, R. W., Forster, J. L., and Snell, M. K. Long-term follow-up of behavioral treatment for obesity: Patterns of weight regain among men and women. *International Journal of Obesity,* 1989, *13,* 123–136.

Kramer, M. S., Cutler, N., Feighner, J., Shrivastava, R., Carman, J., Sramek, J. J., Reines, S. A., Liu, G., Snavely, D., Wyatt-Knowles, E., Hale, J. J., Mills, S. G., MacCoss, M., Swain, C. J., Harrison, T., Hill, R. G., Hefti, F., Scolnick, E. M., Cascieri, M. A., Chicchi, G. G., Sadowski, S., Williams, A. R., Hewson, L., Smith, D., Carlson, E. J., Hargreaves, R. J., and Rupniak, N. M. Distinct mechanism for antidepressant activity by blockade of central substance P receptors. *Science,* 1998, *281,* 1640–1645.

Kranzler, H. R., Modesto-Lowe, V., and Nuwayser, E. S. Sustained-release naltrexone for alcoholism treatment: A preliminary study. *Alcoholism: Clinical and Experimental Research,* 1998, *22,* 1074–1079.

Krause, K. H., Dresel, S. H., Krause, J., Kung, H. F., and Tatsch, K. Increased striatal dopamine transporter in adult patients with attention deficit hyperactivity disorder: Effects of methylphenidate as measured by single photon emission computed tomography. *Neuroscience Letters,* 2000, *285,* 107–110.

Kraut, R. E., and Johnston, R. Social and emotional messages of smiling: An ethological approach. *Journal of Personality and Social Psychology,* 1979, *37,* 1539–1553.

Kress, M., and Zeilhofer, H. U. Capsaicin, protons and heat: New excitement about nociceptors. *Trends in Pharmacological Science,* 1999, *20,* 112–118.

Kristensen, P., Judge, M. E., Thim, L. Ribel, U. Christjansen, K. N., Wulff, B. S., Clausen, J. T., Jensen, P. B., Madsen, O. D., Vrang, N., Larsen, P. J., and Hastrup, S. Hypothalamic CART is a new anorectic peptide regulated by leptin. *Nature,* 1998, *393,* 72–76.

Krubitzer, L. Constructing the neocortex: Influences on the pattern of organization in mammals. In *Brain and Mind: Evolutionary Perspectives,* edited by M. S. Gazzaniga and J. S. Altmann. Strasbourg, France: Human Frontier Science Program, 1998.

Krukoff, T. L., MacTavish, D., and Jhamandas, J. H. Hypertensive rats exhibit heightened expression of corticotropin-releasing factor in activated central neurons in response to restraint stress. *Molecular Brain Research,* 1999, *65,* 70–79.

Kuffler, S. W. Neurons in the retina. Organization, inhibition and excitation problems. *Cold Spring Harbor Symposium on Quantitative Biology,* 1952, *17,* 281–292.

Kuffler, S. W. Discharge patterns and functional organization of mammalian retina. *Journal of Neurophysiology,* 1953, *16,* 37–68.

Kumar, K., Wyant, G. M., and Nath, R. Deep brain stimulation for control of intractable pain in humans, present and future: A ten-year follow-up. *Neurosurgery,* 1990, *26,* 774–782.

Kumar, M. V., Shimokawa, T., Nagy, T. R., and Lane, M. D. Differential effects of a centrally acting fatty acid synthase inhibitor in lean and obese mice. *Proceedings of the National Academy of Science, USA,* 2002, *99,* 1921–1925.

Kunos, G., and Batkai, S. Novel physiologic functions of endocannabinoids as revealed through the use of mutant mice. *Neurochemical Research,* 2001, *26,* 1015–1021.

Kunugi, H., Nanko, S., and Murray, R. M. Obstetric complications and schizophrenia: Prenatal underdevelopment and subsequent neurodevelopmental impairment. *British Journal of Psychiatry,* 2001, *40,* S25–S29.

Kupfer, D. J. REM latency: A psychobiologic marker for primary depressive disease. *Biological Psychiatry,* 1976, *11,* 159–174.

Kupfer, D. J., Ehlers, C. L., Frank, E., Grochocinski, V. J., McEachran, A. B., and Buhari, A. Persistent effects of antidepressants: EEG sleep studies in depressed patients during maintenance treatment. *Biological Psychiatry,* 1994, *35,* 781–793.

Kurata, K., and Hoffman, D. S. Differential effects of muscimol microinjection into dorsal and ventral aspects of the premotor cortex of monkeys. *Journal of Neurophysiology,* 1994, *71,* 1151–1164.

Kurihara, K. Recent progress in taste receptor mechanisms. In *Umami: A Basic Taste,* edited by Y. Kawamura and M. R. Kare. New York: Dekker, 1987.

Kuriki, S., Mori, T., and Hirata, Y. Motor planning center for speech articulation in the normal human brain. *Neuroreport,* 1999, *10,* 765–769.

LaBar, K. S., LeDoux, J. E., Spencer, D. D., and Phelps, E. A. Impaired fear conditioning following unilateral temporal lobectomy in humans. *Journal of Neuroscience,* 1995, *15,* 6846–6855.

Lahti, A. C., Weiler, M. A., Michaelidis, T., Parwani, A., and Tamminga, C. A. Effects of ketamine in normal and schizophrenic volunteers. *Neuropsychopharmacology*, 2001, *25*, 455–467.

Laitinen, L. V., Bergenheim, A. T., and Hariz, M. I. Leksell's posteroventral pallidotomy in the treatment of Parkinson's disease. *Journal of Neurosurgery*, 1992, *76*, 53–61.

Lange, C. G. *Über Gemüthsbewegungen*. Leipzig, Germany: T. Thomas, 1887.

Langston, J. W., and Ballard, P. Parkinsonism induced by 1-methyl-4-phenyl-1,2,3,6-tetrahydropyridine (MPTP): Implications for treatment and the pathogenesis of Parkinson's disease. *Canadian Journal of Neurological Science*, 1984, *11* (1 Suppl.), 160–165.

Langston, J. W., Ballard, P., Tetrud, J., and Irwin, I. Chronic parkinsonism in humans due to a product of meperidine-analog synthesis. *Science*, 1983, *219*, 979–980.

Langston, J. W., Irwin, I., Langston, E. B., and Forno, L. S. Pargyline prevents MPTP-induced parkinsonism in primates. *Science*, 1984, *225*, 1480–1482.

Laruelle, M., Abi-Dargham, A., Van Dyck, C. H., Gil, R., D'Souza, C. D., Erdos, J., McCance, E., Rosenblatt, W., Fingado, C., Zoghbi, S. S., Baldwin, R. M., Seibyl, J. P., Krystal, J. H., Charney, D. S., and Innis, R. B. Single photon emission computerized tomography imaging of amphetamine-induced dopamine release in drug-free schizophrenic subjects. *Proceedings of the National Academy of Sciences, USA*, 1996, *93*, 9235–9240.

Laschet, U. Antiandrogen in the treatment of sex offenders: Mode of action and therapeutic outcome. In *Contemporary Sexual Behavior: Critical Issues in the 1970's*, edited by J. Zubin and J. Money. Baltimore: Johns Hopkins University Press, 1973.

Lavoie, B., and Parent, A. Immunohistochemical study of the serotoninergic innervation of the basal ganglia in the squirrel monkey. *Journal of Comparative Neurology*, 1990, *299*, 1–16.

Lavond, D. G., Kim, J. J., and Thompson, R. F. Mammalian brain substrates of aversive classical conditioning. *Annual Review of Psychology*, 1993, *44*, 317–342.

Lawrence, D. G., and Kuypers, G. J. M. The functional organization of the motor system in the monkey. I. The effects of bilateral pyramidal lesions. *Brain*, 1968a, *91*, 1–14.

Lawrence, D. G., and Kuypers, G. J. M. The functional organization of the motor system in the monkey. II. The effects of lesions of the descending brain-stem pathways. *Brain*, 1968b, *91*, 15–36.

Lê, S., Cardebat, D., Boulanouar, K., Hénaff, M. A., Michel, F., Milner, D., Dkjkerman, C., Puel, M., and Démonet, J.-F. Seeing, since childhood, without ventral stream: A behavioural study. *Brain*, 2002, *125*, 58–74.

Leblanc, R., Meyer, E., Bub, D., Zatorre, R. J., and Evans, A. C. Language localization with activation positron emission tomography scanning. *Neurosurgery*, 1992, *31*, 369–373.

LeDoux, J. E. Brain mechanisms of emotion and emotional learning. *Current Opinion in Neurobiology*, 1992, *2*, 191–197.

LeDoux, J. E. Emotion: Clues from the brain. *Annual Review of Psychology*, 1995, *46*, 209–235.

LeDoux, J. E., Iwata, J., Cicchetti, P., and Reis, D. J. Different projections of the central amygdaloid nucleus mediate autonomic and behavioral correlates of conditioned fear. *Journal of Neuroscience*, 1988, *8*, 2517–2529.

LeDoux, J. E., Sakaguchi, A., and Reis, D. J. Subcortical efferent projections of the medial geniculate nucleus mediate emotional responses conditioned to acoustic stimuli. *Journal of Neuroscience*, 1984, *4*, 683–698.

Lee, D. W., Smith, G. T., Tramontin, A. D., Soma, K. K., Brenowitz, E. A., and Clayton, N. S. Hippocampal volume does not change seasonally in a non food-storing songbird. *Neuroreport*, 2001, *12*, 1925–1928.

Lee, J.-H., and Beitz, A. J. Electroacupuncture modifies the expression of c-fos in the spinal cord induced by noxious stimulation. *Brain Research*, 1992, *577*, 80–91.

Lehman, C. D., Rodin, J., McEwen, B., and Brinton, R. Impact of environmental stress on the expression of insulin-dependent diabetes mellitus. *Behavioral Neuroscience*, 1991, *105*, 241–245.

Lehman, M. N., and Winans, S. S. Vomeronasal and olfactory pathways to the amygdala controlling male hamster sexual behavior: Autoradiographic and behavioral analyses. *Brain Research*, 1982, *240*, 27–41.

Lehman, M. N., Silver, R., Gladstone, W. R., Kahn, R. M., Gibson, M., and Bittman, E. L. Circadian rhythmicity restored by neural transplant: Immunocytochemical characterization with the host brain. *Journal of Neuroscience*, 1987, *7*, 1626–1638.

Leibenluft, E., and Wehr, T. A. Is sleep deprivation useful in the treatment of depression? *American Journal of Psychiatry*, 1992, *149*, 159–168.

Leibowitz, S. F., Weiss, G. F., and Suh, J. S. Medial hypothalamic nuclei mediate serotonin's inhibitory effect on feeding behavior. *Pharmacology, Biochemistry, and Behavior*, 1990, *37*, 735–742.

Lejeune, F., Gobert, A., and Millan, M. J. The selective neurokinin (NK_1) antagonist, GR205,171, stereospecifically enhances mesocortical dopaminergic transmission in the rat: A combined dialysis and electrophysiological study. *Brain Research*, 2002, *935*, 134–139.

Leon, M. Plasticity of olfactory output circuits related to early olfactory learning. *Trends in Neurosciences*, 1987, *10*, 434–438.

Leonard, C. M., Rolls, E. T., Wilson, F. A. W., and Baylis, G. C. Neurons in the amygdala of the monkey with responses selective for faces. *Behavioral Brain Research*, 1985, *15*, 159–176.

Leonard, C. S., Kerman, I., Blaha, G., Taveras, E., and Taylor, B. Interdigitation of nitric oxide synthase-, tyrosine hydroxylase-, and serotonin-containing neurons in and around the laterodorsal and pedunculopontine tegmental nuclei of the guinea pig. *Journal of Comparative Neurology*, 1995, *362*, 411–432.

Leonard, H. L., Lenane, M. C., Swedo, S. E., Rettew, D. C., and Rapoport, J. L. A double-blind comparison of clomipramine and desipramine treatment of severe onychophagia (nail biting). *Archives of General Psychiatry*, 1992b, *48*, 821–827.

Leonard, H. L., Lenane, M. C., Swedo, S. E., Rettew, D. C., Gershon, E. S. and Rapoport, J. L. Tics and Tourette's disorder: a 2- to 7-year follow-up of 54 obsessive-compulsive children. *American Journal of Psychiatry*, 1992a, *149*, 1244–1251.

Leonard, H. L., Swedo, S. E., Rapoport, J. L., Koby, E. V., Lenane, M. C., Cheslow, D. L., and Hamburger, S. D. Treatment of obsessive-compulsive disorder with clomipramine and desipramine in children and adolescents: A double-blind crossover comparison. *Archives of General Psychiatry*, 1989, *46*, 1088–1092.

Leonard, H. L., Swedo, S. E., Rapoport, J. L., Rickler, K. C., Topol, D., Lee, S., and Rettew, D. Tourette syndrome and obsessive-compulsive disorder. *Advances in Neurology*, 1992c, *58*, 83–93.

Leor, J., Poole, W. K., and Kloner, R. A. Sudden cardiac death triggered by an earthquake. *New England Journal of Medicine*, 1996, *334*, 413–419.

LeSauter, J., and Silver, R. Localization of a suprachiasmatic nucleus subrevion regulating locomotor rhythmicity. *Journal of Neuroscience*, 1999, *19*, 5574–5585.

Lesch, K. P., and Mossner, R. Genetically driven variation in serotonin uptake: Is there a link to affective spectrum, neurodevelopmental, and neurodegenerative disorders? *Biological Psychiatry*, 1988, *44*, 179–192.

Leshner, A. I. Molecular mechanisms of cocaine addiction. *The New England Journal of Medicine*, 1996, *335*, 128–129.

Lesser, R. Selective preservation of oral spelling without semantics in a case of multi-infarct dementia. *Cortex*, 1989, *25*, 239–250.

Lester, L. S., and Fanselow, M. S. Exposure to a cat produces opioid analgesia in rats. *Behavioral Neuroscience*, 1985, *99*, 756–759.

LeVay, S. A difference in hypothalamic structure between heterosexual and homosexual men. *Science*, 1991, *253*, 1034–1037.

Levenson, R. W., Ekman, P., and Friesen, W. V. Voluntary facial action generates emotion-specific autonomic nervous system activity. *Psychophysiology*, 1990, *27*, 363–384.

Levine, J. A., Eberhardt, N. L., and Jensen, M. D. Role of nonexercise activity thermogenesis in resistance to fat gain in humans. *Science*, 1999, *283*, 212–214.

Levine, J. A., Schleusner, S. J., and Jensen, M. D. Energy expenditure of nonexercise activity. *American Journal of Clinical Nutrition*, 2000, *72*, 1451–1454.

Levine, J. D., Gordon, N. C., and Fields, H. L. The role of endorphins in placebo analgesia. In *Advances in Pain Research and Therapy, Vol. 3*, edited by J. J. Bonica, J. C. Liebeskind, and D. Albe-Fessard. New York: Raven Press, 1979.

Levy, F., Hay, D. A., McStephen, M., Wood, C., and Waldman, I. Attention-deficit hyperactivity disorder: a category or a continuum? Genetic analysis of a large-scale twin study. *Journal of the American Academy of Child and Adolescent Psychiatry*, 1997, *36*, 737–744.

Lewin, R. Big first scored with nerve diseases. *Science*, 1989, *245*, 467–468.

Lewis, D. A., and Levitt, P. Schizophrenia as a disorder of neurodevelopment. *Annual Review of Neuroscience*, 2002, *25*, 409–432.

Lewis, D. A., and Smith, R. E. Steroid-induced psychiatric syndromes: A report of 14 cases and a review of the literature. *Journal of the Affective Disorders*, 1983, *5*, 19–32.

Lewis, E. B. Clusters of master control genes regulate the development of higher organisms. *Journal of the American Medical Association*, 1992, *267*, 1524–1531.

Lewy, A. J., Bauer, V. K., Cutler, N. L., Sack, R. L., Ahmed, S., Thomas, K. H., Blood, M. L., Latham Jackson, J. M. Morning vs evening light treatment of patients with winter depression. *Archives of General Psychiatry*, 1998, *55*, 890–896.

Li, B.-H., and Rowland, N. E. Effects of vagotomy on cholecystokinin- and dexfenfluramine-induced fos-like immunoreactivity in the rat brain. *Brain Research Bulletin*, 1995, *37*, 589–593.

Li, B.-H., Spector, A. C., and Rowland, N. E. Reversal of dexfenfluramine-induced anorexia and c-Fos/c-Jun expression by lesion in the lateral parabrachial nucleus. *Brain Research*, 1994, *640*, 255–267.

Li, C., Chen, P., and Smith, M. S. Identification of neuronal input to the arcuate nucleus (ARH) activated during lactation: Implications in the activation of neuropeptide Y neurons. *Brain Research*, 1999, *824*, 267–276.

Li, J. Y., Finniss, S., Yang, Y. K., Zeng, Q., Qu, S. Y., Barsh, G., Dickinson, C., and Gantz, I. Agouti-related protein-like immunoreactivity: characterization of release from hypothalamic tissue and presence in serum. *Endocrinology*, 2000, *141*, 1942–1950.

Li, S.-H., Lam, S., Cheng, A. L., and Li, X.-J. Intranuclear huntingtin increases the expression of caspase-1 and induces apoptosis. *Human Molecular Genetics*, 2000, *9*, 2859–2867.

Li, T.-K., Lumeng, L., and Doolittle, D. P. Selective breeding for alcohol preference and associated responses. *Behavioral Genetics*, 1993, *23*, 163–170.

Li, X.-J., Sharp, A. H., Li, S.-H., Dawson, T. M., Snyder, S. H., and Ross, C. A. Huntingtin-associated protein (HAP1): Discrete neuronal localizations in the brain resemble those of neuronal nitric oxide synthase. *Proceedings of the National Academy of Sciences, USA*, 1996, *93*, 4839–4844.

Li., X.-J., Sharp, A. H., Nucifora, F. C., Schilling, G., Lanahan, A., Worley, P., Snyder, S. H., and Ross, C. A. A huntingtin-associated protein enriched in brain with implications for pathology. *Nature*, 1995, *378*, 398–402.

Li, X.-W., Li, T.-K., and Froelich, J. C. Enhanced sensitivity of the nucleus accumbens proenkephalin system to alcohol in rats selectively bred for alcohol preference. *Brain Research*, 1998, *794*, 35–47.

Liao, D., Hessler, N. A., and Malinow, R. Activation of postsynaptically silent synapses during pairing-induced LTP in CA1 region of hippocampal slice. *Nature*, 1995, *375*, 400–404.

Lidberg, L., Asberg, M., and Sundqvist-Stensman, U. B. 5-Hydroxyindoleacetic acid levels in attempted suicides who have killed their children. *Lancet*, 1984, *2*, 928.

Lidberg, L., Tuck, J. R., Asberg, M., Scalia-Tomba, G. P., and Bertilsson, L. Homicide, suicide and CSF 5-HIAA. *Acta Psychiatrica Scandanavica*, 1985, *71*, 230–236.

Liljequist, S. The competitive NMDA receptor antagonist, CGP 39551, inhibits ethanol withdrawal seizures. *European Journal of Pharmacology*, 1991, *192*, 197–198.

Lin, J. S., Sakai, K., and Jouvet, M. Evidence for histaminergic arousal mechanisms in the hypothalamus of cat. *Neuropharmacology*, 1998, *27*, 111–122.

Lin, L., Faraco, J., Li, R., Kadotani, H., Rogers, W., Lin, X., Qiu, X., de Jong, P. J., Nishino, S., and Mignot, E. The sleep disorder canine narcolepsy is caused by a mutation in the hypocretin (orexin) receptor 2. *Cell*, 1999, *98*, 365–376.

Lindemann, B. Taste reception. *Physiological Reviews*, 1996, *76*, 719–766.

Links, J. M., Zubieta, J. K., Meltzer, C. G., Stumpf, M. J., and Frist, J. J. Influence of spatially heterogenous background activity on "hot object" quantitation in brain emission computed tomography. *Journal of Computer Assisted Tomography*, 1996, *20*, 680–687.

Liotti, M., Mayberg, H. S., McGinnis, S., Brannan, S. L., and Jerabek, P. Unmasking disease-specific cerebral blood flow abnormalities: Mood challenge in patients with remitted unipolar depression. *American Journal of Psychiatry*, 2002, *159*, 1830–1840.

Lisk, R. D., Pretlow, R. A., and Friedman, S. Hormonal stimulation necessary for elicitation of maternal nest-building in the mouse (*Mus musculus*). *Animal Behaviour*, 1969, *17*, 730–737.

Lisman, J. E., and Zhabotinsky, A. M. A model of synaptic memory: a CaMKII/PP1 switch that potentiates transmission by organizing an AMPA receptor anchoring assembly. *Neuron*, 2001, *31*, 191–201.

Liuzzi, F. J., and Lasek, R. J. Astrocytes block axonal regeneration in mammals by activating the physiological stop pathway. *Science*, 1987, *237*, 642–645.

Livingstone, M. S., and Hubel, D. Segregation of form, color, movement, and depth: Anatomy, physiology, and perception. *Science*, 1988, *240*, 740–749.

Livingstone, M. S., and Hubel, D. H. Anatomy and physiology of a color system in the primate visual cortex. *Journal of Neuroscience*, 1984, *4*, 309–356.

Livingstone, M. S., and Hubel, D. H. Psychophysical evidence for separate channels for the perception of form, color, movement, and depth. *Journal of Neuroscience*, 1987, *7*, 3416–3468.

Lledo, P. M., Hjelmstad, G. O., Mukherji, S., Soderling, T. R., Malenka, R. C., and Nicoll, R. A. Calcium/calmodulin-dependent kinase II and long-term potentiation enhance synaptic transmission by the same mechanism. *Proceedings of the National Academy of Scienc, USA*, 1995, *92*, 11175–11179.

Llorca, P. M., Chereau, I., Bayle, F. J., and Lancon, C. Tardive dyskinesias and antipsychotics: A review. *European Psychiatry*, 2002, *17*, 129–138.

Loeb, G. E. Cochlear prosthetics. *Annual Review of Neuroscience*, 1990, *13*, 357–371.

Loewenstein, W. R., and Mendelson, M. Components of receptor adaptation in a Pacinian corpuscle. *Journal of Physiology (London)*, 1965, *177*, 377–397.

Loftus, T. M., Jaworsky, D. E., Frehywot, G. L., Townsend, C. A., Ronnett, G. V., Lane, M. D., and Kuhajda, F. P. Reduced food intake and body weight in mice treated with fatty acid synthase inhibitors. *Science*, 2000, *288*, 2379–2381.

Logan, F. A. Decision making by rats: Delay versus amount of reward. *Journal of Comparative and Physiological Psychology*, 1965, *59*, 1–12.

Logothetis, N. K., Pauls, J., and Poggio, T. Shape representation in the inferior temporal cortex of monkeys. *Current Biology*, 1995, *5*, 552–563.

Lohr, J. B., Caligiuri, M. P., Edson, R., Lavori, P., Adler, L. A., Rotrosen, J., and Hitzemann, R. Treatment predictors of extrapyramidal side effects in patients with tardive dyskinesia: Results from Veterans Affairs Cooperative Study 394. *Journal of Clinical Psychopharmacology*, 2002, *22*, 196–200.

Lohse, P., Lohse, P., Chahrokh-Zadeh, S., and Seidel, D. The acid lipase family: Three enzymes, one highly conserved gene structure. *Journal of Lipid Research*, 1997, *38*, 880–891.

Lømo, T. Frequency potentiation of excitatory synaptic activity in the dentate area of the hippocampal formation. *Acta Physiologica Scandinavica*, 1966, *68* (Suppl. 227), 128.

Lopez, M., Seoane, L., Garcia, M. C., Lago, F., Casanueva, F. F., Senaris, R., and Dieguez, C. Leptin regulation of prepro-orexin and orexin receptor mRNA levels in the hypothalamus. *Biochemistry and Biophysics Research Communications*, 2000, *269*, 41–45.

Loscher, W., Annies, R., and Honack, D. The N-methyl-D-aspartate receptor antagonist MK-801 induces increases in dopamine and serotonin metabolism in several brain regions of rats. *Neuroscience Letters*, 1991, *128*, 191–194.

Lowe, T. L., Tanaka, K., Seashore, M. R., Young, J. G., and Cohen, D. J. Detection of phenylketonuria in autistic and psychotic children. *Journal of the American Medical Association*, 1980, *243*, 126–128.

Lu, E., Willard, D., Patel, I. R., Kadwell, S., Overton, L., Kost, T., Luther, M., Chen, W., Woychik, R. P., and Wilkison, W. O. Agouti protein is an antagonist of the melanocyte-stimulating-hormone receptor. *Nature*, 1994, *371*, 799–802.

Lu, J., Greco, M. A., Shiromani, P., and Saper, C. B. Effect of lesions of the ventrolateral preoptic nucleus on NREM and REM sleep. *Journal of Neuroscience*, 2000, *20*, 3830–3842.

Lu, J., Zhang, Y.-H., Chou, T. C., Gaus, S. E., Elmquist, J. K., Shiromani, P., and Saper, C. B. Contrasting effects of ibotenate lesions of the paraventricular nucleus and subparaventricular zone on sleep-wake cycle and temperature regulation. *Journal of Neuroscience*, 2001, *21*, 4864–4874.

Lu, X.-C. M., and Slotnick, B. M. Olfaction in rats with extensive lesions of the olfactory bulbs: Implications for odor coding. *Neuroscience*, 1998, *84*, 849–866.

Lucas, B. K., Ormandy, C. J., Binart, N., Bridges, R. S., and Kelley, P. A. Null mutation of the prolactin receptor gene produces a defect in maternal behavior. *Endocrinology*, 1998, *139*, 4102–4107.

Lupien, S., Lecours, A. R., Schwartz, G., Sharma, S., Hauger, R. L., Meaney, M. J., and Nair, N. P. V. Longitudinal study of basal cortixol levels in healthy elderly subjects: Evidence for subgroups. *Neurobiology of Aging*, 1996, *17*, 95–105.

Luppino, G., Matelli, M., Camarda, R., and Rizzolatti, G. Corticocortical connections of area F3 (SMA proper) and area F6 (pre-SMA) in the macaque monkey. *Journal of Comparative Neurology*, 1993, *228*, 114–140.

Luquin, M. R., Montoro, R. J., Guillen, J., Saldise, L., Insausti, R., Del Rio, J., and Lopez-Barneo, J. Recovery of chronic parkinsonian monkeys by autotransplants of carotid-body cell aggregates into the putamen. *Neuron*, 1999, *22*, 743–750.

Lüscher, C., Xia, H., Beattie, E. C., Carroll, R. C., von Zastrow, M., Malenka, R. C., and Nicoll, R. A. Role of AMPA receptor cycling in synaptic transmission and plasticity. *Neuron*, 1999, *24*, 649–658.

Lutz, T. A., Diener, M., and Scharrer, E. Introportal mercaptoacetate infusion increases afferent activity in the common hepatic vagus branch of the rat. *American Journal of Physiology*, 1997, *273*, R442–R445.

Luzzi, S., Pucci, E., Di Bella, P., and Piccirilli, M. Topographical disorientation consequent to amnesia of spatial location in a patient with right parahippocampal damage. *Cortex*, 2000, *36*, 427–434.

Lydic, R., Baghdoyan, H. A., Hibbard, L., Bonyak, E. V., DeJoseph, M. R., and Hawkins, R. A. Regional brain glucose metabolism is altered during rapid eye movement sleep in the cat: A preliminary study. *Journal of Comparative Neurology,* 1991, *304,* 517–529.

Lydic, R., McCarley, R. W., and Hobson, J. A. The time-course of dorsal raphe discharge, PGO waves and muscle tone averaged across multiple sleep cycles. *Brain Research,* 1983, *274,* 365–370.

Lydon, J. P., DeMayo, F. J., Funk, C. R., Mani, S. K., Hughes, A. R., Montgomery, C. A., Shyamala, G., Conneely, O. M., and O'Malley, B. W. Mice lacking progesterone receptor exhibit pleitropic reproductive abnormalities. *Genes and Development,* 1995, *15,* 2266–2278.

Lynch, G., Larson, J., Kelso, S., Barrionuevo, G., and Schottler, F. Intracellular injections of EGTA block induction of long-term potentiation. *Nature,* 1984, *305,* 719–721.

Lynch, G., Larson, J., Staubli, U., and Granger, R. Variants of synaptic potentiation and different types of memory operations in hippocampus and related structures. In *Memory: Organization and Locus of Change,* edited by L. R. Squire, N. M. Weinberger, G. Lynch, and J. L. McGaugh. New York: Oxford University Press, 1991.

Lytton, W. W., and Brust, J. C. M. Direct dyslexia: Preserved oral reading of real words in Wernicke's aphasia. *Brain,* 1989, *112,* 583–594.

Ma, W., Miao, Z., and Novotny, M. Induction of estrus in grouped female mice (*Mus domesticus*) by synthetic analogs of preputial gland constituents. *Chemical Senses,* 1999, *24,* 289–293.

MacKinnon, D. F., Jamison, K. R., and DePaulo, J. R. Genetics of manic depressive illness. *Annual Review of Neuroscience,* 1997, *20,* 355–373.

MacLean, H. E., Warne, G. L., and Zajac, J. D. Defects of androgen receptor function: From sex reversal to motor-neuron disease. *Molecular and cellular Endocrinology,* 1995, *112,* 133–141.

MacLean, P. D. Psychosomatic disease and the "visceral brain": Recent developments bearing on the Papez theory of emotion. *Psychosomatic Medicine,* 1949, *11,* 338–353.

Madden, P. A. F., Heath, A. C., Rosenthal, N. E., and Martin, N. G. Seasonal changes in mood and behavior: The role of genetic factors. *Archives of General Psychiatry,* 1996, *53,* 47–55.

Madsen, P. L., Holm, S., Vorstrup, S., Friberg, L., Lassen, N. A., and Wildschiodtz, G. Human regional cerebral blood flow during rapid-eye-movement sleep. *Journal of Cerebral Blood Flow and Metabolism,* 1991, *11,* 502–507.

Magee, J. C., and Johnston, D. A synaptically controlled, associative signal for Hebbian plasticity in hippocampal neurons. *Science,* 1997, *275,* 209–213.

Magert, H. J., Cieslak, A., Alkan, O., Luscher, B., Kauffels, W., and Forssmann, W. G. The golden hamster aphrodisin gene: Structure, expression in parotid glands of female animals, and comparison with a similar murine gene. *Journal of Biological Chemistry,* 1999, *274,* 444–450.

Magistretti, P. J., Pellerin, L., Rothman, D. L., and Shulman, R. G. Energy on demand. *Science,* 1999, *283,* 496–497.

Maguire, E. A., Burgess, N., Donnett, J. G., Frackowiak, R. S. J., Frith, C. D., and O'Keefe, J. Knowing where and getting there: A human navigation network. *Science,* 1998, *280,* 921–924.

Maguire, E. A., Frackowiak, R. S. J., and Frith, C. D. Recalling routes around London: Activation of the right hippocampus in taxi drivers. *Journal of Neuroscience,* 1997, *17,* 7103–7110.

Maguire, E. A., Gadian, D. G., Johnsrude, I. S., Good, C. D., Ashburner, J., Frackowiak, R. S. J., and Frith, C. D. Navigation-related structural change in the hippocampi of taxi drivers. *Proceedings of the National Academy of Science, USA,* 2000, *97,* 4398–4403.

Maier, S. F., Drugan, R. C., and Grau, J. W. Controllability, coping behavior, and stress-induced analgesia in the rat. *Pain,* 1982, *12,* 47–56.

Maksay, G., and Ticku, M. K. Dissociation of [^{35}S]t-butylbicyclophosphorothionate binding differentiates convulsant and depressant drugs that modulate GABAergic transmission. *Journal of Neurochemistry,* 1985, *44,* 480–486.

Malach, R., Reppas, J. B., Benson, R. R., Kwong, K. K., Jiang, H., Kennedy, W. A., Ledden, P. J., Brady, T. J., Rosen, B. R., and Tootell, R. B. H. Object-related activity revealed by functional magnetic resonance imaging in human occipital cortex. *Proceedings of the National Academy of Sciences, USA,* 1995, *92,* 8135–8139.

Malamut, B. L., Graff-Radford, N., Chawluk, J., Grossman, R. I., and Gur, R. C. Memory in a case of bilateral thalamic infarction. *Neurology,* 1992, *42,* 163–169.

Malaspina, D., Harlap, S., Fenning, S., Heiman, D., Nahon, D., Feldman, D., and Susser, E. S. Advancing paternal age and the risk of schizophrenia. *Archives of General Psychiatry,* 2001, *58,* 361–367.

Maldonado, R., and Koob, G. F. Destruction of the locus coeruleus decreases physical signs of opiate withdrawal. *Brain Research,* 1993, *605,* 128–138.

Maldonado, R., and Rodriguez de Fonseca, F. Cannabinoid addiction: Behavioral models and neural correlates. *Journal of Neuroscience,* 2002, *22,* 3326–3331.

Maldonado, R., Blendy, J. A., Tzavara, E., Gass, P., Roques, B. P., Hanoune, J., and Schutz, G. Reduction of morphine abstinence in mice with a mutation in the gene encoding CREB. *Science,* 1996, *273,* 657–659.

Maldonado, R., Stinus, L., Gold, L. H., and Koob, G. F. Role of different brain structures in the expression of the physical morphine-withdrawal syndrome. *Journal of Pharmacology and Experimental Therapeutics,* 1992, *261,* 669–677.

Malhotra, A. K., Adler, C. M., Kennison, S. D., Elman, I., Pickar, D., and Breier, A. Clozapine blunts N-methyl-D-aspartate antagonist-induced psychosis: a study with ketamine. *Biological Psychiatry,* 1997, *42,* 664–668.

Malizia, A. L., Cunningham, V. J., Bell, C. J., Liddle, P. F., Jones, T., and Nutt, D. J. Decreased brain GABA(A)-benzodiazepine receptor binding in panic disorder: Preliminary results from a quantitative PET study. *Archives of General Psychiatry,* 1998, *55,* 15–20.

Mallow, G. K. The relationship between aggression and cycle stage in adult female rhesus monkeys (*Macaca mulatta*). *Dissertation Abstracts,* 1979, *39,* 3194.

Malnic, B., Hirono, J., Sato, T., and Buck, L. B. Combinatorial receptor codes for odors. *Cell,* 1999, *96,* 713–723.

Malsbury, C. W. Facilitation of male rat copulatory behavior by electrical stimulation of the medial preoptic area. *Physiology and Behavior,* 1971, *7,* 797–805.

Manji, H. K., and Lenox, R. H. Lithium: A molecular transducer of mood-stabilization in the treatment of bipolar disorder. *Neuropsychopharmacology*, 1998, *19*, 161–166.

Manji, H. K., Moore, G. J., and Chen, G. Bipolar disorder: Leads from the molecular and cellular mechanisms of action of mood stabilisers. *British Journal of Psychiatry*, 2001, *178* (Suppl. 41), S107–S109.

Mann, J. J., Malone, K. M., Diehl, D. J., Perel, J., Nichols, T. E., and Mintun, M. A. positron emission tomographic imaging of serotonin activation effects on prefrontal cortex in healthy volunteers. *Journal of Cerebral Blood Flow and Metabolism*, 1996, *16*, 418–426.

Mann, M. A., Konen, C., and Svare, B. The role of progesterone in pregnancy-induced aggression in mice. *Hormones and Behavior*, 1984, *18*, 140–160.

Manning, L., and Campbell, R. Optic aphasia with spared action naming: A description and possible loci of impairment. *Neuropsychologia*, 1992, *30*, 587–592.

Mansvelder, H. D., and McGehee, D. S. Long-term potentiation of excitatory inputs to brain reward areas by nicotine. *Neuron*, 2000, *27*, 349–357.

Mantyh, P. W. Connections of midbrain periaqueductal gray in the monkey. II. Descending efferent projections. *Journal of Neurophysiology*, 1983, *49*, 582–594.

Mantyh, P. W., Hunt, S. P., and Maggio, J. E. Substance P receptors: Localization by light microscopic autoradiography in rat brain using [3H]SP as the radioligand. *Brain Research*, 1984, *30*, 147–165.

Mantzoros, C., Flier, J. S., Lesem, M. D., Brewerton, T. D., and Jimerson, D. C. Cerebrospinal fluid leptin in anorexia nervosa: Correlation with nutritional status and potential role in resistance to weight gain. *Journal of Clinical Endocrinology and Metabolism*, 1997, *82*, 1845–1851.

Manuck, S. B., Kaplan, J. R., and Clarkson, T. B. Behaviorally-induced heart rate reactivity and atherosclerosis in cynomolgous monkeys. *Psychosomatic Medicine*, 1983, *45*, 95–108.

Manuck, S. B., Kaplan, J. R., and Matthews, K. A. Behavioral antecedents of coronary heart disease and atherosclerosis. *Arteriosclerosis*, 1986, *6*, 1–14.

Maquet, P. Sleep function(s) and cerebral metabolism. *Behavioural Brain Research*, 1995, *69*, 75–83.

Maquet, P., Dive, D., Salmon, E., Sadzot, B., Franco, G., Poirrier, R., Von Frenckell, R., and Franck, G. Cerebral glucose utilization during sleep-wake cycle in man determined by positron emission tomography and [18F]2-fluoro-2-deoxy-D-glucose method. *Brain Research*, 1990, *513*, 136–143.

Marcotte, D. Use of topiramate, a new anti-epileptic as a mood stabilizer. *Journal of Affective Disorders*, 1998, *50*, 245–251.

Maren, S. Auditory fear conditioning increases CS-elicited spike firing in lateral amygdala neurons even after extensive overtraining. *European Journal of Neuroscience*, 2000, *12*, 4047–4054.

Maret, G., Testa, B., Jenner, P., el Tayar, N., and Carrupt, P. A. The MPTP story: MAO activates tetrahydropyridine derivatives to toxins causing parkinsonism. *Drug Metabolism Review*, 1990, *22*, 291–332.

Margolin, D. I., and Goodman-Schulman, R. Oral and written spelling impairments. In *Cognitive Neuropsychology in Clinical Prac-*

tice, edited by D. I. Margolin. New York: Oxford University Press, 1992.

Margolin, D. I., and Walker, J. A. Personal communication, 1981.

Margolin, D. I., Marcel, A. J., and Carlson, N. R. Common mechanisms in dysnomia and post-semantic surface dyslexia: Processing deficits and selective attention. In *Surface Dyslexia: Neuropsychological and Cognitive Studies of Phonological Reading*, edited by M. Coltheart. London: Lawrence Erlbaum Associates, 1985.

Marrocco, R. T., Witte, E. A., and Davidson, M. C. Arousal systems. *Current Opinion in Neurobiology*, 1994, *4*, 166–170.

Marshall, B. E., and Longnecker, D. E. General anesthetics. In *The Pharmacological Basis of Therapeutics*, edited by Goodman, L. S., Gilman, A., Rall, T. W., Nies, A. S., and Taylor, P. New York: Pergamon Press, 1990.

Marshall, J. C., and Newcombe, F. Patterns of paralexia: A psycholinguistic approach. *Journal of Psycholinguistic Research*, 1973, *2*, 175–199.

Marson, L. Central nervous system neurons identified after injection of pseudorabies virus into the rat clitoris. *Neuroscience Letters*, 1995, *190*, 41–44.

Marson, L., and McKenna, K. E. CNS cell groups involved in the control of the ishiocavernosus and bulbospongiosus muscles: A transneuronal tracing study using pseudorabies virus. *Journal of Comparative Neurology*, 1996, *374*, 161–179.

Martin, A., Wiggs, C. L., Ungerleider, L. G., and Haxby, J. V. Neural correlates of category-specific knowledge. *Nature*, 1996, *379*, 649–652.

Martin, P. R., White, A. J., Goodchild, A. K., Wilder, H. D., and Sefton, A. E. *European Journal of Neuroscience*, 1997, *9*, 1536–1541.

Martin-Santos, R., Bulbena, A., Porta, M., Gago, J., Molina, L., and Duro, J. C. Association between joint hypermobility syndrome and panic disorder. *American Journal of Psychiatry*, 1998, *155*, 1578–1583.

Mas, M. Neurobiological correlates of masculine sexual behavior. *Neuroscience and Biobehavioral Reviews*, 1995, *19*, 261–277.

Masland, R. H. Neuronal diversity in the retina. *Current Opinion in Neurobiology*, 2001, *11*, 431–436.

Mather, P., Nicolaïdis, S., and Booth, D. A. Compensatory and conditioned feeding responses to scheduled glucose infusions in the rat. *Nature*, 1978, *273*, 461–463.

Matsuda, L. A., Lolait, S. J., Brownstein, M. J., Young, A. C., and Bonner, T. I. Structure of a cannabinoid receptor and functional expression of the cloned cDNA. *Nature*, 1990, *346*, 561–564.

Matsunami, H., Montmayeur, J.-P., and Buck, L. B. A family of candidate taste receptors in human and mouse. *Nature*, 2000, *404*, 601–604.

Matteo, S., and Rissman, E. F. Increased sexual activity during the midcycle portion of the human menstrual cycle. *Hormones and Behavior*, 1984, *18*, 249 255.

Matthes, H. W. D., Maldonado, R., Simonin, F., Valverde, O., Slowe, S., Kitchen, I., Befort, K., Dierich, A., Le Meur, M., Dolle, P., Tzavara, E., Hanoune, J., Roques, B. P., and Kieffer, B. L. Loss of morphine-induced analgesia, reward effect and withdrawal symptoms in mice lacking the Mu-opioid-receptor gene. *Nature*, 1996, *383*, 819–823.

Matthews, D. B., Simson, P. E., and Best, P. J. Ethanol alters spatial processing of hippocampal place cells: A mechanism for impaired navigation when intoxicated. *Alcoholism: Clinical and Experimental Research,* 1996, *20,* 404–407.

Matuzawa, R. Colour naming and classification in a chimpanzee. *Journal of Human Evolution,* 1985, *14,* 283–291.

Maunsell, J. H. R. Functional visual streams. *Current Opinion in Neurobiology,* 1992, *2,* 506–510.

Mawson, A. R. Anorexia nervosa and the regulation of intake: A review. *Psychological Medicine,* 1974, *4,* 289–308.

Mayer, D. J., and Liebeskind, J. C. Pain reduction by focal electrical stimulation of the brain: An anatomical and behavioral analysis. *Brain Research,* 1974, *68,* 73–93.

Mayer, D. J., Price, D. D., Rafii, A., and Barber, J. Acupuncture hypalgesia: Evidence for activation of a central control system as a mechanism of action. In *Advances in Pain Research and Therapy, Vol. 1,* edited by J. J. Bonica and D. Albe-Fessard. New York: Raven Press, 1976.

Mazur, A. Hormones, aggression, and dominance in humans. In *Hormones and Aggressive Behavior,* edited by B. B. Svare. New York: Plenum Press, 1983.

Mazur, A., and Booth, A. Testosterone and dominance in men. *Behavioral and Brain Sciences,* 1998, *21,* 353–397.

Mazur, A., and Lamb, T. Testosterone, status, and mood in human males. *Hormones and Behavior,* 1980, *14,* 236–246.

McBride, W. J., Bodart, B., Lumeng, L., and Li, T. K. Association between low contents of dopamine and serotonin in the nucleus accumbens and high alcohol preference. *Alcoholism: Clinical and Experimental Research,* 1995, *19,* 1420–1422.

McBride, W. J., Murphy, J. M., Gatto, G. J., Levy, A. D., Lumeng, L., and Li, T.-K. Serotonin and dopamine systems regulating alcohol self-administration. *Alcohol and Alcoholism* (Suppl.), 1991, *1,* 411–416.

McCann, U. D., Wong, D. F., Yokoi, F., Villemagne, V., Dannls, R. F., and Ricaurte, G. A. Reduced striatal dopamine transporter density in abstinent methamphetamine and methcathinone users: Evidence from positron emossion tomography studies with [^{11}C]WIN-35,428. *Journal of Neuroscience,* 1998, *18,* 8417–8422.

McCarley, R. W., and Hobson, J. A. The form of dreams and the biology of sleep. In *Handbook of Dreams: Research, Theory, and Applications,* edited by B. Wolman. New York: Van Nostrand Reinhold, 1979.

McCarthy, G., Blamire, A. M., Rothman, D. L., Gruetter, R., and Shulman, R. G. Echo-planat magnetic resonance imaging studies of frontal cortex activation during word generation in humans. *Proceedings of the National Academy of Sciences, USA,* 1993, *90,* 4952–4956.

McCarthy, R. A., and Warrington, E. K. Evidence for modality-specific meaning systems in the brain. *Nature,* 1988, *334,* 428–435.

McCarthy, R. A., and Warrington, E. K. *Cognitive Neuropsychology: A Clinical Introduction.* San Diego: Academic Press, 1990.

McCaul, K. D., Gladue, B. A., and Joppa, M. Winning, losing, mood, and testosterone. *Hormones and Behavior,* 1992, *26,* 486–504.

McCleod, P., Dittrich, W., Driver, J., Perret, D., and Zihl, J. Preserved and impaired detection of structure from motion by a "motion blind" patient. *Vision and Cognition,* 1996, *3,* 363–391.

McClintock, M. K. Menstrual synchrony and suppression. *Nature,* 1971, *229,* 244–245.

McClintock, M. K., and Adler, N. T. The role of the female during copulation in wild and domestic Norway rats (*Rattus norvegicus*). *Behaviour,* 1978, *67,* 67–96.

McCormick, D. A. Neurotransmitter actions in the thalamus and cerebral cortex. *Journal of Clinical Neurophysiology,* 1992, *9,* 212–223.

McCoy, N. L., and Pitino, L. Pheromonal influences on sociosexual behavior in young women. *Physiology and Behavior,* 2002, *75,* 367–375.

McDonald, R. J., and White, N. M. A triple dissociation of memory systems: Hippocampus, amygdala, and dorsal striatum. *Behavioral Neuroscience,* 1993, *107,* 3–22.

McEwen, B. S., and Sapolsky, R. M. Stress and cognitive function. *Current Biology,* 1995, *5,* 205–216.

McFarland, K., and Kalivas, P. W. The circuitry mediating cocaine-induced reinstatement of drug-seeking behavior. *Journal of Neuroscience,* 2001, *21,* 8655–8663.

McFarlane, A. C., Atchison, M., and Yehuda, R. The acute stress response following motor vehicle accidents and its relation to PTSD. *Annals of the New York Academy of Science,* 1997, *821,* 437–441.

McGinty, D. J., and Sterman, M. B. Sleep suppression after basal forebrain lesions in the cat. *Science,* 1968, *160,* 1253–1255.

McGrath, J. Hypothesis: Is low prenatal vitamin D a risk-modifying factor for schizophrenia? *Schizophrenia Research,* 1999, *40,* 173–177.

McGrath, J., Welham, J., and Pemberton, M. Month of birth, hemisphere of birth and schizophrenia. *British Journal of Psychiatry,* 1995, *167,* 783–785.

McGregor, A., and Roberts, D. C. S. Dopaminergic antagonism within the nucleus accumbens or the amygdala produces differential effects on intravenous cocaine self-administration under fixed and progressive ratio schedules of reinforcement. *Brain Research,* 1993, *624,* 245–252.

McHugh, T. J., Blum, K. I., Tsien, J. Z., Tonegawa, S., and Wilson, M. A. Impaired hippocampal representation of space in CA1-specific NMDAR1 knockout mice. *Cell,* 1996, *87,* 1339–1349.

McIver, B., Connacher, A., Whittle, I., Baylis, P., and Thompson, C. Adipsic hypothalamic diabetes insipidus after clipping of anterior communicating artery aneurysm. *British Medical Journal,* 1991, *303,* 1465–1467.

McKenna, T. M., Weinberger, N. M., and Diamond, D. M. Responses of single auditory cortical neurons to tone sequences. *Brain Research,* 1989, *481,* 142–153.

McLaughlin, S. K., McKinnon, P. J., Robichon, A., Spickofsky, N., and Margolskee, R. F. Gustducin and transducin: A tale of 2 G-proteins. *CIBA Foundation Symposia,* 1993, *179,* 186–200.

McMackin, D., Cockburn, J., Anslow, P., and Gaffan, D. Correlation of fornix damage with memory impairment in 6 cases of colloid cyst removal. *Acta Neurochirurigica,* 1995, *135,* 12–18.

McNaughton, B. L., Leonard, B., and Chen, L. Cortical-hippocampal interactions and cognitive mapping: A hypothesis based on reintegration of the parietal and inferotemporal pathways for visual processing. *Psychobiology,* 1989, *17,* 230–235.

Mechoulam, R., Ben-Shabat, S., Hanus, L., Ligumsky, M., Kaminski, N. E., Schatz, A. T., Gopher, A., Almog, S., Martin, B. R., Compton, D. R., Pertwee, R. G., Griffin, G., Bayewitch, M., Barg, J., and Vogel, Z. Identification of an endogenous 2-monoglyceride, present in canine gut, that binds to cannabinoid receptors. *Biochemical Pharmacology,* 1995, *50,* 83–90.

Mechoulam, R., Hanus, L., and Fride, E. Towards cannabinoid drugs—Revisited. *Progress in Medicinal Chemistry,* 1998, *35,* 200–243.

Mednick, S. A., Machon, R. A., and Huttunen, M. O. An update on the Helsinki influenza project. *Archives of General Psychiatry,* 1990, *47,* 292.

Meesters, Y., Jansen, J. H. C., Beersma, D. G. M., Bouhuys, A. L., and Van den Hoofdakker, R. H. Light therapy for seasonal affective disorder. The effects of timing. *British Journal of Psychiatry,* 1995, *166,* 607–612.

Mehlman, P. T., Higley, J. D., Faucher, I., Lilly, A. A., Taub, D. M., Vickers, J., Suomi, S. J., and Linnoila, M. Correlation of CSF 5-HIAA concentration with sociality and the timing of emigration in free-ranging primates. *American Journal of Psychiatry,* 1995, *152,* 907–913.

Meijer, J. H., and Rietveld, W. J. Neurophysiology of the suprachiasmatic circadian pacemaker in rodents. *Physiological Reviews,* 1989, *69,* 671–707.

Melges, F. T. *Time and the Inner Future: A Temporal Approach to Psychiatric Disorders.* New York: John Wiley & Sons, 1982.

Mellet, E., Tzourio, N., Crivello, F., Jolio, M., Denis, M., and Mazoyer, B. Functional anatomy of spatial mental imagery generated from verbal instructions. *Journal of Neuroscience,* 1996, *16,* 6504–6512.

Melzak, R. Phantom limbs. *Scientific American,* 1992, *266(4),* 120–126.

Menco, B. P. M., Bruch, R. C., Dau, B., and Danho, W. Ultrastructural localization of olfactory transduction components: The G protein subunit G_{olf} and type III adenylyl cyclase. *Neuron,* 1992, *8,* 441–453.

Mercer, J. G., Hoggard, N., Williams, L. M., Lawrence, C. B., Hannah, L. T., Morgan, P. J., and Trayhurn, P. Coexpression of leptin receptor and preproneuropeptide Y mRNA in arcuate nucleus of mouse hypothalamus. *Journal of Neuroendocrinology,* 1996, *8,* 733–735.

Meredith, M. Chronic recording of vomeronasal pump activation in awake behaving hamsters. *Physiology and Behavior,* 1994, *56,* 345–354.

Meredith, M., and O'Connell, R. J. Efferent control of stimulus access to the hamster vomeronasal organ. *Journal of Physiology,* 1979, *286,* 301–316.

Mereu, G., Yoon, K.-W. P., Boi, V., Gessa, G. L., Naes, L., and Westfall, T. C. Preferential stimulation of ventral tegmental area dopaminergic neurons by nicotine. *European Journal of Pharmacology,* 1987, *111,* 395–400.

Mesches, M. H., Fleshner, M., Heman, K. L., Rose, G. M., and Diamond, D. M. Exposing rats to a predator blocks primed burst potentiation in the hippocampus *in vitro. Journal of Neuroscience,* 1999, *19,* RC18(1–5).

Mesulam, M.-M. Frontal cortex and behavior. *Annals of Neurology,* 1986, *19,* 320–325.

Meyer-Bahlburg, H. F. L. Psychoendocrine research on sexual orientation: Current status and future options. *Progress in Brain Research,* 1984, *63,* 375–398.

Meyer-Bahlburg, H. F. L. Gender and sexuality in classic congenital adrenal hyperplasia. *Endocrinology and Metabolism clinics of North America,* 2001, *30,* 155–171.

Mignot, E. Genetic and familial aspects of narcolepsy. *Neurology,* 1998, *50,* S16–S22.

Miller, E. K., Erickson, C. A., and Desimone, R. Neural mechanisms of visual working memory in prefrontal cortex of the macaque. *Journal of Neuroscience,* 1996, *16,* 5154–5167.

Miller, M. T., and Strömland, K. Thalidomide embryopathy: An insight into autism. *Teratology,* 1993, *47,* 387–388.

Miller, N. E. Understanding the use of animals in behavioral research: Some critical issues. *Annals of the New York Academy of Sciences,* 1983, *406,* 113–118.

Miller, V. M., and Best, P. J. Spatial correlates of hippocampal unit activity are altered by lesions of the fornix and entorhinal cortex. *Brain Research,* 1980, *194,* 311–323.

Milner, A. D., Perrett, D. I., Johnston, R. S., and Benson, P. J. Perception and action in "visual form agnosia." *Brain,* 1991, *114,* 405–428.

Milner, B. Memory disturbance after bilateral hippocampal lesions. In *Cognitive Processes and the Brain,* edited by P. Milner and S. Glickman. Princeton, N.J.: Van Nostrand, 1965.

Milner, B. Memory and the temporal regions of the brain. In *Biology of Memory,* edited by K. H. Pribram and D. E. Broadbent. New York: Academic Press, 1970.

Milner, B., Corkin, S., and Teuber, H.-L. Further analysis of the hippocampal amnesic syndrome: 14-year follow-up study of H. M. *Neuropsychologia,* 1968, *6,* 317–338.

Mindus, P., Rasmussen, S. A., and Lindquist, C. Neurosurgical treatment for refractory obsessive-compulsive disorder: Implications for understanding frontal lobe function. *Journal of Neuropsychiatry and Clinical Neurosciences,* 1994, *6,* 467–477.

Mirenowicz, J., and Schultz, W. Importance of unpredictability for reward responses in primate dopamine neurons. *Journal of neurophysiology,* 1994, *72,* 1024–1027.

Mirenowicz, J., and Schultz, W. Preferential activation of midbrain dopamine neurons by appetitive rather than aversive stimuli. *Nature,* 1996, *379,* 449–451.

Mishkin, M. Visual mechanisms beyond the striate cortex. In *Frontiers in Physiological Psychology,* edited by R. W. Russell. New York: Academic Press, 1966.

Mishkin, M., Ungerleider, L. G., and Macko, K. Object vision and spatial vision: Two cortical pathways. *Trends in Neuroscience,* 1983, *6,* 414–417.

Mitchell, J. E. Psychopharmacology of eating disorders. *Annals of the New York Academy of Sciences,* 1989, *575,* 41–49.

Mitler, M. M. Evaluation of treatment with stimulants in narcolepsy. *Sleep,* 1994, *17,* S103–S106.

Mitsuno, K., Sasa, M., Ishihara, I., Ishikawa, M., and Kikuchi, H. LTP of mossy fiber-stimulated potentials in CA3 during learning in rats. *Physiology and Behavior,* 1994, *55,* 633–638.

Miyauchi, S., Takino, R., and Azakami, M. Evoked potentials during REM sleep reflect dreaming. *Electroencephalography and Clinical Neurophysiology,* 1990, *76,* 19–28.

Moghaddam, B., and Bunney, B. S. Differential effect of cocaine on extracellular dopamine levels in rat medial prefrontal cortex and nucleus accumbens: Comparison to amphetamine. *Synapse,* 1989, *4,* 156–161.

Moldin, S. O., Reich, T., and Rice, J. P. Current perspectives on the genetics of unipolar depression. *Behavioral Genetics,* 1991, *21,* 211–242.

Mollon, J. D. "Tho' she kneel'd in that place where they grew . . .": The uses and origins of primate colour vision. *Journal of Experimental Biology,* 1989, *146,* 21–38.

Moltz, H., Lubin, M., Leon, M., and Numan, M. Hormonal induction of maternal behavior in the ovariectomized nulliparous rat. *Physiology and Behavior,* 1970, *5,* 1373–1377.

Mombaerts, P. Molecular biology of odorant receptors in vertebrates. *Annual Review of Neuroscience,* 1999, *22,* 487–510.

Monaghan, D. T., and Cotman, C. W. Distribution of NMDA-sensitive $L^{-3}H$-glutamate binding sites in rat brain as determined by quantitative autoradiography. *Journal of Neuroscience,* 1985, *5,* 2909–2919.

Money, J. Components of eroticism in man: Cognitional rehearsals. In *Recent Advances in Biological Psychiatry,* edited by J. Wortis. New York: Grune & Stratton, 1960.

Money, J., and Ehrhardt, A. *Man & Woman, Boy & Girl.* Baltimore: Johns Hopkins University Press, 1972.

Money, J., Schwartz, M., and Lewis, V. G. Adult erotosexual status and fetal hormonal masculinization and demasculinization: 46,XX congenital virilizing adrenal hyperplasia and 46,XY androgen-insensitivity syndrome compared. *Psychoneuroendocrinology,* 1984, *9,* 405–414.

Montague, C. T., Farooqi, I. S., Whitehead, J. P., Soos, M. A., Rau, H., Wareham, N. J., Sewter, C. P., Digby, J. E., Mohammed, S. N., Hurst, J. A., Cheetham, C. H., Earley, A. R., Barnett, A. H., Prins, J. B., and O'Rahilly, S. Congenital leptin deficiency is associated with severe early-onset obesity in humans. *Nature,* 1997, *387,* 903–908.

Montero, S., Fuentes, J. A., and Fernandez-Tome, P. Lesions of the ventral noradrenergic bundle prevent the rise in blood pressure induced by social deprivation stress in the rat. *Cellular and Molecular Neurobiology,* 1990, *10,* 497–505.

Moore, B. O., and Deutsch, J. A. An antiemetic is antidotal to the satiety effects of cholecystokinin. *Nature,* 1985, *315,* 321–322.

Moore, C. L. Interaction of species-typical environmental and hormonal factors in sexual differentiation of behavior. *Annals of the New York Academy of Sciences,* 1986, *474,* 108–119.

Moore, C. L., Dou, H., and Juraska, J. M. Maternal stimulation affects the number of motor neurons in a sexually dimorphic nucleus of the lumbar spinal cord. *Brain Research,* 1992, *572,* 52–56.

Moore, G. J., Bebchuk, J. M., Wilds, I. B., Chen, G., and Manji, H. K. Lithium-induced increase in human brain grey matter. *Lancet,* 2000, *356,* 1241–1242.

Moore, R. Y., and Card, J. P. Intergeniculate leaflet: An anatomically and functionally distinct subdivision of the lateral geniculate complex. *Journal of Comparative Neurology,* 1994, *344,* 403–430.

Moore, R. Y., and Eichler, V. B. Loss of a circadian adrenal corticosterone rhythm following suprachiasmatic lesions in the rat. *Brain Research,* 1972, *42,* 201–206.

Moore, R. Y., Card, J. P., and Riley, J. N. The suprachiasmatic hypothalamic nucleus: Neuronal ultrastructure. *Neuroscience Abstracts,* 1980, *6,* 758.

Morales, F. R., Boxer, P. A., and Chase, M. H. Behavioral state-specific inhibitory postsynaptic potentials impinge on cat lumbar motoneurons during active sleep. *Experimental Neurology,* 1987, *98,* 418–435.

Moran, T. H., Shnayder, L., Hostetler, A. M., and McHugh, P. R. Pylorectomy reduces the satiety action of cholecystokinin. *American Journal of Physiology,* 1989, *255,* R1059–R1063.

Morgan, D., Grant, K. A., Gage, H. D., Mach, R. H., Kaplan, J. R., Prioleau, O., Nader, S. H., Buchheimer, N., Ehrenkaufer, R. L., and Nader, M. A. Social dominance in monkeys: Dopamine D2 receptors and cocaine self-administration. *Nature Neuroscience,* 2002, *5,* 169–174.

Mori, E., Ikeda, M., Hirono, N., Kitagaki, H., Imamura, T., and Shimomura, T. Amygdalar volume and emotional memory in Alzheimer's disease. *American Journal of Psychiatry,* 1999, *156,* 216–222.

Morris, J. S., de Gelder, B., Weiskrantz, L., and Dolan, R. J. Differential extrageniculostriate and amygdala responses to presentation of emotional faces in a cortically blind field. *Brain,* 2001, *124,* 1241–1252.

Morris, J. S., Frith, C. D., Perrett, D. I., Rowland, D., Young, A. W., Calder, A. J., and Dolan, R. J. A differential neural response in the human amygdala to fearful and happy facial expressions. *Nature,* 1996, *383,* 812–815.

Morris, N. M., Udry, J. R., Khan-Dawood, F., and Dawood, M. Y. Marital sex frequency and midcycle female testosterone. *Archives of Sexual Behavior,* 1987, *16,* 27–37.

Morris, R. G. M., Garrud, P., Rawlins, J. N. P., and O'Keefe, J. Place navigation impaired in rats with hippocampal lesions. *Nature,* 1982, *297,* 681–683.

Moscovitch, M., and Olds, J. Asymmetries in emotional facial expressions and their possible relation to hemispheric specialization. *Neuropsychologia,* 1982, *20,* 71–81.

Moscovitch, M., Kapur, S., Koehler, S., and Houle, S. Distinct neural correlates of visual long-term memory for spatial location and object identity: A positron emission tomography study in humans. *Proceedings of the National Academy of Sciences,* 1995, *92,* 3721–3725.

Moscovitch, M., Winocur, G., and Behrmann, M. What is special about face recognition? Nineteen experiments on a person with visual object agnosia and dyslexia but normal face recognition. *Journal of Cognitive Neuroscience,* 1997, *9,* 555–604.

Motta, V., Penha, K., and Brandao, M. L. Effects of microinjections of mu-receptor and kappa-receptor agonists into the dorsal periaqueductal gray of rats submitted to the plus-maze test. *Psychopharmacology,* 1995, *120,* 470–474.

Mountcastle, V. B. Modality and topographic properties of single neurons of cat's somatic sensory cortex. *Journal of Neurophysiology,* 1957, *20,* 408–434.

Mountcastle, V. B., Lynch, J. C., Georgopoulos, A., Sakata, H., and Acuna, C. Posterior parietal association cortex: Command functions for operations within extra-personal space. *Journal of Neurophysiology,* 1975, *38,* 871–908.

Mountjoy, K. G., Mortrud, M. T., Low, M. J., Simerly, R. B., and Cone, R. D. Localization of the melanocortin-r receptor (MC4-R) in neuroendocrine and autonomic control circuits in the brain. *Molecular Endocrinology,* 1994, *8,* 1298–1308.

Mucha, R. F., and Herz, A. Motivational properties of kappa and mu opioid receptor agonists studied with place and taste preference conditioning. *Psychopharmacology,* 1985, *86,* 274–280.

Mukhametov, L. M. Sleep in marine mammals. In *Sleep Mechanisms,* edited by A. A. Borbély and J. L. Valatx. Munich: Springer-Verlag, 1984.

Munro, J. F., Stewart, I. C., Seidelin, P. H., Mackenzie, H. S., and Dewhurst, N. E. Mechanical treatment for obesity. *Annals of the New York Academy of Sciences,* 1987, *499,* 305–312.

Murakami, N., Hayashida, T., Kuroiwa, T., Nakahara, K., Ida, T., Mondal, M. S., Nakazato, M., Kojima, M., and Kangawa, K. Role for central ghrelin in food intake and secretion profile of stomach ghrelin in rats. *Journal of Endocrinology,* 2002, *174,* 283–288.

Murphy, A. Z., and Hoffman, G. E. Distribution of gonadal steroid receptor-containing neurons in the preoptic-periaqueductal gray-brainstem pathway: A potential circuit for the initiation of male sexual behavior. *Journal of Comparative Neurology,* 2001 *438,* 191–212.

Murphy, J. M., McBride, W. J., Lumeng, L., and Li, T.-K. Contents of monoamines in forebrain regions of alcohol-preferring (P) and-nonpreferring (NP) lines of rats. *Pharmacology, Biochemistry and Behavior,* 1987, *26,* 389–392.

Murray, A. M., Hyde, T. M., Knable, M. B., Herman, M. M., Bigelow, L. B., Carter, J. M., Weinberger, D. R., and Kleinman, J. E. Distribution of putative D4 dopamine receptors in postmortem striatum from patients with schizophrenia. *Journal of Neuroscience,* 1995, *15,* 2186–2191.

Murray, A. M., Ryoo, H., Gurevich, E., and Joyce, J. N. Localization of dopamine D_3 receptors to mesolimbic and D_2 receptors to mesostriatal regions of human forebrain. *Proceedings of the National Academy of Sciences, USA,* 1994, *91,* 11271–11275.

Murray, C. J., and Lopez, A. D. Alternative projections of mortality and disability by cause 1990–2020: Global Burden of Disease Study. *Lancet,* 1997, *349,* 180–183.

Murre, J. M. J., Graham, K. S., and Hodges, J. R. Semantic dementia: Relevance to connectionist models of long-term memory. *Brain,* 2001, *124,* 647–675.

Museo, G., and Wise, R. A. Place preference conditioning with ventral tegmental injections of cystine. *Life Sciences,* 1994, *55,* 1179–1186.

Mushiake, H., Inase, M., and Tanji, J. Neuronal activity in the primate premotor, supplementary, and precentral motor cortex during visually guided and internally determined sequential movements. *Journal of Neurophysiology,* 1991, *66,* 705–718.

Must, A., Spadano, J., Coakley, E. H., Field, A. E., Colditz, G., and Dietz, W. H. The disease burden associated with overweight and obesity. *Journal of the American Medical Association,* 1999, *282,* 1523–1529.

Myers, R. D., and Robinson, D. E. μ and D_2 receptor antisense oligonucleotides injected in nucleus accumbens suppress high alcohol intake in genetic drinking HEP rats. *Alcohol,* 1999, *18,* 225–233.

Myers, R. D., Wooten, M. H., Ames, C. D., and Nyce, J. W. Anorexic action of a new potential neuropeptide Y antagonist

[D-Tyr27,36,D-Thr32]-NPY (27–36) infused into the hypothalamus of the rat. *Brain Research Bulletin,* 1995, *37,* 237–245.

Nadeau, S. E. Impaired grammar with normal fluency and phonology. *Brain,* 1988, *111,* 1111–1137.

Nader, K., Majidishad, P., Amorapanth, P., and LeDoux, J. E. Damage to the lateral and central, but not other, amygdaloid nuclei prevents the acquisition of auditory fear conditioning. *Learning and Memory,* 2001, *8,* 156–163.

Naeser, M. A., Palumbo, C. L., Helm-Estabrooks, N., Stiassny-Eder, D., and Albert, M. L. Severe nonfluency in aphasia: Role of the medial subcallosal fasciculus and other white matter pathways in recovery of spontaneous speech. *Brain,* 1989, *112,* 1–38.

Nafe, J. P., and Wagoner, K. S. The nature of pressure adaptation. *Journal of General Psychology,* 1941, *25,* 323–351.

Nakahara, D., Ozaki, N., Miura, Y., Miura, H., and Nagatsu, T. Increased dopamine and serotonin metabolism in rat nucleus accumbens produced by intracranial self-stimulation of medial forebrain bundle as measured by in vivo microdialysis. *Brain Research,* 1989, *495,* 178–181.

Nakamura, J., Endo, K., Sumida, T., and Hasegawa, T. Bilateral tactile agnosia: A case report. *Cortex,* 1998, *34,* 375–388.

Nakamura, T., and Gold, G. A cyclic nucleotide-gated conductance in olfactory receptor cilia. *Nature,* 1987, *325,* 442–444.

Nakazato, M., Mauakami, N., Date, Y., Kojima, M., Matsuo, H., Kangawa, K., and Matsukura, S. A role for ghrelin in the central regulation of feeding. *Nature,* 2001, *409,* 194–198.

Nambu, T., Sakurai, T., Mizukami, K., Hosoya, Y., Yanagisawa, M., and Goto, K. Distribution of orexin neurons in the adult rat brain. *Brain Research,* 1999, *827,* 243–260.

Naranjo, C. A., Poulos, C. X., Bremner, K. E., and Lanctot, K. L. Citalopram decreases desirability, liking, and consumption of alcohol in alcohol-dependent drinkers. *Clinical Pharmacology and Therapeutics,* 1992, *51,* 729–739.

Narayan, S. S., Temchin, A. N., Recio, A., and Ruggero, M. A. Frequency tuning of basilar membrane and auditory nerve fibers in the same cochlae. *Science,* 1998, *282,* 1882–1884.

Nathans, J., Piantanida, T. P., Eddy, R. L., Shows, T. B., and Hogness, D. S. Molecular genetics of inherited variation in human color vision. *Science,* 1986, *232,* 203–210.

Nauta, W. J. H. Hypothalamic regulation of sleep in rats: Experimental study. *Journal of Neurophysiology,* 1946, *9,* 285–316.

Nauta, W. J. H. Some efferent connections of the prefrontal cortex in the monkey. In *The Frontal Granular Cortex and Behavior,* edited by J. M. Warren and K. Akert. New York: McGraw-Hill, 1964.

Navarro, M., Carrera, M. R. A., Fratta, W., Valverde, O., Cossu, G., Fattore, L., Chowen, J. A., Gómez, R., del Arco, I., Vallanúa, M. A., Maldonado, R., Koob, G. F., and Rodriguez de Fonseca, F. Functional interaction between opioid and cannabinoid receptors in drug self-administration. *Journal of Neuroscience,* 2001, *21,* 5344–5350.

Nef, P., Hermansborgmeyer, I., Artierespin, H., Beasley, L., Dionne, V. E., and Heinemann, S. F. Spatial pattern of receptor expression in the olfactory epithelium. *Proceedings of the National Academy of Sciences (USA),* 1992, *89,* 8948–8952.

Nestler, E. J. Under siege: The brain on opiates. *Neuron,* 1996, *16,* 897–900.

Neumeister, A., Goessler, R., Lucht, M., Kapitany, T., Bamas, C., and Kasper, S. Bright light therapy stabilizes the antidepressant effect of partial sleep deprivation. *Biological Psychiatry,* 1996, *39,* 16–21.

New, A. S., Hazlett, E. A., Buchsbaum, M. S., Goodman, M., Reynolds, D., Mitropoulou, V., Sprung, L., Shaw, R. B., Koenigsberg, H., Platholi, J., Silverman, J., and Siever, L. J. Blunted prefrontal cortical 18fluorodeoxyglucose positron emission tomography response to meta-chlorophenylpiperazine in impulsive aggression. *Archives of General Psychiatry,* 2002, *59,* 621–629.

Nichelli, P., Grafman, J., Pietrini, P., Clark, K., Lee, K. Y., and Miletich, R. Where the brain appreciates the moral of a story. *NeuroReport,* 1995, *6,* 2309–2313.

Nicholl, C. S., and Russell, R. M. Analysis of animal rights literature reveals the underlying motives of the movement: Ammunition for counter offensive by scientists. *Endocrinology,* 1990, *127,* 985–989.

Nicholls, P., and Wenner, C. E. Release of respiratory control by uncouplers: The question of stoichiometry. *Archives of Biochemistry and Biophysics,* 1972, *151,* 206–215.

Nicolas, A., Petit, D., Rompre, S., and Montplaisir, J. Sleep spindle characteristics in healthy subjects of different age groups. *Clinical Neurophysiology,* 2001, *112,* 521–527.

Nicoll, R. A., and Malenka, R. C. A tale of two transmitters. *Science,* 1998, *281,* 360–361.

Nicoll, R. A., Alger, B. E., and Jarh, C. E. Enkephalin blocks inhibitory pathways in the vertebrate CNS. *Nature,* 1980, *287,* 22–25.

Nilsson, O. G., Shapiro, M. L., Gage, F. H., Olton, D. S., and Björklund, A. Spatial learning and memory following fimbria-fornix transection and grafting of fetal septal neurons to the hippocampus. *Experimental Brain Research,* 1987, *67,* 195–215.

Nisell, M., Nomikos, G. G., and Svensson, T. H. Systemic nicotine-induced dopamine release in the rat nucleus accumbens is regulated by nicotinic receptors in the ventral tegmental area. *Synapse,* 1994, *16,* 36–44.

Nishino, S., Ripley, B., Overeem, S., Lammers, G. J., and Mignot, E. Hypocretin (orexin) deficiency in human narcolepsy. *Lancet,* 2000, *355,* 39–40.

Noirot, E. Selective priming of maternal responses by auditory and olfactory cues from mouse pups. *Developmental Psychobiology,* 1972, *5,* 371–387.

Nonogaki, K., Strack, A. M., Dallman, M. F., and Tecott, L. H. Leptin-independent hyperphagia and type 2 diabetes in mice with a mutated serotonin 5-HT$_{2C}$ receptor gene. *Nature Medicine,* 1998, *4,* 1152–1156.

Norgren, R., and Grill, H. Brain-stem control of ingestive behavior. In *The Physiological Mechanisms of Motivation,* edited by D. W. Pfaff. New York: Springer-Verlag, 1982.

Novin, D., VanderWeele, D. A., and Rezek, M. Hepatic-portal 2-deoxy-D-glucose infusion causes eating: Evidence for peripheral glucoreceptors. *Science,* 1973, *181,* 858–860.

Novotny, M. V., Ma, W., Wiesler, D., and Zidek, L. Positive identification of the puberty-accelerating pheromone of the house mouse: The volatile ligands associating with the major urinary protein. *Proceedings of the Royal Society of London [B],* 1999, *266,* 2017–2022.

Nowlis, G. H., and Frank, M. Qualities in hamster taste: Behavioral and neural evidence. In *Olfaction and Taste, Vol. 6,* edited by J. LeMagnen and P. MacLeod. Washington, D.C.: Information Retrieval, 1977.

Numan, M. Medial preoptic area and maternal behavior in the female rat. *Journal of Comparative and Physiological Psychology,* 1974, *87,* 746–759.

Numan, M., and Numan, M. J. Projection sites of medial preoptic area and ventral bed nucleus of the stria terminalis neurons that express Fos during maternal behavior in female rats. *Journal of Neuroendocrinology,* 1997, *9,* 369–384.

Numan, M., and Smith, H. G. Maternal behavior in rats: Evidence for the involvement of preoptic projections to the ventral tegmental area. *Behavioral Neuroscience,* 1984, *98,* 712–727.

Numan, M., Rosenblatt, J. S., and Komisaruk, B. R. Medial preoptic area and onset of maternal behavior in the rat. *Journal of Comparative and Physiological Psychology,* 1977, *91,* 146–164.

Nunn, J. A., Graydon, F. J. X., Polkey, C. E., and Morris, R. G. Differential spatial memory impairment after right temporal lobectomy demonstrated using temporal titration. *Brain,* 1999, *122,* 47–59.

Nutt, D. J., Glue, P., Lawson, C. W., and Wilson, S. Flumazenil provocation of panic attacks: Evidence for altered benzodiazepine receptor sensitivity in panic disorders. *Archives of General Psychiatry,* 1990, *47,* 917–925.

Oaknin, S., Rodriguez del Castillo, A., Guerra, M., Battaner, E., and Mas, M. Change in forebrain Na,K-ATPase activity and serum hormone levels during sexual behavior in male rats. *Physiology and Behavior,* 1989, *45,* 407–410.

Obler, L. K., and Gjerlow, K. *Language and the Brain.* Cambridge, England: Cambridge University Press, 1999.

O'Brien, C. P., Volpicelli, L. A., and Volpicelli, J. R. Naltrexone in the treatment of alcoholism: A clinical review. *Alcohol,* 1996, *13,* 35–39.

O'Callaghan, E., Gibson, T., Colohan, H. A., Buckley, P., Walshe, D. G., Larkin, C., and Waddington, J. L. Risk of schizophrenia in adults born after obstetric complications and their association with early onset of illness: A controlled study. *British Medical Journal,* 1992, *305,* 1256–1259.

O'Carroll, R., Shapiro, C., and Bancroft, J. Androgens, behavior and nocturnal erection in hypogonadal men: The effects of varying the replacement dose. *Clinical Endocrinology,* 1985, *23,* 527–538.

O'Connor, M., Walbridge, M., Sandson, T., and Alexander, M. A neuropsychological analysis of Capgras syndrome. *Neuropsychiatry, Neuropsychology, and Behavioral Neurology,* 1996, *9,* 265–271.

O'Dell, T. J., Hawkins, R. D., Kandel, E. R., and Arancio, O. Tests of the roles of two diffusible substances in long-term potentiation: Evidence for nitric oxide as a possible early retrograde messenger. *Proceedings of the National Academy of Sciences, USA,* 1991, *88,* 11285–11289.

Ogawa, S., Olazabal, U. E., Parhar, I. S., and Pfaff, D. W. Effects of intrahypothalamic administration of antisense DNA for progesterone receptor mRNA on reproductive behavior and progesterone receptor immunoreactivity in female rat. *Journal of Neuroscience,* 1994, *14,* 1766–1774.

O'Keefe, J., and Bouma, H. Complex sensory properties of certain amygdala units in the freely moving cat. *Experimental Neurology,* 1969, *23,* 384–398.

O'Keefe, J., and Dostrovsky, T. The hippocampus as a spatial map: Preliminary evidence from unit activity in the freely moving rat. *Brain Research,* 1971, *34,* 171–175.

Olausson, H., Lamarre, Y., Backlund, H., Morin, C., Wallin, B. G., Starck, G., Ekholm, S., Strigo, I., Worsley, K., Vallbo, Å. B., Bushnell, M. C. Unmyelinated tactile afferents signal touch and project to insular cortex. *Nature Neuroscience,* 2002, *5,* 900–904.

Olds, J. Commentary. In *Brain Stimulation and Motivation,* edited by E. S. Valenstein. Glenview, Ill.: Scott, Foresman, 1973.

Olds, M. E., and Fobes, J. L. The central basis of motivation: Intracranial self-stimulation studies. *Annual Review of Psychology,* 1981, *32,* 523–574.

Oleksenko, A. I., Mukhametov, L. M., Polyakova, I. G., Supin, A. Y., and Kovalzon, V. M. Unihemispheric sleep deprivation in bottlenose dolphins. *Journal of Sleep Research,* 1992, *1,* 40–44.

Oliveri, M., Turriziani, P., Carlesimo, G. A., Koch, G., Tomaiuolo, F., Panella, M., and Caltagirone, C. Parieto-frontal interactions in visual-object and visual-spatial working memory: Evidence from transcranial magnetic stimulation. *Cerebral Cortex,* 2001, *11,* 606–618.

Olmstead, M. C., and Franklin, K. B. J. Differential effects of ventral striatal lesions on the conditioned place preference induced by morphine or amphetamine. *Neuroscience,* 1996, *71,* 701–708.

Olton, D. S. Memory functions and the hippocampus. In *Neurobiology of the Hippocampus,* edited by W. Siefert. New York: Academic Press, 1983.

Olton, D. S., and Papas, B. C. Spatial memory and hippocampal function. *Neuropsychologia,* 1979, *17,* 669–682.

Olton, D. S., and Samuelson, R. J. Remembrance of places past: Spatial memory in rats. *Journal of Experimental Psychology: Animal Behavior Processes,* 1976, *2,* 97–116.

Olton, D. S., Collison, C., and Werz, M. A. Spatial memory and radial arm maze performance in rats. *Learning and Motivation,* 1977, *8,* 289–314.

O'Mara, S. M., Rolls, E. T., Berthoz, A., and Kesner, R. P. Neurons responding to whole-body motion in the primate hippocampus. *Journal of Neuroscience,* 1994, *14,* 6511–6523.

Öngür, D., Drevets, W. C., and Price, J. L. Glial reduction in the subgenual prefrontal cortex in mood disorders. *Proceedings of the National Academy of Science, USA,* 1998, *95,* 13290–13295.

Ossebaard, C. A., Polet, I. A., and Smith, D. V. Amiloride effects on taste quality: Comparison of single and multiple response category procedures. *Chemical Senses,* 1997, *22,* 267–275.

Ostrowsky, K., Magnin, M., Tyvlin, P., Isnard, J., Guenot, M., and Mauguière, F. Representation of pain and somatic sensation in the human insula: A study of responses to direct electrical cortical stimulation. *Cerebral Cortex,* 2002, *12,* 376–385.

Otsuki, M., Soma, Y., Arihiro, S., Watanabe, Y., Moriwaki, H., and Naritomi, H. Dystypia: Isolated typing impairment without aphasia, apraxia or visuospatial impairment. *European Neurology,* 2002, *47,* 136–140.

Owen, A. M., James, M., Leigh, P. N., Summers, B. A., Marsden, C. D., Quinn, N. P., Lange, K. W., and Robbins, T. W.

Fronto-striatal cognitive deficits at different stages of Parkinson's disease. *Brain,* 1992, *115,* 1727–1751.

Ozata, M., Ozdemir, I. C., and Licinio, J. Human leptin deficiency caused by a missense mutation: Multiple endocrine defects, decreased sympathetic tone, and immune system dysfunction indicate new targets for leptin action, greater central than peripheral resistance to the effects of leptin, and spontaneous correction of leptin-mediated defects. *Journal of Clinical Endocrinology and Metabolism,* 1999, *84,* 3686–3695.

Packard, M. G., and Teather, L. A. Double dissociation of hippocampal and dorsal-striatal memory systems by posttraining intracerebral injections of 2-amino-5-phosphonopentanoic acid. *Behavioral Neuroscience,* 1997, *111,* 543–551.

Packard, M. G., Hirsh, R., and White, N. M. Differential effects of fornix and caudate nucleus lesions on two radial maze tasks: Evidence for multiple memory systems. *Journal of Neuroscience,* 1989, *9,* 1465–1472.

Pallast, E. G. M., Jongbloet, P. H., Straatman, H. M., and Zeilhuis, G. A. Excess of seasonality of births among patients with schizophrenia and seasonal ovopathy. *Schizophrenia Bulletin,* 1994, *20,* 269–276.

Papadimitriou, G. N., Christodoulou, G. N., Katsouyanni, K., and Stefanis, C. N. Therapy and prevention of affective illness by total sleep deprivation. *Journal of the Affective Disorders,* 1993, *27,* 107–116.

Papez, J. W. A proposed mechanism of emotion. *Archives of Neurology and Psychiatry,* 1937, *38,* 725–744.

Park, W.-K., Bari, A. A., Jey, A. R., Anderson, S. M., Spealman, R. D., Rowlett, J. K., and Pierce, R. C. Cocaine administered into the medial prefrontal cortex reinstates cocaine-seeking behavior by increasing AMPA receptor-mediated glutamate transmission in the nucleus accumbens. *Journal of Neuroscience,* 2002, *22,* 2916–2925.

Parkinson, J. A., Crofts, H. S., McGuigan, M., Tomic, D. L., Everitt, B. J., and Roberts, A. C. The role of the primate amygdala in conditioned reinforcement. *Journal of Neuroscience,* 2001, *21,* 7770–7780.

Parr, L. A., and Hopkins, W. D. Brain temperature asymmetries and emotional perception in chimpanzees, *Pan troglodytes. Physiology and Behavior,* 2000, *71,* 363–371.

Partiot, A., Verin, M., Pillon, B., Teixeira-Ferreira, C., Agid, Y., and Dubois, B. Delayed response tasks in basal ganglia lesions in man: further evidence for a striato-frontal cooperation in behavioural adaptation. *Neuropsychologia,* 1996, *34,* 709–721.

Pascoe, J. P., and Kapp, B. S. Electrophysiological characteristics of amygdaloid central nucleus neurons during Pavlovian fear conditioning in the rabbit. *Behavioural Brain Research,* 1985, *16,* 117–133.

Passingham, R. Delayed matching after selective prefrontal lesions in monkeys (Macaca mulatta). *Brain Research,* 1975, *92,* 89–102.

Pattatucci, A. M. L., and Hamer, D. H. Development and familiality of sexual orientation in females. *Behavior Genetics,* 1995, *25,* 407–420.

Patterson, K., and Kay, J. A. How word-form dyslexics form words. Paper presented at the meeting of the British Psychological Society Conference on Reading, Exeter, England, 1980.

Patterson, K., and Ralph, M. A. L. Selective disorders of reading? *Current Opinion in Neurobiology,* 1999, *9,* 235–239.

Paulesu, E., Démonet, J.-F., Fazio, F., McCrory, E., Chanoine, V., Brunswick, N., Cappa, S. F., Cossu, G., Habib, M., Frith, C. D., and Frith, U. *Science,* 2001, *291,* 2165–2167.

Paulesu, E., Frith, C. D., and Frackowiak, R. S. J. The neural correlates of the verbal component of working memory. *Nature,* 1993, *362,* 342–345.

Pauls, D. L., and Leckman, J. F. The inheritance of Gilles de la Tourette's syndrome and associated behaviors. *New England Journal of Medicine,* 1986, *315,* 993–997.

Pauls, D. L., Towbin, K. E., Leckman, J. F., Zahner, G. E., and Cohen, D. J. Gilles de la Tourette's syndrome and obsessive-compulsive disorder. Evidence supporting a genetic relationship. *Archives of General Psychiatry,* 1986, *43,* 1180–1182.

Pavlides, C., Greenstein, Y. J., Grudman, M., and Winson, J. Long-term potentiation in the dentate gyrus is induced preferentially on the positive phase of theta rhythms. *Brain Research,* 1988, *439,* 383–387.

Peck, B. K., and Vanderwolf, C. H. Effects of raphe stimulation on hippocampal and neocortical activity and behaviour. *Brain Research,* 1991, *568,* 244–252.

Pedersen, C. B., and Mortensen, P. B. Evidence of a dose-response relationship between urbanicity during upbringing and schizophrenia risk. *Archives of General Psychiatry,* 2001, *58,* 1039–1046.

Pedersen-Bjergaard, U., Host, U., Kelbaek, H., Schifter, S., Rehfeld, J. F., Faber, J., and Christensen, N. J. Influence of meal composition on postprandial peripheral plasma concentrations of vasoactive peptides in man. *Scandanavian Journal of Clinical and Laboratory Investigation,* 1996, *56,* 497–503.

Pelleymounter, M. A., Cullen, M. J., Baker, M. B., Hecht, R., Winters, D., Boone, T., and Collins, F. Effects of the obese gene product on body weight regulation in ob/ob mice. *Science,* 1995, *269,* 540–543.

Penfield, W., and Jasper, H. *Epilepsy and the Functional Anatomy of the Human Brain.* Boston: Little, Brown & Co., 1954.

Penfield, W., and Perot, P. The brain's record of auditory and visual experience: A final summary and discussion. *Brain,* 1963, *86,* 595–697.

Penfield, W., and Rasmussen, T. *The Cerebral Cortex of Man: A Clinical Study of Localization.* Boston: Little, Brown & Co., 1950.

Pennington, B. F., Gilger, J. W., Pauls, D., Smith, S. A., Smith, S. D., and DeFries, J. C. Evidence for major gene transmission of developmental dyslexia. *Journal of the American Medical Association,* 1991, *266,* 1527–1534.

Perkel, D. J., and Farries, M. A. Complementary 'bottom-up' and 'top-down' approaches to basal ganglia function. *Current Opinions in Neurobiology,* 2000, *19,* 725–731.

Perlmutter, S. J., Garvey, M. A., Castellanos, X., Mittleman, B. B., Giedd, J., Rapoport, J. L., and Swedo, S. E. A case of pediatric autoimmune neuropsychiatric disorders associated with streptococcal infections. *American Journal of Psychiatry,* 1998, *155,* 1592–1598.

Perrett, D. I., Hietanen, J. K., Oram, M. W., and Benson, P. J. Organization and functions of cells responsive to faces in the temporal cortex. *Philosophical Transactions of the Royal Society of London [B],* 1992, *335,* 23–30.

Pert, C. B., Snowman, A. M., and Snyder, S. H. Localization of opiate receptor binding in presynaptic membranes of rat brain. *Brain Research,* 1974, *70,* 184–188.

Pes, D., Mameli, M., Andreini, I., Krieger, J., Weber, M., Breer, H., and Pelosi, P. Cloning and expression of odorant-binding proteins Ia and Ib from mouse nasal tissue. *Gene,* 1998, *212,* 49–55.

Petersen, S. E., Fox, P. T., Posner, M. I., Mintun, M., and Raichle, M. W. Positron emission tomographic studies of the cortical anatomy of single-word processing. *Nature,* 1988, *331,* 585–589.

Petersen, S. E., Fox, P. T., Snyder, A. Z., and Raichle, M. E. Activation of extrastriate and frontal cortical areas by visual words and word-like stimuli. *Science,* 1990, *249,* 1041–1044.

Petersen, S. E., Miezin, F. M., and Allman, J. M. Transient and sustained responses in four extrastriate visual areas of the owl monkey. *Experimental Brain Research,* 1988, *70,* 55–60.

Petit, H. O., and Justice, J. B. Dopamine in the nucleus accumbens during cocaine self-administration as studied by in vivo microdialysis. *Pharmacology, Biochemistry and Behavior,* 1989, *23,* 899–904.

Petre Quadens, O., and De Lee, C. Eye movement frequencies and related paradoxical sleep cycles: Developmental changes. *Chronobiologia,* 1974, *1,* 347–355.

Petrovitch, H., Ross. G. W., Abbott, R. D., Sanderson, W. T., Sharp, D. S., Tanner, C. D., Mansaki, K. H., Blanchette, P. L., Popper, J. S., Foley, D., Launer, L., and White, L. R. Plantation work and risk of Parkinson disease in a population-based longitudinal study. *Archives of Neurology,* 2002, *59,* 1787–1792.

Petryshen, T. L., Kaplan, B. J., Fu, L. M., de French, N. S., Tobias, R., Hughes, M., and Leigh, F. L. Evidence for a susceptibility locus on chromosome 6q influencing phonological coding dyslexia. *American Journal of Medical Genetics,* 2001, *105,* 507–517.

Pettito, L. A., Zatorre, R. J., Gauna, K., Nikelski, E. J., Dostie, D., and Evans, A. C. Speech-like cerebral activity in profoundly deaf people processing signed languages: Implications for the neural basis of human language. *Proceedings of the National Academy of Science, USA,* 2000, *97,* 13961–13966.

Peuskens, H., Sunaert, S., Dupont, P., Van Hecke, P., and Orban, G. A. Human brain regions involved in heading estimation. *Journal of Neuroscience,* 2001, *21,* 2451–2461.

Peyron, C., Faraco, J., Rogers, W., Ripley, B., Overeem, S., Charnay, Y., Nevismalova, S., Aldrich, M., Reynolds, D., Albin, R., Li, R., Hungs, M., Pedrazzoli, M., Padigaru, M., Kucherlapati, M., Fan, J., Maki, R., Lammers, G. J., Bouras, C., Kucherlapati, R., Nishino, S., and Mignot, E. A mutation in a case of early onset narcolepsy and a generalized absence of hypocretin peptides in human narcoleptic brains. *Nature Medicine,* 2002, *6,* 991–997.

Pfaff, D. W., and Keiner, M. Atlas of estradiol-concentrating cells in the central nervous system of the female rat. *Journal of Comparative Neurology,* 1973, *151,* 121–158.

Pfaff, D. W., and Sakuma, Y. Deficit in the lordosis reflex of female rats caused by lesions in the ventromedial nucleus of the hypothalamus. *Journal of Physiology,* 1979, *288,* 203–210.

Pfaus, J. G., Kleopoulos, S. P., Mobbs, C. V., Gibbs, R. B., and Pfaff, D. W. Sexual stimulation activates c-fos within estrogen-concentrating regions of the female rat forebrain. *Brain Research,* 1993, *624,* 253–267.

Phiel, C. J., and Klein, P. S. Molecular targets of lithium action. *Annual Review of Pharmacology and Toxicology,* 2001, *41,* 789–813.

Phillips, D. P., and Farmer, M. E. Acquired word deafness, and the temporal grain of sound representation in the primary auditory cortex. *Behavioural Brain Research,* 1990, *40,* 85–94.

Phillips, M. I., and Felix, D. Specific angiotensin II receptive neurons in the cat subfornical organ. *Brain Research,* 1976, *109,* 531–540.

Phillips, M. L., Young, A. W., Scott, S. K., Calder, A. J., Andrew, G., Giampietro, V., Williams, S. C. R., Bullmore, E. T., Brammer, M., and Gray, J. A. Neural responses to facial and vocal expressions of fear and disgust. *Proceedings of the Royal Society of London [B],* 1998, *265,* 1809–1817.

Phillips, R. G., and LeDoux, J. E. Differential contribution of amygdala and hippocampus to cued and contextual fear conditioning. *Behavioral Neuroscience,* 1992, *106,* 274–285.

Piccirillo, J. F., Duntley, S., and Schotland, H. Obstructive sleep apnea. *Journal of the American Medical Association,* 2000, *284,* 1492–1494.

Pickar, D. Prospects for pharmacotherapy of schizophrenia. *Lancet,* 1995, *345,* 557–562.

Pickles, J. O., and Corey, D. P. Mechanoelectrical transduction by hair cells. *Trends in Neuroscience,* 1992, *15,* 254–259.

Pierce, K., Müller, R.-A., Ambrose, J., Allen, G., and Courchesne, E. Face processing occurs outside the fusiform "face area" in autism: Evidence from functional MRI. *Brain,* 2001, *124,* 2059–2073.

Pijl, S., and Schwarz, D. W. F. Intonation of musical intervals by musical intervals by deaf subjects stimulated with single bipolar cochlear implant electrodes. *Hearing Research,* 1995a, *89,* 203–211.

Pijl, S., and Schwartz, D. W. F. Melody recognition and musical interval perception by deaf subjects stimulated with electrical pulse trains through single cochlear implant electrodes. *Journal of the Acoustical Society of America,* 1995b, *98,* 886–895.

Pilla, M., Perachon, S., Sautel, F., Garrido, F., Mann, A., Wermuth, C. G., Schwartz, J. C., Everitt, B. J., and Sokoloff, P. Selective inhibition of cocaine-seeking behaviour by a partial dopamine D_3 receptor agonist. *Nature,* 1999, *400,* 371–375.

Pilleri, G. The blind Indus dolphin, *Platanista indi. Endeavours,* 1979, *3,* 48–56.

Pitkänen, A., Savander, V., and LeDoux, J. L. Organization of intra-amygdaloid circuits: An emerging framework for understanding functions of the amygdala. *Trends in Neuroscience,* 1997, *20,* 517–523.

Pleim, E. T., and Barfield, R. J. Progesterone versus estrogen facilitation of female sexual behavior by intracranial administration to female rats. *Hormones and Behavior,* 1988, *22,* 150–159.

Plenz, D., and Kitai, S. T. A basal ganglia pacemaker formed by the subthalamic nucleus and external globus pallidus. *Nature,* 1999, *400,* 677–682.

Poggio, G. F., and Poggio, T. The analysis of stereopsis. *Annual Review of Neuroscience,* 1984, *7,* 379–412.

Poizner, H., Feldman, A. G., Levin, M. F., Berkinblit, M. B., Hening, W. A., Patel, A., and Adamovich, S. V. The timing of arm-trunk coordination is deficient and vision-dependent in Parkinson's patients during reaching movements. *Experimental Brain Research,* 2000, *133,* 279–292.

Pomp, D., and Nielsen, M. K. Quantitative genetics of energy balance: Lessons from animal models. *Obesity Research,* 1999, *7,* 106–110.

Porkka-Heiskanen, T., Strecker, R. E., and McCarley, R. W. Brain site-specificity of extracellular adenosine concentration changes during sleep deprivation and spontaneous sleep: An *in vivo* microdialysis study. *Neuroscience,* 2000, *99,* 507–517.

Portas, C. M., Thakkar, M., Rainnie, D., and McCarley, R. W. Microdialysis perfusion of 8-hydroxy-2-(di-n-propylamino) tetralin (8-OH-DPAT) in the dorsal raphe nucleus decreases serotonin release and increases rapid eye movement sleep in the freely moving cat. *Journal of Neuroscience,* 1996, *16,* 2820–2828.

Post, R. M., Ballenger, J. C., Uhde, T., and Bunney, W. Efficacy of carbamazepine in manic-depressive illness: Implications for underlying mechanisms. In *Neurobiology of Mood Disorders,* edited by R. M. Post and C. Ballenger. Baltimore, Md.: Williams and Wilkins, 1984.

Post, R. M., Denicoff, K. D., Frye, M. A., Dunn, R. T., Leverich, G. S., Osuch, E., and Speer, A. A history of the use of anticonvulsants as mood stabilizers in the last two decades of the 20th century. *Neuropsychobiology,* 1998, *38,* 152–166.

Post, R. M., Leverich, G. S., Altshuler, L., and Mikalauskas, K. Lithium-discontinuation-induced refractoriness: Preliminary observations. *Americal Journal of Psychiatry,* 1992, *149,* 1727–1729.

Post, R. M., Weiss, S. R. B., and Chuang, D.-M. Mechanisms of action of anticonvulsants in affective disorders: Comparison with lithium. *Journal of Clinical Psychopharmacology,* 1992, *12,* 23S–35S.

Powers, J. B., and Winans, S. S. Vomeronasal organ: Critical role in mediating sexual behavior of the male hamster. *Science,* 1975, *187,* 961–963.

Price, C. The functional anatomy of word comprehension and production. *Trends in Cognitive Science,* 1998, *2,* 281–288.

Price, D. B. Psychological and neural mechanisms of the affective dimension of pain. *Science,* 2000, *288,* 1769–1772.

Price, J. The genetics of depressive behavior. *British Journal of Psychiatry,* 1968, *2,* 37–45.

Price, L. H., and Heninger, G. R. Drug therapy: Lithium in the treatment of mood disorders. *New England Journal of Medicine,* 1994, *331,* 591–598.

Price, R. A., and Gottesman, I. I. Body fat in identical twins reared apart: Roles for genes and environment. *Behavioral Genetics,* 1991, *21,* 1–7.

Pritchard, T. C., Hamilton, R. B., Morse, J. R., and Norgren, R. Projections of thalamic gustatory and lingual areas in the monkey, *Macaca fascicularis. Journal of Comparative Neurology,* 1986, *244,* 213–228.

Proctor, W. R., Soldo, B. L., Allan, A. M., and Dunwiddie, T. V. Ethanol enhances synaptically evoked GABAA receptor-mediated responses in cerebral cortical neurons in rat brain slices. *Brain Research,* 1992, *595,* 220–227.

Propping, P., Kruger, J., and Janah, A. Effect of alcohol on genetically determined variants of the normal electroencephalogram. *Psychiatry Research,* 1980, *2,* 85–98.

Propping, P., Kruger, J., and Mark, N. Genetic disposition to alcoholism: An EEG study in alcoholics and their relatives. *Human Genetics,* 1981, *59,* 51–59.

Provencio, I., Rodriguez, I. R., Jiang, G., Hayes, W. P., Moreira, E. F., and Rollag, M. D. A novel human opsin in the inner retinal *Journal of Neuroscience*, 2000, *20*, 600–605.

Proverbio, A. M., Lilli, S., Semenza, C., and Zani, A. ERP indexes of functional differences in brain activation during proper and common names retrieval. *Neuropsychologia*, 2001, *39*, 815–827.

Pulvermüller, F. Words in the brain's language. *Behavioral and Brain Sciences*, 1999, *22*, 253–279; Peer commentary and author's replies, pp. 280–336.

Pulvermüller, F., Harle, M., and Hummel, F. Neurophysiological distinction of verb categories. *Neuroreport*, 2000, *11*, 2789–2793.

Qu, D., Ludwig, D. S., Gammeltoft, S., Piper, M., Pelleymounter, M. A., Cullen, M. J., Mathes, W. F., Przypek, R., Kanarek, R., and Maratos-Flier, E. A role for melanin concentrating hormone in the central regulation of feeding behaviour. *Nature*, 1996, *380*, 243–247.

Quattrochi, J. J., Mamelak, A. N., Madison, R. D., Macklis, J. D., and Hobson, J. A. Mapping neuronal inputs to REM sleep induction sites with carbachol-fluorescent microspheres. *Science*, 1989, *245*, 984–986.

Quillen, E. W., Keil, L. C., and Reid, I. A. Effects of baroreceptor denervation on endocrine and drinking responses to caval constriction in dogs. *American Journal of Physiology*, 1990, *259*, R618–R626.

Quintana, J., and Fuster, J. M. Mnemonic and predictive functions of cortical neurons in a memory task. *Neuroreport*, 1992, *3*, 721–724.

Quirk, G. J., Muller, R. U., Kubie, J. L., and Ranck, J. B. The positional firing properties of medial entorhinal neurons: Description and comparison with hippocampal place cells. *Journal of Neuroscience*, 1992, *12*, 1945–1963.

Quirk, G. J., Repa, J. C., and LeDoux, J. E. Fear conditioning enhances short-latency auditory responses of lateral amygdala neurons: Parallel recordings in the freely behaving rat. *Neuron*, 1995, *15*, 1029–1039.

Quirk, G. J., Russo, G. K., Barron, J. L., and Lebron, K. The role of ventromedial prefrontal cortex in the recovery of extinguished fear. *Journal of Neuroscience*, 2000, *20*, 6225–6231.

Raine, A., Lencz, T., Bihrle, S., LaCasse, L., and Colletti, P. Reduced prefrontal gray matter volume and reduced autonomic activity in antisocial personality disorder. *Archives of General Psychiatry*, 2002, *57*, 119–127.

Raine, A., Meloy, J. R., Bihrle, S., Stoddard, J., LaCasse, L., and Buchsbaum, M. S. Reduced prefrontal and increased subcortical brain functioning assessed using positron emission tomography in predatory and affective murderers. *Behavioral Science and the Law*, 1998, *16*, 319–332.

Rainer, G., Rao, S. C., and Miller, E. K. Prospective coding for objects in primate prefrontal cortex. *Journal of Neuroscience*, 1999, *19*, 5493–5505.

Rainville, P., Duncan, G. H., Price, D. D., Carrier, B., and Bushnell, M. C. Pain affect encoded in human anterior cingulate but not somatosensory cortex. *Science*, 1997, *277*, 968–971.

Rakic, P. Mode of cell migration to the superficial layers of fetal monkey neocortex. *Journal of Comparative Neurology*, 1972, *145*, 61–83.

Rakic, P. Specification of cerebral cortical areas. *Science*, 1988, *241*, 170–176.

Raleigh, M. J., McGuire, M. T., Brammer, G. L., Pollack, D. B., and Yuwiler, A. Serotonergic mechanisms promote dominance acquisition in adult male vervet monkeys. *Brain Research*, 1991, *559*, 181–190.

Ralph, M. R., and Lehman, M. N. Transplantation: A new tool in the analysis of the mammalian hypothalamic circadian pacemaker. *Trends in Neuroscience*, 1991, *14*, 362–366.

Ramirez, I. Why do sugars taste good? *Neuroscience and Biobehavioral Reviews*, 1990, *14*, 125–134.

Rapin, I. Autistic regression and disintegrative disorder: How important the role of epilepsy? *Seminars in Pediatric Neurology*, 1995, *2*, 278–285.

Rapin, I. Autism in search of a home in the brain. *Neurology*, 1999, *52*, 902–904.

Rapoport, J. L. Recent advances in obsessive-compulsive disorder. *Neuropsychopharmacology*, 1991, *5*, 1–10.

Rapoport, J. L., Ryland, D. H., and Kriete, M. Drug treatment of canine acral lick: An animal model of obsessive-compulsive disorder. *Archives of General Psychiatry*, 1992, *49*, 517–521.

Rasmusson, D. D., Clow, K., and Szerb, J. C. Modification of neocortical acetylcholine release and electroencephalogram desynchronization due to brain stem stimulation by drugs applied to the basal forebrain. *Neuroscience*, 1994, *60*, 665–677.

Ratcliff, G., and Newcombe, F. Object recognition: Some deductions from the clinical evidence. In *Normality and Pathology in Cognitive Functions*, edited by A. W. Ellis. London: Academic Press, 1982.

Ratnasuriya, R. H., Eisler, I., Szmukler, G. I., and Russell, G. F. M. Anorexia nervosa: Outcome and prognostic factors after 20 years. *British Journal of Psychiatry*, 1991, *158*, 495–502.

Rauschecker, J. P., and Tian, B. Mechanisms and streams for processing of "what" and "where" in auditory cortex. *Proceedings of the National Academy of Science (USA)*, 2000, *97*, 11800–11806.

Rauschecker, J. P., Tian, B., and Hauser, M. Processing of complex sounds in the macaque nonprimary auditory cortex. *Science*, 1995, *268*, 111–114.

Ravussin, E., Valencia, M. E., Esparza, J., Bennett, P. H., Schulz, L. O. Effects of a traditional lifestyle on obesity in Pima Indians. *Diabetes Care*, 1994, *17*, 1067–1074.

Reber, P. J., and Squire, L. R. Encapsulation of implicit and explicit memory in sequence learning. *Journal of Cognitive Neuroscience*, 1998, *10*, 248–263.

Recer, P. Study: English is a factor in dyslexia. Washington, D.C.: Associated Press, 16 March 2001.

Rechtschaffen, A., and Bergmann, B. M. Sleep deprivation in the rat by the disk-over-water method. *Behavioural Brain Research*, 1995, *69*, 55–63.

Rechtschaffen, A., and Bergmann, B. M. Sleep deprivation in the rat: An update of the 1989 paper. *Sleep*, 2002, *25*, 18–24.

Rechtschaffen, A., Bergmann, B. M., Everson, C. A., Kushida, C. A., and Gilliland, M. A. Sleep deprivation in the rat. X. Integration and discussion of the findings. *Sleep*, 1989, *12*, 68–87.

Rechtschaffen, A., Gilliland, M. A., Bergmann, B. M., and Winter, J. B. Physiological correlates of prolonged sleep deprivation in rats. *Science*, 1983, *221*, 182–184.

Reebs, S., and Mrosovsky, N. Effects of induced wheel running on the circadian activity rhythms of the Syrian hamster: Entrainment and phase response curve. *Journal of Biological Rhythms,* 1989, *4,* 39–48.

Reed, C. L., Caselli, R. J., and Farah, M. J. Tactile agnosia: Underlying impairment and implications for normal tactile object recognition. *Brain,* 1996, *119,* 875–888.

Reed, J. M., and Squire, L. R. Retrograde amnesia for facts and events: Findings from four new cases. *Journal of Neuroscience,* 1998, *18,* 3943–3954.

Regan, B. C., Julliot, C., Simmen, B., Vienot, F., Charles-Dominique, P., and Mollon, J. D. Fruits, foliage and the evolution of primate colour vision. *Philosophical Transactions of the Royal Society of London [B],* 2001, *356,* 229–283.

Rehkämper, G., Haase, E., and Frahm, H. D. Allometric comparison of brain weight and brain structure volumes in different breeds of the domestic pigeon, *Columbia livia f. d.* (fantails, homing pigeons, strassers). *Brain, Behavior and Evolution,* 1988, *31,* 141–149.

Reid, L. D. Endogenous opioids and alcohol dependence: Opioid alkaloids and the propensity to drink alcoholic beverages. *Alcohol,* 1996, *13,* 5–11.

Reid, M. S., Mickalian, J. D., Delucchi, K. L., and Berger, S. P. A nicotine antagonist, mecamylamine, reduced cue-induced cocaine craving in cocaine-dependent subjects. *Neuropsychopharmacology,* 1999, *20,* 297–307.

Rempel-Clower, N. L., Zola, S. M., Squire, L. R., and Amaral, D. G. Three cases of enduring memory impairment after bilateral damage limited to the hippocampal formation. *Journal of Neuroscience,* 1996, *16,* 5233–5255.

Reppert, S. M., and Weaver, D. R. Molecular analysis of mammalian circadian rhythms. *Annual Review of Physiology,* 2001, *63,* 647–676.

Resnick, H. S., Yehuda, R., Pitman, R. K., and Foy, D. W. Effect of previous trauma on acute plasma cortisol level following rape. *American Journal of Psychiatry,* 1995, *152,* 1675–1677.

Ressler, K. J., Sullivan, S. L., and Buck, L. A molecular dissection of spatial patterning in the olfactory system. *Current Opinion in Neurobiology,* 1994a, *4,* 588–596.

Ressler, K. J., Sullivan, S. L., and Buck, L. Information coding in the olfactory system: Evidence for a stereotyped and highly organized epitope map in the olfactory bulb. *Cell,* 1994b, *79,* 1245–1255.

Reynolds, D. V. Surgery in the rat during electrical analgesia induced by focal brain stimulation. *Science,* 1969, *164,* 444–445.

Rhees, R. W., Shryne, J. E., and Gorski, R. A. Termination of the hormone-sensitive period for differentiation of the sexually dimorphic nucleus of the preoptic area in male and female rats. *Developmental Brain Research,* 1990, *52,* 17–23.

Richter, R. M., and Weiss, F. In vivo CRF release in rat amygdala is increased during cocaine withdrawal in self-administering rats. *Synapse,* 1999, *32,* 254–261.

Ridley, R. M., Thornley, H. D., Baker, H. F., and Fine, A. Cholinergic neural transplants into hippocampus restore learning ability in monkeys with fornix transections. *Experimental Brain Research,* 1991, *83,* 533–538.

Riedel, G., Micheau, J., Lam, A. G., Roloff, E., Martin, S. J., Bridge, H., Hoz, L., Poeschel, B., McCulloch, J., and Morris, R. G. Reversible neural inactivation reveals hippocampal participation in several memory processes. *Nature Neuroscience,* 1999, *2,* 898–905.

Riemann, D., Berger, M., and Voderholzer, U. Sleep and depression—Results from psychobiological studies: An overview. *Biological Psychiatry,* 2001, *57,* 67–103.

Riemann, D., König, A., Hohagen, F., Kiemen, A., Voderholzer, U., Backhaus, J., Bunz, J., Wesiak, B., Hermie, L., and Berger, M. How to preserve the antidepressive effect of sleep deprivation: A comparison of sleep phase advance and sleep phase delay. *European Archives of Psychiatry and Clinical Neuroscience,* 1999, *249,* 231–237.

Riemann, D., Wiegand, M., and Berger, M. Are there predictors for sleep deprivation response in depressive patients? *Biological Psychiatry,* 1991, *29,* 707–710.

Rissman, E. F., Early, A. H., Taylor, J. A., Korach, K. S., and Lubahn, D. B. Estrogen receptors are essential for female sexual receptivity. *Endocrinology,* 1997, *138,* 507–510.

Ritter, R. C., Brenner, L., and Yox, D. P. Participation of vagal sensory neurons in putative satiety signals from the upper gastrointestinal tract. In *Neuroanatomy and Physiology of Abdominal Vagal Afferents,* edited by S. Ritter, R. C. Ritter, and C. D. Barnes. Boca Raton, Fla.: CRC Press, 1992.

Ritter, R. C., Slusser, P. G., and Stone, S. Glucoreceptors controlling feeding and blood glucose: Location in the hindbrain. *Science,* 1981, *213,* 451–453.

Ritter, S., and Taylor, J. S. Vagal sensory neurons are required for lipoprivic but not glucoprivic feeding in rats. *American Journal of Physiology,* 1990, *258,* R1395–R1401.

Ritter, S., Dinh, T. T., and Friedman, M. I. Induction of Fos-like immunoreactivity (Fos-li) and stimulation of feeding by 2,5-anhydro-D-mannitol (2,5-AM) require the vagus nerve. *Brain Research,* 1994, *646,* 53–64.

Rizzo, M., and Robin, D. A. Simultanagnosia: A defect of sustained attention yields insights on visual information processing. *Neurology,* 1990, *40,* 447–455.

Rizzolatti, G., and Arbib, M. A. Language within our grasp. *Trends in Neurosciences,* 1998, *21,* 188–194.

Rizzolatti, G., Fadiga, L., Gallese, V., and Fogassi, L. Premotor cortex and the recognition of motor actions. *Cognitive Brain Research,* 1996, *3,* 131–141.

Robbins, L. N., Helzer, J. E., Weissman, M. M., Orvaschel, H., Gruenberg, E., Burke, J. D., and Regier, D. A. Lifetime prevalence of specific psychiatric disorders in three sites. *Archives of General Psychiatry,* 1984, *41,* 949–958.

Robertson, G. S., Pfaus, J. G., Atkinson, L. J., Matsumura, H., Phillips, A. G., and Fibiger, H. C. Sexual behavior increases c-fos expression in the forebrain of the male rat. *Brain Research,* 1991, *564,* 352–357.

Robinson, D., Wu, H., Munne, R. A., Ashtari, M., Alvir, J. M., Lerner, G., Koreen, A., Cole, K., and Bogerts, B. Reduced caudate nucleus volume in obsessive-compulsive disorder. *Archives of General Psychiatry,* 1995, *52,* 393–398.

Robinson, F. R. Role of the cerebellum in movement control and adaptation. *Current Opinion in Neurobiology,* 1995, *5,* 755–762.

Robinson, T. E., and Berridge, K. C. The neural basis of drug craving: An incentive-sensitization theory of addiction. *Brain Research Reviews,* 1993, *18,* 247–291.

Robinson, T. E., Gorny, G., Mitton, E., and Kolb, B. Cocaine self-administration alters the morphology of dendrites and dendritic spines in the nucleus accumbens and neocortex. *Synapse,* 2001, *39,* 256–266.

Rockland, K. S., Andresen, J., Cowie, R. J., and Robinson, D. L. Single axon analysis of pulvinocortical connections to several visual areas in the macaque. *Journal of Comparative Neurology,* 1999, *406,* 221–250.

Rodieck, R. W. *The First Steps in Seeing.* Sunderland, MA: Sinauer Associates, 1998.

Rodier, P. M., Ingram, J. L., Tisdale, B., Nelson, S., and Romano, J. Embryological origin for autism: Developmental anomalies of the cranial nerve motor nuclei. *Journal of Comparative Neurology,* 1996, *370,* 247–261.

Rodman, H. R., Gross, C. G., and Albright, T. D. Afferent basis of visual response properties in area MT of the macaque. I. Effects of striate cortex removal. *Journal of Neuroscience,* 1989, *9,* 2033–2050.

Rodman, H. R., Gross, C. G., and Albright, T. D. Afferent basis of visual response properties in area MT of the macaque. II. Effects of superior colliculus removal. *Journal of Neuroscience,* 1990, *10,* 1154–1164.

Rodrigues, S. M., Schafe, G. E., and LeDoux, J. E. Intra-amygdala blockade of the NR2B subunit of the NMDA receptor disrupts the acquisition but not the expression of fear conditioning. *Journal of Neuroscience,* 2001, *21,* 6889–6896.

Rodriguez de Fonseca, F., Carrera, M. R., Navarro, M., Koob, G. F., and Weiss, F. Activation of corticotropin-releasing factor in the limbic system during cannabinoid withdrawal. *Science,* 1997, *276,* 2050–2054.

Roeltgen, D. P., Rothi, L. H., and Heilman, K. M. Linguistic semantic apraphia: A dissociation of the lexical spelling system from semantics. *Brain and Language,* 1986, *27,* 257–280.

Roffwarg, H. P., Dement, W. C., Muzio, J. N., and Fisher, C. Dream imagery: Relation to rapid eye movements of sleep. *Archives of General Psychiatry,* 1962, *7,* 235–258.

Roffwarg, H. P., Muzio, J. N., and Dement, W. C. Ontogenetic development of human sleep-dream cycle. *Science,* 1966, *152,* 604–619.

Rogan, M. T., and LeDoux, J. E. LTP is accompanied by commensurate enhancement of auditory-evoked responses in a fear conditioning circuit. *Neuron,* 1995, *15,* 127–136.

Rogers, M. P., Trentham, D. E., McCune, W. J., Ginsberg, B. I., Rennke, H. G., Reike, P., and David, J. R. Effect of psychological stress on the induction of arthritis in rats. *Arthritis and Rheumatology,* 1980, *23,* 1337–1342.

Rogers, R. D., and Robbins, T. W. Investigating the neurocognitive deficits associated with chronic drug misuse. *Current Opinion in Neurobiology,* 2001, *11,* 250–257.

Rogers, R. D., Owen, A. M., Middleton, H. C., Williams, E. J., Pickard, J. D., Sahakian, B. J., and Robbins, T. W. Choosing between small, likely rewards and large, unlikely rewards activates inferior and orbital prefrontal cortex. *Journal of Neuroscience,* 1999, *20,* 9029–9038.

Roland, P. E. Metabolic measurements of the working frontal cortex in man. *Trends in Neurosciences,* 1984, *7,* 430–435.

Rolls, E. T. Feeding and reward. In *The Neural Basis of Feeding and Reward,* edited by B. G. Hobel and D. Novin. Brunswick, Me.: Haer Institute, 1982.

Rolls, E. T. Functions of the primate hippocampus in spatial processing and memory. In *Neurobiology of Comparative Cognition,* edited by D. S. Olton and R. P. Kesner. Hillsdale, N.J.: Lawrence Erlbaum Associates, 1989.

Rolls, E. T. Central taste anatomy and neurophysiology. In *Handbook of Olfaction and Gustation,* edited by R. L. Doty. New York: Dekker, 1995a.

Rolls, E. T. Learning mechanisms in the temporal lobe visual cortex. *Behavioural Brain Research,* 1995b, *66,* 177–185.

Rolls, E. T. A theory of hippocampal function in memory. *Hippocampus,* 1996, *6,* 601–620.

Rolls, E. T., and Baylis, G. C. Size and contrast have only small effects on the responses to faces of neurons in the cortex of the superior temporal sulcus of the monkey. *Experimental Brain Research,* 1986, *65,* 38–48.

Rolls, E. T., Murzi, E., Yaxley, S., Thorpe, S. J., and Simpson, S. J. *Brain Research,* 2986, *368,* 79–86.

Rolls, E. T., Yaxley, S., and Sienkiewicz, Z. J. Gustatory responses of single neurons in the orbitofrontal cortex of the macaque monkey. *Journal of Neurophysiology,* 1990, *64,* 1055–1066.

Romanski, L. M., Tian, B., Fritz, J., Mishkin, M., Goldman-Rakic, P. S., and Rauschecker, J. P. Dual streams of auditory afferents target multiple domains in the primate prefrontal cortex. *Nature Neuroscience,* 1999, *12,* 1131–1136.

Romero, P. R., Beltramino, C. A., and Carrer, H. F. Participation of the olfactory system in the control of approach behavior of the female rat to the male. *Physiology and Behavior,* 1990, *47,* 685–690.

Rosa, R. R., and Bonnet, M. H. Reported chronic insomnia is independent of poor sleep as measured by electroencephalography. *Psychosomatic Medicine,* 2000, *62,* 474–482.

Rose, J. D. Changes in hypothalamic neuronal function related to hormonal induction of lordosis in behaving hamsters. *Physiology and Behavior,* 1990, *47,* 1201–1212.

Rose, J. E., Westman, E. C., Behm, F. M., Johnson, M. P., and Goldberg, J. S. Blockade of smoking satisfaction using the peripheral nicotinic antagonist trimethaphan. *Pharmacology, Biochemistry and Behavior,* 1999, *62,* 165–172.

Rosén, I., and Asanuma, H. Peripheral inputs to the forelimb area of the monkey motor cortex: Input-output relations. *Experimental Brain Research,* 1972, *14,* 257–273.

Rosenblatt, J. S., Hazelwood, S., and Poole, J. Maternal behavior in male rats: effects of medial preoptic area lesions and presence of maternal aggression. *Hormones and Behavior,* 1996, *30,* 201–215.

Rosenkranz, J. A., and Grace, A. A. Modulation of basolateral amygdala neuronal firing and afferent drive by dopamine receptor activation in vivo. *Journal of Neuroscience,* 1999, *19,* 11027–11039.

Rosenthal, D. A program of research on heredity in schizophrenia. *Behavioral Science,* 1971, *16,* 191–201.

Rosenthal, N. E., Sack, D. A., Gillin, C., Lewy, A. J., Goodwin, F. K., Davenport, Y., Mueller, P. S., Newsome, D. A., and Wehr, T. A. Seasonal affective disorder: A description of the syndrome and preliminary findings with light therapy. *Archives of General Psychiatry*, 1984, *41*, 72–80.

Rosenthal, N. E., Sack, D. A., James, S. P., Parry, B. L., Mendelson, W. B., Tamarkin, L., and Wehr, T. A. Seasonal affective disorder and phototherapy. *Annals of the New York Academy of Sciences*, 1985, *453*, 260–269.

Ross, E. D., Homan, R. W., and Buck, R. Differential hemispheric lateralization of primary and social emotions. *Neuropsychiatry, Neuropsychology, and Behavioral Neurology*, 1994, 7, 1–19.

Rosser, A. E., and Keverne, E. B. The importance of central noradrenergic neurons in the formation of an olfactory memory in the prevention of pregnancy block. *Neuroscience*, 1985, *16*, 1141–1147.

Rossetti, A. L., Hmaidan, Y., and Gessa, G. L. Marked inhibition of mesolimbic dopamine release: A common feature of ethanol, morphine, cocaine and amphetamine abstinence in rats. *European Journal of Pharmacology*, 1992, *221*, 227–234.

Roth, M., Decery, J., Raybaudi, M., Massarelli, R., Delon-Martin, C., Segebarth, C., Morand, S., Gemignani, A., Décorps, M., and Jeannerod, M. Possible involvement of primary motor cortex in mentally simulated movement: A functional magnetic resonance imaging study. *Neuroreport*, 1996, 7, 1280–1284.

Rothman, S. M., and Olney, J. W. Excitotoxicity and the NMDA receptor. *Trends in Neurosciences*, 1987, *10*, 299–302.

Routtenberg, A. "Self-starvation" of rats living in activity wheels: Adaptation effects. *Journal of Comparative Psychology*, 1968, *66*, 234–238.

Routtenberg, A., and Malsbury, C. Brainstem pathways of reward. *Journal of Comparative and Physiological Psychology*, 1969, *68*, 22–30.

Roy, A., De Jong, J., and Linnoila, M. Cerebrospinal fluid monoamine metabolites and suicidal behavior in depressed patients. *Archives of General Psychiatry*, 1989, *46*, 609–612.

Rozanski, A., Blumenthal, J. A., and Kaplan, J. Impact of psychological factors in the pathogenesis of cardiovascular disease and implications for therapy. *Circulation*, 1999, *99*, 2192–2217.

Rubin, B. D., and Katz, L. C. Optical imaging of odorant representations in the mammalian olfactory bulb. *Neuron*, 1999, *23*, 499–511.

Rubin, B. S., and Barfield, R. J. Priming of estrous responsiveness by implants of 17B-estradiol in the ventromedial hypothalamic nucleus of female rats. *Endocrinology*, 1980, *106*, 504–509.

Rubin, L. L., and Staddon, J. M. The cell biology of the blood–brain barrier. *Annual Review of Neuroscience*, 1999, *22*, 111–128.

Ruggero, M. A. Responses to sound of the basilar membrane of the mammalian cochlea. *Current Opinion in Neurobiology*, 1992, *2*, 449–456.

Rusak, B., and Morin, L. P. Testicular responses to photoperiod are blocked by lesions of the suprachiasmatic nuclei in golden hamsters. *Biology of Reproduction*, 1976, *15*, 366–374.

Rusak, B., McNaughton, L., Robertson, H. A., and Hunt, S. P. Circadian variation in photic regulation of immediate-early gene mRNAs in rat suprachiasmatic nucleus cells. *Molecular Brain Research*, 1992, *14*, 124–130.

Rusak, B., Meijer, J. H., and Harrington, M. E. Hamster circadian rhythms are phase-shifted by electrical stimulation of the geniculohypothalamic tract. *Brain Research*, 1989, *493*, 283–291.

Rusak, B., Robertson, H. A., Wisden, W., and Hunt, S. P. Light pulses that shift rhythms induce gene expression in the suprachiasmatic nucleus. *Science*, 1990, *248*, 1237–1240.

Russchen, F. T., Amaral, D. G., and Price, J. L. The afferent connections of the substantia innominata in the monkey, *Macaca fascicularis*. *Journal of Comparative Neurology*, 1986, *242*, 1–27.

Russell, G. F. M., and Treasure, J. The modern history of anorexia nervosa: An interpretation of why the illness has changed. *Annals of the New York Academy of Sciences*, 1989, *575*, 13–30.

Russell, M. J. Human olfactory communication. *Nature*, 1976, *260*, 520–522.

Russell, M. J., Switz, G. M., and Thompson, K. Olfactory influences on the human menstrual cycle. Paper presented at the meeting of the American Association for the Advancement of Science, San Francisco, June 1977.

Rutter, M. Cognitive deficits in the pathogenesis of autism. *Journal of Child Psychology and Psychiatry*, 1983, *24*, 513–531.

Ryba, N. J., and Tirindelli, R. A new multigene family of putative pheromone receptors. *Neuron*, 1997, *19*, 371–392.

Ryback, R. S., and Lewis, O. F. Effects of prolonged bed rest on EEG sleep patterns in young, healthy volunteers. *Electroencephalography and Clinical Neurophysiology*, 1971, *31*, 395–399.

Saayman, G. S. Aggressive behaviour in free-ranging chacma baboons (*Papio ursinus*). *Journal of Behavioral Science*, 1971, *1*, 77–83.

Sachar, E. J., and Baron, M. The biology of affective disorders. *Annual Review of Neuroscience*, 1979, *2*, 505–518.

Sachdev, P., and Hay, P. Does neurosurgery for obsessive-compulsive disorder produce personality change? *Journal of Nervous and Mental Disease*, 1995, *183*, 408–413.

Sackeim, H. A., and Gur, R. C. Lateral asymmetry in intensity of emotional expression. *Neuropsychologia*, 1978, *16*, 473–482.

Sackeim, H. A., Decina, P., Prohovnik, I., Malitz, S., and Resor, S. R. Anticonvulsant and antidepressant properties of electroconvulsive therapy: A proposed mechanism of action. *Biological Psychiatry*, 1983, *18*, 1301–1310.

Sadato, N., Pascualleone, A., Grafman, J., Ibanez, V., Deiber, M. P., Dold, G., and Hallett, M. Activation of the primary visual cortex by Braille reading in blind subjects. *Nature*, 1996, *380*, 526–528.

Saffran, E. M., Marin, O. S. M., and Yeni-Komshian, G. H. An analysis of speech perception in word deafness. *Brain and Language*, 1976, *3*, 209–228.

Saffran, E. M., Schwartz, M. F., and Marin, O. S. M. Evidence from aphasia: Isolating the components of a production model. In *Language Production*, edited by B. Butterworth. London: Academic Press, 1980.

Sagvolden, T., Aase, H., Zeiner, P., and Berger, D. Altered reinforcement mechanisms in attention-deficit/hyperactivity disorder. *Behavioural Brain Research*, 1998, *94*, 61–71.

Sagvolden, T., and Sergeant, J. A. Attention deficit/hyperactivity disorder: From brain dysfunctions to behaviour. *Behavioural Brain Research*, 1998, *94*, 1–10.

Sahu, A., Kalra, P. S., and Kalra, S. P. Food deprivation and ingestion induce reciprocal changes in neuropeptide Y concentrations in the paraventricular nucleus. *Peptides*, 1988, *9*, 83–86.

Saitoh, K., Maruyama, N., and Kudoh, M. Sustained response of auditory cortex units in the cat. In *Brain Mechanisms of Sensation*, edited by Y. Katsuki, R. Norgren, and M. Sato. New York: John Wiley & Sons, 1981.

Sakai, F., Meyer, J. S., Karacan, I., Derman, S., and Yamamoto, M. Normal human sleep: Regional cerebral haemodynamics. *Annals of Neurology*, 1979, *7*, 471–478.

Sakai, K. Some anatomical and physiological properties of pontomesencephalic tegmental neurons with special reference to the PGO waves and postural atonia during paradoxical sleep in the cat. In *The Reticular Formation Revisited*, edited by J. A. Hobson and M. A. Brazier. New York: Raven Press, 1980.

Sakai, K., and Jouvet, M. Brain stem PGO-on cells projecting directly to the cat dorsal lateral geniculate nucleus. *Brain Research*, 1980, *194*, 500–505.

Sakuma, Y., and Pfaff, D. W. Facilitation of female reproductive behavior from mesencephalic central grey in the rat. *American Journal of Physiology,* 1979a, *237*, R278–R284.

Sakuma, Y., and Pfaff, D. W. Mesencephalic mechanisms for integration of female reproductive behavior in the rat. *American Journal of Physiology*, 1979b, *237*, R285–R290.

Sakuma, Y., and Pfaff, D. W. Convergent effects of lordosis-relevant somatosensory and hypothalamic influences on central gray cells in the rat mesencephalon. *Experimental Neurology*, 1980a, *70*, 269–281.

Sakuma, Y., and Pfaff, D. W. Excitability of female rat central gray cells with medullary projections: Changes produced by hypothalamic stimulation and estrogen treatment. *Journal of Neurophysiology*, 1980b, *44*, 1012–1023.

Sakurai, T., Amemiya, A., Ishii, M., Matsuzaki, I., Chemelli, R. M., Tanaka, H., Williams, S. C., Richardson, J. A., Kozlowski, G. P., Wilson, S., Arch, J. R., Buckingham, R. E., Haynes, A. C., Carr, S. A., Annan, R. S., McNulty, D. E., Liu, W. S., Terrett, J. A., Elshourbagy, N. A., Bergsma, D. J., and Yanagisawa, M. Orexins and orexin receptors: A family of hypothalamic neuropeptides and G protein-coupled receptors that regulate feeding behavior. *Cell*, 1998, *20*, 573–585.

Sakurai, Y., Ichikawa, Y., and Mannen, T. Pure alexia from a posterior occipital lesion. *Neurology*, 2001, *56*, 778–781.

Sakurai, Y., Momose, T., Iwata, M., Sudo, Y., Ohtomo, K., and Kanazawa, I. Different cortical activity in reading of Kanji words, Kana words and Kana nonwords. *Cognitive Brain Research*, 2000, *9*, 111–115.

Sakurai, Y., Sakai, K., Sakuta, M., and Iwata, M. Naming difficulties in alexia with agraphia for kanji after a left posterior inferior temporal lesion. *Journal of Neurology, Neurosurgery, and Psychiatry*, 1994, *57*, 609–613.

Salamone, J. D. Complex motor and sensorimotor function of striatal and accumbens dopamine: Involvement in instrumental behavior processes. *Psychopharmacology*, 1992, *107*, 160–174.

Saller, C. F., and Stricker, E. M. Hyperphagia and increased growth in rats after intraventricular injection of 5,7-dihydroxytryptamine. *Science,* 1976, *192*, 385–387.

Samson, H. H., Hodge, C. W., Tolliver, G. A., and Haraguchi, M. Effect of dopamine agonists and antagonists on ethanol rein-forced behavior: The involvement of the nucleus accumbens. *Brain Research Bulletin*, 1993, *30*, 133–141.

Sananes, C. B., and Campbell, B. A. Role of the central nucleus of the amygdala in olfactory heart rate conditioning. *Behavioral Neuroscience*, 1989, *103*, 519–525.

Sanders, S. K., and Shekhar, A. Anxiolytic effects of chlordiazepoxide blocked by injection of $GABA_A$ and benzodiazepine receptor antagonists in the region of the anterior basolateral amygdala of rats. *Biological Psychiatry*, 1995, *37*, 473–476.

Sandler, V. M., and Ross, W. N. Serotonin modulates spike back-propagation and associated [Ca2+]i changes in the apical dendrites of hippocampal CA1 pyramidal neurons. *Journal of Neurophysiology*, 1999, *81*, 216–224.

Santini, E., Muller, R. U., and Quirk, G. J. Consolidation of extinction learning involves transfer from NMDA-independent to NMDA-dependent memory. *Journal of Neuroscience*, 2001, *21*, 9009–9017.

Saper, C. B., Chou, T. C., and Scammell, T. E. The sleep switch: Hypothalamic control of sleep and wakefulness. *Trends in Neurosciences*, 2001, *24*, 726–731.

Sapolsky, R. *Stress, the Aging Brain and the Mechanisms of Neuron Death*. Cambridge, Mass.: MIT Press, 1992.

Sapolsky, R. M. Social subordinance as a marker of hypercortisolism: Some unexpected subtleties. *Annals of the New York Academy of Science*, 1995, *771*, 626–639.

Sassenrath, E. N., Powell, T. E., and Hendrickx, A. G. Perimenstrual aggression in groups of female rhesus monkeys. *Journal of Reproduction and Fertility*, 1973, *34*, 509–511.

Saudou, F., Amara, D. A., Dierich, A., Lemeur, M., Ramboz, S., Segu, L., Buhot, M. C., and Hen, R. Enhanced aggressive behavior in mice lacking $5\text{-}HT_{1B}$ receptor. *Science*, 1994, *265*, 1875–1878.

Savic, I., Berglund, H., Gulyas, B., and Roland, P. Smelling of odorous sex hormone-like compounds causes sex-differentiated hypothalamic activations in humans. *Neuron*, 2001, *31*, 661–668.

Sawaguchi, T., and Goldman-Rakic, P. S. The role of D1-dopamine receptor in working memory: Local injections of dopamine antagonists into the prefrontal cortex of rhesus monkeys performing an oculomotor delayed-response task. *Journal of Neurophysiology*, 1994, *71*, 515–528.

Sawchenko, P. E. Toward a new neurobiology of energy balance, appetite, and obesity: The anatomist weigh in. *Journal of Comparative Neurology*, 1998, *402*, 435–441.

Saxena, S., Brody, A. L., Schwartz, J. M., and Baxter, L. R. Neuroimaging and frontal-subcortical circuitry in obsessive-compulsive disorder. *British Journal of Psychiatry*, 1998, *173*, 26–37.

Scammell, T. E., Gerashchenko, D. Y., Mochizuki, T., McCarthy, M. T., Estabrooke, I. V., Sears, C. A., Saper, C. B., Urade, Y., and Hayaishi, O. An adenosine A2a agonist increases sleep and induces Fos in ventrolateral preoptic neurons. *Neuroscience*, 2001, *107*, 653–663.

Scammell, T. W., Estabrooke, I. V., McCarthy, M. T., Chemelli, R. M., Yanagisawa, M., Miller, M. S., and Saper, C. B. Hypothalamic arousal regions are activated during modafinil-induced wakefulness. *Journal of Neuroscience*, 2000, *20*, 8620–8628.

Scarpace, P. J., Matheny, M., and Tümer, N. Hypothalamic leptin resistance is associated with impaired leptin signal transduction in aged obese rats. *Neuroscience*, 2001, *104*, 1111–1117.

Schacter, D. L., Alpert, N. M., Savage, C. R., Rauch, S. L., and Albert, M. S. Conscious recollection and the human hippocampal formation: Evidence from positron emission tomography. *Proceedings of the National Academy of Sciences, USA,* 1996, *93,* 321–325.

Schafe, G. E., and LeDoux, J. E. Memory consolidation of auditory pavlovian fear conditioning requires protein synthesis and protein kinase A in the amygdala. *Journal of Neuroscience,* 2000, *20,* RC96 (1–5).

Schein, S. J., and Desimone, R. Spectral properties of V4 neurons in the macaque. *Journal of Neuroscience,* 1990, *10,* 3369–3389.

Schenck, C. H., and Mahowald, M. W. Motor dyscontrol in narcolepsy: Rapid-eye-movement (REM) sleep without atonia and REM sleep behavior disorder. *Annals of Neurology,* 1992, *32,* 3–10.

Schenck, C. H., Bundlie, S. R., Ettinger, M. G., and Mahowald, M. W. Chronic behavioral disorders of human REM sleep: A new category of parasomnia. *Sleep,* 1986, *9,* 293–308.

Schenck, C. H., Hurwitz, T. D., and Mahowald, M. W. REM-sleep behavior disorder: An update on a series of 96 patients and a review of the world literature. *Journal of Sleep Research,* 1993, *2,* 224–231.

Schenkel, E., and Siegel, J. M. REM sleep without atonia after lesions of the medial medulla. *Neuroscience Letters,* 1989, *98,* 159–165.

Scherschlicht, R., Polc, P., Schneeberger, J., Steiner, M., and Haefely, W. Selective suppression of rapid eye movement sleep (REMS) in cats by typical and atypical antidepressants. In *Typical and Atypical Antidepressants: Molecular Mechanisms,* edited by E. Costa and G. Racagni. New York: Raven Press, 1982.

Schiffman, J., Ekstrom, M., LaBrie, J., Schulsinger, F., Sorensen, H., and Mednick, S. Minor physical anomalies and schizophrenia spectrum disorders: A prospective investigation. *American Journal of Psychiatry,* 2002, *159,* 238–243.

Schiffman, S. S., Lockhead, E., and Maes, F. W. Amiloride reduces the taste intensity of Na⁺ and Li⁺ salts and sweeteners. *Proceedings of the National Academy of Sciences, USA,* 1983, *80,* 6136–6140.

Schiller, P. H. The ON and OFF channels of the visual system. *Trends in Neuroscience,* 1992, *15,* 86–92.

Schiller, P. H., and Malpeli, J. G. Properties and tectal projections of monkey retinal ganglion cells. *Journal of Neurophysiology,* 1977, *40,* 428–445.

Schiller, P. H., Sandell, J. H., and Maunsell, J. H. R. Functions of the ON and OFF channels of the visual system. *Nature,* 1986, *322,* 824–825.

Schleifer, S. J., Keller, S. E., Camerino, M., Thornton, J. C., and Stein, M. Suppression of lymphocyte stimulation following bereavement. *Journal of the American Medical Association,* 1983, *15,* 374–377.

Schmidt, M. H., Valatx, J.-L., Sakai, K., Fort, P., and Jouvet, M. Role of the lateral preoptic area in sleep-related erectile mechanisms and sleep generation in the rat. *Journal of Neuroscience,* 2000, *20,* 6640–6647.

Schneider, B., Muller, M. J., and Philipp, M. Mortality in affective disorders. *Journal of the Affective Disorders,* 2001, *65,* 263–274.

Schneider, F., Gur, R. E., Alavi, A., Seligman, M. E. P., Mozley, L. H., Smith, R. J., Mozley, P. D., and Gur, R. C. Cerebral blood flow changes in limbic regions induced by unsolvable anagram tasks. *American Journal of Psychiatry,* 1996, *153,* 206–212.

Schrauwen, P., Xia, J., Bogardus, C., Pratley, R. E., and Ravussin, E. Skeletal muscle uncoupling protein 3 expression is a determinant of energy expenditure in Pima Indians. *Diabetes,* 1999, *48,* 146–149.

Schuman, E. R., and Madison, D. V. A requirement for the intercellular messenger nitric oxide in long-term potentiation. *Science,* 1991, *254,* 1503–1506.

Schuster, C. R., and Balster, R. L. The discriminative stimulus properties of drugs. *Advances in Behavioral Pharmacology,* 1977, *1,* 85–138.

Schwartz, M. F., Marin, O. S. M., and Saffran, E. M. Dissociations of language function in dementia: A case study. *Brain and Language,* 1979, *7,* 277–306.

Schwartz, M. F., Saffran, E. M., and Marin, O. S. M. The word order problem in agrammatism. I. Comprehension. *Brain and Language,* 1980, *10,* 249–262.

Schwartz, M. W., Peskind, E., Raskind, M., Boyko, E. J., and Porte, D. Cerebrospinal fluid leptin levels: Relationship to plasma levels and to adiposity in humans. *Nature Medicine,* 1996, *2,* 589–593.

Schwartz, W. J., and Gainer, H. Suprachiasmatic nucleus: Use of ¹⁴C-labelled deoxyglucose uptake as a functional marker. *Science,* 1977, *197,* 1089–1091.

Schwartz, W. J., Reppert, S. M., Eagan, S. M., and Moore-Ede, M. C. In vivo metabolic activity of the suprachiasmatic nuclei: A comparative study. *Brain Research,* 1983, *274,* 184–187.

Schwarzkopf, S. B., Nasrallah, H. A., Olson, S. C., Coffman, J. A., and McLaughlin, J. A. Perinatal complications and genetic loading in schizophrenia: Preliminary findings. *Psychiatry Research,* 1989, *27,* 233–239.

Scott, S. K., Blank, E. C., Rosen, S., and Wise, R. J. S. Identification of a pathway for intelligible speech in the left temporal lobe. *Brain,* 2000, *123,* 2400–2406.

Scott, T. R., and Plata-Salaman, C. R. Coding of taste quality. In *Smell and Taste in Health and Disease,* edited by T. N. Getchell. New York: Raven Press, 1991.

Scott, T. R., Plata-Salaman, C. R., Smith, V. L., and Giza, B. K. Gustatory neural coding in the monkey cortex: Stimulus intensity. *Journal of Neurophysiology,* 1991, *65,* 76–86.

Scott, T. R., Yaxley, S., Sienkiewicz, Z. J., and Rolls, E. T. Gustatory responses in the nucleus tractus solitarius of the alert cynomolgus monkey. *Journal of Neurophysiology,* 1986, *55,* 182–200.

Scoville, W. B., and Milner, B. Loss of recent memory after bilateral hippocampal lesions. *Journal of Neurology, Neurosurgery and Psychiatry,* 1957, *20,* 11–21.

Seagraves, M. A., Goldberg, M. E., Deny, S., Bruce, C. J., Ungerleider, L. G., and Mishkin, M. The role of striate cortex in the guidance of eye movements in the monkey. *The Journal of Neuroscience,* 1987, *7,* 3040–3058.

Sedvall, G., Fyrö, B., Gullberg, B., Nybäck, H., Wiesel, F.-A., and Wode-Helgodt, B. Relationship in healthy volunteers between concentrations of monoamine metabolites in cerebrospinal fluid and family history of psychiatric morbidity. *British Journal of Psychiatry,* 1980, *136,* 366–374.

Seidman, L. J., Biederman, J., Weber, W., Hatch, M., and Faraone, S. V. Neuropsychological function in adults with attention-deficit hyperactivity disorder. *Biological Psychiatry,* 1998, *44,* 260–268.

Selye, H. *The Stress of Life.* New York: McGraw-Hill, 1976.

Semba, K. Aminergic and cholinergic afferents to REM sleep induction regions of the pontine reticular formation of the rat. *Journal of Comparative Neurology,* 1993, *330,* 543–556.

Semenza, C., and Zettin, M. Evidence from aphasia for the role of proper names as pure referring expressions. *Nature,* 1989, *342,* 678–679.

Semenza, C., Cipolotti, L., and Denes, G. Reading aloud in jargonaphasia: An unusual dissociation in speech output. *Journal of Neurology, Neurosurgery, and Psychiatry,* 1992, *55,* 205–208.

Sergent, J., and Signoret, J.-L. Functional and anatomical decomposition of face processing: Evidence from prosopagnosia and PET study of normal subjects. *Philosophical Transactions of the Royal Society of London [B],* 1992, *335,* 55–62.

Service, R. F. Probing alcoholism's "dark side." *Science,* 1999, *285,* 1473.

Sforza, E., Montagna, P., Tinuper, P., Cortelli, P., Avoni, P., Ferrillo, F., Petersen, R., Gambetti, P., and Lagaresi, E. Sleep-wake cycle abnormalities in fatal familial insomnia: Evidence of the role of the thalamus in sleep regulation. *Electroencephalography and Clinical Neurophysiology,* 1995, *94,* 398–405.

Shalev, U., Grimm, J. W., and Shaham, Y. Neurobiology of relapse to heroin and cocaine seeking: A review. *Pharmacological Reviews,* 2002, *54,* 1–42.

Shallice, T. Phonological agraphia and the lexical route in writing. *Brain,* 1981, *104,* 413–429.

Sham, P. C., O'Callaghan, E., Takei, N., Murray, G. K., Hare, E. H., and Murray, R. M. Schizophrenia following pre-natal exposure to influenza epidemics between 1939 and 1960. *British Journal of Psychiatry,* 1992, *160,* 461–466.

Shammi, P., and Stuss, D. T. Humor appreciation: A role of the right frontal lobe. *Brain,* 1999, *122,* 657–666.

Shapiro, L. E., Leonard, C. M., Sessions, C. E., Dewsbury, D. A., and Insel, T. R. Comparative neuroanatomy of the sexually dimorphic hypothalamus in monogamous and polygamous voles. *Brain Research,* 1991, *541,* 232–240.

Shapiro, M. L., Simon, D. K., Olton, D. S., Gage, F. H., Nilsson, O., and Björklund, A. Intrahippocampal grafts of fetal basal forebrain tissue alter place fields in the hippocampus of rats with fimbria-fornix lesions. *Neuroscience,* 1989, *32,* 1–18.

Sharp, F. R., Sagar, S. M., Hicks, K., Lowenstein, D., and Hisanaga, K. C-fos mRNA, Fos, and Fos-related antigen induction by hypertonic saline and stress. *Journal of Neuroscience,* 1991, *11,* 2321–2331.

Shastry, B. S. Schizophrenia: A genetic perspective (review). *Internal Journal of Molecular Medicine,* 2002, *9,* 207–212.

Shavit, Y., Lewis, J. W., Terman, G. W., Gale, R. P., and Liebeskind, J. C. Opioid peptides mediate the suppressive effect of stress on natural killer cell cytotoxicity. *Science,* 1984, *223,* 188–190.

Shaywitz, B. A., Shaywitz, S. E., Pugh, K. R., Mencl, W. E., Fulbright, R. K., Skudlarski P., Constable, R. T., Marchione, K. E., Fletcher, J. M., Lyon, G. R., and Gore, J. C. Disruption of posterior brain systems for reading in children with developmental dyslexia. *Biological Psychiatry,* 2002, *52,* 101–110.

Shearman, L. P., Sriram, S., Weaver, D. R., Maywood, E. S., Chaves, I., Zheng, B., Kume, K., Lee, C. C., van der Horst, G. T., Hastings, M. H., and Reppert, S. M. Interacting molecular loops in the mammalian circadian clock. *Science,* 2000, *288,* 1013–1019.

Shelton, K. L., and Balster, R. L. Ethanol drug discrimination in rats: Substitution with GABA agonists and NMDA antagonists. *Behavioural Pharmacology,* 1994, *5,* 441–450.

Shen, K., and Meyer, T. Dynamic control of CaMKII translocation and localization in hippocampal neurons by NMDA stimulation. *Science,* 1999, *284,* 162–166.

Shenton, M. E., Dickey, C. C., Frumin, M., and McCarley, R. W. A review of MRI findings in schizophrenia. *Schizophrenia Research,* 2001, *49,* 1–52.

Shepherd, G. M. Discrimination of molecular signals by the olfactory receptor neuron. *Neuron,* 1994, *13,* 771–790.

Sher, A. E. Surgery for obstructive sleep apnea. *Progress in Clinical Biology Research,* 1990, *345,* 407–415.

Sher, L., Goldman, D., Ozaki, N., and Rosenthal, N. E. The role of genetic factors in the etiology of seasonal affective disorder and seasonality. *Journal of Affective Disorders,* 1999, *53,* 203–210.

Sherin, J. E., Elmquist, J. K., Torrealba, F., and Saper, C. B. Innervation of histaminergic tuberomammillary neurons by GABAergic and galaninergic neurons in the ventrolateral preoptic nucleus of the rat. *Journal of Neuroscience,* 1998, *18,* 4705–4721.

Sherin, J. E., Shiromani, P. J., McCarley, R. W., and Saper, C. B. Activation of ventrolateral preoptic neurons during sleep. *Science,* 1996, *271,* 216–219.

Sherry, D. F., Jacobs, L. F., and Gaulin, S. J. C. Spatial memory and adaptive specialization of the hippocampus. *Trends in Neuroscience,* 1992, *15,* 298–303.

Shi, S.-H., Hayashi, Y., Petralia, R. S., Zaman, S. H., Wenthold, R. J., Svoboda, K., and Malinow, R. Rapid spine delivery and redistribution of ampa receptors after synaptic NMDA receptor activation. *Science,* 1999, *284,* 1811–1816.

Shifren, J. L., Braunstein, G. D., Simon, J. A., Casson, P. R., Buster, J. E., Redmond, G. P., Burki, R. E., Ginsburg, E. S., Rosen, R. C., Leiblum, S. R., Caramelli, K. E., and Mazer, N. A. Transdermal testosterone treatment in women with impaired sexual function after oophorectomy. *New England Journal of Medicine,* 2000, *343,* 682–688.

Shik, M. L., and Orlovsky, G. N. Neurophysiology of locomotor automatism. *Physiological Review,* 1976, *56,* 465–501.

Shima, K., and Tanji, J. Both supplementary and presupplementary motor areas are crucial for the temporal organization of multiple movements. *Journal of Neurophysiology,* 1998, *80,* 3247–3260.

Shima, K., and Tanji, J. Neuronal activity in the supplementary and presupplementary motor areas for temporal organization of multiple movements. *Journal of Neurophysiology,* 2000, *84,* 2148–2160.

Shimada, M., Tritos, N. A., Lowell, B. B., Flier, J. S., and Maratos-Flier, E. Mice lacking melanin-concentrating hormone are hypophagic and lean. *Nature,* 1998, *396,* 670–674.

Shimokawa, T., Kumar, M. V., and Lane, M. D. Effect of a fatty acid synthase inhibitor in food intake and expression of hypothalamic neuropeptides. *Proceedings of the National Academy of Science, USA*, 2002, *99*, 66–71.

Shimura, T., Yamamoto, T., and Shimokochi, M. The medial pre-optic area is involved in both sexual arousal and performance in male rats: Re-evaluation of neuron activity in freely moving animals. *Brain Research*, 1994, *640*, 215–222.

Shindy, W. W., Posley, K. A., and Fuster, J. M. Reversible deficit in haptic delay tasks from cooling prefrontal cortex. *Cerebral Cortex*, 1994, *4*, 443–450.

Shinohara, K., Morofushi, M., Funabashi, T., and Kimura, F. Axillary pheromones modulate pulsatile LH secretion in humans. *Neuroreport*, 2001, *12*, 893–895.

Shipley, M. T., and Ennis, M. Functional organization of the olfactory system. *Journal of Neurobiology*, 1996, *30*, 123–176.

Shirayama, Y., Mitsuchio, H., Takashima, M., Ichikawa, H., and Takahashi, K. Reduction of substance P after chronic antidepressants treatment in the striatum, substantia nigra and amygdala of the rat. *Brain Research*, 1996, *739*, 70–78.

Shors, T. J., Seib, T. B., Levine, S., and Thompson, R. F. Inescapable versus escapable shock modulates long-term potentiation in the rat hippocampus. *Science*, 1989, *244*, 224–226.

Shoulson, I., Oakes, D., Fahn, S., Lang, A., Langston, J. W., LeWitt, P., Olanow, C. W., Penney, J. B., Tanner, C., Kieburtz, K., and Rudolph, A. Parkinson Study Group. Impact of sustained deprenyl (selegiline) in levodopa-treated Parkinson's disease: A randomized placebo-controlled extension of the deprenyl and tocopherol antioxidative therapy of parkinsonism trial. *Annals of Neurology*, 2002, *51*, 604–612.

Shouse, M. N., and Siegel, J. M. Pontine regulation of REM sleep components in cats: Integrity of the pedunculopontine tegmentum (PPT) is important for phasic events but unnecessary for atonia during REM sleep. *Brain Research*, 1992, *571*, 50–63.

Shuto, Y., Shibasaki, T., Otagiri, A., Kuriyama, H., Ohata, H., Tamura, H., Kamegai, J., Sugihara, H., Oikawa, S., and Wakabayashi, I. Hypothalamic growth hormone secretagogue receptor regulates growth hormone secretion, feeding, and adiposity. *Journal of Clinical Investigation*, 2002, *109*, 1429–1436.

Siciliano, D., and Smith, R. F. Preadolescent alcohol alters adult behavioral characteristics in the rat. *Physiology and Behavior*, 2001, *74*, 637–643.

Sidman, M., Stoddard, L. T., and Mohr, J. P. Some additional quantitative observations of immediate memory in a patient with bilateral hippocampal lesions. *Neuropsychologia*, 1968, *6*, 245–254.

Siegel, A., Roeling, T. A. P., Gregg, T. R., and Kruk, M. R. Neuropharmacology of brain-stimulation-evoked aggression. *Neuroscience and Biobehavioral Reviews*, 1999, *23*, 359–389.

Siegel, J. M. Brainstem mechanisms generating REM sleep. In *Principles and Practice of Sleep Medicine*, edited by M. H. Kryger, T. Roth, and W. C. Dement. Philadelphia: W. B. Saunders, 1989.

Siegel, J. M., and McGinty, D. J. Pontine reticular formation neurons: Relationship of discharge to motor activity. *Science*, 1977, *196*, 678–680.

Siegel, R. M., and Andersen, R. A. Motion perceptual deficits following ibotenic acid lesions of the middle temporal area (MT) in the behaving monkey. *Society for Neuroscience Abstracts*, 1986, *12*, 1183.

Siever, L. J., Kahn, R. S., Lawlor, B. A., Trestman, R. L., Lawrence, T. L., and Coccaro, E. F. Critical issues in defining the role of serotonin in psychiatric disorders. *Pharmacological Reviews*, 1991, *43*, 509–526.

Sigvardsson, S., Bohman, M., and Cloninger, R. Replication of the Stockholm adoption study of alcoholism. *Archives of General Psychiatry*, 1996, *53*, 681–687.

Silva, A. J., Paylor, R., Wehner, J. M., and Tonegawa, S. Impaired spatial learning in α-calcium-calmodulin kinase II mutant mice. *Science*, 1992b, *257*, 206–211.

Silva, A. J., Stevens, C. F., Tonegawa, S., and Wang, Y. Deficient hippocampal long-term potentiation in α-calcium-calmodulin kinase II mutant mice. *Science*, 1992, *257*, 201–206.

Silver, R., LeSauter, J., Tresco, P. A., and Lehman, M. N. A diffusible coupling signal from the transplanted suprachiasmatic nucleus controlling circadian locomotor rhythms. *Nature*, 1996, *382*, 810–813.

Silveri, M. C. Peripheral aspects of writing can be differentially affected by sensorial and attentional defect: Evidence from a patient with afferent dysgraphia and case dissociation. *Cortex*, 1996, *32*, 155–172.

Simos, P. G., Castillo, E. M., Fletcher, J. M., Francis, D. J., Maestu, F., Breier, J. I., Maggio, W. W., and Papanicolaou, A. C. Mapping of receptive language cortex in bilingual volunteers by using magnetic source imaging. *Journal of Neurosurgery*, 2001, *95*, 76–81.

Simpson, J. B., Epstein, A. N., and Camardo, J. S. The localization of dipsogenic receptors for angiotensin II in the subfornical organ. *Journal of Comparative and Physiological Psychology*, 1978, *92*, 581–608.

Simuni, T., Jaggi, J. L., Mulholland, H., Hurtig, H. I., Colcher, A., Siderowf, A. D., Ravina, B., Skolnick, B. E., Goldstein, R., Stern, M. B., and Baltuch, G. H. Bilateral stimulation of the subthalamic nucleus in patients with Parkinson disease: A study of efficacy and safety. *Journal of Neurosurgery*, 2002, *96*, 666–672.

Sinclair, A. H., Berta, P., Palmer, M. S., Hawkins, J. R., Griffiths, B. L., Smith, M. J., Foster, J. W., Frischauf, A. M., Lovell-Badge, R., and Goodfellow, P. N. A gene frrom the human sex-determining region encodes a protein with homology to a conserved DNA-binding motif. *Nature*, 1990, *346*, 240–244.

Singer, A. G. A chemistry of mammalian pheromones. *Journal of Steroid Biochemistry and Molecular Biology*, 1991, *39*, 627–632.

Singer, A. G., Macrides, F., Clancy, A. N., and Agosta, W. C. Purification and analysis of a proteinaceous aphrodisiac pheromone from hamster vaginal discharge. *Journal of Biological Chemistry*, 1986, *261*, 13323–13326.

Singer, C., and Weiner, W. J. Male sexual dysfunction. *Neurologist*, 1996, *2*, 119–129.

Singer, F., and Zumoff, B. Subnormal serum testosterone levels in male internal medicine residents. *Steroids*, 1992, *57*, 86–89.

Singer, L. K., and Ritter, S. Intraventricular glucose blocks feeding induced by 2-deoxy-D-glucose but not mercaptoacetate. *Physiology and Behavior*, 1996, *59*, 921–923.

Singh, N. A., Clements, K. M., and Fiatarone, M. A. Sleep, sleep deprivation, and daytime activities: A randomized controlled trial of the effect of exercise on sleep. *Sleep*, 1997, *20*, 95–101.

Sipos, M. L., and Nyby, J. G. Concurrent androgenic stimulation of the ventral tegmental area and medial preoptic area:

Synergistic effects on male-typical reproductive behaviors in house mice. *Brain Research*, 1996, *729*, 29–44.

Sirigu, A., Duhamel, J.-R., and Poncet, M. The role of sensorimotor experience in object recognition: A case of multimodal agnosia. *Brain*, 1991, *114*, 2555–2573.

Sitaram, N., Moore, A. M., and Gillin, J. C. Experimental acceleration and slowing of REM ultradian rhythm by cholinergic agonist and antagonist. *Nature*, 1978, *274*, 490–492.

Skaggs, W. E., and McNaughton, B. L. Spatial firing properties of hippocampal CA1 populations in an environment containing two visually identical regions. *Journal of Neuroscience*, 1998, *18*, 8455–8466.

Skakkebaek, N. E., Bancroft, J., Davidson, D. W., and Warner, P. Androgen replacement with oral testosterone undecanoate in hypogonadal men: A double blind controlled study. *Clinical Endocrinology*, 1981, *14*, 49–61.

Skene, D. J., Lockley, S. W., and Arendt, J. Melatonin in circadian sleep disorders in the blind. *Biological Signals and Receptors*, 1999, *8*, 90–95.

Skutella, T., Criswell, H., Moy, S., Probst, J. C., Breese, G. R., Jirikowski, G. F., and Holsboer, F. Corticotropin-releasing hormone (CRH) antisense oligodeoxynucleotide induces anxiolytic effects in rats. *Neuroreport*, 1994, *5*, 2181–2185.

Slotkin, T. A. Fetal nicotine or cocaine exposure: Which one is worse? *Journal of Pharmacology and Experimental Therapeutics*, 1998, *22*, 521–527.

Smith, C. Sleep states, memory processes and synaptic plasticity. *Behavioural Brain Research*, 1996, *78*, 49–56.

Smith, C., and Lapp, L. Increased number of REMs following an intensive learning. *Sleep*, 1991, *14*, 325–330.

Smith, G. P., Gibbs, J., and Kulkosky, P. J. Relationships between brain-gut peptides and neurons in the control of food intake. In *The Neural Basis of Feeding and Reward*, edited by B. G. Hoebel and D. Novin. Brunswick, Me.: Haer Institute, 1982.

Smith, K. A., Morris, J. S., Friston, K. J., Cower, P. J., and Dolar, R. J. Brain mechanisms associated with depressive relapse and associated cognitive impairment following acute tryptophan depletion. *British Journal of Psychiatry*, 1999, *174*, 525–529.

Smith, M. J. Sex determination: Turning on sex. *Current Biology*, 1994, *4*, 1003–1005.

Smith-Roe, S. L., and Kelley, A. E. Coincident activation of NMDA and dopamine D_1 receptors within the nucleus accumbens core is required for appetitive instrumental learning. *Journal of Neuroscience*, 2000, *20*, 7737–7742.

Smith-Swintosky, V. L., Plata-Salaman, C. R., and Scott, T. R. Gustatory neural coding in the monkey cortex: Stimulus quality. *Journal of Neurophysiology*, 1991, *66*, 1156–1165.

Smulders, T. V., Sasson, A. D., and DeVoogd, T. J. Seasonal variation in hippocampal volume in a food-storing bird, the black-capped chickadee. *Journal of Neurobiology*, 1995, *27*, 15–25.

Snyder, S. H. *Madness and the Brain.* New York: McGraw-Hill, 1974.

Soares, J. C., and Gershon, S. The lithium ion: A foundation for psychopharmacological specificity. *Neuropsychopharmacology*, 1998, *19*, 167–182.

Soares, J. C., and Mann, J. J. The anatomy of mood disorders: Review of structural neuroimaging studies. *Biological Psychiatry*, 1997, *42*, 86–106.

Solyom, L., Turnbull, I. M., and Wilensky, M. A case of self-inflicted leucotomy. *British Journal of Psychiatry*, 1987, *151*, 855–857.

Sørensen, T. I. A., Price, R. A., Stunkard, A. J., and Schulsinger, F. Genetics of obesity in adult adoptees and their biological siblings. *British Medical Journal*, 1989, *298*, 87–90.

Speelman, J. D., Schuurman, R., de Bie, R. M., Esselink, R. A., and Bosch, D. A. Stereotactic neurosurgery for tremor. *Movement Disorders*, 2002, *17*, S84–S88.

Spence, M. A., Flodman, P. L., Sadovnick, A. D., Bailey-Wilson, J. E., Ameli, H., and Remick, R. A. Bipolar disorder: Evidence for a major locus. *American Journal of Medical Genetics*, 1995, *60*, 370–376.

Sperry, R. W. Brain bisection and consciousness. In *Brain and Conscious Experience*, edited by J. Eccles. New York: Springer-Verlag, 1966.

Spiegler, B. J., and Mishkin, M. Evidence for the sequential participation of inferior temporal cortex and amygdala in the acquisition of stimulus-reward associations. *Behavioural Brain Research*, 1981, *3*, 303–317.

Spiers, H. J., Maguire, E. A., and Burgess, N. Hippocampal amnesia. *Neurocase*, 2001, *7*, 357–382.

Spitzer, M., Kwong, K. K., Kennedy, W., Rosen, B. R., and Belliveau, J. W. Category-specific brain activation in fMRI during picture naming. *NeuroReport*, 1995, *6*, 2109–2112.

Spray, D. C. Cutaneous temperature receptors. *Annual Review of Physiology*, 1986, *48*, 625–638.

Sprengelmeyer, R., Rausch, M., Eysel, U. T., and Przuntek, H. Neural structures associated with recognition of facial expressions of basic emotions. *Proceedings of the Royal Society of London [B]*, 1998, *265*, 1927–1931.

Sprengelmeyer, R., Young, A. W., Calder, A. J., Karnat, A., Lange, H., Hömberg, V., Perrett, D. I., and Rowland, D. Loss of disgust: Perception of faces and emotions in Huntington's disease. *Brain*. 1996, *119*, 1647–1665.

Sprengelmeyer, R., Young, A. W., Pundt, I., Sprengelmeyer, A., Calder, A. J., Berrios, G., Winkel, R., Vollmöeller, W., Kuhn, W., Sartory, G., and Przuntek, H. Disgust implicated in obsessive-compulsive disorder. *Proceedings of the Royal Society of London [B]*, 1997, *264*, 1767–1773.

Squire, L. R. Stable impairment in remote memory following electroconvulsive therapy. *Neuropsychologia*, 1974, *13*, 51–58.

Squire, L. R. Memory and the hippocampus: A synthesis from findings with rats, monkeys, and humans. *Psychological Review*, 1992, *99*, 195–231.

Squire, L. R., Shimamura, A. P., and Amaral, D. G. Memory and the hippocampus. In *Neural Models of Plasticity: Experimental and Theoretical Approaches*, edited by J. H. Byrne and W. O. Berry. San Diego: Academic Press, 1989.

Squires, R. F. How a poliovirus might cause schizophrenia: A commentary on Eagles' hypothesis. *Neurochemical Research*, 1997, *22*, 647–656.

Stallone, D., and Nicolaïdis, S. Increased food intake and carbohydrate preference in the rat following treatment with the serotonin antagonist metergoline. *Neuroscience Letters*, 1989, *102*, 319–324.

Standing, L. Learning 10,000 pictures. *Quarterly Journal of Experimental Psychology*, 1973, *25*, 207–222.

Stanley, B. G., Magdalin, W., Seirafi, A., Thomas, W. J., and Leibowitz, S. F. The perifornical area: The major focus of (a) patchily distributed hypothalamic neuropeptide Y-sensitive feeding system(s). *Brain Research,* 1993b, *604,* 304–317.

Stanley, B. G., Willett V. L., Donias, H. W., Dee, M. G., and Duva, M. A. Lateral hypothalamic NMDA receptors and glutamate as physiological mediators of eating and weight control. *American Journal of Physiology: Regulatory, Integrative and Comparative Physiology,* 1996, *270,* R443–R449.

Stanley, B. G., Willett, V. L., Donias, H. W., Ha, L. H., and Spears, L. C. The lateral hypothalamus: A primary site mediating excitatory amino acid-elicited eating. *Brain Research,* 1993a, *630,* 41–44.

Stanton, P. K., and Sejnowski, T. J. Associative long-term depression in the hippocampus induced by Hebbian covariance. *Nature,* 1989, *339,* 215–218.

Starkey, S. J., Walker, M. P., Beresford, I. J. M., and Hagan, R. M. Modulation of the rat suprachiasmatic circadian clock by melatonin in-vitro. *Neuroreport,* 1995, *6,* 1947–1951.

Stebbins, W. C., Miller, J. M., Johnsson, L.-G., and Hawkins, J. E. Ototoxic hearing loss and cochlear pathology in the monkey. *Annals of Otology, Rhinology and Laryngology,* 1969, *78,* 1007–1026.

Stein, J., and Walsh, V. To see but not to read: The magnocellular theory of dyslexia. *Trends in Neuroscience,* 1997, *20,* 147–152.

Stein, L., and Belluzzi, J. D. Cellular investigations of behavioral reinforcement. *Neuroscience and Biobehavioral Reviews,* 1989, *13,* 69–80.

Stein, M. B., Jang, K. L., Taylor, S., Vernon, P. A., and Livesley, W. J. Genetic and environmental influences on trauma exposure and posttraumatic stress disorder symptoms: A twin study. *American Journal of Psychiatry,* 2002, *159,* 1675–1681.

Steiner, H., and Gerfen, C. R. Dynorphin opioid inhibition of cocaine-induced, D_1 dopamine receptor-mediated immediate-early gene expression in the striatum. *Journal of Comparative Neurology,* 1995, *353,* 200–212.

Steininger, R. L., Alam, M. N., Szymusiak, R., and McGinty, D. State dependent discharge of ruberomammillary neurons in the rat hypothalamus. *Sleep Research,* 1996, *25,* 28.

Stellar, J. R., Kelley, A. E., and Corbett, D. Effects of peripheral and central dopamine blockade on lateral hypothalamic self-stimulation: Evidence for both reward and motor deficits. *Pharmacology, Biochemistry, and Behavior,* 1983, *18,* 433–442.

Stephan, F. K., and Nuñez, A. A. Elimination of circadian rhythms in drinking activity, sleep, and temperature by isolation of the suprachiasmatic nuclei. *Behavioral Biology,* 1977, *20,* 1–16.

Stephan, F. K., and Zucker, I. Circadian rhythms in drinking behavior and locomotor activity of rats are eliminated by hypothalamic lesion. *Proceedings of the National Academy of Sciences, USA,* 1972, *69,* 1583–1586.

Steriade, M. Basic mechanisms of sleep generation. *Neurology,* 1992, *42* (Suppl. 6), 9–18.

Steriade, M. Arousal: Revisiting the reticular activating system. *Science,* 1996, *272,* 225–226.

Steriade, M., Paré, D., Datta, S., Oakson, G., and Curró Dossi, R. Different cellular types in mesopontine cholinergic nuclei related to ponto-geniculo-occipital waves. *Journal of Neuroscience,* 1990, *8,* 2560–2579.

Sterman, M. B., and Clemente, C. D. Forebrain inhibitory mechanisms: Cortical synchronization induced by basal forebrain stimulation. *Experimental Neurology,* 1962a, *6,* 91–102.

Sterman, M. B., and Clemente, C. D. Forebrain inhibitory mechanisms: Sleep patterns induced by basal forebrain stimulation in the behaving cat. *Experimental Neurology,* 1962b, *6,* 103–117.

Stern, K., and McClintock, M. K. Regulation of ovulation by human pheromones. *Nature,* 1998, *392,* 177–178.

Sternbach, R. A. *Pain: A Psychophysiological Analysis.* New York: Academic Press, 1968.

Stevens, J. R. Neurology and neuropathology of schizophrenia. In *Schizophrenia as a Brain Disease,* edited by F. A. Henn and H. A. Nasrallah. New York: Oxford University Press, 1982.

Stevens, J. R. Schizophrenia and multiple sclerosis. *Schizophrenia Bulletin,* 1988, *14,* 231–241.

Steward, O., and Schuman, E. M. Protein synthesis at synaptic sites on dendrites. *Annual Review of Neuroscience,* 2001, *24,* 299–325.

Stewart, M., and Fox, S. E. Do septal neurons pace the hippocampal theta rhythm? *Trends in Neuroscience,* 1990, *13,* 163–168.

Stewart, R. B., Russell, R. N., Lumeng, L., Li, T.-K., and Murphy, J. M. Consumption of sweet, salty, sour, and bitter solutions by selectively bred alcohol-preferring and alcohol-nonpreferring lines of rats. *Alcoholism: Clinical and Experimental Research,* 1994, *18,* 375–381.

Stinson, D., and Thompson, C. Clinical experience with phototherapy. *Journal of the Affective Disorders,* 1990, *18,* 129–135.

Stolerman, I. P., and Jarvis, M. J. The scientific case that nicotine is addictive. *Psychopharmacology,* 1995, *117,* 2–10.

Stone, A. A., Reed, B. R., and Neale, J. M. Changes in daily event frequency precede episodes of physical symptoms. *Journal of Human Stress,* 1987, *13,* 70–74.

Stout, S. C., Owens, M. J., and Nemeroff, C. B. Neurokinin$_1$ receptor antagonists as potential antidepressants. *Annual Review of Pharmacology and Toxicology,* 2001, *41,* 877–906.

Stowers, L., Holy, T. E., Meister, M., Dulac, C., and Koentges, G. Loss of sex discrimination of male-male aggression in mice deficient for TRP2. *Science,* 2002, *295,* 1493–1500.

Stoyva, J., and Metcalf, D. Sleep patterns following chronic exposure to cholinesterase-inhibiting organophosphate compounds. *Psychophysiology,* 1968, *5,* 206.

Strakowski, S. M., DelBello, M. P., Zimmerman, M. E., Getz, G. E., Mills, N. P., Ret, J., Shear, P., and Adler, C. M. Ventricular and periventricular structural volumes in first- versus multiple-episode bipolar disorder. *American Journal of Psychiatry,* 2002, *11,* 1841–1847.

Strecker, R. E., Morairty, S., Thakkar, M. M., Porkka-Heiskanen, T., Basheer, R., Dauphin, L. J., Rainnie, D. G., Portas, C. M., Greene, R. W., and McCarley, R. W. Adenosinergic modulation of basal forebrain and preoptic/anterior hypothalamic neuronal activity in the control of behavioral state. *Behavioural Brain Research,* 2000, *115,* 183–204.

Stricker, E. M., Swerdloff, A. F., and Zigmond, M. J. Intrahypothalamic injections of kainic acid produces feeding and drinking deficits in rats. *Brain Research,* 1978, *158,* 470–473.

Strobel, A., Issad, T., Camoin, L., Ozata, M., and Strosberg, A. D. A leptin missense mutation associated with hypogonadism and morbid obesity. *Nature Genetics,* 1998, *18,* 213–215.

Strömland, K., Nordin, V., Miller, M., Akerstrom, B., and Gillberg, C. Autism in thalidomide embryopathy: A population study. *Developmental Medicine and Child Neurology,* 1994, *36,* 351–356.

Stromswold, K., Kaplan, D., Alpert, N., and Rauch, S. Localization of syntactic comprehension by positron emission tomography. *Brain and Language,* 1996, *52,* 452–473.

Stunkard, A. J., Sørensen, T. I. A., Harris, C., Teasdale, T. W., Chakraborty, R., Schull, W. J., and Schulsinger, F. An adoption study of human obesity. *New England Journal of Medicine,* 1986, *314,* 193–198.

Sturgis, J. D., and Bridges, R. S. N-methyl-DL-aspartic acid lesions of the medial preoptic area disrupt ongoing parental behavior in male rats. *Physiology and Behavior,* 1997, *62,* 305–310.

Sturup, G. K. Correctional treatment and the criminal sexual offender. *Canadian Journal of Correction,* 1961, *3,* 250–265.

Su, T.-P., Pagliaro, M., Schmidt, P. J., Pickar, D., Wolkowitz, O., and Rubinow, D. R. Neuropsychiatric effects of anabolic steroids in male normal volunteers. *Journal of the American Medical Association,* 1993, *269,* 2760–2764.

Suddath, R. L., Christison, G. W., Torrey, E. F., Casanova, M. F., and Weinberger, D. R. Anatomical abnormalities in the brains of monozygotic twins discordant for schizophrenia. *The New England Journal of Medicine,* 1990, *322,* 789–794.

Sullivan, E. V., Land, B., Deshmukh, A., Rosenbloom, M. J., Desmond, J. E., Lim, K. O., and Pfefferbaum, A. In vivo mammillary body volume deficits in amnesic and nonamnesic alcoholics. *Alcoholism: Clinical and Experimental Research,* 1999, *23,* 1629–1636.

Suppes, T., Baldessarini, R. J., Faedda, G. L., and Tohen, M. Risk of recurrence following discontinuation of lithium treatment in bipolar disorder. *Archives of General Psychiatry,* 1991, *48,* 1082–1088.

Susser, E., Neugebauer, R., Hoek, H. W., Brown, A. S., Lin, S., Labovitz, D., and Gorman, J. M. Schizophrenia after prenatal famine: Further evidence. *Archives of General Psychiatry,* 1996, *53,* 25–31.

Susser, E. S., and Lin, S. P. Schizophrenia after prenatal exposure to the Dutch Hunger Winter of 1944–1945. *Archives of General Psychiatry,* 1992, *49,* 983–988.

Suzdak, P. D., Glowa, J. R., Crawley, J. N., Schwartz, R. D., Skolnick, P., and Paul, S. M. A selective imidazobenzodiazepine antagonist of ethanol in the rat. *Science,* 1986, *234,* 1243–1247.

Suzuki, T., Funada, M., Narita, M., Misawa, M., and Nagase, H. Morphine-induced place preference in the CXBK mouse: Characteristics of mu-opioid receptor subtypes. *Brain Research,* 1993, *602,* 45–52.

Svare, B. Psychobiological determinants of maternal aggressive behavior. In *Aggressive Behavior: Genetic and Neural Approaches,* edited by E. C. Simmel, M. E. Hahn, and J. K. Walters. Hillsdale, N. J.: Lawrence Erlbaum Associates, 1983.

Svare, B. Recent advances in the study of female aggressive behavior in mice. In *House Mouse Aggression: A Model for Understanding the Evolution of Social Behavior,* edited by S. Parmigiani, D. Mainardi, and P. Brain. London: Gordon and Breach, 1989.

Svare, B., and Gandelman, R. Postpartum aggression in mice: The influence of suckling stimulation. *Hormones and Behavior,* 1976, *7,* 407–416.

Svare, B., Betteridge, C., Katz, D., and Samuels, O. Some situational and experiential determinants of maternal aggression in mice. *Physiology and Behavior,* 1981, *26,* 253–258.

Svare, B., Mann, M. A., Broida, J., and Michael, S. Maternal aggression exhibited by hypophysectomized parturient mice. *Hormones and Behavior,* 1982, *16,* 455–461.

Svennilson, E., Torvik, A., Lowe, R., and Leksell, L. Treatment of Parkinsonism by stereotactic thermolesions in the pallidal region. *Neurologica Scandanavica,* 1960, *35,* 358–377.

Swaab, D. F., and Hofman, M. A. An enlarged suprachiasmatic nucleus in homosexual men. *Brain Research,* 1990, *537,* 141–148.

Swaab, D. F., Gooren, L. J. G., and Hofman, M. A. Brain research, gender, and sexual orientation. *Journal of Homosexuality,* 1995, *28,* 283–301.

Swanson, L. W., Köhler, C., and Björklund, A. The limbic region. I. The septohippocampal system. In *Handbook of Chemical Neuroanatomy. Vol. 5: Integrated Systems of the CNS, Part I,* edited by A. Björklund, T. Hökfelt, and L. W. Swanson. Amsterdam: Elsevier, 1987.

Swanson, R. A. Physiologic coupling of glial glycogen metabolism to neuronal activity in brain. *Canadian Journal of Physiology and Pharmacology,* 1992, *70,* S138–S144.

Swanson, R. A., and Choi, D. W. Glial glycogen stores affect neuronal survival during glucose deprivation in vitro. *Journal of Cerebral Blood Flow and Metabolism,* 1993, *13,* 162–169.

Sweet, W. H. Participant in brain stimulation in behaving subjects. Neurosciences Research Program Workshop, 1966.

Swerdlow, N. R. Obsessive-compulsive disorder and tic syndromes. *Medical Clinics of North America,* 2001, *85,* 735–755.

Swerdlow, N. R., Geyer, M. A., Vale, W. W., and Koob, G. F. Corticotropin-releasing factor potentiates acoustic startle in rats: Blockade by chlordiazepoxide. *Psychopharmacology,* 1986, *88,* 147–152.

Szuba, M. P., Baxter, L. R., and Fairbanks, L. A. Effects of partial sleep deprivation on the diurnal variation of mood and motor activity in major depression. *Biological Psychiatry,* 1991, *30,* 817–829.

Szuba, M. P., O'Reardon, J. P., Rai, A. S., Snyder-Kastenberg, J., Amsterdam, J. D., Gettes, D. R., Wassermann, E., and Evans, D. L. Acute mood and thyroid stimulating hormone effects of transcranial magnetic stimulation in major depression. *Biological Psychiatry,* 2001, *50,* 22–27.

Szymusiak, R., Alam, N., Steininger, T. L., and McGinty, D. Sleep-waking discharge patterns of ventrolateral preoptic/anterior hypothalamic neurons in rats. *Brain Research,* 1998, *803,* 178–188.

Tabakoff, B., and Hoffman, P. L. Alcohol addiction: An enigma among us. *Neuron,* 1996, *16,* 909–912.

Takahashi, L. K. Hormonal regulation of sociosexual behavior in female mammals. *Neuroscience and Biobehavioral Reviews,* 1990, *14,* 403–413.

Takahashi, L. K., Turner, J. G., and Kalin, N. H. Prenatal stress alters brain catecholaminergic activity and potentiates stress-induced behavior in adult rats. *Brain Research,* 1992, *574,* 131–137.

Takahashi, N., Kawamura, M., Shinotou, H., Hirayama, K., Kaga, K., and Shindo, M. Pure word deafness due to left hemisphere damage. *Cortex,* 1992, *28,* 295–303.

Takei, N., Sham, P. C., O'Callaghan, E., Glover, G., and Murray, R. M. Early risk factors in schizophrenia: Place and season of birth. *European Psychiatry,* 1995, *10,* 165–170.

Tam, W.-C. C., and Sewell, K. W. Seasonality of birth in schizophrenia in Taiwan. *Schizophrenia Bulletin,* 1995, *21,* 117–127.

Tamminga, C. A., Burrows, G. H., Chase, T. N., Alphs, L. D., and Thaker, G. K. Dopamine neuronal tracts in schizophrenia: Their pharmacology and *in vivo* glucose metabolism. *Annals of the New York Academy of Sciences,* 1988, *537,* 443–450.

Tan, S. E., and Liang, K. C. Spatial learning alters hippocampal calcium calmodulin-dependent protein kinase II activity in rats. *Brain Research,* 1996, *711,* 234–240.

Tanaka, K. Inferotemporal cortex and object vision. *Annual Review of Neuroscience,* 1996, *19,* 109–139.

Tang, Y.-P., Shimizu, E., Dube, G. R., Rampon, C., Kerchner, G. A., Zhuo, M., Lium, G., and Tsien, J. Z. Genetic enhancement of learning and memory in mice. *Nature,* 1999, *401,* 63–69.

Tanne, J., Boussaoud, D., Boyer-Zeller, N., and Rouiller, E. M. Direct visual pathways for reaching movements in the macaque monkey. *Neuroreport,* 1995, *7,* 267–272.

Tanner, C. M. The role of environmental toxins in the etiology of Parkinson's disease. *Trends in Neuroscience,* 1989, 12, *49–54.*

Tarsy, D., Baldessarini, R. J., and Tarazi, F. I. Effects of newer antipsychotics on extrapyramidal function. *CNS Drugs,* 2002, *16,* 23–45.

Taylor, B., Miller, E., Lingam, R., Andrews, N., Simmons, A., and Stowe, J. Measles, mumps, and rubella vaccination and bowel problems or developmental regression in children with autism: Population study. *British Medical Journal,* 2002, *324,* 393–396.

Taylor, S. F. Cerebral blood flow activation and functional lesions in schizophrenia. *Schizophrenia Research,* 1996, *19,* 129–140.

Tei, H., Soma, Y., and Maruyama, S. Right unilateral agraphia following callosal infarction in a left-hander. *European Neurology,* 1994, *34,* 168–172.

Teicher, M. H., Anderson, C. M., Polcari, A., Glod, C. A., Maas, L. C., and Renshaw, P. F. Functional deficits in basal ganglia of children with attention-deficit/hyperactivity disorder shown with functional magnetic resonance imaging relaxometry. *Nature Medicine,* 2000, *6,* 470–473.

Teitelbaum, P., and Stellar, E. Recovery from the failure to eat produced by hypothalamic lesions. *Science,* 1954, *120,* 894–895.

Terenius, L., and Wahlström, A. Morphine-like ligand for opiate receptors in human CSF. *Life Sciences,* 1975, *16,* 1759–1764.

Terman, T., Terman, J. S., and Ross, D. C. A controlled trial of timed bright light and negative air ionization for treatment of winter depression, *Archives of General Psychiatry,* 1998, *55,* 875–882.

Tetel, M. J., Celentano, D. C., and Blaustein, J. D. Intraneuronal convergence of tactile and hormonal stimuli associated with female reproduction in rats. *Journal of Neuroendocrinology,* 1994, *6,* 211–216.

Tetel, M. J., Getzinger, M. J., and Blaustein, J. D. Fos expression in the rat brain following vaginal-cervical stimulation by mating and manual probing. *Journal of Neuroendocrinology,* 1993, *5,* 397–404.

Tetrud, J. W., and Langston, J. W. The effect of deprenyl (Selegiline) on the natural history of Parkinson's disease. *Science,* 1989, *245,* 519–522.

Thach, W. T. Correlation of neural discharge with pattern and force of muscular activity, joint position, and direction of intended movement in motor cortex and cerebellum. *Journal of Neurophysiology,* 1978, *41,* 654–676.

Thaker, G. K., and Carpenter, W. T. Advances in schizophrenia. *Nature Medicine,* 2001, *7,* 667–671.

Thakkar, M. M., Winston, S., and McCarley, R. W. Orexin neurons of the hypothalamus express adenosine A1 receptors. *Brain Research,* 2002, *944,* 190–194.

Theorell, T., Leymann, H., Jodko, M., Konarski, K., Norbeck, H. E., and Eneroth, P. "Person under train" incidents: Medical consequences for subway drivers. *Psychosomatic Medicine,* 1992, *54,* 480–488.

Thiels, E., Xie, X. P., Yeckel, M. F., Barrionuevo, G., and Berger, T. W. NMDA receptor-dependent LTD in different subfields of hippocampus in vivo and in vitro. *Hippocampus,* 1996, *6,* 43–51.

Thier, P., Haarmeier, T., Chakraborty, S., Lindner, A., and Tikhonov, A. Cortical substrates of perceptual stability during eye movements. *Neuroimage,* 2001, *14,* S33–S39.

Thompson, L. T., and Best, P. J. Long-term stability of the place-field activity of single units recorded from the dorsal hippocampus of freely behaving rats. *Brain Research,* 1990, *509,* 299–308.

Thompson, P. M., Vidal, C., Giedd, J. N., Gochman, P., Blumenthal, J., Nicolson, R., Toga, A. W., and Rapoport, J. L. Mapping adolescent brain change reveals dynamic wave of accelerated gray matter loss in very early-onset schizophrenia. *Proceedings of the National Academy of Science, USA,* 2001, *98,* 11650–11655.

Thrasher, T. N. Role of forebrain circumventricular organs in body fluid balance. *Acta Physiologica Scandanavica,* 1989, *136* (Suppl. 583), 141–150.

Thrasher, T. N., and Keil, L. C. Regulation of drinking and vasopressin secretion: Role of organum vasculosum laminae terminalis. *American Journal of Physiology,* 1987, *253,* R108–R120.

Tiedge, H., and Brosius, J. Translational machinery in dendrites of hippocampal neurons in culture. *Journal of Neuroscience,* 1996, *16,* 7171–7181.

Timmann, D., Watts, S., and Hore, J. Failure of cerebellar patients to time finger opening precisely causes ball high-low inaccuracy in overarm throws. *Journal of Neurophysiology,* 1999, *82,* 103–114.

Toh, K. L., Jones, C. R., He, Y., Eide, E. J., Hinz, W. A., Virshup, D. M., Ptacek, L. J., and Fu, Y.-H. An h*Per2* phosphorylation site mutation in familial advanced sleep phase syndrome. *Science,* 2001, *291,* 1040–1043.

Toledo-Aral, J. J., Mendez-Ferrer, S., Pardal, R., and Lopez-Barneo, J. Dopaminergic cells of the carotid body: Physiological significance and possible therapeutic applications in Parkinson's disease. *Brain Research Bulletin,* 2002, *57,* 847–853.

Toni, N., Buchs, P.-A., Nikonenko, I., Bron, C. R., and Muller, D. LTP promotes formation of multiple spine synapses between a single axon terminal and a dendrite. *Nature,* 1999, *402,* 421–425.

Topper, R., Kosinski, C., and Mull, M. Volitional type of facial palsy associated with pontine ischemia. *Journal of Neurology, Neurosurgery, and Psychiatry*, 1995, *58*, 732–734.

Tordoff, M. G., and Friedman, M. I. Hepatic control of feeding: Effect of glucose, fructose, and mannitol. *American Journal of Physiology*, 1988, *254*, R969–R976.

Tordoff, M. G., Hopfenbeck, J., and Novin, D. Hepatic vagotomy (partial hepatic denervation) does not alter ingestive responses to metabolic challenges. *Physiology and Behavior*, 1982, *28*, 417–424.

Torrey, E. F., Torrey, B. B., and Peterson, M. R. Seasonality of schizophrenic births in the United States. *Archives of General Psychiatry*, 1979, *34*, 1065–1070.

Träskmann, L., Åsberg, M., Bertilsson, L., and Sjöstrand, L. Monoamine metabolites in CSF and suicidal behavior. *Archives of General Psychiatry*, 1981, *38*, 631–636.

True, W. R., Xian, H., Scherrer, J. F., Madden, P. A., Bucholz, K. K., Heath, A. C., Eisen, S. A., Lyons, M. J., Goldberg, J., and Tsuang, M. Common genetic vulnerability for nicotine and alcohol dependence in men. *Archives of General Psychiatry*, 1999, *56*, 655–661.

Trulson, M. E., and Jacobs, B. L. Raphe unit activity in freely moving cats: Correlation with level of behavioral arousal. *Brain Research*, 1979, *163*, 135–150.

Trussell, L. O. Synaptic mechanisms for coding timing in auditory neurons. *Annual Review of Physiology*, 1999, *61*, 477–496.

Tsacopoulos, M., and Magistretti, P. J. Metabolic coupling between glia and neurons. *Journal of Neuroscience*, 1996, *16*, 877–885.

Tsai, G., and Coyle, J. T. Glutamatergic mechanisms in schizophrenia. *Annual Review of Pharmacology and Toxicology*, 2002, *42*, 165–179.

Tschöp, M., Smiley, D. L., and Heiman, M. L. Ghrelin induces adiposity in rodents. *Nature*, 2000, *407*, 908–913.

Tsien, J. Z., Huerta, P. T., and Tonegawa, S. The essential role of hippocampal CA1 NMDA receptor-dependent synaptic plasticity in spatial memory. *Cell*, 1996, *87*, 1327–1338.

Tsuang, M. T., Gilbertson, M. W., and Faraone, S. V. The genetics of schizophrenia: Current knowledge and future directions. *Schizophrenia Research*, 1991, *4*, 157–171.

Turner, S. M., Beidel, D. C., and Nathan, R. S. Biological factors in obsessive-compulsive disorders. *Psychological Bulletin*, 1985, *97*, 430–450.

Turrone, P., Remington, G., and Nobrega, J. N. The vacuous chewing movement (VCM) model of tardive dyskinesia revisited: Is there a relationship to dopamine D_2 receptor occupancy? *Neuroscience and Biobehavioral Reviews*, 2002, *26*, 361–380.

Tyrell, J. B., and Baxter, J. D. Glucocorticoid therapy. In *Endocrinology and Metabolism*, edited by P. Felig, J. D. Baxter, A. E. Broadus, and L. A. Frohman. New York: McGraw-Hill, 1981.

Uchikawa, K., and Boynton, R. M. Categorical color perception of Japanese observers: Comparison with that of Americans. *Vision Research*, 1987, *27*, 1825–1833.

Unger, J., McNeill, T. H., Moxley, R. T., White, M., Moss, A., and Livingston, J. N. Distribution of insulin receptor-like immunoreactivity in the rat forebrain. *Neuroscience*, 1989, *31*, 143–157.

Ungerleider, L. G., and Mishkin, M. Two cortical visual systems. In *Analysis of Visual Behavior*, edited by D. J. Ingle, M. A. Goodale, and R. J. W. Mansfield. Cambridge, Mass.: MIT Press, 1982.

Ungless, M. A., Whistler, J. L., Malenka, R. C., and Bonci, A. Single cocaine exposure in vivo induces long-term potentiation in dopamine neurons. *Nature*, 2001, *411*, 583–587.

Uno, H., Tarara, R., Else, J. G., Suleman, M. A., and Sapolsky, R. M. Hippocampal damage associated with prolonged and fatal stress in primates. *Journal of Neuroscience*, 1989, *9*, 1705–1711.

Urban, P. P., Wicht, S., Marx, J., Mitrovic, S., Fitzek, C., and Hopf, H. C. Isolated voluntary facial paresis due to pontine ischemia. *Neurology*, 1998, *50*, 1859–1862.

Vaina, L. M. Complex motion perception and its deficits. *Current Opinion in Neurobiology*, 1998, *8*, 494–502.

Vaisse, C., Clément, K., Guy-Grand, B., and Froguel, P. A frameshift mutation in human MC4R is associated with a dominant form of obesity. *Nature Genetics*, 1998, *20*, 113–114.

Valenstein, E. S. *Brain Control*. New York: John Wiley & Sons, 1973.

Valenstein, E. S. *Great and Desperate Cures: The Rise and Decline of Psychosurgery and Other Radical Treatments for Mental Illness*. New York: Basic Books, 1986.

Valenza, N., Ptak, R., Zimine, I., Badan, M., Lazeyras, F., and Schnider, A. Dissociated active and passive tactile shape recognition: A case study of pure tactile apraxia. *Brain*, 2001, *124*, 2287–2298.

Valverius, P., Crabbe, J. C., Hoffman, P. L., and Tabakoff, B. NMDA receptors in mice bred to be prone or resistant to ethanol withdrawal seizures. *European Journal of Pharmacology*, 1990, *184*, 185–189.

Van Bockstaele, E. J., Bajic, D., Proudfit, H., and Valentino, R. J. Topographic architecture of stress-related pathways targeting the noradrenergic locus coeruleus. *Physiology and Behavior*, 2001, *73*, 273–283.

van de Poll, N. E., Taminiau, M. S., Endert, E., and Louwerse, A. L. Gonadal steroid influence upon sexual and aggressive behavior of female rats. *International Journal of Neuroscience*, 1988, *41*, 271–286.

Van der Does, A. J. W. The effects of tryptophan depletion on mood and psychiatric symptoms. *Journal of Affective Disorders*, 2001, *64*, 107–119.

van der Lee, S., and Boot, L. M. Spontaneous pseudopregnancy in mice. *Acta Physiologica et Pharmacologica Néerlandica*, 1955, *4*, 442–444.

van Dyck, C. H., Quinlan, D. M., Staley, J. K., Malison, R. T., Baldwin, R. M., Seibyl, J. P., and Innis, R. B. Unaltered dopamine transporter availability in adult attention deficit hyperactivity disorder. *American Journal of Psychiatry*, 2002, *159*, 309–312.

Van Essen, D. C., Anderson, C. H., and Felleman, D. J. Information processing in the primate visual system: An integrated systems perspective. *Science*, 1992, *255*, 419–423.

Van Goozen, S., Wiegant, V., Endert, E., Helmond, F., and Van de Poll, N. Psychoendrocrinological assessments of the menstrual cycle: The relationship between hormones, sexuality, and mood. *Archives of Sexual Behavior*, 1997, *26*, 359–382.

Van Tol, H. H. M., Bunzow, J. R., Hong-Chang, G., Sunahara, R. K., Seeman, P., Niznik, H. B., and Civelli, O. Cloning of the gene for a human dopamine D4 receptor with high affinity for the antipsychotic clozapine. *Nature,* 1991, *350,* 614–619.

Vandenbergh, J. G., Whitsett, J. M., and Lombardi, J. R. Partial isolation of a pheromone accelerating puberty in female mice. *Journal of Reproductive Fertility,* 1975, *43,* 515–523.

Vanderwolf, C. H. Hippocampal electrical activity and voluntary movement in the rat. *Electroencephalography and Clinical Neurophysiology,* 1969, *26,* 407–418.

Vanderwolf, C. H. The electrocorticogam in relation to physiology and behavior: A new analysis. *Electroencephalography and Clinical Neurophysiology,* 1992, *82,* 165–175.

Vanderwolf, C. H., Kramis, R., Gillespie, L. A., and Bland, B. G. Hippocampal rhythmical slow activity and neocortical low voltage fast activity: Relations to behavior. In *The Hippocampus. Vol. 2: Neurophysiology and Behavior,* edited by R. L. Isaacson and K. H. Pribram. New York: Plenum Press, 1975.

Vargha-Khadem, F., Gadian, D. G., Watkins, K. E., Connelly, A., Van Paesschen, W., and Mishkin, W. Differential effects of early hippocampal pathology on episodic and semantic memory. *Science,* 1997, *277,* 376–380.

Vassar, R., Ngai, J., and Axel, R. Spatial segregation of odorant receptor expression in the mammalian olfactory epithelium. *Cell,* 1993, *74,* 309–318.

Veldman, B. A., Wijn, A. M., Knoers, N., Praamstra, P., and Horstink, M. W. Genetic and environmental risk factors in Parkinson's disease. *Clinical Neurology and Neurosurgery,* 1998, *100,* 15–26.

Vergnes, M., Depaulis, A., Boehrer, A., and Kempf, E. Selective increase of offensive behavior in the rat following intrahypothalamic 5,7-DHT-induced serotonin depletion. *Brain Research,* 1988, *29,* 85–91.

Verney, E. B. The antidiuretic hormone and the factors which determine its release. *Proceedings of the Royal Society of London [B],* 1947, *135,* 25–106.

Vewers, M. E., Dhatt, R., and Tejwani, G. A. Naltrexone administration affects ad libitum smoking behavior. *Psychopharmacology,* 1998, *140,* 185–190.

Vgontzas, A. N., and Kales, A. Sleep and its disorders. *Annual Review of Medicine,* 1999, *50,* 387–400.

Victor, M., and Agamanolis, J. Amnesia due to lesions confined to the hippocampus: A clinical-pathological study. *Journal of Cognitive Neuroscience,* 1990, *2,* 246–257.

Vikingstad, E. M., Cao, Y., Thomas, A. J., Johnson, A. F., Malik, G. M., Welch, K. M. A. Language hemispheric dominance in patients with congenital lesions of eloquent brain. *Neurosurgery,* 2000, *47,* 562–570.

Vindlacheruvu, R. R., Ebling, F. J. P., Maywood, E. S., and Hastings, M. H. Blockade of glutamatergic neurotransmission in the suprachiasmatic nucleus prevents cellular and behavioural responses of the circadian system to light. *European Journal of Neuroscience,* 1992, *4,* 673–679.

Virkkunen, M., De Jong, J., Bartko, J., and Linnoila, M. Psychobiological concomitants of history of suicide attempts among violent offenders and impulsive fire setters. *Archives of General Psychiatry,* 1989, *46,* 604–606.

Voci, V. E., and Carlson, N. R. Enhancement of maternal behavior and nest behavior following systemic and diencephalic administration of prolactin and progesterone in the mouse. *Journal of Comparative and Physiological Psychology,* 1973, *83,* 388–393.

Vogel, G., Cohen, J., Mullis, D., Kensler, T., and Kaplita, S. Nefazodone and REM sleep: How do antidepressant drugs decrease REM sleep? *Sleep,* 1998, *21,* 70–77.

Vogel, G. W., Buffenstein, A., Minter, K., and Hennessey, A. Drug effects on REM sleep and on endogenous depression. *Neuroscience and Biobehavioral Reviews,* 1990, *14,* 49–63.

Vogel, G. W., Thurmond, A., Gibbons, P., Sloan, K., Boyd, M., and Walker, M. REM sleep reduction effects on depression syndromes. *Archives of General Psychiatry,* 1975, *32,* 765–777.

Vogel, G. W., Vogel, F., McAbee, R. S., and Thurmond, A. J. Improvement of depression by REM sleep deprivation: New findings and a theory. *Archives of General Psychiatry,* 1980, *37,* 247–253.

Volkow, N. D., Hitzemann, R., Wang, G.-J., Fowler, J. S., Wolf, A. P., Dewey, S. L., and Handlesman, L. Long-term frontal brain metabolic changes in cocaine abusers. *Synapse,* 1992, *11,* 184–190.

Volpe, B. T., LeDoux, J. E., and Gazzaniga, M. S. Information processing of visual stimuli in an "extinguished" field. *Nature,* 1979, *282,* 722–724.

vom Saal, F. S. Models of early hormonal effects on intrasex aggression in mice. In *Hormones and Aggressive Behavior,* edited by B. B. Svare. New York: Plenum Press, 1983.

vom Saal, F. S., and Bronson, F. H. *In utero* proximity of female mouse fetuses to males: Effect on reproductive performance during later life. *Biology of Reproduction,* 1980, *22,* 777–780.

von Békésy, G. *Experiments in Hearing.* New York: McGraw-Hill, 1960.

von der Heydt, R., Peterhans, E., and Duersteler, M. R. Periodic-pattern-selective cells in monkey visual cortex. *Journal of Neuroscience,* 1992, *12,* 1416–1434.

von Meduna, L. General discussion of the cardiazol therapy. *American Journal of Psychiatry (Supplement),* 1938, *94,* 40–50.

Vorel, S. R., Liu, X., Hayes, R. J., Spector, J. A., and Gardner, E. L. Relapse to cocaine-seeking after hippocampal theta burst stimulation, *Science,* 2001, *292,* 1175–1178.

Wada, Y., and Yamamoto, T. Selective impairment of facial recognition due to a haematoma restricted to the right fusiform and lateral occipital region. *Journal of Neurology, Neurosurgery and Psychiatry,* 2001, *71,* 254–257.

Wada, H., Inagaki, N., Itowi, N., and Yamatodani, A. Histaminergic neuron systems in the brain: Distribution and possible functions. *Brain Research Bulletin,* 1991, *27,* 367–370.

Wahlbeck, K., Forsén, T., Osmond, C., Barker, D. J. P., and Eriksson, J. G. Association of schizophrenia with low maternal body mass index, small size at birth, and thinness during childhood. *Archives of General Psychiatry,* 2001, *58,* 48–52.

Wahlestedt, C., Skagerberg, G., Edman, R., Heilig, M., Sundler, F., and Hakanson, R. Neuropeptide Y (NPY) in the area of the paraventricular nucleus activates the pituitary-adrenocortical axis in the rat. *Brain Research,* 1987, *417,* 33–38.

Walker, E. F., Lewine, R. R. J., and Neumann, C. Childhood behavioral characteristics and adult brain morphology in schizophrenia. *Schizophrenia Research,* 1996, *22,* 93–101.

Walker, E. F., Savoie, T., and Davis, D. Neuromotor precursors of schizophrenia. *Schizophrenia Bulletin,* 1994, *20,* 441–451.

Walker, P. A., and Meyer, W. J. Medroxyprogesterone acetate for paraphiliac sex offender. In *Violence and the Violent Individual,* edited by J. R. Hays, T. K. Roberts, and T. S. Solway. New York: SP Medical and Scientific Books, 1981.

Wallen, K. Desire and ability: Hormones and the regulation of female sexual behavior. *Neuroscience and Biobehavioral Reviews,* 1990, *14,* 233–241.

Wallen, K. Sex and context: Hormones and primate sexual motivation. *Hormones and Behavior,* 2001, *40,* 339–357.

Wallen, K., Eisler, J. A., Tannenbaum, P. L., Nagell, K. M., and Mann, D. R. Antide (Nal-Lys GnRH antagonist) suppression of pituitary-testicular function and sexual behavior in group-living rhesus monkeys. *Physiology and Behavior,* 1991, *50,* 429–435.

Wallen, K., Mann, D. R., Davis-DaSilva, M., Gaventa, S., Lovejoy, J. C., and Collins, D. C. Chronic gonadotropin-releasing hormone agonist treatment suppresses ovulation and sexual behavior in group-living female rhesus monkeys (*macaca mulatta*). *Animal Behaviour,* 1986, *36,* 369–375.

Walsh, B. T., and Devlin, M. J. Eating disorders: Progress and problems. *Science,* 1998, *280,* 1387–1390.

Walsh, V., Carden, D., Butler, S. R., and Kulikowski, J. J. The effects of V4 lesions on the visual abilities of macaques: Hue discrimination and color constancy. *Behavioural Brain Research,* 1993, *53,* 51–62.

Walsh, V., Ellison, A., Battelli, L., and Cowey, A. Task-specific impairments and enhancements induced by magnetic stimulation of human visual area V5. *Proceedings of the Royal Society of London [B],* 1998, *265,* 537–543.

Walters, E. E., and Kendler, K. S. Anorexia nervosa and anorexic-like syndromes in a population-based female twin sample. *American Journal of Psychiatry,* 1995, *152,* 64–71.

Wang, G., Tanaka, K., and Tanifuji, M. Optical imaging of functional organization in the monkey inferotemporal cortex. *Science,* 1996, *272,* 1665–1668.

Wang, G.-J., Volkow, N. D., Fowler, J. S., Cervany, P., Hitzemann, R. J., Pappas, N. R., Wong, C. T., and Felder, C. Regional brain metabolic activation during craving elicited by recall of previous drug experiences. *Life Sciences,* 1999, *64,* 775–784.

Wang, Q., Bing, C., Al-Barazanji, K., Mossakowaska, D. E., Wang, X. M., McBay, D. L., Neville, W. A., Taddayon, M., Pickavance, L., Dryden, S. Thomas, M. E., McHale, M. T., Gloyer, I. S., Wilson, S., Buckingham, R., Arch, J. R., Trayhurn, P., and Williams, G. Interactions between leptin and hypothalamic neuropeptide Y neurons in the control of food intake and energy homeostasis in the rat. *Diabetes,* 1997, *46,* 335–341.

Ward, I. Prenatal stress feminizes and demasculinizes the behavior of males. *Science,* 1972, *175,* 82–84.

Ward, I. L., and Stehm, K. E. Prenatal stress feminizes juvenile play patterns in male rats. *Physiology and Behavior,* 1991, *50,* 601–605.

Warne, G. L., and Zajac, J. D. Disorders of sexual differentiation. *Endocrinology and Metabolism Clinics of North America,* 1998, *27,* 945–967.

Warrington, E. K., and Shallice, T. Word-form dyslexia. *Brain,* 1980, *103,* 99–112.

Wassink, T. H., Piven, J., Vieland, V. J., Huang, J., Swiderski, R. E., Pietila, J., Braun, T., Beck, G., Folstein, S. E., Haines, J. L., and Sheffield, V. C. Evidence supporting WNT2 as an autism susceptibility gene. *American Journal of Medical Genetics,* 2001, *105,* 406–413.

Watkins, K. E., Dronkers, N. F., and Vargha-Khadem, F. Behavioural analysis of an inherited speech and language disorder: Comparison with acquired aphasia. *Brain,* 2002a, *125,* 452–464.

Watkins, K. E., Vargha-Khadem, F., Ashburner, J., Passingham, R. E., Connelly, A., Friston, K. J., Frackowiak, R. S. J., Mishkin, M., and Gadian, D. G. MRI analysis of an inherited speech and language disorder: Structural brain abnormalities. *Brain,* 2002b, *125,* 465–478.

Webster, H. H., and Jones, B. E. Neurotoxic lesions of the dorsolateral pontomesencephalic tegmentum-cholinergic cell area in the cat. II. Effects upon sleep-waking states. *Brain Research,* 1988, *458,* 285–302.

Wehr, T. A. Improvement of depression and triggering of mania by sleep deprivation. *Journal of the American Medical Association,* 1992, *267,* 548–551.

Wehr, T. A., Giesen, H. A., Schulz, P. M., Anderson, J. L., Joseph-Vanderpool, J. R., Kelly, K., Kasper, S., and Rosenthal, N. E. Contrasts between symptoms of summer depression and winter depression. *Journal of the Affective Disorders,* 1991, *23,* 173–183.

Wehr, T. A., Sack, D. A., and Rosenthal, N. E. Seasonal affective disorder with summer depression and winter hypomania. *American Journal of Psychiatry,* 1987, *114,* 1602–1603.

Weinberger, D. R. Schizophrenia and the frontal lobe. *Trends in Neurosciences,* 1988, *11,* 367–370.

Weinberger, D. R., and Wyatt, R. J. Brain morphology in schizophrenia: *In vivo* studies. In *Schizophrenia as a Brain Disease,* edited by F. A. Henn and H. A. Nasrallah. New York: Oxford University Press, 1982.

Weiner, R. D., and Krystal, A. D. The present use of electroconvulsive therapy. *Annual Review of Medicine,* 1994, *45,* 273–281.

Weintraub, S., Mesulam, M.-M., and Kramer, L. Disturbances in prosody: A right-hemisphere contribution to language. *Archives of Neurology,* 1981, *38,* 742–744.

Weiskrantz, L. Residual vision in a scotoma: A follow-up study of "form" discrimination. *Brain,* 1987, *110,* 77–92.

Weiskrantz, L., Warrington, E. K., Sanders, M. D., and Marshall, J. Visual capacity in the hemianopic field following a restricted occipital ablation. *Brain,* 1974, *97,* 709–728.

Weiss, J. M. Effects of coping response on stress. *Journal of Comparative and Physiological Psychology,* 1968, *65,* 251–260.

Weissman, M. M., Canino, G. J., Greenwald, S., Joyce, P. R., Karam, E. G., Lee, C. K., Rubio-Stipec, M., Wells, J. E., Wickramaratne, P. J., and Wittchen, H. U. Current rates and symptom profiles of panic disorder in six cross-national studies. *Clinical Neuropharmacology,* 1995, *18* (Suppl. 2), S1–S6.

Weitzman, E. D. Sleep and its disorders. *Annual Review of Neuroscience,* 1981, *4,* 381–418.

Welsh, D. K., Logothetis, D. E., Meister, M., and Reppert, S. M. Individual neurons dissociated from rat suprachiasmatic nucleus express independently phased circadian firing rhythms. *Neuron,* 1995, *14,* 697–706.

Weltzin, T. E., Hsu, L. K. G., Pollice, C., and Kaye, W. H. Feeding patterns in bulimia nervosa. *Biological Psychiatry,* 1991, *30,* 1093–1110.

Wernicke, C. *Der Aphasische Symptomenkomplex*. Breslau, Poland: Cohn & Weigert, 1874.

West, D. B., Fey, D., and Woods, S. C. Cholecystokinin persistently suppresses meal size but not food intake in free-feeding rats. *American Journal of Physiology,* 1984, *246,* R776–R787.

Whalen, P. J., Rauch, S. L., Etcoff, N. L., McInerney, S. C., Lee, M. B., and Jenike, M. A. Masked presentations of emotional facial expressions modulate amygdala activity without explicit knowledge. *Journal of Neuroscience,* 1998, *18,* 411–418.

Wheeler, M. E., Petersen, S. E., and Buckner, R. L. Memory's echo: Vivid remembering reactivates sensory-specific cortex. *Proceedings of the National Academy of Science, USA,* 2000, *97,* 11125–11129.

Whipple, B., and Komisaruk, B. R. Analgesia produced in women by genital self-stimulation. *Journal of Sex Research,* 1988, *24,* 130–140.

White, F. J. Synaptic regulation of mesocorticolimbic dopamine neurons. *Annual Review of Neuroscience,* 1996, *19,* 405–436.

White, J. Autonomic discharge from stimulation of the hypothalamus in man. *Association for Research in Nervous and Mental Disorders,* 1940, *20,* 854–863.

Whitfield, I. C., and Evans, E. F. Responses of auditory cortical neurons to stimuli of changing frequency. *Journal of Neurophysiology,* 1965, *28,* 655–672.

Whitten, W. K. Occurrence of anestrus in mice caged in groups. *Journal of Endocrinology,* 1959, *18,* 102–107.

Wickelgren, I. Drug may suppress the craving for nicotine. *Science,* 1998, *282,* 1797–1798.

Wickland, C., and Turek, F. W. Lesions of the thalamic intergeniculate leaflet block activity-induced phase shifts in the circadian activity rhythm of the golden hamster. *Brain Research,* 1994, *660,* 293–300.

Wickland, C. R., and Turek, F. W. Phase-shifting effects of acute increases in activity on circadian locomotor rhythms in hamsters. *American Journal of Physiology,* 1991, *261,* R1109–R1117.

Wiener, S. I., Paul, C. A., and Eichenbaum, H. Spatial and behavioral correlates of hippocampal neuronal activity. *Journal of Neuroscience,* 1989, *9,* 2737–2763.

Wiesner, B. P., and Sheard, N. *Maternal Behaviour in the Rat.* London: Oliver and Brody, 1933.

Wilckens, T., Schweiger, U., and Pirke, K. M. Activation of 5-HT1C-receptors suppresses excessive wheel running induced by semi-starvation in the rat. *Psychopharmacology (Berlin),* 1992, *109,* 77–84.

Wilens, T. E., Biederman, J., and Spencer, T. J. Attention deficit/hyperactivity disorder across the lifespan. *Annual Review of Medicine,* 2002, *53,* 113–131.

Wilensky, A. E., Schafe, G. E., and LeDoux, J. E. Functional inactivation of the amygdala before but not after auditory fear conditioning prevents memory formation. *Journal of Neuroscience,* 1999, *19,* RC48 (1–5).

Willesen, M. G., Kristensen, P., and Romer, J. Co-localization of growth hormone secretagogue receptor and NPY mRNA in the arcuate nucleus of the rat. *Neuroendocrinology,* 1999, *70,* 306–316.

Wilska, A. Eine Methode zur Bestimmung der Horschwellenamplituden der Tromenfells bei verscheideden Frequenzen. *Skandinavisches Archiv für Physiologie,* 1935, *72,* 161–165.

Wilson, B. E., Meyer, G. E., Cleveland, J. C., and Weigle, D. S. Identification of candidate genes for a factor regulating body weight in primates. *American Journal of Physiology,* 1990, *259,* R1148–R1155.

Wilson, F. A. W., Ó Scalaidhe, S. P. O., and Goldman-Rakic, P. S. Dissociation of object and spatial processing domains in primate prefrontal cortex. *Science,* 1993, *260,* 1955–1958.

Winans, S. S., and Powers, J. B. Olfactory and vomeronasal deafferentation of male hamsters: Histological and behavioral analyses. *Brain Research,* 1977, *126,* 325–344.

Winslow, J. T., and Miczek, K. A. Social status as determinants of alcohol effects on aggressive behavior in squirrel monkeys (*Saimiri sciureus*). *Psychopharmacology,* 1985, *85,* 167–172.

Winslow, J. T., and Miczek, K. A. Androgen dependency of alcohol effects on aggressive behavior: A seasonal rhythm in high-ranking squirrel monkeys. *Psychopharmacology,* 1988, *95,* 92–98.

Winslow, J. T., Ellingoe, J., and Miczek, K. A. Effects of alcohol on aggressive behavior in squirrel monkeys: Influence of testosterone and social context. *Psychopharmacology,* 1988, *95,* 356–363.

Winter, P., and Funkenstein, H. The auditory cortex of the squirrel monkey: Neuronal discharge patterns to auditory stimuli. *Proceedings of the 3rd Congress of Primatology, Zurich,* 1971, *2,* 24–28.

Wirz-Justice, A., and Van den Hoofdakker, R. H. Sleep deprivation in depression: What do we know, where do we go? *Biological Psychiatry,* 1999, *46,* 445–453.

Wirz-Justice, A., Graw, P., Kraeuchi, K., Gisin, B., Jochum, A., Arendt, J., Fisch, H.-U., Buddeberg, C., and Poeldinger, W. Light therapy in seasonal affective disorder is independent of time of day or circadian phase. *Archives of General Psychiatry,* 1993, *50,* 929–937.

Wirz-Justice, A., Graw, P., Kraeuchi, K., Sarrafzadeh, A., English, J., Arendt, J., and Sand, L. 'Natural' light treatment of seasonal affective disorder. *Journal of Affective Disorders,* 1996, *37,* 109–120.

Wise, R., Chollet, F., Hadar, U., Friston, K., Hoffner, E., and Frackowiak, R. Distribution of cortical neural networks involved in word comprehension and word retrieval. *Brain,* 1991, *114,* 1803–1817.

Wise, R. A. Psychomotor stimulant properties of addictive drugs. *Annals of the New York Academy of Sciences,* 1988, *537,* 228–234.

Wise, R. A., Leone, P., Rivest, R., and Leeb, K. Elevations of nucleus accumbens dopamine and DOPAC levels during intravenous heroin self-administration. *Synapse,* 1995, *21,* 140–148.

Wise, R. J. S., Greene, J., Buchel, C., and Scott, S. K. Brain regions involved in articulation. *Lancet,* 1999, *353,* 1057–1061.

Wise, S. P., and Rapoport, J. L. Obsessive compulsive disorder: Is it a basal ganglia dysfunction? *Psychopharmacology Bulletin,* 1988, *24,* 380–384.

Wissinger, B., and Sharpe, L. T. New aspects of an old theme: The genetic basis of human color vision. *American Journal of Human Genetics,* 1998, *63,* 1257–1262.

Wolff, P. H., and Melngailis, I. Family patterns of developmental dyslexia: Clinical findings. *American Journal of Medical Genetics,* 1994, *54,* 122–131.

Wong, G. T., Gannon, K. S., and Margolskee, R. F. Transduction of bitter and sweet taste by gustducin. *Nature*, 1996, *381*, 796–800.

Wong-Riley, M. Personal communication, 1978. Cited by Livingstone, M. S., and Hubel, D. H. Thalamic inputs to cytochrome oxidase-rich regions in monkey visual cortex. *Proceedings of the National Academy of Sciences, USA*, 1982, *79*, 6098–6101.

Wood, D. L., Sheps, S. G., Elveback, L. R., and Schirder, A. Cold pressor test as a predictor of hypertension. *Hypertension*, 1984, *6*, 301–306.

Wood, E. R., Dudchenko, P. A., Robitsek, R. J., and Eichenbaum, H. Hippocampal neurons encode information about different types of memory episodes occurring in the same location. *Neuron*, 2000, *27*, 623–633.

Wood, R. I., and Newman, S. W. Mating activates androgen receptor-containing neurons in chemosensory pathways of the male Syrian hamster brain. *Brain Research*, 1993, *614*, 65–77.

Woodruff-Pak, D. S. Eyeblink classical conditioning in H. M.: Delay and trace paradigms. *Behavioral Neuroscience*, 1993, *107*, 911–925.

Woods, B. T. Is schizophrenia a progressive neurodevelopmental disorder? Toward a unitary pathogenetic mechanism. *American Journal of Psychiatry*, 1998, *155*, 1661–1670.

Woods, S. C., Lotter, E. C., McKay, L. D., and Porte, D. Chronic intracerebroventricular infusion of insulin reduces food intake and body weight of baboons. *Nature*, 1979, *282*, 503–505.

Woodworth, R. S., and Schlosberg, H. *Experimental Psychology.* New York: Holt, Rinehart and Winston, 1954.

Wooley, S. C., and Garner, D. M. Controversies in management: Should obesity be treated? Dietary treatments for obesity are ineffective. *British Medical Journal*, 1994, *309*, 655–656.

World Health Organization. *Tobacco or Health, a Global Status Report.* Geneva, Switzerland: World Health Organization Publications, 1997.

Wright, B. A., Bowen, R. W., and Zecker, S. G. Nonlinguistic perceptual deficits associated with reading and language disorders. *Current Opinion in Neurobiology*, 2000, *10*, 483–485.

Wu, J. C., and Bunney, W. E. The biological basis of an antidepressant response to sleep deprivation and relapse: Review and hypothesis. *American Journal of Psychiatry*, 1990, *147*, 14–21.

Wu, J. C., Buchsbaum, M. S., and Bunney, W. E. Positron emission tomography study of phencyclidine users as a possible drug model of schizophrenia. *Yakubutsu Seishin Kodo*, 1991, *11*, 47–48

Wysocki, C. J. Neurobehavioral evidence for the involvement of the vomeronasal system in mammalian reproduction. *Neuroscience and Biobehavioral Reviews*, 1979, *3*, 301–341.

Xu, M., Moratalla, R., Gold, L. H., Hiroi, N., Koob, G. F., Graybiel, A. M., and Tonegawa, S. Dopamine D_1 receptor mutant mice are deficient in striatal expression of dynorphin and in dopamine-mediated behavioral responses. *Cell*, 1994, *79*, 729–742.

Yadin, E., Thomas, E., Strickland, C. E., and Grishkat, H. L. Anxiolytic effects of benzodiazepines in amygdala-lesioned rats. *Psychopharmacology*, 1991, *103*, 473–479.

Yamashita, H., Fukikawa, T., Yanai, I., Morinobu, S., and Yamawaki, S. Clinical features and treatment response of patients with major depression and silent cerebral infarction. *Neuropsychobiology*, 2001, *44*, 176–182.

Yang, T. T., Gallen, C. C., Ramachandran, V. S., Cobb, S., Schwartz, B. J., and Bloom, F. E. Noninvasive detection of cerebral plasticity in adult human somatosensory cortex. *Neuroreport*, 1994, *5*, 701–704.

Yanovski, J. A., and Yanovski, S. Z. Recent advances in basic obesity research. *Journal of the American Medical Association*, 1999, *282*, 1504–1506.

Yates, W. R., Perry, P., and Murray, S. Aggression and hostility in anabolic steroid users. *Biological Psychiatry*, 1992, *31*, 1232–1234.

Yatham, L. N., Liddle, P. F., Shiah, I. S., Scarrow, G., Lam, R. W., Adam, M. J., Zis, A. P., and Ruth, T. J. Brain serotonin-2 receptors in major depression: A positron emission tomography study. *Archives of General Psychiatry*, 2000, *57*, 850–858.

Yehuda, R. Are glucocorticoids responsible for putative hippocampal damage in PTSD? How and when to decide. *Hippocampus*, 2001, *11*, 85–90.

Yeo, G. S. H., Farooqi, I. S., Aminian, S., Halsall, D. J., Stanhope, R. G., and O'Rahilly, S. A frameshift mutation in MC4R associated with dominantly inherited human obesity. *Nature Genetics*, 1998, *20*, 111–112.

Yeo, J. A. G., and Keverne, E. B. The importance of vaginal-cervical stimulation for maternal behaviour in the rat. *Physiology and Behavior*, 1986, *37*, 23–26.

Yettefti, K., Orsini, J. C., and Perrin, J. Characteristics of glycemia-sensitive neurons in the nucleus tractus solitarii: Possible involvement in nutritional regulation. *Physiology and Behavior*, 1997, *61*, 93–100.

Yokoo, H., Tanaka, M., Yoshida, M., Tsuda, A., Tanaka, T., and Mizoguchi, K. Direct evidence of conditioned fear-elicited enhancement of noradrenaline release in the rat hypothalamus assessed by intracranial microdialysis. *Brain Research*, 1990, *536*, 305–308.

Yokota, T., Ishiai, S., Furukawa, T., and Tsukagoshi, H. Pure agraphia of kanji due to thrombosis of the Labbe vein. *Journal of Neurology, Neurosurgery, and Psychiatry*, 1990, *53*, 335–338.

Yost, W. A. Auditory image perception and analysis: The basis for hearing. *Hearing Research*, 1991, *56*, 8–18.

Young, A. W., Aggleton, J. P., Hellawell, D. J., Johnson, M., Broks, P., and Hanley, J. R. Face processing impairments after amygdalotomy. *Brain*, 1995, *118*, 15–24.

Young, S. N., and Leyton, M. The role of serotonin in human mood and social interaction: Insight from altered tryptophan levels. *Pharmacology, Biochemistry and Behavior*, 2002, *71*, 857–865.

Youngren, K. D., Inglis, F. M., Pivirotto, P. J., Jedema, H. P., Bradberry, C. W., Goldman-Rakic, P. S., Roth, R. H., and Moghaddam, B. Clozapine preferentially increases dopamine release in the rhesus monkey prefrontal cortex compared with the caudate nucleus. *Neuropsychopharmacology*, 1999, *20*, 403–412.

Yuste, R., and Denk, W. Dendritic spines as basic functional units of neuronal integration. *Nature*, 1995, *375*, 682–684.

Yuste, R., Majewska, A., Cash, S. S., and Denk, W. Mechanisms of calcium influx into hippocampal spines: Heterogeneity among spines, coincidence detection by NMDA receptors, and optical quantal analysis. *Journal of Neuroscience*, 1999, *19*, 1976–1987.

Zayfert, C., Dums, A. R., Ferguson, R. J., and Hegel, M. T. Health functioning impairments associated with posttraumatic stress disorder, anxiety disorders, and depression. *Journal of Nervous and Mental Disease,* 2002, *190,* 233–240.

Zeki, S. The representation of colours in the cerebral cortex. *Nature,* 1980, *284,* 412–418.

Zeki, S., and Shipp, S. The functional logic of cortical connections. *Nature, 1988, 335,* 311–317.

Zeki, S., Aglioti, S., McKeefry, D., and Berlucchi, G. The neurological basis of conscious color perception in a blind patient. *Proceedings of the National Academy of Science, USA,* 1999, *96,* 14124–14129.

Zenner, H.-P., Zimmermann, U., and Schmitt, U. Reversible contraction of isolated mammalian cochlear hair cells. *Hearing Research,* 1985, *18,* 127–133.

Zhang, C. Y., and Wong-Riley, M. T. Do nitric oxide synthase, NMDA receptor subunit R1 and cytochrome oxidase co-localize in the rat central nervous system? *Brain Research,* 1996, *729,* 205–215.

Zhou, F. C., Zhang, J. K., Lumeng, L., and Li, T. K. Mesolimbic dopamine system in alcohol-preferring rats. *Alcohol,* 1995, *12,* 403–412.

Zhuang, X., Oosting, R. S., Jones, S. R., Gainetdinov, R. R., Miller, G. W., Caron, M. G., and Hen, R. Hyperactivity and impaired response habituation in hyperdopaminergic mice. *Proceedings of the National Academy of Science, USA,* 2001, *98,* 1982–1987.

Zihl, J., Von Cramon, D., Mai, N., and Schmid, C. Disturbance of movement vision after bilateral posterior brain damage: Further evidence and follow up observations. *Brain,* 1991, *114,* 2235–2252.

Zola-Morgan, S., Squire, L. R., and Amaral, D. G. Human amnesia and the medial temporal region: Enduring memory impairment following a bilateral lesion limited to field CA1 of the hippocampus. *Journal of Neuroscience,* 1986, *6,* 2950–2967.

Zola-Morgan, S., Squire, L., Rempel, N. L., Clower, R. P., and Amaral, D. G. Enduring memory impairment in monkeys after ischemic damage to the hippocampus. *Journal of Neuroscience,* 1992, *12,* 2582–2596.

Zola, S. M., Squire, L. R., Teng, E., Stenfanacci, L., Buffalo, E. A., and Clark, R. E. Impaired recognition memory in monkeys after damage limited to the hippocampal region. *Journal of Neuroscience,* 2000, *20,* 451–463.

Zou, Z., Horowitz, L. F., Montmayeur, J.-P., Snapper, S., and Buck, L. B. Genetic tracing reveals a stereotyped sensory map in the olfactory cortex. *Nature,* 2001, *414,* 173–179.

Zumpe, D., Bonsall, R. W., Kutner, M. H., and Michael, R. P. Medroxyprogesterone acetate, aggression, and sexual behavior in male cynomolgus monkeys (Macaca fascicularis). *Hormones and Behavior,* 1991, *25,* 394–409.

Zwiers, M. P., Van Opstal, A. J., and Cruysberg, J. R. M. A spatial hearing deficit in early-blind humans. *Journal of Neuroscience,* 2001, *21,* RC142 (1–5).

Name Index

Abe, H., 302
Abe, M., 396
Abel, E. L., 588
Abercrombie, H. C., 539
Abolmaali, N. D., 323
Abrahamov, A., 127
Adams, H. P., 484
Adams, L. A., 324, 453, 524
Adamson, K. L., 587
Adey, W. R., 286
Adieh, H. B., 340
Adler, C. M., 522, 529
Adler, N. T., 318
Adolphs, R., 363–364
Advokat, C., 407
Agamanolis, J., 461
Aggleton, J. P., 464
Aghajanian, G. K., 583
Agmo, A., 582
Aharon, Etcoff, N., 445
Ait-Daoud, N., 599
Akhtar, S., 550
Akil, M., 530
Alain, C., 218
Albers, H. E., 302
Albrecht, D. G., 180
Albright, T. D., 194
Alexander, G. M., 324
Alexander, M. P., 509
Alger, B. E., 230
Alkire, M. T., 460
Allen, L. S., 328, 333
Allison, D. B., 402
Allison, D. W., 424
Allison, T., 191
Allman, J. M., 80, 193
Almers, W., 54–55
Altschuler, H. L., 591
Amaral, D. G., 237, 344, 457, 460
Amen, D. G., 354
Anand, B. K., 394
Ancoli-Israel, S., 280
Andersen, R. A., 193
Anderson, A. K., 363, 368
Anderson, C. H., 185
Anderson, C. M., 559
Anderson, R. H., 329, 332
Anderson, S. W., 354
Anderson-Hunt, M., 325
Andreasen, N. C., 517
Andres, K. H., 223
Andrews, N., 557
Angrilli, A., 347
Annies, R., 590
Arbib, M. A., 197, 443
Archer, J., 357

Arendt, J., 306
Arnold, A. P., 331
Aroniadou, V. A., 428
Aronson, B. D., 301–302
Arroyo, S., 366
Artmann, H., 406
Asanuma, H., 256
Aschoff, J., 300
Aslin, R. N., 79
Asnis, G. M., 549
Aston-Jones, G., 291
Atack, J. R., 536
Atchison, M., 565
Attia, E., 407
Auer, R. N., 461
Avenet, P., 234
Avery, D. H., 543
Avila, M. T., 529
Axel, R., 240, 320
Azakami, M., 279

Büchel, C., 505
Bacher-Svendsen, K., 476
Baddeley, A. D., 494
Baer, L., 553
Bagatell, C. J., 325
Bai, F. L., 396
Bailey, A., 557
Bailey, A. J., 330, 556
Bailey, J. M., 330
Baizer, J. S., 186
Bak, T. H., 496
Baker, D. G., 565
Baldessarini, R. J., 519, 522, 535
Baldwin, A. E., 448
Balint, R., 198
Ballantine, H. T., 553
Ballard, P., 101
Balon, R., 549
Balskubik, R., 581
Balster, R. L., 590
Bancroft, J., 358
Banks, M. S., 79
Banks, W. A., 403
Baranaga, M., 127
Baranyi, A., 428
Barbazanges, A., 564
Barclay, C. D., 196
Barfield, R. J., 334, 338
Baron, M., 537
Barr, L. C., 554
Barsh, G. S., 403
Bartness, T. J., 305
Basbaum, A. I., 229, 230
Batkai, S., 127, 592
Batterham, R. L., 390, 399

Bauer, R. H., 434
Baum, A., 567
Baum, M. J., 318, 321–322
Baxter, J. D., 561
Baxter, L. R., 543
Baylis, G. C., 189, 430
Baylor, D., 168
Bazett, H. C., 226
Beach, F. A., 331
Beam, K. G., 235
Beamer, W., 317
Bean, N. J., 355–356
Bear, M. F., 427
Beaudet, A., 295–296
Beauregard, M., 354
Beauvois, M. F., 506, 510
Bechara, A., 347, 353, 456, 539
Beckstead, R. M., 237–238
Beecher, H. K., 229
Beeman, E. A., 355
Behan, P. O., 513
Behrmann, M., 191, 505
Beidel, D. C., 550
Beidler, L. M., 234
Beitz, A. J., 231–232
Belin, P., 488
Bell, A. P., 326
Bellugi, U., 498
Belluzzi, J. D., 448
Beltramo, M., 593
Benington, J. H., 288
Benson, D. F., 467, 510
Benson, D. L., 78
Bercovitch, F. B., 327
Bergenheim, A. T., 266
Berger, M., 542–543
Bergmann, B. M., 285
Bermant, G., 317–318
Bernhardt, P. C., 358
Berns, G. S., 446
Bernstein, I. L., 406
Berrettini, W., 534
Berridge, K. C., 577
Berson, D. M., 302
Bertelsen, A., 518
Berthier, M., 229, 551
Bertini, M., 277
Berwick, G. S., 56
Best, P. J., 473–474, 590
Bettelheim, B., 556
Betteridge, C., 357
Betz, W. J., 56
Beversdorf, D. Q., 505
Biederman, J., 558
Bier, M. J., 298
Bierut, L. J., 594

Bigiani, A., 236
Bingman, V. P., 471
Bini, L., 534
Birch, L. L., 401
Bird, E., 387
Bischofberger, J., 126
Bisiach, E., 7
Blair, R. J., 353
Blake, R., 196
Blanchard, R., 329
Blaustein, J. D., 319, 334–335
Blest, A. D., 14
Bleuler, E., 517
Blier, P., 554
Bliss, T. V. P., 417
Bloch, V., 287
Blonder, L. X., 362
Bloom, F. E., 291, 586
Blum, K., 596
Blumenthal, J. A., 566
Blundell, J. E., 399, 401, 405
Boatman, D., 490
Bodner, M., 434
Bodner, S. M., 552
Boeve, B. F., 283
Bohman, M., 594
Boller, F., 486
Bolton, R. F., 296
Bon, C., 426
Bonnet, M. H., 280
Bontempi, B., 471
Boot, L. M., 320
Booth, A., 358
Booth, D. A., 388
Borbély, A. A., 286
Born, R. T., 183, 194
Bornstein, B., 192
Borod, J. C., 367
Bors, E., 286
Bottini, G., 493
Boulos, Z., 306
Bouma, H., 344
Bourgouin, P., 354
Boussaoud, D., 188
Bouwknecht, J. A., 350
Bowen, R. W., 512
Bowers, D., 362–363
Bowersox, S. S., 277
Boxer, P. A., 297
Boynton, R. M., 175, 187
Bozarth, M. A., 583–584
Brüning, J. C., 390
Bracha, H. S., 525, 527
Bradbury, M. W. B., 38
Bradley, D. C., 194
Bradley, S. J., 328
Bramham, C. R., 476

Brandao, M. L., 581
Bray, G. A., 405
Brecher, E. M., 586
Breedlove, S. M., 319, 328, 331
Breier, A., 520
Breisch, S. T., 399
Breiter, H. C., 552
Bremner, J. D., 538, 565
Brewer, J. B., 460
Brickner, R. M., 547
Bridges, R. S., 339–340
Britten, K. H., 195
Britton, K., 561
Brobeck, J. R., 394
Broberg, D. J., 406
Broberger, C., 396
Broca, P., 483
Bronson, F. H., 356–357
Brosius, J., 427
Brossaud, D., 199
Broughton, H. B., 536
Brown, A. S., 518
Brown, R. E., 292, 511
Brown, T. H., 418–419
Brownell, H. H., 493
Brownell, W. E., 213
Brozowski, T. J., 529
Bruce, H. M., 320
Brun, V. J., 474
Bruno, J. P., 337
Brust, J. C. M., 508
Bryant, D. N., 303
Bryden, M. P., 362
Buchs, P. A., 425
Buchsbaum, M. S., 284, 529
Buck, L. B., 235, 240, 367
Budka, H., 286
Buggy, J., 378
Bunney, B. S., 445
Bunney, W. E., 529, 541–542
Bunyard, L. B., 405
Burgess, N., 454
Burke, J. R., 268
Burnstock, G., 226
Burt, A. D., 324
Burt, D. R., 519
Burton, M. J., 447
Buxbaum, L. J., 191
Buzsaki, G., 476–477
Byne, W., 328
Bystritsky, A., 549

Cabanac, M., 390
Cahill, L., 347
Cain, W. S., 242
Caine, S. B., 585
Calabrese, J. R., 536
Calabrese, P., 464, 466
Calder, A. J., 363
Callaway, C. W., 297
Camardo, J. S., 380
Cameron, H. A., 79
Campbell, B. A., 347
Campbell, C. S., 388
Campbell, R., 364, 496

Campeau, S., 344
Campfield, L. A., 391
Cannon, M., 526, 528
Cannon, W. B., 370
Card, J. P., 301–302
Cardone, C. C., 387
Carew, T. J., 436
Carlson, N. R., 339, 495, 508
Carmichael, M. S., 318
Caro, J. F., 403
Carpenter, C. R., 356
Carpenter, W. T., 517
Carr, C. E., 216
Carr, D. B., 530
Carrera, M. R., 597
Carroll, R. C., 428
Carter, C. S., 318–319
Caselli, R. J., 227
Castellanos, F. X., 559
Castles, A., 511
Caterina, M. J., 226
Cavada, C., 199
Cecil, J. E., 388
Celentano, D. C., 334
Cenci, M. A., 561
Cerletti, U., 534–535
Chandler, L. J., 590
Channabasavanna, S., 550
Chapman, P. F., 426
Charney, D. S., 538
Chase, M. H., 297
Chaudhari, N., 236
Chehab, F. F., 314
Chemelli, R. M., 282, 396
Chen, G., 536
Chen, J., 591–592
Chen, P., 397
Chen, W. R., 428
Chen, Y.-C., 442
Chen, Y. W., 533
Cherry, J. A., 321–322
Choi, D. W., 288
Chou, T. C., 292–293
Chuang, D.-M., 536
Chun, M. M., 191
Cipolotti, L., 502, 510
Clapham, J. C., 404
Clark, J. T., 396
Clegg, M. T., 317
Clemente, C. D., 293
Clements, K. M., 544
Climent, K., 403
Cloninger, C. R., 594–595
Clow, K., 289
Clugnet, M.-C., 428, 438
Cobb, S., 562
Coble, P. A., 541
Coccaro, E. F., 351
Coen, K. M., 587
Cohen, E. A., 562
Cohen, N. J., 457–458
Cohen, S., 570
Colapinto, J., 309
Cole, B. J., 561
Colledge, E., 353
Collins, C. E., 183

Collins, D. R., 437
Collison, C., 461
Colman, D. R., 78
Coltheart, M., 511
Comarr, A. E., 331
Comuzzie, A. G., 402
Conner, R., 355
Constantinidis, C., 433
Contreras, R. J., 387
Coolen, L. M., 333
Cooper, J. D., 296
Coover, G. D., 345
Corbett, D., 445
Corey, D. P., 208
Corkin, S., 453, 458
Cornwall, J., 296
Corrigall, W. A., 587
Corwin, J. T., 213
Coscina, D. V., 396
Coslett, H. B., 191
Cossu, G., 127, 592
Cotman, C. W., 428
Cottingham, S. L., 333
Couceyro, P., 398
Courchesne, E., 557
Courtney, S. M., 435
Covington, H. E., 579
Cowan, W. M., 301
Cowey, A., 184, 187–188, 364
Cox, A., 556
Coyle, J. T., 531
Crabbe, J. C., 591
Crane, G. E., 534
Creese, I., 519
Crews, F. T., 590
Crick, F., 287
Crow, T. J., 445, 517
Cruysberg, J. R. M., 217
Cubelli, R., 509
Culebras, A., 283
Culotta, E., 128, 426
Cummings, D. E., 397
Cummings, T. A., 234
Currie, P. J., 396
Currs Dossi, R., 297
Cutler, W. B., 322
Cutting, J. E., 196
Czopf, J., 476

Dabbs, J. M., 357–358
Dahl, D., 476
Dalen, P., 524
Dallos, P., 209
Damasio, A. R., 188, 192, 198, 352, 363, 493–494, 496
Damasio, H., 192, 352, 484, 494, 502
Damsma, G., 289, 587
Dani, J. A., 588
Daniel, D. G., 529
Daniele, A., 496
Daniels, D., 142, 335
Darwin, C., 360
Datta, S., 297
Davidowa, H., 402
Davidson, D., 591, 598

Davidson, J. M., 318
Davidson, M. C., 289
Davidson, R. J., 365
Davis, D., 526
Davis, J. D., 388
Davis, J. O., 525, 527
Davis, M., 345, 347, 438
Davison, G. C., 550
Daw, N. W., 176
Day, J., 289, 587
De Biasi, M., 588
de Castro, E. S., 385
de Castro, J. M., 385–386
de Gelder, B., 364
De Gennaro, L., 277
De Jong, J., 537
De Jonge, F. H., 332–333
de la Riva, C., 321
De Lee, C., 287
De Long, G. R., 557
De Valois, K. K., 180, 183
De Valois, R. L., 180, 183
de Wit, H., 590
Deacon, S., 306
Deadwyler, S. A., 592
Dean, P., 188
Debanne, D., 428
Dehaene, S., 498
Dejerine, J., 502
Del Cerro, M. C. R., 339
Delay, J., 519
Delgado, P. L., 537–538
Dement, W. C., 277, 281, 284, 286–287
Denes, G., 502
Deniker, P., 519
Denk, W., 420
Dennerstein, L., 325
Dennis, M., 486
Deol, M. S., 210
DePaulo, J. R., 534
Desimone, R., 186–189, 194, 435
D'Esposito, M., 464
Deutch, A. Y., 530
Deutsch, J. A., 389
Devane, W. A., 127
Devine, D. P., 582
Devinsky, O., 481
Devlin, M. J., 406
DeVoogd, T. J., 471
Dewey, S. L., 598
Dhatt, R., 599
Di Chiara, G., 576, 590
Di Ciano, P., 584
Di Monte, D. A., 267
di Pellegrino, G., 199
di Tomaso, E., 593
Diamond, D. M., 217, 309, 563
Diamond, I. T., 182
Diana, M., 590
Diener, M., 386
Digiovanni, M., 489
Dijk, D. J., 286, 306
Dilsaver, S. C., 533

Dinh, T. T., 394
Dionne, V. E., 235
Dérouesné, J., 506, 510
Divac, I., 440
Dixon, A. K., 356
Does, A. J. W., 537
Doherty, P. C., 318, 559
Dolan, R. J., 366
Dolan, R. P., 173
Dominguez, J., 333
Donnelly, N., 363
Donny, E. C., 587
Doolittle, D. P., 596
Dosemeci, A., 424
Dostrovsky, T., 471
Doty, R. L., 323
Dou, H., 331
Dougherty, D. D., 354, 553
Douglass, J., 398
Dresel, S., 559
Drevets, W. C., 539–540
Dronkers, N. F., 485
Drugan, R. C., 231
Dryden, S., 399
Dube, M. G., 395
Duchenne, G.-B., 365
Dudek, S. M., 427
Due, D. L., 588
Duersteler, M. R., 181
Duhamel, J.-R., 199
Dujardin, K., 287
Dulac, C., 320
Dunn, F. A., 302
Dunnett, S. B., 395
Duntley, S., 280
Dunwiddie, T. V., 294
Durie, D. J., 283
Duva, M. A., 395
Duvauchelle, C. L., 448
Dyck, C. H., 559
Dykes, R. W., 227

Eacott, M. J., 440
Eaton, W. W., 524, 548
Eberhardt, N. L., 401
Eckel, L. S., 391
Eddy, N. B., 574
Eden, G. F., 511
Edwards, D. P., 183, 425
Edwards, G. L., 380
Egeland, J. A., 533
Ehrhardt, A. A., 309, 312, 325–326, 328
Eichenbaum, H., 457, 470, 476
Eichler, V. B., 301
Eilam, R., 566
Ekman, P., 360–361, 365
El Mansari, M., 296, 554
Elbert, T., 79
Elias, C. F., 396, 398
Elias, M., 358
Elkis, H., 539
Ellingoe, J., 358
Ellsworth, P., 361
Elmquist, J. K., 398

Ende, G., 535
Endenberg, H. J., 596
Endoh, M., 426
Engber, T. M., 586
Enggasser, J. L., 590
Ennis, M., 240
Epstein, A. N., 380
Erb, S., 579
Erickson, C. A., 434–435
Ernst, M., 353, 558
Ernulf, K. E., 330
Eslinger, P., 484
Eslinger, P. J., 352
Esposito, M., 486
Estabrooke, I. V., 292, 294
Ettenberg, A., 448
Evans, E. F., 212, 217
Evarts, E. V., 256
Everitt, B. J., 578
Everson, C. A., 286

Fabbro, F., 498
Fagg, A. H., 443
Fairbanks, L. A., 543
Falls, W. A., 438
Fanselow, M. S., 231
Farah, M. J., 227
Faraone, S., 558
Faraone, S. V., 518
Farber, N. B., 531
Farmer, M. E., 489
Farooqi, I. S., 402–403
Farries, M. A., 266
Farrington, C. P., 557
Fava, M., 406
Feder, H. H., 318, 335
Feigenbaum, S. L., 569
Feinhandler, D. A., 591
Feinle, C., 389
Felix, D., 380
Felleman, D. J., 185
Fernandez-Ruiz, J., 441
Fernandez-Tome, P., 561
Ferrara, M., 277
Ferris, C. F., 302
Fey, D., 389
Fiatarone, M. A., 544
Fibiger, H. C., 289, 519, 587
Field, T., 371
Fields, H. L., 230, 232
Fieve, R. R., 535
Fiez, J. A., 494, 496, 507
Filipek, P. A., 511
Finger, S., 9
Firestein, S., 240
Fischer, H., 549
Fisher, C., 278–279
Fisher, S. E., 511
Fishman, P. S., 267
Fiske, A. P., 550
Fitz, E., 591, 598
Fitzpatrick, D., 182
Fitzsimons, J. T., 380
Flanagan-Cato, L. M., 142, 335
Flaum, M., 517

Fletcher, J. M., 592
Fletcher, P. J., 399
Flock, A., 208
Flood, J. F., 396
Fobes, J. L., 444–445
Folstein, S. E., 556–557
Fombonne, E., 555
Fornal, C. A., 291
Fort, P., 298
Foster, D. L., 314, 318
Foundas, A. L., 482
Fox, S. E., 476
Foy, M. R., 567
Frackowiak, R. S., 464, 494
Frahm, H. D., 471
Francis, J., 388
Frank, G., 213
Frank, M., 237
Franklin, K. B. J., 582
Freed, C. R., 265
Freedman, M. S., 301
Freeman, W. J., 321
Freund, H. J., 443
Frey, U., 426
Fride, E., 127
Friedman, J., 390
Friedman, M. I., 337, 394
Friedman, S., 338
Friedmann, E., 322
Friesen, H. G., 370
Friesen, W. V., 360–361
Frisch, R. E., 314
Friston, K., 505
Frith, C. D., 464, 494
Frith, U., 556
Froelich, J. C., 596
Frost, A. S., 530
Fry, J. M., 282
Frydenberg, M., 524
Fuentes, J. A., 561
Fujikawa, T., 540
Fukuwatari, T., 237
Fullerton, C. S., 564
Fulton, J. F., 547
Fung, Y. K., 588
Funkenstein, H., 217
Fuster, J. M., 433–435

Gabrieli, J. D. E., 458
Gaffan, D., 187–188, 440
Gaffan, E. A., 447
Gage, F. H., 80, 476
Gagliardo, A., 471
Gainer, H., 304
Galaburda, A. M., 482, 512
Gallassi, R., 285
Gallese, V., 195, 497
Galuske, R. A. W., 482
Gandelman, R., 357
Gannon, K. S., 236
Ganong, A. H., 418
Garcia-Velasco, J., 323
Gardner, H., 482
Gariano, R. F., 448
Garner, C., 534
Garner, D. M., 404

Gasbarri, A., 476
Gatchel, R. J., 567
Gaulin, S. J. C., 471
Gauthier, I., 192
Gayan, J., 511
Gazzaniga, M. S., 5, 7
Gähwiler, B. H., 428
Geary, N., 584
Gehring, W. J., 353
Genefke, I., 564
Gentili, B., 235
Gentilucci, M., 199
George, M. S., 362–363, 535
Georges-Françios, P., 474
Gerashchenko, D., 282
Gerbino, L., 535
Gerfen, C. R., 586
Gerhand, S., 508
Gerren, R., 428
Gerrits, M. A. F. M., 582
Gershon, E. S., 533
Gershon, S., 534–535
Geschwind, N., 490, 510, 513
Gessa, G. L., 586, 590
Getzinger, M. J., 334
Ghiraldi, L., 357
Gibbs, J., 389
Gibbs, W. W., 402
Giedd, J. N., 551
Gilbert, B. O., 594
Gilbert, D. G., 519, 594
Gilbertson, M. W., 518
Gilbertson, T. A., 237
Giles, D. E., 541
Gillespie, P. G., 208
Gillette, M. U., 306
Gillin, J. C., 295
Giordano, A. L., 340
Givens, B., 590
Givens, B. S., 476
Gjerlow, K., 483
Gladue, B. A., 358
Glaser, J. K., 569
Glaser, R., 568
Glaum, S. R., 398
Gloor, P., 347
Glosser, G., 191
Gluecksohn-Waelsch, S., 210
Gobert, A., 538
Goddard, A. W., 549
Goeders, N. E., 582
Goel, V., 366
Goff, D. C., 531
Golby, A. J., 192
Gold, A. R., 324
Gold, G., 240
Golden, P. L., 403
Goldman-Rakic, P. S., 199, 434, 529
Goldstein, R. Z., 578
Golgi, C., 35
Gongwer, M. A., 596
Gonzalez, M. F., 389
Goodale, M. A., 199
Goodglass, H., 499
Goodman-Schulman, R., 509

Gooren, L. J. G., 328
Gordon, B., 6
Gordon, N. C., 232
Goris, A. H. C., 401
Gorski, R. A., 328, 332–333
Gottesman, I. I., 402, 518
Gouras, P., 176
Goy, R. W., 327
Graber, G. C., 338
Grabowski, T. J., 493
Grace, A. A., 449, 530
Grados, M. A., 551
Graf, P., 457
Grafton, S. T., 266, 443
Graham, K. S., 466
Grant, S. G. N., 475
Gratacos, M., 549
Grattan, D. R., 339
Grau, J. W., 231
Gray, Z., 321
Graybiel, A. M., 266
Green, E. J., 474
Greenberg, D., 389
Greenberg, R., 287
Greene, J. D., 354
Greenough, W. T., 474
Grelotti, D. J., 192
Grico, B., 333
Grigorenko, E. L., 511
Grijalva, C. V., 347
Grill, H. J., 393
Grimm, J. W., 577
Gross, C. G., 188, 194
Gross, J., 278
Grossman, E. D., 196
Groves, P. M., 448
Grundy, D., 389
Grunhaus, L., 541
Guerin, G. F., 445
Guerrien, A., 287
Guilleminault, C., 281
Gulevich, G., 284
Gummer, A. W., 213
Gur, R. C., 367
Gura, T., 403
Gurd, J. M., 506
Gurden, H., 448–449
Gurevich, E. V., 521
Guridi, J., 266
Gurin, B., 405
Gurvits, T. V., 565

Haarmeier, T., 197
Haas, H. L., 292
Haas, R. H., 453
Haase, E., 471
Habib, M., 511
Hackett, R. A., 211
Hadjikhani, N., 188
Hahn, T. M., 396
Hajak, G., 280
Hakansson, M. L., 398
Halaas, J. L., 391
Halem, H. A., 321–322
Haley, J. E., 426
Halford, J. C. G., 399, 405

Halgren, E., 347
Hall, W., 592
Halmi, K. A., 406–407
Halpern, M., 321
Halsband, U., 443
Hamberger, M. J., 493
Hamer, D. H., 330
Hammersmith, S. K., 326
Hampson, R. E., 592
Hara, J., 282
Hari, R., 511
Hariri, A. R., 351
Hariz, M. I., 266
Harle, M., 496
Harley, C. W., 476
Harmon, L. D., 181
Harries, M. H., 364
Harrington, M. E., 302
Harris, G. W., 314
Harris, J. A., 434
Harris, R. A., 590
Harrison, S., 440, 447
Harrison, Y., 284
Hart, B., 331
Hartline, H. K., 172
Harvey, S. M., 324
Haslam, N., 550
Hatfield, T., 447
Hattar, S., 302
Haug, H.-J., 542
Hauser, M., 217
Hauser, M. D., 367
Havel, P. J., 403
Hawke, C., 357
Haxby, J. V., 198
Hay, P., 553
Hazelwood, S., 340
Heath, A. C., 594–595
Hebb, D. O., 413
Heckler, M. M., 594
Heffner, H. E., 217
Heffner, R. S., 217
Heilman, K. M., 259–260,
   362–363, 505
Heiman, M. L., 397
Heimer, L., 332
Heinrichs, S. C., 561
Helenius, P., 511
Heller, H. C., 288
Hellhammer, D. H., 325
Helmuth, L., 512
Hemmert, W., 213
Hendrickson, A. E., 182, 301
Hendrickx, A. G., 356
Hendrie, C. A., 231
Hendry, S. H. C., 183
Heninger, G. R., 535, 538
Henke, P. G., 345
Hennessey, A. C., 335
Hennevin, E., 287
Heresco-Levy, U., 531
Herholz, K., 406
Hering, E., 174
Hernan, M. S., 267
Hernandez, L., 448
Hertzmann, M., 529

Herz, A., 581
Hessler, N. A., 422
Hetherington, A. W., 394
Hettema, J. M., 549–550
Heuser, J. E., 53, 55
Heywood, C. A., 187–188,
   364
Hickok, G., 498, 504
Higley, J. D., 349, 596
Hikosaka, O., 442
Hilditch-Maguire, P., 268
Hill, A. J., 473
Hill, J. P., 405
Hines, M., 333
Hinjo, S., 550
Hirata, Y., 486
Hirayama, K., 510
Hirsch, J., 400
Hirsh, R., 440
Hitchcock, J., 347
Hmaidan, Y., 586
Hobson, J. A., 279, 282, 298
Hodge, C. W., 590
Hodges, J. R., 465–466
Hoebel, B. G., 399, 445, 448
Hofbauer, R. K., 230
Hofer, M. A., 338
Hoffman, D. J., 402
Hoffman, D. S., 443
Hoffman, G. E., 334
Hoffman, P. L., 590
Hofman, M. A., 328
Hohman, G. W., 370
Holahan, M. R., 448
Holden, C., 350
Hollander, E., 551, 554, 557
Hollister, J. M., 525
Hollup, S. A., 473
Holmes, G., 270
Homan, R. W., 367
Honack, D., 590
Honda, T., 298
Honda, Y., 297
Hong, C. C. H., 279
Hopf, H. C., 365
Hopfenbeck, J., 387
Hopkins, W. D., 362
Hore, J., 270
Horikoshi, T., 505
Horne, J. A., 284, 286
Horner, P. H., 80
Horowitz, R. M., 235
Horowitz, T. S., 306
Horton, J. C., 182
Howard, G., 540
Howland, J. G., 447
Hubel, D. H., 178, 182–183
Hubert, W., 325
Hublin, C., 282
Hudspeth, A. J., 208, 213
Huerta, P. T., 474, 476
Huestis, M. A., 591
Hughes, J., 126
Hughes, J. R., 588
Hull, E. M., 333
Hulshoff-Pol, H. E., 523

Humm, J. L., 332
Hummel, F., 496
Humphrey, A. L., 182
Humphreys, G. W., 363
Hungs, M., 289
Hunt, M., 174, 385, 538
Huntley, G. W., 78
Hurwitz, T. D., 283
Huszar, D., 399
Huttunen, M. O., 524–525
Hwa, J. J., 399
Hyldebrandt, N., 564
Hyman, S. E., 575, 578, 583,
   586–587

Iacoboni, M., 497
Ibuka, N., 301
Ichikawa, Y., 507
Iggo, A., 223
Ihnat, R., 338
Iijima, M., 326
Ikonomidou, C., 588
Imaki, T., 569
Imperato, A., 590
Inase, M., 442
Ingelfinger, F. J., 388
Innala, S. M., 330
Inoue, M., 287
Insel, T. R., 340
Inui, T., 486
Ioali, P., 471
Irwin, I., 101
Isenberg, N., 348
Itoh, K., 182
Iwai, E., 188
Iwata, M., 507, 510
Izard, C. E., 361

Jürgens, U., 486
Jackson, J. M., 530, 547
Jacob, S., 322
Jacobs, B., 487
Jacobs, B. L., 291, 344
Jacobs, G. H., 174
Jacobs, L. F., 471
Jacobsen, C. F., 547
Jacobsohn, D., 314
Jahr, C. E., 230
Jakobson, L. S., 199, 444
James, W., 369
James, W. P. T., 402
Jamison, K. R., 534
Janah, A., 595
Jang, T., 321
Jaramillo, F., 208
Jarvis, M. J., 586, 598
Jasper, J. H., 295
Javitt, D. C., 529
Jay, T. M., 448–449
Jaynes, J., 10
Jeffery, K. J., 472
Jeffress, L. A., 215
Jellestad, F. K., 345
Jensen, M. D., 401–402
Jensen, M. L., 461
Jensen, T., 564

Jentsch, J. D., 529–530
Jervey, J. P., 433
Jeste, D. V., 517
Jewett, D. C., 396
Jhamandas, J. H., 566
Jiang, C. L., 385
Jodo, E., 296
Johanson, A., 549
Johansson, G., 196
Johnson, A. K., 380
Johnson, B. A., 599
Johnson, L., 284
Johnson, M. K., 455, 467
Johnson, S. W., 582
Johnston, D., 421
Johnston, R., 361
Jonas, P., 126
Jones, G., 240, 289, 295–297, 361, 556
Jope, R. S., 536
Joppa, M., 358
Jordan, C. L., 331
Jornales, V. E., 196
Jouvet, M., 292, 296–298
Julesz, B., 181
Juraska, J. M., 331
Justice, J. B., 584

Kaas, J. H., 183, 211
Kahler, A., 391
Kaitin, K. I., 277
Kakei, S., 443
Kales, A., 280, 282, 284
Kalin, N. H., 561
Kalivas, P. W., 577
Kalra, P. S., 395–396
Kalra, S. P., 395–396
Kanamori, N., 298
Kanner, L., 555
Kanwisher, N., 191, 432
Kaplan, E., 499
Kaplan, J., 566
Kaplan, J. M., 393
Kaplan, R., 183
Kaplan, S. B., 569
Kapp, B. S., 344, 347, 437
Kaptchuk, T. J., 231
Kapur, N., 466
Karacan, I., 278, 288
Karlson, P., 320
Kartsounis, L. D., 461
Kasper, S., 543–544
Katayama, Y., 297
Kattler, H., 286
Katz, D., 357
Katz, L. C., 242
Kavaliers, M., 231
Kavoussi, R. J., 351
Kawamura, H., 301
Kawamura, M., 510
Kawauchi, H., 395
Kay, J. A., 508
Kayama, Y., 296
Kaye, W. H., 406–407
Kehoe, P., 579
Keil, L. C., 379–380

Keiner, M., 340
Keller, S. E., 569
Kelley, A. E., 445, 448
Kelso, S. R., 418
Kelsoe, J. R., 533
Kendell, R. E., 524
Kendler, K. S., 406, 549–550
Kennard, C., 188
Kentros, C., 475
Kertesz, A., 259–260, 487
Kestler, L. P., 520
Kety, S. S., 518
Keverne, E. B., 321, 338
Kew, J. J. M., 79
Khanna, S., 550
Khateb, A., 292
Kiang, N. Y.-S., 213
Kiecolt-Glaser, J. K., 562, 568
Kim, J. J., 436, 563
Kim, J. K., 455
Kim, J. W., 340
King, G. A., 405
Kingston, K., 406
Kinnamon, S. C., 234–235
Kinney, D. K., 540
Kinon, B. J., 520
Kinsey, A. C., 326
Kinsley, C., 355
Kinsley, C. H., 332, 357
Kirkpatrick, B., 340
Kitada, T., 267
Kitai, S. T., 266
Kitchener, E. G., 465
Klein, E., 535
Klein, P. S., 536
Kleitman, N., 278
Klima, E. S., 498
Kloner, R. A., 566
Klukowski, G., 476
Knapp, P. H., 569
Knebelmann, B., 313
Knecht, S., 482
Knowlton, B. J., 441
Knutson, B., 445
Kobatake, E., 190
Kodali, S. K., 289
Kodama, T., 297
Koenen, K. C., 565
Kogan, J. H., 583
Kojima, M., 397
Komatsu, H., 183, 187
Komisaruk, B. R., 232, 340
Konen, C., 357
Konen, C. M., 357
Konishi, M., 216
Koob, G. F., 561, 577, 583, 585–586, 589
Koopman, P., 310
Kopelman, M. D., 463
Kornhuber, H. H., 270
Kortegaard, L. S., 406
Koshland, D. E., 128, 426
Kosten, T. A., 579
Kotlyarov, E. V., 529
Kourtzi, A., 432
Kovacs, G., 189

Koylu, E. O., 398
Kozlowski, L. T., 196
Kramer, F. M., 404
Kramer, L., 500
Kramer, M. S., 538
Krantz, D. S., 567
Kranzler, H. R., 599
Krause, K. H., 559
Kraut, R. E., 361
Kress, M., 226
Kriete, M., 554
Kristal, M. B., 338
Kristensen, P., 397–398
Kroger, J., 434
Krubitzer, L., 79
Kruger, J., 595
Krukoff, T. L., 566
Krystal, A. D., 535
Kudoh, M., 217
Kuffler, S. W., 172
Kulkosky, P. J., 389
Kumar, K., 230
Kumar, M. V., 392, 399
Kunos, G., 127, 592
Kunugi, H., 525
Kupfer, D. J., 541
Kurata, K., 443
Kurihara, K., 236
Kuriki, S., 486
Kutlesic, V., 407
Kuypers, G. J. M., 258–259

Lüscher, C., 428
LaBar, K. S., 347
Lafrance, L., 390
Lahti, A. C., 529
Laing, P., 525
Laitinen, L. V., 266
Lamb, T., 358
Lambert, K. G., 332
Lane, D. M., 395
Lane, J. D., 582
Lane, M. D., 399
Lange, C. G., 369
Langston, J. W., 101, 119–120, 267
Lapp, L., 287
Larsson, K., 232, 332
Laruelle, M., 520
Laschet, U., 357
Lasek, R. J., 37
Lavasani, M., 267
Lavoie, B., 554
Lavond, D. G., 436
Lawrence, D. G., 258–259
Leblanc, R., 484
Leckman, J. F., 550
Leconte, P., 287
LeDoux, J. E., 5, 7, 345–346, 428, 438
Lee, C., 232, 471
Lehman, C. D., 569
Lehman, M. N., 302, 306, 321
Leibenluft, E., 543
Leibowitz, S. F., 399

Leiguarda, R., 229
Lejeune, F., 538
Lenox, R. H., 536
Leon, M., 321, 339
Leonard, C. M., 344, 430
Leonard, C. S., 298
Leonard, H. L., 551, 553–554
Leor, J., 566
LeSauter, J., 303
Lesch, K. P., 351
Leshner, A. I., 598
Leslie, A. M., 556
Lesser, R., 511
Lester, L. S., 231
Letson, R. D., 79
LeVay, S., 328
Levenson, R. W., 370
Levine, J. A., 401–402
Levine, J. D., 232
Levitt, P., 528
Levy, U., 441, 558
Lewin, R., 101
Lewine, R. R. J., 526
Lewis, D. A., 528, 562
Lewis, E. B., 80
Lewis, O. F., 286
Lewis, V. G., 326
Lewy, A. J., 543
Ley, R. G., 362
Leyton, M., 537
Li, B.-H., 400
Li, C., 397
Li, J. Y., 398
Li, S.-H., 268
Li, T.-. K., 596
Li, X.-J., 268
Li, X.-W., 596
Liang, K. C., 475
Liao, D., 422
Licinio, J., 402
Lidberg, L., 351
Lieberman, J. A., 520
Liebeskind, J. C., 230
Liljequist, S., 591
Lin, J. S., 292
Lin, L., 282
Lin, S. P., 525
Lindemann, B., 234, 236
Lindquist, C., 553
Links, J. M., 539
Linnoila, M., 537, 596
Liotti, M., 539
Lisk, R. D., 338
Lisman, J. E., 424, 476
Liuzzi, F. J., 37
Livesque, J., 354
Livingstone, M. S., 182–183, 512
Lj, S., 196
Lledo, P. M., 423
Llorca, P. M., 522
Lockhead, E., 234
Lockley, S. W., 306
Loeb, G. E., 212
Loewenstein, W. R., 224
Loftus, T. M., 392

Logan, F. A., 575
Logothetis, N. K., 190
Lohr, J. B., 522
Lohse, P., 237
Lombardi, J. R., 320
Longnecker, D. E., 531
Lopez, A. D., 586
Lopez, M., 398
Loscher, W., 590
Lowe, V., 557
Lu, E., 398
Lu, J., 293, 302–303, 396
Lu, X-C. M., 242
Lubin, M., 339
Lucas, B. K., 339
Lumeng, L., 596
Lupien, S., 563
Luppino, G., 443
Luquin, M. R., 265
Luscher, B., 320
Lutz, T. A., 386
Luzzatti, C., 7
Luzzi, S., 464
Lømo, T., 415, 417
Lydic, R., 295, 298
Lydon, J. P., 318
Lynch, G., 420, 428
Lytton, W. W., 508

Ma, W., 320
MacCagnan, T. J., 403
Machon, R. A., 524
MacKinnon, D. F., 534
Mackintosh, J. H., 356
Macko, K., 188
MacLean, H. E., 312
MacLean, P. D., 86
MacTavish, D., 566
Madden, P. A. F., 543
Madison, D. V., 426
Madsen, P. L., 279
Maes, F. W., 234
Magee, J. C., 421
Magert, H. J., 322
Maggio, J. E., 538
Magistretti, P. J., 35
Maguire, P., 454, 464, 471
Mahowald, M. W., 283
Maier, S. F., 231
Maiese, K., 426
Maksay, G., 591
Malach, R., 195
Malamut, B. L., 464
Malaspina, D., 518
Maldonado, R., 583, 592
Malenka, R. C., 126, 575, 578, 587
Malhotra, A. K., 530
Malinow, R., 422
Malizia, A. L., 549
Mallow, G. K., 356
Malnic, B., 241
Malpeli, J. G., 173
Malsbury, C. W., 332, 445
Mandler, G., 457
Mangels, J. A., 441

Manji, H. K., 536
Mann, J. J., 354, 539
Mann, M. A., 357
Mannen, T., 507
Manning, L., 496
Manning-Bog, A. B., 267
Mansvelder, H. D., 588
Mantyh, P. W., 231, 538
Mantzoros, C., 407
Manuck, S. B., 566
Maquet, P., 284, 295
Marcel, A. J., 495, 508
Marcotte, D., 536
Maren, S., 437
Maret, G., 119
Margolin, D. I., 494–495, 508–509
Margolskee, R. F., 236
Marin, O. S. M., 484–485, 488
Mark, N., 595
Marrocco, R. T., 289
Marshall, B. E., 531
Marshall, J. C., 506
Marson, L., 334, 336
Martin, C., 183, 496
Martin-Santos, R., 549
Maruyama, N., 217
Maruyama, S., 510
Mas, M., 318, 332
Masi, A. T., 569
Masino, S. A., 294
Masland, R. H., 168
Matheny, M., 403
Mather, P., 388
Matsuda, L. A., 127
Matsunami, H., 235
Matteo, S., 324
Matthes, H. W. D., 581
Matthews, D. B., 590
Matuzawa, R., 187
Maunsell, J. H. R., 173, 186
Mawson, A. R., 406
Mayer, A. D., 340
Mayer, D. J., 230–231
Mazur, A., 357–358
McArthur, A. J., 306
McBrair, M. C., 327
McBride, W. J., 596
McCann, U. D., 584
McCarley, R. W., 279, 282, 294, 298
McCarthy, G., 496
McCarthy, R. A., 465, 492, 506
McCaul, K. D., 358
McCleod, P., 196
McClintock, M. K., 318, 322
McCormick, D. A., 289
McCoy, N. L., 322
McDermott, J., 191
McDonald, R. J., 440
McEwen, B. S., 562
McFarland, K., 577
McFarlane, A. C., 565
McGehee, D. S., 588

McGinty, D. J., 271, 293, 344
McGrath, J., 524–525
McGregor, A., 585
McHugh, T. J., 474
McIver, B., 381
McKay, R. D. G., 80
McKenna, K. E., 334
McKenna, T. M., 217
McKinzie, A. A., 398
McLaughlin, S. K., 236
McMackin, D., 464
McMahon, K., 590
McNaughton, B. L., 473–474
Mechoulam, R., 127
Mednick, S. A., 524–525
Meesters, Y., 543
Mehlman, P. T., 349–350
Meijer, J. H., 301–302
Melges, F. T., 279
Mellet, E., 198
Melngailis, I., 511
Melzak, R., 230
Menco, B. P. M., 240
Mendelson, M., 224
Mercer, J. G., 398
Meredith, M., 320
Mereu, G., 587
Mesches, M. H., 563
Mesulam, M.-M., 448, 500
Metcalf, D., 295
Meyer, T., 423
Meyer, W. J., 357
Meyer-Bahlburg, H. F. L., 326–327
Miao, Z., 320
Miczek, K. A., 358, 579
Miele, L., 357
Miezin, F. M., 193
Mignot, E., 281, 289
Millan, M. J., 538
Miller, L., 21, 434–435, 474
Milner, A. D., 199
Milner, B., 452–453, 455
Minai, A., 473
Minard, A., 286
Mindus, P., 553
Mirenowicz, J., 446
Miselis, R. R., 142, 335
Miserendino, M. J. D., 438, 579
Mishkin, M., 186, 188, 198–199, 430
Mitchell, D. G., 353
Mitchell, J. E., 407
Mitchison, G., 287
Mitler, M. M., 282
Mitsuno, K., 474
Miyauchi, S., 279
Modesto-Lowe, V., 599
Moghaddam, B., 445, 530, 583
Mohr, J. P., 455, 477
Moldin, S. O., 533
Mollon, J. D., 174
Moltz, H., 339
Mombaerts, P., 240

Monaghan, D. T., 428
Mondragon, M., 323
Money, J., 309, 312, 325–326, 328
Montague, C. T., 402
Montero, S., 561
Montmayeur, J.-P., 235
Moore, R. M., 283, 295, 301–302, 305, 331, 536
Moore-Gillon, M. J., 380
Mora, F., 447
Morales, F. R., 297
Moran, T. H., 389
Mordan, D., 579
Mori, T., 486
Mori, E., 347
Morin, L. P., 305
Morley, J. E., 396
Morris, J. S., 363–364
Morris, N. M., 324
Morris, R., 357
Morris, R. G. M., 426, 469–470
Morse, J. R., 237–238
Morshed, S. A., 552
Mortensen, P. B., 524
Morton, J., 556
Moscovitch, M., 191, 367, 432
Mossner, R., 351
Motta, V., 581
Mountcastle, V. B., 227, 261
Mountjoy, K. G., 398
Mrosovsky, N., 302
Mucha, R. F., 581
Mukhametov, L. M., 284, 288
Muller, D., 425
Muller, M. J., 533
Muller, R. U., 438
Munitz, H., 192
Munro, J. F., 404
Murakami, N., 397
Murison, R., 345
Murphy, A. Z., 334
Murphy, J. M., 596
Murray, A. M., 520–521
Murray, C. J., 586
Murray, R. M., 525, 528
Murray, S., 358
Murre, J. M. J., 466
Museo, G., 587
Mushiake, H., 442
Must, A., 400
Muzio, J. N., 286–287
Myers, R. D., 396, 596

Nadeau, S. E., 484
Nader, K., 437
Naeser, M. A., 484
Nafe, J. P., 225
Nagatani, S., 314
Nakahara, D., 445
Nakamura, J., 227
Nakamura, Y., 240
Nakazato, M., 397
Nambu, T., 396
Nanko, S., 525

Naranjo, C. A., 598
Narayan, S. S., 212
Nath, R., 230
Nathan, R. S., 550
Nathans, J., 175
Nauta, W. J. H., 237, 292
Navarro, M., 592
Neale, J. M., 550, 569
Neale, M. C., 549–550
Nef, P., 240
Nelson, J., 505
Nemeroff, C. B., 538
Nestler, E. J., 583
Neumann, C., 526
Neumeister, A., 543
New, A. S., 355
Newcombe, F., 192, 506
Newman, S. W., 332–333
Ngai, J., 240
Nichelli, P., 493
Nicholl, C. S., 21
Nicholls, P., 403
Nicolaodis, S., 388, 399
Nicolas, A., 277
Nicoll, R. A., 126, 230
Nielsen, M. K., 401
Nilsson, O. G., 476
Nisell, M., 587
Nishino, S., 282
Niskanen, P., 525
Nobrega, J. N., 522
Noirot, E., 338
Nomikos, G. G., 587
Nonogaki, K., 399
Norgren, R., 237–238, 393
North, R. A., 582
Novin, D., 386–387
Novotny, M. V., 320
Nowlis, G. H., 237
Numan, M., 339–340
Numan, M. J., 340
Nunn, J. A., 465
Nuñez, A. A., 301
Nutt, D. J., 549
Nuwayser, E. S., 599
Nyby, J. G., 333

Oaknin, S., 318, 332
Oakson, G., 297
Obeso, J. A., 266
Obler, L. K., 483
O'Brien, C. P., 599
O'Callaghan, E., 528
O'Carroll, R., 358
O'Connell, R. J., 320–321
O'Connor, M., 467
O'Dell, T. J., 426
Ogawa, S., 334
Ohta, M., 296
O'Keefe, J. M., 344, 471–472
Olausson, H., 224–225
Olds, J., 367, 411
Olds, M. E., 444–445
Oleksenko, A. I., 288
Oleshansky, M., 535
Oliveri, M., 433

Olmstead, M. C., 582
Olney, J. W., 462
Olson, C. X., 187
Olster, D. H., 319
Olton, D. S., 461, 469, 476
O'Mara, S. M., 474
O'Rahilly, S., 403
Orban, G. A., 189
Orlovsky, G. N., 271
Orsini, J. C., 387
Ó Scalaidhe, S. P. O., 434
Ossebaard, C. A., 234
Ostrowsky, K., 229
Otsuki, M., 509
Otto, T., 457
Owen, A. M., 441
Owens, S., 538
Oyler, G. A., 267
Ozata, M., 402
Ozdemir, I. C., 402

Packard, M. G., 440–441
Pallast, E. G. M., 524
Papadimitriou, G. N., 543
Papas, B. C., 469
Papez, J. W., 86
Pardridge, W. M., 403
Parent, A., 554
Paré, D., 297, 437
Park, W.-K., 577
Parkinson, J. A., 447
Parr, L., 362
Partiot, A., 441
Pascoe, J. P., 344
Passingham, R. E., 434
Pattatucci, A. M. L., 330
Patterson, K., 504, 506, 508
Paul, C. A., 476
Paulesu, E., 494, 512
Pauls, D. L., 550
Pauls, J., 190
Pavlides, C., 476
Pearlman, C. A., 287
Peck, B. K., 291
Pedersen, D., 524
Pedersen-Bjergaard, U., 390
Pelleymounter, M. A., 391
Penfield, W., 255, 431
Penha, K., 581
Pennington, B. F., 511
Perkel, D. J., 266
Perlmutter, S. J., 552
Perot, P., 431
Perrett, D. I., 364
Perrin, J., 387
Perry, P., 358
Pert, C. B., 126
Pes, D., 322
Peterhans, E., 181
Petersen, S. E., 193, 496, 503, 507
Peterson, B. S., 552
Peterson, M. R., 524
Petit, H. O., 584
Petre-Quadens, O., 287

Petrovitch, H., 267
Petryshen, T. L., 511
Pettito, L. A., 498
Peuskens, H., 196
Peyron, C., 282
Pfaff, D. W., 333–335, 340
Pfaus, J. G., 334
Phelps, E. A., 363, 368
Phelps, J. A., 527
Phiel, C. J., 536
Philipp, M., 533
Phillips, A. G., 447
Phillips, D. P., 489
Phillips, M. I., 380
Phillips, M. L., 365
Phillips, P. E., 591
Phillips, R. G., 445
Phillipson, O. R., 296
Piccirillo, J. F., 280
Pickar, D., 520
Pickles, J. O., 208
Pierce, K., 556
Pijl, S., 213
Pilla, M., 597
Pillard, R. C., 330
Pilleri, G., 284
Piomelli, D., 593
Pirke, K. M., 406
Pitino, L., 322
Pitkänen, A., 344
Piven, J., 556
Plagemann, A., 402
Plata-Salaman, C. R., 236, 238
Pleim, E. T., 334
Plenz, D., 266
Poggio, G. F., 79, 182
Poggio, T., 79, 182, 190
Poizner, H., 264
Polet, I. A., 234
Pollack, S. J., 536
Pomp, D., 401
Poncet, M., 199
Poole, J., 340
Poole, W. K., 566
Porkka-Heiskanen, T., 294
Portas, C. M., 298
Porter, R. W., 286
Posley, K. A., 434
Post, R. M., 536
Powell, T. E., 356
Powers, J. B., 321
Pretlow, R. A., 338
Preuss, T. M., 211
Price, C., 505, 507
Price, D. B., 229
Price, J. L., 237, 533, 540
Price, L. H., 535
Price, R. A., 402
Pritchard, T. C., 237
Proctor, W. R., 591
Propping, P., 595
Provencio, I., 301
Proverbio, A. M., 493
Pulvermüller, F., 492, 496
Purpura, K. P., 183

Qu, D., 395
Quadfasel, F. A., 490
Quattrochi, J. J., 297
Quillen, E. W., 380
Quintana, J., 435
Quirk, G. J., 437–438, 473

Raine, A., 353–354
Rainer, G., 435
Rainville, P., 229
Rakic, P., 77, 81
Raleigh, M. J., 350
Ralph, M. R., 306, 504, 506
Ramirez, I., 233
Ranson, S. W., 394
Rao, S. C., 435
Rapin, I., 555, 557
Rapoport, J. L., 550, 554
Rasmussen, S. A., 553
Rasmussen, T., 255
Rasmusson, D. D., 289
Ratcliff, G., 192
Ratnasuriya, R. H., 406
Rauschecker, J. P., 211, 217–218
Ravussin, E., 402
Raye, C. L., 467
Read, N. W., 388–389
Reba, R. C., 529
Reber, P. J., 455
Recer, P., 513
Rechtschaffen, A., 285
Reebs, S., 302
Reed, B. R., 569
Reed, C. L., 227
Reed, J. M., 465
Reed, R. R., 240
Reese, T. S., 55
Regan, B. C., 174
Rehkämper, G., 471
Reich, T., 533
Reid, I. A., 380
Reid, L. D., 590–591
Reid, M. S., 588
Remington, G., 522
Rempel-Clower, N. L., 461, 465
Repa, J. C., 437
Reppert, S. M., 305
Resnick, H. S., 565
Ressler, K. J., 240
Reynolds, D. V., 230
Rezek, M., 386
Rhees, R. W., 332
Rice, J. P., 533
Richter, R. M., 583
Riddoch, M. J., 363
Ridley, R. M., 476
Riedel, G., 471
Riemann, D., 542–543
Rietveld, W. J., 301
Riley, M. T., 301
Risse, G., 455
Rissman, E. F., 318, 324
Ritter, R. C., 387, 389
Ritter, S., 386–387, 394

Rizzo, M., 198
Rizzolatti, G., 195, 197, 199, 497
Robbins, L. N., 550
Robbins, T. W., 592
Roberts, D. C. S., 585
Robertson, G. S., 332
Robertson, H. A., 302
Robertson, R. G., 474
Robin, D. A., 198
Robinson, D., 268, 551
Robinson, D. E., 596
Robinson, T. E., 577–578
Rockland, K. S., 184
Rodieck, R. W., 169, 176
Rodier, P. M., 557
Rodman, H. R., 194
Rodrigues, S. M., 438
Rodriguez de Fonseca, F., 583, 592
Roeltgen, D. P., 511
Roffwarg, H. P., 279, 286–287, 541
Rogan, M. T., 438
Rogers, M. P., 569
Rogers, R. D., 353, 592
Roland, P. E., 286
Rolls, E. T., 189, 237–238, 344, 447–448, 474
Romanski, L. M., 218
Romer, J., 397
Romero, P. R., 322
Rosa, R. R., 280
Rose, J. D., 334
Rose, J. E., 587
Rose, R. M., 562
Rosen, G. D., 482
Rosenblatt, J. S., 340
Rosenkranz, J. A., 449
Rosen-Sheidley, B., 557
Rosenthal, D., 533
Rosenthal, N. E., 543
Rosin, I., 256
Ross, D. C., 543
Ross, E. D., 367
Ross, W. N., 475
Rosser, A. E., 321
Rossetti, A. L., 586
Rosvold, H. E., 440
Roth, M., 255
Roth, R. H., 529
Roth, T., 280
Rothi, L. H., 259–260, 511
Rothman, S. M., 462
Routtenberg, A., 406, 445
Rowland, N. E., 400
Roy, A., 537
Rozanski, A., 566
Rubin, B. D., 242
Rubin, B. S., 334
Rubin, D. C., 38
Rudge, P., 461
Ruggero, M. A., 212
Rusak, B., 302, 305
Rush, A. J., 541
Russchen, F. T., 237

Russell, G. F. M., 406
Russell, M. J., 322–323
Russell, R. M., 21
Rutter, M., 556
Rutter, M. L., 557
Ryba, N. J., 320
Ryback, R. S., 286
Ryland, D. H., 554

Saayman, G. S., 356
Sachar, E. J., 537
Sachdev, P., 553
Sack, D. A., 543
Sackeim, H. A., 367, 536
Sadato, N., 79
Saffran, E. M., 484–485, 488
Sagvolden, T., 558–559
Sahu, A., 396
Saito, M., 396
Saitoh, K., 217
Sakai, F., 284
Sakai, K., 292, 296–298
Sakuma, Y., 334–335
Sakurai, T., 395
Sakurai, Y., 507
Salamone, J. D., 446, 576
Salis, P. J., 278
Saller, C. F., 399
Samson, H. H., 590
Samuels, O., 357
Samuelson, R. J., 461
Sananes, C. B., 347
Sandell, J. H., 173
Sanders, S. K., 347
Sandkühler, J., 126
Sandler, V. M., 475
Sanna, P. P., 586
Santini, E., 438
Saper, C. B., 292–293, 398
Sapolsky, R. M., 562, 568
Sarvey, J. M., 476
Sassenrath, E. N., 356
Sasson, A. D., 471
Saudou, F., 350
Savic, I., 322
Savoie, T., 526
Sawaguchi, T., 529
Sawchenko, P. E., 396
Saxena, S., 552–553
Scammell, T. E., 282, 292, 294
Scarpace, P. J., 403
Schacter, D. L., 467
Schafe, G. E., 437–438
Schall, M., 487
Scharrer, E., 386
Scheibel, A. B., 487
Schein, S. J., 187
Schenck, C. H., 282–283
Schenkel, E., 298
Scherschlicht, R., 541
Schiffman, J., 526
Schiffman, S. S., 234
Schiller, P. H., 173
Schleifer, S. J., 568
Schleusner, S. J., 402

Schlosberg, H., 361
Schmidt, M. H., 297
Schmitt, U., 213
Schneider, B., 533
Schneider, F., 348
Scholes, R., 362
Schotland, H., 280
Schrauwen, P., 404
Schultz, R. T., 192
Schultz, W., 446
Schuman, E. M., 427
Schuman, E. R., 426
Schurmeyer, T., 325
Schuster, C. R., 590
Schwartz, D. W. F., 213
Schwartz, M., 326
Schwartz, M. F., 484–485, 508
Schwartz, M. W., 398, 403
Schwartz, W. J., 304
Schwarzkopf, S. B., 528
Schweiger, U., 406
Scott, S. K., 488
Scott, T. M., 238
Scott, T. R., 236, 238
Scoville, W. B., 453
Seagraves, M. A., 194
Sedvall, G., 537
See, R. E., 577
Segarra, J. M., 490
Seidman, L. J., 558
Sejnowski, T. J., 428
Sekuler, E. B., 505
Selye, H., 562
Semba, K., 298
Semenza, C., 493, 496, 502
Sergeant, J. A., 558
Sergent, J., 193
Service, R. F., 583
Sesack, S. R., 530
Sewell, K. W., 524
Sforza, E., 285
Shaham, Y., 577
Shair, H. N., 338
Shalev, U., 577
Shallice, T., 507, 510
Sham, P. C., 524
Shammi, P., 366
Shapiro, C., 358
Shapiro, L. E., 340
Shapiro, M. L., 476
Sharp, F. R., 569
Sharpe, L. T., 175
Shastry, B. S., 518
Shavit, Y., 569
Shaywitz, B. A., 512
Sheard, N., 338
Shearman, L. P., 305
Shekhar, A., 347
Shelton, K. L., 590
Shen, K., 423
Shenton, M. E., 529
Shepherd, G. M., 240
Sher, A. E., 280
Sher, L., 543
Sherin, J. E., 293
Sherman, G. F., 482

Sherman, J. E., 561
Sherry, D. F., 471
Shi, S.-H., 422
Shields, J., 518
Shifren, J. L., 325
Shik, M. L., 271
Shima, K., 442
Shimada, M., 396
Shimamura, A. P., 457
Shimazu, T., 396
Shimokawa, T., 399
Shimokochi, M., 332
Shimura, T., 332
Shindy, W. W., 434
Shinohara, K., 322
Shipley, M. T., 240
Shipp, S., 185
Shirayama, Y., 538
Shors, T. J., 567
Shoulson, I., 120
Shouse, M. N., 297
Shryne, J. E., 332
Shuto, Y., 397
Siciliano, D., 589
Sidman, M., 455, 477
Siegel, A., 349
Siegel, J. M., 271, 297–298
Siegel, R. M., 193
Sienkiewicz, Z. J., 237
Siever, L. J., 537
Sigmundson, H. K., 309
Signoret, J.-L., 193
Sigvardsson, S., 594
Silva, M., 423, 475
Silver, R., 303
Silveri, M. C., 509
Simon, N. G., 357
Simos, P. G., 498
Simpson, J. B., 380
Simson, P. E., 590
Simuni, T., 266
Sinclair, A. H., 310
Singer, A. G., 321
Singer, C., 278
Singer, F., 561
Singer, L. K., 387
Singh, N. A., 544
Sipos, M. L., 333
Sirigu, A., 199
Sitaram, N., 295
Skaggs, W. E., 473
Skakkebaek, N. E., 358
Skene, D. J., 306
Skinner, J. E., 321
Skutella, T., 561
Slotkin, T. A., 586
Slotnick, B. M., 242
Slusser, P. G., 387
Smiley, D. L., 397
Smith, A. P., 570
Smith, C., 287
Smith, D. V., 234
Smith, G. P., 389
Smith, H. G., 340
Smith, J. E., 582
Smith, K. A., 538

Smith, M. J., 310
Smith, M. S., 397
Smith, R. E., 562
Smith, R. F., 589
Smith-Roe, S. L., 448
Smith-Swintosky, V. L., 238
Smulders, T. V., 471
Snowman, A. M., 126
Snyder, S. H., 126, 519
Soares, J. C., 534–535, 539
Sokol, R. J., 588
Solowij, N., 592
Solyom, L., 553
Soma, Y., 510
Sørensen, T. I. A., 402
Spector, A. C., 400
Speelman, J. D., 266
Spence, M. A., 533
Spencer, T. J., 558
Sperry, R. W., 5–6
Spiegler, B. J., 447
Spiers, H. J., 454, 465
Spitzer, M., 493
Spray, D. C., 226
Sprengelmeyer, R., 365
Squire, L. R., 441, 455, 457, 460, 465, 535
Squires, R. F., 528
Staddon, J. M., 38
Stallone, D., 399
Standing, L., 430
Stanley, B. G., 395–396
Stanton, P. K., 428
Starkey, S. J., 306
Starkstein, S., 229
Stebbins, W. C., 212
Stehm, K. E., 329
Stein, M. A., 448, 512, 564
Steiner, H., 586
Steininger, R. L., 292
Steinman, J. L., 232
Steinmetz, M. A., 433
Stellar, E., 394
Stellar, J. R., 445
Stephan, F. K., 301
Steriade, M., 277, 289, 296–297
Sterman, M. B., 293
Stern, K., 322
Sternbach, R. A., 229
Stevens, D. R., 292
Stevens, J. M., 461
Stevens, J. R., 522, 524
Steward, O., 427
Stewart, C., 470
Stewart, J., 579
Stewart, M., 476
Stewart, R. B., 596
Stinson, D., 543
Stoddard, L. T., 455, 477
Stoerig, P., 184
Stolerman, I. P., 586, 598
Stone, A. A., 569
Stone, S., 387
Stout, S. C., 538
Stowers, L., 356

Stoyva, J., 295
Strakowski, S. M., 539
Strecker, R. E., 294
Strick, P. L., 443
Stricker, E. M., 395, 399
Strobel, A., 402
Stroka, H., 192
Stromswold, K., 486
Strvmland, K., 557
Stunkard, A. J., 402
Sturgis, J. D., 340
Sturup, G. K., 357
Stuss, D. T., 366
Styron, W., 533
Su, T.-. P., 358
Suddath, R. L., 526
Suh, J. S., 399
Sullivan, R. L., 240, 463
Suomi, S. J., 596
Suppes, T., 536
Susser, E. S., 525
Suzdak, P. D., 591
Suzuki, T., 581
Svarc, B., 355, 357
Svennilson, E., 266
Svensson, T. H., 587
Swaab, D. F., 328
Swanson, L. W., 587
Swanson, R. A., 288
Sweet, W. H., 370
Swerdloff, A. F., 395
Swerdlow, N. R., 551, 561
Swift, R., 591, 598
Switz, G. M., 322
Szatmari, P., 556
Szcwarcbart, M. K., 440
Szente, M. B., 428
Szerb, J. C., 289
Szuba, M. P., 535, 543
Szymusiak, R., 293

Tümer, N., 403
Tabakoff, B., 590
Taepavarapruk, P., 447
Takahashi, L. K., 318, 561
Takahashi, N., 489
Takahashi, Y., 297
Takao, M., 302
Takei, N., 524
Takino, R., 279
Takita, M., 449
Tam, W.-. C. C., 524
Tamminga, C. A., 519
Tamori, Y., 190
Tan, S. E., 475
Tanaka, K., 189–190
Tang, Y.-P., 438, 475
Tanifuji, M., 190
Tanji, J., 442
Tanne, J., 444
Tanner, C. M., 120
Tarazi, F. I., 522
Tarsy, D., 522
Tassin, J. P., 448
Taylor, B., 557
Taylor, J. R., 529

Taylor, J. S., 386, 394
Taylor, S. F., 529
Teather, L. A., 441
Tei, H., 510
Teicher, M. H., 559
Teitelbaum, P., 394
Tejwani, G. A., 599
Terenius, L., 126
Terman, J. S., 543
Terman, T., 543
Tessier, J., 295
Tetel, M. J., 334
Tetrud, J. W., 101, 120
Teuber, H.-L., 453
Teyler, T. J., 428
Thach, W. T., 271
Thaker, G. K., 517
Thakkar, M. M., 294
Theorell, T., 562
Thiels, E., 428
Thier, P., 197
Thompson, C., 543
Thompson, D. L., 528
Thompson, K., 322
Thompson, R. F., 436, 473
Thompson, S. M., 428
Thorell, L. G., 180
Thrasher, T. N., 379, 381
Tian, B., 211, 217–218
Ticku, M. K., 591
Tiedge, H., 427
Timmann, D., 270
Tirindelli, R., 320
Todd, D. A., 318
Toh, K. L., 305
Toledo-Aral, J. J., 265
Tonegawa, S., 474
Toni, N., 425
Tootell, R. B. H., 183
Topper, R., 365
Tordoff, M. G., 387, 390
Torrey, B. B., 524
Torrey, E. F., 524
Touhouda, Y., 540
Tramo, M. J., 211
Tranel, D., 363, 496
Trayhurn, P., 402
Trdskmann, L., 537
Treasure, J., 406
True, W. R., 594
Trulson, M. E., 291
Trussell, L. O., 217
Tsacopoulos, M., 35
Tsai, G., 531
Tschöp, M., 397
Tsien, J. Z., 474
Tsuang, M. T., 518
Turek, F. W., 302
Turnbull, I. M., 553
Turner, S. M., 550
Turrone, P., 522
Tyrell, J. B., 561
Tyrrell, D. A. J., 570

Uchikawa, K., 187
Unger, J., 390

Ungerleider, L. G., 186, 188, 198–199
Ungless, M. A., 578
Uno, H., 563
Urban, P. P., 365
Uutela, K., 511

Vaina, L. M., 194, 196
Vaisse, C., 403
Valenstein, E. S., 411, 534, 547
Valenza, N., 228
Valverius, P., 591
Van Bockstaele, E. J., 561
Van de Poll, N., 356
Van den Hoofdakker, R. H., 542
van der Lee, S., 320
Van Essen, D. C., 185
Van Goozen, S., 324
Van Hoesen, G. W., 192
Van Opstal, A. J., 217
Van Tol, H. H. M., 520
van Wezel, R. J., 195
Vandenbergh, J. G., 320
VanderWeele, D. A., 386
Vanderwolf, C. H., 289, 291, 476
Vanree, J. M., 582
Vargha-Khadem, F., 462–463
Vassar, R., 240
Vega, E. M., 520
Veldman, B. A., 120
Vergnes, M., 349
Verney, E. B., 377
Vewers, M. E., 599
Vgontzas, A. N., 282
Victor, M., 461
Vikingstad, E. M., 482
Vindlacheruvu, R. R., 302
Virkkunen, M., 351
Voci, V. E., 339
Voderholzer, U., 543
Vogel, G. W., 541
Vogels, R., 189
Volkow, N. D., 578
Volkow, N. F., 578
Volpe, B. T., 7
Volpicelli, J. R., 599
Volpicelli, L. A., 599
vom Saal, F. S., 355–357
von Bikisy, G., 206
von der Heydt, R., 181
von Meduna, L., 534
Vorel, S. R., 578

Wada, H., 289
Wada, Y., 191
Wagner, J. A., 426
Wagoner, K. S., 225
Wagoner, N., 301
Wahlbeck, K., 525
Wahlestedt, C., 396
Wahlstrvm, A., 126
Walker, E., 520
Walker, E. F., 526

Walker, J. A., 494
Walker, P. A., 357
Wallen, K., 323–325
Walsh, B. T., 406
Walsh, V., 187, 195, 512
Walters, E. E., 406
Wang, G., 190
Wang, G.-J., 578
Wang, Q., 398
Warchol, M. E., 213
Ward, I. L., 329
Warne, G. L., 310, 312
Warrington, E. K., 492,
  506–507, 510
Wassink, T. H., 557
Watkins, K. E., 484
Watson, R. T., 362–363
Watts, S., 270
Weaver, D. R., 305
Webster, H. H., 296–297
Wehr, T. A., 286, 542–543
Weinberg, M. S., 326
Weinberger, D. R., 522,
  529–530
Weinberger, N. M., 217,
  428
Weiner, R. D., 535
Weiner, W. J., 278
Weintraub, S., 500
Weiskrantz, L., 184
Weiss, F., 583
Weiss, G. F., 399
Weiss, J. M., 567
Weiss, S. R. B., 536
Weissman, M. M., 548
Weitzman, E. D., 280
Welham, J., 524
Welsh, D. K., 304
Weltzin, T. E., 406
Wenner, C. E., 403
Wernicke, C., 484
Werz, M. A., 461

West, D. B., 389
Westerterp, K. R., 401
Westerterp-Plantenga, M. S.,
  401
Whalen, P. J., 363
Wheeler, M. E., 431
Whipple, B., 232
Whishaw, I. Q., 461
Whitam, F. L., 330
White, A. M., 473
White, F. J., 576
White, J., 347
White, N. M., 440
White, N. R., 338
Whitfield, I. C., 217
Whitsett, J. M., 320
Whitten, W. K., 320
Wickelgren, I., 599
Wickland, C., 302
Wiegand, M., 542
Wiener, S. I., 476
Wiesel, T. N., 178
Wiesner, B. P., 338
Wilckens, T., 406
Wilcox, G. L., 426
Wilens, T. E., 558
Wilensky, A. E., 437
Wilensky, M., 553
Wilkinson, L. O., 291
Willesen, M. G., 397
Williams, R. L., 278
Willoughby, A. R., 353
Wilska, A., 213
Wilson, J. E., 281, 390, 434
Winans, S. S., 321
Winn, P., 395
Winocur, G., 191
Winslow, J. T., 358
Winston, S., 294
Winter, P., 217
Wirz-Justice, A., 542–544
Wise, R., 496

Wise, R. A., 582, 584–585,
  587–588
Wise, R. J. S., 486
Wise, S. P., 199, 550
Wissinger, B., 175
Witte, E. A., 289
Wolf, M. E., 578
Wolfe, J. B., 547
Wolff, P. H., 511
Wong, G. T., 236
Wong-Riley, M. T., 182, 426
Wood, D. L., 566
Wood, E. R., 474
Wood, J. N., 226
Wood, R. I., 332–333
Woodruff-Pak, D. S., 455
Woods, B. T., 528
Woods, S. C., 389–390
Woodworth, R. S., 361
Woody, C. D., 428
Wooley, S. C., 404
Woolf, C. J., 229
Wright, B. A., 512
Wu, J. C., 529, 541–542
Wyant, G. M., 230
Wyatt, R. J., 522
Wysocki, C. J., 320

Xu, M., 586

Yadin, E., 347
Yamamoto, H., 510
Yamamoto, T., 191, 332
Yamashita, H., 541
Yamawaki, S., 540
Yang, T. T., 79
Yanovski, J. A., 400
Yanovski, S. Z., 400
Yates, W. R., 358
Yatham, L. N., 537
Yaxley, S., 237
Yehuda, R., 565

Yeni-Komshian, G. H., 488
Yeo, G. S. H., 403
Yeo, J. A. G., 338
Yettefti, K., 387
Yokoo, H., 561
Yokota, T., 510
Yoshioka, T., 183
Yost, W. A., 217
Young, A. W., 363
Young, R. C., 389
Young, S. N., 537
Youngren, K. D., 530
Yuste, R., 420

Zajac, J. D., 310, 312
Zayfert, C., 564
Zecker, S. G., 512
Zeffiro, T. A., 511
Zeilhofer, H. U., 226
Zeki, S., 185–186, 188
Zemlan, F. P., 399
Zenner, H.-P., 213
Zettin, M., 493, 496
Zhabotinsky, A. M., 424
Zhang, C. Y., 426
Zhou, F. C., 328, 596
Zhuang, X., 559
Zigmond, M. J., 395
Zihl, J., 195–196
Zimmermann, U., 213
Zola, S. M., 463
Zola-Morgan, S., 460–461
Zou, Z., 241
Zuch, J., 278
Zucker, I., 301
Zufall, F., 240
Zukin, S. R., 529
Zumoff, B., 561
Zumpe, D., 357
Zwiers, M. P., 217

Subject Index

Note: Page numbers in **bold** refer to pages with definitions. Page numbers followed by letters *f* and *t* indicate figures and tables, respectively.

A

Abducens nerve, 95*f*
Ablation. *See* Experimental ablation
Absorptive phase, of metabolism, 384*f*, **384**–385, 390
Abstract concepts, speech conveying, 493
Acamprosate, 599
Accessory olfactory bulb, 320*f*, **320**–322
Accommodation, of eyes, **166**
Acetylcholine (ACh), 56, **59**–60, 112–115, 126
  and arousal, 289–290
  biosynthesis of, 112–113, 113*f*
  components of, 112
  deactivation of, 114–115, 115*f*
  localization in brain, 156, 157*f*
  postsynaptic potential produced by, 59–60
  during REM sleep, measuring, 151
  secretion of, 98
  and sleep, 295–298
Acetylcholine receptors, 115
  nicotine and stimulation of, 587–588
Acetylcholinergic neurons, 112–113, 113*f*
  and arousal, 289–290
  drugs affecting, 109*f*, 113–115, 129*t*
  and hippocampal activity, 475–477
  in Huntington's disease, 267
  in peribrachial area, 295–296, 296*f*
  and REM sleep, 295–298, 296*f*, 297*f*
Acetylcholinesterase (AChE), 59–**60**, 111, 114–115, 115*f*, 588
Acetylcholinesterase inhibitors, 156
Acetyl-CoA, 112–**113**, 113*f*
ACh. *See* Acetylcholine
AChE. *See* Acetylcholinesterase
Achromatopsia, 187–**188**
Acquired dyslexia, 506–508
Acquired immunodeficiency syndrome (AIDS), 22
Acral lick dermatitis, 554
ACTH. *See* Adrenocorticotropic hormone
Actin, **247**
Actin filaments
  in auditory cilia, 208, 208*f*
  in muscle contraction, 247, 247*f*
  in muscle fiber, 246*f*

Action potential, 30, **42**, 43*f*, 45–47
  all-or-none law, **48**
  conduction of, 30, 47–49, 48*f*, 49*f*, 50*f*
  in dendrites, 420–421, 422*f*
  full-strength, 30
  membrane permeability during, 46–47, 47*f*
  movement of ions during, 45–47, 47*f*
  in muscle contraction, 247–248, 248*f*
  and neurotransmitter release, 53–55
  production of, 45–48
  rate law, **48**, 48*f*
Activational effect, of hormones, **310**, 316
  on aggressive behavior, 355*f*
  on men's sexual behavior, 325–326
  on women's sexual behavior, 323–325
Acuity, visual, 166
Acupuncture, analgesic effects of, 231–232
Adaptation
  to ambient temperature, 226
  to pressure, 225
Adaptive traits, 13–15, 14*f*, 15*f*
Addiction, 573–580
  common features of, 573–580
  craving and relapse in, 577–579
  historical perspective on, 573–574
  negative reinforcement and, 576–577
  physical *versus psychological*, 574–575
  positive reinforcement and, 575–576
Addictive drugs, 574*t*
Adenosine, **127**–128, 129*t*
  and sleep control, 289, 294, 294*f*
Adenosine triphosphate (ATP), **33**
  in muscle contraction, 247
  pain receptors sensitive to, 226
  in sodium-potassium pump, 45
Adipose tissue, 383
  satiety signals from, 388, 390–392
Adipsia, 381
Adoption studies, 160
  of alcoholism, 594, 595
Adrenalin. *See* Epinephrine
Adrenal insufficiency, 380
Adrenal medulla, **98**
Adrenergic receptors, 121
Adrenocorticotropic hormone (ACTH), **561**, 561*f*
Affect, 532

Affective disorders, major, **532**–544
  brain abnormalities in, evidence for, 538–541
  heritability of, 533–534
  physiological treatments for, 534–536
Afferent axons, **94**, 94*f*
  in cochlear nerve, 209–210
  in muscle, 248, 249*f*
  tracing, 142*f*, 142–143, 143*f*
  of vestibular nerve, 221
Affinity, **106**
Afterimage, negative, 176–177, 177*f*
2-AG (2-arachidonyl glycerol), 591
Aggressive behavior, 348–359
  alcohol and, 358*f*, 358–359
  in females, 356*f*, 356–357
  hormonal control of, 355–359
  in males, 355–356
  maternal, 356–357
  neural control of, 349*f*, 349–355
  prefrontal cortex and, 351–355
  research with humans, 350–351
  research with laboratory animals, 349*f*, 349–350
  serotonin and inhibition of, 349–351, 350*f*
Agnosia, 190
  auditory, 218
  tactile, 227–228, 228*f*
  visual, **190**–193
    apperceptive, **190**–192
    associative, 190, **192**–193, 193*f*, 199–200
    versus pure alexia, 504
    and verbal mechanisms, 199–200
Agonist(s), **108**–110
  direct, **109**, 109*f*, 110*f*
  indirect, **110**, 110*f*
Agonist (muscle), **253**
Agoraphobia, **548**
Agouti mouse, **398**
Agouti-related peptide (AGRP), **396**
  and eating behavior, 396–399
  leptin receptors in, 398
Agrammatism, **484**–485, 486
AGRP. *See* Agouti-related peptide
AIDS, 22
Akinetopsia, **195**
Albumin, **104**
  and depot binding of drugs, 104, 104*f*

Alcohol, 574*t*, 588–591
  and aggression, 358*f*, 358–359
  anxiolytic effect of, 589, 591
  and apoptosis, 588, 589*f*
  discovery of, 573
  fetal effects of, 588, 589*f*
  harmful effects of, 573
  intoxication, drug reversing, 591, 591*f*
  and memory deficits, 476, 590
  reinforcing effects of, 589–590, 591, 596, 598
  sites of action, 574*t*, 588, 590, 591
  withdrawal effects of, 583, 590–591
Alcoholism
  animal models of, 596*f*, 596–597
  binge drinking, 594–595, 595*t*
  heritability of, 594–596
    evidence for, 594–595
    possible mechanisms of, 595–596
  and Korsakoff's syndrome, 452–453, 573
    personality differences and, 595
    steady drinking, 594–595, 595*t*
    treatment of, 591, 596, 598–599, 599*f*
Aldosterone, and fluid balance, 380
Alexia, pure, 502*f*, **502**–505, 503*f*, 514*t*
All-or-none law, **48**
Allostasis, 577
Allylglycine, **124**, 129*t*
Alpha activity, **276**, 276*f*
Alpha motor neurons, **246**, 246*f*, 252, 252*f*, 252–254, 253*f*
Amacrine cells, 167*f*, **168**
American Sign Language (ASL), 497–498
Amino acids
  lesions produced with, 133–134, 134*f*
  as neurotransmitters, 123–127
Ammon's horn, 416. *See also* Hippocampal formation/hippocampus
Amnesia
  anterograde, **452**–468, 477
  retrograde, **452**, 465
AMPA, effect on glutamate receptors, 124, 129*t*
AMPA receptors, **123**–124, **419**
  long-term depression and, 428
  long-term potentiation and, 419, 422, 423*f*, 424, 424*f*, 425, 427, 427*f*
Amphetamine(s), 584–586
  addiction, 574*t*
  for attention-deficit/hyperactivity disorder, 558
  effects of, 118–119, 129*t*
  long-term effects on brain, 584, 584*f*
  psychotic effects of, 584
  reinforcing effects of, 445, 584–586
  and schizophrenia symptoms, 519
  site of action, 574*t*, 584
Amphibians, 16–17
AMPT, **118**, 129*t*, 537
Ampulla, **220**, 220*f*

Amygdala, 67, **86**, 86*f*, 321*f*
  and aggressive behavior, 349, 349*f*, 354
  and anxiety disorders, 347
  basal nucleus of, **344**, 345*f*
  basolateral, 447*f*, 447–448
  central nucleus of, **344**–347, 345*f*, 436–437, 437*f*
  and conditioned emotional response, 436–438, 437*f*, 456
  and conditioned reinforcement, 447–448
  and depression, 539, 539*f*
  in differential classical conditioning, 437–438, 438*f*
  and emotional recognition, 351, 363–364, 368, 368*f*
  and emotional responses, 344–348, 345*f*, 348*f*, 436
  and fear, 344
  in gustatory pathway, 237, 237*f*
  in instrumental conditioning, 448
  lateral nucleus of, **344**, 345*f*
  lesions of, effects of, 347
  long-term potentiation in, 428, 438
  major divisions and connections of, 344, 345*f*
  medial. *See* Medial nucleus of amygdala
  in olfactory pathway, 240
  and sexual behavior, 333, 334*f*, 336*f*
  sexual dimorphism of, 333
  and withdrawal symptoms, 582–583
Anabolic steroids, and aggressiveness, 358
Analgesia
  biological significance of, 231–232
  neural circuits producing, 230–231, 231*f*
  opiates for, 126, 581
Anandamide, **127**, 591
Anapsids, 16, 16*f*
Androgen(s), **311**–312, 315*t*, 316
  and aggression, 355–356, 356, 356*f*, 357–359
  and female sexual behavior, 324–325
  organizational effects of, 319, 319*f*, 355, 355*f*, 356
  prenatal, and sexual orientation, 326–327
  and sexual dimorphism of brain, 328
Androgen insensitivity syndrome, **312**, 312*f*, 313, 327–328
Androgen receptors, 312
Androstenedione, 315*t*, 322, 325
Angel dust. *See* PCP (phencyclidine)
Anger, 348, 370. *See also* Aggressive behavior
Angiotensin, 126–127, **379**, 380–381
  effects of, 379*f*, 379–381, 381*f*
  and salt appetite, 379
Angiotensinogen, 379
Angular gyrus damage, behavioral effects of, 227–228
Animal research, ethical issues in, 21–22

Animism, 2
Anions, 43
  organic, 44, 44*f*
Anisomycin, 438
Anomia, 484–**485**
Anomic aphasia, 495–497, 496*f*, 501*t*
Anorexia nervosa, **405**–407
Anorexigens, 398
Anosmia, 233
Anoxia, and hippocampal damage, 461*f*, 461–462
ANS. *See* Autonomic nervous system
Antagonist(s), **108**–110
  direct, **109**, 109*f*, 110*f*
  indirect, **109**–110, 110*f*
Antagonist (muscle), **253**
Antagonist-precipitated withdrawal, **583**
Anterior, **68**, 68*f*
Anterior cingulate cortex
  and drug abuse, 578, 578*f*
  and laughter, 366
  and pain perception, 229*f*, 229–230
Anterior commissure, sexual dimorphism of, 328
Anterior pituitary gland, **88**, 89*f*, 314
Anterograde, **34**, 140
Anterograde amnesia, **452**–468, 477
  anatomy of, 459–464
  basis description of, 453–454
  as failure of relational learning, 458–459
  hippocampal damage and, 459, 460–462, 461*f*, 465
  limbic damage and, 462–463
  retrograde amnesia with, 465–466
  spared learning abilities and, 454–456
Anterograde axoplasmic transport, 34–35
Anterograde labeling method, **140**–143, 141*f*, 143*f*, 145*t*
  combined with immunocytochemical methods, 158, 159*t*, 159*f*
Anteroventral tip of the third ventricle (AV3V), and drinking behavior, 378, 380–381, 381*f*
Antibodies, 140–142, **567**–568, 568*f*
Anticipatory anxiety, **548**
Anticonvulsant drugs, for bipolar disorder, 534, 536, 536*f*
Antidepressant medications, 534
  for narcolepsy, 282
Antidiuretic hormone. *See* Vasopressin
Antigens, 140–142, **567**–568, 568*f*
Antigravity muscles, 246
Antihistamines, and drowsiness, 292
Anti-Müllerian hormone, **311**, 312
Antipsychotic medications
  for anorexia nervosa, 407
  atypical, 520, 522
  problems with, 522
Antisocial behavior, 350–351, 353–355
Anxiety, anticipatory, **548**

Anxiety disorders, **548**–555
  amygdala and, 347
  serotonin in, 122, 549
  treatment of, 125, 347, 549
Anxiolytic(s), **125**, 549
  alcohol as, 589, 591
  effects of, neural basis of, 347
AP5, **123**, 129*t*, **419**, 420, 422, 423*f*, 438,
    448, 449*f*
Aphasia(s), **482**, 501*t*
  anomic, 495–497, 496*f*, 501*t*
  Broca's, 483*f*, **483**–486, 499–500, 501,
    501*t*
  conduction, **493**–495, 494*f*, 495*f*,
    501*t*, 501–502
  in deaf people, 497–498
  fluent, 499
  and reading and writing skills,
    501–502
  receptive, 487
  transcortical sensory, 489–**490**, 490*f*,
    491*f*, 501*t*
  Wernicke's, 367, **487**–495, 499, 501,
    501*t*
Aphrodisin, 321–322
Apomorphine, **118**, 118*f*
Apoptosis, **78**, 265
  drugs causing, 588, 589*f*
Apperceptive tactile agnosia, 228
Apperceptive visual agnosia, **190**–192
Appetite-inducing chemicals, 395
Appetite-suppressing chemicals, 398
Apraxia, 228, **259**–262
  callosal, **260**–261, 261*f*
  constructional, 260, **262**, 262*f*
  left parietal, 261*f*, **261**–262
  limb, 259–262
  ocular, **198**–199
  oral, 260
  of speech, **485**–486, 486*f*
  sympathetic, **261**, 261*f*
  tactile, 228
Apraxic agraphia, 260
2-Arachidonyl glycerol, 591
Arachnoid granulations, 72*f*, **73**
Arachnoid membrane, **70**, 71*f*, 93*f*, 94*f*
Arachnoid trabeculae, 70, 71*f*
Arcuate fasciculus, **493**–494, 494*f*, 495*f*,
    501*t*
Arcuate nucleus, 394*f*, **396**
  CART neurons in, 398, 399*f*
  and eating behavior, 396–397, 398,
    399*f*
  NPY neurons in, 397, 397*f*, 398
Area postrema, **38**–39, 378, 378*f*
  and eating behavior, 393–394, 394*f*,
    400
  nutrient receptors in, 387
Arginine, 128
Aristotle, 9
Arousal, neural control of, 91, 289–292
Arrival times, of sound waves, 214
  localization by means of, 214–216,
    215*f*
Articulation difficulties, 484–486

Artificial selection, 14
ASL. *See* American sign language
Asperger's disorder, 555
Association areas, cortical, 83*f*, 83–85
Associative long-term depression, 428
Associative long-term potentiation, **418**,
    418*f*, 421, 422*f*
Associative tactile agnosia, 228
Associative visual agnosia, 190,
    192–193, 193*f*, 199–200
Astrocytes (astroglia), 35*f*, **35**–36, 289
Asymmetrical division, 77–79
ATP. *See* Adenosine triphosphate
Atrial baroreceptors, 380, 381*f*
Atropine, **115**, 129*t*
Attention, brain areas responsible for,
    91
Attention-deficit/hyperactivity disorder,
    558–560
  delay of reinforcement gradient and,
    558–559, 559*f*
  possible causes of, 558–559
  treatment of, 558
Attractiveness, 318
Audition, 203–219
  behavioral functions of, 217–218
  central system, 210*f*, 210–211
  ear anatomy, 204–207, 205*f*
  and loudness perception, 213
  and maternal behavior, 338
  neural pathway for, 209–211, 210*f*,
    211*f*
  and pitch perception, 211–213
  and recognition of emotions, 361–365
  and spatial location perception,
    214–217
  and speech comprehension, 486–488
  stimulus for, 203–204, 204*f*
  and timbre perception, 213–214, 214*f*
  transduction of auditory information,
    207–208, 208*f*, 209*f*
Auditory agnosia, 218
Auditory association cortex, 83*f*, 84, 211,
    211*f*
  damage to, 218
  and perceptual memory, 431, 431*f*
  in phonological loop, 494–495, 495*f*
  and speech comprehension, 487–488
Auditory cortex. *See* Auditory
    association cortex; Primary
    auditory cortex
Auditory learning, 431, 431*f*
Auditory nerve, 95*f*, 209–210, 221
Autistic disorder, **555**–558
  brain pathology in, 557
  description of, 555–556
  and facial recognition, 192, 556, 556*f*
  heritability of, 556–557
  possible causes of, 556–557
  streptococcal infection and, 557
Autoassociative network, 477–478
Autoimmune disease, 60
Autolysis, halting, in histologic samples,
    137–138
Automatic movements, 257

Autonomic nervous system, **96**, 97*f*, 98*t*
  in emotional response, 370–371
  parasympathetic division of, 96, 97*f*,
    98, 98*t*
  sympathetic division of, **96**–98, 97*f*,
    98*t*
Autoradiography, **149**, 149*f*, 155*t*,
    157–158, 158*f*, 159*t*
  in instrumental conditioning, 441
  of suprachiasmatic nucleus, 304, 304*f*
Autoreceptors, **61**–62
  dendritic, 110, 111*f*
  dopaminergic, 118
  drug effects on, 110, 111*f*
Autosomal recessive juvenile
    parkinsonism, 267
Autotopagnosia, 84, **492**–493
AV3V, and drinking behavior, 378,
    380–381, 381*f*
Axoaxonic synapse, 51, 52*f*, 62, 62*f*,
    110
Axodendritic synapse, 51–52, 52*f*
Axon(s), 29*f*, **29**–30, 30*f*
  afferent, **94**, 94*f*
    in cochlear nerve, 209–210
    in muscle, 248, 249*f*
    tracing, 142*f*, 142–143, 143*f*
    of vestibular nerve, 221
  all-or-none law, **48**
  cable properties of, **49**
  conduction of action potential
    through, 30, 47–49, 48*f*
  development of, 37–38, 78
  efferent, 94*f*, 94–**95**
    in cochlear nerve, 210
    tracing, 140–142, 141*f*, 143*f*
  growth of, 87
  length of, 34
  measuring electrical potential of, 41*f*,
    41–42
  rate law, **48**, 48*f*
  rate of firing, 48, 60
Axonal varicosities, **121**, 121–122
Axon hillock, 60, 61*f*
Axoplasm, 34
Axoplasmic transport, 34*f*, **34**–35
  anterograde, 34–35
  retrograde, 34–35
Axosomatic synapse, 51, 52*f*
Azimuth, 214

B

BA37, 505, 505*f*, 507
Balint's syndrome, **198**–199
Ballistic movement, 270
Barbiturate(s), 125, 591
  addiction, 574*t*
  sites of action, 574*t*
  withdrawal effects of, 590–591
Basal ganglia, 81, **86**, 87*f*, 262–268
  anatomy and function of, 262–264,
    263*f*, 440, 440*f*
  and attention-deficit/hyperactivity
    disorder, 559
  direct pathway in, 263*f*, **264**, 553

Basal ganglia *(continued)*
  diseases of, 264–267, 364–365, 441–442, 442*f*
  and emotional recognition, 364–365
  indirect pathway in, 263*f*, **264**, 553
  and instrumental conditioning, 439–442
  and obsessive-compulsive disorder, 551–554, 552*f*
  and speech deficits, 484
  and tardive dyskinesia, 522
Basal nucleus of amygdala, 344, 345*f*
Basic rest-activity cycle, **278**, 299
Basilar membrane, **205**–207, 206*f*, 207*f*, 208, 210
  pitch coding in, 211*f*, 211–212
  and timbre perception, 214
Basolateral amygdala, and conditioned reinforcement, 447*f*, 447–448
Bed nucleus of stria terminalis (BNST), 328–329, 329*f*, 333, 333*f*, 579
Bedwetting (nocturnal enuresis), 283
Behavioral neuroscience, 23
Belladonna alkaloids, 115
Belt region, **211**, 211*f*
Benzodiazepines, **125**
  addiction, 574*t*
  in alcohol withdrawal, 590
  anxiolytic effects of, 549
  effects of, 129*t*
    brain regions responsible for, 347
  for REM sleep behavior disorder, 283
  sites of action, 574*t*
  and sleep, 289
Bernard, Claude, 374
Beta activity, **276**, 276*f*, 277
Bicuculline, **125**, 129*t*
Bilingual brain, 498–499, 499*f*
Binaural sounds, 214
Binding
  competitive, 110*f*
  depot, **104**, 104*f*
  noncompetitive, **109**–110, 110*f*
Binding site, **51**
Binge drinking, 594–596, 595*t*
Binocular vision, 182, 183
Biological clocks, 299–307
  circadian rhythms, 300*f*, **300**–301
  and depression, 541–544
  seasonal rhythms, 305–306
  suprachiasmatic nucleus and, 301–305
Biological psychology, 23
Biopsychology, 23
Bipedalism, evolutionary advantage of, 19
Bipolar cells, 167*f*, 167–169, **168**, 169*f*
Bipolar disorder, **533**
  brain abnormalities in, evidence for, 538–541
  heritability of, 533–534
  physiological treatments for, 534–536
  sleep deprivation and, 542
  treatment compliance in, 536
Bipolar neurons, **30**, 30*f*

Bitterness, 233
  neurons sensitive to, 238
  trandsduction of, 235*f*, 235–236
Black widow spider venom, 109*f*, 113–**114**, 129*t*
Blest, 14
Bleuler, Eugen, 517
Blindness
  cortical, **184**
  word, 502, 504
Blindsight, **3**–4, 5*f*, **184**
Blind spot, 167, 167*f*
Blood-brain barrier, 38*f*, **38**–39, 103, 104
  insulin transport across, 390
  leptin transport across, 403
Blood plasma. *See* Intravascular fluid
Blood supply, to brain, 70
B-lymphocytes, **567**–568, 568*f*
BNST. *See* Bed nucleus of stria terminalis
Body mass index (BMI), 400
Body weight
  loss of, 405
  relative stability of, 390–391, 391*f*
Boston Diagnostic Aphasia Test, 483*f*
Bottlenose dolphin, sleep in, 284, 289
Botulinum toxin, 109*f*, **113**–114, 129*t*
Bouton. *See* Terminal buttons
Brachium conjunctivum, 295–296, 296*f*
Braille, recognition of, brain region responsible for, 505, 505*f*
Brain, 70. *See also specific cerebral structures*
  adult, neurogenesis in, 79–80, 80*f*
  anatomical subdivisions of, 76*f*, 76–77, 77*t*
  bilingual, 498–499, 499*f*
  blood supply to, 70
  connections with eyes, 170*f*, 170–172
  cross sections of, 69, 69*f*
  Descartes's theory of, 10*f*, 10–11
  development of, 75–80
    details of, 76–80
    experience and, 79
    overview of, 75*f*, 75–76, 76*f*
    REM sleep and, 286–287
  drug administration into, 103
  functional division of, Müller on, 11
  glucose sparing for, 383
  Hippocrates on, 9
  human, evolution of, 19–20, 80–81
  metabolic activity of, 149*f*, 149–151, 150*f*, 155*t*, 284, 295
  midsagittal view of, 85, 85*f*
  models of, 10–11
  and movement control, 82–83, 254–272
  neurotransmitters in
    localizing, 155–157, 156*f*, 157*f*, 159*t*
    measuring, 151–152, 155*t*
  nutrient detectors in, 386–387, 387*f*
  primary function of, 8, 28
  receptors in, localization of, 157–159, 158*f*, 159*t*
  relation to rest of body, 70, 71*f*

  secretions of, measuring, 151–152
  sexual differentiation of, 328–329
  sexual responses controlled by, 332–334
  size of
    determinants of, 80–81
    as function of body weight, 20, 20*f*
    subcortical regions of, **81**
Brain damage. *See also* Brain lesions
  in autistic disorder, 557
  in schizophrenia, 522–531
  stress and, 562–564, 563*f*
Brain imaging
  autoradiography, **149**, 149*f*, 155*t*, 159*t*
  computerized tomography (CT), 143*f*, **143**–144, 144*f*, 145*t*
  functional magnetic resonance imaging (fMRI), **150**–151, 151*f*, 155*t*
  magnetic resonance imaging (MRI), **144**, 144*f*, 145*t*
  positron emission tomography (PET), **150**, 150*f*, 151–152, 152*f*, 155*t*
Brain lesions
  evaluating behavioral effects of, 133–134
  excitotoxic, 134*f*, **134**–135, 145*t*
  histologic methods in, 137–139
  production of, 134–135
  radio frequency, 134*f*, **134**–135, 145*t*
  reversible, 135
  sham, **135**
  stereotaxic surgery for, **135**–137, 145*t*
  studies of, 132–145, **133**
Brain stem, **89**–90, 90*f*
  and autistic disorder, 557
  and ingestive behaviors, 393–394, 394*f*
Brain studies
  chemical stimulation, 152–153, 155*t*
  double labeling, **158**, 159*f*
  electrical stimulation, 11, 12, 152, 153–154, 155*t*. *See also* Electrical brain stimulation
  labeling, 77, 80*f*. *See also* Labeling studies
  lesion, 132–145, **133**
  recording of neural activity, 144–152, 155*t*
  split-brain, 4–6, 5*f*, 6*f*
  stimulation of neural activity, 152–153, 155*t*
Breeding cycles, 299–300
Bregma, **136**, 137*f*
Brightness, **164**, 165*f*
Broca, Paul, 11–12
Broca's aphasia, 483*f*, **483**–486, 499–500, 501*t*
  reading and writing skills in, 501
Broca's area, 11–12, 12*f*, 483*f*, **483**–484, 484*f*, 486
  and auditory association complex, 494–495, 495*f*
  in bilingual brain, 499
  and sign language, 497*f*, 497–498

and verb production, 496
and Wernicke's area, connection between, 490, 490*f*, 493–494, 494*f*
Broken drawings, 454–455, 455*f*
Brood nest, 337, 337*f*
Bruce effect, **320**
Bulimia nervosa, **405–407**
Butterflies, eyespots on, 14, 14*f*

C

C75, 392, 392*f*, 399
Cable properties, of axon, **49**
Caffeine, **128,** 129*t*
food content, 128*t*
CAH. *See* Congenital adrenal hyperplasia
Calbindin D$_{28K}$, 303, 303f
Calcarine fissure, **82,** 82*f*, 170–**171**
Calcium channels, 55, 58*f*, 58–59
in muscle contraction, 247
NMDA receptor and, 123–124, 124*f*
and taste perception, 235*f*, 236
Calcium ions, in long-term potentiation, 418–421, 420*f*, 422–423, 427, 427*f*
Callosal apraxia, **260**–261, 261*f*
CaM-KII, **422**
in spatial learning, 475
in synaptic plasticity, 422–424, 423*f*, 424*f*, 427*f*
Canine narcolepsy, 281*f*, 281–282
Cannabinoid receptors, **127,** 127*f*, 592–593
and reinforcing effects of opiates, 592, 592*f*
Cannabis, 574, 574*t*, 591–593
and cognitive impairment, 592–593, 593*f*
long-term use of, damaging effects of, 592–593
sites of action, 574*t*
withdrawal effects of, 583
Cannon, Walter, 370, 560
Cannula electrodes, 349
Capsaicin, 226, 228
Captopril, for hypertension, 379
Carbachol, **296**–297
Carbamazepine, **536**
for bipolar disorder, 536, 536*f*
Carbohydrate reservoir, 382–383, 384
Cardiac muscle, **249**
Cardiovascular disease, stress and, 566, 566*f*
Careers, in neuroscience, 22–23
Caregiver stress, 562, 562*f*, 568*f*, 568–569
Carotid body, as source of dopamine-secreting neurons, 265
CART, **398**–399, 405
CART neurons
in arcuate nucleus, 398, 399*f*
connections of, 398, 399*f*
Cataplexy, **281,** 281*f*, 282

Catecholamine(s), **116,** 116*t*. *See also* Dopamine; Epinephrine; Norepinephrine
biosynthesis of, 116, 116*f*
Cations, 43
Cauchemar (nightmare), 279, 279*f*
Cauda equina, 71*f*, **91**
Caudal, **68,** 68*f*
Caudal block, **91**
Caudal medulla, 237*f*
Caudate nucleus, 86, 87*f*, 262, **263,** 263*f*, 264, 440, 440*f*
electrical stimulation of, 153–154
in Huntington's disease, 267, 267*f*
in instrumental conditioning, 440–441
and obsessive-compulsive disorder, 552–553
in Parkinson's disease, 265
CB1 receptor, 591–592
Cell(s)
founder, **77**–79
nerve. *See* Neurons
supporting, 35–38
Cell assembly, 492
Cell body (soma), **29,** 29*f*, 30*f*
Cell-body stain, 138, 178
Center of expansion, 194
Central nervous system (CNS), **29,** 70, 70*t*, 74–94. *See also* Brain; Spinal cord
development of, 75–94
major divisions of, 70*t*
planes of section of, 69*f*
regenerative properties of, 37–38
supporting cells of, 35–37
Central nucleus of amygdala, **344,** 345*f*, 436
and anxiety disorders, 347
brain regions receiving input from, 345*f*
and classical conditioning, 436
and conditioned emotional response, 346*f*, 346–347, 436–437, 437*f*
damage, effects of, 344–345
and fear, 344–345
Central sulcus, **82,** 82*f*, 83
Central tegmental field, and male sexual behavior, 334*f*
Central (foveal) vision, 172, 172*f*
Cerebellar cortex, **91**
Cerebellar peduncles, 90*f*, **91**
Cerebellum, 85*f*, 90*f*, **91**
damage to, 91
and autistic disorder, 557
and movement control, 268–271, 269*f*, 270
Cerebral aqueduct, 72*f*, **73,** 90*f*
Cerebral cortex, 67, **76,** 81*f*, 81–86, 82*f*, 83*f*
association areas of, 83*f*, 83–85
development of, 76–80
sensory areas of, 82*f*–83*f*, 82–84
specialized regions of, 79, 79*f*
surface area of, 81

Cerebral hemisphere(s), **5, 81,** 82*f*
lateralized functions of, 84–85, 482
left, 84–85
damage to, 261–262
perceptual functions of, 482
speech specialization of, 5–6, 11–12, 12*f*, 482
and olfaction control, 5
right, 84
and comprehension of figurative speech, 493
damage to, effects of, 262, 262*f*, 482
and emotional expression, 367*f*, 367–368
and emotional recognition, 361–363, 363*f*
perceptual functions of, 482
and prosody, 500
and speech control, 5
Cerebrospinal fluid, **70,** 71*f*
circulation and reabsorption of, 72*f*, 73–74
obstruction of flow, 73–74, 74*f*
production of, 70–74, 72*f*
Cerebrovascular accident (stroke), 22, 84, 245, 342, **481**
Cerletti, Ugo, 534–535
Cervical vertebrae, 91, 91*f*
ChAT. *See* Choline acetyltransferase
Cheese effect, of MAOIs, 534
Chemical stimulation, of brain, 152–153, 153*f*, 155*t*
Chemical transmission
concept of, 51
nonsynaptic, 62–63
synaptic, 53–63
Childhood disintegrative disorder, 555
Chimerical faces, 367, 367*f*
Chlordiazepoxide (Librium), 125, 347
Chloride channels, 58, 58*f*
Chloride ions (Cl-), 44, 44*f*
Chlorpromazine, **119,** 129*t*, 519
antipsychotic effects of, 516, 519
Chocolate
anandamidelike chemicals in, 593
caffeine in, 128*t*
Cholecystokinin (CCK), **389,** 405
Choline acetyltransferase (ChAT), **113,** 113*f*, 156, 157*f*
Chorda tympani, **236,** 237, 237*f*
Choroid plexus, 72*f*, **73,** 73*f*, 85*f*
Chromosomes, 15, **32**
human, 309
sex, **309**–310, 310*f*
Cilium (cilia)
auditory, **207**–208, 208*f*, 209*f*
gustatory, 233
olfactory, 239, 239*f*, 240
vestibular, 220–221, 221*f*
Cingulate gyrus, **85,** 85*f*
and obsessive-compulsive disorder, 551–553
Cingulotomy, **553**

Circadian rhythms, 300*f,* **300**–301
  changes in, 306
  and depression, 541–544
  suprachiasmatic nucleus and,
    301–303, 302*f,* 303*f*
Circumlocutions, **495**
Circumstriate cortex. *See* Extrastriate
  cortex
Circumvallate papillae, 233
Circumventricular organs, 378*f,* 378–379
Cisterna(e), **52,** 53*f*
  membrane recycling in, 55–56, 56*f*
Clasp-knife reflex, **253**
Classical conditioning, 8, 346, **412**–413,
  436–439
  conditioned emotional response, 346*f,*
    346–347, 436–438, 437*f*
  differential, 437–438, 438*f*
  and drug craving, 577
  extinction of, **438**
  neural model of, 412, 412*f,* 436–438,
    437*f*
Clitoris, development of, 313, 313*f*
Clomipramine, for obsessive-
  compulsive disorder, 553, 554,
  554*f*
Clonazepam, for REM sleep behavior
  disorder, 283
Clonidine, **121,** 129*t,* 551
Clozapine, **119,** 129*t,* **520,** 530
CNS. *See* Central nervous system
CO blobs. *See* Cytochrome oxidase
  blobs
Cocaine, 119, 129*t,* 584–586
  addiction, 574*t,* 575
    treatment of, 597–598
  concentration in blood plasma, routes
    of administration and, 103, 103*f*
  craving and relapse, 577–579, 578*f,*
    597
  cross-priming effect of nicotine on,
    588
  harmful effects of, 573
  long-term effects on brain, 584
  psychotic effects of, 584
  reinforcing effects of, 445, 584–586
  and schizophrenia symptoms, 519
  self-administration of, 584, 584*f*
  site of action, 574*t,* 584
  social stress and intake of, 579, 579*f*
  withdrawal effects of, 583, 586
Cocaine- and amphetamine-regulated
  transcript. *See* CART
Cochlea, 205*f,* **205**–207, 206*f,* 220, 220*f*
  cross section through, 206*f*
  and loudness perception, 213
  uncurled, 207*f*
Cochlear implants, **212**
Cochlear nerve, **209,** 221
  connections with, 209–210
  and loudness perception, 213
Cochlear nerve (spiral) ganglion, 206*f,*
  209
Cochlear nucleus, **210**
Coenzymes, 113
Cognitive neuroscience, 23

Coincidence detector, auditory, 215*f,*
  215–216, 216*f*
Cold pressor test, 566
Colds, stress and, 570, 570*f*
Color(s)
  coding in retina, 174–178, 177*f*
  complementary, **176**
  dimensions of, 164, 165*f*
  opponent, 174, 176
  primary, 174
  trichromatic coding of, 174–176
Color constancy, **187**
Color mixing, 174–175, 175*f*
Color vision, 166
  evolutionary advantage of, 19
  genetic defects in, 175–176
  opponent-process coding in, 176
  striate cortex and, 182–183
  trichromatic theory of, 174
  visual association cortex and, 186–188
    studies in laboratory animals,
      186–187
    studies with humans, 187–188
Communication, 480–514
  consciousness and, 3
  of emotions, 360–369
    emotional expression, 365–368
    emotional recognition, 361–365
    neural basis of, 361–368
  neural. *See* Neural communication
  verbal, 481. *See also* Language; Speech
Competitive binding, 110*f*
Complementary colors, **176**
Complex cells, **179,** 179*f,* 183
Comprehension without reading, 508,
  509*f*
Compulsions, **550,** 551*t*
Computerized tomography, 143*f,*
  143–144, 144*f,* 145*t*
Concordance rate, 160, 330
Conditional response (CR), **412**
Conditional stimulus (CS), **412**
Conditioned emotional response,
  346–347, 436–438, 437*f,* 456
  testing of, 346, 346*f*
Conditioned place preference, **582,**
  582*f,* 598
Conditioned punisher, **446**
Conditioned reinforcement, 446–448
Conditioned reinforcer, **446**
Conditioning. *See* Classical
  conditioning; Instrumental
  conditioning
Conduction, of action potential, 30,
  47–49, 48*f*
  decremental, 48–49, 49*f*
  saltatory, 49, 50*f*
Conduction aphasia, **493**–495, 494*f,*
  495*f,* 501*t*
  reading and writing skills in, 501–502
Cones, 166*t,* **166**–168, 168*f*
  absorption characteristics of, 175, 175*f*
Confabulation, **453,** 466–467
Congenital adrenal hyperplasia (CAH),
  326–327, 327*f,* 329
Conjunctiva, 165, 165*f*

Consciousness
  blindsight and, 3–4
  physiological approach to, 3–8
  during sleep, 278–279
  split brains and, 4–6
  term, 3
  unilateral neglect and, 6–7
Consolidation, memory, **454,** 454*f*
  hippocampal formation and, 471
Constructional apraxia, 260, **262,** 262*f*
Content words, **483,** 487
Contralateral, **69**
Contrast enhancement, 173*f,* 173–174
Control, delusions of, 517
Coolidge effect, **317**
Coolness, sensation of, 225–226
Coordinated limb movements, 256
Coping response, **346,** 566–567
Core region, auditory, **211**
Cornea, 165*f,* 166
Cornu ammonis. *See* Hippocampal
  formation/hippocampus
Corpulent rat, 403
Corpus callosum, **4, 85,** 85*f,* 86*f*
  anterior, damage to, 260–261, 261*f*
  cutting, in split-brain operation, 4–5,
    5*f,* 6*f*
  and Japanese writing deficits, 510*f,*
    510–511
  posterior, damage to, reading deficits
    with, 502–503, 503*f*
  sexual dimorphism of, 328
Corpus luteum, **316**
Correctional mechanism, **372,** 373
Cortical-basal ganglia loop, 263*f,* 264
Cortical blindness, **184**
Corticobulbar tract, 256, 257*f,* **258,** 260*t*
Corticorubral tract, 257*f,* **258**
Corticospinal tract, 256–258, **257,** 257*f*
  lateral, **257,** 257*f,* 260*t*
  ventral, 257*f,* **257**–258, 260*t*
Corticotropin-releasing hormone
  (CRH), **561,** 561*f,* 566
  and drug craving, 579
  in posttraumatic stress disorder, 565,
    565*f*
Cortisol, 561
  in posttraumatic stress disorder, 565,
    565*f*
CR (conditional response), **412**
Cranial nerve ganglia, 226
Cranial nerves, 70, 71*f,* 95*f,* **95**–96, 98*t*
Craniosacral system, 98. *See also*
  Parasympathetic division, of
  ANS
Craving, drug abuse and, 577–579
CREB (cyclic AMP-responsive element-
  binding protein), **583**
  and withdrawal symptoms, 583, 583*f*
Cresyl violet, 138, 139*f*
Cribriform plate, 239
Cristae, 32–33
Cross section, **69,** 69*f*
Cryoloop, 135, 135*f,* 145*t*
CS (conditional stimulus), **412**
CSF. *See* Cerebrospinal fluid

CT. *See* Computerized tomography
Culture, and display rules, 361
Cupula, **220,** 220*f*
Curare, 60, **115,** 129*t*
Cutaneous senses, **222,** 222–226
Cyclic AMP, 57
  and taste perception, 235*f,* 236
Cyclic GMP, 128, 168, 169*f*
Cyclotron, 150
Cynodont, 16, 16*f*
Cyproheptadine, 407
Cytochrome oxidase (CO) blobs, 182*f,*
  182–183, 186
Cytokines, **568**
Cytoplasm, **32,** 32*f*
Cytoskeleton, **34**

D

DA. *See* Dopamine
Darwin, Charles, 13*f,* 13–15, 360
Dawn simulation, 543
db mouse, 403
Deaf community, opposition to cochlear
  implants, 212
Deaf people
  aphasia in, 497–498
  inability to comprehend sign
    language by, 504
Decerebrate, **253**
Decerebrate rigidity, **253**
Decerebration, **393,** 393*f*
Declarative memory, 456–458, **457,**
  458*t,* 477
  hippocampus and, 460, 460*f*
  retrieval of, 465–466
Decomposition of movement, 270
Decremental conduction, 48–49, 49*f*
Deep brain stimulation, 266, 266*f*
Deep cerebellar nuclei, **91**
Defeminization, behavioral, 319, 319*f*
Defeminizing effect, **311**
Defensive behavior, **348**
  neural control of, 349, 349*f*
Delayed matching-to-sample task,
  433–435, 434*f*
Delay of reinforcement gradient, and
  attention-deficit/hyperactivity
    disorder, 558–559, 559*f*
Delta activity, 276*f,* **277,** 284, 286, 289
Delusions, **517,** 519, 584
Dendrites, **29,** 29*f,* 30*f*
  action potentials in, 420–421, 422*f*
  development of, 78
  protein synthesis in, 427
Dendritic autoreceptors, 110, 111*f*
  drug effects on, 110, 111*f*
Dendritic spikes, **420**–421, 421*f,* 422*f*
Dendritic spine, **51**–52, 52*f,* 53*f*
Dendrodendritic synapse, 62
Dentate gyrus, **416,** 416*f,* 417, 417*f,* 428,
  459
Dentate nucleus, **268**–270, 270*f,* 271
2-Deoxyglucose (2-DG), 149*f,* **149**–150,
  150*f,* 155*t,* 304, 304*f,* 339–340,
  386, 387, 441
Deoxyribonucleic acid (DNA), **32**

Depolarization, **42,** 43*f,* 169, 169*f*
  of postsynaptic neurons, in long-term
    potentiation, 418, 419*f*
  weak, transmission of, 48–49, 49*f*
Depot binding, **104,** 104*f*
Deprenyl, 119*f,* **119**–120, 129*t*
Depression, 533
  brain abnormalities in, evidence for,
    538–541
  circadian rhythms and, 541–544
  heritability of, 533–534
  late-onset, 540
  long-term. *See* Long-term depression
  monoamine hypothesis of, **536**–538
  physiological treatments for, 534–536
  seasonal affective disorder, **543**–544
  serotonin in, 122
  silent cerebral infarctions and,
    540–541
  sleep deprivation as treatment of,
    541–542, 542*f*
  sleep patterns in, 541, 541*f*
  substance P in, 538, 538*f*
  summer, **543**
  unipolar, **533**
Depth perception, 79, 182
Descartes, René, 9–10
  theory of brain, 10*f,* 10–11
Desensitization, drug abuse and, 588
Designer drugs, 573
Desipramine, 129*t*
  for obsessive-compulsive disorder,
    553, 554*f*
Desynchrony, EEG, during sleep, 277,
  278*t,* 295, 295*f*
Detector, **372,** 373
Deuteranopia, **175**
Development dyslexias, 506, **511**–513
  in different languages, 512–513
2-DG. *See* 2-Deoxyglucose
Diacetylmorphine. *See* Heroin
Dialysis, 151
Diapsids, 16, 16*f*
Diazepam (Valium), 125
Diazepoxide (Librium), 125, 347
Dichorionic twins, 526–527, 527*f*
Diencephalon, 76*f,* 77, 77*t,* 86–89, 89
Dieters's cells, **205**
Differential classical conditioning,
  437–438, 438*f*
Diffusion, **43**
Dihydromorphine. *See* Heroin
Dihydrotestosterone, 311–**312,** 315*t*
Dinosaurs, 16
Direct agonist, **109,** 109*f,* 110*f*
Direct antagonist, **109,** 109*f,* 110*f*
Direct dysgraphia, 511
Direct dyslexia, **508,** 514*t*
Direct pathway, in basal ganglia, 263*f,*
  264, 553
Disgust, recognition of, 364–365
Display rules, **361**
Dizygotic (fraternal) twins, 160, 316
DNA (deoxyribonucleic acid), **32**
Doctrine of specific nerve energies, **11**
Dogs, narcolepsy in, 281*f,* 281–282

Dolphins, sleep in, 284, 284*f,* 289
Dominance
  versus aggression, 350
  alcohol and, 358*f,* 358–359
  androgens and, 358
  serotonin and, 350
DOPA decarboxylase, 116, 116*f*
Dopamine (DA), 112, 116, **116**–120
  activating effect in prefrontal cortex,
    529
  in attention-deficit/hyperactivity
    disorder, 559
  biosynthesis of, 116, 116*f*
  and hippocampal functions, 476
  reinforcing effects of, 444–446, 519,
    522, 576
  release of
    alcohol and, 590
    cocaine/amphetamine and,
      584–586, 585*f*
    cocaine and, 577
    dynorphin and, 586, 586*f*
    nicotine and, 587, 587*f*
    opiates and, 582
    and positive reinforcement,
      576
    THC and, 591–592, 592*f*
  and synaptic plasticity, 448–449
  transmission, in schizophrenia, 520*t,*
    520–521, 521*f*
Dopamine agonists, and schizophrenia
  symptoms, 519, 529–531
Dopamine antagonists, and
  schizophrenia symptoms, 519
Dopamine b-hydroxylase, 116,
  116*f,* 120
Dopamine hypothesis, of schizophrenia,
  119, 519–522, 529, 530, 530*f*
Dopamine receptors, 118
  effects of drugs on, 118–119
  in schizophrenia, 520–521, 521*f*
  supersensitivity of, 522
Dopaminergic neurons, 117, 117*f*
  activation in ventral tegmental area,
    446
  drugs affecting, 117–120, 129*t*
  and male sexual behavior, 333,
    333*f*
  mesocortical system of, **117,** 117*f,*
    444–446
  mesolimbic system of, **117,** 117*f,* 444,
    519, 530, 576, 582
  nigrostriatal system of, **117,** 117*f,* 264,
    444
  overactivity of, and schizophrenia,
    119, 519–522, 529, 530, 530*f*
  in Parkinson's disease, 117, 119–120,
    152, 152*f,* 265–267
  and reinforcement, 444–446, 445*f*
Dorsal, **68,** 68*f*
Dorsal columns, of spinal cord, 226
Dorsal lateral geniculate nucleus, **170,**
  170*f,* 178, 183
Dorsal raphe nucleus, 121–122
Dorsal root(s), **91,** 92*f,* 94*f*
Dorsal root ganglia, 93*f,* **94,** 94*f,* 226

Dorsal stream
  auditory, 211, 218, 218*f*
  visual, 185–**186,** 186*f,* 198–199, 430,
    430*f*
Dorsolateral prefrontal cortex, and
    schizophrenia, 528, 529–531,
    530*f*
Dose-response curve, **105,** 105*f*
Double-jointedness, and panic disorder,
    549
Double labeling, **158,** 159*f*
Downregulation, 583
Dreaming, 277, 279, 279*f,* 298, 379
  organophosphates and, 155–156
Drinking, 375*f,* 376–382
  as correctional mechanism, 375, 375*f*
  neural control of, 380–381, 381*f*
  osmometric thirst and, **377**–379
  satiety mechanism, 375, 375*f*
  volumetric thirst and, **379**–380
Drug(s). *See also specific drugs*
  addictive, 574*t*
  commonly abused, 580–594
  definition of, 101
  depot binding of, **104,** 104*f*
  designer, 573
  distribution within body, 103–105
  dose-response curve for, **105,** 105*f*
  effectiveness of, 105–106
  effects on neurotransmitters, 108,
    109*f,* 110–111, 129*t*
    acetylcholinergic, 109*f,* 111,
      113–115, 129*t*
    dopaminergic, 117–120, 129*t*
    noradrenergic, 120–121, 129*t*
    serotonergic, 121–123, 129*t*
  effects on receptors, 108–110, 109*f,*
    129*t*
    GABA, 125, 129*t*
    glutamate, 123–124, 129*t*
  effects on reuptake, 109*f,* 110–111
  effects on synaptic transmission,
    108–111, 109*f*
  inactivation and excretion of, 105
  margin of safety for, 105–106
  recreational, 573–574. *See also* Drug
    abuse
  reinforcing effects of, 445
  repeated administration of, effects of,
    106–107
  routes of administration, 102–103
  sites of action, **101,** 102, 103–104, 106,
    107, 108–111, 156
Drug abuse, 572–600. *See also specific
    drugs*
  animal models of, 596–597
  craving and relapse and, 577–579
  heredity and, 594–596
  historical perspective on, 573–574
  and long-term changes in brain, 578*f,*
    578–579
  models for schizophrenia, 529–531
  negative reinforcement and, 576–577
  positive reinforcement and, 573,
    575–576

  stress and, 579, 579*f*
  therapy for, 597–599
  tolerance in, **574**–575
  withdrawal symptoms in, **574**–575
Drug dependency insomnia, **280**
Drug discrimination procedure, **590**
Drug effects, **101**
Drug-seeking behavior, 577–579
D system, **121**–122, 122*f*
Dualism, **3,** 10
Duchenne de Boulogne, Guillaume-
    Benjamin, 365, 365*f*
Duchenne's muscle, 365, 365*f,* 368
Duodenum, **388,** 389
Dura mater, **70,** 71*f,* 93*f,* 94*f*
Dynein, 34
Dynorphin, **581**
  and dopamine release, 586, 586*f*
Dysgraphia(s), 510
  direct, 511
  orthographic, **510,** 514*t*
  phonological, 509–**510,** 514*t*
Dyskinesia, 265
Dyslexia(s)
  acquired, 506–508
  developmental, 506, **511**–513
    in different languages, 512–513
  direct, **508,** 514*t*
  phonological, **506**–507, 507*f,* 514*t*
  spelling (word-form), **507**–508, 508*f,*
    509, 514*t*
  surface, **506,** 507*f,* 514*t*
Dysphoria, 106
Dystonia, 265
Dystypia, 509

E
Ear(s)
  as analytical organ, 204
  anatomy of, 204–207, 205*f*
Eating, 382–407
  brain mechanisms in, 393–400
  brain stem and, 393–394, 394*f*
  as correctional mechanism, 375
  disorders of, 400–407
  hypothalamus and, 394*f,* 394–400
  physiological hunger signals for,
    386–387
  satiety mechanisms, 388–393
  social and environmental factors in,
    385–386
  stimuli for, 385–388
Ecstasy (MDMA), **123,** 129*t*
ECT. *See* Electroconvulsive therapy
EEGs. *See* Electroencephalograms
Effector cells, 210
Efferent axons, 94*f,* 94–**95**
  in cochlear nerve, 210
  tracing, **140**–142, 141*f,* 143*f*
EGTA, 420
Ehrlich, Paul, 38
Ejaculation, 317, 332
Electrical brain stimulation, 11, 12, 152,
    155*t*
  and analgesia, 230

  behavioral effects of, 153–154
  deep, for Parkinson's disease, 266,
    266*f*
  and reinforcement, 411, 444–445,
    445*f*
Electrical potentials. *See also specific
    potentials*
  measuring, 41*f,* 41–42
  recording, 146–149
Electrical synapses, 62, 63*f*
Electric ray, 56
Electroconvulsive therapy (ECT),
    534–**535,** 535*f,* 536, 541
Electrode(s), **41**
  cannula, 349
Electroencephalograms (EEGs),
    147–148
  sleeping patterns, 276*f,* 276–278
  waking patterns, 276, 276*f*
Electrolytes, **43**
Electromagnetic spectrum, 164, 164*f*
Electromyogram (EMG), **276**
  during sleep, 276–277
Electron microscopy, 139, 139*f*
Electro-oculogram (EOG), **276**
  during sleep, 276–277
Electrostatic pressure, **43**
EMG. *See* Electromyogram
Emotion(s), 342–372
  amygdala and, 344–348, 345*f,* 348*f*
  brain structures responsible for, 86
  communication of, 360–369
    neural basis of, 361–368
  components of, 342–343
  definitions of, 342
  facial expression of, 351, 351*f,*
    365–368
    hemispheric specialization for, 367*f,*
    367–368
    innate responses, 360*f,* 360–361
    in schizophrenia, 522, 526
  feelings of, 369–372
  imitation of, 371, 371*f*
  James-Lange theory of, 369*f,*
    369–370
  pain and, 229*f,* 229–230
  primary, 368
  recognition of, 351, 351*f,* 361–365,
    368, 368*f*
  as response patterns, 342–360
  stimulated, feedback from, 370–371
Emotional facial paresis, **366,** 366*f*
Emotional memory, 456
Emotional response, conditioned,
    346–347, 436–438, 437*f,* 456
  testing of, 346, 346*f*
Endocrine glands, **51**
Endogenous opioids, **126,** 129*t*
  alcohol and, 591
  analgesia produced by, neural circuit
    mediating, 230–231, 231*f*
  in eating disorders, 406
  and reinforcement, 581, 582
  stress response and, 569
Endolymph, 220, 220*f*

Gray matter, 81
   periaqueductal. *See* Periaqueductal
      gray matter
   in schizophrenia, 523, 523f, 528, 528f,
      530
   in spinal cord, 92–93, 93f
Growth cones, 78
Growth hormone, 88
Gustation, 233–238
   anatomy of taste buds and gustatory
      cells, 233–234, 234f
   neural pathways for, 237, 237f
   perception of gustatory information,
      234–236, 235f
   stimuli for, 233
Gustducin, 235f, **236**
GVG. *See* Gamma-vinyl GABA
Gyrus (gyri), **81,** 81f

H
Hair cells
   auditory, **205**–207, 206f
      connections with cochlear nerve,
         209–210
      damage to, 212
      inner, 208f, 210
      ion channels in, 208, 209f
      outer, 208f, 210, 212–213
      transduction apparatus in, 208f
      and transduction of auditory
         information, 207–208, 208f, 209f
   vestibular, 221, 221f
Hairless (glabrous) skin, 223f, 223–224
   mechanoreceptors in, 224, 224t
Hairy skin, 223, 223f
Hallucinations, **517,** 584
   hypnagogic, **281**
Haloperidol, 551
Handel, George Frideric, 533
Hand movement, control of, 255, 256f,
   258
Hangul language, 504
HAP1 (Huntington-associated protein
   1), 268
6-HD. *See* 6-Hydroxydopamine
Head factors, for satiety, 388
Healing, stress and, 562, 562f
Hearing. *See* Audition
Heart, thirst receptors in, 380
Hebb rule, **413,** 415, 418, 428
   and word acquisition and meaning,
      491–492
Helmholtz, Hermann von, 12
Hemicholinium, **115,** 129t
Hemisphere. *See* Cerebral hemisphere(s)
Hepatic portal vein, **386,** 387f
Hering, Ewald, 174
Heritability, 13–15
   of alcoholism, 594–596
   of autistic disorder, 556–557
   of drug abuse, 594–596
   of major affective disorders, 533–534
   of schizophrenia, 518, 518f, 523
   of smoking habit, 594

Heroin (dihydromorphine), 580–583
   addiction to, 573, 574–575
      treatment of, 597
   as analgesic, 126
   cross-priming effect of nicotine on,
      588
   intoxication, 126
   lipid solubility of, 104, 575
   versus morphine, 104, 575–576
   tolerance to, 574–575
   withdrawal effects of, 106, 574–575
Herpes encephalitis, prenatal, and
   autistic disorder, 557
Hertz, **204**
Hertz, Heinrich, 204
5-HIAA, **537**
   in alcoholism, 597
Hindbrain, 76f, 76–77, 77t, 89, **91**–92
Hippocampal formation/hippocampus,
   67, **86,** 86f, **416**–417
   anterior, in schizophrenia, 526
   cannabis and, 592
   components of, connections of, 416f
   cortical connections of, 459f, 459–460
   damage to
      and anterograde amnesia, 453–454,
         459, 460–462, 461f, 465
      and posttraumatic stress disorder,
         565
      stress and, 562–564, 563f
   functions of
      monoaminergic and
         acetylcholinergic modulation of,
         475–477
      theoretical explanations of,
         477–478
   limbic cortex and, 462, 462f
   long-term potentiation in, 415–418,
      428, 474–475, 475–476
   and memory, 453, 458, 460, 460f,
      477–478
      consolidation, 471
      retrieval of, 465–466
      spatial, 464f, 464–465
   NMDA receptors in, 428
   in olfactory pathway, 240
   place cells in, 471–474, 473f, 590
   and relational learning, 468–479,
      477–478
   and spatial learning, 469–471, 470f
   subcortical connections of, 460,
      461f
   theta activity of, 476f, **476**–477
Hippocrates, 9
Histamine, and arousal, 292
Histaminergic neurons, 292
Histologic methods, 137–139
Hitzig, Eduard, 12
Homeostasis, **374**
Hominids, 17–18
   brain size as function of body weight,
      20, 20f
   percentage differences in DNA
      among, 18f

Homo erectus, 18
   brain size as function of body weight,
      20f
Homo neanderthalis, 18
Homo sapiens, 18
   brain size as function of body weight,
      20f
   migration routes of, 18–19, 19f
Homosexuality, 326–330
   birth order of male siblings
      and, 329
   brain and, 328–329
   heredity and, 329–330
   prenatal androgens and, 326–327
   prenatal stress and, 329
Homunculus, motor, 254, 255f
Horizontal cells, 167f, **168**–169
Horizontal sections, **69,** 69f
Hormones. *See also specific hormones*
   activational effects of, **310,** 316
   and aggressive behavior, 355–359
   anterior pituitary, 88, 314
   distribution of, 51
   lactogenic, 339
   organizational effect of, **310,** 316
   peptide, 63, 126–127
   posterior pituitary, 88–89, 318
   production of, 51
   sex. *See* Sex hormones
   and sexual behavior, 316–331
   steroid, **63,** 63f, 125
   stress, 560–562
5-HT. *See* Serotonin
5-HTP (5-hydroxytryptophan), 121, 121f
5-HTP decarboxylase, 121, 121f
Hubel, David, 178
Hue, **164**
Humans
   advantages of, 19
   brain of
      compared with other animals,
         19–20
      evolution of, 19–20, 80–81
   circadian rhythms in, 300–301
   evolution of, 16–19, 18f
   sexual behavior of, 323–326
Humor, brain mechanisms involved in,
   366–367
Hunger
   brain stem and, 393–394
   lateral hypothalamus and, 394,
      395–397
   physiological signals for, 386–387
Hunger Winter, 525
Huntingtin, 267–268
Huntington's disease, 128, 264, 267f,
   267–268
   and emotional recognition, 364–365
   learning deficits in, 441
Hydrocephalus, obstructive, **73**
   surgical correction of, 73–74, 74f
6-Hydroxydopamine (6-HD), **135,** 145t
5-Hydroxytryptamine (5-HT). *See*
   Serotonin

5-Hydroxytryptamine. *See* Serotonin
5-Hydroxytryptophan (5-HTP), 121, 121*f*
Hypercomplex cells, **179**, 179*f*
Hyperpolarization, **42**
Hyperprolactinemia, 318
Hypertension, 379
  stress and, 562, 562*f*, 566, 566*f*
Hypertonic solution, **376**
Hypnagogic hallucination, **281**
Hypocretin, 395
  and arousal, 292
  and narcolepsy, 282
  and sleep/waking flip-flop, 293–294, 294*f*
Hypofrontality, 529–531
Hypoglossal nerve, 95*f*
Hypoglycemia, 386
Hypogonadal syndrome, 358
Hypothalamic hormones, 315*t*
Hypothalamus, 87*f*, **87**–88, 88*f*
  and aggressive behavior, 349, 349*f*
  and conditioned reinforcement, 447–448
  and drinking behavior, 378
  and eating behavior, 394*f*, 394–400
  electrical stimulation of, 153
  and emotional response, 346–347
  in gustatory pathway, 237, 237*f*
  lateral, 394, 394*f*. *See also* Lateral hypothalamus
  nuclei of, 88*f*
  in olfactory pathway, 240
  paraventricular nucleus of. *See* Paraventricular nucleus
  and seasonal rhythms, 305–306
  suprachiasmatic nucleus of. *See* Suprachiasmatic nucleus
  third interstitial nucleus of (INAH-3), 328
  tuberomammillary nucleus of, **292**, 293, 294
  ventromedial nucleus of. *See* Ventromedial nucleus of the hypothalamus (VMH)
Hypothermia, opiates and, 581
Hypotonic solution, **376**, 376*f*
Hypovolemia, **376**–377, 379
  detection of, 379*f*, 379–380

I
"Ice pick" procedure, 547
ICV administration, **103**
Identical twins. *See* Monozygotic twins
Ifenprodil, 438
IGL (intergeniculate leaflet), **302**
IM injection, **102**
Imitation, and communication of emotions, 371, 371*f*
Immediate early genes, 149
Immune reactions
  cell-mediated, 567–568, 568*f*
  chemically mediated, 567–568, 568*f*

Immune system, 567–568
  neural control of, 568–569
  stress and, 567, 568*f*, 568–570
Immunocytochemical methods, **140**
  combined with anterograde or retrograde tracers, 158, 159*t*, 159*f*
  for localizing neurotransmitters, 156, 157*f*, 159*t*
  for localizing receptors, 158, 159*t*
  for tracing efferent axons, 140–142
Immunoglobulin(s), **567**–568, 568*f*
Immunoglobulin A (IgA), 569
Implicit memory, 457, 457*f*
Impotence, testing for, 278
INAH-3. *See* Third interstitial nucleus of anterior hypothalamus
Incentive salience, 577
Incubus, 279, 279*f*
Incus, 17*f*, 204–**205**, 205*f*, 207*f*
Independent limb movements, 256
Indirect agonist, **110**, 110*f*
Indirect antagonist, **109**–110, 110*f*
Indirect pathway, in basal ganglia, 263*f*, **264**, 553
Indolamines, 116*t*
Infectious disease, stress and, 569*f*, 569–570, 570*f*
Inferior (term), 68–69
Inferior colliculi, 89–90, 90*f*
Inferior temporal cortex, **188**, 188*f*, 189*f*, 430, 430*f*
  color-sensitive region in, 187
  and form analysis, 188–190, 190*f*
  and recognition of visual stimuli, 430
  regions of, 188, 188*f*
  and spatial location perception, 197–198
  and visual pattern discrimination, 430, 431*f*
Influenza, and schizophrenia, 524, 525*f*
Ingestive behavior, **374**. *See also* Drinking; Eating
Inhalation, **103**
Inhibition, neural, 40*f*, 40–41
  versus behavioral, 60–61
  first evidence of, 252–253
  presynaptic, **62**, 62*f*
Inhibitory neurotransmitters, 112, 123
Inhibitory postsynaptic potential (IPSP), 57–**58**, 58*f*, 60–61, 61*f*
Inhibitory synapses, 40*f*, 40–41, 60–61, 61*f*
Ink-writing oscillograph, 147, 147*f*
Inner ear, 205
Insertional plaques, **208**, 208*f*, 209*f*
In situ hybridization, **156**–157, 157*f*
Insomnia, 280
  drug dependency, **280**
  fatal familial, **285**, 286
Instrumental conditioning, 412, **413**–414, 414*f*, 439–449
  neural pathways in, 439–442
  strengthening neural connections, 448–449, 449*f*
Insufflation, 103

Insular cortex, **82**, 82*f*, 224–225, 485, 486*f*
  and pain perception, 229, 229*f*
  and speech articulation, 485–486, 486*f*
Insulin, **382**–383, 383*f*
  administration of, 103
  in anorexia nervosa, 406, 406*f*
  in fasting phase of metabolism, 384, 384*f*
  as satiety signal, 390
Insulin receptors, 383, 390
Intensity differences, localization of sounds through, 216
Intergeniculate leaflet (IGL), **302**
Interleukins, 568
Interneuron(s), **28**
  excitatory, 40, 40*f*
  inhibitory, 40*f*, 40–41
  local, 28
  relay, 28
Interposed nuclei, **268**, 269*f*
Interstitial fluid, **376**, 376*f*
  loss of, 377, 377*f*
  regulation of concentration, 376, 377–379
  relative volume of, 376*f*
Intestinal bypass surgery, 404–405
Intestinal factors, in satiety, 389–390
Intracellular fluid, **43**, **376**, 376*f*
  ions in, 43–45, 44*f*
  loss of, 377
  regulation of concentration of, 376*f*, 376–377
  relative volume of, 376*f*
Intracerebral administration, **103**
Intracerebroventricular (ICV) administration, **103**
Intrafusal muscle fibers, **246**, 246*f*, 248, 252
Intralipid, 389
Intramuscular (IM) injection, **102**
Intraperitoneal (IP) injection, **102**
Intrarectal administration, **103**
Intravascular fluid (blood plasma), **376**, 376*f*
  loss of, 377
  regulation of volume, 376–377, 379–380
  relative volume of, 376*f*
Intravenous (IV) injection, **102**
Intromission, 317, 318, 324
Ion(s), **43**
  in extracellular and intracellular fluid, 43–45, 44*f*
  movement through membrane, during action potential, 45–47, 47*f*
Ion channels, **45**–47, 46*f*
  in auditory system, 208, 209*f*, 217–218
  neurotransmitter-dependent, 56*f*, **56**–57, 57*f*
  major types of, 58–59
  refractory, 46

in somatosensory transduction, 224, 225*f*
and taste perception, 234–236, 235*f*
in vestibular hair cells, 221
voltage-dependent, **46,** 55
Ionotropic receptors, **56,** 56*f*
IP injection, **102**
Iproniazid, 534
Ipsilateral, **69**
IPSP. *See* Inhibitory postsynaptic potential
Iris, 165*f*, 166
Ischemia, 226
Isotonic solution, **376**
Italian language, and dyslexia, 512–513
IV injection, **102**

J
James, William, 369
James-Lange theory, 369*f*, **369**–370
Japanese language
brain mechanisms involved in reading, 507
and dyslexia, 513
writing deficits in, 510*f*, 510–511
Jaw wiring, in obesity treatment, 404
Jet lag, 306
Joint hypermobility syndrome, and panic disorder, 549

K
Kainate receptors, **123**–124
Kainic acid, 124, 129*t*, 134–135, 145*t*, 152
Kanamycin, and auditory hair cell damage, 212
Kana symbols, in Japanese writing, 507, 510, 510*f*
Kanji symbols, in Japanese writing, 507, 510, 510*f*
Kanner, Leo, 555–556
K complexes, 276*f*, 277
Ketamine
addiction to, 574*t*
and schizophrenia symptoms, 529, 531
site of action, 574*t*
Kidneys, renin-angiotensin system of, 379, 379*f*
Kinesin, 34, 34*f*
Kinesthesia, **222**
Koniocellular layers, **170,** 170*f*, 182–183
properties of, 186, 187*t*
Korsakoff, Sergei, 452
Korsakoff's syndrome, **452**–453, 573
anatomy of, 463*f*, 463–464
confabulation in, 453, 467
retrograde amnesia with, 466

L
Labeling studies, 77, 80*f*
anterograde method, **140**–143, 141*f*, 143*f*, 145*t*
combined with immunocytochemical methods, 158, 159*t*, 159*f*

double labeling, **158,** 159*f*
retrograde method, 142*f*, **142**–143, 143*f*, 145*t*
Labia, development of, 313, 313*f*
Laborit, Henri, 519
Lactate, 35
and panic disorder, 549
Lactogenic hormones, 339
Lamellae, **168,** 168*f*
Lamina terminalis, organum vasculosum of. *See* OVLT
Lange, Carl, 369. *See also* James-Lange theory
Language. *See also* Speech
impairments, brain region involved in, 9
physiology of, 481–482
Late-onset depression, 540
Lateral, 68*f*, **69**
Lateral corticospinal tract, **257,** 257*f*, 260*t*
Lateral fissure, **82,** 82*f*
Lateral geniculate nucleus, **87,** 171*f*, 430
dorsal, **170,** 170*f*, 178, 183
intergeniculate leaflet (IGL) of, **302**
magnocellular system of, **170,** 170*f*, 178, 186, 187*t*, 512
parvocellular system of, **170,** 170*f*, 178, 182–183, 186, 187*t*, 512
Lateral group, of descending motor tracts, **256**–258, 257*f*, 260*t*
Lateral hypothalamus, 394, 394*f*
and conditioned reinforcement, 447–448
and eating behavior, 394–397
Lateral lemniscus, **210,** 210*f*
Lateral nucleus of amygdala, **344,** 345*f*
and conditioned emotional response, 436–438, 437*f*
in differential classical conditioning, 437–438, 438*f*
in long-term potentiation, 438
synaptic changes in, 437, 437*f*
Lateral ventricles, 72*f*, **72**–73
Laterodorsal tegmental nucleus (LTN), 295
Latitude effect, in schizophrenia, **524**–525
Laughter, brain mechanism involved in, 366–367
L-DOPA, **116,** 116*f*, 120, 129*t*
for anorexia nervosa, 407
for Parkinson's disease, 101, 117, 152, 152*f*, 265–266
and schizophrenia symptoms, 519
and tardive dyskinesia, 522
Learning, 411. *See also* Classical conditioning; Instrumental conditioning
aversive emotional, 345
basal ganglia and, 439–442
basic forms of, 412
brain structures responsible for, 86
episodic, 414–415, 429, 440
long-term potentiation and, 429
motor, 412, **414,** 415*f*, 439, 442–444

nature of, 411–415
nitric oxide and, 128
observational, 415
perceptual, **412,** 414, 415*f*, 477–478
premotor cortex and, 442–444
primary function of, 412
relational, 412, 414–415, 452–479
in laboratory animals, 468–479
long-term potentiation in, 474–475
REM sleep and, 287, 287*f*
spared abilities in anterograde amnesia, 454–456
spatial, 414, 469–471, 470*f*, 477
stimulus-response, **412**–414, 415*f*, 436
strategies for, 24–25
synaptic plasticity and, 415–429
Lectins, 140
Lee-Boot effect, **320**
Left-handedness, and dyslexia, 513
Left parietal apraxia, 261*f*, **261**–262
Lens (eye), 166
Leptin, 314, **391**
high-fat diet and, 403, 403*f*
and obesity, 402–403
reduced sensitivity to, 403
and satiety signals, 391*f*, 391–392, 392*f*, 398–399, 405
stimulating effects of, 399
transport across blood-brain barrier, 403
Lesion studies, 132–145, **133,** 145*t*
evaluating behavioral effects of, 133–134
histologic methods in, 137–139
of living human brain, 143–144
producing brain lesions for, 134–135
stereotaxic surgery for, **135**–137, 145*t*
and tracing of neural connections, 139–143
Levorphanol. *See* Percodan
Levorphanol (Percodan), 126
LH. *See* Luteinizing hormone
Librium, 125, 347
Ligand, **51**
Light, 164
electromagnetic spectrum, 164, 164*f*
perceptual dimensions of, 164, 165*f*, 204
as zeitgeber, 300–301, 302, 306
Light and dark, coding of, 172–174, 173*f*, 174*f*
Light therapy, 542–544
Limb apraxia, 259–262
Limbic cortex, **85,** 459, 459*f*
damage to, amnesia caused by, 462–463
and hippocampus, 462, 462*f*
Limbic system, 81, **86,** 86*f*
Lingual lipase, 236
Lipid neurotransmitters, 127
Lipid solubility, 104–105
Lipoprivation, **386**–387, 394*f*, 396
Lithium, **535**
for bipolar disorder, 534, 535–536, 536*f*

Liver
 carbohydrate reservoir in, 382–383
 hepatic portal blood supply to, 386, 387*f*
 metabolic functions of, 382–384
 nutrient detectors in, 386–387, 387*f*
 satiety signals from, 390
L–NAME, 128, 129*t*
Lobotomies, 547
Local interneurons, 28
Lockjaw. *See* Tetanus
Locus coeruleus, 120*f*, **120–121**, **290**, 293
 and arousal, 290*f*, 290–291, 291*f*
 and REM sleep, 295, 298, 299*f*
 and withdrawal symptoms, 582–583
Long-term depression, 418, **427–428**
 drug abuse and, 578–579
 versus long-term potentiation, 427–428, 428*f*
 theta rhythm in, 476, 476*f*
Long-term memory, **454**
 conversion of short-term memory into, 454, 454*f*
Long-term potentiation, 415–**416**, 427*f*
 alcohol and, 590
 AMPA receptors and, 419, 422, 423*f*, 424, 424*f*, 425, 427, 427*f*
 associative, **418**, 418*f*, 421, 422*f*
 CaM-KII and, 422–424, 423*f*, 424*f*, 427, 427*f*
 cannabis and, 592
 and classical conditioning, 438
 dendritic spikes and, 420–421, 421*f*
 dopamine and, 448, 476
 drug abuse and, 578–579
 forms of, 428–429
 induction of, 415–418
 and instrumental conditioning, 441, 448
 and learning, 429
 long-lasting, 426–427
 versus long-term depression, 427–428, 428*f*
 nicotine and, 588
 NMDA receptors and, 418–421, 420*f*, 422*f*, 427, 427*f*, 438, 474–475, 475*f*
 nonassociative, 418
 postsynaptic changes involved in, 422–425, 425*f*, 426*f*
 presynaptic changes in, 426–427
 procedure for producing, 417, 417*f*
 protein synthesis and, 426–427, 438
 in relational learning, 474–475
 serotonin and, 475–476
 stress and, 563, 563*f*, 567
 summation and, 418, 419*f*
 theta rhythm in, 476, 476*f*
Lordosis, **318**, 324, 335
Loudness, **204**
 perception of, 213
LSD (lysergic acid diethylamide), **122**, 129*t*, 580
Lumbar vertebrae, 91, 91*f*

Luteinizing hormone, 314, 315*t*
 and menstrual cycle, 316, 317*f*
 stress and, 561
Lysergic acid diethylamide, 129*t*
Lysergic acid diethylamide (LSD), **122**, 580
Lysosomes, 32*f*, **33–34**

M

MA (mercaptoacetate), **386**
Macroelectrode(s), **147**
 recording neural activity with, 147*f*, 147–148, 155*t*
Magnetic resonance imaging (MRI), **144**, 144*f*, 145*t*
 functional (fMRI), **150–151**, 151*f*, 155*t*
Magnetoencephalography, 148–**149**, 149*f*, 154, 155*t*, 498, 499*f*
Magnocellular layers, **170**, 170*f*, 178, 512
 and developmental dyslexia, 512
 properties of, 186, 187*t*
Magnocellular nucleus, **297–298**
Major affective disorders, **532–544**
 brain abnormalities in, evidence for, 538–541
 heritability of, 533–534
 physiological treatments for, 534–536
Males
 aggression in, 355–356
 external sex organs in, 313, 313*f*
 genetic, failure of androgenization in, 313, 327–328
 internal sex organs in, 310–312, 311*f*
 prenatal sexual development in, 310–313
 sexual behavior in
  hormonal control of, 317–318, 325–326
  neural control of, 331–334, 334*f*
 sexual maturation of, 314, 314*f*
Malleus, 17*f*, **204–205**, 205*f*, 207*f*
Malonyl-CoA, as satiety factor, 391–392, 392*f*, 399
Mammals
 evolution of, 16*f*, 16–17
 middle ear in, 17, 17*f*
Mammillary bodies, **86**, 86*f*, 89*f*
 degeneration of, amnesia caused by, 463*f*, 463–464, 466
Mania, 533. *See also* Bipolar disorder
 sleep deprivation and, 542
 treatment of, 535–536
MAO. *See* Monoamine oxidase
Margolin, David, 193
Marijuana, 127, 407, 574, 574*t*, 583, 591–593
Masculinization
 behavioral, 319, 319*f*
 in congenital adrenal hyperplasia, 326–327
Masculinizing effect, **311–312**
Massa intermedia, 72*f*, 73, 85*f*, 87, 87*f*
Master genes, 80

Maternal behavior
 aggression, 356–357
 hormonal control of, 338–339, 339*f*
 neural control of, 339–340
 of rodents, 337*f*, 337–338, 338*f*
Maternal stress, 564, 564*f*
 and brain development, 329
 and reduction in aggression, 355
MCH. *See* Melanin-concentrating hormone
MC4-R. *See* Melanocortin-4 receptor
MDMA, **123**, 129*t*
Meal schedule, 385
Meaning, of words, 490–493
 dictionary analogy for, 491*f*, 491–492
Mechanoreceptors, in skin, 224, 224*t*
Medial, 68*f*, **69**
Medial forebrain bundle (MFB), **444**
 in reinforcement, 444–445, 445*f*
Medial geniculate nucleus, **87**
 in auditory pathway, 210, 210*f*
Medial lemniscus, 226–227, 227*f*
Medial nucleus of amygdala, **321**, 321*f*, **344**, 345*f*
 and female sexual behavior, 336*f*
 and male sexual behavior, 333, 333*f*, 334*f*
 sexual dimorphism of, 333
Medial pontine reticular formation (MPRF), 296–**297**, 297*f*, 298–299
Medial preoptic area (MPA), **332**
 and intermale aggression, 355–356
 and male sexual behavior, 332–334, 334*f*
 and maternal behavior, 339–340
 and parental/paternal behavior, 340
Medial temporal lobe
 limbic cortex of. *See* Limbic cortex
 and memory retrieval, 465–466
 in spatial memory, 464–465
Median preoptic nucleus, 378*f*, **380**
 and drinking behavior, 380–381, 381*f*
Median raphe nucleus, 121–122
Medulla (medulla oblongata), 85*f*, 90*f*, **91**
Meissner's corpuscles, 223*f*, **223–224**, 224*t*
Melanin-concentrating hormone (MCH), **395–397**, 405
 connections of, 398
Melanin-concentrating neurons
 connections of, 396, 396*f*
 location of, 395, 395*f*
Melanocortin-4 receptor, **398**
 and eating behavior, 398–399, 403
a-Melanocyte-stimulating hormone (a-MSH), **398**
 and eating behavior, 398–399
Melanopsin, **301–302**, 302*f*
Melatonin, **305–306**
Membrane
 ion channels in, 45–47, 46*f*
 of neuron, **31**, 32*f*
 permeability, action potential and, 46–47, 47*f*

of photoreceptors, 168
postsynaptic, **52,** 53, 53*f*
presynaptic, **52,** 53*f*
sodium-potassium transporters in, 45, 45*f*
Membrane potential, 41–42. *See also* Action potential; Resting potential
forces responsible for, 42–45
recording of, 42, 42*f*
Memory/memories, 411–412
alcohol and, 476, 590
auditory, 431, 431*f*
automated, basal ganglia and, 441–442
brain structures responsible for, 84–86
cannabis and, 592
confabulation of, 466–467
consolidation of, **454,** 454*f*
hippocampal formation and, 471
declarative, 456–458, **457,** 458*t,* 477
effect of emotions on, 347
emotional, 456
episodic, 439, 456, **458,** 465–466
explicit, 457, 457*f*
implicit, 457, 457*f*
lesion studies of, 133
long-term, **454**
motor, 484
nondeclarative, 456–458, **457,** 458*t*
olfactory, 238, 240
perceptual, 431*f,* 431–433, 432*f,* 433*f*
short-term, 433–436
REM sleep and, 287
retrieval of, medial temporal lobe and, 465–466
semantic, **462**–463, 466
in amnestic patients, 462, 463*t*
short-term, **433**–436, **454**
spatial, medial temporal lobe in, 464–465
stress and, 563
visual, 431*f,* 431–433, 432*f*
of words, 495–497
Men. *See* Males
Meninges, **70,** 71*f,* 85*f*
Menstrual cycle, **316**
and aggression, 356
anorexia nervosa and, 406–407
neuroendocrine control of, 316–317, 317*f*
and sexual behavior, 324, 324*f*
synchronization of, 322
Mental images, construction of, 198, 199*f*
Mental retardation, alcohol and, 588, 589*f*
Mercaptoacetate (MA), **386**
Merkel's disks, 223*f,* **224,** 224*t*
Mesencephalic locomotor region, **271**
Mesencephalon, 76*f,* 77, 77*t,* **89**–91
Mesocortical system, **117,** 117*f,* 444
in reinforcement, 444–446

Mesolimbic system, **117,** 117*f,* 444
drug abuse and, 576
opiate use and, 582
and schizophrenia symptoms, 519, 530
Messenger ribonucleic acid (mRNA), **32**
and localization of neurochemicals, 156–157, 157*f*
in protein synthesis, 32, 33*f*
Metabolic activity of brain
recording of, 149*f,* 149–151, 150*f,* 151*f,* 155*t*
sleep/sleep deprivation and, 284, 295
Metabolic disorders, 401
Metabolism, 382–385
absorptive phase of, 384*f,* **384**–385, 390
efficiency of, differences in, 401–402
fasting phase of, **384,** 384*f*
and satiety, 390
Metabotropic glutamate receptors, **123**
Metabotropic receptors, **57,** 57*f*
Metencephalon, 76*f,* 77, 77*t,* 91
Methadone, 576, 597
Methamphetamine, 584, 584*f*
Method acting, 365
Methylene blue, 138
Methyl palmoxirate (MP), **386**
Methylphenidate (Ritalin), 118–**119,** 129*t*
for attention-deficit/hyperactivity disorder, 558, 559
for narcolepsy, 282
and schizophrenia symptoms, 519
Methysergide, 399
MFB. *See* Medial forebrain bundle
Microdialysis, **151,** 151*f,* 155*t*
Microelectrode(s), **41,** 41*f,* 42*f,* **146,** 153
construction of, 146, 146*f*
recording neural activity with, 146–147, 147*f,* 155*t*
Microelectrode puller, 146
Microglia, 35–**36**
Microiontophoresis, 152–**153,** 153*f*
Micrometer, 36
Micropipette, multibarreled, **153,** 153*f*
Microtome, 138–**139,** 138*f*
Microtubules, 32*f,* **34,** 34*f*
Midbrain, 76*f,* 76–77, 77*t,* 85*f,* **89**–91, 90*f. See also* Mesencephalon
Middle ear, 204–205, 205*f*
disease, 207
evolution of, 17, 17*f*
Midsagittal plane, **69**
Milner, Peter, 411
Mind-body question, 2–3
Mirror-drawing task, 455, 455*f*
Mirror neurons, 195, 197, 497
Mitochondria, 32*f,* **32**–33
Mitral cells, **240**
MK-801, 531
MK-869, effects on depression, 538, 538*f*
MK-901, 589*f*
Moclobemide, **120,** 129*t*

Modafinil, for narcolepsy, 282
Model (scientific), **10**–11
Monism, **3**
Moniz, Egas, 547
Monoamine(s), 116*t,* **116**–123. *See also* Dopamine; Epinephrine; Norepinephrine; Serotonin
Monoamine hypothesis, of depression, **536**–538
Monoamine oxidase (MAO), **119,** 119*f,* 120
Monoamine oxidase inhibitors (MAOIs), 119–120, 534
Monoaminergic neurons, 116
Monochorionic twins, 526–527, 527*f*
Monosodium glutamate, taste of, 236
Monosynaptic stretch reflex, **250,** 251*f*
role in postural control, 250, 251*f*
Monozygotic (identical) twins, 160, 526–527, 527*f*
Mood disorders, 532. *See also* Bipolar disorder; Depression
Moral judgment, prefrontal cortex and, 353–355
Morphine
dose-response curve for, 105, 105*f*
versus heroin, 104, 575–576
Morris water maze, 469–470, 470*f,* 471, 475, 476
Motion sickness, 222
Motivation, brain structures responsible for, 86
Motor association cortex (premotor cortex), 83*f,* 84, **84, 254,** 255*f,* 442, 442*f*
connections with sensory association cortex, 439
and learning, 442–444
in Parkinson's disease, 266
Motor control, of writing, 508–509
Motor cortex. *See also* Motor association cortex; Primary motor cortex
firing of single neurons, effect on hand movement, 256*f*
long-term potentiation in, 428
organization of, 255–256, 255*f*
Motor endplates, **247**
Motor homunculus, 254, 254*f*
Motor learning, 412, **414,** 415*f,* 439
neural pathways in, 442–444
spared, in anterograde amnesia, 455*f,* 455–456, 456*f*
Motor memories, in Broca's area, 484
Motor neurons, **28**
alpha, **246,** 246*f,* 252, 252*f,* 252–254, 253*f*
gamma, 246*f,* **246**–247, 250–252, 271
Motor pathways, 260*t*
descending, 256–259
lateral group, **256**–258, 257*f,* 260*t*
ventromedial group, **256**–259, 259*f,* 260*t*
Motor unit, **247**
Mounting medium, 138

Movement
  ballistic, 270
  control of, 244–273
    basal ganglia and, 262–268
    brain structures responsible for, 82–83, 254–272
    cerebellar, 268–271, 269f, 270
    cortical, 255f, 256–259
    reflex, 250–254
    reticular formation and, 271
  decomposition of, 270
  perception of, 179, 193–197, 195f
    studies with laboratory animals, 193–195
  sequences, integration of, 270–271
  verbally controlled, deficits of (apraxias), 259–262
  visual memories of, 432, 432f
Moving stimuli, somatosensory responsiveness to, 225
MP. See Methyl palmoxirate
MPA. See Medial preoptic area
MPRF. See Medial pontine reticular formation
MPTP, 101, 119, 132, 265, 266–267
MRI. See Magnetic resonance imaging
mRNA. See Messenger ribonucleic acid
MSG (monosodium glutamate), taste of, 236
a-MSH. See a-Melanocyte-stimulating hormone
MST area, 194–197, 432
M system, 122, 122f
Müller, Johannes, 11, 11f
Müllerian system, 310–312, 311f
Multibarreled micropipette, 153, 153f
Multiple sclerosis, 36–37, 524–525
Multipolar neurons, 29f, 30
  internal structure of, 31, 32f
Multiunit smooth muscle, 248
Muscarine, 115, 129t
Muscarinic receptors, 115
Muscimol, 125, 129t, 135, 437, 442
Muscle(s), 245–250
  cardiac, 249
  contraction of
    physical basis of, 247f, 247–248, 248f
    timing, cerebellum and, 270
  facial
    and emotional expression, 365, 365f
    and emotional response, 370–371
  paralysis, during REM sleep, 277, 278, 281, 295, 297–298
  sensory feedback from, 248, 249f
  skeletal, 245–248
    anatomy of, 246f, 246–247
  smooth, 248–249
  striated, 247
Muscle length detectors, 248
Muscle spindles, 246, 246f
  efferent control of, 250–252
Mutations, 15, 15f
  of extra gene, 80
  targeted, 160

Myasthenia gravis, 60, 114
  case study of, 28
Myelencephalon, 76f, 77, 77t, 92
Myelin sheath, 29f, 29–30, 32f, 36
  conduction of action potential in, 49–50, 50f
  formation of, 36f, 36–38
Myofibrils, 247
Myosin, 247
Myosin cross bridges, 247, 247f
Myosin filaments
  in muscle, 246f
  in muscle contraction, 247, 247f

N
Naloxone, 126, 129t, 582, 583
  in addiction therapy, 583, 591, 599
Naltrexone, in addiction therapy, 591, 597, 598–599, 599f
Naming
  brain regions activated by, 496, 497f
  deficits in, 492–493, 493f
Narcolepsy, 275, 280–282
  canine models of, 281f, 281–282
Natural selection, 13, 14–15
Nauru islanders, obesity in, 402
Navigational tasks, 464f, 464–465, 468–474
NE. See Norepinephrine
Neanderthals, 18
NEAT. See Nonexercise activity thermogenesis
Negative afterimage, 176–177, 177f
Negative feedback, 372, 373, 373f
Negative reinforcement, 576
  and drug addiction, 576–577
Negative symptoms of schizophrenia, 517t, 517–518, 522
  drugs causing, 529
  relationship with positive symptoms, 529–531
Neocortex, 85
  and perceptual learning, 477
Neomycin, and auditory hair cell damage, 212
Neostigmine, 114, 129t
Neostriatum, 264, 440, 440f
Neoteny, 20
  in evolution of human skull, 20, 20f
Nerve(s), 30f, 30–31
  doctrine of specific energies, 11
  messages of, interpretation of, 11
  and message transmission, 10
  speed of conduction through, 12
Nerve cells. See Neurons
Nervous system, 66–99
  basic divisions of, 29
  basic features of, 67–74
  cells of, 29–39
  major divisions of, 70, 70t
  overview of, 70
  relation to rest of body, 70, 71f
  terms associated with, 67–79, 68f, 69f
Nesting behavior, 337, 337f, 338–339

Neural activity
  recording, 146–149, 155t
  stimulating, 152–153
Neural communication, 39–41
  within neuron, 39–50
  between neurons, 50–64
    synaptic, 53–63
    nonsynaptic, 62–63
  synaptic, 31, 31f
Neural connections, tracing, 139–143, 140f
  anterograde labeling method of, 140–143, 141f, 143f, 145t
  immunocytochemical methods of, 140–142
  retrograde labeling method of, 142f, 142–143, 143f, 145t
  transneuronal methods of, 142–143, 145t
Neural integration, 60–61
Neural rewiring, in adult brain, 79–80, 80f
Neural tube, 75f, 75–76
Neuraxis, 67–68, 68f
Neurogenesis, in adult brain, 79–80, 80f
Neuroglia (glia), 35–37
  development of, 77–79, 78f
  scanning electron micrograph of, 139f
Neurokinin, 538
Neurology, 23
Neuromas, 230
Neuromodulators, 51, 62–63
  localizing, 156
  measuring, 151–152
  peptides as, 126
Neuromuscular junction, 247
Neurons, 28–35
  basic structure of, 29f, 29–31
  bipolar, 30, 30f
  communication. See Neural communication
  development of, 77–79, 78f
    in adult brain, 79–80, 80f
  hormone receptors in, 51
  internal structure of, 31–35, 32f
  motor, 28
  multipolar, 29f, 30, 31, 32f
  neurotransmitter-producing, localizing, 155–157, 156f, 157f, 159t
  number in nervous system, 28–29
  postganglionic, 96, 97f
  postsynaptic, 51, 52
  preganglionic, 96, 97f
  regenerative properties of, 37–38
  scanning electron micrograph of, 139f
  sensory, 28
  supporting cells of, 35–38
  unipolar, 30, 30f
Neuropeptide Y (NPY), 396
  in anorexia nervosa, 406–407
  and eating behavior, 396–399, 405
  leptin receptors in, 398
Neuropeptide Y neurons, connections of, 397f

Neuropil, lost volume in schizophrenia, 528
Neuroscience, 23
   careers in, 22–23
Neuroscience research, goal of, 67
Neurosecretory cells, **88**, 89f
Neurotransmitter(s), **31**, 51, 112–129. See also specific neurotransmitters
   amino acid, 123–127
   autoreceptors for, **61**–62
   in brain
      localizing, 155–157, 156f, 157f, 159t
      measuring, 151–152, 155t
   drug effects on, 108, 109f, 110–111, 129t
   excitatory, 112, 123
   inhibitory, 112, 123
   lipid, 127
   nucleoside, 127–128
   peptide, 126–127
   release of, 40, 51, 53–56
      regulation of, 62, 62f
   reuptake of, **59**, 59f
      drug effects on, 109f, 110–111
   soluble gas, 128
Neurotransmitter-dependent ion channels, 56f, **56**–57, 57f
   major types of, 58–59
Nicotine, 586–588
   addiction, 573, 574t, 586–587
      genetic factors in, 594
      treatment for, 576, 598, 598f
   cross-priming effect on other drugs, 588
   effects of, 129t
   sites of action, 574t
   topical administration of, 103
   withdrawal effects of, 588
Nicotine patches, 576
Nicotinic receptors, **115**, 587–588
Nightmares, 279, 279f
Night terrors (pavor nocturnus), 283
Nigrostriatal system, **117**, 117f, 444
   degeneration of, 264
Nimiety, 404
Nissl, Franz, 138
Nissl substance, 138
Nitric oxide (NO), **128**, 129t
   in long-term potentiation, 426, 427, 427f
Nitric oxide synthase (NOS), **128, 426,** 427, 427f
Nitroglycerine, sublingual administration of, 103
NK₁ receptor, 538
NMDA, effect on glutamate receptors, 124, 129t
NMDA-R2B, 475
NMDA receptors, **123**–124, 124f, **418**
   alcohol and, 588, 590–591, 599
   anoxia and, 461f, 461–462
   CaM-KII binding to, 424, 424f
   and classical conditioning, 438
   in hippocampal formation, 428
   and instrumental conditioning, 448

and long-term potentiation, 418–421, 420f, 422f, 427, 427f, 474–475, 475f
   and operant conditioning, 441
   and schizophrenia symptoms, 530–531
NO. See Nitric oxide
Nociceptors, 226, 228
Nocturnal emissions, 278
Nocturnal enuresis, 283
Node of Ranvier, **36**, 36f, 49, 50f
Noncompetitive binding, **109**–110, 110f
Nondeclarative memory, 456–458, **457,** 458t
Nonexercise activity thermogenesis (NEAT), 402
Non-REM sleep, **277**
Nontheta behaviors, 476
Noradrenalin. See Norepinephrine
Noradrenergic neurons, 120f, 120–121
   and arousal, 290f, 290–291, 291f
   drugs affecting, 120–121, 129t
   and REM sleep, 146–147, 295, 298–299, 299f
Noradrenergic receptors, 121
Norepinephrine (NE), 112, 116, **120**–121
   and arousal, 290–291
   behavioral effects of, 121
   biosynthesis of, 116, 116f, 120
   in depression, 536–537
   in eating disorders, 406
   and hippocampal functions, modulation of, 475–476
   and olfactory memory, 240
   secretion of, 98
   and sleep, 298–299
   in stress response, 560–561, 561f
Norepinephrine reuptake inhibitors, 534, 537–538, 538f
Nouns, anomia for, 496
Novelty seeking, and drug abuse, 595
NPY. See Neuropeptide Y
Nucleolus, **31**–32
Nucleosides, 127–128
Nucleus, of neuron, **31**, 32f
Nucleus accumbens, **444,** 444f
   dopamine release by
      alcohol and, 590
      cocaine/amphetamine and, 584–586, 585f
      dynorphin and, 586, 586f
      nicotine and, 587, 587f
      opiates and, 582
      and positive reinforcement, 576
      THC and, 591–592, 592f
   in instrumental conditioning, 448, 449f
   and reinforcement, 444–447
Nucleus/nuclei (collection of neurons), **86.** See also specific nuclei
Nucleus of the solitary tract, **236**–237, 236f, 238, **380**
   and drinking behavior, 380–381, 381f

and eating behavior, 393–394, 394f, 400
   nutrient receptors in, 387
Nucleus paragigantocellularis (PGi), 333–**334,** 334f
Nucleus raphe magnus, **230**–231
Nucleus ruber (red nucleus), 90f, **91,** 257f, 258, 269f, 269–270, 270f
Nutrient reservoirs, 382–385, 386
   and obesity, 401–402
Nystagmus, 219

O

Obesity, 400–405
   fat storage and, 391
   health hazards of, 400
   incidence of, 400
   possible causes of, 400–404
   and sexual maturation, 314
   treatment of, 392, 404–405
OB gene, 391
Object(s)
   spatial arrangements of, memory for, 465, 465f
   visual recognition of, 192, 192f
Object-memory retrieval task, 432f, 432–433, 433f
ob mouse, **391,** 391f, 402
Observational learning, 415
Obsessions, **550,** 551t
Obsessive-compulsive disorder, 534, **550**–554
   description of, 550
   and emotional recognition, 364–365
   possible causes of, 550–554
   serotonin in, 122
   streptococcal infection and, 552, 552f
   treatment of, 553–554, 554f
Obstetric complications
   and bipolar disorder, 540
   and schizophrenia, 528
Obstructive hydrocephalus, **73**
   surgical correction of, 73–74, 74f
Occipital lobe, **83,** 83f
Occipitotemporal cortex, left, and reading, 512, 512f
OCD. See Obsessive-compulsive disorder
Ocular apraxia, **198**–199
Ocular dominance, **183**
Oculomotor nerve, 95f
Odor(s)
   and maternal aggression, 357
   perception of, 240–242, 241f
   as pheromones, 319–323
Odorants, 238
Olds, James, 411
Oleic acid, 383
Olfaction, 238–242
   anatomy of olfactory apparatus, 239f, 239–240
   pattern recognition in, 241–242, 241f–242f
   and sexual behavior, 319–323
   split brain and, 6, 6f

Olfaction *(continued)*
  stimulus for, 238–239
  transduction of olfactory information, 240
Olfactory bulb, **96,** 239*f,* **240,** 241, 241*f*
  patterns of activation, 241–242, 242*f*
Olfactory epithelium, **239,** 239*f*
Olfactory glomeruli, 239*f,* **240**–241
  patterns of activation, 241–242, 242*f*
Olfactory memories, 238, 240
Olfactory nerve, 95*f*
Oligodendrocytes, 35–**36,** 36*f*
  Schwann cells *versus,* 37–38
Olivocochlear bundle, **210**
Onychophagia, 554
Operant conditioning, 413. *See also* Instrumental conditioning
Ophthalmoscope, 12
Opiate(s), 126–127, 580–583
  addiction to, 573, 574*t,* 580
    treatment for, 576, 597
  cross-priming effect of nicotine on, 588
  effects of, 129*t,* 581
    neural basis of, 347, 581–583
  intoxication, 126
  reinforcing effects of, 126, 127, 581–582
    cannabinoid receptors and, 592, 592*f*
  sites of action, 574*t*
  withdrawal effects of, 582–583
Opiate blockers, 596, 597, 598–599
Opiate receptors, 126, 581*f,* 581–583
  localization in brain, 158, 158*f*
  and pain perception, 230, 232
Opioids. *See* Endogenous opioids
Opium, 574, 580
Opossum, cerebral cortex of, 79, 79*f*
Opponent colors, 174, 176
Opponent-process coding, 176
Opsin, **168,** 175
Optic ataxia, **198**–199
Optic chiasm, **88,** 88*f,* **171,** 171*f*
Optic disk, **166**–167
Optic flow, **194,** 196–197
Optic nerve, 95*f,* 165, 165*f,* 171*f*
Optic radiations, 170–171
Oral administration, **102**–103
Oral apraxia, 260
Orbitofrontal cortex, 240, **351**–352, 352*f*
  and aggressive behavior, 352–355
  damage to, effects of, 352*f,* 352–353
  and depression, 539, 539*f*
  and drug abuse, 578, 578*f*
  and obsessive-compulsive disorder, 552–554
Orbits (eye), 165
Orexigens, 395
Orexin, 282, **395**–397, 405
Orexin A, 395
Orexin B, 395

Orexin neurons
  connections of, 396, 396*f,* 398
  location of, 395, 395*f*
Organelle, 32
Organic anions, 44, 44*f*
Organic senses, **222**
Organizational effect, of hormones, **310,** 316
  on aggressive behavior, 355*f,* 355–356, 356
  on sexual behavior, 319, 319*f,* 323
Organ of Corti, **205,** 206*f*
Organophosphates, effects on dreaming, 155–156
Organum vasculosum of the lamina terminalis. *See* OVLT
Orientation sensitivity, 179, 179*f*
  and ocular dominance, 183
Orlistat, in obesity therapy, 405
Orthographic dysgraphia, **510**
Oscillograph, ink-writing, 147, 147*f*
Oscilloscope, **42,** 43*f*
Osmometric thirst, **377**–379
  neural mechanisms of, 380–381
Osmoreceptors, **377**–378
  hypothetical explanation of action, 378*f*
  location of, 378*f,* 378–379
Osmosis, 377, 377*f*
Ossicles, **204**–205, 205*f*
  evolution of, 17, 17*f*
Otoconia, 221, 221*f*
Ouabain, 226
Oval window, **205,** 205*f,* 206, 207*f*
Ovarian follicles, **316**
Ovaries, development of, 310, 311*f*
Overtones, **213**–214
OVLT (organum vasculosum of the lamina terminalis), 378*f,* 378–**379,** 380
  and drinking behavior, 380–381, 381*f*
  osmoreceptors in, 378–379
Ovulation, 316
  and aggression, 356
Oxytocin, 89, 315*t,* **318**
  and female sexual behavior, 325
  and male sexual behavior, 318, 326

P

Pacemaker, cardiac, 249
Pacemaker potentials, 249
Pacinian corpuscles, **223,** 223*f,* 224, 224*t,* 227, 246*f*
PAG. *See* Periaqueductal gray matter
Pain, 222, 226
  constructive role of, 228
  endogenous modification of sensitivity to, 230–231, 231*f*
  perception of, 203, 228–232
  perceptual and behavioral effects of, 228–229
  sensory and emotional components of, 229*f,* 229–230
Paired-associate task, **435**

Pallidotomies, for Parkinson's disease, 263*f,* 265–266
Palmitic acid, 383
Panic disorder, **548**–549
  description of, 548
  gender differences in, 548, 548*f*
  possible causes of, 548–549
Papillae, tongue, 233, 234*f*
Parabelt region, **211,** 211*f*
Paradoxical sleep, 277. *See also* REM sleep
Parahippocampal cortex, **459,** 459*f*
Paranoid delusions, 519
Parasympathetic division, of ANS, 96, 97*f,* **98,** 98*t*
Parasympathetic ganglia, 98
Paraventricular nucleus (PVN) of hypothalamus, 306, 394*f,* **396,** 398, 399–400
  and eating behavior, 396
  and glucocorticoid secretion, 561
Parental behavior, 337–340
  neural control of, 340
Paresis
  emotional facial, **366,** 366*f*
  volitional facial, **365**–366, 366*f*
Parietal lobe, **83,** 83*f*
  damage
    and apraxia, 259, 261*f,* 261–262
    behavioral effects of, 6–7, 133, 197–198, 227–228, 245
  functions of, 254–255, 255*f*
  left, command apparatus of, 261–262, 262*f*
  right, damage, 262, 262*f*
  spatial-memory retrieval and, 432, 433*f*
Parkin gene, 267
Parkinson's disease, **117,** 264–267
  brain imaging in, 152, 152*f*
  cause of, 86, 91, 117, 264, 266–267
  drug abuse and, 573, 584, 584*f*
  learning deficits in, 441–442, 442*f*
  stereotaxic surgery for, 263*f,* 265–266, 266*f*
  symptoms of, 86, 264–265
  treatment of, 22, 101, 117, 119–120, 132, 152, 263*f,* 265–266
Paroxetine, effects on depression, 538, 538*f*
Parturition, **337**
  and maternal behavior, 339–340
Parvocellular layers, **170,** 170*f,* 178, 182–183, 512
  properties of, 186, 187*t*
Patellar reflex, 250
Paternal age, and schizophrenia, 518
Paternal behavior, neural control of, 340
Pattern completion, 478
Pattern recognition
  auditory system and, 217–218
  olfactory system and, 241–242, 241*f*–242*f*
  visual system and, 430, 431*f*
Pavor nocturnus (night terrors), 283

PCP (phencyclidine), **124,** 580
  addiction to, 574*t*
  behavioral symptoms of, 124*t*
  and schizophrenia symptoms, 529*f,*
      529–531
  site of action, 530–531, 574*t*
PCPA, **121,** 129*t*
Pedunculopontine tegmental nucleus
      (PPT), 295, 296*f*
Pelvic thrusting, 317
Penile erections
  hormonal control of, 317
  neural control of, 331, 332
  nitric oxide and, 128
  during REM sleep, 278, 297
Penis, development of, 311*f,* 313, 313*f*
Peptide(s), 51, **62**–63
  localization in brain, 156*f,* 156–157,
      157*f*
  neurotransmitters, 126–127
Peptide bonds, 62, 126
Peptide YY$_{3-36}$ (PYY), **390,** 399
Perception
  basic function of, 8
  brain areas responsible for, 84–85
Perceptual learning, **412,** 414, 415*f,*
      429–436, 477–478
  auditory, 431, 431*f*
  spared, in anterograde amnesia,
      454–456, 457
  visual, 430–433
Perceptual memory, 431*f,* 431–433,
      432*f,* 433*f*
  short-term, 433–436
Percodan (levorphanol), 126
Perforant path, **416,** 416*f*
Perforated synapses, 425, 425*f*
Perfusion, 138–**139**
Periaqueductal gray matter (PAG), 90*f,*
      91, 141*f,* 142, **333**
  and aggressive behavior, 349, 349*f*
  and emotional response, 346–347
  and female sexual behavior, 335, 336*f*
  and male sexual behavior, 333–334
  opiate receptors in, 581, 582–583
  and pain perception, 231–232
  and speech production, 486
  and withdrawal symptoms, 582–583
Peribrachial area, **295**
  acetylcholinergic neurons in,
      295–296, 296*f*
  and REM sleep, 295–298, 299
Periodic patterns, visual perception of,
      181–182
Peripheral ganglia, 70
Peripheral nervous system (PNS), **29,**
      70, 70*t,* 94–98
  autonomic, **96**–98, 97*f*
  major divisions of, 70*t,* 98*t*
  regenerative properties of, 37–38
  somatic, **96**
  supporting cells of, 37–38
Peripheral vision, 172, 172*f*
Perirhinal cortex, **459,** 459*f*
Peritoneal cavity, 102

Persecution, delusions of, 517
Persistent Müllerian duct syndrome, **312**
Pervasive developmental disorders, 555
PET. *See* Positron emission tomography
PGi. *See* Nucleus paragigantocellularis
PGO waves, **295,** 297, 298, 298*f*
Phagocytosis, **36**
PHA-L, **140**
  in double labeling, 158, 159*f*
  in tracing efferent axons, 140–142,
      141*f*
Phantom erection, 331
Phantom limb, **230**
Pharmacokinetics, **102**–105
Pharmacology, 100–130. *See also* Drug(s)
  of schizophrenia, 519–522
Phase differences, **214**–215
  localization of sounds through,
      214–215, 215*f*
Phencyclidine. *See* PCP
Phenylketonuria, **557**
Pheromones, **319,** 334*f*
  effects of, 319–323
  and intermale aggression, 356
Phonetic reading, **505**–506, 506*f*
  deficits in, 506–508, 511
Phonological awareness, deficient, 511
Phonological dysgraphia, 509–**510**
Phonological dyslexia, **506**–507, 507*f,*
      514*t*
Phonological loop, 494–495, 495*f*
Phosphodiesterase, 168, 169*f*
  and taste perception, 235*f,* 236
Phosphoinositide system, 536
Photopigments, **168,** 174
Photoreceptors, **166**–169, 169*f*
  absorption characteristics of, 175, 175*f*
  locations and response characteristics
      of, 166*t*
  and synchronization of daily rhythms,
      301–302
  trichromatic coding in, 175–176
Phototherapy, **543**–544
Physical dependence, 574
Physiological psychologists, 22–**23**
Physiological psychology
  biological roots of, 9–12
  careers in, 22–23
  on mind-body question, 2–3
  nature of, 8–13
  research goals in, 8–9
Physiological regulatory mechanisms,
      375, 375*f*
Physostigmine, 60
Pia mater, **70,** 71*f,* 93*f,* 94*f*
Picrotoxin, 125
Pigment mixing, 174
Piloerection, 96, 248
Pima Indians, obesity in, 402, 404
Pimozide, 551, **582**
Pineal body, 90*f*
  Descartes's theory of, 10*f,* 10–11
Pineal gland, **305**
  and seasonal rhythms, 305–306
Pinna (external ear), 204

Pinocytosis, **55**–56, 56*f*
Piriform cortex, long-term potentiation
      in, 428
Pitch, **204**
  perception of, 211–213
  place coding of, 211*f,* 211–212
  rate coding of, **213**
Pituitary gland, 85*f,* 86*f,* 88, 88*f,* 89*f*
  anterior, **88,** 89*f,* 314
  posterior, **88**–89, 89*f,* 318
PKU. *See* Phenylketonuria
Placebo, **107**
Placebo effects, 107, 232
Place cells, **471**
  alcohol and, 590
  in hippocampal formation, 471–474,
      473*f*
  response to environmental cues, 472,
      472*f*
Place coding, of pitch, 211*f,* 211–212
Placenta, and prenatal development,
      526–527, 527*f*
Places visited, remembering, 468*f,*
      468–469, 469*f*
Plants, evolution of, 17
Plasma. *See* Intravascular fluid
PNS. *See* Peripheral nervous system
Polyamines, 124
Polygraph, 147
Polysynaptic reflexes, 252–254
  inhibitory, 252*f,* 252–253
Pons, 67, 85*f,* 90*f,* **91**
  acetylcholinergic neurons in,
      295–296, 296*f*
  and REM sleep, 295–298, 296*f,* 297*f*
Pontine nucleus, **268,** 270*f*
Pontine tegmental reticular nucleus,
      268, 269*f*
Population EPSP, **417,** 417*f*
Positive reinforcement
  and drug addiction, 573, 575–576
  neural mechanisms of, 576
Positive symptoms of schizophrenia,
      517, 517*t*
  drugs producing, 519, 529–531
  relationship with negative symptoms,
      529–531
Positron emission tomography (PET),
      150, 150*f,* 151–152, 152*f,* 155*t*
Posterior, **68,** 68*f*
Posterior language area, 489–491, 490*f,*
      491*f,* 496, 501*t*
Posterior pituitary gland, 88–89, 89*f,* 318
Postganglionic neurons, **96,** 97*f*
Postsynaptic density, 423–424, 424*f,* 427
Postsynaptic membrane, **52,** 53, 53*f*
Postsynaptic neurons, 51, 52
  depolarization, in long-term
      potentiation, 418, 419*f*
Postsynaptic potential(s), **51,** 57–59
  effects of, 60–61
  excitatory (EPSP), 57–**58,** 58*f,* 60–61,
      61*f*
  inhibitory (IPSP), 57–**58,** 58*f,* 60–61,
      61*f*

Postsynaptic potential(s) *(continued)*
  ion movement during, 58*f*, 58–59
  termination of, 59–60
Postsynaptic receptor, **56**
  drug effects on, 108–110, 109*f*
Posttraumatic stress disorder, **564**–565
Posture, control of
  cerebellar, 268, 270
  cortical, 259
  in Parkinson's disease, 265
  reflex, 250, 251*f*
Potassium channels, 58, 58*f*
  in auditory system, 208, 209*f*,
    217–218
  and taste perception, 234–235, 235*f*
  in vestibular hair cells, 221
Potassium ions (K+), 44*f*, 44–45
Potential(s)
  electrical. *See* Electrical potentials
  pacemaker, 249
  receptor, **164**
    auditory, 208
    production of, 169*f*
  term, 41
Potentiation, long-term. *See* Long-term
    potentiation
Prader-Willi syndrome, 374
Predation, **348**
  neural control of, 349, 349*f*
Prefrontal cortex, **84**
  and aggressive behavior, 351–355
  connections with visual association
    cortex, 434, 434*f*
  damage to
    and confabulation, 466–467
    effects of, 366
  and depression, 539–540, 540*f*
  as dopaminergic target, 448
  and drug abuse, 578, 578*f*
  hypofrontality of, **529**–531
  long-term potentiation in, 428,
    448–449
  and moral judgment, 353–355
  and obsessive-compulsive disorder,
    551, 553
  and pain perception, 229*f*,
    229–230
  in perceptual short-term memory,
    434*f*, 434–436, 435*f*
  and reinforcement, 448
  and schizophrenia, 528, 529–531,
    530*f*
  and sexual arousal, 354
  ventromedial, and appreciation of
    humor, 366–367
Prefrontal lobotomies, 547
Preganglionic neurons, **96**, 97*f*
Pregnancy, 316
Premotor cortex (motor association
    cortex), 83*f*, 84, **84, 255,** 255*f*,
    442, 442*f*
  connections with sensory association
    cortex, 439
  and learning, 442–444
  in Parkinson's disease, 266

Preoptic area
  medial (MPA), **332**
    and intermale aggression, 355–356
    and male sexual behavior,
      332–334, 334*f*
    and maternal behavior, 339–340
    and parental/paternal behavior,
      340
  ventrolateral, **292**
    role in sleep, 292–294, 293*f*, 294*f*,
      299
Pressor amines, 534
Pressure, sensitivity to, 222, 224
Prestriate cortex. *See* Extrastriate cortex
Presynaptic facilitation, **62,** 62*f*
Presynaptic heteroreceptors, **110,** 111*f*
Presynaptic inhibition, **62,** 62*f*
Presynaptic membrane, **52,** 53*f*
  fusion of synaptic vesicle with, 53–55,
    54*f*
Presynaptic receptor, drug effects on,
    109*f*, 110
Primary auditory cortex, **82,** 82*f*, 83*f*,
    211, 211*f*
Primary colors, 174
Primary gustatory cortex, 237, 237*f*
Primary motor cortex, 12, 82*f*, **82**–83,
    83*f*, 254–256, 255*f*
  connections with primary
    somatosensory cortex, 256
Primary olfactory cortex, 239*f*, 240
Primary sex characteristics, 314
Primary somatosensory cortex, **82,** 82*f*,
    83*f*, 227, 227*f*
  connections with primary motor
    cortex, 256
  and pain perception, 229*f*, 229–230
Primary visual cortex, **82,** 82*f*, 83*f*, 171*f*,
    430, 430*f*. *See also* Striate cortex
  long-term potentiation in, 428
Primates, evolution of, 18*f*, 18–19
Primed-burst potentiation, stress and,
    563, 563*f*
Priming, 579
Principal sulcus, 434, 434*f*
Principles of Physiological Psychology
    (Wundt), 8
Probability learning task, 441*f*, 441–442
Proceptivity, 318
Progesterone, 315*t*, **316**
  and female sexual behavior, 318–319,
    323–324, 335, 336*f*
  and maternal behavior, 338–339,
    339*f*, 357
  and menstrual cycle, 316–317, 317*f*
Progesterone receptors, estradiol and,
    335, 335*f*
Projection fibers, **87**
Prolactin, 88, 315*t*, **318**
  and male sexual behavior, 318, 326
  and maternal behavior, 339, 339*f*,
    340
Prosody, 482, 489, **499**–501
Prosopagnosia, **190**–192, 193, 363
Protanopia, **175**

Protein(s)
  in cytoskeleton, 34
  enzymes, **32**
  in membrane of nucleus, 31
  synthesis of, 31–32, 33*f*
    and long-term potentiation,
      426–427, 438
Proteosomes, in Parkinson's disease, 267
Prozac. *See* Fluoxetine
PSD95, 424
Pseudopodia, 35–36
Pseudorabies virus, **142**–143, 335–336
Psychic dependence, 574
Psychobiology, 23
Psychoneuroimmunology, **567**–570
Psychopharmacology, 100–130, **101.** *See
    also* Drug(s); *specific drugs*
  principles of, 102–107
Puberty, 314*f*, 314–315
  emergence of schizophrenia
    symptoms during, 528, 531
Pulvinar, 364
Punishing stimuli, **413**
Punishment
  versus negative reinforcement,
    576–577
  oversensitive mechanism, in binge
    drinkers, 595–596
  undersensitive mechanism, in steady
    drinkers, 595
Pupil (eye), 165*f*, 166
Pure alexia, 502*f*, **502**–505, 503*f*, 514*t*
Pure word blindness, 502
Pure word deafness, 362, 488–489, 501*t*
  brain damage responsible for, 489,
    489*f*
Purkinje cells, in autistic disorder, 557
Pursuit movement, 165–**166**
Putamen, 86, 87*f*, 262, **263,** 263*f*, 264,
    440*f*, 440–441
  in Huntington's disease, 267
  in Parkinson's disease, 265
PVN. *See* Paraventricular nucleus
Pyramidal cells, **416**–417
Pyramidal tracts, **257,** 257*f*, 258, 259
Pyriform cortex, 239*f*, 240
PYY, **390,** 399

R

Radial-arm-maze task, 468*f*, 468–469,
    469*f*, 471–472, 472*f*
Radial glia, **77**–79, 78*f*
Radio frequency (RF) lesion, 134*f*,
    134–135, 145*t*
Raphe nuclei, **291,** 291*f*, 293
  serotonergic neurons of, 291, 291*f*
    and arousal, 291, 292*f*
    and REM sleep, 295, 298, 298*f*,
      299*f*
Rapid eye movement. *See* REM sleep
Rate coding, of pitch, **213**
Rate law, **48,** 48*f*
Reading
  aphasia and, 501–502
  comprehension, two routes of, 9

disorders, 501–513, 514*t*
understanding process of, 505–508, 506*f*
Rebound effect, visual, 173, 176–177
Rebound phenomenon, **286**
after REM sleep deprivation, 286
Receptive aphasia, 487
Receptive fields, of visual system neurons, 172*f*, **172–174**
color-sensitive ganglion cells, 176, 176*f*
light-sensitive ganglion cells, 172–174, 173*f*, 174*f*
overlap of, 183
Receptivity, to sexual behavior, 318
Receptor(s), 51. *See also specific receptors*
activation of, 56–57
binding site of, **51**
drug effects on, 108–110, 109*f*, 129*t*
for hormones, 51, 63, 63*f*
ionotropic, **56,** 56*f*
localization of, 157–159, 158*f*, 159*t*
metabotropic, **57,** 57*f*
postsynaptic, 53, **56**
sensory, **163**
Receptor blocker (direct antagonist), **109,** 109*f*, 110*f*
Receptor potentials, **164**
auditory, 208
production of, 169*f*
Recreational drugs, 573–574
Recurrent collaterals, **477**
Red nucleus, 90*f*, **91,** 257*f*, 258, 269*f*, 269–270, 270*f*
Reduction, **8**–9, 169, 169*f*
Reflex(es), **9,** 250–254
clasp-knife, **253**
Descartes's theory of, 9–10, 10*f*
monosynpatic stretch, **250,** 251*f*
patellar, 250
polysynaptic, 252*f*, 252–254
secondary, 253, 253*f*
vestibulo-ocular, 222
withdrawal, 39–40, 40*f*
Refractory ion channels, 46
Refractory period, **317,** 318
Regulatory mechanisms, 375
example of, 375, 375*f*
Reinforcement, 413–414, 444–449
conditioned, 446–448
dopamine and, 448–449, 449*f*
endogenous opioids and, 126, 127
functions of system, 446–449
in gustation, 237
immediacy of, and addiction, 575–576
negative, **576**
and drug addiction, 576–577
versus punishment, 576–577
neural circuits involved in, 444*f*, 444–446
positive
and drug addiction, 573, 575–576
neural mechanisms of, 576
and schizophrenia, 519, 522

Reinforcement gradient, delay of, and attention-deficit/hyperactivity disorder, 558–559, 559*f*
Reinforcing stimuli, 411, **413**
delay of, and attention-deficit/hyperactivity disorder, 558–559, 559*f*
detecting, 446–448
expected *versus* unexpected, 446, 447*f*
Reinstatement model, of drug seeking, 577
Relapse, in drug addiction, 577–579
Relational learning, 412, 414–415, 452–479
anterograde amnesia as failure of, 458–459
hippocampus and, 468–479
in laboratory animals, 468–479
long-term potentiation in, 474–475
Relay interneurons, 28
Release zone, of synapse, **52,** 53*f*, 55
REM-ON cell, 296, 296*f*
REM sleep, **277**–278
acetylcholine during, measuring, 151
amount per night, 277–278
and brain development, 286–287
depression and, 541, 541*f*
deprivation effects, 286–287
antidepressant, 541
EEG patterns during, 276*f*, 277–278, 278*f*
executive mechanism of, 295–298
eye movements during, 279, 295
functions of, 286–287
and learning, 287, 287*f*
mental activity during, 279
muscular paralysis during, 277, 278, 281, 295, 297–298
neural control of, 146–147, 295–299, 298*f*
onset of, 298, 298*f*
principal characteristics of, 278*t*
REM sleep behavior disorder, **282**–283
Repetition of speech, disorders of, 493–495
Reproductive behavior, 308–341
and aggression, 355–356
biological clocks and, 299–300
hormonal control of, 316–331
and pain perception, 232
pheromones and, 319–323
Research, 131–161
animal, ethical issues in, 21–22
genetic methods of, 159–160
goals of, 8–9, 67
lesion method (experimental ablation), 132–145
neurochemical methods of, 155–159
physiological psychologists and, 23
recording and stimulating neural activity, 146–155
Reserpine, **118,** 129*t*, 519, 537
Resting potential, **42**

Reticular formation, 90*f*, 90–**91,** 91
and learning, 411
motor functions of, 259, 271
Reticular membrane, 205
Reticulospinal tract, 257, **258**–259, 259*f*, 260*t*
Retina, 165*f*, 165–169, **166**
center of, receptive field in, 172, 172*f*
and circadian rhythms, 301–302, 302*f*
coding of visual information in, 172–178
color, 174–178, 177*f*
light and dark, 172–174, 173*f*, 174*f*
neural circuitry in, 167*f*, 167–169, 169*f*
periphery of, receptive field in, 172, 172*f*
Retinal, **168**
Retinal disparity, **182**
Retinohypothalamic pathway, 301–302, 302*f*
Retrograde, **34,** 142
Retrograde amnesia, **452,** 465–466
Retrograde axoplasmic transport, 34–35
Retrograde labeling method, 142*f*, 142–143, 143*f*, 145*t*
combined with immunocytochemical methods, 158, 159*t*
Rett's disorder, 555
Reuptake, **59,** 59*f*
drug effects on, 109*f*, 110–111
Reversible brain lesions, 135
RF lesion. *See* Radio frequency lesion
Rh incompatibility, and schizophrenia, 525
Rhodopsin, **168,** 169*f*
Rhombencephalon, 80
Rhombomeres, 80, 80*f*
Ribosomes, **31**–32
Risky behavior, serotonin and inhibition of, 350, 354–355
Risperidone, 551
Ritalin. *See* Methylphenidate
Ro15-4513, 591, 591*f*
Rods, 166*t*, **166**–168, 168*f*
absorption characteristics of, 175, 175*f*
Rostral, **68,** 68*f*
Rough endoplasmic reticulum, 32*f*, 33, 301
Round window, 205*f*, **206,** 207*f*
Rubella, prenatal, and autistic disorder, 557
Rubrospinal tract, 256, 257*f*, **258,** 260*t*
Ruffini corpuscles, **223,** 223*f*, 224*t*

S
Saccadic movements, 165–**166**
Saccule, 220*f*, **220**–221, 221*f*
Sacral vertebrae, 91, 91*f*
Sagittal sections, **69,** 69*f*
Salt appetite, 377, 379
Saltatory conduction, **49,** 50*f*
Saltiness, 233
neurons sensitive to, 238
receptors for, 234

Saltiness *(continued)*
 reinforcing effects of, 237
 transduction of, 234, 235*f*
Satiety, 388–393
 adipose tissue and, 388, 390–392
 gastric factors in, 388–389
 head factors for, 388
 intestinal factors in, 389–390
 leptin and, 391*f*, 391–392, 392*f*,
  398–399, 405
 liver factors in, 390
 long-term, 390–392
 metabolic factors for, 390
 ventromedial nucleus of
  hypothalamus and, 394,
  397–400
Satiety mechanism, **372,** 373
 in drinking, 375, 375*f*
 in eating, 388–393
Saturation, **164,** 165*f*
Scala media, 205, 206*f*
Scala tympani, 205, 206*f*
Scala vestibuli, 205, 206*f*
Scanning electron microscope, **139,** 139*f*
Schaffer collateral axon, 416*f*, 427–428,
 428*f*
Schaffer commissura axon, 416*f*
Schizophrenia, 516, **517**–532
 brain abnormalities in, 522–531
  evidence for, 522–523, 525–528
  possible causes of, 523–528
 description of, 517–518
 dopamine agonists and antagonists in,
  519
 dopamine hypothesis of, 119,
  519–522, 529, 530, 530*f*
 dopamine transmission in, 520*t*,
  520–521, 521*f*
 drug abuse and symptoms of, 584
 drug abuse models of, 529–531
 early-onset, 528
 electroconvulsive therapy for,
  534–535
 epidemiological studies of, 523–525
 heritability of, 518, 518*f*, 523
 latitude effect in, **524**–525
 long-term drug treatment of,
  consequences of, 521–522
 minor physical anomalies associated
  with, 526, 526*t*
 negative symptoms of, 517*t*, **517**–518,
  522
  drugs causing, 529
 as neurological disorder, 522–531
 nutritional factors and, 525
 onset of, 527*f*, 527–528, 528*f*
 pharmacology of, 519–522
 positive symptoms of, **517,** 517*t*
  drugs producing, 519, 529–531
  relationship with negative
   symptoms, 529–531
 prefrontal cortex and, 528, 529–531,
  530*f*
 seasonality effect in, 524*f*, **524**–525
 susceptibility hypothesis of, 518

 twin studies of, 160, 518, 518*f*, 526*f*,
  526–527, 528
 viral hypothesis of, 524, 525*f*, 528
Schwann cells, 36*f*, **37**–38, 49
 versus oligodendrocytes, 37–38
SCI. *See* Silent cerebral infarctions
SC injection, **102**
Sclera, 165*f*, 165–166
SCN. *See* Suprachiasmatic nucleus
Scopolamine, 476
Scrotum, development of, 311*f*, 313, 313*f*
SDN. *See* Sexually dimorphic nucleus
Seasonal affective disorder, **543**–544
Seasonality effect
 in schizophrenia, 524*f*, **524**–525
 viral hypothesis of, 524, 525*f*
Seasonal rhythms, 305–306
Secondary sex characteristics, 314–315,
 315
Second-color defect (deuteranopia), **175**
Second messenger, **57,** 57*f*, 63, 420
 functions of, 57
Sectioning, 137–138
Sedation, opiates and, 581
Seizure(s), 124. *See also* Epilepsy
 alcohol withdrawal and, 590–591
 surgery for, 67
  information obtained from, 481,
  490
Selective advantage, **15,** 15*f*
Semantic agraphia, 511
Semantic dementia, **466**
Semantic memory, **462**–463, 466
 in amnestic patients, 462, 463*t*
Semantic paraphasias, 501–502
Semicircular canals, **219**–221, 220*f*, 221*f*
Seminal vesicles, 311, 311*f*, 312
Senses, 164
Sensitization, drug, **106**–107
Sensory association cortex, 83*f*, **84**
 connections with motor association
  cortex, 439
 and meaning of words, 492
 and perceptual learning, 429
 and perceptual memory, 431–433
Sensory component, of pain, 229, 229*f*
Sensory information, crossed brain
  representation of, 5–6, 82
Sensory neurons, **28**
Sensory receptors, **163**
Sensory transduction, **163**–164
Septum, damage to, behavioral effects
 of, 133–134
Sequoyah, 504
Serial functions, of left hemisphere,
 84–85
Serotonergic agonists, 122
 for bulimia nervosa, 407
 for obesity, 405
Serotonergic antagonists, 122
Serotonergic neurons, 121–122, 122*f*
 and arousal, 291, 291*f*
 drugs affecting, 121–123, 129*t*
 D system of, **121**–122, 122*f*
 M system of, **122,** 122*f*

 in prefrontal cortex, 354–355
 and REM sleep, 146–147, 295,
  298–299, 299*f*
Serotonin (5-HT), 112, 116, **121**–123
 and alcoholism, 597
 and anxiety disorders, 122, 549
 and arousal, 291
 behavioral effects of, 121
 biosynthesis of, 121, 121*f*
 and depression, 122, 536–538
 in eating disorders, 406
 and emotional recognition, 351, 351*f*
 and hippocampal functions,
  modulation of, 475–476
 and inhibition of aggression, 349–351,
  350*f*, 354–355
 and long-term potentiation, 475–476
 and obsessive-compulsive disorder,
  122, 554
 satiating effects of, 399–400, 405
 and sleep, 298–299
Serotonin receptors, 122
Serotonin reuptake inhibitors, **534,**
 537–538, 538*f*
 for alcoholism, 598
 for anxiety disorders, 549, 549*f*
 for obsessive-compulsive disorder,
  554
 for panic disorder, 549, 549*f*
Set point, **372,** 373
Sex chromosomes, **309**–310, 310*f*
Sex hormones, 314–315, 315*t*. *See also*
 specific hormones
 activational effects on sexual behavior
  in men, 325–326
  in women, 323–325
 classification of, 315*t*
 and female reproductive cycles,
  316–317, 317*f*
 and gender development, 311–313
 and maternal behavior, 338–339,
  339*f*
 organization effects on sexual
  behavior, 319, 319*f*, 323
 and reproductive behavior, 316–331
 and sexual maturation, 314*f*, 314–315
Sex organs
 development of, 310–313
 external, 313, 313*f*
 internal, 310–313, 311*f*, 313*f*
Sexual arousal, prefrontal cortex and,
 354
Sexual behavior
 hormonal control of, 316–331
 human, 323–326
 of laboratory animals, 317–319
 neural control of, 331–337
 pheromones and, 319–323
Sexual development, 309–316
Sexual dimorphism, 309, 316
 of brain, 328–329
 prenatal androgens and, 326–327,
  327*f*
Sexual identity, 309, 328–329
Sexually dimorphic behavior, **309**

Sexually dimorphic nucleus (SDN) of preoptic area, **332,** 332*f*
Sexual maturation, 314*f*, 314–315
Sexual orientation, 309, 326–330
    brain and, 328–329
    heredity and, 329–330
    prenatal androgens and, 326–327
SFO. *See* Subfornical organ
Sham feeding, **389**
Sham lesions, **135**
Shift work, 306
Short-term memory, **433–436, 454**
    conversion into long-term memory, 454, 454*f*
    perceptual, 433–436
Sibutramine, for obesity, 405
Sign language, 497–498
    brain regions activated in, 497, 497*f*
    inability to comprehend, brain damage responsible for, 504
Silent cerebral infarctions (SCIs), **540**
    depression caused by, 540–541
Simple cells, **179,** 179*f*, 183
Simultanagnosia, **198–199**
Sine-wave gratings, 180*f*, **180–181,** 181*f*
Single-unit recording, **146**
Single-unit smooth muscle, 249–250
Sites of action, drug, **101,** 102, 103–104, 106, 107, 108–111, 156
Skeletal muscle, **245–248**
    anatomy of, 246*f*, 246–247
Skin
    anatomy of, 223*f*, 223–224
    mechanoreceptors in, 224, 224*t*
Skin (cutaneous) senses, 222–226
Skull, human, neoteny in evolution of, 20, 20*f*
Sleep, 275–299
    brain areas responsible for, 91
    chemical control of, 288*f*, 288–289
    effects of exercise on, 286
    effects of mental activity on, 286
    functions of, 283–288
    mental activity during, 278–279
    physiological and behavioral description of, 275–279
    physiological mechanisms of, 288–299
    REM. *See* REM sleep
    slow-wave. *See* Slow-wave sleep
    stages of, 276*f*, 276–278, 278*f*
Sleep apnea, **280**
Sleep attack, **281,** 282
Sleep deprivation
    antidepressant effects of, 541–543, 542*f*
    effects of, 284–286
        studies with humans, 284–285
        studies with laboratory animals, 285*f*, 285–286
    REM, effects of, 286–287, 541
    total, 541–543, 542*f*
Sleeping medication, as cause of insomnia, 280
Sleep laboratory, 276, 276*f*

Sleep paralysis, **281**
Sleep-promoting substances, 288, 288*f*
Sleep spindles, 276*f*, 277
Sleep/waking flip-flop, 293*f*, 293–294, 294*f*
Sleepwalking (somnambulism), 283
Slow-wave sleep, **277–278**
    amount per night, 277–278
    depression and, 541, 541*f*
    effects of exercise on, 286
    effects of mental activity on, 286
    functions of, 283–288
    mental activity during, 279
    neural control of, 292–294
    principal characteristics of, 278*t*
    problems associated with, 283
Smile, 365, 365*f*, 368
Smoking, 573, 586–588. *See also* Nicotine
    heritability of, 594
Smooth endoplasmic reticulum, 32*f*, 33
Smooth muscle, 96, **248–249**
SNB. *See* Spinal nucleus of the bulbocavernosus
Social factors, for eating behavior, 385–386
Social phobia, 534
Social stress, and drug abuse, 579, 579*f*
Sodium, in fluid balance, 377, 379, 382
Sodium channels, 58, 58*f*
    and olfaction, 240
    and taste perception, 234, 235*f*
Sodium ions (Na+), 44*f*, 44–45
Sodium-potassium pump, 44
    and temperature transduction, 226
Sodium-potassium transporters, 44*f*, **45,** 46, 58
Solitary tract, nucleus of. *See* Nucleus of the solitary tract
Soluble gases, as neurotransmitters, 128
Solutes, 376
Soma (cell body), **29,** 29*f*, 30*f*
Somatic nervous system, **96,** 98*t*
Somatization disorder, 595
Somatosensation, 222–233
    adaptation in, 225
    and emotional recognition, 363
    neural pathways of, 226–228, 227*f*
    perception of cutaneous stimulation, 224–226
    perception of pain, 228–232
    responsiveness to moving stimuli, 225
    skin anatomy, 223*f*, 223–224
    stimuli for, 222
    transduction of somatosensory information, 224, 225*f*
Somatosensory association cortex, 83*f*, 84
Somatosensory cortex. *See* Primary somatosensory cortex; Somatosensory association cortex
Somatotopic organization, **255**
Somatotropic hormone, 88
Somnambulism, 283

Sound waves, 203–204, 204*f*
    arrival times of, 214
        localization by means of, 214–216, 215*f*
    physical and perceptual dimensions of, 204, 204*f*
    response to, 206–207, 207*f*, 208
Sourness, 233
    neurons sensitive to, 238
    receptors for, 234
    transduction of, 234–235, 235*f*
Spatial filtering, 181, 181*f*
Spatial frequency, 180*f*, **180–181,** 181*f*, 183–184, 184*f*
Spatial learning, 414, 469–471, 470*f*, 477
Spatial location, perception of
    auditory system and, 214–217
    brain lesions and, 133–134
    and learning, 469–471, 470*f*
    visual association cortex and, 197–200, 198*f*
Spatial memory, medial temporal lobe in, 464–465
Spatial-memory retrieval task, 432*f*, 432–433, 433*f*
Spatial receptive fields, 471–474, 475
    alcohol and, 590
Spatial view cells, 474
Specific serotonin reuptake inhibitor, **534**
    for obsessive-compulsive disorder, 554
    for panic disorder, 549, 549*f*
Speech, 481–501
    apraxia of, **485–486,** 486*f*
    articulation of, control of, 485–486
    bilingual, brain mechanisms of, 498–499, 499*f*
    brain lateralization in, 5–6, 11–12, 12*f*, 482
    comprehension, 486–496
        in Broca's aphasia, 485, 485*f*
        disorders of, 487–495
        meaning and, 490–493
        versus recognition, 486
    production of, 482–486
        disorders of, 483–486
    prosody of, 482, 489, **499–501**
    repetition of, disorders of, 493–495
Speech sounds
    recognition of, 488*f*, 488–489
    temporal structure of, 488–489
Spelling, methods of, 509–510
Spelling dyslexia, **507–508,** 508*f*, 509, 514*t*
Spendthrift phenotype, 401, 404, 405
Sphincter vaginae, 331
Spinal accessory nerve, 95*f*
Spinal cord, 70, 71*f*, 91*f*, **91–92,** 92*f*
    and control of sexual responses, 331–332
    cross sections of, 69
    damage to, and feelings of emotion, 370
    development of, 75*f*

Spinal cord *(continued)*
  pathways to somatosensory cortex, 226–228, 227*f*
  relation to rest of body, 70, 71*f*
Spinal foramens, 91, 91*f*
Spinal nerves, 70, 71*f*, 91, 92*f*, 94*f*, 94–95, 98*t*, 226
Spinal nucleus of the bulbocavernosus (SNB), **331**
Spinal roots, **91**
Spinothalamic tract, 227, 227*f*
Spiral ganglion, 206*f*, 209
Split brain, 4–6
  and olfaction, 6, 6*f*
Split-brain operation, 4–**5**, 5*f*
Squid, giant axon of, 42*f*
S-R learning. *See* Stimulus-response learning
Sry gene, 310
Staining, 138, 139*f*
Stanislavsky, Konstantin, 365
Stapes, 17, 17*f*, 204–**205**, 205*f*, 206–207, 207*f*
Steady drinking, 594–595, 595*t*
Stearic acid, 383
Stem cells, 79, 132, 265
Stereopsis (stereoscopic vision), 79, 182
Stereotaxic apparatus, 136, **137**, 137*f*
Stereotaxic atlas, **136**, 136*f*
Stereotaxic surgery, **135**–137, 145*t*, 146
  for obsessive-compulsive disorder, 553
  for Parkinson's disease, 263*f*, 265–266, 266*f*
Stereotaxis, definition of, 135–136
Steroids, **63**, 63*f*, 125
Stimulus-response learning, **412**–414, 415*f*, 436
  spared, in anterograde amnesia, 455–456
Stomach, and satiety signals, 388–389
Streptococcal infection, group A b-hemolytic
  and autistic disorder, 557
  and obsessive-compulsive disorder, 552, 552*f*
Stress, **560**
  and brain damage, 562–564, 563*f*
  and cardiovascular disease, 566, 566*f*
  and coping response, 566–567
  disorders related to, 560–570
  and drug abuse, 579, 579*f*
  effects on immune system, 567, 568*f*, 568–570
  and infectious disease, 569*f*, 569–570, 570*f*
  long-term, health effects of, 562*f*, 562–564
  and long-term potentiation, 563, 563*f*, 567
  prenatal, 564, 564*f*
    and brain development, 329
    and reduction in aggression, 355
  and schizophrenia, 525
Stressors, **560**

Stress response, **560**
  physiology of, 560–562
Stretch receptors, 248
Stretch reflex, monosynaptic, **250**, 251*f*
  role in postural control, 250, 251*f*
Striate cortex, **171**, 185*f*. *See also* Primary visual cortex
  analysis of visual information in, 178–185
  anatomy of, 178, 178*f*
  and blindsight, 184
  and color vision, 182–183
  and depth perception, 182
  modular organization of, 183*f*, 183–184
  and orientation sensitivity, 179, 179*f*
  and spatial frequency, 180–181, 183–184, 184*f*
  and texture sensitivity, 181–182
Striated muscle, **247**. *See also* Skeletal muscle
Stroke (cerebrovascular accident), 22, 84, 245, 342, **481**
Strychnine, **126**, 129*t*
Studying, strategies for, 24–25
Subarachnoid space, **70**, 71, 71*f*, 72*f*, 93*f*, 94*f*
Subcortical regions, **81**
Subcutaneous (SC) injection, **102**
Subfornical organ, 378, 378*f*
  and drinking behavior, 380–381, 381*f*
Subgenual prefrontal cortex, and depression, 539–540, 540*f*
Subicular complex, 416, 416*f*, 459
Sublingual administration, **103**
Submissive behavior, **348**
Subparaventricular zone, 302
Substance P, **538**
  and depression, 538, 538*f*
Substantia innominata, 447–448
Substantia nigra, 90*f*, **91**, 117, 117*f*, 262–263, 263*f*
  in Parkinson's disease, 266–267
  in schizophrenia, 519
Subthalamic nucleus, 264
  in Parkinson's disease, 266, 266*f*
Suckling, and maternal aggression, 357
Suicide, 533, 537
Sulcus (sulci), 81*f*, **81**–82
  central, **82**, 82*f*, 83
Summation, and long-term potentiation, 418, 419*f*
Summer depression, **543**
Superconducting quantum interference devices (SQUIDS), 148
Superior (term), 68–69
Superior colliculi, **89**–90, 90*f*
Superior olivary complex, **210**, 210*f*, 216
Superior sagittal sinus, 72*f*, **73**
Superior temporal gyrus, and speech comprehension, 486–487, 488, 501*t*
Supersensitivity, **522**
Supplementary motor area, **255**, 255*f*, 442, 442*f*
  and learning, 442–443
  in Parkinson's disease, 266

Supporting cells, 35–38
Suprachiasmatic nucleus (SCN) of hypothalamus, **301**, 301*f*
  activity cycle of neurons in, 304, 304*f*
  biological clock in, nature of, 304–305, 305*f*
  chemical control by, 302–303
  and circadian rhythms, 301–303, 302*f*, 303*f*
  metabolic activity of, 304, 304*f*
  and seasonal rhythms, 305
  sexual dimorphism of, 328
  synaptic connections with retina, 301–302, 302*f*
Surface dyslexia, **506**, 507*f*, 514*t*
Surgery
  cingulotomy, **553**
  for obesity, 404–405
  for obstructive hydrocephalus, 73–74, 74*f*
  prefrontal lobotomy, 547
  seizure, 67
    information obtained from, 481, 490
  stereotaxic, **135**–137, 145*t*, 146
    for obsessive-compulsive disorder, 553
    for Parkinson's disease, 263*f*, 265–266, 266*f*
Sutures, 136
Sweetness, 233
  neurons sensitive to, 238
  reinforcing effects of, 237
  trandsduction of, 235*f*, 235–236
Symmetrical division, **77**, 81
Sympathetic apraxia, **261**, 261*f*
Sympathetic division, of ANS, **96**–98, 97*f*, 98*t*
Sympathetic ganglion, **96**, 97*f*
Sympathetic ganglion chain, **96**
Synapse(s), **29**, 29*f*, 31, 31*f*
  activity, recording of, 149–151
  axoaxonic, 51, 52*f*, 62, 62*f*, 110
  axodendritic, 51–52, 52*f*
  axosomatic, 51, 52*f*
  dendrodendritic, 62
  development of, 78
  effects of drugs on, 108–111, 109*f*, 129*t*
  electrical, 62, 63*f*
  excitatory, 39–40, 40*f*, 60–61, 61*f*
  Hebb rule of, **413**, 415, 418, 428, 491–492
  inhibitory, 40*f*, 40–41, 60–61, 61*f*
  locations of, 51
  perforated, 425, 425*f*
  structure of, 51–53, 53*f*
Synapsids, 16, 16*f*
Synaptic cleft, **52**, 53*f*
Synaptic plasticity
  dopamine and, 448–449
  and learning, 415–429
  mechanisms of, 422–427
Synaptic vesicles, **52**, 53*f*
  docking of, 54, 54*f*
  fusion with presynaptic membrane, 53–55, 54*f*

recycling membrane of, 55–56, 56*f*
  storage in, drugs affecting, 108, 109*f*
Synchrony, EEG, during sleep, 278*t*
Synpatic pruning, and onset of
  schizophrenia, 528
Synthesis, in right hemisphere, 85
Synucleinopathies, 283
System variable, **372,** 373

T
Tactile agnosia, 227–228, 228*f*
Tactile apraxia, 228
Tardive dyskinesia, **522**
Target cells, **51,** 63*f*
Targeted mutations, **160**
Taste
  ipsilateral representation in brain, 237
  neural coding of, 237*f,* 237–238
  qualities of, 233
  transduction of, 234–236, 235*f*
Taste buds, 233–234, 234*f*
Taste receptors, 234, 234*f*
TE area, 188*f,* 188–190, 189*f*
  response characteristics of neurons in,
    189, 189*f*
Tectorial membrane, 205–206, 206*f,*
  208
Tectospinal tract, 257, **258**–259, 259*f,*
  260*t*
Tectum, **89**–90
Tegmentum, **90**–91
Tegretol. *See* Carbamazepine
Telencephalon, 76*f,* 77, 77*t,* 81–86
Temperature
  circadian rhythms of, 302, 303*f*
  sensation of, 225–226
  transduction of changes in, 226
Temporal lobe, **83,** 83*f*
  damage to, and anterograde amnesia,
    453
  medial. *See* Medial temporal lobe
Tendons, 245, 248, 249*f*
Tentorium, 85*f*
TEO area, 187, 188, 188*f,* 189*f*
Terminal buttons (terminals), 29*f,* 30*f,*
  31, 31*f*
  autoreceptors on, 61–62
  neurotransmitter release by, 51,
    53–55
  synaptic vesicles in, 52, 53*f*
Testes, development of, 310, 311*f*
Testis-determining factor, 310
Testosterone, **311**–312, 314, 315*t*
  and aggression, 355*f,* 355–356, 356,
    356*f,* 357–359
  and female sexual behavior, 324–325
  levels of
    stress and, 561
    winning or losing and, 358
  and male sexual behavior, 318, 325
  organizational effects on sexual
    behavior, 319, 319*f*
Tetanus (lockjaw), 125
Tetrahydrocannibinal. *See* THC
Tetrodotoxin. *See* TTX
Texture sensitivity, 181*f,* 181–182

5-TG, 386, 387
Thalamus, 79, 85*f,* **87,** 87*f,* 90*f*
  long-term potentiation in, 428
  ventral anterior nucleus of, 264*f,*
    264–**265**
    in Parkinson's disease, 265
  ventral posterior nuclei of
    and pain perception, 229, 229*f*
    and somatosensation, 226–227
  ventral posteromedial nucleus of, and
    gustation, 236–237, 237*f*
  ventrolateral nucleus of, **87,** 264*f,*
    264–**265**
    in Parkinson's disease, 265
Thalidomide, prenatal exposure to, and
  autistic disorder, 557
THC (tetrahydrocannibinal), 127, 127*f,*
  407, 591–593
Theory of mind, autistic disorder and,
  556
Therapeutic index, **105**–106
Therapsids, 16, 16*f*
Theta activity, during sleep, 276*f,*
  277
Theta behaviors, 476
Theta rhythm, 476*f,* **476**–477
Thiamine. *See* Vitamin B$_1$
Thiopental, lipid solubility of, 104
Third-color defect (tritanopia), **176**
Third interstitial nucleus of anterior
  hypothalamus (INAH-3), 328
Third ventricle, 72*f,* **72**–73, 85*f*
Thirst
  definition of, 377
  neural mechanisms of, 380–381,
    381*f*
  osmometric, **377**–379
  types of, 377–380
  volumetric, 377, **379**–380
Thoracic vertebrae, 91, 91*f*
Thoracolumbar system, 96. *See also*
  Sympathetic division, of ANS
Thought disorder, **517**
Threat behavior, **348**
Threshold of excitation, **42**
Thrifty phenotype, 401
Tic disorders, 550–551
Timbre, **204**
  perception of, 213–214, 214*f*
  sound localization by means of,
    216–217
Tip links, **208,** 208*f,* 209*f*
  ion channels at, 208, 209*f*
  regulation of tension of, 208, 209*f*
T-lymphocytes, **568,** 568*f*
T-maze task, 474, 474*f*
TMS. *See* Transcranial magnetic
  stimulation
Tolerance, drug, 106–107, **574**–575
Tongue, anatomy of, 233–234, 234*f*
Tonotopic representation, 210
Topical administration, **103**
Touch, 222, 224–225
Tourette's syndrome, 550–**551**
Tranquilizers, effects of, brain regions
  responsible for, 347

Transcortical sensory aphasia, 489–**490,**
  491*f,* 501*t*
  brain damage responsible for, 490,
    490*f*
Transcranial magnetic stimulation, **154,**
  154*f,* 155*t,* 433–434
  for depression, 535
  during movement perception,
    195–196
Transducin, 168, 169*f*
Transmitter substance. *See*
  Neurotransmitter(s)
Transneuronal tracing methods,
  142–143, 145*t*
Transorbital leucotome, 547
Transverse plane, 69*f*
Trichotillomania, 554
Trichromatic coding, in photoreceptors,
  174–176
Trichromatic theory, of color vision, 174
Tricycle antidepressants, **534**
Trigeminal nerve, 95*f,* 226, 236–237
Triglycerides, 236
  taste receptors for, 236
Tritanopia, **176**
Trochlear nerve, 95*f*
Tryptophan, 121, 121*f*
Tryptophan depletion procedure, **537,**
  549
  in depression, 537–538, 538*f*
Tryptophan hydroxylase, 121, 121*f*
TTX (tetrodotoxin), 421, 421*f*
Tuberomammillary nucleus, of
  hypothalamus, **292,** 293, 294
Tuberous sclerosis, and autistic disorder,
  557
Turner's syndrome, **312**–313
Twin studies, 160
  of affective disorders, 533
  of alcoholism, 594
  of anorexia nervosa, 406
  of attention-deficit/hyperactivity
    disorder, 558
  of autistic disorder, 556–557
  of homosexuality, 329–330
  of obesity, 402
  of obsessive-compulsive disorder,
    550
  of posttraumatic stress disorder,
    564–565
  of schizophrenia, 160, 518, 518*f,* 526*f,*
    526–527, 528
Two-photon laser scanning microscopy,
  420, 422, 423*f*
Tympanic membrane (eardrum), **204,**
  205*f,* 207*f*
Tyrosine, 116, 116*f*
Tyrosine hydroxylase, 116, 116*f*

U
UCP. *See* Uncoupling protein
Umami, 233, **236**
Unconditional response (UR), **412**
Unconditional stimulus (US), **412**
Uncoupling protein (UCP), **403**–404
Uncus, 67

Unilateral neglect, 6–7
case study of, 2
Unipolar depression, **533.** *See also*
Depression
Unipolar neuron, **30,** 30*f*
Upper respiratory infection, stress and,
569, 569*f*
UR (unconditional response), **412**
US (unconditional stimulus), **412**
Uterus, 310, 311*f*
Utricle, 220*f,* **220**–221, 221*f*

V

Vagina, 310, 311*f,* 313, 313*f*
Vagus nerve, **95,** 95*f,* 236
and hunger, 386, 387
Valium. *See* Diazepam
Vandenbergh effect, **320**
V4 area, 187, 194*f*
V5 area, and movement perception,
193–194, 194*f*
Varicosities, axonal, **121,** 121–122
Vas deferens, 311, 311*f,* 312
Vasoactive intestinal peptide (VIP),
126
Vasopressin, 89
localization in brain, 156*f,* 156–157,
157*f*
Ventral, **68,** 68*f*
Ventral anterior nucleus, of thalamus,
264*f,* 264–**265**
in Parkinson's disease, 265
Ventral corticospinal tract, 257*f,*
257–258, 260*t*
Ventral posterior nuclei, of thalamus
and pain perception, 229, 229*f*
and somatosensation, 226–227
Ventral posteromedial nucleus, of
thalamus, and gustation,
236–237, 237*f*
Ventral roots, **91,** 92*f,* 94*f*
Ventral stream
auditory, 211, 218, 218*f*
visual, 185–**186,** 186*f,* 199–200, 430,
430*f*
Ventral tegmental area, 91, **444,** 444*f*
nicotine and, 587, 587*f*
and reinforcement, 444–448
in schizophrenia, 519
Ventricles, brain, 10, 72*f,* **72**–73
in bipolar disorder, 539, 539*f*
development of, 75–76
in schizophrenia, 522–523, 523*f,* 526,
526*f*
Ventricular zone, **76**–80, 78*f,* 81
Ventrolateral nucleus, of thalamus, **87,**
264*f,* 264–**265**
in Parkinson's disease, 265
Ventrolateral preoptic area (VLPA),
292
role in sleep, 292–294, 293*f,* 294*f,*
299
Ventromedial group, of descending
motor tracts, **256**–259,
259*f,* 260*t*

Ventromedial nucleus of the
hypothalamus (VMH)
role in female sexual behavior,
334–335, 335*f,* 336*f*
animal study of, 139–143, 141*f,*
142*f,* 143*f,* 158
and satiety, 394, 397–400
stimulation of, 152–153
Ventromedial prefrontal cortex
and appreciation of humor, 366–367
and emotional reactions, 353
Verbal communication, 481. *See also*
Language; Speech
Verbally controlled movements, deficits
of (apraxias), 259–262
Verbal mechanisms, visual agnosia and,
199–200
Verbs, anomia for, 496, 496*f*
Vergence movements, 165–**166**
Vermis, **268,** 269*f*
and attention-deficit/hyperactivity
disorder, 559
and autistic disorder, 557
Vertebral column, 91, 91*f*
Vertebrates
brain evolution in, 80
evolution of, 16, 16*f*
Vesalius, Andreas, *On the Workings of the
Human Body,* 3*f*
Vesicles. *See* Synaptic vesicles
Vestibular ganglion, **221**
Vestibular nerve, 220*f,* 221, 221*f*
Vestibular sacs, **219**–221, 220*f*
receptive tissue of, 221, 221*f*
Vestibular system, 164, 219–**222**
anatomy of, 220*f,* 220–221
neural pathway of, 221–222
receptor cells of, 221, 221*f*
Vestibulo-ocular reflex, 222
Vestibulospinal tract, 257, **258**–259,
259*f,* 260*t*
Vibration, sensation of, 222, 224
Vietnam Era Twin Registry, 565
VIP, 126
Viral hypothesis, of schizophrenia, 524,
525*f,* 528
Vision, 162–201
analysis of visual information
striate cortex and, 178–185
two streams of, 185–186, 186*f*
visual association cortex and,
185–201
anatomy of visual system, 165–172
binocular, 182, 183
coding of light and dark, 172–174,
173*f,* 174*f*
coding of visual information in retina,
172–178
color, 166, 174–178, 177*f*
evolutionary advantage of, 19
genetic defects in, 175–176
opponent-process coding in, 176
striate cortex and, 182–183
visual association cortex and,
186–188

foveal (central), 172, 172*f*
and hippocampal place cells, 473–474
mammalian system of, 4, 5*f*
peripheral, 172, 172*f*
primitive system of, 4
and recognition of emotions,
361–365
stereoscopic, 79, 182
stimulus for, 164
Visual agnosia, **190**–193
apperceptive, **190**–192
associative, 190, **192**–193, 193*f,*
199–200
versus pure alexia, 504
and verbal mechanisms, 199–200
Visual association cortex, 83*f,* 84, 178,
185–201, 430
and color perception, 186–188
studies in laboratory animals,
186–187
studies with humans, 187–188
connections with prefrontal cortex,
434, 434*f*
damage to, 84, 190–193, 195
dorsal stream of, 185–**186,** 186*f,*
198–199, 430, 430*f*
and dreaming, 279
and form analysis, 188–193
studies with humans, 190–193
studies with laboratory animals,
188–190
fusiform face area of, 191*f,* **191**–192
and movement perception,
193–197
studies with laboratory animals,
193–195
and perceptual learning, 430–433
and reading, 503
in short-term memory, 434–435
and spatial location perception,
197–199
transcranial magnetic stimulation of,
433–434
ventral stream of, 185–**186,** 186*f,*
199–200, 430, 430*f*
Visual cortex. *See also* Primary visual
cortex; Visual association cortex
major divisions of, 430, 430*f*
Visual stimuli, learning to recognize,
430–433
Vitamin B$_1$ (thiamine) deficiency
alcoholism and, 452–453
and schizophrenia, 525
Vitreous humor, 165*f,* 166
VLPA. *See* Ventrolateral preoptic area
VMH. *See* Ventromedial nucleus of the
hypothalamus
Voles, parental behavior in, 340
Volitional facial paresis, **365**–366,
366*f*
Voltage-dependent ion channel,
46, 55
Volumetric thirst, 377, **379**–380
neural mechanisms of, 380–381
receptors for, 379–380

Vomeronasal organ, 240, 320*f,* **320**–323,
    322*f,* 356
  human, 323, 323*f*
von Békésy, Georg, 206
VR1 receptors, 226, 228

W

Wada test, **367**–368
Wakefulness-promoting substances, 288,
    288*f*
Waking (wakefulness)
  chemical control of, 288*f,* 288–289
  EEG patterns during, 276, 276*f*
  neural control of, 91, 289–292
Walker, Mary, 60
Warmth, sensation of, 225–226
Water, body loss of, 377, 377*f,* 379
Wernicke's aphasia, 367, **487**–495, 499,
    501*t*
  analysis of, 487–495
  description of, 487
  reading and writing skills in, 501
Wernicke's area, 482, 483*f,* 486–**487,**
    491, 491*f,* 492
  and Broca's area, connection
    between, 490, 490*f,* 493–494,
    494*f*
  damage to, 487–495
Wet dreams, 278

White matter, 81*f,* 82
  in spinal cord, 92–93, 93*f*
Whitten effect, **320**
Whole-word reading, **505**–506, 506*f*
  deficits in, 506–508, 511
Wiesel, Torsten, 178
Withdrawal reflex, 39–40, 40*f*
Withdrawal-seizure prone (WSP) rats,
    591
Withdrawal symptoms, **106**–107,
    574–575
  alcohol and, 590–591
  barbiturates and, 590–591
  brain structures involved in, 578
  cocaine and, 586
  CREB and, 583, 583*f*
  as negative reinforcement, 577
  nicotine and, 588
  opiates and, 582–583
Wolffian system, **311,** 311*f*
Women. *See* Females
Word(s)
  content, **483,** 487
  difficulty finding (anomia), 485–486
  function, **483,** 487
  meaning of, 490–493
    dictionary analogy for, 491*f,*
      491–492
  memory of, 495–497

  recognition, disorders of, 488–489
  written, perceptual mechanisms for
    identifying, 504–505
Word blindness, 502, 504
Word-form dyslexia, **507**–508, 508*f,*
    509, 514*t*
Word order, 485
Writing
  aphasia and, 501–502
  disorders, 501–513, 514*t*
  perceptual mechanisms for
    identifying, 504–505
  understanding process of, 508–511
Wundt, Wilhelm, 8

X

X chromosomes, 309–310, 310*f*

Y

Y chromosomes, 309–310, 310*f*
Yoked-control procedure, 285
Young, Thomas, 174

Z

Zeitgebers, **300**–301, 302
  and depression, 543–544
  in treatment of jet lag, 306
Zucker rat, 403